NEW HORIZONS

1927–1950

Prepared under the Auspices of the
BUSINESS HISTORY FOUNDATION, INC.

New Horizons

1927-1950

by HENRIETTA M. LARSON

EVELYN H. KNOWLTON

and CHARLES S. POPPLE

1817

HARPER & ROW, PUBLISHERS

NEW YORK, EVANSTON, SAN FRANCISCO, LONDON

FIRST EDITION

STANDARD BOOK NUMBER: 06-012527-6

LIBRARY OF CONGRESS CATALOG CARD NUMBER: 55–8055

Contents

v

Appendices

Tables in Text

Maps

Charts and Diagrams

Illustrations

Tía Juana field in Lake Maracaibo, a major source of oil for war
Sungei Gerong refinery in Sumatra
Fiery destruction of the Sungei Gerong refinery
Oil well in the Jusepin field in eastern Venezuela
Driller stabbing fishtail bit into a bit-break-out lock
Rotary men bringing drill pipe out of the hole
Drilling rig on the bluffs at Elk Basin, Wyoming
Derrick man steadying pipe in the elevator
Roughnecks unscrewing section of drill pipe
Fractionating unit at Humble's Baytown refinery
General view of the Baytown refinery in 1944
Spheroid tanks containing butadiene
Fluid catalytic cracking units at the Baton Rouge refinery
Plantation pipeline manifold for switching products to tanks
Carter well in Illinois being pumped to raise wartime production
The Hungarian company's pipeline, which ran from the field to Budapest
Tanker fueling Navy ship at sea
The Esso tanker *Utica* loading its decks with planes and plane parts
Grease from the Pittsburgh plant for military equipment
Wartime operator of a milling machine at the Gilbert & Barker plant
Trains of tank cars being made up in the Potomac railroad yards
Tank cars and catalytic cracking units at the Baytown refinery
Geologists surveying along the Mackenzie River in Canada
Oil train crossing the Montana prairie in August, 1944
Rock cores from wells filed for study in geological laboratory
Geologist with gravity meter
"The Four Horsemen," the inventors of fluid catalytic cracking
At the Perbunan plant, synthetic rubber rolling out in giant sheets
Truck being loaded with lubricants from the Baltimore plant

*Photographs of the following subjects, for the years 1945–1950, will be
    found in a group after page 644:*

Eugene Holman
Frank W. Abrams
President Holman and Chairman Abrams in 1947
Board of Directors in October, 1949
Producing well at El Centro, Colombia
Humble rig at Weeks Island, Louisiana
Oklahoma wells on 40-acre spacing plan
Derrick among sand dunes in Saudi Arabia
Christmas tree, over an Oklahoma well, to control the flow of oil
Drilling an Imperial well during harvest in an Alberta field
A Stanvac derrick in Sumatra
Indonesian driller on a well near the Pendopo field camp
A Humble well in the Gulf of Mexico

These illustrations came from the photographic collections of Standard Oil Company (New Jersey) and its affiliates in the United States and other countries. Most of the photographs from the parent company's files are in the collection now at the University of Louisville; some were reproduced directly from printed copies of *The Lamp*, the magazine of Standard Oil Company (New Jersey).

Foreword

WITH THIS BOOK the three-volume *History of Standard Oil Company (New Jersey)* is brought to a close. Into the series has gone the labor of more than a score of researchers and writers; the man-years of effort have been incalculably greater than N. S. B. Gras and Henrietta M. Larson could have imagined in 1947 when they agreed to guide and supervise the project under the sponsorship of the Business History Foundation, Inc.

From the beginning of the undertaking, the Foundation's Trustees hoped the product would contribute to an improved understanding of the historic role of large-scale enterprise, especially that of Standard Oil Company (New Jersey), in the petroleum industry as well as in the economies of the United States and of the world. That the preceding volumes in the series have moved toward that goal has been demonstrated. This volume adds an analysis of changes in that role since 1927 and illumines the significance of decisions made by leaders of an international business dealing with problems ranging from its organizational structure to improvement of the general welfare in underdeveloped areas in the world.

To the authors of Volume III, which carries the detailed history of the Jersey group to 1950, the Trustees give thanks and credit for surmounting many obstacles. The extensive files of documentary materials imposed the necessity of devoting a massive amount of time to research. Charles Sterling Popple, now deceased, and, later, Evelyn Knowlton did most of the "digging"; they pored over vast collections of correspondence, exercised excellent discrimination in selecting meaningful data, and wrote early drafts of many chapters. Their task became heavier as they moved nearer the present; the most significant actions became more difficult to determine and objectivity more difficult to maintain. Meanwhile, the preparation of the publishable manuscript had to wait for the editor to complete other tasks with higher priority.

After the death of Professor Gras, the full burden of editing and revising all manuscripts fell upon Professor Larson. The Trustees called on her to fuse early drafts of chapters with her own research and writing to produce a unified, balanced Volume III. She has borne the responsibility steadily and has given unstintingly of her time and energy. Without her devotion to the task, the Trustees would have had great difficulty in meeting their obligation to produce this study. They gratefully acknowledge their debt to her and take pride in presenting this result of the joint efforts of the three authors.

The foregoing statements are made in the name of a ten-person Board of Trustees. The members are: Ray Palmer Baker, Chairman, Vice-President Emeritus of Rensselaer Polytechnic Institute; Alfred D. Chandler, Jr., Professor of History, The Johns Hopkins University; W. Thomas Easterbrook, Professor of Political Economy, University of Toronto; Herbert Heaton, Professor of Economic History Emeritus, University of Minnesota; Ralph W. Hidy, Straus Professor of Business History, Harvard University; Ralph M. Hower, Professor of Business Administration, Harvard University; John G. B. Hutchins, Professor of Business History and Transportation, Cornell University; Henrietta M. Larson, Professor of Business History Emerita, Harvard University; Ross M. Robertson, Professor of Business Economics and Public Policy, Indiana University; and Harold F. Williamson, Professor of Economics, Northwestern University, and Secretary of the American Economic Association.

RALPH W. HIDY
President, Business History
Foundation, Inc.

August, 1969

Authors' Preface

THE UNDERSIGNED authors of this volume hope that, like the earlier volumes in the series, this study will contribute toward a better understanding of the historic role of big business, especially of the multinational type of enterprise. The span of years covered by *New Horizons: 1927–1950* was an especially fluid time, a time when the demand for petroleum products rose steeply around the globe and basic transformations came in the world's economies, governments, and societies. In the circumstances, the survival and growth of Standard Oil Company (New Jersey) were not automatic. Indeed, there was no formula for long-term success except the constant exercise of rational calculations and of timely, informed, and broadly based judgments, together with discriminating and vigilant implementation of policies and plans. The result was not a static company but one that brought about significant changes in its organization, personnel, operations, and products and, indeed, in the concept of its obligations to the diverse peoples whom it served.

The arrangements with Standard Oil Company (New Jersey) under which this project was carried on are described in the introductory statements of the preceding volumes: *Pioneering in Big Business: 1882–1911,* by Ralph W. Hidy and Muriel E. Hidy, and *The Resurgent Years: 1911– 1927,* by George Sweet Gibb and Evelyn H. Knowlton. The company, in accordance with these arrangements, extended to the authors of this third volume the same helpfulness and the same freedoms that the authors of the first two volumes enjoyed: to use its records and to interview its personnel, as well as to publish without restriction.

It is impossible to acknowledge by name the many individuals within the parent company and affiliates who gave us assistance. Those who provided specific data or insights are named in the notes to chapters. Officers and directors, active or retired, and also managers and specialists in technology, law, and other areas read chapters and made valuable suggestions for additions or changes. George H. Freyermuth, Stewart Schackne, and William P. Headden of the Public Relations Department were, successively, our official liaison with the company. For many years, the late Dr. Frank M. Surface served as our contact with company personnel and departments, read the manuscript, and gave us help in other ways. More recently, Charles E. Springhorn has similarly served. He has also supervised the preparation of charts, maps, and illustrations in accordance with our specifications.

Many individuals who from time to time were associated with the Business History Foundation contributed to this project. John S. Ewing prepared reports on the history of Imperial Oil Limited from his research in that company's records. Helen I. Cowan searched records of International Petroleum Company, Limited. A. John Fair and Herbert Kip assisted Dr. Popple in research on the parent company, Esso Standard Oil Company, and The Carter Oil Company. The *History of Humble Oil & Refining Company,* by Henrietta M. Larson and Kenneth Wiggins Porter, provided information about that important affiliate. Professor William T. Baxter of the London School of Economics—who spent a summer in the parent company's offices in New York studying its financial organization, policies, and procedures—in a consulting capacity gave us valuable insights into the complex subject of company finance.

Throughout the years, we had the support and assistance of the Trustees of the Business History Foundation. Ray Palmer Baker and Ralph W. Hidy, as officers of the Foundation, encouraged us at times when the going seemed especially difficult. Professors John G. B. Hutchins, Ross M. Robertson, and Harold F. Williamson read all or large parts of the manuscript; Professor Hidy, together with Dr. Muriel E. Hidy, read two drafts of all the chapters. These readers not only gave most helpful suggestions but also the encouragement that such assistance affords.

Although he had no official connection with the project, Professor Richard S. Meriam of the Harvard Graduate School of Business Administration read many chapters and gave invaluable advice on particular issues. He thus gave us the benefit of his knowledge of contemporary business and its historical background and of his observations as a consultant to Standard Oil Company (New Jersey) for many of the years covered by this volume.

Many contributed to the work of typing and of seeing the manuscript through the press. Florence Glynn and Marian L. Anderson, successively, typed chapters with patience and intelligence. Elsie Hight Bishop gave a high level of editorial assistance in the preparation of early chapters. Professor Ralph L. Henry served as an understanding critic and as editor of the whole manuscript.

We are deeply grateful to all who gave us assistance, counsel, and support. We regret that Dr. Charles Sterling Popple did not live to read the later drafts of chapters and thus to share with us further the knowledge of the company which he had gained from his work on this volume and from the years he spent writing *Standard Oil Company (New Jersey) in World War II.*

HENRIETTA M. LARSON
Professor of Business History, Emerita
Graduate School of Business Administration
Harvard University
EVELYN H. KNOWLTON
Formerly, Associate of the
Business History Foundation, Inc.

August, 1969

NEW HORIZONS

1927–1950

Chapter 1

Standard Oil Company (New Jersey) in 1927

I N THE LONG HISTORY of Standard Oil Company (New Jersey), the year 1927 marks an important turning point. In that year its Board of Directors decided that, as then constituted and administered, the company could not cope adequately with trends in the oil industry that were challenging its competitive position and profits. The board therefore initiated a series of changes in its structure and policies. These, as they developed, radically transformed the company and its operations.

Although it was the world's largest oil concern, the Jersey Company* faced a difficult competitive situation in 1927. It had extensive capital and managerial resources, relatively advanced refining processes, vast outlets for products at home and abroad, and the highest standing as a commercial concern. Its chief executive, President Walter C. Teagle, was widely known as one of the industry's leading administrators. But it was predominantly a refiner and a volume marketer at a time when competitive advantage was shifting to concerns performing the various oil-industry operations and selling a large percentage of their products in the mass consumer market.

The company's relative weakness in oil producing and mass marketing had deep roots in the past.[1] Especially important was the dissolution of the Standard Oil combination in 1911 as a result of a decision of the United States Supreme Court under the Sherman Antitrust Act. As the parent company of the group, Standard Oil Company (New Jersey) then lost nearly all its domestic producing, pipeline, and marketing affiliates and also those selling products in Great Britain and the Orient. It thus became essentially a domestic refiner with plants principally on the Atlantic Coast and a large part of its market for products outside the United States.

---

* Throughout this volume, "Jersey" and "Jersey Company" are used frequently instead of Standard Oil Company (New Jersey).

The funetional specialization of the company resulting from the dissolution of 1911 was contrary to Standard Oil policy of a quarter of a century, as well as to the then current movement among oil companies toward performing all the various oil operations—that is, toward vertical or functional integration. By 1911 Jersey's largest foreign competitor, Royal Dutch–Shell, and the Gulf Oil Corporation and The Texas Company in the United States had already moved extensively forward from production into refining and marketing or were in the process of so doing.

During the years from 1911 to 1927 the company had made persistent efforts to regain a more nearly balanced functional structure, particularly to expand its oil reserves and production.[2] Its first acquisition was an oil producing property in Peru, the ownership of which was lodged in a corporation owned by Imperial Oil Limited, Jersey's Canadian affiliate.* The initial step taken at home was to shift the chief production of The Carter Oil Company from the Appalachian region to the Mid-Continent. After World War I had demonstrated the strategic importance of petroleum products to national defense and the United States government had begun to encourage American companies to participate in the international race for the acquisition of petroleum reserves, Jersey spurred its efforts. In a few years, beginning in 1917, it acquired oil production in Sumatra and ownership in oil producing companies in Mexico, Colombia, and Russia. It tried without success to find oil in other foreign countries, its greatest effort and disappointment being in Venezuela. It also engaged in long and difficult negotiations to gain entry into Middle East production. In 1919, still fearing antitrust action, it cautiously entered Texas by acquiring a half-interest in Humble Oil & Refining Company, a vigorous and promising oil producer operating principally in that state. By such efforts Jersey advanced from a net crude oil production at home and abroad averaging 11,000 barrels daily in 1911 to an average of 139,200 barrels in 1926.[3]

However, the ratio of Jersey's production to its refinery crude oil runs was still far below that of several of its competitors. In the foreign market, where the company was then selling nearly half its products, it had to meet the competition of the Royal Dutch–Shell group and Anglo-Persian Oil Company, Limited. Both of these concerns had large foreign concessions in which oil production could be developed more economi-

---

* For the sake of simplicity, all the companies in which Jersey had a considerable ownership interest, directly or indirectly, including those in which it held all the stock, are in this volume referred to as affiliates.

cally and efficiently than under the system of competitive development of oil fields in the United States. In addition, Royal Dutch–Shell had a transportation cost advantage in European markets because of its large production near tidewater in Venezuela, with shorter tanker routes to Europe than those from the United States ports on the Gulf of Mexico. Gulf Oil Corporation, one of the most dynamic refiners and marketers in the United States, in 1926 produced more oil at home and in Venezuela than it refined. The Texas Company, despite its then recent expansion in refining and marketing, was producing more than half of its refinery crude runs.

The Jersey Company in 1926 had a net production of 39 per cent of its refinery crude runs. Its domestic affiliates, although they provided 14.3 per cent of the country's refined products, contributed about 5 per cent of the total crude production in the United States.[4] Sir John Cadman, chairman of Anglo-Persian and one of the world's leading oil executives, stated in that year that Standard Oil Company (New Jersey) "owned production as a precautionary measure and collateral to its main policy."[5]

President Teagle and several top executives of Jersey and Humble had become concerned that the Jersey Company did not have a sufficient owned production in relation to the needs of its refineries. They had learned from experience with alternate periods of feast and famine that in times of oversupply the purchase of crude involved serious difficulties in maintaining the good will of producers, and that in times of real or threatened shortages Jersey refineries faced the possibility of insufficient oil. These executives knew that dependence on other producers necessitated carrying huge inventories, with high costs, much waste of oil, and considerable risk of loss from price decline.[6]

Moreover, heavy reliance on domestic oil production for refining for foreign markets meant competing with products made from lower-cost oil produced on large concessions abroad. American oil, to be sure, still had substantial markets outside the United States. The test would come if foreign production should become more aggressive in displacing American products in Eastern Hemisphere markets.

At home and abroad Jersey's own market outlets were still nearly limited to those retained in 1911. Its former associates, lacking producing and refining facilities of their own, had continued to purchase products from Jersey refineries.[7] But they also had begun to acquire production and refining, or to look for lower-cost supplies to purchase.[8] Although Jersey's total sales continued to expand, the time was clearly coming when nonaffiliates would not provide an adequate outlet for a large part of the products of Jersey refineries. An obvious solution would be for Jersey to move more extensively into the mass consumer market.

By the middle 1920's, however, there was a strong movement on the part of oil companies into jobber and retail distribution in the United States. With the rapid multiplication of automobiles in this country, the filling station—as retail outlets were then called—became especially attractive as an outlet for gasoline, the more so because refinery expansion and improved refining methods had led to a surplus output of that product. Standard Oil Company (Indiana), which was especially strong in the jobber and retail markets, entered into Jersey's marketing territory. Another former Jersey affiliate, The Atlantic Refining Company, also extended its marketing beyond its original territory. The Gulf Oil Corporation, with a high ratio of oil production to refining and up-to-date refineries, was very actively expanding in the mass market, as also were Shell Oil Company and The Texas Company. These three, unlike Jersey and its former affiliates with Standard Oil names, were moving toward becoming national marketers.[9]

Standard Oil Company (New Jersey) was slow to expand in the growing mass market for gasoline and other products. Many of its own bulk outlets in the Middle Atlantic states, which had been established in earlier decades when kerosene was the main product and distribution was mostly by horse-drawn wagons, were obsolete and badly located for the new gasoline business. In addition, fear of antitrust law placed a restraining hand on the company in the early and middle 1920's. Because the courts, congressional committees, and the Federal Trade Commission were actively seeking evidence of practices in restraint of trade in the oil industry in the middle 1920's, the legal counsel of Jersey and Humble advised against adopting certain methods then being widely used by oil companies to improve their position in jobbing and retailing. These advisers were especially fearful of the lease-and-license system for service stations—whereby, without much outlay of capital, a company could tie independent gasoline distributors to itself. They also opposed the growing practice of furnishing independent dealers with pumping equipment at a nominal charge and of granting discounts to selected jobbers, retail distributors, and other customers. Handicapped by these restraints and restrictions, Jersey and its domestic affiliates expanded only modestly in the middle 1920's through owned outlets.[10]

None of these developments had been serious for Jersey so long as the supply of oil stayed generally below demand, and the trend of prices for crude oil and products was upward. But the rapid expansion of oil production and refining capacity in the 1920's tended to outrace the rise in demand. In 1926 a steep increase in production brought an unprecedented surplus. From Russia, Persia, Sumatra, Colombia, and Venezuela abroad, and from Oklahoma, Texas, and California in the United States, came a flood of oil which intensified competition and started a severe price decline late in the year.

This decline buffeted Jersey in the old bulwark of its strength—refining—which, like the industry's refining, had been expanded beyond the needs of the market. The resultant narrowing of refinery and wholesale margins, as well as the prospect of decline in the volume of Jersey's refinery crude runs and product sales, gave warning of the great reduction in the company's net earnings that actually came in 1927.

Some of Jersey's executives believed that the price decline of late 1926 was the beginning of a long downtrend in petroleum prices. In such a situation competitors with a high ratio of low-cost crude oil production to refinery runs and a firm position in mass markets would have great advantages over Jersey. It was a question whether the company would have to yield here and there to its chief foreign rivals, Royal Dutch–Shell and Anglo-Persian, or to such American concerns as Gulf Oil Corporation, Standard Oil Company of New York, The Atlantic Refining Company, Standard Oil Company (Indiana), and The Texas Company. Since World War I, several of these American oil companies had consistently averaged higher annual net earnings relative to net worth than had Jersey itself.[11]

The company's top administrators recognized that an important factor in Jersey's current difficulties was the overcapacity of the oil industry, especially in the United States. Normally, overexpansion corrected itself, although not without bringing trouble in the industry. The current overproduction, however, revealed the unique vulnerability of the American oil industry, with its erratic and unstable production and its economic and physical waste. Because of their heavy fixed investments and their responsibilities to economies that were increasingly dependent on petroleum products, oil companies had to have assurance of supplies for the future. And if the American companies were to continue to compete outside the United States with others selling products made from lower-cost foreign oil, they would have to acquire large oil production abroad and also set their domestic house in better order.

Among the Jersey officers, President Walter C. Teagle of the parent company and President William S. Farish of Humble, especially, had come to believe that it was necessary to make a frontal attack on the instability and waste of the American oil industry. Both men were becoming convinced that the solution lay in the study of oil reservoirs and in such regulation of production as would minimize the uncertainties and check the excesses resulting from the competitive development of oil fields.[12] But how could such study be carried on? And what system of regulation could be devised that would be effective and also be sound so far as the industry, the long-run social good, and American constitutional law were concerned?

As for Jersey itself, several of its executives were convinced that the company's structure was not such as to enable it to cope effectively with its many problems.[13] Its organizational weaknesses were comparable, although on a larger scale, to those faced by John D. Rockefeller and his associates during the years from 1879 to 1882. Someone likened Jersey at this later time to a mastodon that could not flick a fly off its back. The company had a clumsy and poorly coordinated corporate, administrative, and operational structure. It had remained essentially as it had been left by the dismemberment of 1911, but since then it had grown greatly in size and had expanded both geographically and functionally. It obviously did not have the flexibility and coordination required in the oil industry of the late 1920's.

The Jersey Company was made up of a maze of corporate relationships. At the beginning of 1927, the parent company itself had a direct ownership in more than ninety corporations. It had a minority interest in about forty of them, and in the remainder its share ranged from a bare majority to complete ownership. Many of the companies in which it had a direct interest also had investments in other corporations—in more than eighty at this time. Some of those, again, had wholly or partially owned affiliates, a few of which, in turn, had investments in other companies. Thus many, and even important, companies were far removed from Jersey's direct ownership and hence had no legal or administrative relationship with the parent corporation. Actually, Jersey had a direct majority interest in less than a third of the companies with which it had a corporate relationship. This corporate network had become so involved that probably no one executive, not even President Teagle, knew all its ramifications.[14]

Even with the companies in which it had a direct majority ownership,

Jersey had a varied relationship. Some new and completely owned corporations—mostly engaged in exploration for oil in foreign countries— were managed from headquarters in New York. Others had a large measure of autonomy because of an influential outside ownership, the circumstances of their origin, local conditions bearing upon them, or location far from New York. The balance sheets and income statements of only those majority-owned companies that were sufficiently developed to have profitable operations were consolidated with those of the parent. Almost fifty in number, this consolidated group constituted the principal part of the operations of the Jersey Company.

Further complicating this maze of relationships was the fact that Jersey itself was an operating as well as a holding company. It had been established as a refining concern under the old Standard Oil Trust and had continued its operating functions after it became a holding company in the 1890's. In 1927 it had refineries and marketing activities on the Atlantic Coast, a marine department, and a department engaged in research and development. Jersey thus, as an operating company, had commercial relations with affiliates for which it also had varying degrees of responsibility as a holding company.

In the judgment of several of its top executives in 1926 and 1927, the over-all administration of the company's complex holdings was weakened by lack of administration in the general interest and inadequate coordination of the various specialized operations of parent company and affiliates. These weaknesses were also largely results of the dissolution of 1911. This event had destroyed the company's unique administrative organization with its committee system and large supply of capable administrators. Because Jersey had survived that fateful year principally as a refining concern, most of its later directors had spent their careers in that field. Moreover, competition in oil refining after 1911 and the drive to expand sales had encouraged a high degree of specialization among its executives. This tendency, which was industry-wide, was described in 1927 by Jersey's house organ, *The Lamp:*

As in other industries, the trend of the times was strongly in the direction of the creation of specialists. Problems of manufacturing and marketing had become more intricate as refining practice advanced, the variety of products multiplied, and better acquaintance with local conditions became necessary to the conduct of business in foreign countries; and these problems called for specialists. As vacancies on the board occurred through death or retirement, they were for the most part filled by the election of specialists, whose experience qualified them

to supervise particular branches of the business. The exercise of these specialized functions was so exacting that it became impossible for these men to find
time to devote to the general problems of the industry.[15]

Although such executive specialization was common in large corporations at the time, it had struck Standard Oil Company (New Jersey)
especially hard. Of its pre-1911 directors—men with broad experience—
only two remained by 1927. One, Walter Jennings, was inactive except for
attendance at occasional meetings of the Board of Directors. President
Teagle was the only active member with a long and varied career in the
company. The other directors, who had risen to the board after 1911,
were men of outstanding ability, but they were all specialists, with a
preponderant representation from domestic refining.[16] Charles G. Black
and Daniel R. Weller were old-time refiners, Seth B. Hunt had risen in
refining, and Edgar M. Clark had come to Jersey in 1919 as an expert in
the new refining technology. James A. Moffett, Jr., was in charge of
marketing. Everit J. Sadler, the only director besides Teagle who had had
much foreign experience, had been absorbed in the search for new oil
properties and production abroad. George H. Jones had spent his career
in company corporate finance. Clearly, President Teagle was the only
member of the Jersey board who had both the broad experience and the
relative freedom from other responsibilities that enabled him to serve the
general interest.

However, the burden of top administration had become far too heavy
for one man to carry. Teagle actually had become the only effective
channel of communication between headquarters and some of the larger
affiliates. In addition, he had carried on most of the negotiations concerning Jersey's Russian properties, which had been lost to the Communists
by 1927. He had been representing Jersey abroad in prolonged negotiations for participation in oil production in the Middle East. He had also
been in frequent communication with officials of the United States
concerning the company's expanding foreign interests. He had similarly
participated in an endless series of conferences in Washington on domestic crude oil production and reserves, first occasioned by a fear of
scarcity and later by threat of a surplus. These negotiations and conferences abroad and at home left Teagle insufficient time to keep fully
informed about the problems and operations of the Jersey interests. Yet
he also carried responsibilities for operational details and routines and for
negotiations for crude-supply and product-sales contracts. By 1927 he
had become deeply dismayed by his inability to fulfill all the responsibil-

ities that centered in the presidency of the Jersey Company as then constituted.[17]

The company had tried after World War I to improve its over-all planning and operations. One set of innovations had looked toward better coordination of individual functions through the creation of the Marketing Committee and the Foreign Producing Department (which in 1926 became the Producing Department). The Board of European Executives, with headquarters in Paris, had been established in 1924 to advise European affiliates on marketing and producing problems and, in general, to help overcome the fragmentation among them which had occurred during and after World War I. A statistical committee had been set up in 1922 to correlate the reports prepared by each operating division and to furnish the Board of Directors with summaries of the business as a whole. The Budget Department had been established in 1926 to bring about more uniformity in the financial reporting and planning of the affiliates. The most imaginative innovation had been the Coordination Committee established in 1925. Made up of members of the Board of Directors and assisted by a staff department, this committee was intended to gather information about all Jersey interests, to analyze the whole range of operations, and to provide information necessary for the planning of over-all activities.[18]

Contrary to expectations, these departments and committees had not contributed much to better coordination; they had actually had an opposite effect. The responsibilities of the individual directors as members of committees or departments concerned with specific operations had tended to focus their interest on their one specialty rather than on the whole. The Coordination Committee, especially designed to consider all areas of operations, had not succeeded in raising the gathering and analyzing of information above the specialized interests of individual directors. Indeed, this new committee had actually become subordinate to the Manufacturing Committee.

Men with insight into the internal problems of the company and into the great forces bearing upon it from the outside had come to see by 1927 that changes had to be made in Jersey's administrative organization. President Teagle was convinced that the responsibilities forced upon him were more than any one executive could carry. Director Sadler urged better over-all planning and coordination at the top. Frank A. Howard, manager of the Development Department, stressed the necessity of separating the functions best performed by operating companies from those properly belonging to a holding company.[19]

The Jersey Company's administrative problems, it may be noted, were not unique. Few companies—if indeed any—had so diverse and scattered operations and so complex a corporate structure as Jersey, but many were facing somewhat similar difficulties in administration. Lever Brothers experienced a crisis in administration in 1925,[20] and Royal Dutch–Shell's top organization was under strain. General Motors—which had somewhat simpler problems than those of Jersey but had met a critical situation in the early 1920's—was making progress in improving its top administrative structure.[21] Generally speaking, business concerns in growing large had not developed a top organization suited to new needs.

Jersey's leaders, however, looked upon the company's current problems as only another set of difficulties to be overcome. They were sanguine about the future of the oil industry and confident that Jersey would maintain a leading position in it. A basically favorable factor in the future of both industry and company was the prospect of a continuing upward trend in the demand for petroleum products. The United States was increasing its utilization of such products, especially to provide industrial energy and to fuel automobiles. This expanding need meant a rapidly growing and year-round market. Ships of the leading maritime countries were using more and more oil for fuel; Jersey's own tankers had by this time been converted from coal to oil. Many foreign countries were expected to increase their demand for oil products as soon as they overcame their postwar problems of inflation and readjustment. Latin America, which lacked coal and water power, was finding oil an important source of energy. Industry research was also contributing to the manufacture of a wider range and a higher quality of products. And the emerging conservation movement, supported by research in the problems of oil recovery, gave promise of less wasteful and better regulated production of oil in the United States. On the whole, Jersey's leaders had reason to feel that, if solutions could be found for current difficulties, both the company and its industry should advance and prosper in the future.

The years of the company's history with which this volume is principally concerned are hereafter considered in three periods. The first, 1927 to 1939, was essentially a time of transition in Jersey's administration and technology and of both geographic and functional expansion. It was also a time of significant developments in the oil industry's relations with governments. The second period deals with the war years 1939 to 1945, when the parent company and the affiliates not under enemy domination were concerned principally with serving the war effort—on both the military and the home front—of the United States and the Allies. The third period, 1946 to 1950, was a time of recovery from war and of reconversion to the serving of civilian needs, of great expansion, and of new departures in policy and practice. Notable during those postwar years was the continued change in relations with peoples and governments in many countries.

In fact, to emphasize the company as an entity to the exclusion of the society and the economy in which it operated would be to overlook a great reality in business. Individual firms and the institution of private business typically survive and grow only as they adjust to change. By employing old and shaping new policies and practices, they contribute constructively to meeting the needs of the societies of which they are a functional part. The quarter-century after 1927 was a time of important advances in science and engineering, of economic instability, of limited aggression and worldwide war, of shifts in power relationships among national states and classes, and of modifications in the basic values that give societies purpose and direction. This complex of change gave rise to unusual business risks, but it also afforded great opportunities to business concerns that could adjust to change and maintain their competitive ability throughout their operations.

This volume ends with the year 1950. That particular year marks no such break in the company's history as does 1927, although by 1950 significant postwar developments in Jersey had taken definite form. Some of these were still in process, and the unprecedented growth that had begun after the war's end was unchecked. However, the years 1927 to 1950 as a whole do have an essential unity. The developments within Jersey during this period constituted the company's response to the mounting demand for petroleum products and to a changing social and political order throughout the world. In a larger sense, the story of these developments illuminates a new era in the history of private business.

Chapter 2

Creating a New Administrative System,
1927–1939

THIS CHAPTER deals with the evolution of a new administrative leadership, structure, and techniques within Standard Oil Company (New Jersey). By 1927, the Board of Directors of the parent company had become cognizant of the need to ease the load carried by its officers and directors and to bring about a better coordination of the planning and operations of the whole Jersey Company. It consequently took action designed to decentralize the management of operations and to improve central policy making, planning, and control in the general interest. In so doing, the board applied no particular theory or master plan but instead followed the experienced and informed judgment of its officers and directors about what needed to be done and how it could best be accomplished.[1]

The departures then taken were only a beginning, but they set the general direction of later innovations. The objectives of 1927 proved sound over the years, but the means provided were found to be inadequate. In its traditionally pragmatic way, the Board of Directors therefore made further changes. They thereby developed an administrative system better suited than the old to deal with an expanding and increasingly complex aggregation of affiliates and operations.

FIRST STEPS IN ADMINISTRATIVE CHANGE, 1927–1933

Before the annual stockholders' meeting in June, 1927, Jersey's Board of Directors prepared proposals for altering the corporate and administrative structure of the Jersey companies. Their guiding concept was to separate essential holding-company functions from the management of operations. The parent company was to transfer its various operations to appropriate affiliates to be created or reorganized, and to devote itself

12

entirely to matters of policy, planning, and supervision in the general interest. In order to bring about a better coordination of decentralized management, the top executives of the principal affiliates and others responsible for groups of companies would be elected to the Jersey board. An executive committee would be established, and the two principal committees—the Board of European Executives and the Co-ordination Committee—would be retained.

Action at the annual stockholders' meeting was a mere legal formality because, except for a few company employees and one outsider, stockholders did not attend the meeting but sent their proxies to designated Jersey executives.[2] In this way, the proposals that required authorization by stockholders were approved, and eight new directors were elected in addition to nine who were re-elected. (See Table 1.)

The Board of Directors acted at once to make Standard Oil Company (New Jersey) a holding company only. Jersey transferred to a new affiliated company, incorporated in Delaware, its refining and marketing in the Middle Atlantic states and its holdings in The Carter Oil Company, Tuscarora Oil Company, Limited, and six Mexican companies. It also transferred to this new affiliate its Producing Department, the handling of the large-volume sales of affiliates, and the staff groups having to do with employee relations. This corporation, Standard Oil Company of New Jersey, was organized in August, 1927, with a capital stock of $200,000,-000, then the largest capitalization among all the affiliates. At the same time, Jersey transferred its Marine Department to the Standard Shipping Company, capitalized at $25,000,000. It turned its Development Department and Inspection Laboratory over to Standard Development Company, the name of which was changed to Standard Oil Development Company by a revision of its charter in October, 1927. In December it lodged the preparation of specialty products in Stanco, Incorporated, a new company with a capital stock of $10,000,000.[3] Thus by the end of the year, for the first time in its long history, the parent company was without operating properties and activities.

The enlargement of the Jersey Board of Directors was designed to bring about a better coordination of the planning and operations of the whole Jersey Company. Many of the new directors elected in 1927 or in the next few years were heads of affiliates in North America or Europe: one with each of Standard of Louisiana, Humble in Texas, and Imperial in Canada, and five with European affiliates. Directors with managerial responsibilities hundreds or even thousands of miles from New York obviously could not be expected to attend board meetings frequently in those days of travel by train or ship. But they could at all times be brought into the consideration of matters of policy and general interest by correspondence and consultation. The members who were chief executives of affiliates with headquarters in New York or managers of corporate departments of Jersey itself could generally attend meetings of the board. A regular nucleus for meetings was provided by the four or five who were officers of the parent company.[4]

Most of these directors were specialists who had spent the greater part of their careers in a given operation and in one region or country. They had been successful managers of affiliates, largely in refining and marketing, in which management had to a considerable extent settled into traditional patterns. Among the specialists in refining, Edgar M. Clark was an exception in that he was an advocate of the emerging new technology and would fight hard for the improvement of processes.

Only four of the seventeen board members could be regarded as effective planners, policy makers, and executives on the level required by so large and complex a concern as Jersey had become. These were President Teagle, Heinrich Riedemann, Everit J. Sadler, and William S. Farish. All four had had considerable formal education and broad experience, the first three internationally and Farish in the domestic oil industry.

Beyond question, the outstanding general administrator in the group was President Teagle. He combined a rare physical vitality with a phenomenal grasp of the oil business, an unusual ability to make decisions, and a capacity to change with the times. He remained for many years a major contributor to Jersey's advance and to its leadership in both the American and the international oil industry.

Born into a family of English origin engaged in the oil business in Cleveland, Teagle, after his graduation from Cornell University in 1899, had worked in his father's business for two years before it was sold to Standard Oil. He had then transferred to the Standard Oil group of companies, which he served first in domestic operations and later in European marketing. He had been elected a director of Jersey in 1909, and in 1914 he had moved to Canada as president of Imperial. In that capacity, he had had principal charge of Jersey's then newly acquired producing interest in Peru. Late in 1917, when the parent company had been in great need of new administrative talent to assist in supplying the Allies with oil products, he had been called back to New York to become the company's president.[5] Teagle's background and his experience in two business worlds—American and European—undoubtedly had an influence on Jersey policy in the years before World War II.[6]

Farish was the Board of Director's authority on domestic production. As president of Humble Oil & Refining Company, he led that affiliate in greatly expanding its reserves and production, improving its production technology, and promoting the oil conservation movement. From his knowledge and experience, Farish contributed substantially to Jersey's promotion of more efficient, less wasteful methods in the affiliates' producing operations and to its support of governmental regulation in the interest of conservation.[7]

For the worldwide range of Jersey's interests, Teagle, Riedemann, and Sadler were the best informed and the most dynamic among the Jersey directors. Riedemann and Sadler, each of whom represented certain characteristics or convictions of the respective regions of their origin, Europe and America, reinforced Teagle's duality of background and experience.

Born and educated in Germany, Heinrich Riedemann was the son of one of the original promoters of the business which became Jersey's Deutsch-Amerikanische Petroleum-Gesellschaft. He was his father's successor as general manager of this German affiliate. After World War I, having moved his office to Liechtenstein, he had played an important role as a negotiator and contact man for Jersey in Europe and as an adviser on foreign marketing policy. He had been influential in the company's decision to invest in Nobel properties in Poland and Russia, and to seek entry into oil production in the old Turkish Empire. Riedemann was a close adviser of Teagle in matters relating to its international competitors. He believed it desirable to cooperate in certain markets with rival companies when such a policy would further Jersey's interests. He was a master of strategic planning.[8]

Director Sadler, the general manager of the Producing Department—in 1927 transferred from the parent company to Standard Oil Company of New Jersey—was primarily occupied with obtaining new oil properties and production in foreign countries and in general with reducing costs throughout producing operations. "Sad," as he was known to his peers— or "Don Triste," as his younger associates called him—like Teagle and Riedemann, came from a family in the oil business. His mother as well as his father had been oil producers in the Mid-Continent of the United States. Sadler had entered the oil business after a short period of service in the Navy following his graduation from the United States Naval

Academy. He had served Jersey's producing interests in Romania before World War I, and for many years during and after the war he had directed the company's efforts to obtain concessions and to search for oil abroad.[9] Sadler held that the Jersey Company's success could be maintained only by operating as efficiently and economically as possible and by deriving supplies from the most advantageously located sources at the lowest costs. He had little patience with other considerations, whether they involved the conservation movement and government regulation of the oil industry in the United States or marketing agreements abroad.

Because of its own large and widely scattered membership and the executive responsibilities of many of its members for particular affiliates, the Board of Directors set up the Executive Committee to assume the board's administrative functions between its infrequent meetings. This committee had five members, none of whom had regular responsibilities for affiliates. It met on every business day except when the full board met. Its legal quorum was three members, but the board could appoint a director temporarily to fill a vacancy. Actually, because any director could attend meetings whenever he chose, directors were usually present who were not committee members.[10]

The Executive Committee was composed of men whose official concern was with Jersey itself. The members of the 1927 committee were Chairman Jones, President Teagle, Vice-President and Treasurer Hunt, Vice-President Moffett, and General Counsel Swain. After Jones's death in 1928, no one was elected to fill his place, but President Teagle presided at meetings. Nor was anyone added after Hunt resigned all his positions with Jersey in April, 1933.[11]

The committee was not originally intended to share directly in carrying the responsibilities of the president. Its members, as directors and officers, assisted President Teagle in various negotiations and took part in discussions with representatives of industry and government concerning oil-industry problems.[12] But Teagle carried nearly all the executive load and even at times acted for the Executive Committee. He was a strong administrator and had long held the reins firmly in his own hands.

It soon became evident that the changes initiated in 1927 had not brought the intended improvement in the company's administration. Organizational defects were manifest almost at once. So also was the plain fact that even successful business leaders have difficulty in changing their attitudes, accustomed ways, and old relationships.

The decentralization of the management of operations met with only partial success. Old patterns were not easily changed, especially when the same men continued to occupy top positions. Before 1927 the relations of Jersey directors with affiliates had been on a functional basis. Director Moffett, for example, had been responsible for relations with the marketing operations of domestic and foreign affiliates; he had had a marketing committee and a department to advise him on domestic matters and a foreign sales department in New York and the Board of European Executives to advise on marketing in Europe. Director Clark had similarly been responsible for domestic and foreign refineries and for research on refining. Black had directed the operations of the American tanker fleet, and Sadler had been the chief administrative officer for foreign producing. Although these men generally had other assignments after 1927, they did not at once change to conform to the new pattern. Consequently, the arrangement whereby other directors as heads of affiliates were to manage their own companies and report directly to the Jersey board was not fully observed.

Nor did the desired coordination in the general interest materialize at the board level. Former refining or marketing managers, for instance, could not easily shed their preoccupation with the particular operations to which they had devoted their careers and in which they had acquired high competence. It was understandably difficult for them, after decades of specialization, to extend their thinking to encompass the wide range of Jersey's functions and operations in many countries.[13] It was not strange that board meetings lost time in prolonged discussions between a few members, and that they considered details which should have been left to the officers of affiliates.[14] More serious still was the tendency of each Jersey director who headed an affiliate to promote the interest of that particular company above the general interest. One example of this tendency occurred in refining; when the business decline of the late 1920's gave Jersey a surplus refining capacity, no action was taken to concentrate operations in the lower-cost locations.[15]

Two committees helped to remedy these organizational weaknesses. One was the Committee of European Directors, which took precedence over the old Board of European Executives. The other was the Coordination Committee.

The Committee of European Directors improved communication among Jersey's directors in Europe and between them and headquarters in New York. In 1929, Riedemann became chairman of the group, with headquarters in London. He was a logical choice in view of his close

Table 1: **DIRECTORS OF STANDARD OIL COMPANY (NEW JERSEY) AND THEIR PRINCIPAL RESPONSIBILITIES, 1927–1939**
(Unless otherwise indicated, positions listed were in the parent company.)

Director	Year Elected	Principal Responsibilities	Location of Office
Walter Jennings	1903	Inactive. (Died in 1933.)	New York
Walter C. Teagle	1909ª	President and chairman of Executive Committee to 1937; chairman of the Board of Directors from 1937.	New York
Seth B. Hunt	1914	Vice-president; treasurer; member of Executive Committee. (Retired in 1933.)	New York
George H. Jones	1917	Chairman of the board; member of Executive Committee. (Died in 1928.)	New York
James A. Moffett, Jr.	1919	Vice-president; member of Executive Committee. (Resigned as director in 1933.)	New York
Charles G. Black	1920	Vice-president from 1930; president, Standard Oil Company of New Jersey. (Retired in 1933.)	New York
Edgar M. Clark	1920	Vice-president from 1930; president of Standard Oil Development Company and Standard Shipping Company. (Retired in 1933.)	New York
Everlt J. Sadler	1920	Vice-president from 1930; general manager to 1933 of Producing Department of Standard Oil Company of New Jersey; president of Creole Petroleum Corporation, 1928–1933; supervisor of Jersey integrated affiliates in the United States; chairman of Coordination Committee from 1933.	New York
Daniel R. Weller	1926	President of Standard Oil Company of Louisiana, 1927–1931. (Resigned as director in 1931.)	Baton Rouge
Frederick H. Bedford, Jr.	1927	President of specialty companies to 1933 and supervisor from 1933.	New York
William S. Farish	1927	President of Humble until 1933; chairman of board, 1933–1937; member of Executive Committee from 1933; president and chairman of Executive Committee from 1937.	New York
John A. Mowinckel	1927	General manager of Società Italo-Americana. (Resigned as director in 1934.)	Paris
Christy Payne	1927	General manager of natural gas business to 1933; treasurer, vice-president, and member of Executive Committee from 1933. (Retired in 1935.)	New York
Heinrich Riedemann	1927	Member of shareholders' committee of Deutsch-Amerikanische Petroleum-Gesellschaft; chairman of Committee of European Directors. (Retired in 1933 but later served on the London Council of the International Association [Petroleum Industry] Limited.)	London
Joseph H. Senior	1927	President of West India Oil Company and other affiliates marketing in Latin America. (Retired in 1933.)	New York
G. Harrison Smith	1927	Vice-president of Imperial Oil Limited; president of Imperial from 1933.	Toronto
Chester O. Swain	1927	General counsel to 1935; member of Executive Committee from 1927; vice-president from 1935. (Died in 1937.)	New York
Peter Hurll	1928	Managing director of Bedford Petroleum Company; chairman of Agwi Petroleum Corporation, Ltd. (Retired in 1934.)	London
Orville Harden	1929	Member of Coordination Committee, 1928–1934; supervisor of Latin American affiliates, 1934–1936; vice-president and member of Executive Committee from 1935.	New York
Harry G. Seidel	1929	Managing director of Romãno-Americana; member of Committee of European Directors. (Resigned as director in 1934.)	Paris
Francis E. Powell	1930	Chairman of Anglo-American Oil Company, Ltd. (Retired in 1931.)	London

Table 1 *(cont.):* **DIRECTORS OF STANDARD OIL COMPANY (NEW JERSEY) AND THEIR PRINCIPAL RESPONSIBILITIES, 1927–1939**

Director	Year Elected	Principal Responsibilities	Location of Office
Robert G. Stewart	1932	President of Pan American Foreign Corporation, 1932–1933; general manager of marketing, four domestic affiliates, 1933–1935. (Resigned as director in 1935.)	New York
Ralph W. Gallagher	1933	Supervisor of natural gas companies, 1933–1937; vice-president and member of Executive Committee from 1937.	New York
Donald L. Harper	1935	Contact director for International Association (Petroleum Industry) Limited; president of Standard Oil Export Corporation.	New York
Thomas C. McCobb	1935	Comptroller; supervisory responsibility for finance.	New York
Wallace E. Pratt	1937	Member of Executive Committee from 1937.	New York

[a] Teagle served as director from 1909 to 1914 and from 1917 to 1942.
Source: Standard Oil Company (New Jersey): Directors' and Stockholders' Minutes, 1903–1939; Personnel records; *Annual Report*, 1927–1939; *The Lamp*, various issues from 1927 to 1939.

relations with President Teagle, his important part in planning new arrangements for foreign operations, and his administrative capacity. He discussed company matters with the other European directors—Peter Hurll and Francis E. Powell of British affiliates, Harry G. Seidel of Româno-Americana, and John A. Mowinckel of the Italian affiliate.[16] The committee held occasional meetings, and its members corresponded frequently with one another and with directors in New York.

No significant change was made in the Coordination Committee during this period. After 1927, as before, it was a committee of directors—Chairman Jones, President Teagle, and directors Black, Clark, and Sadler—with Orville Harden as secretary until he became a regular member on the death of Jones in 1928. This committee was still handicapped by the fact that its members, except Harden, were fully occupied with other responsibilities within Jersey itself or as heads of affiliates. Hence the group's work depended mostly on Harden as operating head of the staff department, a post he retained even after he was elected to the Jersey board in 1929.[17] Despite Riedemann's urging in 1931 that, because of his great administrative potential, this young director should be given "a broader education" than that of "routine worker," Harden continued to carry the load as head of the staff until 1933.[18]

Actually, it was Harden who raised the committee's level above routine by developing staff studies. He slowly extended the committee's interests and activities beyond the original objective of bringing about a closer physical coordination between crude supply, transportation, refining, and marketing. He had begun before 1927 to study the costs of various domestic refineries belonging to the Jersey companies. He had found that the New Jersey plants were operating at much higher costs than the refineries at Baton Rouge and Baytown on the Gulf Coast, a fact that had not been apparent from reports of the Manufacturing Committee.[19] After 1927, at a time of intensifying competition, he endeavored to obtain from the heads of the various affiliates—and even from individual departments —information needed for determining the operating costs of the various refinery units.

The Coordination Committee's study of costs revealed serious short-comings in the affiliates' accounting methods which made comparative cost studies virtually impossible: a lack of realistic accounting within affiliates and of uniformity in accounting methods among them. Accounting had generally not kept up with the need for better records brought by increasing competition, the more rapid obsolescence of equipment, and the corporate income tax. For example, neither Jersey nor its affiliates had the necessary accounting records for making adequate cost studies to assist in adjusting to the narrowing spread between refining expenditures and income in the later 1920's. The affiliates encountered special problems in the valuation of reserves in the earth and in figuring depletion charges for producing wells and fields. The parent company had employed tax consultants to assist in developing more precise accounting for tax purposes. But on the whole the affiliates had been left to cope with their own accounting problems themselves with whatever help they could get from Jersey's traveling auditors and a twenty-page revision of its accounting manual issued in 1926.

More realistic and more nearly uniform accounting among the affiliates was obviously essential to Jersey's system of decentralized management and central planning and control. The lack of uniformity as well as of adequate accounting records became embarrassingly apparent in the early 1930's during the negotiations for a possible merger with Standard Oil Company of California. Jersey, therefore, asked Price Waterhouse & Co., an accounting firm with offices in many parts of the world, to prepare a comprehensive accounting manual for the parent company and its affiliates and to serve as public auditor for the group as a whole. The *Accounting Manual* was completed in 1934.[20]

The budgeting system which had been adopted in 1926 also proved unworkable, but little progress was made in improving it. Under this system, operating affiliates were requested to prepare statements covering the next year's expected gross income and operating expenses, capital receipts and expenditures, and cash balances at the end of the year. Because of declining prices and volumes and of depression conditions, it would have been difficult at best to make usable forecasts for even a year ahead. However, the affiliates' method of drawing up budgets was still casual and subjective. Budgets were made by department managers and officers who used their own judgment and statistics gathered by assistants generally untrained in statistical techniques. The process, in fact, consisted of the extrapolation of past figures as modified by the individuals' judgment as to trends. When an affiliate's budget had been passed upon by its board of directors, the practice was for an executive to go to the Jersey Board of Directors and, depending not a little on his individual persuasiveness, to obtain or fail to obtain approval for the proposed expenditures.

Although some of Jersey's organizational concepts and managerial arrangements were inadequate, the company nevertheless expanded substantially from 1927 to 1933 and greatly improved its competitive stance. This was accomplished under the leadership of a few men in the parent company and affiliates who had a keen grasp of petroleum logistics and of competitive strategy within the industry. Because of the company's financial strength, the Jersey Board of Directors was able to move boldly when certain circumstances (noted in later chapters) made properties available on what Jersey men believed to be satisfactory terms. However, the greater size and diversity of investments and operations intensified some of the problems faced in 1927. The necessity of consolidating the gains being made obviously required more effective administration of the Jersey Company than was being achieved.

As depression deepened and chaos ruled in a large part of the world oil industry—especially in the United States—the Board of Directors recognized that the reorganization of 1927 had not achieved the intended improvement in the company's administration. Accordingly, in June, 1932, a special committee of five executives below the board level was appointed to suggest "improvements in organization which would increase efficiency and economy."[21] This committee, headed by Frank W. Pierce, submitted its report in January, 1933, in which it criticized past performance and suggested possible improvements. It was especially critical of Standard Oil Company of New Jersey, which operated ineffectively with a large board of directors that often was not consulted on important matters. The report revealed that the president of this affiliate, instead of consulting his company's board, brought matters up for consideration at the daily meetings of the parent company's Executive Committee.[22]

President Teagle, disturbed by the ineffectiveness of the daily meetings at 26 Broadway and aroused by this special report, drafted a memorandum suggesting major changes in the top administrative organization. He introduced it with the following statement of his concept as to how a large organization should function:

The problem which confronts every large organization, particularly one that spreads over various countries and for which it must find a solution, is the difficulty of keeping informed about conditions and of details vital to the conduct of the business sufficiently to manage the business from the head office. Finally, there will come a stage when it is impossible for the head office to keep the actual control necessary for the successful operation of the business. When this stage is reached, there is only one solution, and that is to delegate the actual control of the business to independently operated units, making each unit responsible for its operations in a given territory. It will then be the obligation of the head office to lay down the policy for the various operating units and to control the manner in which the directions so given are carried out. In order to be in a position to do so, the head office must be kept informed currently of conditions existing wherever the units operate and must receive from the operating units information which will enable it to exercise the necessary control. Furthermore, if every operating unit is to be responsible for the operations in its territory, the head office must not interfere with the actual management of any unit.

These are conditions governing the operations of the Jersey Company [Standard Oil Company (New Jersey)]. In addition it is a holding company and should function exclusively as such, delegating to its subsidiary companies the management of and the responsibility for the business in their respective spheres of operation. To do this effectively necessitates the Jersey Board's delegating the responsibility for the actual management of the business to the various subsidiary units, and confining its own activities solely to decisions as to the general policy to be followed by the units and the control of the business as a whole.[23]

Teagle then stated what he thought the duties and responsibilities of the Jersey directors, Executive Committee, and Coordination Committee should be.[24]

After being revised in certain details by the Executive Committee, the memorandum was sent to the other directors in New York for their consideration. They discussed it at meetings held during office hours at 26 Broadway and evenings at the University Club. The directors agreed with the general purposes of the memorandum, but they differed regarding the means of carrying them out.[25] Sadler held that the Jersey board should consist of seven or eight members, from two to four of whom should be "business executives" and the remainder practical operators. He maintained that "decision as to policy made without the advice or thought of the practical operators is one of the greatest dangers of the Jersey Company." Sadler differed with Teagle's recommendation that individual directors should be assigned responsibility for maintaining contact with all the business in given geographic areas. He stood firmly for review by operating functions rather than by areas.[26] A compromise was finally agreed upon whereby advisory or supervisory responsibilities were to be by areas and the Coordination Committee was to analyze and plan operations by functions.

On the very day of the annual stockholders' meeting in June, 1933, a final draft was completed (which will be referred to in later pages as the Memorandum of 1933).[27] It was, in effect, a blueprint for radical revisions of the administrative organization of the Jersey Company with special reference to the parent concern.

ADMINISTRATIVE PERSONNEL, ORGANIZATION, AND TECHNIQUES, 1933–1939

Again the Board of Directors proposed changes in the company's top administration to the annual stockholders' meeting. This was still little more than a formality; as in the recent past, few stockholders attended the meeting. The proposals included lowering the retirement age of men employed by the company, reducing the membership of the board, and changing the responsibilities of the directors. And, as if to symbolize the new relationship of the Jersey board with affiliates, plans were announced for moving the company's headquarters from 26 Broadway to the new Rockefeller Center in midtown Manhattan.[28]

Circumstances did not allow the full realization of the plan to separate the parent-company offices from those of most of the affiliates in New York by moving them to the new RCA Building. The intention had been that most of the departments of the local affiliates and the New York offices of other affiliates should remain at 26 Broadway, but Socony-Vacuum Oil Company, Inc., which owned the building, had an increasing need for space. Because of this situation, many employees of the largest affiliate, Standard Oil Company of New Jersey, were moved to the new location. That company's top administrative offices and many departments, however, remained in lower Manhattan. The New York offices of a number of affiliates operating elsewhere were also moved uptown. This transfer to 30 Rockefeller Plaza was completed by the end of 1933. At that time about 900 men and women, approximately two-thirds of the employees of Jersey and affiliates formerly at the historic home of Standard Oil, were established in new quarters in Rockefeller Center.[29]

Some of the changes recommended in the Memorandum of 1933 were put into effect at the next directors' meeting.[30] Although the new plan encountered objections and was subsequently modified in certain respects, it was generally acceptable because it gave promise of being more suitable for a company with widely scattered affiliates than the former organization had been. Its essential features were derived from one underlying purpose: to separate the parent company administration altogether from the management of operating affiliates.

The adoption of a change in the retirement age for men brought a reduction in the number of directors. It also expedited the transition throughout the Jersey companies from the traditional ways of many older executives to the scientific methods of younger and more highly trained men. The age of retirement was lowered from sixty-five to sixty, with the provision that individuals might be retained until they reached sixty-two years, which then became the mandatory retirement age. Four Jersey directors—Black, Clark, Riedemann, and Senior—as well as many executives in key positions had to retire in 1933 because of this new rule. However, the plan lasted only six months; at the end of 1933, the limits were raised to voluntary retirement at sixty-two and mandatory retirement at sixty-five years.[31]

In accordance with the Memorandum of 1933, all but one of the Jersey directors who also were executives of affiliates resigned from the latter positions. The exception was G. Harrison Smith, who became Imperial's president in 1933 but continued until 1940 to hold his parent-company directorship. President Farish resigned as president of Humble Oil & Refining Company and moved to New York. Those directors who had top executive responsibilities for affiliates having their offices in New York City similarly gave up their posts in the affiliates. The three remaining European directors also resigned from their positions as officers of affiliates.[32]

Within a year more changes were made in the membership of the Jersey board. James A. Moffett, Jr., resigned in July, 1933. The reason for his resignation as stated in the press was the inadvisability of having two directors, Teagle and Moffett, on one government committee in Washington. Another consideration was Moffett's disagreement with the rest of the board over the question of price fixing for the petroleum industry under the National Industrial Recovery Act, then a subject of controversy in both industrial and governmental circles. In November, 1933, Ralph W. Gallagher was elected director. He was president of the East Ohio Gas Company and had recently been given charge of the natural gas business of Jersey interests in the Northeast. He promptly resigned these responsibilities in conformance with the new policy.[33] In the spring of 1934 the three remaining European directors left the Jersey board. Hurll retired because of ill health. Mowinckel and Seidel left to devote their full time to an organization to be set up under the International Association (Petroleum Industry) Limited, incorporated in August, 1934, to assist Jersey's foreign affiliates.[34]

By June, 1934, the Jersey Board of Directors consisted of only ten members, which was to be the number for the next five years. When Christy Payne retired and Robert G. Stewart resigned in 1935, their places were filled by two specialists with long records of Jersey service: Donald L. Harper, who had been associated with foreign sales for many years and since 1929 had been president of Standard Oil Export Corporation; and Thomas C. McCobb, who had risen to the Jersey comptrollership. After Director Swain's death in 1937, Wallace E. Pratt was elected a director of the company. Pratt then gave up a vice-presidency in Humble Oil & Refining Company and moved to New York. This was the last addition to the board in the 1930's.[35]

The Board of Directors thus was gradually becoming a "mix" of men well suited to governing a company with such large and diverse operations in an industry and a world in transition. Producing had the strongest representation: Sadler, Farish, and Pratt had been concerned principally in the exploration and production branch of the oil business. Marketing also had a considerable representation on the board: Teagle, Smith, and Harper had risen in that field. Bedford's experience had been mostly in the promotion and sale of specialty products. Refining after 1933 came to be represented only by Harden, who was not a refiner but had served with the Manufacturing Committee of the early 1920's and later with the Coordination Committee. Director McCobb had been a leader in accounting, and Gallagher, as noted, had been an executive in the natural gas companies.

Most of these directors had risen above their specialties to attain a comprehensive view of the company's interests. Most of them were committed to the technological change then under way in the oil industry. Some also proved to be especially sensitive to the shifts in public opinion and government policy that were going on in the 1930's. Teagle and Sadler had long been progressive leaders in the company. Farish, a lawyer by training, had presided over Humble during years of notable growth and technological development and had become a national leader in the conservation movement. Pratt had a distinguished reputation as a petroleum geologist and had been one of Humble's outstanding executives.[36] He was a creative thinker with a broad view of the company's functions and responsibilities. Gallagher brought special assets from his long experience with natural gas companies, which because of their public-utility character had to maintain close relations with both public and government. He was also conscious of the need for regular reports on operations and for observing organization patterns and lines of authority.

Teagle continued to serve as Jersey's president until 1937. He then retired officially on an annuity but remained with the company as director and chairman of the Board of Directors. Farish, who had been chairman of the board and member of the Executive Committee since 1933, succeeded Teagle as president and as chairman of that committee.

In 1933 the Board of Directors was relieved of a large part of its former load by the assignment of more responsibility to the Executive Committee. The committee took over much of the board's work of making day-to-day decisions and of gathering information to guide its action. In fact, the committee rose to a position of central importance. This change was in accordance with the Memorandum of 1933, which gave it broad responsibility and authority and specifically assigned the latter to the committee as a unit. The memorandum stated: "The authority of the Executive Committee shall rest with the committee as a whole, and not with its members acting as individuals. Correspondence for the committee shall be addressed 'Executive Committee,' and not to individual members thereof; likewise, outgoing correspondence shall be signed in the name of the committee."[37]

According to the memorandum, the committee should represent the general interest of Jersey and its affiliates. No individual member should have any managerial duty or function as the head or adviser of any department. This restriction was deemed necessary because the committee "must consider all questions from the standpoint of the general interest of the company, and must devote its time to the study of all conditions affecting the oil industry worldwide, as well as of existing and potential problems in order to plan the future of the company."[38] The memorandum further strengthened the committee's hand by providing that in the absence of a member the committee itself—not members of the board, as previously—be empowered to "designate an alternate to serve as a substitute, such substitute to have the same duties and responsibilities as a regular member."[39]

The memorandum spelled out these duties and responsibilities: First of all, "within the limits of the general policy as agreed upon from time to time by the Board," the committee was "to decide all questions directly or indirectly affecting the interests of the company." It was also to "keep informed of the world petroleum situation and conditions affecting the same, and to formulate for Board approval the general policies of the company." It was to keep "in close and constant touch, through the Treasurer and Comptroller, with questions involving the finance of the company, advising the Board currently on all matters of importance in that connection." It was to pass on all budget expenditures, "in line with general policy approved of by the Board." It was to be responsible for all matters affecting the public relations of the company and relations with stockholders. It was to "pass upon recommendations as to executive personnel and to handle important salary and wage questions, current annuities and pensions." It was to be "responsible for the corporate structure of all subsidiaries." And it was to have authority to assign specific areas of responsibility to individual members of the Jersey board.[40]

After the reorganization of 1933, the Executive Committee included all the senior officers of the company except Sadler, who was chairman of the Coordination Committee. The resignation of Moffett left four members. The limiting of its membership to directors without departmental responsibilities was finally achieved in 1935, when Payne retired and Swain gave up his post as general counsel to become vice-president.[41] The retirement of Teagle from the committee and the death of Swain in 1937 left two vacancies. Pratt and Gallagher then became members. Henceforth, the Executive Committee consisted of Farish as chairman, Harden as vice-chairman, Gallagher, and Pratt.[42]

The practice of keeping a regular record of the daily meetings of the Executive Committee was introduced by its secretary, Adrian C. Minton, who also served as Jersey's corporate secretary. Earlier, only brief minutes were kept of formal action that for legal reasons had to be recorded.

Secretary Minton went beyond this legal requirement and included short statements about matters discussed and action taken.[43]

The Executive Committee, operating under broader and more clearly defined powers and with a changed membership, functioned far more effectively after 1933 than it had in the preceding six years.[44] The members could give more time to the committee because they were called away less frequently than earlier to serve on governmental committees in Washington and to participate in discussions and negotiations having to do with the acquisition of companies. The committee also had far better information about affiliates and operations because of improved reports from the companies and the assistance of the Coordination Committee with its greater attention to the compilation of exact data and to more precise economic analysis. With new authority, new personnel, and new assistance, the Executive Committee assumed leadership in changing the Jersey companies from an unwieldy conglomeration to a more closely knit whole.

The Memorandum of 1933 made a specific recommendation as to the means by which the Board of Directors should maintain contact with affiliates: "Each member of the Board not a regular member of the Executive Committee shall be charged with supervisory responsibility in connection with the activities of operating affiliates." This recommendation was based on the following concept of decentralization:

It is the clear intent that intracorporate operations . . . shall be conducted by the respective Boards of Directors and executives of the operating subsidiaries; in this way, subject to the general policy agreed upon from time to time by the Jersey Board, authority and responsibility for the details of current operations shall rest where the law places them—and, furthermore, individual initiative will be built up and executive experience acquired. It is obvious that successful management of the current business cannot be assured in any given area unless all interests such as producing, refining, and marketing in such area are placed under one managing control.[45]

Several directors were given such individual assignments. Bedford was made responsible for contact with the specialty companies; Sadler for two integrated domestic affiliates, Standard Oil Company of New Jersey and Standard Oil Company of Louisiana; Harden for the Latin American companies other than those belonging to Imperial; and Gallagher for the natural gas companies. The three European directors constituted a committee to advise the managers of affiliates in Europe. Director Smith, as president of Imperial and International, represented the Canadian, Peruvian, and Colombian affiliates on the Jersey board.[46]

However, this design for contact with affiliates through individual directors was not fully carried out in the 1930's. Not enough directors were available after Harden and Gallagher became members of the Executive Committee and the three European executives left the Jersey board. Also, the new organization set up in London in 1936 under the International Association (Petroleum Industry) Limited thereafter performed for the foreign companies—except Imperial and its Latin American affiliates—the functions which individual directors and the Coordination Committee performed for the domestic ones. (See Chapter 11.) Harper of the Jersey board was the contact director for this association until his retirement.[47] By late 1937, only two directors, Bedford and Sadler, continued to supervise individual affiliates.

The principle of decentralization of the management of operations adopted in 1927 gradually became more widely effective throughout the Jersey companies. Some affiliates, which had formerly maintained a considerable measure of independence of Jersey, became better informed about the general policies of the parent company. Others, which had leaned heavily on Jersey, became more experienced in handling their own affairs. Certain conflicts of interest also were resolved. For example, in the operation of domestic refineries, such difficulties were lessened by electing directors in common for Standard Oil Company of New Jersey and Standard of Louisiana and by drawing up a contract covering the sale of Humble's refinery products to the former.[48]

An investigation of the parent company–affiliate relationship was undertaken in 1936.[49] A group of representatives of the Coordination Committee and affiliates subsequently met with the Executive Committee, as reported in the committee's minutes, "to discuss the corporate relationship which should be maintained by the company with its subsidiaries." The minutes stated: "Particular emphasis was placed upon the fact that since 1927 subsidiary companies have been adequately staffed with personnel to perform all functions pertaining to operating management, leaving to the Jersey Company [the parent] the assumption only of functions inherent in its status as a shareholder."[50] It was recognized that management had not always assumed its full responsibilities, but that progress had been made.

Side by side with the broader application of the principle of decentralization of management—and as a necessary corollary to it—came more rational planning and closer coordination of the operations of all Jersey affiliates under the policies determined by the parent company's Board of Directors. In this development, the Coordination Committee played a major role. Its action was in line with its responsibility, as defined by the Memorandum of 1933, for "coordinating the activities of all producing and refining units, coordinating supplies to marketing companies, and currently compiling such information on producing and refining as is necessary for a complete picture of the company's entire operations."[51]

The Coordination Committee's membership was a significant departure from the old committee composed of directors. With Director Sadler as chairman, the group was still tied closely to the company's top governing body. Two other directors, one also a manager in operations, were members for a short time. But all the other members were either officers or managers of operating affiliates or full-time specialists. They were expected to devote more time to the work of the committee than the directors had been able to do. This change in membership reflected Sadler's conviction that operating men should have a strong hand in planning, and also his concern that operations be carried on with the lowest cost and greatest efficiency possible.

Table 2:   **MEMBERS OF THE COORDINATION COMMITTEE AND THEIR PRINCIPAL RESPONSIBILITIES, 1933–1939**

Member	Year Appointed	Principal Responsibilities
Everit J. Sadler	1925	Chairman of the committee; vice-president and director, Standard Oil Company (New Jersey).
Orville Harden	1928	Director, Standard Oil Company (New Jersey). (Membership terminated in 1934.)
Harry L. Shoemaker	1930	Secretary of the committee; general manager, Coordination Department.
Stewart P. Coleman	1933	Economic analyst under title of Manufacturing Representative.
Frank A. Howard	1933	President, Standard Oil Development Company.
Robert G. Stewart	1933	Director, Standard Oil Company (New Jersey); general manager of marketing for four domestic affiliates (left the company in 1935).
Frank W. Abrams	1934	President, Standard Oil Company of New Jersey.
Harry H. Hill	1934	Staff member of the Producing Department in New York.
Robert T. Haslam	1935	General manager of marketing for four domestic affiliates. (Membership terminated in 1936.)
George W. Gordon	1936	New York head of foreign refining.
Edgar A. Holbein	1936	Manager of tank-car sales for four domestic affiliates.
Eugene Holman	1936	General manager of the Producing Department in New York.
W. R. Mook	1936	New York head of foreign marketing.
Clarence H. Lieb	1938	Assistant manager of the Producing Department in New York.

Source: Standard Oil Company (New Jersey): Coordination Committee Membership, 1931–1952, by H. L. Shoemaker, Jan. 17, 1952; Organization Manual, for the years from 1943 to 1950, inclusive; circular letters, 1925–1950.

Various branches of operations were represented on the committee. Among the members were men who held high managerial posts in production, refining research, refinery operations, and marketing.[52] Three members headed departments in New York with over-all supervisory and advisory responsibilities in production, foreign refining, and foreign marketing.

The rising importance of staff functions to the work of the committee is indicated by the fact that three members were staff specialists. Harry L. Shoemaker, who continued to serve as the committee's secretary, was also general manager of the growing group known as the Coordination Department. Harry H. Hill, who had been a research engineer in the Bureau of Mines and had joined the Producing Department in New York to report on petroleum engineering and on production statistics, became a member in 1934. Dr. Stewart P. Coleman, formerly head of research and economic analysis with Humble, was brought to New York in 1933, with the title of Manufacturing Representative, to institute procedures in economic analysis similar to those developed within Humble.[53]

In only a few years, the Coordination Committee rose to a strategic position in the company's administration. Sadler, its chairman, came to be known as "the father of coordination." More than any other executive, he influenced Jersey's then unique philosophy of coordination, which has been characterized as "the systematic application of group executive judgment to long-range problems."[54] Sadler himself described the Coordination Committee as an "advisory, analytical body from an economic and technical standpoint."[55] He held that its general function should be to help plan supplies that would meet estimated product requirements at the lowest cost on delivery at the point of consumption. The function being worldwide in scope, the committee gradually became more than a planning body in New York and began to gather representatives of affiliates from around the world in annual conferences to discuss matters of importance to the parent company and its affiliates.[56] This type of conference became an essential part of the coordination effort.

The core function of the Coordination Committee was to serve as an analytical and advisory group for current operations and long-range planning. The committee met regularly once a week in New York and held additional meetings whenever necessary. It studied current levels of performance, as compared with past experience and future expectations, so that it could watch the flow of supplies and inform operating groups of possible shortages or proposed changes in sources or outlets. It furnished the Executive Committee and the Board of Directors with information and recommendations essential to decisions on capital expenditures.

The procedures for drawing up the over-all annual capital budget of the Jersey companies gradually became more formal and more analytical than they had been. The affiliates prepared their own budgets, arranged by departments, and submitted them to the parent company. By the later 1930's, their budgeting was becoming more soundly based than earlier. For example, Humble in 1937 adopted a formal procedure for preparing both its operating and its capital budget. Under this plan, the top management of the individual departments, consulting with the director in charge, prepared the departments' budgets, which included estimates of the amount of business for the budget year and of capital and operating expenditures. In 1939 Humble began to use forecasts based on statistical studies of trends in the oil industry and the general economy that would have a bearing on the company's business. Standard Oil Company of New Jersey similarly in the 1930's established more rational procedures for preparing its budgets.

The affiliates submitted their capital budgets to Jersey's Budget Department, of which Richardson Pratt became head in 1934. These were combined by functions and also into a single budget. This combining of many budgets was made practicable by the affiliates' adoption of the accounting standards and procedures laid down by the new *Accounting Manual* of 1934.[57]

The Coordination Committee made an intensive examination of the comprehensive functional budgets and the total budget. In this process of study it conferred with officers and other representatives of affiliates. For the cost studies and the economic analyses which it needed in order to evaluate planned expenditures and to draw up alternate plans, the Coordination Committee looked to the Coordination Department.

Dr. Coleman and his staff of that department applied and further refined the techniques of economic analysis developed at Humble by Coleman and such engineering associates as H. W. Ferguson and J. W. Harrell with the advice of Dr. W. K. Lewis of the Massachusetts Institute of Technology. Utilizing these techniques, the department's staff could weigh possible alternate sources and methods. It made studies of the cost of different crude oils, plants, and processes. It studied incremental costs for various volume levels of operations and the replacement cost of the crude oil used. It calculated the allocation of costs to joint products, employing the replacement (or opportunity) cost method developed at

Humble—for example, instead of assigning a cost to heating oil in proportion to its sales value as compared with that of gasoline, the cost was figured in terms of the gasoline that might have been made instead. The group also analyzed various combinations of crude supply, processes, plants, and other factors through the successive steps from the crude source to the consumers' market in order to find the lowest-cost combination of factors.

The staff group did not, however, seek the elusive goal of the least expensive and most efficient operation at every step and in every place. It considered competition and the state of the market, but new capital expenditures had to offer sufficiently lower operating expense to justify the increase in fixed costs that would be incurred. No situation was considered static. The general goal was to operate at the lowest over-all cost in a dynamic situation.[58]

A constant problem of the Coordination Committee was how best to obtain estimates of future demand and supply. As already noted, forecasts of the demand for and supply of oil products had in the past been made by the officers and managers of Jersey and its affiliates on the basis of statistics gathered by assistants and of their own judgment. The Coordination Committee for a time depended on the estimates drawn up by functional groups for their particular operations: by Harper's office for foreign marketing and by the Producing Department and the Coordination Department of Standard Oil Company of New Jersey. This method proved unsatisfactory.[59] To be sure, any forecasting was precarious in the 1930's, especially for foreign countries, where it was virtually impossible to estimate the direction of political and economic change. In addition, there was a lack of uniformity and depth in the ways estimates were arrived at; it was still a common practice to extrapolate past statistical series, a method especially unsatisfactory in the unstable oil industry and economies of the time. The Producing Department in New York in the late 1930's developed a sounder procedure, which involved estimating the trends of those factors that would affect future supply and demand. The marketing group in New York also improved its estimates of sales, a result to which the new marketing research organization contributed. (See Chapter 10.) In 1937 the Coordination Committee was given responsibility for making the estimates if the various functional groups could not work out satisfactory figures in cooperation with each other.[60]

The Department of Economics, established in 1940 under Dr. Coleman, was to provide a more sophisticated and uniform handling of this problem. Coleman was then instructed "to assemble, consolidate, analyze, and interpret information relating to the petroleum industry, and more particularly to the business of company interests, worldwide." Departments or sections of affiliates were invited to cooperate closely with the Department of Economics.[61] Although this was a step toward the better forecasting that was essential to sound planning, World War II interrupted the development of new procedures by shifting control of oil-industry operations to government agencies.

The Coordination Committee submitted its findings and recommendations on budgets to the Executive Committee. This committee studied the proposed capital budgets in the light of the estimates of future business and the recommendations of the Coordination Committee. It also consulted with representatives of leading affiliates. The functional totals and the grand totals were then considered in relation to available funds. There was as yet no systematic procedure for forecasting what the Jersey Company's financial resources would be in the year or years ahead; the funds available were generally thought of as current depreciation and depletion charges plus one-half of net earnings. Further funds could be obtained by borrowing outside the companies, but Jersey was conservative in assuming long-term loan obligations.

The Executive Committee reported its findings and recommendations to the Board of Directors, which made the final examination of the proposed budgets. The directors gave their views to the affiliates. But they left to each company the final decisions about its budget. Although the parent company board obviously influenced the decisions of the affiliates, actually it preferred to do so by an extensive system of consultation and "education" rather than by exercising its prerogative as a stockholder or by bringing pressure as a creditor.

Such consultation and education took many forms. The advisory directors and the London Council of the International Association (Petroleum Industry) Limited had these functions as their special responsibilities. The Executive Committee and the Coordination Committee, as observed above, conferred with officers and others representing affiliates, particularly on budgets. The Coordination Committee helped train young men in its ideas and techniques and also sponsored general conferences of representatives of affiliates.

This method of training merits emphasis. Sadler was especially concerned with the training of young men. As chairman of the Coordination Committee, he encouraged the members to bring their assistants to the committee's weekly meetings; the visitors lined the walls of the conference room while the members sat around the table. The committee's staff department also worked with young men, teaching them methods of economic analysis. This practice of exposing nonmembers to the thinking and the techniques of the Coordination Committee and its staff department proved valuable in preparing them for similar work in affiliates. It was to demonstrate its practical value further in later years in staffing the various functional coordination departments established within the parent company.

Of signal value from the very first were the annual conferences arranged by the Coordination Committee. These meetings of top-level officers, managers, and specialists from the affiliates and the parent company became an important instrument for coordinating the thinking and experience of the whole Jersey Company. At these conferences major problems were discussed, important innovations were made known, and experience and ideas were exchanged. Chairman Sadler believed that such communication was essential to the achievement of maximum decentralization, and this became the general attitude of Jersey's leaders.

The first meeting was held at the University Club in New York in October, 1934, and subsequent meetings followed each spring. For many years, they were held in the New York area. These conferences lasted a week, with three sessions each day. Many of the sessions were held in two sections. One, concerned mostly with producing, was led by Eugene Holman, manager of the Producing Department in New York. The other, headed by President Frank W. Abrams of Standard Oil Company of New Jersey, considered refining and marketing. General problems were discussed and possible future programs were outlined during the week. The number attending the conference in 1939—the last meeting before World War II—was 132.[62]

By 1939 the coordination of the activities of Jersey's affiliates had made great strides. At the sixth annual conference in that year, Director Sadler recalled how "years ago our business was handled in a very secretive manner" and a "relatively small group knew all about the business and the other executives were simply told what to do." Although this system worked fairly well when the operations were smaller, the "growing complexity of the business was recognized" and the methods were changed. The first general meeting at the University Club, Sadler said, had shown that executives in the various branches were hampered by a "considerable lack of understanding of the problems of others." As a result of this discovery, he added, "it was decided to furnish from a central office to our key men all information pertaining to the business." The Jersey Board of Directors decided "to give out our most confidential information" in order to help men throughout the organization increase their effectiveness in their own areas of responsibility as well as to cooperate more fully and effectively in the general interest. From such beginnings had grown a method of communication which was contributing increasingly to the unity in diversity—or coordinated decentralization —that had been attained within the Jersey Company.[63]

By the outbreak of war in 1939, Standard Oil Company (New Jersey) had greatly improved its system for administering its large and diverse interests. The management of operations had become decentralized. All but one member of the Board of Directors were associated with the parent company only and hence could devote their full attention to matters of over-all concern. The Executive Committee acted for the board in day-to-day administrative matters and made investigations preliminary to board action. The Coordination Committee served as an indispensable arm of these top governing bodies in planning and coordination. Both parent company and affiliates benefited from better methods of cost analysis and more careful planning of capital expenditures and from group-wide communication of ideas, experiences, and methods. But there was one serious weakness: inadequate liaison with affiliates by members of the Board of Directors.

Important revisions in Jersey policy and in all branches of operations paralleled these developments in administration. Changes in all branches of operations went on simultaneously over the years. These were meshed in a related network of adjustment and innovation. But for the sake of clarity, they can best be considered separately. Attention is directed first to developments in production, a branch of operations that was of special concern to the parent company's leaders in 1927.

Chapter 3

Producing Policies and Programs, 1927–1939

IT MAY SEEM PARADOXICAL that, when oil was abundant and the industry's inventories were rising and prices falling, the major concern of President Teagle and his associates in 1927 was with their company's crude oil supply. Actually, their concern was based on a realistic estimation of Jersey's long-term profit opportunities. The most urgent need of the company, they believed, was assurance for the future of adequate supplies of crude oil at competitive costs.[1]

This assurance was important to all operations. Because storage tanks, pipelines, tankers, refineries, and other facilities operated, up to their optimum capacity, at diminishing unit costs with increasing volume, it was important to utilize those facilities as near to capacity as possible. And since crude oil constituted so large a part of the total expense of refineries, even a small disadvantage in its price might make the difference between refining profit and loss. Finally, supplying marketers with products at costs that would make possible a profit margin was essential to maintaining Jersey's position in the market.

The men who led in shaping new policies and programs to solve the problems of the Jersey Company's oil supply were President Teagle and directors Sadler and Farish, with Riedemann playing an influential secondary role. Teagle, who had a world view of the oil industry, was a farsighted planner and the company's chief negotiator in the acquisition of foreign producing properties. Sadler was its leader in foreign exploration and production. Farish was its outstanding authority on the domestic producing industry. All were strong advocates of the expansion of Jersey's oil reserves and production. Sadler, however, maintained that the solution of the problems of crude oil supply should be sought in the area of competitive costs; Teagle and Farish held that broad attacks on certain industry problems were also required; Riedemann stressed strategic considerations in terms of worldwide competition.

In 1927 these leaders and their associates on the Board of Directors set the company on virtually a new course. In the next few years they greatly expanded Jersey's foreign producing properties by purchasing companies that already had crude oil reserves and producing operations. They supported the affiliates in the United States in increasing their reserves and production. And they participated both at home and abroad in efforts to solve industry problems. Over the years, they also developed a more effective organization for coordinating production and advising affiliates in this branch of operations.[2]

INVESTMENTS IN TWO HEMISPHERES, 1927–1939

The Jersey Company in 1927 produced approximately 6.5 per cent of the world's crude oil, but supplied between 12 and 13 per cent of the products sold in world markets. The average daily net production of its affiliates was 189,900 barrels, of which 112,400 were produced in the United States and 77,500 in foreign countries. Of this foreign production, 36,700 barrels were produced in Colombia, 21,300 in Peru, 9,800 in Mexico, 4,200 in Romania, and 3,400 in the Dutch East Indies. In the same year, Jersey sold a daily average of approximately 430,000 barrels of products—245,000 at home and 185,000 abroad.[3]

The company's output of crude oil was far below that of its leading international competitor and less advantageously located with respect to markets. The Royal Dutch–Shell group averaged 328,000 barrels a day in 1927. Their production was favorably located with respect to markets: 127,000 barrels in the United States, 83,000 in Venezuela, 29,000 in Mexico, 12,000 in Romania, 61,000 in the Dutch East Indies, 13,000 in Sarawak, and 3,000 elsewhere. This British-Dutch group was utilizing its Mexican and Venezuelan oil to compete with Jersey in North American, South American, and European markets. Anglo-Persian Oil Company, Limited, with a daily production of 112,000 barrels in Persia (later Iran), also surpassed Jersey's foreign production. The Burmah Oil Company, Limited, a stockholder in Anglo-Persian, was itself averaging about 22,000 barrels a day in Burma. These three companies were combining their selling in much of Asia, and Royal Dutch–Shell and Anglo-Persian were marketing jointly in Europe; all drew upon the most favorably located sources of supply.[4]

Two American companies had larger production abroad than Jersey. Standard Oil Company (Indiana), with an average daily production in

1927 of 44,000 barrels in Venezuela and 68,000 in Mexico, was a rival of Anglo-Persian for second place in foreign production. Gulf Oil Corporation produced a daily average of 38,000 barrels in Venezuela and 8,000 in Mexico. Both companies were somewhat of a threat to established foreign marketers: inasmuch as their outlets were inadequate to absorb their rapidly increasing supplies, they were driving hard to acquire new markets.[5]

Jersey itself as the parent company, although interested in acquiring new producing properties wherever feasible, focused its own efforts mainly on the expansion of its producing interests abroad. It attempted, unsuccessfully, to negotiate a merger with Standard Oil Company of California, which had extensive production on the Pacific Coast of the United States. On the whole, however, it left the expansion of reserves and production at home to its experienced affiliates, particularly depending on Humble Oil & Refining Company, which was operating in the most dynamic oil region in the United States.[6] Abroad, Jersey looked primarily to the Middle East and Venezuela, two oil provinces of great promise.

By a strange turn of fate, at the very time when the company was planning a stepped-up search for oil properties outside the United States, it missed an opportunity that might have given it a firm foothold in the Middle East. Early in 1927 the head of the Producing Department in New York refused an offer of options on government concessions in that region.[7]

These options had been obtained by Major Frank Holmes as a representative of the Eastern and General Syndicate, Ltd., a group of London mining engineers. Holmes, a New Zealand veteran of the British campaign in the Middle East in World War I, had been commissioned by the London syndicate in 1920 to search for potential mining or oil lands in the region of the Persian Gulf. He armed himself with all the information he could obtain on possible prospects in that part of the world. He learned of a report of a promising anticline on Bahrain Islands—issued in 1908 by the Indian Geological Survey—by Dr. Guy Ellcock Pilgrim, a scientist of international reputation. He had the advice of Professor T. George Madgwick of Birmingham University, who had had wide experience in the search for oil. After several years in the Middle East, Holmes returned to London at the end of 1925 with an option on an oil concession on the Bahrain Islands, on which Professor Madgwick had examined the surface structure. He had also obtained options on al-Hasa in Saudi Arabia and the Neutral Zone between Saudi Arabia and Kuwait. In addition he had established good relations with the Sheik of Kuwait. Options on nearly all of the Persian Gulf region were subject to the approval of the British government.

Major Holmes and his principals offered their options to several oil companies. They first attempted to sell them in London, but neither Anglo-Persian nor Royal Dutch–Shell was interested. The heads of these two companies may well have been influenced by the fact that their concerns had heavy obligations to develop concessions they already held, especially in the Middle East, at the very time when there was a growing threat of a world oversupply of petroleum. They maintained, however, that there was no prospect of oil on Bahrain, the only area on which Holmes presented any geologic data—the report of a surface survey by Professor Madgwick.

Having failed to sell the syndicate's options in London, Holmes went to New York. The validity of the al-Hasa and Neutral Zone options was by that time questionable, and negotiations with Kuwait had not been completed. The Bahrain option was clearly valid. Holmes, together with an associate in New York, first approached Gulf Oil Corporation. Gulf was interested, but it refused the offer. The geologic information provided by Professor Madgwick was not sufficient to justify the investment.

In January, 1927, Holmes's associate offered the options to C. Stuart Morgan, Jersey's special adviser on the region. Morgan had come to New York in 1922, on the invitation of President Teagle, to join Jersey as an expert adviser on its contemplated entry into what was then called the Near East. A British officer in Africa and the Near East in World War I, Morgan immediately after the war had joined the executive staff of Anglo-Persian's operating management in Persia. He was engaged in that capacity when Teagle first came to know of him. His early contact as adviser to Jersey in New York was with President Teagle, but he soon became associated with Director Sadler inasmuch as foreign exploration came under the Producing Department.

Morgan was impressed by the possibilities of the Holmes offer, and he recommended to the Producing Department that a Jersey geologic party, then on a field trip in Somaliland in eastern Africa, be sent to Bahrain to make a survey. However, Director Sadler knew that companies with long experience in the Middle East had already turned down the offer, and other members of the department were similarly not impressed by the prospect—one reason given was that Bahrain was too small to be worth the expense and risk involved. There was the further consideration that

Bahrain was under British control. At this time, Jersey's own interest was focused on Latin America, especially Venezuela, and the company was also negotiating for participation in Turkish Petroleum Company. The offer of the Holmes options was refused, and the matter was dropped without further consideration.

In November of the same year, Gulf Oil, which had sent an exploration party to Bahrain, signed two contracts with the Eastern and General Syndicate which Holmes represented. One was for the purchase of the Bahrain option for $50,000 and an overriding royalty to the syndicate on commercial production. The other contract gave Gulf options—if revalidated or completed—on al-Hasa, the Neutral Zone, and Kuwait. This was the first in a series of developments that were later to become of great importance to Standard Oil Company (New Jersey).

Jersey's first successful move after 1927 to expand its foreign producing interests came in Venezuela, a country with large known oil resources well located with respect to markets in the United States and Europe. Through its affiliate, Standard Oil Company of Venezuela, the parent company had spent more than $27,000,000 without developing any commercial production, and President Teagle and his associates were no longer willing to wait while geologists explored and drillers drilled wells in search of oil.[8] They wanted new production at once, even the heavy crude from the Maracaibo basin in Venezuela, to replace the oil they could no longer obtain in sufficient quantity from the shrinking output of Mexican operations. Hence they began to look for a successful independent company with producing properties in Venezuela that might be purchased on reasonable terms.

A promising prospect at the end of 1927 was The Creole Syndicate, which had production from fields on the edge of Lake Maracaibo. This company, incorporated in Delaware in 1920 by a group of promoters in New York, had been fortunate in the acquisition and development of government concessions in Venezuela. It had financed itself largely by the sale of stock through Naphen & Company and Blair & Company, Inc., in New York. Not being an operating concern, Creole had arranged with Venezuela Gulf Oil Corporation to drill on its narrow strip off the shore of Lake Maracaibo. When commercial quantities had been discovered in 1925, Creole had sold its share of the oil to Venezuela Gulf. This successful development had led the company to plan to acquire more Venezuelan concessions and to seek to obtain better prices for oil than it was receiving under its contract with Gulf. In order to get such prices, however, it would have to provide transportation from Lake Maracaibo to a terminal where ocean-going tankers could dock. Creole's officers learned that they could arrange with Lago Oil & Transport Company, Limited, for the use of certain facilities on the Dutch island of Aruba. By the end of 1927 they were looking for funds with which to purchase tankers as well as to acquire new concessions.[9]

Knowing of Creole's need, Jersey opened negotiations for the purchase of the company. The discussions progressed rapidly. In February, 1928, the Creole board considered Jersey's proposals favorably; it called a stockholders' meeting in March to approve them. The terms proposed included changing the company's name to Creole Petroleum Corporation, increasing the number of its authorized shares to 6,000,000, and discussing its acquisition of Standard Oil Company of Venezuela. When the stockholders had approved these and other terms, Creole's officers completed the transaction.

The two parties signed a contract on June 30, 1928, retroactive to April 1. In order to provide working capital, Jersey agreed to purchase, over a period of five years, 800,000 shares of the newly created Creole stock at $10 a share; it also agreed to transfer all the shares of the Standard Oil Company of Venezuela to Creole in exchange for 2,225,000 shares of the latter. This at once gave Jersey a majority ownership. The net value of the consolidated company at the end of 1928 amounted to nearly $55,000,000, two-thirds representing the value of the original Creole Syndicate and the remainder that of Standard of Venezuela and its concession-holding affiliate, the American British Oil Company.[10]

As agreed, during the negotiations, Jersey took over the management of Creole and provided most of its directors. Jersey's Sadler was elected president, an office which he continued to hold until 1933.[11]

In 1928 Jersey also acquired a small company operating on the British island of Trinidad, the Trinidad Oil Fields Operating Company, Limited. It arranged to purchase this concern for $2,000,000 through Beacon Oil Company, which Jersey was then negotiating to buy. (See Chapter 10.) With its many surface evidences of petroleum, including seepages and pitch lakes, Trinidad had interested oilmen for more than six decades. After the discovery of a commercial field there in 1907, production had grown steadily on the island; it exceeded that of Venezuela until 1923. The southwestern tip of Trinidad and the waters of the shallow Gulf of Paria were thought to have as great promise as Lake Maracaibo's eastern shore and contiguous waters. Whatever its oil potential, Trinidad was favorably located for the development of the business of supplying fuel oil for ships, which would utilize a large portion of the products refined from its heavy oil.[12]

Only about a month after the Creole purchase, Jersey also obtained an interest in a company with oil production in the Middle East. This was the Turkish Petroleum Company, Limited—later to become the Iraq Petroleum Company, Limited. In 1925 Turkish Petroleum had obtained confirmation of a large concession in the Kingdom of Iraq, which had formerly been a part of the Turkish Empire, and two years later it had discovered the great Kirkuk field.* Jersey was one of five American companies that obtained ownership participation in this Middle East concern through Near East Development Corporation.[13]

The entry of the American companies into this enterprise in the Middle East culminated long negotiations with the owners of the Turkish Petroleum Company.[14] The company's original owners were an individual, Calouste S. Gulbenkian, and three companies: Royal Dutch–Shell, Anglo-Persian, and Compagnie Française des Pétroles. In the last two of these companies, their respective home governments had a large ownership interest. Gulbenkian had conducted the early negotiations among these owners and with the Turkish government and had subscribed for 15 per cent of the company's original stock. Later, however, he had exchanged his stock for a 5 per cent "beneficial interest"—that is, 5 per cent of all future benefits flowing to the company with no further cost to him.

The United States government had supported the efforts of the American companies to enter this oil enterprise. Its interest sprang especially from the fact that the United States Navy had been converted to burning oil, which made it almost imperative to have that fuel available in the Orient as well as in the Western Hemisphere. This country had still a broader motivation, however: ever since World War I it had been seeking to persuade the British and Netherlands governments to accept the open-door policy in the territories they controlled in the Middle East and the Far East.

Because of its support of this policy, the United States Department of State had opposed one condition of the American companies' entry into

* For an account of the international rivalries and the complex issues involved in the organization of the Turkish Petroleum Company, Limited, and also for the negotiations leading to the American companies' participation, see Chapter 11 of *History of Standard Oil Company (New Jersey), 1911–1927, The Resurgent Years,* by George Sweet Gibb and Evelyn H. Knowlton.

Turkish Petroleum: that they agree not to obtain, independently of the other owners of the company, oil or concessions in the vast area formerly within the boundaries of the old Turkish Empire. This condition had been agreed upon by the original owners of Turkish Petroleum in 1914; it was essentially a compromise between conflicting national interests in the region. This self-denying restriction had thus originated long before the Americans took an active interest in Turkish Petroleum Company. Moreover, it applied only to those who subscribed to it as participants in the company and did not mean closing the region to others who might obtain concessions there. However, so strong was Britain's position under treaties with local rulers that the entry of an American company into most parts of the Middle East would require approval of the British.

The Department of State finally unconditionally agreed to the acceptance by the American companies of this restrictive provision. The five corporations organized Near East Development Corporation to represent their participation in Turkish Petroleum. Jersey and Standard Oil Company of New York each took a 25 per cent interest in this new enterprise, and The Atlantic Refining Company, Gulf Oil Corporation, and Pan American Petroleum & Transport Company each took 16⅔ per cent.

In July, 1928, Near East Development and the other owners of the Turkish Petroleum Company entered into a working agreement.[15] The American corporation, Anglo-Persian, Royal Dutch–Shell, and Compagnie Française were each to have a 23¾ per cent participation. Gulbenkian retained his 5 per cent beneficial interest, and the other participants, under a private understanding, agreed to purchase his share of the oil at market value. Anglo-Persian, because it relinquished a part of its prior share in the company, was to receive a 10 per cent royalty on all production—later reduced to 7½ per cent. Each of the four corporate owners was to take its share of the oil at cost. The owners of the Turkish Petroleum Company bound themselves, with certain qualifications, not to operate independently without the others' permission within a large area designated on a map by a red line that embraced virtually all of the old Turkish Empire. Because of this provision, the agreement of 1928 came to be known as the Red Line Agreement.

The American companies' acceptance of the Red Line provision was a measure not only of their interest in getting a foothold in a promising oil province but also—especially on the part of Jersey and Standard of New York—of their need for crude. The former had to have products for its large market in Europe, and the latter needed supplies as an extensive marketer south and east of Suez. When the other three American participants for various reasons chose to withdraw, Jersey and Standard of New York purchased their interests. By October, 1934, these two companies each owned 50 per cent of Near East Development and thus 11⅞ per cent of Iraq Petroleum. They had only limited influence on the latter company's management, in which the British and British-Dutch companies occupied a dominant position.

A much-considered question among the Jersey directors in the late 1920's and early 1930's was what general policy to follow in the search for further reserves and production abroad. Two directors especially concerned with this issue were Sadler and Riedemann. Sadler, as already noted, believed that the most important consideration was low-cost crude from which to manufacture products for specific markets. Riedemann's focus was not so much on individual markets as on the relative strength around the globe of Jersey and its leading competitor, Royal Dutch–Shell. Believing that the American concern should be in a position to compete with the British-Dutch company in any part of the non-Communist world, he proposed that the Jersey Company merge with some of the affiliates it had lost in 1911. Within the old Standard Oil combination, the various companies had had complementary properties and operations. If combined again, especially abroad, they could meet Royal Dutch–Shell on more nearly equal terms in all regions.[16]

There was much economic sense in this proposal as well as a keen perception of the strategic problems involved. In fact, one reason why the British-Dutch group had grown so strong was the breakup of the Standard Oil combination in 1911. The dissolution not only had separated functionally complementary parts of Standard Oil but also had more or less divided them geographically. These functional and geographic divisions still largely prevailed two decades later. As a result, Standard Oil Company of California had excess crude from fields in its home state which it had to sell elsewhere. Standard of Indiana had large surplus production in Latin America but no appreciable foreign markets. Jersey had production in the East Indies but no marketing in the Orient. Standard of New York had extensive markets in the Orient but had to purchase its supplies, buying from both Jersey and Standard of California. Vacuum Oil Company was a large marketer of lubricants, which it manufactured from purchased crude. In Latin America and Europe, as well as at home, Jersey had large markets for gasoline and kerosene which it had to supply largely from purchased crude.

By 1930, circumstances were already inclining the thinking of officers of some of these companies in the direction of union. Standard of New York and Vacuum were negotiating a merger. Standard of California approached Jersey about a possible uniting of their two companies, and Standard of Indiana informed Jersey and other concerns that it might sell its foreign properties. At the same time, pressure from the government of the Netherlands was making Jersey and Standard of New York consider the merger of their interests in the Orient. Jersey entered into discussions with all these companies.

When President Kenneth R. Kingsbury of Standard Oil Company of California in 1929 approached President Teagle about a possible merger, the Jersey president's first concern was with the legality of the proposed combination. The two companies were competitive only to a minor extent, but the legality of the reunion of a former American affiliate with Jersey had never been tested. President Teagle submitted the question to the distinguished New York attorney John W. Davis. After consulting the Department of Justice in Washington, Davis advised against the union.[17] The two companies thereupon decided to await the outcome of a suit brought by the United States over the merger of Standard Oil Company of New York and Vacuum Oil Company. When a federal court in 1931 handed down a decision favorable to this combination, the discussions of Jersey and the California company were renewed in earnest.[18]

The discussions progressed so well that in the summer of 1931 the presidents of the two companies issued a press release stating the reasons for considering a merger:

The California Company has important domestic crude oil reserves but no important foreign reserves and only limited foreign distributing facilities. The Jersey Company has limited domestic crude oil reserves but has large foreign reserves and an important foreign system of distribution. The Jersey Company operates on the Atlantic Seaboard and in the Gulf Coast states, the California Company in the states and territories west of the Rocky Mountains. Therefore the operations of the two companies are in effect complementary and the merger would make possible the most economic use of their reserves and facilities.[19]

However, the negotiations ran into too many hurdles to be successful. Serious difficulties arose over the valuation of the respective properties of the two companies—particularly oil and gas reserves. The two largest single items on which there was prolonged discussion were Humble's holdings in the new East Texas field and those of Standard of California in the new North Kettleman Hills field. The Humble executives finally accepted a material reduction of their estimate of Humble's reserves in the East Texas field—though time has since proved their original estimate correct. Other differences might also have been compromised had there been firm support on both sides. However, there was disagreement among Jersey and Humble executives as to the advisability of the union. Director Sadler, for example, could see no advantage in having supplies of crude on the Pacific Coast that normally would be high-cost oil in Jersey's markets in eastern and southern sections of the United States and in Europe. Moreover, there was personal antipathy between certain men on both sides, involving especially Jersey's Sadler and President Farish of Humble, on the one side, and President Kingsbury of Standard of California, on the other. When it finally became clear that the differences could not be reconciled, a statement was issued late in 1933 to the effect that the two companies had decided to discontinue their discussions.[20]

Negotiations with Standard of Indiana had in the meantime proceeded more smoothly and rapidly. These had to do with the Indiana company's ownership of 96 per cent of the shares of Pan American Petroleum & Transport Company, which had a fleet of ocean tankers and held stock in many companies. Among them were corporations operating in several countries: Mexican Petroleum Company and Huasteca Petroleum Company, both producing and the latter also refining and marketing in Mexico; Lago Petroleum Corporation, producing in Venezuela; Lago Oil & Transport Company, Limited, with extensive storage and a large refinery on the Dutch island of Aruba; Lago Shipping Company, Limited, which carried oil from Lake Maracaibo to Aruba by tanker; Tide Water Export Corporation and the Caloric Company, both marketing in South America; and Ebano Asphalt Werke, A.G., in Germany.[21] Jersey acquired control of Pan American's foreign interests by purchase in 1932.

The authoritative history of Standard of Indiana characterized the sale of those interests as a "casualty of the depression and an outstanding event in the history of Standard [of Indiana]."[22] Pan American had been spending heavily on building a foreign marketing organization since 1929, and in 1931 the prospect was that it would have to spend many additional millions. It was questionable, however, whether heavy investments would provide adequate foreign outlets under depression conditions and intense competition for markets. The situation was not especially critical so long as Pan American could dispose within the United States of the larger part of the crude and products of its affiliates. But the tremendous oversupply of oil in 1931, particularly from the prolific new East Texas field, led domestic producers to demand an import tariff or embargo on foreign oil. Such a restrictive measure would have involved Pan American in serious difficulty. Exclusion from the United States market might indeed have jeopardized the sale of its large output in Venezuela and especially the sale of the products of the Aruba refinery. The directors of the Indiana company were also well aware of the possibility that oil properties in Mexico might be nationalized.[23]

The problem of Indiana's officers was to find a buyer for so large a property on terms their company would accept. Two requirements were essential: the buyer had to have adequate foreign markets; and, at least for a time, it had to assume responsibility in the United States for Pan American's supply contracts for gasoline with American Oil Company and for fuel oil with Petroleum Heat and Power Company. Standard of Indiana approached Jersey, Royal Dutch–Shell, and The Texas Company. The only one interested was Jersey.[24]

Jersey's leaders were concerned about the possible effect on their own company of acquiring an enterprise which, directly or indirectly, had been involved in much adverse publicity in the 1920's. Edward L. Doheny, head of Pan American until 1925, and Robert W. Stewart, president of Standard of Indiana, which had purchased the former company, had been charged with participating in unethical deals. Doheny, who early in the decade had obtained leases from the Department of the Interior on naval oil reserves in California, was found to have "loaned" a substantial sum to the department's head, Secretary Albert B. Fall. Stewart had been a party to a deal that was profitable to himself at the expense of the company of which he was president. He failed of re-election in 1929 after a long and highly publicized proxy fight led by John D. Rockefeller, Jr. More immediately serious was the poor reputation of the Pan American affiliates in Mexico, which intensified the unfortunate relations of foreign oil concerns with the Mexican government. Despite these unfavorable considerations, Jersey executives were impressed by the advisability of acquiring Standard of Indiana's interest in the foreign holdings of Pan American Petroleum & Transport Company.[25]

Complications in determining the value of the properties were inevitable in so large a trade. A major difficulty arose from the fact that the valuation of Pan American's holdings—contrary to Jersey's practice of carrying producing properties at cost—had been revised upward three times in the past to reflect the increased value of oil concessions in

Mexico and Venezuela. The legality of certain concessions in Venezuela was also questioned, but the conclusion was that they seemed to be well authenticated.[26]

Although differences arose as to the valuation of specific Pan American properties,[27] there was essential agreement as to their over-all value. Director Sadler wrote in a memorandum in March, 1932: "We would say that the book values even written up as shown are far below actual values in Venezuela, whereas we believe on the other hand that the book values as shown for the Mexican properties are far above the values of the properties in Mexico."[28] Eugene Holman of the Producing Department in New York, like Wallace E. Pratt of Humble, was enthusiastic about acquiring the Venezuelan properties. Holman wrote in reply to Sadler's memorandum: "Using the appraised value of the refining, marketing, and transportation facilities and appraising the Venezuelan producing properties" with a 75-cent price at tidewater for each barrel of crude and the Mexican with a 71-cent price, with future production discounted to present values, "we come to a total value of approximately $140,000,000." Holman, therefore, believed that "the property would be a good buy on a $125,000,000 basis."[29] The higher of these two figures became approximately the agreed price for the transfer.[30]

The contract with Standard of Indiana was signed April 30, 1932. The two companies therein agreed that the seller should transfer the foreign properties and American tankers of Pan American Petroleum & Transport to a new holding company, Pan American Foreign Corporation. Jersey was to purchase Indiana's 96 per cent of the shares of this new company at 87.15 per cent of the net book value of its foreign properties and ships; the total cost was $140,453,000. The buyer was to pay this sum in five annual installments, one-third in cash and two-thirds in 1,788,973 shares of its own stock at book value as of December 31.[31]

Both parties to this exchange obtained what they sought. Jersey acquired a substantial addition to its foreign properties, notably in producing. Especially pleasing were the Venezuelan production, averaging 88,000 barrels daily in 1931, and the estimated Venezuelan reserves of 550,000,000 barrels.[32] Production in Mexico averaged 16,000 barrels daily in the same year. Jersey obtained a large refinery on the island of Aruba in the Caribbean, conveniently located for processing Venezuelan crude. It acquired other properties in Latin America and Europe. Through its Jersey stock, Standard of Indiana retained an indirect interest in these foreign properties. (It later distributed that stock to its stockholders.) It received a substantial cash payment, which it could use in acquiring production at home. It was relieved of its foreign marketing problems and gained contracts with Humble Oil & Refining Company for meeting the supply obligations of one of its affiliates in the United States until it could develop an adequate supply of its own. Indiana's sale of its foreign interests was well timed. About a month after the consummation of the trade, the new tariff on oil imports almost shut foreign gasoline and lubricants out of the United States, and reduced crude and fuel oil imports greatly. A few years later, the properties of its former Mexican affiliates were nationalized.[33]

As in the Creole purchase, several Jersey executives became directors and officers of the newly acquired Pan American companies. Eugene Holman was elected president of Lago Petroleum in 1932, of Pan American Foreign and of Huasteca Petroleum in 1933, and of Mexican Petroleum in 1934. Holman also in 1933 succeeded to the presidency of Creole. He thus became the chief executive of Jersey's most important producing affiliates in Latin America. The former president of Pan American Petroleum & Transport, Robert G. Stewart, was elected to the Jersey Board of Directors in June, 1932.[34]

With these additions to its foreign reserves and production, Jersey had reached a position where it no longer had to depend appreciably on others for its supply of foreign oil. Its gross production—that is, its total production including royalty oil, which it purchased—was sufficient to supply its foreign markets. Since much of this oil was relatively low in cost, Jersey could compete with the low-cost oil of other companies. In addition, it had built up its reserves so that its potential supply in foreign countries was believed to be as great as that of Anglo-Persian or Royal Dutch–Shell.[35]

Heinrich Riedemann was still not satisfied. In a letter to President Teagle in November, 1934, he wrote:

I cannot get over the firm conviction that our position abroad, to the extent that it is not world-wide, is inferior to that of the Shell. I do not care when I am told that we match the Shell barrel for barrel in the costs of production, the costs of refining, and the amount of reserves we have in the way of crude. We cannot hit them *everywhere,* if it should ever come to a fight entailing supremacy. In my mind, it is a question of time and circumstances before we slip from the position we hold, if we face an antagonist who is in a superior position so far as marketing outlets are concerned. That is why I was and am still for nothing but a world-wide position, and consequently for nothing but a world-wide merger.[36]

A DEFENSIVE MOVE IN THE MIDDLE EAST, 1934–1937

Even with its large acquisitions in Latin America and its entry into Iraq Petroleum, Jersey was still weak east of Suez compared to its leading international competitors. Its only holding in the Middle East was its minor share in Iraq Petroleum through Near East Development. Anglo-Persian not only owned a far larger share in that company and had a royalty claim in addition but also had extensive production in Persia and an affiliate with substantial production in Burma. Jersey's affiliate in the Dutch East Indies—N. V. Nederlandsche Koloniale Petroleum Maat-schappij—had some production, but this was far surpassed by that of Royal Dutch–Shell, which also owned nearly a fourth of Iraq Petroleum.

Over the years, Jersey and its competitors had arrived at something of a truce in markets in the Eastern Hemisphere (see Chapter 11), but in the early 1930's the equilibrium that had been established was threatened by the growing activities of certain American companies in the Middle East. This situation rose out of the Holmes options purchased by Gulf Oil Corporation late in 1927.

In 1928, when the European owners of Iraq Petroleum had taken the position that the Bahrain concession on which Gulf Oil had purchased the option was within the Red Line, this company—as one owner of Near East Development—had offered to sell that option at cost to Iraq Petroleum Company. The American companies bound by the Red Line Agreement had urged accepting the offer, and Jersey's Stuart Morgan, who had become a member of the board of Near East Development, was sent to London to obtain the approval of the other owners of Iraq Petroleum. But again Anglo-Persian and Royal Dutch–Shell refused their assent. In London and later in New York, Sir John Cadman, the highly influential head of Anglo-Persian, still maintained that there was no prospect of oil in Bahrain. Late in the year Gulf Oil sold its option to Standard of California.[37]

With the support of the United States Department of State, the California company obtained approval from the British government for the Bahrain concession to be issued to an affiliate to be chartered in Canada. This company, Bahrain Petroleum Company, Limited,* began to drill in 1929 and completed a commercial well in 1932.[38] The question was then

---

* Its name was originally Bahrein Petroleum Company, Limited; it was changed to the above name in 1952.

raised among Jersey executives as to what could be done about the company's participation in the Bahrain concession if the negotiations between Jersey and Standard of California should lead to the merger of the two companies. This never became an issue, however, inasmuch as the negotiations ended in 1933.[39]

The discovery of oil deposits on Bahrain improved the prospects of similar strikes elsewhere in the region. The California company consequently opened negotiations with Saudi Arabia—which in 1927 had gained release from its status as a British protectorate—and in 1933 obtained concessions in the al-Hasa province. Gulf Oil, with the cooperation of the United States Department of State, sought to obtain approval from the British for its Kuwait option, Kuwait being outside the Red Line. Finally, late in 1934, the ruling sheik, with the approval of the British government, awarded the concession to Gulf Oil and Anglo-Persian for the Kuwait Oil Company, which they organized and owned in equal shares.[40]

These developments threatened to reduce Jersey to a minor position—among American as well as European companies—in what was coming to be a very productive oil region. The company could not afford such a position, for by 1934 Middle East oil had become important to supply not only Jersey's European markets but also markets in eastern Africa and Asia in which it had acquired an interest.

This interest came from the merger in 1934 of Jersey's producing affiliate in the Dutch East Indies with Socony-Vacuum's marketing operations in the Orient. Such a union had been discussed for some time by Jersey and Socony, but it probably would not have come about at this time, if at all, had not the Dutch government virtually forced the merger in order to increase its tax revenue. (See Chapter 11.) The two companies worked out a plan to organize Standard-Vacuum Oil Company and transfer to it their affiliates and properties in the East at the beginning of 1934.[41]

This merger gave Jersey, together with Socony, immediate reasons for being interested in the Bahrain operations of Standard of California. They now saw in Bahrain a possible source of oil for their markets—particularly for those south and east of Suez and west of the Dutch East Indies. They were also especially concerned over the prospect of new competition.[42] Standard of California was not an immediate threat because it had no market for its prospective production, and it could not easily acquire new outlets in markets so tightly controlled and so largely dominated by Anglo-Persian and Royal Dutch–Shell. However, executives of Jersey and Socony and their jointly owned affiliate were apprehensive that some aggressive new marketing company drawing supplies from Bahrain and possibly Saudi Arabia might cultivate some of the promising markets where they hoped Standard-Vacuum would grow. Consequently, the two companies began to consider the possibility of obtaining participation in Bahrain's production, either as owner or partial owner of the California company's properties or as purchaser of oil under a long-term contract.

Standard of California was obviously in need of some assistance in developing its concessions, or at least in disposing of whatever oil they might yield. It not only had no suitable marketing outlets but it also had no adequate organization experienced in foreign production and sales. And it would require tremendous capital to develop its immense concessions on the Bahrain Islands and in Saudi Arabia. Here was the kind of opportunity that under normal circumstances would have been most attractive to Jersey as well as to Socony.

However, circumstances in the Middle East were not normal for them because both companies were tied to their Iraq associates by the Red Line Agreement. As the only remaining members of the American group in Iraq Petroleum in 1934, they were presumably barred from entering any agreement with respect to Bahrain independently of the other owners of that company.[43] One possible exception was a contract by Standard-Vacuum to purchase oil from the Bahrain Petroleum Company.[44]

For about three years, executives of Jersey and Socony, in search of some way to get a foot in the Bahrain door, carried on discussions with their associates in Iraq Petroleum and with executives of Standard of California. Correspondence, reports, and memoranda in the Jersey files record the moves made and the problems met, together with comments by various executives on given situations.

The problems came from the divergent interests of the parties to the Red Line Agreement. Gulbenkian had no need for oil and no markets to protect. His price for consenting to a change was expected to be steep.[45] Compagnie Française needed oil in France, but to bring it from Iraq by pipeline to the Mediterranean and thence by tanker would cost less than to transport it from Bahrain by tanker. The French company, consequently, could not be expected to agree to anything that might reduce the desire of its associates to develop production rapidly in Iraq. Executives of Anglo-Persian and of Royal Dutch–Shell, according to Jersey's Seidel, feared that the French company, supported by the government of

France, would use any Bahrain oil that it might obtain to monopolize markets in French Indochina. Underlying this concern was the rivalry of British, Dutch, and French imperial interests in the Middle East and the Far East, a situation intensified in this instance by the fact that the government of Great Britain owned half of Anglo-Persian and that of France owned a large part of Compagnie Française. The situation was especially threatening to the British and Dutch interests because they were having difficulty in disposing of the production they already had in the Middle East.[46]

THE MIDDLE EAST AND THE RED LINE AS OF 1928

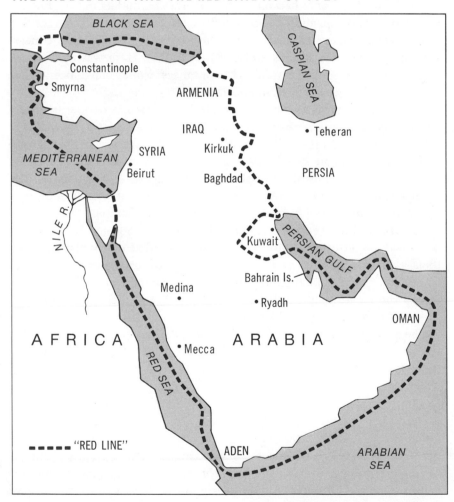

Like Jersey and Socony, the British and British-Dutch companies foresaw competition in their markets from the California company's concessions on Bahrain and in Saudi Arabia. These European concerns had no special need to obtain more oil; but they thought that the prospective production on Bahrain, if controlled by a new marketer, would disturb their strong position in Oriental markets at a time when they needed to sell more oil. Anglo-Persian and Royal Dutch–Shell had far larger sales in those markets than Standard-Vacuum; in November, 1935, for instance, "Stanvac" was reported to have only 9 per cent of the total industrial and diesel business in its territory, excluding Japan, as compared to Royal Dutch–Shell's 64 per cent.[47] With their large sales, the European companies were more concerned with maintaining the existing equilibrium than were Stanvac's owners, who were chafing because they were virtually quota-bound to a minor role.[48]

Such was the maelstrom of conflicting interests within which the executives of Jersey, Socony, and Standard-Vacuum, with considerable support and assistance from the British and British-Dutch companies, explored various possibilities. Their preference was to obtain participation as owners in the California company's concessions. If this could not be done, they hoped at least to be able to contract for the purchase of oil produced from these concessions.

The first move of Jersey and Socony was to discuss the possibility that all the Iraq Petroleum owners might join in some arrangement. In July, 1934, these owners authorized the two American companies and Anglo-Persian to explore with Standard Oil Company of California the terms under which the Bahrain or the Saudi Arabian concession, or both, might be purchased or a contract entered into for buying crude oil. If the concessions could be acquired, an operating affiliate would be organized by Iraq Petroleum. Jersey representatives examined the pertinent records in the offices of Standard Oil Company of California in San Francisco, and Anglo-Persian sent an inspection party to investigate the Bahrain properties and operations. Before the end of the year, however, the negotiations foundered on the restrictions imposed by the Iraq associates, including the British group's low valuation of the properties.[49]

The two American companies, meanwhile, had become still more impressed by what they had learned about the concessions, as well as by the progress of the California company's developments on Bahrain. They therefore decided to try another course. In this they were joined by Anglo-Iranian (the new name of Anglo-Persian adopted in 1935) and Royal

Dutch–Shell, whose executives were reported to favor the exclusion of Gulbenkian and the French company from any deal over Bahrain and Saudi Arabia. The American companies first tried to find some way of negotiating an amendment to the Red Line Agreement with Gulbenkian and the French. What Jersey and Socony tentatively suggested included redrawing the line to go directly from Suez to Baghdad, thus excluding Bahrain and Saudi Arabia. The records do not reveal what they proposed to give for such a change in the original agreement. Royal Dutch–Shell urged a revision. But the French refused to yield—one reason was said to be that they opposed British participation. Gulbenkian also proved to be uncooperative. In addition, Jersey and Socony found that the British and British-Dutch groups still placed a lower valuation on the concessions and the Bahrain oil reserves than the California company would accept— even considerably less than the values estimated by the American companies' own experts. As for the benefits to accrue to each of the three groups, the British maintained that Standard-Vacuum should be held to its current percentage of the market. Amending the agreement proved impossible.[50]

As a last resort, Jersey and Socony attempted to negotiate some arrangement whereby they might obtain clearance from their Iraq associates for a trade between themselves and the California company. They discussed several possibilities with Standard of California. These included offering a stock interest in Standard-Vacuum, or the outright purchase of the Bahrain properties and a half-interest in the concession in Saudi Arabia for cash and a royalty on oil produced. But Anglo-Iranian's Sir John Cadman insisted that no deal would be accepted unless it made "a clean sweep" of the California company. The British and British-Dutch groups, on the strength of previous marketing agreements with Jersey, also tried to apply quota restrictions on the proposed American combination. With Jersey under restraint and Standard of California under no restrictions, this may have been one of the rocks on which this latest effort foundered. This plan was apparently never proposed to Gulbenkian and the French. The records of this negotiation end in March, 1936.[51]

In the second half of that year, the whole situation changed. Bahrain Petroleum Company having by then developed a substantial production, the inevitable happened: Standard of California found a partner outside the Iraq groups. It merged its Middle East holdings with those of another American "interloper" in the Orient, The Texas Company, in a new corporation. The new concern was called the California-Texas Oil Company, Ltd. From an economic point of view, this was a happy union because one company had markets but no crude in the East and the other had crude and products but still no markets of its own in that region.[52] This "Caltex" combination greatly increased the rivalry for the outlets of the leading marketing concerns in the Orient.

The question again arose as to whether Jersey and Socony should make still another attempt to gain participation in what by 1937 was not only a serious threat to Standard-Vacuum's markets but also a very promising producing and refining operation. The president of Standard-Vacuum now suggested that Anglo-Iranian and Royal Dutch–Shell "might waive their rights under the Red Line Agreement *provided* some commitment was made by the American group whereby the properties that might be acquired would not be used to affect their interests detrimentally." However, there was the contrary possibility that if Caltex did not become too active the British and British-Dutch groups would not agree to a revision of the Red Line Agreement because they would not want to strengthen Standard-Vacuum's position in the Orient. It would be necessary also to reckon with the French company—and with Gulbenkian, whom President Teagle in February, 1937, described as "most difficult in a difficult situation." The records reveal no progress. President Teagle had become discouraged. In his judgment, insuperable obstacles prevented negotiating any arrangement by which the other Iraq Petroleum associates might allow the American companies to join Caltex.[53]

The record of these Jersey efforts closes with a memorandum of January 8, 1938, written by a member of the Jersey Producing Department in New York. The Caltex men in New York, the memorandum states, were "sitting on the edge of their chairs" awaiting news of a well in Saudi Arabia which had reached the same deep horizon that was producing oil on Bahrain. The memorandum also noted that the Bahrain refinery had topping stills with a daily capacity of 30,000 barrels, two Dubbs cracking units of 5,000-barrel capacity, a re-forming unit, and a sulfur-dioxide plant. The refinery, according to reports, was making quality gasoline, kerosene for heating and illumination, and fuel and diesel oil for industrial plants and ships.

In losing an opportunity to participate in the California company's concessions, Jersey clearly paid a high price for its 11⅞ per cent ownership in Iraq Petroleum. Although no novice in the strategy of competition and the power plays of European cartels, Jersey had placed itself in a highly vulnerable position by becoming involved with such seasoned

strategists as its European associates in Iraq Petroleum, most of whom
had strong government support. But for its shortage of crude and its
comparatively weak position in Eastern Hemisphere markets in 1928, the
American company would probably not have compromised its independence by becoming a party to the Red Line Agreement. However, the
year 1937 was not to mark the end of its efforts to improve its position in
oil production in the Middle East.

NEW PRODUCTION IN VENEZUELA
AND EUROPE

Although its Bahrain negotiations in the Middle East failed, Jersey was
making progress elsewhere. Advance was being achieved partly by the
purchase of an interest in an operating company and partly through the
work of European affiliates organized to explore for oil, acquire concessions, and develop production.

In 1937 International Petroleum acquired a half-interest in the concessions, plant, and equipment of Mene Grande Oil Company, a wholly
owned affiliate of Gulf Oil Corporation in Venezuela. International was
chosen to make this purchase, rather than Creole or Lago, mainly because
it had the required funds, but also because, as a Canadian company, it
seemed less vulnerable to the anti-big-business attitude then prevailing in
Washington. International agreed to pay Gulf $100,000,000 for its partici-
pation in Mene Grande and to reimburse the company for half of all
expenditures to be incurred in exploring and developing the concessions.
Half of all the oil produced by Mene Grande would accrue to each of the
participating companies.

Despite the prospects of success, it soon became apparent that very
large expenditures would be required to explore and develop Mene
Grande's Venezuelan concessions adequately. Therefore, in 1938 International Petroleum decided to reduce its potential obligations. Late in the
year, for $50,000,000 and the assumption of half its future obligations
under the 1937 purchase, it sold half of its interest in Mene Grande to an
affiliate of Royal Dutch–Shell.[54]

Although Jersey followed the policy of purchasing companies having
producing properties and operations, it did not abandon its own search
for oil. The Producing Department sent geologists to Africa and Europe
to explore for oil, and it had test drilling done in several countries in
Europe.

One promising addition to its production in Europe was the discovery of oil in Hungary on the eve of World War II. In 1933 a partly owned affiliate organized for this purpose, European Gas & Electric, had acquired a concession of 8,000,000 acres from the Hungarian government. This company found oil in commercial quantities near the Yugoslav border in 1937. At last Jersey was to achieve successful production in Central Europe.[55] (See Chapter 5.)

Other efforts to find oil in Europe were less successful. Anglo-American searched in Great Britain with only token success. Because the government of France did not grant exploration permits to private companies at the time, virtually nothing was accomplished in that country.[56] In a letter to Eugene Holman in June, 1939, Director Sadler summarized his attitude toward efforts in both countries: "Except for advertising value, my own feeling is that producing efforts in Great Britain and France are doomed to failure."[57] At about this time, Jersey acquired a minor interest in a company that discovered oil in Germany.[58]

Besides "advertising value," Jersey's leaders found other grounds to justify the search for oil in some European countries. Sadler in June, 1939, took the position that it was better to utilize frozen marks for exploring in Germany than for other projects.[59] Director Pratt frankly stated that "a producing effort in Europe on our part is justified as a defensive measure for the purpose of safeguarding our marketing in various countries there."[60]

These statements by Jersey executives give a clue to the state of mind then existing among the governments of countries in Europe which had no oil production. They were determined to make every effort to develop indigenous sources of petroleum products and even to become self-sufficient so far as possible. They would assist exploration for petroleum and give marked preference to domestic sources of supply.

RESPONSES TO INDUSTRIAL INSTABILITY

While striving to expand its production around the globe, Jersey also participated in efforts to overcome the worldwide malaise of the oil industry basically arising from the overproduction of crude.* In 1927 world production rose to 1,260,000,000 barrels, an increase of about 17

---

* "Overproduction," as herein used, represents a condition of the oil industry characterized by the building up of inventories far beyond normal requirements, a decline in prices to the level below that necessary to cover cost of production plus a profit margin, and an increase in the waste of oil.

per cent over the output of the preceding year. Storage stocks reached unprecedented levels, totaling some 600,000,000 barrels in the United States at the end of the year.[61] The annual average price of a barrel of crude in the United States fell from $1.88 in 1926 to $1.30 in 1927. Both the rise in production and the fall in prices continued for several years thereafter.

Excess production outside the United States presented some especially difficult problems for Jersey and other companies in the late 1920's. In several countries, operations were on concessions granted by national governments; no nation wanted its production reduced or even the rate of development of new production slowed down. With no way of promoting an agreement among the oil-producing countries, the oil companies faced two alternatives: (1) to enter upon potentially destructive competition or (2) to come to some understanding among themselves to limit output.

Until it acquired considerable foreign production, Jersey would be under serious handicaps in an open competitive struggle. In such a conflict, it would be at a disadvantage in its foreign markets, especially as compared to Royal Dutch–Shell and Anglo-Persian. These two companies, as already observed, could bring large supplies of comparatively low-cost oil to the markets in which Jersey had large outlets.[62]

Late in the summer of 1928, President Teagle met with Sir Henri Deterding of Royal Dutch–Shell and Sir John Cadman of Anglo-Persian at Deterding's Achnacarry Castle in Scotland to consider the problems of the oil industry. The heads of the three leading international oil companies deliberated on methods of avoiding a world oil conflict. They discussed "the acceptance by the units of their present volume of business and their proportion of any future increase of production" with "only such facilities to be added as are necessary to supply the public with its increased requirements of petroleum products in the most efficient manner."[63] (See Chapter 11.)

It is impossible to assess the effect of the Achnacarry meeting on production, but it is clear that the decline in demand brought by the depression necessitated some reduction in both oil production and new expenditures. The large international companies curtailed their exploration and drilling in many countries for several years; where they held large fields, they reduced the output of the wells. At the same time, however, many smaller companies were striving to maintain and even to increase their production. As world demand recovered from the depression and the production of crude oil was brought into better balance with demand in the United States, the large companies increased their output in foreign countries, generally in accordance with the rise in demand.[64]

Overproduction had become especially serious in the United States, where, until well into the 1930's, there was no effective regulation of crude oil output. Many independent producers, helpless before the flood pouring out of prolific new fields, looked to the large, integrated companies for some solution of their difficulties. The urgency of the situation is expressed in a letter of President Teagle to President Farish of Humble dated May 13, 1927:

I have put in a hectic week, and am leaving for a few days in Canada, ostensibly to catch a few trout, but in reality to try to forget the complications of the present situation. All last week people seemed to be drifting in from different parts of the country, all singing the same kind of swan song, namely that they thought it was up to some of the larger companies to do something constructive in the present overproduction situation; that for prices to go lower . . . would mean elimination or financial difficulty to a great many of the smaller operators.

Not only was there trouble from a deluge of oil at home, but the rapid rise of production abroad at the same time threatened to make petroleum products from the United States marginal or even submarginal in foreign markets. This situation illuminates some of the weaknesses of the domestic producing industry, which both economically and physically was unstable and wasteful. The volume of production depended on the discovery and competitive development of new fields rather than on sound production practices and the demand for products.

Heavily dependent on purchased domestic crude, Jersey had an interest not only in a sound American oil industry but also in the well-being of the independent producer whose oil and good will it so badly needed. Ever since the late 1880's—the days of prolific production in the Bradford field in Pennsylvania—Jersey had been cognizant of the need in times of overproduction for a large purchaser to buy the oil of independent producers. This the company judged to be necessary even when it meant cutting back on its own production or putting oil into expensive storage. To follow this policy had not been easy, or even physically possible, in all instances of high production from new fields. In fact, in the first decade of the twentieth century, the prolific output from new fields in Kansas had started the movement that had led to the dissolution of the Standard Oil combination in 1911. Humble had faced the same problem when the production of "fault-line" fields in Texas in 1923 and 1924 had increased

so rapidly that the company had been unable to build storage or pipelines fast enough to take all the oil offered from wells connected with its
gathering lines. It had then begun to take proportionately as much oil
from other producers' wells connected with its outlets as it took from its
own, a practice that came to be known as ratable taking. Nevertheless,
suit had been brought against Humble for alleged violation of Texas
antitrust law, litigation which had threatened the cancellation of the
company's Texas charter. Although Humble won the case, the experience
demonstrated how vulnerable a large purchaser was to political attack
when there was a great surplus of oil.[65]

In January, 1927, Jersey recommended to its domestic crude oil purchasing affiliates a course of action to protect relations with their suppliers. The parent company proposed that the affiliates continue to take
oil from other wells connected with their outlets as from their own wells.
Its Coordination Committee held that the affiliates "could not play fast
and loose with the connections with producers, and in sound business
practice were obliged to take their oil through thick and thin."[66] In view
of the downward trend of prices, purchasing much more than was normally required would be risky; but for the large concern to have refused
to take the oil might have had serious political consequences. This
dilemma provided a major motive impelling Jersey and its affiliates to
search for ways to make the crude supply more responsive to the market.

The lack of balance between oil supply and demand in the United
States was rooted in the American law of ownership of gas and oil and in
federal and state antitrust statutes. The "rule of capture"—under which
oil belonged to anyone who could gain possession of it through wells
drilled on land he owned or leased—prevented individual producers
from adjusting their own production either to their market outlets or to
the requirements of efficient recovery. At the same time, antitrust law
prevented producers in a given field from pooling their holdings so as to
achieve these same ends. Instead, each operator had to drill at once when
oil was discovered in his vicinity in order to recover any oil in place under
his land before it was drained underground by wells on neighboring
leases. This contingency led to the drilling of many unnecessary wells in
each oil-bearing structure. The consequence was a period of flush production followed by rapid decline resulting from the exhaustion of the
natural energy driving the oil to the surface. The reduction in reservoir
energy soon necessitated expensive pumping and reduced the amount of
oil ultimately recoverable.[67]

From the beginning of the oil industry, American producers had had some awareness of the waste, inequities, and uncertainties that accompanied their system of production, but not until the prospect of a shortage appeared soon after World War I had a movement arisen to promote effective regulation. It was led by a few oilmen—notably Henry L. Doherty—and individuals in the federal government who had become convinced that remedial action was necessary and that such action would be effective only if based on some knowledge of oil reservoirs and of the natural factors governing the recovery of the resource.

Study of those factors had already begun when the conservation movement arose. For several years, it had been carried on by Doherty's engineers and the United States Bureau of Mines at Bartlesville, Oklahoma. Their research, together with the establishment of the Federal Oil Conservation Board in 1924 and the beginnings of reservoir research by educational institutions and a few oil companies, had focused attention on basic scientific problems. It contributed greatly, although for some time tentatively, to a better understanding of the natural factors involved in production. By 1927, many of those who were familiar with this research had come to believe that the primary lifting agent in the recovery of oil from a reservoir was gas in solution in the oil. They held that the most efficient use of the energy provided by gas could be made by developing each reservoir as a unit. Although gas was later found to be only one of several energy factors affecting oil recovery, recognition of the reservoir as a unit was a fundamental contribution to the revolution in production that was to come in later years.[68]

This pioneering research had a profound effect on Jersey policy. President Farish of Humble brought to the company's directors, and especially to President Teagle, knowledge of the new reservoir concepts and of their significance to production. Several Humble executives had followed reservoir research with great interest. Vice-President Pratt, in charge of exploration, had early become convinced of its importance, and Vice-President Wiess, in charge of refining, had lent several refinery research men to reservoir research projects. Farish himself had become a firm believer in the efficient use of gas in oil recovery.

Farish was an early advocate of the unit plan—that is, developing and operating an oil field as an entity under one management. He held that unit operation would contribute to the solution of three basic problems of the American oil industry: (1) it would reduce costs by making possible efficient recovery with fewer wells and the use of a reservoir's natural energy instead of pumping; (2) it would give a measure of control over the rate of production from a reservoir and thus help to reduce the extreme fluctuation in prices, the need for costly storage, and the above-ground waste of oil resulting from flush production; and (3) it would reduce underground waste resulting from competitive field development and the consequent dissipation of reservoir energy, and thus make possible a greater ultimate recovery of oil from a reservoir.[69]

In the light of these concepts, the Jersey Board of Directors in June, 1927, adopted a new policy with respect to the leasing of prospective oil lands or the purchase of developed properties by affiliates. The directors decided, as stated by Director Sadler, "that the Jersey Company would be interested in purchasing properties or prospective properties, wherever they are able to be so blocked up as to control an entire structure, so that the oil could be produced slowly or rapidly as the conditions warranted." It was the wish of the Jersey directors, Sadler wrote to Humble, "that this view be passed to all directors having producing properties under their charge."[70]

Since it was often impossible to obtain an entire structure because of competition in leasing, the Jersey directors also tried to promote unit development and production by pooling individual holdings in a proved or prospective field. Here antitrust law stood in the way, but in May, 1927, the presidents of Jersey and Humble presented to the chairman of the Federal Oil Conservation Board a "unitizing" plan that they believed would not violate the law. This plan, originated by Humble, provided for the complete merging, prior to the discovery of oil, of all interests in an area that was believed to be a prospective field. If oil was found, each participant would receive a percentage of the production of each well in accordance with a formula stated in the unitization agreement. A weakness of this plan was that operators might hesitate to enter such an agreement before a property had been developed lest their percentages prove too small, a situation that might arise because of variations in the amount of oil in different parts of a reservoir. Although it was hoped that some way might be worked out to adjust percentages after a field had been developed, antitrust laws cast a shadow over any such procedure.[71]

Teagle was in complete agreement with Farish on the need for legislation to permit cooperative development of oil fields, but that was as far as the Jersey president would go in advocating legislation at the time. He believed—as Farish had previously, and as most oil executives apparently still did—that the industry's problems could be solved by the industry itself and that legislation should go only so far as to make possible, under proper safeguards, the necessary agreements among oil producers. Farish had progressed further in his consideration of the problem: by 1927 he had come to believe that some regulation by states was necessary and that only state agencies could effectively administer any regulatory law under the many different conditions that characterized oil production. When it became clear that nothing could be done about antitrust law, President Teagle also began to see that some kind of state regulation was necessary. But he held, correctly as it proved, that a great deal of study of oil reservoirs and of law—as well as education of oilmen, government officials, and the public—would be required before effective legislation could be enacted and applied to production.[72]

The company's leaders could fully subscribe to an address given in the autumn of 1927 before a meeting of the American Bar Association by James A. Veasey, legal counsel of Jersey's Carter Oil Company. If conservation could not be effected by voluntary action of the industry, Veasey said, compulsory legislation should be enacted if it could be "upheld under any theory of constitutional law." He explored such fundamental questions of law as the source of authority to regulate oil production and the powers under which such authority might be exercised. He suggested that measures under the police powers of states might be upheld by the courts, and he called upon the bar to give careful and studious attention to the problem.[73]

Jersey left participation in such a study and in the education of oilmen, government officials, and the public mostly to its domestic affiliates, but it gave them counsel and firm support. Not being an operating company itself, it was not so close to the legal, economic, and technological problems of production as were the producing companies. Besides, tarred with the reputation of the old oil trust, it might be looked upon by the public with deep suspicion if it tried to assert leadership. For all these reasons, the company did not take a conspicuous public stand on the various issues. Any position it did take was usually concerned with national policy and was expressed in association with representatives of many companies.

One such step resulted from the crisis in production following the discovery in the late 1920's of such prolific fields in the United States as Seminole and Oklahoma City in Oklahoma, Yates in Texas, and Ventura in California.[74] A committee of the American Petroleum Institute consisting of eighty oil executives—including President Teagle and directors

Sadler, Farish, and Smith of Jersey—endeavored to meet this crisis by suggesting a plan for setting production levels for the whole country. The committee's report of March, 1929, recommended that production in that year be held to the level of 1928. However, when presented for the approval of the American Petroleum Institute, the Federal Oil Conservation Board, and state regulatory agencies, the report immediately ran into legal difficulties. The Attorney General of the United States informed the chairman of the federal board that that agency had no power to approve agreements among producers but could only investigate and recommend action. The board's chairman himself stated that "in the long view the positive method of conservation is the initial control of development through the control of drilling" and the "sole legal authority for such action lies within the state governments themselves."[75]

A different method of dealing with the problem of oversupply was the reduction of oil imports. As requested by President Hoover, the large American companies with foreign production agreed to reduce their imports of crude. Jersey favored such reduction by voluntary action; even Director Farish, who was president of the largest domestic producing affiliate, for a time supported this approach to the problem. But with a further cut in prices in 1930, the Independent Petroleum Association of America started a campaign for a tariff. The movement was accelerated by the vast flood of oil from the East Texas field—the largest problem field in the whole history of the American oil industry. In 1931 the sudden increase in the field's production drove the average price of crude in the United States down to 65 cents a barrel. When the board of directors of the American Petroleum Institute endorsed a petroleum tariff in principle in November, 1931, Farish voted affirmatively. An act of Congress effective in June, 1932, set import taxes ranging from half a cent per gallon on crude oil to 4 cents a gallon on lubricants. This was the proverbial ill wind that blew Jersey the good of helping it to acquire Standard of Indiana's foreign properties.[76]

A test of the company's position with respect to national oil policy came in 1933. Jersey supported the drawing up, under the New Deal's National Industrial Recovery Act, of a code that had as one of its objectives the bringing of oil production into balance with consumption. Members of the industry, however, did not agree on what should be included in the petroleum code. At one extreme were those who held that, if the production of oil were brought into line with demand, the other operations of the industry would work satisfactorily; at the other extreme were the advocates of price fixing at every point from producing wells to sale to consumers. Both extremes were represented on the Jersey board, but Vice-President James A. Moffett, Jr., was alone in favoring price controls.[77]

Farish, by that time chairman of the Jersey Board of Directors, wrote to the chairman of the federal government's Petroleum Administrative Board outlining the directors' diagnosis of the situation. Their view was that "the basic trouble with the oil industry in recent years has been that the control of production was uncertain and ineffective, and in important areas production was in excess of consumer demand." They believed that "if an equilibrium is achieved and maintained . . . prices will take care of themselves and will reach levels at the same time reasonably compensatory to the industry and fair to the consuming public." They considered "the fixation of prices for petroleum and its products by government decree to be economically unsound, incapable of enforcement and of doubtful legality."[78]

The company's *Annual Report* for 1933 contained a summation of its position:

This company adheres to its long-time conviction that the solution to the industry's troubles lies in a rigid control of the crude oil supply and welcomes the cooperation of the Government in that field. It has supported and will continue to support all sound measures to that end, with reasonable provisions for inquiry and enforcement. It is believed, however, that the continuance of the industry on a self-governing basis should be assured at all cost, and that any policy approaching complete regimentation, whether temporary or permanent, will prove fatal to the best interests of the public and the oil industry alike.

The attempt under the National Industrial Recovery Act to solve the problems of an oversupply of oil was short-lived. In January and May of 1935 the Supreme Court of the United States in three cases invalidated individual sections and finally the whole of the act.[79] This left the regulation of the oil industry primarily with the states.

By that time, a few states had made progress in developing regulation that was making a rational and effective attack on the peculiar problems of the oil industry in the United States. Although Jersey looked to its affiliates to act on the local and state level, on the national level it supported the establishment of An Interstate Compact to Conserve Oil and Gas and the enactment of the Connally Act of February, 1935. This last measure was designed to buttress state regulation by forbidding the shipment across state boundaries of oil produced in violation of state law.[80] When the form of regulation known as proration was challenged in the hearings of the Temporary National Economic Committee (TNEC) in 1939, Farish, then president of Jersey, although recognizing weaknesses in the administration of proration law, expressed his vigorous support of that type of regulation of production.[81] (See Chapter 4.)

Basic to these efforts to rationalize and stabilize oil production in the United States and elsewhere were the great improvements made in reservoir and production technology and in the management of operations. In all these areas, Jersey had left action primarily to the operating companies. However, over the same years the parent company had developed organizations and techniques for more effectively guiding and coordinating the efforts of its affiliates in the production of crude oil.

THE EVOLUTION OF PRODUCING COORDINATION

The parent company's development of more effective ways to guide and coordinate producing operations was a gradual process. The direction of change was, on the one hand, away from the direct involvement of Jersey's own administrative personnel with the management of operations and, on the other hand, toward the improvement and better coordination of the total producing effort.

From 1927 to 1933, the producing activities of the affiliates were represented on the Jersey Board of Directors by top executives of producing companies. They included President Farish of Humble and Sadler as a director and officer of several Latin American affiliates. Other directors from companies with producing interests were the chief executives of Standard of Louisiana, Standard Oil Company of New Jersey (which held the stock of Carter Oil and Mexican affiliates), Imperial (with affiliates in Peru and Colombia), and Româno-Americana. Actually, board responsibility for production was left almost wholly to President Teagle and directors Farish and Sadler.

The Producing Department—in 1927 transferred to Standard Oil Company of New Jersey—was for several years principally concerned with assisting Jersey's search for new production possibilities abroad. It had little direct contact with the operations of Humble and Imperial, which were largely independent of New York. Director Sadler was the department's head. Next in rank was Thomas R. Armstrong, an attorney fluent in Spanish and familiar with the petroleum laws and the customs of Latin American countries. Armstrong specialized in negotiating concession contracts with governments on behalf of certain affiliates in the southern continent. Charles F. Bowen headed a group of geologists active in making surveys in countries in both the Eastern and the Western Hemisphere where Jersey had no affiliates or its affiliates had no geologists of their own. George S. Walden served as chief liaison officer with foreign producing operations until he became managing director in 1929 of the affiliate in the Dutch East Indies which was then actively developing its production. Walden's successor was Eugene Holman, formerly Humble's chief geologist. Harry H. Hill, member of the new division of production engineering established in Standard Oil Development Company in 1928, served as the connecting link between this research affiliate and the Producing Department; he also prepared monthly reports on petroleum engineering and compiled statistics on the world oil industry.[82]

Upon the parent company's acquisition of large foreign producing interests in 1928 and the early 1930's, members of the Producing Department of Standard Oil Company of New Jersey were assigned managerial positions in the new affiliates. Sadler, until 1933, and Eugene Holman served as presidents of several Latin American producing companies. Other members of the same department also held positions with the newly acquired foreign affiliates. All such assignments with affiliates were discontinued, however, as soon as qualified men from the operating companies themselves became available to fill them.[83]

After the reorganization of 1933, production gained stronger representation on the Jersey board, a logical consequence of the company's rising investment in producing properties and the affiliates' expanding production. Because of the decision that Jersey directors should generally no longer serve as chief executives of affiliates, both Sadler and Farish resigned from their official positions with operating companies. Thenceforth, they devoted their full attention and energy to Jersey's general administration. Sadler became chairman of the Coordination Committee and Farish chairman of the Board of Directors and a member of the Executive Committee. When Farish was elected its president in 1937, the parent company for the first time had as its chief executive a man who had risen in the production branch of operations. In the same year, the election of Humble's Wallace E. Pratt to the Board of Directors and to the Executive Committee raised the competence of both groups to deal with production. During the remainder of the decade, four forceful members of the board, three out of four members of the Executive Committee, and the head of the Coordination Committee were notably knowledgeable and experienced in the production branch of the oil business.

In the late 1930's, the trend of the Producing Department—of which Eugene Holman had become manager as successor to Sadler—was away from managerial involvement with producing affiliates and toward having its leaders serve as advisers, supervisors, and general coordinators of production. By 1939, according to Holman, the Producing Department's relations with affiliates were entirely supervisory and not managerial.[84]

The department's internal organization also underwent substantial change. This was no doubt owing in part to Holman's administrative capacity; it was also a response to the expansion and increasing diversity of Jersey's producing interests and to the need for technologically competent and more efficient management. Although the personnel of the department increased only modestly—from seventy in 1933 to ninety in 1939—the responsibilities of individual executives were more clearly defined. In 1935, members of the department were assigned responsibility for contact with producing affiliates in five areas or groups of countries: the United States; Mexico, Cuba, Brazil, and Iraq; Venezuela; Europe; and Canada, Peru, Colombia, and the East Indies. Holman and Armstrong, because of particular problems in Argentina, corresponded with affiliates in that country. New advisory divisions were also established in the department; by 1939 these had to do with such matters as personnel, medical care, storage, contracts and law, pipelines, and coordination. The work of some of the older groups was maintained, but with a different emphasis. For example, the geologists—instead of heading exploration parties sent to Africa, Europe, Latin America, or other parts of the world—were concentrating on worldwide studies of sedimentary basins. In addition, the division served the affiliates as a clearinghouse for geologic information and exploration methods and techniques.[85]

The Producing Department also provided liaison between producing operations and the Executive Committee and Coordination Committee. It had at times as many as three representatives in the latter group, and it furnished both committees with information about the producing activities of the whole industry as well as of Jersey affiliates.

In fact, by the later 1930's better communication had been established widely among Jersey producing interests, both vertically and horizontally. Relations between the Producing Department in New York and operating managers had been improved by increased correspondence, regular reports, and the more frequent two-way travel made possible by airplanes. Members of the department made trips to producing locations to observe and discuss at first hand the problems of operating men and to inform them of new developments of possible use in their operations. The managers of producing operations came to New York at least twice a year. They came in the fall, when budgets were discussed with the Coordination Committee, and in the spring, when a conference of producing men was held close to the annual conference sponsored by the Coordination Committee.[86]

The transfer of greater responsibility for management to local producing executives and managers paralleled the gradual change within Jersey's top administrative organization. In the Producing Department, it reflected the move from managerial to advisory functions. This shift of function did not directly affect Humble, Imperial, or the latter's affiliates; all of these companies had for some time been operating with a great deal of autonomy. However, throughout producing operations, the administrative groups in New York—from the Producing Department to the Jersey Board of Directors—used their influence to bring about the selection of production managers who were qualified in the new reservoir science and petroleum engineering.

As the parent company, Jersey itself had thus made great progress in the late 1920's and the 1930's in expanding its producing properties and potential. It had acquired new producing affiliates in foreign countries, which gave it sources of supply for markets abroad comparable to those of its leading international competitors. It had participated at home and abroad, with limited success on the international level, in efforts to reduce the glut in the oil market. It had encouraged and assisted its affiliates in developing and applying new scientific concepts to exploration and production. And it had made changes in its administrative personnel and organization that contributed to improving the producing operations of its affiliates.

Under Jersey's system of decentralized management, the affiliates were responsible for operations. The next two chapters deal with the producing policies and activities of the affiliates in the United States and abroad and with actual results in terms of estimated reserves and the volume of crude output.

Chapter 4

Domestic Production in Transition

THE DECADE before the outbreak of World War II brought a revolution in oil finding and production in the United States. The immediate pressures behind this development were the conservation movement of the 1920's and the worldwide overproduction of oil which threw the industry into disorder and threatened to become especially disruptive in the United States. A more basic, long-range factor was the accelerating shift around the globe toward the use of petroleum as a source of energy to turn wheels, propel ships and aircraft, and furnish power for industrial plants.

The American economy had become especially dependent on a reliable supply of petroleum products. However, under the system of competitive development of oil fields in the United States, oil production was highly unstable and wasteful, and prices and profits generally fluctuated widely. Both the economy and the oil industry had to have assurance of a stable and adequate supply, and the industry must have profits to help expand reserves and production to serve a rising consumption. Hence, the needs of the economy and of the industry combined to spur the search for ways to conserve the nation's petroleum resources and to make their recovery more efficient—both physically and economically—and more closely responsive to market demand.

The industry itself played the major role in this search. Jersey's producing affiliates, especially Humble Oil & Refining Company, were among the leaders. They acquired large reserves of oil and gas, joined in developing and applying new concepts in exploration and production, reduced producing costs, and applied old legal principles to overcome the instability, waste, and inequities that characterized American oil production.

POLICIES AND TECHNIQUES IN
EXPLORATION AND LEASING

Contrary to its policy abroad of purchasing companies with already developed producing properties, Jersey left the acquisition of new reserves at home to affiliates. However, it helped shape their policies, and it gave them firm financial support even in years when many other companies were hesitant or unable to invest heavily in reserves.

Humble Oil & Refining Company, with headquarters in Houston, was the most vigorous and the most advantageously situated of the domestic affiliates. Its successful producing operations in 1927 were located principally in eastern and coastal Texas, an oil region soon to become the most prolific the United States had ever known. This region was close to tidewater, and Humble had a pipeline system of its own to carry crude to its Baytown refinery or to tankers at a terminal on the Gulf of Mexico. The company also had some production in other parts of Texas and in southern Oklahoma and western Louisiana. The Carter Oil Company, with producing properties in the Mid-Continent, and Standard Oil Company of Louisiana, which had operations in its home state and Arkansas, were also located in important producing regions. These, however, were at the time less promising than Humble's. Unlike Humble and Carter, which were primarily producing companies, Standard of Louisiana was principally a refiner and marketer.

Strength in production was a result not only of location but also of policy. In the early decisive years of this period, Humble had four directors (including President Farish) who favored an aggressive reserves-acquisition program and were committed to applying scientific knowledge to exploration and production. Carter in the years after 1932, when Clarence H. Lieb was transferred from Venezuela to become the company's chief executive, gained renewed vitality and greatly improved its reserves. Carter missed the opportunity—which Humble seized—to expand its reserves greatly during the depression of the early 1930's. But in the years that followed, it successfully applied the same policies to the acquisition of reserves that Humble had pioneered: employing scientific methods in exploration, spending heavily for proved or prospective oil lands, and leasing land in large blocks.[1]

The key Humble administrator in the formulation and application of exploration and leasing policies was Wallace E. Pratt, director, vice-president, and head of the Geologic, Lease and Scouting Department. One of the country's leading petroleum geologists, Pratt was completely committed to utilizing the resources of science in the search for oil. At a time when many oilmen doubted the wisdom of investing heavily in building up reserves, he was an uncompromising expansionist. Even when the risks seemed heavy, he persuaded the directors of Humble as well as those of Jersey that the company should invest large sums in proved and unproved properties. He developed an unusually able group of men to search for oil. In negotiations for properties, his reputation for fair dealing and sound judgment is said to have contributed greatly to the company's success in obtaining leases. More than anyone else, Pratt was responsible for Humble's acquisition of tremendous reserves.[2]

Indispensable to Humble's achievements in adding to its reserves in the years 1927 through 1939—and to Carter's success in the later years of this period—were the new geophysical techniques utilized in exploring for oil. Leadership in this field was provided by a handful of companies. Humble's geologists had been highly successful in the early 1920's with the technology of that time, which depended for evidence of subsurface structures either on surface manifestations or on cuttings or cores brought up in drilling. When Rycade Oil Company, of which E. L. DeGolyer was manager, and a few other companies began to experiment with geophysical techniques, Pratt was at first skeptical. He was convinced that the theory involved was valid; but he had little confidence in the first fumbling attempts to apply it to deeply buried geological structures, and he was suspicious of the German-speaking crews employed by the geophysical contractor. However, when Rycade and Gulf in 1924 succeeded in mapping shallow salt domes, Pratt recommended that Humble proceed at once to build its own seismograph and to develop its own geophysical staff.[3] By so doing, Humble became the first American company to obtain seismic equipment and staff of its own. It had its seismic crews on the Gulf Coast early in 1925, a time when the only other parties in the field were manned from Europe.

Three early geophysical instruments were used in oil exploration. The torsion balance measured the pull of gravity, which varied with the density of rocks; the magnetometer, which measured variations in the earth's magnetic field, gave clues to differences in the subsurface structures. The refraction seismograph, which recorded sound waves sent into the earth by an explosion and refracted to the surface, gave an indication of the nature of the strata shot. By using records made by these instruments at various points in an area, geophysicists skilled in the interpretation of the data could determine much about the density, depth, and horizontal extent of individual subsurface structures. These instruments had been known to scientists for some time, especially in Europe, but not until the 1920's were they used in oil exploration in the United States. Although it took time to adapt them to the search for the types of structures that might contain oil and to learn to use them under varying geologic conditions, by 1927 their utility had been proved.

The significance of the use of geology and geophysics is shown by historical statistics on the discovery of new oil fields in the United States. In sixty years before 1920, sixty-eight major fields had been discovered. "Practical men," as the old-fashioned unscientific prospectors were called, had made most of the discoveries for several decades, but geologists had gradually risen to considerable importance. The two groups ·were probably about equally responsible for discoveries made during World War I. In the years 1920 through 1926, geologists had been more productive than practical men; they had found two-thirds of seventy major fields. From 1927 through 1939, of 171 major discoveries, geophysicists found 65, geologists 77, and the old type of prospector found 29. It is significant also that practical men had only one successful strike out of seventeen wells drilled, as compared to the technologists' one in every 7.5.[4]

Humble's first discovery with the new geophysical equipment, a refraction seismograph, was a salt dome found in 1926 at Moss Bluff on the Texas coastal plain. Carter geologists in that same year began to use the torsion balance and the magnetometer. But the early geophysical equipment was less useful to them than to Humble's exploration crews. This was true because, in most of Carter's territory, the instruments could not distinguish one layer from another in the uniformly dense and compact strata of the geologically much older rocks with which oil fields were associated.[5]

Late in 1927 Humble geophysicists scored their first important discovery. Using the refraction seismograph, they found indications of a salt dome at Sugarland, a few miles southwest of Houston. A test well drilled there discovered oil. Sugarland was the first major oil field of which there is record discovered on the basis of the findings of the new technique of seismic surveying, and it was the first fairly deep salt dome discovered by the use of geophysical instruments. Humble and other companies had explored this area before, even with geophysical instruments. However, the successful crew used larger charges of explosives and longer shot lines than had been employed earlier. This greater distance on the surface from the explosion to the recording instrument was soon recognized as necessary in the search for the deeper salt domes.

In the next two years, Humble's geophysicists found several salt domes, but their success did not long continue. Although the instruments and their use were improved, by the end of the 1920's the limits of the utility of the refraction seismograph seemed to have been reached. It was found not to be useful in locating structures more than 5,000 feet below the surface.[6]

Humble's response to this limitation was to devise more effective instruments. It put an expanded research staff to work in 1929 improving its geophysical equipment and the recording and interpretation of geophysical data. In a few years, the research group greatly improved the torsion balance. Early in the 1930's it perfected what geophysicists generally regard as the first effective gravity meter, a device which made an important contribution to geophysical exploration. This instrument proved so useful in the rapid surveying of an area that by 1939 it had entirely superseded the more cumbersome torsion instrument. For more detailed study of an area, Humble principally used the reflection seismograph developed by the Geophysical Research Corporation under the sponsorship of E. L. DeGolyer. This type of seismograph recorded sound waves reflected (not refracted, as in the early instrument) from successive subsurface formations. Humble's seismic crews had all been outfitted with reflection equipment by 1931.[7]

The company's early adoption of geophysical techniques proved important to its own operations and to those of several other Jersey affiliates. Records of the crew-months of geophysical exploration by various companies in Texas, beginning with 1932, show that in that year Humble crews did 42 per cent of the geophysical field work done in that state. The company discovered three major fields, besides a number of small ones, on the basis of data collected by its reflection crews: Means in western Texas in 1934, Anahuac in the eastern coastal area in 1935, and Friendswood on the Gulf Coast near Houston in 1937. Beginning in 1929, the company's geophysical research findings were made available to all Jersey affiliates through Standard Oil Development Company, and for a number of years Humble contracted crews to Carter and to affiliates in Europe, Latin America, and even the Dutch East Indies. One such crew working for Carter in 1933 located the structure on which the Keokuk field was discovered in the Seminole district of Oklahoma.[8]

Starting in 1935, Carter expanded its own geophysical work. Its seismic crews were responsible for the discovery in Illinois of the Loudon field late in 1937 and the Dix field two years later. About the same time, working for Standard of Louisiana, they also located the structure on which the Buckner field in Arkansas was discovered. In 1939 Carter—with a record of successful field work and an active research group—through its research center at Tulsa took over responsibility for providing other Jersey affiliates with geophysical equipment, personnel, and research, and with advisory service.[9]

The geologists, in the meantime, continued to play an important part in the exploration carried on by Jersey affiliates. They ranged everywhere within the areas in which the companies operated, making both surface and subsurface studies. In regions where geophysical methods were not

HOW A REFLECTION SEISMOGRAPH WORKS

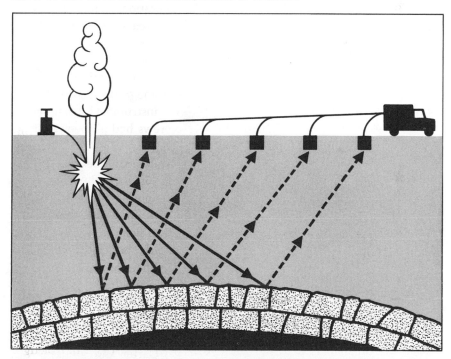

This diagram shows sound waves sent downward in the earth by a seismic explosion and reflected to geophones and a recording truck. A seismograph in the truck records the reflections on sensitized paper. Data thus gathered from various depths and over a wide area help find geologic structures that may be traps for underground oil.

yet effective, they had full responsibility for exploration. It was largely as a result of their work, for example, that Humble gained a substantial position in the East Texas field. The company had leased large blocks in the area and had gathered information on which to base the acquisition of more acreage before oil was discovered by a "wildcatter" in 1930. Its holdings in that field, although amounting to only about one-sixth of the acreage, resulted in the largest estimated reserve that Humble had ever obtained in any one field.[10]

The affiliates also experimented with other exploration techniques. In the later 1930's, for example, they tried gamma rays, hired electron crews to measure electrical transients in the earth, and drilled slim holes from which data could be obtained at a lower cost than from the drilling of full-scale wells. None of these attempts proved successful; even slim-hole drilling was practicable only to moderate depths. An important new technique adopted by the affiliates was Schlumberger electrical well-logging, a method for recording the nature and thickness of successive formations penetrated in drilling. An importation from France, this technique came to be widely used by the oil industry.[11]

Armed with these increasingly potent technical advances in exploration, the affiliates leased and explored extensive areas in the years 1927 through 1939. Beginning in the late 1920's, Humble was the first to step up its activity. The company was motivated at first by a shortage of reserves, and, during the years of deep depression, by the availability of both proved and unproved properties at costs which were believed to be below their future value. In those years, some of Humble's major competitors and many smaller operators lacked either sufficient funds or the necessary confidence in the future value of oil lands to invest substantially. Competition for leases and, accordingly, the prices asked were considerably reduced. Even so, some of Humble's individual trades involved large investments. For one purchase in 1932, in addition to the commitment on royalties, Humble paid $3,000,000 in cash and pledged additional payments as oil was produced, which eventually amounted to $17,000,000. Its direct annual cash payments for new acreage reached $13,500,000 in 1934—besides unknown millions to be paid in royalties and in "oil money" (bonuses to be paid if oil were found).[12]

Competition increased in the later years of the decade, but Humble continued to buy heavily, with greater emphasis on untested and unproved land but not excluding the purchase of strategically located proved tracts—as in the great West Ranch purchase in fee in 1938.

During this period as a whole, Humble spent $85,000,000 in cash for leases in various sections of Texas, across the state boundary in New Mexico, and in coastal Louisiana. Despite a continuous surveying and testing of lands, with a consequent dropping of leases on an extensive acreage that did not prove promising, Humble from 1927 to the end of 1939 doubled its holdings to a total of 8,000,000 acres.

The other affiliates were later in entering upon vigorous leasing programs. Carter—which had a surplus of oil for some time after it lost its outlet to the Baton Rouge refinery when Humble developed prolific properties in eastern Texas—did not undertake an extensive leasing campaign until after the depression of the 1930's. Its total leased lands at the end of 1939 amounted to 1,500,000 acres. An important departure was its leasing in south-central Illinois, a new oil region. Standard of Louisiana, which had previously relied upon the purchase of proved property, also entered upon a leasing and exploration campaign later than Humble. Beginning in 1935, exploration parties provided by Carter scouted for promising areas for the Louisiana affiliate to lease and test.[13]

The policy of block leasing was followed by Humble throughout the period and by Carter in the later 1930's. By controlling all or nearly all of a field, a company could reduce costs through wide spacing of wells and—within the limits of its lease contracts and state regulatory orders—it could also adjust the rate of production to reduce surface and underground waste.

Although block leasing was difficult in the older and more competitive regions, both Humble and Carter were successful in obtaining large tracts. Because of its early entry into Illinois, Carter was able to lease nearly all the productive acreage of what became the major Loudon field and a large portion of the smaller Dix field. Humble had leases running from 90 per cent to 100 per cent of the acreage of a number of major fields in Texas and also of smaller fields in that state and Louisiana. These fields included Sugarland, Raccoon Bend, Means, Anahuac, and Friendswood in Texas. In many others—some of major importance, such as Tomball, Thompsons, Conroe, and Tomoconnor—the affiliate acquired approximately half of the productive acreage. It obtained smaller percentages in many others, including the great East Texas field.[14]

The most spectacular block acquired by a Jersey affiliate in the United States was the King Ranch of more than a million acres in southwestern Texas. This was offered to Humble when the King heirs needed funds for paying estate taxes. Most of the land was then still unexplored, and oil had not been discovered. However, Pratt had such faith in the possibilities of the King Ranch that he finally persuaded the Humble directors to sign contracts for the lands. The major lease, which initially ran for twenty years but was later extended to the year 2000, was for the King Estate lands, with an annual rental of $127,800 and the customary royalty of one-eighth. Two other leases on King lands, owned by a daughter of the original owner and her son, gave Humble the right to explore and develop another 160,000 acres. Because of the long term allowed for exploration and development at a time when the market was still oversupplied, Humble did not at once undertake to test these lands, but substantial production was later obtained from the King blocks.[15]

The Jersey affiliates followed a moderately conservative policy during the depression in testing and developing their leased lands, but in few instances could they delay such operations to conform to the actual demand for oil. Heavy lease obligations, high rentals, and drilling by others in competitively leased fields, as well as the need to increase reserves, somewhat forced the pace of Humble's wildcatting and development. In the years from 1927 to 1939, it drilled 408 wildcats, of which 35 discovered oil in sufficient quantity for commercial development. In several fields it acquired estimated reserves of 100,000,000 barrels or more. Carter's largest single acquisition was in the Loudon field in Illinois, which was one of the ten largest discoveries in the United States in the later 1930's. Standard of Louisiana's largest was the Buckner field in Arkansas.[16]

The reserve acquisitions of Jersey's domestic affiliates added up to a notable accomplishment. At the beginning of the period, Humble had estimated reserves of only about 55,000,000 barrels; Carter and Standard of Louisiana each had even less. At the end of 1939, despite a large volume of production during the period, Humble had gross estimated oil reserves of 2.4 billion barrels; the three companies had a total of 2.6 billion. In the same period, the estimated reserves of the whole American oil industry approximately doubled to 18.5 billion barrels.[17]

DEVELOPING NEW SCIENTIFIC CONCEPTS IN PRODUCTION

This increase in the reserves of Jersey affiliates was in part a result of reservoir research leading to new production methods which made possible a great increase in the amount of oil that could be recovered from each reservoir. This research and development work was carried on intensively, beginning late in the 1920's, by Humble and Carter and by several other companies, as well as by research groups and individuals in academic institutions.[18]

The producing affiliates, as noted in Chapter 3, had by 1927 adopted two concepts concerning production that had come out of the early reservoir research: (1) that gas in solution in oil in a reservoir is the primary source of the pressure or "drive" that lifts oil in a well, and (2) that, in order to make the best use of gas as an energy factor, a field must be developed as a unit. Both Carter and Humble had begun to experiment in the 1920's with the injection of gas into wells to increase recovery. This was not a new principle, but Carter employed it on a large scale to stimulate declining wells at Seminole. To plan and supervise the operation, it engaged S. F. Shaw, an engineer who had done important work in forcing water out of flooded mines owned by the Guggenheim interests in Mexico. He succeeded so brilliantly that Carter's production, and indeed the field's, exceeded the output in Seminole's initial flush period. This experiment indicated, however, that in order to use gas efficiently much more had to be learned than was then known about how it functioned in the recovery of oil.[19] Although Carter did not enter upon a comprehensive production research program until the later 1930's, Humble began serious research at once.

Under John R. Suman as director in charge from 1927 on, and with W. W. Scott as head of petroleum engineering and Dr. W. K. Lewis of the Massachusetts Institute of Technology as consultant, a small but able research group began to study gas as a factor in oil recovery. This team was headed by Dr. Stewart P. Coleman and H. Dayton Wilde. The objective was to learn how gas could be used most efficiently in producing oil from a reservoir—and particularly what ratio of gas to oil obtained from wells in a field would best maintain the reservoir's natural energy and result in the greatest ultimate recovery.[20]

Although the Humble group did some basic research, its most important early contributions were quantitative studies of actual reservoirs.[21] By correlating data on the volume of production, the ratio of gas to oil produced, and reservoir pressures, it soon drew some important conclusions. Several years' study of the Desdemona field, where production was declining, indicated that with uncontrolled production from wells only a small percentage of the oil in a reservoir was actually produced. The rest was lost because of inefficient use of reservoir energy. In the small Olney field, where depletion of the oil sand had already advanced so far that commercial production had ceased, gas was injected from another field to restore the reservoir's pressure. Production was then resumed through wells so spaced and controlled as to make the most efficient use of the gas to lift the oil. This process doubled the recoverable oil in the field—a truly sensational result giving incontrovertible evidence that under old methods great quantities of oil were being left in the producing sand. The Olney study also demonstrated the savings that could be achieved by the use of a field's natural energy rather than by the customary resort to pumping. Study of the Sugarland field demonstrated how controlled production in a new field could maintain a relatively stable flow of oil by utilizing the reservoir's own energy.[22]

This study of Humble's completely owned Sugarland field, initiated soon after development was begun in 1928, was the first attempt in the industry to investigate quantitatively the causes of pressure decline in a reservoir as oil was withdrawn. Wells were carefully spaced, and records were kept of bottom-hole pressures and of the gas-oil ratio for different rates of production. The objective was to find the rate at which the most efficient use could be made of gas as the energy source for driving the oil to the surface. In 1930 a plant was built for returning gas to the reservoir to help maintain pressure. By controlling the rate of production and returning nearly all the gas, 12,000 barrels of oil could be recovered per day with a very small waste of gas in proportion to the oil produced. This was the beginning of the application at Sugarland of a producing method which—with later refinements as more was learned about the natural energy source of the reservoir—has made possible the continuing production of oil from that field by means of its own energy.[23]

In the autumn of 1929 Humble research men presented, at a meeting of the American Institute of Mining and Metallurgical Engineers, a paper based on the Sugarland experiment entitled "Quantitative Effect of Gas-Oil Ratios on Decline of Average Rock Pressure." The appearance of this paper in the Institute's *Transactions* marks the beginning of the publication of quantitative studies of reservoir behavior during production.[24]

Professional and industry organizations, such as the American Institute of Mining and Metallurgical Engineers and the American Petroleum Institute, and also the Federal Oil Conservation Board provided means for presenting new research findings and studying production problems. Humble's men at first, and Carter's later, participated in this broad study effort. Farish of Humble served on the Committee of Seven of the American Petroleum Institute, which, aided by a technical subcommittee, reported in favor of gas conservation and unit operations.[25] A volume entitled *Function of Natural Gas in the Production of Oil,* edited by H. C. Miller and published in 1929 under the joint sponsorship of the American Petroleum Institute and the United States Bureau of Mines, brought together the findings of research men and petroleum engineers on oil and gas reservoirs. This publication presented the accomplishments of the first phase of the scientific study of oil production. It demonstrated the importance of gas in oil recovery and the possibilities of reducing costs and conserving the resource by controlled production of a reservoir as a unit.

Sound as far as it went, the early research was merely a beginning. It was soon discovered that water was a more important energy source in reservoirs than had previously been realized. To be sure, scientists, including Gulf research men in Pittsburgh, had been working in laboratories on the behavior and function of water in oil recovery. Conclusions from the study of the great East Texas field, as it was being developed in the 1930's, led to an important new concept. Several research groups, interested in determining the source of the energy of this field, tested and discarded various hypotheses. When it had been determined that neither the gas in solution in the oil nor the water moving through the producing formation from where it outcropped on the surface provided sufficient energy to lift the volume of oil being produced, Humble's research engineers began to study the possible effect of compressed water beneath the oil in the reservoir. Their findings demonstrated that oil in the East Texas field was driven to the surface principally by the energy provided by the elastic expansion of the compressed water underlying the oil zone.[26] This discovery contributed to the more efficient use of the field's energy and to a better understanding of water as an energy factor in oil reservoirs in general.

Meanwhile, other key questions were being studied by Humble, other oil companies, industry groups, governmental agencies, and educational institutions.[27] At what rate should oil be produced in a field in order to maximize ultimate recovery? What was the best spacing of wells for both maximum recovery and economy of operations? In a field having more than one producer, how could the amount of oil under each lease be determined as a basis for allocating equitably the allowable production rate of each participant? What could be done, within economic limits, to maintain reservoir pressure by reinjecting gas and water produced with the oil? Humble's research staff was in a particularly good position for studying such questions because the company virtually controlled the entire acreage of several large fields.

The developing knowledge was made widely available through addresses, publications, meetings of professional and industry associations, and government hearings. The research scientists, engineers, and executives of Jersey's affiliates participated extensively in this educational process.

In turn, the new developments were made known to all the Jersey affiliates engaged in production. The accomplishments of any one affiliate were communicated through such formal channels as the Producing Engineering Department of Standard Oil Development and the conferences sponsored by Jersey's Coordination Committee. Informal communication throughout the Jersey producing affiliates also aided in the dissemination of valuable new ideas and techniques. In 1940 Humble assembled the results of the work of its own research men and engineers, other Jersey affiliates, and the industry generally in a book entitled *Principles of Reservoir Behavior*. This volume was prepared for use by its own personnel and that of other Jersey affiliates.

A REVOLUTION IN OIL PRODUCTION

The study of reservoirs provided clues to the solution of the problems of high cost, waste of the resource, and oversupply that were plaguing the American oil industry. It did not, however, immediately solve these problems. Carter and Humble applied the new technical advances so as greatly to improve their own production and also advocated their use by the whole industry. In so doing, they helped to bring about basic changes in the technology and law of the American oil industry in the late 1920's and the 1930's.

Because it early began to lease large blocks on prospective oil lands and in a few years obtained all or nearly all the acreage of several large fields, Humble was by far the most successful practitioner among the Jersey affiliates of this new producing technology, which depended so greatly on the control of entire reservoirs. It was not until the late 1930's that Carter, in its Loudon and Dix fields, effectively applied the same progressive methods. In order to determine the best practices, Humble's research scientists and engineers—within the limits set by lease contracts and regulatory agencies—studied each field as it was being developed.

The methods adopted changed with the growth of knowledge and experience. At first, on the assumption that gas in solution in the oil was the principal energy factor in production, Humble's engineers were chiefly concerned with the efficient use of the gas; they concentrated their efforts on attaining low ratios of gas to the oil recovered and on returning gas to the producing formation in order to help maintain pressure. But soon they came to recognize that other energy factors might also be important, particularly a cap of free gas pressing down on the oil in a reservoir or a water table pressing upward from under the oil zone. They found that if the rate of production was too high the gas cap would be dissipated and the water would rise unevenly and would permanently shut off the flow of oil through the reservoir. As it came to be recognized that most fields were "driven" by more than one energy factor, the engineers tried to establish the rate of production that would most efficiently utilize the factors in combination. In time, they also gave consideration to other phenomena—such as the structural characteristics of a reservoir, the chemical composition of the liquids and gases within it, and the permeability of the reservoir rock to oil. By the late 1930's Humble's development of new fields was being preceded and accompanied by the investigation of many such reservoir phenomena.[28]

The development of many wholly or largely controlled fields brought important results. The control of a whole field made possible the reduction of costs and of the waste of the natural resource. Even in wholly controlled fields, it is true, the company's freedom was limited by the terms of its leases and by the rulings of state regulatory agencies. But, as evidence supporting the new methods accumulated, royalty owners and regulatory commissions became more receptive to proposals based upon these new methods. The effect on reserves was to be demonstrated during World War II by the notable increase in the volume of production in Humble's wholly controlled fields without exceeding the MER, that is, the maximum efficient rate.[29] (See Chapter 17.)

A far more difficult set of problems had to be faced where the Jersey affiliates owned scattered acreage. Humble had interests in a large number of fields where many companies operated. Carter and Standard of Louisiana derived most of their production from fields in which they held checkerboarded leases. In such fields, before regulation was established, Jersey affiliates had to conform, both in their own interest and that of their royalty owners, to the prevailing practices.[30]

By 1927 the Jersey affiliates had envisioned two possible ways of attacking the problem of waste resulting from competitive operation of fields: (1) state regulation of both physical and economic waste, underground and aboveground; (2) agreements among the operators in a given field to develop production in accordance with some plan that considered the whole as a unit. Several difficulties stood in the way of such attacks on the problem. There had long been a lack of agreement as to what constituted waste and how it could be reduced. Moreover, many operators were more interested in the short term than in the long term; they believed that competitive production in a field would yield them larger profits. Also, as observed in Chapter 3, antitrust laws—both state and federal—stood in the way of cooperative field development.

The approach through state law and regulation had little by way of precedent. No state in 1927 had any provision in law either for voluntary cooperation among the operators in an oil field or for effective governmental regulation of fields under competitive development. Oklahoma had a law enacted in 1915 which contained three important conservation features: (1) the definition of waste as both economic and physical and both surface and underground, (2) regulation of production to prevent waste, and (3) provision for the prorating of production among operators in a field in accordance with the market demand for its oil. This law, which recognized the basic physical problems of production, met its first real test when the enormous flood of oil from Seminole in 1926 and 1927 called forth efforts to prorate the field's production. In this situation, the law proved of little use because too little was known about reservoir conditions to apply it.

In Texas and Louisiana, the law was still less developed. Texas had a constitutional provision to prevent waste of natural resources, laws prohibiting waste of oil and gas, and an administrative agency—the Railroad Commission—to formulate and administer regulations applying to the production of oil and gas. But Texas law and regulations had been almost exclusively concerned with the more obvious aboveground physical waste. In Louisiana, too, the applicable laws and regulations were chiefly concerned with the prevention of surface waste.[31]

Humble and Carter and Standard of Louisiana to a lesser extent took an active part in an industry-wide effort to work out an adequate system of law and regulation. The address given by Carter's general counsel, James A. Veasey, at the meeting of the American Bar Association in 1927 (referred to in Chapter 3) is a landmark in the development of the study of American petroleum law.[32] In the late 1920's, committees of the American Petroleum Institute, the American Bar Association, and the Federal Oil Conservation Board, many attorneys in the employ of oil companies or in private practice, and members of law school faculties all studied problems of oil and gas law and regulation. Carter's Veasey and Humble's Hines H. Baker led their companies in this field of investigation and were influential in their own states and in the industry. These men and others from their companies and from Jersey served as members of various national committees concerned with all phases of the over-all problem.[33]

Among the affiliates, it was again Humble that took the most active part in these efforts. This assumption of leadership was partly because Humble faced more critical situations in Texas, whose regulatory system was less advanced than that of Oklahoma, where Carter had most of its operations. Carter's concern with petroleum law increased in the later 1930's after it had acquired large operations in other states.

As the Humble executives' thinking on the problem progressed, they gave central importance to a principle of American law known as "ownership in place." Under this principle, oil and gas in the earth belong to whoever owns the overlying surface. Because of the migratory nature of these materials and the poor early knowledge of reservoirs, the courts had long found it impossible to follow this principle. Instead they had adopted, as a rule of convenience, the common-law "rule of capture" under which oil belongs to whoever produces it. But the law of ownership in place still stood as the preferred principle, waiting only for practical means of application. It had played an important part in the Supreme Court decision of 1900 in *State* v. *Ohio Oil Company*. This decision asserted the right of a state, under its police power, to protect both its natural resources and the correlative rights of the various owners of a field.[34] Although the application of this decision was narrowly limited for a long time by the lack of knowledge of reservoirs, it remained as a potential legal basis for greater control by states in the interest of conservation—that is, the prevention of both physical and economic waste—and of equity among operators in a pool.

Humble's leaders by 1929 had come to regard the principle of ownership in place as fundamental to any effective regulation of oil production.[35] However, progress in the actual adoption of state laws and regulations was slow in coming. An early accomplishment in Texas was in the field of gas conservation—which Humble's executives had advocated, along with unit development of oil fields, before either had gained much support among industry leaders. But by the time a gas conservation act was passed in Texas in 1929, Humble's executives had concluded that this step, however important, would not be effective unless each producing reservoir could be treated as a unit by all the owners.

Indeed, Humble for several years had urged the "unitization" of fields with divided ownership, and it had even made a proposal designed to accomplish this objective without violating antitrust law. The plan provided for the agreement of landowners and lessees in a prospective field to pool operations before oil was found. In March, 1928, five operators, including Humble, entered into such an agreement for a tract in west-central Texas.[36]

It was clear that new legislation was necessary to safeguard such plans from attack under antitrust law. Humble, as well as other affiliates and Jersey itself, believed that such unitization laws should be permissive, not compulsory. Humble's Farish, Pratt, and Suman all participated in the work of a committee of the American Petroleum Institute which in 1927 recommended such legislation, but the board of directors of the institute did not accept the recommendation. Farish, as a member of the important Committee of Nine established in 1927 under federal auspices to study the need for legislation, again urged unit operations. In 1929 Humble strongly advocated the adoption by the Texas legislature of a conservation bill that included provision for unit operations; but, because of the opposition of a number of large companies and a majority of the independents, the bill was passed without the provision for unitization.[37]

Despite this failure, Humble, Pure Oil, Sun, Texas, and Shell in the fall of 1929 entered into an agreement for the development of the Van field, in northeastern Texas, where oil had already then been discovered. President Farish continued to advocate unit operations as a means for holding reserves in the earth and solving the problem of overproduction, and as "the only method of reducing costs to a point where we can meet the competition of cheap foreign oil, itself a product of oil pools owned and operated as individual units." Few operators, however, were willing to go so far in risking antitrust prosecution, and most producers apparently still believed that competitive development and operations promised the larger profits. Because of this attitude, experience soon proved that even with permissive legislation it would be impossible to effect many agreements to unitize fields.[38]

In this situation, another method, proration in accordance with market demand, gradually became the conservation principle most strongly urged by the Jersey affiliates. Humble took the lead in the first successful attempt to prorate the production from a large oil field among the various operators there. This was the Yates field in West Texas, discovered in 1926 but still in September of the next year without a pipeline outlet for its large daily production. Humble was interested in proration in West Texas not only as a producer but also as a purchaser forced at the time to take more oil than it could handle properly. Accordingly, it offered to extend its pipeline to the Yates field if the producers would agree to ratable sharing of the outlet: that is, each producer would supply his agreed share of all the oil taken. After some difficulty, a workable system of apportioning the pipeline capacity among the individual leases was devised by a committee of operators.[39]

This Yates effort stands as something of a milestone in American oil conservation history. It demonstrated (1) the possibility of limiting a field's production to the capacity of its pipeline outlet or market, (2) the feasibility and the economy of wide spacing of wells, and (3) the value of controlled production, based on the study of individual wells, in conserving a field's energy.[40]

So successful was this experiment that many companies, including Pan American (an affiliate of Standard of Indiana), Marland, Shell, Humble, and a number of West Texas independents, joined in supporting a wide application of proration in the region. In 1928 the Texas Railroad Commission, under its authority to act to conserve oil and gas, established proration in several prolific fields in the vast stretches of West Texas and assumed the administration of the prorating of the Yates field. Similar efforts were made to unitize and prorate production in several other fields in Texas and in California and the Mid-Continent.[41]

Although voluntary prorating of individual fields demonstrated the utility of proration, it was obvious that such action in a few fields or even in a few states would not solve the problems of competitive production for the whole domestic industry. Out of the work of a committee of the American Petroleum Institute to study oil supply in 1928 and 1929 came the idea of an interstate oil compact. Humble's Farish was an active member of this committee, and Humble and the other Jersey producing affiliates gave the idea enthusiastic support.

A plan for such a compact was drawn up in 1929 by Hines H. Baker of Humble's Law Department. Under this plan, the member states could establish a fact-finding agency to determine and allocate among the states the amount of oil required to meet market demand; they could encourage states and Congress to remove the restraints of antitrust law in order to make possible unit development and operation of fields; and they could stimulate states to provide legislation and administrative machinery to promote conservation. This Humble plan unequivocally stated that such a compact should have no legislative or enforcement powers, and that the authority to regulate production within a state rested solely with its own police powers. Thus Humble took a position in support of a form of compact in general similar to the one adopted in 1935 by several oil states.[42]

Proration, which late in the 1920's had made such promising beginnings, was nearly swamped by the oversupply of oil in the early 1930's. In 1931 the efforts of the Texas Railroad Commission to prorate production from individual fields were weakened by court decisions and injunctions. The commission failed to establish any effective control of production in the new crisis-producing East Texas field. And the Texas legislature, in opposition to Humble's advocacy of a market-demand law, passed a measure specifically forbidding the limitation of the production of oil to market demand.[43]

The executives of the affiliates thenceforth took no active part in urging conservation legislation. Speaking as chairman of the Board of Directors of Jersey, Farish explained their reticence to a congressional committee in 1934: "We have learned from experience . . . that one of the easiest ways to defeat a thing is for us to ask for it."[44] But executives and engineers of the affiliates did participate, whenever the opportunity arose, in hearings of administrative agencies and in proposals to such agencies, in legislative hearings and investigations, and in litigation in state and federal courts. Their testimony carried weight because of their leading position in the new producing technology. Meanwhile, Humble, although at some cost to its public relations, did not hesitate to enter suit when a conservation issue of importance to its operations was involved.[45] By such means, rather than by public advocacy of legislation or defense of their position, the Jersey affiliates in the 1930's helped to strengthen oil conservation in general and proration in particular.

Depression and the prolific production of the East Texas field finally combined to bring the conservation issue to a crisis, which began in 1932. This difficult situation brought support for government regulation in legislatures and courts as well as within the oil industry. Accompanied by great controversy, efforts were made to bring about some improvement through the federal government, but regulation was left mostly to the state governments.[46]

The principal issue in Texas and, indeed, in some other states was the regulation of production in accordance with market demand, that is, proration. In the spring of 1932, the United States Supreme Court, in *Champlin Refining Company* v. *Oklahoma Corporation Commission,* upheld Oklahoma's conservation statutes and orders.[47] This was followed in the autumn by the passing of the so-called market-demand bill by a special session of the Texas legislature, after bitter controversy and by a close vote. This law specifically included in its definition of waste "the production of crude petroleum oil in excess of transportation or market facilities or reasonable market demand." Signed by the governor of Texas, the new law authorized the state's administrative agency to regulate the volume of production and to prorate that production among producers in a field. A federal court subsequently upheld the constitutionality of the Texas market-demand statute and the authority of the state's agency to administer it. The opinion in *Amazon Petroleum Corporation* v. *Railroad Commission*[48] was written by the same judge who in 1931 had referred to the evidence of engineers as mere theory and speculation. At this later time, the statement of the court referred to their evidence in this more liberal way: ". . . we are bound to say that all this vast amount of evidence, submitted in favor of the Commission's findings, is too ponderable to be brushed aside as no evidence at all." Thus, the growing knowledge of oil reservoirs and of their behavior under the production process contributed to the development of American law governing oil production. The other states in which Jersey's producing affiliates operated, with one exception, adopted regulatory measures similar to those of Oklahoma and Texas. That exception was Illinois.

Regulation by states was in 1935 supplemented by two other developments that gave support to the efforts of the states. One was the enactment of a federal law known as the Connally Act. This measure provided a means by which it was possible virtually to stop the shipment out of a state of crude and products produced in violation of the state's laws. The other one was An Interstate Compact to Conserve Oil and Gas. This compact—approved by nearly all the states in which Jersey affiliates produced oil and by the Congress and President of the United States— provided for a voluntary organization of the member states to consider and advise on conservation matters. Although it had no legislative or enforcement powers, this body proved an influential agency for education in the new technology and in oil and gas conservation, and also for promoting cooperation among the states. An important result was the designation of the United States Bureau of Mines as the agency to compile statistics on the consumptive demand for petroleum products in the United States and to recommend the portion of the national total to be supplied by individual states. These statistics were to serve as a basis for a state's regulatory agency to use in determining the state's total production and in allocating it among fields and among the operators in each field.[49]

Regulation to bring about less wasteful production thus became established by law, and agencies empowered to administer it were created. But many questions still remained in regard to the interpretation and application of the laws. For example, how should a given field's allowable production be determined? What should be the spacing pattern for wells in a field? Under what conditions might exceptions to a field's spacing rule be made for individual wells or tracts? What factor or combination of factors—such as acreage, bottom-hole pressure, thickness of the oil sand, or just the well itself—should be considered in determining the allowable production for the wells in a field?

Jersey affiliates, especially Humble, took a firm stand on such issues and continued to add to the knowledge concerning reservoirs that was an essential basis for decisions. After the Bureau of Mines, in conformance with the Interstate Oil Compact, began to recommend to oil-producing states their allowable production based on the estimated national demand, Humble men urged, with certain qualifications, that the distribution of the Texas allowable among fields be proportionate to the individual field's estimated reserves relative to the state's total. Humble was especially active in the later 1930's in promoting wide spacing of wells as economical and efficient from the viewpoint of oil recovery; it held that actual spacing in a field should be determined on the basis of engineering data as to how wide an area the individual wells could drain efficiently. It maintained that exceptions to the administrative agency's rules in favor of small tracts were inequitable, since their owners would thereby recover more than their share of the oil in the reservoir. In addition, such exceptions were wasteful because the resulting uneven production and the upsetting of the balance of various reservoir factors would reduce ultimate recovery. Humble men urged that, as far as was reasonably possible, a field's allowable production should be allocated among leases and wells in accordance with engineering evidence about the oil in place under the surface area they represented.[50]

Although most oil states had by 1939 made progress in developing regulation of production, not all the problems that had plagued the

American industry had been solved. Proration especially remained a controversial issue. It had not been adopted in California, an important oil state, or in Illinois, a recently burgeoning one. And it was opposed by many small producers. This became a pressing issue in 1938, when, because of the flood of oil coming largely from the unregulated development of production in prolific fields in Illinois, the major oil companies reduced their posted prices, and regulatory agencies in Texas and Oklahoma shut down production for several days.

The proration issue was examined in 1939 at the hearings of the Temporary National Economic Committee investigating alleged monopolistic practices of large oil companies. In his testimony, as noted in Chapter 3, President Farish of Jersey unequivocally stated the company's position on the crucial proration issue and on conservation in general. He acknowledged that, because the country's producing capacity exceeded market demand, production had often been held below the maximum daily output consistent with good conservation practice. To the charge that allocation to individual fields, leases, or wells was inequitable, he replied that equitable allocation was difficult to achieve and could come only with the growth of an appreciation of conservation throughout the industry and among the general public. Humble, he said, had stood for reasonable equity. He urged that more "attention must be given to the proper spacing of wells to get optimum production in each field with minimum drilling expenditure." He expressed the conviction that the administration of proration law by states was a "sound concept" and that progress was being made. He held that proration was for the good of all and that its establishment "was an important act of real industrial statesmanship."[51]

Meanwhile, petroleum engineers were making further important contributions to producing technology. The problems on which they worked became more serious as prices fell. These also grew with the greater depth of wells, which increased the per-foot cost of drilling and brought new or greatly increased drilling difficulties. These problems of deep drilling became especially serious on the Gulf Coast, where Humble had most of its operations. Wells there were deeper than in some other regions, gas pressure was frequently heavy, and heaving shales were troublesome. In addition, underwater drilling brought new problems.

The petroleum engineers of Humble and Carter contributed to the solution of various problems. For overcoming difficulties encountered in deep drilling, they asked manufacturers for—and obtained—sturdier equipment, including seamless pipe and stronger steel alloys. They devised ways of reducing the number of blowouts and of coping with them more successfully when they did occur; they made some progress in drilling through heaving shales; and they improved the cementing of deep wells.[52] They also designed faster drilling bits and a unitized drilling rig. The latter, which shortened the time required to dismantle

STATES IN WHICH JERSEY AFFILIATES HAD CRUDE OIL PRODUCTION IN 1939

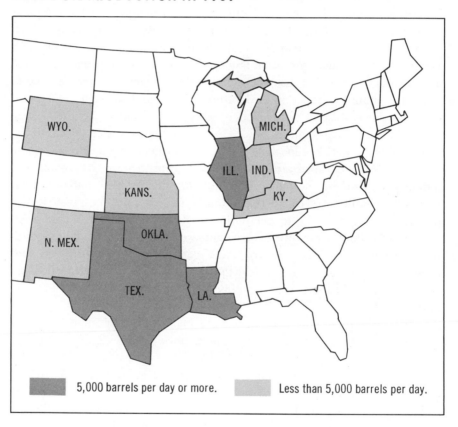

5,000 barrels per day or more.   Less than 5,000 barrels per day.

and move rigs and to set them up in new locations, was the forerunner of the present-day draw works. The engineers, in addition, made progress in drilling under water. They also standardized a wide range of drilling equipment and established better inventory controls for materials and equipment. In general, they raised the efficiency of all aspects of producing operations.[53]

For the same purposes of efficiency and economy, Jersey affiliates transferred among themselves the ownership and management of some of their producing properties. In 1929 Humble turned over to Carter or Standard of Louisiana its scattered properties in Oklahoma, Arkansas, and northern Louisiana. The Louisiana company in 1940 transferred all its producing properties, organization, and operations to Carter, which had begun exploring for the company on contract in 1935. This change enabled the Louisiana affiliate to devote its resources to refining and marketing.

The merger of the Carter-Louisiana properties placed nearly all the domestic oil producing operations of the Jersey affiliates under two companies. Humble was still the larger at the end of the thirties, but Carter's expansion, especially into Illinois, and the improvement of its production methods had gone far to raise it to a position in the Mid-Continent comparable to Humble's in the South and the Southwest.[54]

By the time of the outbreak of World War II, Jersey's domestic producing affiliates had made the transition from empirical to rational, technical operations. More than a decade of oversupply of oil, plus a growing understanding of reservoirs, had brought into being a new production technology and better government regulation. In place of the wasteful, erratic, high-cost industry that had prevailed in the United States since the beginning of oil production in Pennsylvania, most oil states had achieved a more stable and efficient production which promised the ultimate recovery of a far larger percentage of the oil in each reservoir than had been possible in earlier times.

OIL SUPPLY: PRODUCING AND PURCHASING

While improving their methods, the domestic affiliates made substantial progress toward achieving a better ratio of owned production to refinery runs. Humble, Carter, and Standard of Louisiana—together with the natural gas companies in the Northeast, which produced some oil—in 1939 had a combined net* daily average crude oil production of approximately 185,100 barrels. This was sufficient to supply nearly half the requirements of the refineries of the domestic affiliates, compared to providing just over a third of the runs in 1927. The net crude output of the

---

* Net production is the total or gross production minus royalty oil or any other oil produced from wells or leases to which some individual or other company is entitled. Royalty oil is the fraction, customarily one-eighth, belonging to the lessor of the producing property as a condition of the lease. The producer usually purchased the royalty oil or sold it for the account of the lessor.

Table 3: **DAILY AVERAGE NET CRUDE OIL PRODUCTION, PURCHASES, SALES, AND NET AVAILABLE, 1927–1939**

Domestic Affiliates of Standard Oil Company (New Jersey)

(In thousands of 42-gallon barrels)

Net Production

Year	Carter	Humble	Standard of Louisiana	Other Companies	Total United States
1927	61.3	35.2	12.8	3.0	112.4
1928	40.6	42.4	10.1	2.7	95.7
1929	37.0	64.2	10.5	3.2	114.9
1930	29.9	71.8	11.0	3.2	116.0
1931	20.1	78.7	8.9	3.0	110.8
1932	17.5	70.8	6.6	2.7	97.6
1933	16.5	95.9	6.1	2.3	120.8
1934	27.6	95.6	6.0	2.2	131.4
1935	31.1	100.7	5.3	1.9	139.1
1936	34.3	111.3	7.8	1.8	155.3
1937	37.0	138.7	8.8	1.8	186.2
1938	28.3	127.0	9.0	1.7	166.1
1939	44.6	130.4	8.6	1.5	185.1

Purchases from Nonaffiliates[a]

Year	Carter	Humble	Standard of New Jersey	Standard of Louisiana	Other Companies	Total United States
1927	46.2	166.0	23.1	13.8	0.4	249.5
1928	49.5	191.5	11.3	22.3	0.4	275.0
1929	67.3	216.0	12.1	17.3	12.5	325.3
1930	63.5	177.7	13.4	23.0	5.8	283.4
1931	42.6	159.1	7.4	33.2	3.8	246.1
1932	48.2	166.4	7.9	28.4	0.0[b]	250.8
1933	53.6	156.9	2.6	30.6	0.0[b]	243.8
1934	54.5	136.1	2.6	29.6	0.0[b]	222.8
1935	48.6	140.2	7.8	28.9	0.0[b]	225.6
1936	53.9	164.8	8.9	42.6	0.0[b]	270.1
1937	54.4	228.0	7.9	49.9	0.5	340.7
1938	35.2	222.4	9.7	52.7	0.0[b]	319.9
1939	24.6	241.9	7.0	55.4	0.6	329.5

NOTE: Because of the rounding of the numbers, totals are not in all cases the exact sum of individual company figures.

[a] Purchases include royalty oil and oil produced by companies and individuals outside the Jersey Company. Some of the purchases represented one side of the exchange of oil with other companies to save on transportation or to obtain particular kinds of crude; the exact amounts cannot be determined.

[b] Purchases were less than twenty barrels.

affiliates was 64 per cent larger in 1939 than in 1927, while the domestic industry as a whole had increased its volume by 40 per cent. Moreover, the potential production of the affiliates in the United States was considerably larger than their actual output.[55] In 1939, their total estimated oil reserves constituted approximately one-seventh of the estimated reserves of the whole United States, but their crude oil production was less than one-sixteenth of the country's volume.[56]

Table 3 (*cont.*): **DAILY AVERAGE NET CRUDE OIL PRODUCTION, PURCHASES, SALES, AND NET AVAILABLE, 1927–1939**
Domestic Affiliates of Standard Oil Company (New Jersey)
(In thousands of 42-gallon barrels)

		Sales to Nonaffiliates[c]			
Carter	Humble	Standard of New Jersey	Standard of Louisiana	Other Companies	Total United States
5.7	38.8	1.1	1.1	0.8	47.4
13.0	34.9	0.1	0.4	0.6	48.9
21.7	50.5	11.9	0.7	0.8	85.6
20.9	48.9	—	1.2	1.6	67.6
46.3	41.6	—	0.9	1.5	90.3
41.2	39.2	0.7	0.5	1.3	82.9
40.9	28.2	—	0.7	1.0	70.8
45.7	34.8	—	0.7	0.8	82.0
47.0	54.4	0.4	1.8	0.6	104.2
66.6	68.2	0.1	2.3	0.6	137.9
62.1	83.6	0.0[d]	1.7	0.5	147.9
43.4	78.9	1.0	2.6	0.5	126.4
46.5	76.8	1.1	4.2	1.1	129.8

		Net Crude Available to Refineries of Affiliates			
Carter	Humble	Standard of New Jersey	Standard of Louisiana	Other Companies	Total United States
101.9	162.3	22.0	25.6	2.6	314.4
77.1	198.9	11.3	32.0	2.5	321.8
82.6	229.8	0.1	27.1	14.9	354.6
72.4	205.6	13.4	32.9	7.5	331.8
16.4	196.3	7.4	41.2	5.3	266.6
24.4	198.0	7.2	34.5	1.4	265.5
29.3	224.5	2.6	36.0	1.3	293.8
36.4	196.9	2.6	34.9	1.4	272.2
32.7	186.6	7.4	32.5	1.3	260.5
21.5	207.9	8.8	48.1	1.3	287.6
29.2	283.1	7.9	57.0	1.8	378.9
20.1	270.5	8.6	59.1	1.3	359.6
22.6	295.5	5.9	59.7	1.0	384.7

[c] Some of these sales to nonaffiliates were the other side of exchange transactions referred to in note a.

[d] Twenty-one barrels.
Source: Statistical records of Standard Oil Company (New Jersey).

The domestic affiliates were still large buyers of crude oil. In 1939 they purchased a daily average of nearly 329,500 barrels, which was approximately 130,000 more than was needed by the Jersey refineries. They might at times purchase oil beyond the requirements of the refineries in order to keep the Jersey pipelines filled as near to optimum capacity as possible, to supply nonaffiliates on contract, or even to keep the good will of producers when there was a surplus of oil. From the 1920's, the affiliates had followed the policy, whenever production exceeded pipeline or storage capacity, of taking proportionately as much oil from the wells of other producers connected with their pipelines as from their own.[57]

Overproduction posed serious problems for the large purchaser pursuing such a policy. Prorating its purchases, Humble late in the 1920's acquired large storage stocks, which it sold on a declining market at a heavy loss. It attempted to reduce purchases, but within a year its inventories rose by more than 4,000,000 barrels to nearly 17,000,000. The company reduced this amount by selling 5,000,000 barrels, again at a large loss. Instead of refusing to purchase oil in the East Texas field, where it had large production of its own, it then qualified, under a new state regulation, as a public storer; it proposed to store, at a charge, oil offered by its regular suppliers beyond what it purchased. However, this proved an unsatisfactory solution to the problem of surplus oil: the owners objected to paying storage charges and, facing the prospect of selling their oil on a declining market, they vented their resentment against the company. Humble eventually absorbed some of the producers' loss, but it ceased to operate as a public storer. It continued to follow the policy of purchasing ratably when production got out of bounds. It was proration that eventually enabled Humble and other affiliates to keep their inventories down to more manageable proportions. In the later 1930's, they aimed to keep enough storage stocks to supply the refining needs of the domestic affiliates for approximately fifty days. However, not until the long period of overabundance of oil ended in 1941 with the rise in the demand for national defense did the pressure from surplus oil entirely abate.[58]

For the large purchaser, the basic problems after 1926 were the decline in prices and the instability of prices. The general downward trend was worldwide, but in the United States the extreme declines resulted from the rapid competitive development of particular oil fields. A series of annual average field prices for domestic crude compiled by the United States Bureau of Mines gives a general view of the trend. The average of $1.88 per barrel in 1926—the highest since $3.07 in 1920—fell to $1.30 in 1927 and to 65 cents in 1931. Thereafter, it rose to the decade's high of $1.18 in 1937, but declined again to $1.02 in 1939. In Texas, the annual average field price for crude was $1.85 in 1926, 99 cents in 1930, 51 in 1931, 83 in 1932, 56 in 1933, and 95 in 1934; thereafter it rose again until 1937, but then began a decline that continued through 1939. Within these years, fluctuations were sometimes extreme, especially when high production in the East Texas field and later the Loudon field in Illinois upset the market. In East Texas in May, 1931, Humble paid 15 cents a barrel, and "spot sales" were reported as low as 2 cents.[59]

In a price situation so destructive of normal values, conflict between oil producer and purchaser was almost inevitable. The Jersey producing and purchasing affiliates, along with other large purchasers, had to bear much of the onus of transmitting to independent producers the evil tidings of a long-term price decline. On occasions, when Humble initiated reductions or refused to raise prices under strong pressure from producers, it was severely criticized and even attacked in courts and legislative hearings. Many independent producers tended to blame their financial troubles on the foreign crude imported by Jersey and other international companies and urged a tariff on imports. Faced with the superior numbers of the independent producers and with political pressures, the large integrated companies in such circumstances were relatively ineffective in their public and governmental relations.[60]

Humble was in something of a dilemma concerning its policy on crude prices. As a large producer it was interested in high prices; as a heavy purchaser it was cognizant of price as a factor in holding the good will of suppliers. Yet, as a wholesaler and as a supplier to its own refineries, it had little choice because of competition. Its specific decisions were generally based on the economics of a situation, principally because paying more would be unprofitable but also because of its belief that unrealistic pricing would unduly inflate production and lead to a further decline in prices. Only on rare occasions did Humble yield to pressure for higher prices than it believed economically sound. One of its policies made friends, however. It never bought oil at less than its posted prices— those formally offered by posting them in the fields—even when much crude was being sold below postings.[61]

As the years passed, Humble became so sensitive to the effect of price changes on its relations with producers and with the public that it tended to leave the initiation of such changes to others. In the late 1930's, in the bitter controversy over reductions caused by the unregulated flood of oil from new fields in Illinois, the company became cognizant of the necessity for informing producers and public of the reasons for changing its posted prices. Thus Humble came to recognize in Texas, as the Standard Oil combination had done in Pennsylvania half a century earlier, that a large company must justify its actions to others in its own industry and even to the general public.[62]

EXPANSION OF THE NATURAL GAS
BUSINESS OF AFFILIATES

Like oil production, the natural gas business of Jersey affiliates experienced great changes in the late 1920's and the 1930's. Jersey had long had integrated gas operations in western Pennsylvania, eastern Ohio, and West Virginia. These now had to be adjusted to changing conditions, one being the failure to increase the supply of gas commensurate with the increase in demand. In the South and Southwest, on the contrary, the parent company and its affiliates had to strive to find outlets for mounting supplies.

Jersey had made few changes in its natural gas interests in the Appalachian region since the dissolution in 1911, when it had been permitted to retain its gas properties and operations. It had subsequently disposed of a few small companies and had organized the remaining holdings into a system of affiliates for producing, transporting, and marketing. The largest among these affiliates were marketing companies: The East Ohio Gas Company, which served eastern Ohio; Hope Natural Gas Company, which operated in West Virginia; and The Peoples Natural Gas Company, which supplied western Pennsylvania.

In 1927 the gas-producing affiliates had almost 2,700,000 acres under lease. They had 10,000 wells, of which two-thirds produced gas and the remaining third yielded either oil or a combination of the two. Their many small casinghead plants in the fields, for extracting gasoline from the gas at the wellhead, had a daily output of 2,500 barrels of gasoline. Their major business was to provide the marketing affiliates with gas, the volume being approximately 98 billion cubic feet in a year. About a quarter of this amount went directly to industry; another quarter was sold at wholesale to other distributors; and the remaining half was distributed to households and commercial consumers.[63]

Jersey before 1927 had also become interested in the natural gas business in the South. Its first venture in commercial production and transmission outside the Appalachian region was its participation in a company organized in Louisiana in 1926. This venture grew out of a suggestion made by a member of Ford, Bacon & Davis, an engineering firm which for several years had been appraising properties of Jersey's natural gas affiliates in the Northeast. These engineers had done their work in connection with rate hearings, and in 1925 they had made a study of the Monroe field in northern Louisiana as a possible source of fuel for a projected electric generating plant. They had suggested that Jersey acquire leases in that field and build a pipeline to supply gas for the proposed power plant and also for the Baton Rouge refinery.

The company's administrators were then interested in the possibility of reducing refinery operating costs by substituting other fuel for oil at Baton Rouge. They therefore had arranged with the engineering firm to prepare a detailed report for their consideration. They had also called upon one of the leading executives in Jersey's gas operations in the Northeast, Ralph W. Gallagher, to prepare, with the assistance of H. C. Cooper, a separate study of the costs and possible markets for such a venture. The resulting reports had convinced the Board of Directors that the proposal was a promising one. Accordingly, in October, 1925, Jersey had signed a contract with Ford, Bacon & Davis calling for that firm to obtain leases, lay a pipeline to Baton Rouge, and manage operations.[64]

Progress in carrying out the contract was rapid. Interstate Natural Gas Company, Incorporated, was organized in April, 1926. Jersey originally took 37.5 per cent of the initial issue of $3,000,000 in common stock, but it eventually increased its holding to 54 per cent of an enlarged capitalization. Several Jersey men, including Christy Payne, Gallagher, and Cooper, were among the company's directors and officers. Interstate Natural Gas acquired leases on 60,000 acres in the Monroe field, in which twelve wells had already been completed. By the end of 1926, a 170-mile pipeline had been built to Baton Rouge. The company had contracted with Standard of Louisiana to supply up to 30 billion cubic feet of gas a year for ten years at 15 cents per thousand cubic feet.[65]

The growing importance of this product in Jersey's operations in 1927 led to the election of Christy Payne to its Board of Directors. This officer was the leading executive among the old gas affiliates in the Northeast. His duties as director were later enlarged to include advising several natural gas transmission companies in which Jersey acquired a part interest. After Payne became the parent company's treasurer in 1933, Gallagher, who was elected Jersey director in the same year, succeeded him as adviser to the gas companies.

Gallagher had been engaged for many years in Jersey's operations in the Northeast. Although not an engineer by formal training, he had played an important part in the construction of a number of gas transmission lines and in the establishment of safety standards for the industry. His leadership was recognized in 1933 by his election to the presidency of the American Gas Association. As noted in Chapter 2, he became a Jersey vice-president and a member of the Executive Committee in 1937.[66]

In the years from 1927 to 1939, many difficulties arose for the gas affiliates in the Northeast. The main problem was in maintaining an adequate supply. Although the demand for natural gas declined during the depression years, in the longer term demand tended to exceed supply as production declined in old fields and few new productive areas were discovered. The Jersey affiliates in the region barely maintained their supply at approximately an even level by participating in several new fields. In 1939 they sold only slightly more gas than they had sold in 1927; however, their sales in the later year amounted to 28 per cent of the industry's sales in the region, a figure which was about the percentage of the market they had supplied in the earlier year. At the same time, they were squeezed between prices set by governmental agencies and rising costs. They succeeded in reducing costs by consolidating companies and raising operating efficiency.[67]

Although their profits were reduced in the 1930's, the affiliates in which Jersey had a majority interest had earnings in the black every year. In 1933 their combined net earnings dropped to less than 4 per cent of the total in 1929, which was their most profitable year from 1927 to 1939. The earnings rose after 1933, but at no time in the decade did they reach the record level of the thirteen-year period.[68] However, the gas business of the affiliates in the Northeast in 1939 was still a substantial operation earning moderate profits.

The Federal Public Utility Holding Company Act of 1935 introduced a new problem which was still unresolved at the end of the thirties. Companies selling gas directly to consumers had long been subject to municipal and state regulation, but this new act placed under federal control companies in which gas activities of a public utility nature constituted a large part of their total business. Since Jersey, as a stockholder in several such companies, might be classified as a public utility and its entire operation regulated, it applied to the Securities and Exchange Commission for exemption on the ground that the public utility business constituted only a very small part of its total operations. It did not obtain a ruling on this issue until the early 1940's.[69]

In the South and Southwest, Jersey's natural gas interests expanded substantially in the years 1927–1939. The affiliates greatly increased their production, and Jersey acquired ownership in several transmission lines. These lines were a part of a movement that began to develop late in the 1920's to transmit natural gas by pipeline from producing fields in the South and Southwest to distant consumers.

Interstate Natural Gas, organized in Louisiana in 1926, in its first year of operation (1927) delivered 23 billion cubic feet of gas to the Baton Rouge refinery, its largest customer. The company continued to drill new wells, increased the power of two compressor stations on its transmission lines, and doubled parts of the lines in order to serve new customers—including industrial, public utility, and transmission companies. Within two years, it had among its outlets five transmission companies serving large cities in the South. However, the decline in crude prices in the late twenties and the depression of the thirties brought difficulties. When the price of crude fell to a point where it was more economical for the Baton Rouge refinery to burn oil rather than gas, Standard of Louisiana obtained a revision of its purchase contract with Interstate. Other customers also reduced their purchases. But with the help of loans from Jersey and a New York bank, the company weathered the depression and paid off its ten-year mortgage. In 1936 it began to pay regular dividends. Jersey men became active in the company's management on the expiration of the Ford, Bacon & Davis contract in 1935. In 1939 Interstate sold 52 billion cubic feet of natural gas and carried 24 billion for another company.[70]

Louisiana laws and regulations helped to assure a steady supply of gas. The state had enacted a number of laws to reduce the waste of this natural resource; three passed in 1924 had been especially designed to safeguard the Monroe field. In the 1930's other laws were passed to reduce the waste of natural gas from the Rodessa field and of the distillates from deep formations in the Cotton Valley field.[71]

Because of its success in planning and financing Interstate with its pipeline from the Monroe field, Jersey was asked by Prairie Oil & Gas Company and Cities Service Oil Company to join them in providing an outlet for gas from the Texas Panhandle. They offered to supply the product and arrange sales if Jersey would plan the transportation line and furnish the necessary funds. Again the company turned to Ford, Bacon & Davis and to Gallagher and Cooper to make studies of the situation. Satisfied with the prospect of a substantial outlet to the city of Denver and to a steel plant in Pueblo, Colorado, the three oil companies in 1927 incorporated Colorado Interstate Gas Company to build a 250-mile pipeline through New Mexico and Colorado. Jersey subscribed to 42.5 per cent of the common stock and half of the preferred. Meanwhile, its two partners incorporated Canadian River Fuel Corporation to take ownership of leases on about 300,000 acres in the Panhandle field and to provide a pipeline to connect with Colorado Interstate's line at the Texas–New Mexico boundary. These steps bore fruit in 1928, when

Colorado Interstate began to take gas from Canadian River, delivering the fuel to the steel mill in Pueblo and to a distributor in Denver. In 1935 the company paid accumulated preferred dividends, and the next year it began to pay dividends on its common stock. In 1939 it transmitted 42 billion cubic feet of gas.[72]

LONG-DISTANCE NATURAL GAS TRANSMISSION LINES IN WHICH JERSEY HAD AN INTEREST, AS OF 1929

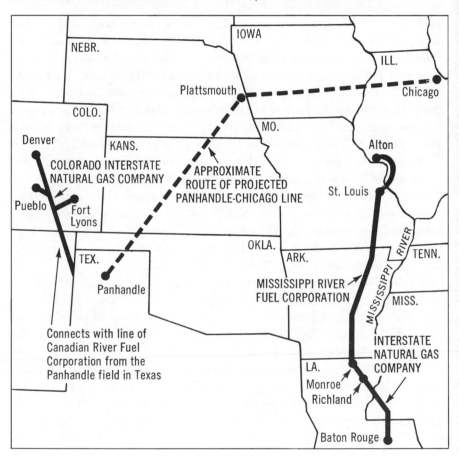

At the urging of five other companies with leases in the Monroe field in Louisiana, Jersey in 1928 joined them in organizing Mississippi River Fuel Corporation to build a 430-mile pipeline to St. Louis. Jersey took 22.5 per cent of the company's stock and mortgage bonds totaling $22,500,000, and, like the other companies, it agreed to furnish the same percentage of the gas required as its percentage of the total of the company's capital stock and bonds. Not being certain that Interstate would have sufficient gas to supply Mississippi River Fuel Corporation and its other customers, Jersey organized Hope Producing Company to acquire acreage in the Monroe and Richland fields. Mississippi River Fuel encountered financial difficulties during the depression, but it paid dividends from 1936 on. Three years later it was carrying about 33 billion cubic feet of natural gas per annum.[73]

Jersey next obtained a minor participation in a still more ambitious venture, the construction of a transmission line to reach the thousand miles from the Texas Panhandle to Chicago. Preliminary surveys had indicated that such a line would not be economically feasible unless it could be made of a thin steel pipe of large diameter and able to withstand double the usual pressure of 400 pounds per square inch. No such pipe was obtainable until 1929, when two manufacturing concerns offered to supply it in 24-inch diameter. One company proposed to manufacture an electric-weld pipe and the other a seamless pipe. These proposals opened the way for organizing a new company, Natural Gas Pipeline Company of America, in which Jersey subscribed to about 13 per cent of the stock and the same percentage of mortgage bonds. The resulting transmission line obtained its supplies from the Texoma Natural Gas Company. In 1939 it delivered 75 billion cubic feet of gas.[74]

Other companies were also building long-distance gas transmission lines in the late 1920's, especially to the north and northeast of the Texas Panhandle and the Hugoton field in Kansas. Among them were two lines built from Texas. One belonged to Panhandle Eastern Pipe Line Company, which delivered gas at the Illinois-Indiana boundary to an affiliate of Columbia Gas & Electric Corporation. This concern served the Northeast, including several states where Jersey affiliates were engaged in the same business. Another long transmission line, owned by Northern Natural Gas Company, reached from Texas to Minnesota.[75]

Humble's role in this growth of the natural gas business for some years was much less than might have been expected from its prominence in the industry. There were special reasons for this. In the mid-1920's, the company had concentrated on oil production; it had assigned its rights in gas fields and had sold gas produced by its oil wells to other concerns—such as oil companies in the gas business, local gas concerns, or carbon-black plants. Then, in 1928, when the Raccoon Bend field on the Texas Gulf Coast gave Humble its first important gas production, an obstacle arose. To dispose of this new supply, Humble signed a contract to sell gas at the field to a pipeline company. But the Texas Railroad Commission, ruling that this contract made Humble a gas utility, promptly reduced the selling price below that stipulated in the contract.[76]

This setback delayed for several years Humble's large-scale entry into the natural gas business. In the meantime, much of the company's gas produced in oil fields was being accounted for by the new practice of reinjecting the gas into the producing formation. Humble had long followed the practice of separating from the gas at the wellhead whatever gasoline it contained. In 1932, the company built two combination casing-head gasoline and repressuring plants in the East Texas field. It enlarged these plants in 1933 and built another plant in the Conroe field in 1934. By that time, it had also acquired large reserves in several other fields. The discovery of the Katy field in the next year increased Humble's gas reserves to an estimated 3 trillion cubic feet.[77]

These enormous reserves, plus the increased production of gas in oil fields, virtually forced Humble to enter heavily into the production and sale of natural gas. It hesitated for a time because of proposals before the Texas legislature to divorce gas and oil properties. The legislature took no action on this issue in 1935, but instead passed the Gas Waste Act, which Humble executives believed to be an improvement over prior legislation. The company thereupon established a separate gas division within the Production Department and set out to find buyers among large industrial consumers and commercial distributors. Its first contract, effective January 1, 1936, was with the Texas Gulf Sulphur Company, which agreed to purchase gas for its plants for ten years at 9 cents per thousand cubic feet. Although much lower than the price the purchaser had been paying to others, this price was estimated to yield Humble a profit.[78]

In the same month the Raccoon Bend problem was resolved, and thus the last important obstacle to Humble's large-scale commercial sale of gas was removed. The solution took the form of an injunction against the enforcement of the Railroad Commission's order of 1928. This decision, affirmed by the Texas Court of Civil Appeals in 1939, established that under Texas law the sale of gas to a utility at the point of origin did not make the seller a public utility.[79]

Attracted by Humble's potential as a supplier of natural gas, other large consumers began to approach the company in 1936. It then explored every possibility for sale at the well, particularly for contracts with large industrial concerns. It had no intention, however, of selling gas for household use or entering into the general purchase and sale of the product. In the autumn of the year, it entered into agreements to process gas to sell to The Texas Company. This step necessitated building a casinghead plant in the large Tomball field and a system of transmission lines leading to refineries at Houston, Port Arthur, and Port Neches in Texas. Humble also entered into other contracts for the sale of gas for fuel to public utilities and industrial plants.[80]

After the middle thirties, a substantial market for natural gas developed as a result of advances in technology and refining. This grew out of the use of butane, propane, and other light hydrocarbons in refinery processing, especially for the manufacture of high-octane gasoline. Humble consequently expanded its plant facilities for providing these lighter hydrocarbons.[81]

But the company's sales—like those of the entire industry in Oklahoma, Louisiana, and Texas—could not keep up with increased gas production. Humble, with its large oil production and enormous gas reserves, was in a worse situation than most companies. It was able to take care of the larger part of the gas produced with oil by increasing processing in natural gasoline plants and by reinjecting it to help maintain reservoir pressures. But the company still flared some gas from oil fields and had a surplus in gas fields. Its building of plants to produce a marketable product in the latter was yet to come.[82] In fact, the industry generally did not at this time find it wise to process gas in gas fields in the uncertain hope of finding markets. The obvious solution was to sell more for transmission to centers of population and industry, but most of these were far from the main producing regions.

Although by the end of the thirties progress had been made in long-distance transmission, only a small part of the potential gas market had yet been reached. In 1939, of a total consumption of natural gas in the United States, less than a fourth was carried by interstate pipelines. Wide regional variations in supply gave rise to great variations in price. Average prices of natural gas at the well in 1939 ranged from 1.5 cents per thousand cubic feet in New Mexico and 2.1 cents in Texas to 18.5 cents in Pennsylvania. Average prices at the points of consumption were as low as 11.2 cents per thousand cubic feet in Oklahoma and as high as 93.7 cents in Washington; in Pennsylvania the average was 37.5 cents.[83]

The natural gas industry obviously needed to build an extensive network of efficient long-distance pipelines in order to connect the producing regions with the great consuming sections of the country. The lines laid by the late 1930's had demonstrated the physical and economic feasibility of gas transmission to distant markets.

However, other roadblocks appeared late in the 1930's. One was the prospect of changes in federal policies following the passage of the Natural Gas Act of 1938. Humble's administrators, uncertain how this law would be applied, were hesitant to sell their company's gas in interstate commerce. They feared that federal regulation of interstate transmission might lead to setting prices at the wellhead, which might in turn bring some federal control over the production of gas and of its joint product, oil.[84] World War II delayed the clarification of federal policy on these questions as well as the building of gas transmission lines.

By the outbreak of war in 1939, Jersey's domestic affiliates had progressed far toward overcoming the weaknesses of their earlier producing and supply operations. They had greatly increased their reserves and had raised substantially the ratio of their owned production to the requirements of their refineries. They had achieved a more stable crude oil production relative to market demand. They had made more effective use of new exploration techniques. By improvements in drilling, they had countered somewhat the rising cost of drilling wells. Taking advantage of new laws and regulations, they had reduced costs by wider spacing of wells and by utilizing the natural energy in the reservoirs to bring oil to the surface. They had also made better use of the natural gas produced. Except in 1931, the producing affiliates as a whole showed a profit in every year of the depression—a better record than that of some years in the 1920's.

Most important was the fact that Jersey's domestic affiliates ended the decade with increased assurance of oil for the future. This assurance came partly from the acquisition of large reserves and from more efficient recovery of oil. But it also reflected the entire industry's greater ability to control the rate of production, to cushion it from the impact of new discoveries, and to make it more rationally responsive to demand and to the long-range needs of the industry.

Chapter 5

Expansion of Foreign Production, 1927–1939

IN EXPANDING its oil production abroad, Standard Oil Company (New Jersey) assumed large risks and commonly operated under conditions far different from those at home. But in many countries there was promise of oil for the future at costs that would be competitive in foreign markets. That promise drew Jersey capital and management into areas geologically unknown, into subtropical and tropical lands, into economically underdeveloped countries, into regions with social and political environments unlike the predominantly North European culture of the United States, and into countries in a state of political ferment and flux.

After 1927, the company's foreign producing organizations were at work in nearly all parts of the non-Communist world. Its Canadian affiliate continued its search for new oil fields. Jersey's own principal focus was on South America, where it acquired its largest operations in Venezuela. Its affiliates also looked for new producing properties in Eastern Europe. It did not participate in the management of Iraq Petroleum Company operating in the Middle East, in which it acquired a minority ownership in 1928. In the Dutch East Indies, however, its affiliate made considerable progress in obtaining concessions and finding new oil fields.

THE IMPERIAL GROUP IN THE AMERICAS

Imperial Oil Limited and its Latin American affiliates—International Petroleum Company, Limited, and The Tropical Oil Company—were largely independent of Jersey's Executive Committee* and of the Produc-

* Imperial's relative independence from New York came partly from the fact that it had a strong Canadian minority ownership. There were also other reasons—psychological, political, and practical—which had helped to shape the relationship of parent company and affiliate over the years. Humble in Texas and certain European affiliates similarly had a large measure of independence.

ing Department in New York. Jersey's Director G. Harrison Smith was an officer of these companies; he became president of International in 1927 and of Imperial in 1933. With headquarters in Toronto, Smith was virtually a one-man organization; he not infrequently made decisions even concerning operating details. Working closely with him on issues concerned with production were R. V. LeSueur, director of Imperial in charge of legal matters, and the successive heads of production, O. B. Hopkins and A. M. McQueen.[1]

Despite many years of a nearly fruitless effort to find oil in Canada, Imperial continued its search in that country. This work was carried on principally by its exploration affiliate, Northwest Company, Limited, which had been organized in 1917 to explore in the province of Alberta. The examination of oil seepages near Fort Norman some ninety miles south of the Arctic Circle, undertaken in 1919 by a 22-year-old geologist, Theodore Link, had led to the discovery of oil in a Devonian reef. Although the test well had been shut in for lack of a profitable outlet, the discovery had helped to defeat the plan of Royal Dutch–Shell's Sir Henri Deterding to obtain a profit-sharing concession from the Canadian government on a large part of northwestern Canada.[2]

Jersey's President Teagle, who as chief executive of Imperial from 1914 to 1917 had promoted the search in Alberta, still held to his conviction that great oil fields were to be found in the vast reaches of western Canada. In fact, it was at his urging that Wallace E. Pratt in 1937 made that region his first field investigation as a Jersey director. "I returned convinced," Pratt recalled in 1963, "that Mr. Teagle's faith was justified concerning the potential hydrocarbon resources of western Canada."[3]

During the years from 1927 until World War II, Imperial's only active producing operation in Canada, except waning production in the old oil region around Petrolia, Ontario, was in the Turner Valley field in Alberta.[4] The company had entered this field after independent operators had developed production. Because these producers were strongly entrenched, it had acquired leases and producing operations by organizing several small companies with the independents as minority owners. The first was Royalite Oil Company, Limited, incorporated in 1921. This company, together with several others in which Imperial held a major interest, by 1929 controlled three-fourths of the Turner Valley field.[5]

Turner Valley was primarily a gas field until 1936. As the gas poured from the wells, it was run through absorption plants to strip it of its liquid content. Most of the resulting distillate was purchased for the

Imperial refinery at Calgary, the only one in the area. Because this light oil was not suited to making the full range of products required by the local market, Imperial brought heavy crude from the United States to help round out the products line of the Calgary plant. Some of Turner Valley's gas was piped to Calgary and other towns for illuminating purposes.

Since these towns did not take all the production, the excess gas was burned in the field. In 1929 a leading Canadian authority on gas called attention to this waste.[6] The following year the Parliamentary Committee on Conservation and Utilization of Natural Gas in Turner Valley reported that 90 per cent of the heat and power value of the gas produced was being wasted.[7] Frantic competition by some forty licensed companies to maximize their production had brought on this condition; little thought had been given to curtailing the waste of gas or prolonging the life of wells. Because attempts to get producers to cooperate in working out a conservation plan had failed, the Parliamentary Committee suggested legislation to be uniformly administered throughout the area.

Imperial—familiar with the objectives and progress of conservation in the United States—had announced its willingness to cooperate in carrying out any conservation measures that might be adopted. In fact, ever since bringing in the important Royalite Number Four in 1924,[8] it had equipped its wells with means for shutting them off in order to conserve gas. But it was not prepared to stop producing in order to save gas when neighboring wells were permitted to run without restraint.[9] However, when the demand for gas and its liquid contents fell drastically in 1931 as a result of the depression, Imperial prorated its own production and its purchases to half the potential of the wells.[10]

Wise though this was as a conservation measure, it had some adverse results. When a provincial conservation committee set production allowables on the basis of current production, Imperial's wells were assigned lower quotas than those of the independent producers. The company also came under severe criticism for reducing its purchases.[11]

Although the government of Alberta was unsuccessful until 1938 in bringing about conservation in the Turner Valley field, Imperial took several measures to reduce waste. It continued to seek the cooperation of other producers in making efficient use of the resource. In 1933, in order to increase naphtha recovery, it put into operation a high-pressure natural gas plant, the first in Canada; two years later it constructed another absorption plant to serve the southern end of the Turner Valley field.

These plants were built to utilize the natural resource to the fullest extent economically feasible. But they did not solve the gas problem.

The discovery of crude oil in the Turner Valley field in June, 1936, and the ensuing boom in production heightened the need for effective government regulation.[12] Imperial, which had normally purchased the field's distillate for its Calgary refinery, was unable to handle the rising volume of crude oil. Therefore, in the fall of 1937, it asked the Alberta government to establish potentials for individual wells so that it could prorate its crude purchases. When the government complied with this request, the company announced that it would purchase not more than 65 per cent of the potential production of any one well. This raised a storm of criticism—reminiscent of early Standard Oil experience—by newspapers, politicians, and independent producers.[13] The producers even considered building their own refinery. The basic trouble, however, was not a lack of refining capacity but the inability of the local market to absorb all the production. Charges for transport to other markets were too high to justify shipment.

In order to reach more distant markets, Imperial in 1937 entered negotiations with Canadian railway companies that resulted in a reduction in freight rates on crude from Calgary to Regina and Moose Jaw in Saskatchewan. Imperial then began to ship oil to its Regina refinery, and British-American Oil Company to ship to its plant in Moose Jaw.[14] But competition with imports from Montana brought a decline in the price of oil from both regions. In January, 1938, Imperial reduced its charge for Turner Valley crude from $1.42 per barrel to the Montana price of $1.20.[15]

Finally, recognizing that the basic problem was the production of too much oil for their available market, the majority of the Turner Valley producers became reconciled to reducing output.[16] In April, 1938, a proration law, known as the Alberta Oil and Gas Act, was passed. A board with supervisory and enforcement powers was established to administer the act, provision was made for production quotas, and a proration formula was adopted. Thus, Alberta, without the enormous waste that for decades had preceded the establishment of effective legislation in the United States, acquired a system of regulation well in advance of the great postwar discoveries in that province.

The war at once brought an increased demand, and late in 1939 the situation of oversupply in the Turner Valley field began to change. During 1940 the demand for oil rose beyond the field's capacity to produce, and frantic drilling was undertaken to extend the limits of the producing area and to increase its output. But the output declined. The bitter truth was that the earlier profligate production had depleted Turner Valley's underground energy.

Imperial's search for new oil fields in the 1930's was disappointing, and by the end of the decade the company still had little production outside Turner Valley. It had increased its small output of 1927 to a daily average of only 2,500 barrels of crude oil in 1939, or a mere one-ninth of Canada's entire production. Consequently, Imperial had to depend on purchases from others for the major portion of the daily average of approximately 60,000 barrels of crude required by its refineries in the 1930's. Its purchases from nonaffiliates in the Dominion over the years ranged between the high daily average of 37,000 barrels in 1929 and the low average of 14,000 in 1934. Carter Oil in the Mid-Continent of the United States and Jersey companies in South America supplied most of the remainder. Among the latter were Imperial's directly owned affiliate in Peru and that company's affiliate in Colombia.

These companies in the southern continent had operations on large tracts.[17] International Petroleum, Limited, had both developed and undeveloped acreage in its big La Brea y Pariñas Estate located in the extreme northwestern part of Peru and served by the port of Talara. The company produced oil on its estate under agreements made in 1922 with the government for a specific annual surface tax to run for fifty years and an export tax fixed for a period of twenty years. Tropical Oil Company operated on its large De Mares concession in Colombia. Managers with headquarters at Talara in Peru and Barrancabermeja in Colombia directed operations. Company representatives in Lima and Bogotá handled relations with governments. Officers in Toronto made the major decisions.

The basic work of the two companies was oil production, but both carried on integrated operations. International had a refinery and tanker loading facilities at Talara from whence it shipped crude for export and products for Peruvian and foreign markets. Tropical's refinery on the Magdalena River supplied products that were shipped by barge and truck to Colombian markets. The pipeline of its affiliate, Andian National Corporation, Limited, carried crude oil for export through lowland jungle to a tanker loading terminal on the Caribbean.

The producing operations of the two affiliates followed similar patterns. Because holdings were large and fields could be operated as units, it was possible to employ production methods similar to those being developed in the United States. Wells were widely spaced and operated so as to avoid unnecessary reduction of reservoir pressure. In the absence of sufficient outlets, much of the gas produced was stripped of its liquid content and returned to the reservoir.

Because the companies operated in regions where few skilled workers were available, they had to provide living facilities. International had the advantage of a better climate and of longer experience in developing a working force and an industrial relations program. Tropical's operations were in humid jungle where health hazards were extreme. Although the company at first had a poor medical record, it became a creditable example of what could be done in overcoming health problems in a difficult environment. Both companies had labor troubles, including strikes. Both made changes in their employee management to improve their labor force and to promote workers to skilled jobs as well as to comply with new legislation.[18]

International Petroleum had special problems in its public relations. The government of Peru was unstable, and there was widespread political unrest. Finding itself in serious financial difficulties, the national administration in Lima sought substantial assistance from foreign companies. It asked for help in developing the port of Callao and in building roads, and it requested funds to stabilize the Peruvian pound. International made several loans to Peru, usually under arrangements that were more advantageous to the country than normal commercial terms. In order to encourage repayment before the expiration in 1942 of the export tax agreement, some loan contracts carried the stipulation that export tariffs would not be increased before the loans were repaid.[19]

Tropical met somewhat different problems in Colombia. The government it dealt with, although more stable, was highly sensitive to public opinion. A persistent cause of friction in employee and public relations was the company's employment of managers and skilled workers from North America. International in Peru also employed outsiders, but they had less impact on the public because they were fewer in number and the company communities were isolated. The fact that Tropical, as the only oil producer and refiner in Colombia until late in 1939, supplied products to the national market contributed to the Colombians' suspicions that the company was charging too much for oil products. The basic prices of the principal products were determined according to a formula—based on prices in New York—agreed upon with the government, but differences arose over certain costs.[20]

Table 4: **DAILY AVERAGE NET CRUDE OIL PRODUCTION, BY COUNTRIES, 1927–1939**

Foreign Affiliates of Standard Oil Company (New Jersey)

(In thousands of 42-gallon barrels)

WESTERN HEMISPHERE

Latin America

Year	Canada[a]	Peru[b]	Colombia[c]	Mexico[d]	Trinidad[e]	Bolivia[f]	Argentina[g]	Venezuela[h]	Total Latin America
1927	0.6	21.3	36.7	9.8	—	0.1	0.8	0.1	68.6
1928	0.9	26.0	48.2	6.4	0.3	0.0	1.2	14.2	96.3
1929	1.9	29.6	49.3	5.0	0.9	0.2	1.9	18.6	105.5
1930	2.2	26.8	49.1	4.5	1.5	0.1	2.1	17.1	101.1
1931	1.6	21.0	43.8	4.1	0.7	0.1	3.3	20.4	93.4
1932	1.1	20.9	39.3	13.5	0.8	0.1	4.7	82.4	161.8
1933	1.0	30.7	31.6	21.3	0.6	0.3	6.4	123.9	214.8
1934	0.8	38.7	41.6	27.3	0.4	0.4	6.6	160.4	275.5
1935	0.6	40.4	42.3	18.6	0.6	0.4	5.8	181.1	289.3
1936	0.4	41.3	45.3	11.9	0.6	0.3	5.2	198.6	303.2
1937	1.6	40.3	49.5	16.1	0.5	0.0	5.2	236.6	348.2
1938	2.4	36.0	52.5	2.0	0.5	—	4.9	233.3	329.2
1939	2.5	29.6	54.5	—	0.9	—	4.6	273.0	362.5

EASTERN HEMISPHERE

	Romania[i]	Poland[j]	Italy[k]	Hungary[l]	Germany[m]	Great Britain[n]	Iraq[o]	Dutch East Indies[p]	Total Eastern Hemisphere	Total Both Hemispheres
1927	4.2	0.7	0.0	—	—	—	—	3.4	8.3	77.5
1928	7.1	0.9	0.0	—	—	—	—	4.5	12.4	109.6
1929	7.4	0.7	0.0	—	—	—	—	7.0	16.0	122.6
1930	8.3	0.6	0.1	—	—	—	—	11.9	20.9	124.2
1931	12.1	0.6	0.3	—	—	—	—	15.1	27.9	122.9
1932	13.8	0.4	0.4	—	—	—	—	17.7	32.4	195.3
1933	13.2	0.4	0.4	—	—	—	—	23.9	38.0	253.8
1934	17.0	0.3	0.3	—	—	—	2.2	27.9	47.8	324.0
1935	14.1	0.3	0.2	—	—	—	8.2	36.1	58.9	348.8
1936	13.7	0.3	0.2	—	—	—	9.0	40.9	64.0	367.6
1937	13.4	0.2	0.2	0.0	—	—	9.0	43.0	65.8	415.6
1938	13.7	—	0.2	0.7	0.0	—	9.5	39.7	63.8	395.4
1939	11.9	—	0.2	2.6	0.2	0.0	8.6	42.3	65.6	430.6

NOTE: 0.0 represents an average daily production of less than 51 barrels. Because of the rounding of numbers, the totals are not in all cases the exact sum of the individual figures.
[a] Imperial Oil Limited and its Canadian affiliates.
[b] International Petroleum Company, Limited.
[c] Tropical Oil Company, The.
[d] Compañía Transcontinental de Petroleo, S.A., 1927–1938; Huasteca Petroleum Company and Mexican Petroleum Company, 1932–1938.
[e] Standard Oil Company of Trinidad.
[f] Standard Oil Company of Bolivia.
[g] Standard Oil Company, S.A., Argentina, and Compañía de Petroleos La Republica, Ltd.
[h] Creole Petroleum Corporation: Standard Oil Company of Venezuela, 1927–1939; Lago Petroleum Corporation, 1932–1939; Compañía de

Petroleo Lago, 1935–1939. Also International Petroleum Company, Limited's, share of Venezuelan oil, 1935–1939.
[i] Romāno-Americana Societa Anonima pentru Industria.
[j] Standard-Nobel w Polsce.
[k] Società Petrolifera Italiana per Azioni.
[l] Magyar Amerikai Olajipari Részvénytársaság.
[m] Gewerkschaft Brigitta.
[n] Anglo-American Oil Company, Ltd.
[o] Jersey's share of oil produced by Iraq Petroleum Company.
[p] Total production of N.V. Nederlandsche Koloniale Petroleum Maatschappij, of which Jersey's share was half from 1934.
Source: Production records of Standard Oil Company (New Jersey).

The situation was extremely complex. Besides differences on economic issues, there were others less tangible and even more difficult to handle. The managers of Tropical apparently did not recognize the extent of the social and psychological problems arising from the fact that aliens were developing the country's natural resources and living among a people of a different culture. According to local standards, the company was a good employer, but for a time it was conservative in its expenditure for improving living facilities for Colombian employees and in its provisions for training and education to enable them to rise more rapidly to higher levels. Moreover, the Canadians had a minimum of communication with the nationals outside the necessary work and government relations. Even the higher-ranking national employees had to live in workers' camps rather than in staff camps. This separateness understandably led to suspicion and resentment that tended to overshadow the company's real virtues and its contributions to the development of a valuable natural resource in Colombia.[21]

One striking aspect of the operations of these companies in both Peru and Colombia was the fact that they did not expand into new areas. Late in the 1920's, International Petroleum, as well as two small producing concerns in Peru, was exploring areas near its operations. But it had ceased doing so by 1931, when the world oversupply of oil made the less promising concessions unattractive. Standard Oil Company (New Jersey) had another affiliate, Standard Oil Company of Peru, which some years earlier had acquired an exploration concession in the Montaña, Peru's territory in the Amazon basin. After the government failed to adopt what the executives in New York considered a satisfactory petroleum law, the affiliate ceased to explore in what would be a high-cost producing region relative to the trend in world oil prices. The government finally passed a new law in 1937, but the company considered its provisions too onerous to justify operations under the difficult conditions in the Montaña. Jersey's officials decided that developing production in that area and building a pipeline to a shipping point on the Pacific would require more capital than they should invest in the region.[22]

After the middle 1930's, however, International and Tropical entered upon exploration programs because they believed their reserves were inadequate to meet future needs. Both companies hired seismograph, gravity-meter, and magnetometer crews to explore their host countries for likely oil-bearing structures.[23] International had an exploration concession and did some geologic and geophysical work in Ecuador.[24] It also entered negotiations with the government of Peru for a concession in the Sechura Desert, just south of its La Brea y Pariñas Estate. Jersey, however, questioned the authority of the government to enter into such a concession contract, and the negotiations finally broke down. International looked into the possibility of obtaining an interest in a large tract, known as the Barco concession, in northeastern Colombia; but, foreseeing high development costs, it did not meet the terms of the concession's owners.[25]

From the standpoint of current operating results, however, both the Peruvian and the Colombian ventures were moderately successful. The volume trend of the oil production of the two companies was upward. Tropical's output rose to a daily average of nearly 54,500 barrels in 1939. International's volume moved upward until 1937, when it averaged more than 40,300 barrels daily, but it declined during the next two years. The Peruvian operations made satisfactory profits. Tropical's producing in Colombia yielded net returns through 1930, although not as high profits as those of its pipeline affiliate. The net earnings of both Colombian companies declined in the 1930's, but their combined earnings were good in those years.[26]

On the whole, there were neither bright lights nor heavy shadows in the experience of the affiliates in Peru and Colombia in the late twenties and the thirties. Would a more perceptive, flexible, and courageous group of administrators have improved the position of the companies despite the difficulties encountered? Or were International and Tropical marooned in an economic and political backwater where progress was difficult? Still, by comparison with certain other affiliates abroad, these two fared reasonably well. They expanded their output modestly, turned in profits, and survived at a time when producing affiliates in one country in Latin America were severely restrained by government regulations and those in two other countries were expropriated.

RETREAT IN ARGENTINA, BOLIVIA, AND MEXICO

Jersey felt the full force of rising economic nationalism and revolution in some countries. The impact on its affiliates was increased by the changing relations of the United States government with Latin America. These developments raised many difficulties and some fundamental questions of policy for both parent company and affiliates.

The producing operations in Argentina were affected by the efforts of a national company to develop production. The leader in this movement was General Enrique Mosconi, who had headed the Argentine petroleum concern, Yacimientos Petroliferos Fiscales (YPF), since its establishment in 1923.[27] General Mosconi was Argentina's chief promoter of government operation of oil production and an outspoken opponent of foreign oil companies. His influence was felt also in other Latin American countries. For example, on a visit to Mexico in 1928, at the invitation of President Calles, he was reported to have recommended the exploitation of Mexico's petroleum resources by a mixed company—with governmental and private ownership—in which the government would have a majority interest. He was quoted as referring to Jersey as a hempen and to Royal Dutch–Shell as a silken rope; both companies, he said, "might hang us."[28]

But Jersey's difficulties in Argentina came from more than the opposition of one leader. The operations of foreign oil companies there were caught in a struggle between the federal and provincial governments for control of oil production. They were also affected by strife between rival factions on the national political stage, as well as by a rising spirit of economic nationalism.[29] Being an American company, Jersey was probably also affected by Argentina's traditional European orientation, which became especially influential in the 1930's under the leadership of Dr. Carlos Saavedra Lamas. In addition, the company's position may have been weakened by Foreign Minister Saavedra's efforts to promote Argentina's leadership among its neighbors.[30]

Over the years, YPF obtained strategic advantages from both the federal and provincial governments. In 1932 it was granted a huge territory in the national reserves and was incorporated as a government-owned corporation. Two years later it was also granted large concessions in the most promising provincial reserves. A Jersey representative in Argentina later reported that the lands held by the national company totaled nearly 167,000,000 hectares (one hectare equals 2.471 acres), "covering every area in Argentina which could by any stretch of the imagination be of interest to a prospector for oil."[31] The explorations of YPF also benefited from the requirement that private companies should report to the government all their own geologic and geophysical information and supply complete records of their drilling operations.[32]

At the same time, the Argentine government placed severe limitations on foreign companies. A law of 1935 prohibited them from obtaining new concessions unless the federal government held half their stock and had a dominant voice in determining their policies. The government also limited the foreign companies—affiliates of Jersey and Royal Dutch–Shell were the largest—to operations in areas already developed by them. Production there was dwindling despite efforts to increase it.[33] In addition, taking advantage of a provision in Argentina's mining code, the government recovered a large part of the concessions held by Jersey affiliates.[34] For example, Standard Oil Company of Argentina, after having spent $5,000,000 on exploration in the Comodoro Rivadavia and Plaza Huincul districts, was entirely eliminated from the former and was reduced to a thousand-hectare concession in the latter.[35]

The effect of these measures is shown by production figures. The highest net crude output of Standard Oil Company, S.A., Argentina, and its small leaseholding affiliate in any year in the 1930's was the daily average of 6,600 barrels in 1934. YPF had an average production of 14,600 barrels daily in that year, and it then held a far larger crude oil reserve than did the Jersey affiliates.[36] Since they obtained less than half the products which they sold in Argentina from oil produced in the country, the Jersey affiliates had to supply the rest from abroad and pay a tariff on the imports.

Despite its favored position, the national company was in a weak financial condition as compared to the affiliates of the leading foreign concerns. Apparently recognizing that YPF could not compete with these two, in 1936 the Argentine government granted the national company the right to determine the volume of oil which the privately owned companies could import. This ruling was modified the next year to allow the affiliates of Jersey and Royal Dutch–Shell, after giving up some of their market outlets, to keep their sales volume as of that time; but it required that for any increase they had to obtain supplies from the national company.[37]

Jersey, nevertheless, maintained its producing operations in Argentina. Its policy was not to withdraw from a country under pressure but rather to continue operations in the hope that conditions would eventually improve. Its executives believed that the efficiency and general superiority of the operations of the affiliates in Argentina, as compared to the performance of the national concern, would eventually be recognized. They overlooked the extent to which a public concern could draw on the national treasury to cover its deficits. Later in the 1930's, any expectation of winning on the strength of performance was dampened by developments in Bolivia and Mexico.

In 1937 Jersey experienced in Bolivia the first nationalization of its foreign properties in the Western Hemisphere—the first in the world except for the early loss in Russia of Nobel properties of which Jersey had become a part owner in 1920.* This experience in Bolivia was of importance not so much because of the loss of investments and oil reserves but because of the way expropriation came about and its implications for the security of foreign investments in the future. This episode was also significant as a challenge to the Good Neighbor Policy of the United States and a test of this country's obligations under the Protocol Relative to Nonintervention signed in the Inter-American Conference at Buenos Aires in 1936.[38]

Standard Oil Company (New Jersey) had acquired a large concession in Bolivia in the early 1920's, at the height of its drive to acquire prospective oil lands in foreign countries. This was a government concession for oil exploration and exploitation which it had purchased in 1921 from Richmond Levering Company, an American concern dealing in foreign concessions. Jersey's executives, having sent high-level operating men to explore the possibilities in Bolivia, were well aware of the difficulties to be overcome in developing operations in that landlocked, mountainous, and undeveloped country with little demand for oil itself and located far from substantial foreign markets.[39] In order to safeguard its heavy prospective investments there, the company requested a new concession contract from the government. This was obtained in 1922.[40]

Standard Oil Company of Bolivia, organized in 1921, began to explore for likely places to drill as soon as the new contract was in effect. During the next ten years, it did a great deal of geologic work, located several areas to be tested, and drilled many wells. Its first discovery was in the Villa Montes–Tarija area near the Bermejo River, which at that point marks the international boundary between Bolivia and Argentina. The Bermejo wells were in an almost inaccessible region near the eastern foothills of the Andes, an area quite incapable of consuming any sizable volume of petroleum products. The prospect of successful development depended on finding a sufficiently large production to justify building a pipeline for transporting oil to consuming centers or shipping points.[41] While exploring for new fields and drilling more wells, the company used its small Bermejo output as fuel for drilling and for operating a still to

---

* For an account of this ill-fated investment, see *History of Standard Oil Company (New Jersey), The Resurgent Years, 1911–1927*, by George Sweet Gibb and Evelyn H. Knowlton, pp. 328–358.

supply gasoline for its automobiles and trucks. During a number of months in 1925 and 1926, the local manager of the operation allowed some oil to be pumped through a two-inch pipe a few hundred yards to the Argentine side of the Bermejo River for use as fuel by a wildcat drilling outfit of Standard Oil Company of Argentina.

Actual production raised the question as to when the increased surface rentals, under the concession contract of 1922, should become effective. This agreement called for higher rentals when operations reached the state of "production," but it did not define the term. T. R. Armstrong of the Producing Department in New York, who had participated in drawing up the contract of 1922, held that, when it was drafted, both parties had understood that commercial production was meant. After discussions between representatives of the company and the government, the latter issued a presidential decree in 1928 declaring that rentals should begin January 1, 1930, regardless of whether or not commercial production had been developed. The company paid the surface rental in accordance with this decree.[42]

In 1931, however, a new *de facto* Bolivian government revoked the decree of 1928 and ordered the company to pay surface charges as if commercial production had begun in 1924. This the company refused to do. It filed with the Supreme Court of Bolivia an appeal attacking the substance of the resolution of 1931 and asking for its cancellation. The court did not act on this appeal, and the issue was still unresolved when the company's concession was canceled and its properties were seized in March, 1937.[43]

Standard Oil Company of Bolivia reduced its drilling program in 1932 and soon ceased to look for more oil. Its highest annual output in the 1930's averaged around 450 barrels a day. Two small plants supplied local markets. During the Chaco War between Bolivia and Paraguay from 1932 to 1935, the Bolivian army authorities took possession of these plants and disposed of their output. The Bolivian authorities returned control to the company after the termination of hostilities, but Standard of Bolivia did not resume its effort to expand operations.[44]

Economics, Bolivian politics, and international relations all contributed to the relaxation of the company's search for more oil. The need to obtain production in Latin America that had motivated Jersey's entry into Bolivia in the early 1920's was no longer urgent; oil production had been developed in more favorably located countries. A more important factor was the situation within Bolivia itself. Because of the disappointing results of the expenditures already made, it had become economically unattractive for the company to incur the further cost of expanding production and constructing the necessary oil carriers. Neither roads nor rivers offered means of transport within Bolivia, and to reach outside markets had become economically impracticable and, apparently, even politically impossible. To have built a pipeline over the high Andes to the Pacific would have been inordinately expensive. Argentina's high rates on oil shipment by railroad from the Bolivian boundary and its refusal to grant a right of way for a pipeline to the Paraná River made virtually impossible the sale of Bolivian oil in Argentina or transport across the northern part of that country for shipment to other markets.[45] Ironically, Bolivia itself, because of its long-standing dispute with Paraguay over the Chaco, had refused to grant a right of way through that region for a pipeline to carry oil to the Paraguay River. The Chaco War, of course, made transport over the disputed territory impossible.[46] The increasing political insecurity of foreign investments in Bolivia in itself discouraged further investing there.

A foreshadowing of trouble appeared in 1935. It was then charged in the Argentine Congress that Standard Oil Company of Argentina was smuggling oil into that country from Bolivia. The accusation was widely publicized, but the Argentine authorities investigated and found it without foundation.[47] In Bolivia itself, a critical attitude toward Standard of Bolivia, which had arisen because of the latter's reduction of its exploration and development, had been heightened by claims that the company did not support that country adequately in the war with Paraguay. Among other charges, Standard of Bolivia was accused of supplying Paraguay with 9,000,000 gallons of gasoline by way of Argentina—at a time when the output was actually controlled by the Bolivian army.[48] The company was also severely criticized for refusing to loan several million dollars to the government during the Chaco War.[49]

Just before the scheduled Bolivian election of May 30, 1936, a military junta ousted the government—a result of the disastrous effect of the war, which had ended in a truce. The country's army was defeated and demoralized, its social and economic institutions were shattered, and its old leadership was discredited. Discontent in the army and among civilians, particularly university students, had led to the formation of the National Socialist Party. The party's leader, Colonel David Toro, was proclaimed provisional president of the new "socialist republic." This government appealed to a growing nationalist sentiment and to labor discontent. It had the support of Tristan Maroff, the leading Bolivian Communist, and his followers, who controlled the Confederación Sindical de Trabajadores de Bolivia.[50]

Despite its nationalist orientation to the left, the Toro government in November, 1936, took action reassuring to Standard Oil Company of Bolivia. It returned the fund that the oil concern had pledged as a guaranty of the observance of the terms of its concession contract. The government's "supreme resolution" ordering the refund of the 250,000 bolivianos stated that the company had fully met the obligations covered by the fund. The resolution was signed by President Toro and all the members of his cabinet.[51]

In December, however, the same government initiated a series of acts that ended in seizure of the company's properties and operations.[52] First, the junta created a national oil enterprise, called Yacimientos Petroliferos Fiscales Bolivianos (YPFB), modeled after Argentina's YPF. Bolivian officials and newspapers immediately launched a campaign of vituperation against Standard Oil Company of Bolivia. In January, 1937, the constitutionally elected Supreme Court was replaced by a new group of judges. And, on March 13, 1937, the regime issued a decree canceling the affiliate's concession contract and confiscating its properties.[53] The government based this action on the allegation that the company had defrauded Bolivia by its export of petroleum in 1925 and its failure to pay increased surface rentals from 1931. The government declared the concession and properties forfeit under Richmond Levering's concession contract of 1920. Two days later, representatives of the newly established YPFB, accompanied by police, appeared at Standard's headquarters, turned the employees out of the offices, and took possession of all files, books, office equipment, bank accounts, and accounts receivable. The government also seized the company's oil wells and other physical assets.[54]

Jersey rightly denied that it was a party to the 1920 contract of Richmond Levering and maintained that its affiliate was governed by the concession contract of 1922 with the government of Bolivia. Unlike that of 1920, which gave the government the right to cancel the concession in case of fraud, Jersey's contract provided that the government should give six months' notice of any allegation of default before taking action; it also gave the company recourse to the courts in its own defense.[55]

Standard of Bolivia denied the validity of the technicalities on which the allegation of fraud was based. It had refused to pay surface rentals under the decree of 1931 until the Supreme Court rendered a decision on its appeal, but it pointed out that it had stood ready to pay rentals in accordance with the court's decision. It also maintained that it was legally clear of the charge of defrauding Bolivia by the export of petroleum. It admitted that over several months in 1925 and 1926 it had piped a total of close to 5,000 barrels of oil from its Bolivian operations across the river to the wildcat drilling of Standard of Argentina, but it held that the matter had been duly settled with the government.[56]

According to correspondence in the Jersey files concerning the oil, in brief this is what had happened.[57] When the oil had been transferred to the Argentine side of the Bermejo River, the operations on the Bolivian side had been in an early developmental stage and without a commercial outlet. The transfer had been reported at the time to the local Argentine customs official. But Armstrong, the legal expert of the Foreign Producing Department in New York, had advised that it should not be formally reported to the Bolivian government. He held that it was not necessary to report the transfer because there was no Bolivian export tax, the company had a right to export oil under its concession contract, and the transfer was merely a loan and not a commercial transaction. Armstrong held that the government might make this use of the oil the basis for levying higher surface rentals on what was too small a production to be classed as a commercial operation. However, the transfer of the oil was known at the time by the local Bolivian customs authority and was discussed informally with a national officer in La Paz. When the Argentine charges in 1935 again had raised the issue, executives in New York had decided to make a formal report of the matter. This had been done, and, on the basis of the 1922 contract, the Bolivian government had charged royalty against the oil amounting to less than a thousand dollars. Company executives then believed that this had closed the affair. Their interpretation had been confirmed by the government's subsequent return of the guaranty fund to the company.

Recent historical research has thrown light on this Bolivian affair. *The Making of the Good Neighbor Policy* by Bryce Wood is especially illuminating in what it reveals from the records of the United States Department of State.[58]

These records give some insight into the considerations motivating the action of the Bolivian government. Foreign Minister Enrique Finot is quoted as having said to the United States Minister to Bolivia that, aside from legal grounds, there was "a moral justification arising from the company's noncooperative attitude during the Chaco War," and that it was "a natural aspiration of a country to control its own petroleum resources."[59] Beyond these were other motives or objectives. One was Minister Finot's own political ambitions. More significant was Bolivia's desire to win Argentina's support to its side in the forthcoming Chaco Peace Conference. Minister Finot was reported to have learned late in 1936 from discussions with Foreign Minister Carlos Saavedra Lamas of Argentina that this neighboring country demanded access to Bolivia's oil resources in return for its support of Bolivia at the peace conference. Soon after the meeting of the two ministers, indeed, Argentina agreed to extend its railway into Bolivia from the frontier railhead at Yacuiba in return for arrangements for joint exploitation of Bolivian oil fields. It was at this very time that the Bolivian national oil company was established. The fact that the only oil fields in Bolivia belonged to the Jersey affiliate indicates that the immediate fulfillment of the objective of this Argentine-Bolivian convention necessitated control of that company's properties and operations.[60]

These developments came at about the time when the United States signed the Protocol Relative to Nonintervention at Buenos Aires in December, 1936.[61] After the seizure of Standard Oil properties, the United States Minister to Bolivia reported that Bolivian Foreign Minister Finot had little fear of diplomatic pressure from Washington, "for he had repeatedly asserted to friends that the policy of the United States is to let American investments abroad take care of themselves."[62]

The Bolivian seizure, as already noted, was the first test of the United States' interpretation of its 1936 commitment. When Jersey consulted the Department of State, it was informed that the United States government could take no action until the company had exhausted all possible remedies in Bolivia. The department did, however, instruct the United States Minister to inform the Bolivian Foreign Minister that it regretted "to see difficulties arise" out of the interpretation of contracts between United States companies and foreign governments—and that it hoped for an equitable settlement based on friendly discussions. In the interview that followed, Minister Finot asserted that "we had to drive the Standard Oil Company out of Bolivia for political reasons." He also said to the United States representative later: "As I always contended, the American Government will never lift a finger in defense of the Standard Oil Company; the informal presentation of the views of your Government proves this."[63]

Jersey itself entered discussions with the Bolivian government. It had no desire to resume operations in Bolivia, but it considered the removal of the allegation of fraud as important to its good standing generally. It also hoped to receive some compensation for its investment of $17,000,-000, from which it had derived no profits. It therefore sent one of its attorneys, F. C. Pannill, who was familiar with operations in Latin America, to discuss the matter with Foreign Minister Finot. During the course of their conference, according to Pannill, Minister Finot showed him a letter from Sumner Welles of the Department of State indicating that the United States government would not intervene if Bolivia should take action against Standard Oil.[64] Jersey continued to maintain communications with Bolivian officials, but no progress was made.

In the meantime, Secretary Cordell Hull of the Department of State, whose Good Neighbor Policy was involved, tried to bring about an amicable settlement on the basis of mutual confidence. When no progress was made, the Department of State finally proposed arbitration, but to no avail. The Bolivian government was willing to make a cash settlement, but it would make no compromise as to the validity of the decree canceling the company's concessions and confiscating its properties. In fact, it had already made agreements with Argentina and Brazil which assumed the validity of the seizure.[65] The company on its part would not accept any settlement that might establish a precedent for expropriation by other countries.[66]

Jersey's only remaining recourse was to appeal to the Bolivian Supreme Court. It hesitated to do so because it believed the court to consist of members arbitrarily chosen by the military junta governing the country. Because the Bolivian statute of limitations allowed thirty years in which to seek redress, the company could postpone such an appeal in the hope that the country's leadership would change. But events forced Jersey to act. A revolt overthrew the Toro government and established a new *de facto* administration headed by Colonel Germán Busch. In October, 1937, this government issued a decree stating that appeal must be made within ninety days; this time limit was extended by sixty more days on request from the United States Department of State. The company filed its appeal on March 21, 1938.[67]

In the meantime, a campaign of intimidation had been started against Standard of Bolivia. Its Bolivian counsel, Dr. Carlos Calvo, was taken to the Argentine border and ordered out of the country. It was proposed in newspapers and over the radio that eight Bolivian lawyers who had expressed the opinion that the decree was arbitrary and illegal should lose their citizenship. How extreme this campaign became is illustrated by a statement made by the Director General of the National Police in a radio broadcast delivered in February, 1939: "It is precisely in these moments that we should make known to the justices of the Supreme Court our decision to tear out their entrails and burn their blood if perchance they should rule against the sacred interests of the Nation and in favor of the Standard Oil Company." One member of the court resigned in protest against attempts to intimidate the justices.[68]

The decision of the Supreme Court was handed down on March 8, 1939. The court, whose membership had been completely changed by Busch, avoided a decision on the legality of the decree by merely ruling that the company did not have legal status in Bolivia and hence could not enter suit against the state. This ruling was based on two technicalities: that the transfer of the contract from the Richmond Levering Company to Standard Oil Company of Bolivia had not had the approval of the government, and that the power of attorney from the company executed by its president in 1921 had not been accompanied by a certified copy of the minutes of the directors' meeting which elected him president.[69] Actually, both these alleged irregularities had been followed by the new concession contract of 1922. Although the court's decision left the basic issues unresolved, it left the company without further recourse in Bolivia.

Following this development, the United States Department of State took the controversy in hand, but for some time it made no progress. The settlement eventually made was influenced by the pressures resulting from the outbreak of World War II in 1939. (See Chapter 15.) By that time, both the Department of State and Jersey, together with other American oil companies, had virtually met defeat at the hands of another Latin American country, Mexico.

In 1938, only a year after the cancellation of the concession of Standard Oil Company of Bolivia, President Lázaro Cárdenas of Mexico expropriated the properties of Jersey and other foreign oil companies in that country. This was the Mexican president's response to the refusal of the companies to meet fully the government's terms in a labor dispute. Actually, it climaxed a struggle between foreign oil companies and the government of Mexico during a quarter-century of revolution in that country.

Controversy lasting a decade over the nationalization of oil in the subsoil under Article 27 of the Mexican Constitution of 1917 was ostensibly resolved for the American companies as a result of the discussions in 1927 between President Plutarco E. Calles of Mexico and Ambassador Dwight W. Morrow of the United States.[70] Uncertainty as to its rights had caused Jersey to liquidate much of its investment in oil production in Mexico. Under the new agreement, companies could obtain confirmatory concessions for lands owned or leased before May 1, 1917, on which work had actually been done or the intent to explore and exploit had been expressed; they could also apply for new concessions on lands leased or purchased after that date. The Department of State completed the structure of the new relationship with Mexico by issuing a statement to the effect that in the future questions could be left for determination by the courts of Mexico.[71]

Jersey's Compañía Transcontinental de Petroleo, S.A., and smaller Mexican affiliates forthwith applied for and received concessions on both pre- and post-constitutional leases.[72] However, the concessions on the latter obligated the company to heavy payments for exploration and exploitation privileges. Richardson Pratt, an executive of Transcontinental in Mexico, wrote with reference to the leases obtained after May 1, 1917: "We know now that the government has recognized them but has made the terms so drastic that unless low-cost production is found somewhat similar to Panuco and Southern field production the leases cannot be operated profitably at anywhere near today's market." Concerning northern Mexico, on which the eyes of Jersey interests had long been fixed and where some exploratory work had been done, Pratt held that oil could not be produced there profitably "under the present tax, royalty and other obligations that the Mexican Government imposes"; hence he indicated that he "would not spend good money after bad."[73]

This restrictive consideration came to govern Jersey policy in Mexico, and operations as well as investments were reduced. But a considerable acreage was retained in the hope that the American oil companies and the government might some day come to a workable understanding. Jersey then invested its capital in more promising countries, notably Venezuela, and transferred its ablest executives in Mexico to more active operations. Among others, C. H. Lieb, president and general manager of Transcontinental, was transferred to Venezuela.

Thus poor prospects brought an attrition of Jersey management as well as of investments and operations in Mexico. The same policy of curtailment was followed by other companies. This in turn weakened the operations of the Mexican oil industry and contributed to increasing criticism of foreign companies in that country. A vicious circle was generated that brought a progressive decline in the industry and diminished its standing in Mexico.

With the acquisition of Huasteca Petroleum and Mexican Petroleum through its purchase of the foreign properties of Standard Oil Company (Indiana) in 1932, Jersey, despite its policy of withdrawal, became heavily involved in oil operations in Mexico. Consequently it was affected by a series of adverse developments. These grew out of a renewed nationalist and antiforeign movement. After the ratification by the United States in 1934 of the Montevideo Treaty on the Rights and Duties of States and the coming into power of both the labor-oriented government of Lázaro Cárdenas in Mexico and the New Deal administration in the United States, the relationship under the Calles-Morrow compromises broke down altogether. Mexico then again expropriated the lands of United States citizens—as it had done in the 1920's—in order to carry forward a program of collective farming and ranching. But it made no provision for compensation.[74]

President Cárdenas' position was greatly strengthened in the middle 1930's. By deporting two of his leading opponents, former President Calles and Luis Morones, head of a moderate party of the left, he weakened his opposition. He also won support from another quarter. Although apparently not then a Communist himself, in 1935 the president legalized the Mexican Communist Party, which, in keeping with the new policy of the Communist International, had turned itself into a popular-front movement. Early in 1936, Cárdenas' firm supporter, Communist Vicente Lombardo Toledano, consolidated his hold on Mexican labor by becoming general secretary of the Confederación de Trabajadores de Mexico.[75] Two laws passed late in 1936 greatly increased the powers of the Cárdenas administration. One authorized the expropriation of private property of a public utility nature—broadly defined—"to satisfy collective necessities in the case of war or interior upheaval."[76] The other reduced the terms of justices of the Supreme Court of Mexico from life to the tenure of the president who appointed them.[77]

On the very day in November, 1936, when the Senate of Mexico approved the law authorizing the expropriation of private property, trouble began for the oil companies. The Oil Workers' Syndicate then requested the foreign oil concerns operating in Mexico to agree to a new contract.

The union's demands, if agreed to by the American companies, would have meant both high additional labor costs and participation in management by representatives of the labor organization. Among the proposed provisions that would have increased costs were the following: a substantial raise in wages; double pay for working in rain; heavy layoff allowances; liberal pensions after twenty years of employment; private cars and chauffeurs for labor leaders; payment of the expenses of delegates to labor syndicate conventions; free overalls and laundry service for workmen; free medical, dental, and surgical services for employees and their families and a wide range of relatives; paid annual vacations of from four to six weeks for employees; payment of first-class railway accommodations to whatever place an employee chose to go for vacation; payment for 365 days a year for only 233 days of actual work; and pay for 56 hours for a 40-hour week. Bearing on the prerogatives of management were the demands that no employees be discharged or transferred without the union's permission and that the union should appoint from its own membership assistant general managers of production and sales and also executives next in rank to other important managers. In the judgment of Jersey's leaders, if these demands were granted, the number of administrative positions left to the control of company management would be so limited as to make proper supervision and management impossible.[78]

A series of meetings followed between representatives of the foreign oil companies and of the Mexican government. During several months of negotiations, the oilmen offered substantial wage increases. They refused other syndicate demands. In consequence, the union called a strike to begin May 28, 1937. The government took action at once and terminated the strike. Alleging that a dangerous state of disorder existed, it filed with the Mexican Labor Board "a suit of an economic order" under the expropriation law of 1936.[79]

Among other considerations, the Labor Board had to judge the financial capacity of the companies to pay. A committee appointed to study the question submitted, after only thirty days of investigation, a 1,500-page report on its examination of the accounting records of all the companies covering a period of several years. On the basis of this report, the Labor Board decided, contrary to the position taken by the foreign oil interests, that the syndicate's demands did not exceed the companies' capacity to pay. The companies appealed, but the Supreme Court of Mexico upheld the Labor Board's decision and denied any rights to the foreign concerns in this suit.[80]

After the court had ruled on the issue, the companies on March 16,

1938, offered to pay the amount of the new awards under the Labor Board's decision—26,000,000 pesos per year—in addition to continuing payments under existing contracts. However, they did not agree to other requirements of the Labor Board, some of which would have seriously weakened management.[81] Two days later, Cárdenas signed the expropriation decree, and the government seized the properties of the foreign companies and turned them over to Petróleos Mexicanos, the national oil company, which held very large national land reserves but had found no oil. On December 3, 1939, the Supreme Court of Mexico upheld the expropriation decree.[82]

Opinion differed as to whether expropriation was the result of a deliberate policy of President Cárdenas or he was driven to it by the intransigence of the oil companies. There were those who believed that the oilmen might have fared better if they had been less determined to stand on their rights as they saw them and more appreciative of the pressures bearing upon the president of Mexico. Others felt that the president was so heavily committed in advance to the nationalization of Mexico's natural resources that whatever the companies had done would have been of little avail. Most if not all of Jersey's top executives held that expropriation was the objective of President Cárdenas from the beginning. Josephus Daniels, the United States Ambassador to Mexico, maintained that the primary issue was the labor dispute and that Cárdenas' original objective was not expropriation.[83]

The governments of the United States and the United Kingdom both protested. The Mexican government severed diplomatic relations with the latter but not with the United States—which, it apparently believed, would do no more than protest. Somewhat at odds among themselves and uncertain over what course to take, the members of the Department of State and Ambassador Josephus Daniels pursued a policy which from one point of view led to a series of retreats and, from another, was a triumph for the Good Neighbor Policy. Secretary of State Cordell Hull believed that good-neighborliness was reciprocal. And, although he fully recognized the right to expropriate, he took a firm stand for compensation. He stated in a note to the Mexican government: "The taking of property without compensation is not expropriation. It is confiscation. It is no less confiscation because there may be an expressed intent to pay at some time in the future."[84]

Standard Oil Company (New Jersey) and the other American oil companies, except Sinclair Oil & Refining Company, failed to come to any settlement with the Mexican government. They held out for arbitration, with the support for some time of Secretary Hull and other members of the Department of State. Arbitration, however, which for decades had been recognized as a proper procedure for settling international disputes involving one or more sovereign states, was no more acceptable to Mexico than it was to Bolivia. Mexico proposed settlement by a commission of two members, one to be appointed by the Mexican and the other by the United States government. The economic adviser of the Department of State, Herbert Feis, and the petroleum adviser, Max Thornburg, both recommended that settlement be deferred. They held that leaving it to the commission proposed by Mexico would establish a dangerous precedent.[85] Jersey's top executives—advised by Edwin Borchard of Yale University, an authority on international law, to hold out for arbitration—refused to yield, as also did officers of other American oil companies. This left the final negotiation of a settlement to the Department of State. Some observers believed that the companies might have strengthened their moral position had they continued, despite a lack of progress, to carry on discussions with representatives of the Mexican government.

As in the 1927 climax of the controversy over their rights under the Mexican Constitution of 1917, the oil companies at this later time had held to their contractual and property rights as they interpreted them. On the other hand, the United States government had acted in accordance with its policy of improving the international standing of the United States. At first guided by its commitment to promote a viable Good Neighbor Policy, the Department of State eventually became committed to building Western Hemisphere solidarity in defense of the Allies in World War II. (See Chapter 15.)

SUCCESS IN VENEZUELA

Jersey's position in Venezuela in the 1930's was in striking contrast to its standing in Argentina, Bolivia, and Mexico. Not only did it greatly expand its reserves and production in Venezuela but it also maintained sound relations with the government and with its own employees.

Venezuela had great natural advantages for the crude oil producer. Like Mexico, it had rich petroleum resources not far from tidewater and favorably located with relation to markets. Venezuela's long coastline faces the Caribbean to the north and the Atlantic to the northeast. Its coast is closer to American North Atlantic and European markets than is the Gulf Coast of Texas.

In Venezuela as in most Latin American countries, many obstacles had to be overcome in developing oil production. Except in the highlands, the tropical climate ranged from arid semidesert to humid jungle. When Jersey began to explore for oil there in the 1920's, Venezuela was still largely an undeveloped country. Only a modest number of roads were usable at all times, and in the interior they became mere trails passable only by oxcart or pack mule—and not even by them in rainy periods. Lake Maracaibo in western Venezuela and the San Juan and Orinoco rivers in the eastern part were navigable by fairly large craft, but sand bars obstructed outlets to the sea. Almost no skilled labor was available, and the attitudes and social structure of the mass of the population made adjustment to the organization and discipline of a modern industrial enterprise difficult. Nearly all of the occupied area was held by large landowners; only a small part of it was cultivated, and that by peons using primitive methods and living in small villages on vast estates. Large parts of Venezuela were inhabited only by Indians still living in tribal units. Much of the country's population was poverty-stricken, illiterate, and superstitious. The poorer classes suffered from malnutrition and disease; only the wealthy were served by the country's inadequate medical and educational facilities.

Jersey's affiliates could deal with such conditions if they had some assurance of security for the large and long-term investments required. They did have a considerable measure of security in Venezuela. Ironically, however, for many years their relatively safe position was under an ironhanded military dictatorship. General Juan Vicente Gómez, an Indian from the Andean highlands, had seized power in 1908, and he held it without effective opposition until his death late in 1935. Gómez, who controlled congress, courts, and administrative officers, in fact was the government, arbitrary and tyrannical; under him individual rights did not exist except as he granted them. He ran the country for the benefit of himself, his family, and members of his military clique. But his government maintained strict civil order of a kind.

As Díaz of Mexico had been, Gómez was friendly to foreign capital and business as means to obtain wealth from the natural resources of his backward country. By adopting the new petroleum code of 1922 and setting up a competent agency to administer the law, his government encouraged foreign interests to develop Venezuela's petroleum resources. Oilmen soon learned that Gómez respected contracts.

Venezuelan oil law was the most favorable in Latin America to the development of the industry. In contrast with Mexico's, the law on the ownership of oil was indisputably clear: minerals in the subsoil belonged to the state and not to the surface owner. The petroleum law of 1922, drawn up with the advice of experts in the oil law of the United States, defined the conditions under which concessions would be granted and operations carried on.[86] It also specifically stated the obligations of the concessionaires to the government. This law governed oil operations in Venezuela for more than two decades.

The Petroleum Bureau set up by the Venezuelan government had supervision of the administration of the petroleum code. This agency came to be staffed by experts, including geologists and petroleum engineers, who had an understanding of oil exploration and production and of the oil business in general. With such representatives of the government, oil company executives could discuss difficulties and differences on a high level of understanding and confidence, a relationship that was then almost unique in Jersey's experience in the southern part of the Western Hemisphere.[87] The situation in Venezuela was in striking contrast to that in some countries, where issues that should have been settled on the basis of facts became the subject of emotional debate in the national congress.

Standard Oil Company of Venezuela in 1928 completed its first well to promise commercial production. Prior to this discovery, the company had to show for its investment of $27,000,000 over nearly a decade of time only unexplored concessions, inland water craft, drilling rigs, much disappointing experience, miscellaneous camp facilities, and forty-two dry holes.[88] One of those dry holes was Moneb No. 1 in Quiriquire in eastern Venezuela, which had been drilled by a cable rig. In June, 1928, a rotary rig struck oil in this very well, thus making the first commercial discovery in the eastern part of the country and initiating an important development there.[89] It was at the end of the same month that Jersey signed the contract for the acquisition of Creole Petroleum Corporation, which already had production in western Venezuela. (See Chapter 3.)

In order to introduce economies and to meet certain provisions in recent laws of Venezuela, Jersey simplified the corporate structure of its affiliates operating in that country. Creole Petroleum Corporation became a holding company, and Standard Oil Company of Venezuela was made the operating company. The physical assets of the former were transferred to the latter, and several affiliates that had been set up to hold concessions were by 1931 merged with Standard Oil Company of Venezuela.[90] By that time, Jersey had bought enough additional shares from individual owners to raise its original bare majority to 64.8 per cent of the capital stock of Creole Petroleum Corporation.

On Jersey's acquisition of its Creole interest in 1928, Director Sadler became the new affiliate's president. Three other Jersey men became vice-presidents: T. R. Armstrong, legal counsel; Eugene Holman, from 1929 head of the division for relations with foreign producing affiliates of the Producing Department in New York; and C. H. Lieb, an engineer in charge of producing operations in Mexico. L. C. Booker, formerly with Standard Oil of Venezuela, continued to represent Jersey's interests with the Venezuelan government. The top executives, who remained in New York, corresponded regularly with local managers, received periodic reports from them, and made frequent visits to Venezuela to talk with local managers and groups and to examine conditions at first hand.

In 1929 Lieb was named president and general manager of Standard Oil Company of Venezuela. He immediately set about raising the quality and morale of the employee organization; in addition, he got under way extensive programs for exploration and development. Henry E. Linam, who had come to Venezuela as a driller in 1925, was appointed superintendent of the eastern division. Tough with his men and quick to discharge the unfit, Linam built up a driving supervisory force of North Americans. He was merciless with others, as he was with himself, and he was disliked by many. Nevertheless, the Venezuelans liked him because he learned to speak Spanish and so could communicate with them directly. Linam became Lieb's successor as president and general manager when the latter returned to the United States in 1932 to become president of Carter.[91]

Aside from Creole's "lake parcels," developed and operated by the Venezuelan affiliate of Gulf Oil Corporation, Standard of Venezuela at the end of 1928 had only one producing well, the one in which oil had been discovered at Quiriquire. But it had nearly 11,000,000 acres in concessions, mostly subject to increasing annual rentals.[92] These had to be explored in order to find likely places to drill and to determine what areas should be "renounced" in order to reduce rental costs.

The exploration program required an able organization. Because the land was in large part geologically blind, being covered with dense jungle and having little in the way of visible outcropping of strata, geology was of limited value for surface exploration. Standard of Venezuela therefore turned to geophysics. Having no geophysical organization itself, it hired crews from the large affiliate in Texas. The first Humble unit arrived in eastern Venezuela late in 1928, and others followed in the next few years. Standard's own crews did geologic surveying where such operations were feasible and also did aerial surveying. G. Moses Knebel of Humble became the company's chief geologist.[93]

The first producing field to be developed was Quiriquire. Wells were drilled to stake out its limits. At the end of 1930 it was estimated to contain reserves of 80,000,000 barrels and to extend over more than 40,000 acres. The company built roads and laid a pipeline to the San Juan River at Caripito. This pipeline was ready for use when production was begun in 1931. The oil was carried from Caripito by partially filled tankers and barges to beyond the Maturin Bar, where the tankers were filled for their ocean voyage. Because of the promise of this area, the headquarters of Standard of Venezuela was moved to Caripito.[94]

As a result of extensive surveying and wildcatting, the company discovered three fields in the early 1930's. Two were in the state of Falcón in western Venezuela. One proved disappointing and was shut in, but the other, near the coast at Cumarebo, yielded a desirable light oil. The third discovery was at Pedernales, on the Gulf of Paria near Trinidad, in the Venezuelan territory known as Delta Amacuro. This field yielded oil with a high sulfur content, a disadvantage that was offset in part by its favorable location.

On the basis of the findings of its exploration crews, Standard of Venezuela gave up a tremendous amount of acreage. From 1929 through 1932, it reduced its concession acreage from 11,000,000 to 5,250,000. By the end of 1932, Creole's executives in New York were reasonably satisfied with the affiliate's holdings, but were again interested in acquiring new concessions.[95] President Linam's close relationship with members of the ruling clique in the government undoubtedly was a factor in the company's acquisition of additional concessions until the death of Gómez in 1935.

The 1932 purchase of the foreign properties of Standard of Indiana greatly extended Jersey's holdings in Venezuela. Lago Petroleum Corporation had extensive concessions, reserves, and production in the great Maracaibo basin and some concessions in other parts of the country. Especially valuable were its production on the so-called maritime strip on Lake Maracaibo and its large undeveloped concessions in the lake. The latter were believed to be extensions of geologic formations from which oil was already being produced.

Again Jersey made changes in its Venezuelan organization. Because both Creole and Lago had some minority ownership, it was not practicable to merge the two in one corporation. But executives of the parent company in New York established a large measure of administrative unity by making its own men top officers of both. Although Lago Petroleum was a more important producer than Creole, it was not Lago's chief executive but Jersey's Eugene Holman who became the company's president in 1932. The next year Holman also became president of Creole. The two companies thereafter had the same chief executive. Frank C. Laurie, Lago's former head, continued to serve as that company's general man-

HOLDINGS OF JERSEY AFFILIATES IN VENEZUELA AND ARUBA IN 1939

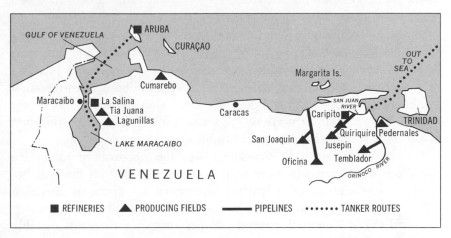

ager. In March, 1937, the Creole directors in New York officially designated Linam as the senior officer in Venezuela with headquarters in Caracas.

Creole gradually simplified the operating management of these affiliates. Although it could not merge Standard of Venezuela and Lago into one corporation because of minority ownership in the latter, it transferred operating responsibility in particular situations to whichever company could best handle the operation. The affiliates had to reflect in their account books the participation of each company in a given operation. In 1937 Creole separated operations into the eastern and the western division. It assigned management of the former to Standard of Venezuela and of the latter to Lago Petroleum. Before the end of the decade, it centered the top management of all operations in Caracas. Actual corporate merger did not come until later.[96]

Lago Petroleum greatly extended its Lake Maracaibo operations. For some time it confined itself mainly to operating developed fields and drilling on the down-dip to the southeast of the huge stratigraphic trap from which it was already obtaining oil. It hired exploration crews to carry out geophysical and core-drilling programs on its lake concessions. On the basis of their findings, Lago surrendered nearly half its concession acreage in 1934 and 1935; these reductions included its holdings in Lake Maracaibo where the depth was more than 75 feet, then the limit of effective drilling in water. Information obtained from these explorations in the mid-1930's led to Lago's important discovery of oil in the Eocene sands; these lay below the Miocene, in which the earlier discoveries had been made in Lake Maracaibo.

Standard of Venezuela found several fields on the llanos (great plains) of the eastern part of the country in the later 1930's. By this time G. Moses Knebel was second in command of the company and John W. Brice had succeeded him as chief geologist. On the basis of information obtained from geophysical and geologic surveys, the company discovered the Temblador field just north of the Orinoco River, Jusepin in the state of Monagas, and San Joaquin and El Roble in Anzoátegui.

A distinct advantage in Venezuela was the opportunity to unitize operations in fields where more than one company had an interest. Because there was no antitrust law in that country, the operators in such a field could pool their interests under the management of one company.[97] Standard Oil of Venezuela owned 100 per cent of some fields, notably Quiriquire. In other producing fields in eastern Venezuela in which ownership was divided, it joined with whatever company or companies had interests there—affiliates of Royal Dutch–Shell or Gulf Oil Corporation—in pooling operations under one management, each company receiving oil proportionate to its ownership. In western Venezuela, the Jersey affiliates in the Lake Maracaibo fields and at Cumarebo entered into similar arrangements. Thus it was possible to apply the growing knowledge of the nature and mechanics of oil reservoirs and the new production engineering to reducing costs and ensuring more efficient production.

Efficient operations were a necessity in a country where the development of oil fields was virtually a colonizing operation. When geologists had indicated likely places for drilling, wildcat rigs were brought to such sites by water, where possible, or by oxcart, muleback, or even human carriers. Whenever a new field was discovered on land, roads and bridges had to be constructed and pipelines laid to a refinery or shipping terminal. Often they were built through deep and even swampy jungle. They also had to be maintained; and transport equipment, which was subjected to the unbelievable wear and tear of extremely difficult operating conditions, had to be kept in repair at high cost.[98]

Because oil was usually discovered in more or less isolated areas, it was necessary to supply living facilities for the working crews.[99] When a field was being developed, housing, food, and potable water had to be provided. The accommodations in the early years were generally quite primitive. The sickness rate was always high in such camps, and as a result a doctor had to be secured and a first-aid station set up. As permanent operations became established, the Venezuelan workers began to bring in their women and children. At first the affiliates allowed the families to live in huts built just outside company camps; but the resulting filth and disease soon necessitated providing special quarters, with supervised sanitation and medical care, for the Venezuelan employees. It was only with much effort that the companies succeeded in breaking down prejudices against doctors and inoculations and in raising sanitary standards to tolerable levels.

To provide medical care in Venezuela, where there were no adequate facilities, the affiliates built area hospitals and recruited a staff of doctors and nurses to care for major illnesses and accidents. Company employees, brought from camps to such medical centers, were given free care; but others were charged nominal amounts if they were able to pay. Resistance to the bringing in of medical men from the United States soon necessitated the employment of Venezuelans. The Jersey affiliates solved the problem of providing competent medical services by sending national doctors and medical students to the United States for training. Registered nurses had to be brought from the United States because there was no training school for nurses in Venezuela.

The companies had to make each oil field something of a community in itself. As operations grew and the original camps developed into permanent communities, the companies' responsibilities became fixed. This situation not only was costly; it also led to extreme paternalism on the part of management. Expensive and troublesome as it was, to provide housing and community facilities was commonly a necessary condition of operations in underdeveloped countries.

The Jersey affiliates had to build up an effective working force. In the early years, skilled oil-field workers simply were not available in Venezuela and, as a matter of course, they had to be imported from North America. It was Jersey policy everywhere to utilize as many national personnel as possible—both law and cost differentials encouraged local employment—but for years most Venezuelan workers qualified only for common labor. They were basically illiterate, undernourished, and accustomed only to the use of hoe, spade, and machete.

In a letter written in 1930 to President Lieb of Standard of Venezuela, Eugene Holman advised employing Venezuelans wherever they could do as good a job as North Americans. Holman wrote that on his inspection trips he had been impressed with the native ability of the national employees; he felt that the problem was primarily one of training and education. He suggested to Lieb that he give thought to this matter, particularly that he consider the possibility of selecting a group of young Venezuelans to be sent to the United States for schooling and for a period of training in some of Jersey's domestic affiliates in order to prepare them for taking over technical and managerial jobs.[100]

Many years later Eugene Holman told, as an example of the potential of illiterate and unskilled nationals, of the rise of one young Venezuelan employee. On a trip to an eastern Venezuelan operation in about 1930, Holman had been impressed by the look of amazement and admiration with which a young warehouse employee watched the visiting executive utilize the principle of the lever, in the form of a plank and a large rock, in lifting a 100-pound drilling bit to the level of a truck's floor. This principle was completely new to the young worker. On a visit to the same warehouse two years later, Holman found that this same young man was then an efficient warehouse clerk—the North American in charge had taught him enough reading, writing, and arithmetic to keep records.[101]

Training in skills was not the only requirement; attitudes also had to be changed and motivations developed. At first the individual workers were reluctant to accept promotion to supervisory jobs because doing so would raise them above their social group. This attitude, of course, was not limited to Venezuelans; elsewhere in Latin America and also in Asia, oil companies met the same reluctance to rise above one's peers. The short-term solution was to bring in outsiders to fill supervisory posts. For this reason, as well as because of the lack of skills among the nationals, Jersey's Venezuelan operations for many years employed North Americans for even the lowest supervisory jobs in the fields. It is said that the nationals first employed in such capacities were not from among the majority of local lowland workers but were outsiders—sturdy native Indians from the Andean highlands and pearl divers from the coastal island of Margarita.[102]

Some formal, organized training of Venezuelan employees was established in the early years, but it was at first mainly on the job. As well-established and profitable operations were developed, more and more attention was given to specialized training. As long as Gómez lived, however, such programs were limited by his opposition. The dictator discouraged company practices that might encourage independence on the part of the workers.

In fact, Gómez did not allow labor to organize or any agitator from another country to appear in Venezuela. The government also outlawed Communists. It brutally crushed any effort to start a labor movement by exiling, imprisoning, or even executing labor leaders or agitators. It forbade strikes. The police handled any labor unrest.

The death of Gómez in December, 1935, changed this situation. Then came an opportunity for the people to make known their long-suppressed aspirations and grievances. Radicals and reformers flocked to Venezuela. But when the deadly calm that had prevailed under Gómez seemed about to explode into bloody revolution, martial law was declared. To fill the unexpired "term" of President Gómez, the Venezuelan Congress elected the acting Minister of War; he was later elected for a constitutional term of five years.[103]

The new president, General Eleazar López Contreras, immediately demonstrated a liberal tendency. His government restored civil rights and freedom of speech. It encouraged the organization of labor syndicates. It also generally maintained civil order.

This new freedom led to the rapid unionization of workers and the fall of the unions into hands of radical leaders. Serious disturbances arose, including strikes in oil centers, during which the workers made extreme demands for wage raises and privileges. They soon began to demonstrate a rebellious spirit. The lives of supervisors of Standard of Venezuela and Lago Petroleum were threatened, and several foremen were severely beaten. In December, 1936, Lago unions began to strike. However, widespread chaos in labor-management relations in Venezuela finally led the political leaders to take a hand in the situation. A presidential decree dictated the terms of strike settlements, and the government deported some radical leaders and agitators and suppressed communications media that were allegedly subversive. It also organized a new body of national police for patrol duty.[104]

In the meantime, Jersey's Venezuelan affiliates had taken measures to improve relations with their national employees. After the death of Gómez, they were free to adapt to their own needs the programs and practices employed by Jersey companies in other countries. In 1936 they undertook a program to improve their employee force and their relations with it. Operating units then began to experiment with employee representation.[105] The affiliates in 1937 introduced several employee benefits plans, including a life insurance program, a sickness benefit plan, and a voluntary thrift plan based on contributions by both company and participating workers. The employees at first looked upon the savings plan with some suspicion: labor unions in the Western Division started a whispering campaign to the effect that the employee would not see his money again. However, as experience demonstrated the good faith of the companies, the thrift plan won support among the workers. The companies also attempted to establish better communication with employees. This necessitated special training of the North American foremen—to encourage them to act as schoolmasters rather than as bosses and to learn the language of the national employees.[106]

Officers in New York urged that every effort be made to build an understanding and loyal labor force. In 1937 Creole's President Holman warned the general manager of one affiliate that larger reserves, lower costs, and better techniques were not enough. He wrote:

Assuming that our crude reserves and prospects are sufficient to support a successful producing effort in the years to come, it is up to us to continue our efforts in the building of an efficient and loyal organization that will function harmoniously in our producing activity. This leads us to the main point which we wish to emphasize more strongly in this letter. We do not think any manager has a more important problem before him today than this all-important one. Nationalistic and radical trends are rampant throughout the world today, and scholars well versed in world affairs point out the dangers to modern business in such trends. . . . If we have an understanding management which an employee can consult on problems that may arise, our experience leads us to believe that most complaints, which are in the beginning trivial, can be solved to the satisfaction of the employer and the employee.[107]

T. R. Armstrong, undoubtedly mindful of current labor difficulties in Mexico, went even further in a letter to an executive in Venezuela. Good employee relations, he wrote, might well be the decisive factor in determining whether or not the company could continue to operate as a private enterprise in Venezuela.[108]

A new labor law enacted by the Venezuelan Congress in 1936 greatly advanced the cause of labor and labor organizations and spurred the affiliates' efforts, already under way, to improve their employee relations. Although some of the changes envisaged by the new law were long overdue and others were admirable from a social point of view, many provisions were far too advanced for the state of Venezuela's commercial and industrial development. Drawn up under the influence of Mexican labor legislation and the social ideas of a liberal British representative from the International Labor Organization, the new law embodied the most radical developments in legislation in the New World and the most advanced thinking on labor problems in Europe. The law provided for the formation of labor syndicates, empowered to represent a company's workers if 75 per cent joined the union; it also provided for a system of national and local labor boards to administer the law and of special courts to try cases rising under it.[109]

Meeting the requirements of this new law was not too difficult for the Jersey affiliates. The board that drew up the regulations to govern the application of the law sought to make it workable and consequently softened its impact. This was especially important to companies not well established or with very limited resources. The Jersey affiliates were already operating extensively and were generally in advance of the requirements for housing, schooling, scholarships, and worker training. What the law did in such matters was to give the workers of Jersey's affiliates legal rights to benefits they already were receiving.[110]

However, one *reglamento* that became effective in 1938 caused the Jersey affiliates some trouble: the requirement that 75 per cent of the employees by different classes or levels of employment be Venezuelan nationals. On an over-all basis, the companies met the percentage requirement by a wide margin; to employ that proportion of nationals in all classes was another matter. But the Labor Department, when it learned that a sufficient number of Venezuelans to fill the jobs requiring higher skills simply did not exist, allowed the companies an extension of time in which to comply with the rule.[111]

The Jersey companies thereupon increased the range and tempo of their educational program for Venezuelan nationals. Elementary schooling beyond the four grades required by the law was provided for the children of employees, and further education—including advanced training in schools in Venezuela or the United States—was made available for the most promising candidates. In order to raise the literacy rate of the employees, classes for adults were also started, and night schools were organized to train them for skilled producing and refining jobs or for typing, stenography, comptometer operating, and other kinds of office work. The students were promised assignment to appropriate jobs as these became available.[112]

The company viewed with some apprehension the provision of the law for so-called profit sharing (*utilidades*). An executive decree of December, 1938, established the rate of sharing by ordering that each employee, in addition to his regular earnings, should receive for the previous twelve-month period 12.45 per cent of his total wages or salary for the year. Although the amount paid by the Jersey interests was large, it was well within their ability to pay. This was not profit sharing in the usual sense, however, because it meant an obligation to pay even if the company had no profit.[113]

The functioning of the labor laws obviously depended on the new Labor Ministry, with its regional branches, and on the new system of labor courts, which were a part of the national judiciary. The administrative machinery had some jurisdiction over the unions as well as over the application of the law to the companies. The early operation of the agency, as expressed in the *reglamento* of 1938, gave promise of a realistic handling of problems. In fact, the establishment of the labor agency and courts promised an orderly administration of labor law.

Everything considered, Jersey was well established in Venezuela by the time of the outbreak of World War II. Progress had been made in building an effective labor force, and on the whole relations with the government were good. The crude oil production of affiliates in Venezuela had increased from almost nothing in 1927 to a daily average of 273,000 barrels in 1939. This volume then accounted for about two-thirds of Jersey's foreign and two-fifths of its total production. The estimated gross crude oil reserves of the Venezuelan affiliates, not counting the recently acquired interest in Mene Grande, had risen from virtually zero in 1927 to approximately 2½ billion barrels at the end of 1939.[114]

SLOW PROGRESS IN THE EASTERN HEMISPHERE

Jersey's rising oil production in Venezuela was a boon to its marketing in the Eastern Hemisphere, especially in Europe. For reasons of cost and competitive strategy, the company also sought to expand its crude oil production in that part of the world. Some additional production was acquired in Europe, but results there were mixed. Progress was made in the Dutch East Indies, although problems were also encountered there.

In Romania, which was believed to have substantial undiscovered oil resources, the political situation was unfavorable. Româno-Americana's report to Jersey for 1930 noted: "The untiring ingenuity of the politicians and journalists in endeavoring to create an unfavorable atmosphere about the government results in a life that is diversified by incidents, scandals and alarms." Members of the royal family, notably King Carol, might have led their country, which was greatly favored by nature, to a relatively high state of economic development. Unfortunately they were not cast in the mold of King Charles and Queen Elizabeth ("Carmen Sylva"), their royal forebears of the early years of the century.[115]

A new mining law passed in Romania in 1929 gave some spur to the oil industry by placing foreign oil companies on the same basis as nationals in applying for new holdings. However, the small size and the high cost of concessions made exploration attractive only in areas close to proved production. In fact, only three fields of major importance were discovered in Romania in two decades, the last being Buscani in 1934. A mining law of 1937 imposed onerous and uncertain conditions, especially upon foreign companies. The political climate under the dictatorial rule of King Carol had become highly unfavorable to the development of oil concessions.[116]

Româno-Americana remained a weak company during most of this period although it did improve somewhat after Ralph P. Bolton became manager in 1937. Its estimated reserves totaled about 90,000,000 barrels in 1939, but its crude production had declined to a daily average of 11,900 barrels. Româno's income barely covered operating expenditures and thus did not pay for administrative and other nonoperating charges.[117] Despite its difficulties, the company followed the general Jersey pattern of providing some benefits for its employees that were not required by law.

The condition of the producing affiliate in Poland was even more discouraging. There was no change in the downward trend of production which had been going on since 1909. Work in the fields north of the Carpathian Mountains was confined largely to deepening existing wells or drilling additional ones in proved territory. The government's control of the industry and the country's economic difficulties compounded the troubles of the oil companies. Standard–Nobel w Polsce, Jersey's affiliate, therefore gave up its struggle to increase its production after 1927 and began a gradual liquidation of its operations. In 1937 it sold its remaining properties to Socony-Vacuum. Thus ended a once-promising operation which for many years had brought only declining production and loss.[118]

In Italy, the small production of Società Petrolifera Italiana in the Po Valley rose until 1932, but thereafter it went into a decline. Jersey retained a controlling interest in the company in the hope that a concession for a substantial acreage might be obtained. From 1927 to 1939 there were more unprofitable than profitable years.[119]

The most promising Jersey producing operation in Europe on the eve of World War II was a new development in Hungary. Here, after oil was found in commercial quantities near the Yugoslav border in 1937, the European Gas & Electric Company—in which Jersey had acquired a 90 per cent interest—organized an operating company, Magyar Amerikai Olajipari Részvénytársaság (MAORT). Paul Ruedemann, an American of German birth, was manager of operations. Drilling extended this field to a net production of 2,600 barrels daily in 1939. Jersey had spent more than $10,000,000 in Hungary when it received its first dividend of $206,000 in 1939. At last in Central Europe the company was meeting with promise for the future.[120]

In the Middle East, Jersey obtained its first crude oil from Iraq Petroleum in 1934. Although the affiliate had discovered the Kirkuk field in 1927, commercial production had had to await the building of pipeline outlets. It was not until 1934 that lines were completed to Haifa and Tripoli on the Mediterranean Coast. The owners of Iraq Petroleum extended their holdings to a complete coverage of Iraq and acquired additional concessions within the boundaries of the old Turkish Empire. They organized affiliates to explore for oil and to develop production outside the concessions of Iraq Petroleum itself. One company operating in Qatar, a small peninsula jutting out into the Persian Gulf, discovered oil in 1939. In that year, Jersey's one-eighth share of the crude production of Iraq Petroleum rose to a daily average of 8,600 barrels; its share of the estimated reserves was approximately 360,000,000 barrels.[121]

Jersey's largest crude production in the Eastern Hemisphere before World War II was in the Dutch East Indies. Its affiliate—N.V. Nederlandsche Koloniale Petroleum Maatschappij (NKPM)—in 1927, after fifteen years of exploration and wildcatting, had just entered upon commercial production on lands which it had acquired from private holders. By that time, it had completed a pipeline from its Talang Akar field in South Sumatra to a refinery at Sungei Gerong on the Moesi River near Palembang.[122] Since it had no market outlets of its own in the East, it entered into a contract with Standard of New York for the sale of the products of the refinery.

By obtaining a 600,000-acre concession from the Dutch, NKPM in July, 1928, broke through the colonial barrier that the Dutch and British governments had raised against American producing companies in the Far East. This grant was the crowning achievement in the long career of Frederick Horstmann, one of the company's managing directors, himself a native of the Netherlands. The concession was to run for forty years, with the obligation to pay an annual rental, a royalty, and a share of profits up to a maximum of 20 per cent of the net profit.[123] Trouble soon arose over what was meant by net profits. The Dutch government understood that the amounts to be used in figuring payments to itself included net earnings from all aspects of oil-industry operations minus a 5 per cent marketing commission. But, under the contract with Standard of New York (which became Socony-Vacuum in 1931), the marketer earned the marketing profit. This meant less income for the government. The final solution was the merger of the interests of Jersey and Socony-Vacuum in Africa and the Far East to form Standard-Vacuum Oil Company.[124] (See Chapter 11.)

NKPM's operations, under Lloyd W. Elliott as local manager, increased substantially between 1927 and 1939. The company applied for additional concessions and, in conjunction with Royal Dutch–Shell and Standard of California, in 1935 obtained a 25,000,000-acre concession in Dutch New Guinea on which it discovered oil in 1937. Despite its exploratory and drilling program, NKPM made no important addition to its reserves in Sumatra until it discovered the Lirik field in 1939. But its discovery that the Talang Akar field extended into its large new Pendopo concession was fortunate because little addition of facilities was necessary to develop this holding. NKPM increased its output from a daily average of 3,400 barrels in 1927 to the prewar high of 43,000 in 1937. Its reserves declined, but additions were expected from the development of the Lirik discovery. Despite successful expansion, NKPM's producing and refining were kept to fairly modest profits; the company met severe competition in Oriental markets in the later 1930's from products from other sources, including Iran, Burma, and Bahrain.[125]

Jersey's success in increasing its production in the Eastern Hemisphere obviously was not to be compared to its expansion in the Americas. Its increase in Europe, the Middle East, and the Far East was from an average of 8,300 barrels daily in 1927 to 44,500 in 1939 (including its 50 per cent of NKPM's production in the latter year). This was a substantial rise in percentage, but not a large increase in volume.

JERSEY'S PRODUCTION IN 1939, DOMESTIC AND FOREIGN

By the outbreak of World War II, Standard Oil Company (New Jersey) had overcome the imbalance in its operations that had led its administrators in 1927 to adopt the policy of vigorous expansion of production at home and abroad. It had shed its earlier preoccupation with refining and marketing and had become the world's leading oil producer. It had even surpassed its great rivals, Royal Dutch–Shell and Anglo-Iranian.

Figures give a striking measure of growth. By 1939 the company's investment in production at home and abroad had become approximately

Table 5: **DAILY AVERAGE NET CRUDE OIL PRODUCTION, PURCHASES, SALES, AND NET AVAILABLE IN THE UNITED STATES, ABROAD, AND WORLDWIDE, 1927–1939**
Affiliates of Standard Oil Company (New Jersey)
(In thousands of 42-gallon barrels)

	Net Production of Affiliates[a]			Purchases from Nonaffiliates[b]			Sales to Nonaffiliates			Net Available to Affiliates' Refineries		
	United States	Foreign	World	United States	Foreign	World	United States	Foreign	World	United States	Foreign	World
1927	112.4	77.5	189.9	249.5	54.5	304.0	47.4	2.9	50.3	314.4	129.2	443.6
1928	95.7	109.6	205.4	275.0	54.5	329.5	48.9	21.8	70.7	321.8	142.4	464.2
1929	114.9	122.6	237.6	325.3	64.2	389.4	85.6	6.7	92.3	354.6	180.1	534.7
1930	116.0	124.2	240.1	283.4	58.1	341.6	67.6	7.1	74.7	331.8	175.2	507.0
1931	110.8	122.9	233.7	246.1	40.3	286.4	90.3	4.3	94.5	266.6	159.0	425.6
1932	97.6	195.3	292.9	250.8	38.4	289.2	82.9	4.5	87.3	265.5	229.2	494.8
1933	120.8	253.8	374.6	243.8	39.2	282.9	70.8	9.3	80.0	293.8	283.7	577.5
1934	131.4	324.0	455.5	222.8	45.7	268.5	82.0	10.7	92.7	272.2	359.1	631.3
1935	139.1	348.8	487.9	225.6	50.6	276.2	104.2	12.5	116.7	260.5	386.9	647.4
1936	155.3	367.6	523.0	270.1	51.3	321.4	137.9	11.5	149.4	287.6	407.5	695.0
1937	186.2	415.6	601.9	340.7	54.4	395.0	147.9	13.1	161.1	378.9	456.8	835.7
1938	166.1	395.4	561.5	319.9	52.5	372.3	126.4	17.4	143.6	359.6	430.6	790.1
1939	185.1	430.6	615.7	329.5	62.7	392.2	129.8	34.7	164.5	384.7	458.5	843.3

NOTE: Because of rounding, the totals under *World* are not in all cases the exact sum of the two preceding figures.
[a] Net production is gross production minus royalty oil or oil belonging to other interests.

[b] Includes royalty oil purchased and purchases from nonaffiliates.
Source: Statistical records of Standard Oil Company (New Jersey).

equal to that in all the other functions combined. Its total of approximately half a billion dollars in producing properties was nearly equally divided between domestic and foreign.[126] The total net crude output of the Jersey companies (gross production minus chiefly royalty oil) had risen from a daily average of 189,900 barrels in 1927 to an average of 615,700 in 1939. The net production of the foreign affiliates had risen from a daily average of 77,500 barrels in 1927 to 430,600 in 1939. This foreign production in 1939 was sufficient to provide approximately nine-tenths of the products required to supply Jersey's markets abroad. The company's total estimated reserves had increased from slightly over a billion barrels at the end of 1927 to 6 billion at the end of 1939.[127] Thus, while the output had slightly more than tripled, the reserves had multiplied nearly sixfold. During the same period, refinery crude runs had increased from an average of 434,300 barrels daily in 1927 to 849,800 in 1939. In the latter year, the group produced 72 per cent of the requirements of its refineries.

Other less tangible gains also had been made, gains that were basic from the standpoint of costs and the value of reserves. Certain Jersey affiliates had been among the leaders in production research and in generally raising the efficiency of oil recovery. The companies had profited from the fact that production practices could be employed which meant lower costs and a larger ultimate recovery from individual fields. Jersey and its affiliates had also made progress in upgrading their operating personnel and in raising the effectiveness of their employee force. Further, they had learned much about how to build an effective working force among illiterate peoples without the skills and disciplines required by large industrial undertakings.

One problem, however, loomed larger at the end of this period than at its beginning: that of relations with governments and with peoples outside the direct reach of operations. Rising nationalism abroad and changing concepts of the relations of government to economic life were challenging the moral and legal bases of private enterprise. The expropriation of the properties of Jersey in Bolivia and of foreign companies in Mexico dramatized the growing desire of underdeveloped countries for a larger share of the profits from the exploitation of their oil resources. The Jersey leaders were aware of the portentous nature of this problem, but by the outbreak of World War II they had found no effective ways of dealing with it.

Chapter 6

Refining Research and Development, 1927–1939

W HILE THE JERSEY COMPANY was expanding and transforming its production of crude oil, its refining was undergoing similar changes.
There was entry into new regions, expansion of operations, and advance
in technology.

The immediate spur to change at the beginning of this period was the
unsatisfactory profit record of the Jersey refineries over a number of
years, which culminated in heavy losses in 1927. Among the factors
contributing to this situation were overcapacity in Jersey's and the
industry's refining, rising competition, and declining prices.

Action along several lines was clearly necessary—in the supply of raw
materials, in transportation, and in marketing, as well as in refining. The
refineries, on their part, had to be able to manufacture products that
would meet quality competition at costs which, despite declining prices,
would leave a profit margin. The officers and directors of the parent
company had become convinced by 1927 that it was necessary to advance
the technology of the Jersey refineries and to raise the efficiency of their
management.

Believing that a greater emphasis on science and engineering was
essential to such improvement, the Board of Directors decided to promote
programs to intensify research and development among the affiliates.
They believed that progress could best be made by an organized system
that combined collaborative activity and competition. The Jersey Company already had the beginnings of such a system in various research
units within the parent company itself and a few affiliates. The new
program looked toward expanding this research organization and making
it a more effective instrument for advancing the refining technology of the
whole company.

THE RESEARCH ORGANIZATION

In the reorganization of 1927, the parent company's development, engineering, and inspection departments were transferred to the patent-holding affiliate, whose functions were broadened and whose name was changed to Standard Oil Development Company. The Jersey directors planned that this company should perform two functions: to carry on research and to coordinate a program of technical progress among the affiliates.

The offices of Standard Oil Development were in New York City and its laboratories in Linden, New Jersey. From 1927 to 1933 its president was Edgar M. Clark, who had joined the parent company in 1918 to lead in improving its refining technology and who had become a Jersey director late in 1920. Clark was not an engineer by formal training, but he was a man of broad experience and of imagination and courage in promoting new methods. Before coming to Jersey from the refining organization of Standard of Indiana, he had established his reputation as an inventor and as a business manager in guiding the development and industry-wide acceptance of the Burton-Clark cracking still (an improvement on the original Burton still). The general manager of Standard Oil Development was Frank A. Howard, engineer and patent attorney; he had been in charge of the Burton-Clark patent and licensing program and had joined Jersey in 1919 to head its Development Department. The research affiliate had 150 employees in 1927.[1]

Humble and Imperial also had groups working on refining research. Humble's Development Department was headed by Dr. Stewart P. Coleman, a chemical engineer trained at the Massachusetts Institute of Technology. This department had played an increasingly important role in the Baytown refinery; in 1927 its research staff was expanded.[2] Imperial had a small research group at its refinery at Sarnia, Ontario.

These research departments of the affiliates were an outgrowth of nearly a decade of experience. The work of Jersey's own Development Department and similar undertakings by Humble had made considerable progress. With Dr. Warren K. Lewis of Massachusetts Institute of Technology as consultant and Carleton Ellis—an independent inventor—as collaborator, these departments had developed an effective continuous cracking process (the tube-and-tank process) and also commercially feasible continuous vacuum distillation. At the same time, the Development Department in New York had set up one of the first special research libraries in the petroleum industry, and its staffs had kept abreast of the developing research and literature in their field. They had also become acquainted with German industrial research which had potential value for the petroleum industry. By 1927 Jersey was ready for a wider application of science and engineering to the problems of its refineries.[3]

A new research staff was organized early in that year to work principally on hydrogenation. On the advice of Dr. Lewis and with the enthusiastic support of Director Farish, this group was located at the refinery at Baton Rouge, Louisiana, in the Gulf Coast region. This location was chosen in order to bring Standard of Louisiana into contact with up-to-date chemical engineering and also because of the plentiful supply of natural gas and crude oil in the vicinity of its refinery. Robert T. Haslam of MIT was persuaded to take a leave of absence—a leave that became permanent—to start the new organization at Baton Rouge. He was professor of chemical engineering at MIT and director of the Institute's School of Chemical Engineering Practice and of its Research Laboratory of Applied Chemistry. Haslam chose Robert P. Russell to head the new research staff; at age 29 Russell was assistant director of the laboratory at MIT directed by Haslam. Russell and twelve other young men, most of whom were chemical engineers from the same school, made up the first research group at Baton Rouge. The addition of these scientists and engineers enlarged Jersey's already established association with MIT and brought into the company several men who became invaluable to the Jersey Company's research and its refinery management.[4]

The plan under which Standard Oil Development Company had been organized—the so-called Mutual Plan—contemplated the use of the company as a vehicle for coordinating and distributing the cost of all the research and development efforts of general interest to the Jersey affiliates. The formal implementation of this plan was made in 1928 in what was known as the Mutualization Agreement. Under this agreement, the other affiliates contracted with Standard Oil Development for the exchange of licenses under patents and for the sharing of the cost of research.[5]

The existence of these separate research organizations resulted in both competition and cooperation. A healthy rivalry developed among them. Although virtually free to plan their own operations, they challenged and stimulated one another. But they also worked together to further the research effort of the whole group. Representatives of these staffs constituted a technical committee, which held periodic meetings to discuss new developments or other matters of interest to their work. As the technical meetings became more widely attended and the subjects more involved, another committee was formed. The original one became the leader of the theorists, and a manufacturing technical committee was set up for those specially interested in the practical aspects of applied research.

Association with a leading German research group gave new stimulus and direction to Jersey's own research organization in 1927 and subsequent years. Germany was by far the world's leader in industrial research in the 1920's, and American companies in various lines of manufacture were then turning to their German counterparts for whatever assistance they might obtain. Jersey established contact with Interessen Gemeinschaft-Farbenindustrie Aktiengesellschaft—variously referred to as I.G. Farbenindustrie, I.G. Farben, Farben, or only I.G. This concern, a combination of German companies organized in 1926, was the most advanced in the world in the chemical research industry. Jersey's relations with Farben were to become important to the American company's progress in research and refining in the 1930's. But they also led to serious attacks on Jersey after America's entry into World War II, as will be seen in a later chapter.

EARLY RELATIONS WITH I.G. FARBEN

For several years, Jersey's executives had been following the progress of research in Germany relating to oil. They had become especially interested in the efforts of Badische Anilin und Soda Fabrik, a notably successful chemical company, to find a commercially practicable way to convert coal into oil.[6] Badische held the patents for a process, invented by Professor Friedrich Bergius before World War I, for converting coal into a liquid resembling crude oil by subjecting powdered coal to the action of hydrogen at high pressures and temperatures. The meeting of Jersey directors and Frank A. Howard of Standard Oil Development with some Badische directors who in 1925 were on tour of American industrial plants had led to an invitation from the German company for Howard to visit its research laboratories at Ludwigshafen.

Howard went to Ludwigshafen in April, 1926. There, as he wrote later, "I was plunged into a world of research and development on a gigantic scale such as I had never seen." After studying progress at the hydrogenation pilot plant, he suggested to President Teagle, who was then in Paris with a number of other senior officers of Jersey, that he come to Ludwigshafen for a personal inspection. Teagle promptly came, accompanied by Director Moffett. The three Jersey men, as recorded by Howard, "met in the lovely medieval town of Heidelberg and sat down together there to ponder the effect the startling developments at Ludwigshafen, ten miles away, would have on the world's oil industry."[7]

Although the Jersey executives found Badische's coal hydrogenation process still too costly for large-scale commercial use, they concluded that an inexpensive way would eventually be developed. They were especially interested in the possibility of using the Badische process to convert the worst types of crude oil and even tar into gasoline. This was an intriguing prospect at a time when the demand for gasoline was rising, but, even using the more highly developed current methods, as much as two barrels of crude were required to make a barrel of gasoline. In addition, in the event of an actual shortage of crude, the Badische hydrogenation process might be used to convert coal to oil. At that very time, indeed, Jersey—as a hedge against a possible future shortage—was looking into the feasibility of deriving oil from shale in Colorado.[8]

After a full examination of the situation and much discussion in New York, Jersey entered into negotiations with the Germans. These negotiations were with I.G. Farbenindustrie, into which concern the Badische organization had been merged in the summer of 1926. In the autumn of 1927, the two parties reached an understanding and drew up and signed a twenty-five-year contract. At the request of Farben, this contract was supplemented by an exchange of letters expressing the good intentions of each company in the event of developments which could not then be foreseen. John W. Davis, former Solicitor General of the United States, represented Jersey as its general counsel in these negotiations.[9]

Under this contract, Jersey undertook to carry on research and development designed to adapt the hydrogenation process to oil operations. It agreed to erect and operate an oil hydrogenation plant having an output of 40,000 tons of products per year, using the Badische patents without paying royalty. It also arranged that, if it so desired, it could build and operate additional plants in this country by the payment of fair royalties. I.G. Farben was to retain all its United States patents and to control the licensing of them to others; but, in compensation for Jersey's expenditures, Farben was to pay to Jersey one-half of any American royalties. The latter, in turn, would own the patents on any of its improvements on Farben's hydrogenation process and retain full control of their licensing; but it would pay the German concern half of whatever royalties it collected in the United States.[10]

As soon as this understanding had been reached, the research group that had already been set up at Baton Rouge went to work on the problem of applying hydrogenation to petroleum. The first step was to develop an economic method for making hydrogen. The scientists next began to work on the project of making gasoline by hydrogenating heavy oils. Numerous minor difficulties were experienced, but one by one they were overcome. When it became clear that the researchers were moving toward success, the team's enthusiasm ran high. Many of the men reported for work early and stayed long into the night; often they paid no attention to Sundays or holidays.

Toward the end of 1928, the research staff became convinced that hydrogenation was the most important scientific development that had ever occurred in the oil industry. With its use, refiners could convert heavy crude into light oil, even into gasoline. In fact, out of a barrel of crude oil they could make more than a barrel of high-grade gasoline. They could also make better lubricants. The prospect was that they no longer would be plagued with unwanted by-products. The entire Jersey high command followed the progress of the research at Baton Rouge with great enthusiasm.

In the meantime, Jersey officials became somewhat anxious over their relationship with I.G. Farben. The two companies were to cooperate in their research on hydrogenation and to exchange information, but there was suspicion on both sides that full and frank disclosures were not being made. On its part, Farben followed with some concern the progress of Jersey's hydrogenation research. Despite its ownership of the basic patents, Farben was afraid that the American company was gaining such a strong position that it might use its knowledge to launch itself into new fields of activity without the German company's getting adequate compensation. Jersey, on its part, wanted its foreign as well as its domestic affiliates to obtain licenses. Consequently, neither party was satisfied with the 1927 agreement.[11]

Early in 1929 Frank A. Howard entered into discussions with I.G. Farben officials in Germany intended to facilitate working out a new arrangement to cover the hydrogenation patents. In March, a meeting of directors of Jersey and of Farben was held in New York. After further negotiation, the German concern agreed to sell its hydrogenation and other oil-refining patents, including those based on inventions that might be made during the next seventeen years, for the whole world except Germany—Farben to retain an overriding interest of 20 per cent in gross royalties. The two parties also agreed to exchange technical knowledge and experience on matters within the scope of the agreement. Jersey was to pay Farben $35,000,000, which at the latter's request was paid in the former's stock; 546,011 shares were delivered in November. The patent rights were lodged in Standard-I.G. Company, organized for this purpose; Jersey held 800 and Farben 200 shares of this new company. The dividend rights of these shares were of nominal value since Jersey was entitled by contract to substantially all the income after Farben's 20 per cent override.[12]

In the discussions over these patents, the Germans expressed fear that Jersey would make use of them for the manufacture of chemical products in competition with I.G. Farben; they proposed that their company be protected against this possibility. Howard assured them that Jersey was an oil and not a chemical company, but discussion indicated that borderline cases might arise. Accordingly, an arrangement was decided upon whereby the American company was to offer to Farben, on fair and reasonable terms, control of any new chemical development it made that was not closely related to the oil business. Farben similarly agreed to offer, on the same terms, control outside Germany of any chemical development that could not be carried on advantageously except as part of an oil or natural gas business. At the same time, the Germans promised to allow the Americans minority participation in any new process which they developed for making chemical products from oil or natural gas. This part of the agreement was later to enable Jersey to share in Farben's process for making synthetic rubber.[13]

Within a year, this 1929 arrangement was found to be inadequate. It was recognized, as urged by Farben, that numerous processes and products might not be subject to definite classification and that disagreement might arise as to whether they were to be classified as oil or chemical. The parties therefore agreed to organize a company to be owned jointly, to which each would assign borderline processes. Every such process would be handled as a separate project, and the company turning over an invention would retain control of it as well as a five-eighths financial interest. The new company was incorporated in October, 1930, as Jasco, Incorporated (Joint American Study Company). Farben lodged in Jasco its worldwide rights, outside Germany, under numerous patents, such as those pertaining to paraffin oxidation, acetylene arc, Oppanol, and Buna processes. Jersey had none to contribute.[14]

After the relationship with I.G. Farben had thus been further defined in 1929, Jersey affiliates began to construct both pilot-scale and commercial hydrogenation plants. The building of a unit at Baton Rouge capable of handling half a barrel per day was followed before the end of 1929 by another with a daily capacity of 100 barrels. The construction of plants to produce 5,000 barrels daily was started at about the same time at Baton Rouge and at Bayway, New Jersey. The Bayway plant, the first to be completed—at a cost of $5,000,000—was ready for operation in August, 1930. The building of another of similar capacity was begun at Baytown. The successful development and operation of such large-scale hydrogenation plants meant that the engineers of Jersey affiliates, with the help of Farben "know-how," had mastered a new, difficult, and promising process.[15]

The interest of other companies in the hydrogenation of petroleum led Jersey to organize several corporations to make its process and know-how available to others. It realized that any attempt to monopolize the technique would create antagonism; it also desired to obtain some immediate cash returns on its immense investment and to maximize future royalty income. Consequently, in 1930 it organized the Hydro Patents Company for licensing in the United States. Standard Oil Development Company took 10,000 shares, thirteen other large oil companies 1,000 each, and four smaller ones 500 each. In order to furnish technical knowledge on this process to Hydro Patents' stockholders and licensees, Jersey in 1931 formed its wholly owned Hydro Engineering and Chemical Company. It organized similar companies abroad. One was the International Hydrogenation Patents Company, Limited—incorporated in Liechtenstein—of which Jersey and Royal Dutch–Shell, through affiliates, held all the stock. Another was the International Hydrogenation Engineering and Chemical Company—incorporated in the Netherlands—in which the Liechtenstein company held the entire stock except 10 per cent of the preference shares, which were taken by Imperial Chemical Industries, Limited, the leading British chemical company. Still another concern, the Hydrogenation Construction and Service Company, was formed in 1935 for consulting, designing, and construction engineering; its stock was held equally by International Hydrogenation Patents and I.G. Farben.[16]

Ironically, these developments in the hydrogenation of petroleum came during years when the discovery of new oil fields in eastern Texas and elsewhere flooded the industry with cheap oil and gave assurance of adequate reserves for many years to come. There was then no need to manufacture products synthetically at higher costs, unless the resulting products contained some quality lacking in those made by simpler processes. Such an exception was lubricants, but larger supplies of Pennsylvania and other crudes were then providing good lubricants at lower costs. So even for this purpose the new hydrogenation process, although useful, was not so vital as had been anticipated. For the major product—gasoline—hydrogenation certainly was not needed at a time when existing equipment could easily produce all that was required to meet the demand.

Therefore, even after more than $30,000,000 had been spent on research and on experimental and commercial plants—in addition to the $35,000,000 payment in Jersey stock to I.G. Farben—the decision was made to suspend the completion of the Baytown unit, except the power plant, and to use the Baton Rouge and Bayway installations for improving lubricating stocks. In 1933 even Bayway's use of the process was reduced, and the operation was concentrated at Baton Rouge.[17]

From the point of view of the original objective, this venture had been expensive indeed, but out of these early experiments was later to come a whole line of important hydrogenation and dehydrogenation processes. Some of these are described in subsequent pages of this chapter and others in later chapters dealing with research and refining. The first iso-octane used in making 100-octane aviation fuel was produced by the hydrogenation of di-isobutylene. Later outgrowths were catalytic reforming processes, such as hydroforming and power forming, for improving the quality of gasoline. Hydroforming was applied in making nitration-grade toluene in 1940; its use was extended to the production of high-quality gasoline fractions after World War II. Other outgrowths were hydrofining and related hydrogen treating processes to remove sulfur and improve the quality of fuels, lubricants, and waxes. Widespread commercial use of the hydrofining process was begun in 1954.

Perhaps the most important result of the early work in hydrogenation was the interest it stimulated among Jersey researchers in catalysis and catalytic processing. This impetus helped pave the way toward the development of fluid catalytic cracking, which was one of the most important—probably the most important—development in the history of Jersey's affiliate for refining research and engineering. Catalytic research also aroused the company's interest in the synthesis of hydrocarbons from carbon monoxide and hydrogen derived from natural gas or coal.

Jersey derived other benefits besides research concepts and techniques from its relations with Farben. A general early gain of long-range value was the stimulus that contributed to the building up of a large research staff soundly trained in chemistry and chemical engineering. More specific gains were the data obtained from Farben from time to time on various products and processes which the American company could adapt in its own research to the improvement of old products and the development of new ones.

IMPROVING LUBRICANTS AND GASOLINES

Severe competition and the requirements of higher-compression motors necessitated continuing improvements in lubricants and gasolines. Many oil companies were doing research on product improvement, and patent complexities were so numerous that it is difficult to say in some cases what was the actual contribution of any one company. However, in the broad forward movement in research, important advances can be attributed to the Jersey affiliates; these enabled the parent company steadily to meet rising quality competition and at times to lead it.

A great deal of attention was given to lubricants. The quality requirements of this class of products were rising in the early 1930's. Some companies had been buying lubricants made from oil from Pennsylvania crudes in order to supply their customers with the highest-quality product. But with an abundance of crude available elsewhere and a growing market for lubricants, it became economically advantageous for a company to use its own oil. Jersey's dependence on Mid-Continent and especially Texas crudes made it desirable to find ways of using those oils as well as to improve lubricants generally in order to meet rising standards. Hydrogenation was helpful; but, as already observed, it was an expensive process.

An important discovery for improving lubricants was made by Garland Davis of Jersey's Baton Rouge laboratory. Having seen in the Farben plant at Ludwigshafen a bottle of synthetic lubricating oil obtained by the condensation of naphthalene and paraffin, he drew upon this observation to develop an additive that inhibited the solidifying of wax in lubricants. Jersey put this additive on the market in 1932 as Paraflow. The new product brought an early test of Jersey's relations with Farben. The American company claimed that Paraflow was closely related to its oil business and thus within its field as agreed upon in 1929. The German concern accepted this interpretation.[18]

Within a short time, Standard Oil Development acquired information from Farben about two other additives for lubricants. One, called

Oppanol in Germany, came to be known in the United States by various trade names, including Vistanex and Paratone. When added in small amounts to a thin oil, this additive improved the viscosity index of the oil—that is, it reduced the range of changes in viscosity caused by variations in temperature. Jersey's affiliates used this product, which it called Paratone, in their high-quality lubricant, Uniflo. From 1936 on, they used in lubricants another additive whose production was based on information obtained from Farben. Paranox, as it was called, made oil resistant to oxidation and to the tendency to sludge, and it reduced the corrosion of hard-alloy bearings.[19]

Still another discovery, made by Dr. R. K. Stratford of Imperial, reduced the reliance of Jersey affiliates on expensive hydrogenation for producing high-quality lubricants. The Stratford process improved the viscosity index of motor oils by treating them with phenol. In 1934 this method was adopted by Standard of Louisiana, which then discontinued using the hydrogenation plant at Baton Rouge for work on lubricants. The company converted this unit to producing high-quality naphtha and gas oil for the European trade. In the same year, Humble also built a phenol treating plant at Baytown, Baton Rouge added a second unit in 1938, and the Port Jérôme refinery in France acquired one in 1939.[20]

The Humble laboratories in the meantime developed still another treating process, one that became especially important in improving the quality of lubricants made from Texas Panhandle crudes. These crudes had certain natural qualities favorable for making high-quality lubricants, but they also had a high content of asphalt and wax, which precluded processing by conventional methods. The Baytown laboratory gave attention to the newer techniques of propane deasphalting, acid treating, and dewaxing then being worked on by several companies. After nearly a year of experimentation with a pilot project, Humble built a plant for propane deasphalting, dewaxing, and acid treating of lube distillates and residues obtained primarily from Panhandle and Ranger crudes.[21]

The propane treating process had several advantages over the older methods used in making lubricants, but it also had definite limitations. It made possible the utilization of distillates of crudes having some naturally poor lubricating qualities. This resulted not only in higher yields and a better quality of finished oils but also in reduced manufacturing costs. Alone, however, the propane process did not materially improve the viscosity index of nonwaxy lube distillates. A distinct improvement in this direction was accomplished by using Imperial's phenol extraction process.

The use of these two processes together enabled Humble by 1939 to make lubricants from its own cheaper crudes that were competitive in quality with those made from Pennsylvania oils.[22]

Although giving much attention to lubricants, the research groups of Jersey affiliates in the late 1920's and the 1930's placed major emphasis on the improvement of gasoline. This effort was in response to the need for a certain quality in gasoline for engines being built with higher compression ratios for automobiles and especially for airplanes. Such engines tended to "knock" more than earlier engines had done. This knocking—or detonation—could be reduced by using gasolines that exploded more slowly than other types.

Knocking could also be reduced by mixing tetraethyl lead with the gasoline. This method of raising the antiknock quality of the motor fuel had been discovered in 1921 by Thomas Midgley, Jr., of the research division of General Motors Corporation. A low-cost process for making this additive had later been developed by Professor Charles A. Kraus of Clark University, who was working with Standard Oil Development on this problem. The product was manufactured by Ethyl Gasoline Corporation, which was organized by General Motors and Jersey in 1924 for this purpose.[23] For a time, tetraethyl lead raised the antiknock quality of gasoline sufficiently. With the rise in the compression ratio of engines, however, the knocking tendency increased to a point where the problem could not be solved by adding more tetraethyl lead.

Before this limit was reached, objective standards for testing gasolines had been developed. Up to 1926, they had been tested in engines with varying compression ratios, and individual judgment had played a part in determining the degree of knocking. In September, 1926, Dr. Graham Edgar, an officer in charge of the research of Ethyl Gasoline Corporation, reported at the annual meeting of the American Chemical Society the discovery of a method for setting antiknock standards by using two hydrocarbons, normal heptane and iso-octane.[24] Any engine using only heptane knocked, but one using only iso-octane* did not knock. The antiknock quality of a given fuel could be matched against blends of these two standard reference fuels and reduced to a numerical value. The percentage of iso-octane in the blend with heptane established a standard called octane rating, a high rating meaning low detonation. Some of the commercial gasolines that ranged up to 75 on the octane scale at the time

---

* Actually, this is one of a large number of iso-octanes. In the oil industry it is usually called iso-octane, although its specific chemical name is trimethyl pentane.

could be raised experimentally to a maximum of 87 by the addition of a small amount of the newly discovered iso-octane.[25]

The announcement of the new octane scale in 1926 immediately created a demand for iso-octane and normal heptane for testing and rating commercial gasolines, but no process for the manufacture of the former was available outside the laboratory. Ethyl Gasoline Corporation turned to Arthur D. Little, Inc., a research concern, to work out a commercial method. By the middle of 1927, this company had produced only a hundred gallons of pure iso-octane, which it sold to Ethyl Gasoline for $2,500.[26] The Ethyl Gasoline Corporation also asked Jersey for help in making this product.

Jersey research groups thereupon set about finding a way to make iso-octane in quantity. They knew that it could be made by hydrogenating di-isobutylene, a combination of two isobutylene molecules. They also knew that isobutylene appeared in small quantities in mixtures of gases resulting from the cracking of petroleum under heat and pressure. The problems were how to obtain sufficient isobutylene and to develop commercially usable processes for converting it into di-isobutylene and hydrogenating the latter. In 1929, by using sulfuric acid as a catalyst, they succeeded in converting isobutylene, obtained from mixtures of gases generated in synthetic alcohol operations at Bayway, into di-isobutylene. This process involved the then little-known technique called polymerization—a chemical reaction combining two or more molecules, usually with the help of a catalyst, to form a larger molecule known as a polymer. In 1929 and 1930, Jersey delivered a thousand gallons of di-isobutylene to Ethyl Gasoline Corporation. The di-isobutylene was purified by the Ethyl Gasoline Corporation and hydrogenated, and the resulting synthetic iso-octane was sold for use in setting octane standards. Since isobutylene was available in only small amounts in refinery gases, the quantity of iso-octane that could be made in this way was much too limited for mixture with gasoline for general commercial use.[27]

In 1930 the United States Army Air Corps adopted the octane scale for rating the antiknock quality of gasolines and made 87-octane the grade for combat planes.[28] This grade could then—and for some time thereafter—be obtained only by using selected gasoline fractions that exploded slowly and adding tetraethyl lead to retard the explosion still further. As the compression ratio of airplane engines rose, so did the demand for better fuels.

The Army Air Corps, in fact, provided the principal stimulus to the development of the commercial manufacture of iso-octane. Jersey had continued to manufacture small amounts, which were sold to the Ethyl Corporation for use as a reference fuel. Shell Chemical Company (an American Shell), utilizing processes similar to Jersey's, had also begun to make the product. It did so on the urging of Shell's aviation manager, James H. Doolittle, an aeronautical engineer with a degree of doctor of science from the Massachusetts Institute of Technology and a reputation as a flyer.* In May, 1934, the Matériel Command of the Army Air Corps purchased 1,000 gallons of hydrogenated di-isobutylene from Shell at $2 per gallon. At Wright Field in Ohio, this iso-octane was blended with high-quality aviation gasoline, and enough tetraethyl lead was added to bring the octane rating of the mixture up to 100.[29]

The success of the Army Air Corps in experimenting with 100-octane fuel led Jersey to construct facilities for making iso-octane. In June, 1934, it decided to convert an old alcohol plant at the Bayway refinery to the manufacture of di-isobutylene. Work was begun in 1935 on building permanent facilities for its production at the Bayway and Baytown refineries. The plants went into operation late in the spring of that year. They utilized the process employed by Standard Oil Development in 1929—that is, they converted isobutylene from a refinery gas mixture into di-isobutylene with the aid of cold sulfuric acid as a catalyst. The purified di-isobutylene was shipped to Baton Rouge for hydrogenation to form iso-octane by utilizing a slightly modified I.G. Farben method. However, the use of this process was still limited by the small amount of isobutylene available in refinery gases.[30]

These developments made Jersey a commercial producer of 100-octane aviation gasoline. On June 26, 1935, ten drums of superior aviation gasoline were shipped from Baton Rouge to Tulsa, Oklahoma, for sale to participants in the Southwest Air Races. Soon thereafter Standard of Louisiana entered into a contract to supply, at 30 cents a gallon, approximately a third of the nearly 1,000,000 gallons of 100-octane aviation gasoline required by the Army Air Corps in the second half of 1935—Shell contracted to supply the remainder. The first delivery from Baton Rouge was a tank-car shipment in September. Sales records show that Standard of Louisiana sold 370,513 gallons in 1935.[31]

* This was the famous "Jimmy" Doolittle. He had started his career as a flyer with the United States Army in 1917 and had later won many trophies as an aviator. He was with Shell from 1930 to 1940. He entered active service with the Army Air Corps and served as commander in both North Africa and the Western Pacific.

The experience of the Army Air Corps with 100-octane gasoline proved that this product was superior to other aviation fuels. Planes utilizing it had more power relative to engine weight and a greater flying range in proportion to the amount of fuel carried than planes using lower-octane fuels. This combination of 100-octane fuel and high-compression engines would clearly give an air force an immense advantage in combat over an enemy with planes using inferior fuels. The Army Air Corps used 100-octane gasoline to the extent that iso-octane was available and continued to urge its adoption for general combat use. After much controversy, investigation, and a hearing held at Wright Field late in 1936, the decision was finally made to adopt 100-octane gasoline for combat planes.[32]

In the meantime, search went on for means of making iso-octane in larger quantity, and a new method was discovered: the hot sulfuric acid catalytic process. Jersey's research staffs, as well as those of other companies, had been at work on this project, but the new process was developed mainly by Shell. By using a strong sulfuric acid solution heated to at least 140° F., both isobutylene and normal butylene were absorbed from unsaturated refinery gases. Applying a still higher heat to this mixture brought about the union of isobutylene molecules with normal butylene molecules. The product, called a copolymer, was then hydrogenated. The result was the virtual doubling of the iso-octane yield from the refinery gas fraction utilized.[33]

In 1938, copolymer plants, designed by technical staffs of the affiliates, were completed at Baytown and Baton Rouge; their product was hydrogenated at the latter refinery. At the same time, Jersey's Lago Oil & Transport, after entry into an agreement with the government of Great Britain, built both a copolymer and a hydrogenation plant at its refinery on Aruba, an island in the Caribbean owned by the Netherlands. The British were then becoming uneasy over Germany's increasing aggressiveness and military preparation. Because of the neutrality legislation of the United States, they were fearful that, in the event of war, Britain might not be able to obtain aviation gasoline from this country.[34]

By this time Humble had developed a third catalytic polymerization method for producing iso-octane, one that had the special advantage over the cold-acid and hot-acid methods in that hydrogenation was not required. This process was sulfuric acid alkylation. Its theoretical basis had been worked out by the research department of Anglo-Iranian Oil Company, Limited, but that company had not put the theory to practical use. An article describing the process, which appeared in *Petroleum*

1927 to 1939

Heinrich Riedemann

Walter C. Teagle

Frank A. Howard

Wallace E. Pratt

William S. Farish

Ralph W. Gallagher

Everit J. Sadler

Henry A. Church, retired businessman, flanked by Jersey officers, was the stockholder who attended the 1927 annual meeting.

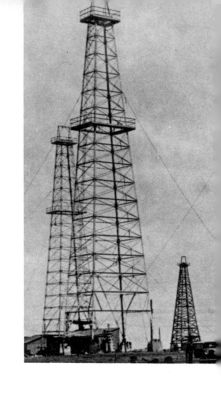

The RCA Building in Rockefeller Center became headquarters for the Jersey Company in 1933.

Barber's Hill field, crowded with derricks, produced more than 120,000,000 barrels of oil since 1928.

The early refinery at Fawley, England, where Anglo-American later built a large, new refinery.

The Eagle Works at Jersey City, New Jersey, on Upper New York Bay, in 1937.

The plant at Baton Rouge where Jersey first tried hydrogenation process.

This pipe still at Port Jérôme in France was built in 1932-1933.

Anglo-American tanker *Cheyenne*, built in 1930, as it appeared in 1934.

This type of tank truck was used in the United States from 1927 to the middle 1930's.

Humble used this type of tank truck in the middle 1930's.

Anglo-American Oil Company introduced the Esso brand name to British motorists in 1935.

In 1936 Anglo-American used this Bedford chassis with a composite tank body.

Motorship *Harry G. Seidel* ready for European service in 1930.

Battery of rerun stills at the Bayway refinery in 1930.

Colonial Beacon introduced this type of service station in New England in 1933.

The large refinery at Aruba at the time of purchase from Standard of Indiana.

In downtown Tunis a double gasoline pump provided Esso premium and Standard regular.

Esso advertisement in Italy in 1927.

A kerosene cart in Holland about 1935.

Technology in June, 1938, caught the attention of Humble's research staff. When preliminary experiments indicated that a practicable method could be developed, patent and royalty arrangements were made with Anglo-Iranian. By this process, isobutane (separated from uncracked field gases) and butylene (extracted from cracked refinery gas) were passed at low pressure and low temperature through a bath of strong sulfuric acid. The acid acted as a catalyst to promote a chemical reaction resulting in a molecule of isobutane combining with a molecule of butylene to form a heavier molecule of alkylate, which consisted largely of iso-octane. Later it was found that amylene or pentylene, as well as butylene, could be used in this process.[35]

The first commercial production of alkylate was begun at a plant at Baytown before the end of 1938. Two years later, units went into operation at Baton Rouge, Aruba, and Sungei Gerong (on the Dutch island of Sumatra in the Far East). The last two were built especially to supply Great Britain. Because of the contributions and conflicting patent claims of several companies which had worked on some aspect of alkylation, an agreement was made by Jersey, Shell, Anglo-Iranian, The Texas Company, and Universal Oil Products Company to license the alkylation process. Alkylation made possible the manufacture of iso-octane in virtually unlimited quantities and at far less cost than by any other method of producing antiknock components of high-octane aviation fuels.[36]

To provide adequate supplies of the gases required for the plants manufacturing iso-octane, the Jersey affiliates found it necessary to build additional facilities. By 1935 Standard of Louisiana, Humble, and Lago had built gas absorption and gasoline recovery plants which saved the now valuable light fractions that had previously been wasted or burned as fuel by the refineries. With rising needs, still other units of this type were built.[37]

Steadily, year by year, the amount of iso-octane manufactured by Jersey affiliates increased. By 1935 their actual output had averaged 27 barrels daily—all hydrogenated at Baton Rouge. It rose to a daily average of 208 barrels in 1936, and to 326 in 1937—all still from Baton Rouge. In 1938 alkylation at Baton Rouge, Baytown, and Aruba raised the total daily average to 1,455 barrels. The next year the average production by Jersey affiliates reached 4,350 barrels per day. These volumes represented a substantial percentage of the total output of iso-octane by the oil industry of the entire world.[38]

Their rising iso-octane production enabled the Jersey affiliates to increase greatly their production of aviation gasoline. In the last full year before World War II, with a refining capacity of one-sixth of the world total, they were supplying approximately a quarter of the total supply for military airplanes. From the beginning of 1939, alkylation raised their capacity for making 100-octane gasoline. The problem was now coming to be, not how to provide the high-octane component, but rather how to manufacture enough high-quality base stock. This had become a pressing problem for the whole oil industry.[39]

FLUID CATALYTIC CRACKING, TOLUENE, AND RUBBER

On the eve of World War II, Jersey contributed to the development of processes for manufacturing other products that were to prove of vital importance to the United States and its Allies. The research laboratories discovered ways to provide in large volume base stocks for making aviation gasoline and other essential products. They also developed a process for making synthetically a necessary component of the explosive, TNT. And they made basic contributions to the manufacture of synthetic rubber.

To provide sufficient gasoline of the quality required—that is, high-octane—to serve as a base stock for making gasoline for aircraft and other high-compression engines had become the most urgent need. For several years a full-scale, high-pressure catalytic hydrogenation plant that went into operation at Baton Rouge in June, 1937, was an important source of such stock. Standard Oil Development had been doing research for many years on the catalytic cracking of oil, the process of breaking up oil molecules in the presence of a catalyst which alters the reaction involved in cracking under pressure at high temperature. By 1934 Jersey had made sufficient progress with the use of a powdered catalyst to consider building a plant to carry on a continuous process called suspensoid cracking. A plant was designed, but it was not built because of a certain technical difficulty and the seeming inadvisability of making the investment in a time of depression.[40]

In 1936, Eugene P. Houdry, a Frenchman, who for several years had been working to develop a catalytic method, introduced a new process. Sun Oil Company and Socony-Vacuum, which had given Houdry financial aid, built units employing this discovery which proved capable of producing gasoline with a higher octane rating and yield than was generally obtained from old-time thermal cracking.

The Houdry method used a fixed-bed catalyst placed in a cracking tower. The oil vapor to be cracked was forced into the tower under heat and pressure, held in contact with the catalyst until cracking occurred, and then withdrawn for fractionation. In this reaction, the catalyst lost activity rapidly, but it could be restored, or regenerated, by controlled burning to clean its surface. When the catalyst had been cleaned, oil vapor was again introduced. In order to keep the process continuous, each Houdry unit consisted of two or three chambers, and the oil vapor stream was switched from one to the other.

Late in 1937, President Howard of Standard Oil Development, President Abrams of Standard Oil Company of New Jersey, and President Wiess of Humble opened discussions with Sun Oil executives concerning the possibility of obtaining a license to use the Houdry process. During these discussions the representatives of that process suggested substantial cash payments for licensing fees, but these payments would not give the Jersey companies any participation in the Houdry patents. Jersey considered the terms exorbitant, and no agreement was reached.[41]

The Jersey Company was not alone in the search for a different catalytic cracking process. Several other oil companies and also engineering firms were studying the matter. One of the latter, the M. W. Kellogg Company, had become highly interested in developing a competitive method. Having learned from Farben that Jersey controlled the German concern's patents relating to petroleum, Kellogg approached the company and suggested that they cooperate in a project to develop another process. Jersey countered by proposing a broader effort in which all the "have-nots" in the catalytic cracking field should join forces and attempt to develop an independent process.

At a meeting held in London in October, 1938, representatives of the M. W. Kellogg Company, Standard-I.G. Company, Standard Oil Company (New Jersey), Standard Oil Company (Indiana), and I.G. Farben-industrie organized a group called the Catalytic Research Associates. They were soon joined by Anglo-Iranian Oil Company, Limited, Royal Dutch–Shell Company, The Texas Company, and Universal Oil Products Company. The purpose of the associates was to develop a process that would not infringe the Houdry patents which covered only one method and not the general principle of cracking with a catalyst.

The Catalytic Research Associates generated a tremendous research effort. The participating groups of the associated companies totaled about a thousand men. According to an authoritative writer on process innovation in the refining industry, this "represented probably the largest single concentration of scientific manpower in the world . . . and would be surpassed only by the development of the atomic bomb."[42] The companies individually undertook to do research on special aspects of the problem or on particular approaches to its solution. About 400 men in Standard Oil Development worked on the project. The leaders among them were E. V. Murphree, D. L. Campbell, H. Z. Martin, and C. W. Tyson—known to their associates as "The Four Horsemen."

Like others working on the project, this group at first tried to design a fixed-bed-catalyst process. But they and their company's executives soon came to the conclusion that a continuous process would be better, less costly, and safer from attack for patent infringement.

As a result of this decision, the Standard Oil Development men began to concentrate on searching for a satisfactory continuous process utilizing a moving catalyst. While they were working on the many problems involved, Professors W. K. Lewis and E. R. Gilliland of the Massachusetts Institute of Technology, as Jersey consultants, initiated research at the institute on the use of a continuous flow of catalyst. Using a catalyst and air, two graduate students, John Chambers and Scott Walker, experimented with some of the engineering principles underlying the fluid technique. Within six months, the Jersey research men were cracking oil in the presence of a fluid catalyst. But they still had to find ways to remove the catalyst from the reactor, burn off the carbon that had collected on it, and then return it to the reactor without interrupting the cracking process. They finally worked out a design which they tested in 1940 in a pilot unit built at Baton Rouge with a daily capacity of one hundred barrels. The plant worked well and provided the basis for the designing of commercial-size equipment.[43]

The successful method employed a powdered catalyst. After being aerated, this powder was placed in a tall standpipe which produced such a pressure build-up that the catalyst flowed into and through the reactor with the oil vapor. Because the aerated catalyst acted more like a fluid than a powder, the operation came to be known as fluid catalytic cracking. As the mixture emerged from the reactor, the catalyst was separated out of the cracked oil vapor, which was then sent to the fractionating tower to be divided into its various components. The spent catalyst dropped into a hopper, whence it flowed into the regenerator to have the carbon burned off. It was then returned to the standpipe. This process was continuous; it had to be interrupted only for cleaning and repairing the equipment.

Fluid catalytic cracking was not yet operating on a commercial scale when Hitler invaded Poland in September, 1939. However, it was developed in time to play a strategic role in supplying high-quality base stock for aviation gasoline, as well as other vital products, for the Allies. From this type of cracking, several other processes were also to be developed later, including fluid coking, fluid hydroforming, fluid iron-ore reduction, and other nonpetroleum applications of fluidized solids.

Jersey sought still other methods for making motor fuels of high quality. For example, it investigated the Fischer-Tropsch hydrocarbon synthesis process, developed by Ruhrchemie, A.G., which converted brown coal into liquid fuel. In 1938 and 1939, patents for this process outside Germany were transferred by Ruhrchemie to Hydrocarbon Synthesis Corporation, in which Standard Oil Development took 680 shares, Shell and Kellogg 425 each, and I.G. Farben 170. Both Great Britain and France considered the building of plants using this synthetic process for producing aviation gasoline, but they had been unable to accomplish anything definite by the time the war broke out in Europe in 1939.[44]

Another innovation that was to contribute to the success of the Allies was a process for the manufacture of synthetic toluene. Essential to the manufacture of TNT (trinitrotoluene), toluene could be made from coal and petroleum. However, because these materials had not yielded a sufficient quantity of natural toluene during World War I, the United States Army Ordnance Department had subsequently investigated possible new sources of the chemical. The first indication of the feasibility of producing it synthetically occurred to the scientists at Baton Rouge. Working in the laboratory on hydrogenation, they found that toluene appeared in the product although it was not in the feed stock. When in January, 1933, R. T. Haslam informed the Ordnance Department in Washington of this discovery, the department immediately indicated its interest.[45]

The project to find a practicable process for producing synthetic toluene was assigned to the Baton Rouge research group. Its work on this task was expanded in 1938, when Jersey's officers realized that the international situation was worsening. Using the hydroforming process—that is, cracking and dehydrogenation (the elimination of hydrogen from a molecule) in the presence of a catalyst and hydrogen—the researchers finally were able to produce synthetic toluene in quantity. However, the product contained impurities that boiled at the same temperature as the toluene, thus preventing its purification by ordinary distillation methods.[46]

Humble research men, who also had undertaken research on toluene, solved this problem. They succeeded in extracting nitration-grade (99+ per cent pure) toluene from naphtha by utilizing a process known as SO_2 (sulfur dioxide) extraction. After this discovery, the Humble research group and other Jersey laboratories developed a commercially feasible method for producing synthetic toluene of sufficient purity for the manufacture of TNT. The process was complete by the time war broke out in 1939.[47]

The Jersey laboratories in the 1930's contributed to the development of still another product that was to become vital to the war effort: synthetic rubber. Again, important new processes were in part the result of co-operation with I. G. Farben. Ever since World War I, German scientists had been trying to find some way of manufacturing rubber from raw materials readily available in their country. By 1927 Farben had made definite progress. Since the process it had discovered did not utilize petroleum, it seemed to have no possible connection with the oil industry. Jersey, nevertheless, followed this development closely.[48]

Farben was primarily concerned with the manufacture of a synthetic rubber called Buna-S. This was obtained by combining butadiene and styrene. Styrene was relatively easy to produce; Farben had a process for making it in ample quantities at low cost. Butadiene was definitely another matter. The Germans manufactured it from acetylene gas, which they produced from calcium carbide made in an electric furnace from coal and limestone. But the product was very expensive. Recognizing that the cost of Buna-S would remain high unless the cost of making acetylene could be reduced, they began to experiment with other ways of manufacturing this component. One of their projects, in the course of time, had to do with manufacturing acetylene from hydrocarbon gases by passing them through an electric arc. Since production from hydrocarbons fell in the borderline field under the Farben-Jersey agreement of 1929, the Germans soon turned the project, with all research data, processes, and ideas, over to Jasco, Incorporated, for further development.[49]

Once the project had become the property of Jasco, the Jersey research organization began to work on it. An experimental electric-arc plant was constructed late in 1932 at the Baton Rouge refinery to process either natural or refinery gases into acetylene. From the outset, the researchers experienced difficulties, which were referred to either Standard Oil Development or I.G. Farben for solution. Within two years, most technical problems had been solved, and the plant was able to convert natural or refinery gas into acetylene or acetic acid. By using the Farben process, the acetylene could be converted into butadiene and the latter into synthetic rubber. The Baton Rouge unit continued to produce acetylene in 1936 and early 1937. But the costs proved excessive, and the decision was made to close it. Jersey and Farben shared equally the accrued cost of $1,600,000. However, this experiment had important results: it demonstrated that rubber could be produced from petroleum, and it focused the attention of Jersey scientists on the possibility of discovering an economically feasible process.[50]

In the meantime, Jersey research men had made an interesting discovery. In experimenting with high-temperature, low-pressure steam cracking of petroleum fractions—in trying to produce light hydrocarbon gases as part of the process of manufacturing alcohol—they had found that this method produced butadiene. The amount was so small that the discovery seemed of little use in providing the needed chemical. However, this process was to become of great value. It was soon found that light naphthas from crude oil could be cracked, at low pressure in the presence of steam, to produce good yields of such olefins as ethylene, propylene, and butylenes, and also a reasonable yield of butadiene. Steam cracking eventually became the most important process for producing a wide range of chemical raw materials from petroleum.

While searching for some practicable way to make Buna-S from petroleum, the Jersey research organization observed the progress of I. G. Farben's efforts to make it from coal. In 1933 the German concern took out United States patents on its process, but within the next year experiments by Goodyear Tire & Rubber Co., Inc., using Farben's Buna-S, proved unsatisfactory. Farben made some headway in the later 1930's under pressure from the National Socialist government, which endeavored to stimulate the development and production of synthetic rubber by offering subsidies to German chemical companies for absorbing the heavy production costs and by requiring all manufacturers using rubber to buy and use the new product. Farben improved the quality of this synthetic so that, in some limited respects, it was even superior to the natural substance. Jersey was eager for the new rubber to be tested again by American tire companies. But Farben, the holder of the patents, had to obtain the assent of the German government, which had subsidized its research on Buna-S. In fact, Farben had to obtain from the government—principally the *Wehrmacht*—permission to send to other countries information that had to do with matters in which the military had an interest.[51]

This situation created certain difficulties for Jersey and other American concerns having relations with Farben. It was especially important to Jersey in connection with Buna-S in 1938. On May 3, a Farben representative in New York cabled to an officer of that company in Germany that at the request of Orville Harden and F. H. Bedford, Jersey directors, he had had a conference with them concerning Buna. "It appears," he cabled, "that Board of Directors of Standard Oil Co. of New Jersey has not been thoroughly informed about the entire situation. . . . Those directors emphasized necessity to hasten plans for development and discussions here." Apparently in reply, Dr. Fritz ter Meer, who was in charge of Farben's rubber development, cabled: "Everything must be avoided which may interfere with current negotiations we are carrying on with government agencies. There must be absolutely no publicity in regard to the steps we want to take in the U S A before our government has given its permission."[52]

Jersey continued to urge action with Farben, and in December, 1938, Dr. ter Meer himself, at the American company's instance, came to the United States to discuss the matter with five rubber companies. As a result of these conferences, Farben provided samples of Buna-S for rubber companies to test. The tests were under way when the war broke out in 1939. Jersey sent a summary of the results of the tests to the Army and Navy Munitions Board in November, 1939. By that time, the German concern had agreed to turn over control of the Buna patents to Jersey.[53] (See Chapter 14.)

Although its major effort had been directed toward producing the general-purpose Buna-S rubber, Farben at the same time had conducted numerous experiments on other synthetic rubbers. In one of these, it had created a new product by combining butadiene with acrylonitrile, the basic material again being coal. In 1934 Farben patented this type, known as Buna-N, in the United States. Buna-N proved unsuitable for general use; but, since it was far more resistant to oil than natural rubber, it could be used in the manufacture of specialty products, such as gasoline hoses. This synthetic was relatively expensive; but, nevertheless, the Germans in 1937 began to export it to the United States, where it met a small demand.[54]

Jersey men watched this development in synthetic rubber production with great interest because they thought that the new product might provide an outlet for butadiene made from petroleum in high-temperature, low-pressure steam cracking operations. However, not until I.G. Farben gave up to Jersey its Buna rights in the United States after the outbreak of war was the American company free to enter into the production of Buna-N.[55]

Late in the 1930's, the laboratories of Standard Oil Development made a discovery that was eventually to lead to the production of still another type of synthetic rubber.[56] In 1932 I.G. Farben had informed Jersey that it had polymerized isobutylene with boron fluoride to form a tough and resilient plastic resembling rubber. However, the Germans had not succeeded in vulcanizing it. This was Vistanex, which, as noted earlier, was used as an additive to improve lubricants. Since isobutylene was a petroleum derivative, Farben turned the process over to Jasco, Inc., and Standard Oil Development undertook a program of experimentation. Its research staff succeeded in producing pure isobutylene as a by-product of cold-acid polymerization in making iso-octane, and it polymerized this isobutylene to form a tough, resilient product much like natural rubber. The research staff was highly enthusiastic over the possibility of developing this product into synthetic rubber, but these scientists, also, were at first unable to vulcanize it.

Despite this early failure, Standard Oil Development continued to experiment with Vistanex. The bulk of the work was carried on by R. M. Thomas and Dr. W. J. Sparks. Eventually, with the help of others in the chemical division, they solved the problem. Combining a small amount of butadiene with the isobutylene resulted in a new polymer that could be vulcanized. This new rubber product, made in the laboratory in the summer of 1937, was called Butyl. The next year Jersey took out patents on the process in many countries. It informed Farben of its discovery, in accordance with their agreements, but by the outbreak of the war it had not turned the process over to Jasco. This synthetic was not yet in commercial production; and, because of difficulties met in developing production, it was not to be available for many years.

No solution had been found by the end of the decade for the basic problem of producing butadiene in large quantities at low cost. The electric-arc process could produce large amounts of acetylene for making butadiene, but the cost was prohibitive. The high-temperature, low-pressure steam cracking process was less expensive, but was strictly limited in output. Still another method was tested by I.G. Farben shortly before the war, a new chlorination process for converting butylene into butadiene. Farben obtained fairly satisfactory results with a pilot plant using by-product butylene from Jersey refineries in the United States. None of the various processes, however, gave promise of large-scale, low-cost production. The Jersey organization therefore kept on searching. Its successful method for catalytically dehydrogenating butylene to butadiene was not finally achieved until 1941. The incentive for this invention had to await the availability of large quantities of butylene, which turned out to be a by-product of the fluid catalytic cracking process.

During the later 1930's, Jersey kept the United States government informed of progress with synthetic rubber. In the fall of 1938, President Howard of Standard Oil Development reviewed with the United States Ambassador in Berlin the progress of Germany in the production of raw materials normally imported, noting among other developments I.G. Farben's success in the production of synthetic rubber.[57] This report was transmitted by the Ambassador to the Secretary of State in Washington.[58] Early in 1939, on the initiative of Standard Oil Development, a meeting was held, attended by representatives of the company and of the Army and Navy Munitions Board, at which company men presented a report of the production possibilities of Buna-N, Buna-S, and Butyl. The representatives of the military services were interested, but their main concern was with the quality of the synthetic, as compared to natural rubber, rather than with the availability of a supply. Again in May of the same year, men from Standard Oil Development discussed the manufacture of synthetic rubber with representatives of the same military board. Out of this meeting came the suggestion that Jersey should arrange with tire manufacturers to test samples of Butyl. Such arrangements were made in June, 1939, with Firestone and United States Rubber, but the plan was to be of little value because of difficulties met in the manufacture of Butyl.[59]

By the end of 1939, the Jersey organization had become one of the world's leading industrial research institutions. The staff of Standard Oil Development alone numbered 1,364. This affiliate's laboratories in New Jersey had evolved into eleven different groups, including a small but active chemical division headed by Dr. Per K. Frolich. The laboratory at Baton Rouge had a staff of 248 employees. The total research expenditures of the New Jersey and Baton Rouge laboratories in 1939 amounted to more than $4,500,000. Humble's research staff was approximately the same size as that at Baton Rouge; Imperial's at Sarnia was somewhat smaller. Altogether these research groups constituted a large and effective system within which they worked cooperatively and competitively to advance the whole Jersey refining operation.[60]

Institutionalized research and development carried on by a large organization had become essential in the 1930's in an industry where progress in technology required large resources of highly trained men and capital. The day of the lone inventor and innovator was all but gone. Indeed, even teamwork within a large organization was not enough. Commonly, oil companies gained from one another's discoveries. Sometimes, when the problems were especially large and solutions urgent, collaboration among companies took place—even among competitors. At all times, research in academic institutions was followed closely. Advancing the field of petroleum chemistry was basic, but to apply knowledge, old and new, to the problems of the oil industry so as to find workable solutions was essential to progress.

It was in this particular area that the Jersey organization for refining research and development made its most important contribution. By their innovations, Jersey research scientists and engineers in the 1930's helped to bring about a revolution in the oil-refining industry and to advance greatly their own company's manufacturing operations and products.

Chapter 7

A Time of Transition in Refinery Operations, 1927–1939

I N THE HISTORY of the Jersey Company's refining, the late 1920's and the 1930's mark a clear transition from old to new. The old refining was carried on in plants located mostly in the United States, particularly in New Jersey but with expanding operations on the Gulf Coast; the new was marked by notable expansion abroad. The old was the work of practical men operating largely by rule-of-thumb as guided primarily by experience; the new was characterized by the influence of scientists, engineers, and economists working with changing concepts, equipment, and processes. The old could be carried on efficiently in small plants with simple equipment; the new required higher capital expenditures and larger-volume operations to be profitable. The results were a general rise in the quality of products and much product innovation.[1]

These developments did not spread equally to all Jersey refineries in the 1930's. In some instances, it was not economically feasible to install the new equipment, for example, in small plants near producing fields that were serving local markets. In others, tariffs and government regulations affecting refining made it virtually necessary to set up plants which, because total sales were relatively small, could not bear the cost of the new equipment and processes. Such national barriers in many countries prevented Jersey from fully utilizing the developing technology and taking advantage of the potential economies of scale.

THE COMPANY'S REFINERIES IN 1927

Jersey's plants in 1927 constituted a substantial part of the world's refining industry. Their total worldwide capacity was larger than that of any other concern. The capacity at home exceeded that of the largest competitors, but abroad it was smaller than both Royal Dutch–Shell's and

Anglo-Persian's. The total crude processing or runs of the Jersey plants in 1927 averaged 434,300 barrels daily, of which 85,000 barrels were processed outside the United States. (See Table 6.) The volume at home amounted to 15 per cent of the domestic industry's total; abroad it was 11 per cent of all the refining. Jersey's domestic and foreign runs totaled 14 per cent of the crude oil processed by the oil industry of the whole world.

The location of Jersey's refineries in the United States, which on the whole had originally been sound and forward-looking, was not altogether favorable in 1927. The individual plants had generally been built at points that afforded the lowest transportation cost from crude source to product market. A few small ones—inland or on waterways—served nearby markets. The large refineries were on tidewater because Jersey's markets were mainly in coastal regions. Thus tankers, the cheapest form of transportation, could carry their products to marketing areas. Some refineries, both inland and coastal, were losing business to others more favorably located.

Problems of high cost and reduced volume had especially struck the refineries transferred in 1927 to Standard Oil Company of New Jersey. These included small plants at Parkersburg in West Virginia, Baltimore in Maryland, and Charleston in South Carolina, and also the New Jersey Works consisting of the Bayonne and Bayway refineries and the Eagle Works. These three plants near New York Harbor constituted the largest refining operation among all the affiliates at this time.

The New Jersey Works, however, was losing some of its outlets—especially foreign markets—to the refineries of Standard of Louisiana and Humble on the Gulf Coast. These southern plants had lower operating costs, mainly because of their location near fields yielding oil and the cheap natural gas used as refinery fuel. They also had lower wages and taxes than the New Jersey Works. Plants on the Gulf Coast had the further advantage of transportation routes to Europe that were shorter than the distance involved in shipping crude oil from the Gulf Coast to New Jersey for making products to be shipped to Europe. Standard Oil Company of New Jersey was trying to counter the northern plants' loss of foreign outlets by enlarging sales in its own markets in the Middle Atlantic states. It was finding such expansion difficult.[2]

The principal refineries on the Gulf Coast were Standard of Louisiana's at Baton Rouge, at the head of tanker navigation on the Mississippi, and Humble's at Baytown on the Houston Ship Channel. The former refinery was next in size to the New Jersey Works, and the Baytown plant was third; both were expanding at the time. These refineries supplied local and especially distant American and foreign markets. Humble also had a small refinery at San Antonio to supply southwestern Texas. Unlike the New Jersey Works and the Baton Rouge refinery, the plant at Baytown, with its more up-to-date equipment and its proximity to oil fields, made a modest profit in 1927.

Although the refineries of Imperial Oil Limited were unprofitable in competition with the growing import of products from the United States and Latin America, the company was increasing its refining operations in 1927. In that year its total crude runs averaged 48,500 barrels daily. The oldest and largest refinery, located at Sarnia near the southern tip of Lake Huron, obtained crude by pipeline from Mid-Continent fields in the United States. The three on tidewater—at Halifax, Montreal, and Ioco (near Vancouver)—processed crude brought by tanker, principally from Latin America. The two small inland plants—at Regina and Calgary—got oil from Turner Valley and distant fields in the United States by pipeline and railroad. Imperial also had two smaller units in operation, one a fuel-oil supplier and the other a general supplier. In 1927 this affiliate owned nearly 90 per cent of the refining capacity in Canada.

The refineries of Jersey affiliates in Latin America had been built in large part to supply markets in the countries where they were located. The small plant in Cuba, where there was no oil production, was protected by a tariff on products. Even with such protection, the old refinery at Belot near Havana, which processed imported crude, was not profitable. A tariff on products also helped the Campaña refinery, near Buenos Aires, which imported crude oil to supplement that produced by affiliates in Argentina. Operating conditions were good in Peru and Colombia, where the production of Imperial's associates exceeded their refining capacity and the refineries were protected by import tariffs on products. The International Petroleum Company was processing about half of its crude output at the Talara refinery for supplying Peruvian markets and for export to other countries in Latin America. In 1927 it had daily average runs of 13,000 barrels. The Tropical Oil Company's smaller refinery at Barrancabermeja, up the Magdalena River, was increasing its operations to supply Colombian markets. In Mexico, because of uncertain relations with the government and generally disturbed conditions, Jersey in 1927 decided to shut down the Tampico refinery of Compañía Transcontinental de Petróleo.

The refineries of Jersey affiliates in Europe, although small, were on the whole operating profitably in 1927. Four were protected by tariffs, but they were affected by the competition of Russian products and by the regulations of various governments. The largest was the Teleajen refinery in Romania with average daily crude runs of 6,200 barrels in 1927. This plant processed Româno-Americana's own production and some purchased crude; it supplied products to local and distant markets. The plant at Libusza in Poland was processing a daily average of 700 barrels, the total production of Standard–Nobel; to comply with governmental regulations, this affiliate was exporting products at a loss. The Trieste refinery of Triestina Olii Minerali had become separated by new national boundaries and by tariff walls from its former source of crude—distant oil fields formerly in Austria-Hungary but now in Poland. This refinery and the plant in Norway of Aktieselskabet Vallö Oljeraffineri were processing a few hundred barrels daily of special crudes or distillates to provide products on which import duties were high. The refinery of Agwi Petroleum Corporation, Limited, at Fawley on the south coast of England was operating at about half its capacity. It was running a daily average of 2,500 barrels of heavy Latin American crude to produce fuel oil for the bunkering trade and asphalt for surfacing roads.[3]

In the Orient, Jersey's affiliate, Nederlandsche Koloniale Petroleum Maatschappij, had a refinery at Sungei Gerong on the island of Sumatra. This plant, which in 1927 processed a daily average of 3,400 barrels of crude brought by pipeline from fields in southern Sumatra, was being expanded to run the rising production of the Talang Akar field. Its products were sold to Standard Oil of New York in competition with supplies from California and Russia. An older unit of NKPM at Kapoean in Java was maintaining a low level of operation.

In addition to these refineries, Jersey affiliates had a few small rerunning and special compounding plants more closely allied with marketing than with production or refining. They were the Pittsburgh Grease Works, a small specialty plant in Boston, the Bremen works of the old Mineraloel-Raffinerie vorm. August Korff, a lubricating plant in Belgium, and a few small units in Germany processing imported naphtha to meet local requirements.

The years from 1927 to 1939 were to bring significant developments in Jersey's refineries and their operations. An immediate spur to change came from operating losses over several years which reached a record high in 1927. Thereafter, new problems, new opportunities, and new knowledge had an impact on both plants and operations. These developments brought changes in refinery location, management, and equipment which radically transformed this branch of Jersey's operations.

THE CHANGING PATTERN OF REFINERY LOCATION

Nothing shows more clearly the break of Jersey's refining with the past than the changes in the location and size of the refineries of the affiliates. New plants were acquired, the operations of old ones were reduced or increased, and some were dismantled or sold. These shifts were in response to a complexity of factors: the development of new oil regions, the growth of certain markets, an oversupply of crude and products, the depression, and rising economic nationalism in many countries.

The addition of new plants at home came as a result of Jersey's and Humble's decision of 1927 to expand their marketing in the United States. One of these plants was located at Everett, Massachusetts, on Boston Harbor; the others were in Texas.

The Everett refinery was acquired in 1929 with Jersey's purchase of Beacon Oil Company in order to obtain marketing facilities and operations in New England. This firm had originally built its plant to process Mexican crude for providing fuel and gas oils for industrial use in New England. It had extended operations to include gasoline which was sold by a marketing affiliate. Although Colonial Beacon—the new name of Beacon Oil—extended Jersey's markets, the additional outlets were not at once sufficient to keep the Everett refinery and the New Jersey Works operating at full capacity.[4]

Humble Oil & Refining Company constructed several small plants to help carry out the 1927 program to expand its marketing in Texas. These were in sections of the state where products from Baytown, because of high transportation costs, could not compete with those of plants processing crude from nearby fields. One plant was at Ingleside, near the terminus of Humble's Southwest Texas pipeline system to the Gulf. Another was at McCamey, an oil-boom town on a belated frontier in rough country in West Texas. However, these and other new plants with one exception were short-lived; only the one at Ingleside survived the depression. The others became uneconomical to operate after their crude processing was greatly reduced in the early 1930's by the competition of small local plants making low-grade products from "bootleg" or other cheap crudes.[5]

As the crude production of foreign affiliates increased in the years from

1927 to 1931, the Jersey Company expanded its processing abroad. It added to existing facilities and built new plants near producing fields. The capacity of the Sungei Gerong refinery in Sumatra reached a daily average of 16,000 barrels in 1931. Small plants were built in Europe, one by Romåno-Americana in the Moreno field and another at Fornovo by the Italian producing affiliate, Società Petrolifera Italiana. Several new ones were also acquired in South America: the La Brea plant in Trinidad of

LOCATION OF AFFILIATES' REFINERIES IN NORTH AMERICA AND THE CARIBBEAN IN 1939

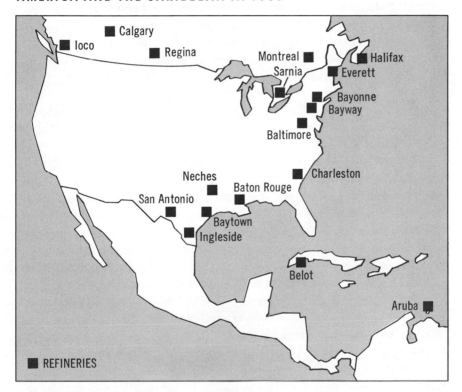

the newly purchased Trinidad Oil Fields Operating Company; one belonging to the West India Oil Company at La Arriaga on the western shore of Lake Maracaibo, which ran crude produced by Jersey's new affiliate, Creole Petroleum Corporation; the Caripito refinery of Standard Oil of Venezuela in the eastern part of the country; three very small units of Standard Oil of Bolivia; and three small plants of local affiliates in Argentina.[6]

Notable expansion of Jersey's foreign refining began in 1932 with the purchase of the Pan American properties of Standard of Indiana. This acquisition, the principal objective of which was to acquire oil reserves in Venezuela's Maracaibo basin, brought Jersey a major addition to its refining. The refineries thereby acquired were valued at $29,000,000. One unit was a small plant at La Salina on the eastern shore of Lake Maracaibo. Another, at Tampico in Mexico, belonged to the Huasteca Petroleum Company, the operations of which had been greatly reduced in recent years. Still another was at Hamburg, Germany, the property of Ebano Asphalt Werke, A.G., which produced a line of heavy petroleum products. The most important was the refinery of Lago Oil & Transport Company, Limited, on the Caribbean island of Aruba.[7]

This Lago refinery was in an exceptionally favorable location. The island was a possession of the Netherlands and thus under a stable and dependable government, an important consideration in view of the instability of governments and uncertainty about their policies in many countries at that time. Because Aruba had no import duty on crude oil, the location had a distinct advantage over plants processing imported oil in the United States after its new tariff went into effect in 1932. To be sure, oil to be processed for export could be brought into the United States under bond without paying the duty; but the amount of red tape involved and the difficulty of segregating products in the bonded manufacturing operation reduced the value of this privilege. The Aruba refinery, moreover, could get crude in virtually unlimited quantity from nearby Latin American fields, especially from the Lake Maracaibo basin. In addition, the island had a harbor deep enough for large ocean tankers and was on direct tanker routes to Western Europe from fields in western Venezuela, Colombia, and Mexico. In fact, Aruba was a little closer to Europe than Jersey's Gulf Coast refineries in the United States. This location had one disadvantage compared to Jersey's refineries in the United States: nearly all provisions had to be brought in by ship, mainly from North America. Even water of potable quality for employees' homes and for certain needs of the refinery had to be brought by tanker from the United States, where it was purchased from the state of New Jersey.[8]

The Aruba refinery was the largest addition of the 1930's to Jersey's foreign refining. Under its Jersey ownership in the last half of 1932, this plant ran an average of 87,500 barrels of crude per day (an average of 58,300 barrels under Jersey ownership, for the whole year).[9] The refinery was of recent construction and efficient by current standards, and it had excellent facilities for handling large quantities of heavy Lake Maracaibo crude. It had eight pipe stills for separating the lighter oil fractions from the crude; each still could run a daily average of 6,500 barrels. It also had eight so-called combination units, each with three separate parts or circuits. The first circuit could run as much as 20,000 barrels of crude oil daily; the second cracked or reduced the residual from the first; and the third cracked the gas oil from the first and second. Combining several operations, these units represented a major advance in refinery design, one that brought many economies in operations. In fact, this was Jersey's first foreign plant with operations of a sufficient size to make the use of expensive new equipment economically feasible.[10]

Heavy fuel oil was the main product of the Aruba refinery in the 1930's. It made up approximately 45 per cent of the plant's total output. Gasoline was a poor second, and diesel oil was third. These products represented adjustment to the refinery's markets at the time, the demand for residual fuels being proportionately far larger in foreign markets than in the United States. Aruba's concentration on these three products was similar to that of its rivals, Royal Dutch–Shell's refinery on the nearby island of Curaçao and Anglo-Iranian's at Abadan at the head of the Persian Gulf.[11]

In the late 1930's the Aruba refinery grew increasingly important. As observed in Chapter 6, it came to occupy a strategic position among Jersey's refineries in preparation for war in Europe. This fact, together with the rising demand for the plant's products, brought marked expansion of its equipment and operations. In 1939 it averaged a daily crude run of 227,600 barrels, an average affected adversely by the loss of market outlets in Europe after the outbreak of war in the third quarter of the year. With all equipment operating fully, it could have processed as much as 323,000 barrels per day. This refinery, from the time of its acquisition by Jersey to the end of the 1930's, had far larger crude runs than even Humble's at Baytown.

In the later 1930's Jersey also increased its refining operations in Venezuela, where its producing was mounting rapidly but local markets remained small. The government of President López Contreras, after the death of Gómez in 1935, called for greater economic development within the country. It particularly asked the foreign oil companies to process more of their production within Venezuela. By this time Jersey affiliates had three small refineries there. Gulf Oil also had a small plant; Royal Dutch–Shell had the largest, one capable of running 17,000 barrels daily. The Jersey affiliates moved to comply with the government's request. They enlarged the refinery at La Salina on Lake Maracaibo, but shut down the less favorably located one at La Arriaga. They added to the capacity of the plant at Caripito, which could supply products economically to various markets along the eastern coast of South America. The Caripito expansion was completed before the end of 1939 after an expenditure of more than $6,000,000. The refinery was then capable of processing 35,000 barrels of crude daily, a sufficient capacity to make possible efficient operations using up-to-date equipment.[12]

Imperial in Canada and its affiliates in South America also increased the facilities and crude runs of their refineries. At the Talara plant in Peru, the production of fuel oil for the international bunkering business was expanded. The Colombian refinery at Barrancabermeja was enlarged. Despite Canada's 1936 reduction of its tariff on imported products, Imperial added to its existing refineries; it could import crude at a lower cost by tanker or pipeline than its competitors could bring products from the United States by tank car.[13]

Governmental action determined the fate of Jersey's refining in several countries in Latin America. Bolivia's seizure of Jersey properties in 1937 and Mexico's forcible take-over of the foreign oil companies' properties in 1938 ended the operations of Jersey affiliates in those countries. (See Chapter 5.) In Argentina, the government set strict limits on the capacity and output of the affiliates' plants.[14]

A new refinery of Standard Oil Company of Brazil ran into an unusual situation. It was only after some hesitation that the administrators in New York had decided to build a plant in that country. Brazil had no oil production, but the levying of a tariff on imported products had encouraged Jersey to investigate the feasibility of operating a refinery there. In 1937, after the local manager had received official approval of the construction of a small plant at São Paulo, the Brazilian affiliate began to construct one with a daily capacity of 2,160 barrels at an estimated cost of about $500,000. The work was proceeding satisfactorily when in April, 1938, the National Department of Mineral Production published a decree-law limiting refining to companies whose capital was entirely national. Accordingly, the government notified Standard Oil Company of Brazil that its construction must be suspended at once. Although the company obtained permission to complete it, the plant stood idle until it was dismantled during World War II for use elsewhere.[15]

In Europe, both economic and political considerations made the acquisition of new refineries by Jersey interests advisable in the 1930's. This would undoubtedly have come eventually as the consumption of oil products increased and crude oil became available in the Middle East. But its coming was hastened by rising economic nationalism and, late in the 1930's, by the drive of several countries to increase refining within their boundaries in preparation for a possible war.

One addition to Jersey's European refining interests came in France in response to a shift in the government's policy with regard to the importing of crude oil. The 1927 discovery of oil by the Iraq Petroleum Company, in which Compagnie Française des Pétroles was a large owner, touched off a movement for the government to encourage the building of refineries. France enacted legislation and issued decrees making it advisable for foreign marketers within that country to build refineries to supply products for national outlets. Anglo-Persian and Royal Dutch–Shell soon built refineries there. Representatives of the leading American companies—Jersey, Gulf Oil, Atlantic Refining, and Vacuum—discussed various plans for meeting the new situation. To the companies selling a range of products, this posed the problem that the individual concern had insufficient sales to build a refinery approaching efficient size. Three of these American companies agreed on joint action.[16]

In 1929 these three—Jersey, Gulf Oil, and Atlantic Refining—organized the United Petroleum Securities Corporation, an American holding company with a capital of $15,000,000. This union of competing interests was possible under the Webb-Pomerene Act of the United States, which under certain conditions allowed competitors at home to join in carrying on foreign operations.[17] Jersey received 67½ per cent of the corporation's stock, Gulf Oil 22½, and Atlantic 10. The three companies turned over to the new holding company 70 per cent of their shares in their marketing affiliates in France; Jersey in addition contributed 45 per cent of its former holding company, Compagnie Standard Franco-Américaine S.A., which obtained the remaining 30 per cent of the stock of the French marketing affiliates. French nationals who owned shares in these marketing affiliates exchanged their holdings for 55 per cent of the stock of Franco-Américaine. The American companies also created a refining affiliate, Société Franco-Américaine de Raffinage (later called Standard Franco-Américaine de Raffinage S.A.); this corporation was owned directly by the marketing companies and indirectly by the French and American holding companies. This complicated set of holdings arose from difficulties in transferring ownership and at the same time meeting the country's legal requirements. The law specified that owners of stock in French refining companies must be French nationals or companies, but it did not require that the ultimate principal owner be an individual or corporate citizen of France.[18]

Because Jersey had a majority interest in United Petroleum Securities Corporation, it was entitled to provide four of the company's seven directors and to take a leading part in planning the French refinery. Jersey men supervised the construction by American engineering firms. A maximum capacity of 17,000 barrels daily was originally planned. This refinery was located at Port Jérôme, twenty-five miles up the Seine River from Le Havre.

The refinery began to operate on May 1, 1933. At first it processed Colombian and Peruvian crudes, but it used some Iraqi crude after that Middle East oil became available late the next year. The managers of the new refinery also had charge of the old La Mailleraye plant, which was equipped to run 750 barrels daily of lubricating distillates. By 1939, the Port Jérôme refinery had been expanded to provide for a daily capacity of 25,000 barrels.[19] This was a fair capacity for a plant in France; and for the types of products it made, it was probably close to the minimum efficient size of that time.

The location at Port Jérôme conformed to the plan of the country's leading foreign marketers to build plants of moderate size at various coastal points for supplying nearby markets. This program would enable them to carry out an elaborate system for exchanging products in order to provide products as economically as possible in all parts of France. Royal Dutch–Shell and Anglo-Persian each built an additional refinery; Vacuum constructed a second; and The Texas Company, one. Compagnie Française de Raffinage built two.[20]

Compagnie Française de Raffinage was in a favored position. It was partly owned by the French government. Another French concern, Compagnie Française des Pétroles, provided it with nearly a quarter of all the crude produced by Iraq Petroleum Company. Further, the government-sponsored refining company was guaranteed a quarter of the domestic market, which it supplied through independent French marketing firms. The affiliates of the international groups were required to take any surplus, and they were prevented by their refining licenses from expanding independently. In 1938 the refineries in France were averaging a total output of 139,000 barrels daily, which was sufficient, with the addition of synthetic products, to supply the national demand. These refineries were protected by tariffs on imported products amounting in 1937 to the equivalent of 17.7 cents per American gallon of gasoline.[21]

In contrast to France, the United Kingdom—the largest and most concentrated market for oil products in Europe—did little to promote the expansion of refining. At various times from 1928, the government levied small taxes on imports, whether crude or products, but these were designed to provide revenue and to give aid to coal and shale industries rather than to stimulate the oil-refining industry in Britain. In 1934 the government guaranteed a tax differential of fourpence per gallon in favor of products made from indigenous materials. This differential served to strengthen the shale oil industry, increase the production of benzole, step up the search for petroleum in Britain, and start the hydrogenation of British coal. However, supplies from local sources in 1936 provided only 8 per cent of the national consumption of motor fuel.[22]

The refining within the United Kingdom was actually supplying a declining percentage of the consumption of petroleum products. After World War I, Anglo-Persian Oil Company, Limited—in which the government had majority ownership—had built plants to utilize some of its Persian crude. Other companies, especially affiliates of Royal Dutch–Shell and the American Doheny interests, had followed Anglo-Persian's example by refining in Britain crude oil from Mexico and Venezuela to supplement products they imported from those countries. After pipelines were completed from Iraq to the Mediterranean in 1934, the major refineries obtained low-cost crude produced by Iraq Petroleum Company and another concern organized by its owners. Even so, the refining industry in Britain, which in 1925 had averaged total runs of approximately 44,000 barrels daily—sufficient to supply about a quarter of the demand—in 1938 was running an average of only 46,500 barrels daily, or less than one-fifth of the consumption.[23]

In 1937 a government committee headed by Lord Falmouth investigated various possibilities for assuring fuel supplies for Britain in the event of war. The committee reported in 1938 that "in general a policy of depending on imported [petroleum] supplies with adequate storage is the most economical means of providing for an emergency. . . ."[24] As the committee recommended, the tax was raised to ninepence per gallon (the equivalent of 15.4 cents for an American gallon in 1937) on products made from foreign petroleum and used for road transport; only one penny had to be paid on those made from indigenous materials, such as shale. The refining of petroleum was given no tariff protection in Great Britain, and taxes on oil products continued to be looked upon principally as a source of revenue.[25]

In Germany, on the contrary, Hitler promoted programs for making his country as independent as possible of outside fuel sources. He fostered not only local production and manufacture but also the development of substitutes from indigenous materials, especially from brown coal (an intermediate between peat and bituminous coal containing much volatile matter). High tariffs—the equivalent of 36.2 cents on the American gallon of gasoline in 1937—and other inducements brought about local production of a substantial portion of the nation's requirement for motor fuels and a small part of the demand for other products. Jersey's affiliates in Germany were forced to enlarge their existing refineries and to invest in synthetic plants. Accordingly, the old August Korff plant at Bremen and that of Ebano Asphalt Werke at Hamburg added such equipment. The total output of petroleum products within Germany in 1938 amounted to an average of 36,000 barrels daily; this was still far short of the national requirement of 152,000 barrels daily.[26]

Italy under Mussolini combined parts of the programs of both France and Germany, although it was even more deficient than these countries in natural resources and had less investment in producing companies elsewhere. In 1937 it raised the tariff on gasoline to the equivalent of 49.1 cents on the American gallon, then the highest rate in Europe. It also encouraged the production of synthetics and provided assistance for government-controlled refineries. Jersey's affiliates expanded the old Trieste plant and the one at Fornovo; their combined runs averaged only 2,100 barrels daily in 1938. These two units represented only a small fraction of the Italian refining industry, which in the same year was averaging runs of 29,800 barrels daily. This was nearly half the volume of the nation's daily product requirement.[27]

Jersey and its affiliates also made changes in their refining in other European countries. Discouraged over the possibility of developing profitable integrated operations in Poland, the parent company sold its Polish affiliate to Socony-Vacuum in 1937. The next year it organized a Danish company, A/S Kalundborg Oljeraffinaderi, which acquired a small unit to provide asphalt and other heavy products for a growing market. Affiliates increased slightly the output of the Teleajen plant in Romania and equipped the old Atlas plant in Belgium and the Vallö refinery in Norway to provide a wider range of products than they had been making.[28]

Contrary to Jersey's experience in several countries in Europe, economic considerations were the most important in determining policies with respect to the Sungei Gerong refinery in the Dutch East Indies. Under joint ownership by Jersey and Socony, the capacity of this Standard-Vacuum plant was raised from 25,000 to 45,000 barrels daily, which was about a quarter of the total refining capacity in the Dutch East Indies. Altogether, by 1940 expenditures on the Sungei Gerong plant totaled $33,000,000. Next to that at Aruba, this was the largest foreign refinery among the Jersey affiliates. In size and equipment it was an efficient, up-to-date refinery.[29]

In Japan, Standard-Vacuum was under some pressure from the government to enter refining. Officials in that country imposed many controls upon the petroleum industry in the 1930's and looked with favor upon joint efforts by foreigners and nationals to build up processing there. Royal Dutch–Shell—whose two home governments were fearful of Japanese aggression on the mainland and in the islands—did not favor participation with Japanese interests in refining. After discussions with Japanese officials, Standard-Vacuum came to a similar conclusion.[30]

The large net increase in Jersey's foreign refining held down the rate of expansion at home. In contrast to the whole domestic refining industry's 30 per cent increase in processing from 1929 to 1939,[31] the total average daily crude runs of Jersey's domestic refineries rose only about 9 per cent. Affiliates made adjustments primarily on the basis of opportunities in the markets within the regions where they sold products—that is, largely sales within the United States. The capacity of a few plants was increased, including that at Baytown, which became the largest refinery owned by Jersey affiliates in the United States and indeed the largest in the country. The capacity of some other refineries was reduced, especially that of the New Jersey Works, which lost most of its export market. In the volume of their crude runs, this group of plants fell to third rank among the domestic refineries of Jersey affiliates. In 1936 Standard Oil Company of New Jersey shut down the old Parkersburg refinery because the markets it served could be supplied more economically by pipeline from the New Jersey Works and by Mississippi River barges from Baton Rouge. That old plant could no longer hold out against the growth of large refineries with their newer equipment and economies of scale.[32]

As a result of changes in their markets, the domestic refineries had to adjust their equipment to the production of different yields of major products. After 1932 they increased their output of gasoline, kerosene, distillates, and lubricants, but they greatly reduced their production of residual fuel oils. The increase in distillates was largely due to the expanding market for light fuel oils for heating homes and for use in certain types of motors. The decline in the output of residual fuels came because of the shifting of much of the bunkering of foreign ships to foreign ports and the importing under bond of fuel oil for such bunkering in ports of the United States.[33]

The growth of the Jersey Company's foreign refining was of basic importance to its total operation. It necessitated finding new markets at home to take the place of the domestic refineries' loss of a large part of their foreign outlets. It gave the company's refining abroad a dimension comparable to its foreign production and marketing. It also necessitated changing Jersey's policies and management in the refining branch of its business from a predominantly American orientation to one that could work effectively within different cultures and with various peoples and governments.

REFINERY MANAGEMENT IN TRANSITION

Refining operations themselves increasingly called for professionally trained men employing the tools of science and engineering. The demand for products of higher quality and greater diversity and the contributions of research were making it both necessary and possible to change the character of the operations. The result was a gradual transformation in the management personnel of Jersey's refineries.

In 1927 the traditional leadership in Jersey's refining was still that of men who had learned the art in the school of experience and who had worked almost entirely within the United States. The president and the vice-president for refining of Standard Oil Company of New Jersey both had exactly such backgrounds. Among the four directors of the company who had spent their careers in refining, only Frank W. Abrams was a trained engineer. The top managers of Standard of Louisiana and also of Imperial were of the old school. Humble had a graduate in civil engineering, Director Harry C. Wiess, in charge of refining. But, as in other affiliates, this company's processing operations were still under managers who had risen from the ranks without formal training in any engineering field. They were men who, at the most, had taken correspondence courses in subjects related to their work.[34]

As the older managers retired and operations expanded, engineers and scientists were gradually appointed to managerial positions throughout Jersey's refining organization. In New York, William J. Haley, a graduate in mechanical engineering from the University of Pennsylvania, was in 1929 made assistant to George W. Gordon, the parent company's executive for refining in the Far East and Latin America (except in Peru and Colombia). After J. C. Hilton—a general purchasing agent in New York—was appointed chief executive of Standard of Louisiana in 1931, several retirements at Baton Rouge made room for the advancement of younger men to managerial posts. Henry H. Hewetson, who had started work as a student engineer at Sarnia after World War I, was made general manager of the refinery in 1931. Monroe J. Rathbone, a 1921 graduate in chemical engineering from Lehigh University, became general superintendent.[35]

Change was accelerated in 1933, when retirement throughout the domestic affiliates was temporarily made optional at 60 years of age and mandatory at 62. Many men who had done good work according to old standards then passed off the scene after decades of empirical approaches to refining problems. The pioneer of the new age in Jersey's refining, Director Edgar M. Clark, also retired at this time.

In only a few years the new type of executive rose to leadership in the affiliates' refineries. In 1933 Frank W. Abrams was promoted to the presidency of Standard Oil Company of New Jersey, and Chester F. Smith, a chemical engineer who had started his career at Bayonne, became vice-president. In 1934 Lloyd G. Smith, a 1913 graduate in chemical engineering from the University of Illinois, was appointed manager of the Aruba refinery. When Hewetson was transferred to Imperial in 1935, Rathbone was elected vice-president of Standard of Louisiana and general manager at Baton Rouge. A year later, he became president of the company and Marion W. Boyer rose to the general managership of that plant. With a bachelor's and a master's degree from the Massachusetts Institute of Technology, Boyer had been a member of the research group established at Baton Rouge in 1927; since 1931 he had been next in line to Rathbone in the management of the refinery. In 1935 Brian Mead became technical adviser at the Port Jérôme refinery. An Englishman who had become an American citizen, Mead had come to this country to study chemical engineering at MIT and had joined the Humble research staff in 1926.[36]

In Humble also, chemical engineers were promoted to higher posts in the refining organization in the 1930's. Dr. E. F. Voss, who had joined Humble's research staff in 1924, became a member of the company's Manufacturing Committee in 1935, and Gordon L. Farned, superintendent of the small Ingleside refinery, was appointed superintendent at Baytown. Two years later, Harry W. Ferguson, who had become a member of Humble's research staff in 1924 and had served for several years as head of technical service at the Baytown refinery, was appointed assistant general manager of refining.[37]

Even before the rise of these professionally trained men to managerial posts in refining, staffs made up of scientists and engineers had begun to bring the developing technology into processing operations. In fact, the parent company had long utilized such groups; its General Engineering Department had been in existence many years before the organization of the Development Department in 1919. Within the latter had been set up almost at once a technical service division under Dr. N. E. Loomis to assist in manufacturing development. When the engineering and technical service staffs were transferred to Standard Oil Development in 1927, the latter group became the Technical Service Department of Standard Oil Company of New Jersey. Its members served as consultants to advise the operating organizations of the company's refineries and also of the Everett plant after its acquisition in 1929. In Humble, a similar advisory function was first performed by the Development Department, but in 1929 a special division was set up; the two were later merged as the Technical Service and Development Department. Somewhat later than Humble, Standard of Louisiana also organized such a technical staff.[38]

Like the research groups, these service staffs were very much influenced by Professor Warren K. Lewis of the Massachusetts Institute of Technology. A large percentage of the scientists and engineers who were employed by Jersey and its affiliates from the early 1920's were from MIT and many of them had been drawn to that institution by Dr. Lewis, who was an unusually creative teacher. Lewis had become a consultant to Jersey in 1920 and soon thereafter to Humble. His influence, directly and through his students, entered into the whole stream of thinking of the Jersey refining organization.[39]

Dr. Lewis questioned many existing practices in operations. For instance, he held that, instead of permitting unexplained losses to occur during processing, there should be a full accounting for the crude oil and its products at all times—that is, a materials balance. As an essential of good engineering, he also stressed a thorough analysis of costs for each process. He urged that when the addition of new equipment was considered economic analyses be made as a basis for estimating the market probabilities of the resulting product. This approach, he maintained, should replace the old practice of relying on extrapolations of past trends. In general, he stimulated an attitude that led to the questioning of the old and a search for better ways.[40]

The technical service staffs advised on both physical and economic aspects of refining technology. They were concerned with plant design and equipment, with costs, and with the development and application of standards. They planned alternate ways of accomplishing given results, devised methods of using equipment more economically from the point of view of the whole refinery, and studied the processing of crudes of different qualities in order to use the ones that would yield the largest amount of given products at the lowest cost. They also developed the principle of replacement or opportunity cost for determining the cost of specific products.

Out of technical service grew special groups concerned with process control. Their function was to make thorough studies of actual operations in order to establish standards and controls through the application of engineering principles. In 1934 a process division was formed in Standard Oil Development. Its duties were to assist operating groups with process or quality problems, to work on improving yields and quality and reducing costs, and to help develop new ways that might have promise for the future. In 1934 a process-control system was established at the Baltimore refinery. Its first assignment was to determine whether the consumption of steam, fuel, and chemicals could be reduced by applying a technical approach to the problem and, at the same time, to arrive at cost standards for each operation. After six months, it was estimated that an annual saving of $200,000 could be made on utilities alone. Executives at Baton Rouge were quick to see the value of this work; in 1936, according to the Annual Report of Standard of Louisiana, process control was being applied in seven out of fourteen areas in the company's refinery. A process control group was set up at Baytown in 1937.[41]

Giving attention to costs was not new to Jersey; indeed, it was an old practice in the company's operations. It had been an important factor in the growth of the Standard Oil combination in the 1870's and 1880's.[42] The techniques used in the old days were crude compared with those developed in the 1930's and thereafter, but even those simple methods had been more or less submerged under the demands of expansion and readjustment during and immediately after World War I. From 1925 on, the Coordination Committee had provided for a more comprehensive examination of refining costs on the part of the parent company than had previously been made under the Manufacturing Committee. Because the Atlantic Coast refineries were losing money at the time, studies of their operations were made with a view to determining what their future should be. These studies revealed the need to improve the management of these refineries and led to the merging of the plants' management and the appointment of Abrams as general manager.[43]

Both short- and long-term considerations made cost reduction necessary. Unsatisfactory refinery earnings in 1926 and 1927, declining prices, and shrinking refinery margins made it imperative. Later, during the depression years, especially from 1930 through 1933, costs had to be cut because of a decline in demand as well as in prices. A particular problem rose in the United States from the competition of small refiners utilizing "bootleg" crude from the East Texas field. For the short run, the problem of high unit costs could be met in part by taking the less efficient equipment out of operations. But anticipated long-term competition motivated managers to reduce costs as much as possible and generally to raise the efficiency of equipment and operations.

The economic analysis staff of Humble's Technical Service and Development Department took the lead among Jersey affiliates in developing sophisticated techniques for study of economic aspects of refining operations and particularly for the planning of new equipment and expansion. This group was under the direction of Dr. Stewart P. Coleman, a former student of Dr. Lewis at MIT. In 1933, principally because of his work in directing Humble's application of economic and engineering analysis to problems of cost, Coleman was invited to join the Coordination Committee in New York to head a new staff group specializing in economic analysis.[44]

In the course of time, the results of the work of research men and engineers spread throughout the Jersey refining organization. The developing system of communication facilitated the cooperation of the various groups in advancing refining technology and managerial techniques and in spreading word of the progress being made. Not all the refineries—especially the smaller ones—came to be managed by technically trained men at this time; innovations in leadership and technology came first in the large refineries of the affiliates in the United States. But the progress made became known and new practices were gradually introduced throughout a large part of the Jersey Company's refining operations, foreign as well as domestic. Standard Oil Development and the parent company's Coordination Committee by means of the conferences it sponsored spread information about new processes, equipment, techniques, and standards and generally promoted more effective controls. Helpful also were committees made up of representatives of research and technical staffs among the affiliates. In addition, personal communication between individuals throughout Jersey's refining aided greatly in the process of effective modernization.

More than top leadership was required, however, to make the developing technology effective in operations; a measure of adaptation to the new by operating employees on all levels was also necessary. With changes in equipment and processes—especially in the large refineries and those with advanced equipment—refinery workers had to have skills and be able to take responsibility beyond the requirements of the less complex operations of former times. More and more attention was therefore given in the later 1930's to improving operating personnel, especially to training foremen. Extensive programs were developed for supervisory training and conferences. These were concerned with employee relations and safety in general and also with the handling of the more volatile materials and new equipment being utilized in refinery processing. (See Chapter 12.)

INNOVATIONS IN REFINERY EQUIPMENT

Before new managers and staff technologists became widely established in the refineries of Jersey affiliates, significant changes had already been initiated in the equipment used in two basic processes: distilling and cracking. In fact, this development had come well under way before 1927; it spread among the Jersey refineries in the next few years. More revolutionary, however, were the new facilities resulting from the extensive research and development carried on after 1927.

For several years the Jersey affiliates made distinct improvements in distillation equipment, that is, the units performing the basic function of separating different types of oil molecules—or fractions of crude oil— from one another. Many refineries had depended on the use of batch stills, but these necessitated time out for cleaning; others had used batteries of continuous shell stills. Both required much labor. For some time the companies experimented with pipe stills—so called because oil was heated as it passed through pipes instead of in a tank; this method had proved its value in California for handling heavy oils. These stills had several advantages: continuous operation, more economical utilization of heat, and much lower labor requirements. Fractionating columns (bubble towers), which the Jersey refineries had utilized for several years, were used with this equipment to separate the various fractions from each other. By 1931 Bayway, Baytown, and Baton Rouge had acquired pipe stills with improved bubble towers capable of more precise fractionating than the old columns and able to handle from 10,000 to 20,000 barrels daily.[45]

The affiliates in the same years acquired improved cracking equipment. By 1927 the old Burton-Clark stills were already being superseded by the tube-and-tank cracking facilities, which had lower unit costs than the earlier stills. This tube-and-tank equipment was improved as experience and new knowledge of metallurgy made it possible to operate with pressures up to 1,000 pounds per square inch; the new units yielded a larger proportion of gasoline from crudes than did the old ones operating with lower pressures. By 1931 the three major Jersey refineries were equipped with advanced thermal cracking equipment; Baytown alone had spent about $8,000,000 in constructing new Cross cracking coils and revamping old tube-and-tank units. A few of the smaller refineries—those having a capacity of at least 12,000 barrels per day and supplying an active gasoline market—also obtained new equipment.[46]

The addition of improved cracking equipment in Jersey refineries had run its course by 1931. That year's decision of the Supreme Court of the United States in a long-standing suit over cross-licensing of patents—in which Jersey, Standard of Indiana, and other companies were involved—cleared an obstacle to the installation of such facilities.*[47] However, by that time further additions had been reduced by overcapacity, the flow of cheap crude from the East Texas field, and the general business depression. Indeed, the type of cracking that used heat and pressure had become well established throughout the oil industry in the United States. In 1931, such cracking constituted 40 per cent of the total, a sizable increase over 30 per cent in 1927.[48]

Before the end of 1931, other kinds of equipment had also been added at the large domestic refineries of the Jersey affiliates. These additions were mainly used for finishing products and improving their quality.[49] The only radically new type resulting from the research undertaken by Jersey laboratories in 1927 was the hydrogenation plant. Although an

---

* After long negotiations but shortly before the decision of the court, these and other large refining companies purchased Universal Oil Products Company; this concern held patents relating to cracking for the use of which the companies were paying royalties.

oversupply of oil soon made the use of such plants uneconomic for producing a higher yield of gasoline from crude, they were important as forerunners of a new era in refining.

For several years after 1931, the addition of new refining equipment came mostly abroad, where Jersey was acquiring new plants and expanding old ones. The combination unit was especially important at Aruba. Three such units were added to those already in use when the refinery was taken over by Jersey. This kind of equipment, which performed several basic steps in the refining process, foreshadowed the obsolescence of such old types as tube-and-tank cracking units. At home, however, the depression and the loss of foreign markets delayed for a time the addition of new equipment. The installation of combination units at Baytown—although recommended by the Jersey Coordination Committee as having lower operating costs—was postponed in the middle 1930's because Humble's administrators believed the condition of the market did not justify the investment at the time.[50]

In the later 1930's the addition of new equipment was stepped up at the domestic refineries and was continued abroad, especially at the Aruba plant. Additions were spurred by several developments. Basic was the rising demand for oil products resulting from general economic improvement and from the preparation of certain foreign countries for a possible emergency. There was also rising pressure to produce certain new products and to raise the quality of old ones, especially gasoline. The need to reduce costs was a continuing spur to installing more efficient equipment.

In several refineries, additions were made for expanding and improving the basic processes of distillation and cracking. One type was a two-unit pipe still built at Baytown: (1) an atmospheric unit to produce a high yield of gasoline, kerosene, and light oils; and (2) a vacuum unit to produce gas oil and lubricating oil. Combination units, like those at Aruba, were built at Bayway and Everett in the United States, Calgary in Canada, and Caripito in Venezuela. These new ones ranged in daily capacity from the 7,500 barrels at Calgary to 38,000 at Caripito. They required less outlay of capital and also had lower operating costs than conventional equipment of equivalent capacity.[51] In other refineries, the managers generally modernized old facilities with a minimum amount of expenditures.[52]

Other types of new equipment, designed to improve old products or to make new ones, were the result principally of work done by Standard Oil

Development Company and the research staffs of other affiliates. (See Chapter 6.) For improving lubricants, phenol treating plants were built at several Jersey refineries from 1934 to 1939 and a propane treating plant was constructed at Baytown in 1937.[53] The various types of equipment installed in several large refineries to produce iso-octane for 100-octane gasoline were especially important. Plants for making di-isobutylene—to be hydrogenated at Baton Rouge so as to make iso-octane—were built at Bayway and Baytown in 1935. In 1938, copolymer plants, utilizing an improved process for making di-isobutylene, were constructed at Baytown and Baton Rouge, the product being hydrogenated at the latter refinery. In the same year a copolymer and a hydro plant were built at Aruba. In 1938, also, the first alkylation plant for manufacturing iso-octane—the most efficient process developed up to that time for making this product—was built at Baytown, and plans were made for erecting similar ones in other refineries. In order to provide enough of the gases required by the new processes, units were also built at these refineries to separate from mixtures of wasted refinery gases the light hydrocarbons that were needed.[54]

Although they did not bulk large in terms of cost or volume as compared to traditional equipment, these facilities for carrying on new processes made important contributions to what may rightly be called a revolution in refining, one that was to be accelerated in the early years of World War II. The new equipment utilizing the techniques of hydrogenation, catalysis, and polymerization took molecules apart and out of the parts made larger molecules of the same kind or altogether different ones. These operations can be designated as manufacture as distinguished from the traditional refining, which was mostly concerned with separating crude oils into various fractions by distillation and with making lighter fractions by thermal cracking.

Despite these many additions and changes, the capital expenditures to improve the Jersey Company's refineries during the years from 1927 through 1939 were not large compared to investments for increasing oil reserves and production. In fact, they totaled slightly less than depreciation charges amounting to $166,000,000. To some extent this was in response to low refinery earnings. However, Jersey's refining did not require the expansion that came in production. The only substantial increase in capacity came abroad, particularly at Aruba with its favorable location in regard to foreign crude supply and markets. There and elsewhere new types of equipment were added as they reached a practicable stage of development and came to be economically justifiable. Dollar figures, however, do not measure fully the improvement in the plants because much of it came from the modernization and more efficient use of old equipment. At the end of 1939 the net value of the refineries of Jersey affiliates was $188,000,000. More than 60 per cent of this total represented domestic plants. These generally called for a larger investment in new equipment relative to capacity than the foreign refineries because they had to supply a wider range of products and a larger proportion of gasoline for the American market.[55]

In brief, during this period the petroleum chemist and engineer, with the help of improved techniques of cost analysis, brought vital changes in both the refineries and their operations. Among the results were the improvement of product quality, the utilization of light hydrocarbons formerly to a large extent wasted, the raising of. the efficiency of equipment and men, and a general reduction of unit costs.

OPERATING RESULTS, 1927–1939

The results of much of the progress made during the thirteen years were not to be clearly evident before the wartime demand raised the output of the refineries to unprecedented levels in volume, range of products, and quality. But throughout the period, this progress enabled Jersey products to maintain their position in the market.

Table 6 presents a statistical picture of the expansion in the volume of crude oil processed. Total crude runs nearly doubled from 1927 to 1939. They rose steeply through 1929, declined in the next two years, in 1933 moved above those of 1929, and thereafter, except in 1938, grew larger every year to the end of the decade. Despite this substantial increase in volume, Jersey only a little more than maintained the relative position it had held in 1927 in world refining; its share of worldwide crude runs rose only from 14 per cent in 1927 to 15 per cent in 1939.[56]

However, a notable rise came in the size of Jersey's foreign refinery runs as compared to its domestic ones. While the company's total processing in the United States increased from a daily average of 349,300 barrels in 1927 to 389,400 in 1939, that abroad rose from a daily average of 85,000 in the former year to 460,400 in the latter. At home the runs declined from 15 per cent to 11 per cent of the industry total, but abroad they increased from 11 to 21 per cent of the whole industry's runs.[57]

Although Jersey was only one of several large refiners in the United States in 1939, no other American company approached the volume of its

Table 6: **DAILY AVERAGE CRUDE OIL RUNS BY REFINERIES OF AFFILIATES, 1927–1939**
Standard Oil Company (New Jersey)
(In thousands of 42-gallon barrels)

Refinery Location	1927	1928	1929	1930	1931
United States[a]					
Everett	—	—	28.2	23.6	20.7
Bayway and Bayonne	123.2	113.2	112.8	97.3	96.6
Baltimore	25.6	27.8	27.2	24.7	22.8
Parkersburg and Charleston[b]	14.2	9.3	7.2	7.4	6.3
Baton Rouge	98.7	105.6	99.4	90.8	84.4
Baytown	77.6	99.6	111.8	99.8	90.8
Ingleside	—	2.9	9.3	8.8	9.5
Others in Texas[c]	10.0	16.4	13.2	11.3	5.1
Total United States	349.3	394.9	409.1	363.7	336.2
Canada[d]					
Halifax	8.3	9.3	10.2	9.9	9.1
Montreal	12.0	13.1	17.5	14.5	14.8
Sarnia	12.2	14.5	18.3	18.3	19.0
Regina	3.8	5.2	6.5	5.6	4.5
Calgary	4.0	4.5	4.7	5.0	4.6
Ioco	8.2	9.8	13.3	13.0	11.5
Coutts	—	—	—	—	—
Total Canada	48.5	56.4	70.5	66.3	63.5
Latin America					
Tampico, Mexico	0.5	—	—	—	—
Aruba, N.W.I.	—	—	—	—	—
Venezuela[e]	—	—	0.7	1.5	2.0
Talara, Peru	13.0	14.9	15.6	14.2	12.0
Barrancabermeja, Colombia	3.3	4.0	4.7	3.4	3.5
Belot, Cuba	1.5	2.0	2.0	1.6	1.9
La Brea, Trinidad	—	—	0.1	0.6	0.8
Argentina[f]	4.7	5.9	9.7	11.1	9.6
Bolivia[g]	—	0.1	0.1	0.0	0.0
Total Latin America	23.0	26.9	32.9	32.4	29.8
Europe					
Fawley, England	2.5	3.5	7.2	6.2	6.5
Italy[h]	0.4	0.4	0.6	0.9	1.1
Vallö, Norway	0.3	0.5	0.5	0.7	0.7
Libusza, Poland	0.7	0.7	0.7	0.7	0.7
Teleajen, Romania[i]	6.2	9.1	10.8	11.7	14.4
Hamburg, Germany	—	—	—	—	—
Port Jérôme, France[j]	—	—	—	—	—
Belgium[k]	—	—	—	—	—
Kalundborg, Denmark	—	—	—	—	—
Total Europe	10.1	14.2	19.8	20.2	23.4
Far East					
Sungei Gerong, Sumatra[l]	3.4	4.6	6.9	12.5	15.8
Total Foreign	85.0	112.2	130.1	131.4	132.5
Total World	434.3	497.1	539.2	495.1	468.7

NOTE: Because of the rounding of numbers, totals are not in all cases the exact sum of the numbers added. 0.0 means less than 51 barrels.
[a] Does not include reprocessed crude in refineries of Standard Oil Company of New Jersey: 9,500 barrels in 1936, 9,500 in 1937, 14,800 in 1938, and 15,200 in 1939.
[b] Parkersburg was closed in 1936.

[c] Includes: Burkburnett, 1927; McCamey, 1927 to 1932; Chilton, 1927–1932; Breckenridge, 1927–1931; San Antonio, 1927–1939; and Neches, 1929–1939.
[d] Figures for a few other small refineries not available.
[e] Includes: La Arriaga, 1929–1939; Caripito, 1932–1939; La Salina, 1932–1939.

Table 6 (cont.): **DAILY AVERAGE CRUDE OIL RUNS BY REFINERIES OF AFFILIATES, 1927–1939**
Standard Oil Company (New Jersey)
(In thousands of 42-gallon barrels)

1932	1933	1934	1935	1936	1937	1938	1939
20.2	19.6	19.7	17.5	19.7	16.2	13.9	21.4
97.2	90.0	94.3	78.6	82.7	104.0	80.4	87.0
22.1	21.2	23.1	23.5	28.0	28.2	23.8	24.8
5.5	5.6	6.2	5.6	2.7	2.6	2.5	2.5
78.3	82.0	84.4	81.8	93.3	103.0	96.6	101.4
85.6	86.8	86.3	101.3	115.1	124.7	131.2	126.5
8.7	12.2	8.9	7.3	9.9	18.5	20.9	23.0
2.3	2.4	2.7	2.9	3.3	3.8	3.9	2.8
319.9	319.8	325.6	318.5	354.7	401.0	373.2	389.4
6.1	8.9	8.9	9.4	9.9	12.8	9.7	11.5
9.8	12.8	12.4	13.0	14.8	14.9	15.0	14.9
17.0	17.7	17.1	18.2	19.2	21.8	19.8	22.7
4.0	3.6	2.6	2.0	3.1	3.6	5.4	5.2
3.0	3.1	4.7	4.7	4.6	5.6	7.8	7.3
10.5	8.8	9.2	9.6	9.8	11.2	10.0	9.8
—	0.9	0.6	0.5	0.5	—	—	—
50.4	55.8	55.5	57.4	61.9	69.9	67.6	71.4
4.6	9.9	16.8	8.3	10.1	8.3	1.2	—
58.3	109.1	138.1	162.8	185.3	226.5	221.7	227.6
4.9	6.8	8.8	10.0	10.6	10.7	11.8	15.9
14.0	15.2	16.8	16.8	16.7	16.7	17.4	18.3
2.6	2.1	3.8	3.9	5.6	6.5	7.6	7.7
1.7	1.6	2.0	2.1	2.4	2.7	3.2	3.3
0.9	0.7	0.9	1.0	1.0	1.1	0.9	0.5
7.9	9.0	8.7	10.4	9.7	11.2	13.3	13.6
0.1	0.3	0.4	0.4	0.3	0.1	—	—
95.0	154.7	196.3	215.7	241.7	283.8	277.1	286.9
8.4	9.3	9.7	9.3	10.1	10.8	10.4	9.5
1.7	1.7	1.5	1.5	1.5	1.8	2.1	2.4
0.6	0.5	0.6	0.4	0.5	0.4	0.5	0.4
0.7	0.6	0.6	0.6	0.6	0.3	—	—
16.0	15.2	18.8	19.7	19.0	17.0	18.3	16.1
2.4	3.3	3.5	4.2	5.3	5.4	4.9	5.3
—	3.8	16.5	23.6	23.6	21.6	22.1	23.4
—	—	1.8	1.3	1.0	1.1	1.2	0.9
—	—	—	—	—	—	—	0.2
29.8	34.4	53.0	60.6	61.6	58.4	59.5	58.3
18.6	24.4	28.7	37.1	42.2	43.5	40.6	43.8
193.8	269.3	333.5	370.8	407.4	455.6	444.9	460.4
513.7	589.1	659.1	689.3	762.1	856.6	818.1	849.8

f Includes: Campaña, 1927–1939; Bahiá Blanca and Embarcación, 1928–1939; and Dadin, 1931–1939.
g Includes: Lobitos, 1928–1937; Camiri, 1931–1937; and San Andita, 1930–1937.
h Includes: Trieste, 1927–1939; Fornovo, 1930–1939.
i Teleajen includes small runs by Moreni refinery from 1927 to 1929.

j Port Jérôme includes operations of La Mailleraye.
k Includes: Belgo, 1934–1937; Atlas, 1934–1939.
l Includes small runs of less than 300 barrels daily of refinery in Java. Although Jersey owned only a half-interest from 1934 to 1939, full runs are shown here.
Source: Statistics on crude runs of affiliates' refineries, Standard Oil Company (New Jersey).

refining abroad. At the outbreak of World War II—counting half of the crude runs of Standard-Vacuum and the total of the refineries in which Jersey owned a majority of the stock—the company accounted for about 83 per cent of American participation in foreign refining. Socony-Vacuum had approximately 6 per cent. Standard of California and The Texas Company together accounted for approximately 9 per cent; however, their potential growth had then recently been greatly increased by the merger of their marketing, producing, and refining interests in the Middle and the Far East and by the expansion of their oil production and refining in Bahrain. Gulf, Union of California, Pure Oil, Tidewater, and a few others had a combined total of about 2 per cent of American refining abroad.[58]

It is impossible to arrive at any specific conclusions about the over-all profits from refining, or to compare the profits of different plants during the years from 1927 to 1939. In the later years of the period, the two largest refineries operated under contractual arrangements with affiliates that virtually guaranteed them a definite return on their investment. In 1934 Humble made a sales contract with Standard Oil Company of New Jersey under which the latter agreed to purchase from the former, for a period of fifteen years, large volumes of products at prices that would cover costs plus a given rate of return on the company's investment in refining.[59] In 1935 Lago Oil & Transport entered into a contract with the two producing affiliates in Venezuela to process their crude at Aruba and arrange for outlets at a specified rate of return on its investment in the refinery.[60] In view of these contracts, the profits of the two large refineries cannot be compared with the net earnings of other Jersey refineries.

However, it seems fair to conclude that over-all profits from 1927 to 1939 were not large. Such operating figures as are available for the earlier years—when accounting practices varied considerably from company to company—indicate that the refineries generally operated at a loss in 1927 and in the years from 1930 through 1933.[61] A study made within Jersey itself of earnings from 1934 through 1940 found that even in those years refining had the lowest rate of earnings of the various operating functions.[62]

Jersey's Director Sadler viewed these relatively low profits as a result of the lesser amount of risk borne by refining as compared to other functions, particularly production. In a long memorandum which he wrote to President Teagle and the Board of Directors in June, 1936, he took the position that only two things in the oil industry could not be obtained at a predetermined cost: reserves in the earth and the good will of marketers. "Transportation facilities and refineries," he maintained, "may well be looked upon as service units . . . entitled merely to a definite, fixed return on investment rather than allowing them either too great a profit or a participation in the speculative part of the business."[63]

Neither volume of output nor profits provide adequate standards for measuring accomplishment in Jersey refining during the years from 1927 through 1939. As these years passed, the essential measure was the contribution made by refinery operations to the company's success in meeting competition in the world market for petroleum products. The general achievement of long-term significance was the transition made from the largely traditional-empirical refining of 1927 to the rational-technical organization and operations of 1939. In the near future, the new organization and operations were to be tested by the unprecedented requirements of the Allies in World War II.

Chapter 8

Expanding the Tanker Fleet, 1927–1939

V ITAL TO THE SMOOTH FUNCTIONING of the producing, refining, and
marketing operations of Jersey affiliates was efficient transportation
of crude oil from fields to refineries and of products from refineries to
markets. In 1927 the transportation systems supplying these services—
principally tankers and pipelines—were in good condition and were generally earning well when they were being used to capacity or near capacity. They were under no difficulties comparable to those affecting producing, refining, and even marketing.

The tanker fleets of the Jersey organization provided physical links
between affiliates on different continents and, being the lowest-cost
carriers of oil, they also transported supplies between distant ports of a
continent. From 1927 to 1939 the Jersey fleet—that is, the tankers of
affiliates in which the parent company owned the majority of the stock—
was substantially expanded, especially the foreign-flag fleet. This was
in response to the worldwide increase in the consumption of petroleum
products and the expansion of the foreign production of Jersey affiliates.
Like other branches of operations, however, tanker transportation in the
early 1930's had to adjust to a decline in the demand for petroleum
products and a general worldwide depression and to a rise in the later
years. Since the demand for ship tonnage in the short run is highly
inelastic, the tankers had difficulty in adjusting to the ups and downs of
the oil industry in the late 1920's and the 1930's.

THE JERSEY FLEET IN 1927

On October 1, 1927, the Jersey Company owned 92 tankers—ocean-
going, coastal, and inland deepwater vessels—totaling 960,000 deadweight tons. These tankers were operated by various affiliates and were
based at ports around the globe. By far the largest fleet of a single

affiliate, in both number of ships and tonnage, was that of Standard Shipping, consisting of 38 tankers, of 481,000 tons, flying the flag of the United States. The next largest in tonnage was that of Baltisch-Amerikanische Petroleum-Import-Gesellschaft, mbH (known as Bapico), which had 13 ships, totaling 161,000 tons, registered in Danzig.* Next in line was Imperial's fleet of 15 ships of 113,000 tons under the British flag. The remaining foreign tankers were 22 ships of 195,000 tons owned by eight affiliates on the European Continent, three small ships totaling 7,000 tons belonging to affiliates in Peru and Argentina, and one of 3,000 tons owned by N.V. Nederlandsche Koloniale Petroleum Maatschappij in the Dutch East Indies.

The Jersey fleet ranked second in tonnage among the world's tanker fleets in private hands. It was outranked by the Royal Dutch–Shell group, which owned 145 tankers of 1,047,000 deadweight tons operating under British, Dutch, and Mexican flags. Third in rank was Anglo-Persian Oil Company, Limited, with 83 tankers of 735,000 deadweight tons, all ships of British registry.[1]

Within the broad policy limits set by the Jersey Board of Directors, the affiliates were left to manage their own shipping affairs. The foreign companies had had virtually full autonomy in tanker matters, an independence that generally had extended to all the operations of the European companies and to Imperial and its affiliates in the Americas. This independence was reinforced by differences in the laws, regulations, and economic circumstances affecting the tankers flying different flags. The lack of coordination went so far that, when an affiliate needed tonnage beyond its own, it commonly turned to the charter market for ships rather than to another Jersey company. There was, in fact, no organization for coordinating the utilization and operations of the affiliates' fleets.

These tankers were not common carriers; they transported crude or products for their owners or other Jersey affiliates. Many served their corporate owners only, but Standard Shipping and Bapico specialized in transportation and worked for other affiliates. The former principally carried crude oil and products for Jersey affiliates between ports on the Gulf and Atlantic coasts of the United States. Its ships brought crude oil

---

* This company had been organized in 1919 to take over the tankers being built for Jersey's German affiliate. Because of its domicile in what became the Free City of Danzig in January, 1920, under the Treaty of Versailles, its tankers were immune from seizure under the reparations provisions of that treaty.

from Humble tanker terminals to Jersey refineries on the Atlantic Coast or products from Baytown and Baton Rouge for Standard Oil Company of New Jersey to sell in its markets. It chartered foreign-flag tankers of affiliates or of independent tanker owners to transport crude oil from foreign fields to domestic and foreign refineries and to carry products to markets outside the United States; foreign ships could not be used in coastwise trade within the United States. Bapico's thirteen tankers were engaged in the transatlantic trade and in the coastal trade in the Western Hemisphere outside the United States. The tankers of other European affiliates transported products to the markets of the various companies from refineries in both hemispheres. More than half of Imperial's tankers distributed products to Canadian ports on the Great Lakes; the rest brought crude from Colombia, Mexico, and the United States to the company's refineries on the Atlantic and Pacific coasts of Canada. Two river and coastal vessels carried products to various points in Argentina, and a coastal tanker handled products from the Talara refinery in Peru. The lone tanker in the Far East performed a similar service from the Sungei Gerong refinery to nearby bulk terminals.

A varying tonnage of chartered ships was employed by Jersey companies from time to time. The larger tanker-owning affiliates chartered a small percentage of their requirements in normal times. They reduced the chartered tonnage so far as possible in slack times and increased it when their need rose sharply. In 1927 Standard Shipping was using in its foreign operations an average of ten tankers chartered from affiliates in Germany and Danzig and twenty-six vessels of independent owners.[2]

This chartering of foreign tankers resulted from the fact that ships flying the United States flag were handicapped in foreign trade by their high construction and operating costs as compared to those of foreign-flag carriers. However, the difference was not serious for American ships so long as European fleets had not sufficiently recovered from their losses in World War I to keep up with the growth of the demand, with the result that tanker rates were high enough to support American costs.

American companies could register at home ships built abroad, but their use had certain limitations. They were not allowed to operate between ports in the United States, and when they sailed to foreign ports they still had to observe the regulations of the United States as to officers and crews. All ships of United States registry, whether built at home or abroad, were required to employ officers of American citizenship, and at least three-fourths of their crew members had to be able to speak

Table 7: **TANKER FLEETS OF AFFILIATES OF STANDARD OIL COMPANY (NEW JERSEY), 1927, 1935, AND 1939**
Number and Deadweight Tonnage (in thousands)
of Ocean, Lake, and Special-Service Tankers

Affiliates	October 1, 1927		December 31, 1935		September 3, 1939		Flag of Fleet
	Number	Tons	Number	Tons	Number	Tons	
Western Hemisphere							
United States							
Standard Shipping Co.	38	481					United States
Standard Oil Co. of New Jersey			63	837	71	965	United States
Other Countries							
Imperial Oil Ltd.	15	113	21	152	22	159	Canadian[a]
International Petroleum Co., Ltd.	1	3	2	27	—	—	Peruvian[b]
Cia. Transportadora de Petroleos, S.A.	2	4	4	16	5	14	Argentine
Creole Petroleum Corp.[c]	—	—	4	31	4	20	Venezuelan
Lago Petroleum Corp.							
Cia. de Petroleo Lago	—	—	1	2	4	13	Venezuelan
Lago Shipping Co., Ltd.	—	—	19	70	23	95	British
Panama Transport Co.	—	—	25	373	29	440	Panamanian
Total	18	120	76	671	87	741	
Total Western Hemisphere	56	601	139	1,508	158	1,706	
Eastern Hemisphere							
Anglo-American Oil Co., Ltd.[d]	—	—	21	243	21	203	British
Ostlandske Petroleumscompagni, Akt.	2	6	2	16	2	16	Norwegian
Baltisch-Amerikanische Petroleum-Import-Ges.	13	161	—	—	—	—	Danzig
Det Danske Petroleums-Akt.	1	12	4	44	4	44	Danish
Deutsch-Amerikanische Petroleum-Ges.[e]	2	27	2	31	4	61	German
Krooks Petroleum & Oljeakt.	1	9	—	—	—	—	Swedish
"La Columbia," Società Marittima	6	49	6	51	6	51	Italian
N.V. Petroleum Industrie Maat.	3	34	3	37	3	37	Dutch
American Petroleum Co., S.A.	2	23	2	26	2	29	Belgian
Standard Française des Pétroles, S.A.	5	35	5	31	5	32	French
N.V. Nederlandsche Koloniale Petroleum Maat.	1	3	—	—	—	—	Dutch
Standard-Vacuum Oil Co.[f]							
N.V. Nederlandsche Koloniale Tankvaart Maat.	—	—	4	21	4	21	Dutch
Oriental Tankers, Ltd.	—	—	2	30	10	153	British
Total Eastern Hemisphere	36	359	51	530	61	647	
Total Foreign	54	479	127	1,201	148	1,388	
Total World	92	960	190	2,038	219	2,353	

[a] Changed from British to Canadian flag by 1935.
[b] Changed from British to Peruvian flag by 1935.
[c] In 1935 and 1939, tankers of Standard Oil Company of Venezuela.
[d] Includes fleet of its affiliate, The British-Mexican Petroleum Company, Limited.
[e] Includes fleet of Waried Tankschiff Rhederei Ges. mbH. in 1935 and 1939.

[f] Total number and tonnage but Jersey owned only a half-interest.
Source: Esso Shipping Company, Statement of Number and Tonnage for October 1, 1927; Standard Oil Company (New Jersey), Annual Statistical Review, 1943 and 1945, and a compilation prepared October 1, 1949. *Register of Tank Vessels of the World,* June, 1934.

English. Hence, American ships had higher employment costs than did their foreign counterparts. Only in load-line regulations did the former have an advantage over the latter; and, under the new navigation rules instituted in 1927, that advantage applied only to newer ships meeting certain requirements.[3]

In 1927, and for several years thereafter, the affiliates generally charged the going commercial rates for the use of their tankers. The management of Standard Shipping, for instance, kept itself informed by a regular flow of information about charter rates in New York, London, and the Hanseatic ports. This was used in determining charges for carrying oil for affiliates as well as in negotiating short- and long-term charters.

Standard Shipping was the leading tanker organization among the Jersey affiliates in 1927 and the one in closest communication with the parent company. It had its head office in New York and branches—equipped to dispatch or receive bulk shipments—in various ports in the United States where affiliates operated. It had a total of 250 office employees and 500 licensed or unlicensed officers.[4] The performance of this domestic marine organization had been greatly enhanced after World War I by the improvement of its management and operations and by the employment of men capable of advising on technical aspects of tanker construction at home and abroad. Although the whole fleet had not been brought up to the most advanced standards, in 1927 nearly four-fifths of Standard Shipping's tankers were less than ten years old and a third were diesel-propelled.[5]

Robert L. Hague, since 1920 the general manager of Jersey's Marine Department, was elected director and vice-president of Standard Shipping on its incorporation. He continued to serve as general manager. Hague was of the old school, an individualist who kept his hands on all aspects of operations and who maintained personal relations with the staffs in company offices and with officers and crews on the tankers. Within Standard Shipping Company, he was largely a law unto himself. Until 1933 he reported to Edgar M. Clark of the Jersey board; after Clark's retirement in 1933, he reported to Jersey's Director Orville Harden. Both directors allowed him virtually a free hand.[6]

IMPROVING TANKER OPERATIONS, 1927–1929

There was no immediate prospect in 1927 of a need for an over-all expansion of the Jersey fleet. To add a ship here and there for special reasons, or to transfer ships from one service or affiliate to another, was of course a normal part of Jersey tanker management. The program that the company had initiated early in the 1920's to raise the efficiency of vessels and their operations generally was still being followed. This included substituting new ships for old ones that were becoming obsolete and hence carried oil at higher unit costs than those of new tankers of larger size and improved design.

Orders were placed for the construction of several tankers in 1927. Imperial, then meeting rising market competition from imported oil products, needed crude at the lowest possible cost for its coastal refineries. It therefore contracted for two new ships to be delivered the next year. At this time two of its old tankers were transferred to Standard Shipping. In 1928 International Petroleum, Imperial's affiliate, launched a tanker built on its order. This was the *C. O. Stillman,* a diesel motor ship of 24,185 deadweight tons. This tanker was a little larger than Jersey's *John D. Archbold,* which for several years had been the world's largest tanker.[7]

In 1928, also, affiliates entered into contracts for the building of tankers to serve special purposes. Bapico ordered two designed to carry such heavy products as asphalt and lubricants; these were launched the next year. Jersey's purchase of Creole Petroleum Corporation necessitated providing tankers to transport crude from Lake Maracaibo to a nearby port. The parent company provided funds for Creole to acquire three new Venezuelan-flag ships, the first of its so-called lake tankers.

By 1929 Jersey's top administrators had concluded that it had become necessary to both expand and upgrade the fleet. They believed that, with new field discoveries in the region of the Gulf Coast and rising production in Venezuela, more tonnage would be required; also, that, with declining prices, old tankers with high unit costs could not compete with the larger new ships of improved design. They therefore adopted a large program to build new ships and dispose of tankers that were becoming obsolete.

Standard Shipping placed orders for two tankers to be delivered in 1930. This first addition of new ships to the United States–flag fleet since 1921 was planned to increase the company's tonnage and also to displace some obsolete vessels. Although not so large as International Petroleum's *C. O. Stillman,* these two vessels of 20,615 deadweight tons were comparatively large for that time.[8] Standard Shipping utilized the latest advances in design in planning these oil carriers. One was the world's first high-pressure steam-propelled tanker.[9]

In both the specifications for new ships and the maintenance of tankers

ings. The next few years brought a falling demand for its services, a rising surplus of tonnage, and reduced earnings. The fleet's growing surplus was a result not only of a drop in demand; it also came from the delivery of new ships ordered late in the 1920's and from the acquisition of others through the purchase of companies.

The delivery of new ships began in 1930. In that year, Standard Shipping got two new tankers, Imperial four, Anglo-American two, an affiliate in Italy and NKPM one each, and Bapico five. During the next three years, Det Danske and Standard Française each launched one ship, and Bapico nine. Within four years, new tankers totaling 344,000 deadweight tons were added to the Jersey fleet. This was an annual average of 86,000 tons; the additions during the last three years of the 1920's had averaged 52,000 tons.[19]

Additions to the Jersey fleet by the purchase of two companies raised the tonnage substantially; they did not bring a disproportionate increase of the surplus because these new affiliates continued to use their ships in their own service. Anglo-American Oil Company, Limited, maintained a large fleet to bring crude oil and products from across the ocean and to carry products to its various markets. The company itself owned fourteen ocean-going and four coastal vessels; and its affiliate, British-Mexican Petroleum Company, Limited, owned eight tankers for bringing oil to Great Britain and for supplying British bunkering stations in Europe.[20] Lago Shipping Company, Limited, which Jersey acquired in 1932 with the purchase of the foreign properties of Standard of Indiana, had twenty-one tankers for carrying crude oil from Lake Maracaibo to the Aruba refinery. Two of its largest ships were transferred to Standard of Venezuela for service in eastern Venezuela. Lago used the others in its former service and also for carrying Creole's oil from Lake Maracaibo to Aruba. It thereafter handled all the Jersey crude shipped from the lake to the island. Lago remained for several years under the management of an agent of a British company resident in Aruba.[21]

It was the acquisition of two other companies from Standard of Indiana that seriously increased Jersey's tanker surplus. One was Pan American Trade & Transport Company, which had a fleet of twenty-seven United States–flag tankers of 291,000 deadweight tons—valued by its former owner at $20,000,000. These were older ships. Two were disposed of, and twenty-five were chartered to Standard Shipping Company. The other company was Huasteca Petroleum Company, which had time charters on five recently built Norwegian tankers; these charters were also transferred to Standard Shipping. The Pan American and Huasteca tankers virtually lost their trade—transporting oil to the United States—when the tariff of 1932 eliminated much of that service.[22]

The downward turn of the net operating earnings of the Jersey fleet in 1930 started remedial action on the part of parent company and affiliates. The tanker managers worked on the reduction of costs. But their immediate concern was their rising oversupply of tonnage at a time when the demand for oil products and for tanker transport was falling.

Standard Shipping began to take action at once to reduce its tonnage. It ceased to enter long-term charters when existing ones expired. Thereafter, for the duration of the oversupply, it chartered only a few ships for special needs on a limited-time or a voyage basis. It reduced the speed of its tankers in operation in order to spread the work and thus to minimize the laying up of tonnage—which would require costly reconditioning when returned to service. Late in the year, however, because the demand for tankers continued to fall, the company finally tied up twenty-two of its United States–flag ships and five of its chartered foreign ones.[23]

The surplus that developed in 1930 spurred the movement, under the leadership of B. B. Howard in London, to bring about better coordination of the use of the tankers of European affiliates. During 1930, the pooling of the ocean-going carriers was promoted in order that the combined fleet might be utilized most efficiently. All the affiliates having tankers, except Anglo-American, became members of a European consortium in 1931. They chartered their ocean-going tankers to International Co. (Vaduz). This Jersey affiliate, organized in Liechtenstein in 1922, had taken over the insuring of the European tankers; self-insurance, an old company practice, reduced the cost of insurance because the loss rate of the Jersey fleet was lower than that of the tanker industry generally.[24]

The terms of the consortium were spelled out in the 1931 agreement of its members, which provided for a two-year pooling of tonnage—both owned and chartered ships. In general, the provisions tied the consortium rates to market charges for time and voyage charters. They provided for each member to share in net earnings or losses in proportion to the cargo carried for its account. A second agreement to run for five years from the beginning of 1933 also included Anglo-American. Its provisions were similar to those in the first agreement. The rates charged under the consortium were normally more sensitive to changes in economic conditions and fluctuated more widely than rates on the Atlantic Coast of the United States.[25]

The Jersey affiliates made no substantial reduction in their tonnage; indeed, that of Standard Shipping was greatly increased by its taking over of the tankers of Pan American and Huasteca in 1932. At the end of 1934, the tonnage of the Jersey fleet was approximately double that of 1927.[26] However, the lodging of most of the Western Hemisphere tankers in Standard Shipping and the pooling of the European tankers had made possible the utilization of the ships with the lower unit costs. Some obsolete ships were scrapped; others that could not be kept in operation were tied up (that is, if they could not earn at least enough to cover their variable, or out-of-pocket, costs).

It is not possible to come to any specific conclusion about the earnings of the Jersey fleet in these depression years. Bapico and the small tanker affiliate of DAPG had operating losses from 1931 through 1934. Separate income statements for the other Eastern Hemisphere affiliates are not available. Neither Imperial nor Standard Shipping had net operating losses on transportation in the years 1930 to 1934. Imperial's transportation earnings fell slightly in the first of these years and in 1933 declined to its lowest figure during the period. The net earnings of the United States–flag fleet were much lower in 1930 than in 1929; they recovered substantially in 1931 but fell to new lows in 1933 and 1934.[27]

Standard Shipping was virtually protected from actual loss by its 1929 rate agreement with its refining and marketing customers. Under its rate formula, which covered actual operating costs plus depreciation and interest on the book value of the fleet, the refiners and marketers in the depression years generally paid more than the prevailing tanker rates. The charges on both "clean" and "dirty" cargoes from the United States Gulf ports to New York Harbor varied from 27.3 cents per barrel in the early part of 1931 to 19.9 cents in the first half of 1934. The rates for other trades fluctuated similarly. The high figure in 1931 reflected the expenses of many idle tankers added to the charges of those continuing in service. The managers of Jersey refining and marketing operations—many with operating losses—in the early thirties requested lower charges from Standard Shipping. A new rate formula was agreed upon, to become effective in July, 1934. Under this agreement, charges were to be based on current commercial tanker rates but were not to be lower than costs, including those for the tied-up ships, or higher than 23 cents per barrel, unless costs were higher.[28]

In 1934 the business of the tankers began to improve. The first upturn came on the Venezuela-Aruba-Europe route. The one new tanker added to the whole Jersey fleet in that year was a ship of 5,000 deadweight tons to carry crude oil from Lake Maracaibo to Aruba. Traffic on some routes was slow to recover, but a general upward trend began late in 1934.

FLEET MANAGEMENT IN RECOVERY AND RECESSION, 1935–1939

In the second half of the 1930's, when the petroleum trade was again increasing and business was generally improving, the concern of the managers of the affiliates' tankers was no longer largely with an over-capacity of tonnage. It was rather with adjusting to certain external developments affecting the ships and to rising competition in an expand-ing trade.

Of special concern to Jersey's administrators in New York was the fact that half of the carrying capacity of the European affiliates' tankers was domiciled in Danzig—twenty-five tankers representing an investment of $25,000,000. Registering the Bapico fleet in Danzig had originally been fully justified by the neutral position of the free city, the favorable tax situation there, and relatively low operating costs under its flag. By 1935, however, Jersey's leaders saw in Hitler and his Nazi program a growing threat to Danzig—which could easily lose its neutral status and be taken over by Germany—and indeed a threat to the peace of Europe.[29]

Jersey's leaders decided to take action to protect the company from suffering loss by the alienation of a large part of its fleet in the event of war. The question was to what country to transfer the tankers in order to assure both reasonable security and economical operations. Vice-Presi-dent Hague of Standard Shipping took the position that "the present European political situation would make any European fleet subject to most of the disadvantages presented by the Danzig registry."[30] To transfer the ships' registry to the Western Hemisphere was desirable for security, but to register them in the United States was economically not feasible. Hence some location outside the United States was necessary.

Hague proposed that the Bapico fleet be transferred to Panamanian registry, "subject to being able to make a satisfactory agreement with the Panamanian government on taxes and maritime regulations generally." These should include "complete freedom of nationality of licensed and unlicensed personnel and complete freedom to transfer the vessels to other registry when desired." It was contemplated, he stated, "that these vessels could be manned by Germans or other nationals, thereby main-taining equal efficiency."[31] Hague believed that in the case of a major war Panama and the United States might agree to the transfer of the ships to the latter's registry in order to provide adequate protection for these Panamanian tankers. He also suggested that the operation of the company be under direct supervision of the New York office, that manning and provisioning be carried out in the cheapest market, and that previous loans by Jersey for the construction of many of Bapico's tankers be taken over by the new Panamanian company, which in time would repay the parent.[32]

In making these suggestions, Hague was in effect proposing that Jersey follow the example of several companies in their search, after World War I, for a flag that would enable ships owned in the United States to compete on equal terms with ships of other flags. To register ships outside the country of their owner was, indeed, an old practice in international trade, one that had grown as international business under corporate ownership had developed. Certain South and Central American countries, in order to attract foreign capital, had long allowed the registry of merchant ships owned in other countries. In the 1920's, several American concerns—especially oil companies—had transferred their ships to Panamanian registry in order to be able to employ comparatively low-cost foreign crews.[33]

On May 31, 1935, the Bapico fleet was transferred to Panamanian registry and to a new affiliate, Panama Transport Company, incorporated under the liberal incorporation laws of Panama. This transfer placed Jersey's largest European fleet under the laws of a country which allowed foreign ownership and virtually full employment of crews from other countries and also called for low taxes. The tankers continued to be staffed by German crews. Their salaries and wages were paid by Jersey's German affiliate, DAPG, one of the roundabout means by which the dividends of the German company in marks were converted into dollars. As in the past, the ships were chartered and insured by International Co. (Vaduz) and thus remained within the consortium. The New York office had charge of the management of the fleet.[34]

In fact, New York had become the headquarters of the management of the largest part of the Jersey fleet. As of the end of 1935, Standard Oil Company of New Jersey owned 44 per cent of the fleet's total tonnage; the companies in the Western Hemisphere owned 75 per cent of the total, and the total in the Americas outside the United States was much larger than that of affiliates in Europe. (See Table 7.) Moreover, in 1935 nearly all the petroleum supplies for Europe came from across the Atlantic;

Jersey's European refineries had begun to get Iraqi crude in 1934, but the volume was small compared to that from the Western Hemisphere.

An important development in the administration of the fleets of the foreign affiliates had occurred in 1934. B. B. Howard had then been brought back to New York from London to assume major responsibility for the coordination of the planning and operations of the foreign fleets. A graduate in 1911 of the United States Naval Academy, Howard had served in the Navy until he had joined Jersey in 1920. He had served abroad in various capacities from 1922 to 1934. His training and experience had given him a knowledge of Jersey's and the oil industry's tanker fleets and operations which qualified him for his new responsibilities for the foreign tankers and for advising the Jersey Board of Directors on worldwide tanker matters. The actual management of the ships' operations remained with the affiliates.

Tax regulations and the need to reduce costs in 1935 also brought shifts in the corporate domicile and management of several fleets. Because the Internal Revenue Act of 1934 did not allow offsetting the profits from one corporation within an integrated group with losses from another, as had previously been permitted, the marine properties of Pan American Foreign Corporation and the properties and organization of Standard Shipping Company were joined to form the Marine Department of Standard Oil Company of New Jersey. The next year Imperial, also in order to reduce its tax liability under Canadian law, transferred its tankers to a separate company, Imperial Oil Shipping Company, Limited. This company thereafter handled Imperial's and International Petroleum's tanker transport. In the same year, in order to eliminate duplication of management on the Lake Maracaibo-Aruba-Europe route, the managing of Lago Shipping was transferred to Anglo-American.[35]

In the Orient, 1935 also brought new developments under Standard-Vacuum Oil Company. N.V. Nederlandsche Koloniale Tankvaart Maatschappij was organized under NKPM to take over the latter's tankers. At the same time, Oriental Tankers, Limited, was organized as a direct affiliate of Stanvac itself. This company, domiciled in Hong Kong, was organized in order to build up an ocean-going fleet under the British flag. Marketing operations in the Orient under Socony had formerly depended on the small tankers of NKPM for transporting products in the Dutch East Indies and on ships of American and British affiliates and chartered tankers and cargo ships to bring products from Romania, Russia, Persia (Iran), Burma, and California to its many marketing stations. By the end of 1935, NKTM had three tankers transferred from NKPM and a new one; Oriental Tankers, Limited, had two new tankers.[36]

In the second half of the 1930's, the Jersey affiliates' tankers met increasing competition from the European tanker industry. For many years after World War I, the construction of new ships had boomed in the United States while European tanker concerns were still handicapped by war losses and the slow recovery of shipbuilding. Despite high costs, the United States for many years was the leader in the world tanker industry. However, as the Europeans rebuilt their fleets, the American tankers met rising competition from new ships with lower costs than those of a large part of the United States tanker industry. German shipping did not recover before World War II, but by the late 1930's several European countries and Japan had acquired many vessels of advanced design. By the beginning of the war, Britain had 424 tankers with a total deadweight tonnage of 4,380,000, an amount nearly equal to the tonnage under the United States flag. The most remarkable growth was that of Norway, which by 1939 had a total tonnage equal to two-thirds of the tonnage under the United States or the British flag; Norway's tonnage was owned by firms chartering vessels to oil companies. The Netherlands also had acquired a good-sized fleet, and Italy, France, and Japan each a modest one. Approximately three-fourths of the world's tankers then flew the flag of the United States, Great Britain, or Norway.[37]

The growing strength of these European fleets spurred Jersey's program late in the 1930's to improve the affiliates' fleets by disposing of old tankers and acquiring new ones. The problem of surplus tankers was finally solved. Some obsolete tankers were scrapped. Others were demoted to shorter and less demanding hauls when larger new tankers became available for the longest and most competitive ocean routes. Those demoted might take the place of older or smaller ships, serve an increased trade, or even go where the deepening of channels or other improvements made possible the use of the old tankers of larger capacity. In fact, what had once been an outstanding ocean carrier might, after fifteen or twenty years of service, be working under a new name in coastal waters or on deep lakes or rivers.[38]

Upgrading the fleets was accomplished principally by the construction of new ships. Thirty-nine new ocean tankers—including eight for Standard-Vacuum's Oriental Tankers, Limited—were added to the affiliates' fleets between January 1, 1936, and September 3, 1939, when war broke out in Europe. These additions totaled 440,000 deadweight tons, an average of 13,600 tons per ship.[39] Thirteen ships—the largest number—were added to the United States–flag fleet. Jersey's top administrators and the domestic fleet's managers had long known that many old tankers must be replaced. At the end of 1935, the average age of the vessels was 16½ years—old age for a tanker. The trade between American ports was increasing with the improvement of business and the growing dependence of the refineries and marketers of Standard Oil Company of New Jersey on crude and products from the Gulf Coast of the United States. Ships of American construction and under the United States flag were required to handle the coastwise business—about 90 per cent of the fleet's trade with foreign ports was being carried by tankers chartered from foreign affiliates.[40]

The first new tankers of Standard Oil Company of New Jersey were two purchased in 1936 from Federal Shipbuilding and Dry Dock Company. The hulls of these ships were welded; only about a third the usual number of rivets was used. This innovation reduced the cost of both construction and repairs. In April, 1936, General Manager Hague reported that the performance of one of these new American tankers had "exceeded our expectations and is far beyond [that of] any vessel previously constructed for our account."[41] Before the end of the year, Jersey placed orders with three American shipyards for ten more tankers to be completed within two and a half years. All had been delivered by July, 1938. Two of the ten were named for Jersey men, in accordance with company tradition, but the other eight were called *Esso* plus the name of a refinery or terminal important in Jersey operations.[42]

An entirely new development affected Jersey's building of tankers late in the decade. Concern in the United States over the lack of a modern merchant marine led to the passing of the Merchant Marine Act of 1936. This measure provided for establishing the Maritime Commission to work out a long-range program for enlarging the country's merchant marine. The act authorized arranging with private industry to build ships capable of serving as naval and military auxiliaries in the event of an emergency. The commission took action to meet a special need of the United States Navy. By 1937 the entire fleet was burning oil, but its fueling facilities were far short of permitting the maximum mobility of the fleet in its worldwide operations. The Navy in cooperation with the Maritime Commission chose to arrange with private industry to build tankers convertible to naval use if needed.[43]

Officials of the United States Navy and of the Maritime Commission approached the Marine Department of Standard Oil Company of New Jersey. As a result of conferences between government officials and General Manager Hague, the Jersey organization in January, 1938, placed orders for the building of twelve national defense tankers, each of about 16,300 deadweight tons and with a speed of 16½ knots instead of the usual 12 or 13. The cost to the company was $27,000,000; the government was to pay the additional cost of special features on each tanker to meet the Navy's requirements. The contracts carried a proviso that, with government approval, Jersey could sell some of these tankers to other companies. One of the vessels was delivered to the Marine Department early in the spring of 1939; a second was delivered late in the year. The other ten were not completed until 1940.[44] (See Chapter 14.)

By the time of the outbreak of war in September, 1939, the tonnage of the United States–flag fleet was up to 965,000 tons, but the number of the tankers was not much larger than that of 1935. This tonnage conformed to the company's objective of maintaining sufficient American tankers to cover fully its transportation requirements in American waters, the level set being 110 per cent of average needs.

Several of the foreign affiliates had also added new ships to their fleets. Jersey's administrators aimed to have approximately three-fourths of the foreign requirements covered by the tankers of foreign affiliates by 1942; additional long-term chartering was to be relied on to assure a total tonnage sufficient for 90 per cent of normal needs. Uncertainties in Europe, however, delayed the placing of contracts, and therefore only eight tankers were delivered to European affiliates from 1936 to September, 1939. In the Western Hemisphere, Panama Transport acquired only one new tanker, but a large percentage of its ships were only a few years old. Toward the end of the decade, Imperial added two new ships to its fleet, Lago Shipping launched eight, and Jersey's half-owned affiliate in the Orient also got eight new ones under Oriental Tankers.[45]

In the Western Hemisphere, the need for tankers for local or short routes was increasing. The trade of Imperial Oil Limited necessitated more shipping on the Great Lakes. In Venezuela and Argentina, more vessels were required for use in supplying a rising demand. However, the main expansion of oil transportation in South America came with the rise in the crude oil production of Jersey affiliates in Venezuela. There two outlets by water to the Caribbean came to be used by more tankers and by ships of greater tonnage. In the late 1930's, the continuous dredging of the shifting sand bar at the outlet from Lake Maracaibo to the Gulf of

Venezuela made possible the use of larger transports to carry crude from shipping terminals on the lake to Aruba. By 1939 Lago Shipping's fleet included nine tankers capable of carrying 30,000 barrels and fourteen with a capacity of 20,000 barrels. As a result of the dredging of the Maturin bar in the San Juan River in the eastern part of the country, Standard Oil Company of Venezuela, which had been using shallow-draft tankers and others only partially loaded until over the bar, by 1939 had turned to the more economical use of ocean-going tankers to transport crude or products from the refinery and pipeline terminal at Caripito on that river to the Caribbean and deepwater terminals.[46]

More ships were also required in the Eastern Hemisphere for carrying products from one deepwater terminal to another. In 1939 Anglo-American had six coastal tankers, the French affiliate had three, an Italian affiliate had two, the Danish company had one, and the Dutch shipping affiliate in the Far East had four. The demand for these local carriers— like that for their larger sisters on the ocean—had expanded in response to the growth of the petroleum trade in the second half of the decade.[47]

New agreements were again required in order to make tanker rates satisfactory to both the owners of the tankers and the refining or marketing interests served. Both the United States–flag marine organization and its affiliated customers and the members of the European consortium now agreed upon new formulas.

The rate agreement that had become effective in July, 1934, governed the charges of Standard Shipping (later the Marine Department of Standard Oil Company of New Jersey) until 1938. Under the accepted formula, the rates for dirty cargoes—crude oil and heavy fuel oil— shipped from ports on the Gulf of Mexico to Atlantic Coast ports in the United States varied from a low of 15 cents per barrel during August and September, 1935, to a high of 23 cents in December of the same year. They remained at this level until September, 1937, except for a drop to 16 cents during the summer of 1936. Inasmuch as these charges for many months were lower than the prevailing market rates, this arrangement worked out to the advantage of refiners and marketers.[48]

In 1937 a new arrangement was made in order to establish rates more nearly equitable to both sides. The formula agreed upon based charges on the cost of owned vessels plus 10 per cent of their book value, and on the cost of ships chartered by the Marine Department plus 2 per cent for management services. Under a special proviso, any loss from idle vessels would be applied to the composite rate. This formula became effective in

1938. The resulting charges from the Gulf to Atlantic ports, which were fairly close to outside tanker rates, fluctuated between 19.4 and 24.7 cents per barrel in the months until the outbreak of World War II.[49]

In the meantime, the agreement of July, 1934, covering the rates of affiliates participating in the European consortium, was revised several times to adjust to changing conditions. For example, in the spring of 1937 tanker rates were changed to reflect the current rise in freight rates. Under the European Tanker Chartering Agreement of the affiliates effective at the beginning of 1938, independent brokers were selected to determine, every six months, the voyage freight rates to be used as bases for charges. This arrangement was also revised after six months to set up annual rates and was abrogated by the majority of the affiliates in September, 1939.[50]

Charges from Caribbean to United States ports varied in accordance with the rates for trade between the ports on the United States Gulf and the Atlantic Coast. From the end of 1935, freight rates paid by Latin American affiliates were determined in the same way as those under the European consortium and tanker chartering agreement, except that marketing affiliates not owning ocean-going tankers did not share in the profit or loss. Imperial, since it handled all the intercontinental transportation for its Canadian refineries and operated a local tanker fleet on the Great Lakes, remained a law unto itself.[51]

The scheduled freight rates for European companies fluctuated more widely than those paid by American affiliates. For each ton of dirty cargo in a tanker of specified capacity, the Europeans, who had paid as low as $1.41 in January, 1933, were charged as high as $6.12 in June, 1937. Converted into barrels at seven and a half American barrels per ton, these rates ranged from the equivalent of 19 to 83 cents per barrel. The American range for shorter hauls was from 15 to 27.3 cents per barrel. This difference in fluctuations between American and European rates was to be expected because there was much more chartering from outside sources in the foreign trades. However, seasonal and cyclical patterns were evident in both sets of rates.[52]

One development in the operation of the United States–flag ships merits attention as a break with the past and a move in the direction of achieving a more stable operating personnel. This had to do with the relations of management with officers and crews—which had been generally unsatisfactory for many years. This situation was a reflection of depressed conditions in the American shipping industry since 1921 and also a result of the reluctance of Jersey's general manager of marine activities to depart from traditional practices except in dealing with tanker officers.

In the early 1920's, under Hague's management, some changes had been made to improve conditions for the officers and to raise their efficiency, but little had been done for the unlicensed seamen. Through the marine house organ, *The Bulletin* (after 1936, *The Ships' Bulletin*), Hague encouraged the officers to take advantage of several of Jersey's benefits plans. He offered bonuses for efficient and continuous service and furnished information and instruction. These efforts were appreciated by the officers, many of whom worked regularly and were entitled to a month's vacation following a year of service. The unlicensed seamen, however, worked long hours, earned low wages, lived in cramped quarters, and ate poor food. These men usually served for only one voyage, signing on and off in accordance with archaic shipping practices. An indication of the difference in the treatment of the two groups was the turnover in 1928 of 447 per cent for the unlicensed seamen and 86 per cent for the licensed officers.[53]

American seamen, generally, became restless and assertive in the 1930's. Like American labor after the enactment of New Deal legislation, they tried, through strikes and other organized activities, to improve the conditions of their employment. From 1934 to 1937, strikes and threatened strikes of longshoremen and seagoing personnel and the rise of rival unions kept the American shipping industry in turmoil. An insurgent group in 1937 formed the National Maritime Union (NMU), which became affiliated with the Congress of Industrial Organizations (CIO). In elections held under the National Labor Relations Board to determine the proper bargaining agency for unlicensed marine employees, this maritime union received an overwhelming majority.

Soon thereafter, the NMU signed a temporary agreement with a group of tanker operators, including Standard Oil Company of New Jersey, which was followed by a regular agreement in 1938. The union obtained many of its demands, which included an eight-hour day, fresh food, better living conditions, and preferential consideration of union members in the hiring of seamen.[54]

These contracts for unlicensed personnel increased the efforts of labor organizers to get officers to join unions. In fact, union agents even used physical force upon the officers when they resisted, and the agents encouraged unlicensed personnel to exert other pressures while at work.

Jersey's tanker officers—even those men who formerly had been union members—resented these tactics. They realized that, because their wages and fringe benefits were well above average, they had little to gain from joining national unions. They also knew that if they joined a union they would lose their continuity of employment with Jersey because it was union practice to assign an officer on his return from vacation to the tanker of any company that was available.[55]

The officers on Jersey tankers felt that they needed a union to represent them, but they preferred an organization of their own. They discussed the possibilities on board the tankers and with officers of other fleets when in port. They learned that Socony's officers had been successful in establishing their own independent union. This information convinced two members of the Jersey group, Andrew S. Jakobsen and Carl Stevens, that they could form a similar union. Accordingly, they took an unpaid leave in February, 1938, borrowed money from another officer to pay their living expenses, and sought the assistance of John J. Collins, adviser to the Socony-Vacuum Tanker Officers Association. Jakobsen and Stevens talked with various tanker officers of their own company as they came into port, sent letters to others, and soon came to believe that the majority wanted an independent union. They drew up a constitution and bylaws, which the officers approved; then they asked the National Labor Relations Board to hold an election to determine whether the Jersey Standard Tanker Officers Association represented the majority. This election took place late in 1938. A large majority of the nearly 700 officers, according to the official count on February 1, 1939, voted for the new association.[56]

In June, 1938, those who had agreed to become members had elected four officers to form the union's executive committee. These four were to consist always of one master, one chief engineer, one mate, and one assistant engineer, so that all ranks would be represented. They were to maintain contact with members of other tankers of the company through a ship's representative, who was chosen by the members of each tanker.[57]

The first executive committee had responsibility for negotiating with the Marine Department of Standard Oil Company of New Jersey. The two groups met in February, 1939, and drew up an agreement that provided for somewhat improved conditions, including a month's vacation within a year's service—instead of after the year's end—and payment for overtime work when in port. These provisions solved only two of the many problems that troubled the men, but the union's executive committee realized that this was not the time to press further demands, because the shipping industry was then depressed and the company had recently increased wage rates. The members of the association ratified the agreement soon thereafter. News concerning this achievement spread to officers of fleets of other major tanker concerns in the oil industry and led to the formation of similar independent unions in some other companies.[58]

This association of Jersey tanker officers also influenced the formation of an organization by the unlicensed personnel, who numbered more than 2,000 in 1939. The National Maritime Union in the spring of that year had called a strike on the Atlantic Coast, demanding that all hiring be carried on through the union's hiring halls. Jersey and other companies were unwilling to grant this demand. Many of the seamen themselves were unsympathetic toward the proposed hiring procedure; they walked back on the tankers during the strike, which lasted almost two months. Leaders among Jersey's unlicensed seamen thereupon formed their own union with the assistance of John J. Collins. They called for an election by the National Labor Relations Board. Finally that body in March, 1941, certified the Esso Tanker Men's Association as representing a majority on Jersey's United States–flag tankers.[59]

These developments speak well for the leaders and members of the tanker groups and for the fairness of Jersey's executives. Events might well have turned out quite differently if the parent company's industrial relations experts had not participated in the joint meetings and explained their views to the marine managers. The latter moved from their formerly independent position to closer conformity with Jersey's employee relations policies. The company's relations with its seagoing employees were thereby greatly improved.

The operating earnings of the tankers improved in the second half of the 1930's, but the upturn was neither steady over the years nor even throughout the whole Jersey fleet. A study of Jersey's departmental operations for the years from 1934 through 1939 presents some figures on the net operating earnings (net income before administrative costs and income taxes were charged) of the Jersey fleet. The United States–flag fleet in no year from 1935 through 1939 lost on actual operations; its highest net operating income as a percentage of net investment was earned in 1936 and its lowest in 1939. Some foreign affiliates, especially those in Germany, had operating losses in one or more years; the total net foreign marine operating earnings, however, were in the black every year. Before 1939 the lowest earnings as a percentage of net investment occurred in 1935 and the highest in 1938. In 1939 the domestic and foreign fleets suffered from the disruption of trade at the outbreak of the war in Europe.[60]

Robert L. Hague served as the key executive in Jersey's tanker operations until his death in March, 1939. He was succeeded by Robert F. Hand, who had been his assistant for many years. When Hand retired in October of the same year, B. B. Howard was made general manager of the Marine Department of Standard Oil Company of New Jersey.[61] This marked the rise to the most influential position in the whole Jersey fleet of a new type of executive, one who had had professional training, was widely experienced in tanker management at home and abroad, and looked upon the fleet as an integral part of the whole operation of the Jersey Company.

Signal progress had been made since 1927 in the direction of the more effective coordination and the strengthening of the worldwide Jersey fleet. Although the individual fleets belonged to many affiliates, flew many flags, and still had a great deal of independence, they were all parts of one large organization serving the expanding needs of the whole Jersey Company at home and abroad. The outbreak of war in 1939 proved the wisdom of transferring the largest European fleet to the Western Hemisphere—and indeed to Panama, as will be noted in a later chapter.

Chapter 9

Continental Transportation on Land and Water, 1927–1939

A VARIETY OF TRANSPORT FACILITIES besides tankers made up the vast network of Jersey carriers that brought crude oil from producing fields to refineries and products to markets. These included barges and smaller craft on inland and coastal waters, tank cars, and pipelines. In terms of the amount of oil transported and cost per barrel-mile, pipelines were by far the most important of these oil carriers. They provided mass transportation at relatively low cost.

For several years after 1927, these transport facilities did not encounter as difficult problems as did refining and production. In fact, for a time they profited from the rising demand for their services that came with the expansion of crude oil production. Eventually, however, they too were severely affected by a decline in both prices and demand which reduced rates and volume. The domestic pipelines in addition came under heavy political attacks. Their managers had to cope with both falling income and increasing regulation by state and federal governments.

THE PIPELINES OF DOMESTIC AFFILIATES IN 1927

At the beginning of 1927, the domestic crude oil pipeline affiliates had approximately 4,000 miles of gathering lines and 3,000 of trunk lines.[1] This was 7½ per cent of the total national pipeline mileage.[2] The pipeline companies managed their operations quite independently of one another and of Jersey itself except in financial matters. Whatever communication they had with the parent company in New York was generally between their own and Jersey's top officers on matters of policy. The latter kept themselves informed through an office that gathered statistical records of the lines and their operations.

Several domestic affiliates owned pipelines that were segments of a system of such oil carriers, largely belonging to nonaffiliates, which reached from the Mid-Continent to the Atlantic Coast with branches along the way. In the Mid-Continent, the Jersey-owned Oklahoma Pipe Line Company gathered oil from the leases of The Carter Oil Company and other producers in Oklahoma and Kansas for movement eastward. This company's trunk line delivered the crude to Prairie Pipe Line Company, a pre-1911 Jersey affiliate. Prairie and other nonaffiliates in turn carried it eastward. At Cygnet in Ohio, Transit & Storage Company, owned by Imperial in Canada, picked up oil for transport across northern Ohio and Michigan to the international boundary just below Lake Huron. There it was delivered to Imperial's refinery at Sarnia, Ontario. At the Ohio-Pennsylvania line, Tuscarora Oil Company, Limited, a Jersey-owned pipeline, received crude destined for the New Jersey Works and transported it to those plants on New York Harbor.

Most of the Jersey pipelines in 1927 carried oil to refineries or terminals on the Gulf Coast. Oklahoma Pipe Line delivered the larger part of the crude it gathered to Standard Pipe Line Company of Standard of Louisiana. The latter's lines brought oil from the Oklahoma-Arkansas boundary and from fields in Arkansas and Louisiana to the Baton Rouge refinery. Humble Pipe Line Company, an affiliate of Humble Oil & Refining Company, had the largest total mileage among the domestic affiliates. At the beginning of 1927, it had 3,500 miles of gathering and trunk lines in two separate systems. The larger system gathered oil from fields in North and West Texas and on the Gulf Coast and moved it to the Baytown refinery or to a Humble tanker terminal at Texas City. The smaller one reached from fields in Southwest Texas to Ingleside on the Gulf of Mexico. Besides transporting oil, Humble Pipe Line Company, as agent of Humble Oil & Refining Company, purchased oil in the fields at posted prices determined by the crude oil committee and the board of directors of the latter company.[3]

The pipelines generally derived income from several sources. They charged specific rates for gathering and transporting crude and for such other services as loading it on tankers. They were also customarily allowed a 2 per cent deduction on the volume of oil carried to cover losses in transport and storage. Although subject to some governmental regulation, this was not very effective until later. In fact, the charges in 1927 and for a number of years thereafter were generally determined by competition with other pipelines or with tankers, barges, and tank cars.[4]

Although the pipelines were common carriers under state and federal law, in 1927 the affiliates' lines were doing little work for nonaffiliated interests. Most of the charges, except the volume deduction on crude purchases from independent producers, consequently were paid by other Jersey companies.

Given specific rates and allowances, the pipeline affiliates' gross revenue was determined by the volume of oil carried. Because these lines did a relatively small amount of carrying for outsiders, their volume depended largely on the crude production and purchases of affiliated companies and on the general situation in regard to supply and demand.

A line's net income varied with the volume moved up to its optimum capacity, which was determined by both the diameter of the pipe and the pumping power of the line. Because the cost of operating a pipeline varied little with variations in the volume carried (throughput), up to capacity the transportation cost per barrel decreased as the throughput increased. To assure themselves of capacity operations, companies therefore normally extended their lines to new producing fields. So long as competitive development of oil fields prevailed in the United States, they were under a special need to do so because the individual field normally had a short period of peak production followed by a steep decline. Pipelines usually moved on to new fields or producing regions almost regardless of the condition of the oil market.

Most of the lines of Jersey affiliates were in a flourishing condition in 1927. Although the Tuscarora in Pennsylvania was suffering from the competition of tankers from the Gulf in supplying the New Jersey Works, the three companies in the oil-producing regions were still successfully riding the wave of expansion and high profits that had carried them forward in the years since World War I. Inasmuch as Standard Pipe Line in 1926 and Humble and Oklahoma in 1927 recorded the highest net pipeline earnings in their experience, these transport companies were relatively free from the financial difficulties that then troubled refiners and marketers among Jersey affiliates.[5]

EXPANSION AND SHIFTING TRAFFIC OF DOMESTIC PIPELINES, 1927–1930

For several years after 1927, the domestic pipelines continued to expand and to operate profitably. Their substantial profits led to demands for reducing their rates. The outstanding development in most of these carriers late in the 1920's was the building of lines to serve new fields in the large oil region within the geographic triangle having its northern point in Kansas, its western in New Mexico, and its eastern on the Gulf Coast of Louisiana.

Of all the pipeline systems of Jersey's domestic affiliates, Humble's expanded the most in the years from 1927 to 1930. Humble Pipe Line Company operated in a highly dynamic oil region at the time, and it had lines that led to Gulf ports from which tankers carried crude oil to Atlantic Coast refineries and products to American and European markets. Humble's pipelines thus were part of a system of economical transport that connected the prolific oil regions of Texas with markets at home and abroad.

In the years from 1926 through 1930, Humble Pipe Line Company, under President Ralph V. Hanrahan, approximately doubled its mileage, at a cost of $47,000,000. Close on the heels of new field discoveries, the company extended its major system in East Texas and into New Mexico and the Texas Panhandle. It constructed a connecting link from West Texas to its Southwest Texas line reaching to the Gulf of Mexico, where it built a new tanker terminal on Harbor Island just outside Corpus Christi. It also laid a line in eastern Texas to the Louisiana boundary to bring oil from highly productive fields to a pipeline of Standard Pipe Line Company for delivery to the Baton Rouge refinery. After 1930 Humble added little to its mileage until late in the decade.[6]

Standard Pipe Line Company, under F. Ray McGrew as president, in only a few years had to adjust to major changes in the sources of crude oil for the Baton Rouge refinery. The rapid decline in the production of the Smackover field in Arkansas after 1927 reduced the volume carried by pipeline to the Mississippi River for transport south by barge. Increased production in Oklahoma, on the other hand, necessitated stepping up the flow of oil in the line from the Oklahoma-Arkansas boundary to Baton Rouge, which was done by adding more power at the pumping stations. Late in 1930, a pipeline was laid to connect with the new Humble line at the Texas-Louisiana boundary. So large was the volume delivered from Texas that the next year Standard Pipe Line built a parallel line to carry oil produced by the new East Texas field. Texas oil then nearly supplanted Mid-Continent crude brought by pipeline through Arkansas and Louisiana to Baton Rouge. In fact, in the summer of 1931 Standard Pipe Line, with its multiple-line system, even began to carry some East Texas crude northward for delivery to Oklahoma Pipe Line.[7]

This company, under E. H. Leroux as president, had to make similar alterations in its lines. Until 1930 it built new lines or increased the power of its old ones in order to transport Carter's production and purchases from two large new fields. To carry oil from the Seminole field, it added booster stations in 1927 to a pipeline built in 1926 and also laid a new 10-inch line. This was large-diameter pipe for that time and continued to be so until welded pipe of greater strength was made to meet the general

PRINCIPAL CRUDE OIL PIPELINES OF DOMESTIC AFFILIATES IN 1940

need among pipelines for larger capacity. Discovery of the Oklahoma City field in 1928 necessitated laying a 50-mile, 8-inch line to connect with the Oklahoma company's trunk system.[8]

The year 1930 brought a radical change in Oklahoma Pipe Line's operations. This came when crude from eastern Texas began to replace oil from the state of Oklahoma at the Baton Rouge refinery. Serious difficulty was averted by turning northeastward most of the crude gathered in Oklahoma. Jersey affiliates had long been shipping some oil in that direction by pipelines of Prairie Pipe Line Company, but this outlet had become relatively costly as the price of crude declined in the later 1920's and Prairie did not reduce its rates—not a part of an integrated system and unable to get sufficient common-carrier work, this company's gross income had fallen seriously. Because Prairie continued to charge its customary rates when oil prices fell drastically, several of its shipper-customers decided to acquire lines themselves. Standard of Indiana was the first to do so.[9]

In 1930 Jersey joined Standard Oil Company of Ohio and Pure Oil Company in organizing the Ajax Pipe Line Company to construct a pipeline northeastward from Oklahoma. Built by new methods, including mechanical ditching and acetylene welding of pipe joints, this 400-mile line was completed in five months. It started to carry oil in December, 1930—only a few weeks after the discovery of the East Texas field. It provided a comparatively economical outlet for oil gathered by Oklahoma Pipe Line when it lost most of its business to the south.[10]

The Ajax Pipe Line Company had two parallel lines, with a combined daily capacity of 65,000 barrels, from Glenn Pool station in eastern Oklahoma to Wood River, Illinois, on the east bank of the Mississippi River north of St. Louis. These pipelines were built with funds borrowed from Jersey. They were constructed under the supervision of one of Oklahoma Pipe Line's few engineers, H. S. Austin, who had specialized in this type of construction. The three owners originally held the stock of the company through the Ajax Corporation, which was later merged with the operating company. Jersey itself owned 81.7 per cent of the preferred stock, and three affiliates—Carter, Imperial, and Standard Oil Company of New Jersey—took a total of 53.1 per cent of the common and 40 per cent of the management stock. Oklahoma Pipe Line, on contract, provided top management for the Ajax Pipe Line Company.[11]

The building of these lines as a joint venture in order to assure sufficient volume for economical transport was a departure from Jersey's general policy. Partly out of fear of antitrust action, the parent company and its affiliates had formerly refrained from joining others in building pipelines in the United States. This fear, which was shared by other companies as well, accounted in part for the relatively small diameter, and hence the higher operating costs, of domestic pipelines as compared to those built abroad.

Jersey's Canadian affiliate, which was buying a rising volume of crude from within the United States, expanded its pipeline interests in this country. Imperial Pipe Line Company, Limited, raised the capacity of its Transit & Storage Company pipeline, which transported oil for the Sarnia refinery from Cygnet, Ohio, on the trunk line from Oklahoma of which Ajax owned 400 miles. Imperial Pipe Line also acquired a small line in Montana to bring oil from the western plains country of the United States to the Canadian boundary for shipment by railroad to refineries at Calgary and Regina.[12]

The old Tuscarora Oil Company, Limited, experienced what was at that time a radical transformation: from a crude oil to a products line. It had virtually lost its old business because the New Jersey Works was getting crude from Gulf ports at lower cost by tanker than from the Mid-Continent by pipelines. Jersey's administrators, therefore, decided to convert most of Tuscarora's multiple lines from carrying crude eastward to transporting gasoline inland from Bayway in order to supply a new marketing affiliate, Standard Oil Company of Pennsylvania. (Short lines of this company's system continued to carry crude.) This reversal of the flow through Pennsylvania and the need for more power to carry a larger volume of oil necessitated not only reversing the drive of the old pumping stations but also building thirteen new stations. When Tuscarora began to carry gasoline in October, 1930, it was the first pipeline in the United States to deliver refined oil products to the consumers' market. Only a few months later, however, pipelines of Sun Oil Company and The Atlantic Refining Company began to carry gasoline northwestward from the refineries of these companies in the vicinity of Philadelphia. Only a year later, the Great Lakes Pipe Line Company—jointly owned by six smaller firms—started carrying gasoline from the Mid-Continent to the Chicago and Minneapolis areas.[13]

The Jersey companies in the later 1920's made improvements in both their technology and employee relations in the building and operating of pipelines. They began to contract with specialized construction firms. These firms used new machinery far too costly for the companies to purchase for only occasional or short-term use. The pipeline affiliates themselves utilized welding more extensively for joining pipe lengths and repairing leaks caused by corrosion. They also began to install all-welded steel bottoms in tanks. By reducing their employment of temporary construction workers, they were able to develop a more stable operating organization. At the same time, they improved their operating forces by providing better training, extending the benefits program for their employees, and adopting the Jersey system of employee representation on some lines. On the whole, however, the condition of employee relations on the pipelines at the end of the 1920's was still largely determined by the managers and the supervisory force, who themselves had risen from the ranks. The successful foreman was the man who could be fair without weakness and firm without tyranny.[14]

The financial results of the domestic pipeline operations were generally excellent for several years; earnings corresponded roughly with changes in the volume carried. Tuscarora operated at a loss until it began to carry gasoline. Standard Pipe Line's net earnings in 1927 fell sharply from the record high of 1926, but were satisfactory until the early 1930's. Oklahoma's net declined after high earnings in 1927, but still remained substantial well into the 1930's. Ajax started out with excellent earnings. Humble Pipe Line's net income reached its highest for the period in 1929, but fell considerably in 1930. So large were Humble's pipeline earnings in the 1920's that they financed the major part of the growth of Humble Oil & Refining Company in those years; from 1919 through 1930, the pipeline company provided its parent with $124,000,000 out of the latter's net income of $140,000,000.[15]

The high profits in a time of declining prices for crude oil and products brought suggestions from Humble's large stockholder for reducing rates. The parent company's executives were especially concerned over Humble's charges because Standard Oil Company of New Jersey, which lost heavily on its refining in 1927, purchased most of the crude oil sold by Humble. For oil delivered to tankers, the Texas affiliate charged the refining company the posted field price plus a purchasing commission, the usual gathering and trunk-line rates and volume discounts to cover evaporation and leakage in trunk lines, and a charge for loading the oil on tankers.

President Teagle, who was concerned over the high cost of crude for the New Jersey refineries, was also conscious of the possible effect of high pipeline profits on Jersey's and Humble's public relations. In 1928 he urged the Texas affiliate to reduce its charges. In a letter to President Farish of that company, he said: "I have felt, and have so expressed to you on one or two occasions, that the holding up of pipeline rates in order to exact the fullest possible earnings in the transportation end of the business might not be the wisest policy to pursue."[16]

In reply, President Farish emphasized the problems of the pipelines, but he also pointed out that their high profits had facilitated the rapid development of the oil industry in Texas. The pipeline managers, wrote Humble's president, were then finding it difficult and expensive to obtain enough oil to keep the lines operating at capacity or near capacity; in order to fill the lines, they were continually forced to expend a large part of their earnings in extending them to new fields. These facts, he urged, would have to be weighed in any consideration of the reduction of tariffs.[17]

There was no general reduction in the pipeline affiliates' charges during these years of expansion. Standard Pipe Line Company reduced its gathering charge at Smackover in Arkansas in 1930, but that was because of special circumstances in the particular field. A drive for lower rates came only with the extreme overproduction and price decline ushered in by the development of the East Texas field.

DOMESTIC LINES UNDER ECONOMIC AND POLITICAL PRESSURES, 1931–1935

The unprecedented rise in oil production in the United States in the early 1930's, with the consequent flooding of a declining market and the further depressing of prices, threatened to end the high profits of the domestic pipelines. The price of crude oil fell drastically in Texas, then the world's most prolific oil region and crude oil market leader. The average annual price, which had fallen from $1.85 per barrel in 1926 to 99 cents in 1930, fell to 51 cents the next year. This latest decline was caused principally by the virtually unregulated development of the East Texas field. This field could have supplied—at least for a short time, although with great waste—nearly all, if not all, the demand for oil in the United States. So large was its production that, until it was finally brought under state control in 1935, it affected crude prices in all oil regions in the United States and, because the Gulf Coast market was the largest in the world, in foreign countries as well.

Humble's experience shows how this one field affected pipeline operations. Itself a substantial producer in the East Texas field, Humble also began to purchase oil there in April, 1931. Its first posted price was 65 cents a barrel. But on May 26 it reduced that price to 35 cents when a flood of oil resulted from the producers' disregard of the proration orders of the state administrative agency. A week later it reduced its posted price to 15 cents per barrel; "spot" sales were then reported as low as 2 cents a barrel. Delivered to tankers on the Gulf, the 15-cent oil cost 50 cents.[18]

This low delivery cost of high-quality oil at the Gulf brought serious problems for producers in distant regions, especially in West Texas, as well as to the pipelines providing outlets for their oil. When superior crude from the East Texas field could be loaded on tankers at a total cost of 50 cents per barrel, Humble could not continue to purchase oil to fill its West Texas line and maintain the old charge of 52.5 cents per barrel for gathering, transporting, and loading the oil on tankers at the Texas City terminal.[19]

Obviously, the economics of the situation made a reduction in pipeline charges imperative. Consequently, on June 6, 1931, Humble announced the first general reduction it had ever made in its pipeline charges: "a general reduction in rates approximating 20 per cent . . . in order to increase the demand and stimulate the movement from fields more distantly located than the East Texas field." In fields far from shipping terminals on the Gulf, the company also reduced its gathering charges from the traditional 20 cents per barrel to as low as 7.5 cents. As did other companies, it cut its posted price outside the East Texas field.[20]

At the same time, the continuing decline in the field prices of crude oil brought widespread demands from independent producers for lower pipeline charges. Actually, the Jersey affiliates were virtually the only shippers over the Humble, Oklahoma, and Standard of Louisiana pipeline systems. However, the independent producers, who generally sold their output in the field, had come to believe that lower rates would mean higher field prices. In fact, their demands varied with fluctuations in the volume of production and the resulting price. These factors, in turn, varied not only with the discovery of new fields—which again and again raised crude oil output and inventories above current needs—but also with the ups and downs in efforts to establish regulation of production by states and the federal government. The oil markets of the Gulf Coast and Mid-Continent continued to be highly unstable until an effective system of regulation of production was finally established in 1935. The East Texas field was for several years the most disturbing element.[21]

Historically, independent producers had generally attacked large crude oil purchasers and pipelines when the volume of production had become so large as to depress prices and to exceed the capacity of the purchasers and transporters to handle all the oil offered. It was such a situation in Kansas that had started a movement which led to the dissolution of Standard Oil Company (New Jersey) in 1911.[22] Many producers, especially the smaller ones, in the early thirties attacked both pipeline charges and field prices. Humble Pipe Line was particularly subject to such attacks because it was the largest carrier in Texas and was making good profits and Humble Oil & Refining Company was the leading crude oil purchaser in the state.

Criticism of pipeline profits and demands for lower rates brought action by both the federal and state governments. Important to Humble was a new Texas statute that became effective in August, 1931. It classified pipelines as public utilities and gave the Railroad Commission authority to set maximum charges. This statute for the first time provided for a workable system of regulation of pipelines in Texas. The federal Internal Revenue Act of 1932, although designed primarily to bring in much-needed revenue for the government during the depression, struck pipelines in two ways. It levied a 4 per cent tax on their transportation of crude and products and by so doing reduced the value of high rates.[23]

The first move of the Texas Railroad Commission of particular importance to Humble Pipe Line had to do with a general industry practice which added considerably to the income of pipelines. This was the deduction on the volume of oil accepted for transport to compensate for losses from leakage and evaporation in pipelines and storage tanks. The deduction had become more serious for the producers who sold their oil in the field as prices declined; it came to be regarded as especially onerous when the gross tax on production in Texas was changed from a percentage to a flat per-barrel charge. This meant not only that the producers continued to pay a tax on the customary 2 per cent deduction on deliveries to pipelines but also that the tax remained the same regardless of the price. Humble Pipe Line Company, because of the large volume it transported, had been deriving annual profits of between one and two million dollars from the sale of "surplus" oil. When the Railroad Commission ordered the pipeline companies operating in the state to report the situation as to the need for the 2 per cent allowance, the deduction was found to be larger than actual losses. Consequently, in December, 1933, the commission ordered it reduced to 1 per cent; in 1937, after a series of court tests, it was abolished altogether.[24]

In 1933 and even more extensively in 1934, small refiners joined the independent producers in attacks on pipelines in particular and large integrated oil companies in general. Small plants had mushroomed throughout the oil regions, especially in Texas, when independent refiners were able to obtain low-cost crude from prolific fields and could produce gasolines of marketable quality with simple equipment. The East Texas field had proved a source of cheap crude through theft of oil from pipelines, evasion of state taxes, production beyond allowables set for individual wells under proration law, and spot purchases below posted prices. Low-cost oil obtained in the field by one or more of these means was trucked far and wide to small refineries. However, these plants were adversely affected by the reduction in the crude available at "distress" prices resulting from the temporarily successful efforts of regulatory agencies to apply prorating programs. In addition, these plants also in time suffered from the growing demand for gasolines of higher quality than they could produce with their simple equipment. Although not directly affected by crude oil pipeline rates, operators of such small plants became active participants in a general attack on integrated companies. They claimed that high pipeline profits subsidized other operations of the integrated companies. This claim became the basis for advocating the divorcement of pipelines from the integrated concerns of which they were a part.

This issue was one of many relating to the oil industry that came under federal investigation and action. The findings of such an investigation of pipelines, under the House Committee on Interstate and Foreign Commerce, were reported early in 1933. The report concluded that pipelines were essentially plant facilities in an integrated industry. However, it recommended that, in instances where relief might be needed, the Interstate Commerce Commission consider what it could do, under its authority, to help the small operators. The National Industrial Recovery Act of 1933 provided a statutory basis for action. It authorized the President of the United States to initiate proceedings before the Interstate Commerce Commission to bring about reasonable rates and also to start action to divorce a pipeline concern from its parent company if the line tended, by unfair practices or excessive rates, to create a monopoly. Pipeline issues were also covered by a comprehensive investigation of the oil industry in 1934 by a subcommittee of the House Committee on Interstate and Foreign Commerce. Representatives of integrated companies, including Humble Oil & Refining Company, defended the integrated structure as beneficial to the independent producers. They also held that the Interstate Commerce Commission was the proper agency to take whatever action might be necessary. The independents were not all of one mind. Some held that the profits of the pipelines of integrated companies were in effect rebates that subsidized other operations and thus gave those concerns an advantage over nonintegrated or specialized companies. Others defended the pipelines against this and other allegations. The Cole Committee Report of January, 1935, recommended no federal legislation. In May, the Supreme Court of the United States invalidated the National Industrial Recovery Act. Pipeline issues were thus left to the Interstate Commerce Commission.[25]

Political attacks and the prospect of new government regulation, together with declining oil prices and demand, led the Jersey pipeline companies to reduce their rates. In 1932 the parent company and its pipeline affiliates began to make a study of rates. In 1933, after the National Industrial Recovery Act had been passed, President Hilton of Standard of Louisiana proposed the reduction of Standard Pipe Line's trunk-line rates by 25 per cent and its gathering charges from 12.5 cents to 10 cents a barrel. He also proposed that the minimum tender requirement (the least amount in one batch that would be accepted from an independent producer for transport) be reduced from 100,000 barrels to 10,000. Hilton pointed out that, because of the federal transportation tax, the actual loss of revenue would not be large. The Jersey executives in New York did not favor a general reduction in rates at the time. However, Oklahoma Pipe Line reduced its gathering charge from 20 to 15 cents a barrel.[26]

In 1934 the affiliates made across-the-board reductions in their rates. Standard Pipe Line and Oklahoma Pipe Line reduced their gathering charges to 10 cents per barrel; Humble cut the same charge to a range of from 10 to 5 cents. Reductions in trunk-line rates depended on the origin and destination of crude oil transported. Humble cut its charges ranging from 50 to 15 cents to a range of from 22.5 to 5 cents. Standard and Oklahoma lowered their rates by from 5 to 7.5 cents per barrel. Oklahoma Pipe Line and Standard Pipe Line reduced their joint rate from Drumright, Oklahoma, to Baton Rouge from 37.5 to 33 cents per barrel. Oklahoma, Ajax, Imperial, and other companies reduced their joint rate from the state of Oklahoma to the Canadian boundary in Michigan from 62.5 cents to 55 cents per barrel. Tuscarora cut from 40 to 34 cents its per-barrel charge for carrying gasoline from Bayway, New Jersey, to Midland, Pennsylvania.[27]

The pipeline affiliates attempted to make up for the lowering of their gross revenue resulting from the reduction in charges and in the deduction for wastage. They worked on reducing costs, but their first line of defense was to maintain operations as near to capacity as possible. This they did in two ways.

One way was to eliminate low-volume operations as far as possible and to keep the lines that brought the largest revenue per barrel-mile. All the Jersey pipeline affiliates operating in producing regions cut losses—as other companies were doing—by abandoning some pipelines operating far below capacity and salvaging as much of the abandoned pipe and stations as possible; Oklahoma Pipe Line and Standard Pipe Line had already made shifts in their carriers to conform to changing oil traffic patterns. In 1934 these companies and Humble gave up some of their low-volume lines, the latter especially in East Texas and the Panhandle. Sometimes two companies with competing lines operating with small volumes relative to their capacity exchanged lease connections and ceased operating their lines from fields where they gave up their leases. In this way, they eliminated some wasteful and high-cost duplication—thus necessity reduced the overcapacity resulting from the excessive competitive construction of lines in the 1920's. Humble also gave up some of its short lines; long ones not only yielded more revenue because of their length but, everything else being equal, were more profitable per barrel-mile of oil carried. It was not by chance that Humble's purchases in West Texas and New Mexico came to range from about a third to nearly half of its total purchases, nor that from a fourth to nearly half of the total volume carried by its trunk lines came from the same region.[28]

The other means by which pipeline managers strove to reach capacity or near-capacity operations was to increase the total volume carried by the individual lines. Success in this direction, of course, depended on whether or not there was an adequate demand as well as supply. Standard Pipe Line had a sharp drop in its deliveries during the depression years. Oklahoma Pipe Line was unable to maintain its volume at the level of the 1920's, but it was more successful than the Louisiana company. Humble Pipe Line, which was more fortunately located with respect to outlets and whose parent was increasing its sales, was actually able to increase its deliveries even though it reduced its gathering lines and only slightly increased its trunk-line mileage.[29]

The net earnings of the domestic pipelines declined in the early 1930's and reached a low point in 1935. Even Humble, which operated in a very productive oil region better located with respect to markets than the Mid-Continent, did not increase its runs sufficiently to make up for reductions in its charges and crude-oil deductions and for rising transportation and income taxes. In 1935 Humble's trunk lines delivered nearly twice as much crude as they had delivered in 1927, but the pipeline company's net income was only half that of the former year. Its net income, which had reached its record high of nearly $24,000,000 in 1929, was $6,700,000 in 1935.[30] Standard Pipe Line and Oklahoma were affected by both reduced charges for their services and lower volume. Standard, which had had an annual average profit of $7,200,000 in the last three years of the 1920's, in 1935 had a net income of only $710,000. Oklahoma Pipe Line's profits, which had been $7,632,000 in 1927 and $4,500,000 in 1930, fell to $1,465,000 in 1935.[31]

DOMESTIC PIPELINES IN RECOVERY AND RECESSION, 1935–1939

By 1935 prospects were improving for the pipelines. Petroleum prices and the demand for products had turned upward. The Cole Committee's report of its investigation of the American oil industry recommended no federal legislation, and the Supreme Court declared unconstitutional the National Industrial Recovery Act with its threat of pipeline divorcement. One development in federal and state policies bore positive promise for pipelines: the foundation had been laid, in law and to some extent in its administration, for effective regulation of oil production in the Mid-Continent and the Gulf Coast region. Such regulation would make possible more rational long-term planning for pipelines and also more efficient management.[32]

However, the prospects were not all favorable. The Interstate Commerce Commission and state regulatory agencies were keeping a close watch on pipeline operations and earnings. There remained much opposition on the part of the independents within the oil industry to integrated companies and their pipeline systems. Further, competition itself was rising to a higher level of managerial and technological competence. Indeed, the pipelines were clearly undergoing a transition from their headlong expansion of the 1920's to a greater effort to maintain volume and reduce costs and from a relative freedom from government regulation to extensive controls.

The Jersey officers and directors in New York were cognizant of the growing problems of pipelines and new demands on their management.

In the past several years they had been occupied with planning and implementing programs for the expansion and improvement of other branches of the Jersey Company's operations. But the difficulties of the companies and the decline of their earnings had led those administrators to give more attention to the pipelines. They were not especially concerned with Tuscarora, which was close to Standard Oil Company of New Jersey, nor with Humble Pipe Line, which like its parent, Humble Oil & Refining Company, was largely independent of Jersey's administrators in New York. Their special concern was with Standard Pipe Line and Oklahoma Pipe Line. No longer were these companies, as an old-time pipeliner later said, Jersey's "orphan child."[33]

The major move of the company's leaders was to bring a new top executive into the management of the domestic crude oil pipeline systems other than Humble's. In 1936, Wallace R. Finney was elected president of Oklahoma Pipe Line Company and vice-president of Ajax Pipe Line Company. He was also appointed as coordinator for the Oklahoma company, the Pipeline Department (formerly Standard Pipe Line Company) of Standard of Louisiana, and Jersey's interest in Ajax.[34] His appointment as coordinator for the three companies was comparable to the beginnings of the relations of supervisory and advisory staffs in New York with Jersey affiliates in other branches of operations.

Finney's election to these posts introduced a new type of top manager and a new concept of management into Jersey's pipeline systems. Finney was a professionally trained and widely experienced executive. He had received a degree in mechanical engineering at Stanford University in 1912, and he had had managerial experience in several oil companies and oil-industry functions abroad as well as at home. He had come to Jersey with its purchase in 1932 of the foreign properties of Standard of Indiana. Transferred to the Producing Department in New York, he had been assigned to engineering work with the production and transportation of oil and gas in foreign countries.

According to the author of the history of Interstate Oil Pipe Line Company and its predecessors, "Finney's advent as president of the [Oklahoma] company marked the beginning of the use of more engineers, the better utilization of their services, the adoption of a broader view of pipeline operations, and a more wide-ranging and sophisticated search for means to improve them."[35] There was considerable opposition within the pipeline organizations to one who in this case was also looked upon as an outsider. But effective cooperation was soon achieved.

The new president of the Oklahoma company began at once to have studies made to guide in making improvements in the company's physical facilities and operations. He started research to learn where and by what means costs could be reduced. This included study of the cost of constructing and operating lines of different diameters and of pumping stations of varying horsepower relative to capacity. Study was also made of the carrying of different types of crude, and a uniform system of sampling the oil was developed. Research on how to measure the amount of basic sediment and water in crude enabled the company to make allowances in crude-oil accounting for these nonoil components of the oil transported.[36]

Finney also made some progress in coordinating the planning and budgeting of the three pipeline systems which he served as coordinator. He consulted closely with the top managers of the Baton Rouge refinery and The Carter Oil Company. The latter, which in 1936 took over the management of Standard of Louisiana's producing operations in Arkansas and Louisiana, managed all the producing and purchasing of crude oil for Jersey interests in the regions where the pipelines of the Louisiana and Oklahoma companies operated. Finney also participated in the preparation of budgets for these two pipeline systems and Ajax, and he represented the companies in the presentation of their budgets for examination at headquarters in New York.[37]

The president of Oklahoma Pipe Line had barely had time to begin to introduce improved managerial methods and to install more efficient equipment when a crisis again struck the pipeline companies. In 1937 and 1938 the expectation of improvement and expansion, under a relatively stable condition of the oil industry, grew dim. The industry was again struck by economic recession and by the discovery and development of highly productive new fields, especially in Illinois. Because that state had no effective regulation of oil production, discoveries there—notably the Loudon field—led to the same kind of rapid exploitation that had historically caused extreme fluctuations in crude oil production throughout the United States. New fields in Louisiana and Texas added to this condition of oversupply, but in those states the volume produced was restrained somewhat by rulings of regulatory agencies. Even the discovery of crude oil in Turner Valley in Canada had an effect in the United States; it brought about the closing of Imperial's pipeline in Montana which had carried crude to the Canadian boundary for shipment to refineries in Saskatchewan. This new flood of oil upset the whole supply pattern in the

Mid-Continent, brought a general decline in petroleum prices, increased the pressure for further reduction of pipeline rates, and raised more forcefully than ever before the issue of pipeline divorcement.

Oklahoma Pipe Line and Ajax—like other companies similarly located —were drastically affected by the flood of oil from Illinois. That oil displaced much of the crude formerly shipped eastward from Oklahoma. It had two competitive advantages over Mid-Continent crude: (1) it was produced closer to the refineries of the Great Lakes region and hence could be delivered at a lower transport cost, and (2) it was a lighter oil—an especially important consideration for refineries serving an expanding gasoline market.

Because former buyers of Oklahoma crude were beginning to purchase Illinois oil, the affiliates of the three corporate owners of Ajax late in 1937 began to reduce their purchases in Oklahoma. This led to a serious drop in the volume transported by Oklahoma Pipe Line and Ajax. In 1938 the latter, which had a daily capacity of 65,000 barrels, carried an average of only 31,000 barrels and was operating at a loss. It closed some of its pumping stations and laid off many employees, some of whom it was able to transfer to affiliates. In the same year, Oklahoma Pipe Line's trunk-line deliveries fell to the lowest point since 1922 and to approximately half the volume carried in 1927. In 1939, its deliveries to Ajax averaged only 10,000 barrels daily, which was far below Oklahoma's break-even point. The company had a net loss on its operations in that year.[38]

The decline in its throughput made the Oklahoma company take drastic action. It retired two long lines: one from Augusta, Kansas, to Drumright, Oklahoma; and the other from Hewitt in the southern part of the state to the Arkansas boundary, where the pipeline of Standard of Louisiana was taking a greatly reduced volume of Mid-Continent crude. Because the reduced volume on its other lines required less power, Oklahoma Pipe Line also took out of service several pumping stations on pipelines kept in operation. Even the important Glenn Pool station was demoted to a stand-by basis.[39]

More difficult to deal with than pipelines and pumping stations was the resulting surplus of employees.[40] For a time, the company was able to transfer men to other work. In the spring of 1938, however, it started to lay off workers. It began by dismissing those with less than four years of service, and from time to time it laid off employees with longer service until in 1939 men with service of less than fourteen years and three months were dismissed. The company tried to cushion the impact of its dismissals on employees. It gave them help in looking for other jobs. And it made cash severance payments—then rare in American industry—proportionate to the individual's length of service with the company. It also offered pensions to men with longer service who retired voluntarily.

The dismissals had a disastrous effect on management-employee relations and affected operations. The morale of the whole organization was shattered. Accident and sickness rates rose on the pipelines. Employees maintained that, because of the company's former good profits, at least the men with many years of service should be kept on the payroll. They also pointed to the profits of Jersey itself as justifying the retention of surplus employees. They complained that construction work was being contracted on the company's pipeline to new fields in Illinois. The employees talked of the independent union's affiliating with the national oil workers' union, and they drew up a long list of complaints against the company under its latest agreement with the employees' association.

President Finney and his associates toured the lines to talk with employees. The president explained the company's situation. He said that it had retained more men than it needed by operating pumping stations beyond power requirements and doing other unnecessary work. It had tried to place employees with other affiliates. As for construction contracting in Illinois, for the company to do this work was impracticable. Profits, Finney said, had been used to finance expansion and improvement and to enable Jersey to pay dividends, without which stockholders would not continue to invest in the company.

Not until the war brought improvement in the operations of Oklahoma Pipe Line did its relations with employees approach normal, but some improvement came in 1940. Although their morale was then still low, the majority of the employees recognized that the company's situation was serious and that it had handled its employee problems relatively well. The majority voted against joining a national labor organization. As for those laid off in the field, one employee said that they "always speak a good word for the company." He added, "It has been the [Oklahoma] management with the Standard of New Jersey policies that has done it."[41]

The other Jersey pipelines fared better than the Oklahoma company. None was directly affected by the Illinois development. However, all felt the effect of economic recession and of the overproduction of oil.

Tuscarora was in a special situation. As a gasoline line, it had no common-carrier business but transported that product from the refineries of its corporate owner in New Jersey to distribution points under the

Esso Marketers. Its volume depended on the requirements of the marketers. In order to help the New Jersey Works and the Esso Marketers to maintain their sales in the region—and hence its own business—Tuscarora had to keep its costs and rates competitive.

Standard Pipe Line Company in 1936 lost its corporate existence by becoming a department of its parent company. For a number of years Standard of Louisiana had been supervising many of its affiliate's staff functions, and the union of the two companies reduced duplication and costs still further. The chief motive for the merger, however, was to save on corporate income taxes. Under the Internal Revenue Act of 1934, these companies could no longer follow their long-standing practice of consolidating their income tax returns and thereby offsetting Standard of Louisiana's losses with the pipeline affiliate's earnings. After study by the law departments of Jersey and of these two affiliates had ascertained that there would be no difficulties under the new rules of the Interstate Commerce Commission for pipeline reporting, nor under the reporting requirements of the regulatory agencies of Arkansas and Louisiana, it was decided to merge the two companies.[42]

The pipeline business of Standard of Louisiana held up well, principally because of extension to productive new fields. The largest trunk-line addition was the southwest Louisiana system. The main line was built in 1937 from near Baton Rouge into that section of the state where French exiles from Nova Scotia had settled in the eighteenth century. The company met unusual and difficult problems in obtaining rights of way and constructing the pipelines in the backward and watery bayou country. In the next two years, the company added lines to still more fields in both southern and northern Louisiana and also in southwestern Arkansas. The southwest Louisiana system and the other new lines raised the volume transported to an annual average of well over 40,000,000 barrels in the last three years of the decade. This was substantially above the low point of the early 1930's, but still far from the record volume of 54,290,-000 barrels delivered in 1926.[43]

Humble Pipe Line Company, which was by far the largest of Jersey's pipeline affiliates, from 1935 operated under far more stable conditions than either the Oklahoma or Louisiana system. It built more trunk lines than in the first half of the decade; but, even so, in the last five years it added only 750 miles to its 4,300 miles as of the end of 1934. The additions consisted of extensions in areas where Humble Oil & Refining Company already had producing operations. The most important new field was Friendswood near Houston.

The major concern of Humble Pipe Line at this time was to keep its operations as near to optimum capacity as possible. As before, it gave up some short lines; it also withdrew entirely from North Texas because of the small volume obtainable there. It raised its trunk-line deliveries proportionately more than the increase in mileage—from a daily average of 287,600 barrels in 1934 to 382,200 in 1939. This rise in volume came from only a moderate increase in Humble's own production plus a substantially larger addition to its crude oil purchases and a small rise in the volume carried for nonaffiliates. By raising the total crude handled relative to its mileage, Humble utilized its pipeline capacity closer to the optimum than in the depression years.[44]

While making every effort to raise the percentage of the capacity utilized, Humble was also trying to reduce costs. One cost that was rising was that of maintaining the pipelines and storage tanks in good condition. Maintenance had always been relatively costly on pipelines, but some of Humble's lines were reaching an age when much mending and replacing were necessary. Where corrosion was especially severe, sections of lines had to be replaced. In addition, old and obsolete power equipment made some of Humble's pumping stations inefficient compared to those on new lines.

Corrosion was a major maintenance problem for both pipelines and storage tanks. The oil industry and the United States Bureau of Standards had been doing research on corrosion for several years; Humble had its own research group working on this problem. Electrolytic action—especially on pipe in wet soil or swampy land—was found to be the chief cause of external corrosion. The main culprits inside pipes and tanks were water and hydrogen sulphide in the crude.

Humble began to make real progress in corrosion control in the later 1930's. It applied improved coatings to old pipelines requiring repairs and to new ones that were built. In 1935 it began to install along its pipelines what soon proved to be the most important preventive: cathodic units. It first utilized wind-driven generators to provide electric current, but winds proved both inadequate and irregular. It found public utilities to be the most economical source of electricity as transmission lines were extended to rural areas. In order to reduce corrosion inside pipe, Humble installed better equipment in the producing fields for separating water and hydrogen sulphide from the crude before it entered the pipeline. To protect the inside of tank roofs, it used floating roofs as a means to reduce the vapor space above the oil, which was conducive to evaporation and corrosion.[45]

Humble also worked on raising the operating efficiency of its pipeline system. It made studies of costs. In some old and in new pumping stations, it installed lighter and smoother-running multiple-cylinder vertical engines and lightweight, quiet centrifugal pumps. It followed the general Humble program to raise the quality and morale of employees and to strengthen the operating organization. It placed particular emphasis on safety training and on the instruction of foremen. And it stabilized the employee force by contracting temporary work, a practice started in the 1920's, and by less transferring of men from one place to another as producing operations were stabilized.[46]

Gains from efforts to reduce maintenance work and raise operating efficiency were largely canceled out by higher costs and taxes. New equipment to take the place of old was more expensive. Wages and salaries rose. And taxes in the later 1930's took a larger portion of net earnings than a decade earlier. The extent of the rise in taxes may be indicated by the experience of Humble Oil & Refining Company, including its pipeline affiliate: while the company's total net income for the last three years of the 1930's was nearly twice that for the same years in the 1920's, the total tax—not counting sales taxes on gasoline and other products—in the later period was nearly three times that of the earlier.[47]

The efforts of Jersey's pipeline affiliates to reduce unit costs by increasing volume, relative to capacity, and reducing operating and maintenance costs were spurred by declining petroleum prices and rising pressure from both inside and outside the oil industry to reduce pipeline charges. The investigations carried on by the Interstate Commerce Commission and state agencies, as well as criticism from within the oil industry of pipeline rates and earnings, focused attention on pipeline charges. However, the need to maintain operations as near to capacity as possible was still the principal factor affecting pipeline rates in the later 1930's.

The first rate reduction after 1934 among Jersey's pipeline affiliates was Tuscarora's in April, 1936. In order to keep its charges to Esso Marketers competitive—especially with those of barges transporting products northeastward by rivers—this gasoline line reduced from 34 to 29 cents per barrel its rate from Bayway, New Jersey, to Midland, Pennsylvania. Reductions by the crude pipelines came with the price decline, overproduction, and general economic recession beginning in 1937. In the next year, Oklahoma Pipe Line, Ajax, and owners of segments of the trunk line carrying crude from Oklahoma eastward cut from 55 to 45 cents per barrel their joint rate from the state of Oklahoma to the Canadian boundary near Sarnia. Oklahoma and Standard of Louisiana reduced from 33 to 25 cents per barrel their joint tariff from Drumright, Oklahoma, to Baton Rouge. These two companies and Humble also cut some of their intrastate rates and their charges for gathering oil in the fields.[48]

In the second half of the 1930's, lower rates tended to offset gains from larger volume. Tuscarora was the one exception that had larger operating earnings despite lower rates, but this came from greatly increased sales of gasoline in its territory. Oklahoma Pipe Line's operating earnings rose from its low of 1935 through 1937, but declined steeply in 1938 and turned into a net loss in 1939. Standard of Louisiana had good profits on its pipelines after 1935, but its lines had greatly increased their volume and mostly served the company's own needs at Baton Rouge. Humble Pipe Line's net earnings in 1935 were the lowest since 1924, rose substantially the next two years, and then declined so that the earnings in 1939 were approximately half those of 1937 but were a moderate gain over 1935. According to a memorandum prepared within Jersey in 1940, the net rate of returns on the net plant investment of the pipelines of domestic affiliates in 1939 was 10.5 per cent after taxes. Pipelines were still the most profitable of the operations of Jersey's domestic affiliates.[49]

Generally high earnings throughout the American pipeline industry made these oil carriers especially vulnerable to renewed political attacks on large integrated oil companies after 1937. The earnings were undergoing continuous study by the Interstate Commerce Commission, but no definite conclusions were reached until 1940. In 1939, however, came the decade's most extensive examination of the oil industry. This was a part of the investigation of concentration of control in the American economy—resulting from a growing antimonopoly movement—by the Temporary National Economic Committee (TNEC) of the United States Congress.[50]

Pipelines were given a comprehensive examination by the TNEC. The principal issue was rebates. Historically, rebates on oil shipments had been a very controversial subject. In its early decades, Standard Oil had been charged with benefiting from railroad rates lower than those granted to smaller companies. The Elkins Act had been passed in 1903 to prevent such discrimination by common carriers, and the Hepburn Act of 1906 had classed as common carriers the pipelines crossing state lines or supplying oil to others at state lines—a classification later upheld by the United States Supreme Court. Under neither act, however, had it been claimed that dividends from pipeline affiliates constituted rebates to owners carrying on an integrated business. But in the 1930's, critics of pipelines argued that such dividends were in effect rebates, and that they gave an unfair competitive advantage to the other operations of owners of pipelines—that they actually subsidized the other operations. This argument was used to justify the demand for the divorcement of pipelines from integrated companies.[51]

In the TNEC hearings, oil-company executives, including Jersey officials, took a firm stand on the issue of rebates and divorcement. They contended that a fair return on pipeline investments did not constitute a rebate, even when outsiders used the lines. This was true, they said, because in the existing economic system a return on the capital required was essential under any ownership. As for divorcement, they held that experience had demonstrated the impracticability of such a separation.[52]

No congressional action was taken on this issue in 1939, but the political thrust was toward curbing oil pipelines. Given the prevailing political climate, the general profitability of these oil carriers, and the opposition of a large number of independent producers and refiners to integrated companies, greater regulation was clearly foreshadowed. It was actually to come in 1941, but then in the form of a ceiling on profits rather than divorcement. (See Chapter 15.) In fact, the Splawn, Cole, and TNEC investigations of the 1930's, as well as the extensive examinations carried on for many years by the Interstate Commerce Commission, had on the whole not supported divorcement. The ICC had, in fact, taken a position in favor of a ceiling of 8 per cent on profits.

As so often in such investigations, much weight was given to the past. Actually, reductions that had come in pipeline rates in the 1930's had substantially reduced the pipelines' gross margin and net profits. For example, Humble Pipe Line's gathering charges, which had been 20 cents in the 1920's, in 1939 ranged from 10 to 5 cents; its trunk-line charges, which at the beginning of the period had ranged from 50 to 15 cents, had fallen to a range from 22½ to 5 cents.[53] In addition, allowances on the volume of oil gathered had been discontinued altogether. The other Jersey pipeline companies had similarly reduced their tariffs severely.

Comparison of net earnings and volumes carried in 1927 and 1939 is illuminating. In the first year of this period, Humble Pipe Line had made trunk deliveries of 56,000,000 barrels and had had net earnings of $13,100,000; in 1939 it delivered 139,000,000 for $7,600,000. Standard of Louisiana, which had delivered 41,000,000 barrels and had earned a net of $7,500,000 in 1927, delivered approximately the same amount in 1939 at a net profit of about $2,800,000. Oklahoma Pipe Line, which had delivered 40,600,000 barrels and had had net earnings of $7,600,000 in

1927, registered a net loss of over $300,000 on 16,600,000 barrels delivered in 1939.[54]

The downward trend of pipeline earnings, as well as the threat of severe governmental action, led Jersey's directors and officers and the managers of pipeline companies to proceed further with the improvement of the operations of these transportation interests. In cooperation with the affiliates, Jersey set up a committee to develop plans for reducing costs and achieving greater efficiency generally. In 1939, Wallace R. Finney was again transferred to the Producing Department in New York to coordinate the operations of several domestic pipeline affiliates. The outbreak of World War II, however, delayed the carrying out of a coordinated program. During the war, Finney was associated with the building and managing of new pipelines.

OTHER OIL CARRIERS IN THE UNITED STATES

Barges and other watercraft carried oil in large volume on deep rivers and coastal waters, while tank cars and tank trucks transported it on land to points which pipelines did not reach. Some of these facilities were operated by producing companies and others by the traffic departments of refining and marketing affiliates. Generally, because of the high cost of trucking and relatively high railroad tariffs, the companies used other means as far as possible.[55]

Among Jersey's domestic affiliates, Standard of Louisiana with its refinery on the lower Mississippi River had the best opportunity to utilize inland waterways. It kept in use the large old towboat, the *Sprague*, which pushed barges carrying crude from the Arkansas pipeline terminal to the refinery at Baton Rouge and products from Baton Rouge to bulk stations up the Mississippi and Ohio rivers. Having for many years after 1927 made few attempts to reduce costs and charges on these operations, the company lost business when prices and demand fell and competition increased. From 1936, however, when Harry Graham—formerly of Standard Oil Company of New Jersey—became its traffic manager, it made studies of costs and took measures to lower them. The Louisiana company then added new facilities, including the river steamer *Jack Rathbone*. With more efficient operations as well as a rise in demand, the volume transported within one year increased by almost 27 per cent to a daily average of approximately 31,000 barrels in 1937.[56]

The Baltimore office of Standard Shipping Company—later Marine

Department of Standard Oil Company of New Jersey—managed several operations. It carried on a lighterage business around Chesapeake Bay and up nearby rivers by tugboats and barges, a few of the latter being self-propelled. Until the plant at Parkersburg, West Virginia, was shut down, Standard Shipping also directed deliveries from that refinery by way of the Ohio River and three tributaries that had been deepened in 1927. The business on the Ohio and its tributaries was expanded in 1930 after the Tuscarora line began to pump gasoline from the New Jersey Works to the line's river terminal on the western boundary of Pennsylvania. Although the lower cost by pipeline and barge did not result in a proportionate increase in profits, it did improve the competitive position of Jersey interests in the markets reached.[57]

The acquisition of Beacon Oil Company in 1929 added to Jersey's domestic river operations and especially to its coastal shipping. Colonial Beacon's facilities reduced dependence on Standard of New York for handling lighterage operations in New York Harbor. Tankers also carried products from the New Jersey Works up the Hudson River to a terminal at Albany; from there on, barges took products by the Erie Canal westward across New York state and by another canal northward from the Hudson to Lake Champlain. Both tankers and small coastal craft supplied Colonial Beacon's bulk stations on the New England coast. Low transportation costs by water were of vital importance to the company in the years when it was trying to advance its position as a marketer in competition with Standard of New York and its successor, Socony-Vacuum, then the leading gasoline marketer in both New York and New England.[58]

The shipping of products by leased railroad tank cars, although declining, remained important. Standard of Louisiana, for instance, with considerable product sales in thinly populated areas in the South, depended on railroads for shipment to points that could not be reached directly by river or coastal transport. In 1939 it was sending products by tank cars from the Baton Rouge refinery and river bulk plants in Louisiana, Tennessee, and Arkansas. In that year the volume it sent by rail averaged more than 25,000 barrels daily, or about a quarter of the output of the Baton Rouge refinery. Because railroad charges on a ton-mile basis were several times the cost of transporting products by barge or pipeline, Standard of Louisiana and other affiliates held their tank-car business to a minimum by utilizing their own lower-cost facilities so far as possible.[59]

The carrying of products to American markets in 1936 became subject to the same type of scrutiny within the Jersey Company that other functional divisions among the affiliates had already experienced. A transportation committee, with headquarters in New York, then began to study various methods of reducing the cost of transportation from refineries to consuming centers. Members of this committee, headed by H. S. Austin, represented traffic and marine departments, pipelines, and marketing organizations of Jersey's domestic affiliates. Subsequently, another committee was established to study the transportation problems of Standard of Louisiana. Within a few months, the main committee had made much progress, particularly in recommending bulk terminals in key places that could be supplied by large tankers. As reported to the general Coordination Committee meeting in May, 1937, it had become convinced that "untold opportunities, for betterment in our transportation methods and activities related thereto, are probably existing throughout the entire field of Company operations."[60]

Among the proposals considered in 1937 as a result of the committee's findings was a products pipeline northeastward from Baton Rouge—to extend as far as western North Carolina—to take the place of higher-cost shipment by railroad. However, Jersey turned down the proposal. It was believed that, under North Carolina's price regulation, product prices would soon be forced down to the level of reduced costs, and that as a result such new facilities would yield little return on the investment. The suggestion was advanced that, instead, efforts be made to get railroads to reduce their tariffs in North Carolina. In the other states, the railroads, because of the proposed line's threat to their business of carrying oil products, opposed granting permission to cross their right of way.[61]

The political climate in 1939 was hardly favorable to Jersey's building of products pipelines. Such projects were not in keeping with the current inclination of the federal government to aid small enterprises in their competition with large concerns. The Federal Coordinator of Transportation, in the interest of small shippers, was at the time proposing ways to reduce railroad rates on oil.[62]

CRUDE PIPELINES AND OTHER TRANSPORT IN FOREIGN COUNTRIES

Abroad, Jersey's affiliates used pipelines only for transporting crude oil. They moved products by various types of land vehicles and watercraft— even employing donkeys on jungle and mountain trails in some countries. The parent company had close relations with the few foreign pipeline affiliates of which it was directly or indirectly the major owner; it had little to do with the management of other lines.

The pipelines in oil-producing countries abroad were far different from the network of competing systems in the United States. These foreign lines were generally built to provide exclusive outlets from an oil region to refineries or to rail or water terminals. This made possible larger-diameter lines and gave assurance of more stable volume. Risks abroad were almost wholly political.

In 1927 only a few foreign affiliates had pipelines of any importance, but more lines were constructed as Jersey's producing interests abroad grew. Except a small mileage in Canada, these carriers were mostly built through tropical jungles and barren deserts to distant coastal terminals.

One line was in Sumatra. NKPM had constructed in 1926 a 6-inch pipeline through eighty miles of wet jungle from the Talang Akar field to the Sungei Gerong refinery. Later in the decade it laid two parallel 8-inch lines for moving the rising volume of crude oil from fields in the central part of the island to the refinery. Since the greater part of the way was through swampy jungle, the pipe was laid in dikes built up above the swamp.[63]

Another pipeline of international interest and of importance as a carrier was built by the Andian National Corporation, Limited, in Colombia. This 335-mile line of 10-inch pipe with nine pumping stations reached from El Centro, where The Tropical Oil Company had oil producing fields, through swampy jungle along the Magdalena River to a point near its mouth; from thence it ran westward to Mamonal, a few miles south of Cartagena, on the northern coast. This long system, with 280 miles of loops (parallel pipe) added to increase its capacity, in 1927 had a maximum daily capacity of 51,000 barrels; this was later increased by still further looping. Jersey's Medical Department rendered splendid service in connection with this construction. Its doctors applied the knowledge of how to cope with the health menaces of tropical jungles learned from the earlier development of production in Colombia and from such other sources as the Panama Canal experience of the United States government and the work of the Rockefeller Institute. The results were almost unbelievably good.[64]

The president of Andian was James W. Flanagan. A complex personality, Flanagan became a controversial figure within the Jersey Company, as indeed among the Colombian public. In recognition of his contribution to the promotion of Colombian business and his gifts to charitable institutions, he was awarded the Cross of Boyaca by the Colombian government in 1935, an honor which had been conferred on only one other American citizen, Colonel Charles A. Lindbergh. Andian's president was a demanding but humane employer. He called for strict application to work, but took a personal interest in each worker and his family; he commonly attended weddings, baptisms, and funerals in the families of national employees. Flanagan won the loyal support of many workers of different ranks. A generous spender of company funds as well as his own, he did not heed the suggestions made in 1929 by his superiors—G. Harrison Smith in Toronto and Walter C. Teagle in New York—that the expenses of the pipeline company "be cut to the bone." Andian's gross and net revenues remained high, although in 1931 the trunk-line tariff was reduced from 65 cents a barrel to 55 cents—against which had to be charged the monthly allowance of eighteen hours of free passage for government royalty oil. Until his retirement in 1942, Flanagan opposed reductions in pipeline rates as well as in his business expenditures. Although the tariff was wholly a Jersey Company matter, the president's spending and Andian's high profits gave Colombians an exaggerated idea of the earnings of Jersey's affiliates in that country.[65]

From 1927 to 1939, both The Tropical Oil Company in Colombia and International Petroleum Company, Limited, in Peru kept on laying pipelines from wells to refineries or terminals on lands which they owned or held under long-term concessions. The gathering lines in Peru were again surveyed and were relaid during the depression. This work provided employment for Peruvians during difficult years and resulted in an excellent system of lines. Crude from the wells was pumped to tank farms on the plateau; thence it flowed by gravity to the refinery on the coast.[66]

Larger but widely scattered production in Venezuela necessitated the building of several pipelines, which were laid through roadless jungle or semidesert to some shipping point. The discovery of the Quiriquire field in eastern Venezuela in 1928 led to the building of an 8-inch line, with a daily capacity of 18,000 barrels, to Caripito on the San Juan River and the construction of a tanker terminal there. Before this pipeline could be laid, a road had to be built through twenty miles of swampy and almost impenetrable jungle. A 10-inch line was added in 1933 to carry increased production. The development of production in the Temblador field near the Orinoco River brought the building in 1937 of a 42-mile pipeline to a shipping point on the Caño Mánamo, one of the mouths of the Orinoco. Two short lines were also built to the Caribbean from oil fields in western Venezuela. Late in the decade a 16-inch pipeline, built jointly by Standard of Venezuela and an affiliate of Gulf Oil Corporation, was laid the hundred miles from the Oficina field in eastern Venezuela to Puerto La Cruz on the Caribbean.[67]

In other countries in the Western Hemisphere, Jersey affiliates laid few lines and these were usually short. After the discovery of crude oil in the Turner Valley field in 1936, Imperial converted a part of its system for transporting gas and naphtha to carrying the heavier oil to the Calgary refinery. In Trinidad and Bolivia affiliates laid only short lines from fields to small plants. Limited by the government's restrictions on foreign companies, Standard Oil Company of Argentina could only build small-diameter lines from fields to plants or rail or water shipping points.[68]

The world's most outstanding pipeline achievement within the years 1927–1939 was the construction of two lines from the Kirkuk field in Iraq to the Mediterranean Coast. These carriers were built by the Mediterranean Pipe Line Company, which was organized by the owners of Iraq Petroleum Company to build and operate pipelines to transport the company's crude to Mediterranean terminals. Both companies were owned by several corporate owners, including British, British-Dutch, French, and American companies. Through the Near East Development Corporation, Jersey owned 11⅞ per cent of the stock of the Middle East producing and pipeline companies and a like proportion of the crude oil produced by Iraq Petroleum. Jersey itself had no direct participation in the management of Middle East Pipe Line Company, but it contributed expert and experienced personnel to the planning and building of the lines.

This was a truly international undertaking. The problem of getting the right of way in regions where few records of ownership existed was solved by obtaining the right of eminent domain from the government of Iraq and from the mandatory powers of the area—Great Britain and France. Plans were made for the Mediterranean Pipe Line Company to build lines to terminals at Tripoli in Lebanon and Haifa in Palestine. Jersey's H. S. Austin participated in preparing plans for the surveying of routes. Construction was begun in 1933 on what proved to be an incredible undertaking to lay pipe over hundreds of miles of rough semidesert terrain. Experienced personnel were drawn from pipeline organizations in the United States, Latin America, and Europe; unskilled workers came from several countries in the Middle East. At one time, more than 10,000 men were on the company's payroll. Seamless 10-inch and 12-inch steel pipe and also equipment for thirteen pumping stations came from England, Germany, France, and the United States. Because both harbors on the Mediterranean were too shallow for large tankers, sea lines almost a mile long had to be built. The first delivery of oil was made at Tripoli on July 14, 1934, and the first at Haifa on October 14 of the same year, which was just seven years and a day after the discovery of oil in the great Kirkuk field.[69]

Many difficulties had to be surmounted in managing these lines—at first by Middle East Pipe Line Company and from 1936 on by Iraq Petroleum, which purchased the pipeline properties of the Middle East company. The Iraqi crude was highly sulfurous, and the employee force of varied national origin was difficult to handle. A large repair organization had to be maintained, especially because of frequent sabotage in Palestine by the shooting of holes in the pipe. English and French air transport companies patrolled the lines and transported men between stations and terminals. The income-tax complexities of this line owned by companies from different countries—particularly the prospect of the British and French governments' taxing its income—were solved by operating virtually at cost. The corporate owners, who received crude at the Mediterranean terminals, paid the prorated cost plus a shilling per ton. Despite such unusual circumstances, until World War II this pipeline system delivered a daily average of approximately 84,000 barrels through the two lines, in which almost £ 37,500,000 had been invested.[70]

The pipeline accomplishments of Jersey's affiliates in Europe were minor and were complicated by government policies. Nationalism in Romania and low production elsewhere limited the building and operating of lines. An affiliate in France constructed a 23-mile pipeline to carry crude oil from the harbor at Le Havre to its Port Jérôme refinery. In Italy and Poland, affiliates shipped oil by railroad from gathering lines to a small refinery in each country. In Romania, Româno-Americana made short additions to its crude, gas, and products lines within the areas where oil was being produced. But the Romanian government required that both crude and products be carried by its own railroads or pipelines from the oil regions to terminals on the Danube or the Black Sea. In order to obtain more revenue, the government raised its transportation charges; it increased the tariff on products shipped from the Teleajen refinery to the Black Sea from the equivalent of 19 cents a barrel in 1928 to 41.5 cents in 1938. Nationalism proved less restrictive in Hungary, where a Jersey affiliate found considerable oil late in the 1930's. The company constructed a short pipeline to a railroad and planned extension to Budapest, where affiliates of Royal Dutch–Shell and Socony-Vacuum had refineries.[71]

To arrive at even a general conclusion as to the relative costs or earnings of these foreign pipelines is impossible. Nearly all were service facilities for their owners and not common carriers. Their operations— except in the case of Andian National—were generally so closely integrated with producing or marketing activities that separate expense and income data are not available. Moreover, differences in accounting practices and government regulations, including depreciation rates, would make generalization nearly worthless.[72] In some countries, national regulations raised costs so high as to make profits unattainable; in others, expropriation brought about the loss of properties. The pipeline system carrying crude from Iraq to the Mediterranean operated on a cost basis. Andian National in Colombia did make high profits, but one affiliate paid another the high rates that made the profits possible.

The method of transporting products from refineries to bulk stations outside the United States varied from country to country. This was partly because of differences in the volume of products to be transported. It was also a result of variations in geography, in the state of economic development, and in governmental regulations.

In the Caribbean islands and the countries of Central and South America, which had few railroads, products were transported in the main by small ships or barges from refineries to bulk stations. For example, coastal tankers and ships carrying packaged goods brought products from the refinery at Talara, Peru, to ports on the west coast of South America, including Callao, the port serving the capital city of Peru. In Colombia, specially constructed stern-wheel steamers, towing barges on the shallow and twisting Magdalena River, carried products downstream from the Barrancabermeja refinery; they brought fuel oil in bulk for river vessels and products in cans for depots on the Magdalena.[73]

In the Eastern Hemisphere, Jersey's affiliates, many serving highly developed areas, used railroad tank cars as well as coastal and river craft to supply bulk plants. Generally they owned the railroad cars as well as the watercraft. Anglo-American, the most important marketer among the European affiliates, in 1938 had 88 barges and 1,886 tank cars besides coastal tankers. French and German affiliates had somewhat less equipment of these types, except that the German operations required a large number of tank cars. In the Far East, Standard-Vacuum, in which Jersey and Socony-Vacuum merged their properties in the Orient in 1934, used both railroad and water carriers, the latter including steamers, lighters, tugs, launches, junks, and sampans.[74]

Jersey had little influence on these miscellaneous carriers of its foreign affiliates, particularly in the Eastern Hemisphere, and it did not take action to improve transportation methods abroad as it did in the United States. The many different government regulations and restrictions and the varying conditions under which foreign affiliates operated made such efforts difficult if not impossible. The traditionally greater independence of many of the foreign affiliates also interfered with the upgrading of transportation operations. In addition, there was the practical consideration that during most of the 1930's the parent company was occupied with more urgent problems.

Standard Oil Company (New Jersey) did not establish as close coordinating and advisory relations with the affiliates' various modes of transportation as it did with other operations, but the carriers still did well in meeting the company's over-all expanding needs. However, the decline in the net earnings of transport operations generally led to a search for ways to increase their efficiency, especially that of the tanker fleets and of pipelines operating within the United States. The affiliates themselves made some improvements, but over-all coordinated efforts to improve transport facilities and management were delayed by World War II.

Chapter 10

Selling Domestic Refined Products, 1927–1939

LIKE PRODUCTION, REFINING, and transportation, the sale of Jersey Company products—the crucial front line of the oil business—experienced basic changes in the years from 1927 to 1939. Initiated as defensive measures to meet the challenge of certain emerging problems, the early efforts to strengthen the company's position prepared Jersey and its affiliates for a more aggressive role in the expanding world oil market of the late 1930's.

Altogether, this span of thirteen years presented both great problems and great opportunities. This was a period of rising competition in the world oil industry, competition which affected sales on all levels from that of the large contract buyer to the small-volume consumer. It was a time when foreign production and refining were displacing petroleum products from the United States in markets abroad. It was a time when many countries put limits on the free working of market forces, and when overproduction, price decline, and general economic deterioration had a disturbing effect on the market. But—except during a few years of deep depression—it was also a time of a strong upward trend in the use of oil products and of important shifts in the pattern of their consumption. There was a rising demand for fuel oil to furnish power for industrial plants and transport facilities and to provide heat for buildings. Especially dynamic was the demand for gasoline coming from the proliferation of automobiles, trucks, and airplanes. Late in the 1920's gasoline rose to first rank in the United States in the percentage it represented of the total consumption of products made from petroleum.[1]

This chapter and the next deal with the response of Standard Oil Company (New Jersey) and its affiliates to the problems affecting their sales operations and organizations and to the potentials of a highly dynamic market in this period. Consideration of the distribution of refinery products made in the United States comes first. Then follows a chapter dealing with adjustment and growth in foreign markets.

ORGANIZATION, PROBLEMS, AND POLICIES IN 1927

The Board of Directors of the parent company elected in 1927 had a broad representation of interests directly concerned with the sale of products. Among its members was Heinrich Riedemann, Jersey's leading authority on European markets and foreign competition in general. Directors Black, Farish, and Weller were chief executives of three domestic affiliates having substantial refining and marketing operations. Director Bedford was the head of domestic and foreign companies preparing and marketing lubricants and specialty products. President Teagle himself had had much experience in foreign trade.

The products of Jersey refineries were distributed through two different channels. One was large-volume transactions—known as contract, general office, or refinery sales—arranged by high executives, commonly by officers and directors of the parent company. Such sales were made to affiliates, to nonaffiliated oil companies, or to large industrial and commercial consumers. The handling of this business—both domestic and export—was in 1927 assigned to Standard Oil Company of New Jersey, but within a year the export trade was transferred to a new company, Standard Oil Export Corporation. The other channel was sales to jobbers, retailers, and consumers, including the smaller-volume or local industrial and commercial users of oil products. This type of distribution was the function of specialized marketing companies and of departments of other affiliates. In the reorganization of 1927, the parent company's own marketing was transferred to Standard Oil Company of New Jersey.

These marketing organizations, like other branches of operations, functioned essentially as independent units. They had their own managers and employees, they were allotted their own capital, and they were expected to make profits. They normally purchased their supplies from affiliated refiners at the same prices as were paid by independent marketers. Products were moved from refineries to bulk plants at the expense of the marketers; in accordance with Jersey accounting practice, the refinery price plus the transportation cost and handling charges represented the bulk plant cost. The marketers used tank trucks to move products from bulk plants to their customers. These buyers paid the so-called tank-wagon price, which was adjusted to market conditions. The difference between the bulk plant cost and the tank-wagon price had to cover the cost of wholesale distribution as well as to provide a profit. Service stations added their own margins, which depended on competitive retail prices.

Statistics for the year 1927 indicate the volume of products sold by the Jersey group of companies and the types of outlets to which these went. Of the planned worldwide deliveries for the year, totaling 156,500,000 barrels, 129,000,000 barrels were provided by refineries in the United States. Approximately 120,000,000 barrels of the domestic products came from Jersey refineries; the remainder was purchased from nonaffiliates. Nearly a third of these domestic supplies—40,000,000 barrels—was sold on contract for export. These exports in 1927 constituted 41 per cent of the total exports of the American oil industry. Approximately 45,000,000 barrels of domestic products were sold on contract in the United States, the larger part going to nonaffiliated oil concerns and the remainder to large consumers, principally shipping companies. The remaining 44,000,- 000 barrels were sold by the marketing organizations of affiliates in the United States to jobbers, retailers, and consumers. Thus in 1927 approximately two-thirds of the total output of Jersey's domestic refineries went to large-volume buyers—divided about equally between the foreign and the domestic market. The remaining one-third was sold in the domestic wholesale and retail market.[2]

As noted in Chapter 1, there were potentially serious weaknesses in Jersey's position in the market for oil products. One was its large dependence on exports at a time when competition abroad was increasing. Especially important to Jersey were its large sales to its pre-1911 affiliate, the Anglo-American Oil Company. It was a question how long domestic products could compete abroad with oil from large government concessions in Venezuela and Persia or from the expropriated properties of oil companies in Russia. At home, the movement toward functionally integrated operations was of particular concern to Jersey because of its sales to other oil companies with large marketing operations. Its former affiliate, Standard of New York, which after 1911 had continued to purchase from Jersey a large part of the products it distributed, was building up substantial production and refining of its own. As late as 1924, this company had purchased approximately 48 per cent of the gasoline sold by Jersey in the United States.[3]

Although the domestic affiliates had profitable marketing operations and had been selling a larger volume year after year, by 1927 they were in an exposed position. They were not as strong as some of their competitors in supplying the burgeoning demand of automobiles and trucks for gasoline, and they served only very limited territories.

A warning had come in the form of a considerable decline in the percentage of the gasoline demand supplied by Jersey marketing organizations in their operating areas—a warning all the more serious because gasoline had become such an important product. To be sure, in a rapidly expanding industry in which the demand generally was rising, no company could expect to hold the same percentage that it had held as an early leader. Standard of Indiana, Standard of New York, and Standard of California had suffered even larger percentage declines than Jersey. In 1926 Jersey, although it was still the largest supplier, had sold only 43 per cent of total gasoline sales in its marketing area as against 77 per cent in 1912, and gasoline sales of Standard of Louisiana in its territory had gone down from 82 per cent in 1912 to 35.5 per cent in 1926.

Since World War I, Jersey like its former affiliates had faced aggressive competition from younger companies, particularly from those with a strong base in oil production in Texas. Notable among them were The Texas Company and Gulf Oil Corporation. These and other so-called independent companies had had distinct advantages over the Jersey group. They had a larger ratio of production to the volume of their refining and sales, a situation which gave them assurance of supplies at relatively steady costs. Unlike Jersey, they were not particularly inhibited by fear of prosecution under antitrust law or other form of government regulation.[4] And being younger, they were more flexible in a dynamic situation where flexibility was an asset.

Especially portentous for Jersey's future was the limited geographic reach within the United States of the marketing operations of its affiliates as compared to that of most of their competitors. In 1911, the Jersey organizations selling the general line of petroleum products to jobbers, retailers, and consumers had been left with outlets in only six states and the District of Columbia. Even by 1927 they operated in only ten states and the federal district, and most of these areas were relatively small consumers of oil products. Standard Oil Company of New Jersey in 1927 took over the parent corporation's marketing in New Jersey, Maryland, Virginia, West Virginia, the District of Columbia, and North and South Carolina. Standard of Louisiana had charge of distribution in Louisiana, Arkansas, and Tennessee. Humble marketed in its home state of Texas. Stanco Distributors, Inc., was a wholesaler; it sold such products as Flit,

Mistol, Nujol, alcohol, and white oils, sales which made up only a minor portion of the total business of the Jersey marketers.

According to figures compiled for the year 1926, many oil companies were marketing in more states than the Jersey affiliates. In that year, The Texas Company had marketing organizations in forty-four states, Consolidated Oil Corporation (Sinclair) in thirty, Cities Service in twenty-five, and Gulf Oil in twenty-four. Several other companies also had a wider geographic distribution in the United States than did the whole Jersey organization.[5]

Although most of those companies did not sell a percentage of the total national sales of gasoline commensurate with the territorial extent of their operations, several in 1926 sold a larger portion of that total than did Jersey. In 1926 the parent company and its affiliates had 5.7 per cent of national gasoline sales. Consolidated Oil sold 6 per cent, The Texas Company 6.5 per cent, and Gulf Oil 7 per cent. Standard of Indiana, which marketed in only eleven states, accounted for 10.2 per cent; Standard of New York, in second rank, sold 9.5 per cent of the national total in fifteen states.[6] Although some of those companies obviously handled a small volume in many states and hence had high unit costs, their extensive territory gave them a broad base for expansion.

In 1927 the Jersey Company acted decisively to overcome weaknesses in its distribution of oil products. For several years, President Teagle and his associates had been well aware of the need to improve their marketing operations. But the old channels and outlets had enabled the group to dispose of its products at a profit so long as the demand was tending to exceed supply and the general price trend was upward. In 1927, however, the prospect of a long-term overproduction and price decline, accompanied by intensive competition, made imperative the attainment of a strong position in the market for products. Hence the Jersey Board of Directors decided that—in addition to maintaining its traditional position in the volume market—the company should enter upon a vigorous program to increase sales to jobbers, retailers, and consumers generally in the United States.

EXPANDING JERSEY'S MARKETING TERRITORY, 1927–1933

An important part of the company's program was to extend the operations of the domestic marketing organizations into more states. The expansion then undertaken continued until it was checked by the impact of the depression of the early 1930's.

The initial move of the Board of Directors of the parent company was to recommend the extension of the marketing territory of Standard Oil Company of New Jersey into states that could conveniently be supplied by its refineries on the Atlantic Coast. This was the first time since the dissolution that the Jersey Company had adopted the policy of territorial expansion along the Atlantic.

In accordance with this recommendation, Standard Oil Company of New Jersey in October, 1927, entered Delaware. Here it was fairly simple to start operations because district and division offices and bulk stations a few miles away in neighboring states could send in salesmen and supplies. In most instances the brands carried by Jersey's former affiliate, The Atlantic Refining Company (then the dominant marketer in Delaware), were different; hence there was no difficulty in using Standard, Esso, and other Jersey brand names. By 1933 Standard Oil Company of New Jersey had achieved second place in gasoline sales in Delaware; it had almost 14 per cent of total sales in the state.[7]

Entry into Pennsylvania came at about the same time. At first, facilities close by in other states were used. But it soon became evident that, if more than commercial business around Philadelphia was to be obtained, a separate organization would be necessary. Consequently, in July, 1928, Standard Oil Company of Pennsylvania was incorporated in Delaware. Its head office was established in Philadelphia and a branch office in Pittsburgh. Grant McCargo, who for many years had been president of the Pennsylvania Lubricating Company, Incorporated, became the new company's president. J. A. Van Wynan and F. H. Bedford, Jr., were elected its vice-presidents, the former as general manager and the latter as representative of the Jersey board.[8]

Standard of Pennsylvania developed slowly in its first two years. The parent company was at the time investigating the feasibility of reversing the flow of the pipeline of the Tuscarora Oil Company, Limited, and changing it from a crude to a gasoline carrier. The eventual decision was to use the line to carry products inland from the coastal refineries in New Jersey. The first gasoline entered the Tuscarora at Bayway in February, 1930. The use of this new method of transporting products gave Standard of Pennsylvania a considerable cost advantage in transporting gasoline through the southern part of the state as far as the terminal at Midland on the Ohio River. This was the first large gasoline pipeline from the coast to the interior, but it was not long before competitors acquired similar facilities.[9]

The new Pennsylvania affiliate sought to obtain good outlets at reasonable costs. At places that could be supplied advantageously by bulk plants on the Tuscarora line or on navigable rivers, it built some facilities, including service stations. It leased others, and also bought chains of stations. It gained good will by replacing old hand pumps in retail outlets with new electric pumps, an innovation not yet much used in the area by such well-established competitors as Atlantic Refining, Gulf Oil, Pure Oil, The Texas Company, Tide Water, Sun Oil, Cities Service, and Sinclair.

Standard of Pennsylvania increased its sales in spite of the competition of these companies as well as of such newcomers in Pennsylvania as Socony-Vacuum, Shell, and the American Oil Company (which in 1923 had become an affiliate of Standard of Indiana). In 1933 Standard of Pennsylvania had about 9 per cent of the gasoline sales of the state.[10]

Expansion into New England and New York came about in a different way. Although Jersey had lost its marketing organization in these important regions in 1911, it had continued to supply a large portion of the products sold there by Standard of New York.[11] But the prospect that the New York company would derive increasing supplies from its own producing and refining made it advisable for Jersey to acquire outlets in the northeastern states. This was a natural field for it to enter because of the large market and the favorable location with reference to the New Jersey Works. However, because both companies bore the Standard Oil name, Jersey could enter New England and New York only through a company with a different title. One possibility was the Beacon Oil Company. Jersey had already established relations with this concern by leasing to it the tube-and-tank patent for cracking gas oil.

In 1928 Clifford M. Leonard, a promoter, large stockholder, and director of the Beacon Oil Company, was looking for a source of funds with which to meet urgent needs. He had been a member of the group which had started the company in 1919. At that time, the plan was to exploit the possibility of profit from distilling top fractions of Mexican crude to produce fuel oil, for which the Boston area offered a good market. Within a short time, the company had built a refinery at Everett, Massachusetts, acquired tank cars and ocean-going tankers, invested in an oil concession in Venezuela, and built up a marketing system in various areas in New England and New York through an affiliate, Colonial Filling Stations, Inc. As of November 30, 1928, this marketing company controlled extensive facilities; it had 354 owned or leased service stations, 4,458 pumps leased to retail dealers, and 77 bulk plants with a storage capacity of 320,000 barrels. By 1928 Beacon Oil had obtained more than $12,000,000 from subscriptions to about two-thirds of its authorized common stock and $3,000,000 from subscriptions to 7½ per cent preferred stock—and it had borrowed almost $8,000,000. However, the stockholders, who had received no cash dividends since 1922, were not then interested in subscribing to additional shares of common. Leonard consequently had to seek funds elsewhere.[12]

Officers of Standard Oil Company (New Jersey) and Beacon Oil Company agreed on a plan for the former to acquire the major part of the latter's closely held stock. On January 4, 1929, Jersey made a firm offer to buy 350,000 shares of unissued common stock at $19.10 per share, provided the Beacon stockholders would exchange 300,000 additional shares at the ratio of one share of Jersey stock for 2¼ shares of Beacon. Since this ratio represented approximately the market value of the shares of the two companies and since Beacon had not been paying cash dividends while the other company had paid dividends regularly, most of Beacon's stockholders, including Leonard, were willing to exchange shares. By the end of January, 1929, Jersey had acquired more than 75 per cent of the total shares outstanding.[13]

Two Jersey men were elected to Beacon Oil's board, Director F. H. Bedford, Jr., and J. A. Van Wynan. The former had responsibility for supervision but was not the new affiliate's top officer. Richard B. Kahle continued to serve as the company's president.[14]

Jersey further extended its marketing area by arranging for Beacon Oil—whose coverage of the market in New England and New York was spotty—to purchase going concerns. In February, 1929, Beacon purchased the Monroe Oil Company, which operated in and around Rochester, New York. In September it bought a controlling interest in the Sylvestre Utilities Companies, Inc., which had a subsidiary marketing fuel oil in New York City and Westchester County. In 1931, it acquired 75 per cent of the stock of Kesbec, Inc., a company owning and operating fifty-five service stations in Westchester County, in the boroughs of Manhattan and the Bronx in New York City, and on Long Island. By 1935 Beacon Oil—its name changed to Colonial Beacon—had greatly increased its business in New England and New York; its gasoline sales were then nearly 7 per cent of the total in these areas.[15]

The Jersey Board of Directors did not confine its plans for expansion to territories contiguous to the company's old marketing operations. It also tried to negotiate a merger with Standard Oil Company of California, a former affiliate on the Pacific Coast. A press release issued by the presidents of the two companies in August, 1931, disclosed the point of view of their directors not only concerning this possible merger but also with regard to future market expansion. It reads in part:

Each of the two companies is today handicapped by being able to meet only locally the competition of other oil companies having nationwide systems of distribution. To meet the competition of such corporations each of the two companies feels the necessity for enlarging the territory in which it distributes. This can be accomplished by expanding separately or by merger. Expansion separately would involve costly duplication of existing facilities which are already more than adequate with consequent economic waste and with no compensating benefit; while a merger would accomplish the same result without such duplication and would utilize the complementary facilities of the two companies. In addition the merger would result in many important economies such as the use of more accessible points of supply and the elimination of crosshauls.[16]

Several directors who had had successful careers in marketing favored this merger. F. H. Bedford, Jr., who approved of it from beginning to end, wrote in 1933: "We undoubtedly will ultimately have to meet our competitors by becoming nation-wide in our activities and there is no way we can accomplish this so well and so cheaply and so quickly as by combination with a company having a Standard name and brand."[17] Heinrich Riedemann, who had had long experience in European marketing, wrote Teagle that "my heart is set on this merger with California strongly."[18] However, as noted in Chapter 3, negotiations between the two companies were terminated late in 1933 because of certain differences which could not be reconciled.

No doubt the executives' joint press release concerning the contemplated merger and the advisability of nationwide marketing brought about unforeseen, if delayed, complications. It certainly gave notice to Standard Oil Company (Indiana) that Jersey might be planning to enter the Middle West. The Indiana company had lost heavily in relative position in the United States since 1910; naturally, it was opposed to Jersey's entry into its home territory. However, it was itself invading the eastern states through its affiliate, American Oil Company, and it had entered the South through another affiliate, Pan American Petroleum Corporation. Jersey did not at this time set up a marketing organization in the territory of Standard of Indiana, although many of that company's marketing areas close to the Mississippi River were attractive as possible outlets for the products of the Baton Rouge refinery.[19]

While this varied program of expansion was being carried forward, Humble Oil & Refining Company was at work extending its operations in Texas. The company's board, of which Jersey's Director Farish was president, decided that Humble should enter more heavily into retailing and should expand its marketing operations throughout the state wherever its principal competitors could not supply products more cheaply than it could. Poor roads and the scarcity of rail lines—and the high cost of transportation by both—posed serious cost problems in supplying distant markets, such as those in West Texas a thousand miles from the Baytown refinery.

However, Humble was able to overcome most of its cost handicap in

STATES IN WHICH DOMESTIC AFFILIATES
HAD MARKETING OPERATIONS IN 1939

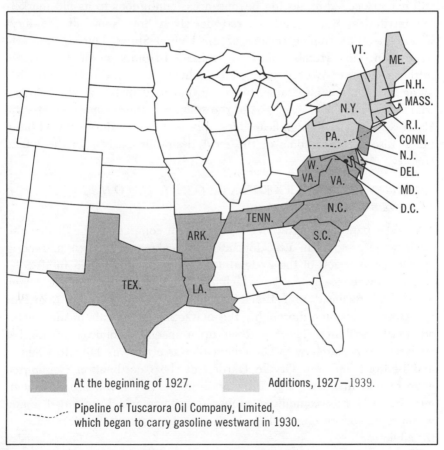

At the beginning of 1927.   Additions, 1927–1939.

Pipeline of Tuscarora Oil Company, Limited,
which began to carry gasoline westward in 1930.

the Beaumont–Port Arthur and the Fort Worth–Dallas areas and also in West Texas either by setting up small refineries where crude was available or by purchasing or exchanging products. The company added to its bulk and service stations until the onset of the depression in 1930. It increased the number of the former from 68 early in 1927 to 143 in 1930, and its service stations from three at the beginning of expansion to 220 owned and 56 on long-term leases in 1930. With all this expansion, Humble in 1929 raised its proportion of the total gasoline sales in Texas to just above 6 per cent. Even so, it remained in a very bad fifth place as compared to its leading competitors.[20]

Thus in only a few years the Jersey Company had greatly extended its marketing territory in the United States, thereby retrieving some of its markets lost in 1911. When the drive had spent itself, the company had still not succeeded in moving beyond areas contiguous to its old marketing territories. But it had entered decisively into some of the most important oil-consuming regions of the United States. During the early depression years, Humble marketers retreated from some of the sparsely settled sections of West Texas, where declining sales and rising unit costs made operations unprofitable, but they remained in the growing industrial sections of the eastern part of the state. Advances along the Atlantic Coast were especially significant; not only was the territory entered large but it also included some of the most desirable markets in the whole country.

IMPROVING MARKETING OPERATIONS, 1928–1933

While expanding geographically, the parent company and affiliates also made some progress in attacking internal weaknesses of their marketing operations. A report of the Federal Trade Commission issued in 1928[21]— which showed the extent to which the relative position of the Jersey group had declined in national gasoline sales—spurred the Board of Directors to examine thoroughly the marketing organizations and methods of the affiliates. The board set up a special committee on market analysis and research, with Director Sadler as chairman. Directors Senior and Bedford and also Orville Harden of the Coordination Committee were regular members, and Director Black served as an informal member. In 1929 this committee prepared reports which revealed many weaknesses and recommended changes to improve the performance of the affiliates.[22]

The committee made recommendations which had to do with nearly all aspects of marketing. It proposed that the efficiency and effectiveness of the organizations be raised. It held that the quality of many of their products must be improved. It stressed the need to revise the pricing policies of the companies. And, recognizing the slow progress made in acquiring service stations, it proposed that more such retail outlets be obtained.

Before much had been accomplished in carrying out the committee's recommendations, the depression was severely affecting marketing operations. The volume of sales held up fairly well for some time. But prices fell, the decline in 1930 and 1931 being especially steep. A study of prices in Baltimore, where Standard Oil Company of New Jersey was the leading marketer, reveals a drastic reduction. The average industry tank-wagon price per gallon of house-brand gasoline (exclusive of taxes), which had fallen from 17.58 cents in 1926 to 10.85 cents in 1930, fell to an average of 7.75 cents in 1931. As prices dropped, the gross margins of the marketers became narrower.[23]

A complicating factor was the increase in state, federal, and local taxes on gasoline. In fifty representative cities in the United States, state excises in 1932 averaged about 4 cents a gallon; the figure climbed steadily until the 1940's. Added to the state tax was the federal tax of 1 cent per gallon beginning in June, 1932, which rose to a cent and a half a year later. It fell back to 1 cent at the beginning of 1934, at which level it remained for several years. Four of the fifty cities selected as representative had also themselves levied taxes on gasoline in 1931. Altogether, the state, federal, and municipal taxes added an average of almost 5½ cents to the retail price of a gallon of gasoline in 1933. Their total represented 30 per cent of the price charged the consumer.[24]

The recommendation of the directors' committee to raise the effectiveness of the management and sales personnel of the marketing organizations was a direct result of the changes that were going on in the market. The relative importance of major products was changing and competition was becoming more intense. Nearly all the marketers then in high positions in Standard Oil Company of New Jersey and Standard of Louisiana were men whose early experience had largely been in selling kerosene and who were oriented toward the wholesale rather than the retail market. Four directors of the East Coast affiliate had had such a background as had also the vice-president in charge of marketing for Standard of Louisiana. There were, in fact, few top officers capable of managing new operations. In general, the marketing organizations were found to be both inefficient and overstaffed.[25]

The parent company's board consequently elected new directors in three of the marketing affiliates, and these men were given high executive positions. When the president of Colonial Beacon resigned at the end of 1930, A. Clarke Bedford was made a director and subsequently became president. In 1931 two outstanding young marketers from Standard of Louisiana were added to Colonial Beacon's board: A. C. Minton and J. R. Riddell, the latter being elected vice-president. In the Louisiana company, J. C. Hilton and J. E. Skehan were chosen to fill vacancies on the board. Hilton, a purchasing agent in New York, was elected president; Skehan, who had been manager of the Newark (New Jersey) sales division, was made a vice-president and later in the year, on the retirement of the former head, was put in charge of marketing. When two officers and veteran marketers retired from Standard of Pennsylvania in 1932, Jersey's Director Senior and two successful marketers with Standard Oil Company of New Jersey, C. G. Sheffield and E. A. Holbein, were elected to the board. Senior became president and the other two were elected vice-presidents.[26]

The recently elected executives began at once to upgrade the marketing personnel of the companies. The newcomers on Colonial Beacon's board initiated changes that were in time to transform that company into an effective organization. More new men were added by these marketing affiliates, but the number of sales personnel was cut during the depression in accordance with Jersey's policy of curtailment. This reduction was most severe in Standard of Louisiana.[27]

Upgrading the quality of gasolines was a special problem on which research staffs and refiners were working. The marketing organizations of each affiliate then had two grades of gasoline, regular and premium. The former was called Standard by the three companies bearing the Standard Oil name, Colonial by Colonial Beacon, and Humble Flashlike and later Humble Gasoline by the Texas affiliate. The premium grade contained tetraethyl lead. At first selling for 5 cents per gallon more than the regular, it was called Esso by three affiliates and Colonial Ethyl and Humble Flashlike Ethyl by the other two until they agreed in 1931 to name their premiums Esso. In 1930 and 1931, affiliates tried to increase the sale of the premium grade by reducing the price differential between the two grades to 3 cents. However, for by far the larger part of their sales, they depended on the regular product. Several other companies were then selling a regular gasoline of higher quality, among them Sun Oil Company, a vigorous competitor of Standard Oil Company of New Jersey.

The latter company's marketers were not at once able to obtain from the refiners a better grade of gasoline; they therefore turned to other methods to improve the sale of their major product.[28]

The affiliates also encountered quality problems in selling motor lubricants, but they made early progress toward solving them. The companies bearing the Standard Oil name were handling their own regular motor oil—Standard, introduced in 1926—and a premium made by Vacuum which was in great demand all over the country. Colonial Beacon was distributing two grades, Beacon and Beacon Penn, whereas Humble had only one grade, Velvet. The Texas affiliate undertook in 1930 to market Vacuum's Mobiloil, but in 1931 it introduced one of its own products, named "997," after its research group had worked for several years on the task of producing from Texas crudes a grade of oil that could compete with Pennsylvania oils. Jersey's new Essolube, introduced in 1932, came to be accepted by the market, especially by industrial and commercial consumers. All the affiliates then discontinued the sale of Mobiloil.[29]

The special 1929 committee on marketing analysis and research proposed several changes in the price policies of the marketing companies. In earlier years, the executives of the parent company and affiliates had hesitated to reduce prices as a means of holding or increasing their share of the business. Before the dissolution, Standard Oil had been criticized severely for its price cutting, and in the 1920's Jersey's legal counsel advised that local price reductions were not defensible under the federal Clayton Act and state statutes on price discrimination. The principal marketing affiliate—by ordering late in 1928 that no discounts should be granted and that the tank-wagon price should be 15 cents everywhere— had actually reduced the price of regular gasoline about one cent per gallon. However, all affiliates had included in their prices a wide margin for the marketers. They had thereby provided an umbrella for competitors, who understandably had set their prices lower than those of the Jersey companies. In the hope that before long the competitors would have to raise prices again, the Jersey marketers had not reduced theirs. Further, they had hesitated to adopt certain other devices used by competing concerns for obtaining the business of jobbers who had previously bought in tank-car lots from the Jersey companies. In their efforts to obtain the business of independent service-station owners, the affiliates had also refrained from utilizing such practices of competitors as supplying the dealers with tanks, pumps, and other equipment on various special terms.[30]

The committee recommended the reduction from 8 to 7 cents of the differential between the tank-car prices of gasoline charged jobbers and the service-station price to motorists. This should be done by cutting the margin allowed the jobber to 3 cents. It was expected, however, that the differential would continue to be split about equally—as had been the common practice—between the middleman and the retailer who purchased from the former at tank-wagon prices. The jobber might of course retain the 4-cent margin, thus reducing that of the retailer to 3 cents; but independent jobbers were competing against large companies which sold to wholesalers, to retailers, and to consumers at service stations.[31] A compilation of industry prices for house-brand gasolines in 1929 shows that in Baltimore the average tank-wagon price to dealers was 14.33 cents and the service-station price was 17.83. This left a margin of 3.5 cents for the retailer. Comparable averages for fifty representative cities in the United States were 15.58 cents for the tank-wagon price and 17.92 for the service-station price, leaving 2.34 for the retailer's margin.[32]

Additional changes were also recommended by the committee. One was to grant a 2-cent discount from tank-wagon prices in places where competition was especially keen, a reversal of the former policy of granting no discounts. Another was to establish the tank-wagon and service-station price of a product as the price at the supply point plus the cost of transport to the bulk or service station. This was contrary to the practice, adopted by Standard Oil Company of New Jersey in 1928, of maintaining uniform prices throughout a territory.

The affiliates followed several of the recommendations of the committee. Early in 1930 Standard Oil Company of New Jersey announced a new price policy. The resulting reductions probably met the prices of competitors except those who set their prices below costs or whose costs were much lower than those of the Jersey affiliate. This marketer was actually later in closing its price umbrella over competitors than was another company, Standard of Ohio, which had followed a similar policy but had announced in 1928 that it would meet its competitors' prices.[33] Humble late in 1929 adopted the policy of aiding its dealer-customers to meet competition by agreeing to compensate them for discounts on gasoline which they had to grant to hold certain customers, especially commercial ones. As a result, the Texas affiliate soon established a general 4-cent differential between its tank-wagon charge to service-station dealers and the retail price posted in its own stations.[34]

The marketing organizations also expanded their retailing by acquiring additional service stations. Humble had begun in 1927 to add to its original three such outlets—located in Houston—with the result, as already noted, that by the end of 1930 it had 220 owned stations and 56 on long-term leases.[35] The aim of Standard Oil Company of New Jersey had been to obtain a sufficient number of company-owned retail outlets to handle 30 per cent of its gasoline sales. But in 1929 that affiliate was making only 18 per cent of its gasoline sales through its own service stations. Standard of Louisiana was retailing only 8 per cent of the gasoline it sold. After 1929 these two affiliates invested in more retail stations. By 1932 the Jersey companies owned and operated 2,500 such outlets. These service stations marketed 25 per cent of the gasoline bearing the affiliates' brands that was sold in their territories. More than 25,000 other retail dealers sold the remaining 75 per cent.[36]

Efforts were also made in the meantime to raise standards in the operation of service stations. Control over the outlets had been inadequate in the first stage of expansion. After a survey in 1927, a manual of procedures and standards was prepared for general use. It stressed economy, efficiency, neatness, and courtesy. The affiliates started various campaigns to encourage greater efforts by service-station attendants to meet these standards. Standard Oil Company of New Jersey also adopted the practice of having supervisors visit its stations to call attention to the need for improvement and to advise on how it could be brought about. Articles in *The Salesmotor*, the company magazine for the sales force, discussed these needs. J. M. Winchester, who had been hired as an automobile expert in 1913 and had become the head of the Automotive Department in 1931, often gave suggestions for better operation of company trucks and automobiles.[37]

An industry-wide attack on certain competitive practices also was helpful to the Jersey marketers. In December, 1928, the American Petroleum Institute announced a code of fair practices designed to eliminate such methods as loaning and leasing equipment to dealer-owned outlets and paying for the construction of stations, advertising, or a part of the rent on sites. This code had some effect at once. In 1931, however, the Federal Trade Commission withdrew its approval. Hearings subsequently took place in Washington. Edwin S. Hall, legal counsel of Standard Oil Company of New Jersey, was a member of the committee to represent the oil industry. A revised code, approved by the federal agency, was then set up. Although carrying no power of enforcement, the code established standards which had the support of a large part of the industry.

An innovation introduced in 1929 was expected to add income without an appreciable increase in expense: the selling of private-brand merchandise, that is, tires under the Atlas brand. The venture grew out of Beacon Oil's experiment with selling tires. To provide the product, the Atlas Supply Company, incorporated in Delaware, was organized jointly by Standard Oil Company of New Jersey, Beacon Oil, Standard of Louisiana, and four pre-1911 Jersey affiliates—the Standard Oil companies of Ohio, Indiana, Kentucky, and California. This new company was not itself a manufacturer but contracted for the products it handled. Atlas thus provided its corporate owners with a tire of uniform quality to sell nationwide under the same brand. Batteries were added in 1932. Soon thereafter other products were made available, under the Atlas brand, at service stations for the convenience of motorists and, it was hoped, with profit to the companies.[38]

The domestic marketing organizations also undertook to increase their sale of fuel oil for households. President Teagle in the 1920's had opposed promoting the sale of heating oil for home furnaces. His objection rested principally on the ground that the available crude oil—at a time when many oilmen believed a shortage was in prospect—should rather be used to increase the supply of gasoline. When it became evident, however, that oil supplies would be adequate for many years—especially with the overproduction of the early 1930's—Teagle and other Jersey executives saw in the sale of kerosene or other grades of heating oil a potentially large market. The marketing organizations therefore turned to promoting this type of business. These fuels not only provided new sales opportunities for oil but also increased the demand for the tanks and burners manufactured by Jersey's affiliate, Gilbert & Barker.[39]

An important development in the make-up of the sales force of the marketing organizations came in the early 1930's: the introduction of sales engineering. This came first in the sale of industrial lubricants. Walter E. Lee, the assistant director of research on fuels and lubricants in Standard Oil Development, was given the assignment to find ways to improve the performance of lubricating-oil salesmen. He found that the men were largely order takers. They would visit a plant, chat with the manager in charge, and before leaving write out an order for supplies that was generally similar to past orders. If some objection was made to a product, the salesman might suggest a substitute, but he commonly did not attempt to determine the reason for the complaint. It became obvious that the field representatives of the company who had been adequate in the past could not judge satisfactorily the kinds of products needed for lubricating more complex machinery and meeting competition.

It was clearly necessary to adopt the engineering approach to industrial sales, a method which Vacuum Oil had successfully employed for many years in handling its extensive commercial, marine, and industrial accounts at home and abroad. The first move by the Jersey Company in this direction was the compilation of a manual, called *Lubetext*. This publication, introduced in 1931, informed the sales force about the machines and processes of industrial consumers, the lubrication requirements of these customers, and the qualities of the products the salesmen were selling.[40]

As prices fell, more attention was also given to selling costs. Some progress was made, but there was no comprehensive approach to the particular difficulties involved. In this area as in others, advances were in the direction of learning something about the problems to be met and of experimenting with ways to solve them rather than with specific programs to reduce costs. Small savings were made here and there in some operations, and as employees retired or resigned they generally were not replaced. The average cost per gallon of distributing gasoline by Standard Oil Company of New Jersey, Colonial Beacon, Standard of Pennsylvania, and Standard of Louisiana was reduced from 3.09 cents in 1931 to 3 cents in 1932 and to 2.82 cents in 1933.[41] Humble in the early 1930's reduced its average cost of selling gasoline by abandoning its recently entered marketing territory, where—with severe competition from local plants processing cheap crude—the volume of its sales was low and unit costs were high.[42]

The domestic marketers were unable to reduce costs or to increase the volume sold sufficiently to make up for the general narrowing of their gross margin that came with declining prices. The result was that their operating earnings declined.* The earnings from domestic marketing operations, as a whole, fell from a substantial gain in 1927 to a large loss in 1933. Standard of Louisiana had the poorest record of all the marketers; it had a heavy loss on its marketing operations in 1930 and large losses in the next two years. The new marketing affiliates—as is not

---

* That is, departmental earnings from which administrative and other general charges and income taxes had not been deducted. These earnings are not net earnings, but they are useful for making comparisons within the Jersey marketing group.

uncommon for such operations—had operating losses every year except for Colonial Beacon's nominal earnings in 1929. Humble showed small losses in 1930 and 1931. However, the specialty companies as a group and Standard Oil Company of New Jersey, which continued to sell along the Atlantic seaboard, operated in the black. Their operating earnings, however, also trended downward and in 1933 amounted to less than 8 per cent of those earnings for 1927.[43]

GENERAL OFFICE SALES, 1927–1933

Inasmuch as the domestic marketing organizations were able to maintain the volume of their sales, except for a drop in 1931 and 1932, they provided a fairly stable outlet for the products of the affiliates' refineries. The same was true of large-volume contract sales from 1927 to 1933. That is, with the exception of the decline in the early 1930's, these sales also held up fairly well. Certain developments in the 1930's, however, were to bring important changes.

Sales to old customers among oil companies within the United States not affiliated with Jersey declined. The downward trend resulted from the movement toward functional integration and self-sufficiency of supply among oil companies as well as from the depression of the 1930's. Standard of New York was receiving a rising volume from its affiliates in Texas and California. After the merger of the New York company with Vacuum Oil Company in 1932 to form Socony-Vacuum, the combination obtained products from Vacuum's refining in the Northeast. Jersey's sales to Standard of New York in 1930 averaged 30,000 barrels daily; those to Socony-Vacuum in 1933 averaged 20,000 barrels. Its sales to Standard of Kentucky—a specialized marketer largely dependent on Jersey for supplies—also declined, from a daily average of 25,000 barrels in 1930 to 18,000 in 1933.[44]

The Jersey companies continued to sell to their large industrial and commercial contract customers, such as shipping companies. But these concerns were also affected by the depression. However, one large new contract and the beginning of recovery helped to generate a considerable rise in sales in 1933. (See Table 8.)

Jersey also looked for new types of customers. Its purchase of Daggett & Ramsdell, a leading manufacturer of cold creams and related cosmetic preparations, provided an outlet for such refinery products as white oils and petrolatums used as basic ingredients. While this company at best would not use large volumes of refined products, it at least provided an additional controlled outlet. More important for the future were Jersey's efforts to improve its position in supplying the growing aviation industry.

In 1928 Standard Oil Development Company undertook special research to provide products to meet the rising quality requirements of airplane engines. But even with the best products, Jersey was handicapped in trying to obtain contracts to supply airline companies because of the limited territorial reach of its marketing at home and abroad. Not being able to assure such companies of uniform products everywhere, it was in danger of losing out altogether in supplying this developing demand. It therefore proposed to other oil concerns similarly handicapped that they adopt uniform specifications to enable them to supply the aviation industry with standardized products throughout their operating territories. Because Standard Oil Company (Indiana) and Standard Oil Company of California faced the same problem of limited marketing territories, they readily accepted Jersey's suggestion. Late in 1929, these two companies joined Standard Oil Company of·New Jersey in creating Stanavo Specifications Board, Inc., with offices at 26 Broadway in New York City. Stanavo had two specific purposes: to correlate the research of the three companies on gasolines, oils, and greases for use in aeronautical engines; and to establish product specifications so that the aviation industry could obtain a similar quality under the various brands of the companies in different places.[45]

Jersey at the same time worked to establish itself as a supplier to the developing aviation market in the regions where it had marketing operations. The demand was small at first. But by the steps taken in the late 1920's and early 1930's, the company gained a stronger position from which to compete for sales to the aviation industry when it became a large consumer of high-quality oil products.

The most vulnerable of the outlets for the products of the domestic refineries was their export sales. Prior to 1930 Jersey still had secure sales to affiliates abroad. It also sold substantial amounts for export to non-affiliated French marketers, to Vacuum Oil Company, and especially to Anglo-American Oil Company, its former associate and its largest foreign customer. In addition, it had fuel-supply contracts with foreign navies and commercial shipping lines.

This export trade was meeting stiff competition from products manufactured abroad. Jersey's officers and directors first became concerned that Anglo-American might not be able to maintain its customary position in competition with such vigorous marketers as Royal Dutch–Shell and Anglo-Persian. They also foresaw that their company itself might find it impossible to compete for very long with products made from the oil produced on expropriated properties (of which Jersey had been one of the owners) in Russia and offered by the Soviet at lower prices than a private company could afford.

Relations with Anglo-American became critical in 1928. This development was of special concern to Humble, a large supplier for the British company through Standard Oil Company of New Jersey. A gasoline price war was then going on in England between Royal Dutch–Shell and the Russians, and other companies had to meet their prices or take a serious decline in sales. In consideration of Russian competition, the Jersey affiliate handling exports to the British company had agreed to assume the loss under certain conditions. During the first five months of 1928, the sales of Standard Oil Company of New Jersey to Anglo-American resulted in a deficit of $1,000,000; in the sixth month alone, the loss was $1,500,000. It was then estimated that the loss for the rest of the year would average nearly $1,000,000 each month. Under its arrangements with Standard Oil Company of New Jersey, Humble had to assume half of such losses. President Farish of the Texas affiliate declared that Humble's monthly share of the adverse balance on sales to Anglo-American was more than the profits on the Baytown refinery's other business could be "with everything working right." He said: "A few more contracts like this, and we will all be sick or in our graves. . . . We are not in position here to judge the value of the future business with Anglo, but it will have to be extremely valuable to stand this kind of pressure."[46]

The situation raised the not uncommon question as to what the terms of Humble's sales to or through Standard Oil Company of New Jersey should be, but the interest here is in the problem that this intense competition posed for Jersey. In the belief that it could hold this outlet only by purchasing Anglo-American and thereby entering directly and vigorously into the British market, Jersey opened negotiations with the company which led to its purchase in 1930. (See Chapter 11.)

Rising economic nationalism abroad also affected the export of the products of Jersey's domestic affiliates. This movement led to the development of refining within several European countries which had long been supplied at least in part from the United States. National regulation to encourage refining within a country first manifested itself in France, but Italy and later Germany under the Nazis also promoted refining within their national boundaries. (See Chapter 7.)

Before this movement had advanced very far, however, other developments brought a radical change in Jersey's export sales. Especially important was the parent company's acquisition of extensive producing properties in Venezuela and the Aruba refinery. (See Chapters 3 and 7.) Because that plant, by processing Venezuelan crude, could supply most of Jersey's European markets at lower costs than could refineries in the United States, it became the leading supplier of the company's foreign markets.

The United States tariff of 1932 also reduced the import of heavy Latin American crude to the New Jersey Works for making bunker oil and other heavy fuels. Crude to process for foreign markets could be imported under bond, but to segregate imported crude in refining operations was not very practical. The result was that Jersey's business of bunkering ships in East Coast ports began to utilize products imported under bond.

The effect of this shift to foreign supplies for customers outside the United States was felt by the three large coastal refineries of Jersey affiliates—but most severely by Humble. During 1930 this company had contributed more than 20,000,000 barrels of products to Jersey's foreign trade, or 55 per cent of the total export of the domestic affiliates; in 1933 it supplied 8,000,000 barrels, which was 47 per cent of a greatly reduced export. The decline in Humble's sale of gasoline for shipment abroad was especially severe—from more than 10,000,000 barrels, or 61 per cent of Jersey's gasoline exports, to less than 2,000,000 barrels, or 37 per cent. The Texas affiliate's contribution to Jersey's foreign sales thereafter consisted principally of lubricants and gas oil.[47]

Humble was in an especially difficult situation because it was dependent on other affiliates for outlets for approximately 80 per cent of the products of the Baytown refinery; in addition, it did not have any immediate prospect of increasing its sales in Texas. Its executives therefore took the position that the parent company, which had encouraged them to expand the Baytown refinery, had to take responsibility for supplying outlets for the plant's products. Even before the reduction of foreign sales—that is, after the intense competition that accompanied the development of the East Texas field—Humble's Wiess, its director in charge of refining, had suggested that the company's Baytown and Ingleside refineries be put on a cost-plus basis. No decision concerning what steps to take was then reached. It was only after the severe decline in Humble's sales in 1934 that a contract was drawn up between the Texas affiliate and Standard Oil Company of New Jersey. The latter company agreed to purchase from Humble substantial volumes of refined products at prices that would cover costs plus a fair return on Humble's investment, the rate agreed upon being 5.75 per cent.[48]

Because Jersey had to shift so much of its processing for European markets to the Aruba refinery and to a lesser extent to smaller foreign refineries, the affiliates in the United States had to build up their markets at home or reduce the output of their refineries. There was not much prospect of increasing sales substantially, if at all, to nonaffiliated oil companies. It was therefore necessary to promote sales in other directions. One way was to increase the operations of the marketing organizations serving a growing mass consumer market.

THE ESSO MARKETERS, 1933–1939

Although changes in their marketing policies and practices in the years from 1927 to 1933 had not particularly increased sales or substantially reduced costs, Jersey and its domestic affiliates had made some important breaks with the past and had adopted a more critical and flexible attitude in regard to marketing operations. In 1933 their executives decided to act vigorously to raise the effectiveness of their sales efforts.

Leadership was provided by the Esso Marketers. This was an organization established in 1933 to centralize the administration of the marketing operations of Standard Oil Company of New Jersey, Colonial Beacon, Standard of Pennsylvania, and Standard of Louisiana. The Humble Sales Department—inasmuch as Humble for special reasons was virtually independent—was not a member of this group and hence remained outside the mainstream of Jersey's marketing at this time.

In fact, Humble had obtained assurance of other outlets for the products of its refineries, particularly the one at Baytown. It had large processing contracts with several companies not affiliated with Jersey; these were especially important in the years from 1934 through 1937. The relationship of Humble's Refining Department with Standard Oil Company of New Jersey, which had previously been close, was strengthened by the product sales contract of 1934. Humble continued to sell to that affiliate around 80 per cent of its output of products. As a matter of fact, from 1934 on, Humble's capital expenditures on refining were determined principally by the product requirements of its largest customer.[49]

As a practical matter, therefore, there was no great advantage for Humble in carrying on an expensive campaign to expand its sales in the mass market. The company's marketing operations—especially from 1932 on—were cost- rather than volume-oriented. Humble continued to close small refineries, bulk plants, and service stations in order to eliminate operations in unprofitable areas where the volume of sales was small or where competition from other refineries was extremely keen. It considerably reduced the number of its company-operated outlets. It put many of its bulk stations in the hands of commission agents and also converted a large number of its service stations to operations by dealers buying on contract from Humble. However, it continued to operate more service stations than did the other Jersey affiliates. Humble's administrators believed that clean stations offering excellent service had a high public relations value.[50]

Although Humble reversed its earlier policy of territorial expansion, it nevertheless promoted sales vigorously in Texas. As before, it put special effort into the distribution of industrial lubricants. It increased the number of its specialty products. After its legal counsel in 1934 advised that it could safely do so, it began to handle TBA products (tires, batteries, and accessories). In 1937 it added liquefied gas and asphalt to its products line. Humble put a strong emphasis on the quality of products and on cleanliness and service in its stations. It advertised moderately; the radio broadcasting of the Southwest Conference football games which it began to sponsor in 1934 was especially popular.[51]

Altogether, Humble's sales in Texas increased only modestly, but they became profitable. Its total sales in 1939 (the record year of the decade) were only 353,000 barrels more than the 2,219,000 barrels sold in 1929 (the record year of the 1920's). Its gasoline sales in 1939 represented 5.8 per cent of the industry's total in Texas as against 5.9 per cent in 1933. The company's sale of industrial lubricants, however, was 20 per cent of total sales in Texas in 1939. In 1936 its operating earnings (before administrative and other charges) changed from red to black. The percentage of return on gross investment in marketing facilities rose fairly steadily in the late 1930's.[52]

The experience of the Esso Marketers in the 1930's is of greater importance in the history of the Jersey Company than are the immediate results in volume sold or profits earned. As Standard Oil Development took the lead in research on refinery products and processes and as Humble became the leader in production research and engineering, so the Esso Marketers developed ways of raising the effectiveness and efficiency of marketing operations that set a pattern for other Jersey companies.

The first manager of the Esso Marketers was Robert G. Stewart, son of a long-time chief executive officer of Standard Oil Company (Indiana).

After attending medical school, young Stewart had begun in 1914 to work for his father's company as a specialty salesman. He had risen rapidly; in 1927 he had been elected president of Pan American Petroleum & Transport Company. In that capacity, he had had charge of negotiating the sale of Pan American's foreign properties to Jersey and had arranged his own transfer to the purchasing company.[53]

Because of the retirement of many old-timers and the resignation of Director Moffett in the summer of 1933, Stewart had a freer hand in building up a new sales organization than he would probably have had previously. His efforts were affected, however, by the National Industrial Recovery Act and by the oil-industry code drawn up under that act. There was controversy for a time over the proposal that the administration in Washington be authorized to set oil prices, a suggestion which Jersey's President Teagle and Chairman Farish strongly opposed.[54]

In September, 1933, Harold L. Ickes, the Petroleum Administrator, put the Code of Fair Competition for the industry into effect, but suspended the price-fixing provision pending hearings on its advisability. The final decision was to omit this provision except in California. The oil-industry code helped to improve competitive practices in marketing throughout the country; many of its rules were similar to those the industry itself had drawn up in 1929. But Ickes had difficulty in enforcing its various provisions. There were still many violators of proration and conservation laws; they bought "bootleg" oil, carried it across state lines, and sold it in other states. This illegal activity did much to demoralize the market, and as a result the marketing sections of the code were widely violated.[55]

It was at this difficult time that the marketing operations of the four Jersey affiliates were centralized under Stewart's management. Sales personnel thereafter reported to the New York office and not to one of the four companies.[56] This change met some opposition. A dissenting officer of Colonial Beacon took the position that "control and supervision along departmental lines was ineffective and costly." He held that the company should be treated as a unit, as it had been in the past.[57]

Three separate divisions were set up at the headquarters of the Esso Marketers to have charge of sales to different types of outlets. The tank-car division, headed by Director Holbein of Standard of Pennsylvania, managed sales in tank-car lots. This business, which had suffered the most from competition, was handled by salesmen sent out from New York to call on jobbers, owners of service stations, and others purchasing in tank-car volume. The wholesale division was headed by Director Skehan of Standard of Louisiana and the retail division by Director Sheffield of Standard Oil Company of New Jersey.[58]

Departments were also established for special purposes. A consolidated fuel oil department—a line of business then being vigorously promoted—was established with J. W. Connolly, formerly of Pan American Petroleum, as manager. The lubricating sales organizations of the four companies were merged, with Robert T. Haslam in charge. He devoted half of his time to this work and half to Standard Oil Development, of which he remained executive vice-president and general manager. A technical group headed by Walter E. Lee was transferred from Standard Oil Development to serve as the sales engineering department. Haslam and Lee and their departments brought a strong engineering interest into the Esso Marketers.[59]

Under this top organization in New York, the wholesale and retail operations of the four companies were organized in geographic divisions. By June, 1934, there were thirteen such divisions covering eighteen states and the District of Columbia. Each division had a head office, at first with separate wholesale and retail managers with their own staffs. Within a year, however, one man was put in charge with a wholesale and a retail specialist under him.[60]

These managers were given scope for initiative and drive. They deferred to New York on questions of policy, but handled other matters themselves. They were all "practical" men who had begun as salesmen and had steadily moved up the managerial ladder. A major function of the office in New York was to help them learn how to do a better job. In general, this set-up represented a change in managerial philosophy: the managers in the field were no longer given detailed orders from headquarters but were expected to assume a wide range of responsibilities. At the same time, they had more rigorous general direction and more effective help from the top.[61]

The name Esso now came to be applied extensively throughout operations. Service stations owned and operated by affiliates under the Esso Marketers were called either "Standard Esso" or "Colonial Esso" stations, the latter under Colonial Beacon. Stations selling Jersey products but operated by independent managers were designated as "Standard Esso Dealer" or "Colonial Esso Dealer." Esso, a name first given to the premium-grade gasoline introduced in 1926, was at this time used extensively where Standard had been used previously. Jersey preferred Esso as a brand name to distinguish its products from those of nonaffiliates using the Standard name.[62]

On Stewart's recommendation, an important addition was made to the headquarters organization in New York: a research group to determine the strengths and weaknesses of current practices and to recommend improvements. Dr. Frank M. Surface, who had been in charge of market research in the United States Department of Commerce during President Hoover's administration, was engaged to head this new staff. A leader in the founding of the American Management Association, he was known as an advocate of the improvement of management generally.

Dr. Surface set up a combined sales research and statistical department. In cooperation with J. C. Anderson, who was in charge of sales accounting for the four companies, he soon changed the methods of reporting so as to make current figures available. Each month the division managers submitted statements on costs and on profit and loss; every six months they supplemented these by detailed reports. As a result of this information and of the constant stressing of economy and profit by the New York office, the sales managers were gradually changed from being volume-minded to being profit-minded, a shift that eventually revitalized the whole sales organization.[63]

Formal cost surveys as a basis for determining where reductions might be made were also undertaken. These began in 1933 with time studies of the activities of the personnel in six New Jersey service stations. It was found that about three-fifths of the employees' time was unproductive. Tank-truck costs were investigated in the next year. These indicated that better scheduling of deliveries to service stations and the installation of more suitable tanks for storing gasoline would reduce costs. These were only the beginnings of a whole series of studies planned for the next few years.[64]

Consumer surveys to determine the attitude of the public toward the gasolines of Jersey's affiliates were also started in 1933 under Dr. Surface's direction. J. David Hauser Associates, who were among the pioneers in the field of measuring consumer attitudes, were employed. Their investigators found that people generally believed that there was little quality difference among leading brands. The surveys indicated that Jersey would have to take positive action to improve its marketing position. It should do more extensive advertising and should emphasize better service at stations.[65]

The research staff also set up quotas for each sales division. These formed the basis for contests running from the middle of 1933 to the end of 1934. *The Salesmotor* reported division sales monthly. In January, 1935, the New York division was announced the winner. This type of contest was used for several years. Others were also started, such as the "Sales for Safety" campaign in 1933 and a drive to improve the cleanliness of rest rooms in service stations in 1934.[66]

Stewart also initiated a plan for improving the performance of the individual salesman. Arrangements were made with the La Salle Extension University (a correspondence school in Chicago) to handle a new training program based on data obtained from Jersey and other companies in the oil industry. The courses offered were designed to give salesmen the type of training needed by each individual for his particular work. Many of the men were astounded by this plan to "make them go back to school"; some even left the company rather than take the prescribed courses. Generally, however, they recognized the advisability of participating, and after a few weeks there was a rush to enroll. But the general effect on the morale of the salesmen was not good.[67]

The work of the sales engineering department became of special importance. This department established a close and continuing liaison between the marketing organization and the research and engineering groups in Standard Oil Development; such communication enabled the former to bring to the latter's attention the need for new products and for improving old ones to meet service requirements. Manager Lee also headed up a formal recruitment program. He visited colleges and universities to hire promising young men. The new employees were given an intensive three-month course in fuels and lubricants engineering. Some men who completed the work remained as sales engineers, but most of them became salesmen. This department also brought with it from Standard Oil Development the publication of *Lubetext,* the manual introduced in 1931. And in 1934 the engineering group collaborated with the advertising staff in introducing *Esso Oilways,* a company periodical devoted to industrial lubrication problems and methods. Thus, technical training, thinking, and practice were being introduced into organizations formerly known for their pragmatic ways.[68]

The sales organizations were greatly helped by improvements in the quality of products. The refineries in 1933 produced a new regular gasoline, Essolene, and in 1934 a new premium grade, Aerotype Esso. Both Essolene, which contained tetraethyl lead, and the new grade, which met specifications for aviation gasoline (except for a modification in its volatility), ranked high in quality. These two gasolines gave the Esso Marketers an advantage that helped them not only to increase their sales but also to improve their relative position. They gained a larger percentage of the total business in their old marketing areas.[69]

The introduction of Essolene was accompanied by an important statement of policy by Jersey directors. They pledged that the quality of the products of the affiliates would henceforth be kept as high as, if not higher than, that of the products of their competitors. This pledge was published in *The Salesmotor* in August, 1933, as follows: "The company has assumed the quality leadership in the production of petroleum products and intends to hold that leadership against all comers. Today we have the best products on the market, bar none, and the Standard Oil Company has determined that when it is possible to produce better products they will carry its labels and trademarks." Copies were distributed throughout the sales territory and posted in offices and service stations.

In 1934, as compared to a decline in 1932 and a small gain in 1933, the sales of the companies whose marketing was managed by the Esso Marketers rose considerably in volume. However, in 1934 this marketing group was still operating at a loss. The heaviest losses occurred in the territory of Standard of Louisiana and of the new affiliates, Colonial Beacon and Standard of Pennsylvania.[70]

Stewart's role as director in charge of the marketing of the four companies lasted less than two years. He resigned in February, 1935, because of conflicts between his personal life and his own business dealings, on the one hand, and his responsibilities as a Jersey director, on the other. In his short term as manager, he had started important developments in organization and operations. His successor as general sales manager of the Esso Marketers was Robert T. Haslam, who reported directly to Jersey's Executive Committee.[71]

At the time Haslam became manager, conditions were growing more favorable for the marketers. Economic recovery was getting under way. Crude oil production was coming under more effective control in several states. The more normal relations between supply and demand were helping to stabilize the market. Competition continued to be intense, but it was depending less on extreme price cutting and more on the quality of products, improved service, and advertising. Prices were rising, a trend that was to last until economic recession and an oversupply again struck the oil industry in 1937. Prices then again turned downward; by 1939 they were down to approximately the 1934 level.[72]

Haslam's talent for understanding and handling men solved a critical problem soon after he became head of the marketers. Knowing that the morale of the employees had been badly shattered by the turmoil of the immediately preceding years, he saw the need to establish closer relations and a better rapport between headquarters and men in the field. One of his first undertakings was a three-week tour of operations accompanied by a group of sales executives. This trip was followed by similar visits to other parts of the territory of the Esso Marketers. Haslam also provided opportunities at sales meetings for salesmen to tell of their progress in the presence of top marketing officials. These tours and meetings did much to raise the morale of the marketing organization—salesmen are on record with statements revealing how the general manager raised their confidence in themselves and gave them a sense of the importance of their jobs.[73]

Haslam also made changes in the organization of the Esso Marketers in order to bring about better supervision as well as a more effective handling of particular operations. He decentralized responsibility still further by setting up four or more districts in each sales division, each headed by a manager who reported to the division head. At the same time the tank-car business was decentralized to the extent of assigning a representative to each field division. But a national-accounts group was set up in New York to correct the situation in which customers' firms operating in more than one sales area were being solicited by salesmen from each area. A liquefied-gas division was also established in the New York office to handle the promotion of the sale of bottled gas to homes and industry.[74]

A radical change in marketing policy, organization, and operations came as a result of a movement that was started in 1935. This was action on the part of states to tax chain stores after such a tax in West Virginia had been declared constitutional. Although such laws were originally aimed at grocery chains, they came to be applied to other types, including service stations. The response of Standard of Indiana to such a tax law in Iowa set a pattern that was followed extensively throughout the oil industry. Indiana's innovation, known as the Iowa Plan, was to lease its stations to men who would operate them as independent businessmen, setting their own retail prices but buying products from the company. Other large companies adopted a similar procedure—even in states where such tax legislation had not yet been passed—in the belief that such laws would be enacted later or that the federal government might take action against companies setting prices from the well to the ultimate consumer.[75] Undoubtedly there was another contributing factor: federal regulation of hours of work and rates of pay, regulations which increased the difficulty and cost of operating service stations.[76]

Jersey's affiliates were among those who turned over the operation of service stations to individuals. Standard Oil Company of New Jersey negotiated such transfers in the states in which it operated, and Standard of Louisiana, Standard of Pennsylvania, and Colonial Beacon followed suit. Humble, alone among the affiliates, held out against this movement, but because of high operating costs it also eventually reduced the number of its company-operated stations.[77]

The companies whose marketing was handled by the Esso Marketers leased their stations to individuals, who then purchased their supplies from the lessor but operated independently. Although the operation of service stations had generally been profitable for the companies, representatives of the New York office tried to convince managers of local Esso outlets that it was better for them to become independent businessmen. Many were reluctant to give up their equity and security as Jersey employees. However, by the end of 1936, only eight of the stations formerly owned and operated by Jersey's affiliates (not including Humble) were still managed by the companies themselves. Several were kept as training stations for sales personnel and as a source of information on service-station standards, methods, and costs.[78]

Before Jersey had begun to study the plan of Standard of Indiana for leasing service stations to independent operators, the chief executives of the two companies had been discussing the possibility of making available in the Middle West two of Jersey's lubricants, Essomarine and Essolube. The Indiana company then maintained that the Esso brand name would encroach on its own Standard Oil brands because the pronunciation of "S.O." was identical with that of Esso. Jersey therefore did not move to introduce Esso in Indiana's operating territory.[79]

In March, 1935, however, Haslam unexpectedly heard of a prospective change in brand name by Standard of Indiana that was highly significant to Jersey. He added the following as a postscript to a letter of March 15 to President Teagle:

Since writing the foregoing, I have talked with Mr. Stewart who tells me he recently heard that the Indiana Company, who used to put out a Gasoline called "Solite," are now preparing to change the name of that product to

ESSOLITE and are going to start quite an advertising campaign. If the Indiana Company moves along these lines, we feel confident that we will lose our rights to the name ESSO in their territory, and our only hope of maintaining this right will be by aggressive action which will put the Indiana Company on the defensive. The safest method that appeals to me of protecting our trade mark in the Indiana territory is the suggestion previously made: that we put in a small string of stations in some city like Chicago with all of our regular identification and product names, with the station carrying in a prominent position the statement that it is in no wise connected with the Standard Oil Company (Indiana). It is our positive feeling that if this situation is temporized any longer we will be outmaneuvered and lose our rights to the ESSO trade mark in the Indiana territory.

Jersey's directors acted at once to put the Esso brand to a test. Esso, Incorporated, which had been formed in 1932 to sell Esso Handy Oil to distributors in all parts of the United States, became the corporate vehicle for the test. On April 16, 1935, this corporation opened three service stations and a bulk plant in St. Louis. These outlets offered Esso brands and advertised extensively.

Standard of Indiana thereupon brought suit to enjoin the company from marketing under Esso, Standard, or any similar name in the territory in which Indiana itself carried on business. Its complaint was that, since Esso was obviously an abbreviation for Standard Oil, Jersey was capitalizing on the Standard Oil name in Indiana's own territory. The judge of the District Court in St. Louis upheld this contention in July, 1937, and enjoined Jersey from using Esso in Indiana's territory. The case was appealed to the Circuit Court, which in July, 1938, affirmed the injunction. Esso, Incorporated, consequently had to dispose of its properties in St. Louis, and Jersey did not again in the 1930's try to establish operations in the Middle West.[80]

At the same time, Haslam was rearranging the chains of command in the marketing organization. The retail and wholesale divisions at headquarters in New York were merged in July, 1936, a change brought about as a result of the virtual disappearance of retail gasoline sales. In addition, the territory covered by the Esso Marketers from Maine to Louisiana was divided into two parts, the northern under C. G. Sheffield and the southern under J. E. Skehan. Each of these areas was divided into two regions, each in turn having two or more local districts.[81]

The virtual elimination of the retail selling of the major product and the accompanying organizational changes in 1935 and 1936 marked an important change in policy at home. Ever since the Standard Oil group had been formed, it had tried to get closer to the ultimate consumer. The last step had been taken before the turn of the century through peddling kerosene on city streets and later, with the coming of the gasoline age, through selling gasoline in company-operated stations. The company's virtual retreat from supplying motorists directly ended its program of only about a decade to expand in a market in which some of its competitors had become strong. At this later time, however, the general withdrawal of large, integrated oil companies from service-station operation changed the competitive situation from what it had been earlier.

Other changes were brought about in the organization of the Esso Marketers under Haslam as manager. By 1938 there were sixteen special groups or divisions in the New York office, some old and familiar but others representing new developments or a greater emphasis on certain services. Among the special products or consumer outlets handled by separate divisions were asphalt, automotive, aviation, fuel oil, lubricants, oil burners, railroads, and TBA. Relating to services or functions applying to the whole marketing effort were divisions having to do with advertising and sales promotion, construction and maintenance, personnel and training, research, and costs and operations.[82]

The increase in the number of headquarters divisions devoted to individual products illustrates the greater number sold in substantial volume. Such old majors as gasoline, kerosene, fuel oil, and lubricants were still the most important in terms of both volume and dollar sales, but the distribution of other products was also being successfully promoted by the Esso Marketers. A special group for asphalt sales was needed in order to keep up with the tremendous expansion of road construction and with the increasing manufacture of roofing and other materials derived from petroleum that were utilized in building construction. The addition of an aviation department indicated the growing importance of supplying that industry with high-octane gasoline and suitable lubricants. The consumption of fuel oil by railroads was rising, and so also was the use of kerosene (range oil) in homes and of other fuel oils for heating dwellings and commercial and public buildings. The sale of oil burners also increased with the rise in the use of oil as fuel. To promote the use of household fuels, the Esso Marketers carried on contests for salesmen. The winners in 1936 and in 1937 were given trips to Bermuda and in the next two years to Miami.[83]

A vigorous campaign was carried on to make the Esso brand more widely known and its products favorably regarded. In the 1930's this brand was being applied to a greater range of products. For example, Essoleum was being used for greases, and Essolite, Essowax, Essoburner, Essotane, Essofleet, and Solvesso for various other products. The brand itself was intended to stand as a symbol of high quality.[84]

Indeed, as the price situation became more or less stabilized and competition shifted more and more to the quality of products, it became essential to stress quality in sales. Haslam urged the necessity of keeping Jersey's pledge to maintain the company's leading branded products at a level as good as, if not better than, that of the products of competitors. However, quality was not a static thing. The competitive striving to improve it, together with the growing demand for products tailored to changing needs, necessitated constant attention to defining and meeting new standards. The sales engineers were equipped to work with the refiners in analyzing such needs and setting new objectives.[85]

The refiners made notable improvements in various products, including lubricants, but upgrading the quality of gasoline, as the major product sold by the marketers, became especially important. For some time in the late 1930's, Essolene, the regular grade of gasoline sold by the Esso Marketers, was surpassed in volatility and antiknock performance by the product of certain competitors. Jersey affiliates raised the performance of both the regular and the premium grade by blending selected petroleum fractions to improve volatility and adding more tetraethyl lead to raise the octane rating. The resulting regular grade actually met the minimum standards for the premium grade that had been set by Ethyl Gasoline Corporation. Both grades were renamed, becoming Esso and Esso Extra in 1939. By that time, however, the race was on to produce high-octane gasoline in large quantity by the use of catalytic cracking.[86]

To guide the marketers in sales promotion campaigns, Dr. Surface's research staff continued to make studies of consumer purchasing and of various media for making Esso products and brand names better known. These provided definite guidance as to the usefulness of different kinds of advertising. They showed that more than 50 per cent of the individuals approached remembered either radio or billboard advertising, whereas only from 2 to 5 per cent recalled newspaper advertising. The Esso Marketers were spending considerable sums on the first two of these media. In 1935, although McCann-Erickson, Inc., was still retained for billboard and newspaper advertising, the firm of Marschalk & Pratt was engaged to prepare commercials for a radio program called "The Esso Reporter." Arrangements were made with the United Press to be responsible for the news portion of the broadcast. It was said that this program represented the first combination of commercial sponsoring and straight news reporting in the United States. Some newsmen doubted that the United Press would have complete freedom in the broadcasts, but the service maintained its independence. In 1939 "The Esso Reporter" was reaching all the territory of the Esso Marketers; it was on the air for five-minute periods four times a day and six days a week. Consumers remembered this program, and the Esso Marketers obtained a suitable kind of advertising at a reasonable cost.[87]

Various means, new and old, were used to raise the effectiveness of the sales personnel. The effort to select employees more carefully that had been started by Lee under Stewart was maintained. The controversial correspondence courses were dropped. Instead, Esso employees and dealers attended field meetings, special courses lasting a few days, or a series of weekly discussion meetings. These ways of giving further training—similar in some respects to the customary conventions of business-men—were acceptable to the sales force and resulted in greater efficiency and drive on their part.[88]

The engineers became a vital part of the marketing organization under Haslam. Trained in scientific methods, these specialists sought a logical analysis and rational solution of marketing problems, and they helped to define the qualities required in products designed for specific purposes and machines. This approach had been applied in the two preceding years by Surface in research and by Lee in sales engineering, but under Haslam it came to have a greater influence throughout the organization. More and more, men with engineering training took the place of those who retired. This change from the leadership of practical men to that of others trained in science and engineering came later in marketing than in production and refining. However, it was a necessary development if the products offered were to be suited to the special needs of the market, and if they were to be supplied efficiently and economically to the benefit of the consumer and of the company itself.

A major concern of the Esso Marketers was the reduction of costs. This was necessary as price competition pressed on their gross margin, that is, on the spread between the bulk-station cost and the tank-wagon price to service stations. This spread, which had been 5 cents per gallon of gasoline in 1929 and 3 cents in 1932, narrowed to 2.75 cents in 1938 and 2 cents in 1939. The marketers' gross margin had to cover all costs from refinery to service station, general administrative expenses—and (it was

hoped) profits. Various staff divisions at headquarters worked with the
operating organizations on cost problems.

Guided by the recommendations of the sales research department
under Dr. Surface and assisted by J. R. Riddell, who was in charge of
cost and operations work, the marketers succeeded in reducing bulk-
station and delivery costs. They rearranged the routing of trucks so as to
eliminate waste in driving. They also introduced the use of larger trucks
for long hauls from bulk plants to service stations and installed larger
storage tanks at the stations in order to make less frequent deliveries
possible. Such measures had produced real economies by 1939 and were
to bring even greater results later.[89] The Esso Marketers reduced average
selling costs, which had been 3.09 cents per gallon of gasoline in 1931, to
1.89 cents—almost a 40 per cent cut. Standard Oil Company of New
Jersey ranked first in the reductions made, Colonial Beacon second,
Standard of Pennsylvania third, and Standard of Louisiana fourth.[90]

In a letter to Jersey's comptroller in April, 1936, President Teagle called
attention to one cost increase in offices: the cost of meeting a greater
demand for reporting to company offices and the government. The Jersey
executive expressed his feeling of frustration over the development in this
way: "It sort of struck me that between the multiplication of reports to
the government and to our various departments, the time might not be
far distant when our products could go forward to consumers by mail
and our report forms by freight in car-load lots."[91]

Increased attention was given to the cost of stations. The construction and maintenance staff at headquarters worked on plans and specifications for new bulk and service stations. Under Haslam's management, a
way to expand the number of dealer outlets without requiring company
funds was adopted. A landowner would be located who was willing to
build a station and supply the capital. His expenditure was protected by
a lease to the affiliate engaged in marketing in that particular area, and
the affiliate in turn leased the station to the operator, who became the
Esso dealer.[92]

A reduction in the total cost of products delivered to the bulk stations
of the marketers was also made in some regions by reducing the expense
of transporting products from refineries to bulk stations. However,
greater efficiency in this operation was the responsibility of the transportation organizations and not of the marketers. Standard of Pennsylvania for a short time had an advantage over competitors because of the
economies effected by the Tuscarora pipeline, and other companies

whose marketing was handled by the Esso Marketers had similar advantages in tanker and barge transportation to bulk terminals. But some of the affiliates were at a disadvantage because they were not served by product pipelines or deepwater terminals to the extent that certain competitors were. A beginning was made toward providing new product carriers by the planning of the Plantation Pipe Line Company in 1939. The opening of a new deepwater terminal at Albany in December, 1937, reduced the cost of handling products on the way to bulk stations for a large area. Another such terminal was constructed in Portland, Maine.[93]

The Esso Marketers made substantial progress toward realizing the objectives for which they were organized. They greatly increased the sales volume of the marketing departments of the affiliates under their management. And they improved the earnings of those departments.

Table 8 shows total annual sales of the Esso Marketers. The total was 76.6 per cent larger in 1939 than in 1933. Similar statistics are not avail-

Table 8:   **ANNUAL PRODUCT SALES BY AFFILIATES IN THE UNITED STATES, 1927–1939**
Standard Oil Company (New Jersey)
(In thousands of 42-gallon barrels)

Year	Four Marketing Departments and the Esso Marketers[a]	Marketing Organizations of Other Companies[b]	General Office Sales[c]	Total
1927	d	4,015	d	89,425
1928	d	7,320	d	92,598
1929	d	7,300	d	102,200
1930	43,435	6,935	50,005	100,375
1931	41,975	4,745	42,340	89,060
1932	38,796	5,490	50,508	94,794
1933	40,515	5,840	60,225	106,580
1934	45,260	4,015	48,910	98,185
1935	47,450	2,190	52,925	102,565
1936	54,168	4,392	56,730	115,290
1937	58,765	5,840	64,605	129,210
1938	62,415	5,840	60,955	129,210
1939	71,540	5,475	64,240	141,255

ª Sales by companies whose marketing came under the Esso Marketers in 1934: Standard Oil Company (N.J.) and its 1927 successor in operations, Standard Oil Company of New Jersey; Standard Oil Company of Louisiana; Standard Oil Company of Pennsylvania after its organization in 1928; and Colonial Beacon Oil Company after a majority of its stock was acquired in 1929. Included also are sales of lubricating oils and greases of Pennsylvania Lubricating Company, which was renamed Penola Inc. in 1934.
ᵇ Includes specialty companies and Humble Oil & Refining Company.

ᶜ Sales at the refineries on contract to large accounts in the United States. Does not include Humble's sales to Jersey's affiliates for their own marketing or export sales.
ᵈ Figures not available. Estimates for 1927 are 40,150,000 barrels for the Marketing Departments and 45,260,000 barrels for General Office Sales.
Sources: Standard Oil Company (N.J.): Statistics on deliveries of products; Annual Statistical Review, 1950. Esso Standard Oil Company: Contract sales statistics, 1930–1939.

able for the whole oil industry in the same area. However, comparison with the increase in the national distribution of major refinery products—motor fuels, kerosene, lubricating oil, and fuel oil—has some significance: total sales under the Esso Marketers were 5.3 per cent of total national sales of the four products in 1933 and 6 per cent in 1939.[94]

On a nationwide basis, Jersey improved its position in the sale of gasoline. Its share of the national market rose from 6 per cent in 1933 to 6.9 per cent in 1939. This gain included Humble's business also, but actually this affiliate lost slightly in its marketing territory. Jersey's total still ranked below that of Socony-Vacuum, Standard of Indiana, and The Texas Company.

Jersey was keeping up with what was virtually an oil-industry movement in the direction of nationwide distribution. At the end of the 1930's, it was competing in many states with one or more of its former affiliates, some of which had expanded beyond their 1911 boundaries. It was also competing with other large marketers, ten of which had increased the number of states in which they were operating from an average of fifteen in 1926 to twenty-eight in 1939. A number of other concerns were active in several states, these smaller companies having almost 30 per cent of the national gasoline business in 1939.

The total marketing earnings of the operations under the Esso Marketers improved in the later 1930's, but varied from company to company. Standard Oil Company of New Jersey had a good increase in net earnings on its marketing operations. Standard of Pennsylvania and Colonial Beacon failed to achieve satisfactory records. These two companies still had many problems to solve before their products could be sold profitably throughout their territories. As Farish stated before a subcommittee of the House Judiciary Committee in Washington in June, 1939, "Seldom can a company in any industry break into a new territory already well developed by important competitors without a considerable period of substantial losses." He mentioned that Colonial Beacon was at a transportation disadvantage in many areas and that many of its leases for stations were too costly. He also pointed to the fact that Standard of Pennsylvania had made large investments to extend its operations. A disadvantage of Colonial Beacon was the large proportion of its sales of fuel oils and heavier products—and indeed of all products—made to large accounts on which the margin was narrow.[95] Earnings on marketing operations, before administrative costs and other charges and income taxes, averaged approximately 1.25 per cent on the affiliates' net investment in marketing properties from 1934 through 1939.[96]

In January, 1940, Haslam wrote a letter to two members of the Esso Marketers organization which summarized the gains made through 1939 and looked to the future for continued improvement. He noted that domestic marketing profits had risen steadily from 1934 and that this rise had been accompanied by a gain in position in the market. His purpose in reviewing these accomplishments, he wrote, was "not only to acknowledge the splendid work done by the entire organization" but also to "demonstrate the possibility of piling improved performance on improved performance to an extent not normally dreamed of." Their goal for 1940, Haslam concluded, should be to overcome obstacles and achieve new records.[97]

GENERAL OFFICE SALES, 1933–1939

Although the total contract sales of the domestic affiliates did not rise as much as the sales of the marketing organizations in the 1930's, they nevertheless increased substantially. They were affected by two unfavorable developments: a severe decline in exports and the growing self-sufficiency of Jersey's customers among oil companies outside its own group. But the contract business operated within a rising general demand for petroleum products.

Jersey's domestic affiliates lost much of their export market—mostly to other Jersey companies abroad. According to company statistics on exports, the total export of major products in 1939 was approximately 40 per cent of the total in 1927. The export total in 1939 furnished only about 10 per cent of the whole Jersey Company's sales abroad in 1939, whereas exports had provided 60 per cent of foreign sales in 1927.

Sales to nonaffiliated oil companies in the United States—Jersey's large traditional outlets outside its own affiliates—constituted a decreasing percentage of total contract sales. Socony-Vacuum, with which Standard of New York had merged, took the low daily average of 7,500 barrels in 1939. However, another old customer, Standard of Kentucky, kept Jersey's total sales to its former affiliates from slumping badly; in 1939 the Kentucky company purchased a daily average of 42,000 barrels.[98] This company, in fact, represented the exception to the rule that marketers among oil companies were obtaining more and more of their products from their own operations. The terms of the contracts with this concern in the 1930's have not been ascertained, but it is said that Standard of

Kentucky was a firm negotiator and sometimes obtained products from Standard of Louisiana at lower prices than those paid by Jersey affiliates.

New contract customers were also obtained, but the most important one purchased large amounts for only a limited number of years: the Mexican Petroleum Company, an affiliate of Standard of Indiana. This company had heavy supply obligations to the American Oil Company, but lost its source of products when Jersey purchased Indiana's foreign properties in 1932. Under the tariff act of 1932, it could not have profitably imported what it needed. This enabled Jersey to negotiate a contract to supply gasoline from its domestic refineries with which Mexican Petroleum could meet its obligations to its large customer. Jersey also undertook to furnish that company with Bunker C fuel. Under these contracts, the buyer took an average of 73,000 barrels daily in 1933 and declining amounts thereafter, the daily average in 1939 being 22,000 barrels. A new customer—Fleetwing, an affiliate of Standard of Ohio— took a daily average of 2,000 barrels in 1937 and continued to purchase the same amount through 1938 and 1939.[99]

Shipping concerns remained good customers. But great quantities of fuel oil came to be imported in bond to bunker ships in ports on the East Coast engaged in foreign trade. In 1939 such bunkering was supplied from Aruba to the extent of 15,000,000 barrels (a daily average of approximately 41,000 barrels).[100]

In terms of volume, other types of outlets were of less importance, but one was believed to have great potential for growth. In 1935 the success of Jersey's research and refining organizations in the production of high-octane gasoline enabled the company to obtain contracts to supply the United States Army Air Corps with this fuel. The first 100-octane contract was entered into in 1935. The business thereafter grew as fast as Jersey affiliates could supply the gasoline. Even before they could make the 100-octane grade in large quantities, they supplied rising amounts of high-quality aviation fuel. In 1938 Humble sold to the Army Air Corps 70 per cent of its requirements for its extensive training operations in Texas. Humble also had a large part of the commercial aviation business in that state.[101]

The general sales offices sold relatively small amounts of products to consumers among the Jersey companies. For example, Standard Shipping and its successor, the Marine Department of Standard Oil Company of New Jersey, raised its purchases from 3,400 barrels daily in 1933 to 7,300 in 1939. And the specialty companies also bought whatever petroleum ingredients they needed in manufacturing their types of products.[102] The larger portion of the sales of Jersey's domestic refineries was transfers between affiliates and between departments within an affiliate for distribution by the marketing organizations of the companies themselves. These were not considered in the same category as general office sales to outside distributors or to consumers inside or outside the Jersey group.

Despite shifts in the outlets through large-volume contracts, such sales by Jersey affiliates within the United States rose substantially from 1927 to 1939. Although affected by the depression, they were approximately 5 per cent higher in 1933 than in 1927. In 1939 they were larger by about 40 per cent than in 1927. But they had yielded first rank in both volume and rate of growth to the marketing organizations of the domestic affiliates.

THE SPECIALTY COMPANIES, 1927–1939

A varied group of companies marketed outside the organizations selling the major petroleum products and, in fact, operated more or less independently. Jersey's Director Bedford had particular administrative responsibility for these companies, first as chief executive officer and, after the reorganization of 1933, as supervisory representative of the parent company's Board of Directors.[103]

In December, 1927, Jersey organized Stanco, Incorporated, to coordinate this business. Stanco was both a wholesaler and a holding company. It sold to distributors in scores of countries, and it held the stock of several domestic affiliates. One company was Stanco Distributors, Inc., which had been organized in 1925 to sell specialty products to wholesalers and retailers in states where Jersey was not authorized to sell. Another was Daggett & Ramsdell, Inc., the compounder and distributor of cosmetics purchased by Jersey in 1928. A third was Esso, Incorporated, organized in 1932 to sell Esso Handy Oil nationwide.

The specialties made and sold by these companies used petroleum ingredients, but were outside the usual range of oil products. Among them were the well-known insecticide called Flit, a mineral oil sold under the brand name of Nujol, synthetic alcohols for various uses, cosmetics under the Daggett & Ramsdell name, and the household lubricant named Esso Handy Oil. Under Bedford's direction, the number and variety of these specialties were increased, and their manufacture benefited from the substitution of scientific principles for the rule-of-thumb methods formerly used.

The specialty companies had their own sales organizations.[104] They were wholesale distributors selling to jobbers and retailers. Their products reached the consumers through such retail outlets as drug, hardware, and general stores. Flit was also sold in service stations. Having no direct contact with the retail customers, these concerns advertised extensively in popular magazines in order to stimulate the demand for their special products.

In fact, the specialty affiliates as a group were quite different from the organizations primarily engaged in the mass production, transportation, and distribution of products for which there was a large demand. Their products had a very limited market compared with that of the major petroleum products. On the whole, the volume sold by the specialty companies even declined, and they had a poor record of earnings in the later 1930's.[105] However, they provided outlets, although in relatively small volume, for various kinds of refinery products. They also furnished means for introducing new ones, some of which in time became important, and they extended the sales of the Jersey companies into sections of the United States where the affiliates could not themselves operate.

In this period, the Jersey Company adjusted well to shifts in the market for the products of the oil industry of the United States. Although its domestic affiliates lost a large part of their foreign outlets, they became more important as suppliers within the United States. They significantly won a stronger position in the domestic mass market for major petroleum products. This development in distribution gave Jersey what may be called a complete domestic oil circuit. That is, the affiliates produced and purchased within the United States most of the crude oil processed by their refineries, and they sold the products principally at home to the whole range of customers from large-volume contract buyers to service stations supplying the individual motorist.

The record of Jersey's domestic marketers shows significant accomplishments. Like other branches of operations, marketing experienced important developments in location, management, and technology. Geographic expansion extended the affiliates' marketing into the Middle Atlantic and northeastern states that were high-per-capita consumers of petroleum products. The thrust of change in management was in the direction of better coordination at the top and a greater decentralization in operations. Along with these developments went the adoption of an engineering approach to selling, the employment of better statistical and research techniques, and the improvement of the general competence of managerial and sales personnel. Under new leadership and new disciplines, the marketers changed from conservative and cautious to driving organizations ready to consider innovations of all kinds.

Selected statistics give a rough measure of their accomplishments. In 1939 they sold 80 per cent more products than they had sold in 1927, but their net operating earnings in the later year were only about half those of the earlier one.[106] Some light is shed on their earnings by the gross margin and cost in the marketing of gasoline. In 1939, the gross margin of the marketers was down to 2 cents a gallon, and the average selling cost per gallon was 1.89 cents. Accordingly, operating earnings on the sale of gasoline averaged 0.11 cent per gallon.[107]

In marketing as in other branches of operations, improved methods contributed to a decline in costs which enabled the company to earn profits despite a severe reduction in the prices of products. Gasoline provides illuminating data on the price decline. The average tank-wagon price in Baltimore in 1939 was down to 47 per cent of the 1926 level; in fifty representative cities in the United States, the 1939 price was 51 per cent of the 1926 figure.[108] In the later year, the Wholesale Commodity Price Index of the United States Bureau of Labor Statistics stood at 77 per cent of the 1926 index. It is a fair conclusion that the Jersey Company and its industry in the United States had served both themselves and the consumer well.[109]

Chapter 11

Readjustment and Growth in Foreign Markets, 1927–1939

I N THE FOREIGN MARKET as at home, Standard Oil Company (New Jersey) was meeting rising competition. Although its percentage of total sales abroad had been falling since 1911 despite a large increase in volume, in 1927 it was still one of the three leading suppliers of oil products outside the United States. Jersey's top administrators recognized, however, that in an intense struggle for foreign markets, the company would be in a weaker position than its leading international competitors.

In order to maintain Jersey's position abroad, the company's policy makers and planners after 1927 moved forward along several lines. Advances in production, refining, and transportation have been considered in earlier chapters. The focus of this chapter is on the efforts of the parent company and its affiliates to improve their sales organizations and operations and generally to adjust to changing conditions affecting the sale of oil products outside the United States.

COMPETITION AND COOPERATION IN FOREIGN MARKETS, 1927–1939

In 1927 Jersey had affiliates marketing in Canada, in all parts of Latin America, and throughout Continental Europe.[1] It did not carry on such operations in Great Britain or in the Middle East or Far East, in all of which it had lost its affiliates in the dissolution of 1911. Although the company had increased its total sales abroad by nearly 150 per cent from 1911 to 1927, it no longer commanded the percentage of the business in markets outside the United States that it had once held. After World War I, its affiliates in many countries, especially in Europe, had had to cope with depressed economic conditions, increasing governmental regulations, and growing competition.

The basic weakness of the foreign marketing affiliates was their dependence upon American products while their leading competitors sold products made from lower-cost crude oils produced on large concessions in Venezuela, Persia, and other countries. Jersey had tried for many years to build up its foreign production, but it had had only limited success. For some years after 1911, it had been able to purchase crude in any amount at favorable prices, especially in Mexico. But its sources had become less dependable as production in that country had declined and as producing companies generally had gone into refining and marketing and others specializing in selling products had acquired their own production and refining.

Anglo-Persian Oil Company had become one of Jersey's two rivals in the international oil market. After World War I, under the management of Sir John Cadman, it had upset the old competitive order. Not only was it strong in itself, but it also had the support of Great Britain. The British government owned half of its stock, and Anglo-Persian had a contract to furnish much of the oil required by His Majesty's Navy. In addition, the company worked closely with Burmah Oil Company, Limited, an integrated concern which had production and markets in the Far East and which owned a third of Anglo-Persian's stock.[2]

Anglo-Persian had a firm base in crude oil production in the Middle East. In 1927 its output from a large field in Persia reached 41,000,000 barrels, or three times its production in 1920.[3] Most of this Persian crude production was processed at the Abadan refinery to provide fuel oil and also light products that were distributed by both the company itself and by Royal Dutch–Shell. Some of the Persian crude was refined in Wales, Scotland, France, and Australia; the products were marketed by many companies. Although the shipping distance from Abadan to Northern Europe was much greater than from the Gulf of Mexico, Persian oil was produced at costs that were low enough so that it could compete with American oil in European markets.

The Royal Dutch–Shell group of companies, of which Sir Henri Deterding had been the managing director for many years and which had long had a firm position in European and Oriental markets, had also expanded greatly after World War I. This group—40 per cent owned by The Shell Transport & Trading Company, Limited, and 60 per cent by N.V. Koninklijke Nederlandsche Petroleum Maatschappij—had been fortunate in its ties with two imperial powers and as a beneficiary of British influence in many countries. Royal Dutch–Shell had invested in all types of oil properties in the most promising parts of the world. It had production in all the important oil-producing regions except in Russia, where its properties had been seized by the Communists.[4]

American companies—a few with considerable production abroad—had been expanding in foreign markets, especially after 1925, when they began to have difficulty disposing of all their products in the United States. These concerns included Gulf Oil and Standard of Indiana, both of which had production in Venezuela, and also Atlantic Refining, Sinclair, Cities Service, Tide Water Associated, The Texas Company, and smaller companies depending on domestic production. All were endeavoring in the later 1920's to find outlets in Europe and Latin America. Pacific Coast companies, such as Standard of California and Union Oil, were seeking larger markets in Asia and on the west coast of the Americas. As a whole, these Americans, through their foreign affiliates or through sales to marketing concerns abroad, were depressing prices and making competition more intense.

Two other American companies were in different circumstances: Standard Oil Company of New York and Vacuum Oil Company, both of which had for decades been successful marketers in various parts of the world. For its markets in the Far East, the former was depending only slightly on products from its own affiliates in California and Texas; it was purchasing supplies from the most advantageous sources—California, Romania, Russia, Persia, Burma, and the Dutch East Indies. Vacuum Oil Company—which through affiliates, other companies, or independent agents marketed in Europe and Asia Minor—was meeting rising competition from other distributors of its specialty, lubricants.[5]

Soviet Russia was a serious disturber of the established marketing pattern. In order to realize funds with which to purchase capital equipment, the Soviets were selling petroleum products from confiscated properties at lower prices than those of established companies. Russia had recovered sufficiently from its demoralization and destruction resulting from World War I and revolution to produce 75,000,000 barrels of oil and to export 20,000,000 in 1927. It sought outlets in England, where the major marketers cooperated in efforts to minimize the effects of this new Russian competition. Its oil was also upsetting the *status quo* in the East, especially in India, where Standard of New York was selling some of its purchased Russian products. This action of the American company greatly disturbed Deterding of Royal Dutch–Shell, who had been endeavoring to maintain a boycott of Russian oil until some arrangement could be made for the return of, or payment for, the oil properties seized from private owners in the 1920's. A fierce price war raged for a time in India between the American company selling Soviet oil and British and Dutch interests.[6]

As long as gross margins were sufficiently high, Jersey could make satisfactory profits from foreign marketing. But in a competitive struggle, declining prices would wipe out its margins sooner than those of companies whose products were made from lower-cost foreign crude oils. At the end of 1927, world crude inventories were at record levels.[7] Jersey's leading administrators believed that, in the prospective long-term overproduction and price decline, a company depending on American oil would be at a serious cost disadvantage.

Inasmuch as building up foreign production would take time, the immediately pressing question with regard to Jersey's foreign sales in the late 1920's was how best to meet at once the intense competition that was developing. The first moves of the company's officers and Board of Directors were defensive, both at home and abroad.

Jersey joined in an attempt to form an export association in the United States, still the largest source of supplies for many foreign markets. The formation of such an association had been made possible by the Webb-Pomerene Export Trade Act of 1918. This measure had been enacted to permit competing American companies to form associations for the sole purpose of engaging in export trade, provided that they did not thereby restrain that trade of any domestic competitor or commit any act that enhanced or depressed prices or substantially lessened competition within the United States. A letter written by the acting chairman of the Federal Trade Commission, in answer to an inquiry from the silver industry in 1924, had seemed to indicate the legality of such action.[8] This was the position taken by Gilbert H. Montague, a recognized specialist in the law bearing on export associations.[9]

The possibility of joint action interested many American oil industry leaders, including President Teagle. In the spring of 1928, Jersey's Director Riedemann prepared a draft of rules for such an association. After careful study by the company's other directors and revision with the help of Montague, the draft was presented by President Teagle at a meeting of the executives of the leading American oil concerns at 26 Broadway in October, 1928. Several companies decided to become members of the proposed Export Petroleum Association, Inc. However, although their desire to do something to relieve the serious oversupply in the oil market grew greater day by day, differences soon arose over prices and quotas. No agreement was ever reached, and participation by the American companies in this effort ceased late in 1930.[10]

British and British-Dutch companies, driven by the discovery and development of big fields in Persia and Venezuela in 1928, were also adjusting their operations to the changing situation. Anglo-Persian pressed for and received an outlet for its Persian oil in nearby India, a market which had previously been supplied mostly by Burmah Oil and Royal Dutch–Shell. Anglo-Persian and Royal Dutch–Shell agreed to combine their sales activities in Egypt, Palestine, Ceylon, East and South Africa, and along the Red Sea. They also merged their marketing companies in Great Britain to form The Shell-Mex & British Petroleum Company, Limited. At the same time, Burmah Oil tied the three groups more closely together by acquiring a million shares of The Shell Transport & Trading Company, Limited, and by taking a half-interest in a new company for selling products, the Burmah-Shell Oil Storage and Distributing Company of India, Limited. This closer cooperation of its leading foreign competitors did not augur well for Jersey's interests in the Eastern Hemisphere.[11]

Joint action by Jersey and Royal Dutch–Shell in the summer of 1928 relieved somewhat the troublesome situation that had arisen from the expropriation of oil properties in Russia. The two companies made arrangements for the purchase of quantities of Russian products for the British market; the purchasers were to contribute 5 per cent of the price to the Construction & Development Company, in which Royal Dutch–Shell took a half-interest and the Nobels and Jersey each a quarter-interest. The proceeds were to constitute a fund for compensating the companies for their expropriated properties in Russia. Although this arrangement did not solve the problem of Russian competition everywhere, it lessened the difficulties in England, where Soviet oil had been the most disturbing element in the market.[12]

Such efforts obviously could not solve the problems stemming from the worldwide overproduction of crude oil. Leaders in the international oil industry came to the conclusion that, in attempting to solve the problem of too much oil, they had to choose between a competitive fight and cooperation.

The weight of tradition and experience in foreign markets seemed to favor the second course.[13] Indeed, at that very time European companies in certain other industries were seeking to solve many of their problems by joint action. One method was to form associations of companies, that is, cartels, for one or more of the avowed purposes of fixing prices, allotting markets, and restricting production. Companies also sought such other solutions as entering into local marketing agreements, merging, becoming affiliates of holding companies, and licensing their patents, perhaps with provisions for restriction by areas. Governments, too, became active in making restrictive agreements, the most notable being the one made later by Great Britain, France, India, the Netherlands, and Siam (Thailand from 1949 on) for curtailing worldwide production of natural rubber.

In August, 1928, the heads of the three leading international oil companies, as noted in Chapter 3, met in Scotland at the Achnacarry castle of Sir Henri Deterding of Royal Dutch–Shell. Jersey's Director Riedemann, who had been active in formulating plans, accompanied President Teagle, as also did directors Moffett and Mowinckel.[14] The executives of the three companies reportedly met to shoot grouse, but their real purpose was to discuss the world oil situation. On September 17, 1928, Teagle, Deterding, and Cadman approved a statement of principles entitled "Pool Association." Although they did not sign the statement, it came to be known as the "Achnacarry Agreement" or the "As-Is Agreement." The preamble, which set forth the difficulties existing in the world oil industry, expressed their conception of the problems they were considering:

Since its inception, the oil industry has looked forward with apprehension to the gradual depletion and final exhaustion of its supplies of crude oil. The temporary shortage of supplies that existed in certain countries during the great war further accentuated this fear and caused vast sums of good money to be expended to locate and develop reserves in all parts of the world where petroleum potentialities appeared, as well as in accumulating large reserve stocks above ground.

Now the situation has changed. An adequate supply for a long time to come is assured. This is the result of the application of science to the petroleum industry. More effective methods of handling crude have been developed so that the yield of gasoline from a given amount of crude has been enormously increased. . . .

Excessive competition has resulted in the tremendous overproduction today, when over the world the shut-in production amounts to approximately 60% of the production actually going into consumption. In other branches of the business, overcompetition has had a similar result, so that it may be fairly said that money has been poured into manufacturing and marketing facilities so prodigally that those now available are far in excess of those required to handle efficiently the present world's consumption.

Up to the present each large unit has tried to take care of its own over-production and tried to increase its sales at the expense of someone else. The effect has been destructive rather than constructive competition, resulting in much higher operating costs. Certainly no company can expect to obtain an increased outlet for its own production when all companies have a surplus for which they are desirous of securing a market. . . .

The petroleum industry has not of late years earned a return on its investment sufficient to enable it to continue to carry in the future the burden and responsibilities placed upon it in the public's interest, and it would seem impossible that it can do so unless present conditions are changed. Recognizing this, economies must be effected, waste must be eliminated, the expensive duplication of facilities curtailed, and the following sets out the more important principles for bringing this about in all countries other than the domestic market in the U.S.A. and imports into the U.S.[15]

The "Achnacarry Agreement" proposed general principles for the companies individually to follow: accept the same proportion of the business in the future as they currently held; share existing facilities wherever advisable, payments for their use to be based on demonstrated costs; add facilities only when necessary to handle increased requirements by the public; retain for oil-producing operations in any given place the advantage of their geographical location; draw supplies for markets from the nearest producing area in order to obtain maximum efficiency and economy in transportation; handle excess local production either by shutting in oil wells or offering the oil at a price that would make it competitive with production from other geographical areas; and, finally, hold down costs to the benefit of all interests.[16]

The implementation of these principles met with unexpected complications. Among them was the continuing increase of American production, the major disturbing element in the world oil industry. Excess American production to a great extent nullified the efforts of companies to curtail their production in foreign countries where they had fields on large concessions operated as units. Difficulties in the establishment of the Export Petroleum Association complicated the situation. American oil continued to flow unabated to foreign markets.[17]

As a result of the failure of these American efforts, top executives of Jersey, Royal Dutch–Shell, and Anglo-Persian reconsidered the application of the principles they had drawn up at Achnacarry in 1928. Since the attempt to handle the problem of oversupply by focusing on production had failed, they discussed establishing marketing quotas within countries outside the United States. They were in agreement that each of the three international groups should be entitled to the share of national markets that it had held in 1928; adjustments should be made and penalties paid when one took business from either of the other two. In order that supplies might be made available as economically as possible to the affiliates of their companies, these executives tried to work out a method of exchanges, such as that outlined at Achnacarry, so that supplies for a given place would come from the nearest source. They also suggested that, in order to provide for the economical use of tankers, if one company was short of tankers it should use the others' idle tonnage rather than charter outside tankers. Prices should be based on those posted in American ports on the Gulf of Mexico—then the leading world oil market—adjusted according to freight charges from the Gulf to the point of sale.[18]

Some progress was made in several areas. Early in 1930 the leaders of the three international companies drafted a new set of principles called "Memorandum for European Marketing." They endeavored to set up production schedules for the affiliates of their companies so that supplies of crude oil would not be far in excess of demand. They also established quotas for the sale of gasoline, kerosene, and gas oil in European markets. Deterding wanted lubricating oils placed under quotas, but Teagle felt that he could not take action regarding that product inasmuch as Vacuum Oil Company was the most important American supplier of lubricants in foreign markets. These leaders also gave attention to problems in the Orient. By the spring of 1930, Royal Dutch–Shell and Standard of New York had worked out a price agreement for parts of the Orient, and the latter had agreed to draw a portion of its supplies for the Indian market from the Abadan refinery. A disturbing element in the Far East—besides Russian oil—was abundant supplies at low prices from California. Jersey's Riedemann proposed working for a worldwide agreement, but Director Sadler maintained that it was economically more sound to attempt local solutions of marketing problems.[19]

The three companies continued to work for some control over disturbing elements in foreign markets. After 1930 supplies from Romania became especially troublesome in European markets; several companies not affiliated with the large international groups had sizable production in that country. In 1932 Royal Dutch–Shell and Jersey made arrangements with the Romanian producers which gave those independents a larger outlet than they had had in 1928—the base years for the other companies' quotas—but at the same time brought them under some control. The international companies also entered negotiations for the purchase of Russian oil, but they were unable to reach agreement with the Russians on terms. Two American companies withdrew from foreign marketing in 1932: Continental Oil Company, which sold its British affiliate to Anglo-American and its chief competitors; and Standard of Indiana, which sold all its foreign properties to Jersey. This latter transaction, although primarily motivated on Jersey's part by a desire to increase its production, eliminated a potentially strong competitor in foreign markets. The leading proponents of cooperation brought into their discussions several American oil companies engaged in marketing abroad. This led to a meeting in December, 1932, in which executives of Jersey, Royal Dutch–Shell, and Anglo-Persian were joined by representatives of Socony-Vacuum, Atlantic Refining, Gulf Oil, Sinclair, and Texaco. This group drafted "Heads of Agreement for Distribution" to guide in setting up local agreements for markets outside the United States.[20]

The movement thus set under way was not very effective, however, principally because world production got far out of hand. The most disturbing development was the unprecedented rise in crude output in the United States resulting mostly from the development of the prolific East Texas field. The decline in prices on the American Gulf Coast—the basis for the pricing of the Romanian producers' crude under their agreement with the international companies—led those producers to withdraw from their agreement of 1932. In fact, both the Romanians and Russia increased their exports in 1933.[21]

Some uncertainty arose out of Anglo-Persian's difficulty with the Persian government over royalties, which had declined because of reduced production in Persia and lower prices for its oil. Although the cancellation of the company's concession was threatened in 1933, a revised contract for a longer period was drawn up; it granted a smaller concession area to the company and provided for larger royalty payments to the government and also lower prices for consumers in Persia. Because there was no competitive local market, the prices were to be set at the level of those prevailing at American ports on the Gulf of Mexico or at Constantsa in Romania, whichever was the lower.[22]

Some improvement in the demand-supply situation in world markets came late in 1933. There was an upward turn in the demand for petroleum products nearly everywhere. Important supply developments came in the United States. The tariff of 1932 and the domestic companies' voluntary restriction on the volume of their imports reduced foreign imports and consequently the export of oil produced within the United

States. Especially effective on the supply side of the market were certain advances in government regulation late in 1933. The chaos that developed in the oil market during the early months of 1933 led to efforts to establish effective government controls in the United States through (1) the Code of Fair Competition for the Petroleum Industry under the National Industrial Recovery Act, (2) the banning by the federal government of the shipment—interstate or abroad—of oil produced contrary to state laws, and (3) a stiffening of conservation law and its administration in Texas and other states. (See Chapter 4.) These developments helped, but achieving really effective regulation of oil production in the United States was still in the future.

In 1934 the international companies took still further action. They did not overlook the possibility that Standard of California would develop large production on Bahrain Islands in the Persian Gulf. (See Chapter 3.) Their immediate need, however, was to deal with the many complexities that had risen in the working out of local marketing arrangements under the Heads of Agreement of 1932. They therefore drew up a new set of principles and procedures, to guide the relations of the cooperating companies, known as "Draft Memorandum of Principles." When this effort proved inadequate in subsequent months, various addenda were agreed upon.[23]

By such means, between 1928 and 1939 a measure of cooperation was achieved among many companies operating outside the United States. This collective action did not include all companies at any time, and competition still existed in many countries. Each of the participating concerns also sought, within the existing framework at any given time, to improve its own situation. For example, the companies worked to raise the demand for their products by improving quality; each company knew that quota adjustments would be made in accordance with the individual concern's capacity. However, Jersey's European affiliates, although raising the volume of their sales, experienced a decline in their share of the market in some countries; they dropped to second place in all except Denmark, Norway, Germany, Switzerland, and Tunisia. They were generally outranked by Royal Dutch–Shell and in England by the combined affiliate of that company and Anglo-Persian (Anglo-Iranian from 1935 on). By early 1938, when signs of increasing military preparations had become evident throughout Europe, the leading companies realized that joint efforts in several countries might soon become subject to the control of the various governments.[24]

It is impossible to assess with any certainty the effect of these cooperative efforts of the leaders in the international oil industry. Although their primary objective was to preserve their own interests, they apparently also contributed to preserving those of the whole petroleum industry and indeed of the consumer. Prices may have been higher for the short run in some markets than strictly competitive prices would have been, but the moves made subsequent to the Achnacarry meeting helped to stabilize the industry and to prevent the chaos that might have become serious for all interests. The movement was actually an attempt to establish something in the way of a counterpart to proration in the United States. Both brought a measure of stability and reduced waste, but apparently neither completely solved the problem of oversupply or of equity among the various companies and interests concerned.

Cooperation among the leading companies had definitely come to an end by September, 1939. The outbreak of war dissolved agreements still in effect. It brought the control of petroleum supplies in belligerent countries under governmental bodies and introduced greater regulation elsewhere. It also postponed the declaration of new policies for foreign marketing by Jersey's top officials.[25]

By that time, however, various events had already greatly weakened whatever cooperation had existed in international markets. All but one of its principal architects had given place to other leaders. Heinrich Riedemann had retired from active service with Jersey. In 1936, Sir Henri Deterding, at the age of 70, had stepped down as managing director of Royal Dutch–Shell, although he remained a director until his death in February, 1939. Sir John Cadman remained for a time at the helm of Anglo-Iranian. Teagle in 1937 exchanged the duties of chief executive for those of the chairmanship of the Jersey Board of Directors; thereafter he served as senior adviser. Of those who had met at Achnacarry in 1928, only Cadman remained in a key position at the end of 1939.[26]

The influence of new leaders, as well as the many difficulties inherent in carrying out specific arrangements, had for several years strained the fabric of cooperation. W. S. Farish, who succeeded Teagle as Jersey's chief executive, believed in competition among companies as well as freedom from governmental regulation except as necessary to conserve a natural resource. Within the Jersey Company, younger executives—some of whom had risen through the producing side of the business—were taking over management. These men saw that through a variety of circumstances production had become fairly well adjusted to world

the operations of Jersey's affiliate, N.V. Nederlandsche Koloniale Petroleum Maatschappij.

NKPM, with rising production and a new refinery in Sumatra but no
markets in the Orient, had made a contract in 1927 for the sale of all its
products to Standard Oil Company of New York. Because this company
had alternate supply sources while Jersey's affiliate was in need of an
outlet for its products, the terms of the sales contract did not provide for
the customary commission of 5 per cent. Instead it called for outright sale
at a delivered price equal to that for supplies from California minus
transportation charges from the Sungei Gerong refinery to the point of
delivery. This arrangement resulted in a larger margin of profit for the
marketing company and less for Jersey's producing and refining affiliate
than would have been the case if the latter had received the customary
commission. Consequently, the local Dutch government obtained a
smaller revenue from taxing the profits of NKPM than it would have had
under the commission arrangement—or than it might have received if the
company itself had marketed the products.[31]

There seemed to be only two ways for NKPM to escape from a situation so unsatisfactory to the Dutch government. One possible way was
for the affiliate to undertake to do its own marketing. However, that
would involve large expenditures for new facilities and possibly would
bring no more revenue to the Dutch government because of a probable
reduction of prices by all other companies while NKPM was attempting
to break into the market. An alternative was to merge NKPM with a
marketing company. Jersey approached Standard of New York, but this
company, being in a good position with plentiful supplies from California
at comparatively low prices, was not interested in the terms offered. The
possibility of merging with the Royal Dutch–Shell group was discussed,
but there obviously were many obstacles to such a solution.[32]

It appeared that, unless an arrangement was made to broaden the
taxable base for the Dutch government, NKPM might not have an opportunity to get new concessions or it might even lose the large concession it
had obtained in 1928. The situation remained uncertain until June, 1933,
when Jersey decided to initiate marketing in the Far East by purchasing
from Atlantic Refining and Union Oil Company of California their joint
marketing company in Australia and New Zealand. Then Socony-
Vacuum, the recent combination of Standard of New York and Vacuum
Oil, decided that a merger with Jersey would be to its advantage.

Jersey and Socony each took a half-interest in Standard-Vacuum Oil

AREAS IN WHICH STANDARD-VACUUM HAD PRODUCING, REFINING, AND MARKETING OPERATIONS AFTER THE MERGER OF 1934

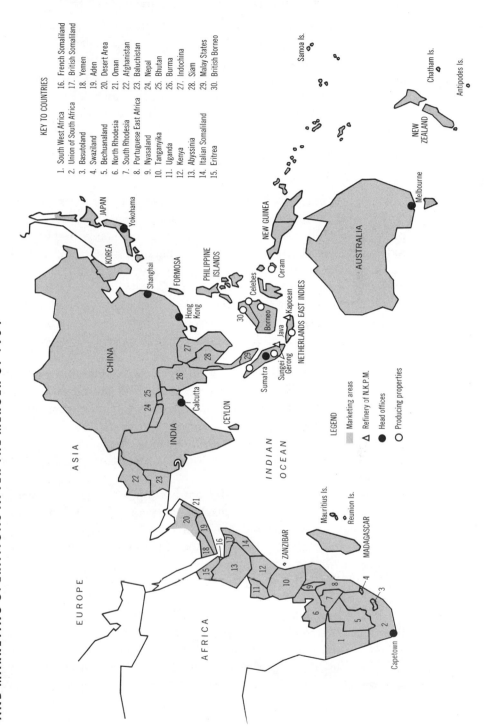

KEY TO COUNTRIES

1. South West Africa
2. Union of South Africa
3. Basutoland
4. Swaziland
5. Bechuanaland
6. North Rhodesia
7. South Rhodesia
8. Portuguese East Africa
9. Nyasaland
10. Tanganyika
11. Uganda
12. Kenya
13. Abyssinia
14. Italian Somaliland
15. Eritrea
16. French Somaliland
17. British Somaliland
18. Yemen
19. Aden
20. Desert Area
21. Oman
22. Afghanistan
23. Baluchistan
24. Nepal
25. Bhutan
26. Burma
27. Indochina
28. Siam
29. Malay States
30. British Borneo

LEGEND

Marketing areas
△ Refinery of N.K.P.M.
● Head offices
○ Producing properties

Company, which they incorporated in the United States in 1934. They turned over to this company all their producing, refining, transporting, and marketing interests south and east of Suez. They agreed on a wide area for Standard-Vacuum's operations in which they themselves would not individually carry on any business. This area included East and South Africa, Australia, New Zealand, the Dutch East Indies, Malaya, India, the Philippine Islands, China, and Japan.[33]

DIVIDED RESPONSIBILITIES FOR FOREIGN MARKETING

At the beginning of 1927 Jersey had no effective over-all system of liaison with its foreign marketing affiliates. Indeed, many of the companies had achieved a large measure of autonomy because of their independent origin, their considerable national ownership, or their particular circumstances and leadership. Several European companies were in this position, and so was Imperial in Canada with its affiliates operating in Colombia and Peru. Even West India Oil Company—a directly owned affiliate marketing in most countries in Central and South America —had acquired a great deal of independence under its chief executive, Joseph H. Senior.

Jersey, of course, had regular channels of communication with its foreign marketing affiliates. President Teagle had direct relations with the leading executives. He was in especially close communication with Heinrich Riedemann, who was very influential among the European marketers, and with G. Harrison Smith of Imperial. James A. Moffett, Jr., as a Jersey director, had responsibility for relations with domestic and foreign marketing.

But such personal contacts did not add up to an effective, systematic organization for coordinating marketing operations or for such advisory or supervisory relations with the affiliates as were implicit in the parent company's investment in them. Although the existing system had worked satisfactorily in the more distant past, in recent years Jersey's officers and directors had decided that Jersey needed closer relations with the foreign marketing organizations.

By adding four leading executives of foreign marketing affiliates to its Board of Directors in 1927, the parent company sought to bring that widely scattered operation into direct association with its policy making and planning. These executives were Heinrich Riedemann, John A. Mowinckel of Società Italo-Americana, head of the Board of European

Executives, G. Harrison Smith of Imperial, and Joseph H. Senior of West India Oil Company.

As an officer of Imperial, Smith was associated with marketing in Canada, Colombia, and Peru. In 1927 Imperial and its affiliates were providing a large share of the oil products consumed in the three countries. The Canadian affiliate, which distributed throughout the southern part of the Dominion, had adopted many of the methods developed earlier in the United States. In Peru, International Petroleum Company left the distribution of a considerable part of the products of the Talara refinery to a commission agent; the company itself handled marketing in Lima, the Peruvian capital, and in the neighboring port of Callao. The Tropical Oil Company in Colombia was utilizing its own marketing organization to provide products for local agents, depending upon difficult and costly transportation from bulk plants on the Magdalena River and tidewater.[34]

Director Senior was responsible for Jersey's marketing—together with a little refining—in other Latin American countries. He was the chief executive of several affiliates, the most important of which was West India Oil Company. This affiliate's northern division included Central America, the northern coast of South America, and islands in the Caribbean; the southern division included Argentina, Paraguay, Uruguay, Bolivia, and Chile. Senior was also president of Standard Oil Company of Brazil, which marketed in that country alone, and of Standard Oil Company of Cuba, which refined imported crude and sold the products on the island.

These companies had recently been improving their marketing facilities. They had introduced pumps for gasoline in the major cities of Latin America and had acquired bulk plants. They had also set up canning factories at the principal ports for transferring a large part of the bulk kerosene and gasoline to cases and cans for handling by agents in the back country. This was still the prevailing method of distribution for extensive areas with a relatively small demand. However, the marketing affiliates still held to their old questionable course of charging high prices. This policy resulted in big profits, but it raised considerable resentment among Latin Americans.[35]

In 1927 Jersey had marketing operations in nearly all countries on the European Continent, with one or more affiliates in each country. The managers of many of these companies, who were sons of founders or of early managers, maintained a high degree of independence. The splintering

of old companies and stockholdings and the formation of new corporations after World War I, because of increasing nationalism, had dispersed even more than before the management of Jersey's marketing in
Europe. The result was that the company had many affiliates on the
Continent that were quite independent of New York and, in fact, of one
another's operations.

In 1927 the new European directors of the Jersey board were given
responsibility for representing various interests in Europe with a view to
bringing about better coordination of European operations, especially
marketing. John A. Mowinckel, managing director of the Italian affiliate,
was to represent the marketing affiliates. Heinrich Riedemann, a director
of several German and Swiss affiliates, had responsibility for contact with
other oil companies and for carrying on important negotiations.[36] These
two men differed on matters of policy. In the hope that a larger group
would make a more harmonious committee, the number of European
executives on the Jersey board was increased and the Committee of
European Directors thereby enlarged. The new members, as noted in
Chapter 2, were executives of Bedford Petroleum, Româno-Americana,
and Anglo-American. Riedemann became chairman of the committee. The
group endeavored to improve marketing in Europe. But differences in
personality and on policy, together with the location of the members at
considerable distances from each other, resulted in this regional committee being far less effective than had been planned.[37] With changes in the
Jersey Board of Directors in 1933, the committee was weakened by
Riedemann's retirement and by the other members' resignation as chief
executives of European affiliates. The next year, they also left the Jersey
board. By that time, plans were under way for a new organization to
advise foreign marketers in both Europe and Latin America.

Senior's retirement in 1933 left a special problem in the Latin American
marketing affiliates which he had long headed. He had generally made
decisions himself and had not encouraged operating managers to assume
much beyond routine responsibilities. Now those men, accustomed to
looking to New York for leadership, were promoted to chief executive in
their organizations. In their new posts they had to assume responsibilities
which they had had little experience in carrying. Director Orville Harden
was given the temporary assignment of assisting them until a new system
for advising foreign marketing affiliates could be established.[38]

Beginning in 1934, West India Oil Company, which for thirty years had
been Jersey's leading marketing affiliate in Central and South America

and adjacent islands, was broken up into several companies. This move was made advisable by rising nationalism in some countries and also by the change at home in the rules for reporting consolidated earnings of affiliates for income-tax purposes so that profits in one no longer could offset losses in another. New affiliates were established in several countries where the business was large enough to make a separate organization practicable. In West India's northern division, its properties and operations were transferred to five companies: one in Puerto Rico, in Trinidad, in Venezuela, and in the Dutch islands in the Caribbean, and one operating in four countries in Central America, the three Guianas in northern South America, and several islands off the coast. In the old company's southern division, its properties and operations were transferred to a new corporation in Chile in 1934, to another in Uruguay in the same year, and to a third in Argentina and Paraguay in 1937. In the latter year, West India ceased operating in Bolivia. All its other properties having been transferred to various corporations, the old West India Oil Company was liquidated.[39]

The new organization for advising the foreign affiliates was established in London in 1936 under the International Association (Petroleum Industry) Limited, incorporated in Great Britain. This organization, which bears the imprint of the ingenuity of Heinrich Riedemann, took over the responsibilities earlier borne by the Committee of European Directors and by Director Harden for Latin American affiliates; it had no relations with the Imperial group in Canada, Colombia, and Peru. Its organization had been discussed with representatives of the British government to ascertain that the earnings of companies operating in other countries would not be taxed in the United Kingdom. (Customarily, any company whose "mind and management" resided there was subject to British taxation.) When the International Association was established, many men were transferred to London to go on its payroll with others already there. Men whose duties were not purely advisory were transferred to another Jersey affiliate, the Overseas Service Corporation, Limited.[40]

The International Association was for Jersey an unusual type of organization. Its members consisted of the heads of the foreign affiliates engaged in marketing, except the Imperial group, in which Jersey held more than half the stock. The association had no capital and therefore no stockholders; its expenses were assessed against the companies represented. Its administrative body was known as the London Council. In 1936 Heinrich Riedemann was its chairman and Harry G. Seidel was vice-chairman; other members were Henry E. Bedford, Jr., Gordon H. Michler, and Emile E. Soubry. Soubry and Peter T. Lamont were in charge of advising the European marketing companies, and Michler had a similar relation with the Latin American affiliates. Bedford headed a department called Company Relations, which was concerned with marketing problems and policies. W. R. Carlisle was general counsel, and R. H. Porters was financial adviser to the association. These men had all had long experience in marketing in Great Britain or on the European Continent except Michler, whose career had been spent largely in Latin America, and Carlisle, who had worked in the United States. Jersey's contact director for the London Council was Donald L. Harper, former head of the Foreign Sales Department, who had been elected a Jersey director in 1935.[41]

The principal responsibility of the London Council was to assist the executives of foreign affiliates. This included advising them about their relations with governments as well as on matters that had to do directly with marketing operations. The council worked with the European companies to achieve some uniformity in corporate titles and brands; these were to indicate the affiliates' connection with Jersey and thus associate their products with the established reputation in the United States of its widely known motor fuels, lubricants, and other products. The London Council also assisted the affiliates in obtaining adequate supplies as economically as possible, a matter of concern to company executives on both sides of the Atlantic. It arranged for products of the Aruba refinery to supply a large part of the British market and for crude oil from the United States, Latin America, and Iraq to be used in processing by local refineries. In order to assist in planning for both supplies and capital expenditures, the London Council asked executives of the foreign affiliates for forecasts of future requirements. Because the officers and managers of many European affiliates were not accustomed to such planning, these requests started them on the educational process of studying the possibilities of their business for several years ahead.[42]

These efforts to bring about more efficient operations were hampered in many places by adherence to customary practices, by governmental regulations, and by restraints imposed by local marketing arrangements. However, the foreign marketers' activities were on the whole improved. But the war broke out before the full possibilities for improvement under the direction of the London Council could be realized.

The International Association became inactive with the outbreak of

World War II.[43] Some members of its staff of more than a hundred were transferred to Anglo-American, but most of them left London. Nearly all the Americans returned to the United States; many of the British personnel joined the military services. The affiliates in belligerent countries were thereafter regulated by their individual governments.

ACHIEVEMENTS OF AFFILIATES IN THE WESTERN HEMISPHERE

Although Jersey could plan and execute grand strategy and contribute toward the development of more effective management and methods, in the final analysis success or failure depended on the operating affiliates themselves and on the conditions under which they carried on their work.

In 1927 Imperial was by far Jersey's most important foreign marketing company, and it was the largest distributor of oil products in Canada. In the next few years, it carried out a plan for retail expansion which increased the number of its service stations from 239 in 1927 to 628 in 1930. In the latter year, its investments in marketing properties totaled $14,000,000. Thereafter, however, Imperial's administrators, affected by the depression of the early 1930's and Jersey's drive for increased dividends from its affiliates, reduced the company's capital expenditures.[44]

Imperial made a cautious response to the depression. It relied on several marketing concerns in which it had an undisclosed interest to assist it in holding a high percentage of the Canadian market. A new tariff of 2½ cents per gallon on imported gasoline was temporarily helpful to the company, but other concerns soon began to build refineries in Canada. The tariff on petroleum products was reduced in 1936, thus again encouraging their importation. Imperial's attempts to economize and to maintain prices brought intensified competition with extensive price cutting. The company increased its product sales in the 1930's, but its percentage of total sales in Canada was reduced. Its share of the gasoline market fell from two-thirds in 1927 to less than half in 1938. The parent company in New York transferred Henry H. Hewetson from Louisiana to Canada to look over the Canadian marketing situation.[45]

The Canadian company's South American affiliates made few changes in their marketing operations. Tropical in Colombia was the more successful in increasing its product sales. But International in Peru sold a larger volume than the Colombian company.

Tropical had some difficulty over product prices. The only crude oil

Table 9: **ANNUAL PRODUCT SALES BY THE PRINCIPAL AFFILIATES[a] IN FOREIGN COUNTRIES, 1927 AND 1938**
Standard Oil Company (New Jersey)
(In thousands of 42-gallon barrels)

1927		1938	
Western Hemisphere		**Western Hemisphere**	
Imperial Oil Ltd., Canada	14,600	Imperial Oil Ltd., Canada	22,800
Tropical Oil Co., The, Colombia	1,300	Tropical Oil Co., The, Colombia	2,600
International Petroleum Co., Ltd., Peru[b]	2,500	International Petroleum Co., Ltd., Peru	3,100
Standard Oil Co. of Brazil	1,400	Standard Oil Co. of Brazil	4,100
Standard Oil Co. of Cuba	1,500	Standard Oil Co. of Cuba	1,600
		Cia. de Petroleo Lago, Venezuela	700
		Lago Oil & Transport Co., Ltd., N.W.I.	5,100
West India Oil Co., Northern Division	3,100	West India Oil Co. (Puerto Rico)	1,300
		West India Oil Co., S.A., Panama	2,200
West India Oil Co., Southern Division	3,500	West India Oil Co., S.A., Argentina	5,100
		West India Oil Co., S.A., Uruguay	600
		West India Oil Co., S.A., Chile	1,700
Total	27,900	**Total**	50,900
Eastern Hemisphere		**Eastern Hemisphere**	
American Petroleum Co., S.A., Belgium	900	Standard American Petroleum Co., S.A., Belgium	1,300
American Petroleum Co., Netherlands	1,800	N.V. Standard American Petroleum Co., Netherlands	2,700
Det Danske Petroleums-Akt., Denmark and Sweden	2,800	Det Danske Petroleums-Akt., Denmark	2,600
Ostlandske Petroleumscompagni, Akt., and others, Norway	600	Ostlandske Petroleumscompagni, Akt., Norway	1,200
		Svenska Petroleum Akt. Standard, Sweden	2,500
Finska Akt. Nobel-Standard, Finland	400	Finska Akt. Nobel-Standard, Finland	800
Standard-Nobel w Polsce, Poland	500		
Deutsch-Amerikanische Petroleum-Ges., Germany	4,900	Deutsch-Amerikanische Petroleum-Ges., Germany	16,000
Petroleum Import Cie., Switzerland	600	Standard Mineraloel Produkte, Switzerland	1,200
Società Italo-Americana pel Petrolio, Italy, Algeria, Tunis, and Malta	3,400	Standard Società Italo-Americana pel Petrolio, Italy	5,000
		Société Tunisienne des Pétroles, Tunis, Algeria, Malta	1,000
L'Economique, S.A., France	4,600	Standard Française des Pétroles, S.A., France	8,000
Româno-Americana, Romania	400	Româno-Americana, Romania	1,600
Industrias Babel y Nervión, Cia. A., Spain	1,100	Société Bedford Ibérique, Spain	100
		Anglo-American Oil Co., Ltd., United Kingdom	22,200
		Standard-Vacuum Oil Co., Asia, Australia, South Africa[c]	22,700
		Other affiliates[d]	800
Total	22,000	**Total**	89,700
Sales to Nonaffiliates[e]	17,600	Sales to Nonaffiliates	21,700
Total Foreign Sales	67,500	**Total Foreign Sales**	162,300

[a] Sales by affiliates include those to local agents but not usually to general agents and other marketing companies.
[b] Includes sales to agent for Peru.
[c] Entire sales given, although Jersey had only a half-interest in the company.
[d] Includes sales in Egypt, Czechoslovakia, and Hungary, and sales of British-Mexican Petroleum Company, Limited, outside the United Kingdom.

[e] About 15,000,000 estimated for Eastern Hemisphere, including 11,000,000 to Anglo-American. Sales to affiliates, not listed above, are also included.
Source: Statistical records of Standard Oil Company (New Jersey): product sales, deliveries into consumption, and report of worldwide sales; Supplement to the Annual Statistical Review, 1946.

producer in Colombia, it was protected by import duties and had little competition. Its concession contract contained a general formula governing charges for products, but differences arose over the application of the formula. The company's President Smith in 1937 denied the statement of a citizen of Colombia visiting in New York that the prices of oil products were unduly high in his home country—a common Colombian complaint. Smith stated that the price of gasoline in bulk in Bogotá was 13.7 cents a gallon without the tax, a price that was next to the lowest in consuming centers in South America; only International's 12.7 cents a gallon at Lima was lower. He explained that the charges for freight to Bogotá plus the dealer's differential, or gross margin, took 6.4 cents. This left less than 7.3 cents per gallon for producing, refining, handling, and storing several months' stocks to take care of the seasonal interruption in river shipments. Moreover, Smith said, the company had not increased the prices of its products when the value of the Colombian peso, in relation to the American dollar, had dropped by 60 per cent. Prices had not been raised despite the provision in the concession contract that prices of products at the local refinery destined for the Colombian market should be in line with those in New York.

In Peru, International had no formal agreement with the government covering local prices, but the company usually set prices at Talara at the level of those on the Atlantic Coast. Like Tropical, International was protected in its home markets by import duties, which resulted in its supplying most of the demand in Peru. Only lubricants, which International was late in manufacturing, met much competition; outsiders took somewhat less than half of that business. Fuel oils for bunkering and industrial uses remained in good demand and accounted for more than half the total volume of the products the company sold.[46]

International was hampered by an old contractual relationship that made it employ an antiquated system of marketing. When Jersey had negotiated the purchase of producing properties in Peru in 1913, a condition of the sale had been that Balfour, Williamson & Company of London and its South American agents should market for the company along the west coast of South America. In 1927 these local agents were Milne & Company of Lima, Peru, and Williamson & Company of Valparaiso, Chile.

Relying on general merchants of this old type had proved ineffective in promoting and even holding sales against rising competition. International had been able to obtain changes in the former contract with Milne & Company, which operated in Peru and Ecuador. When it had taken over marketing in Lima and the port of Callao, the Jersey affiliate—in return for this change in the old relationship—had agreed to allow the Milne firm a commission of 1 per cent on sales which International itself made in these two places and a 2.5 per cent general commission on Milne's own sales elsewhere in Peru and Ecuador. The old mercantile firm was to continue to furnish products to large industrial consumers, railroads, shipping companies, and local subagents. These subagents generally received an additional 2.5 per cent commission. In 1930 another change was made in the sales contract; under the new arrangement, the Milne firm supplied Ecuador with local products instead of Peruvian, drawing them from a recently constructed refinery of Anglo-Ecuadorean Oilfields, Limited. A 1931 restriction on imports into Ecuador gave still further protection to local supplies.[47]

Williamson & Company, the agent for Chile and northern Bolivia, was beset with many difficulties in its old business of supplying Peruvian fuel and diesel oils to large consumers and other products to various agents. It lost nitrate companies as customers during the depression, when many firms were combined into three large units, which then sought supplies on the open market and not on long-term contracts with an agent. West India Oil, marketing various petroleum products in Chile and southern Bolivia, was among the successful bidders for the business. This added to the strain between Williamson & Company and West India over arrangements made in 1927 for the latter to obtain lubricants from International's refinery at Talara for selling in Chile without paying any commission to the Williamsons. The agency also objected to the introduction of salesmen to assist it in developing the lubricating business in Chile and Bolivia and to the deduction of the salesmen's expenses from its own commission. Williamson's petroleum business in those countries shrank steadily during the 1930's. The system of marketing which Milne and Williamson employed was unaggressive and costly.[48]

At various times, officers in Toronto and managers in Peru considered taking over all the marketing of International's products in that country in order to provide better service at lower cost. A survey made in 1933 showed that half the products were sold in cases and cans and that there were few curb pumps and no service stations in all of Peru. International was restrained from taking over, however, by the established position of its agents and subagents. Many of them were prominent in commercial and political circles, and their good will was important at a time when a national petroleum monopoly was being advocated. The company consequently retained the old system of agents and subagents instead of introducing the more effective marketing organizations and operations being developed by Jersey's other affiliates on the same continent.

As a result of retaining the traditional agency system on the west coast and of the narrow marketing margins in Colombia, International and Tropical had little or no net earnings from these operations. In fact, after 1932 they turned in no operating profits from marketing.[49]

The operations of other affiliates in Latin America were under greater influence from New York or London than were the companies in Colombia and Peru. Jersey's Director Senior was the chief officer in charge of the distribution of Jersey products in most of Latin America until his retirement in 1933. Thereafter, Director Harden supervised those operations from New York until that function was taken over by the London Council in 1936.[50]

Under new leadership and the pressure of price decline, some changes were made in the policies affecting the marketing operations of these Latin American affiliates. The old policy of maintaining wide margins was dropped. Instead, the margins were reduced and more emphasis was placed on increasing the volume of sales and reducing costs. However, the affiliates' policies and operations were affected by matters not subject to their control, such as old contractual relations with agents, quota arrangements, and rising economic nationalism. The result was a lack of over-all unity in policy and practice.

In the later 1930's the volume of products sold in the Dutch West Indies rose substantially and the much smaller sales in Venezuela increased. This growth came in spite of the more firmly entrenched position of Royal Dutch–Shell in both areas at the beginning of the period—a position protected by the arrangements made to implement the principles drawn up at Achnacarry. Here as elsewhere, there undoubtedly were disagreements between the two international companies over volumes and prices. Jersey men held that prices in countries with local production should be based on local costs and not on prices in the United States plus freight from that country. In the Dutch islands, where West India's marketing had been transferred to Lago Oil & Transport Company, Limited, the latter maintained an old agency arrangement with S. E. L. Maduro & Sons of Curaçao. The Maduros built up such a good business in Aruba and Curaçao—largely in fuel for the ships entering the islands' ports—that Lago Oil & Transport supplied 40 per cent of the requirements. In Venezuela, West India's marketing had been transferred to

Compañía de Petróleo Lago, a new affiliate of Lago Petroleum Corporation. Sales there—principally bunker oils and gasoline—rose to approximately the same percentage of the country's total as on the two Dutch islands. Although the volume of Lago sales rose, profits declined in the later 1930's.[51]

Success varied in other outlets in the lands bordering on the Gulf of Mexico and the Caribbean. The West India Oil Company (Puerto Rico) and West India Oil Company, S.A., Panama, contributed to a tripling of sales in the countries originally included in the northern division of the old West India Company. Standard Oil Company of Cuba, which processed imported crude, held its traditional position as the major marketer of all oil products on the island excepting fuel oil, of which a Sinclair affiliate became an important supplier. However, Standard's sales increased only slightly from 1927 to 1939.[52]

In Mexico, Huasteca Petroleum Company, acquired by Jersey through the purchase of Standard of Indiana's foreign properties in 1932, endeavored to improve its marketing organization and to enlarge its sales volume despite declining production from its wells in old fields. In 1935 the company sold about 6,000,000 barrels of petroleum products, or about three-eighths of the country's total. It supplemented its own supplies from the Tampico refinery with the purchase of more than 2,000,000 barrels of fuel oil from a Royal Dutch–Shell affiliate which had large production from its newly developed Poza Rica field. Huasteca was then selling fuel oil to railroads—its major customers in the past—and was marketing other products through sales agencies and the recently remodeled service stations in Mexico City and its vicinity. It closed many stations, however, as unprofitable under a national order that the price of gasoline be reduced from 20 to 18 centavos per liter. Huasteca's marketing was taken over by the Mexican government with its seizure of foreign oil properties and operations in 1938.[53]

In the southern countries of South America, rising government intervention at a time of depressed economic conditions left its mark on the oil business. Nevertheless, the total sales of Jersey affiliates rose from 1927 to 1938, with approximately the same percentage increase as in the northern Latin American countries and adjacent islands.

Throughout the late 1920's and the next decade, Brazil was one of Jersey's largest outlets in Latin America, but problems also rose there. One was difficulties with the government late in the 1920's over the taxing of consignment agents. This led Standard Oil Company of Brazil to begin to sell products directly to consumers. In the early 1930's, the affiliate ran into trouble with payments for imports because of Brazil's foreign-exchange difficulties. A plan was set up in 1933 for gradual dollar payment to the parent company of accumulated dividends of $6,000,000, but the arrangement proved unworkable.[54]

As in other countries in Latin America, economic nationalism became more marked in Brazil late in the 1930's. In 1938 the government made the marketing of petroleum products a public utility and created the National Petroleum Council—an agency responsible only to the president—with regulatory powers over all aspects of the industry. However, Standard Oil Company of Brazil and also the Caloric Company—acquired in 1932 from Standard of Indiana—still were active marketers in that country; they sold a total of 4,100,000 barrels of products in 1938. Consideration was given to combining these affiliates in order to reduce costs, but merger was given up as unwise at the time because of an outside minority ownership and possible objections by the government.[55]

In Chile, depression in the nitrate and copper industries immediately affected the oil business. Gasoline was rationed in 1931 because of an unfavorable export-import balance. A law was passed in 1932 which authorized reserving to the state alone—or to the state in partnership with Chilean citizens or national companies—the monopoly for importing, distributing, and selling petroleum and its products. The law also authorized the expropriation of distributing equipment. In 1934, the year in which West India Oil Company, Chile, S.A., was organized, a government-sponsored company, Compañía de Petróleos de Chile, was formed. In 1937 West India and Shell, the two leading marketers, at the instance of the government made an agreement with this national company for sharing markets. The government set the prices for products, which allowed only a narrow margin between the cost of the imported oil and the domestic selling price. However, under H. D. Humpstone as manager, West India had the lowest marketing costs and was able to operate with a profit. But because of exchange difficulties, its net earnings had to be retained in the country and could not be paid out in dollar dividends to Jersey.[56]

Uruguay, where the old West India Company operated until West India Oil Company, S.A., Uruguay, was set up in 1934, established even more restrictive regulations than Chile. A monopoly law passed in 1931 created a government industrial organization (ANCAP) to carry on oil operations. The government favored ANCAP, limited the operations of private companies, and exerted coercion, with the result that the companies in 1937 had to enter a marketing agreement with the government company.[57]

Conditions in Argentina, one of Jersey's largest outlets in Latin America, were even more complicated than those in Chile and Uruguay. Argentina's petroleum products came partly from local fields and refineries and partly from imports. Principally as a result of government regulations, Jersey in 1932 was operating through eight affiliates—too many for efficient management. Its efforts to merge these companies were opposed by the public, which feared that any local combination of companies might reduce competition. Because of the public's attitude, the government did not consent to the merger.[58]

Argentina restricted the activities of foreign oil companies in many ways. It put a protective tariff in force in 1931. It ruled that prices be the same throughout the country regardless of transportation costs and thereby discouraged investment in additional facilities in the hinterland. It also favored the state-owned oil concern. Bad feeling grew until a workable solution of differences was finally reached in February, 1937. The new arrangement set up a six-month provisional agreement with the government, which was followed by a three-year agreement, allowing Jersey's affiliates to maintain their existing volume of business. West India Oil Company, S.A., Petrolera, Argentina, incorporated in April, 1937, with G. S. Laing as president, took over the old West India's marketing in Argentina and Paraguay. But the other seven marketing affiliates were retained.[59]

In Bolivia, the Jersey marketers were driven out altogether. With the government's seizure of Standard Oil Company of Bolivia in 1937, West India ceased to operate in the southern part of the country. However, a local subagent in the northern section still sold products from International's refinery in Peru.[60]

In most foreign countries in the Western Hemisphere, Jersey affiliates benefited from one development: a rising demand for oil products. Their combined sales were nearly twice as large in 1938 as in 1927. Although they did not supply as large a percentage of the total demand in 1938 as they had a decade earlier, they still sold an average of approximately 40 per cent of the total product sales in the countries where they had marketing operations. This meant that they were the leading marketers in most of the countries. However, their operating earnings had fallen—in 1938 to approximately a quarter of the earnings in 1927. This decline, of course, was largely a result of the narrowing of profit margins everywhere with declining prices. But it was also a result of both governmental regulation and Jersey policy. In Latin America generally—especially after 1933—Jersey as a matter of policy priced its products lower, relative to prices elsewhere, than it had formerly done.[61]

MARKETING IN THE EASTERN HEMISPHERE

The forces affecting the sale of petroleum products in Europe were somewhat different from those in Latin America. Many European countries were economically highly developed, but some were too small for economic self-sufficiency. In some also, relatively new governments had not yet developed effective ways of dealing with foreign companies. All suffered from depression and foreign-exchange difficulties, thus reflecting a basic imbalance that had existed since World War I. And many were more or less under the influence of social-democratic and even Marxian ideas. These countries sought various ways of sustaining their economies or increasing government participation in business. Some believed that an increase in the local producing and refining of oil was vital; they therefore legislated to favor such development under close government control. Some held that the oil industry should bear a heavy burden of taxation.

Anglo-American was the most important of Jersey's European marketing affiliates after 1930. Ever since World War I, this company had been expanding its operations by organizing or acquiring other companies in keeping with its general policy of maintaining leadership in the United Kingdom. In 1922, it had set up the Irish American Oil Company for marketing in the newly independent Irish Free State. It also had invested in several candle companies. When Doheny's oil properties had been sold in 1925, Anglo-American had acquired the British-Mexican Petroleum Company, Limited, which carried on general marketing in Great Britain through affiliates and conducted a bunkering business. Anglo-American had in 1927 acquired Glico Petroleum Company, which had been established in 1888 for manufacturing benzine; it had merged the company with an affiliate of British-Mexican to form Redline-Glico Limited.[62]

During the period of negotiations preceding its purchase by Jersey, Anglo-American had begun to make changes in its personnel and to carry out recommendations arising out of a survey of its organization. Many employees were found not to be needed and were laid off. The company's three top executives retired before the end of 1931. Frederick J. Wolfe of Imperial, who went to England in the spring of 1931 to be managing director of the company, in August succeeded Francis E. Powell as chairman. Emile E. Soubry, who had started to work for Anglo-American as an office boy at age fifteen and by 1931 had risen to the position of general sales manager, became a member of the board in 1933. After he became a director, Soubry broadened his experience and his knowledge of the operations of Jersey and its affiliates by making trips to the United States and the Far East. He resigned from Anglo-American in the summer of 1936 to become a member of the council of the International Association (Petroleum Industry) Limited.[63]

The British company continued to expand after Jersey obtained control of it. One addition was Cleveland Petroleum Products Company, together with its four affiliated companies marketing in Great Britain, which Jersey had acquired with the purchase of Pan American's foreign properties in 1932. Cleveland was an aggressive marketer; in three years it had cut the price of gasoline and had obtained about 9 per cent of the sales of that particular product in Great Britain. In 1933 Anglo-American also acquired an interest in Sealand Petroleum Company, an affiliate of Continental Oil Company—Royal Dutch–Shell and Anglo-Persian had ownership participation in Sealand as stipulated in marketing agreements. Thus, by the addition of marketing properties and other facilities, Anglo-American within one decade increased considerably the scope of its selling. In the 1930's the volume of its sales grew to about half that of The Shell-Mex & British Petroleum Company, Limited, the merged marketing affiliate of Royal Dutch–Shell and Anglo-Persian.[64]

Anglo-American became a directly owned affiliate of Standard Oil Company (New Jersey) in 1936. This change was deemed advisable because of the 1934 revision of United States regulations concerning consolidated income-tax returns. Also, by 1936 sentiment in the United States had swung away from Webb-Pomerene associations. Standard Oil Export's common stock was transferred to Jersey, its preferred stock was called, and the company was liquidated.* Jersey subsequently transferred to Anglo-American its holdings of other British companies, the most important being Agwi Petroleum Corporation, Limited, which operated a small refinery at Fawley.[65]

Because Great Britain imposed no controls on the operations of the oil industry and because the importation of supplies was affected only

---

* In order to protect the name, another American corporation by the same name was formed at the time.

slightly by exchange problems, the leading international companies' policy of attempting to set quotas in certain markets was more effective there than in most other countries. The quota arrangements came into use in 1931, when Jersey, Royal Dutch–Shell, and Anglo-Persian turned from their unsuccessful efforts to reduce production throughout the world to the level of current demand and instead attempted to set quotas in national markets. Anglo-American's salesmen then began to feel the restraints that their executives imposed upon them to maintain only their former share of the market and not to infringe upon the business of the affiliates of Royal Dutch–Shell and Anglo-Persian. However, with the usual ingenuity of salesmen, they found ways of getting new business. In time, arrangements were made by the cooperating companies to give some incentive to their sales forces by allowing a company—after paying a penalty for exceeding its quota in one year—to have a larger quota thereafter.[66]

Anglo-American proved a valuable addition to Jersey's foreign marketing. Although its share of the total market in the United Kingdom declined from about 29 per cent in 1931 to 27 per cent in 1938, its volume increased, reaching 22,200,000 barrels in 1938. Sales of distillates and fuel oils by British-Mexican outside the United Kingdom amounted to more than 3,000,000 barrels in that year. Kerosene was still used extensively in England for heating and cooking. The demand for gasoline, mainly for small cars and motorcycles, grew modestly. The use of diesel and fuel oils by buses and ships increased. The prices of petroleum products rose in the later 1930's in accordance with the rise in the United States, changes in exchange rates, and new British tax policies. The wholesale price of a gallon of gasoline, for example, increased from a shilling and a halfpenny in 1931 and 1932 to the decade's high of one shilling and six and a half pence in the spring of 1937. Depending mainly on products from the Aruba refinery, Anglo-American on the average enjoyed satisfactory profits after 1933. Problems still existed in marketing in Great Britain, but they were far less critical than in several other European countries.[67]

Jersey's German affiliate, Deutsch-Amerikanische Petroleum-Gesellschaft, advanced rapidly in the 1920's and 1930's. This company was under the local management of Franz Klasen, Heinrich and Frederik Breme, and Albert Spangenberg, Jr., and under the distant but firm influence of Heinrich Riedemann. In 1927 the company, encouraged by Jersey's Director Moffett, began to acquire drive-in filling stations, and during the next five years the number of DAPG stations steadily increased. The years 1927–1933, however, were years of depression, excess supplies, and poor earnings, although the oil business benefited from the general rise of economic activity after Adolf Hitler came into power in January, 1933.

The Nazi regime fostered the building of major road systems and thereby provided a market for asphalt; it also encouraged the use of automobiles, motorcycles, buses, and airplanes, a policy which increased the demand for gasoline greatly. However, in order to make the country independent of outside sources of oil in the event of war, Hitler demanded the development of indigenous supplies through the production and refining of oil within the country, and also the manufacture of oil from coal by hydrogenation. Among the scientific efforts to find a practical method of producing oil synthetically from coal were those of I.G. Farbenindustrie. Farben supplied synthetic fuel to Deutsche Gasolin A.G., in which DAPG had a quarter-interest.[68]

Germany's foreign-exchange problems made it difficult to obtain payment for oil shipped to that country. Because of payments problems, imports came increasingly from countries to which Germany sold manufactured products, including Romania, Peru, the Netherlands, and the United Kingdom. Special arrangements were at times worked out to provide funds to pay for oil imports. Jersey's affiliates in other countries had tankers built in Germany, employed Germans on their ships, or arranged for the sale of German products abroad. Best remembered of efforts to dispose of German goods in countries where they could be sold for dollars, or for currency convertible into dollars, was the plan to ship mouth organs to the United States. This experiment proved unsuccessful because the proposed discount made the arrangement a case of dumping—and therefore illegal under American import regulations. As the foreign-payments problem became severe, the use of German synthetics for mixing with petroleum products helped to supplement imports.[69]

DAPG increased its volume of sales from 4,900,000 barrels in 1927 to 16,000,000 in 1938. The figure for the latter year also included sales in Austria, a neighboring state into which the Nazis had moved and where DAPG had purchased Socony-Vacuum's Austrian company. In Germany, DAPG had 29 per cent of the country's business in 1938 and was still the leading oil marketer.[70]

Although profits were good in the later 1930's, Jersey was unable to convert its dividends from DAPG into dollars because of Germany's unfavorable foreign-exchange balance. The same was true of interest and payments on funds advanced to the company. Much of what was owed to

Jersey therefore had to remain in Germany, where it was invested in various properties. The parent company managed to invest the equivalent of a million dollars of dividends in pipe, which was stored in Romania for future use but was lost when that country was invaded during World War II.[71]

In France, the third European oil market of importance to Jersey, operations were greatly affected by the government's policy of having as much as possible of the petroleum industry carried on by Frenchmen within the country's own boundaries. One manifestation of economic nationalism was the government's sponsoring of Compagnie Française des Pétroles, S.A., for holding the French interest in Iraq Petroleum Company, and of Compagnie Française de Raffinage, S.A., for refining the country's share of Iraqi crude. This refining company supplied about a quarter of the total consumption in France. The fostering of the French oil industry was effected by two laws enacted in 1928, one providing tariff protection for local refineries and the other placing all imports of crude and products of 300 or more tons per month under special licenses. Two kinds of licenses were authorized by decrees: one to marketers for products, limited to not more than three years; the other to refiners, for not more than twenty years. The first license for products was issued to marketers in 1929, and the first for crude oil in 1931 to those willing to construct and operate refineries in France. On the whole, expansion by small businessmen was favored in that they received licenses for amounts of products which exceeded their past volume. The French government also regulated prices. It was reluctant to approve price increases because of consumer opinion, but it also frowned on any reduction because that meant less revenue for the government. Prices, therefore, remained fairly steady. Several large and many small companies were active in marketing in France.[72]

Jersey found the opportunities for profits greatly circumscribed in France. As noted in Chapter 7, it built the Port Jérôme refinery jointly with Gulf Oil and Atlantic Refining, both companies being marketers of lubricants and specialties. It organized a new marketing company in 1929, Standard Française des Pétroles, which together with other companies was merged by 1936 with the holding company, Standard Franco-Américaine. The latter company was then changed to Standard Française des Pétroles, S.A. This affiliate, under the management of Leon Martin and W. D. Crampton, in 1938 accounted for 16.5 per cent of total sales in France and ranked next to Royal Dutch–Shell in volume.[73]

The policies of the Italian government were in many respects similar to those of France and Germany. Jersey's principal affiliate in Italy was its wholly owned Società Italo-Americana pel Petrolio, which in 1928 supplied nearly half of Italy's gasoline and kerosene and large percentages of other major products. The Italian government in 1934 assumed extensive control of the oil industry and established importing and refining quotas. Because Jersey's affiliates in Italy engaged in a little producing and refining as well as marketing, they were able to take advantage of tariff and license regulations which favored the importation of crude as against products. In that country as in France and Germany, the drive for local supplies to provide for a possible emergency became intense.[74]

The eyes of the world were focused on Italy in the fall of 1935, when, contrary to his country's obligations under the League of Nations, Mussolini moved against Ethiopia. Fifty-one countries voted sanctions against Italy and declared an embargo on war supplies—not including oil. The United States, which was not a member of the League, allowed its nationals to carry on trade with Italy at the shipper's own risk. Jersey was in a difficult position; the Italian government was pressing Società for increased supplies, while many Americans demanded that no assistance be given Italy as the aggressor. Jersey decided that, as in similar instances in the past, its policy should be to maintain its normal operations; it would supply its Italian affiliate, but only to the extent of the preceding year. The parent company was criticized in the American press for this operation.[75]

The difficulty over furnishing products to an aggressor was the most striking event in the operations of Società Italo-Americana during the 1930's. Although the company's sale of 5,000,000 barrels of products in 1938 was a considerable increase over sales in 1927 to a market which then also included several North African areas, its portion of the Italian market declined to 21 per cent. Growth had been handicapped by the government's policy of maintaining prices below world parity. The Italian affiliate, whose name was changed in 1938 by prefixing Standard to its old title, remained under the direction of American general managers: John A. Mowinckel through 1931 and R. F. Hawkins thereafter.[76]

The managing directors of affiliates elsewhere in Europe met heightened competition, but generally fared comparatively well. In Belgium and Luxembourg, Jersey's principal marketing company operated through several affiliates. In accordance with the International Association's program, the name of the principal company in 1938 became Standard American Petroleum Company, S.A., Belge. This concern was still managed by members of founders' families, Charles Speth succeeding his kinsman, Maurice Speth, on the latter's death in 1938. Foreign exchange was relatively free in Belgium, and the government imposed few restrictions. But competition was intense. Many companies endeavored to market products in that country, including Sinclair, Gulf, Atlantic, and The Texas Company, in addition to affiliates of the international big three. A special reason for this competition was the fact that Belgian ports served as transshipping points to the interior of Europe, in consequence of which supplies in transit were large and not easily checked for quotas. Standard American Petroleum's share of the market declined from 32 per cent in 1928 to 21 per cent in 1938; its volume, however, increased by 40 per cent.[77]

Jersey's principal marketer in the Netherlands (which in 1938 became N.V. Standard Amerikaansche Petroleum Compagnie) also met increased competition. Abundant supplies in transit forced prices down, and Royal Dutch–Shell's affiliate enjoyed greater popularity because one of its parent companies was Dutch in origin and one of its two main offices was at The Hague. Standard Amerikaansche, although it increased its sales by 50 per cent during this period, was second to the Royal Dutch–Shell company by 1938; it then held 23 per cent of the business as compared to 39 per cent in 1927.[78]

The marketing affiliate in Switzerland, Petroleum Import Compagnie (which in 1938 became Standard Mineraloel Produkte A.G.) was changed in 1931 from Riedemann's direction to that of a combined German and Swiss management under L. Duve and J. Duvoisin. Although the importing of Russian and Romanian supplies by way of the Danube River and also exchange difficulties had reduced its profits, the company nevertheless remained the leading Swiss marketer. It had about a third of the business in Switzerland in 1938.[79]

Conditions in the Scandinavian countries were in many respects similar to those in the Low Countries and Switzerland. Because Denmark favored trade with Great Britain, its largest customer for dairy products, Det Danske Petroleums-Aktieselskab obtained its products from Jersey's Fawley refinery. Independently minded Christian Holm kept his company the leading marketer, with more than 40 per cent of the Danish business in 1938, which was the highest percentage of national totals sold by Jersey affiliates in European countries. The companies in Norway remained the leading marketers in that country, but those in Sweden and Finland yielded first place to affiliates of Royal Dutch–Shell. Jersey's marketing companies in Norway were consolidated under Aktieselskabet Ostlandske Petroleumscompagni as a holding company. Those in Sweden similarly came under a holding company, Svenska Petroleum Aktiebolaget Standard. Competition was especially severe throughout Sweden, where Gulf Oil purchased an interest in a former Nobel affiliate. Jersey's Finska Aktiebolaget Nobel–Standard in Finland was beginning to install service stations during this period, but in this improvement it lagged behind the marketers in other European countries.[80]

The company's sale of products was in a weak position in Romania. This was mainly the result of the government's requirement initiated before World War I that major oil companies sell their general line through a government-controlled company, commonly referred to as Distributia. The government, however, did not apply similar restrictions to the many independents, which during the 1920's and 1930's took over a major share of the business. In fact, in 1938 Romăno-Americana, Jersey's affiliate, was providing through Distributia only 1,600,000 barrels, or about one-eighth of the country's total. The company was using Agentia Americana, set up in 1931, to sell specialty products. Romăno depended mainly upon markets in foreign countries to take the products of its Teleajen refinery.[81]

Affiliates also fared badly in other parts of Europe. Two specialty companies, one in Czechoslovakia and one marketing in both Austria and Hungary, reported losses more often than profits. In Poland, Standard–Nobel w Polsce marketed in the red, averaging annual losses of more than $300,000 for the years 1931 through 1936. Government controls restricted company activities and left little incentive for introducing better distribution methods. However, Jersey sold its Polish properties to Socony-Vacuum.[82]

Several affiliates operated in the islands of the Mediterranean and in countries on the northern coast of Africa. Some of these became direct holdings in 1935 as a result of governmental restrictions on foreign investments of Italian companies. Three affiliates incorporated in Tunisia and Algiers, all having small operations, were transferred to the parent company. Jersey also held an interest in the Tagus Oil Company, a supplier of bunkering fuels in the Azores.[83]

Jersey provided a few supplies for Spain, mostly lubricants and asphalt through Société Bedford Ibérique. In 1927 a royal decree had instructed the government to expropriate all properties of oil companies in that country, and these were subsequently turned over to a petroleum monopoly. When the United States Department of State lodged a protest with the Spanish government, it was assured that compensation would be forthcoming. The company was successful in getting a fairly satisfactory indemnity for its interest in the two marketing companies taken over by the government. The French investors in those companies brought about the payment through their government, which threatened to cut off the rights of Spanish nationals living in France if the rights of French nationals were not respected in Spain.[84]

Comparable in size of operations to Imperial's in Canada and Anglo-American's in Great Britain was Standard-Vacuum's in the Orient. Jersey's contacts with the marketing activities of this affiliate, of which it owned 50 per cent, were far less close than its contacts with the companies in which it was a majority stockholder. This remoteness was partly explained by the fact that "Stanvac's" marketing was directed by men who had grown up in the Socony-Vacuum organization. After President William B. Walker's death in 1934, Philo W. Parker became the new president in charge of marketing. However, Jersey's George S. Walden became chairman. Standard-Vacuum had six sales divisions: India, North China, South China, Japan, Australia, and South Africa. It had 700 service stations in the larger cities and 3,000 agents, who operated almost 17,000 curbside and portable pumps. In the larger ports of the immense regions it served, the company operated canning factories and plants for transferring products in bulk to cases and cans for distribution to retailers and consumers. It was distributing in a market that was vast in terms of population but small in per capita purchasing power. It sold 22,700,000 barrels of products in 1938. Royal Dutch–Shell's affiliates were by far the largest marketers, and the Caltex affiliates, which late in the decade began to draw some of their supplies from their affiliated refineries in Bahrain and Saudi Arabia, were making inroads in Standard-Vacuum's operating territories.[85]

The company inherited marketing difficulties from Standard of New York. Among them were continuing problems in India over Russian supplies. There were also problems in Japan, the most important of the Far Eastern markets. Soon after the Japanese Industry Control Act was passed in August, 1931, the marketing of gasoline was placed under government control. The Japanese Department of Commerce, which was given jurisdiction over prices, set maximums which yielded little if any profit. At the same time, a Japanese firm was importing Russian oil, which it sold at prices below those of established marketers.[86]

It became increasingly difficult in the next few years for foreign companies to operate in Japan because of the government's action to encourage the development of Japanese industry. The Petroleum Industry Control Law, enacted in March, 1934, and effective the following July, imposed greater restrictions than the earlier law. Thereafter, companies planning to refine or import oil had to get a permit and submit plans for governmental approval. Companies also had to obtain permission to make any changes in operations. Most onerous was the requirement that all refiners and importers must keep large stocks in reserve. The government, with full control over prices, made it clear that foreign companies would be given larger quotas when they entered the refining business if they had a Japanese partner. Neither Royal Dutch–Shell nor Standard-Vacuum would agree to all these conditions. Although complying with other regulations, they maintained their supplies for Japan at normal peacetime levels in 1938, when that country was invading China.[87]

Socony-Vacuum and Jersey in the later 1930's moved to increase their marketing of aviation products in the Orient. Jersey's leaders were dissatisfied with arrangements for foreign aviation sales within Standard-Vacuum's marketing area, inasmuch as this new affiliate was not aggressive in getting contracts from international air line companies. A solution to this problem was found in 1936 by setting up International Aviation Associates—known as Intava—as a joint enterprise of Jersey and Socony-Vacuum, with W. W. White in charge at the company's headquarters in London. The two parent companies and their joint affiliate could now operate with a common purpose in getting contracts and servicing international air lines in the Far East.[88]

Affiliates in neutral as well as belligerent countries felt the impact on their petroleum supplies and markets of the outbreak of World War II. For foreign marketing, therefore, this period closes with September, 1939, and figures on volumes and profits end with 1938, the last relatively normal year for all countries. Indeed, the uneasiness of many countries had an effect on the oil business even in 1938, as inventories were being built up in anticipation of an emergency. After the war broke out in September of the next year, the petroleum industry was quickly brought under the control of governmental bodies in belligerent countries.

Jersey's affiliates in the Eastern Hemisphere, as in the Western outside the United States, had operated in the late 1920's and the 1930's under increasing governmental controls of marketing but within a rising demand for products. Counting half of Standard-Vacuum's business, Jersey interests considerably more than tripled their total sales in the Eastern

Hemisphere. In 1938 they sold an average of just less than 30 per cent of the total product sales in the countries where they had marketing operations. They were then still the leading distributor in Germany, Denmark, Norway, Switzerland, and Tunisia, and they were well established in the large British market.

Profits held up better in the Eastern than in the Western Hemisphere. With the tripling of volume, the operating revenue in the former was a little more than twice as large in the highest-income year in the 1930's (1937) as in the comparable year in the late 1920's (1928). Profits increased by approximately one-eighth. The best earner in the Eastern Hemisphere through 1938 was the German affiliate.[89]

A REVIEW OF FOREIGN MARKETING

On balance, Jersey had accomplished its principal 1927 objective in foreign marketing in the succeeding years; that is, it had maintained a firm over-all position abroad. To be sure, its affiliates had been excluded from two countries in the Western Hemisphere. And its relative position had been weakened in certain other countries by government promotion of national concerns—but even in such places, its sales had expanded. At the same time, Jersey had obtained large participation in the United Kingdom, the leading market in Europe, and it had acquired half-ownership in an old marketing operation in the Orient. By these acquisitions it had re-entered marketing territory lost in 1911. The volume of its foreign sales had more than doubled. Although the ratio of Jersey sales to total industry sales had generally declined, this was to be expected in an industry expanding so rapidly by the entry of new companies as well as the growth of well-established ones. In 1938 the affiliates were still the leading marketers in the majority of the countries in the Western Hemisphere outside the United States, but only in Germany and several small countries in Europe did they continue to be the largest suppliers in the Eastern Hemisphere.

Absolutely and relative to the volume of their sales, Jersey's foreign affiliates as a whole earned lower profits in the late 1930's than in the late 1920's. This change was in large part a result of generally lower prices and more intense competition, but it also reflected increased government controls. As a group, however, the affiliates turned in a fair return on invested capital.[90]

Costs were apparently not reduced as much as they might have been under less conservative managers and with more nearly normal conditions of supply and demand. The Jersey Coordination Committee and the

International Association had gathered information that enabled the company's directors to judge better than formerly the points of strength and weakness of the management of foreign marketing operations. However, the Jersey administrators had not had a firm and direct influence on either Imperial and its affiliates or on the companies in the Eastern Hemisphere. In fact, the International Association had become a somewhat independent entity, especially with respect to affiliates that were under the direction of European officers. Moreover, the war came before the potential of that advisory group could be fully realized.

These developments in marketing were significant to Jersey's total world operations. Not only had the company maintained a firm position in sales abroad but it had also increased those sales at a rate that had provided outlets for its rising foreign production and refining. In fact, the rate of its foreign growth had outstripped the rate at home with the result that, whereas in 1927 Jersey's total sales at home were larger than the total abroad, in 1938 total sales to foreign markets surpassed those in the United States. Jersey had in fact developed a large integrated operation outside its home country and had greatly improved itself as a multinational oil company.

With extensive foreign investments and operations, Standard Oil Company (New Jersey) had a special stake in the conflict that broke out in Europe in September, 1939, but it also had at home and in foreign countries the potential to become an important supplier of products for war. The size of that potential can be indicated by statistics on the material resources of Jersey affiliates in 1939. Their total oil reserves were estimated to be approximately 6 billion barrels at the end of the year. Their daily average net production for the year was 615,700 barrels. Their daily average refinery runs in 1939 were 849,800 barrels. And on September 3—the day the war started in Europe—their total tanker deadweight tonnage stood at 2,353,000.

The strength of the company was not only in reserves in the earth and facilities for producing, processing, and transporting petroleum; it was also in the human resources of parent company and affiliates. The creating of a top administration and of managerial organizations capable of directing and managing such diverse operations around the world has been considered in Chapter 2 and in subsequent ones on various branches of operations. The next chapter shows by what means and with what success the Jersey Company had worked to build an efficient and effective employee organization at home and abroad.

Chapter 12

Advancing Jersey's Employee Relations
Policies, 1927–1939

As THE YEARS PASSED, the success of the Jersey Company depended more and more on the soundness of its employee policies and the effectiveness with which they were carried out. New forces at work, both inside and outside the company, required attention to employee relations as never before. Expansion, more complex equipment and operations, greater competition, and shrinking profit margins gradually made necessary more systematic efforts to maintain employee organizations of adequate size and skills and of good morale. At the same time, parent company and affiliates had to adjust their employee policies and practices to mounting pressures from "social evolution at a very rapid pace."[1] Two trends were particularly significant: the movement toward advanced social legislation in the United States and abroad, and rising nationalism in many foreign countries. The company met many employee problems occasioned by its expanding role and by the sweep of events the world around.

ACHIEVEMENTS BY 1927

In shaping its employee programs and practices after 1927, Jersey built on the progressive policies it had formally adopted in 1918 and on the experience gained in applying them in subsequent years. Both the design and the application had been under the guidance of Clarence J. Hicks, who had come to the company as executive assistant to President Teagle to plan a program of what was then called industrial relations and to advise on its implementation. With support from the officers, Hicks already by 1927 had led Jersey to an advanced position in employee relations among American industrial concerns.[2]

Hicks referred to his basic principle as the Golden Rule, but actually it embodied several principles. First of all, he believed in the great potentialities of the individual and in the importance of offering opportunities

343

for the development of his capacities. He believed that sound industrial relations could be achieved only through effective communication between management and employees, and through the cooperation of the latter with management in promoting their own interest as well as that of the company. He also held that the companies should pay adequate salaries and wages, provide good working conditions, and assist employees in building up their own financial security.

The program that Hicks had furthered was expressed in seventeen points. Among them were collective dealing on all matters of mutual interest; submission of grievances to a council made up of representatives of management and employees; provision for death, disability, and sickness benefits; vacations with pay; promotion on the basis of demonstrated ability and length of service; retirement annuities; training to qualify for better positions; and freedom from discrimination on account of race, religion, or membership or nonmembership in a union.[3]

So broad a program required time for implementation. Some parts, such as annuity and benefits plans, depended principally on providing an organization and funds with which to implement them. Other parts, especially the industrial representation plan, safety work, and training, could be made effective only with experience on the part of both management and employees. Most of Hicks's proposals required a break with the past on both sides; essentially, they necessitated the development of new attitudes as well as skills in communication and personal relations. Consequently, even when conditions were most favorable, many changes could be realized only over a period of time. Because of the diversity of conditions under which Jersey's affiliates operated as well as the relative independence of their managers, the extensive program adopted by the parent company had not by 1927 been introduced uniformly throughout the affiliates.

The greatest success had been attained in the parent company's own operations, especially in the refineries in New Jersey. Besides introducing various programs for annuities and benefits, the company had set up an industrial representation system under which representatives of management and employees met in conference to discuss wages, hours, and working conditions. These meetings had provided a fruitful means of communication and had proved helpful in settling grievances before they had become serious.

Further developments had gradually contributed to the growth of mutual confidence between management and employees. Among them were formal programs for training and safety work. Especially conducive to good feeling had been the classification of jobs and the adoption of standard wage scales in the three New Jersey refineries. These reforms had taken the place of the old unsatisfactory system whereby the foreman, for example, could raise the hourly pay of one worker and withhold a raise from another. This new system also provided a form of collective bargaining between representatives of employees and management on the terms of employment. Differences which the two could not resolve had been referred to executives in New York. The local managers who had been unable to adjust to the new ways had gradually been relieved of their duties.

Other segments of Jersey's own operations as well as of its North American affiliates had by 1927 adopted the Hicks program in principle, but had implemented it in varying degrees. They had set up annuity and benefits plans and adopted industrial representation for some of their refinery, marketing, pipeline, and producing units. They had experimented with safety work, and had classified jobs and wages. By 1927, such classifications had been completed at Humble's Baytown refinery and Standard of Louisiana's at Baton Rouge.

Not much had been accomplished outside North America. In older and less fluid societies, as in Europe, long-standing rigidities of both management and worker had prevented affiliates from adopting such a democratic program as the parent company had promoted. Further, in some countries government regulation had already provided for various protective and benefit payments to labor. In the industrially less developed countries, such as the Latin American, the broad programs implicit in Jersey's seventeen points had not been adopted, even where operations had reached the scale required for formal plans. However, the companies had tried to solve urgent problems of health.

By 1927 the foundation had been laid for a wider application of Jersey's employee program among the affiliates. The top administration in New York had become convinced of its value, and the parent company had had enough experience and had acquired a sufficient staff to assist affiliates in developing their own organizations and programs. The leaders of some of the domestic affiliates had also come to see that the old ways of managing operating forces were not adequate in the larger organizations of this later time. At the same time, rising competition and shrinking profit margins focused attention on the need to raise employee productivity.

PROBLEMS AND PROGRESS IN THE
UNITED STATES, 1927–1939

Until his retirement in 1933, Clarence J. Hicks was the leader in interpreting to affiliates the parent company's policies and in advising them in developing appropriate programs. As executive assistant to President Teagle, Hicks had a staff with T. H. A. Tiedemann and Frank W. Pierce as his special assistants. These men, and others, worked closely with the Industrial Relations Department of Standard Oil of New Jersey, which had the active support of Frank W. Abrams, general manager of the New Jersey Works. This affiliate had the first department among Jersey affiliates devoted exclusively to employee relations.[4]

In accordance with the parent company's decision of 1927 to decentralize the management of operations, these men in New York worked in an advisory capacity with affiliates. The companies' top administrators decided upon their own organizations and programs in accordance with their view of needs and how best to meet them. Their practice was generally to adopt specific programs and to fit the men in charge into already existing departments, but within a few years separate industrial relations staffs or departments were set up in several domestic affiliates.

The first affiliate besides Standard Oil of New Jersey to set up a complete industrial relations department was Humble—at the time, by far the largest and unquestionably the most progressive of the domestic affiliates outside the New York–New Jersey area. In 1927 this company, which already had had considerable experience with several programs patterned after Jersey's, saw the need for a more systematic handling of relations with its expanding and widely scattered employee force. In its customary way, Humble's board had a study made of the employee organizations and programs of a number of companies. The directors then formed a committee—consisting of top executives for the company's principal functions—to plan a department to direct in carrying out a formal effort to strengthen the company's employee relations. Organized in 1929, the Industrial Relations Department consisted of groups for annuities and benefits, medical work, safety training, and personnel. Charles E. Shaw, formerly manager of employee relations at Jersey's Bayway refinery, was appointed head of the department. Shaw brought to Humble the philosophy and experience of the older company.[5]

Jersey continued to place special emphasis on the promotion of its industrial representation plan. This form of joint management-employee conference was established in new affiliates and adopted more widely in old ones. By 1930 there were more than thirty such groups, covering at least two-thirds of the total domestic employment roll of 46,000. The members were generally the employees paid by the hour. They elected representatives to meet with a like number of men from management to discuss wages, hours, and working conditions as well as to consider any grievances that might arise.

The most successful joint conference groups for a number of years were those in the New Jersey refineries, where the plan had first been introduced, and General Manager Abrams pioneered in putting into practice the general principles advocated by Hicks. At the other large refineries of the domestic affiliates—at Baton Rouge and Baytown—little progress was made before 1933 in building up the representation system and in achieving real bargaining between management and labor. Local supervisors still dominated the joint conferences. But this was changed as new managers took charge of the refineries and supervisors with new attitudes and skills in human relations replaced the old. In such other operations as production, which covered large areas, regular meetings were not easily arranged and were usually limited to annual dinners. On these occasions representatives of management reported the various changes that had been approved by top executives of Jersey and affiliated companies.[6]

Salaried employees did not for some time participate in this system of representation in joint councils with management, nor did they have the security of job classifications with specific wage scales. Although they experienced the same favoritism and lack of system in establishing their compensation as hourly paid employees had met formerly, they had no regular system for making their grievances heard but had to rely on their particular superiors. The parent company's corporate secretary had kept cards recording the annual remuneration of each salaried individual employed by affiliates, except for such companies as Humble and Imperial, which had sizable minority stockholder interests. Jersey's directors had received monthly and yearly recommendations from affiliates concerning salary increases for some employees. The directors had sometimes approved, but often had slashed, the proposed increases rather arbitrarily in order to bring the total compensation in line with estimated expenditures.

A more satisfactory method of determining salaries was adopted late in the 1920's. A committee had been set up in 1926 to study the remuneration of employees in New York City and to compare their salaries with those paid for comparable work by other companies from which such information could be obtained. This committee drew up classifications of jobs and ranges for salaries up to the $3,000 level, a limit which covered the majority of salaried positions. At the conclusion of the study late in 1928, the parent company left to Standard Oil Company of New Jersey and other affiliates in the New York area responsibility for determining annual raises for their salaried people. As before, Jersey itself approved increases for its own small group and for those holding the more highly paid positions in affiliates in New York City and its vicinity. Other domestic affiliates then made similar studies of job classifications and salary ranges. However, some of these efforts, because they occurred during the downtrend in business in the early 1930's, resulted in considerable employee resentment.[7]

The parent company also took a stand against the nepotism practiced in many offices and recommended the training of promising managerial talent. President Teagle in 1929 called upon executives not to engage relatives to work with them. If such persons desired employment with the company, they should apply to other departments. Teagle urged that hiring and promotion should be solely on the basis of competence.[8] A year later he firmly stated his position with respect to executive posts: "The first duty of an executive is to provide for continuity of efficient management. . . . No executive has fulfilled his duty until he has trained his successor."[9] Although the company's efforts did not meet with immediate success, Jersey men gradually assumed more responsibility for preparing those who were to succeed them.

During the years from 1927 to 1933, the Jersey board and its special committees also investigated the various plans which had been set up previously to provide for contingencies which the individual employee could not normally handle alone. The changes they adopted marked a general movement away from the earlier paternalistic system, under which the companies had provided the benefits, toward joint participation by companies and employees.

Attention was first turned to the reserves for paying annuities to retired personnel. Late in the 1920's, the Board of Directors became concerned that these reserves might not be adequate. Jersey and many of its affiliates had in 1927 set aside $10,355,000 as a reserve for annuities. But the income from these funds was falling while the burden of annuity payments was growing heavier because more employees were staying with the companies until retirement and better records were kept of the length of the individual's service. Jersey therefore had studies made of pension reserves and costs. One study by the Equitable Life Assurance Society showed that the reserves of the parent company and certain affiliates, totaling approximately $10,000,000 at the time, were far short of actual requirements. Consequently, in the three years 1929–1931, the companies increased those reserves to $45,000,000 by transfers from surplus and by higher annual contributions. They made further additions later in the decade.[10]

As the depression grew worse, as annuity payments increased with the rising number of retirements, and as the rate of income from pension funds declined, Jersey's Board of Directors decided in 1932 to alter the plan then in force, under which the companies provided all the funds. The existing Jersey plan, and similar ones adopted by some affiliates, had set annual retirement payments at 2 per cent of an annuitant's average compensation during the last five years of employment multiplied by the number of years of service. In 1932 Jersey recommended changing to a joint company-employee contribution but continuing to hold for each employee's account the credits already accumulated. The parent company and affiliates modified their retirement plans so that the company thereafter provided for each employee a retirement credit of 1 per cent of earnings for each year of service. Employees could build up larger credits by voluntary contributions.[11]

The old employee stock-purchase plan was retained. This program had been instituted in 1921 and modified in 1925 to help promote thrift and provide security. Under successive three-year plans after 1925, the employee could authorize the purchase of company stock from a fund to which he or she could contribute up to 10 per cent of earnings and the company would contribute proportionately up to 5 per cent of the individual's earnings. By the time of the termination of the plans in 1935, the participating employees had received nearly 2,000,000 shares of stock worth more than $60,000,000 at the prices at which they were purchased by the trustees administering the funds.[12]

In 1932, a profit-sharing plan for executives of the parent company and affiliates was terminated. This plan had been approved by Jersey's stockholders in May, 1929. To run for five years, it provided that, when profits exceeded 7 per cent of the net assets of the consolidated group of companies, 5 per cent of the excess should be turned over to a special compensation fund for executives.* Not more than one-half of the

---

* President Teagle favored the plan, but chose not to participate.

amount thus made available was to be paid to the parent company's own directors. Out of $4,535,000 set aside from earnings, payments were made in the years from 1929 through 1931. However, because of a decline in earnings in 1931 and 1932, the plan was terminated in the latter year.[13]

Among other plans that came under the scrutiny of various committees was group life insurance. Until 1932 Jersey and its domestic affiliates laid aside funds for death benefits for employees and annuitants, which were handled by the Equitable Life Assurance Society. This arrangement had been revised in 1925 to provide a full year's pay, with a maximum of $3,000 for those with less than ten years of service at the time of death. In 1932, this company plan was supplemented by a group life insurance arrangement under which employees and annuitants took out life insurance, each individual paying 60 cents a month per $1,000 of coverage. Two years later, the minimum was raised from $1,000 to $1,500, the maximum was set at $20,000, and the rate was raised to 64 cents monthly per $1,000. The companies continued to provide for any totally disabled employees and also for the beneficiaries of any employees who were not covered by group insurance.[14]

Other benefits were changed only slightly, if at all. Paid vacations for salaried and wage employees were continued without change by Standard Oil Company of New Jersey and some other affiliates. As before, the companies provided help in cases of accident and sickness; they made payments in excess of the amounts required by state workmen's compensation laws to employees who were involved in accidents while at work. For those who were not eligible for an annuity but who had had at least ten years of service, the companies considered instances of total disability on their own merits. In 1932 they increased from thirteen to twenty-six weeks the time requirement for eligibility for sickness benefits.[15]

The companies' medical departments added to their services for employees during these years. The parent company employed a few specialists in its office in New York—including Dr. W. J. Denno and Dr. A. W. Schoenleber—to advise affiliates. Standard Oil of New Jersey had a medical staff to serve employees of Jersey and affiliates in and around New York. The parent company's medical men discussed with affiliates their plans for doctors and nurses in locations having large groups of employees and also arrangements for medical staffs on a part-time basis or subject to call in other places. It was expected that applicants for employment would be given a medical examination before they were hired and periodically thereafter. Employees were free to go to the medical staffs for the treatment of illnesses and accidents; but serious cases were referred to outside physicians for diagnosis and treatment. In 1930 the affiliates in the United States had a total of seventeen full-time doctors and eleven nurses. The employees at Baton Rouge made provision for the medical care of their families by maintaining their own organization—the Stanocola Medical and Hospital Association—to which they paid monthly dues and from which they received a wide range of benefits.[16]

In the late 1920's also came greater attention to the prevention of accidents, which in the oil industry were frequent and often severe. The traditional attitude of the oil worker was that accidents were an unavoidable part of the job—a fatalistic attitude which it was difficult to change. This could no longer be tolerated as equipment became more complex and the larger working crews required on many operations made a single accident a possible threat to many employees.

Assisted by the Safety Department in New York, the operating affiliates set up special groups to study and promote ways to reduce accidents. These safety specialists studied the causes of accidents and how to prevent them. They inspected machines and equipment in order to reduce hazards. They distributed safety appliances. And they advised managers and supervisors in setting up and carrying out safety programs.

Safety, however, was a line-management responsibility, and reducing hazards in refinery and field was a function of managers and supervisors. Safety programs became a constant and vital part of operations nearly everywhere among the affiliates. Safety committees were set up and regular meetings were held to interest employees in taking all necessary precautions and to train them in the proper procedures to protect themselves and their co-workers. A significant technique used in training was for the workers themselves to draw up safety rules.

There were both tangible and intangible results of these safety efforts. Attitudes and standards conducive to accident prevention were developed. Accident rates and costs were reduced. And morale was improved. By-products of the regular safety meetings were the easy form of communication they provided between employees and management personnel and the opportunity for developing and recognizing qualities of leadership among the employees. The safety meetings were especially important in regions where no other organized means of communication between management and employees had been established.[17]

Of central importance was the more systematic effort among the affiliates from the late 1920's to raise the quality of the employee force. The parent company for a decade had had a personnel and training department, which in 1927 was transferred to Standard Oil of New Jersey. Similar groups were set up in other affiliates within the next few years.[18] These personnel staffs were designed to help stabilize employment and to make hiring, firing, and promotion more intelligently selective. They also helped develop extensive training programs, including special instruction in industrial processes, particularly for supervisory employees in the refineries. Additional courses were designed for Standard Oil of New Jersey which included the sale of lubricants and specialty products. Humble in 1930 undertook a broad program of training which was made up not only of old courses in office and operating skills but also others in foremanship and engineering and even such technical specialties as geology and geophysics. These efforts to broaden the training of employees had barely come well under way when the deepening depression made it necessary for management to give its major attention to new employee problems.[19]

Surplus labor became a pressing matter as early as 1930 and remained so for several years. The first move was not to undertake new construction after projects already started were completed. Although the contracting of most construction had become both technically and economically advisable in the later 1920's, the affiliates themselves still employed a large number of men on such projects, especially for temporary unskilled work. These short-term unskilled workers were among the first to go. Late in 1930, the companies tried to maintain their employee forces by eliminating overtime work. In the next year, Jersey suggested a general weeding out of the least efficient and the dismissal of the most recently hired workers. Standard Oil of New Jersey, Standard of Louisiana, Carter, Colonial Beacon, and Humble then reduced their employee forces considerably. Humble, which had had extensive construction under way from late in the 1920's, reduced its personnel by 28 per cent in 1930 and 1931. The total number of employees of the parent company and its domestic affiliates declined from 57,865 at the end of 1929 to 46,197 at the end of 1931.[20] (See Appendix 2, Table 6.)

Jersey's directors soon began to consider other ways of reducing payrolls than by laying off employees. In the spring of 1931, Heinrich Riedemann wrote President Teagle from Europe advising that world conditions be considered in determining company policy. He urged that reducing the income of workers would be shortsighted since it would throw the burden on the weakest shoulders. Riedemann wondered whether Americans realized that "if economic conditions the world over continue much longer as they are today this will cease to be one of the periodically returning periods of depression and develop into a critical catastrophe for the past and present order of things." People in Europe, he wrote, did not understand "on what a volcano the European situation really exists."[21]

President Teagle took the initiative in proposing that the workweek be shortened. He had received expressions from many sources of the advisability of sharing the work among employees and cutting the hours of those who so far had not felt the impact of the depression. After discussions early in January, 1932, with Farish, one of his closest advisers, the Jersey president suggested to the Board of Directors that they recommend the sharing of work within the companies.

Teagle particularly favored a reduction of hours and consequently of the total pay of salaried personnel, who so far had not generally been adversely affected. He held that employees on salary should share the reductions of those engaged in operations. The Bayonne refinery had by this time cut its hours per week from forty-eight to forty. Humble had limited its hours so that its weekly schedule early in 1932 called for eight hours daily for five days for refinery process men and pipeline employees, and for four days for refinery mechanics and producing department employees. Teagle believed that a reduction in the hours of salaried persons would result in an increase in the total number of employees, and that this would help to reverse the downtrend of employment. Actually, many on salaries had been benefiting from a higher net purchasing power, inasmuch as the cost-of-living index had declined from 100 in 1926 to 82 in 1932.[22]

The nine directors in New York at first took the position that the president's suggestion to reduce the pay of salaried employees was neither wise nor soundly based. They pointed out that these people had not received the increases that wage earners had obtained, that the company still had a large financial surplus from previous profitable years, and that it was paying regular and extra dividends. They also held that the five-day week which Teagle proposed would raise expenses generally. They proposed various other measures, including intensifying the economy program and making individual adjustments in the payrolls.[23]

However, Teagle persisted in his efforts to bring about a reduction by about one-eleventh in the hours and compensation of salaried workers of Jersey and its domestic affiliates. He pointed out, in support of his proposal, that at least four major oil companies were reducing their hours and salaries. He also informed Clarence J. Hicks of proposals of leading industrialists for the sharing of work in order to prevent the setting up of a dole and for the passing of legislation for shorter hours in the United States. He agreed with the executives who preferred to have industry carry out the adjustment in hours and wages voluntarily, thus making it easier to adapt to future changes in business conditions.

By June, 1932, President Teagle carried a quorum of Jersey's directors with him. He appointed a committee, of which Frank W. Pierce was chairman, to study the equalization of salaries, to survey wage and salary rates, and to recommend adjustments. In an article in the issue of *The Lamp* for June, 1932, Teagle explained the new policy, under which hours were reduced from forty-four to forty and salaries were lowered proportionately, but a minimum salary of $100 per month was maintained. Within a short time, many of the domestic affiliates adopted this rule for their salaried employees.[24]

Teagle carried still further his fight for sharing the work. He conferred with other industry leaders in Washington in August, 1932, and accepted the chairmanship of the national Co-ordination Committee of the Share-the-Work Movement. This was one of six committees set up under the federal government's sponsorship to help bring the country out of the depression. Congress, at President Hoover's urging, passed various measures to ease unemployment throughout the country.[25]

In the spring of 1933, Jersey and its affiliates in the United States adopted still another method to reduce employment. This was the retirement of men between 60 and 62 years of age, to be compulsory at the latter age, throughout the domestic companies. Six months later this was changed to voluntary retirement at 62 years and mandatory at 65. As a result of the 62-year rule, Jersey itself lost Clarence J. Hicks, who more than any one else was responsible for its advanced employee relations. Soon thereafter Hicks and Tiedemann, who resigned at this time, became active in Industrial Relations Counselors, Inc., which the Rockefellers had set up to study labor problems.[26]

Altogether, these attempts by industry and government might have contributed markedly toward lifting the United States out of the depression if 1932 had not been an election year. During the critical months of the campaign and between the election and the inauguration of President Roosevelt, business conditions deteriorated seriously. Nationwide unemployment rose to 24 per cent of the labor force.[27]

At this difficult time, a change came in the leadership of the Jersey employee relations groups in New York. Frank W. Pierce succeeded

Clarence J. Hicks as executive assistant to President Teagle for this work, and Ralph L. Mason became manager of the Industrial Relations Department of Standard Oil Company of New Jersey. Pierce worked closely with Mason and with Frank W. Abrams, who in 1933 became president of Standard Oil Company of New Jersey. With Abrams' support, the two men utilized this company—especially its New Jersey Works—as a proving ground for further developments in Jersey's employee policies and programs.

The year 1933 marks an important turning point in Jersey's—and indeed the country's—relations between employers and employees. From then on for several years, the Roosevelt administration promoted a new national labor policy in the United States, and the federal government became an important factor in determining the conditions of work and the relations between employees and management. This introduced a strong third party into those relations.

The new national administration first took the initiative in drawing up—with the aid of industrial leaders, including President Teagle and other Jersey men—codes of fair-trade practices to improve economic conditions. The National Industrial Recovery Act called upon employees to share the work, setting thirty-six hours as a workweek for wage earners and forty for salaried employees. It also called upon industry to increase hourly rates or weekly salaries so that total weekly earnings, taking into account the decline in the cost of living, were equal to those prevailing for longer hours before the depression. These regulations ended, however, when the Supreme Court in 1935 declared the National Industrial Recovery Act unconstitutional.

The demise of the NIRA was followed by new social security legislation. This included provision for unemployment insurance, for which employers were required to contribute to the federal government 1 per cent of their payroll; the national government utilized its insurance fund in assisting state programs for payment to unemployed workers. Legislation also provided for employers and employees each to contribute 1 per cent of their payroll or pay to the federal government to use in cooperating with the states in assisting needy aged, widows, widowers, and children. The Wagner Act encouraged collective bargaining between companies and unions. And in 1938 the Walsh-Healey Act set up minimum hourly rates and maximum hours, before payment of overtime rates, for companies with government contracts. The number of unemployed, however, remained a serious problem until 1939.[28]

Jersey's domestic affiliates altered their previous employee programs to comply with the new federal measures. They raised average hourly rates in accordance with the NIRA regulations. In the New Jersey Works, for example, a common laborer, who for ten years had earned 57.5 cents an hour, received 64 cents in August, 1933; the average hourly pay, which had been approximately 75 cents, became 83 cents. The new levels for a thirty-six-hour week were accepted by the employees and the companies as providing the same real earnings as with lower rates, longer hours, and higher prices at the end of 1929.[29]

As prices increased during 1934 and succeeding years, Jersey recommended that the domestic affiliates make further adjustments in their wage and salary scales in accordance with the company's general principles. Employee representatives at joint conferences in the New Jersey refineries in 1934 urged that hourly wage rates be raised by 15 per cent because of the rising cost of living. The management representatives pointed out that the company was willing to grant an increase when the federal cost-of-living index rose by 5 per cent. However, the employees doubted the applicability of the Department of Labor index to conditions in New Jersey. The local managers therefore agreed that the company would make an adjustment if a committee of employees and supervisors found that the cost of living in New Jersey had risen appreciably. Twelve from each group were relieved of their regular duties to investigate local prices and living standards and compare them with data obtained from Washington. By early 1935 the employee representatives were satisfied that the federal index adequately reflected changes in local living costs. Jersey, assuming that the rise in the cost of living would amount to 5 per cent by the middle of the year, recommended to its affiliates that they grant a 5 per cent increase in June, 1935. Later, inasmuch as the cost of living was still rising, the parent company recommended still another 5 per cent increase to go into effect late in 1936. In order to meet the prevailing wage rates—another refinery in New Jersey having raised its wages—Jersey also recommended a raise in March, 1937, of 10 cents an hour for wage earners and 10 per cent for salaried personnel up to a salary of $3,000 a year.[30]

By its willingness to submit the question of the cost-of-living index to a joint management-employee committee and by its later increases in wage rates, Standard Oil Company of New Jersey demonstrated to its employees that it was striving to be fair even at a time when it was having difficulty in making profits, especially in the refineries. The position taken by the company in this matter, which reflected the attitude of

Frank W. Abrams, increased the confidence of the employees in the president and managers of the company.

At the same time that these general raises in pay for both wage earners and salaried personnel went into effect, Jersey resumed its former policy of granting merit increases for the latter group. It also proposed in 1935 that the domestic affiliates again grant salary increases to the lower-paid in accordance with ability and responsibility. The next year it announced that its Executive Committee would review only those salaries that were over $5,000. However, the committee would examine statistical reports indicating the general programs of the affiliates.[31]

The chairman of the Coordination Committee, E. J. Sadler, raised a question about payments to those earning more than $25,000, calling attention particularly to the effect of high income taxes in the United States. These executives were then receiving much lower net salaries after taxes than in the past, while the wage earners were getting more. The spread between the two was therefore decreasing. However, Jersey did not raise the salaries of its higher executives to counteract this trend.[32]

The company actually moved in the other direction. In an address to the Academy of Political Science in November, 1933, President Teagle had pointed out that the American economic condition indicated the need for a more equitable distribution of the rewards of industry, the country's productive capacity in the preceding three decades having grown faster than its consumption. Jersey subsequently recommended that affiliates make more nearly equitable the spread between the wages of their lower-paid and higher-paid personnel.[33]

With New Deal legislation, a notable change came in Jersey's employee relations: the old employee-management representation plan was discontinued. This was a result of the National Industrial Recovery Act of 1933 and the Wagner Act of 1935, both of which stated that employees had the right to organize and bargain collectively with managers through units of their own choosing. Because the Jersey Company's employees were satisfied with the industrial representation plan, they did not discard it at once after the first of these laws was passed, but introduced some modifications. However, when the Supreme Court of the United States in 1937 upheld the constitutionality of the Wagner Act, the affiliates' management informed the employees that the old representation plan must be abandoned because it did not conform to the law. It also informed them that the employees themselves would have to decide what they wanted to do. A few representatives from the New Jersey Works went to Washington to consult John L. Lewis, president of the Congress of Industrial Organizations, to learn what the national union might have to offer. Lewis is reported to have said that they already had good conditions and that he could not do more for them.[34]

The employees of Jersey's domestic affiliates then drew up constitutions and bylaws for independent unions. These associations were supported by the majority and were recognized by the companies as the representative groups for the various units. However, they were not unchallenged.

Although the managers of the plants in the New Jersey Works endeavored to stay completely aloof from the action of the employees in setting up independent units, they were accused by outside union organizers of trying to influence employees. The charges were investigated and dismissed by the National Labor Relations Board as based only on hearsay. In subsequent years, however, charges of coercion and intimidation by company officials resulted in investigations and court decisions. These were concluded by a decision in 1944 that another election be held to determine the representative unit. The employees again voted for an independent union.[35]

At Humble's Baytown refinery also, some difficulty was experienced in the transition to employee federations. Here resentment had arisen on the part of a number of skilled men, who, instead of being laid off during the depression and losing their benefits, had been assigned to maintenance and repair work at the rate of 25 cents per hour. Their resentment at this demotion, and a general feeling among the refinery employees that management did not give them adequate recognition, provided an opportunity for a former laboratory worker to build up some support at the refinery for membership in the Oil Workers International Union–CIO. Although this individual was aided by a general drive to organize such locals along the Gulf Coast, his attempt to call a strike in 1936 aroused such an unfavorable reaction in the general community, as well as among refinery personnel, that the strike was called off. The men instead formed an independent union, which became the agency of the refinery employees for collective bargaining with Humble's management.[36]

The Jersey seagoing personnel on United States–flag ships were similarly affected by widespread efforts to organize American marine employees. But both officers and unlicensed seamen eventually chose to set up independent associations. They succeeded in negotiating favorable agreements with the marine executives. (See Chapter 8.)

New Deal legislation in the later 1930's also brought changes in the benefits programs of the parent company and its domestic affiliates. The companies adjusted their arrangements to supplement federal social security measures. Previous annuity plans were frozen, and the stock-purchase arrangement was suspended at the end of 1935. A new thrift plan was set up under which an employee could voluntarily contribute from 3 to 13 per cent of his earnings regularly. The companies would match the first 3 per cent and half of the remainder; they also proposed to share profits with the employees by making special contributions when their net earnings were high. A portion of the thrift fund was to be used to build up annuities. The remainder, in accordance with the individual employee's choice, could be utilized to purchase stock or to serve as collateral for loans, or it could be withdrawn after a time. In 1938 Jersey affiliates also changed sickness benefits and vacations.[37]

As business conditions improved after 1933, Jersey and its domestic affiliates again added to their employee force. At the end of 1939, the regular employment rolls totaled 48,654, but this was lower than in all other years since 1927, except from 1930 through 1933. Reduction in the number of employees of Jersey refineries and the change from company service stations to independently operated ones kept the number of domestic employees from rising to the earlier figure. At the same time, employment became more stable; in 1937 the affiliates' labor turnover was 7.2 per cent of the total number employed. The Jersey companies continued to give special recognition to employees as they reached their tenth, twentieth, thirtieth, and fortieth year of service—fifty-year service was no longer possible after the retirement age was lowered.[38]

In the later 1930's, the companies again began to place emphasis on programs to improve the quality of both the employee force and its performance. Such improvement became increasingly important as the work grew more complex in most operations and the operating organizations became larger. New skills were required to handle the more volatile materials used in refineries, to overcome the difficulties met in drilling deeper wells, and to run the highly mechanized equipment used in nearly all operations. Also, because of the growing need for coordinated effort on a large scale, good teamwork was more important than ever. The Jersey companies, therefore, gave more attention to hiring and retaining men and women of good quality, and they greatly expanded the range of their training programs. At the same time, they improved communication between management and the rank-and-file employees.[39]

Operating management had always had chief responsibility for employees in the Jersey companies. In this later period the concept of the functions and responsibilities of the supervisory force was changing. No longer was the duty of the foreman almost wholly that of getting the work done—to give orders and direct the men under him. He also was given increasingly more responsibility for the safety and morale of the workers.

Maintaining a supervisory force with the qualities required for such leadership was partly a matter of selecting the right type of men, but it also required special supervisory training as well as good communication among the supervisors and between them and the managers. In the later 1930's this training was expanded and improved. In addition, conferences of foremen were held periodically to discuss problems and develop rules and standards and generally to help raise the quality and performance of these responsible overseers of operations. Conferences of supervisors and managers also came to be held regularly throughout the companies.[40]

Thus, from 1927 to 1939, Jersey and its domestic affiliates experienced significant changes in their employee management and relations. With a large measure of success, the companies had put into practice the principles introduced by Clarence J. Hicks. They had worked to develop stable employee forces of the quality required in large and complex operations at a time when technical competence and competition were rising in the oil industry. Many years of effort, based on a constructive attitude on the part of management and spurred by outside pressures and the demands of employees themselves, had eliminated most vestiges of arbitrary dominance and paternalism and had brought instead a large measure of voluntary cooperation between management and employees.

Both companies and employees benefited. The lower-paid workers, especially, gained absolutely and relatively in income. Extensive training programs helped the individual to improve his position and at the same time raised employee productivity. In a period of much turbulence, both the companies and the employees had largely escaped the conflicts that were common in the 1930's and had successfully adjusted to the new federal regulations of the decade. The evidence seems incontrovertible that, at the end of the period, the Jersey companies in the United States had employees of both high quality and high morale.

EMPLOYEE RELATIONS IN CANADA

Imperial Oil Limited and its affiliates in Canada adopted programs similar to those recommended by Jersey. The Canadian group profited by taking advantage of Jersey's extensive experience with progressive employee relations. But it had a different leadership, different needs, and a different social, economic, and political environment. It is, therefore, understandable that Imperial did not progress in the same direction and degree in its employee management and relations as the Jersey companies in the United States.[41]

The system of employee-management councils had taken firm roots in Canadian operations in the 1920's. There had been resistance and distrust at first, but gradually joint councils were developed. As new plants were opened, areas entered, and affiliates organized, the system of representation was explained to employees and, if they so desired, joint councils were established. By September, 1930, Imperial and its affiliates had ninety councils—in its offices and among office maintenance personnel and in refining, producing, pipeline transportation, shipping, and marketing. These councils considered conditions affecting employment, wages, and work, and they also discussed grievances. If no action was taken on an issue, the matter could be referred to the Imperial board in Toronto. Not all the joint councils were successful; their effectiveness, in Canada as elsewhere, varied with the nature of the individual group's leadership.

The economic depression, which became acute in Canada in 1930, provided a test of the soundness of Imperial's relations with its employees as well as of the company's ability to carry out the programs adopted in 1919. Interestingly, at the very time that the depression began to be felt, the work force presented a singular token of appreciation for the half-century of industrial peace in Imperial. The employees across Canada had collected a fund of $35,700, which was presented to the company's directors with the stipulation that the income from it be used for philanthropic purposes outside the company.[42]

The ink was hardly dry on the newspapers that hailed the gift as unique in Canadian and American industrial history when the impact of the depression began to be felt by Imperial. The effect on its employee relations was very similar to that experienced by Jersey and its affiliates in the United States. Because of the high cost of maintaining its insurance and pension plan itself, the company decided that employees also should contribute. It consequently worked out a new insurance arrangement, with the cost partly borne by employees, and made its annuities plan contributory; both plans were similar to those adopted in the United States. As a depression measure, Imperial also instituted the five-day week, with reductions in pay of half a day's wages for hourly workers and one-eleventh of their pay for salaried employees, with no reductions for those earning $100 or less per month. The reductions also applied to officers and directors, whose earnings had already been reduced. When the five-day week proved not to take up the employment slack, Imperial's directors decided to apply the rule to retire men at 65 and women at 55, and also to review, with retirement in mind, the case of each male employee reaching 60 years of age. These efforts did not altogether solve the problem of surplus, and the company also laid off many employees. When layoffs were necessary, so far as possible those were dismissed who had the fewest dependents. When rehiring was done, other things being equal, preference was given to those who needed work the most.[43] The number of employees declined from 20,282 at the end of 1929 to 13,058 at the end of 1932. (See Appendix 2, Table 6.)

Imperial made further changes in its employee programs in the later 1930's. In 1937 it instituted vacations with pay. In 1939 it adopted a thrift plan to take the place of its annuity plan of 1932. Under this new combined pension and savings program, employees could contribute from 3 to 13 per cent of their current compensation, to which the company added the equivalent of from 3 to 8 per cent of the total employee contributions. Four per cent of the amount credited to the individual employee had to be used for the purchase of an annuity, handled by Sun Life Assurance Society. The remainder, in accordance with the individual's wishes, could be held as cash savings to his credit or used for the purchase of Imperial stock, or for both.[44]

Although the company adopted annuities and benefits plans similar to Jersey's and had a large number of joint management-employee councils, it did not in the 1930's make all the changes instituted by the affiliates in the United States. It did not set up a special department at headquarters in Toronto to direct the development of, and to coordinate, employee relations organizations and activities throughout operations. Also, it did not establish the close communication between headquarters and operating units that developed within the Jersey companies in the United States. However, the company's generally satisfactory relations with its employees indicated that it was regarded as a good employer.

LIMITED PROGRESS AMONG EUROPEAN AFFILIATES

The relations of the European affiliates with their employees necessarily differed from those in North America because of the different nature of European societies and the different political and economic developments going on across the Atlantic. Those differences had deep historical roots. Instead of the relatively open society of America, most

European countries had a traditional social stratification that affected all aspects of life. In business, employees on salaries were quite separate from workers on an hourly wage basis; neither had much communication with managing directors. Economic organizations tended to follow class lines. In virtually every country in which Jersey had affiliates, national unions of workers negotiated with national associations of employers. Economic interests also heavily influenced political organizations so that labor unions were closely tied to political parties. Contrary to the traditionally wide range of competition in the United States, supported by the Sherman Antitrust Act and the Clayton Act, monopolies under government protection were common in Europe.[45]

However, conditions were far from static. Social and economic maladjustments after World War I, worldwide depression, and new ideologies were bringing into these structured societies great changes affecting business. These were of a more or less evolutionary character in some countries—the Scandinavian, for instance—and quite revolutionary in others, such as Russia, Italy, and Germany. Governmental regulation and control in most countries was intensified. In some, there was confusion, even chaos. Commonly, intervention by government greatly limited the managers' freedom in dealing with salaried employees and wage workers.

The managers of Jersey's European affiliates consequently faced many difficulties in their employee relations. Some of Jersey's directors who were in charge of foreign operations believed that Europeans could understand and handle these matters more satisfactorily than could the Americans. Consequently, many of the latter were sent home or were transferred to purely advisory or technical positions. When the Europeans later came to recognize that they needed a better understanding of developments in their countries and that their proximity to local problems limited their appreciation of trends, they sought help from others. Better communication was established among themselves through the membership of their companies in the International Association (Petroleum Industry) Limited; a few of the top men in the European affiliates gave up operating responsibilities and moved to London to become members of the association's council. The European managers also in time achieved better communication with their American counterparts, with whom they exchanged views and experiences and from whom they sought advice on particular problems. But the progress that came under way was interrupted by World War II.[46]

Few generalizations on employee relations hold for all the European countries in which Jersey affiliates operated. Legislation for workmen's compensation and welfare, such as pensions and unemployment payments, was widespread. Salaried employees, however, were rarely protected by governments. The right of labor to organize unions and to bargain with management was widely recognized. Although conditions differed greatly from country to country, and the affiliates had to adjust their employee management and relations to conditions within each country, in most countries governments more and more determined relations between managers and employees.

In the 1930's, Jersey's affiliates in France were subjected to growing limitations on their relations with employees and also to rapid social and political change, especially after the middle 1930's. A law that became effective in 1930 set up a compulsory program for the workers on hourly wages, including pensions and sickness and death benefits paid from contributions by industry, labor, and government. A law of 1932 made provision for special payments by employers to workers in amounts proportionate to the number of children in their families. With the coming of the Stavisky scandal, severe unemployment, and riots and general strikes, the Confédération Générale du Travail was revived and a radical labor party, Front Populaire, was formed. This party won control of Parliament in 1936, and a sit-down strike paralyzed French industry in that year. In this atmosphere of labor victory, union leaders and representatives of employers' associations signed the Matignon Agreement, which was incorporated into law under the leadership of Léon Blum. This agreement required immediate resumption of work and entry into collective action by industries for shortening the workweek, raising wages, increasing various benefits, and making collective bargaining with unions effective. Strikes and further concessions to labor, together with a near paralysis of operations and industrial stagnation, led to the rise of Édouard Daladier. His efforts checked the membership and power of labor organizations, but he did not succeed in arresting the decline of morale among both management and workers.[47]

Jersey's affiliates in France, which had virtually been compelled by the government to join industry associations, conformed to the new French policies in 1936 and later years. They participated in drawing up contracts with unions for their labor forces. Before the Matignon Agreement, they had about 5,500 employees on an hourly basis and 3,200 on salaries whose earnings averaged 877 francs ($53.58) and 1,935 francs ($118.23) per month, respectively. These rates of pay were now increased by 15 per cent for the lower-paid and 7 per cent for the higher-paid, and the work-week was reduced from forty-eight to forty hours. The affiliates made other changes, such as establishing overtime rates and providing for vacations with pay for both hourly workers and salaried employees. Because it was not accompanied by corresponding increases in productivity, the nationwide rise in labor costs increased the cost of living, which then called for still higher wages. Late in 1937, Jersey's French affiliates were paying 56 per cent more to their workers than before the sit-down strike of 1936. They continued to contribute, as required by law, for social insurance and family allowances. They also set up a pension plan for the salaried employees and the workers earning more than 25,000 francs a year that was similar to the plan used by the Jersey companies in the United States.[48]

The affiliates in France actually had little scope for independent action. They were limited not only by extensive government regulations but also by the policies of other petroleum companies that were members of the *syndicale*. Any proposed changes had to be cleared with this organization. Having to conform to the practices of other members of the industry was frustrating to the more efficient and aggressive managers, some of whom wished to introduce various measures for their labor forces designed to raise morale and improve the quality of the work done. One means by which Standard Française was trying to develop effective relations with employees and workmen was through safety meetings. At these meetings not only accidents and safety measures were discussed but also many other matters looking toward the building up of confidence between local management and labor. The company was still often disturbed by interruptions of its operations, but these occurred less frequently after the government late in the decade introduced strict measures to deal with industrial difficulties.[49]

The turbulent years in France between 1927 and 1939 were in great contrast to the dull despondency that existed in Great Britain. There industry was in a bad way, and large numbers of people remained unemployed as a result of the country's grave economic conditions after World War I and during the depression of the 1930's. Following the unsuccessful general strike of 1926 and the Trades Dispute Act of 1927, the labor movement suffered an eclipse, which lasted until after World War II. Wage rates remained virtually stationary, and the workweek stayed at forty-seven or forty-eight hours. A large majority of Englishmen received a dole, unemployment insurance payments, or very low wages or salaries.

There was little hope of improvement until the country began to rearm late in the decade.[50]

Jersey's British affiliates made relatively few changes in their employee policies. These affiliates, whose employees numbered 11,000, had the largest total personnel of Jersey interests in any European country. They contributed to workers' benefits as required by law, but did little more.[51] They were members of employers' associations which negotiated with labor unions. They attempted to build a direct relationship with their workmen by setting up works councils similar to the Jersey management-employee conferences. The managers of the Fawley refinery and the marketing divisions assumed that these, rather than the national unions, would become effective means for settling disputes. But they were abruptly disabused when a vote at the refinery showed that the great majority belonged to the Transport and General Workers' Union, the largest labor organization in Britain. The works councils were abandoned at Fawley, where safety groups were developed instead by the spring of 1939. But efforts to build cooperation between management and the sales organizations were continued. These attempts to establish closer relations with the affiliates' own employees were no doubt spurred by the fact that syndicalism, socialism, and fascism were spreading on the Continent.[52]

Jersey's affiliates in Scandinavia, which managed widely scattered marketing organizations throughout the area and small refineries in Norway and Denmark, conformed to the prevailing employee policies in the various countries. In these northern countries, the progress of intervention by governments in matters concerning workers was steady and broad. Legislation provided a wide range of benefits and rights for the working population, with the result that the standard of living rose considerably. In Denmark, Norway, and Sweden, the actual level of living was second only to that in the United States. In these countries also, laws required bargaining of employers' associations with labor federations. Sweden in 1928 established a labor court to handle differences between the two groups. Jersey's Scandinavian affiliates contributed to pensions and other benefits for the hourly paid workers, as determined by various laws, and also voluntarily to pensions for salaried employees. The companies revised their pension programs after the affiliates in the United States had changed theirs to provide that the employees as well as the companies contribute to the supporting funds.[53]

The German affiliates had little freedom to develop their own employee programs during the years from 1927 to 1939. During the first six years, they were members of industry associations which bargained with national unions concerning wages and working conditions. As economic conditions deteriorated after 1929, the German government resorted to awards and decrees to settle difficulties and to reduce wages, thus restricting the freedom of both managers and employees. Unemployment became severe in Germany in 1932, when about one-fifth of those formerly gainfully employed were out of work.[54]

These German affiliates lost their last vestiges of independence in labor matters when Adolf Hitler came into power in 1933. Thereafter they had to conform to his dictates, but they still tried to provide as good conditions as possible for their 6,500 employees. Hitler arrested union leaders, confiscated union property, and ordered the dissolution of unions and employers' associations. The Nazis set up the German labor front, which was devoted to collecting dues, arranging welfare activities, and organizing vacation trips and entertainment. Early in 1934, the government passed an act providing for the national organization of labor. It repealed labor laws and set up a works council for each factory; but, since the determination of all issues involving employees was turned over to appointed trustees, these councils soon became inactive. Jersey's affiliates found that this 1934 measure provided for minute regulation of all aspects of company operations: for the determination, for example, of the exact minute for beginning and ending work in each area. Minimum wages were set in 1935 and maximum wages in 1938. If any worker left voluntarily before payday, his wages were turned over to the labor front to help finance recreational activities.[55]

In Italy, Mussolini moved more slowly to assume control of the economy and the labor force. After four years of resistance beginning in 1922, Italians had generally accepted increasing controls. A labor law passed in 1928 determined the rights and benefits of the workingman—such as sickness funds, to which the workers and companies contributed equally. Although workers and their employer had the right to bargain together, this meant little to either party because workers were not allowed to strike and any difference between labor and management was subject to compulsory arbitration. In 1935, at the time of Italy's aggression in Ethiopia and its participation in the Spanish Civil War, government controls over workers were intensified.[56]

The Italian affiliates tried to maintain good labor conditions despite a difficult economic situation and increasingly restrictive government controls. They altered the pension plan for salaried employees, revising it in

1934 from the former 2 per cent credit for each year of service to 1 per cent. This plan was supplanted in 1935 by a provident fund, to which the employee contributed 5 per cent of his salary and the company added 12 per cent, with extra amounts at times. The Italian affiliates thus followed the system prevailing in Jersey companies in much of Europe, under which the hourly paid worker was covered by the government setup and the salaried employee was provided for by voluntary company plans.[57]

In Romania, where Jersey's affiliate had been operating since the early years of the century, economic conditions were more like those in underdeveloped countries of the Far East and Latin America than in industrial Europe. Since this Eastern European country had been affected only slightly by the Industrial Revolution, Româno-Americana depended upon men from outside Romania for the more skilled positions in fields and refineries. The company provided medical care for all on its payroll and houses for the more skilled workers. Because of economic depression and its serious financial condition, Româno reduced salaries, wages, and the number employed, with the result that in 1932 the rolls listed only 2,100 as compared to the record high of 5,750 in 1929. The unemployed workers came under the influence of Communists; they took part in a disturbance early in 1933 which was put down by the arrest of the leaders.[58]

Difficult adjustments had to be made in Romania after new labor legislation became effective in 1935. This law contained many stipulations, including one that required 80 per cent of the employees and workers in the various categories to be Romanians. Jersey's affiliate then set up a training program for nationals; it sent some men to Humble and Carter for a year and a half, and it retired or transferred as many of the seventy foreign employees as it could spare. The government was not satisfied with this effort and fined Româno-Americana, but the company brought suit against this action and won the return of the fine in 1937.[59]

Româno made other changes in its industrial relations after the labor law of 1935 became effective. Some of the lower-paid workers were covered by pensions required by the law, but the higher-paid employees lacked any definite coverage. Management determined the provision made for anyone who had an accident or was too old to continue working. Ralph P. Bolton, the general manager, in 1937 called for the assistance of specialists from New York to draw up suitable programs for employee benefits. Among these was a pension plan—for both salaried employees and hourly workers—which the former initially turned down because it set 65 as the age for retirement. The age was then lowered to

60, with permissive earlier retirement. The company and the employees contributed under this plan as under the American thrift plan.[60] This was the first pension program in Romania and probably the first among Jersey's European affiliates that did not discriminate between manual laborer and white-collar employee.

To provide a vehicle for discussions between its working force and management, Româno-Americana at the same time drew up a so-called plan of cooperation similar to the industrial representation formerly in wide use within the Jersey companies in the United States and recently adopted by affiliates in a few European countries. This and other programs at the time—such as the medical, safety, and performance rating—were exceptional steps forward in Romania.[61]

Altogether, the affiliates in Europe made some progress in their employee relations in the 1930's. This was especially important inasmuch as Europeans constituted a large segment of the Jersey Company's total employee force. The European personnel numbered about 35,000 in 1939, which was 27 per cent of the world total for Jersey affiliates.[62] But progress was definitely limited; it consisted mostly of pension plans for salaried employees and the organization of industrial representation groups in a few places. Broad advances were hampered by the widespread absence of confidence of employer and worker in each other and by a lack of effective communication between them, and in most countries by a complex system of government regulation and industry-wide bargaining which reduced the scope for effective company action.

CHALLENGE AND RESPONSE IN THE FAR EAST AND LATIN AMERICA

In the largely underdeveloped countries where affiliates operated, problems in relations with employees multiplied. Because of the expansion of operations—particularly of production—and also an advancing technology, to build an adequate working force presented vast problems. In addition, mounting social and political unrest, accompanied by an extreme form of nationalism, presented problems in a number of countries. The situation was made especially difficult by the mass illiteracy and poverty which characterized most of these countries. In order to succeed at all, the companies had to learn to operate under such conditions. For most of the affiliates in underdeveloped countries, the 1930's were a period of experimentation, of learning how to build adequate working forces and to maintain good relations with them.

One obvious need was to improve the health and general well-being of the employees. The affiliates gradually built up various types of medical facilities, as well as some housing, schools, churches, and many recreational facilities, all of which they considered essential in building up a proficient labor force.[63] They also encouraged the nationals to take advanced training and promoted some individuals to responsible positions. Over the years, they increasingly replaced or supplemented the employees who had come from outside the country. These were generally Americans who had been occupying managerial, supervisory, and even skilled operating positions.

Until nationals of adequate training were available, however, it was necessary to depend upon many Americans and a few Europeans who could be induced to leave their home countries and live in uncomfortable quarters and often in debilitating climates while doing pioneer work. These men were willing to undertake such assignments when jobs were scarce at home and pay was high in foreign service. In order to reduce expenses during depression years as well as to comply with various government regulations, the affiliates intensified their drive to train local employees and, in the case of the Dutch East Indies, Dutchmen from the Netherlands.[64]

Managers were assisted in employee matters by specialists in offices in New York and London as well as by local legal experts who served as counsel for the companies in each country. New York contributed medical advisers, employee relations consultants, and lawyers. The London office of the Committee of European Directors and later the International Association (Petroleum Industry) Limited also provided advice to Jersey's majority-owned affiliates in several countries.[65] Although help thus could be obtained from the outside, critical problems that might have an important bearing on the affiliates called for decisions by local managers.

Relations with workers and employees in underdeveloped countries and colonial possessions necessitated recognition of mounting nationalism. Oil-industry executives had not always determined policies for operations in such countries with a view to national interests. Mistakes had been made, for example, in Mexico by operating so as to meet contractual and legal obligations but with little concern for the general well-being or aspirations of the people. In some countries, governments intervened directly in labor matters; in many, they dictated some of the rules but left relations on the whole to management and workers. Generally, however, individual relations with workers and employees were heavily affected by the prevailing political climate.

The first among the less developed regions in which Jersey's affiliates had encountered employee problems was the Dutch East Indies, where NKPM had begun to explore for oil in 1912. This company had been an affiliate of Jersey's American Petroleum Company of Holland until 1926, but had then come under direct Jersey ownership and guidance. Dutchmen had determined many of the policies, although they had hired some Americans and Canadians to carry on exploration and many Eurasians, Malayans, Japanese, and Chinese for manual work. NKPM's health measures had been directed by a Dutch doctor, who had followed the example of the older and larger local affiliate of Royal Dutch–Shell.

Health problems in the Dutch East Indies had grown greatly during the years immediately preceding 1927. During this period the Talang Akar field in the Sumatran jungle was developed, an 80-mile pipeline laid, and a refinery constructed at Sungei Gerong on the Moesi River. All health problems were handled by a staff made up of a doctor and a nurse stationed at a small hospital at the refinery and by local first-aid men elsewhere.

For several years after 1927, according to reports made to New York, the administration of medical and safety programs was satisfactory. For the second half of 1928, the first period for which statistics were prepared, the local Dutch doctor reported the malaria rate—usually high in a tropical country—as only 66 cases among 1,500 Asiatics. He also gave the relatively low accident rate of only 46 per 1,000 workers. The medical staff in New York questioned these remarkable figures; they wondered whether the records were kept on a sound basis.[66] Probably they were not, inasmuch as different standards prevailed in foreign countries. This situation illustrates the need for the closer over-all supervision of health and safety matters which Jersey was extending to foreign affiliates.

Concession contracts for new areas to explore and exploit in the Dutch East Indies required greater participation in the industry by Dutch citizens. NKPM's contracts of 1928 stipulated that at least 75 per cent of the personnel engaged in producing and handling the oil from these concessions be of Dutch citizenship. Compliance with this rule was not too difficult for unskilled jobs, but it was impossible for a time to fill many of the skilled positions with Dutch citizens because of the limited number experienced in oil operations. The company managed to comply with the regulation by classifying most of its Americans working in the Dutch East Indies for two or three years as temporary employees. It also adopted the policy of contracting with technical groups for specific projects. For example, when it was impossible to obtain satisfactory Dutch geologists and geophysicists, NKPM contracted for crews of scientists in these special fields from Humble Oil & Refining Company. In the meantime, it initiated a program to hire and train promising Dutchmen; it sent some men to the United States for further training after they had become acquainted with operations in the Dutch East Indies. As a result, although the total number of salaried employees in NKPM rose from 400 to 500, the number of Americans fell from 128 in 1931 to about half that number in 1939.[67]

Americans, however, remained in top management positions in the Indies. Lloyd W. Elliott, who had come there from Mexico in 1924, was the local general manager during these years. In 1938 he was in charge of more than 8,000 workers and salaried employees in NKPM's producing, refining, and pipeline operations and in its offices. Standard-Vacuum Oil Company, which became this old affiliate's direct parent company in 1934, at that time had 19,000 employees engaged in marketing and shipping in the Far East. The total number employed by Standard-Vacuum and its affiliates increased by 3,000 during the next year as a result of new refinery construction at Sungei Gerong and the launching of additional tankers under the British flag.[68]

NKPM encountered many complications in its employee relations because of its separate programs for American employees, Dutchmen from their home country, and those hired locally—generally workers paid by the hour whose service with the company was usually brief. The benefits for the third group were limited. The Dutch East Indies in 1927 did not have a workmen's compensation law in force, although the Dutch home country did and British India had had one since 1923. NKPM had established annuity and insurance plans for its salaried employees before 1928. In the case of Americans, these benefits, formerly paid for by the company, were changed to joint contributions as in the United States. For Dutchmen, one-third was contributed by the employees and two-thirds by the company in accordance with the Protector Plan in force in the Netherlands. The medical program throughout this period was more generous for Dutch employees and local workers than for Americans in that the company paid for the care of families of the former but not of the latter. Free housing was discontinued in September, 1931, salaries being increased by $30 per month instead.[69]

Because of the more fluid political and social conditions in Latin America, the employee relations of Jersey's affiliates there were more critical than in the Far East. Changes were just beginning in some countries and were reaching fruition in others. These came from nationalist and socialist aspirations that were local expressions of broad international movements. Conditions varied from country to country, but there was a deep stream of similarity in the employee problems that arose. Here too, North Americans were working in cultural and social environments quite different from those at home, and the responses and programs of the oil companies varied from country to country because of differences in local conditions and in the managers of the affiliates themselves.

The most conservative of the Jersey companies in Latin America in these years was the International Petroleum Company, Limited, which had producing and refining operations on its La Brea y Pariñas Estate in northwestern Peru. The company had inherited a British tradition from the preceding organization, a way of doing things which had been maintained in part by the Canadians who had replaced most of the British in key positions. These later managers had pursued a paternalistic policy toward the Peruvian employees. By 1927 the nationals were largely sons of former workers, who had been brought up on the estate and had benefited from medical care, a varied diet, and education in company schools. Although some had risen from the rank of laborers (*obreros*) to that of employees (*empleados*)—particularly as drillers in the fields—the company had had no definite program for training them for still higher positions.

The consequent lack of adequately trained Peruvians led to difficulty when the government in 1930 issued a decree requiring that half of the technical staff must be Peruvian nationals. The country went still further in 1932 and 1933 by requiring that 80 per cent of the labor force and of the total payroll be Peruvian. Immediate conformance being impossible, the government allowed the company time to train national workers and also permitted it to classify as Peruvian those from outside the country who had been working in Peru as long as ten years. International Petroleum immediately reduced the number of expatriates and stepped up its training programs. By 1939 it was employing only 200 non-Peruvians out of nearly 5,000 employees.[70]

This affiliate felt the full force of political instability in Peru; it passed through an especially difficult period from October, 1930, to July, 1931. At this time the presidency of the country changed and, in order to gain popular support, the new president freed many political prisoners. Among them were Communists, who took advantage of the situation to foment trouble in industrial areas. Agitators arrived at Talara and in the producing fields. There they caused unrest which led to three strikes in nine months. This unstable condition ended with a demonstration of force by the government. The company then gave assurance that it would improve certain local conditions.[71]

New social welfare laws in Peru required some changes in International Petroleum's employee programs. In 1928 the company had complied with a new law and decree by taking out group life insurance for all Peruvians on its payroll. On a voluntary and individual basis, at the termination of long periods of employment it paid a pension equal to one or two weeks' pay for each year of service (or a month in a few cases). As part of the strike settlement in 1931, it agreed to pay 66 per cent of annual wages or salaries of Peruvians in cases of total incapacity resulting from an accident at work. In 1936 and 1937, various laws and decrees, providing for payments during illness and old age and to beneficiaries after an *obrero's* death, made obligatory some monetary benefits the company had formerly given voluntarily. One decree stipulated that the companies pay a tax of 2 per cent of the *obreros'* wages in order to take care of these responsibilities. Nothing was stipulated about the pension for the *empleados* or the Canadian employees, a type of assistance which the company provided on an individual basis.[72]

International Petroleum was slow to develop adequate health programs for its labor force in Peru. Because the Humboldt Current shifted its customary course only every seven years, which change raised the amount of illness, there were few crises to meet on account of climate. Occasionally, outsiders brought diseases to the company's camps, such as smallpox in 1928 (for which all were then vaccinated), scarlet fever and diphtheria in 1937, and typhoid in 1938. Whenever Dr. A. W. Schoenleber of the New York office visited Peru, he found conditions to criticize in the handling of normal health hazards. For example, in 1933 he reported that the general sanitation situation at Talara was not as good as it had been a few years previously, largely because of poor inspection by a local official. Again, early in 1937, he found sanitation still unsatisfactory and the hospital at Talara below the standard of Jersey's affiliates in other countries. International Petroleum's management resisted suggestions for larger expenditures and endeavored to keep operating costs as low as possible in order to remain competitive with oil companies in areas more advantageously located. Some improvements in housing had been made, principally by allowing a number of individual families to take over two living units, which had become possible when the labor force had been greatly reduced in 1931.[73]

The company thus moved cautiously. On the whole, it maintained a paternalistic type of management, which usually relied on support from the government, particularly when outside agitators tried to stir up trouble. The government officials in power in Peru represented a relatively small part of the total population. As one means of maintaining its control, the ruling class adopted regulations to provide better conditions for large numbers of their countrymen, generally at the expense of foreign companies. However, the governmental measures in Peru were not so drastic as in some other countries. This difference was partially a result of the cautious management of the leading companies in Peru and the comparatively satisfactory working conditions for their employees.

International Petroleum's affiliate in Colombia, The Tropical Oil Company, was troubled far more than International in developing an adequate, permanent labor force. Tropical Oil had been occupied for a number of years with developing producing fields, building a refinery at Barrancabermeja, and meeting health hazards in tropical jungles in which its operations were located. For its labor supply, it had relied on Colombian nationals who had come from their native villages under short-term contracts. Some of these men recontracted, often bringing their families with them. They found housing in the village of Barrancabermeja; on week ends the workers, who lived in barracks in the producing fields, returned to the central community in a company train. In order to provide for the families of the more skilled nationals and also those of the North Americans, housing was gradually expanded to about 500 family units in the fields and 300 at Barrancabermeja in 1939. These quarters, however, constituted a small percentage of the total housing needed for the producing and refining labor forces, which totaled 200 North Americans and 3,400 Colombians. There were more than 1,000 other nationals employed on river boats, in the marketing organization, and in the office in Bogotá. All these people had to provide their own living arrangements.[74] The housing situation undoubtedly complicated relations with employees; a large proportion of the unskilled workers felt their way of living abnormal and their housing inadequate as compared to the living conditions of the more skilled.

The situation provided fertile ground in which to sow seeds of discontent and to foment strikes. Legislation by a liberal government provided for the organization of labor syndicates and also granted greater benefits to the Colombian worker. The setting up of syndicates increased the opportunities for radical agitation in 1934. Trouble broke out at a time when government policy was uncertain and the company was trying to introduce an employee representation plan (plan of cooperation). Radicals came to Barrancabermeja, organized a local syndicate, and in 1935 called a strike. During this twelve-day strike, staff employees stayed at their posts to protect company property and to keep a part of the refinery in operation. After sending representatives to investigate, the government ended the strike on signing an agreement with Tropical Oil. The company granted an increase in wages, and national officials permitted it to terminate the employment of the strike leaders and to set a limit of forty-eight hours for the other men to return to work if they wished to retain their jobs.[75]

This experience and a subsequent investigation into the nature of the labor force helped to impress upon the company's leaders the need for a generally more enlightened employee policy. The local manager was surprised to find that many of the older and better workers had been among those most eager for a strike—a sad commentary on management. Thereafter, Tropical made a greater effort to provide means for the workers to voice their grievances by developing its plan of cooperation more fully. It also undertook a study of wages and of the cost of living in Colombia, a survey which resulted in granting raises to many nationals. In addition, it classified about 200 Colombian workers as *empleados,* bringing the total in this classification to 300. It also constructed more housing for nationals. These and other measures brought such an improvement in relations that, when another strike was called in 1938, few workers proved sympathetic or left their positions in the refinery.[76]

In the middle 1930's the government of Colombia enacted social security legislation, the provisions of which were more than fulfilled by Tropical Oil Company. Prior to 1934, there was no law providing for thrift plans, severance allowances, or retirement pay. Under an act passed in that year, Colombia in 1935 required the payment to *empleados* of a severance allowance (*cesantía*) equal to one month's salary for each year of service. Although the law required that this allowance be paid only on dismissal without good cause—such as noncompliance with the employment contract or bad conduct—Tropical paid it even if the *empleado* resigned of his own accord. The law made no provision for severance allowances for *obreros,* but the company voluntarily instituted the policy of also paying them a *cesantía*—known as *bonificación de retiro*—amounting to two weeks' pay per year of service.[77]

In 1934 the company voluntarily established the first noncontributory retirement plan in Colombia for its *obreros* and second-class *empleados*. This arrangement provided for a pension to be calculated on a progressive scale according to the number of years of employment. These two classes of employees were entitled to retirement at the age of 45 after ten years of service with the company. But, by agreement with the company, an employee could continue working longer and the amount of his pension would increase with his additional years of service.[78]

Over the years, Tropical Oil conducted training programs to prepare Colombians to take over work being done by foreigners. These ranged from training on the job to sending promising sons of nationals to the United States for further education—Tropical reportedly was the first company in Colombia to do the latter. This was done as a matter of basic policy as well as in preparation for compliance with an anticipated decree requiring that a certain percentage of those employed be nationals. Such a decree in 1936 required that 80 per cent of the *empleados* and *obreros* be Colombians and 70 per cent of the total payroll be paid to Colombian nationals.[79]

Tropical Oil also took measures to improve the health of the *empleados* and of the *obreros* in the fields and at the refinery by carrying out many of the preventive and curative measures which the medical experts in New York thought applicable. From the beginning of Jersey's interest in Colombia, efforts had been made to eliminate malaria among the labor force by clearing the underbrush, ditching around living quarters, disposing of refuse properly, providing suitable storage for food, and boiling drinking water. These improvements had been accompanied by the establishment of a hospital at Barrancabermeja, followed by another in the producing fields. On these beginnings, improvements were made in these later years.

High turnover in the employment of nationals and the increase in their number at certain times added to the difficulty of reducing the incidence of sickness and accident. The malaria rate dropped markedly from 1929 to 1933, when it was ten cases per thousand individuals a year, but it rose to five times this rate in 1939. Hookworm presented another problem, which the medical staff tried to combat. Carelessness—a common and serious difficulty—contributed to a high accident ratio. R. S. Bonsib, safety head in New York, studied hazards to workmen in Colombia in the summer of 1929 and found many ways in which preventive measures and training in safety could reduce the frequency of accidents. Efforts were thereafter made along the remedial lines he proposed, and the accident rate dropped steeply.[80]

Another affiliate in Colombia, the Andian National Corporation, Limited, had relatively few difficulties with its workers. In fact, it had only a small number of employees to man the pumping stations and the coastal terminal, and their living conditions did not present serious problems. Andian's head, James W. Flanagan, won the loyalty of the workers through his interest in their well-being and their personal lives. The pipeline company escaped the strikes which spread to river, railway, and dock workers following the difficulty at Barrancabermeja in 1935.[81]

Far less satisfactory than the condition of employee relations in the Far East, Peru, and Colombia was the situation in Mexico. Here the long conflict between the government and foreign oil interests still prevailed, although after 1927 the object of the controversy shifted from the rights to the subsoil to the rights of labor. The Mexican constitution of 1917 had stated both rights in new terms, but little attention had been paid to labor until the Morrow-Calles agreement in 1927 had quieted the controversy over the subsoil. In the 1930's, under President Lázaro Cárdenas, a dispute developed over labor's demands, which were supported by the government. This difficulty led directly to expropriation of the properties and operations of the foreign oil companies—including Jersey's affiliates. Relations with Mexican labor are considered in connection with that development in Chapter 5.[82]

In Bolivia and Argentina, where Jersey had producing, refining, and marketing interests, affiliates made few advances in employee relations. The small operations in Bolivia ended with expropriation in 1937 after many years of uncertainty. In Argentina, nationalistic movements and legislation prevented foreign companies from developing large operations. Jersey and Royal Dutch–Shell, the two large outsiders, were consequently gradually reducing their operations. One advance made by Jersey's principal affiliate was to establish in 1937 a training course for nurses at Central Camp, Tartagal, which seven Argentinian girls attended. This was a radical experiment in Latin America, where young women were customarily secluded in their homes and where nursing was looked down upon as an occupation for women.[83]

In Venezuela, before and after the death of President Gómez in

December, 1935, labor conditions were gradually getting better with the development of operations. According to contemporary reports, improvements in both safety and health measures and in living conditions had far to go in 1928. At that time, however, Standard Oil Company of Venezuela was exploring for oil in many parts of the country and was employing largely unskilled and inexperienced nationals in regions where disease was more or less endemic. Only as fields were put into commercial production could effective measures be taken to improve conditions for all employees and to build a more stable working force.[84] Unquestionably, Jersey's affiliates advanced further in the 1930's in Venezuela in applying the parent company's employee program than in any other Latin American country. That development, however, is considered elsewhere in connection with the account of the growth of Jersey interests in that country. To the security and successful operations of those interests a large and effective working force was essential. (See Chapter 5.)

Conditions were different at the refinery on the Dutch island of Aruba than in the countries on the mainland. Here an almost total lack of local manpower called for recruitment elsewhere, which meant a veritable babel of tongues and diverse backgrounds. Many Arubans returned home from jobs in other places, and workers from various points in the Caribbean sought employment on the island. Because the Caribbean recruits were generally lacking in industrial training or experience, Americans were employed to fill semiskilled, skilled, and managerial positions. In March, 1936, out of a total labor force of 2,810 at Aruba, about 790 were from outside the Caribbean area and on a contract basis. These outsiders held all nine executive positions and all but two of the 138 supervisory posts. They also filled more than a third of the skilled or semiskilled positions. The Arubans and other islanders held the remainder in these categories as well as the many hundreds of unskilled jobs, an imbalance not conducive to good morale.

Opposition to the employment of so many outsiders was first manifested in the Arubans' resentment toward workers from nearby islands who, because of experience elsewhere or higher qualifications, held better positions than the native islanders. The company therefore instituted a program to reduce immigration and to educate the sons of Aruban workers and train them in the refinery. In addition, it took steps to provide training on the job for the fathers in order to fit them for more responsible positions. Within a year, considerable progress had been made; the number of contract employees from outside Aruba dropped by

156, while the number of those hired locally for skilled and semiskilled positions rose by 160. Increased operations also raised the number hired locally, bringing it to 79 per cent of the total employee roll of nearly 3,000 in 1939.[85]

Management made further attempts to improve relations at Aruba. A system of joint councils was begun; it started with meetings with local workers, who thereby gained group and leadership experience. Housing was improved, and the company assisted many home purchasers by guaranteeing loans granted by a local bank.[86]

In brief, employee relations and conditions in areas in the Far East and Latin America under local or colonial governments were generally improving. The national employee was being better fed and housed and had more medical care than earlier. Better provisions were made for emergencies and retirement. The workers were also being trained and educated for more responsible positions. As a result, qualified nationals were replacing Americans and Europeans as skilled workers and instructors and even as supervisors. Not all the programs were in accordance with the timetable that Jersey might have set up as desirable. Some managers were slow in adopting recommended programs. And several countries legislated changes before it seemed advisable to put them into effect. However, reasonableness on the part of government officials was in evidence in many areas, a situation which allowed a proper period for change-over to a reduced percentage of outsiders in various positions. Except in Mexico and Bolivia, the foreigner remained. Many countries recognized the need for his services and for capital from other countries in utilizing undeveloped resources and contributing to a higher standard of living. But nearly everywhere governments were more and more determining the conditions of employment.

By 1939 the parent company and affiliates had experienced notable transformations in their employee relations. They had had considerable success in putting into wider practice—in ways suited to changing internal needs and external conditions—the principles introduced by Clarence J. Hicks in 1918. At home, the companies' old paternalism was virtually gone; in its place had come a clearer cognizance of the responsibilities and rights of both company and employee and a relationship that was characterized by cooperation in the mutual interest. The result was a stable employee force of the quality and morale required for effective work in large and complex operations. Abroad, especially in producing and refining, the companies had had a varied experience on the frontiers of human relations. They had learned much about how to build and maintain operating forces among peoples lacking the motivations, disciplines, and skills required by large-scale, modern industry.

In most countries, including the United States, the extension of Jersey's policies and programs had been affected by mounting government regulation. The application of new programs had been limited in some countries by communist and fascist ideologies and in many by rising nationalism. Nearly everywhere, company-employee relations had felt the effect of unstable economic and political conditions. Developments in the 1930's had indicated that in the future those relations would not be determined by company and employees alone. Henceforth, they would have to be handled in the larger context of social and political diversity and change.

Chapter 13

Jersey's Involvement in World War II, 1939–1941

THE YEAR 1939 BROUGHT the end of an era for Standard Oil Company (New Jersey). During the years of peace after World War I, the company had been occupied with its own operations and development as a private enterprise. It had grown greatly in size; it had especially expanded its foreign production. It had progressed far toward achieving balanced functional integration. It had made the transition from empirical to technical methods. And it had strengthened its administrative and operating organizations and improved the efficiency of operations. By such advances, the Jersey Company had kept pace with the growth of the dynamic world oil industry. Germany's invasion of Poland in September, 1939, introduced a period of time in which the Jersey Company became increasingly involved in war and in which its energies were turned more and more into supplying Great Britain and its allies and helping to build up the national defenses of the United States.

The leaders of the Jersey Company in America and Europe had observed the growing threat to peace for several years. They had watched with apprehension the rising power of Hitler and his National Socialist Party in Germany. They had seen nationalist and warlike tendencies developing in Europe in 1938 and becoming more ominous during the next year. These developments manifested themselves in political crises, rising military expenditures and government controls, and increasing difficulties with foreign exchange.

Although Jersey's administrators could not know when or where war might come, they made such preparations as they could make to protect their company's interests. Under the system of decentralization and of incorporation of affiliates in foreign countries, they knew that Jersey's influence would at best be limited in countries at war. However, they made some changes in anticipation of trouble. In 1935 they transferred the Bapico fleet from Danzig to Panama registry. In 1938, because of restrictions of American neutrality legislation, they expanded the facilities for the manufacture of aviation gasoline at Aruba. At home, as early as January, 1939, they began to confer with the Munitions Board in Washington. In fact, their research had for several years been concerned with the development of processes for making products for military use in the event of war.

The parent company's leaders knew that Jersey bore risks abroad far beyond those inherent in operations at home. However, there was assurance in the wide distribution of its foreign investments. And, as stated in its *Annual Report* for 1939, "Rendering an indispensable service, which is supported by adequate reserves of raw material, widely placed manufacturing plants, and long established agencies of distribution, we are well prepared for contingencies."

No earlier conflict had placed the oil industry in so strategic a role. This was a war of mobility and speed, and oil was to supply the driving power. Technical progress had raised the military importance of petroleum fuels by increasing the capability of airplanes, submarines, and tanks to inflict destruction upon enemies. This development, together with the use of petroleum in fueling navies, trains, trucks, and other forms of transport and in manufacturing explosives and other products for war, now made the oil industry a vital factor in any such conflict. To obtain supplies and to cut off the enemy's sources of petroleum products became essentials in the strategy of war.

IMPACT OF WAR ON EUROPEAN AFFILIATES

Jersey's European affiliates at once became pawns of the warring powers. In fact, in Germany companies had come under direct governmental control even before the war, and such control had also been applied in other countries that had come under German domination. A similar fate overtook the affiliates in countries that later joined the Axis powers or were conquered by them.

The advance of the Axis in 1939 and 1940 brought most of Continental Europe under the domination of Germany and its allies, and with it nearly all of Jersey's affiliates on the Continent. In 1940 the Russians overcame Finland; Romania, Hungary, and Italy joined Germany; and the Nazis conquered the Netherlands, Belgium, France, Denmark, and Norway. With these countries went control of such important Jersey marketing affiliates as Det Danske, Standard Française, and Società Italo-Americana, and many smaller concerns in Europe and North Africa. In addition, such valuable producing companies as the old Româno-Americana in Romania and the young but growing Magyar Amerikai Olajipari, R.T., in Hungary came under the Nazi yoke. In order to preclude outright seizure of the holdings in countries under German domination, Jersey's directors in 1940 assigned to the executives of its German affiliates the right to vote shares in companies in those countries.[1]

Contact with affiliates in Axis-held lands was virtually broken long before the entry of the United States into the war in 1941. The affiliates outside Axis territory did not supply the German companies after September 3, 1939—when Great Britain and France declared war on Germany—or those in Italy after June 10, 1940.[2] There were several reasons for this break, especially United States shipping regulations and British efforts to stop trade with Axis countries and also the impossibility of getting payment for oil from the Germans and Italians. In the summer of 1941, Jersey might have obtained compensation for one company, the Hungarian producing affiliate, for which I.G. Farbenindustrie offered $24,000,000 in gold to be delivered in Lisbon. The company refused the offer because the United States Interdepartmental Committee on Foreign Funds Control would not authorize the transfer of the gold. This committee stated that its decision was in accordance with government policy "to prevent Germany from acquiring the assets of overrun countries or from being able to make use of any such assets that it may have looted" and "because other American interests might not be able thus to recover their investments."[3]

Most of the Jersey companies in countries dominated by the Axis retained their separate identities, but their administrators had no freedom of action. As President Farish said, when countries in which affiliates were domiciled were "drawn into the orbit of war, neither the operating unit nor the parent company retains any real voice in determining policy."[4] Employees of the affiliates were equally helpless. They were compelled to work long hours, and many in conquered countries were forced into virtual slave labor in German plants.[5]

The Axis-domiciled Jersey affiliates, together with other Axis-controlled oil concerns, were made to exert the greatest possible effort to produce, manufacture, and transport oil and petroleum products for the Axis powers. This was a life-or-death matter for Germany and Italy, which were virtually cut off from overseas supplies. The companies were subjected to heavy pressures to find and produce more crude; the

Hungarian affiliate discovered a new field in 1940.[6] Refinery equipment was transferred from country to country, the better to serve German needs; and affiliates were compelled, as they had been earlier, to invest in plants for manufacturing the synthetic oil products with which Germany planned to meet a large part of its requirements.[7] Transportation equipment was transferred as the Germans directed.[8] Civilian marketing was under complete government control.[9] And the oil products of Jersey companies in storage in conquered countries were seized.

Despite all these controls, Germany eventually began to face the threat of a shortage of petroleum products. The prospect that oil supplies in Europe would not prove sufficient for a long war was one of the reasons for the Nazi change of strategy in 1941. Germany abandoned the plan to use air attacks to bring about the surrender of Great Britain and turned to a policy of gradual attrition, all the while seeking added oil supplies from rich fields in Russia and the Middle East. In June, 1941, violating the agreement with their former ally, the Nazis began a wide-scale invasion of Russia. This attempt, however, was begun with inadequate supplies and too late in the year to assure success before the extreme cold of the Russian winter set in. German motorized equipment, which was using lubricants adversely affected by low temperatures, became virtually immobile in the Russian winter. Unlike the Allies (including Russia later), the Germans did not have lubricants of a type to make possible the operation of motor equipment in the coldest weather. Although by December they were threatening key cities—including Leningrad, Moscow, and Rostov—and were not far from the rich oil fields of the Caucasus, they never reached the first two cities or the productive Baku fields.[10]

In Great Britain—and in France until its surrender in June, 1940—companies in effect became partners of the government in providing oil products for military and civilian use. Before the outbreak of war, British and French officials had met with executives of oil companies to draw up plans for coordinating operations in the event of an emergency. Jersey's British affiliates had representatives on the British Petroleum Board, made up of oil company executives, and on the subsequent Oil Control Board, composed of both government officials and company executives.[11] The latter body, together with its subsidiary agencies, had complete control of British petroleum companies and their operations.

The whole British system for distributing products was under the direction of boards and committees, which pooled available supplies and allotted them to the various distributors in proportion to their established market positions. Civilians were strictly rationed, storage stocks were moved to areas less exposed to bombing or into underground tanks, and aviation gasoline was carefully husbanded for use in fighter planes.[12] For the transport of petroleum from distant sources, the British and French licensed for each voyage vessels flying their flags and belonging to companies operating in their countries.[13] The actual management of operations in carrying out the orders and regulations of the Oil Control Board remained in the hands of the companies' own executives.

All of Jersey's European business with belligerent or neutral countries became affected by the struggle on the seas. From the very first, control of the sea lanes was vital to the Allies because of their dependence on overseas supplies. Immediately after the outbreak of war, Germany began a submarine campaign against all vessels approaching Allied ports; in August, 1940, it announced a total blockade of the British Isles. Britain did not, as in World War I, declare a blockade of Germany but instituted methods that were effective in creating a virtual blockade, particularly of ports in Northwestern Europe. From December 7, 1939, neutral ships, in order to proceed unmolested to their destinations, had to obtain from a British consul a "navicert," a certificate of innocent character. The British also endeavored to stop German exports by detaining all goods of German origin on ships they seized, even when the goods had been bought by neutrals. France followed similar procedures until its fall to the Nazis. The United States in November, 1939, departed from its traditional doctrine of freedom of the seas and forbade American ships to enter belligerent ports or to pass through indicated war zones. Certain other countries in the Western Hemisphere took similar action.[14]

The operations of Jersey companies in most neutral European countries depended on the course of the war on land and sea. In the first year of Nazi advance, only Sweden, Switzerland, Ireland, Spain, and Portugal remained outside the conflict. The affiliates in such countries endeavored to utilize available shipping facilities to bring in as much oil as possible for supplying current needs and building up inventories. However, the losses caused by German submarine attacks and the delays from British regulation of neutral shipping prevented the affiliates from reaching their supply and inventory goals.

Under direction of the governments of these countries, supplies were pooled and markets were shared in proportion to each company's prewar position. In fact, Jersey's affiliates in Sweden distributed only about 50 per cent of their peacetime volume during the early part of 1940 and less than 5 per cent in the early months of the next year. They turned to substitutes, as did those in Switzerland and Ireland. The Swiss affiliates had trees on mountainsides cut down and converted into charcoal for civilian use. The companies provided work for as many employees as possible. In Spain and Portugal, where Jersey had been supplying only specialty products in prewar years, the consumption of petroleum products declined only slightly because the United States declared their ports on the Atlantic Coast to be outside the war zone.[15]

As far as possible, Jersey maintained communications with its European affiliates outside the Axis countries. It had no effective contact with those under Axis control. American personnel remained in conquered countries until the invading armies arrived and in others until the end of the war.

Until the attack on Pearl Harbor, former members of the London Council of the International Association (Petroleum Industry) Limited were active in advising and coordinating operations in countries not under the Axis powers. Chief responsibility for representing the American interest fell on three members from the United States: Harry G. Seidel, Henry E. Bedford, Jr., and Peter T. Lamont. They served as unofficial observers with the British committees and boards. They also participated in planning and directing tanker transport, in controlling inventories in countries threatened by the Axis, in preparing for sabotaging installations belonging to affiliates before the arrival of the Germans, and in keeping oil supplies originating in Europe (especially in Romania) out of the hands of the Axis.

A few executives stayed on in London after the United States entered the war. Seidel, on returning to London from a trip to the Continent in February, 1943, was lost when the commercial plane on which he was traveling crashed at Lisbon. Bedford and Lamont remained in England and served in important capacities. A group belonging to Intava (International Aviation Associates), a company owned jointly by Jersey and Socony, also stayed throughout the war. These men provided liaison between the British Air Ministry and Ministry of Supply and the company's headquarters in New York.

EFFECT OF WAR IN THE MIDDLE AND FAR EAST

The conflict in Europe, together with an undeclared war between Japan and China and uprisings in the Middle East, also brought many complications to Jersey's partly owned affiliates in Asia, of which the Iraq Petroleum Company, Limited, and Standard-Vacuum Oil Company were the most important. Difficulties arose from the fact that these companies supplied crude or products to affiliates in belligerent, conquered, or neutral countries. Other difficulties came because the affiliates were operating in areas more or less controlled by belligerents.

The Iraq Petroleum Company, Limited, in which Jersey owned approximately an eighth interest, was in an especially exposed situation. Its producing and pipeline operations, as well as the refining of some of its crude, were carried on within British or French mandates or spheres of influence which were subjected to intrigues and pressures coming from the Axis powers. The principal markets for Iraqi oil were in Europe, and the route to those markets included shipping on the Mediterranean.

After the war broke out, Iraq Petroleum worked to obtain the maximum output with existing facilities for supplying Britain and France, which were asking for large supplies from the Middle East. Anticipating losing refineries in Europe, the stockholders (including Jersey itself) approved the processing of the company's crude in Tripoli and in a refinery at Haifa owned jointly by Anglo-Iranian and Royal Dutch–Shell. These plants on the Mediterranean Coast received crude by the company's two pipelines, one through Syria and Lebanon and the other through Transjordan and Palestine.[16]

These operations soon met with severe setbacks arising from unrest stimulated by Germany's efforts to gain control of Iraqi oil or to stop its flow to the non-Axis countries in Europe. The pipeline to Tripoli was closed in June, 1940, because of unsettled conditions in French-mandated Syria and Lebanon, which after the German invasion of France came, at least nominally, under the French Vichy government. In the meantime, the Axis-supported prime minister of Iraq had seized control of his country's government. The British, under their treaty rights, sent their own and Indian forces into Iraq and in June, 1941, restored the regent. Syria was brought under Allied control about a month later by a combination of British, Indian, Free French, and Arab Legion forces. The Allies then established relations with friendly governments in Iraq, Syria, and Lebanon.[17]

The fall of France, the entry of Italy into the war, and the closing of the Mediterranean brought even greater difficulties. Because France and Italy were the principal outlets for Jersey's oil from the Middle East, the company was unable to market crude from Iraq after June, 1940. Technically considered enemy aliens under British law, the French interests and Calouste S. Gulbenkian were not allowed to take their share of the oil. The other owners—Socony-Vacuum, Anglo-Iranian, and Royal Dutch–Shell— had markets in the eastern Mediterranean where they could sell products from the refinery at Haifa.

The loss of western Mediterranean outlets for its oil brought some special problems to Iraq Petroleum. One involved the price charged the particular owners of the company who could take their share of the crude oil produced. Since the cost had risen greatly, the question arose as to whether the existing formula of cost plus a shilling per ton should be changed. A new formula was agreed upon. Another problem was the serious dissatisfaction that arose in Iraq because of the decline in annual payments to the government resulting from decreased production. A temporary solution was arrived at with the understanding that a final settlement would be made after the war.[18]

Standard-Vacuum Oil Company was also caught in the vise of war. This affiliate was fully integrated, with production and refining principally on the island of Sumatra in the Dutch East Indies and with marketing in South and East Africa, Southeast Asia, Japan, China, Australia, and islands of the Southwest Pacific and the Indian Ocean. The company's involvement in war was gradual and did not become acutely crippling until 1942.

However, Standard-Vacuum early had to adjust its organization to developing war conditions. In November, 1939, it organized a company in Hong Kong to take over ownership of American products in transit through war zones or in belligerent ports. In May and June, 1940, when the Nazi army overran the Netherlands, Stanvac transferred the main offices of its producing and refining affiliates from The Hague to Batavia in Java. In August, 1940, as a result of growing uncertainty over the future of Hong Kong because of Japanese aggression in China, Standard-Vacuum dissolved its major transportation affiliate, Oriental Tankers, Limited, closed the shipping company's offices in the British crown colony, and transferred its ocean-going ships and other assets to a new Canadian company, Oriental Trade & Transport Company, Limited.[19]

The war greatly affected Standard-Vacuum's sale and shipment of crude and products. A shortage of tankers reduced deliveries, especially to Japan, Australia, continental Asia, and Africa. This shortage resulted from the use of the tankers owned and chartered by Standard-Vacuum's affiliate for carrying oil for the Allies. The situation was relieved for a time in 1941 by using chartered Norwegian tankers, ships of Panama Transport and of Petroleum Shipping Company, Limited (an affiliate organized in Panama to acquire new tankers under construction in American shipyards), and United States–flag tankers belonging to Socony-Vacuum. Standard-Vacuum's deliveries of products were also upset by exchange restrictions throughout its territory—except in the Philippines—and by rationing in parts of the British Empire. Sales to military forces and to Japan, however, helped for a time to keep totals fairly constant at about 22,700,000 barrels a year.[20]

The greatest threat in the Far East came from the Japanese drive for expansion—for the establishment of the Greater East Asia Co-Prosperity Sphere. Japan had been engaged in an undeclared war with China since 1937, but its efforts had not been decisive. Although American sympathies were with China, no action had been taken by the United States government except to protect American citizens in that country. In fact, the Roosevelt administration took no positive stand against the Japanese. Britain did take a stand; but, after it became involved in the war in Europe, there was little it could do to resist Japanese aggression.[21] The Japanese militarists, with virtually no restraint from Western powers and encouraged by the success of the Nazis, became more aggressive. The disturbed situation reduced Standard-Vacuum's marketing in China.

Trade with Japan raised serious questions in the minds of Standard-Vacuum executives. After the United States government terminated its trade treaty with that country early in 1940, the company's managers hesitated to provide the larger quantities of oil demanded by the Japanese. It was known that the latter were determined to purchase crude for government refineries with the obvious intent of stockpiling as well as supplying the current requirements of the home markets. However, although the United States government in the fall of 1940 placed an embargo on the sale to the Japanese of aviation gasoline and other materials with military potential, because of the sensitive nature of its relations with that country it was not ready to have trade with Japan stopped. In November, 1940, Standard-Vacuum and a Royal Dutch–Shell affiliate, with the approval of American and British officials, signed an agreement with Japanese importers to supply them during the next year with approximately 5,000,000 barrels of crude and 4,000,000 barrels of petroleum products. Standard-Vacuum's share was about one-fourth of each total. Because of the tanker shortage, the company actually had furnished less than half of its share before discontinuing shipments when the United States in the middle of 1941 placed an embargo on the sale of petroleum to Japan.[22]

By that time, events were pointing toward the entry of that country into the war as an ally of the European Axis powers. In the fall of 1940, Japan had obtained bases in Indochina and had entered a formal alliance with the Axis, with mutual pledges of support against any attacking power. In April, 1941, it signed a neutrality pact with the Soviet Union. When the Japanese in July entered southern Indochina, Standard-Vacuum's executives, in collaboration with the company's owners in New York and with the Dutch authorities in the East Indies, were already planning for the emergency that seemed to lie ahead. They were especially preparing for a possible invasion of the Dutch East Indies, from which Standard-Vacuum was obtaining a large portion of the products for its markets. Such was the situation at the time of the Japanese attack on Pearl Harbor in December, 1941.

OIL AND TANKERS FOR GREAT BRITAIN AND ITS ALLIES

As a matter of policy, Britain had not stockpiled petroleum products to any considerable extent before the war, but had chosen to depend on obtaining supplies from overseas. With stocks at hand inadequate for long combat, with no crude production, and with small facilities for manufacturing synthetic products, it looked to the Americas and, as long as possible, to the Middle East for oil supplies. It soon came to depend principally on the Western Hemisphere, where it had contracted for products before the outbreak of war.

Two formidable obstacles faced American companies in their efforts to supply the Allies: American neutrality legislation and the German submarine campaign.

The United States government and Latin American countries had raised firm barriers against giving aid to belligerents in the event of war in Europe. In their desire to erect defenses against involvement, these countries through conferences of ministers had arrived at understandings highly unfavorable to sea powers as belligerents. In the United States a series of congressional acts had culminated in the Neutrality Act of 1937, which prohibited the sale of arms and ammunition and the extension of credit to belligerents in the event of war. In the words of an authority on the history of the foreign relations of the United States, "What the Congress of the United States had done was to assure Adolf Hitler . . . that America would interpose no obstacle to his projects of aggression."[23]

Behind this law was a deep-seated spirit of isolationism. Even for a considerable time after the outbreak of war, this spirit prevented any significant modification of neutrality legislation. An influential factor in the development of the isolationist attitude in the 1930's had been the writings of historians, journalists, and others who had held that British propaganda and the influence of American munitions manufacturers and of bankers who had made large loans to the Allies had been responsible for bringing the United States into World War I. The Senate investigation in the middle 1930's of the arms traffic ("the merchants of death") during World War I had given publicity to these views and contributed to popular sentiment against any involvement in war.[24]

Isolationism was still widespread in the United States at the beginning of World War II, but by then President Roosevelt was ready to urge certain changes in neutrality legislation. In September, 1939, he called Congress into special session to enact amendments to eliminate the embargo on arms and ammunition. This was done in November, but belligerents thereafter could obtain these war materials only on a cash-and-carry basis. In exchange for this concession with respect to the embargo, the President was directed to designate war zones which American commercial vessels were forbidden to enter. However, a conference of foreign ministers of the United States and Latin American countries at Panama in October of that year softened the impact of such restrictions by adopting a resolution to the effect that "the transfer of the flag of a merchant vessel to that of any American Republic" should be considered lawful if "made in good faith, without agreement for resale to the vendor, and that it take place within the waters of an American Republic." This resolution made it possible for United States–flag ships to escape the restrictions of the Neutrality Act by transfer to the flags of other countries that did not have such restrictions.[25]

Because its affiliates had producing properties, refineries, and ships in many countries in different parts of the world, Jersey had several product sources and shipping facilities with which to supply the Allies. Consequently, it was not so tightly restrained by American neutrality law as were some other companies. It had a special advantage in that its ships, which at the outbreak of the war constituted the world's largest tanker fleet owned by one concern, were registered in various countries.[26]

The size, registry, and control of the fleets of Jersey affiliates at the beginning of the war are shown in Table 10. Of a total of well over 2,000,000 deadweight tons, more than two-thirds were under neutral Western Hemisphere flags and about one-fourth were under British and Canadian flags. Only four Jersey tankers, of slightly over 15,000 tons each, carried the German flag. By far the largest fleets were those of Standard Oil Company of New Jersey and Panama Transport. The tonnage owned by the former was nearly twice that of the British and Canadian companies combined, but following President Roosevelt's proclamation of November 4, 1939, under revised neutrality legislation, the United States–flag tankers could not operate in designated war zones.

Shortly before the outbreak of war, Jersey had taken action which had placed Panama Transport in a favorable position for service on the side of the Allies. When this fleet had been transferred from Danzig to Panamanian registry in 1935, the German crews had been retained. Beginning in August, 1939, these foreign crews were removed from twenty-seven tankers of Panama Transport. The men were sent back to Europe, and Americans were hired as expeditiously as possible to take their places. At this time also, agreements were made to transfer four Panamanian tankers to British affiliates.[27]

Immediately after the war began, Jersey's affiliates in Great Britain and France appealed to the Marine Department of Standard Oil Company of New Jersey for assurance of additional tonnage by the transfer of flags and rerouting of tanker operations. In September, 1939, ten new tankers of a Standard-Vacuum affiliate were transferred from the Pacific to the Atlantic service under a new company incorporated in Canada, which had declared war on Germany on September 10. Seven Imperial Oil tankers were transferred from Western Hemisphere operations to transatlantic service. In anticipation of the expected banning of vessels under United States registry from belligerent waters in the autumn of 1939, Jersey executives obtained permission from the United States Maritime Commission to transfer fifteen tankers nearing the end of their usefulness from the American to the Panamanian flag, that is, from Standard Oil Company of New Jersey to Panama Transport. The transfers were made between October, 1939, and February, 1940. These ships provided additional tonnage for the Allies at a time when the British government was reluctant to draw heavily upon British investments in the United States to pay for ships under the cash purchase requirement.[28]

Since American neutrality regulations forbade the employment of American crews on ships of foreign registry sailing in belligerent waters, new crews had to be hired for the transferred vessels. American officers and men were removed, and Canadians, Norwegians, and Danes were recruited. This change meant the replacement of regular seamen with less experienced or even inexperienced personnel.

With sufficient tankers and some stocks on hand, the Allies met no real

Table 10: **CHANGES IN FLEETS OF AFFILIATES FROM SEPTEMBER 3, 1939, TO DECEMBER 6, 1941**
Standard Oil Company (New Jersey)

	Number of Ocean, Lake, and Special-Service Tankers			
Affiliates	Owned Sept. 3, 1939	Deliveries and Purchases	Intergroup Transfers In	Out
In Neutral Countries				
Standard Oil Co. of New Jersey	71	12	—	18
Panama Transport Co.	29	1	18	4
Petroleum Shipping Co.c	—	8	—	—
Standard Oil Co. of Venezuela	4	—	—	—
Cia. de Petroleo Lago	4	1	1	1
International Petroleum Co., Ltd.	—	1	—	—
Cia. Transportadora de Petroleos, S.A.	5	—	—	—
Total	113	23	19	23
Under Allied Control				
Anglo-American Oil Co., Ltd.	21	—	4	—
Belgian Overseas Transports, S.A.d	—	—	2	—
Imperial Oil Ltd.	22	—	—	—
Lago Shipping Co., Ltd.	23	—	—	—
Oriental Tankers, Ltd.c	10	—	—	10
Oriental Trade & Transport Co., Ltd.c	—	—	10	—
N.V. Nederlandsche Koloniale Petroleum Maat.cf	4	—	—	—
Standard American Petroleum Co.	2	—	—	2
Total	82	—	16	12
Under Axis Control by 1941				
Deutsch-Amerikanische Petroleum-Ges.	2	1	—	—
Waried Tankschiff Rhederei Ges. mbH.	2	—	—	—
"La Columbia," Soc. Marittima	6	—	—	—
N.V. Petroleum Industrie Maat.	3	—	—	—
Det Danske Petroleums-Akt.	4	—	—	—
Ostlandske Petroleumscompagni, Akt.	2	—	—	—
Standard Française des Pétroles	5	—	—	—
Total	24	1	—	—
Grand Total	219	24	35	35

a Losses from seizures by the enemy, sinkings, collisions, and stranding.
b Eight tankers given provisional British registry during 1941.
c Tankers belonging to affiliates of Standard-Vacuum Oil Co., in which Jersey had a half-interest.
d Tankers were transferred from American Petroleum Co. on Aug. 9, 1940, to Panama Transport Co. and on Feb. 13, 1941, to Belgian Overseas Transports, S.A., but since the former transfer was not deemed valid it has not been included

threat to their petroleum supply in the early months of the conflict. They drew on their accustomed sources, except that, in order to conserve their dollar resources, the British relied almost wholly on oil from countries where payment could be made in sterling. To supply the refineries of European affiliates, especially those in Italy and France, the Jersey

Table 10 (*cont.*): **CHANGES IN FLEETS OF AFFILIATES FROM SEPTEMBER 3, 1939, TO DECEMBER 6, 1941**
Standard Oil Company (New Jersey)

Number of Ocean, Lake, and Special-Service Tankers			Deadweight Tons (in thousands)		Flag of Fleet
Sales to Non-affiliates	Losses[a]	Owned Dec. 6, 1941	Sept. 3, 1939	Dec. 6, 1941	
6	—	59	965	807	United States
—	6	38	440	494	Panamanian[b]
—	—	8	—	122	Panamanian
—	—	4	20	20	Venezuelan
—	—	5	13	20	Venezuelan
—	—	1	—	1	Peruvian
—	—	5	14	14	Argentine
6	6	120	1,452	1,478	
—	8	17	203	178	British
—	—	2	—	28	Belgian[e]
—	1	21	159	142	Canadian
—	—	23	95	95	British
—	—	—	153	—	British
—	4	6	—	92	British
—	—	4	21	21	Belgian
—	—	—	28	—	Dutch
—	13	73	659	556	
—	2	1	31	15	German
—	1	1	30	17	German
—	2	4	51	40	Italian
—	1	2	37	35	Dutch
—	3[g]	1	44	1	Danish
—	2[h]	—	16	—	Norwegian
—	3	2	32	24	French
—	14	11	241	132	
6	33	204	2,352	2,166	

here. Belgian Overseas was an affiliate of Panama Transport Co.
[e] Flag of government in exile in 1941.
[f] Home office transferred in 1940 to the Dutch East Indies.
[g] Two tankers were seized by the British and chartered to Anglo-American Oil Company, Ltd.
[h] One tanker was taken over by the Norwegian Shipping & Trade Mission and chartered to Anglo-American.
Source: Esso Shipping Company, Annual Report of Marine Operations, 1939–1945.

companies drew from Romania as long as possible, and from the parent company's share of the crude produced by Iraq Petroleum. Standard-Vacuum also sent some oil to England from Sumatra.

The closing of the Mediterranean in the summer of 1940 shifted to the Western Hemisphere most of the responsibility for supplying oil to

tankers owned by foreign-flag affiliates seriously reduced the carrying capacity of the whole Jersey fleet and resulted in the loss of many men. The first two oil carriers destroyed by enemy action were the *Kennebec* and the *Cheyenne,* ships owned by Anglo-American that were torpedoed on September 9 and 15, 1939, respectively. Early in 1940 the Danish-flag *Danmark* and the Netherlands-flag *Den Haag* were added to the list of missing vessels. Panama Transport's first loss was the *Joseph Seep,* carrying crude oil from Haifa, Palestine; this vessel was sunk by a mine near Le Havre, France. Many others went down in June, September, and December of 1940.

Even more ships and men were lost in 1941 than in 1940. The toll was especially heavy in the winter and the fall of the year. The number of men lost ranged from none or few on some ships to the total complement of officers and crew on others. Panama Transport's *W. C. Teagle,* chartered to the United States Maritime Commission for service to the United Kingdom, went down with all but one man out of its total officers and crew of forty-five men. By the time the United States entered the war, twenty-six ocean-going tankers belonging to Jersey affiliates had been reported lost, and an additional seven had been seriously damaged by enemy action. Fourteen of those lost were operating under the British flag, and four were of Panamanian registry. At the end of 1941, Jersey's ocean-going fleet consisted of 123 tankers with a total of 1,720,631 deadweight tons.[39]

Standard Oil Company (New Jersey) thus became heavily involved in the war long before the United States entered the conflict. Its affiliates in most countries on the European Continent came under the complete domination of the Axis powers. Those in Great Britain and allied and neutral countries in Europe came under close governmental control. Western Hemisphere affiliates outside the United States served as large suppliers of oil products and transport for Great Britain. While playing a minor role in such supply because of their own country's neutrality law, the Jersey companies in the United States nevertheless were strongly affected by the war.

Chapter 14

Impact of the War on Operations in the Americas, 1939–1941

W HILE PROVIDING THE ALLIES with tankers and oil products, Jersey and its affiliates in the Western Hemisphere continued to supply current needs in countries not at war and to work on programs under way at the beginning of the conflict in Europe. However, all their operations in the Americas were affected by the strife abroad. And, as the war in Europe spread, the Jersey companies in the United States became increasingly involved in preparations for national defense.

THE DEMAND FOR CRUDE AND PRODUCTS

Almost at once after the outbreak of hostilities, the affiliates in the Americas had to adjust to a decreased demand for products for European markets. As already noted, shipments to the large marketing affiliate in Germany ceased on the declaration of war, and Britain's system for regulating trade with the Continent reduced the supplying of oil to European neutrals. The decline in transatlantic passenger-vessel service also reduced demand. The fall of nearly all of the European mainland to the Axis in the summer of 1940 closed almost the entire Continent to the products of Jersey's affiliates.

The effect on Western Hemisphere operations was strong and widespread. Among Jersey refineries, the one on Aruba, which processed principally for European markets, was most severely affected by the loss of former outlets. It averaged daily runs of only 169,000 barrels in 1940, an amount nearly 25 per cent less than the 1939 average. Even the increased shipment of aviation gasoline and other products to England did not make up for the loss of markets on the European Continent. Refineries belonging to Standard Oil Company of New Jersey, Standard of Louisiana, International Petroleum, and the Cuban and Argentine affili-

recommendations of representatives of Jersey's domestic affiliates concerned with tanker transport, the companies introduced at tanker terminals a better arrangement of pipelines and more efficient pumping and other equipment in order to shorten the time required for loading or unloading. On Jersey's advice, subcommittees of the American Tanker Control Board, established in 1941, recommended similar improvements for adoption by other companies.[5]

In 1939 and 1940, Jersey ordered the construction of new tankers for its fleets. It foresaw the need for ships to meet an increasing demand for transport as well as to replace tankers of foreign affiliates, including Panama Transport, destroyed by enemy submarines or mines. Also, it had to provide substitutes for the so-called National Defense Tankers, then nearing completion, when the Maritime Commission and the Navy in 1940 began to exercise their right under agreement with the company to purchase those ships for use as aircraft carriers and, especially, as oilers—by October, 1941, all twelve of Jersey's National Defense Tankers had been taken over by the Navy. By contracting the building of new vessels in American shipyards, Jersey was able, before the shortage of materials became critical, to replace the tankers turned over to the government as well as some of the ships lost by its affiliates in countries at war. Fourteen new ships were actually received by Jersey before the end of 1941. These did not make up for all the tonnage losses of the company's interests, but they went far to close the gap. (See Table 10.) When the United States entered the war in December, 1941, the affiliates' tanker tonnage amounted to more than one-eighth of the world's total and was larger than that of either Royal Dutch–Shell or Anglo-Iranian. This tonnage was under various flags, but by far the larger fleets were those registered in the United States and Panama; only about 6 per cent of the total tonnage was under Axis control.[6]

In 1940 Jersey's executives began to consider ways of increasing the utilization and capacity of other oil carriers in the United States and Canada. The problem became urgent as more Western Hemisphere tankers were required to serve the Allies. A greater use of pipelines appeared to be the principal solution.

The executives first planned to increase the amount of oil transported by existing pipelines. For example, they made arrangements to lighten the burden on Imperial's ocean and lake tankers by shipping Canada-bound crude to Philadelphia instead of Montreal and then transporting it by pipelines to the refinery at Sarnia. These shipments of 10,000 barrels daily did not start until December, 1940, however, and were discontinued a few months later when the decision was made to use all available pipelines for transporting crude oil eastward from the Mid-Continent. This plan provided for greater utilization of the short sections of Tuscarora's old crude oil lines in Pennsylvania, and it also required affiliates to lay some new pipe or improve the old. The daily volume carried in 1941 was greatly increased, particularly that of Ajax Pipe Line from the Mid-Continent.[7]

The Jersey men responsible for oil transport recognized the urgent necessity of providing a substitute for tankers to bring oil from the Gulf Coast to the Atlantic ports and their hinterlands in the United States. This area—which included all the coastal states and also Vermont, Pennsylvania, West Virginia, and the District of Columbia—was in an especially precarious situation because it normally obtained more than 90 per cent of its petroleum by tanker. It contained about half the country's population, approximately two-fifths of its motor vehicles, and a third of its oil burners. This area also had the world's greatest concentration of industrial power, a large part of which used oil for fuel.

Jersey took the initiative in 1940 in planning a products pipeline from Baton Rouge, Louisiana, to Greensboro, North Carolina, with spurs to important cities. The building of this line had been under consideration even before the war as a means of supplying the large region more economically than by the existing combination of tankers and railroad tank cars. (See Chapter 9.) Standard Oil Company of Kentucky and an affiliate of Shell agreed to participate in the Plantation Pipe Line Company. Jersey took 50.4 per cent of the stock, and the other two companies took the remainder. Construction was delayed by the difficulty of obtaining rights of way from certain railroads, especially in Georgia and South Carolina, where state laws did not permit pipelines to exercise the right of eminent domain. In 1941, however, partially in response to the right-of-way difficulties of this company at a time when the transportation shortage was obviously limiting supplies on the market, national legislation came to the rescue. An act of Congress—the so-called Cole Act of July 30—enabled the owners to get the Plantation line declared necessary for national defense and, as such, entitled to the right of eminent domain. Construction was then pressed. The first products were pumped into the line at Baton Rouge on January 1, 1942, and all the pumping stations were completed by April. This twelve-inch line, equipped with automatic controls and electric-powered pumps, had a capacity of 60,000 barrels

daily. The line released other carriers for critical service elsewhere. It
came into operation shortly before the severe German submarine attack
on tankers in the winter of 1942.[8]

A Jersey study made in 1941 of how pipelines could be utilized further
to reduce the Atlantic Coast's dependence on tankers led to the construction of a line from Portland, Maine, to Montreal. This new project was
designed to eliminate a long, hazardous, and seasonally closed portion of
the tanker route from the Gulf or the Caribbean to eastern Canada, that
is, to the Maritime Provinces and up the St. Lawrence River. Jersey
approved the building of the line in February, 1941, and two wholly
owned affiliates were incorporated for this purpose, the Portland Pipe
Line Company and the Montreal Pipe Line Company. This carrier, with a
daily capacity of 80,000 barrels, was designed and laid in record time by
Humble personnel under the supervision of Jersey's pipeline office in
New York. Construction was started in May, 1941, and the line went into
operation shortly before the attack on Pearl Harbor.[9]

Less fortunate was a proposal for another oil carrier by land which
Jersey and other companies were promoting in 1941 to help supply
Atlantic Coast refineries with crude. On May 9, 1941, President Farish,
who in 1937 had succeeded Teagle as chief executive of Jersey, proposed
to seven leading oil companies the construction of a pipeline to bring
crude from Texas to the vicinity of New York Harbor. Representatives of
the companies met to consider the proposal and, under a committee
headed by Jersey's Wallace R. Finney, initiated planning to carry it out.
The result was the incorporation of the National Defense Pipe Lines.
Application was made to the government for permission to acquire pipe
and other equipment. But the agency concerned held that the projected
facility was not required for the defense of the country, and in September
and November, 1941, and again in February, 1942, it refused to grant the
necessary permission. The engineering plans were consequently laid aside
to await later consideration.[10]

Another means of stretching transportation facilities in the United
States was the greater utilization of railroad tank cars. These had been
used principally to carry products to the bulk stations of marketers and in
some places to transport crude oil from fields to refineries. In 1941 oil
companies generally turned over their short hauls to trucks, thus releas-
ing railroad cars for long-distance shipment. Railroads were especially
important for moving oil across Illinois, Ohio, and Pennsylvania, where
pipelines for carrying crude were old and had suffered from disuse for

many years. The Jersey companies increased their tank-car shipments greatly, averaging daily deliveries at East Coast refineries of 38,000 barrels during October, 1941. A reduction in freight rates encouraged this method of moving oil; normally it was much more costly to ship by rail than by pipeline.[11]

Shipment by inland waterways was also increased. Barges came to be used more extensively than at the outbreak of the war. In the United States, Jersey added seven barges, each capable of carrying 8,000 barrels. It also looked into the possibility of having such craft built in shipyards on the Great Lakes for local service in Latin America. In 1941 crude and products carried by lake, river, and coastal vessels increased 20 per cent above the volume in 1940.[12]

As 1941 passed, it became increasingly clear to Jersey executives that oil transport facilities in the Western Hemisphere were insufficient to supply expanding civilian and military needs. Shortages developed despite the fact that tankers were carrying larger volumes of crude and products and that shipment by pipelines, inland and coastal waterways, and railroads had been increased. New and radical expedients were clearly necessary. Indicative of the seriousness of the situation were the conversion of the Bayway plant of Standard Oil Company of New Jersey to the use of coal instead of oil for fuel and the efforts of the federal Office of Petroleum Coordinator to bring about a reduction in the consumption of oil products on the East Coast in the late summer and fall of 1941. Even the oversupply of tankers in November, 1941, was regarded as only temporary. It was obvious to informed oilmen that there was little reserve capacity for emergencies.

CHANGING RELATIONS WITH FARBEN

One problem immediately loomed large when war broke out in Europe in 1939: what to do about Jersey's relations with I.G. Farbenindustrie in Germany.[13] President Frank A. Howard of Standard Oil Development was in France at the time conferring with regard to the installation in that country's refineries of Jersey's latest type of plant designed to produce aviation gasoline. Howard realized that, with Germany at war, complications might arise over the jointly owned Jasco, Incorporated, and the many patents held by Farben under which Jersey had rights. It was also possible that the patents might be confiscated by the belligerents. Howard at once got in touch with Jersey officers in New York. He also conferred in London with W. R. Carlisle—a Jersey attorney who was familiar with the Farben contracts—and with the United States Ambassador. Headquarters in New York made arrangements for Howard to meet Farben representatives at The Hague, and he obtained permission from the British authorities to go there.

On September 22 Howard met at The Hague Dr. Friedrich Ringer, Farben's chief research executive, and a junior patent lawyer. The negotiations first dealt with the Farben patents to which Jersey had rights under the arrangements of 1929 and 1930 between the American and the German company.

The negotiations involved the transfer of record title to a large number of Farben patents relating to oil refining and petrochemicals under which Standard-I.G. or Jasco owned the rights in the principal countries outside Germany. Jersey had not requested the assigning of these patents at any earlier time. Howard expected Farben to be reluctant to transfer the titles. Jersey, of course, had a clear right to their transfer under its agreements with the German company; but the latter, as its correspondence with agencies of the German government reveals, also saw in transfer to the American company a means to protect those rights from seizure in countries which were at war with Germany. On September 24, Dr. Ringer turned over to Howard assignments covering 2,000 patents. He had not brought assignments for the French patents because the French consulate in Berlin had been closed. In a few days, however, the necessary certification was obtained from officials in Paris by arranging with the American consulate in Berlin to send the necessary documents to the Embassy in the French capital and clearing the matter with the Department of State. Nor had Dr. Ringer brought assignments for the Buna rights, which had to await the consent of the German government; they were received by representatives of Standard Oil Development Company in New York on December 15, 1939.[14]

A central problem was how to separate the interests of the two companies in Jasco, a cooperative research company incorporated in the United States in 1930 and owned equally by Jersey and Farben. Both companies, sharing expenses, had carried on research under this corporation. Farben had agreed to assign to Jasco the rights to processes within the range of their agreements which it originated; it had a five-eighths interest in their earnings and Jersey had the remaining three-eighths. The Jasco organization had thus acquired claims to the rights relating to paraffin oxidation and to the acetylene-arc, Oppanol, and Buna processes. (See Chapter 6.) But, as their originator, Farben had the deciding voice with respect to their development and use. The two executives discussed terminating the arrangement in a way that would dissolve the joint ownership.

The obvious solution—that Farben sell its rights to Standard Oil Development—proved not to be feasible. The Germans had spent more on the development of the various processes than had the Americans. But there was actually no basis for placing a value on them; they had earned little or nothing, and their future earnings could not be estimated. Dr. Ringer did quote a price for Farben's rights, but it was higher than Howard would consider. In fact, he doubted that the Jersey Board of Directors would agree to pay a large amount of dollars to Germany when that country was at war with France and England.

After various ways of resolving the matter had been explored, a compromise was worked out: to divide the rights on a territorial basis. Under this settlement, Farben, for a nominal payment, would sell its stock in Jasco to Standard Oil Development Company. Jasco would retain all its rights in the patents for the United States and the British and French empires; it would transfer to Farben its rights in the patents for the rest of the world. However, since Dr. Ringer maintained that this territorial division might prove inequitable, Howard agreed to a periodic review of earnings. If such a review indicated that royalty receipts did not work out in proportion to the original Jasco formula—that is, five-eighths and three-eighths—the two companies would settle the difference in a manner satisfactory to both parties. The two executives on September 30 wrote a memorandum—known as The Hague Memorandum—embodying these points.

In the meantime, Jersey by direct negotiations with Farben had purchased for $20,000 the German company's shares of Standard-I.G. Company, a concern that managed certain oil patents in which both companies had an interest. Although these shares had no particular financial value, participation gave Farben the right to elect two directors and thereby to keep in touch with everything Jersey did with the processes concerned. This situation was clearly undesirable because Farben was under the complete control of the German government.

The conclusion of the negotiations and the acceptance by both Jersey and Farben of the solutions reached by their representatives terminated research relations which had existed for approximately a decade. Certain adjustments remained to be made, and in the process issues rose that had to be resolved. Jersey executives believed that the company had obtained full ownership of Jasco and Standard-I.G. and of the patents involved for the United States and the British and French empires. However, the arrangement for a periodic review of royalty receipts to make adjustments in accordance with the original Jasco formula was later to bring into question the transfer to Jersey in 1939 of Farben's shares in Jasco and its patent rights.[15]

TOLUENE, 100-OCTANE GASOLINE, AND SYNTHETIC RUBBER

On the outbreak of war in Europe in 1939, Jersey's domestic refining research organizations were on the threshold of new developments that were to become of great importance to national defense.

Because of the potentialities of some of the processes developed by affiliates, President Howard of Standard Oil Development and other Jersey executives early in 1939 conferred in Washington on specific matters with representatives of the Munitions Board and other military agencies. Late in the year, arrangements were made for periodic meetings of representatives of Jersey and of various branches of the services to discuss new processes in the light of needs of the United States Army, Navy, and Army Air Corps. Such a meeting was held in December, 1939, and others at about one-year intervals for several years thereafter. The services submitted questions in advance of meetings, and Jersey prepared memoranda on other subjects thought to have a possible military value in the event of war. These meetings kept the government informed of Jersey's potentially useful products, processes, and equipment; and they gave the research staffs guidance about the problems on which to concentrate attention.[16]

The Jersey research and refining groups gave special attention to the development of processes and facilities for the manufacture of certain products that they believed would be of strategic importance in war. Among these were aviation gasoline, synthetic rubber, and synthetic toluene for use in making the explosive, trinitrotoluene (TNT).

Informed in 1939 of the company's discovery of a process for making synthetic toluene of sufficient purity (nitration grade) for use in the manufacture of TNT, the United States Army Ordnance Department inquired of Standard Oil Development whether or not Jersey could produce such toluene with existing commercial equipment. The company replied in the affirmative.[17]

As a result of the conferences that followed, the Army Ordnance

Department requested Jersey to manufacture 20,000 gallons of this product in commercial equipment. Since no refinery had all the facilities necessary for the various steps in its manufacture, the material for the successive stages of processing was shipped from Baytown to Bayway, then back to Baytown, and finally to Baton Rouge. On August 6, 1940, the 20,000 gallons were turned over to the Ordnance Department for transfer to a nitration plant. This was the first nitration-grade toluene ever produced synthetically from petroleum on a commercial scale. Convinced that this method was practicable and that costs would be lower with equipment in one location, the government indicated that it wanted a plant built.[18]

Jersey had made plans for large-scale manufacture of toluene before the initial trial order was filled. A study indicated that the most advantageous location was near Humble's Baytown refinery because the necessary naphtha was plentiful there. In May, 1940, the Texas affiliate began to work on plans with Standard Oil Development. On August 15, 1940, it submitted to the Army Ordnance Department a detailed proposal for building a plant to be owned by the government and operated by itself on the basis of costs plus a fixed fee. Even before negotiations were completed, the company started work on the project, which was well under way before the final contract was signed on October 21, 1940.[19]

The building of the Baytown Ordnance Works proceeded ahead of schedule. Humble staffed the plant with supervisors from the Baytown refinery and trained the necessary operating personnel. On October 21, 1941—only a few weeks before the attack on Pearl Harbor—the first tank-car load of toluene was shipped from Baytown. The Ordnance Works produced more than 2,400,000 gallons of toluene during the last quarter of 1941—nearly 60 per cent of the total produced from petroleum in the United States in that year. The major part of the remainder was made by a Shell affiliate, which had developed a phenol extraction process. A smaller portion was provided by Standard of Indiana, which had been cooperating with Jersey and M. W. Kellogg Company in developing a commercial process for making toluene.[20]

Jersey and its affiliates made plans to expand their production of aviation gasoline. For a number of years before the outbreak of war, several other oil companies also had been conducting research on the improvement of aviation fuels, and various methods had been developed for making 100-octane gasoline. (See Chapter 6.) Both the United States Army Air Corps and the British Royal Air Force had recognized the advantages of this gasoline before 1939, and the Americans and the British had adopted it as their fighting-grade aviation fuel.[21]

Yet, despite the Army Air Corps' recognition in the mid-thirties of the need for high-octane fuel and even after the experience of Britain's Royal Air Force during the late summer and fall of 1940, official planners in the United States set their aviation gasoline sights too low. The amount that would be required depended, of course, on whether or not the United States would be drawn into the war. Even President Roosevelt—who was probably in a better position than any other American to gauge the significance of Nazi conquests in Europe—in one of the last days of the presidential campaign of 1940 explicitly promised that no American boys would be sent into any foreign war. Isolationist and neutralist sentiment in America still affected the government in Washington, and laws still shackled the responsible agencies that favored more aggressive defense efforts. Moreover, many in authority in the government were not familiar with the problems involved and the time required for building new plants to manufacture such complex products as 100-octane gasoline.[22]

Jersey's affiliates had contributed to the development of three processes for obtaining iso-octane to blend with base stocks to produce the desired high-octane rating; the most productive of these processes was alkylation. (See Chapter 6.) The cold- and hot-acid plants at Bayway, Baytown, Baton Rouge, and Aruba had a combined capacity of nearly 2,500 barrels daily. During 1940, alkylation facilities at Baytown were increased to a daily capacity of 2,500 barrels, and new plants were built at Baton Rouge and Aruba, with daily capacities of 1,250 and 500 barrels, respectively. At the end of 1940 the Jersey affiliates in the Western Hemisphere were able to produce a maximum of 6,750 barrels per day of this blending agent. The iso-octane thus provided enabled these refineries to supply in 1940 a total of 2,700,000 barrels of 100-octane gasoline, of which 1,300,000 barrels were shipped to the Allies.[23]

In that same year Jersey decided to expand production of high-octane gasoline by a new process: fluid catalytic cracking. Research on this type of cracking had been nearly completed in 1939. After minor difficulties had been eliminated early in 1940, plans were made for a construction program. On May 9, 1940, the parent company's Executive Committee confirmed the appropriation for the first unit, to be built at Baton Rouge, and on October 21 it took the same action for a unit at Bayway. About the same time, Humble authorized the construction of a similar installation at its Baytown refinery. Each plant was to have a capacity of 12,000 barrels daily and was estimated to cost about $3,500,000. Although construction was started as soon as engineering designs had been completed, the plants were not ready for operation until 1942.[24] These fluid catalytic cracking facilities were to provide a gasoline of high quality that could be used as base stock for aviation gasoline.

Late in 1940, company executives concluded that, although the amount of 100-octane gasoline actually being produced was beyond current requirements in the United States, this would soon be inadequate for military purposes. In December, Dr. Stewart P. Coleman, head of Jersey's Economics Department, advised President Farish that, according to his department's estimates, there would be a surplus of 100-octane in 1941 but a substantial shortage the next year. Coleman especially advised that preparations be made for building additional blending-agent plants on short notice. On December 28, President Farish sent letters to the presidents of fifteen oil companies that were producing 100-octane gasoline. He reviewed the existing capacity, pointed out that it would take from twelve to fourteen months to build new plants, and urged the companies to operate existing facilities at capacity and store the surplus above current consumption. He added, however, that, since current production exceeded demand and the supplies were accumulating, any expansion program would require assurance that the government intended to absorb the new production. However, this guarantee was not forthcoming; the military services did not then have the authority to enter purchasing contracts beyond the current fiscal year.[25]

Principally because of their inability to obtain sufficient materials for the projected construction, the Jersey affiliates were unable to expand their 100-octane output as much as planned. After February 1, 1941, oil companies were not free to construct new facilities without obtaining government priority ratings for scarce materials, an assurance which those in charge of the allocation of priorities did not then give for such plants. Consequently, no important increase was made in 100-octane manufacturing capacity in the United States in 1941.[26]

Even at that late date, according to *A History of the Petroleum Administration for War*, "few in authority in Washington could foresee how pitiably inadequate our 100-octane capacity would be."[27] The Office of Petroleum Coordinator for National Defense, organized in mid-1941, gave promise of improving this situation. The new agency began at once to gather information about existing manufacturing capacity and probable future requirements. In September, it estimated that the current neutral and Allied 100-octane gasoline needs totaled 106,000 barrels daily. In December, daily production in the Western Hemisphere was estimated to be 55,700 barrels. Of this total, the amount supplied by the Jersey affiliates was 13,000 barrels.[28] Such was the situation when the attack on Pearl Harbor brought the United States into the war.

Synthetic rubber was the third strategic wartime petroleum product in the development of which Jersey and its affiliates played an important role. The manufacture of this substitute after the supply of natural rubber was cut off by Japan was to be one of the miracles of American war production. But because of a complication of circumstances, that miracle came almost too late.

Little progress had been made in the United States in the manufacture of synthetic rubber before this country entered the war. Since natural rubber of high quality had always been available, there had been no particular commercial incentive for establishing facilities for making a general-purpose synthetic rubber. The few companies working in this field had been interested mostly in developing types of rubber having qualities not possessed by the natural substance. Three such products were on the American market when war broke out in 1939: neoprene, Thiokol, and Buna-N (Perbunan). These were used mostly where resistance to oil was required. In this respect they were superior to natural rubber, but they were expensive to produce.[29]

Jersey had made noteworthy progress in this field in the 1930's. (See Chapter 6.) Through Jasco it had acquired from Farben an interest in processes for the manufacture of two types of synthetic rubber, and it had itself discovered a process for making a third. Buna-N, made by Farben, was already being imported at the outbreak of war. Buna-S, also developed by the German company, gave promise of serving as a general-purpose rubber. Indeed, tests of Buna-S by American tire manufacturers were under way when the war broke out. Butyl, a Jersey discovery, was based in part on knowledge obtained from Farben, but the process for its manufacture had not been satisfactorily worked out by September, 1939.

The scientists and engineers of Jersey affiliates had also made progress in the production of the components used in these rubber processes, but butadiene required for making Buna-S was still scarce. Jersey research men had developed one process that proved far too expensive, and they had worked on another which they had not succeeded in developing into a large-scale continuous process. They had discovered one method of making butadiene that had real promise—high-temperature, low-pressure steam cracking of petroleum fractions—but this process had the disadvantage that the yield of butadiene was small in proportion to the amount of the petroleum fraction used. Shell Oil also had discovered a method for making butadiene, but this process had not proved practicable for large-scale manufacture. Thus no method was yet available in 1939 for making butadiene in quantities and at costs required for commercial production.[30] However, Jersey did have the one process by which this essential component of Buna-S could be manufactured at high cost as a hedge against an emergency.

By Farben's transfer in September, 1939, of the record title of the Buna patent rights, Jersey acquired full rights within the United States and the British and French empires to the Buna rubber patents and processes. To be sure, Standard Oil Development did not acquire the "know-how" that the German company had gained from its long experience with these synthetics. Henceforth, however, Jersey could proceed not only with further research and development but also with licensing the manufacture of Buna-N and Buna-S.

In October, 1939, immediately after his return from Europe, Frank A. Howard met with representatives of the Army and Navy Munitions Board to inform them of the results of the Farben negotiations and to express his company's increasing concern over the rubber situation. He had found great anxiety in France and England over the supply of essential petroleum products, and he believed the United States should not delay in preparing to meet possible emergencies. The Munitions Board was impressed with the need for action. It suggested that Jersey consult the rubber companies about the progress of their testing of Buna-S and also explore whatever suggestions they might have about how to proceed with manufacture.[31]

After consultation with five rubber companies, Jersey executives again approached the Munitions Board. They had come to the conclusion that under existing circumstances the manufacture of the general-purpose Buna-S by rubber companies could not be self-supporting, and that some form of government cooperation or subsidy would be required. They proposed to the Munitions Board in November, 1939, that Jersey should license certain interested rubber manufacturers to produce Buna-N, for which there was a market, on condition that these companies help to develop the process for manufacturing Buna-S, for which there was no market so long as natural rubber was available. They also suggested that the government assist the rubber companies with a "government subsidy, guarantee, or some sort of outlet for tires fabricated from Buna-S." The decision of the Munitions Board was that no funds were then available. The board added, however, that should funds become available, they would be more readily applicable to a concerted effort than to individual undertakings.[32]

In January, 1940, Jersey drew up a plan for a cooperative company to carry forward research and to make synthetic rubber. Its own particular interest was in the development of Buna-S production. Petroleum, chemical, and rubber concerns were to be invited to lodge their patents with the new company in exchange for stock. Jersey proposed to contribute all its Buna-N, Buna-S, and Butyl knowledge, processes, and rights, in exchange for which it expected to obtain 51 per cent of the stock. This project was probably too ambitious and involved too many commercial rivalries, however, to be acceptable, but it actually foundered on the advice of Jersey's legal counsel. John W. Davis, a prominent New York attorney, as well as the company's own counsel warned of the danger of complications under antitrust law.[33]

In the meantime, the parent company and affiliates made plans to develop the manufacture of butadiene and one type of synthetic rubber. They decided to construct a plant at Baton Rouge for the making of butadiene by the high-temperature, low-pressure steam cracking process —a pioneering step in the development of Jersey's chemical manufacture. They also decided to undertake the building of a small Buna-N plant which could, if needed, also be used as a pilot plant for experimenting with the manufacture of Buna-S. The construction of these plants got under way in the winter of 1940. At about the same time, Standard Oil Development undertook a concerted effort to perfect a process for the production of butadiene by the dehydrogenation of normal butylene, a method the company's research men had discovered previously but had been unable to bring into large-scale production.[34]

By 1940 several rubber companies were interested in Buna-N. Imports from Europe had ceased with the outbreak of war, and the supply in the United States had been sufficient for only a few weeks. Although the demand was small, this rubber was preferable to natural rubber in making certain products. Jersey decided to offer individual licenses for the manufacture of Buna-N to rubber companies that would agree to experiment with Buna-S. Firestone Tire and Rubber Company signed an agreement in March, 1940, and United States Rubber Company in June of that year. B. F. Goodrich Company and Goodyear Tire and Rubber

Co., Inc., were not interested, probably because they were making some progress in developing their own processes. Standard Oil Development's Howard kept Colonel Charles Hines of the Munitions Board advised of what the Jersey affiliates were doing.[35]

In June, 1940, Howard and President Farish appeared before the Senate Committee on Military Affairs at its request. They were asked to give their views on the possibility of using synthetic rubber in an emergency and of furnishing it in quantity. Farish stated that enough progress had been made so that, with adequate financing, petroleum and rubber companies could in two or three years "make all the synthetic rubber that we can use in this country." He believed that the manufactured product would be developed during those years to the point where it could be substituted for 70 per cent or more of the natural rubber in tires. The cost would be high and the risk great because the synthetic would be too expensive to compete with natural rubber if the emergency did not develop. Farish suggested two ways for the government to encourage the manufacture of the synthetic product: by direct subsidy, or by a license-and-import system that would require the purchase of domestic synthetic rubber to the amount of a specified percentage of the natural rubber imported.[36]

By mid-1940 the rubber issue had been taken up by the Advisory Commission to the Council of National Defense. This was a new government agency having a petroleum section which was advised by Dr. R. E. Wilson, an executive of an affiliate of Standard Oil Company (Indiana) and formerly a professor of chemical engineering at Massachusetts Institute of Technology. Jersey executives, like those of other oil and rubber companies, were for several months in communication and consultation with representatives of the commission.

After extensive investigation, this agency decided in July, 1940, to propose a program for government assistance in financing plants. It asked companies to submit preliminary engineering plans for installations capable of producing per annum a total of 10,000 tons of neoprene, 30,000 tons of Butyl, and 60,000 tons of Buna-S. Plans subsequently submitted proposed a total capacity of 150,000 tons. The manufacture of Butyl proving more difficult than had been anticipated, Jersey suggested that this synthetic be eliminated from the government program. However, the company proposed to proceed with the engineering of a Butyl plant at Baton Rouge on its own account. It asked that it be authorized to substitute two plants to produce a total of 30,000 tons of butadiene, one plant at Baton Rouge and another at Baytown. It also suggested that the product be turned over to Firestone and United States Rubber for use in the manufacture of rubber. Humble and Standard of Louisiana made proposals for constructing plants. Early in October, 1940, the commission's program was submitted to Jesse H. Jones as head of the Reconstruction Finance Corporation, which had been given charge of the government's rubber program.[37]

The head of the RFC and President Roosevelt decided not to commit the government to the large expenditures required by the 150,000-ton proposal and instead limited the commitment to $25,000,000. Several considerations probably had a bearing on this decision. There was, of course, no certainty that the supply of natural rubber in Asia would be cut off. Also as a hedge against the possible elimination of that source, Congress in June, 1940, had authorized the government to purchase larger quantities of natural rubber and stockpile it. In addition, the drive of the oil companies to collect used rubber for recapping tires had brought an abundant response. Further, it was believed that the rationing of gasoline would greatly reduce the demand for rubber. There was also the fear that the development of a synthetic industry in the United States might disturb Great Britain and the Netherlands because of the effect on the market for natural rubber from the Orient. The decision may have been affected by the fact that the government officials directly responsible had little comprehension of the possibilities of manufacturing synthetics or of the difficulties to be overcome. Jones may also have been influenced by a belief that Jersey interests had too much to gain from the program. On October 9, 1940, Howard sent a memorandum to Farish suggesting that, because of Jones's attitude toward Jersey, "the only practical basis of reconciliation" would be to adopt a small program for immediate construction and to attempt to secure legislation to encourage a larger program to be financed by private capital, as had been proposed by Farish.[38]

The Reconstruction Finance Corporation then considered scaled-down programs. The first proposal was for building plants to manufacture 40,000 tons of synthetic rubber per year; in March, 1941, this was reduced to 10,000 tons. The RFC next asked four large rubber companies —Firestone, United States Rubber, Goodrich, and Goodyear—each to submit plans for a plant with a potential capacity of 10,000 tons but equipped to produce only 2,500 tons per annum. As requested, Jersey agreed to waive all patent royalties and also any infringement claims that might rise out of the program. However, under pressure from the Office of Production Management—the successor to the Advisory Commission—the RFC finally in the middle of 1941 promised support for the 40,000-ton proposal. Arrangements were then made with the four rubber companies for each to build and operate a 10,000-ton Buna-S plant. These installations were to be owned by the government's Defense Plant Corporation.[39]

To provide butadiene for this rubber program, the RFC authorized Jersey to design a plant of 15,000-ton capacity which would use a petroleum gas. It also authorized Carbide & Carbon Chemical Corporation to design two units with a total capacity of 20,000 tons to use alcohol as a raw material. It was estimated that, because of materials shortages and other problems, from eighteen to thirty months would be required to build these large facilities. The plan was that butadiene from these plants and styrene to be supplied by chemical firms should be polymerized by rubber companies into 40,000 tons of Buna-S rubber, the general-purpose product which these concerns had been testing in tires.[40]

In the spring of 1941, Jersey made plans to increase its own butadiene production by building a second plant at Baton Rouge. Estimated to cost $2,500,000, it was to be larger than the first unit, which had been started in 1940 but was not yet in operation. The second installation was to utilize the same process as the first, that is, high-temperature, low-pressure steam cracking. A still more important move came late in the year as a result of success in research on butylene dehydrogenation. Work on a process for the dehydrogenation of normal butylene in the presence of steam and a catalyst was sufficiently advanced so that the designing of a commercial-scale plant was undertaken. The available butylene was limited, but Jersey engineers were confident that, by the time a plant to use this process could be built, the new fluid catalytic cracking units would be in operation and would supply whatever amount of butylene might be required.[41]

The designing of the government butadiene plant by Jersey engineers was well under way when the rapid progress of the butadiene units of Standard of Louisiana at Baton Rouge caused the Rubber Reserve Company (the federal agency in charge of the rubber program under the RFC) to request suspension of planning for the government plant. Believing that the unit would be required for national defense, Jersey continued to work on the plans on its own account. When in January, 1942, an order to resume work was received, the basic design had been developed, and Jersey was able to provide an engineered process for converting butylene to butadiene which eliminated former difficulties.[42]

The Jersey Company was less fortunate in carrying out its plans to produce Butyl rubber. Butyl had the advantage of requiring relatively little butadiene in its manufacture; it used mostly isobutylene, which was available in large quantities. But in designing the small Butyl plant proposed in mid-1940, the engineers ran into trouble. Standard Oil Development had to do a great deal of additional research before even a small unit could be designed. By the end of 1941, it had spent nearly $800,000 on Butyl research. Progress had been made, but the Butyl process was still far from ready to go into production.[43]

Altogether, only limited advances had been made in the United States toward establishing substantial synthetic rubber manufacture by the time the United States entered the war. Three years of discussion between company men and representatives of the government, and a year and a half of effort on the part of federal defense agencies to develop a program, had resulted in little more than a plan for small plants to be financed by the government. Private industry, however, had made some progress. Jersey, Shell, and a few other companies already had small units in operation, and additional private plants were under construction or planned.[44] Most important was the signal progress made in developing workable processes for the manufacture of butadiene. Jersey's new butylene dehydrogenation process was especially promising.

ORGANIZING FOR DEFENSE

The confusion that attended the forming of a government rubber policy from 1939 through 1941 arose partly out of uncertainties related to that particular issue. Also, no doubt, it grew out of the larger uncertainties and the conflicts that in general attended America's preparation for defense or war. The isolationism of the 1930's had raised a barrier to the recognition of danger to the United States itself, and the movement to curb big business had weakened mutual confidence between large segments of the public and government, on the one hand, and business, on the other. However, the growing threat of the Axis powers eventually began to dissolve isolationism and to bring a realization of the need for cooperation in the interest of national security in the event of actual military involvement. This transition, although only partially achieved by the time of this country's entry into the war, was of great importance to the relations of the government with the oil industry and to the mobilization of that industry for defense.

Neutrality legislation, congressional investigations, and federal suits only slowly gave way to policies favorable to the use of the resources of the oil industry. As a carry-over from the 1930's, a congressional committee in 1941 looked into the advisability of establishing control of crude oil production, and a bill introduced in Congress called for the divorcement of marketing from other functions of integrated companies. Jersey itself was a defendant in two federal suits initiated in 1941, one involving many pipeline companies and the other its own relations with Farben. But, on the whole, the balance was swinging in the other direction. At congressional hearings in April, 1941, the question of laying pipelines by oil companies as a national defense measure was raised, and a subsequent act enabled projected lines vital to national defense to exercise the right of eminent domain. In 1941, the Lend-Lease Act in March, the President's declaration of unlimited emergency in May, and the repeal in November of neutrality legislation—which for the first time allowed American vessels to carry arms and to enter war zones—removed most of the restrictions previously applied to aid for the Allies.

Positive developments had come sooner in the administrative than in the legislative branch of the government. New federal agencies, two of which affected the oil industry, had been established in 1940 to help implement the developing national defense policy. In June of that year the Advisory Commission to the Council of National Defense, already referred to, was set up. This agency was the government's first organization for assisting in mobilizing industry; it was the forerunner of the Office of Production Management, itself the predecessor of the War Production Board. In the same month, Admiral Emory Scott Land of the United States Maritime Commission requested the principal American tanker owners to organize a committee to cooperate with the commission in providing adequate supplies of petroleum products for the Navy. The companies established the four-member Committee of American Tanker Owners, with Jersey's Director Orville Harden as chairman.

This committee arranged with the Maritime Commission for a division of labor between government and tanker owners. The Navy was to requisition tankers for operating with the fleet. The committee was to develop a plan for sharing the requisitioning of company-owned ships for the Navy and for delegating to the principal suppliers of petroleum products and to tanker owners the responsibility for furnishing the Navy with products at American and specified foreign ports. The owners of 85 per cent of the American tanker tonnage above 3,000 gross registered tons per ship agreed to these arrangements. Two additional oil company representatives were added to the committee, and in November, 1940, offices were opened at 30 Rockefeller Plaza in New York. They were staffed in part by the loan of a group from the Marine Department of Standard Oil Company of New Jersey.[45]

In July, 1941, the Committee of American Tanker Owners was merged in the United States Tanker Control Board. The resulting government-industry board was organized by the Office of Petroleum Coordinator for National Defense, with its Deputy Coordinator as chairman. Jersey's Eugene Holman and representatives of two other oil companies were members of the committee.[46]

The establishment of the Office of Petroleum Coordinator for National Defense in May, 1941, was the most comprehensive development in oil industry–government cooperation before America's entry into the war. The general purpose of this agency was to help develop a national defense program for the industry. Harold L. Ickes, Secretary of the Department of the Interior, was appointed Petroleum Coordinator and Ralph K. Davies became Deputy Coordinator.[47] Although the Office of Petroleum Coordinator had only the power of recommendation, it at once began to serve the important functions of gathering and disseminating information about oil matters and of bringing oil company executives together for discussion of problems.

Many top officers of the industry were fearful of organized cooperation among themselves and with the government. They were especially apprehensive that any joint action would lead to difficulties under antitrust law. They also were concerned that a government agency might be used as an instrument for establishing federal regulation of the oil business. They remembered that Coordinator Ickes had been a powerful advocate of federal regulation of this very industry in the middle 1930's.

Ickes and Davies moved rapidly to organize a system of industry-government cooperation. In a meeting on June 19, 1941, oil executives—including representatives of Jersey affiliates—considered the possibility of a serious shortage of petroleum products, especially of aviation gasoline. At this time they drew up a plan for an organization of oilmen to inform and advise the Office of Petroleum Coordinator. Under its provisions, general and functional committees were to be set up to work with head-quarters in Washington; offices were located in the five districts into which the whole country was to be divided. The district committees were set up in the summer, and the general national advisory committee—the Petroleum Industry Council for National Defense—was organized in November, 1941. Its membership was made up of representatives of all branches of the American oil industry and included Jersey's President Farish and Humble's President Wiess.[48]

On the basis of information about current capacity and estimates of future requirements, the Office of Petroleum Coordinator began to urge the expansion of oil-industry facilities. Plans were made for the better use of existing equipment, but the major need was for new construction. Here the OPC ran head-on into the same roadblocks that earlier had made it difficult for Jersey and other oil companies to construct the facilities they had believed necessary. One such obstruction was the government procurement system; under that system the military services could not contract for purchases beyond the current fiscal year. Even had the services foreseen how greatly the requirements would increase, they could not have entered the purchase contracts required to justify the companies in building multimillion-dollar installations. Another restriction was the limitations on the purchase of construction materials. Even companies which decided to construct new plants without government contracts—that is, those who themselves agreed to bear whatever risks were involved—were held back by shortages of materials and the government system for allocating priorities.

The Office of Petroleum Coordinator was able to remove some of these barriers. In November, 1941, the Reconstruction Finance Corporation agreed that it, or its subsidiary agencies, would make long-term contracts for aviation gasoline from new plants constructed by oil companies. In the meantime, studies had been made of plant expansion and authorizations had been obtained from the Supply Priorities and Allocation Board.[49] No system of priorities could supply materials that did not exist; but with its information about needs and its better understanding of construction problems, the OPC could inform the supply board authoritatively of requirements.

Thus, on the eve of Pearl Harbor, the necessity for the rapid expansion of petroleum operations was better understood by both the oil industry and Washington. And an organization was being created that was ready to act effectively when America entered the war.

Jersey's top administration likewise was affected by the pressures of the time. Several changes were made in the membership of the Board of Directors in 1940. W. C. Teagle, who since June, 1937, had been serving as chairman of the board and who felt that the company should have younger directors, submitted a letter of resignation in January, 1940. The other directors, however, recognizing that he could contribute greatly from his experiences during World War I, were not willing to let him step down. They did accept the resignation as Jersey director as of June, 1940, of G. Harrison Smith, president of the Canadian affiliate, in order to uphold the neutral status of the parent company.[50] Two new directors proposed by the Jersey board were elected at the annual stockholders' meeting in June, 1940: Frank W. Abrams, president of Standard Oil Company of New Jersey, and, as already noted, Eugene Holman. Both had demonstrated great executive capacity in the preceding decade. These men served during the remainder of 1940 as members of the Coordination Committee, which was then investigating ways of improving the Jersey organization and of cooperating in national defense efforts. In the same year, Frank A. Howard of Standard Oil Development was elected a vice-president of the parent company, with responsibility for research, development, and chemical manufacturing activities. He continued to act as a member of the Coordination Committee.

The work of the Coordination Committee was adjusted to new needs. The monthly meetings decided upon in 1939 clearly allowed insufficient time for planning the necessary developments in crude oil production and refining. Instead of increasing the number of meetings of the whole group, however, a standing subcommittee called the Supply Committee was formed to meet once a week. As before, the full Coordination Committee examined budgets submitted by the affiliates, but, because of the impossibility of forecasting developments, it virtually ceased to draw up long-range programs.[51] The Department of Economics, headed by Dr. Stewart P. Coleman, was established in 1940 to carry forward the work of preparing forecasts and of making economic studies of actual or possible operations to guide the committee. The Coordination Committee was further assisted by special groups set up to deal with such matters as transportation and manufacturing and to investigate ways of improving operating efficiency.[52]

The attack on Pearl Harbor on December 7, 1941, ended the period of transition from peace to war during which Standard Oil Company (New Jersey) had become increasingly occupied with supplying the Allies and developing new products for national defense or for actual war. Jersey had lost heavily in the Eastern Hemisphere and had been unable to advance as rapidly in preparation for defense as its executives had planned. Nevertheless, the parent company and its Western Hemisphere affiliates were far better prepared late in 1941 than they had been in 1939 for supplying products for military use.

Chapter 15

A Transition in Public Relations, 1941–1942

O N THE FORMAL declaration of war against the Axis by the United States
and other neutrals after the Japanese attack on Pearl Harbor on
December 7, 1941, Standard Oil Company (New Jersey) and many of its
affiliates shifted their operations from a national defense to a war footing.
Like other concerns in the countries which previously had joined the Allies,
these Jersey companies were now to operate not as normal commercial
undertakings but as participants in an international effort under government direction and control. They became merged in a firm alliance whose
resources were mobilized through various boards and committees in what
the Army-Navy Petroleum Board after the war described as "one of the
great industrial enterprises in the history of warfare."[1]

At the very time that Jersey was entering heavily into this industrial
effort, some of its energy was deflected by the need to give attention to
issues that had their origin before the United States entered the war.
Most serious were difficulties in governmental and general public relations. These developments were of great significance to the company and
its operations at the time. They also illuminate the process of change in
company policy and organization. And they afford some insight into the
relations of government and business and into the temper of the country
at the beginning of its participation in the war.

BACKGROUND: CRISIS ABROAD AND
CONFUSION AT HOME

"I have called this volume *The Hinge of Fate* because in it we turn
from almost uninterrupted disaster to almost unbroken success." Britain's
great wartime leader thus explained the title of that part of his history of
World War II which deals with the events of 1942 and the first half of
1943. "For the first six months of this story," Winston Churchill con-

tinued, "all went ill; for the last six months everything went well." It was in those first six months of disaster that America had to face the reality of war and undertake full mobilization of men and resources.

In the Orient, the Japanese in a broad sweep of conquest took Hong Kong, Indochina, the Philippines, the British bastion of Singapore, Malaya, Burma with its overland road to China, and the Dutch East Indies. In the battles of the Java Sea and the Coral Sea, they destroyed a large part of the American and British fleets in the Pacific—the former having been gravely wounded at Pearl Harbor. Not until June, 1942, did the Allies, by destroying many of the enemy's planes and ships at Midway, effectively challenge the Japanese. But months were still to pass before Britain and America could halt the enemy's advance in the Southwest Pacific.

In the first half of 1942, the Allies also suffered severe reverses in Europe and Africa and on the Atlantic. Although the British earlier had succeeded in keeping the Axis out of important areas in the Middle East and in driving the Italians out of eastern Africa, in North Africa they were forced to retreat to El Alamein, only a short distance from the Nile Delta. The Germans also occupied the Crimean Peninsula. They continued to bomb Britain. And their submarines threatened to cut off seaborne supplies for the British Isles and the Atlantic Coast of the United States and Canada.

Not until November, 1942, did the fortunes of the Allies begin to turn for the better. In that month came the stemming of the Axis tide with the great victory of the Americans at Guadalcanal in the Solomons, General Montgomery's break through Rommel's lines in North Africa, the scuttling of the Vichy French fleet, and the Russian defeat of the Nazis at Stalingrad. Although the Allies thus stopped the advance of the Axis, they were still unable to undertake offensive campaigns.

The United States in the meantime was concerned in its own hemisphere with international problems of a different nature, all of which were important both to its military security and to the availability of essential raw materials. These problems rose out of the doubtful support of a number of Latin American countries. That the Nazis had gained a foothold in several countries south of the Rio Grande was well known. Traditional Latin American suspicion of the United States had become less articulate after this country had joined in a common effort to keep the Western Hemisphere out of the war. But a large part of Latin America, where isolationism and neutrality subsided more slowly than in North

America, had opposed the increase in United States aid to the Allies before Pearl Harbor. The instability of some governments heightened the uncertainty over which way their official sympathies might turn. The situation was aggravated by a considerable reduction in demand for raw materials produced in Central and South America, a result of the loss of markets in Europe and of submarine warfare. The entry of the United States into the war made it imperative to counteract forces tending to weaken this country's standing among its southern neighbors.

The unchecked success of the Axis brought shock and confusion in the United States. In addition, the submarine campaign off the Atlantic Coast in the winter of 1942 reduced to dangerous levels the supply of oil products available in the coastal region. The fall to the Japanese of the source of nearly all of America's rubber raised the specter of the immobilization of the country's rubber-tired economy. And the prospect of sending young men into a conflict for which the United States was not prepared raised the question of responsibility for the country's predicament. Consequently, the mobilization of men and resources coincided with a search for explanations of America's unpreparedness. This search brought confusion and delay.

SETTLEMENT OF PREWAR ISSUES

It was to be expected that many old problems would have to be dealt with in order to make way for unified support of the war effort. Standard Oil Company (New Jersey) was a party to several still unresolved differences, abroad as well as at home, which had risen in the 1930's. The settlement of the company's claims against Bolivia and Mexico for properties of affiliates seized in 1937 and 1938 was of immediate concern. At home, suits were pending to determine whether the parent company and certain affiliates had violated federal laws.

Negotiations for the settlement of the claims abroad had been undertaken by the Department of State as a part of its efforts to improve this country's relations with Latin America. These efforts included not only the settlement of claims of American citizens, individual and corporate, but also the support of financially weak countries and governments. Financial aid involved such measures as the agreement of the United States to purchase Mexican silver and the radically new policy of extending government loans to certain other countries in serious need of funds but with little or no standing in private loan markets.[2]

The settlement of Jersey's difficulties with Bolivia was negotiated by

Sumner Welles of the Department of State. The final agreement of February, 1942, took the form of the sale to the Bolivian government of the properties of Standard Oil Company of Bolivia which had been seized in 1937. Jersey was to receive $1,500,000 in cash plus 3 per cent interest from the date of the seizure. The principal sum was 9 per cent of the net worth of the Bolivian assets as recorded on the affiliate's books at the time of the seizure. The Bolivian affiliate was officially dissolved after the transactions had been completed.[3]

As an eminent authority on the history of the Latin American policy of the United States has observed, "Considerations of strategy as well as domestic politics cried imperiously for fraternity with Mexico, a contiguous neighbor."[4] A convention signed by the United States and Mexico in November, 1941, provided for the latter to pay for the expropriated properties of American oil companies in accordance with their value as agreed upon by a commission to be composed of one representative of the government of each country.

The commission's report of April, 1942, awarded the American oil companies a total of approximately $24,000,000 for assets expropriated in 1938 and for interest from that time. As its share, Jersey was awarded $22,332,486, including interest. A part of the amount decided upon was to be paid when the agreement became effective; the balance, bearing 3 per cent interest, was to be due within five years. The award covered approximately the net worth on the holding company's books plus interest from the time of expropriation, but it made no allowance for the considerable oil reserves of Jersey's Mexican affiliates which were not included in their valuation of their assets. A memorandum prepared for the Department of State summarizing editorial comment on the report stated that two-thirds of the United States newspapers from coast to coast held that the report was hard on the companies but of vital importance in maintaining and strengthening friendly relations with Latin America. Excepting Ambassador Josephus Daniels' own paper, which gave it unqualified praise, the other third characterized the report, in effect, as poor precedent with respect to the Good Neighbor Policy. *The New York Times* noted as "dangerous precedent" the fact that the United States (through Export-Import Bank credits) was "furnishing Mexico with the funds to pay for the property it expropriated," but it recognized the need for friendly relations with Latin America. The final agreement was signed in 1943. Jersey's Mexican affiliates were subsequently liquidated.[5]

In these negotiations, in which the companies had no part, corporate interests were apparently subordinated to the effort to win the adherence of Bolivia and Mexico to the Allies and generally to improve the standing of the United States in Latin America. In the circumstances, there could be no quarrel with these objectives. Jersey's executives were concerned, however, that the agreements—which they believed to be highly favorable to the two countries—might encourage others to expropriate the properties of foreign corporations.

At home, a decision of the Securities and Exchange Commission of February 5, 1942, under the Public Utility Holding Company Act of 1935, required Standard Oil Company (New Jersey) to divest itself of its stock ownership in several valuable natural gas utility companies. Jersey had applied for an exemption under the act on the consideration that this operation was only a small part of its total business. Its application was denied on the ground that, because of the size and importance of its gas utility system, exemption was not in the public interest. But the company obtained an extension of time in which to work out a plan to meet the emergency. Its solution was to transfer the stock of the gas companies to a new public-utility holding company and to distribute that concern's stock among Jersey's own shareholders. Accordingly, it transferred to the new Consolidated Natural Gas Company the stock of five companies in as many eastern states—The East Ohio Gas Company, Hope Natural Gas Company, The River Gas Company, The Peoples Natural Gas Company, and New York State Natural Gas Company. It then distributed the stock of this new holding company among its shareholders and charged $48,032,734 to surplus to cover the distribution.[6]

The company also was a party to judicial action initiated by the Department of Justice. Investigators of the department had worked for some time in the offices of the parent company and some of its affiliates. Two suits were of direct concern to Standard Oil Company (New Jersey). One had been filed in September, 1940, and the other shortly before the attack on Pearl Harbor.

The first suit was disposed of without much delay after the United States entered the war. It involved the American Petroleum Institute and a score of major oil companies and fifty-two common-carrier pipelines. Among the corporations were Jersey itself and several of its affiliates.[*] As

---

[*] The issues involved in this case, the long-drawn-out negotiations preceding the settlement, and the terms of the actual settlement are too complex to summarize here. A comprehensive summary is presented in Chapter 16 of Arthur M. Johnson's *Petroleum Pipelines and Public Policy, 1906–1959* (Cambridge, 1967). Chapter 15 presents historical background.

to pipelines, the government claimed that the companies had conspired, contrary to antitrust law, to control petroleum transportation, and that the payment of dividends by pipeline companies to their oil-producing owners constituted the granting of rebates in violation of the Elkins Act— a new interpretation of the statute. Instead of contesting the suit in wartime and in an unfavorable political climate, the defendants had chosen to enter a consent decree. The terms, finally agreed upon after Pearl Harbor, provided that dividends to shipper-owners should be restricted to a maximum of 7 per cent on valuation. This limiting of dividends was an important development in public policy, but it had little immediate significance to pipeline companies because during wartime the government could set rates and hence limit income. The traditional structure of the integrated oil industry remained intact after many years' threat of pipeline divorcement.[7]

The other suit, instituted against Jersey and several affiliates, officers, and executives in November, 1941, charged violation of the Sherman Act. This was one of several suits brought by the Department of Justice as a result of its investigation of the relations of American companies with German concerns. The government was especially concerned over the relations of Jersey and its research affiliate with I.G. Farbenindustrie A.G. Its principal interest was in an extensive and complex system of owning and licensing patents stemming from arrangements between Jersey and Farben, particularly those made in 1929. Investigators of the Department of Justice had worked for more than a year in the offices of the parent company and Standard Oil Development; they had examined countless records and had had copies made of tens of thousands of documents in company files.

The officers of Jersey and Standard Oil Development had maintained over the years that the arrangements made with the German firm in the 1920's and the resulting relations did not violate the Sherman Act or any other antitrust law of the United States. Before these relations with Farben had been entered into, the Jersey companies had been advised by the parent company's own attorneys and also by John W. Davis—outside legal counsel who had formerly been Solicitor General of the United States—that the proposed arrangements did not violate the law. This advice subsequently found support in a decision of the Supreme Court of the United States in 1931 which upheld patent licenses and cross-licenses; another decision in 1940 also allowed such arrangements under certain circumstances.[8] The exact bearing of these decisions on the relationship with Farben may not have been indisputably clear, but Jersey and other companies similarly situated were obviously buffeted by changing concepts of patent law.

Underlying this development was the growing importance of technology in business. A shift in the source of inventions growing out of corporate research and development had brought a considerable change in the ownership of patents from the individual inventor to the corporation. Moreover, when two or more companies had contributed to a single new patentable process, as was often the case, it was difficult to determine which one was the first to develop it. In the oil industry, among others, the difficulty had been overcome to some extent by cross-licensing or by forming a corporation or pool to hold patents on such processes. These solutions were considered valid alternatives to the chaos and high costs that would have resulted from suits over alleged infringement. In the 1930's, such arrangements were recognized by the courts and widely employed by American companies, both among themselves and in relations with foreign concerns.

However, these practices and the court decisions supporting them had come under widespread investigation. The problem was complex. Adjusting patent law to the changing technology was not a simple matter. The new developments invited a re-examination of old concepts and induced the proposal of new ones. This trend may have been a wholesome development in the field of patent law, but it made it difficult if not impossible for a company to determine for itself what was permitted and what was not. The whole subject obviously needed to be given broad and searching study by men with an understanding of the complexities of technology and business as well as competence in patent law.

The patent issue had been given close attention by the Roosevelt administration and Congress. In 1933 President Franklin D. Roosevelt had established the Science Advisory Board, under Dr. Vannevar Bush, to examine the workings of the patent system. This board had recommended certain procedural changes to improve and accelerate patent litigation. The patent system had been thoroughly examined later by the Temporary National Economic Committee. This body had recommended various changes, including the compulsory licensing of future patents, recording of transfers and agreements, limiting of suits for infringement, establishing a single court of patent appeals, shortening the period of patent monopoly, and requiring government approval of both future international cross-licenses and applications for patents in foreign countries. During the TNEC hearings, Congress had passed some patent legislation that had to do with procedural rather than substantive matters. On the eve of America's entry into the war, President Roosevelt appointed another special group—the National Planning Commission, headed by Charles F. Kettering—to study patent problems. An extremely complex issue was thus being investigated from various points of view.[9]

During the 1930's, new attitudes toward patent law had begun to challenge the traditional American position. There was a turning away from the historic concept that patents are rights to a special class of property granted by governments to inventors for a limited period of time as a reward for their contribution to society. The new view was that these rights, when owned by large corporations, made possible the creation of monopolies and that the system of licensing the use of patents brought not a sharing of the exclusive property of the patentee but a withholding of rights from the public. In other words, the American patent system was represented as contributing to the rise of combinations and restraints contrary to American antitrust law. In consequence, it was thought that there should be a differentiation in patent rights as between the individual inventor and the corporation in favor of the former.

This shift was, in fact, part of a broader development in thought about business and law. Among economists, students of law, and officials and agencies in the federal government, there was a growing interest in combinations and cartels, accompanied by a widening view of antitrust law. The principal question was whether new developments in technology and in the structure of business had led to the growth of powers beyond the reach of antitrust law as interpreted up to that time.

This question was especially focused on the relationship that had developed late in the 1920's and in the 1930's between American and German companies. Many of the larger and more progressive corporations in the United States had, like Jersey, established research and patent-holding relations with German concerns which were more advanced than American enterprises in industrial research and in some branches of technology. As a result of new ideas borrowed from these foreign connections, the Americans had accelerated technological change in their own operations, but in return they had given up some of their freedom of action. The arrangements, consequently, made them vulnerable to the charge of participation in foreign cartels. There was no clear precedent or statutory provision, however, under which to apply American antitrust law to such relations outside the United States.

Thurman W. Arnold, head of the Antitrust Division of the Department of Justice and a leading exponent of new views on patents and of a broadened application of antitrust law, proceeded to test the relations of American companies with foreign concerns. Among a number of actions which he instituted against large corporations was a grand jury investigation of Standard Oil Company (New Jersey) with special reference to its connections with I.G. Farbenindustrie. In the prevailing political climate, Assistant Attorney General Arnold's views, as presented earlier in the hearings of the TNEC and in his book, *The Folklore of Capitalism*, foreshadowed a critical treatment of such patent arrangements and research relations between companies.

The members of Jersey's Board of Directors were not of one mind whether or not to challenge the suit growing out of the grand jury investigation. Several of the directors, including Chairman Teagle, wanted to fight it. But those who favored entering a consent decree prevailed, and the Board of Directors chose to work out a negotiated settlement with the Department of Justice. This course was apparently taken to prevent the diversion of the company's energy from the war effort. The decision was also influenced by the recognition that some of Jersey's patent pooling arrangements were vulnerable under current interpretations of antitrust law.

A consent decree was entered, in its words, "without trial or adjudication of any issue of fact or law herein and without admission by any party in respect of such issue. . . ." It was signed on March 25, 1942, by counsel for the company and members of the Department of Justice, including Assistant Attorney General Arnold as head of the Antitrust Division. At the same time, pleas of *nolo contendere* were entered to the information filed by the government and relatively small fines were imposed upon the company and some of its officers as defendants in a criminal action paralleling the civil antitrust suit.

The decree severed any ties of Jersey with Farben that might have remained after the change in the two companies' relations in 1939. The final judgment "ordered, adjudged, and decreed" that "the Court has jurisdiction of the subject matter herein and of all parties hereto" under the Sherman Act and amendments and supplements to that act. The decree required the royalty-free licensing for the duration of the war and six months thereafter of all the patents acquired from the German concern; it also made licensing compulsory for the remainder of the life of the individual patents. In addition, it stipulated that the company should

not enter agreements to restrain trade if such arrangements were in violation of United States antitrust law.* The Alien Property Custodian signed
the decree, as had been requested by the company as protection against
claims that might be entered against Jersey by Farben after the war.[10]

On the day after he signed the decree, Thurman Arnold stated that it
"cured the [patent] situation without a law." Under it, the company
released 2,000 Jersey-Farben patents at a prospective royalty cost which,
Arnold said, possibly would amount to as much as $10,000,000. He also
said that the required licensing after the war would be "at reasonable
rates, which will be fixed on appeal to the court." This freeing of patents,
he added, would mean that Jersey could not dominate the industry in the
future. "I have only one substantial complaint about the Standard decree
which I may take up later," Arnold said, "but aside from that one
complaint, which is a minor detail, it accomplishes everything."[11]

Jersey's executives seemed satisfied with the settlement. The company
had avoided being tied up in a long-drawn-out law suit, and the issues
had been kept on the level of the interpretation of laws. As later stated by
President Farish: "In that consent decree we did not admit—nor were we
asked to admit—that we had violated the antitrust law. We simply
agreed that in the future we would, in respect to these [Farben] contracts,
follow the interpretations now being given by the Antitrust Division to
this country's antitrust law."[12] The restriction on future agreements of
the type affected by the decree was actually in keeping with the opposition to such ties that had risen within the Jersey Board of Directors.[13]
(See Chapter 11.)

On the day the decree was signed, both the Department of Justice and
the company released statements to the press. These were published on
March 26 in various newspapers, including the *Washington Post*. The
Jersey statement contained the following:

The developments made under these agreements [with I.G. Farbenindustrie]
have advanced the progress of American industry and its ability to meet the
war emergency. Nevertheless the company realizes that to obtain vindication
by trying the issue in the courts would involve months of time and energy of its
officers and many of its employees. Its war work is more important than court
vindication. Nor has the company any desire to remain in a position which the
Department of Justice considers in any way questionable.[14]

The company's officers and directors believed that the consent decree
had settled the issues raised by the Department of Justice.[15] But that

---

* This meant that the decree was not applicable to acts and operations outside the
United States not violative of antitrust laws nor to operations and activities authorized
and permitted by the Webb-Pomerene Act of 1918.

was not to be the case. During the next five months, the parent company and its research affiliate were to become deeply involved in hearings of congressional committees. This involvement, in effect, was in the nature of a public trial, widely covered by the press.

JERSEY'S ORDEAL OF 1942

On March 26, 1942, the very day after he had signed the consent decree in the Jersey-Farben suit, Assistant Attorney General Arnold, in open session of the Senate Committee on National Defense, alleged that Jersey's "cartel arrangements with Germany are the principal cause of the shortage of synthetic rubber." He now made charges that had been withdrawn from the original complaint because the company refused to enter a consent decree containing them. The immediate significance of these accusations lay in their bearing on the rubber situation, which, he said, "is in the limelight today because the consumer realizes it more than the shortage of other basic materials."[16]

Rubber was in the limelight, first of all, because of the recent loss to the Japanese of the source of nearly all of this country's natural rubber. The public had come to realize that this material was of such vital importance that without it the Allies might lose the war. People were asking why this contingency had not been foreseen and why provision had not been made for meeting it. The Army, the Navy, and the federal administration and its various agencies were receiving an immense amount of criticism.

The Senate Committee on National Defense had been established in 1941 with Senator Harry S. Truman as chairman. Soon after the attack on Pearl Harbor, this body began to hold hearings on several industries of importance to the United States and its Allies in the conduct of the war. The committee's expressed purpose was to discover ways to improve America's industrial performance. But the records of its hearings and its report lend support to the belief that at least some of the participants, for reasons of their own, may also have been concerned with shifting onto business the responsibility for the country's unpreparedness. Thurman Arnold, judging by his testimony in the hearings of the Committee on National Defense and the hearings of the Senate Committee on Patents, had a special interest in promoting the wide application of antitrust law and the revision of patent law.

Arnold's testimony was not the first public attempt to place blame for the rubber situation on Jersey. A press release issued in New York on January 30 by the Union for Democratic Action[17] had charged the company with primary responsibility for America's lack of large-scale synthetic rubber production. This release was a copy of a letter and a lengthy memorandum sent to Senator Truman. The memorandum, the letter stated, contained data "disclosing the tie-up between the Standard Oil Company of New Jersey and I.G. Farben German Trusts," as a result of which, "according to the material which has been presented to us, the United States is faced with a serious shortage of synthetic rubber." This information was forwarded as "sufficiently important to justify further investigation."[18] In a statement to the press, Jersey described the memorandum as "a garbled and inaccurate version of details of contracts and facts" which had been supplied by the company to the Department of Justice "in the course of the Department's investigation into German chemical interests in the U.S."[19]

The Truman committee's open hearings on the rubber situation had begun on March 5. Testimony on this first day of the open session revealed a dangerously low supply of natural rubber and little immediate prospect of manufacturing any considerable quantity of synthetic substitutes. The testimony on the second day devoted to rubber in open hearings—March 24—told of the long and nearly fruitless efforts of certain individuals and agencies in Washington to get government support for synthetic rubber manufacture as a national defense measure. It also revealed the complex technical problems, shortages of materials, and other difficulties to be overcome in establishing a synthetic rubber industry. The testimony of William Batt of the War Production Board, who in 1940 had been chairman of the rubber committee of the Advisory Commission on National Defense, placed the responsibility for delay in developing synthetic rubber on the government. One member of the committee concluded from Batt's testimony that, if the recommendation made by the Advisory Commission on National Defense "had been followed, as given in September, 1940, the 18 months [required for construction] would now be up and we would presumably be having the plant recommended."[20]

It was at the next session two days later that Arnold declared to the committee that Jersey's arrangements with I.G. Farbenindustrie were the principal cause of the shortage of synthetic rubber. He presented voluminous testimony on the company's relations with the German concern. He said that Jersey had agreed to turn over to Farben its information on synthetic rubber and that, at home, it had neither developed manufacture under its own patents nor allowed other companies to do so. He also stated that Jersey had invented Butyl rubber, had turned full information over to the German concern, but had refused to supply the United States government with information about it. His testimony, in brief, held that the lack of a synthetic rubber industry in the United States was owing to Jersey's restrictive policies.*[21]

The Assistant Attorney General did not limit his discussion to rubber. Using the Jersey Company to illustrate his position that companies in several industries vital to the war effort had stood in the way of war production, he went to great lengths in discussing what he held to be the Jersey-Farben cartel and its effects. He declared: "The sole motive [for the Jersey-Farben relations established late in the 1920's] was an attempt on the part of Standard Oil to get a protected market, to eliminate competition, and, finally, to restrict world production in order to maintain that control." He also said that the company had taken or contemplated other action in its foreign operations contrary to the interests of the United States. It had considered an offer of a German company to purchase its Hungarian properties in 1941, and it had sold gasoline to Axis-controlled Brazilian air lines in the same year contrary to the request of the Department of State. He further alleged that the Jersey-Farben Memorandum drawn up at The Hague in September, 1939, was a "device for the continuation of the conspiracy, at least through the war between Germany and Great Britain."[22] (See Chapter 14.)

The hearings made front-page headlines and were reported in detail in the press. Thurman Arnold specifically disclaimed the belief that the Jersey executives had acted from unpatriotic motives. But Senator Truman, on being asked by a reporter whether he regarded the Hague Memorandum as treasonable, replied, "Why yes, what else is it?"[23] The company was then reported in the press as having committed treason. Highly critical letters at once began to be received in President Farish's office. However, David Lawrence's syndicated column, "Today in Washington," on March 28 placed the responsibility for the lack of American synthetic rubber manufacture on President Roosevelt. *The Christian Science Monitor* said that the charges of "folklorist Arnold" were so sensational as to help the President by turning attention away from a number of "hotly contested discussions" and to introduce "a new news cycle in Washington."[24]

Jersey's President Farish, who began to testify at the next session after Arnold's appearance, was heard and questioned for two days. He pref-

---

* This position, of course, overlooked the fact that other companies also were trying to find ways to make synthetic rubber and that a few had had some success.

aced his discussion by saying that "any charge that the Standard Oil Co. or any of its officers has been in the slightest respect disloyal to the United States is unwarranted and untrue." He said: "I wish to assert with conviction that whether the several contracts made with the I.G. did or did not fall within the borders set by the patent statutes or the Sherman Act they did inure greatly to the advance of American industry and more than any other one thing have made possible our present war activities in aviation gasoline, toluol, and explosives and in synthetic rubber."[25]

Farish considered Arnold's various charges in some detail. As to the charge that "Standard had delayed, or retarded, or stifled the development of synthetic rubber in this country," he said, "This statement has not a shadow of a foundation." He explained that, through its purchase of an interest in Farben patents, the company had obtained a minority interest in the Buna-S process, but that Farben had retained complete control of the patents on this synthetic in the United States. Only after the territorial division of the Jasco patents late in 1939 did Jersey acquire control in the United States of Farben's rubber patents. As for Butyl, said Farish, under the arrangement to exchange research information with Farben (through Jasco, Incorporated), the company had informed the German company of its discovery of Butyl; but Germany did not have the petroleum gases needed for making that synthetic rubber. In regard to Arnold's statement that Jersey had sold aviation fuel to Axis-controlled air lines in Brazil, allegedly contrary to the request of the Department of State, Farish said that that had been done with the approval of the department. He said that the United States officials were then attempting "to get a coordinated political program in South America and particularly in Brazil, and we were acting under their instructions." He referred to an expression in September, 1941, of the department's approval of Jersey's readiness to work with it toward its objectives in other South American republics, mentioning particularly steps taken by the company to control delivery of supplies to air lines. Referring to Arnold's allegation of conspiracy with respect to the Hague Memorandum of September, 1939, Farish testified that the British and American governments had been informed of the negotiations in advance, that the company had offered to conduct the negotiations in the presence of a member of the American Legation at The Hague, and that certain papers involved had actually been carried by a courier of the Department of State.[26]

President Farish was handicapped under questioning because he was not personally acquainted in detail with the earlier negotiations with

Farben or even with later negotiations and had had only a few days in which to prepare for his appearance before the committee. He accordingly had to refer some questions to the chief executive of Jersey's research affiliate. President Howard of Standard Oil Development, who had participated in the negotiations with Farben from the very beginning, assisted Farish in answering questions and in clearing up what they held to be misconceptions arising from Arnold's testimony and interpretation of documents. Both Jersey executives were placed on the defensive, however, by quotations from letters taken out of context and apparently interpreted freely.[27]

Following the testimony of these presidents of the Jersey companies, government witnesses testified concerning Jersey's supplying two Brazilian air lines controlled by German nationals. One line, known as the Lati, operated between Italy and Rio de Janeiro; the other, the Condor, operated within Brazil. The two worked together, so that gasoline and lubricants held in storage by one were known to be available to the other. Standard Oil Company of Brazil supplied both lines and had a supply contract with the Condor. One of two government witnesses, who was chief of the Office of American Republics in the Department of Commerce, firmly contradicted Farish's reply to the charge made by Arnold concerning Jersey's supplying of these lines. He even maintained that nowhere in Latin America had Jersey affiliates cooperated with the efforts of the United States government to weaken Nazi influence. The other government representative, A. A. Berle, Assistant Secretary of State, did not support the charge of noncooperation. The matter is reviewed in detail in his testimony.[28]

A summary of Berle's testimony must suffice here. In order to stop the flow of Nazi influence into and within Brazil through these two air lines, the Department of State in March, 1941, entered discussions with Jersey over the delivery of gasoline to them, which the department wished to have discontinued. In April, Jersey agreed that it would supply the lines through its Brazilian subsidiary and only with the approval of deliveries by the American Ambassador in Rio de Janeiro. The department then sent orders to the Embassy to see that deliveries were so controlled as to reduce the storage stocks of the air lines. The department also tried to arrange cooperative action with the Brazilian government, but it ran into difficulty because the Condor flew 70 per cent of the country's air route mileage and the Brazilians, in Berle's words, "were not philosophical about having their internal communications disrupted. . . ." The United

States government then began to make arrangements for providing a substitute service. In October, presumably because the stocks had become low, the Condor asked for a large delivery of aviation gasoline. A representative of Jersey discussed the matter with the Department of State, but he and Berle disagreed about the responsibility the United States government should take for the breach of contract by the affiliate incorporated in Brazil and hence subject to regulation under Brazilian civil law. Berle thereupon initiated steps to have the Brazilian affiliate blacklisted by the United States. However, the next day President Farish sent a message to the department saying that the company would comply with its request. Berle testified that, so far as he was aware, "there was no departure from the arrangement whereby deliveries, if any, should be controlled by the American Embassy." Immediately after Pearl Harbor, he added, the Condor was shut down because it had no gasoline, and the government of Brazil grounded the Lati line. The United States government then had a substitute service ready to go into operation.

This instance illustrates the dilemma faced—particularly in wartime—by a multinational company like Jersey when the interests of the parent company's home country conflict with those of the foreign corporate home of an affiliate. The issue then arises as to whether or not the operations of the foreign affiliate shall be conducted under the control of, and in the interest of, the host country or be guided primarily by the interest of the United States as viewed by its own government. In this instance involving a Brazilian affiliate, the two governments worked out an arrangement that enabled the company to continue to supply fuel to air lines essential to Brazil. This could be done because both recognized a common threat to their security. Generally in such cases of conflict, whether interests be convergent or divergent, nationalism is an important underlying factor. Such situations are, of course, of importance not only to the company involved; they also have broad implications for American business abroad and indeed for the foreign relations of the United States itself.

In view of the information in other chapters of this volume on Jersey's research on synthetic rubber, it is not necessary to consider at this point Assistant Attorney General Arnold's contention that America lacked a synthetic rubber industry because of Jersey-Farben relations. Those chapters do not, however, contain information concerning one charge that was given special emphasis. This was the allegation that the company had tried to withhold information about Butyl from the United States government in 1939. The event referred to had taken place in November of that year, after the Navy, at the company's request, had made tests on Butyl for which Jersey had supplied samples. A civilian representative of the Navy on the company's invitation came to the laboratories of Standard Oil Development to discuss the results of the tests and to get information about the compounding and handling of synthetic rubber.

A statement in an intracompany report of this visit was the basis for Arnold's charge that Jersey had withheld information from the government. Dr. Per K. Frolich, the head of the chemical division, had reported that the visitor had asked to see the manufacturing process, which was actually still an experimental laboratory operation.[*] Frolich had finally taken him to see it "when it appeared I could not steer his interest away from the process."[29] In his testimony, President Farish explained the reluctance of Dr. Frolich in this way: "The Navy was not, as I understand it, interested in the manufacture of rubber, and as was customary in our laboratory and every laboratory I know of, there is no ready exposition of process work and experimental work that is carried on." He added, "Obviously, anybody who is in our laboratories trying to find out what is going on in experimental work is not shown what is going on."[30] In other words, what had occurred was simply the normal practice of business to protect its trade secrets.

Much of Arnold's position depended on interpretations of certain documents that were different from those of the companies. It was possible, of course, to read various meanings into statements dealing with complex matters and concerned with the uncertainties of the future. Indeed, the meaning found in them could depend on one's basic assumptions and the extent of one's knowledge of the underlying situation.

For example, Thurman Arnold charged that Jersey and Farben in 1929 had made a "coordination agreement" which bound both parties to a cartel to work together, regardless of national laws, to dominate the oil and chemical industries of the world. This charge was based on correspondence between the two companies. Frank A. Howard, who had represented Jersey in the negotiations, explained what had taken place in this way: These were actually letters exchanged in 1927 at the request of Farben; their purpose was to confirm the intention of the two parties to proceed in all good faith in carrying out their twenty-five-year license

---

[*] Dr. Frolich was an associate professor at Massachusetts Institute of Technology before coming to Standard Oil Development Company. In 1942 he was elected president of the American Chemical Society.

arrangement covering hydrogenation processes and extensive technical research. Since each party had to depend upon imperfectly understood laws of a foreign country—subject to change in the future—to get expected benefits from this license agreement, Howard maintained that such personal assurances by the heads of the two companies, that there would be no resort to unfair legal technicalities by either side, seemed reasonable.[31]

Similar differences arose over the Assistant Attorney General's contention as to the arrangements made by Jersey with Farben at The Hague in September, 1939. On the basis of a sentence in Frank A. Howard's report to President Farish concerning the negotiations, Arnold maintained that the result was actually a *modus vivendi* for continuing the cartel throughout the war even should the United States be drawn into it. The company, on the contrary, held that this sentence had to do only with possible payments by Jersey in order to share equitably with Farben royalty income which could not be calculated in advance. This laid the company open to the charge, however, that the transaction was not a bona fide sale. Howard's explanation was that this was the only condition on which Farben would agree to the transfer.[32]

The situation at the beginning of the war was clearly very complex. This procedure may well have been the only way in which Jersey could have saved its ownership rights in a number of important patents from seizure by the belligerents even before the entry of the United States into the European conflict. It was likely the only way Jersey could have acquired rights to other important patents for use in the United States for national defense as well as for commercial manufacture. However, one might ask whether the company could not have protected itself and its rights by informing the Department of State at the time of what had been done and the reasons for it. To be sure, it did not normally inform the department of its business relations abroad, but this was not a normal time or relationship.

The New York Times, in its leading editorial on April 2, 1942, gave an evaluation of the testimony of Arnold, Farish, and Howard. Regarding the cartel issue, it stated that "whether or not the cartel agreement between Standard and I.G. was an 'illegal conspiracy' under the antitrust law cannot be determined for the case has been terminated by a consent decree." The editorial agreed with Arnold's general position that such international patent arrangements as Jersey's with Farben should be cleared with the United States government in the interest of national security. As to his allegation concerning rubber, the editorial, reviewing the charges and the answers of Jersey's executives, concluded: "In the light of this evidence Mr. Arnold's charges that the Standard Oil is responsible for the shortage of synthetic rubber simply evaporate. It is apparent that he did not have the facts."

Among the newspapers that took a contrary position was *PM*, a young New York publication then gaining considerable attention as a promoter of "liberal" causes. In April, 1942, this paper printed a series of "letters" addressed to John D. Rockefeller, Jr. These proposed that Jersey's stockholders should not return signed proxies for the next annual meeting but organize opposition to the company's Board of Directors. They suggested that, although the stockholders might not be able to overthrow the present directors, they could have "a salutary effect on future deals." *PM* supported this challenge with charges against the company, stating that Jersey was in effect "an ally of Hitler, an economic enemy agent" within the United States, and that it had not only helped develop the Axis war machine but had thwarted the production of important materials in the United States.

Jesse H. Jones, who as Secretary of Commerce and head of the Reconstruction Finance Corporation had responsibility—second only to that of President Roosevelt—for the government's rubber program, appeared before the Truman committee on April 7, the last day of the rubber hearings. He stated that he and President Roosevelt had decided not to commit the government to the expense of a large-scale synthetic rubber program before the entry of the United States into the war. He maintained that there was no necessity whatever to develop such an industry except for war.[33] In fact, many informed and responsible individuals, inside and outside the government, believed at the time that Japan would not be able to conquer Southeast Asia even should it be so rash as to risk the attempt.

Senator Joseph C. O'Mahoney, taking a position similar to that taken by Jones, said on April 13: "We know that the Government did not take advantage of the progress of science to make synthetic rubber available to the country."[34]

Before this testimony favorable to the Jersey Company's position was heard, the damage to its reputation and morale had been done. The effect on the personnel of parent company and domestic affiliates was traumatic. The first reaction of Jersey's own leaders was one of nearly paralyzing shock, followed by anger over the misrepresentation of facts and motives and by fear of the results to the company and its many associates. These men desired public respect, and they believed that they merited it. Why, they asked, was Jersey made the whipping boy when the nation came to a full realization of its unpreparedness? Why was the company regarded as monopoly-oriented? Would these attacks lead to another dismemberment of Standard Oil Company (New Jersey)?

The first response of Jersey was to deny the charges. The company issued releases to the press, and on April 9, 1942, it sent out a pamphlet containing the statement President Farish had presented to the Truman committee. The Esso Marketers, on their own initiative, went into action to attempt to counteract the bad effect of the accusations on their sales. The marketing organization had a specific public to which to direct its statements, and its sales promotion staff had had much experience in communicating with that public. Haslam, consequently, arranged to have writers assigned from the Esso Marketers to prepare answers to the charges. These hasty replies, written in a breezy reportorial style, were mailed to all charge customers and handed out at service stations. Typical was a long letter to "Dear Customer" dated April 14, 1942, over the name of Haslam as vice-president of Standard Oil Company of New Jersey.[35] This communication was in question-and-answer form and dealt with the principal issues raised by Thurman Arnold. In keeping with the nature of the man who signed the letter, the answers were direct and emphatic.

The day before this letter was issued, Jersey became involved in another congressional investigation, conducted by the Senate Committee on Patents of which Senator Homer T. Bone was chairman. The stated purpose of the committee's hearings was to consider "a bill to provide for the use of patents in the interest of national defense or the prosecution of the war, and for other purposes."[36]

On the opening day of these new hearings, about a week after the Truman committee's rubber hearings had been completed, Senator Robert M. La Follette, Jr., stated: "I.G. Farben, through its maze of international patents, is the spearhead of Nazi economic warfare. By its cartel agreements with Standard Oil of New Jersey, the United States was effectively prevented from developing or producing any substantial amount of synthetic rubber." Alleging that the consent decree would protect Farben interests during the war, he said: "If this result was due to action in the executive branch of the government, I say let this committee find out who it was that forced its acceptance. . . . In my judgment . . . the people are not in a frame of mind to be gentle with industrial treason at home while American boys die on battlefields scattered all over the globe."[37]

Thurman Arnold represented the problem as one of international patent cartels. To support his charges, he used materials gathered from the files of Jersey and many other large American corporations in connection with the investigations made by the Antitrust Division of the Department of Justice. He asserted that there was a shortage of many basic materials "because of a cartel system that used the patent law not to reward the inventor but as an instrument to establish an antiproductive business policy of high cost and low turnover."[38] Queried on the other side of the patent issue, reward for invention, he replied: "Now, on the question as to . . . what should be the reward to the man spending a lot of money on research, I have not given a great deal of thought to that." His interest, he said, was not only in a stopgap law for the duration of the war but in a reform of the patent system to prevent the postwar use of patent cartels to establish monopolies.[39]

By this time the Jersey Board of Directors had come to believe that the situation was critical. They were alarmed by the effect persistent attacks might have on the company's personnel and operations and on its relations with government, industry, and the public in general. Haslam as general manager of the Esso Marketers informed the board that his organization could not deliver satisfactory sales performance unless something was done to improve Jersey's public relations. John D. Rockefeller, Jr., who had been deeply disturbed by the letters addressed to him in *PM,* emphatically challenged the directors to improve the company's standing with the public. This was the second time the younger Rockefeller had approached Jersey's top executives to urge action in a time of crisis in the affairs of the corporation.[40]

AN EXPLORATION IN PUBLIC RELATIONS

The Jersey directors turned to Haslam to organize a task force to deal with the problem. In no uncertain terms, Director Gallagher, as chairman of the Executive Committee, told him what he was expected to accomplish. Haslam, whose office had been at 26 Broadway, at once moved uptown to 30 Rockefeller Plaza. He recruited a staff from Jersey's publications and the New York sales organizations and hired a few outsiders.

The group's first efforts were strictly defensive. Some members were given the assignment to prepare materials for distribution by the company and to write answers to letters having to do with charges against it. Others were given a training course in preparation for giving speeches before company personnel and outside organizations on issues in controversy. At the same time, arrangements were made for the presentation of Jersey's case at meetings in several cities in the Northeast to which local stockholders and prominent citizens were invited.[41]

Haslam also looked for professional help. On the advice of Gallagher, he consulted "Tommy" Ross of the firm of Ivy Lee and T. J. Ross. Ross suggested that he see Earl Newsom, a public relations consultant. Late in April, 1942, after Haslam had talked with members of several public relations concerns, the company engaged the services of Earl Newsom and his firm.[42]

Haslam and Newsom explored the whole situation with the view to planning an organization and procedures. "I have a growing feeling," the former wrote to Newsom on May 15, 1942, "that the machinery for a modern corporation's contacts with the Public Mind has traditionally been hopelessly minimized in Standard's set-up, and your first job may involve lifting the Company's management out of traditional conceptions." He sketched some preliminary notes on how to proceed, "so that you may see how my mind is running." A comprehensive organization, to meet current onslaughts and "to serve as a constructive force in the future," should be set up "to operate like a well-oiled machine." Means should be provided for "discovering public attitudes—those of a big, broad, general nature which influence basic ideas and those of particular application to the company or its products or its officials or its policies." Trends and factual information published in news media should be called to the attention not only of policy-making officials but also of special individuals—chemists, research men, patent executives, and so on—who should be responsible for reporting immediately to "the Public Relations Office" any incorrect statements against the company. Up-to-the-minute knowledge of charges and insinuations and of actual facts in given cases was essential, wrote Haslam. Working relations should also be established with outside writers and the press.

Haslam was right in his "feeling" that contact with the public mind had traditionally been minimized in the Jersey Company. Why had the parent company not learned its public relations lesson in 1911? Actually, that experience had made the top executives so fearful of the public and the government that for a time they had deliberately avoided publicity. They had still held to the old belief that business is private. And insofar as they had recognized any responsibility to the public, they had envisaged it as primarily industrial. World War I had brought something of a change. A. C. Bedford, company chairman, and Walter C. Teagle, president, had learned to value good relations with the press. But, as was generally true of businessmen at that time, Teagle's concept of public relations had been limited largely to conventional informative releases to the news media.[43]

Even with respect to newspaper publicity, no system had been worked out to provide an effective and continuing effort. An assistant to President Teagle had had as one of his duties to maintain relations with the press. The president held, moreover, that executives throughout the organization had responsibility for similar contact with the public. But this approach had not functioned effectively. Executives had had their hands full with other matters. In addition, the company had grown too large and too complex for any one executive to know much of what was happening outside the area of his own responsibility. Indeed, even the office of the president of the parent company was not organized to answer inquiries from the press.

The trouble ran even deeper. It was not merely that Jersey had had an inadequate organization for handling company publicity. Its top administrators apparently had possessed little conception of the importance of public attitudes toward their company or, indeed, of the implications of the prevailing climate of opinion. Directors and officers generally had maintained outstandingly good relations in their various business contacts. A few had seen clearly that their firm had responsibilities beyond its immediate commercial relations. But the official view of the top administration had continued to be that the company should be judged by its performance as an industrial concern and that no systematic effort was necessary to make that performance known.

In fact, these executives had failed to recognize that a corporation of the size and influence of Jersey had a meaning to the public beyond its immediate industrial operations. Nor had they realized that a large concern cannot safely isolate itself from the society of which it is a part. They had overlooked the fact that recognition of this responsibility to the people is especially important in a country where communication is highly developed and every man as a voter may have a part in determining the conditions under which a large corporation may operate and continue a profitable existence.

Earl Newsom was in complete accord with Haslam's thoughts on what should be done. As a specialist in the field of public relations, he had definite ideas on procedures. He urged that a more positive approach was essential, one that involved a calm and thorough presentation of significant facts. With this objective, he advised the company to ask for an opportunity to be heard at two congressional hearings then going on in Washington. He also suggested that arrangements be made for company personnel to meet the press.

After extended discussion, it was decided to arrange a press conference to announce the completion of the first fluid catalytic cracking plant. The Jersey board was apprehensive of the outcome of the experiment and only with great reluctance agreed to the plan.[44] The conference was scheduled for May 21, 1942.

A few days prior to that date, Jersey again became involved in congressional hearings. On May 16 a special attorney of the Antitrust Division of the Department of Justice referred to Jersey in the hearings of Senator Bone's Committee on Patents which had been going on since April. At this later time, this committee was investigating companies accused of participation in world cartels.[45] On May 19, the cartel issue was raised again, this time in the hearings of Senator Guy M. Gillette's committee, which was investigating the possible use of surplus wheat and other grains for making alcohol to be used in manufacturing butadiene.[46]

On May 20 the Bone committee took up consideration of the Jersey-Farben rubber issue. A special assistant of the Antitrust Division reported on his search of documents in the Jersey files in preparation for the antitrust suit. He repeated, in somewhat greater detail, the testimony presented by Thurman Arnold in the Truman committee hearings in March in support of the charge that Jersey's relations with Farben had delayed the development of synthetic rubber manufacture in the United States.[47]

It was on the second day of these hearings on the Jersey-Farben issue that the company held its press conference. The place of meeting was the board room. The company was represented by President Farish and Robert P. Russell, a former MIT professor then second in command of Standard Oil Development. Although the information to be released to the press had to do with the new fluid catalytic cracking plant at Baton Rouge, the company executives expected that the reporters would be especially interested in synthetic rubber because that subject was then being discussed in the hearings in Washington. The executives were prepared for a tough session. The first question asked by a reporter was a "loaded" one. President Farish did not attempt to reply but only smiled. The newsmen chuckled. And what had been feared as a tense occasion was off to a relaxed start. The press representatives plied Farish and Russell with questions. The event, as had been hoped by the Jersey men, turned out to be somewhat in the nature of an educational seminar. The news of the "cat cracker" got wide publicity in the next day's press.[48]

This successful press conference may have marked a turning point in Jersey's public relations. So far as is known, this was the first time in the history of the company that representatives of the press had been invited into the board room for a free-for-all questioning of the chief executive officer and other officials. Of immediate significance was the fact that the conference gave President Farish a sense of confidence in the press and also that it apparently changed the reporters' attitude toward him. To the Jersey administrators in general, it demonstrated the importance and the feasibility of establishing effective communication through the press with the company's social and political environment.

Only a few days later, the Truman committee issued its report on the rubber investigation. This document stated that there was "no question of moral turpitude or of subjective unpatriotic motivation on the part of Standard or any of its officials." Like Thurman Arnold, it took the position that, as a result of relations with Farben, Jersey had retarded the development and manufacture of synthetic rubber in the United States. However, its statements were less positive and its tone more restrained than Arnold's had been. It recognized that the company had actively participated in conferences with government agencies on synthetic rubber, had made helpful suggestions, and generally had cooperated. But it denied the company's statement that the knowledge and rights derived from Farben had aided in the development of new processes and products important to the war effort of the United States and its Allies.[49]

The report significantly noted "that the principal agreements between Standard and I.G. Farben were made in the 1920's at a time when the possibility of another war was not seriously considered and at a time when the Government had not taken any position with respect to such arrangements with foreign companies." Asserting that basically the fault lay in the patent system, it also stated: "Unless a company in the position of Standard took careful and calculated action to arm itself with the strongest patent structure it could acquire, it would have been apt to find itself either paying an enormous tribute to other companies or being excluded from various fields in which it was legitimately interested." The report further noted that the deliveries to air lines in Brazil had been continued until a substitute air service could be established.

Assistant Attorney General Arnold, in order "to clarify distortions of facts," submitted to the Truman committee a rebuttal to statements made by Jersey executives in the rubber hearings and in Haslam's letter of April 14. This counterargument was accompanied by copies of correspondence and other materials gathered from company files. Arnold took the position that Standard Oil Company (New Jersey) had denied the facts presented with regard to the situation and had attempted to mislead the committee. "This continuing defense of the cartel arrangement with Farben," he stated, "is the most alarming demonstration of the need for immediate legislation."[50] The issue he particularly emphasized in this rebuttal was essentially the same as that being considered by the Bone committee.[51] The rebuttal and the accompanying exhibits were released to the press.

Jersey's Executive Committee decided that Farish should reply to this attack. The president, therefore, wrote to Senator Truman, proposing that "If in your opinion the national interest requires further examination of the whole matter, we will be glad to file with you a documented review of the matters raised in Mr. Arnold's brief." The senator replied:

. . . of course, you and I are not in agreement on just what the facts of our hearings show. I have my views on the subject and, of course, you are entitled to yours. . . . So far as I am personally concerned the record is complete.

I cannot see any reason for further hearings, although if the Standard Oil Company of New Jersey does not feel it has had a square deal a further hearing might be arranged. At this time I cannot see that any good purpose would be served by reopening the case.[52]

Arnold's statement and exhibits were printed—125 pages in length—in the report of the committee's hearings.[53]

These recurring attacks by government officials impressed Jersey's officers and directors with the need for a comprehensive public relations program. They asked Earl Newsom to continue to serve as adviser to the company. Several of the top administrators gave firm support and valuable advice to Newsom and Haslam. President Farish was anxious that no director or executive should ever have to go through the harassing experience he had had in the Truman committee hearings and with the press at that time.[54] Others firmly behind the effort to improve the company's standing were Ralph W. Gallagher, chairman of the Executive Committee in 1942 and later Jersey's president; Wallace E. Pratt, also a member of the Executive Committee; and Frank W. Abrams, a relatively new member of the Board of Directors. For a time, some members of the Jersey board were opposed in principle or were neutral; others were too busy with the company's war work to devote much time to such matters.

In order to learn something about its actual standing with the public, the company engaged Elmo Roper's organization to survey outside opinion concerning the Jersey Company. The survey showed (1) that the company was "currently suffering from the effects of an acute attack of 'Arnolditis' "; (2) that Jersey was disliked not because it was big, but because it was believed to be greedy and had let Germany get the best of America in a business deal; (3) that little was known about its contributions to the war effort; and (4) that there· was a less friendly feeling toward it than toward others among the country's outstanding corporations. Newsom himself, from study of the company's standing with the public, urged a change of policy.[55]

What Newsom proposed essentially meant the application to public relations of the Jersey technique of research and study and a program for establishing effective communication with the public based on incontrovertible information. Hasty denials of charges, such as those made in the first weeks following Thurman Arnold's testimony of March 26, had proved at best ineffective and at worst damaging. They were too brief, they were susceptible to the charge of inconsistency with facts in company documents and testimony, and they were wholly defensive. A more constructive method was clearly required.

In the summer of 1942 it became possible to test a more soundly based procedure. The new approach was followed in the appearance of Jersey men in the later hearings of the same two congressional committees in Washington that had considered the cartel and rubber issues in May— the Bone and Gillette committees. President Farish obtained invitations for the company to be heard. A research staff was set up to prepare statements on matters in controversy. Documents were searched and conferences were held with officers and executives in an effort to prepare full and accurate statements. No incomplete statements or mistakes of any kind could be risked.

Late in July, President Farish and two executives of Standard Oil Development appeared before the Gillette committee. This group was still exploring the possibility of using surplus agricultural products for making synthetic rubber. The Jersey men were hopeful that their appearance would give them an opportunity to tell of their work on this vital material in a less hostile atmosphere than that of the Truman committee. They displayed elaborate exhibits in the room where the hearings were held. President Farish presented a statement explaining what Jersey had done in the synthetic rubber field. Farish and Vice-President E. V. Murphree and W. C. Asbury of Standard Oil Development answered questions, the last two men particularly on technical aspects. The occasion was marked by courtesy and an earnest effort to arrive at an understanding of the issues involved.[56]

The appearance of Jersey representatives before Senator Bone's Committee on Patents was even more significant. The representatives of the Antitrust Division of the Department of Justice had ranged far more widely and had presented evidence concerning the company in greater detail in this investigation than in the Truman committee hearings. Also, the hearings of this committee had been spread over a period of several months and thus had kept the issues before the public throughout the spring and summer. The testimony of the Jersey men extended over three days. Six were heard: President Farish; President Howard of Standard Oil Development; R. T. Haslam, who for several years from 1927 had headed technical relations with Farben; E. V. Murphree of Standard Oil Development; H. W. Fisher, manager of the research affiliate's commercial department; and W. C. Asbury, chemical engineer of the same company. All but President Farish had been associated with Jersey's research and development and with its relations with Farben from some time before 1930 and could thus speak from their own knowledge and experience.[57]

The Jersey executives took up the various issues one by one, each witness dealing principally with matters with which he had been closely associated. A few clashes occurred between the company representatives and the assistant prosecutor for the Department of Justice. As reported by *Time*, there was even "a flurry of anger and a flash of fists" when the Antitrust Division's representative remarked that he would take the word of only one Jersey witness.[58] This time the company representatives generally took a positive stand. They did not hesitate to differ with members of the committee or with its legal counsel. The questions asked by committee members often led to general discussion of the technical situation.

Robert T. Haslam, for example, talked not only of specific details in relations with Farben but also of oil industry problems and the state of scientific and technological development throughout the oil industry. He spoke authoritatively of the advanced condition of German industrial technology and of what Jersey had obtained from Farben. And he could reduce an issue to its essentials, sometimes by a simple analogy. At one point, for instance, Chairman Bone referred to a clause in an agreement of 1929, under which Jersey relinquished to Farben claims to any new chemical product it might discover that was not derived from petroleum. The senator implied that this agreement gave Farben control of the market for that product. Haslam responded that, to the best of his knowledge and belief, Jersey had never made an invention in the non-petroleum chemical field before 1927, and that he knew from his own personal knowledge it had not done so since 1927. "Therefore, to strip it of its legal verbiage," he concluded, "it was somewhat like my saying to you, Senator, that I am willing to sell you my share of the Lincoln Memorial for $25." His testimony, however, like that of the other men speaking for Jersey, was mostly concerned with presenting details on particular matters of controversy and explaining the reasons for the company's actions.[59]

These hearings gave President Farish an opportunity to reply to the charge—made by a government witness early in April and broadcast by the press—that he had misrepresented the facts in the Truman committee hearings with regard to the Brazilian affiliate's supplying Axis-controlled air lines in Brazil with gasoline. When Chairman Bone again introduced this particular issue, Farish offered to read into the record a statement released to the press by the State Department after he had testified in those hearings concerning this controversy.[60] The release contained this introduction:

In connection with the testimony of Mr. Farish, President of the Standard Oil Company of New Jersey, that the American Ambassador in Brazil and several State Department officials had approved the sale of aviation gasoline to an Italian air line in 1941, the following statement is issued for background. Mr. Farish's testimony in this regard is correct.

The statement explained that the department, in its campaign to eliminate Axis control of South American air lines, had dealt with the problem of eliminating such control of a transatlantic line by Italy and another furnishing a large part of air communication within Brazil. Because "Brazil could not be expected to have her internal and external air communications paralyzed," the Department of State had arranged that, while it was making preparations to provide substitute services, Jersey's Brazilian subsidiary should continue to deliver gasoline to these lines under the general supervision of the department and the American Ambassador in Rio de Janeiro.[61]

As the three days of testimony and discussion passed, a change came in the general spirit of the investigation and in the reports in the press. There was a shift of interest from the original emphasis on Jersey's relations with Farben as a commercial cartel to the relationship as a means of advancing the technology of Jersey and the American oil industry. The hearings closed on the last day of the testimony of the company's officers and engineers.

The experiments of the summer of 1942 with a full and calm presentation of facts about the company before congressional committees and to the press demonstrated the value and the possibilities of such an approach. As a result, Jersey proceeded further in its search for ways to improve its relations with government and public.

STUDY AND EXPLORATION UNDER THE PARENT COMPANY

In September, 1942, Robert T. Haslam and his staff were transferred to the parent company organization. They continued to take full advantage of the advice and assistance of Earl Newsom and his staff. Director Gallagher was assigned responsibility for public relations.[62]

Both Haslam and Newsom worked closely with the company's officers and directors. In fact, from the beginning Jersey's top administrators assumed full responsibility in the formulation of policies and programs. Haslam and Newsom also held frequent meetings with the public relations staff. In the autumn of 1942 these conferences considered problems and current activities and explored possibilities for future action.[63]

An immediate need was to establish closer relations with the press. Under the direction of K. E. Cook, company statements and press releases were prepared. Background information was also provided upon the request of members of the press or others outside the company.

The press relations staff soon encountered problems. One was the difficulty of obtaining the release of information from executives and staffs unaccustomed to giving out information about the company and hesitant to assume responsibility for doing so. Support from the Board of Directors helped to solve this difficulty, but even so it took time to win the full cooperation of faithful guardians of Jersey's affairs and records. Achieving objectivity and technical accuracy in the work of writers unfamiliar with the oil business and petroleum technology presented other problems. These were met by the transfer of George H. Freyermuth to the public relations staff to work with the writers. A graduate of the University of California with an M.S. degree in fuels technology from the

The tanker *Charles Pratt* was torpedoed off the west coast of Africa in December, 1940.

Twenty-two survivors from the *Charles Pratt*, after rowing many hours in two lifeboats, were picked up by other ships.

The Tía Juana field under Lake Maracaibo in Venezuela was a major source of oil for the war.

The Sumatra refinery at Sungei Gerong before Japanese paratroopers tried to capture it.

The fiery destruction of the Sungei Gerong refinery spoiled its capture.

Oil well in the Jusepin field in eastern Venezuela, in 1944.

Driller stabs fishtail bit into a bit-break-out-lock.

Rotary men bring drill pipe out of the hole.

Drilling rig on the bluffs at Elk Basin, Wyoming.

Derrick man steadies pipe in the elevator.

Roughnecks unscrew section of drill pipe.

Fractionating unit at Humble's Baytown refinery.

General view of the Baytown refinery in 1944.

Spheroid tanks contain butadiene for the production of synthetic rubber.

Plantation pipeline manifold serves to switch various products to their respective tanks.

Two of three catalytic cracking units built in 1942 and 1943 at the Baton Rouge refinery.

The Carter Oil Company raised wartime oil production in Illinois in some cases by pumping.

The Hungarian company's pipeline ran from oil field to Budapest.

Nearly 1,000 bombs struck the Teleajen refin in Romania. No unit remained intact.

Tankers fueled United States Navy ships at sea.

The Esso tanker *Utica* loaded its decks with planes and plane parts.

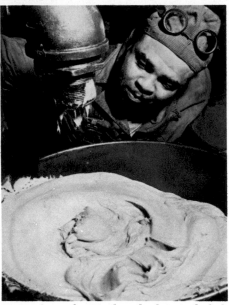

Grease from the Pittsburgh plant included special lubricants for military equipment.

Wartime operator of a milling machine at the Gilbert & Barker plant.

Tank cars and catalytic cracking unit at Humble's Baytown refinery.

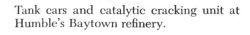

In the Potomac railroad yards trains of tank cars were made up for oil distribution.

In their search for oil, geologists surveyed an area along the Mackenzie River in Canada.

This oil train crossed the Montana prairie in August, 1944.

Rock cores from wells are filed for study in geological laboratory.

Gravity meter measures minute difference in the pull of subsurface geological structure.

Known as "The Four Horsemen," the inventors of fluid catalytic cracking were: (from the lef
Homer Z. Martin, Donald L. Campbell, C. Wesley Tyson, and Eger V. Murphree.

At the Perbunan plant synthetic rubber was rolled out in giant sheets.

Truck being loaded with lubricants from the Baltimore plant.

Massachusetts Institute of Technology, Freyermuth had joined the Baton Rouge research organization in 1928 and had later served for several years as assistant manager of the Sales Engineering Department of Standard Oil Company of New Jersey.[64]

Because the situation required more than good routine press relations, the staff began to look for ways to make known what Jersey and its affiliates were doing to supply products needed to prosecute the war. From the point of view of both employee morale and the need to gain cooperation from government and other sources, it was essential to achieve a better general understanding of the tremendous wartime task the company had been called upon to perform. Various possibilities were explored. The first special occasion arranged was the formal dedication at Bayway on January 11, 1943, of a fluid catalytic cracking plant, the first such plant on the Atlantic Coast. Careful preparations were made. The invited guests included officers of the Army and Navy, sailor heroes from the Southwest Pacific, and many members of the press. The experiment proved highly successful as dramatic proof of the company's contribution to the war effort.[65]

Haslam, Newsom, and the staff in the meantime had studied the public's impression of the company and had explored possible ways of establishing effective, organized work in public relations. In November, Newsom in a long report reviewed what they had learned and made recommendations for action.[66]

A fundamental consideration, the report stated, was that "what people think of the Standard Oil Company should be considered by management as something of vital importance and dealt with accordingly." The company's public, Newsom pointed out, was made up of many different groups, including its own employees, stockholders, and customers, and also leaders of opinion, makers and administrators of law, and people in general. The company had the obligation "(1) to know and understand the changing standards of conduct which symbolize the best interest of the public; (2) to act at all times in the best current tradition of that public interest; (3) to make those actions apparent and keep them from being misinterpreted."

The question was what the company should do to improve its relations with the public. First of all, Newsom advised, management had to recognize that there was no way in which the company could enjoy privacy—a luxury reserved for the obscure. He pointed out that, in the eyes of the American people, "an organization as large and as important

Chapter 16

Wartime Organization: Government, Industry, and Company

THE PRODIGIOUS SUPPLIES of petroleum products required to meet the military and civilian needs of the United States and its allies made necessary the most efficient use of the resources of the oil industry. In planning and coordinating operations, an essential role was played by organizations of government and industry working cooperatively. Responsibility for carrying out the plans was left to the individual companies. The result, as stated by the Army-Navy Petroleum Board of the Joint Chiefs of Staff at the end of the war, was that "at no time did the Services lack for oil in proper quantities, in the proper kinds, and at proper places. . . . No government agency and no branch of American industry achieved a prouder war record."[1]

PRODUCT REQUIREMENTS

From beginning to end, World War II was a war of oil.[2] Petroleum products were vitally necessary to keep civilian economies operating in high gear and to meet the rising needs of the military services. In the United States and in the Western Hemisphere generally, supplies to civilian consumers were kept at approximately an even level throughout the war; worldwide, supplies to the military increased greatly in volume and in kind. Oil constituted more than half the tonnage of shipments overseas. In several invasions, it made up approximately 65 per cent of the total tonnage. So important was oil that, in the words of the executive vice-chairman of the United States War Production Board late in 1943, the responsibility of the petroleum industry was "nothing less than the responsibility for victory."

More than 500 different oil products were used by the military forces. The major requirements were for fueling and lubricating planes, ships, submarines, and motorized equipment on land and inland waters. But oil products for the military did far more than fuel and lubricate the machines of war. As described in *A History of the Petroleum Administration for War*, there was a wide range of other uses:

Oil was also heat and light and comfort and mercy. Out in the field, in the form of gasoline, it fueled the kitchens, it powered the radios and telephones, it warmed and illuminated the hospitals, it refrigerated the life-saving blood plasma, it heated the instrument sterilizers, it ran signal devices, water purification systems, and repair machinery. From oil came the toluene for TNT that went into bombs, the asphalt for airfields, the jellied gasoline for flame throwers, the kerosene for smoke screens, the wax for packaging food and equipment. . . .

From the entry of the United States into the war to the end of the conflict, the world's production of crude oil, excluding Russian and Axis areas, totaled nearly 7⅝ billion barrels. Of this total, about 5½ billion barrels came from the United States; in addition this country produced natural gas equivalent in heat value to 2 billion barrels of oil. Second in rank as an oil producer was the Caribbean area, and third was the Middle East. In the United States, the output of crude was increased during the war by more than 1 million barrels daily, or 27 per cent more than the daily average in 1941. Foreign production was increased by 59 per cent; the largest percentage rise came in the Caribbean area.

The accomplishments of the refining industry involved both large expansion and new products. Refinery runs in the United States rose by more than 1,400,000 barrels daily, or 30 per cent above the average of 1941. Abroad, in the same length of time, they increased by 40 per cent. Besides expansion in the manufacture of the major products, there was a tremendous construction of new plants to produce aviation gasoline, synthetic rubber, and toluene for use in manufacturing explosives. Plants built to manufacture 100-octane gasoline, alone, cost a total of a billion dollars. The staffing of the new plants required the training of large operating forces, especially supervisory personnel.

Transporting the large amount of crude from fields to refineries and of products from refineries to countless places around the globe was in itself a stupendous task. A vast system of transport had to be provided in the United States to take the place of ocean tankers. In this country, alone, pipelines were built, relaid, or reversed, totaling more than 17,600 miles of line; and 75,000 tank cars were mobilized for bringing crude or products to the East Coast. During the war, the United States tanker fleet was tripled in tonnage. This fleet worked with those of other countries to

Table 11: DAILY AVERAGE PRODUCTION, REFINERY RUNS, AND REQUIREMENTS IN ALLIED AND NEUTRAL COUNTRIES,[a] 1942 TO JULY 1, 1945
(In thousands of 42-gallon barrels)

	Year 1942	Year 1943	Year 1944	First Half 1945
Crude Oil Production				
United States	3,795	4,117	4,583	4,806
Caribbean Area[b]	494	584	822	926
Near East and Middle East				
Eastern Mediterranean[c]	73	99	113	121
Persian Gulf and India[d]	246	241	329	385
Other Areas				
Canada	28	26	23	23
Mexico	96	96	104	116
Other Latin American countries[e]	112	116	115	111
United Kingdom and Western Europe	—	2	2	2
Total	4,844	5,281	6,091	6,490
Refinery Crude Runs				
United States	3,654	3,916	4,551	4,815
Caribbean Area[b]	401	500	626	684
Near East and Middle East				
Eastern Mediterranean[c]	83	104	119	120
Persian Gulf and India[d]	254	260	330	392
Other Areas				
Canada	149	162	179	168
Mexico	82	90	94	98
Other Latin American countries[e]	119	119	118	118
United Kingdom and Western Europe	1	3	3	3
Total	4,743	5,154	6,020	6,398
Requirements of Major Products				
By Products				
Aviation gasoline[f]	165	310	566	640
Motor gasoline	1,817	1,673	1,782	1,961
Kerosene	249	253	259	288
Distillates and diesels	723	768	852	980
Residual fuels	1,607	1,784	2,084	2,318
Total	4,561	4,788	5,543	6,187
By Consumers				
Civilian[g]				
United States	3,074	2,833	2,904	3,100
Other Western Hemisphere	402	390	412	429
United Kingdom and Neutral Europe	137	133	143	156
Middle East and Far East and Africa	141	137	143	149
Total	3,754	3,493	3,602	3,834
Indirect military bunkers, ocean vessels				
At United States ports	90	162	235	322
At foreign ports	185	160	230	267
Total	275	322	465	589
Direct military, worldwide	532	963	1,476	1,764
Total	4,561	4,788	5,543	6,187

[a] Russia and certain other countries not included.
[b] Venezuela, Trinidad, Colombia, and N.W.I.
[c] Iraq, Egypt, Syria, and Palestine.
[d] Iran, Bahrain, Saudi Arabia, Kuwait, and India.
[e] Peru, Argentina, Uruguay, Ecuador, Cuba, Brazil, and Bolivia.

[f] Gasoline below 100-octane grade includes, for the above years, respectively, daily averages of 67,000, 122,000, 152,000, and 43,000 barrels.
[g] Includes some indirect military.
Source: PAW, Program Division, World-Wide Petroleum Supply Survey, November, 1945.

supply the civilian and military needs of the Allies. From tanker unload-ing points, oil was distributed by barge, pipeline, or truck. Long pipelines were laid to transport oil from India to China and from the Middle East oil region to Russia; shorter ones were constructed to areas of combat or within a consuming country for safe and efficient oil transport. In addi-tion, facilities had to be built to store products for the use of the military forces. Building pipelines and storage was particularly difficult in tropical and semitropical regions where climate and terrain posed special prob-lems and in countries where construction crews and materials had to be brought long distances by sea.

Supplying the Allies with oil products—in kinds and quantities and at places and times needed—"was a back-breaking task, an around-the-clock task, a task world-wide in scope and bewildering in its complex-ities." This task was accomplished by the oil companies within the system of government-industry cooperation. Because the Jersey group conducted most of its wartime operations under this system of coordination, a brief survey of the system is an essential preliminary to examining the opera-tions themselves.

GOVERNMENT-INDUSTRY COORDINATION OF PLANNING AND OPERATIONS

Because of its military importance, the petroleum industry was one of the few in the United States, Canada, and the United Kingdom to have a wartime system of government agencies and industry committees as-signed exclusively to the over-all planning and directing of its operations. The organizations in the three countries were similar in their underlying principles: these allies placed the direction of oil operations in the hands of civilian agencies and not under the military as in Germany. They staffed the agencies largely with company personnel and set up industry boards and committees to advise the government boards. They worked together through organizations in the capitals, Washington being recog-nized as the most important for this purpose.[3]

The oil control system in the United States, because of the wider range and greater size of oil operations, became far more extensive and complex than that of the United Kingdom or Canada. (See Chapter 13.) The preponderant contribution of petroleum products by this country and the Caribbean area indicates the responsibility borne by the American companies and the special government-industry organization concerned with their operations.

Industrial cooperation had begun in the United States before this country entered the war. The Advisory Commission to the Council of National Defense, with a petroleum section, had been set up in mid-1940. This commission had later become the Office of Production Management, which became the War Production Board. The Office of Petroleum Coordinator for National Defense had been established in May, 1941. It had enlisted the aid of representatives of oil companies in designing an industry organization to work with the government agency. Establishing this body—the Petroleum Industry War Council (PIWC)—was well under way by December of that year. Another government-industry agency, the United States Tanker Control Board, had been organized in July, 1941, with the Deputy Coordinator for National Defense as chairman. (See Chapter 14.)

As the Axis powers extended their conquests in 1942, the organizational structure and activities of the Office of Petroleum Coordinator for National Defense were enlarged and the agency won increasing cooperation from other agencies in Washington. President Roosevelt in December, 1942, officially recognized the extensive authority which it had assumed, and changed its name to the Petroleum Administration for War (PAW). At this time, the fate of the Allies hung in the balance, and military supplies were only sufficient for defensive operations in Europe and Asia and in the Southwest Pacific.

This petroleum agency did not attain complete governmental authority over the oil industry. Although it was the central board for this one industry, in certain areas its decisions were subject to those of other general or special agencies. It could plan and urge the construction of new facilities; but other boards would decide whether materials could be allocated to a given project, and the Reconstruction Finance Corporation determined the allocation of government funds to plants requiring government financing. Other federal agencies determined wages and hours and the prices of oil products. The PAW could only advise concerning operations outside the United States. As to shipping, the petroleum board planned the flow of products by United States–flag tankers, but the War Shipping Administration controlled the ships. In addition, many agencies, domestic and foreign, civilian and military, cooperated in the planning of products and their allocation.[4]

The Petroleum Administration for War had its headquarters in Washington. Both its executive and technical personnel were recruited mainly from oil companies. Its top executives were also members of other federal boards and committees, military and civilian, concerned with petroleum affairs at home and abroad. It had an elaborate organization and a large staff of specialists. In five subsidiary districts in the United States, it had organizations to provide information to headquarters and to administer its programs. It also had representatives in certain foreign areas in the Western Hemisphere where important operations were carried on. These district and area groups, also made up largely of company personnel, worked closely with the companies themselves and with the industry's own district organizations.

The PAW had representatives abroad for maintaining liaison with the petroleum agencies of the other Allies. Relations with Great Britain were especially close. The oil attaché in the United States Embassy in London advised the Oil Control Board and other British agencies having to do with petroleum. The British petroleum representative in Washington similarly served on various committees and boards. Like the PAW in the Western Hemisphere, the British Oil Control Board coordinated all oil operations under the Allies in the Eastern Hemisphere.[5]

The Petroleum Industry War Council assisted the PAW in the development of policies and in planning and carrying out regional, national, and international programs. This agency, which represented the whole domestic oil industry, had its headquarters in Washington with a system of committees similar to that of the PAW. It was originally made up of seventy-eight high executives of large and small companies who also served on many functional and technical committees. It had committees and staffs to parallel the five district organizations of the PAW. The most important were District No. 1, which covered the crucial Atlantic Coast ports and their hinterland, and District No. 3, which included the important Gulf Coast producing and refining region. These regional committees were represented on the national Petroleum Industry War Council and advised the PAW with regard to programs in the various separate districts. Similarly, the Foreign Operations Committee, with headquarters in New York, advised the PAW on the formation and implementation of foreign oil policies and programs.[6]

Like the American oil companies generally, Jersey and its affiliates loaned executive, managerial, and technical personnel to the PAW and the industry organizations. Scores of employees of the parent company and its domestic affiliates served full time in government and industry agencies. To an early request of Coordinator Ickes for nominations for various committees, President Farish replied that Jersey personnel were available at all times, but he asked that the committees be composed "without suggestions from us and without special consideration of our personnel."[7]

Many Jersey executives were members of the high planning and policy echelons of the Petroleum Industry War Council or served the industry or government agencies in other ways.[8] President Farish and directors Gallagher, Harden, and Holman and also Humble's President Wiess were members of the council and of many of its committees. Other executives were on committees in areas where affiliates operated. Jersey furnished an especially large representation on the Foreign Operations Committee, which was headed by Director Orville Harden. Emile E. Soubry of Anglo-American was British representative in Washington until 1943, at which time he was appointed to the new position of Coordinator of Foreign Marketing for the parent company. George S. Walden of Standard-Vacuum was head of the office of the oil attaché in the United States Embassy in London. Jersey's David A. Shepard was one of two other executives who represented the American oil industry in the same office.

The broad functions of the PAW and the PIWC were (1) to plan supplies, (2) to make provisions for adequate manpower and equipment, and (3) to coordinate operations so as to have oil products available as they were required. The PAW had responsibility as the official agency of the United States government. The PIWC, as the industry representative, worked with both the government agency and the companies. Basic to the second and third of these functions was planning, or programming.

Planning, which was essentially a staff function, came to be the work, primarily, of the Program Division of the PAW. This division—consisting of a planning committee and its staff and having no operating responsibilities—was an outgrowth of Jersey's coordination system and of a committee developed within the Petroleum Industry War Council. For some time before the entry of the United States into the war, Jersey's Economics Department had prepared statistical reports for government agencies and industry committees; this it continued to do until a statistical organization was set up under the PIWC. This new unit was the working Subcommittee on Petroleum Economics established in New York in February, 1942, under Stewart P. Coleman. A member of Jersey's Coordination Committee and manager of its Economics Department, Coleman was loaned to the PIWC for full-time work.[9]

The principal function of this subcommittee was to prepare and submit to the main committee of the PIWC suggested operating programs to enable the United States oil industry to meet military and essential civilian requirements with the least expenditure of materials, manpower, and equipment and to do so in the shortest possible time. The group endeavored to outline programs for a year or more in advance. At first, the usual sources of industry statistics were drawn upon, but as soon as available the figures collected by district statistical committees were used. The work was handicapped, however, by the fact that, not being a government agency, this planning group was unable to obtain confidential information from the United States government concerning military requirements. Nevertheless, the information it continued to supply throughout the war was invaluable to the planning of the PAW.[10]

The Program Division of the PAW was formally organized in June, 1943, to carry on this same type of work, but on a broader scale, within the official American petroleum agency. Jersey's Coleman, appointed to be the division's director, left the PIWC subcommittee and took a leave of absence from the company in order that, as a government employee, he could have access to confidential government data. Like the industry committee, this division employed Jersey's coordination concepts and techniques. Several of Coleman's associates in the company's Economics Department—including the assistant directors, J. A. Cogan and H. W. Page—also joined the division. Page succeeded Coleman as director on the latter's return to Jersey at the end of 1944. This new director had begun to work with government agencies early in the war; he had made an especially important contribution to the planning of the Little Big Inch pipeline. The duties of the Program Division were defined as follows:

To formulate integrated, long-range program alternatives for meeting essential world-wide petroleum requirements of the United States and its Allies, to best advantage within the limits of available resources, as a basis for determination of (a) PAW's long-range program objectives, (b) implementing plans and policies, (c) necessary construction programs, (d) operating schedules, and (e) allocations among claimant agencies.[11]

At first the division was severely handicapped by being unable to obtain adequate information from the military services. Army and Navy officials withheld information on tanker operations and the consumption of oil products by destinations. However, when the requirements became critically heavy in the summer of 1943 and comprehensive forward planning became an obvious necessity, the military authorities agreed to provide the information needed to enable the division to formulate a global program. Thereafter, the division was able to project short-term and long-term requirements for military and civilian use. With full cooperation of the PIWC, and with information obtained from British and other foreign sources, it could then make plans on an efficient worldwide basis. To the end of the war, the Program Division carried on a continuous operation of collecting estimates of requirements, capacities, and supplies, and of formulating alternate programs, measuring performance against program commitments, and making adjustments to meet changing situations.[12]

The contributions of the Program Division were acknowledged by Administrator Ickes and Deputy Administrator Davies. In letters written to President Holman after Coleman's return to the company, these executives expressed their appreciation of his efforts in programming operations, stating that no work was more important to the several operating branches.[13]

The complex organization of the PAW and similar units under the PIWC also had responsibility for guiding the carrying out of plans under proper governmental direction and approval.[14] There was an elaborate range of groups in Washington with top responsibility within their particular province. The PAW had divisions having to do with such matters of special importance, owing to wartime shortages, as construction, materials and equipment, and manpower. Other divisions were concerned with particular operating functions at home, with foreign producing and refining, and with supply and transportation. Both at home and in important foreign operations in the Western Hemisphere, committees and staffs advised and assisted in implementing the PAW programs as these applied to particular districts or regions.

THE JERSEY ORGANIZATION FOR WAR

Within the programs and stipulations of government-industry agencies, the individual oil companies were responsible for planning and managing their own operations. This responsibility required not only heightened effort within the Jersey Company but also the adjusting of administrative and operating structures so that they could carry new and heavy burdens of planning, expanding, and operating under the pressures of war. This adjustment had to be made at a time when a considerable portion of company personnel had been drawn into civilian war work outside the companies or had joined the military services.

Certain weaknesses in the functioning of the parent company's top administration became obvious in the first half of 1942. Congressional hearings demonstrated that some of the directors were not well informed on matters involving important policy issues. For example, for many years negotiations with I.G. Farbenindustrie had been conducted principally by President Howard of Standard Oil Development Company. Not infrequently the Board of Directors had been informed after action had been taken. Also, over the years, the Executive Committee had assumed increasing responsibility. The directors now recognized the need to make certain that important policy decisions and large appropriations be acted upon by the entire Board of Directors.

Changes were therefore made to ensure control by the board and to define clearly the functions of the officers, directors, and individual groups within the administrative organization. It was decided in June, 1942, that all matters involving important questions of policy or appropriations in excess of $5,000,000 should be submitted to the Board of Directors. It was also decided that the minutes of meetings of the Executive Committee should be read at subsequent board meetings, followed by an expression of approval or disapproval of the action recorded. The board agreed to meet weekly, on Thursday mornings, instead of once or twice a month as had become its practice.[15] Further, in order to clarify the distribution of authority and responsibility, it made provision for the preparation of an organization manual. The resulting publication, issued in the spring of 1943, defined the duties and responsibilities of the officers and directors, executives, committees, and departments.[16]

The normal attrition of administrative personnel removed several leaders of the parent company late in 1942. Five of the eleven members of the Board of Directors were of an average age of nearly sixty-three years and had an average service in the oil industry of almost forty-two years. Of those five, Chairman Teagle, E. J. Sadler, and D. L. Harper retired at the end of November.

At the same time, new members were added to the board and new officers were named. Ralph W. Gallagher was elected to succeed Teagle as chairman and Wallace E. Pratt and Eugene Holman became vice-presidents as of December 1, 1942. Two younger men were then added to the board: Robert T. Haslam, who had recently been given charge of a new public relations staff; and Frank W. Pierce, who was executive assistant to the president for employee relations.[17] The election of men with special interests in public and employee relations was a significant

Table 12: **WARTIME DIRECTORS OF STANDARD OIL COMPANY (NEW JERSEY) AND THEIR PRINCIPAL RESPONSIBILITIES, 1939–1945**

Director	Year Elected	Principal Responsibilities to 1945
Walter C. Teagle	1909	Chairman of the Board of Directors. (Retired in 1942.)
Everit J. Sadler	1920	Vice-president; chairman of the Coordination Committee. (Retired in 1942.)
William S. Farish	1927	President; chairman of the Executive Committee. (Died in 1942.)
G. Harrison Smith	1927	President of Imperial Oil Limited. (Retired as Jersey director in 1940.)
Frederick H. Bedford, Jr.	1927	Contact director for specialty sales.
Orville Harden	1929	Vice-president; member of the Executive Committee; contact director for overseas marketing, 1943, and for marketing supply and policy, 1944; alternate contact director for domestic marketing, 1943, and for sales and sales promotion, 1944.
Ralph W. Gallagher	1933	Vice-president; member of the Executive Committee and chairman from 1942; chairman of the Board of Directors, December 1, 1942, to January 6, 1943; president, 1943–1944; chairman of the Board of Directors, 1944–1945. (Retired in 1945.)
Donald L. Harper	1935	Contact director for foreign marketing companies. (Retired in 1942.)
Thomas C. McCobb	1935	Comptroller; supervisory responsibility for finance. (Retired in 1944.)
Wallace E. Pratt	1937	Member of the Executive Committee; vice-president from 1942; contact director for producing from 1943. (Retired in 1945.)
Frank W. Abrams	1940	Chairman of the Coordination Committee, 1943–1944; vice-president from 1944.
Eugene Holman	1940	Contact director for marine operations, 1940–1942; vice-president, 1942–1944; member of the Executive Committee from 1943; president from 1944.
Frank W. Pierce	1942	Contact director for employee relations from 1943.
Robert T. Haslam	1942	Contact director for public relations from 1943, for domestic marketing, 1943, and for sales and sales promotion, 1944; alternate contact director for overseas marketing, 1943.
Jay E. Crane	1944	Contact director for Treasurer's, Comptroller's, and Budget departments.
Chester F. Smith	1944	Chairman of the Coordination Committee from 1944.

NOTE: Except for G. Harrison Smith, all responsibilities stated were under the parent company. Walter C. Teagle had retired officially on an annuity in 1937 but had continued to serve without salary.

Source: Standard Oil Company (New Jersey): Stockholders', Directors', and the Executive Committee's Minutes.

development in the composition of the board. Later wartime changes in the membership of the Board of Directors are indicated in Table 12.

Only a few days after the election of new directors and officers, on Sunday morning, November 29, 1942, President Farish died suddenly of a heart attack. He had been in his office as usual on Friday and had taken his briefcase home for work over the week end. It was believed by those close to him that the attack was brought on by overwork and strain. During most of the period of his presidency, beginning with the TNEC investigation, the company had been involved in governmental investigations and suits. Farish had been especially affected by the congressional hearings in the first half of 1942. He had never taken government investigations easily, even Texas legislative hearings. As the chief executive of

Standard Oil Company (New Jersey) and as the father of an only son who had volunteered for service in the Army Air Forces, he was deeply affected by the accusations of lack of patriotism and even of treason made against the company's officers and directors in connection with the hearings of congressional committees in 1942.[18]

The retirement of Teagle and Sadler and the death of Farish removed three great builders from the company's administration. More than anyone else, Teagle was responsible for the notable growth and development of the company for nearly a quarter-century after the dissolution in 1911. A forceful executive, dedicated to the progress of the Jersey Company, he had led it in such new directions as progressive employee relations, a great expansion of oil reserves and production at home and abroad, and a revolution in refining technology. Sadler, who had served as director of foreign production for many years, made his most important contribution as the founder of the parent company's coordination system. Always looking for the lowest-cost combination of functions, he was a great economic rationalist at a time when economic analysis and planning were little practiced even by large corporations. Farish was a founder of Humble Oil & Refining Company and its most forceful executive in the years when its foundations were being laid. He was also an early promoter of the emerging technology of exploration and production, and he became a national leader in the oil conservation movement. He was a leading advocate of the expansion and improvement of Jersey's producing interests and operations.

The mantle of chief executive of Jersey now fell on the shoulders of Ralph W. Gallagher, who served in that capacity as chairman until he was elected president on January 6, 1943. Gallagher is said to have envisaged his role as that of bringing about better coordination in the top administrative organization and of carrying executive responsibility only until another was selected for the presidency. He served until June, 1944, when Eugene Holman was elected president. Gallagher then again became chairman of the board.[19]

The war also brought important changes in Jersey's employee relations. These were instituted in part because of the war and in part in order to erect a more logical administrative structure. Two important organizational developments came in this area. The election of Frank W. Pierce to the Jersey Board of Directors, as already noted, brought into that governing body a specialist in employee relations—the first with this particular background and training to rise to the rank of director. A few months later, the board established within Jersey itself a new department for employee relations. Pierce was made contact director for the new department, and Charles E. Shaw its manager.[20]

A large part of the wartime work of this department was to see that the parent company and its domestic affiliates complied with government regulations. Because of the manpower shortage, the hours of work in essential industries were increased. The War Manpower Commission by 1943 had established a mandatory forty-eight-hour week in a number of areas in which the Jersey companies operated. Wage rates were controlled by the War Labor Board to help brake inflation. In order to compensate for the rise in the cost of living between January 1, 1941, and May 1, 1942, the Labor Board in the spring of 1943 permitted an increase in accordance with the "Little Steel" settlement of June, 1942. The board froze the rates in October, 1943. However, the compensation of the average rank-and-file employee was increased by longer hours and higher overtime rates. Strikes were virtually eliminated by the provision in the Smith-Connally Act for government operation of struck plants. Labor unions kept on with their efforts to organize workers and to get members of independent unions to join the AFL or the CIO, but no important changes came in the Jersey companies. The War Production Board encouraged the formation of labor-management committees to work for the elimination of waste and the reduction of accidents and to consider other matters of common interest.[21]

Jersey took action to protect salaried employees whose compensation did not increase with the longer workweek. The foremen, whose differential over the wages of the rank-and-file workers had begun to shrink in 1940, received some adjustment in 1942 in the form of allowances for extended work schedules. Even under this arrangement, however, at the end of 1943 they were on the average receiving only about 11 per cent more than the workers they supervised. Many became dissatisfied with this small differential, but the government did not allow further changes. Because of this dissatisfaction and the company's general review and revision of the whole administrative structure in 1943, Jersey and its affiliates tried to improve the relative position of the supervisory and executive employees by giving greater attention to these members of their organizations.

Under the leadership of the parent company, the domestic affiliates adopted uniform policies with respect to their regular employees who entered military or civilian government service. They granted leaves of absence to those entering the armed forces and promised them their jobs or equivalent posts on their return. They eased the transfer of employees to the services by paying a month's compensation to men who had been with the company at least six months but less than a year and two months' pay to those with a tenure of a year or more. They also provided for dependents by arranging for supplemental payments, for the duration of the breadwinner's military service, of up to half of each employee's regular pay. The total of government and company payments, however, did not exceed the individual's former earnings with Jersey. The companies also undertook to cover regular thrift and annuity payments—both the employee's and the company's share—for those who were subscribers on entering military service. More than 10,000 domestic employees of Jersey and its affiliates were in military service during all or part of the war; the total had reached 5,029 at the end of 1942.

Inasmuch as civilian government employees were prohibited from accepting pay from a private employer, the benefits granted those in military service could not be extended to the employees who entered other government service. Some men were kept on their company's payroll while on loan to the government. For those who actually transferred to government employment, the company granted leaves of absence with a promise of their jobs or an equivalent on their return.[22]

By these various changes, Jersey adjusted its organization to the necessities of war. Other developments came in the later years of the conflict. These included plans for the selection and training of executives and important changes in the distribution of responsibilities within the parent company's Board of Directors and in its system of coordination. Since these looked more particularly to postwar operations, they are left for consideration in Chapter 22.

Under the direction of the wartime organizations of governments, industry, and parent company, the Jersey affiliates in neutral and Allied countries carried on their various operations. Production, refining, transportation, and the distribution of products are the subjects of the next four chapters.

Chapter 17

Producing Petroleum Raw Materials, 1942–1945

THE PRIMARY ARSENAL of the oil industry was its known reserves of crude oil and natural gas. Two basic questions about its ability to maintain an adequate supply faced the industry during the war. Would the known reserves in the earth and other reserves hopefully to be discovered prove sufficient for developing the additional production that would be required? Would the necessary equipment and manpower be available to drill the new wells and produce the crude oil and gas needed to meet the rising demands of the war?

This chapter deals with the Jersey Company's wartime search for new oil and its production of crude oil and gas. These operations were attended by none of the physical risks or tense drama of the work of the tankers, nor did they have to solve such critical technical problems as were encountered by the refineries. A crucial issue that rose in Venezuela might have had serious consequences if it had not been resolved. On the whole, however, Jersey's producing operations were mainly concerned with a determined and continuous drive to increase the volume of their output.

DRAWING HEAVILY ON CRUDE OIL RESERVES

For nearly two years after the United States entered the war, the industry's oil reserves were adequate without exerting great effort to find new oil fields. During the last two war years, the industry had to drive hard to provide enough raw materials to keep its refineries supplied.

The producing companies operated under the same type of government-industry direction that planned and coordinated other oil operations during the war. The Program Division of the Petroleum Administration for

War provided the information on which this agency, working closely with industry committees, based its plans for the American oil companies and, especially through its liaison with the British, contributed to the coordination of oil production under Allied control. Jersey men served on various committees of the Petroleum Administration for War and the Petroleum Industry War Council that had to do with planning and co-ordinating producing operations. C. H. Lieb, L. F. McCollum, C. S. Morgan, and F. H. Kay were members of the Foreign Producing Committee. J. R. Suman, Humble vice-president for producing, was a member of the committee for the Gulf Coast district; McCollum and O. C. Schorp, as successive presidents of The Carter Oil Company, served on the committee for the Mid-Continent district.[1]

The crude oil producing programs of the Jersey companies in the Western Hemisphere were coordinated by the parent company's Producing Department in New York in accordance with the plans of the PAW and its regional agencies. This department was headed, successively, by Lieb and McCollum. Because of the special need for over-all coordination, it maintained closer relations than in the past with Humble and with Imperial's producing operations in Canada, Colombia, and Peru. It had no connection with whatever remained under the Allies of the production of Jersey's affiliates in the Eastern Hemisphere.

The Jersey Company had its largest reserves in Texas and Venezuela and smaller known resources in several other parts of the Western Hemisphere. The reserves in the Eastern Hemisphere, which were comparatively small, because of enemy action were of little value to Jersey during the war.[2]

The producing operations of the individual affiliates were determined principally by the course of the war. Some companies, especially the Venezuelan, had to reduce their production in 1942, when the success of the German submarine campaign seriously curtailed tanker shipments. But they increased it later as the enemy threat declined and the programs set up by the PAW required ever larger volumes to provide sufficient products for military campaigns. The program of the top petroleum board eventually called not only for producing as much as possible from existing wells but also for vigorous exploration and the development of new oil fields.

Although the oil reserves of the United States—estimated at 20 billion barrels—were approximately the same as the total for foreign countries not including Russia, it was believed that to increase production substantially would be more difficult here than in some other countries. The United States had drawn more heavily on its petroleum resources than had important oil producing regions abroad. In several large proved foreign fields, new wells could be drilled and production stepped up quickly. Accordingly, the expansion program set up in 1943 for the war period established higher rates of increase for such countries as Venezuela, Iran, and Saudi Arabia than for the United States.[3] Jersey affiliates were operating in only the first of these, but Venezuela was then the leading oil producing country outside the United States.

In producing operations as in others, the oil industry in the United States ran into problems of rising costs and shortages of manpower and equipment. The Jersey Company and the industry urged that crude oil prices be increased because of these higher costs, but the request of PAW Administrator Ickes for increases was denied by the Office of Price Administration.[4] The petroleum agency was helpful, however, in obtaining from the Office of War Production priorities for drilling materials, such as steel for rigs, and in ordering that wells be spaced forty acres to a well, which meant a larger tract for each well than had been the rule in many fields in prewar years. This spacing pattern conserved scarce materials, equipment, and labor, and it saved the cost of drilling and operating wells not required for adequate drainage of oil reservoirs. The savings were to some extent canceled, however, by the necessity of drilling progressively deeper wells.[5]

In 1943, in keeping with the PAW program, the Jersey affiliates expanded their search for oil. By so doing, they were able to replace withdrawals with new reserves during the war despite their greatly increased production of crude oil and gas.[6]

Of the additions to the reserves of the affiliates in North America, by far the largest part was discovered by Humble Oil & Refining Company. The Carter Oil Company undertook exploratory programs in several states, but the results were disappointing.[7] In Kansas, Montana, and Wyoming, it added to its reserves by purchases of producing properties from individuals and small companies and by itself drilling extension wells in fields that were already producing. These additions amounted in all to 42,000,000 barrels.[8] Imperial Oil Limited tried to extend the Norman Wells field near the Arctic Circle, and it intensified its exploration in other parts of Canada. But it found no oil. Only in the Turner Valley field, which had been developed before the war, did it produce crude oil in commercial quantities.[9]

In South America, the affiliates sought new concessions and carried on extensive exploration. Their important expansion came in Venezuela. International Petroleum organized International Ecuadorean Petroleum Company to explore a 10,000,000-acre concession obtained from Ecuador in 1939, but this search was not encouraging.[10] Tropical Oil Company began to apply for new concessions in Colombia following the decision of the Colombian government of September, 1944, that the company's De Mares concession would expire in 1951.[11] In other Latin American countries in which Jersey affiliates operated, laws or political conditions were not favorable to obtaining concessions and exploring for oil.[12]

Statistics indicate what was accomplished by the Jersey companies in supplying crude oil during the war years. Table 13 shows the amounts made available by affiliates at home and abroad. All but a relatively small part of the production came from the Western Hemisphere. By far the larger part of both the produced and purchased crude was provided by Humble in North America and by the Venezuelan affiliates in South America. In the United States, because of the decline in the output of the unregulated Illinois fields, Carter's net production fell to a daily average of 58,300 in 1944, but the company greatly increased its purchases from other companies.[13] International increased its net Peruvian production to a daily average of 32,000 barrels in 1944, and Tropical's Colombian net crude output averaged 43,600 barrels per day.[14] The total gross production of domestic and foreign affiliates averaged 752,700 barrels daily in 1941, 534,100 in 1942, and 926,300 in 1944 (the last full year of war).[15]

The wartime experiences of Humble and of Jersey's Venezuelan operations—merged in Creole in 1943—merit examination in fuller detail. These two leading oil producers were the industry's largest in North and South America, respectively, as well as the major contributors to the Jersey group's production. In this conspicuous position, they illustrate significant developments affecting the production of oil. Humble's wartime crude oil production benefited from the recent advances in reservoir research and producing technology. The Venezuelan experience marks a notable adjustment to social and political change in Latin America by both Jersey and the oil industry as a whole.

HUMBLE'S WARTIME PRODUCTION

Humble Oil & Refining Company entered the war with large reserves and with organizations for exploration and production that employed advanced technologies. These were the result of company policies

---

adopted in the 1920's and vigorously implemented throughout the 1930's, and also of the systems of regulation adopted in the 1930's by Texas, Louisiana, and New Mexico. Such regulation enabled companies in those states, to a far greater extent than in some others, to leave the oil in its natural storehouses until needed.[16] (See Chapter 4.)

At the end of 1941, Humble's crude reserves were estimated to be 2.7 billion barrels and its natural gas reserves to be more than 6.5 trillion cubic feet. According to the company's estimates, its holdings in oil reservoirs constituted 19 per cent of the total in its operating territory and more than 13 per cent of the reserves within the United States. Humble had acquired its reserves mostly in the 1930's, when, following a more active acquisition policy than other large companies in the area, it had increased its estimated crude in the earth more than twelvefold. A large part of this total was in fields in which it controlled a major portion of the productive acreage and consequently had been able to follow practices utilizing the natural energy of the fields efficiently.[17]

Because of these reserves and large holdings in a number of major fields, Humble was able with relatively little effort to increase the volume of its production in the early part of the war. In fact, in the three war years 1942–1944, although operating with considerably reduced personnel and drilling far fewer wells than in the three preceding years, Humble doubled its crude oil production. Because of the knowledge gained from extensive studies of individual reservoirs, it increased its output in many fields without reducing the estimated volume of oil ultimately recoverable from the reservoirs. The daily averages of even such comparatively old fields as Raccoon Bend and Sugarland, both operated entirely by Humble, were increased, respectively, from 3,600 to 10,000 barrels and from 1,700 to 7,700 barrels. Had these fields been developed and produced competitively and hence with waste of their natural energy—as was done generally in Texas in the 1920's and to some extent even in the 1930's—those fields would have been reduced to small yields even with pumping. In the Friendswood field discovered in 1937, in which Humble virtually controlled operations, the volume was increased from a daily average of 8,000 barrels in 1941 to 60,000 barrels in March, 1945. In that month, half of Humble's production was coming from five fields. In four of these, its lease holdings ranged from nearly half of Conroe to all but four wells of Friendswood. The fifth was the great East Texas field, in which Humble then had an estimated 14 per cent of the recoverable reserves.[18]

Table 13: **DAILY AVERAGE NET CRUDE OIL PRODUCTION, PURCHASES, SALES, AND NET AVAILABLE TO AFFILIATES' REFINERIES, BY SELECTED AFFILIATES AND AREAS, 1940–1945**
Standard Oil Company (New Jersey)
(In thousands of 42-gallon barrels)

Year	Humble	Total in United States[a]	Imperial in Canada	Affiliates in Venezuela	Total in South America[b]	Total in Western Hemisphere	Total in Eastern Hemisphere[c]	World Total
				Net Production[d]				
1940	134.1	206.1	4.2	237.8	321.0	531.3	60.7	592.0
1941	150.0	219.1	5.8	309.9	392.8	617.7	58.0	675.7
1942	154.2	216.8	6.3	192.6	249.5	472.6	2.9	475.5
1943	236.5	296.2	6.8	231.3	295.8	598.8	0.0[e]	598.8
1944	308.6	366.8	8.8	332.0	410.6	786.2	3.2	789.4
1945	305.0	361.1	6.5	403.1	474.2	841.8	9.3	851.2
				Purchases from Nonaffiliates and Other Outsiders				
1940	235.4	346.2	22.4	25.0	31.7	400.3	4.9	405.2
1941	251.5	382.1	22.4	33.0	41.1	445.6	4.2	449.8
1942	218.0	404.6	25.5	21.2	32.7	462.7	—[f]	462.7
1943	281.3	510.3	24.0	55.5	68.2	602.5	—[f]	602.6
1944	386.6	674.7	23.1	80.0	93.5	791.2	0.5	791.7
1945	399.2	681.0	19.2	105.8	118.0	818.2	0.5	818.7
				Sales to Nonaffiliates				
1940	75.6	139.9	4.6	18.0	24.3	168.9	5.3	174.2
1941	86.8	155.6	4.5	22.9	27.1	187.2	9.2	196.4
1942	108.9	168.5	4.0	14.3	15.5	188.0	0.0[e]	188.0
1943	225.8	294.3	4.5	22.7	24.8	323.6	0.0[e]	323.6
1944	352.3	443.7	7.4	46.9	49.0	500.1	0.0[e]	500.1
1945	353.5	451.7	5.6	81.0	82.6	539.9	0.0[e]	539.9
				Net Crude Available to Affiliates' Refineries				
1940	293.9	412.4	22.0	244.8	328.0	762.5	60.3	822.8
1941	314.7	445.6	23.7	320.0	406.8	876.1	53.0	929.1
1942	263.4	452.9	27.8	199.5	266.7	747.3	2.9	750.2
1943	292.0	512.2	26.3	264.1	339.2	877.7	—[g]	877.7
1944	342.8	597.8	24.5	365.1	455.0	1,077.3	3.7	1,081.0
1945	350.8	590.4	20.1	427.9	509.6	1,120.1	9.8	1,129.9

NOTE: Because of the rounding of numbers, all totals are not the exact sum of the preceding numbers.
[a] Includes operations of Humble Oil & Refining Company and The Carter Oil Company.
[b] Includes affiliates in Venezuela, Trinidad, Colombia, Peru, and Argentina.
[c] Includes Jersey's share of Iraq Petroleum's operations and all of Standard-Vacuum's.
[d] Does not include royalty oil or other oil on which individuals or nonaffiliated companies had a claim.
[e] Only a few barrels daily in England.
[f] No purchases from outsiders.
[g] No crude oil available to affiliates' refineries.
Source: Statistical records of Standard Oil Company (New Jersey).

The wartime production of this East Texas field, great though it was, provides a meaningful contrast with production from the fields in which Humble controlled a large portion of the acreage. Because its natural energy had been reduced, the field had little margin of producing capacity when the war came. In fact, Humble's output there during the years from 1940 through 1945 never reached its daily average of 1939. Experience with this immense field lends emphasis to the fact that the great increase in total oil production came from fields that had been developed in accordance with sound conservation principles and held within their maximum efficient rates (MER) of production—the rate beyond which any increase would reduce the volume of ultimately recoverable oil. Such fields had the necessary reserve of natural energy to drive oil to the surface at a higher rate when increased yields were needed.[19]

By 1943 the demand for crude oil had become so great that the field allowables under state regulation in the regions where Humble operated were approaching the maximum efficient rate. An industry committee had studies made of the individual pools in the entire Gulf Coast district and set the maximum rate of production for each field. Many of Humble's reservoir research personnel and petroleum engineers participated in these studies. In order to ensure adequate production without going beyond the MER, Humble and the industry generally had to step up their search for oil and drill new wells despite wartime shortages of materials.[20]

Humble, therefore, expanded its scouting, leasing, and exploration greatly in 1943. It purchased leases to an extent that raised its undeveloped holdings to nearly 16,000,000 acres in 1944, which was 50 per cent more than its total in 1941. The resulting increase in costs is indicated by the rise in the company's annual rental payments on undeveloped acreage from $3,500,000 in 1941 to $10,000,000 in 1944.[21]

Despite the absence of half of the department's technical personnel and of nearly all its senior geophysicists, who had been released to do government research,[22] the Exploration Department carried out an expanded program. Some additions to the staff were made, research was curtailed, and field work was concentrated on the most promising prospects. Exploration was carried on largely by the junior geophysicists. The geologists were mainly employed in studying the wells being drilled.[23]

In its search for new oil fields, Humble in 1943 entered upon the greatest wildcatting program of its history. In that year, it drilled 55 wildcats, nine of which struck oil. The next year it stepped up its wildcat drilling to 96 wells, 18 of which were producers. In 1945 the number of its wildcats dropped to 80, but 18 found oil. Humble also participated with other companies in joint drilling of a number of test wells.[24]

The drilling of both wildcats and development wells was done mostly where the promise was greatest. This was necessary because of the urgent need to increase production as well as the shortage of men and equipment. A Humble departmental report of the autumn of 1944 stated: "At present large drilling engines, drawworks, and pumps require approximately one year for delivery. Drill pipe with tool joints require nine months to a year." Humble's engineers exercised ingenuity in salvaging old equipment to replace that which was worn out or to meet new needs. The PAW ruling requiring wider spacing of wells was especially helpful because it meant a considerable saving of both men and materials.[25]

New oil became more difficult and more costly to find in the war years. Humble extended its wartime search far beyond the former range of its operations. It reached eastward as far as the southern tip of Florida, where in 1943 it discovered the first field found in that state and the only one up to the present time (1967). Humble also drilled to greater depths: the average of all the wells drilled increased from 5,764 feet in 1942 to 7,445 in 1944. Drilling costs rose sharply: for Humble's producing wells, from an average of $47,000 in 1943 to $66,000 in 1944; and for its dry holes, from an average of $62,000 to $105,000 in the same years.[26]

Humble's discovery of new fields and its acquisition of reserves in fields discovered by others, together with its extension of old fields, resulted in a large addition to its oil and gas reserves during the war years. Despite its greatly increased production, the company was able to raise somewhat the amount of its prewar (1939) reserves; there was an estimated increase of approximately 100,000,000 barrels as of the end of 1945. The company also maintained approximately its prewar percentage of the reserves in its operating territory and in the United States oil industry as a whole. Never during the war was there any real danger that Humble would have to reduce its production or employ practices that would decrease seriously, if at all, the recoverable oil in its reservoirs.[27]

The producing organization greatly increased the volume of Humble's output. From September 1, 1939, to September 1, 1945, it produced more than half a billion barrels of oil. Its daily average net production was 150,000 barrels in 1941 and 308,600 in 1944; its average at the end of the war was well over 300,000 barrels. From 1942 the company was the largest crude oil producer in the United States. Its percentage of the total national production rose from 3.7 in 1939 to 6.7 in 1944. Its increase after 1941 amounted to about 25 per cent of the total domestic increase during the years of this country's participation in the war.[28]

Humble also expanded its operations as a crude oil middleman. It reduced its purchases to a daily average of 251,500 barrels in 1941 and 218,000 in 1942, the time when the submarine campaign was reducing shipping by tanker; during the next three years, however, it raised its purchases to a daily average of 386,600 barrels in 1944 and 399,200 barrels in 1945. At the same time, it increased its sales to Jersey affiliates and other companies from an average of 188,100 barrels daily in 1942 to 466,300 barrels in 1944 and 485,700 in 1945.[29] During the years 1942 to 1945, inclusive, Humble by production and purchase supplied about one-tenth of the crude oil made available to the Allies.[30]

At the same time, the Texas affiliate became a large supplier of the valuable light liquid hydrocarbons recovered from the gas produced in oil and gas fields.[31] Most of the wartime increase came from the Katy cycling plant, which extracted the liquid hydrocarbons from the gas produced. It returned the lighter fractions to the reservoir. The Katy field had been discovered by Stanolind (an affiliate of Standard of Indiana) under a pooling agreement in which Humble was a participant. Humble owned 44.7 per cent of this field. As early as 1940, anticipating a large demand for high-octane gasolines, the operators in the field had made plans for building a cycling plant, for which project they received a high priority rating for materials. In 1941 the Katy owners entered into an agreement for unitizing the field and operating the plant. Stanolind managed field operations until 1944, when Humble became the operator. The Jersey affiliate was given responsibility for the construction and operation of the plant, in which it had a 46.5 per cent interest. It also constructed and operated two four-inch pipelines to carry the product to Baytown.

From January, 1943, through August, 1945, the Katy cycling plant produced 7,500,000 barrels of light liquid hydrocarbons. These included isobutane for use in making alkylate—the high-octane blending agent for aviation gasoline—and also isohexane and isopentane, which were premium-quality base stocks for making that gasoline. Because of its tremendous gas reserves and its location only thirty-five miles from large refineries near Houston, the Katy field was the most important gas condensate field in the United States during the war.[32]

A NEW ERA IN VENEZUELAN RELATIONS

Jersey looked to its affiliates in Venezuela for greatly expanded production. The discovery of a deeper formation in the huge oil fields of the Maracaibo Basin before the war had resulted in a large increase in the estimated oil reserves of the Lago Petroleum Corporation. This vital area was well located for supplying the Aruba refinery with crude oil. In the eastern part of the country, Standard Oil Company of Venezuela was developing new fields itself or jointly with other companies.[33]

Two developments in 1942 for a time put a brake on expansion and production: the German submarine campaign in the Caribbean and on the Atlantic, and the proposal of the Venezuelan government to take action to increase its income from oil production. The volume of oil produced by Jersey affiliates in Venezuela in that year was approximately a third less than the output in 1941; a decline similarly occurred in the output of other companies. This reduction brought severe unemployment. It also substantially reduced the government's income from oil production and Venezuela's foreign balances, on which it was dependent for the larger part of its imports, including food products. The resulting economic difficulties spurred a long-standing effort by the government to obtain a revision of the terms under which foreign oil producing companies were operating in that country; it proposed that the government's share of the profits be increased even under the old concessions issued under the petroleum law of 1922.[34]

Ever since the death of Gómez in 1935, the Venezuelan government had been taking measures to increase the country's income from oil operations. This had been one objective of elaborate labor laws and regulations beginning in 1936. A new petroleum law enacted in 1938 increased royalties on new concessions. However, the oil companies had avoided paying the higher royalties by not applying for concessions after this law went into effect. The government continued to press its case. Although its policy was to gain as large returns as possible from the oil companies' operations, it disclaimed any intent to resort to expropriation, as Bolivia and Mexico had done. Venezuela, to be sure, was in a very different situation as to oil production than were those other Latin American countries. Its government was heavily dependent on the industry for its income, and oil in the late 1930's made up approximately 90 per cent of the country's exports.[35]

Certain developments strengthened the government's position on this issue as the years passed. The oil companies' profits were rising, and the influence of the dominant political element of which Gómez had been the leader was displaced by a developing middle class and organized labor. These groups looked upon the foreign companies as associated with the old oligarchy and as joined with it in exploiting those who did not belong to that closed class. A new nationalism was also growing, and with it an antiforeign attitude especially critical of the foreign oil companies that were drawing on the country's natural resources. The feeling spread that a larger proportion of the companies' profits should go to the people of Venezuela.

This feeling was shared by the new president, General Isaias Medina Angarita, who was elected in 1941. Medina was sympathetic with, and to some extent owed his election to, the growing electorate which represented a shift in the locus of political power in Venezuela. Like his predecessor, Eleazar López Contreras, President Medina was not a radical but stood for the improvement of the Venezuelan people's income generally. Toward that end, among other measures he advocated better statutory control of oil and gas production, provisions to make pipelines common carriers, and especially the stabilization and substantial increase of the nation's income from its petroleum resources.[36]

President Medina and other officials discussed the situation with representatives of the foreign oil companies. Under Jersey's system of decentralization, the company's administrators in New York normally left the conduct of relations with foreign governments to the heads of affiliates in the individual countries. It therefore left relations with the government of Venezuela to its senior executive there, President Henry E. Linam of Standard Oil Company of Venezuela.

Linam, who had come to Venezuela in the 1920's as an oil-well driller, was a self-made man, uneducated but studious, and very able. He was an ardent disciple of Machiavelli, to whose works he had been introduced by Dr. Alejandro Pietri, the company's Venezuelan legal counsel, who was an upper-class Venezuelan with a European cultural background. Linam was opposed to changing the terms of the concession contracts; he believed that he could handle the matter successfully with the Medina government. He was supported by Pietri and Vice-President T. R. Armstrong of Creole, who was a member of the Producing Department in New York. Linam was in an influential position because of the large operations of Jersey in Venezuela. He was looked upon as the leader by the heads of the two other important foreign oil companies, who also were opposed to rewriting the concessions.[37]

When the government made no progress in discussions with oil company officers in Venezuela, it turned to the United States. In 1941, Attorney General Gustavo Manrique Pacanins went to New York to discuss the matter with top officers of the oil companies having operations in his country. Attorney General Manrique was a capable official; he was direct, tactful, and intelligent. He returned to Caracas late in the year without having come to the agreement with the companies that his government desired. In the spring of 1942 he returned to the United States, this time going to Washington. There he discussed the renegotiation of concessions with members of the Department of State. He made it plain that, if the old concessions could not be revised by agreement with the companies, the pressure of public opinion in his country might make unilateral action inevitable.[38]

The Department of State had been concerned for some time over the development of this issue in Venezuela. It had been working for many years to improve the relations of the United States everywhere in Latin America, but it was especially cognizant at this time of the importance of Venezuelan oil to Great Britain and to the defense of the United States. In the circumstances, the department recognized that it should not in this instance follow its policy of noninterference until a crisis had been reached in the difficulties of oil companies as it had done in Bolivia and Mexico late in the 1930's. Instead, it should help to bring about a settlement before the Venezuelan government's position hardened so that no retreat was possible.[39]

Accordingly, in September, 1942, the Department of State arranged for representatives of American oil companies with interests in Venezuela to meet in Washington with Attorney General Manrique. Director Wallace E. Pratt represented Jersey in a conference with Assistant Secretary of State Sumner Welles, the department's adviser on foreign oil matters, Max Thornburg, and Venezuela's attorney general. Then and later these representatives of the Department of State were extremely helpful in guiding the negotiations. In this conference, the Venezuelan again took the position that, unless satisfactory arrangements were made by amicable negotiations, his government would seek its objectives by unilateral action.[40] Director Pratt reported the discussions to Jersey's Executive Committee. Later in the autumn, Attorney General Manrique met with officers of the company in New York.[41]

Jersey's directors and the executives immediately concerned with Venezuelan operations were not all of one mind concerning the position the company should take with regard to the revision of the terms of its old concessions. They believed that they could expect no support from the United States government. They also recognized that nonacceptance of Venezuela's proposals might upset oil operations vital to the Allies and that such a development might even weaken the existing government of Venezuela at a critical time. They were concerned, of course, that the Allies were heavily dependent on Venezuelan oil, but they also knew that the Venezuelan government obtained a large part of its income from oil production and that the country got all but a minor fraction of its foreign exchange from the export of oil. So far as the risks to Jersey's own interests were concerned, these had to be weighed against an important question of policy.

Several company officers at this time stood firmly for the observance of the terms of the old concession contracts, among them being Jersey's Director Sadler and Armstrong, Linam, and Pietri of the Venezuelan affiliates. Their stand was supported by Professor Edwin M. Borchard of Yale University, an authority on international law who was a Jersey consultant. These men held that accepting what in their view would amount to a general weakening of concession contracts would remove an essential safeguard of company interests, an action that might have serious consequences elsewhere as well as in Venezuela. They favored risking loss to the company rather than abandoning the principle of the inviolability of contracts.

Jersey's Vice-President Pratt took a contrary position and in so doing became the leader on the side of revision. He held that the issue was a question of equity because the company was making higher profits than had been expected. He also held that foreign operations in the future would survive not on the strength of contracts but on the basis of recognition by both sides of a mutuality of interest and on an equitable sharing of benefits. Further, he feared that some of the titles to Jersey concessions, which had been acquired by purchase and had originally been negotiated by a third party with Gómez, might be found to be defective and hence were in jeopardy. Moreover, some of Jersey's old concessions, which still had about twenty years to run, would expire by their terms before it would be physically possible to withdraw from them all the gas and oil already developed. Because Venezuela was offering new forty-year concessions in exchange for old ones, there were obvious advantages in converting the old into new concessions.[42]

Why did Pratt take a stand so different from that of several men with long experience in Latin America and with as much knowledge as his own about Jersey's concessions? It is clear, of course, that he was not committed to a particular position by earlier stands in regard to Venezuela. No doubt, also, his position was an expression of his character and general philosophy.[43] Moreover, as an extensive reader, Pratt had a historical perspective on current conditions in the less developed countries and on the relations of industrially developed nations with them. But, like the others, he was also a businessman responsible for finding workable solutions.

Pratt's position was supported by association over nearly three decades with oil operations in underdeveloped countries, largely Spanish and Latin American. As a young man, he had worked for a short time as a geologist in the Orient. He had been in Mexico with The Texas Company shortly before that country's constitution of 1917 was adopted. In the 1920's as an executive with Humble, which had an affiliate in Mexico, he had observed the operations and the government relations of foreign oil companies in that country. He had been asked by Jersey late in the decade to examine the status of Transcontinental Petroleum Company, a Mexican affiliate, which was having difficulties with the government. In Mexico he had heard the views of Ambassador Dwight Morrow, who negotiated the settlement with President Calles in 1927. As an advocate on the Jersey Board of Directors of a somewhat different approach to relations in Latin America than Jersey's with Mexico in 1937 and 1938, in the latter year he had been sent by the parent company on a tour of South American countries in which it had affiliates. On this tour he had conferred with both company men and government officials. In the course of this experience, he had obtained some insight into current problems of Latin American countries and had met with officials who had won his respect and confidence. All this had convinced him of the need and the practicability of change in company relations with certain countries. This conviction was strengthened by discussions in the fall of 1942 with Sumner Welles and Max Thornburg of the Department of State and Attorney General Manrique of Venezuela.[44]

On November 27, 1942, Jersey's Executive Committee decided that the company itself should undertake discussions with the Venezuelan government, and it sent Pratt there with full authority to act as its representative. He spent a month in Caracas, where he conferred with Creole's President Clarence H. Lieb and Vice-President Arthur T. Proudfit and with executives of affiliates of Shell and Gulf Oil as well as with government officials. The Venezuelan government was advised in this matter by

Herbert Hoover, Jr., and his assistant, Duke Curtice, consulting engineers whose firm it had engaged at the suggestion of Sumner Welles.[45]

The conclusions from discussions between representatives of the oil companies and officials of the government were embodied in a new petroleum law effective March 13, 1943, and in changes in the country's corporate income tax. This new statute was applicable to old as well as new concessions. The petroleum law of 1922 had called for royalties ranging from 7.5 to 11 per cent; those on concessions in Lake Maracaibo had been set at the lowest of these rates because of the expected high cost of developing underwater production. The new legislation increased the government's royalty to a uniform 16⅔ per cent and raised the corporate income tax to a normal tax of 2.5 per cent plus a surtax ranging from 2 to 9.5 per cent. This larger percentage of the oil produced—which the companies generally purchased—together with the higher income tax raised the government's income to approximately half of the companies' net earnings from oil production. Certain minor matters of controversy were also settled at the same time. Most important to the companies was the confirmation of old concessions and their renewal for forty years.[46]

The importance of the amicable settlement of the Venezuelan issue can hardly be overstressed. There is no certainty, of course, as to what would have happened if an agreement had not been reached that was reasonably satisfactory to Venezuela's government and people. This is certain: that Venezuelan oil contributed greatly to the cause of the Allies. It may well be said that the sea of oil on which the Allies floated to victory came in large part from Venezuela. As for the oil companies and the country itself, oil production was profitable for both under the new law.

This Venezuelan affair marks an important development in Jersey's position with regard to Latin American governments. The change was somewhat comparable to that which had taken place earlier in the relations of the United States with South American countries.[47] Laws and contracts still defined the terms of the relations of oil companies with national governments. But the company recognized the reality that, in the absence of a resort to force, even laws are only as strong as the opinions and attitudes behind them.

The company's decision to enter direct discussions with Venezuelan officials led to an important change in the leadership of its Venezuelan affiliates. Two executives who had long held key positions resigned: President Linam of Standard Oil Company of Venezuela and Vice-President Armstrong of Creole. As Jersey's senior executive in Venezuela, Linam had been responsible for relations with the government. However, his standing with the government had been predicated on close personal relations with the group in power, with whom he had had considerable influence, but that group had changed since the death of Gómez. Armstrong similarly had long been associated with Jersey interests in Venezuela; it was he who had initiated the negotiations with the dictator Gómez in 1919 that had led to Jersey's entry into that country.[48]

The choice of Arthur T. Proudfit to be Linam's successor as president of Standard Oil Company of Venezuela and also vice-president of Creole introduced a new type of Jersey leadership in that country. Proudfit had qualities of character and personality that were invaluable in so sensitive and important a situation. Besides, he had had nearly a quarter-century of experience in oil production in Latin America, including a number of years in Mexico and a period of service in Argentina. He had become manager of Jersey's operations in eastern Venezuela in 1939. The company's future relations in that country in no small measure depended on this new leader. Elected president of Creole in 1944, he thenceforth had charge of all of Jersey's expanding operations within that country.[49]

By 1944 nearly all the company's Venezuelan holdings had been merged in Creole Petroleum Corporation. An exception was its interest through International Petroleum in Mene Grande Oil Company, for which Creole had no managerial responsibility. Under a plan approved in August, 1943, by majority vote of its stockholders, Creole acquired, in exchange for stock, the Venezuelan assets and properties of Lago Petroleum, with the exception of certain accounts receivable and a stock interest in Lago Oil & Transport.[50] Standard Oil of Venezuela was liquidated. All of the Venezuelan operations were thereafter directly managed by Creole except the shipping in the Caribbean area under Compañía de Petróleo Lago, which had become a wholly owned affiliate of Creole.[51]

Creole Petroleum Corporation applied for the conversion of its old concessions to the new law of 1943. It renounced about one-third of the acreage as being of small promise, but received new titles for the remainder, totaling 3,300,000 acres. During 1943 and 1944, it also applied for concessions in new areas, which brought its net to 4,200,000 acres. High bonuses and as much as a 33⅓ per cent royalty were offered by some companies for concessions subject to competitive bidding on national reserves close to proved fields. The total acreage held by oil companies in Venezuela rose from 13,000,000 acres at the end of 1943 to 26,500,000 acres at the end of 1944.[52]

Because of the need of the Allies for oil and the three-year limit on exploration titles, the companies operating in Venezuela stepped up their exploration and production programs in 1944. They thereby extended old fields and discovered new ones. Creole raised its estimated reserves to over 5 billion barrels by the end of 1945. In that year, it also increased its gross production to an average of 453,000 barrels daily and its net to 373,100 barrels.[53]

During these war years the Jersey affiliates in Venezuela took further measures to improve their employee relations. They extended programs initiated in the 1930's for establishing better living conditions for Venezuelan employees and their families. While this action was in keeping with general Jersey policy to improve the quality and morale of employees, it was spurred by labor unrest resulting from rising living costs, by the growth of labor syndicates, and by the closer relations of the Unión Popular with Communist leaders in other Latin American countries—notably with Lombardo Toledano of Mexico.[54]

Among the wartime changes in Creole's employee programs was the reinstatement late in 1943 of the *Institución Fondo de Ahorros,* a thrift plan which had been discontinued with the beginning of *utilidades* payments late in the 1930's. The employees, few of whom were accustomed to regular saving, were encouraged by the plan to adopt a savings program. Creole also adopted disability, death benefit, and group life insurance plans in 1944 similar to those in effect in the United States. It supported various educational projects not required by law, such as providing schooling for children beyond the stipulated grade and promoting more advanced education. For instance, it maintained scholarships for a few men in the School of Geology of the Central University in Caracas and for others in professional schools, principally in the United States. It also expanded its system of training for workers in various oil operations and maintained courses for adults. The percentage of workers who could read and write rose markedly. More Venezuelans were promoted to responsible positions in Creole as they demonstrated their ability and acquired adequate training. When many employees from the United States were drafted into military service, Venezuelan nationals were ready to take their places. To compensate for higher living costs, Creole and other oil companies, at the government's request, lowered prices at company commissaries instead of raising wages. In general, Creole provided increasing security for its employees, upgraded its whole force, and promoted the more able and promising workers.[55]

The development of employee representation groups, however, made slow progress. This part of the program was at first affected somewhat by the establishment of labor syndicates, a movement which came with industry-wide bargaining. Although perhaps half the workers belonged to the syndicates, Creole for some time did not recognize the unions as representing the majority of its employees. A large number of syndicates were dissolved in 1944 by the government because of their involvement in political affairs. But the increasing political-mindedness of Venezuelan labor made the workers look to political party and government for support. After a constitutional amendment, adopted in May, 1945, permitted the legalization of the Communist Party, the labor syndicates entered into political action; they affiliated with the Acción Democrática and the Communist Unión Popular. Instead of acting as labor organizations, they increasingly devoted themselves to political action. The Medina government, as a result, followed a policy of appeasement.[56]

Creole at the same time took positive action to improve its public relations. Indeed, if it was to maintain good relations in a country where political power was shifting from a narrow group to a broad electorate, it had to make itself better and favorably known to the public. It also had to achieve an understanding in some depth of the economic and social aspirations and the political motivations of the Venezuelan people.[57]

In a few years, Creole made signal progress in its relations. War prosperity, of course, brought an improvement in the company's standing, as also did the amicable solution of the concession issue. President Proudfit proved notably effective in dealing with the higher levels of government, and he was also liked generally and won the people's confidence. Because of his popularity and excellent reputation—and also Henry Pelkey's effectiveness as general press relations and publicity manager—Creole's standing with the Venezuelan press was greatly improved. The company similarly won favor by extending its educational and scholarship programs to students outside its employee groups. In addition, it changed *El Farol*, the house organ established in 1939, into a general cultural magazine which it distributed without charge to Venezuelan subscribers. These various activities were of a nature to make the company better and more favorably known.[58]

The development of greatest immediate wartime importance in Venezuela was the increase in Jersey's crude oil produced there—Creole's production and Jersey's share of Mene Grande's. Table 13 summarizes that production as averaging a net of 192,600 barrels daily in 1942, after which it rose to 332,000 barrels in 1944 and to 403,100 in 1945. The

Venezuelan affiliates also purchased a considerable amount of oil—principally the royalty oil from their own production—which they made available to Jersey refineries and others. The large volume produced by Creole, together with International Petroleum's share of the production of Mene Grande Oil Company, made the net production from Jersey's Venezuelan interests in 1945 larger than the combined net of its affiliates in the United States.

In 1945 the total daily average gross crude oil production of Jersey's affiliates, at home and abroad, for the first time exceeded 1,000,000 barrels. This total was a third larger than that of 1941. The increase represented a rise from 12.4 per cent of the total production of non-Axis countries in 1941 to 13.7 in 1944, and 14.1 per cent in 1945.[59] By raising their production, the Jersey Company and the oil industry generally were able to keep adequate raw materials moving to the refineries supplying the rising wartime demands for oil products.

Chapter 18

Oil Products and Research for War,
1942–1945

O N THE DAY the United States entered the war, the first meeting of the Petroleum Industry War Council was held in Washington. The leaders of the industry, gathered to consider how to organize American oil operations for defense, faced the necessity of mobilizing for war. One immediately critical need was to increase the production of 100-octane aviation gasoline. These men, including Jersey's President Farish and Humble's President Wiess, concluded from surveys already made that the current production of about 40,000 barrels daily could be increased 15 per cent in the next six months and stepped up to an average of 150,000 barrels by not later than July 1, 1943. Raising the amount of tetraethyl lead mixed with aviation-grade gasoline from three cubic centimeters to four per gallon would be of help. But more high-octane gasoline for base stock would be required and especially more iso-octane than was being produced. To obtain these, the necessary immediate steps were the capacity utilization of existing equipment, the quick conversion of certain old units to new uses, and the rapid completion of other facilities then being built.[1]

These planned increases in aviation gasoline were small compared to what actually was soon needed. Toward the end of 1942 the Joint Aeronautical Board estimated that 539,800 barrels per day of 100-octane gasoline would be required.[2] The difference between the increase planned in December, 1941, and the requirements estimated a year later gives an indication of the pressure on the oil industry to provide products for war. The wartime demand for volume expansion and product improvement necessitated planning on a world scale, continuing research and development, new refining facilities, and more trained personnel. This chapter deals with the Jersey Company's response to the problems of product supply.

489

REFINING ORGANIZATION, EQUIPMENT, AND OPERATIONS

Jersey's supply problem was increased by the further reduction of its refining in the Eastern Hemisphere. The two refineries that were still free from control by the Axis powers in December, 1941, ceased to operate a few months after America entered the war. The small Agwi plant at Fawley on the southern coast of England was closed, mainly because it was considered desirable to use available tanker transportation to bring in finished products from Gulf or Caribbean refineries rather than to carry crude oil for processing. The Standard-Vacuum plant on the island of Sumatra in the Dutch East Indies became a casualty of the war.

This Sungei Gerong refinery, which was one of only a few such plants of the Allies in the Orient, fell to the Japanese in February, 1942. In anticipation of its loss, company officials and Dutch military authorities had made plans for wrecking it and for cutting off its supply of raw materials by destroying the oil wells in the company's Sumatran fields. Near the end of 1941, the Dutch authorities gave orders to destroy 173 wells by cementing them in and to make arrangements for the destruction of the remaining wells at a moment's notice. When it became evident by February that the refinery's tanker loading plant at Tandjong Oeban was doomed, that installation was also destroyed. And when the Japanese attempted to drop paratroopers in the vicinity of the refinery, antiaircraft guns protecting the plant kept them away until its demolition had been carried out according to plan. The American employees fled into the jungle and succeeded in making their way to Java, where they left by plane or boarded overcrowded ships for Australia. The ship carrying the general manager, Lloyd W. Elliott, narrowly missed being sunk by a Japanese dive bomber. Several of these men joined the American forces in the Southwest Pacific; Elliott became a brigadier general under General MacArthur.[3]

The only large refinery still held by the Allies in the Middle East and Far East was the plant of Anglo-Iranian at Abadan, at the head of the Persian Gulf. This refinery proved a valuable source of supply for the Russians and also for the forces of the United States and the British in the East, but not until the opening of the Mediterranean by the Allies in 1943 was it to be of help in campaigns against the European Axis powers. A small plant on Bahrain and another built in Saudi Arabia during the war supplied Allied naval forces in the East. After the freeing of the

Mediterranean sea lanes, the three Middle East refineries, together with that at Haifa, increased their runs to a total daily average of 510,000 barrels in the first half of 1945.[4] However, this was far from enough for the Allies in the Eastern Hemisphere.

Most of the responsibility for supplying products for military use fell on the refining industry in the United States and in the Caribbean region. All but a few of the hemisphere's largest and most progressive refineries were on the North American mainland, chiefly in the United States. The financing of the construction of certain types of new plants by the United States government resulted in the further concentration of the manufacture of petroleum products in this country. The most important refineries in the southern part of the hemisphere were two in the Netherlands West Indies.

Consequently, the planning and coordinating of by far the larger part of the refining operations serving the Allies were done by the American Petroleum Administration for War, the Petroleum Industry War Council, and their related boards and committees. National and district committees worked with the refining industry at home, and area subcommittees functioning under the Foreign Operations Committee coordinated the industry's operations abroad. Their plans came to be based primarily on the PAW Program Division's estimates of future needs and its statistics relative to the types and amounts of crude available and the capacity of individual refineries for making given products. Also on the basis of this information, the PAW in consultation with industry boards and committees made provision for new construction and established priority ratings for different products. Early in 1942 this government agency provided for allocating to individual refineries the crude oils best suited to making their specific products.

Representatives of Jersey and its refining and marketing affiliates participated in the system of industrial cooperation both at home and abroad. W. W. White, formerly head in London of Intava—an aviation gasoline sales company in which Jersey owned a half-interest—became aviation officer of the PAW in Washington. He also served as executive secretary of the Aviation Petroleum Products Allocation Committee, which had responsibility for allocating aviation fuels and lubricants for Allied military forces and commercial air lines. Several other men served on important industry committees. William J. Haley, head of Jersey's Foreign Refining Department in New York, and C. E. Lanning, another Jersey authority on refining abroad, were members of the Refining and Specifications Committee of the Foreign Operations Committee. Haley was also chairman and Brian Mead was secretary of the important Caribbean Area Petroleum Committee. Two high executives of Standard Oil Development—Robert P. Russell and Eger V. Murphree—and the manager of Humble's research, H. Dayton Wilde, were members of the Technical Advisory Committee of the Petroleum Industry War Council. Others served on district refining boards. These included Chester F. Smith, president of Standard Oil Company of New Jersey; M. J. Rathbone and M. W. Boyer, president and vice-president of Standard of Louisiana; and Hines H. Baker, vice-president of Humble.[5]

These various committees planned the most productive use of available equipment and raw materials. For example, to obtain the maximum output of the Caribbean refineries as a group, it was necessary to plan operations in the area as a whole and to coordinate their activities as if all the plants belonged to a single corporate entity. An important gain from such cooperation was the greater volume of aviation gasoline obtained by selecting crudes—wherever available in the area's producing regions—that were most suitable for making high-octane gasoline. Another product that benefited from the pooling of resources was fuel oil. Both heavy and light fuel oils were in great demand for ships and land installations. To help meet the demand, the Caribbean refineries processed crude oils that they had not used before in making these products.[6]

After the winter of 1942, all the refining done by Jersey affiliates was in the Western Hemisphere. The smaller plants carried on traditional refining operations and served mostly their old outlets. Nearly all the expansion and the manufacture of new products came at the Lago refinery in Aruba, at the New Jersey Works, Baton Rouge, and Baytown in the United States, and at Sarnia in Canada.

During this era of applied chemistry in refining, the engineers were the key figures in the management of operations as well as in research and development. At the beginning of the war, the managers of the Jersey refineries had to plan for the conversion of old and even obsolete equipment to meet immediate needs; in the next two years much of their activity was similarly concerned with providing means to fill war requirements. In the laboratories they carried on research to improve processes and products and to develop new uses for petroleum in warfare. The affiliates' engineers also designed the new units being built at the refineries and inspected and tested them during construction. In addition, they were responsible for training employees to operate new equipment in the companies' own refineries, and, under the wartime system of exchange of patents and technology throughout the industry, for instructing men from other companies in the processes and techniques developed or improved by Jersey affiliates. Baton Rouge engineers, for example, instructed four hundred men from thirty-six non-Jersey companies in the operation of fluid catalytic cracking plants. Progressing beyond the concepts and techniques of analysis developed in the 1930's, the engineers also established greater control and efficiency in the use of raw materials and equipment.[7]

The outstanding wartime development in the leading Jersey refineries was the introduction of processes for manufacturing new products. In making certain products of vital importance to the war, the refiners projected into large-scale manufacture small-scale operations or laboratory processes developed late in the 1930's and even during the war. They also applied more extensively techniques for the more precise separation of refinery by-product hydrocarbons. Those separated out with a high degree of purity were ethylene, propylene, propane, isobutylene, normal butylene, butane, isobutane, amylene, and isoprene. These hydrocarbons, which had formerly been of low value and largely wasted, were utilized in making many important wartime products.

The expansion of refining and especially the manufacture of new and improved products necessitated a tremendous construction program at the more important Jersey refineries. Outside contractors did most of the building. The principal plants constructed for the affiliates themselves are listed in Table 14; these had to do mostly with the manufacture of aviation gasoline. The Jersey Company spent a total of $104,000,000 on installations built to supply products for war—the larger part being for the aviation-gasoline program. The company spent an additional $51,-000,000 for plants that did not serve specific military needs and would be useful later in providing supplies for the postwar market. Many government plants were also built, especially for the production of toluene at Baton Rouge and Baytown, butadiene at these two refineries and at Sarnia in Canada, and Butyl at Baton Rouge and Sarnia. The most extensive construction was at Baton Rouge, where new plants for the company and for the Defense Plant Corporation cost $90,000,000, about half of the funds being furnished by the affiliate and the rest by the government.[8]

All the wartime construction was planned on the tightest schedules, despite shortages of manpower and materials that sometimes caused a great deal of extra work and seriously disrupted timetables. However, by

Table 14: **REFINERY UNITS CONSTRUCTED, PRINCIPALLY FOR MANUFACTURING AVIATION GASOLINE, BY AFFILIATES OF STANDARD OIL COMPANY (NEW JERSEY), 1942–1943**

Location	Type	Time of Completion	Daily Charging Capacity in Barrels
Construction in the United States			
Baton Rouge, Louisiana	Catalytic cracking	May, 1942	12,000
Baytown, Texas	Catalytic cracking	November, 1942	12,000
Baytown, Texas	Superfractionation	November, 1942	7,500
Baytown, Texas	Isomerization	November, 1942	1,200
Bayway, New Jersey	Catalytic cracking	November, 1942	12,000
Baltimore, Maryland	Alkylation	November, 1942	2,200
Bayway, New Jersey	Light ends plant	February, 1943	9,500
Baton Rouge, Louisiana	Pipe still	March, 1943	40,000
Baton Rouge, Louisiana	Alkylation	March, 1943	3,000
Baytown, Texas	Superfractionation	May, 1943	13,000
Baytown, Texas	Isomerization	May, 1943	800–1,000
Baltimore, Maryland	Pipe still	June, 1943	35,000
Baton Rouge, Louisiana	Catalytic cracking	June, 1943	14,000
Baton Rouge, Louisiana	Catalytic cracking	September, 1943	14,000
Baltimore, Maryland	Catalytic cracking	December, 1943	14,000
Baytown, Texas	Catalytic cracking	February, 1944	14,000
Foreign Construction			
Regina, Saskatchewan	Polymerization	March, 1943	150
Regina, Saskatchewan	Re-forming	March, 1943	2,700
Sarnia, Ontario	Cumene	April, 1943	250
Aruba, Netherlands West Indies	Alkylation	July, 1943	3,300
Aruba, Netherlands West Indies	Isomerization	October, 1943	1,000
Aruba, Netherlands West Indies	Catalytic cracking	December, 1943	14,000

Source: Charles Sterling Popple, *Standard Oil Company (New Jersey) in World War II* (New York, 1952), p. 43.

the end of 1943 the Jersey refineries were operating at nearly full wartime capacity.

So urgent was the need for certain products that facilities to supply them were in some instances built without the normal large-scale pilot-plant testing. In the case of the Butyl rubber units, skipping this particular stage proved unfortunate. Difficulty also arose in putting into operation the first commercial-size fluid catalytic cracking plant, but it was overcome without much delay. Although Jersey had spent many millions of dollars on developing this cracking process, so great was the need for the products that the first unit—built at Baton Rouge—had been designed after testing in only a small pilot plant. When this first "cat cracker" went into operation in May, 1942, seven more such plants were being built by Jersey affiliates, and several were being constructed by other companies. In addition, numerous plants under construction for making aviation-gasoline blending agents, butadiene, and toluene were largely dependent on base stocks from these fluid catalytic cracking plants, and much of the synthetic rubber program depended on butadiene to be made from butylene produced by this process.

Trouble developed at once when the plant at Baton Rouge was put on stream. It was impossible to raise the catalyst temperature high enough in the regenerator for the catalyst to cause cracking to take place in the reactor. The temperature was limited to about 700° F. compared with a desired temperature of 850–900° F.

The engineers in charge—Vice-President M. W. Boyer and H. J. Vorhees—analyzed the problem and came up with an explanation. The plant, 250 feet high, was designed to circulate 40 tons of catalyst per hour. To control the temperature of the regenerator, three huge heat exchangers, connected in parallel and cooled by water, had been placed beneath the regenerator vessel. Increasing the circulation of the catalyst through these heat exchangers should lower the temperature of the catalyst; conversely, decreasing the circulation should raise the temperature. However, it was found that the catalyst did not circulate through the heat exchangers as planned; it was recirculated, and consequently more heat was being removed than was desired. This malfunction was preventing the increase of the catalyst temperature to the planned level for cracking.

Normally the engineers would have taken the problem back to the pilot plant, but, because large-scale pilot-plant testing had not been done, such testing would have meant an especially long delay. Boyer and Vorhees were faced with the choice between postponing the operation of the cat cracker for a considerable time or attempting to find a solution by making changes in the plant itself. They decided to risk such an attempt on the basis of calculations and their own judgment.

They decided that, if the pipes from the catalyst coolers—that is, the heat exchangers—were extended up into the regenerator close to the catalyst distribution grid, the undesired recirculation would stop. As an added improvement, the pipes should be capped and restricting holes provided around the top.

Their solution worked. When these changes had been made, the malfunction in catalyst circulation was corrected and the desired temperature was reached—and invaluable time was saved. Subsequently the efficiency of the original units was raised by further changes, and the design of later units was improved.[9]

Manpower posed continuing problems in most refinery operations. Replacements had to be found for the thousands of men—from research scientists and engineers to rank-and-file workers—who were granted leave to serve the government in civilian posts or to enter military service. Additional thousands were required for new plants. The Baton Rouge and Baytown refineries provided trained technical and operating personnel for government-owned installations, and they absorbed new, untrained workers in their own units. An extended workweek helped to solve the manpower problem, but thousands of inexperienced men and women had to be hired and trained. At Baton Rouge, for example, nearly a fourth of the 4,500 employed at the beginning of the war were granted military leave, and over the war years the total number of employees rose to 8,200.[10]

A serious shortage could have arisen among the supervisory personnel, but this difficulty was minimized by the companies' practice of having available an assistant or alternate capable of taking over each supervisor's job. Even so, the demands on the supervisors were heavy: the existing force had to be spread to cover the new plants, and unfamiliar operations had to be handled. The many new processes and plant units required extensive training even for the experienced workers. Dealing with the more volatile hydrocarbons, operating new equipment, and working under tight schedules increased hazards and necessitated extensive programs of safety training.

Nevertheless, the Jersey refineries had excellent wartime safety records. Accidents did occur. Baytown had nine fatalities during the war years, three each in a butadiene plant, in the Butyl laboratory, and at a cracking coil. The refinery at Everett, Massachusetts, in 1943 won the National Safety Award for Petroleum Group B, and its employees boasted that they would complete the war without a single lost-time accident. But, alas, in September, 1944, a refinery employee smashed his thumb in replacing a heavy manhole cover. Even so, the Everett plant had an unsurpassed safety record. For nearly three years, the men and women at this refinery put one of the most powerful and explosive substances then used in manufacturing plants, under high pressures and high temperatures, through innumerable processing units, pipes, valves, and tanks. The refineries at Baton Rouge and Baytown did not match the record of Everett or that of the New Jersey Works, but they were employing more new processes and handling even more volatile materials than the northern plants. They were carrying on most of the risky development work and the newer operations utilizing gases. In none of the refineries, however, did accidents seriously affect plant units or interfere with refinery operations.[11]

With minor exceptions, the refineries of the affiliates in the United States, despite continued labor unrest and unionization drives in American refining, enjoyed excellent employee relations throughout the war. The attitudes and efforts of the rank-and-file employees as well as of the supervisors contributed to efficient operation. Under government regulations, there could be no disputes over hours of work or rates of pay. For most workers, the normal workweek was 40 hours, with time-and-a-half pay for overtime and double-time rates for Sundays and holidays. The government regulations for the supervisory force, however, made no provision for overtime pay. Thus the supervisors did not receive increased compensation proportionate to that of the employees under them. The affiliates tried to correct this discrepancy as far as possible, one solution being to put the supervisors on extended work schedules, which increased their pay. In a few refineries, issues other than compensation were raised by employee groups under the influence of the wartime drives of the CIO and other labor organizations to unionize employees.

In the New Jersey Works, the representation of employees by independent unions established in the 1930's was challenged by the small minority of the members who belonged to international unions. Following an investigation and decision of the National Labor Relations Board, upheld by the United States Circuit Court of Appeals, the independent unions were dissolved. The employees promptly organized other independent unions, which in 1944 were certified by the NLRB. These employee organizations proved firm bargainers. In contracts signed with Standard Oil Company of New Jersey in 1945, they obtained an irrevocable checkoff—that is, the withholding by the company of union dues from wages. The company would not agree to a maintenance-of-membership clause, which it held to be contrary to the long-established Jersey policy of assuring employees freedom of choice as to union membership.[12]

International unions also endeavored to take over the independent employee organizations in other domestic affiliates of the Jersey group. They were already entrenched in certain skilled trades—such as that of the electrical workers at Baton Rouge and Baytown—and in the small refineries in Montana and Wyoming acquired by The Carter Oil Company during the war. When new contracts were negotiated in these Carter plants in 1944, the question of maintenance of membership was raised, but it was not finally settled until 1945, when a checkoff system was agreed upon.[13]

Only in Humble's small Ingleside refinery did management and employees experience a long-drawn-out conflict. Unionism was then sweeping the Gulf Coast refineries, and the CIO won bargaining rights in large plants of The Texas Company, Shell, and Pan American. No serious difficulties arose in the Baton Rouge and Baytown refineries of Jersey affiliates, but Humble's position on seniority was weakened at Baytown. The CIO was more successful at the small Ingleside refinery, where one employee provided strong leadership and the workers as a group were fearful that the plant might be shut down after the war. In an election to determine the Ingleside bargaining agency in 1942, the CIO won a large majority of the valid votes cast. By the end of April, 1943, all issues except maintenance of membership had been resolved in company-union negotiations, and a contract was signed which left that matter for later decision. The local union threatened to strike despite a no-strike clause in its contract, the government "seized" the plant, and the company exhausted nearly every legal recourse. The issue was still not settled when the war came to an end.[14]

The characteristic Jersey refinery management-employee relationship was not conflict but cooperation. The employees were obviously influenced by the fact that refinery products were vital to the war effort. But it seems fair to conclude that the relatively fortunate relations of management and employees in nearly all the Jersey refineries—as compared with labor unrest in the plants of certain other companies that were also doing important war work—were in large measure the result of employee policies which had been practiced by the company for a quarter of a century.

Table 15 indicates, in terms of refinery crude runs, the expansion of Jersey refining during the war. The decline in 1942 was caused primarily by the German submarine campaign.[15] During 1943 refining operations increased with improvements in tanker and pipeline transportation and with the completion of new plants. The major Jersey refineries established new records in 1944. All efficient units were put into operation on a round-the-clock basis. Old equipment, too high in operating costs in normal times, was returned to use during the last two years of the war. Within the limits established by safety considerations, all were kept in continuous operation as long as they produced satisfactory products.

Table 15: **DAILY AVERAGE REFINERY CRUDE RUNS OF AFFILI-
ATES, 1940–1945**
Standard Oil Company (New Jersey)
(In thousands of 42-gallon barrels)

AFFILIATES	1940	1941	1942	1943	1944	1945
Western Hemisphere						
United States						
Standard Oil Company of New Jersey[a]	109.7	127.0	93.9	124.4	185.5	207.1
Colonial Beacon Oil Company	28.3	27.9	25.9	29.4	31.3	32.4
Standard Oil Company of Louisiana[b]	95.1	111.7	110.9	117.4	132.9	137.2
Humble Oil & Refining Company	161.3	187.2	168.0	192.4	225.9	215.4
Carter Oil Company, The	—	—	—	3.6	10.1	14.3
Total	394.4	453.8	398.7	467.2	585.6	606.4
Other Western Hemisphere						
Imperial Oil Limited	82.4	92.5	87.5	95.4	106.8	104.5
International Petroleum Company, Limited	17.2	21.7	37.3	38.5	37.2	35.9
Tropical Oil Company, The	7.5	8.5	8.3	9.5	10.2	11.2
Standard Oil Company, S.A., Argentina, and Compañía Nacional	10.8	11.4	9.1	6.9	6.5	6.9
Standard Oil Company of Cuba	2.7	3.3	2.6	1.9	1.9	2.3
Compañía de Petroleo Lago[c]	16.2	17.5	7.0	7.4	8.7	20.8
Standard Oil Company of Venezuela[c]	35.2	37.2	28.2	25.4	31.6	33.3
Lago Oil & Transport Company, Limited	168.7	228.0	147.1	222.4	280.7	298.3
Total	340.7	420.1	327.1	407.4	483.6	513.2
Total Western Hemisphere	735.1	873.9	725.8	874.6	1,069.2	1,119.6
Eastern Hemisphere[d]						
Agwi Petroleum Corporation, Limited	7.0	1.8	1.3	—	—	0.8
Norsk Amerikansk Mineraloljecompagni, Aktieselskapet	0.2	—	—	—	—	—
Kalundborg Olïeraffinaderi, Aktieselskabet	0.0[e]	—	—	—	—	—
Standard Française des Pétroles	10.0	—	—	—	—	—
Compagnie Industrielle Atlas	0.4	—	—	—	—	—
Româno-Americana	14.3	14.8	—	—	—	—
Standard Società Italo-Americana pel Petrolio	1.3	—	—	—	—	—
Standard-Vacuum Oil Company	42.2	40.0	2.1	—	—	—
Total Eastern Hemisphere	75.4	56.6	3.4	—	—	0.8
Total of all affiliates	810.5	930.5	729.2	874.6	1,069.2	1,120.4

NOTE: Because of the rounding of numbers, totals are not in all cases the exact sum of the numbers added.
[a] Excluding reruns of reduced crude of 13.3 in 1940, 5.7 in 1941, and 1.5 in 1942.
[b] Became Louisiana Division of Standard Oil Company of New Jersey at the end of 1944.
[c] Merged with Creole Petroleum Corporation in 1943.
[d] Does not include affiliates under Axis control.
[e] Because this refinery ceased operations in 1940, its daily average for the year was 11 barrels.
Source: Statistics of refinery crude runs, Coordination and Economics Department, Standard Oil Company (New Jersey).

Every effort was made to speed up the turnaround time when a unit was taken out of operations for cleaning and repairing.[16] The Jersey refineries, during the years from 1942 to 1945, inclusive, accounted for approximately one-sixth of the average daily crude runs in Allied countries except those under Russian control.[17]

The larger part of the refineries' output consisted of products that fueled civilian airplanes and motorized ground transportation, provided power for industrial establishments, and heated buildings. The many new and improved products of strategic military importance, although less in volume than the familiar nonmilitary fuels, were far more difficult to manufacture. Among them were toluene, aviation gasoline, butadiene, and synthetic rubber.

TOLUENE FOR EXPLOSIVES

Because of the progress made before the entry of the United States into the conflict, the wartime manufacture of toluene from petroleum, for use in the manufacture of TNT, was a singularly smooth operation. As noted in Chapter 14, the Baytown Ordnance Works, the first commercial-scale plant to make synthetic toluene from petroleum, had begun to operate in the fall of 1941. It was using a process developed by Humble, Standard Oil Development, and the research group at Baton Rouge. This was the only method then applicable to large-scale production of nitration-grade toluene. Humble was operating the plant for the government under a cost-plus-fixed-fee contract, which also stipulated the price the company was to receive for prime-cut naphthas supplied to the plant. Shell Oil had built a small unit in 1940 for extracting natural toluene from petroleum, but the process had limited value because the yield was only about 1.5 per cent of the total volume of petroleum used. In 1942 the toluene made from petroleum amounted to about 28 per cent of the total production in the United States. In that year, the Baytown plant produced 50,000,000 gallons. This volume represented 89.5 per cent of the national total for the year made from petroleum; Shell produced most of the remainder.[18]

At the beginning of 1942, the Army Ordnance Department, apprehensive that the Baytown Ordnance Works might not supply sufficient synthetic toluene to supplement the natural product, became interested in having additional plants built. Jersey then made its toluene inventions and processes available to the government without charge and offered to instruct other companies in the techniques of construction and operation. Standard of Louisiana undertook to build a plant for the government and rushed construction. Late in 1942, however, the company was informed that the planned production would not be needed, and it was requested to convert the plant to making components of aviation gasoline. In the meantime, Shell had built a synthetic toluene plant in California that went into operation before the year's end. It used conversion and extraction processes developed by Shell's own research and development organization. At the end of 1942, Baytown's output was still rising; the new California Shell plant was on stream; another was being built by Shell at Wood River, Illinois; and a few other companies, including Standard of Indiana, were planning or building plants to utilize Jersey or Shell processes or a combination of Jersey conversion and Shell extraction.[19]

In 1944 the output of the Baytown Ordnance Works reached nearly 70,000,000 gallons. Other plants also had come into production, so that Baytown in 1943 produced 54.1 per cent of the toluene made from petroleum, and in the next year 38.2 per cent of the total. The importance of this production is indicated by the fact that in 1944 all but 8 per cent of the toluene made in the United States came from petroleum.[20]

The consumption of toluene soared as the war reached its full force in 1944, and toward the end of the year military authorities became concerned that even the substantial stocks available might not be sufficient. Accordingly, in February, 1945, Standard of Louisiana was instructed to reconvert the Baton Rouge unit to toluene production. The reconversion was completed on June 17, 1945. Two days later, because the end of the war in Europe had reduced the need, the Petroleum Administration for War notified the company that, since supplies of toluene were again plentiful and a large surplus was indicated, the plant was not needed for further manufacture of the product. After the capitulation of the Japanese in August, the demand for nitration-grade toluene immediately dropped to zero.[21]

During the war, the Baytown Ordnance Works produced 49.4 per cent of the toluene obtained from petroleum and 41.2 per cent of all the toluene produced in the United States. TNT made of Baytown toluene thus packed more than two out of every five Allied bombs after Pearl Harbor.[22]

GASOLINE FOR THE AIR FORCES

The official *History of the Petroleum Administration for War* notes: "There were only a dozen refiners in the entire country who manufactured 100-octane before the war. They had developed their techniques by many years of research and at a cost of many millions of dollars. Yet, here they were asked to share their expensively acquired skills and knowledge with their competitors, large and small alike, and they did just that."[23]

In producing aviation gasoline, all the domestic refineries operated under close direction from PAW agencies and industry committees. One industry group, the Aviation Gasoline Advisory Committee, of which Dr. H. G. Burks, Jr., of Standard Oil Company of New Jersey was chairman, advised the PAW and drew up schedules for the most effective utilization of the various resources that went into the production of aviation gasoline. One of the committee's particular functions was to furnish blending schedules and plan the exchange of components of aviation gasoline among refineries so as to obtain the greatest volume of output.[24]

The first urgent demand upon the Jersey refineries was to increase production under the "quickie" program agreed upon by the industry leaders in December, 1941. If the war was not to be lost in 1942, the refining industry would have to produce sufficient quantities of 100-octane gasoline to supply the defensive operations of the Allies while also providing fuel for planes used in training men for the expanding air forces.

As noted in Chapter 6, three types of components were required for producing 100-octane gasoline: a base stock of high-grade gasoline, commercial iso-octane to blend with the gasoline to raise its octane rating, and tetraethyl lead to increase the rating to 100. The first two were the products of refining. To provide enough high-quality base stock was a problem, but to manufacture sufficient iso-octane blending agents was the most critical part of the early wartime production.

Several companies—especially Jersey, Shell, and Phillips—had developed processes for producing high-octane mixtures in commercial quantities from a number of hydrocarbons which were refinery by-products. Cold-acid and hot-acid polymerization had largely been superseded by alkylation, a method which did not require expensive hydrogenation and utilized a more plentiful gas. Although the first alkylation plant had gone into operation at Baytown in 1938, not enough of such facilities had been built by December, 1941, to supply the amount of alkylate then required. In addition to the plant at Baytown, the Jersey group had alkylation units at Baton Rouge, Aruba, and Sungei Gerong, as well as facilities for providing the necessary isobutane and butylene.[25]

Since the product of its Western Hemisphere plants was far from sufficient to provide the amount of iso-octane required to carry out Jersey's share of the "quickie" program, it was decided to restore the original polymerization plants to production and to utilize the hydrogenation facilities at Baton Rouge. At first the Jersey refineries—from Everett, Massachusetts, to Baytown, Texas—extracted, purified, and processed isobutylene by the one method and isobutylene and normal butylene by the other to form di-isobutylene (dimer) and codimer, respectively, which were then shipped to Baton Rouge for hydrogenation to produce a high-octane hydrocarbon mixture. The refinery there had to expand its hydrogenation facilities. So great was the need for 100-octane gasoline that in August, 1942, its manufacture was given priority at Baton Rouge and soon thereafter at other refineries.[26]

The Jersey refineries also participated in producing a blending agent for raising the performance of aviation gasoline for limited periods of high power. In the middle of 1942, military authorities asked for fuels that would outperform conventional aviation gasoline during take-off or for quick surges of power in flight. Such an operation is characterized by the use of relatively rich mixtures—that is, with high fuel-air ratios—to provide maximum power and to suppress knocking. The request of the military led to the production of 100/130 grade gasoline—the 100 indicates the octane rating under the cruise or "lean" mixture condition and the 130 the rating of the "rich" or take-off mixtures. This 100/130 rating was reached by adding to the 100-octane fuel a synthetic product known as cumene (isopropyl benzene), which was made by a Shell process offered free to the oil industry. In September, 1942, the first of Jersey's wartime units for cumene production was provided for by converting a nonselective polymer plant at Baton Rouge to the production of this blending agent. This was the beginning of a substantial cumene and 100/130 grade aviation fuel output by Jersey refineries.[27]

As the production of these high-octane mixtures rose, the volume of the base stock also had to be increased. At first, high-grade gasoline made from selected crudes by distillation was used. High-temperature thermal cracking also contributed. Catalytic cracking produced not only more base stock but also gasoline with a higher octane rating. Jersey's fluid catalytic cracking was developed for large-scale production just in time to meet war emergencies. By November, 1942, three affiliates had "cat crackers" in use and several more were being built. By November, 1943, when the first plant of Shell—another leading producer of 100-octane gasoline—was completed, Jersey had five units in operation and three others nearing completion. These produced both high-octane base stock in large volume and increasing amounts of the scarce butylenes for making blending mixtures.[28]

By blending increasing volumes of high-octane hydrocarbon mixtures and four cubic centimeters of tetraethyl lead per gallon with gasolines rating up to 91 octanes, the Jersey refineries were able to exceed their

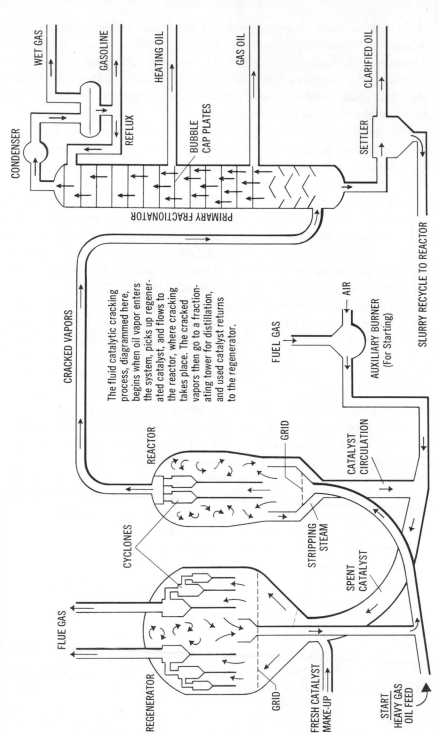

FLUID CATALYTIC CRACKING UNIT

WET GAS

GASOLINE

HEATING OIL

GAS OIL

CLARIFIED OIL

CONDENSER

REFLUX

BUBBLE
CAP PLATES

SETTLER

PRIMARY FRACTIONATOR

SLURRY RECYCLE TO REACTOR

CRACKED VAPORS

The fluid catalytic cracking
process, diagrammed here,
begins when oil vapor enters
the system, picks up regenerated catalyst, and flows to
the reactor, where cracking
takes place. The cracked
vapors then go to a fractionating tower for distillation,
and used catalyst returns
to the regenerator.

AIR

FUEL GAS

AUXILIARY BURNER
(For Starting)

REACTOR

GRID

CATALYST
CIRCULATION

CYCLONES

STRIPPING
STEAM

SPENT
CATALYST

FLUE GAS

REGENERATOR

GRID

FRESH CATALYST
MAKE-UP

START
HEAVY GAS
OIL FEED

original planned 100-octane gasoline production. Their daily production, which was approximately 13,000 barrels at the beginning of 1942, was raised to 43,000 barrels in December. Within the same year, the entire American oil industry, inclusive of Jersey's figure, had increased its 100-octane total; the daily average in December, 1942, was 124,350 barrels. The industry's "quickie" program had succeeded beyond expectations.[29]

By this time, however, the expansion based on refinery facilities existing or nearing completion when the United States entered the war had nearly reached its limit. Some increase was to come from the more efficient utilization of plants and from the modification of processes resulting from more effective control of operations and continued research. But henceforth the greatly increased needs were to be supplied largely by refinery construction undertaken after the attack on Pearl Harbor.

In expanding their production of aviation gasoline, the affiliates were protected by contracts with the Defense Supplies Corporation, a government agency organized to make long-term purchase contracts with companies for military supplies. Those entered into by two Jersey affiliates early in 1942 set goals for 100-octane gasoline manufacture and stated the conditions under which they would supply the government with this product.[30]

As estimates of the requirements of the Allies were raised, the Jersey affiliates made plans to step up their production. Again and again they increased their output. So great was the need that in 1943, despite uncertainty concerning the manufacturing process and even the usefulness of the product as a blending agent, at the Army's urgent request one hydrogenation unit at Baton Rouge was converted to the production of xylidene. This product did not prove a satisfactory substitute for cumene; however, for a time it was blended with gasoline used for training purposes in the United States. In the last quarter of 1943, the affiliates had an "equivalent" production—that is, actual production plus potential production with unblended alkylate—averaging 60,723 barrels daily.[31]

After most of the wartime refinery construction had been completed, there was still demand for additional supplies of aviation gasoline. In April, 1944, the PAW announced that the need was becoming critical. The mounting activity in Europe preceding the invasion of Normandy was consuming 50 per cent more gasoline than had been anticipated, and there was serious danger that military action would be hampered unless additional supplies could be provided. The PAW inquired of Jersey whether a price increase would encourage companies to expand their output; the reply was that the Jersey refineries were already producing the maximum and an increase in the price would be of no avail.[32] The government agency requested all refineries in the United States to take every possible step to ensure maximum production, and the authorities allowed the temporary diversion of butylene feed stocks from the rubber program to the manufacture of aviation gasoline.[33]

By various means, the Jersey affiliates increased their equivalent production to a daily average of 96,290 barrels in the third quarter of 1944. During July their 100-octane gasoline deliveries from refineries in the United States and at Aruba exceeded 100,000 barrels daily, a figure that was surpassed in September and October. However, these deliveries were in excess of what was being currently manufactured and hence reduced inventories. In October industry production finally began to increase faster than consumption, supplies became ample, and modest inventories were accumulated.[34]

With the collapse of Germany in May, 1945, production facilities at last became excessive. The equivalent production of the Jersey affiliates dropped to a daily average of 45,460 barrels in the third quarter of the year. In the fourth quarter, it fell to a daily average of 3,340 barrels.[35]

During the war years, on an equivalent basis the Jersey refineries produced more than a fifth of the 100-octane gasoline consumed by the Allies, not including Russia. As in the case of toluene, their production of aviation fuel relative to the whole industry's was larger in the period of critical shortages in 1942 and 1943 than later. Then, an average of one out of every four Allied planes was fueled by the affiliates' gasoline; toward the war's end affiliates supplied fuel for one out of every five planes. In addition, two of the three refineries in the world that produced as much as a billion gallons of 100-octane fuel during the war belonged to Jersey companies—the Baytown and Baton Rouge refineries. Two of the most important processes involved—fluid catalytic cracking and an alkylation process—were the result in large part of research and development carried on by Jersey affiliates before America entered the conflict. A letter sent after the war by an executive of the Reconstruction Finance Corporation to Standard Oil Company of New Jersey (the contractor for sale to the government of the Jersey refineries' aviation gasoline) expressed appreciation for "the magnificent job you and your associates and employees have done in producing an almost unbelievable quantity of aviation gasoline and lubricants which have contributed so much to an earlier conclusion of both the European and Pacific wars than would otherwise have been possible."[36]

SYNTHETIC RUBBER AND BUTADIENE

Japan's attack on Pearl Harbor did not at once vitalize the government's rubber program; there was still confidence in Britain's Singapore bastion and in the British and American fleets in the Pacific. The small program already decided upon was put into effect. By the end of 1941, however, the government's program for the stockpiling of natural rubber had failed. The total national inventory at the end of the year was little more than 500,000 tons, approximately two-thirds of that year's consumption. In January, with the southward advance of the Japanese, the threat to the source of America's rubber supply became indisputably clear. Obviously the United States would have to furnish the Allies with synthetic rubber.[37]

In January, 1942, the planned program under the Rubber Reserve Company was expanded from 40,000 to 400,000 tons per year. After the fall of Singapore in February, this amount was increased to 805,000 tons annually. This total was to consist of 40,000 tons of Du Pont's neoprene for special uses requiring resistance to oils, 60,000 tons of Jersey's Butyl for fabricating tubes, barrage balloons, and other pneumatic products, and 705,000 tons of Jersey's general-purpose Buna-S. The program provided for qualified companies to construct plants for the Defense Plant Corporation and to operate them and sell the products to the Rubber Reserve Company on the basis of costs plus a fixed fee.[38]

The way was also cleared for a full sharing of rights, knowledge, and techniques having to do with the manufacture of synthetic rubber and its basic components. A few days after America entered the war, Jersey and other companies having processes for the manufacture of the rubber itself signed an agreement providing for the cross-licensing of patents and the interchange of technical information. A committee was set up under the Rubber Reserve Company to administer the exchange. Under the agreement, Standard Oil Development Company was to receive a royalty of 1 per cent on the cost or sale price of Buna. In February, 1942, similar arrangements, in which Jersey and its affiliates participated, were made for companies to make available without remuneration all their processes and technical information bearing on the production of butadiene. On March 11 Jersey proposed to license its Butyl patent, royalty free, to operators under the government program, an offer which was embodied in a formal agreement in May. In March, under the Consent Decree of

1942, the company relinquished for the war period all royalties from its patents having to do with the manufacture of Buna-S rubber.[39] (See Chapter 15.)

It would have been difficult at best to create a whole new rubber industry under war conditions, but the development of the manufacture of synthetic rubber was attended by long and delaying controversy. The congressional hearings in Washington in the spring of 1942, before the Committee on National Defense and the Committee on Patents, raised doubts in the public mind concerning the government's rubber program. A segment of the oil industry urged that a butane-to-butylene process developed by Phillips Petroleum Company be used for making butadiene on the ground that insufficient butylene was available. However, to have built the necessary plants would have taken materials that were in short supply and used up invaluable time. Both Jersey and Shell maintained that the fluid catalytic cracking plant then nearing completion and many similar units under construction would provide sufficient butylene for making butadiene as well as other essential products.[40] The doubts about the government's rubber program encouraged a different group to promote another method of producing synthetic rubber, a diversion which caused a delay of many months in accomplishing anything decisive. This group undertook to bring about the use of alcohol made from surplus grain for the manufacture of butadiene. The resulting investigations by the Subcommittee of the Senate Committee on Agriculture and Forestry—the Gillette Committee noted in Chapter 15—led to legislation that was designed to displace the rubber program already being put into effect by the Rubber Reserve Company.[41]

In August, 1942, Congress passed a bill, known as the Rubber Supply Act of 1942, providing for a new and independent agency with unlimited powers to arrange for the manufacture of an adequate supply of synthetic rubber from agricultural and forest products. By this time, the issue had become so controversial that even America's leading ally had become alarmed. President Roosevelt vetoed the act on August 6.

In order to clarify this dangerously chaotic situation, the President appointed a committee, consisting of Bernard M. Baruch as chairman and two scientists of international reputation—James B. Conant, president of Harvard University, and Karl T. Compton, president of Massachusetts Institute of Technology—"to investigate the whole situation and to recommend such action as will produce the rubber necessary for our total war effort . . . with a minimum interference with the production of other weapons of war."[42]

The Baruch Committee, in its report of September 10, 1942, based on a comprehensive investigation, endorsed the Rubber Reserve Company's program without reservation. The committee recommended certain minor changes, primarily to ensure a supply of synthetic rubber in a shorter time than had been planned. The burden of the report was that the need for rubber was so critically urgent that the production in 1943 of 100,000 tons, more or less, of Buna-S might be the determining factor in the outcome of the war. The committee expressed full confidence in the processes adopted for use in the rubber program and in the men of the industry who were responsible for carrying out the plans. It recommended the appointment of a rubber director to expedite the construction of plants and to speed up operations.[43] This report virtually settled the rubber controversy.[44]

To have charge of "bulling through" (in Baruch's words) the construction of plants and of facilitating the additional research and development still required for converting from a natural to a synthetic rubber industry, President Roosevelt at once established the Office of Rubber Production and gave it broad powers. William M. Jeffers, president of the Union Pacific Railroad, was appointed Rubber Director, and Colonel Bradley Dewey was made operating executive. The Rubber Reserve Company, however, remained the permanent agency responsible for the over-all program, and the Petroleum Administration for War bore responsibility for the coordination of the oil industry's contribution to it.[45]

The government program, as amended in the autumn of 1942, authorized the conversion or building of plants to manufacture 920,000 tons of synthetic rubber per year and also other plants to produce the necessary raw materials. The rubber to be manufactured was to be made up of 739,200 tons of Buna-S and 68,000 of Butyl under Jersey patents, 60,000 tons of neoprene, and 53,000 of Thiokol. Standard of Louisiana and Humble were authorized to build and operate plants to produce the Butyl, but Buna-S production was assigned to rubber companies.[46]

The production of the butadiene required for Buna-S manufacture was assigned to qualified petroleum and chemical companies, which were to operate government-owned plants. Approximately a third of the plant capacity for the manufacture of butadiene was allocated to chemical companies and was planned to use grain alcohol and the alcohol process developed by Carbide & Carbon Chemical Corporation. The remaining capacity was assigned to petroleum companies; they were to utilize principally the Jersey butylene dehydrogenation process and, on a much smaller scale, another Jersey process and the Phillips and Houdry butane processes. The large assignment to butylene dehydrogenation plants was supported by the greatly increased butylene production from the new fluid catalytic plants and by Jersey's discovery that the butylene yield of a catalytic cracker could be multiplied by stepping up the temperature.[47]

Jersey proposed to the government's Rubber Reserve Company a special postwar rubber policy. Under the Consent Decree of 1942, as already noted, its Buna-S patents were made available to the industry without charge during the war. To encourage cooperation with the government program as well as to promote the development of the production of Buna-S—the principal component of which was butadiene—Jersey offered to the Rubber Reserve Company a free license for the life of the Buna-S patents with "the right to issue perpetual free licenses to everyone who cooperates with the Government in its war rubber program, and who reciprocates with similar licenses under its own patents." This offer was made on the condition that "the Government would agree to continue to expand its expenditures for research in the synthetic rubber field up to an aggregate amount of not less than $5,000,000." An agreement embodying this proposal was signed in August, 1943.[48]

The principal contribution of the Jersey affiliates to actual wartime rubber production was in the manufacture of butadiene. When the United States entered the war, one small steam cracking plant was producing this material at Baton Rouge, and plans had been made to build another. Baton Rouge and Humble's Ingleside refinery supplied two of four plants converted by the industry under the "quickie" program to produce butadiene by means of Jersey's process for high-temperature, low-pressure steam cracking of naphtha. The largest units of the Jersey affiliates under the program of the United States government were a butylene dehydrogenation plant at Baton Rouge with an estimated annual capacity of 21,000 tons and another at Baytown intended to produce 42,000 tons. Imperial operated a butylene dehydrogenation unit for the Canadian government at Sarnia, Ontario. The last of the affiliates' plants to be completed went into operation in October, 1943. That at Baton Rouge merits special mention because its successful operation was one of the most critical requirements of the whole Buna-S program. This full-scale plant was constructed on the basis of laboratory-scale data on an entirely new process. Although this was the first such installation built, it performed successfully. It reached capacity operation almost immediately and maintained full production throughout the war period.[49]

The butadiene plants of the affiliates were soon operating in high gear. Standard of Louisiana and Humble provided 32,300 tons of butadiene in 1943, 70,600 tons in 1944, and 85,700 tons in 1945. These two companies produced 14 per cent of all the butadiene made in the United States in these three years and 29.1 per cent of that derived from petroleum.[50]

The manufacture of Butyl by the Jersey affiliates did not progress so smoothly. In getting the process into large-scale production, the engineers ran into difficulties far beyond anything they had anticipated. Although the process was theoretically simple, Jersey had spent large sums on research after it had been discovered—in 1940 and 1941, alone, about a million dollars. The company had undertaken to build a small experimental plant at Baton Rouge. Early in 1942, the Rubber Reserve Company decided to include this unit in the government program and extended it into a three-unit plant with an annual production of 30,000 tons. Rubber Reserve also authorized the building of a large unit at Baytown. These plants were to be built without the regular pilot-plant testing. Further laboratory experimentation convinced the company engineers that the capacity of a plant could be greatly increased by using a cold-screen method of extracting the rubber from the liquid in which it was formed; accordingly, they changed the design to incorporate this feature. But when the first unit at Baton Rouge went into operation at the beginning of 1943, this method proved unsuccessful, and the engineers returned to their original design. Although production was still not satisfactory, the need for rubber was so urgent that the Rubber Reserve Company advised that operations be continued. The managers of the plants found themselves in an impossible situation: production problems could not be solved without experimenting, but government pressure was being exerted to maximize production and minimize experimentation. Finally, in August, 1943, matters reached such a point that the Rubber Director inquired whether there was any justification for continuing this expensive experiment.[51]

Facing the disgrace of a shutdown and under heavy pressure from the government, Jersey executives proposed that one of the three units at Baton Rouge be taken out of production for use as an experimental plant, the cost of operation and of any necessary improvements to be borne by the company. The Rubber Reserve Company agreed to this proposal. Then followed a period of still more discouraging effort. So critical was the need to get manufacture under way that Jersey's President Gallagher requested reports three times a day from Baton Rouge. Not until the end of May, 1944, had all the difficulties been eliminated and a satisfactory process worked out—at a cost to the participating Jersey affiliates of $800,000. The necessary changes were made in the Baton Rouge and Baytown plants, both of which soon operated satisfactorily. They produced 47,800 tons in 1945.[52]

Months before the Butyl problem was fully solved—in fact, by the middle of 1944—the success of the American synthetic rubber program was assured, and the threat of a serious rubber shortage no longer existed. Success came just in time: at the end of 1943, American stocks of natural rubber stood at only 139,500 tons, about a third of the reduced consumption of the previous year. Starting with a very small production in 1942, the output of synthetic rubber in government-owned plants in the United States rose to 737,000 long tons (2,240 pounds per ton) in 1944, the first year when all the plants were in operation.[53]

William Jeffers, the federal Rubber Director, had said in 1943, "Had it not been for the research and engineering work carried on by Standard Oil Company of New Jersey prior to Pearl Harbor, the synthetic rubber program would be one and a half or two years behind what it is now."[54] Jersey's principal direct contributions to this rubber program were its Buna-S and butadiene processes and techniques. Buna-S constituted 90 per cent of the total synthetic rubber made under the government's program. And butadiene made from petroleum provided 46 per cent of that product utilized in the manufacture of Buna-S.[55]

Jersey affiliates also contributed to the production of synthetic rubber in Canada and Russia, the two other allied countries manufacturing this product. The Canadian government financed the building of an integrated rubber project at Sarnia, Ontario. This included a Butyl plant with a rated annual capacity of 7,000 tons and a plant to produce sufficient butadiene for making 30,000 tons of Buna-S. Imperial Oil operated both plants, furnishing butylenes from its own refinery and using Jersey processes. The aid to Russia was at the request of the United States Department of State. A Soviet group visited the Baton Rouge refinery and obtained designs for a plant to manufacture alcohol from petroleum by Jersey's process—it similarly secured from Du Pont a license for manufacturing neoprene. The United States government obtained little of value from the Russians, from whom it had expected to receive data on the production of a Buna-type of rubber from grain alcohol. The Russians, having obtained the Jersey process, could utilize petroleum gases for making alcohol for rubber manufacture and thus save their grain for other purposes.[56]

MAJORS, PETROCHEMICALS, AND SPECIALTY PRODUCTS

Such old majors as gasolines, lubricants, and fuel oils necessarily bulked large in the total wartime output of refineries. There was also a greatly increased demand for industrial alcohols, and for asphalt in large quantities for building military roads and airfield runways. In addition, a wide range of specialties was required; among them were insecticides, jellied gasoline for flame throwers and incendiary bombs, smoke generators for concealing military movements, and also fog dispersers for airfields.[57]

The Jersey affiliates made large volumes of industrial alcohols. Although the synthetic product constituted only approximately one-tenth of the total wartime alcohol output in the United States, it was indispensable because of the greatly enlarged demand. Its production was under strict government regulation. One of the two leading producers of this synthetic from petroleum in the United States, Jersey invested $9,000,000 in alcohol plants during the war. Standard Oil Company of New Jersey, Standard of Louisiana, and Humble produced three types of alcohol and their by-products. These were isopropyl alcohol made from propylene, ethyl alcohol from ethylene, and secondary butyl alcohol from butylenes. In 1942 the capacity of the plants for the manufacture of isopropyl alcohol was increased at the Baton Rouge and Baytown refineries. This type had many uses: as an antifreeze for radiators of motor equipment; as a frost preventive for airplane carburetors, bomber noses, and gun turrets; as a component in the manufacture of cordite (an explosive); and as an ingredient in the making of plastic parts for airplanes. Jersey's first ethyl alcohol plant went into operation at Baton Rouge in March, 1943. This alcohol was used principally in the manufacture of butadiene and gunpowder. Secondary butyl alcohol was especially important in producing methyl ethyl ketone (MEK). This product was used mainly for coating fabrics to enable them to withstand extreme temperatures, dampness, and fungi; it was also used for dewaxing aviation oil. The Bayway refinery produced about half of the total United States output of MEK.[58]

Jersey also participated in adapting the wartime manufacture of lubricants to new needs. Its research men and specialists in this field worked closely with branches of the United States military organization, especially as technical consultants for the Navy and Army air forces. They were sent where difficulties occurred—for example, to Alaska to work on problems involving lubricating oils which were impeding Air Force operations. They similarly cooperated with manufacturers in determining the proper lubricants and rust preventives for such specialized equipment as aircraft flexible cables, resistors, radar, communications equipment, and electrically operated machine-gun turret mounts.

Humble supplied especially large quantities of high-quality lubricants. It had discovered in the 1930's how to make the very best lubes from plentiful crudes that had formerly been unsatisfactory for this purpose. The product proved suitable for use in aviation engines, and for this reason nearly all Humble's output of such lubricants was used for the engines of Army and Navy airplanes.[59]

The Jersey group was the leading supplier of hydraulic oils for the armed services. Univis oils, developed by affiliates before the war, were quickly adapted for use in hydraulic operating mechanisms on military aircraft, in gunfire controls on naval vessels, and in similar equipment on tanks and antiaircraft guns. As operating strains on these mechanisms increased in intensity, Jersey worked on the improvement of the oils. When it became clear to the government late in 1942 that the industry's capacity for producing aircraft hydraulic oil was far short of anticipated needs, Jersey supplied information based on its experience and helped to stimulate production by other companies. The shipments of the affiliates increased from a total of 132,600 gallons in 1942 to 1,179,000 in 1944.[60]

Jersey companies helped solve specific lubricating problems by utilizing certain additives developed on the basis of information received by Standard Oil Development from I.G. Farben in the 1930's. Paraflow inhibited the solidifying of wax in oils in low temperatures. Paratone reduced the change in the viscosity of oils with shifts in temperatures. A wartime improvement on Paranox—known as Paranox 56—reduced oxidation and sludging, thus minimizing the corrosion of hard-alloy bearings. Paranox also contributed to the standardization of lube oils. In 1943 Paranox 56 was improved so that it helped solve a Navy problem by preventing the emulsifying of heavy-duty oils.

The demand for lubricants containing these additives rose throughout the war. The Essolube HD type containing Paranox 56 was used in all kinds of military equipment and marine diesels. As early as 1943, Paranox accounted for 40 per cent of all the lubricating specialties sold by Jersey affiliates. The demand for Paraflow and Paratone also increased, not only because of more extensive military operations but particularly because of the greater range of temperatures in which airplanes and ground automotive equipment had to operate. The United States government restricted the use of Paratone to American military forces and participants in Lend-Lease.[61]

Jersey was called upon by United States government agencies to supply information on lubricants to representatives of the Soviet government. Russia imported Lend-Lease lubricants, but it also manufactured some itself. On the request of the Petroleum Administration for War, Jersey made available to the Russians information on the Voltol process for the manufacture of aviation lubes. And on the advice of the Department of State and the PAW, it acceded to a request for assistance in meeting specific corrosion, gumming, and low-temperature problems.[62]

Associated with work on improving lubricants was the development of preventives of rust and corrosion. Even before the United States entered the war, it was evident that something must be done to prevent Lend-Lease shipments from arriving overseas in a badly rusted condition. The problem became increasingly serious as military equipment was exposed more and more to salt water and salt-laden air and to the humidity of the tropics. Jersey research developed a series of rust preventives marketed under the Rust-Ban trade name. These rust inhibitors were blended with petroleum products, and some were designed to meet special conditions. Rust-Ban 603 and 604, for example, were developed to protect the interior surfaces of internal combustion engines and to neutralize the acidic condition that results from the combustion of most motor fuels. Rust-Ban 392 completely displaced water on the surface of metals and by coating the surface gave excellent protection in indoor storage. Without rust preventives, much overseas war equipment would not have been fit for service on arrival. Jersey affiliates shipped for military use 76,800,000 pounds of these materials.[63]

Among the specialty greases produced by the affiliates, three were particularly important. These were Beacon Lubricant M-285 for antifriction bearings and certain gears at low temperatures, Andok Lubricant C for ball and roller bearings under both high and low temperatures, and what came to be known as "Eisenhower grease."[64]

The making of this grease illustrates how the need for quick action and improvisation could be met. In 1943 General Eisenhower in North Africa dispatched to the Ordnance Department in Washington an urgent request for a large order of an unfamiliar type of grease. At once the request was submitted to Jersey. The grease required was to be similar to an English type containing asbestos. It was needed as soon as possible for use as a sealing compound to prevent the seepage of water into engines during amphibious landings in the projected invasion of Sicily and Italy.

Late on Monday, May 31, 1943, the Esso Laboratories of Standard Oil Development received a sample of the English grease; the last of the grease order was to be delivered the following Sunday. The sample was analyzed, specifications were drawn up, and the purchase of the necessary asbestos was arranged for after several discouraging replies had been received from companies approached. The grease works at the Baltimore refinery, which had been assigned the job, was ready to go ahead as soon as the specifications were available. The basic product was prepared, but the asbestos did not arrive on schedule. It came hours late, at noon on Wednesday, escorted by Maryland State Police called to locate a missing truck on the road and speed its arrival. Trouble was met in working the grease, which was made heavy and claylike by the asbestos. But just before the deadline at 6:00 p.m. on June 6, the last of the 45,000-pound order was delivered by Army trucks, with police escort, at the overseas shipping point in New York. At that time, Army Ordnance had already requested 260,000 additional pounds to be ready for shipment with a convoy leaving New York on June 11. This new order was assigned to Jersey's Pittsburgh Grease Works, which was better equipped than Baltimore to handle heavy greases. Even in the Pittsburgh plant, the strain on the electric motors was so great that they had to be cooled with streams of compressed air. But the grease was delivered on schedule. The last fifty-five drums were rushed to New York by bombers of the Air Transport Command. Still another rush order had to be filled over the Fourth of July week end. The grease performed its function well, and orders continued to come. In 1945 the Pittsburgh works produced more than 3,000,000 pounds of Eisenhower grease.[65]

Table 16 gives a statistical picture of changes in the manufacture of major products by the Jersey refineries. The old majors constituted by far the largest portion of the total volume. The one produced in greatest volume and increasing the most in amount from 1941 to 1944, the last full year of war, was residual fuel, which was used for bunkering ships and providing power for industrial plants. Next in volume was gasoline other than the aviation fuel, but it was made in smaller volume in 1944 than in 1941. Less kerosene was also made in 1944 than in 1941. The output of aviation gasoline, on the contrary, more than quintupled. When the end of the war came at mid-year 1945, however, the drop in requirements for airplane fuels and the rise in the production of other gasolines—as well as

Table 16: **ANNUAL PRODUCTION AND PERCENTAGE YIELDS OF WESTERN HEMISPHERE REFINERIES OF AFFILI- ATES, 1941–1945**
Standard Oil Company (New Jersey)

Products (in thousands of 42-gallon barrels)	1941	1942	1943	1944	1945
Aviation gasoline	6,751	14,314	24,158	39,213	23,985
All other gasoline[a]	98,648	73,065	74,281	86,609	104,868
Total gasoline[a]	105,399	87,379	98,439	125,822	128,853
Kerosene	17,747	12,594	14,657	14,668	18,815
Distillates	56,143	49,674	57,144	59,814	66,897
Residual fuel	114,288	94,610	124,890	161,869	166,527
Lubricating oils	7,319	6,622	6,380	8,095	7,863
Other products and loss	24,290	25,030	32,596	42,312	38,644
Total products[b]	325,186	275,911	334,106	412,580	427,599
Percentage Yields[c]					
Aviation gasoline	2.1	5.3	7.3	9.5	5.6
All other gasoline	29.7	25.6	21.6	20.5	24.1
Total gasoline	31.8	30.9	28.9	30.0	29.7
Kerosene	5.5	4.6	4.4	3.6	4.4
Distillates	17.4	18.2	17.3	14.6	15.7
Residual fuel	35.5	34.7	37.7	39.5	39.2
Lubricating oils	2.3	2.4	1.9	2.0	1.9
Other products and loss	7.5	9.2	9.8	10.3	9.1
Total yields	100.0	100.0	100.0	100.0	100.0

a Includes natural gasoline (thousands of barrels):
1941, 3,044; 1942, 3,278; 1943, 2,667; 1944,
2,350; 1945, 2,466.
b Includes crude oil, process oils, and natural
gasoline blended.

c Calculated on total throughput.
Source: Standard Oil Company (New Jersey),
Annual Statistical Review.

an increase in the output of kerosene—signified a return to supplying products for civilian use on a notably less restricted basis.

MISCELLANEOUS CONTRIBUTIONS TO PRODUCTS FOR WAR

During the war, Jersey affiliates and employees participated in many activities under government contract or sponsorship to provide products not necessarily involving petroleum. Gilbert & Barker Manufacturing Company became fully occupied with the manufacture of military equipment. Standard Oil Development and research groups in other affiliates participated in projects under the war programs of the United States and Britain. In the United States, personnel of the affiliates worked in their own laboratories on special projects under contracts with the Army, the Navy, the National Defense Research Council, or the Office of Scientific Research and Development. In addition, many employees were granted leaves to work in large government-sponsored laboratories manned by scientists and engineers from industrial concerns and educational and research institutions.

Gilbert & Barker, a wholly owned affiliate in Springfield, Massachusetts, which normally manufactured gasoline pumps and oil heating equipment, lost its outlets when the marketers almost ceased to install new oil furnaces in homes and pumps at service stations. Even before the severe drop had come in its normal operations, this company had begun to convert to making parts for military equipment. In 1939 it had undertaken to make fuse adapters for 14-inch and 16-inch projectiles for the Navy; the next year it began to manufacture fire-control equipment for antiaircraft guns for the Frankfort Arsenal.

In 1942 this company discontinued the manufacture of its regular products and converted entirely to war work; it greatly increased its employment and operated its facilities around the clock. The plant became a center for the wartime production of fuse setters. It also manufactured many other parts for military equipment, including cooling equipment and oil gears for antiaircraft guns, steering engines for torpedoes, sights for 6-inch guns on light cruisers, and control parts for Navy Hell Cat and Avenger planes. One of the problems to be met was the rapid obsolescence of many items and the necessity for frequent adjustments to revised designs and schedules. In addition to its manufacturing, Gilbert & Barker served as headquarters for the Remote Control Integrating Committee of the Army Ordnance Association.[66]

Standard Oil Development was active in designing several mechanical specialties. Early in the war, when the Army needed a better smoke generator for concealing troop movements than the one available, the task of developing it was assigned to Jersey's research affiliate and to the research organizations of several other companies. After competitive tests, the Esso Smoke Generator was selected by the Army; it was later designated by the Chemical Warfare Service as the M-1 Smoke Generator. Throughout the war, it was used to blanket movements of the Army and the Navy. The Army used it to provide a screen along a 66-mile battlefront in crossing the Rhine in the spring of 1945. Standard Oil Development also worked with the British on a smokeless and nonluminous gasoline burner for dispersing fog at airports. In addition, company engineers provided consulting services during the designing, installing, and testing of a mile-long fog-dispersal unit at Wright Field in Ohio.[67]

Several months before the attack on Pearl Harbor, the Chemical Warfare Service—through the National Defense Research Council—gave Standard Oil Development an assignment to develop a new incendiary bomb filled with a petroleum product. Gasoline was chosen as the fuel to be used, and experiments at the company's laboratories and at the Massachusetts Institute of Technology indicated that a relatively moderate rate of burning and adhesiveness to the target increased the destructive power of the fuel. It was discovered that gasoline thickened with a jelling agent called napalm, which was made chiefly from naphthenic acid, would burn slowly with intense heat. A bomb was designed to ignite the fuel on landing and to spread the "gel gas" as far as 100 feet. Tests were made under a wide range of conditions, and, less than a year after the project was undertaken, quantity production of the bomb was begun.[68]

In March, 1942, the Chemical Warfare Service gave Standard Oil Development and Gilbert & Barker Manufacturing Company the assignment to improve the Army's flame thrower. The weapon then in use had a maximum range of only 50 feet, and all but from 5 to 10 per cent of the fuel burned before reaching the target. The Jersey engineers, after designing and testing a portable mechanized flame thrower, concluded that the Army's old device could be adapted to the use of thickened gasoline, with a resulting range up to 180 feet and with the added improvement that as much as 70 per cent of the fuel would reach the target. This unit was accepted and standardized by the Army as the M-1 Portable Flame Thrower. It was first used by the Marines at Peleliu.[69]

Humble Oil & Refining Company and The Carter Oil Company also participated in government research. They had highly skilled geophysical staffs which they made available to the government. Men with knowledge of electronics being especially needed, nearly all of Humble's senior geophysicists were granted leaves to work with various government research groups, including the Radio Research Laboratory at Harvard University, the Applied Physics Laboratory at Johns Hopkins University, and the Radiation Laboratory at Massachusetts Institute of Technology. Both Humble and Carter also did research in their own laboratories for the government. Under various contracts, Humble designed and built radar-test and harbor detection equipment and did other highly classified work. Carter converted its entire research organization to war projects. Its laboratories worked on developing safety devices for VTX fuses, self-destruction fuses, general safety devices, and radar equipment, and on measuring the effects of various explosives and missiles.[70]

Two executives of Standard Oil Development Company participated in the administration of government research organizations. Robert P. Russell, president of the company from 1944 on, served as chief of a division of the government's Office of Scientific Research and Development until February, 1943, and later as consultant on various matters. E. V. Murphree, vice-president of the company from 1944 on, served with the Office of Scientific Research and Development as a member of the S-1 Executive Committee headed by James B. Conant, president of Harvard University. Murphree was made chairman of a planning board, organized from this committee, which became responsible for the technical and engineering aspects of the famous Manhattan Project (atomic bomb). This group was responsible for the procurement of the required materials and for the construction of pilot plants and full-sized production facilities. Murphree also directed the construction of a heavy-water plant in British Columbia, which was designed from a process standpoint by Jersey's research organization, and he supervised much of the work on the centrifugal method of separating uranium isotopes.[71]

The contribution of the Jersey group's manufacturing organizations to the cause of the Allies illustrates at its best the notable achievement of the American refining industry during the war. It was difficult enough under war conditions for the industry to expand so greatly the volume of output of petroleum products. A strategic contribution was the tremendous technological and managerial achievement which telescoped into a few crucial years the development of processes and the construction of equipment for producing new products indispensable to the success of the Allies.

Chapter 19

Oil Transport by Land and Sea, 1942–1945

TRANSPORTATION has been called the most critical branch of the oil industry's operations during the war. The situation as to ocean transport was particularly serious. If enough tankers had not come through to areas of combat around the globe, the fighting power of the Allies might have been disastrously weakened. There was never sufficient tonnage to supply military and civilian requirements in the Eastern Hemisphere and at the same time to carry oil by normal sea routes to Western Hemisphere refineries and markets. Hence, so far as possible, tankers had to be released from carrying oil between points in the Americas, particularly from United States ports on the Gulf of Mexico to the Atlantic coastal regions with industries vital to the military forces of the Allies. It became necessary to utilize existing facilities for overland transport to their limit and to build new ones as rapidly as possible. New carriers by land were also required on other continents where ports were seized by the enemy, as in China, or to follow military campaigns inland from tanker unloading points. Despite losses from enemy action and shortages of manpower and materials, oil had to be kept moving in vast quantities from wells to refineries and from refineries to worldwide points of consumption.

JERSEY TANKERS AT WAR

Because of the strategic importance of overseas transport and the consequent need to employ tankers as efficiently as possible regardless of their ownership or the risks involved, the Allies established close governmental controls of tankers and their use. Two major agencies coordinated the shipping of the Allies excepting Russia. The British Ministry of War Transport directed tankers flying the British flag and also those of Norway and other Allies; the companies owning the ships constituted a pool to operate them in the general interest. In the United States the War Shipping Administration, established in February, 1942, was the central agency for controlling the use of ships. The WSA requisitioned all United States–flag tankers of over 3,000 gross tons, and, with the acquiescence of the government of Panama, it similarly requisitioned tankers under that country's flag. The agency also took charge of ships built later during the war for the government or private concerns. WSA tankers were handled by the agency's Tanker Division, which allocated the ships to the military, which had priority, and to other users; it licensed companies as agents of the WSA to operate the tankers, and followed through on their assignments. These British and American agencies cooperated through a combined board that had representation in both London and Washington.

The United States and the United Kingdom also controlled the building of new tankers. Each gave government agencies priority over private companies. In the United States, the Maritime Commission had authority over all tanker construction. It had charge of the government's large building program, under which more than 700 tankers, totaling 11,400,000 deadweight tons, were built in the years from 1939 to 1945.

Marine executives and operating personnel of Jersey affiliates participated in the work of government agencies and related industry bodies having to do with the over-all planning and management of tanker operations under the Allies. B. B. Howard, general manager of the Marine Department in New York, was a member of the tanker-managing subcommittee of the important Atlantic Coast district. W. F. Dunning of Standard-Vacuum served on a foreign shipping committee. J. J. Winterbottom, also of the Marine Department, was for a time tanker expediter in the Caribbean area and later director of the Tanker Division of the WSA. The Marine Department also lent employees to organizations of the government in United States ports. Out of 42 tanker expediters located in various ports around the globe, 26 were from Jersey companies. This system of government expediters was instituted after a six-month experiment in Great Britain carried on by four members of the Marine Department, including B. B. Howard, who had gone to England in July, 1942, to establish the shortest possible turnaround for tankers.[1]

Jersey men also served in ocean transport with the military forces. Many executives and other employees were doing special work in the Navy. One of these was Peter T. Lamont, a former member of the London Council, who was in active service from 1942 to 1945 as Commander in the United States Naval Reserve. He was awarded the Croix de Guerre with Gold Star by General Charles de Gaulle and the Legion of Merit by the United States. His Naval citation, dated May 30, 1945, listed services for which he was responsible as head of the Tanker Control Section of the United States Naval Forces in Europe in support of the invasion of the Continent in June, 1944: developing a program for the delivery of fully assembled aircraft on the decks of tankers; preparing a comprehensive plan for fuel and water supply to all ferry craft operating off United States assault beaches; making possible the rapid utilization of wrecked fuel facilities for servicing the various types of ships using the port of Cherbourg; planning the Le Havre fuel port; and developing the 24-hour turnaround plan for tankers in convoy.

Throughout the war, Jersey men also assisted in the construction and repair of vessels other than those of their own companies. They helped to design 198 tankers for the War Shipping Administration and supervised their construction in United States yards. Company men continued the work, undertaken before our entry into the war, of supervising the repairing of British-controlled tankers in United States yards. They directed approximately a thousand such jobs after Pearl Harbor.[2]

The company also served as an agent of the government in the operation of tankers owned by the United States. It was one of eight concerns which, at the government's request, undertook to operate the War Shipping Administration's new oil carriers as they became ready for service. In 1943 these companies organized a nonprofit corporation for this purpose, War Emergency Tankers, Inc. Each participant subscribed to the same proportion of stock that its own tanker tonnage bore to the total tonnage of the group. Jersey's share was 36.98 per cent. New ships were assigned proportionately for operation by the participating companies. At the end of 1944, an affiliate was operating 25 WSA ships. The Jersey affiliates similarly acted as agents for other government tankers, including several captured by the Allies and assigned to commercial service. Altogether, under arrangements made in 1944, the Jersey group handled more than 1,100 loadings of such vessels before the end of the war.[3]

At the time of the entry of the United States into the war, the Jersey affiliates in Allied or neutral countries had 193 oil ships totaling approximately 2,000,000 deadweight tons. (See Table 10 in Chapter 13.) Of these, 59 belonged to Standard Oil Company of New Jersey, 38 to Panama Transport, 23 to Lago Shipping, 21 to Imperial Oil, and 17 to Anglo-American. The ocean-going tankers were 123 in number with a total of 1,721,000 deadweight tons. Of this tonnage, a total of 86,300 was in the service of the United States Maritime Commission at the time.[4]

The Jersey affiliates operated their own ships within the system of government controls under which they worked. The Marine Department in New York acted as agent of the War Shipping Administration and assumed responsibilities as a time charterer for the large fleets of Standard Oil Company of New Jersey and Panama Transport requisitioned by the government. Government agencies of the United States or the United Kingdom scheduled and routed the ships of Jersey affiliates, which meant that they carried oil between points as directed. Actually, tanker routes were greatly changed during the war to conform to military requirements and the closing for a time of the Mediterranean.

The fastest Jersey tankers accompanied the fighting fleets and saw action in many naval battles, and they fueled ships while traveling on the high seas. Many helped transport the vast amounts of petroleum products needed by the United States expeditionary forces, and others carried Lend-Lease supplies for the military forces of the Allies as well as products for civilian use overseas. At nearly all times, the service was hazardous in the extreme. Ships traveled alone or in convoys. Surface raiders terrorized the sea lanes, enemy planes bombed the vessels, and submarines took their toll.

It is impossible to measure statistically the work done by the entire Jersey fleet. However, existing records show that from the outbreak of the war in 1939 to its end in 1945 the company's tankers of United States and Panamanian registry alone delivered more than 664,500,000 barrels of petroleum for military use.[5] A few examples illustrate the nature of the services performed and the dangers met.

The *Allan Jackson,* owned by Standard Oil Company of New Jersey, was the first tanker of Jersey's Western Hemisphere fleets to be sunk by the enemy after the United States entered the war. Proceeding alone along the Atlantic Coast with thirty-five men aboard and a cargo of Colombian crude, in the early hours of January 18, 1942, it was hit by two torpedoes from a German submarine. The second explosion broke the ship into two parts and set it on fire. Flames swept the decks, and blazing oil from shattered cargo tanks spread over the water. Within ten minutes the ship was gone. Because of fire and damage to gear, only one lifeboat was launched. Eight men escaped in this boat, and several others were thrown by the explosion into the water or jumped overboard and found boards to cling to. One man was picked up by the lifeboat; four others, after surviving for seven hours in the water, were saved by an American destroyer, which also rescued the men in the lifeboat. Twenty-two Americans lost their lives as a result of this attack, and five were critically injured.[6]

This was the first of many sinkings, during the destructive German submarine campaign of 1942, of Jersey tankers flying the flags of the United States and Panama. Other tankers of Standard Oil Company of New Jersey and Panama Transport were sunk on February 3, 23, 25, and 28, and on March 9, 13, 18, and 31, with further losses in subsequent months. Of the 97 ships belonging to these two affiliates on December 7, 1941, a total of 29 had been lost by the end of 1942.[7]

The *George G. Henry,* a sister ship of the *Allan Jackson,* was one of the fortunate tankers that served in dangerous waters but somehow survived mines, submarines, bombers, and other wartime perils of the sea. This vessel belonged to Panama Transport Company and was chartered to Standard-Vacuum until April 15, 1942. Its officers were American citizens—Captain Jens G. Olson, Chief Engineer Joseph E. Jacobs, and Chief Mate Simpson W. Logan—but its crew was made up of Filipinos, Malayans, and others from Allied lands in the Orient. The ship had a close call on December 10, 1941, when Japanese planes dropped bombs on Manila Bay, where it was lying at anchor with a partial load of fuel oil. It continued to lead a charmed life during the next three months and, in fact, throughout the war. It took the last load of fuel oil out of the Royal Dutch–Shell refinery at Balik Papan, Borneo, prior to the blowing up of that plant before the arrival of the Japanese. The tanker then proceeded through mine fields to the Dutch naval base at Soerabaya, Java. The day before that base was captured by the Japanese, the *Henry* left with a naval escort for a new American base at Port Darwin on the northern coast of Australia. There it fueled a warship for what proved to be that vessel's last mission. The tanker departed only a few days before the Japanese destroyed the base. It later fueled other naval vessels on the west coast of Australia, including American transports returning to the United States. It is said to have been the only tanker in the Southwest Pacific besides two Navy oilers to supply fuel oil for Allied warships in the first four months of its war service. In April, 1942, the *Henry* was taken over by the United States Navy, and under the name U.S.S. *Victoria* it served the Allies as an oiler in the Pacific until the end of the war.[8]

The *Esso Baytown* performed another type of war service. A United States–flag ship, it was a long-distance carrier to various theaters of war. This was a vessel of 13,045 deadweight tons and a capacity of 100,000 barrels. It had a succession of American captains with names of such varied national origin as Olaf Anderson, Guy A. Campbell, Walter V. James, Gustave A. Eklund, John O'Kelly, and Karl S. Johansen. Loading at such refineries as those at Caripito in Venezuela, Aruba in the Carib-

Table 17: **CHANGES IN FLEETS OF AFFILIATES, FROM DECEMBER 7, 1941, TO JUNE 30, 1945**
Standard Oil Company (New Jersey)

AFFILIATES	Owned Dec. 7, 1941	Deliveries and Purchases	Intergroup Transfers In	Intergroup Transfers Out	Sales to non-affiliates	Lost[a]	Owned June 30, 1945	Deadweight Tons (in thousands) June 30, 1945	Flag of Fleet
In Allied Countries									
Standard Oil Co. of New Jersey	59	26	1	47	19	20	—	—	United States
Standard Oil Co. (New Jersey)	—	1	45	—	—	—	44	704	United States
Panama Transport Co.	38	—	2	1	—	14	25	331	Panamanian
Petroleum Shipping Co., Ltd.[b]	8	2	—	—	—	4	6	88	Panamanian
Lago Petroleum Corp.	—	1	1	1	—	1	—	—	Panamanian
Creole Petroleum Corp.	—	10	1	—	—	1	10	54	Panamanian
Standard Oil Co. of Venezuela	ˆ4	—	1	5	—	—	—	—	Venezuelan
Cia. de Petroleo Lago	5	—	5	1	—	—	9	40	Venezuelan
International Petroleum Co., Ltd.	1	—	—	—	—	—	1	0[c]	Peruvian
Cia. Transportadora de Petroleos, S. A.[d]	5	—	—	1	—	—	4	10	Argentine
Imperial Oil Ltd.	21	—	—	—	—	3	18	93	Canadian
Lago Shipping Co., Ltd.	23	—	—	—	—	4	19	83	British
Oriental Trade & Transport Co., Ltd.	6	—	—	—	—	—	6	92	British
Anglo-American Oil Co., Ltd.	17	—	—	—	1	2	14	153	British
Belgian Overseas Transports, S.A.	2	—	—	—	—	1	1	15	Belgian
N.V. Nederlandsche Koloniale Tankvaart Maat.	4	—	—	—	—	4	—	—	Dutch
Total	**193**	**40**	**56**	**56**	**20**	**56**	**157**	**1,663**	
In Axis Countries									
Deutsch-Amerikanische Petroleum-Ges.	1	—	—	—	—	1	—	—	German
Waried Tankschiff Rhederei Ges. mbH.	1	—	—	—	—	1	—	—	German
"La Columbia," Società Marittima	4	—	—	—	—	4	—	—	Italian
N.V. Petroleum Industrie Maat.	2	—	—	—	—	2	—	—	Dutch
Det Danske Petroleums-Akt.	1	—	—	—	—	1	—	—	Danish
Standard Française des Pétroles	2	—	—	—	—	2	—	—	French
Total	**11**	**—**	**—**	**—**	**—**	**11**	**—**	**—**	

[a] Losses include sinkings, collisions, strandings, and seizures by the enemy.
[b] Oceangoing tankers belonging to Standard-Vacuum's affiliates, in which Jersey had a half-interest, were operated for the Allies.
[c] One ship of 800 deadweight tons.
[d] Tankers of this Argentine affiliate were outside the Allied effort until March 27, 1945, when Argentina joined the Allies.
Source: Esso Shipping Company, Annual Report of Marine Operations, 1940–1945.

bean, San Pedro in California, and Abadan at the head of the Persian Gulf, the *Baytown* carried cargoes to many places. These included Rio de Janeiro in Brazil, Avonmouth in England, Algiers and Capetown in Africa, Bombay in India, Sydney in Australia, and the Marshall Islands in the Southwest Pacific. On one trip, from Aruba to the Marshall Islands and back, it logged over 15,500 nautical miles in 57 days. From the beginning to the end of the war, this tanker delivered more than 8,500,000 barrels of petroleum products. Thirteen other Esso tankers, some larger and faster than the *Baytown*, carried more oil, but perhaps few if any other ships of the Jersey fleets had a more outstanding record of long-distance transport.[9]

Two Pacific voyages of the *Esso Annapolis* illustrate the tasks and the hazards of tankers at sea. This was a vessel of 16,585 deadweight tons completed for Standard Oil Company of New Jersey in 1942. The *Annapolis* left San Pedro, California, for the Fiji Islands on June 11, 1943, with nearly 100,000 barrels of special Navy fuel. En route it received diversionary orders to meet a French auxiliary cruiser at a certain point. On the way there, soon after dark one night, the watch reported a "life-boat" throwing off flashes of light. Suspecting a submarine, the captain ordered a change in the ship's course. Navy planes a few hours later sighted a submarine on the surface and sank it. After meeting and fueling the French cruiser, the *Annapolis* was ordered to proceed to the New Hebrides, where it fueled a naval task force. Then it was sent back to San Pedro for another cargo. Again it was ordered to proceed to the Fiji Islands, which it reached on November 5. In Captain LeCain's words: "On arrival at Nandi Waters, we were told that a large task force, including the battleships U.S.S. *Washington* and U.S.S. *South Dakota,* was coming in. Some 40 warships steamed into the harbor and formed a huge circle. The *Esso Annapolis,* together with two other commercial tankers and three Navy oilers, fueled the entire force."[10]

The *Beaconoil* can be described as a lifeline to Britain. An old Panama Transport vessel of some 10,000 deadweight tons, it plied the Atlantic from late in 1941 through the remainder of the war. Until July, 1944, it carried cargoes of about 75,000 barrels of fuel, diesel, and gas oil from Corpus Christi, Houston, Aruba, or New York across the Atlantic on 15 successive trips. In these transatlantic voyages, this sturdy ship reached such British ports as Swansea, Glasgow, Liverpool, Avonmouth, Londonderry, Plymouth, Grangemouth, and Scapa Flow. From July, 1944, it carried fuel oil or crude from ports on the Gulf of Mexico and in the

Caribbean to cities on the Atlantic Coast of the United States, and on frequent trips to the Panama Canal Zone.[11]

The *E. G. Seubert*, owned by Standard Oil Company of New Jersey and captained by Ivar Boklund, was one of the few Jersey tankers sunk by enemy action in the last two years of the war. This tanker had plied many seas, brought oil cargoes to many ports, fueled many ships in passage, and carried on its spar deck many fighter planes and other bulky cargo. On its last trip, in February, 1944, it was proceeding in convoy from the Abadan refinery on the Persian Gulf with a cargo of Admiralty fuel for naval operations in the Mediterranean following the Allies' landing at Anzio in Italy. East of Aden, in the dead of night, it was struck by a torpedo and sank in twelve minutes. The chief mate, steward, and boatswain and three armed guards of the United States Navy were lost.

The rescue of the *Seubert*'s clerk illustrates by how fine a thread might hang the fate of a tanker man when his ship went down. This clerk had acquired a Persian deerhound in Abadan. As he told the story later, after the ship was struck he managed to don his life jacket and to free the whimpering dog wedged between a door and a bulkhead. He got into a lifeboat with his dog only to find that the boat could not clear the sinking ship. With the animal's leash tied to his wrist, he jumped into the water. But blinded by oil "several inches deep," he was unable to see in what direction to go, and because of an injured leg he found it difficult to swim. The dog, however, paddled on. Presumably hearing voices, it towed its master safely to a life raft.[12]

Jersey tankers performed other important services besides their primary one of carrying oil. Of the five Lake Maracaibo vessels belonging to the Lago Shipping Company, Limited, which had been requisitioned by the British government, three—the *Bachaquero*, the *Misoa*, and the *Tasajera*—played unusual roles for oil carriers in the Allied war effort. These flat-bottomed tankers were converted into tank landing ships (LST's) and were used in Allied landings in North Africa, Sicily, Italy, and France. The other two, the *Inverrosa* and the *Inverruba*, served for four years as fuel oilers off the coast of West Africa without drydocking or undergoing major repairs. A few of the large and fast new National Defense Tankers sold by Jersey to the government were converted into aircraft carriers for participation in the Pacific campaign; others became Navy oilers. One of these carriers turned in a record of 117 Japanese planes damaged or destroyed and 114 ships damaged or sunk. One of the oilers held the Navy speed record for fueling at sea. Beginning in 1942, tankers in Atlantic or Pacific convoys were equipped with spar decks, on which they carried airplanes and other bulky military equipment for campaigns in Asia, Africa, and Europe. During the war months of 1945 only, Jersey tankers transported almost a thousand planes. This method of transporting aircraft proved extremely valuable. The only alternative was to box the parts and ship them under deck on dry-cargo freighters. The use of spar decks enabled the complete plane to be placed on the vessel and to be promptly taken off at its destination in condition for flying with only a modest amount of preparation.[13]

Table 17 records the number of tankers lost by Jersey affiliates in Allied countries during the period in which the United States participated in the war—a total of 56 ships. Eleven belonging to affiliates in Axis-controlled countries were also lost. All but a few of the losses on the side of the Allies were caused by enemy action.

However, the loss of tankers declined as the war progressed. The ships of Standard Oil Company of New Jersey and Panama Transport destroyed by the enemy, year by year, illustrate the reduction in Allied tanker losses. In 1942 the former company lost 17 ships and Panama Transport 12. In 1943 defensive and offensive measures reduced substantially the number of vessels lost or damaged by enemy action. In that year, the two largest Western Hemisphere fleets had a loss of three ships. In 1944 two United States–flag tankers were sunk but no Panamanian-flag vessel. In 1945 neither Panama Transport nor Standard Oil Company (New Jersey), which had taken over the United States–flag fleet of its domestic affiliate, suffered loss from the enemy.[14]

New tankers were added as fast as possible to offset losses as well as to increase tonnage. Both Great Britain and the United States gave government agencies priorities over private companies in the construction of new tankers. However, before the regulations of the United States government had begun to reduce industry orders for new ships in 1941, Standard Oil Company of New Jersey had contracted for the construction of 20 new tankers—out of an industry total of 71 on order—for completion by the end of 1943. After the new regulations went into effect, American oil companies were permitted to order only a few ocean-going tankers. However, the Jersey affiliate, like other companies, was allowed to purchase several of the government's newly built ships to replace some of those lost as casualties of war or sold to the Maritime Commission when the government was adding to its tanker fleet early in the conflict.

Furthermore, in accordance with prewar legislation, the company exchanged several old tankers for new government vessels.[15]

In 1942, also, Jersey affiliates were permitted to order, for delivery the following year, seven shallow-draft tankers to carry crude from Lake Maracaibo to Aruba. This operation had been affected by the sinking of vessels by the Germans and the requisitioning by the British of five "lakers" for use in the Eastern Hemisphere. So great was the pressure on American shipyards that these ships were built in Duluth, under the supervision of a member of the Marine Department in New York. They were brought by lakes, canals, and rivers to New Orleans, where the high masts, bridges, and other parts of the vessels were added. Several badly damaged tankers belonging to Jersey companies were repaired and returned to service. The addition of new ships and the restoration of damaged ones, however, proved insufficient to maintain the tonnage that the Jersey affiliates had had in December, 1941.[16]

The loss of men on the tankers was high. Of the Americans on Jersey vessels, 334 lost their lives after the United States entered the war. At least as many others—including Canadian, British, Danish, Norwegian, and Dutch subjects and natives of the islands of the Pacific—went down with the foreign-flag tankers. A large number had also perished with the sinking of their ships before the attack on Pearl Harbor.

Some ships were sunk with all or nearly all their officers and men. Among such wartime casualties was the *W. L. Steed*. Northbound with a cargo of Colombian crude, it was torpedoed and shelled off the coast of Florida on a winter night; only 4 of a total of 38 officers and men survived the attack or the long exposure in lifeboats. Another, the *R. P. Resor*, carrying a cargo of fuel oil for Fall River, Massachusetts, was torpedoed in winter off the New Jersey coast. All but 2 of 50 men—officers, crew, and Navy armed guards—were lost. The *L. J. Drake*, bound for Puerto Rico with 35 officers and men and 6 Navy gunners aboard, was sunk without a trace in the Caribbean.[17]

The Jersey tanker crews were insured under company benefit plans, and company executives acted to assure the prompt fulfillment of all obligations under those plans. The companies also kept in communication with the families of those who lost their lives and with injured men and their dependents.[18]

The willingness of the men to face the wartime risks of the ships was a notable aspect of the operations of the tanker fleet. Even when submarine and bomber attacks were heaviest in 1942, survivors of lost tankers signed up for service on other ships. Only a relatively small number left to take jobs on land. To be sure, the tanker crews were paid bonuses for trips in especially dangerous waters and to certain ports. But these alone could hardly have accounted for the perseverance of the men who shared the hazards of the tankers.

The contribution of tanker men received far less recognition than that of their compatriots in the armed forces. Jersey and its shipowning affiliates, together with the Tanker Officers Association, recommended to the United States government that deserving merchant marine personnel be given some recognition. Three types of awards were subsequently established: one for valiant or gallant action, another for action beyond the line of duty, and a third for men on ships attacked by the enemy. Jersey personnel received all three types.[19]

One of the great problems of the marine organizations was to maintain adequate crews. Replacements were urgently needed for those who left for other jobs, joined the armed services, or were lost at sea; and additional men were needed for expanding wartime operations. In the United States, unlicensed seamen were obtained from government training stations and licensed personnel from Fort Trumbull at New London, Connecticut. Specialists were recruited from other places. There was an especially severe shortage of skilled diesel and turbo engineers and of ships' cooks.[20]

Oil companies did not realize high profits from tanker operations during the war, but their financial losses from enemy attack were mostly covered. In order to keep costs down and to help brake inflation, the Allied governments held to the policy of stabilizing tanker rates. Government agencies agreed to underwrite ships transporting oil for the United States at a time when increasing perils were causing war-insurance rates to rise appreciably. The government paid promptly for lost and damaged vessels so insured. Canada and Great Britain similarly covered the loss of ships flying their flags. Payment had also been promised for tankers lost early in the war by Jersey affiliates in countries—Allied or neutral—later occupied by Axis powers. However, there was uncertainty about remuneration for tanker losses of affiliates under Axis control.[21]

EMERGENCY OIL CARRIERS WITHIN THE UNITED STATES

The diversion of tankers from peacetime trades, together with greatly increased requirements for transporting products to war bases and losses from enemy attacks on the ships themselves, brought a radical change in oil transport in North America. Although new facilities also had to be provided in other countries, the heaviest load was laid upon carriers within the United States. Coastal refineries running North American and South American crude oils supplied the major share of Allied needs, and more than 90 per cent of the requirements of Atlantic Coast refineries and markets had previously been supplied by tankers. The first resort was to barges, railroad tank cars, and tank trucks. Among the Jersey men active in these operations were George A. Wilson of Standard of Louisiana and Sherman D. Archbold of Standard Oil Company of New Jersey, specialists in transportation on inland waterways.

Jersey and its affiliates cooperated with industry committees and government boards in using additional local watercraft along coasts and on lakes, rivers, and canals in order to deliver the maximum amounts of crude oil and products. The government, however, allowed only a small increase in the number of petroleum barges by the conversion of old barges from carrying dry cargoes and the construction of new ones. The domestic affiliates, which in 1941 had added seven new barges and one coastal tanker, increased the use of their own equipment and also that hired from outsiders—mainly from Socony-Vacuum—with the result that their total barge deliveries rose approximately 50 per cent from the daily average of 1941 to that of 1944. Some of these oil carriers operated on short routes, for example within the Chesapeake Bay area, but others brought oil from Baton Rouge up the Mississippi and Ohio rivers. Although barges helped, these craft could contribute only to a limited extent to the solution of the problem of long-distance oil movement.[22]

The rapid increase in the use of railroad tank cars was an outstanding wartime achievement of efficient organization. These carriers provided a quick and flexible means of increasing oil transport. They were relieved of their accustomed work of moving crude oil from fields to nearby refineries or products from refineries to markets within a region by the substitution of tank trucks, under government orders, for carrying crude oil and products distances eventually up to 200 miles. In addition, the number of tank cars in petroleum service at the beginning of 1942 was increased by the diversion of other railroad rolling stock to this service and the construction of new cars. But the really important gain was made in expediting the loading, unloading, and moving of cars by methods developed by companies, railroads, industry committees, and government boards.[23]

Jersey's experience illustrates what was accomplished by the industry in providing tank cars for long-distance shipping. In 1941 its affiliates had stopped using railways for distances less than 50 miles, and they were able by other means to release cars for long-distance transport. When the Office of Defense Transportation in May, 1942, ordered that the use of this type of transport for less than 100 miles be discontinued, Jersey's marketers turned to running their trucks both day and night as a means of taking care of the extra work. The company was also able to obtain cars from other districts to serve the crucial Atlantic Coast. By various means, the number of tank cars used by the Jersey affiliates in domestic interdistrict transport was increased from 906 in December, 1941, to 5,613 in July, 1942.[24]

But raising the number of cars was not enough. Jersey also raised the efficiency of its utilization of rail transport. It set up a new division in New York to direct the supply, distribution, and use of tank cars serving the domestic affiliates. Their loading and unloading and their movement were studied, and a 24-hour day and 7-day week were instituted at plants and terminals. The marketers went so far as to refuse further deliveries to dealers who unduly delayed the unloading and returning of cars. The toughest problem was to speed up their movement on railways. The Jersey Traffic Department recognized that moving single cars was wasteful and that great savings could be effected by sorting them by destinations in producing areas or at refineries, combining them into full trainloads, and dispatching them on fixed schedules. In February, 1942, the traffic managers assigned a group of expediters to work with railroads to bring about the most efficient transport of oil. Railroad men, already overburdened with work, understandably looked on these efforts with disfavor at first, but eventually they set up their own expediters at important transfer points.[25]

Practices similar to those which Jersey adopted early in 1942 in connection with the movement of its own oil were established for the whole industry before the end of the year. Railroad expediters at strategic points began to consolidate loaded cars and empties into trainloads, which they sent to their destinations by the shortest routes. In August, railroads established "symbol routes" by which trains were rushed through to their destinations on fixed schedules. Late in the year such routes were extended to cover the whole oil industry, and another group of routes known as "channel routes" was established by which single cars were shipped to assembly points where they were consolidated into "symbol trains." The system was facilitated by pooling the oil to be carried and by the railroads' granting of the highest priority to petroleum trains.

Symbol trains carrying crude oil or products from the Gulf region to the East Coast sometimes made the trip faster than express trains.[26]

Transportation by land also required extensive new loading and un-loading facilities. Humble, with its large crude shipments by tank car—more than 30,000,000 barrels during the war—carried on an especially extensive construction program. Standard of Louisiana also built new facilities for loading cars, and Standard Oil Company of New Jersey constructed a large unloading rack at Bayway. Because this Bayway rack could unload a number of types of products from a hundred cars at one time, these facilities were made available to other companies and to the United States Navy.[27]

The expansion and systemization of tank-car transport contributed vitally to supplying oil for use and shipment on the Atlantic Coast and to meeting war emergencies. In January, 1942, a daily average of about 100,000 barrels reached the East Coast by rail, half of which was for Jersey affiliates. In this same month, when it became impossible to obtain kerosene for New England by tanker or railroad, arrangements were made in Boston to move into public buildings families dependent on this fuel for their "space heaters." Industry committees made plans to supply New England with heating oil by bringing into the area 55-gallon drums in boxcars. By this means, the Esso Marketers in January brought to New England more than half a million gallons of kerosene purchased in Texas. In February they shipped in 3,000,000 gallons in drums from the supplies of Standard of Louisiana at Chalmette and Baton Rouge. From September, 1943, to March, 1944, between one-half and three-quarters of all petroleum shipments to the East Coast came by tank car. For several days in July, 1943, the incredible daily average of approximately a million barrels was delivered in the East, about one-fifth being Jersey's. However, after the completion of new pipelines to the Atlantic Coast, less shipment by railroad was required. Hence many tank cars were released for other service, especially for carrying oil from inland sources to West Coast loading points for military use in the Southwest Pacific. At the end of 1944, Jersey's tank-car deliveries on the East Coast dropped to an average of 15,000 barrels daily.[28]

OLD AND NEW PIPELINES IN THE UNITED STATES

No sooner was the United States in the war than the need for more pipelines became critical. This facility for oil transport became a special concern of the Petroleum Administration for War. An industry subcommittee on pipeline management was set up; its twelve members included directors Gallagher and Holman of the parent company and President Wiess of Humble. Its engineering subcommittee was headed by Jersey's Wallace R. Finney, who also was chairman of an unofficial PAW committee to review the over-all transportation situation in the United States and to analyze problems and proposals.[29]

The recognition by both industry and government agencies of the urgent need for new pipelines and for a more efficient use of existing facilities led in March, 1942, to a meeting in Tulsa of representatives of companies interested in this type of transportation. Jersey's Finney was chairman. The principal object of the meeting was to consider how to increase deliveries by pipeline to the East Coast. Several proposals were drawn up, which came to serve as a program for increasing the capacity of the pipeline network. Old carriers were reconditioned and changed to move oil in directions needed, and new ones were built.[30]

Several changes were made under the Tulsa program in lines owned wholly or partially by Jersey affiliates. The proposal to tie together the old lines of different companies in the Northeast necessitated the reversal and conversion of the Tuscarora to carrying crude eastward again. Its pumping stations were relocated—actually, transferred from one side of a mountain to another—and new pumps and tanks were installed. In November, 1942, the Tuscarora began to send crude oil to Bayway at the rate of 20,000 barrels daily. Also, the pumping capacity of the Ajax pipeline was increased to assist in the movement of oil eastward. The company rehired many of its former employees and others of the Oklahoma Pipe Line Company laid off during the period when flush production in Illinois had reduced the eastward shipment of Mid-Continent crude oil.[31]

Another important proposal of the Tulsa conference was to expand and extend the products line of the Plantation Pipe Line Company which Jersey, Shell, and Standard of Kentucky had built from Baton Rouge as far as Greensboro, North Carolina. Plantation's daily capacity was increased from 60,000 to 90,000 barrels by the installation of additional pumping stations. With the aid of federal funds, inasmuch as the extension had little commercial justification for normal times, the line was extended to Richmond, Virginia. It was ready for operation on April 1, 1943. Deliveries of products to the Plantation at Baton Rouge were supplemented by products from the Houston refineries brought by a line built from old pipe by the Shell Oil Company. This feeder was owned by the Bayou Pipe Line Company, which in turn was owned jointly by several companies, including Humble.[32]

Jersey also participated in carrying out plans recommended by the Tulsa conference for building two large pipelines from Texas to the Atlantic Coast. The government board for allocating materials had turned down three times—the third in February, 1942—a project proposed in May, 1941, by President Farish for building a crude oil line of 20- or 24-inch diameter. (See Chapter 14.) In June, 1942, however, the War Production Board recognized the necessity for building a 24-inch pipeline to Illinois, and in October it approved an extension to Phoenixville, Pennsylvania, with a 20-inch line from Phoenixville to Philadelphia and another to the New York area. Early in 1943 materials were also granted for a parallel products line. The decision to build this 20-inch products facility from Texas to Illinois, with expected extension to the East Coast, was based on a report of preliminary studies written by Jersey's H. W. Page, an analyst in the Transportation Division of the PAW.[33]

The government turned to members of the industry to build these lines for the Defense Plant Corporation—with financing by the Reconstruction Finance Corporation—and also to operate them. Eleven oil companies, including Jersey, became participants in War Emergency Pipe Lines, Inc., a nonprofit corporation. Wallace R. Finney was head of the committee that handled the design and supervised the construction of the two new carriers. Members of Jersey's special engineering section were lent to the project, and several key men of its pipeline affiliates participated in construction. The Big Inch—of 24-inch diameter, then the world's largest petroleum pipeline—was built from East Texas to the Atlantic Coast. It reached Norris City, Illinois, in February, 1943, and Bayway on New York Harbor and Philadelphia on the Delaware River in August. It had a daily crude oil capacity of 320,000 barrels. The 20-inch refined-products line was also laid and operated by War Emergency Pipe Lines, Inc. It reached New York in February, 1944. Its southern terminus was at Beaumont, Texas, where it was supplied by refineries of the region. Its daily capacity was 225,000 barrels.[34]

The Big Inch crude line was supplied in Texas by several feeder lines. Humble Pipe Line Company reversed its own East Texas pipeline so that crude would flow north to Longview, the terminus of the Big Inch, instead of south to the Gulf. The company's most important part in providing feeders, however, was to act as agent of the Defense Plant Corporation in rebuilding and extending an old, badly corroded pipeline to form the Southwest Texas Emergency Pipe Line for carrying crude from Corpus Christi—a terminal for Southwest and West Texas—to the Houston area, whence the oil was piped to Longview. Humble operated the line as agent of the RFC, receiving compensation for costs. Beginning in October, 1943, this emergency pipeline brought 80,000 barrels of crude daily from Southwest Texas to Houston.[35]

The Jersey affiliates made many changes in their own pipeline systems and organizations. Because of shortages, old pipe no longer needed in one place was dug up and laid elsewhere. The systems belonging to Oklahoma Pipe Line Company and Standard Oil Company of Louisiana were consolidated. That is, the former company became the Interstate Oil Pipe Line Company, incorporated in Delaware, and the pipeline assets of Standard of Louisiana were transferred to this new corporation. The combination was a part of the network for moving crude oil from producing regions northward and northeastward. A development of importance to the whole pipeline interest of the Jersey group, foreign as well as domestic, was the setting up of the office of Pipe Line Advisor in New York. Wallace R. Finney was appointed to head this new staff group of the parent company.[36]

Table 18: **MILEAGE AND DAILY AVERAGE AND ANNUAL RUNS OF TRUNK LINES OF DOMESTIC AFFILIATES, 1941, 1943, AND 1945**
Standard Oil Company (New Jersey)

AFFILIATES[a]	Miles Operated			Thousands of 42-gallon Barrels Transported Daily			Billions of Barrel-Miles Transported		
	1941	1943	1945	1941	1943	1945	1941	1943	1945
Humble Pipe Line Co.	5,296	5,367	5,447	380.4	454.0	617.2	32.5	30.0	38.5
Interstate Oil Pipe Line Co.									
Northern Division[b]	1,046	1,031	1,042	75.9	120.3	136.0	2.3	4.9	4.7
Southern Division[c]	1,397	1,523	1,725	125.1	167.8	196.5	8.1	10.1	11.1
Ajax Pipe Line Co.	801	810	819	44.1	82.3	84.8	6.4	11.9	12.2
Transit & Storage Co.	370	370	370	24.5	29.8	30.6	1.4	1.7	1.7
Tuscarora Oil Co.	607	591	591	37.7	51.4	43.0	1.6	2.9	2.4
Portland Pipe Line Co.	166	166	173	3.2	31.7	43.6	0.2	1.9	2.7
Plantation Pipe Line Co.[d]	—	1,261	1,261	—	86.5	86.9	—	21.0	20.1
Yale Pipe Line Co.	—	—	80	—	—	14.6	—	—	0.3
Total[d]	9,683	11,119	11,508	690.9	1,023.8	1,253.2	52.5	84.4	93.7

[a] Bayou Pipe Line Company, in which Humble had a minority interest, is not included.
[b] Oklahoma Pipe Line Company through 1944; thereafter, the Northern Division of Interstate Oil Pipe Line Company.
[c] Pipelines of Standard Oil Company of Louisiana through 1944; thereafter, the Southern Division of Interstate Oil Pipe Line Company.
[d] Figures include the full operation of Plantation, in which Jersey had a 50.4 per cent interest at this time.
Source: Standard Oil Company (New Jersey), Annual Statistical Review, 1943 and 1945.

The volume of oil carried by Jersey's oil pipeline affiliates in the United States is indicated by Table 18. The increase in barrel-miles of oil moved annually from 1941 through 1945—from 52.5 billion to 93.7 billion—was far greater than the expansion in the miles of line operated. Humble's system, the largest among those of the domestic affiliates, carried crude mainly to Texas refineries and shipping points, one exception being the reversal of the line in eastern Texas. The greatest change came in other companies concerned with the eastward flow of oil. The major portion of pipeline deliveries to Jersey's affiliates on the Atlantic Coast was brought by the two big lines of the War Emergency Pipelines, Inc., which went into operation in 1943 and 1944.[37]

BUILDING PIPELINES ABROAD

Jersey men, as members of industry committees and government agencies or in the armed services, also helped to provide pipelines to carry oil products to military forces. In many foreign countries they participated in construction and operations undertaken for purposes directly related to the war effort. Jersey's Finney served in consulting and supervisory capacities for the Navy and was chairman of an Army pipeline committee on foreign projects.[38]

Among the projects were four lines built in 1943 and 1944 in the Panama Canal Zone. These were constructed to ease the burden on the canal by delivering crude from fields along the Gulf of Mexico and the Caribbean and products from the refineries of those regions to tankers at the Pacific terminus—an example of new routes required to serve the military, in this instance in the Southwest Pacific. Engineering designs were made by a Jersey pipeline engineering section in New York, and the lines were constructed and operated under the supervision of L. F. Kahle and L. P. Maier, assisted by a group of specialists from the affiliates. At the Navy's request, company engineers also designed terminals for these pipelines across Panama. Another pipeline manager of a Jersey affiliate, G. B. Randels, supervised the operation of a portion of the overland carrier built from Calcutta in India to Kunming in China. Randels' work had to do with a section of the lines built from Calcutta to the upper part of the Burma Road after the Japanese occupation of southern Burma. This whole undertaking was a heroic effort to supply China with the oil products necessary for resistance to the Japanese; it meant cutting through disease-ridden jungle and going over 8,500-foot mountains.[39]

Jersey pipeliners also participated in laying lines in Africa and Europe to move petroleum products from ports to airfields and areas of combat. These included pipe laid from landing ships to temporary terminals on shore and along the routes of military advance. Such facilities were constructed in North Africa in 1942 by Army men directed by Charles L. Lockett, Jr. Their success resulted in the laying of other lines for campaigns in Sicily and Italy, as well as in southern and northern France, in which the company's personnel similarly participated.[40]

Such in essence was the contribution of the Jersey Company to the industry's transporting of unprecedented quantities of crude oil to refineries and of petroleum products for military and civilian use around the globe. The work of Jersey men, organizations, and carriers illustrates the effectiveness of the petroleum industry's worldwide operations under government direction during the war. The success of the tankers at sea against wartime odds ranks high in the annals of ocean transport. No less an accomplishment was the mobilization of existing facilities and the building of new ones to supply by land essential requirements of industrial and other civilian consumers as well as the military forces of the Allies on all continents.

Chapter 20

The Wartime Distribution of
Petroleum Products

THE PRIMARY FUNCTION of the sales organizations of the Jersey affiliates in the war years was to participate in the cooperative effort of government and industry to distribute limited supplies of oil products where they would make the most effective contribution to the cause of the Allies. As in other phases of their operations, the affiliates had to subordinate their normal commercial objectives to the necessities of war. They made radical alterations in their facilities and operations in order to adjust to changes in the volume of products required, in the points of consumption, and in the conditions under which they operated. The marketers also performed many specialized services for the military forces of the Allies.

GOVERNMENT CONTROL OF DISTRIBUTION

As in other branches of the industry, sales executives and organizations of oil companies operated within systems of government planning and control. A network of special agencies—assisted by industry boards and committees in the United States, the United Kingdom, and Canada—had charge of the allocation of supplies to Allied and neutral countries, with the exception of Russia and the territories under its control. Within the individual countries, governmental agencies regulated the distribution of available products among different types of consumers and determined the conditions of their sale. The military had priority in the allocation of oil products; manufacturing and transportation essential to the war effort came next. Sales to governments for military use were in large part by contract. Those to civilian consumers were regulated by systems of rationing and quality and price controls.

Many executives and marketing specialists of Jersey affiliates served on government and oil industry boards and committees having to do with the distribution of products. Among the foreign affiliates' representatives on such bodies were Anglo-American's E. E. Soubry, Imperial's W. F. Prendergast, and Standard-Vacuum's G. S. Walden. Several executives of Jersey companies who had long been active in foreign sales—including D. L. Harper, L. K. Blood, and G. H. Michler—were members of industry committees under the Petroleum Administration for War which were concerned with the allocation of products distributed outside the United States. Many other marketing men were on district committees in the United States which gathered information concerning civilian requirements for different products and types of consumers and recommended allocations to various uses. Those serving in the very important District No. 1 included Jersey's R. T. Haslam, A. C. Bedford, J. S. Helm, J. W. Connolly, F. M. Surface, and N. H. Seubert.[1]

WORLDWIDE SALES

Table 19 indicates by annual totals the wartime distribution of refined products by Jersey affiliates. These figures do not include such intermediate materials sold to other manufacturers as toluene, butadiene, and Butyl rubber, which were made under special contracts with agencies of the United States government. The products covered by the table range from the majors, which provided energy for various kinds of transportation and for industrial machines, to asphalt and waxes required in lesser volumes.

The annual worldwide product sales of Jersey affiliates rose from 327,900,000 barrels in 1941 to 417,400,000 barrels in 1944—the last full year of war. Because of the lack of consistency in the methods of reporting, the exact amounts supplied for military or other use under governments are not known. The clearly identifiable sales by the affiliates to governments for military and bunkering purposes rose from a total of 38,500,000 barrels in 1941 to 134,500,000 barrels in 1944. These figures represented 13 per cent in 1941 and 22 per cent in 1944 of the Allied totals exclusive of products provided within Russia. Since there was never enough to supply all demands, sales to civilians necessarily depended from time to time on variations in supplies and in military requirements. The sales of the Jersey companies to governments made up 11.7 per cent of their total in 1941 and 32.1 per cent in 1944.[2]

Table 20 indicates by products the annual worldwide sales of Jersey affiliates to civilian and military buyers. A particularly important change

Table 19: **ANNUAL PRODUCT SALES BY AFFILIATES IN ALLIED AND NEUTRAL COUNTRIES, 1940–1945**
Standard Oil Company (New Jersey)
(In millions of 42-gallon barrels)

	1940	1941	1942	1943	1944	1945
By Areas and Sales Organizations						
United States						
Esso Marketers[a] and General Office						
sales of Standard Oil Co. of New Jersey	152.4	179.0	165.4	203.9	258.4	229.7
Humble Oil & Refining Co., in Texas	5.0	4.2	11.6	15.0	17.0	14.3
Carter Oil Co., The, in Mid-Continent	0.0	0.1	0.0	1.2	3.6	5.1
Total	157.5	183.3	177.0	220.1	279.0	249.0
Allied and Neutral Countries						
Imperial Oil Ltd., Canada	28.2	33.0	33.1	33.5	35.0	35.4
Latin American affiliates	31.6	35.9	30.1	29.7	35.3	50.5
European affiliates[b]	34.9	21.8	1.9	0.7	1.2	11.1
Standard-Vacuum Oil Co.[c]	22.7	22.8	13.3	16.4	19.9	23.6
Other outlets, including Lend-Lease	12.5	31.1	35.2	38.3	47.0	70.5
Total	129.9	144.6	113.7	118.5	138.3	191.0
Total	287.4	327.9	290.7	338.6	417.4	440.0
By Consumers[d]						
Civilians						
United States	e	171.3	150.0	149.1	178.3	201.4
Foreign	e	118.1	85.8	92.3	104.5	145.5
Total	e	289.4	235.8	241.4	282.9	346.9
Governments (Military and Bunkering)						
United States[f]	e	12.0	27.0	71.0	100.7	47.6
Foreign	e	26.5	27.9	26.2	33.8	45.5
Total	e	38.5	54.9	97.2	134.5	93.1
Total	287.4	327.9	290.7	338.6	417.4	440.0

NOTE: Because of rounding, totals are not in all cases the exact sum of the figures added. 0.0 represents 50 barrels or less. Does not include natural and cycle plant gasolines and chemical products.

[a] Includes Colonial Beacon Oil Company, Standard Oil Company of New Jersey, Standard Oil Company of Louisiana, Standard Oil Company of Pennsylvania, and Penola Inc., covering marketing territory from Louisiana to Maine.

[b] In countries in Europe and North Africa when neutral or members of the Allies.

[c] Data for Standard-Vacuum Oil Company cover the full amount, although Jersey had a half-interest in this affiliate, which marketed in Asia, Australia, and Africa. Its military sales are included with civilian.

[d] Data for 1945 are not comparable with those for previous war years because of a change in the basis for crediting military sales to domestic and foreign business.

[e] Division between civilian and military is not available for 1940.

[f] Sales to the United States for its use abroad are included with United States figures.

Source: Statistics compiled by the Coordination and Economics Department, Standard Oil Company (New Jersey).

came in the distribution of aviation gasoline: the volume sold was five times as large in 1944 as in 1941, but the amount that went to the military in 1944 was thirteen times that of the earlier year. The distribution of motor gasoline increased relatively little in the years 1941–1944, but

Table 20: **AFFILIATES' ANNUAL WORLDWIDE CIVILIAN[a] AND MILITARY SALES, BY PRODUCTS, 1941–1945**
Standard Oil Company (New Jersey)
(In millions of 42-gallon barrels)

Products	1941 Civilian	1941 Military	1942 Civilian	1942 Military	1943 Civilian	1943 Military	1944 Civilian	1944 Military	1945[b] Civilian	1945[b] Military
Aviation Gasoline	6.0	2.6	7.1	8.2	8.8	20.5	9.6	34.7	8.3	21.3
Other Gasoline[c]	95.0	10.3	73.0	10.3	68.0	15.3	77.9	22.5	96.8	17.9
Kerosene	20.2	2.3	15.8	1.6	14.8	2.9	15.4	2.2	22.4	1.4
Distillates	52.5	8.6	45.5	11.7	45.6	15.5	49.6	19.4	57.1	17.4
Residual Fuels	97.3	13.7	80.8	21.3	91.4	40.8	116.2	52.7	144.7	32.9
Lubricants and Greases	9.5	0.7	7.1	1.6	6.6	1.8	7.5	2.6	8.0	1.7
Wax	0.8	0.0	0.7	0.0	0.7	0.0	0.8	0.1	0.8	0.0
Asphalt	8.0	0.2	5.7	0.2	5.4	0.4	5.9	0.2	7.0	0.3
Liquefied Petroleum Gas[c]	—	—	—	—	—	—	—	—	2.0	—
Total	289.4	38.5	235.8	54.9	241.4	97.2	282.9	134.5	346.9	93.1
Total Civilian and Military	327.9		290.7		338.6		417.4		440.0	

NOTE: Because of rounding, totals are not in all cases the exact sum of the figures added.
[a] The products sold by Standard-Vacuum Oil Company to the military are included in civilian sales.
[b] Data for 1945 are not comparable with those for previous war years because of a change in the basis for crediting military sales to domestic and foreign business.
[c] For the years 1941–1944 liquefied petroleum gases (LPG) are included in Other Gasoline.
Source: Statistics compiled by the Coordination and Economics Department, Standard Oil Company (New Jersey).

military sales grew larger and those to civilians declined. The greatest increase in volume came in residual fuels, including domestic and foreign bunker sales; sales to the military rose more in both volume and percentage than those to civilians.

The affiliates distributed products through various kinds of organizations and channels, with considerable adjustment to meet changing war needs. Most of their sales to governments were under contracts negotiated by company executives and representatives of government agencies, but some sales to military and other government consumers were made by the regular marketing organizations and hence did not come under formal purchasing arrangements. Distribution to private consumers—from large industrial or transportation concerns to the individual motorist and householder—was handled by the marketing organizations. These marketers worked under the particular governmental regulations of the countries where they operated.

Several affiliates entered into contracts to sell products to agencies of the Allied governments. The larger part of such sales was handled by the General Office Sales Department of Standard Oil Company of New Jersey. These included not only sales to the government of the United States but also those under Lend-Lease arrangements with the United Kingdom, Russia, and China. They covered the contract product sales of the Aruba refinery as well as of the refineries of affiliates in the United States. Humble itself negotiated with agencies of the United States for the delivery of products in Texas—principally for use in military training within the state. Imperial and Standard-Vacuum likewise contracted with governments in their operating territories.

SUPPLYING THE UNITED STATES MARKET

As indicated in Table 19, the volume of petroleum products sold each year by the Jersey companies in the United States was far larger than the combined totals of affiliates outside this country. The sales of Standard Oil Company of New Jersey were not wholly for consumption at home; they also included those made to the United States government for bunkering and military use abroad. However, this company and the Esso Marketers sold large quantities for consumption within the country, because they operated in a region which had the greatest concentration of manufacturing and shipping in the United States—which, in fact, was the leader among the Allies in industrial production for the war.

Sales to the United States government rose steeply. The total sold by Standard Oil Company of New Jersey and Humble, the companies that handled such domestic contracts, rose from 12,000,000 barrels in 1941 to 100,700,000 in 1944.

These sales to agencies of the United States, as well as those under Lend-Lease arrangements to its allies, were made under specific contractual terms. Contracts for long or indefinite periods mainly covered such products as were developed during the war to meet special military needs. An outstanding example was aviation gasoline. Early in 1942, representing Jersey refineries in the United States and the one at Aruba, Standard Oil Company of New Jersey entered into a contract with the Defense Supplies Corporation of the United States to supply high-octane aviation gasoline. This agreement was to remain in force until terminated by the government agency on 60-day notice. The stipulated base price was 13 cents per gallon until February 29, 1944, and 12 cents thereafter;

these figures were subject to readjustment in accordance with changes in the cost of raw materials and in the cost-of-living index of the Bureau of Labor Statistics. Most of the sales agreements with government agencies were for products normally made by the companies. These included, among others, motor gasolines, many kinds of lubricants and greases, kerosene, distillate fuels, diesel fuels, residual fuel oils, and heating oils. Generally, contracts covering such supplies ran for short periods and contained fixed prices. In a few instances of long-term arrangements, price readjustments were provided for. In such cases, it was Jersey policy to reduce its prices voluntarily if costs proved substantially lower and profit margins higher than had been anticipated.[3]

The distribution of oil products to civilian consumers in the United States early came under extensive government controls. The hours when retail stations could be open were limited in order to conserve manpower. To brake price inflation, maximum prices were set by the Office of Price Administration, which attempted to prevent increases despite rising costs. Rationing was extended to all consumers, but manufacturing and transportation essential to the war effort had priority. The rationing of gasoline among dealers was first applied to the Atlantic seaboard in March, 1942, when the German submarine campaign caused severe shortages. Because this form of regulation proved inadequate, a system of consumer rationing was established in the summer of 1942. In November, gasoline rationing was extended throughout the country in order to conserve tires as well as to reduce consumption. In the same month, fuel-oil rationing was adopted for the East Coast. Local boards, working under the Office of Price Administration in Washington, handled the allotment of these products to consumers. The amounts allotted to individuals from time to time depended on the supplies available relative to military and other essential requirements.[4]

The allocation of available supplies among the primary distributors raised a problem. In September, 1942, representatives of these distributors in the Northeast met in Washington to consider how to handle the situation. They worked out a general procedure for the efficient use of all facilities for supplying the area. The Petroleum Administration for War issued this plan as Directive 59, which restricted each primary distributor to selling the same percentage of the total available in his zone as his sales had represented in the zone's total in 1941. A supplier had to assign any excess, without a marketing charge, to other distributors who had insufficient volumes to meet their quotas.[5]

Standard Oil Company of New Jersey, Humble, and Carter sold the general line of oil products. Humble increased its sales considerably by supplying essential industries and military training activities in Texas. Carter also entered this branch of the oil business during the war by purchasing marketing facilities and operations in Montana, Idaho, and Washington. This expansion, however, was more important in its geographic extent than in the volume of products sold. In fact, it was the first addition to the marketing territory of the domestic affiliates in more than a decade.[6]

By far the larger part of the sales of the domestic affiliates to private customers was made by the General Office Sales Department of Standard Oil Company of New Jersey and by the Esso Marketers. The former handled contract sales to large-volume buyers, including transportation, industrial, and marketing concerns. Standard of Kentucky remained the largest private contract customer. Many purchasers of fuel oil, which had been making up half of the large-volume business, converted from oil to coal during the war—as did Jersey's own refineries in the state of New Jersey.[7] The Esso Marketers, of which A. C. Bedford became manager as successor to Haslam in 1942, sold in tank-car lots to jobbers and other large noncontract customers and by truck to service stations and to such individual consumers as householders buying in relatively small volume.

The most concentrated market of the domestic affiliates was in the northern half of the region along the Atlantic Coast known as District No. 1 under the Petroleum Administration for War. This northeastern section of the United States had cold winters, a relatively dense population, and extensive war industry and ocean shipping. The region was especially difficult to supply during the war because of transportation problems that were nearly always serious and at times critical.

Throughout the war years, the Esso Marketers also supplied other distributors as well as their own regular jobber customers and other buyers of their products. Because the Jersey companies were bringing crude oil and products to the eastern seaboard by every possible means, the marketers supplied far more than their allotted share of the market under Directive 59. During the period from January 1, 1943, to September 30, 1945, the Esso Marketers assigned to other primary distributors in District No. 1 a net of 33,000,000 barrels of major petroleum products. Thus, without a marketing charge, they furnished large quantities to distributors who had insufficient volume to fill their own sales quotas.[8]

Like oil salesmen generally in the United States, the Jersey marketers were more than distributors during the war. They helped collect information for the government about the amounts of the various oil products needed in an area. They assisted in setting up and handling the rationing system—for this service, the extra accounting required of the average bulk plant was estimated by the PAW as amounting to 20 hours per week.[9] The marketers also performed an important conservation function. They publicized such slogans adopted by oil industry committees as "Sharing the Shortage," "Oil Is Ammunition—Use It Wisely," and "Gasoline Powers the Attack—Don't Waste a Drop." Like the rest of the industry, they urged their customers to convert oil burners to coal—they even stopped selling burners in February, 1942. They trained retail salesmen to show their customers how to make fuel oil and gasoline stretch farther and to reduce the wear and tear of cars and tires, and they prepared conservation booklets for free distribution. The sales organizations also collected, under government programs, scrap aluminum, rubber, iron, and lead—without any remuneration for extra expenditures.[10]

The sales volume of the Esso Marketers fell off as the military demand rose. The marketers' total was approximately 27 per cent lower in 1943 than in 1941; the largest reductions were in fuel for heating and gasoline for private automobiles. The volume decline of these marketers was relatively larger than the average for the whole country, principally because of the disruption of tanker routes but also because of the rising demands to meet military, bunkering, and industrial needs in District No. 1. Like other large distributors, the Esso Marketers reduced the number of their bulk and service-station outlets. Their volume rose again after the overland transportation facilities to the Atlantic Coast were expanded by new pipelines, but even then essential demands for war pressed upon available supplies.[11]

SALES ABROAD

The volume of oil products sold by Jersey affiliates outside the United States was smaller than total sales at home. It decreased substantially in 1942; and, even with increases in the next two years, it did not reach the volume in 1944 that had been sold in 1941. The decline was in distribution to civilians. Although the sale to governments of aviation gasoline and residual fuel oils rose, the increase was not sufficient to maintain the 1941 total.[12]

In Canada, Imperial Oil Limited increased its sales moderately. The company had great difficulty in obtaining sufficient products. But Jersey companies in the United States assisted their Canadian associate in overcoming transportation difficulties and obtaining supplies; and, after the entry of the Dominion's southern neighbor into the war, the two countries jointly allocated their available crude and other petroleum supplies. In Canada as in parts of the United States, transportation remained a problem throughout most of the war period. In the circumstances, priorities cut down the amounts available for civilians. Such sales were under strict rationing and price and other government regulations. Imperial consequently reduced its marketing facilities and operations. Because of the requirements of Canada's Royal Air Force and its training camps, the company's sale of aviation gasoline was thirteen times as large in 1944 as it had been in 1939. Under the government's allocation of responsibility for supplies, this affiliate provided 40 per cent of the high-octane aviation gasoline in Canada outside British Columbia and 60 per cent of the requirements in that province. Its sale of residual fuels also rose substantially throughout the war; these fuels were required by the expanding war industry and for bunkering ships in Atlantic and Pacific ports and on the Great Lakes.[13]

The total sales of Jersey affiliates marketing south of the United States actually declined in 1942 and 1943. In the first of these years, their combined volume was the lowest in seven years, and the total sold in 1943 was still lower. Even the affiliates operating in countries with abundant local supplies—International Petroleum, Tropical, and Creole —felt the depressing effect of higher prices for petroleum products and the scarcity of automobile tires. The Jersey companies in the southern continent were also affected by the rationing programs of the Allies. These were designed generally to provide each country with as large a percentage of their prewar volume as the United States was allowed. This system of allocation was hardest on Argentina and Chile, which did not join the Allies until 1945. In the former country, Jersey was also adversely affected by the government's stipulation that all imported oil products be carried in Argentinian-flag tankers, of which few were available. Inasmuch as its own production within Argentina was far from adequate to provide its allotted share of that country's large market for petroleum products, the company's market position in Argentina declined.[14]

The most severe reduction in the sales of Jersey affiliates came in Europe. The effect of the war is indicated by the decline in the total sold from 34,900,000 barrels in 1940, to 1,900,000 in 1942, and to 700,000 in 1943. By the time the United States entered the conflict, the parent company had contact with only one European affiliate engaged in general marketing, Anglo-American Oil Company, which operated as a member of the British pool under the Oil Control Board in London. Anglo-American did not handle Lend-Lease sales to Great Britain after the entry of the United States into the war. As already noted, these transactions were negotiated by Standard Oil Company of New Jersey under arrangements made by the United States government.

Standard-Vacuum Oil Company—owned in equal parts by Jersey and Socony—operated throughout the war under British regulations. It lost a large part of its marketing territory and personnel as a result of the Japanese conquest of East and Southeast Asia, the Philippines, and the Dutch East Indies. However, the company retained operations in western China, India, New Zealand, Australia, and East and South Africa. It also lost an important source of products in the fall of the Sungei Gerong refinery to Japan. Thereafter it had to depend entirely on products from the Persian Gulf and the Pacific Coast of the United States, areas which themselves had insufficient volume to meet all the demands on them. The long distance from those sources to Standard-Vacuum's outlets increased the company's already serious transport difficulties. As a result, the affiliate's sales to civilians, which were under a rationing system, necessarily declined.

Although Standard-Vacuum lost a large part of its markets early in the war, it was able to recover substantially in volume because of its sales to military forces. It supplied the forces of the Allies—American, British, and Chinese—over an immense area, including East and South Africa, India, China (for transport over The Hump), Australia, and New Zealand. It fueled the planes of the National Chinese Airways Corporation on routes that were moved as the Japanese advanced. It served a large part of the Transport Command of the British Air Force in the China-Burma-India theater of operations. And it furnished fuel for the United States Air Transport Command, which was flying over The Hump to western China. In addition to this direct war service, Standard-Vacuum participated in distributing to civilian markets Lend-Lease and other products under government pooling.[15]

SPECIALIZED SERVICES TO THE MILITARY FORCES

The sales organizations of the Jersey affiliates also served the war effort of the Allies in many special capacities. Managers, specialists, and rank-and-file personnel gave various kinds of help to the military operations of the Allies.

Many employees of the Jersey companies in the United States were lent to the government for special duties. The work of J. B. Adoue, Jr., of Humble illustrates one type of service: he was a member of a committee of the United States government which prepared standard specifications and designs for the construction of oil storage installations for military use. Scott E. Drummond, manager of construction and maintenance for the Sales Department of Standard Oil Company of New Jersey, made a contribution of a different kind. He had become a member in 1940 of an oil industry committee on gasoline storage that later worked closely with the War and Navy departments. Immediately after Pearl Harbor, at the request of the Chief of the United States Army Corps of Engineers, he was granted leave by the company to assist the government engineers in building gasoline storage facilities in the Philippines. When the contemplated construction had to be abandoned, Drummond was lent as a special consultant to the Air Transport Command. He was sent at once to Africa, the Middle East, and India to investigate possibilities and to make recommendations to headquarters in the United States concerning the layout, design, construction, and supervision of installations for storing aviation gasoline on the routes of the Air Transport Command in Africa and the Middle East. After spending several months in Africa and Asia, he returned to the United States. He then went to Greenland on an assignment to investigate aviation-fuel installations there. Late in 1942, he was again sent to Africa and to the Middle East. After his return to the United States, he had to resign in June, 1943, because of a disease contracted in the tropics.[16]

Jersey and Standard-Vacuum both participated in carrying out a large project undertaken by the Air Transport Command late in 1941 to provide additional facilities for fueling planes flying from the United States to India by way of South America, Africa, and Arabia. (Drummond's work in Africa and Asia was related to this undertaking.) After some investigation of the existing situation, the War Department contracted with oil companies already operating in those regions to construct the necessary facilities. Standard Oil Company of Brazil, a Jersey affiliate, assumed responsibility for providing storage for gasoline to fuel planes in Brazil for their flight to Africa. Socony undertook to build such storage in North Africa. Standard-Vacuum did the same for East Africa and India. However, the commanding general of the United States forces in India was subsequently given responsibility for the actual construction in that country.

To coordinate these operations, the participating companies organized the Overseas Engineering Department. The OED agreed to assume over-all responsibility for engineering and design, the procurement and shipping of materials and equipment, construction, and accounting. It also undertook to carry on research on certain special problems. The manager and the majority of the OED staff were Standard-Vacuum men.[17]

One result of the research of this organization was to begin using bolted tanks above ground, instead of underground units, for storing aviation gasoline. Such surface containers were already being utilized for crude and fuel oils, but aviation gasoline contained certain aromatics injurious to rubber gaskets in the tanks. When research developed a satisfactory material for gaskets made from synthetic rubber, and the shortage of steel plate forced the Air Transport Command to give up the building of underground storage for aviation fuel, the OED was requested to substitute bolted tanks. With assembly-line fabrication, ease of transport, and speed and simplicity of construction, these units helped to make possible the rapid provision of liquid fuels for various military campaigns.[18]

Standard-Vacuum, which was an old hand at working in East and South Africa and the Orient, was in a position to make special contributions in those vast regions. It provided storage in Australia for gasoline reserves in cooperation with other oil companies. Most of this storage, because of shortages of materials and skilled labor, consisted of 50-gallon drums filled and stored at company bulk depots. In addition, Stanvac participated with other oil concerns in staffing the Bulk Issue Petrol Oil Depot established in Australia. Experienced company personnel were sworn into the Army for this work and were called to active service as needed. As the Allies advanced, units of this organization were set up in New Guinea and other places in the Southwest Pacific. Employees of Standard-Vacuum also designed and supervised the construction of reserve storage facilities for the Union of South Africa.[19]

The company performed another type of special service in connection with the transport of oil products inside India and across the mountains to China by the British and the Americans. When the military forces found it necessary to carry products other than lubricants in steel drums, Standard-Vacuum set up and operated facilities at several places in India to manufacture these containers. Beginning in January, 1943, it established its own plants at Karachi, Bombay, and Calcutta. These plants turned out a total of 3,250,000 drums of 55-gallon capacity. Stanvac also operated such facilities for the United States Army in its own terminal at

Madras, which provided nearly 3,000,000 drums of 5-gallon and 42-gallon capacity.[20]

With its knowledge of the vast regions that it served, Standard-Vacuum's marketing organization was helpful to the Allied war effort in ways not directly related to supply operations. It provided various kinds of information useful to the military forces in the Orient, including maps and data about routes and transportation facilities, that could be obtained only from men who knew a country or region. Its marketing executives undertook assignments which required familiarity with the people and areas covered. An unusual service was that of C. K. Gamble, the managing director of Standard-Vacuum's marketing subsidiary in Australia. As commissioner of the American Red Cross, he built up and headed the Red Cross organization in the MacArthur Command of the Far Pacific. At the end of the war, this organization had 5,500 employees and 15,000 volunteer workers and a budget that ran into millions of dollars. For this work with the Red Cross, Gamble received the Medal of Merit, the highest American award given to civilians.[21]

As this account of the wartime operations of Standard Oil Company (New Jersey) ends, one question may be asked in review: What in essence were the nature and the extent of the contributions of the parent company and its affiliates to the war effort of the Allies?

Because of its size, the Jersey Company as a matter of course contributed heavily to meeting the wartime requirements of the Allies—both military and civilian—for petroleum products. Except in 1942, when the German submarine campaign and the loss of their East Indian production and refining hit Jersey affiliates hard, the volume of the products they supplied to meet civilian and military needs rose. In 1944 the total averaged more than a million barrels per day. In that same year, the affiliates produced 15.2 per cent of the total world output of petroleum outside Russia and the countries controlled by the Axis powers.* In 1944, also, they ran to refinery stills 17.8 per cent of total world runs excepting runs in Russia and Axis-held countries.[22] With their large tanker fleets and extensive handling and storage facilities around the globe, the affiliates likewise carried heavy responsibilities for transporting and storing products to supply overseas military and civilian needs. At home, the pipeline affiliates—including the Plantation line, of which Jersey owned a

---

* 13.7 per cent of the world total, including an estimated Russian production.

bare majority—doubled the barrel-miles of crude and products they transported during the war.

Besides the large scale of Jersey operations, the company's high capacity for expansion was particularly important at a time when petroleum products in immense volume were essential to the success of the Allies. The totals of the Jersey affiliates in production and refining increased not only substantially but also at a faster rate than did industry totals, even in the United States, where there was no destruction or interruption of operations because of the war. Humble—as noted earlier—doubled its crude output, while the American oil industry raised its production by 19 per cent. No other Jersey affiliate expanded its production at so rapid a rate as did Humble, but Creole's increase in Venezuela was substantial.

This high capacity for expansion—that is, reserve capacity—characterized nearly all the resources of the Jersey Company. The affiliates had comparatively large crude reserves, a fact of special importance inasmuch as there was no assurance that sufficient new petroleum would be found to replace that which was consumed. They also had a pool of skilled managerial, technological, and supervisory personnel, which enabled them to expand and at the same time to release men for service elsewhere without serious loss to their own operations. They contributed research and operating men to assist in meeting many industry and military needs. Their personnel helped to man research laboratories working on military projects, to train supervisors in the use of new processes, to devise systems for expediting the transport of oil, and to provide storage facilities of products for the military around the globe.

The Jersey companies were important contributors to product innovation. In an industry that had become highly research-oriented in the 1930's, they had built up the world's largest petroleum-research organization and had contributed substantially to the development of new knowledge and processes that became indispensable in providing products for war. They developed fluid catalytic cracking, which was the most important single source of base stocks for a number of products of strategic value. They designed—on the basis of theoretical work done by Anglo-Iranian—the first large-scale production of alkylate from petroleum. They also furnished processes for making Butyl, a specialty rubber, and Buna-S, which made up approximately 90 per cent of the total wartime manufacture of synthetic rubber. And they supplied the process for making from petroleum nearly half of the butadiene used in making Buna-S.

The Jersey Company similarly made substantial contributions to the over-all planning and coordination of the oil industry's operations. This service to the Allies took various forms. Accustomed to long-range planning and so situated as to be in a position to observe developments of international significance in various parts of the world, the company's executives early urged the preparation of the oil industry for national defense. The parent company made a unique contribution by making available to the Petroleum Administration for War its own coordination executives, concepts, and techniques. The experience and knowledge gained in the successful operation of one of the world's largest industrial concerns were thereby applied to the continuous planning of the operations of the oil industry under the United States, Canada, and Great Britain.

Less clearly identifiable—because it was merged in the general wartime oil industry effort—was the contribution of the top administrators of parent company and affiliates as members of boards and committees cooperating with government agencies in advisory and liaison capacities. Men of wide experience, they brought to these organizations valuable qualifications. They had a familiarity with the managing of unusually large undertakings and a knowledge of foreign operations and conditions affecting them that were then unequaled by any other American oil company. In addition, their flexibility, derived from working in a large and widely dispersed organization and often under highly dynamic conditions, was of signal value in dealing with rapidly changing and geographically shifting wartime needs.

Chapter 21

Reconversion, Recovery, and Rehabilitation

THE VICTORIOUS DRIVE of the Allies in the spring and summer of 1945, which culminated in the surrender of the Germans in May and of the Japanese in August, brought Standard Oil Company (New Jersey) face to face with stupendous problems of recovery from war and conversion to peace. Its administrators had no illusions about the difficulties that lay ahead or about the risks that would have to be assumed. "There are signs aplenty," said Chairman Gallagher soon after the end of the conflict, "that the problems of peace are no less urgent than those of war."[1]

The company's Board of Directors had begun well before the end of the war to prepare for the return to peace. They had initiated changes in Jersey's administrative structure and techniques. They had begun to study the developing economic, social, and political forces that would affect the postwar world. They had decided to return to the countries lost to the enemy during the war. And they had started to adjust the company's policies and plans so as to meet reviving competition effectively and to take advantage of the opportunities resulting from the expected long-term expansion in the demand for oil products.

The immediate necessity in the late summer of 1945 was to start the processes of rebuilding and of converting to peace. In the areas under Axis or Russian domination, this meant that Jersey had to return as soon as possible to begin the work of restoring corporate organizations, recovering properties, and rehabilitating facilities and personnel. Its eventual goal, of course, was to resume operations. In countries within the orbit of the Western Allies, it was necessary to convert from producing products for war to competing in the civilian market as soon as government regulations were relaxed. The particular interest of this chapter is in how, and with what success, the company proceeded to convert to peace and to regain control of properties lost during the war.

RECONVERSION AT HOME

Nearly all the regulations under the United States government having to do with the petroleum industry were lifted in a few months following the close of the war. The rationing of oil products ceased within 24 hours after the signing of the armistice with Japan. Within a few days, the government rescinded most of its marketing controls—one exception being prices—and canceled nearly all wartime regulation of production and of transportation on land. By October 15, 1945, the Petroleum Administration for War had terminated all orders and directives for the United States, and by November it had removed nearly all those affecting foreign operations. Late in the year, the government began to restore tankers to normal service. The flow of oil through the Big Inch and the Little Big Inch pipelines ceased, and the lines were turned over to the War Assets Administration for disposition.[2]

The Petroleum Administration for War was maintained for some time. One reason was the outbreak of strikes in many refineries. These labor troubles threatened to reduce to dangerous levels the output of products that were still needed in large volume for the armies of occupation and the fleets bringing the servicemen home. Fearing the possible breakdown of supply, the PAW recommended that the government seize and operate the shut-down refineries. This was done by the Secretary of the Navy on orders from President Truman. Other developments combined to create a twofold emergency, which the PAW helped to meet: the enormous increase in the demand for fuel oil for relief ships as well as for combat vessels bringing the servicemen home; and the reduced output of this product after the war. The volume reduction arose from the fact that the prices on fuel oil and gasoline set by the Office of Price Administration had encouraged refiners to make relatively more gasoline and less fuel oil out of a barrel of crude. The Petroleum Administration for War called for more realistic pricing, but the OPA held out for the continuation of wartime controls. The PAW won, and adjustments in price ceilings solved the problem.[3]

In 1946 all the wartime agencies having regulatory powers over the oil industry were closed or changed into bodies with less responsibility and authority. The PAW, which had been limiting the scope of its organization and reducing its personnel since shortly after V-J Day, was terminated in May, 1946. The Petroleum Industry War Council was discontinued, but a new board was set up to advise the Secretary of the

Interior on petroleum matters.[4] The War Production Board was replaced by the Civilian Production Board; this new body maintained control for a time over the domestic use of critical materials in short supply. The authority of the Office of Price Administration was gradually reduced until its demise in the fall of 1946.

The American government soon also disposed of most of its wartime investments in transport facilities and plants by selling them to private companies. Until March, 1946, its tankers were used for providing supplies to war-devastated countries under the United States Maritime Authority organized after the war. In accordance with the Merchant Ship Sales Act of that month, the government began to sell its ships, including tankers, to private companies, domestic and foreign. The Jersey affiliates, which had already received payment for the insured loss of American tankers, in 1947 purchased 23 ocean tankers from the Maritime Commission.[5] The government also offered certain plants and other facilities for sale. Humble purchased the Baytown Ordnance Works at a price based on original cost minus 10 per cent—to cover depreciation and obsolescence—for each year it had been used.[6]

The termination of government contracts had begun even before hostilities ended. With V-J Day in sight, the government canceled its toluene contract with Humble. Upon the ending of the war with Japan, Washington notified the domestic companies of the early cancellation of other war contracts.

The affiliates consequently ceased to manufacture war products and began to convert to peacetime operations. A few plants were placed on a stand-by basis because their immediate conversion proved impossible. Some of the units used in the production of butadiene and two of the Butyl rubber installations at Baton Rouge were closed. But the demand for synthetic rubber was so substantial that the third Butyl unit at Baton Rouge, the one at Baytown, and certain others making butadiene were continued in operation.[7] Humble utilized the Baytown Ordnance Works for the manufacture of aromatic solvents for use in making paints, varnishes, insect sprays, and other products.[8]

The most dramatic change-over was from manufacturing aviation gasoline to making high-octane motor gasoline. With the drop in the demand for the former product and the discontinuance of toluene production, large volumes of light naphtha, copolymer, and alkylate at once became available for producing a superior motor fuel. The units used in making aviation fuel were able with only minor changes to produce large volumes of gasoline superior to the quality required for automobiles. By blending this product with one of lower quality, it was possible to turn out enormous quantities of Esso Extra. Hence on the day after V-J Day, Jersey announced the manufacture of what it called the finest automotive gasoline ever sold under the Esso sign. Placing this 95-octane fuel on the market so soon and without a price increase gave the affiliates a head start in the postwar gasoline market.[9]

The return to the prewar transportation system was accomplished without any serious difficulty. The restoration of tanker transport to serving the Atlantic Coast refineries and markets, although insufficient to meet needs, relieved the pipelines of much of their work. The old Tuscarora no longer had to carry crude eastward; again it was reversed to resume its prewar task of carrying gasoline from the Atlantic Coast westward. On October 5, 1945, Esso gasoline was pumped into this carrier for delivery to inland markets in Pennsylvania.[10] The Portland-Montreal and Plantation pipelines, both built during the war, continued to serve Jersey affiliates.

At the same time, the employee force of the Jersey companies was being put back on a peacetime basis. The change involved shifting from the long workweek with overtime pay to a shorter week and reemploying thousands who had been absent on leave during the war.

The prospect of a shorter week with a reduction in pay from wartime levels brought a general wave of strikes or threats of strikes in American industry. The Oil Workers International Union–CIO demanded that the reduction of hours from 48 to 40 a week should be accompanied by a 30 per cent increase in the hourly wage rate so that take-home pay would not be reduced. When the oil companies refused to meet the demand for so high an increase, the employees in refineries where the oil workers were organized began to strike in the middle of September, 1945. Many of the country's major refineries were closed, but they were "seized" by the Secretary of the Navy and kept in operation under the jurisdiction of the government.[11]

The Jersey affiliates suffered very little from this strike. About September 1, they began to reduce the workweek to 40 hours. Their managers met with unions representing the employees and agreed on an immediate 15 per cent increase in hourly rates and salaries.[12] Only the representatives of the small plant at Ingleside, Texas, refused to accept this offer. On October 3, the CIO local there struck, despite its no-strike contract. Work was resumed when the Secretary of the Navy seized the plant, which then continued to operate under its own management. However, Humble closed the Ingleside refinery permanently in November, 1945. The company was criticized for taking this action, but it announced that, because the cracking facilities there had been converted to other use during the war, the refinery was merely a topping plant and hence was no longer economical to operate after the termination of butadiene production under a government contract.[13]

Although there were no strikes in the other plants of Jersey companies, the managements of the parent organization and its affiliates followed closely the developments in the national strike. When it became clear that the issue would be settled with wage advances of approximately 18 per cent, the Jersey affiliates opened discussions with their employees, with the result that an additional increase of 3 per cent was agreed upon.[14]

Reabsorbing the men on leave during the war proved easier than had been anticipated. A surplus of employees did not materialize, and hence the only real difficulty was to find the right jobs for those who returned. There were several reasons for the absence of any excess in the available labor supply: the shorter workweek, the termination of the employment of many women who had held jobs traditionally filled by men, the large number of retirements, and the great postwar demand for oil products. To find enough employees soon became a problem.

Jersey facilitated the placement of war veterans by setting up on Broad Street in New York a "Veterans' Center," headed by a "Veterans' Administrator," for coordinating and administering policies having to do with the employment, training, and reorientation of returning employees.[15] Every effort was made to place the individuals in positions for which they were best suited and in which they could utilize skills acquired in military service. The Veterans' Center, which was established to fill an advisory function for Jersey's own employees, also assisted a large number of men who had never been with the parent or an affiliate. Although the company had no direct responsibility for these men, the center did not turn away veterans seeking help but gave them access to its trained interviewers and counselors. It inquired about needs among outside employers and sent them suitable applicants. The Veterans' Center thus found jobs with other companies for several hundred veterans.[16]

By the end of 1946, the domestic Jersey companies had hired nearly 20,000 United States veterans. Of their own 10,372 employees who had been on military leave, 174 had been reported dead or missing by the end of 1945. Of the 9,362 released from military service by the end of 1946, a total of 8,260—or 88 per cent—had returned to the payrolls of parent and affiliates. The companies at the same time had hired an additional 11,577 returned servicemen. A survey showed that most of the veterans who had been on leave had been assigned to jobs that represented a definite advance over their prewar work, and they had been rehired at wage rates that included all increases granted those who had stayed at their jobs during the war.[17]

The end of the war likewise brought the return of full-time work for men who had served in part-time advisory capacities or in regular government employment as civilians. Their return was particularly important, for among them were top administrators, managers, scientists, and engineers. They represented a wide range of the experience, knowledge, and skills so greatly needed after the war. Not a few of these men, however, continued to serve the government in a number of advisory capacities.

Jersey was only partially successful in regaining control of properties seized during the war by the United States Alien Property Custodian under the Trading with the Enemy Act.[18] These were patent rights and shares in certain companies—obtained through arrangements with I.G. Farbenindustrie beginning in 1929—of which Jersey claimed to be the owner. (See Chapter 14.) The company had tried unsuccessfully in 1944 to recover these properties, which the Alien Property Custodian maintained were Farben's and which this official was administering with regard to patent rights, royalties, and other matters.[19]

In June, 1945, the company instituted suit under the Trading with the Enemy Act in the District Court of the United States for the Southern District of New York. In a preliminary opinion of November, 1945, Judge Edward Wyzanski, Jr., held that Jersey had a legal right to certain patents and classes of patents and to Farben's 20 per cent interest in Standard–I. G. Company as legitimately purchased in September, 1939. But the judge held that certain other patents were not the property of the company. He ruled that Farben's 1939 sale to Jersey of its 50 per cent interest in Jasco, Incorporated, was not a firm sale and that Farben was left "with unaltered legal and equitable rights in the properties. . . ."[20] The final decree of July 6, 1946, ordered the Alien Property Custodian to return to the parent and Standard Oil Development Company those properties and rights which were ruled as belonging to them.[21]

Both the plaintiff and the defendant appealed to the United States

Circuit Court of Appeals, which in 1947 confirmed the decision of the District Court.[22] The company's application for certiorari was denied in 1948.[23] The final disposition of the case in that year released to Jersey exclusive rights to oil refining processes under 544 patents and restored to the company 100 per cent ownership of Standard Catalytic Company (the new name of the Standard–I. G. Company), which controlled the licensing rights for the processes. The court divided 254 patents between the government and Jasco, Incorporated; Jersey retained its original half-interest but not the other half, which it claimed to have purchased from Farben in 1939.[24]

RECONVERSION ABROAD

Conditions in the Western Hemisphere were generally favorable to the removal of government controls and the return to normal, competitive operations in the oil industry. In the Eastern Hemisphere, however, even in countries that had escaped the worst ravages of war and occupation by the enemy, the restoration of business was generally slow.

The government of Canada, like that of the United States, removed most of its wartime controls soon after the hostilities ceased.[25] The central coordinating committee of oil companies, of which Imperial's H. H. Hewetson had been chairman since its inception in 1942, was dissolved. From V-E Day on, there was a general relaxation in government controls. However, certain regulations remained in effect for some time after the final announcement of victory over Japan.

Jersey's Canadian affiliate operated under a few regulations for about two years. Price controls on petroleum products were retained longer in Canada than in the United States, a result principally of the fact that products were in short supply relative to the rising demand. Early in 1947, these controls were lifted on all kinds of oil except gasoline and tractor distillates; restrictions on these products were removed before the end of the year.[26] In June of the same year, rent regulations on service stations were lifted, as also were other regulations which had affected Imperial's relations with its retail outlets. During the war, for example, the company had been prevented from lending money or equipment to service stations. When this prohibition was discontinued, the dealers, who had been putting up with old or inadequate equipment, could turn to Imperial for help in improving and enlarging their facilities.[27]

Imperial continued to furnish a large part of the substantial quantity of supplies still required by the Canadian government, but this business

Europe, Jersey executives in New York began to receive word from some of the occupied regions. They learned that, although the Nazis had taken complete control of the operations of the affiliates, the corporations still existed and their top managements were more or less intact. In some countries, office buildings, refineries, terminals, bulk stations, and other properties were largely in ruins, and most of the movables that had not been destroyed had been seized by the conquerors. The refineries at Port Jérôme and La Mailleraye in France and Vallö in Norway had been completely demolished; in the occupied countries in Western Europe only the small plant at Kalundborg, Denmark, remained. Employees were scattered if not lost, and many of those who had been located were living in destitution and misery.

There was little difficulty in establishing responsible managements for affiliates in the liberated countries of Western Europe and North Africa. So far as possible, Jersey reinstated its so-called shareholder's representative to advise and assist individual companies and to present claims for the payment of war losses. By V-E Day some progress had been made in Norway, Denmark, the Netherlands, Belgium, France, and North Africa. However, the actual rehabilitation of personnel, properties, and operations was generally to be a long process.

Restoring facilities and operations in France proved especially difficult. After receiving word in March, 1945, that Standard Française and its board of directors had survived, Jersey sent C. G. Irish, an American with experience in European operations, to work with the affiliate's officers. On the basis of his detailed report in April, the parent company authorized the French concern to start rehabilitating its facilities. But because the current official rate for converting dollars to francs greatly overvalued the French monetary unit—and also because of political uncertainty in France—the Jersey Board of Directors advised the affiliate to borrow the necessary funds in that country. Standard Française obtained loans from French banks, recalled a skeleton crew of employees, and started to reconstruct its refining and marketing facilities. It recovered some equipment belonging to the Port Jérôme refinery from hundreds of miles away in Central Europe.[32]

By the autumn of 1945, conditions were such that it was possible to send a party of top Jersey men to visit England and the liberated countries of Western Europe. This group included Robert T. Haslam, Jersey director for marketing; Emile E. Soubry, foreign marketing coordinator; Leo D. Welch, Jersey treasurer; and Edward F. Johnson, head of the

Law Department. David A. Shepard, chairman of the board of Anglo-American, joined them in London.[33] These executives were sent to examine whatever remained of the affiliates' organizations and generally to encourage their leaders. The particular assignments of the visitors were to advise the marketers on compliance with the Consent Decree of 1942, to examine the difficulties that would be met in rebuilding the European marketing setup, and to study the financial situation. Jersey affiliates were already having problems in paying for crude and products: those in Holland and Denmark had asked for permission to pay in pounds sterling, and France was without dollar exchange. The executives in New York were concerned about the development of a sterling bloc and the devaluation of the French franc.[34]

The party visited England, Sweden, and the liberated countries—France, Belgium, Holland, Denmark, and Norway. They were not admitted to countries under military occupation.[35] They found that France was not recovering as rapidly as the others freed from German occupation, but they learned that in general the Jersey organizations in the places visited had come through the war "in pretty good fashion." They reported real progress in the rehabilitation of affiliates. Haslam, however, made two observations about the companies' executives which he considered disturbing: "(1) They are totally unacquainted with modern and competitive marketing; and (2) they are not alert politically." He expressed surprise at finding that these local leaders expected the political swing to the left to be temporary.[36]

The restoration of organizations and the rehabilitation of properties in the liberated countries went forward despite many hindrances. Tight world supplies and exchange controls slowed up the recovery of the oil business. Wartime regulations, including even the pooling of properties and operations, were maintained in most countries for some time. The Belgian government was the first to remove these restrictions and to restore control of operations to the companies. But even Belgium, which gave up the various forms of rationing and pooling in 1946, like other countries continued for some time to set maximum prices for products. In the early months of 1947, sales in Norway and Holland reached prewar totals and those in Belgium were almost back to that level. The volume sold in France and in Denmark was recovering more slowly.[37]

In Italy, Germany, and occupied Austria, the problems met were acute. Jersey turned over to Socony-Vacuum Oil Company its claims in Austria, a country which was partly under Russian occupation and partly under an Allied Control Commission.[38] In Germany and Italy, destruction had been especially severe and morale had been all but destroyed. Economic, social, and political institutions had virtually collapsed. Both countries were under Allied military governments, which for some time continued to manage operations, including the importation and distribution of oil products.

The Jersey representative in Italy, D. H. West—another veteran of the company's European operations—had a special problem. The Italian marketing affiliate had disappeared as a corporation, and its properties had been merged in a government concern. The refineries at Fornovo and Trieste had both been wrecked. The Allied military government had taken over the management of the state oil company. The small producing affiliate, however, had not been sequestered by Italy during the war because it was partly owned by Italians.

West began at once the slow and arduous process of restoring · the marketing affiliate. He set up a temporary office in a part of the wrecked headquarters building in Genoa, which could be repaired sufficiently to provide a shelter. He recruited former executives to constitute a skeleton staff, with Dr. Guido Ringler as the head coordinator. With their help, he set up accounting and fiscal offices and another unit to handle legal matters, including the collection of information necessary for making claims for damages. These men started preparations for reorganizing the corporation and recovering whatever remained of its properties.[39]

In May, 1946, West represented the parent company in the election of members of the board of directors, which then chose executive officers. These executives and Jersey's representative thereafter had charge of the recovery and rehabilitation of the affiliate's properties. By June 8, 1948, the transfer of the assets from the government concern had been completed, but the actual pooling of the distribution of oil products under military control did not end until November. Although the organization and properties were then still far from their prewar level, they were reasonably adequate to service the company's share of the market in Italy.[40]

Not until January, 1946, was Jersey permitted to send anyone to Germany, and then only under a ruling of the British military authorities that allowed each interested oil company to send one representative to Hamburg.[41] However, the officers in New York had by this time received considerable intelligence about the German affiliates. The first information had come in the spring of 1945 from a former employee of Deutsch-

Amerikanische Petroleum-Gesellschaft who, as a prisoner of war, had been allowed to write to Standard Oil Company (New Jersey) concerning the affiliate.[42] The board of managers of DAPG had sent its first communication to New York in June of 1945 and a full report in August.[43] These accounts gave information about the condition of both DAPG and the refining affiliate, Ebano Asphalt Werke, A.G.

In the August report, the board of managers informed New York that it had set up offices in a bombed-out warehouse in Hamburg. (The company headquarters building had survived but was occupied by the British Military Government.[44]) Although the board as yet had no control of operations, it reported that the British had removed the former German government trustee and had appointed Gerhard Geyer, one of the affiliate's senior officers, to have charge of DAPG and Ebano. According to the bits of information which the managers had been able to collect, the operating organization was a wreck and plants and bulk stations had been badly damaged or destroyed. Nearly all transportation equipment had fallen into the hands of the Russians, who also controlled DAPG's property in their military occupation zone. Many employees had been lost in the war or were prisoners, some were accused of membership in the Nazi party, and even those who were working on pooled operations under military governments were in poor physical condition.

Further details were reported later as the board of managers learned more about conditions in the English, French, and American zones. In the autumn of 1945, two company executives from Hamburg, with permits to visit all Allied zones except the Russian, set out to see what they could learn about marketing personnel and properties. They carried knapsacks containing blankets and dehydrated foods, and they traveled by train or army truck or on foot. By this laborious process, they gathered information about employees, plants, and equipment. They found out nothing about the part of Germany occupied by the Russians, where 40 per cent of DAPG's assets had been located before the war.[45]

By the time Jersey's representative, W. A. Greeven, arrived in Hamburg in January, 1946, the board of managers of DAPG was ready to carry out emergency reconstruction plans. Once a nucleus of employees had been gathered and food, clothing, and shelter provided, the work of reconstruction, beginning with pick and shovel, got under way in earnest. Greeven kept in close communication with New York, where the Executive Committee appropriated funds for food and clothing for the German employees. At first they sent this assistance through CARE, but in 1947

Jersey provided funds directly for serving hot, high-calorie meals to several thousand employees at noon of each working day.[46]

DAPG and Ebano gradually restored plants and equipment and rebuilt their organizations. As their recovery progressed, they expanded operations under military control. In March, 1948, they obtained full legal possession of their properties in Germany outside the Russian zone. They regained control of operations in April, but gasoline and gas oil continued to be rationed and handled by a government pool until 1951. Although all phases of the business were under close government regulation and serious obstacles still remained, recovery in Germany outside the Russian zone can be said to have been well under way by the middle of 1948. The Ebano refinery was then functioning; DAPG's bulk plants, depots, and bunker stations in the French, English, and American zones had been partially restored to operations; despite a shortage of equipment, retailing had been resumed.[47]

Developments in Romania and Hungary were not so favorable. By the time operations had been re-established in all of Western Europe, the Iron Curtain had been completely drawn on Jersey interests in those two countries.[48]

Romania, which had signed an armistice with the Allies in 1944, was in a state of unrest and political instability and her economy was shattered. The national officers of Jersey's wholly owned Româno-Americana were in nominal charge when New York established contact with them late in 1945, but on every hand the company was dominated by the Russians. Although the latter had failed to obtain full political domination of Romania, they were in virtual economic control. At this time, Russia was exacting reparations contrary to the recent Potsdam Agreement of the Allies. Româno was required to produce and process the maximum amount of crude oil because, under an arrangement with the Soviets, the government had agreed to deliver annually to Russia 1,250,000 tons of petroleum products as reparations and 250,000 tons for sale. The Jersey affiliate supplied about one-seventh of this total.[49] For this oil, the company received payment in paper *lei* at a price set so low by the Romanian government that it barely covered the company's out-of-pocket expenses.[50]

V. C. Georgescu, a Romanian with a long record of service with the company, was elected in 1946 to succeed its wartime head.[51] He and his associates made every effort to bring crude oil production back to sound practices and to replace badly damaged or destroyed plants and equipment. They could not export products in order to obtain funds for the purchase of new equipment outside Romania, and because of the obvious risk Jersey's directors decided not to advance dollars to Romåno for purchases abroad.[52] The managers tried to rehabilitate their employees, many of whom were in a state of destitution. They helped the workers by purchasing food and clothing for the most needy cases, and they kept individuals on the payroll who were not fit for work. As the rebuilding process began, the managers estimated employee efficiency to be below 50 per cent.[53]

Despite a general good feeling between management and employees, Romåno experienced constant trouble with labor groups. The unions, influenced by the Communists and backed by the Russian army until the peace treaty of 1947, opposed everything the affiliate was trying to do and continually interfered with management. Early in 1947 a union of the company's workers arbitrarily ordered the discharge of thirty employees. These individuals included the heads of the personnel and accounting departments, a field superintendent, an engineer in charge of a gas-absorption plant, and a company doctor. In each instance, the labor leaders decided, regardless of the applicants' qualifications, who should fill these vacancies. The company's officers were helpless.[54]

The Romanian government on July 12, 1947, issued a decree authorizing the discharge of surplus employees.[55] When the regional commission that had been established to pass on discharges requested Romåno to supply a list of employees for discharge, the company replied that it had no excess personnel and that it wanted to hire 77 skilled men. The workers' union thereupon supplied the commission with the names of 209 persons who, it alleged, were useless to the company. This list included the president of the affiliate, all the officers and members of the board of directors, all executives and supervisors, and everyone who spoke English. The commission immediately ordered the entire group to be barred from setting foot on Romåno's property or from handling any of its papers or documents. The company's officers appealed to the central commission. This higher government body ruled that the regional board had gone too far in including 37 minor technicians, but it ordered the discharge of the others on the list.[56] Despite its original assertion that executive employees were unnecessary, the union immediately filled all the vacated positions, chiefly with its own officers.

The discharged employees were in a precarious situation. Some of them abandoned everything and fled from the country. When they were beyond the reach of Communist power, they appealed to Jersey. The company advanced them funds and helped them to get re-established elsewhere. American citizens were brought back to the United States and given new jobs. Others were offered work in foreign countries. In spite of the barriers raised by nationalistic labor laws, the employees were eventually resettled in other countries.

The discharged employees who chose to stay in Romania met serious trouble. They were barred from holding the skilled positions for which they had been trained, and many of them were physically unable to perform common labor. Some were arrested on fictitious charges, some went into hiding, and some disappeared. Little could be learned of their fate.

The Romanian government early in 1948 appointed a supervisory administrator for Român̂o-Americana. It also named a sales manager for Distributia, a marketing company in which Jersey owned a one-third interest. Român̂o's Managing Director Georgescu resigned in March. After a long separation and some bitter experiences, he and his family were finally reunited in the United States. The general manager, A. Christodu, was accused of sabotage in April, and in July he was tried by "popular" judges. He was fined and ordered imprisoned for a year.[57]

On June 12, 1948, the government nationalized the properties and operations of Român̂o-Americana.[58] Jersey had no legal recourse in Romania. It kept the Department of State of the United States informed. It advised executives and departments in New York to cease trying to communicate with Român̂o and prepared claims for compensation.[59]

Developments in Hungary followed a similarly discouraging course. The armistice signed early in 1945 provided for the establishment of an Allied Control Commission and for the return to their owners of the properties sequestered by the Hungarian government. Although the national authorities returned to Jersey the assets of its affiliate, Magyar Amerikai Olajipari, R.T. (MAORT),[60] actually the Russian armies remained in control of the company's properties. They already had carried off all movables—drilling machines, trucks, and telephone wires. Whatever remained of the affiliate's organization was completely demoralized. With inflation rampant, the whole country was in the same condition.

Paul Ruedemann, the American president of MAORT before the entry of the United States into the war, was allowed to come back to Hungary late in 1945. George Bannantine, a former director and technical adviser, was given permission to return in January, 1946.[61] Ruedemann was a geologist who had studied at the University of Michigan and at Cambridge University in England and who had served overseas in a machine-gun battalion in World War I. He had been with the Hungarian affiliate from its beginning. On his return, he was permitted to occupy the company's offices in Budapest.

In January, 1946, however, a Russian delegation called to inform President Ruedemann that, by authority of the Allied Control Commission, the Russians had taken possession of MAORT's oil fields. The commission had no such authority, and it was learned later that its non-Russian members knew nothing of the alleged authorization. In a few days, a Soviet army captain appeared at the company's offices with an order from Marshal K. Voroshilov to assume control and a directive to the board of directors to obey his instructions and demands.[62] Ruedemann immediately protested this additional invasion of MAORT's rights, but without effect.[63] The Department of State of the United States also protested in vain to the Russian government.[64] The Soviets in control employed obsolete and wasteful methods in order to produce the maximum volume of oil for shipment to Russia, contrary to the Potsdam Agreement of the Allies. The inability of the Americans to gain control of production was shattering to the morale of the employees who were not pro-Communist.

This particular situation came to an end in February, 1947. At that time, after the Allies had signed a peace treaty with Hungary, the Russian army withdrew from MAORT's oil fields and offices. The company's management then proceeded to restore sound producing rates and to drill exploratory wells. But in May the Small-Holders Party was eliminated from the Hungarian government by the Russian-backed Communist Party. The new government immediately drew up a three-year plan for the development of Hungarian industry.

In the winter months of 1948, MAORT again began to experience serious trouble, this time from interference with management by Communist-controlled Hungarian labor unions. The first activities of these organizations were restricted to dismissing capable employees who were loyal to MAORT or to the democratic way of life—or who were suspected of being sympathetic with the Americans. Spite, envy, stupidity, incompetence, and ambition to rise in the party—according to Ruedemann—all played their part in building up the power of the unions. One by one the best men among the non-Communists were eliminated and replaced by active Communists, a tragic process which Ruedemann has described in some detail.[65] The officers of the company decided not to interfere, because a policy of resistance would only have further endangered the physical safety of the employees. It was far kinder to give the discharged men a chance to slip quietly out of sight. Management was powerless.

Over Easter week end, 1948, the government in Budapest signed an edict for the nationalizing of industrial undertakings with more than a hundred employees. MAORT was not nationalized at once because major foreign interests were exempted. But in May the government appointed an active Hungarian Communist to be "controller" of the company. Despite Ruedemann's protests, Paul Szekely, an old-line Communist, assumed full authority.[66]

Apparently the Communists felt the need to justify their arbitrary actions. During the summer of 1948, a committee appointed by the Hungarian government reviewed MAORT's previous activities and made allegations against the company's management that would have been ridiculous if the situation had not been so critical. The gist of the charges was that the Americans had attempted to sabotage the Three-Year Plan by slowing down production. The committee charged them with failing to install new equipment; the fact was that postwar shortages and controls had made it impossible to obtain equipment. It also alleged that the managers had had wells drilled where there was little possibility of finding oil—in effect, they blamed the Americans for carrying on ordinary exploration for new oil. The government committee further accused the company's managers of preventing new wells from producing their full potential. This charge condemned MAORT's efforts to reduce the wasteful Russian production to rates that would conserve the natural energy of the reservoirs, a reduction made at the urging of the Hungarian government after the Russian army withdrew early in 1947.[67]

These false charges were used to justify attacks on MAORT's officers and managers. By late summer of 1948, all of the company's Hungarian executives had been arrested or had fled, and management was in the hands of Hungarian Communists—by "wholly arbitrary and unwarrantable" action, according to the United States Department of State.[68] President Paul Ruedemann and Director George Bannantine were not allowed to set foot in the company's offices or on any of its other properties. But they stayed on in Budapest, living in a *pension* run by an order of Catholic nuns. On September 18, 1948, they were arrested and placed in solitary confinement in dungeons.[69] When representatives of the American Legation came to the *pension* to determine the facts of the arrest of Ruedemann and Bannantine, they were driven off by the police.

The two Americans were kept in solitary confinement and were allowed little food and almost no sleep. They were taken from their dungeons only for long periods of protracted questioning. The police attempted to get them to confess that they were trying to reduce oil production that would be of strategic importance to the Soviets in the inevitable war with the West. They were confronted with the alleged confessions of a Hungarian official, which implicated them in planning to sabotage operations. They were required to stand facing a wall, with their hands stretched above their heads, until they collapsed. They were then returned to their cold and damp cells for a few hours and again brought out for further questioning. This treatment continued without relief until September 22, when the two American executives, having decided that nothing was to be gained by holding out any longer, consented to signing a statement. The police gave them typed versions of the desired confessions, which they were required to copy in longhand and which they signed on September 23. They admitted in these confessions the sabotage of which they were accused. Under pressure from the American Legation, the Communists took Ruedemann and Bannantine to the Austrian border on September 25. On arriving in Vienna, Ruedemann made a sworn statement repudiating the "confession" he had made under duress.[70]

On the very day the Americans left Budapest, the government of Hungary issued a decree by which it nationalized MAORT.[71] And on September 28 it published in English a "Gray Book" which attempted to justify the confiscation.[72] This statement had obviously been prepared in advance and had been held up until facsimiles of the handwritten confessions of Ruedemann and Bannantine could be made public. The Gray Book was distributed gratis by the Hungarian authorities to a number of public libraries and individuals in the United States.

The Jersey Company could do nothing but keep the American government advised of the situation and present claims for remuneration for the confiscation of a valuable affiliate. The United States denied the accusations of sabotage and informed the Hungarian government that it must bear full legal and financial responsibility for nationalizing MAORT.[73]

In the Orient, Standard-Vacuum established contact with its lost properties as the Japanese were driven out. When the United States military government came into control in a country, it usually turned the recovered American plants and equipment over to custodians who operated them under military supervision.

The first such national area to which Standard-Vacuum was allowed to send representatives was the Philippines. The company dispatched two men there in April, 1945, to work with the military. In the autumn it sent a party of eighteen to the Philippines. These early representatives found that everything movable—including tugs, ships, tank cars, and tank trucks—had disappeared. Terminals and storage facilities had been wrecked. All equipment for distribution and storage would have to be restored or rebuilt.[74]

After the Japanese surrender in August, 1945, the Petroleum Administration for War requested each of the American oil companies which had operated in Japan before the war to send two experienced oil men to Japan and Korea, at company expense, to work with the military in distributing petroleum products. Standard-Vacuum assigned to this mission two of its marketers who were familiar with the area. They found it impossible to have anything to do with the company's former Japanese organization, but they were able to furnish accurate accounts of its condition. They reported that with some exceptions the properties of Standard-Vacuum in Japan had come through the war fairly well.[75]

As soon as the Allies recovered enemy-held areas on the Asiatic mainland, Standard-Vacuum sent men back to countries from which its marketers had been driven out. One was China, where its organization had had to leave when the Japanese had taken over all but the western section under Chiang Kai-shek. Although Japan's hold was broken, there was unbelievable chaos in China. The advance of the Communists and rampant inflation made the restoration of Stanvac's marketing operations extremely difficult. (See Chapter 29.) Conditions were also bad in other countries to the south invaded by Japan.

Standard-Vacuum's return to the Dutch East Indies was particularly important because its prewar crude oil production and refining had been located there. In October a small party of American Stanvac men reached the headquarters in Batavia of Nederlandsche Koloniale Petroleum Maatschappij, the producing affiliate; and two men made a hurried visit to southern Sumatra, which was still controlled by remnants of the Japanese army. In view of the unsettled conditions after the new Republic of Indonesia declared its independence of the Netherlands, Standard-Vacuum had to decide whether or not it should risk the heavy investments required to rebuild its physical facilities and personnel in that country. Its decision was to take the risks.[76]

The restoration of the operations of NKPM in Sumatra was in fact urgent. This affiliate had furnished, from its oil fields in southern Sumatra and its refining plant at Sungei Gerong, a large part of the products marketed by Standard-Vacuum. The return to the refinery was literally a beachhead operation. Although the plant itself was not in so bad a condition as had been expected, it took company men nearly a year to restore partial operations after they assumed control in October, 1946. Not until July, 1947, was NKPM able to return to the Talang Akar–Pendopo fields.[77]

Rebuilding the employee organization proved difficult because of the miserable condition of those workers who could be located and because of the special skills required for effective operations in producing fields and refinery. The Netherlands employees who were found were all in urgent need of food, clothing, and medical care. Those in serious condition were sent to Holland or the United States on rehabilitation furloughs; those who were better off were provided with food, clothes, and shelter. All were given compensation for losses and other types of assistance; in addition, they were paid full salaries for six months from October 1, 1945, and 60 per cent thereafter until they returned to work.[78] Prewar Asiatic employees who were located were returned to the payroll, and additional workers were hired. The number of such employees rose from 179 at the end of 1945 to 9,500 at the end of 1947. Because of the scarcity of food and clothing, the company purchased rice in South America and other foods and clothing in the United States for shipment to Sumatra. By such relief operations, NKPM was able to rehabilitate its working force while it was rebuilding its refinery, restoring its oil wells, and training old and new employees.[79]

The company started production in the Talang Akar–Pendopo fields in August, 1947, and began pipeline runs to the refinery in October. The Sungei Gerong plant was restored to operation in the autumn, and by the end of 1947 it was working at 50 per cent of capacity. Conditions in the Talang Akar–Pendopo fields were by then fairly satisfactory, but the back country was still in such an unsettled condition that no effort was made to enter the other Sumatran oil fields.[80]

By the beginning of 1948, the recovery and rehabilitation of the properties and organizations of Eastern Hemisphere affiliates and the restoration of their operations had made considerable progress in many countries from which Jersey interests had been driven by the war. Control had not been restored, nor was it to be, in the Baltic territories seized by the Russians or in East Germany, Czechoslovakia, Romania, and Hungary. The Communist hold on China was spreading. The affiliates were also encountering problems elsewhere, but these were more particularly the result of such economic, social, and political difficulties as affected much of Europe and the Orient after the war. Once the companies were again in operation, manifold and difficult internal problems became the immediate concern of their operating managers. Planning for the future became merged with the over-all plans for Jersey interests. For several years, however, the work of both managers and policy makers was made difficult by the breakdown of the normal system of international payments. (See Chapter 26.)

WAR LOSSES: CLAIMS AND COMPENSATION

The preparation of claims for compensation for losses from wartime destruction and from the nationalization of properties has been an arduous process, and success in obtaining reparations has varied from country to country. Certain losses were covered by war-risk insurance. Compensation for others depended on provisions in peace treaties or agreements made by the Allies. In some instances, recovery was governed by laws passed by the countries themselves or by negotiations with their governments. In 1962 the Congress of the United States enacted legislation having to do with payment for losses sustained in Germany and in certain other countries attacked or occupied by Germany and Japan.

Tanker losses were to a large extent covered by insurance, and compensation was received promptly. Under war-risk insurance, the United States and Canadian governments and outside underwriters paid a total of $53,700,000 for 41 ships lost by Standard Oil Company of New Jersey, Panama Transport, and Imperial. European governments—principally that of the United Kingdom—under similar insurance arrangements paid $21,000,000 for 24 tankers of affiliates. These countries also paid a part of the cost of repairing 25 badly damaged vessels. Reimbursement was not obtained for the tankers of certain affiliates under Axis control, but they represented a minor part of the total loss of such ships. Tanker losses not covered by insurance came under laws enacted by Congress in 1962.[81]

The countries in Western Europe that had been occupied by the Germans during the war passed laws to govern compensation for destroyed or damaged properties. Jersey affiliates received payments from the Scandinavian countries, the Netherlands, Belgium, and France. The investments in these countries, excepting France, were largely in marketing properties, and hence losses were not large. Far greater damage had been sustained in France: the destruction of the Port Jérôme refinery was the largest single loss suffered by Jersey in Allied countries. France compensated Standard Française at the same rate as was granted to its own nationals.[82]

The Allies, including Russia, made agreements at Potsdam and Paris in 1945 concerning reparations for losses in enemy countries in Europe. Under the Paris Agreement on Reparation from Germany, effective January 14, 1946, nationals of the Western Allies could claim compensation only from their own country's share of German-owned assets seized in Germany during the war or within the nationals' own countries. Jersey filed claims under legislation passed by Congress to provide for the payment of reparations out of German assets seized in this country. The Foreign Claims Settlement Commission in 1967 awarded about $38,000,-000, not including interest. When the amount available in the War Claims Fund was divided in accordance with law in October, 1967, Jersey received $23,000,000. Under the same 1962 legislation, Humble and Creole received awards of approximately $2,200,000 and $400,000, respectively; in 1967 they collected about $1,300,000 and $260,000 on these claims.[83]

Provisions for reparations applicable to foreign-owned companies were included in peace treaties made before the end of 1947 with Italy, Romania, Hungary, and Bulgaria. Jersey received compensation from Italy under the treaty's provision for payment in that country's currency to the amount of two-thirds of the replacement cost, at the time of payment, of the properties destroyed. But the company received no compensation from Russia for losses in the areas it controlled. These included parts of Germany and Finland seized by Russia, the small Baltic states, Poland, Czechoslovakia, Bulgaria, Romania, and Hungary.[84]

The company submitted claims for losses in certain countries dominated by the Communists to the United States Foreign Claims Settlement Commission, which passed on them but could pay awards only on a pro rata basis from funds derived from the liquidation of seized assets held by this country. The commission awarded a total of about $45,000,000, including interest, on claims filed for losses in Romania; of this award less than $11,000,000 had been paid by 1968. It allowed about $39,000,-000, including interest, on similar claims filed for losses in Hungary, of which less than $1,000,000 had been paid to the company by 1968.[85]

Both Czechoslovakia and Poland made lump-sum settlements with the United States for nationalized American properties. Jersey received an award from the Foreign Claims Settlement Commission of about

$390,000, including interest, on its Czechoslovakian claim, of which only about $22,000 had been paid as of 1968. The commission awarded $1,700,000, including interest, on the company's Polish claim, and as of September, 1968, Jersey had received about $100,000.[86]

Standard-Vacuum's compensation for war losses in the Orient also varied from country to country. The process of settling claims has been long-drawn-out and has involved litigation in the United States and the United Kingdom. As of August, 1968, Stanvac had received reparations for wartime losses totaling close to $35,000,000.[87]

The losses in countries where Stanvac was concerned principally with marketing operations were not so large as those where it had producing and refining. Under legislation provided for in the United States' peace treaty with Japan, the company has been paid approximately $2,380,000 on claims for properties destroyed and *yen* accounts in that country. In addition, after twenty years of litigation reaching to the United States Supreme Court, it has received over $1,000,000 in a suit against the New York Superintendent of Banks as liquidator of the assets of the New York City agency of the Yokohama Specie Bank. Stanvac has also been paid more than $4,000,000 for losses in the Philippines on claims presented to the Philippine War Damage Commission set up by the Congress of the United States. Under prewar insurance programs of local governments in Malaya and Singapore, it has obtained a total compensation of $2,500,-000. It has received no reparation for losses in China.[88]

Stanvac suffered the largest part of its loss from the war in the Dutch East Indies in the planned destruction of its producing and refining properties in Sumatra before occupation by the Japanese. After the war, the new Republic of Indonesia repealed the regulations of the former government, which had authorized compensation for such "scorched-earth" losses. However, under the 1962 legislation of the United States, the company presented claims for over $100,000,000. It was awarded an aggregate of $36,700,000, against which a payment of $22,500,000 was received in 1967.[89]

Besides wartime destruction in many countries and the seizure of properties after the war, Jersey for many years received no income from its affiliates under Axis or Russian domination. This fact must be considered in the total picture of the company's losses resulting from the war. Even where business was resumed with the advent of peace, profitable operations were not restored for some time. The amount of income thus cut off cannot be estimated even roughly, but it should at least be recognized that this type of loss was a war cost which companies operating abroad, particularly in war-ravaged countries, had to bear.

The slow economic recovery in the Eastern Hemisphere and difficulties in international exchange delayed and complicated the restoration of the Jersey Company's business abroad. The problems which the parent company and its affiliates encountered as a result of these conditions were great and long-enduring. This aspect of Jersey's ultimate recovery will be considered in a later chapter.

Chapter 22

A New Era in Administration, 1943–1950

I N 1943 THE Board of Directors initiated in Jersey's administrative structure and procedures a series of changes that constitute one of the most significant developments in the history of the company's top government. These changes were designed to raise the effectiveness of central planning, policy making, and control for the whole Jersey Company with its decentralized management of operations.

The parent company had changed both the structure of its organization and the membership of its Board of Directors in 1927 and 1933. The changes made in 1933, like those of 1927, had proved inadequate. The greater size and diversity of Jersey's interests and operations had made contacts with affiliates insufficient at a time when the level of the oil industry's technology and managerial efficiency was rising. Other complicating factors had developed new importance in the 1930's. One was the growing independence and assertiveness of employees nearly everywhere at the very time when high skills and morale were required for efficient operations. Another was the more complex relations with governments, which both at home and abroad were introducing greater controls over oil industry operations.

Certain events in 1942 brought into sharp focus the administrative problems of the Jersey Company and the need for closer relations of the parent with its affiliates. Trouble over Venezuelan concessions showed that a new approach was called for in relations with government and general public in foreign countries. At home the hearings of the Senate Committee on National Defense in the same year showed a lack of knowledge on the part of Jersey's chief executive—and especially of its directors—concerning what had been going on in certain affiliates. The testimony of witnesses for the government, together with the resulting publicity, also revealed an unsatisfactory relationship with the government and the public. These developments brought about a movement for further change in Jersey's top administration.

ADMINISTRATIVE LEADERSHIP

Change has not always come in business organizations when it has been needed. In Jersey at this time, however, as so often in the past, the need coincided with a leadership that had the wisdom and the flexibility to meet problems by even radical moves. The company then had a governing body which represented a wide range of professional competence and a rising concern for the many relations of the Jersey Company inside and outside its operational reach.[1]

As compared with the Jersey Board of Directors of the 1920's, that of the 1940's reflected a new era. The directors who had served before 1927 were all gone by 1943—even the great builders, Teagle and Sadler. Like most of their forerunners, the officers and directors were employees who had risen through many years of employment with one or more Jersey companies. Unlike their predecessors, however, most of them were scientists or engineers by training; a few had been educated in the school of experience. All had been tempered by the depression and the intense competition of the 1930's. They had felt the impact on business of the prewar movements for social and political reform and also of the rising expectations of the lower economic classes and national groups in many parts of the world. They had encountered the intense challenges of war.

Only two members had served on the Jersey board from the 1920's. Frederick H. Bedford, Jr., who had become a director in 1927, came from a family prominent in the company's early history. He had worked in marketing at home and abroad and was the company's leading authority on the manufacture and sale of specialty products. Elected to the board in 1929, Orville Harden had spent his whole career with the parent company and had developed into a general administrator with an over-all view of its interests. He knew the company's business in greater detail over a longer period of time than any other director. He was a man with a superior intellectual endowment. He became one of Jersey's leaders in conducting important negotiations regarding foreign investments and operations.

Three members, who had been elected in the 1930's, were nearing retirement. Thomas C. McCobb, who had risen to the position of comptroller, represented that aspect of the company's business until his retirement. Ralph W. Gallagher, the board's authority on natural gas, was

Table 21: **DIRECTORS OF STANDARD OIL COMPANY (NEW JERSEY) AND THEIR PRINCIPAL RESPONSIBILITIES, 1943–1950**

Director	Year Elected	Principal Responsibilities to 1950
Frederick H. Bedford, Jr.	1927	Contact director for specialty sales and for Gilbert & Barker Manufacturing Company.
Orville Harden	1929	Vice-president; vice-chairman of the Executive Committee; contact director for overseas marketing, 1943; contact director for Law Department, Standard-Vacuum Oil Company, and Arabian American Oil Company.
Ralph W. Gallagher	1933	President, 1943–1944; chairman of the Executive Committee, 1943–1945; chairman of the Board of Directors, 1944–1945. (Retired in 1945.)
Thomas C. McCobb	1935	Supervisory responsibility for finance. (Retired in 1944.)
Wallace E. Pratt	1937	Member of the Executive Committee; vice-president; contact director for producing, 1943–1944. (Retired in 1945.)
Frank W. Abrams	1940	Chairman of the Coordination Committee, 1943–1944; vice-president, 1944–1945; member of the Executive Committee from 1945; chairman of the Board of Directors from 1946.
Eugene Holman	1940	Vice-president, 1942–1944; president from 1944; member of the Executive Committee from 1943 and chairman from 1946.
Robert T. Haslam	1942	Contact director for domestic marketing, 1943, and for sales and sales promotion, 1944; contact director for public relations, 1943–1945; contact director for marketing, 1945–1948; vice-president from 1946.
Frank W. Pierce	1942	Contact director for employee relations to 1949; contact director for public relations, 1946–1949; contact director for Imperial Oil from 1945.
Jay E. Crane	1944	Contact director for Comptroller's, Treasurer's, Tax, and Budget departments; member of the Executive Committee from 1949; vice-president from 1950.
Chester F. Smith	1944	Chairman of the Coordination Committee from 1946; vice-president from 1946; contact director for refining and for Esso Standard Oil Company to 1949 and for Lago Oil & Transport Company, Limited.
Bushrod B. Howard	1945	Contact director for transportation and for tanker and pipeline affiliates.
John R. Suman	1945	Vice-president from 1945; member of the Executive Committee from 1946; contact director for producing, 1945–1948; contact director for Humble Oil & Refining Company and The Carter Oil Company.
Stewart P. Coleman	1946	Vice-chairman of the Coordination Committee; contact director for Standard Oil Development Company.
John W. Brice	1949	Contact director for producing and for affiliates operating in Latin America except in Colombia and Peru.
Monroe J. Rathbone	1949	Contact director for employee relations, public relations, and Esso Standard Oil Company.
Emile E. Soubry	1949	Contact director for marketing, and for affiliates operating in Europe and North Africa excepting Esso Transportation Company.
Henry H. Hewetson	1950	Alternate contact director for marketing and for Imperial Oil and Latin America.

NOTE: Not all the responsibilities of the individual directors are indicated above, particularly assignments as alternate contact directors.

Source: Standard Oil Company (New Jersey); Stockholders', Directors', and Executive Committee's Minutes.

particularly cognizant of the importance of clear definitions of responsibility and authority in an organization, and of good relations with government officials and the public generally. Wallace E. Pratt was the company's leading authority on petroleum geology and its top adviser on exploration as well as its strongest advocate of the expansion of Jersey's oil reserves and production wherever oil fields could be found around the globe. In addition to his eminence in petroleum geology and his knowledge of production generally, he had a high sensitivity to, and comprehension of, the social and political currents affecting Jersey's investments and operations. Both Gallagher and Pratt were influential in extending the company's horizons in the general area of governmental and public relations.

The four other members of the board in 1943, who had joined it in 1940 or later, similarly represented a broadening of the interests of Jersey's governing body. Frank W. Abrams, an engineer who had spent much of his career in refining, possessed skill in relations with people that had become company legend. As manager of the New Jersey Works from late in the 1920's, he had given firm support to efforts to improve employee relations in the refineries. He had later become president of the large affiliate on the Atlantic Coast. Eugene Holman, trained as a geologist, had been president of important affiliates in Latin America and manager of the Producing Department in New York. He had proved himself an able administrator and a farsighted advocate of the acquisition of low-cost oil reserves with which to protect the Jersey Company's future. Robert T. Haslam, a chemical engineer, had held high executive posts in Jersey's research affiliate and had been manager of the Esso Marketers when that organization had led in modernizing the domestic affiliates' marketing operations. He had later been put in charge of developing public relations policies and programs for the parent company. In these various fields, he had shown great resourcefulness as an innovator and manager. Frank W. Pierce, who had worked with Clarence J. Hicks in introducing new concepts, objectives, and methods in employee relations, was the company's leader in that general field. He was also a strong advocate of decentralization of responsibility.

Within two years after 1943, McCobb, Gallagher, and Pratt retired and two new members were added to the board. Jay E. Crane became a director in 1944. Under his leadership the Treasurer's Department had grown to greater importance in the company's administration. Because of his extensive experience in international finance, his election to the board was particularly fortuitous at a time when Jersey faced the prospect of critical problems in foreign exchange after the war. The company, under his direction, developed a group of experts in this field of finance. (See Chapter 26.) In 1944 also, Chester F. Smith was made a director. Trained as a mechanical engineer, he had spent his whole career in Jersey refining until he had advanced to the presidency of Standard Oil Company of New Jersey.

Three new members completed the Board of Directors of the immediate postwar years. John R. Suman became a director and vice-president in 1945. A petroleum engineer with a reputation as a progressive oil production manager, he had joined Humble as a director in 1927 to introduce petroleum engineering into the company's operations. This he had done with notable success. He had been effective also in employee, industry, and government relations. Elected director in 1945, Bushrod B. Howard was the first general manager of Jersey's marine operations to join the board. A graduate of the United States Naval Academy, he had been with the company for twenty-five years in the management of marine operations at home and abroad; since 1939 he had served as manager of its American tanker fleet. During the war, he had performed outstanding service for the United States Maritime Commission in connection with tanker operations of the Allies. Dr. Stewart P. Coleman, a chemical engineer and economist who became a director in 1946, was the first expert in the latter field to serve on the Jersey board. He had had many years of experience with Humble and Jersey in economic analysis, planning, and coordination. He had organized the Program Division of the United States Petroleum Administration for War and had served as its manager until 1944.

Four directors elected in 1949 and 1950 had risen in various branches of the business at home and abroad. Monroe J. Rathbone, a chemical engineer by training, had served many years as an executive of domestic refining and marketing affiliates; since 1944 he had been president of Standard Oil Company of New Jersey. John W. Brice had served affiliates from the 1920's as geologist and executive in the United States and Venezuela and since 1947 had been head of the Producing Coordination Department in New York. Emile E. Soubry had joined Anglo-American in 1911, had been a member of the London Council in the 1930's, had risen to the chairmanship of Anglo-American, and in 1943 had become head of Jersey's Foreign Marketing Coordination Department. Henry H. Hewetson, who had entered the employment of Imperial after World War I, had served marketing and refining affiliates in North and South America. He had been president of Imperial and came to the Jersey board from the chairmanship of the Canadian affiliate.

At the forefront of the movement to improve the parent company's administration, beginning in 1943 and progressing through the decade, were the company's top officers: Ralph W. Gallagher, Eugene Holman, and Frank W. Abrams. Each in his particular office and term contributed progressive leadership.[2]

Chairman Gallagher became chief executive of Jersey after the death of President Farish late in 1942; he was elected president in January, 1943, and held that office until June, 1944. He thereafter served as chairman of the Board of Directors until his retirement in 1945. Gallagher had qualities of personality and character as well as experience which uniquely fitted him for leadership in the company at this particular time. He was a man of firm convictions, but he was also essentially a modest man. He had a practical wisdom derived from his experience as a veteran executive in the natural gas industry. He won the confidence of those with whom he worked by his integrity, intelligence, fairness, and sound judgment. He encouraged free communication and full discussion with his associates individually or in formal meetings of Executive Committee and Board of Directors. He had positive ideas about administrative arrangements and procedures and about public relations.

During his short tenure as chief executive, a time when the war responsibilities of the Jersey Company were particularly heavy, Gallagher led the Board of Directors in making important changes in the company's administration. First of all, he did much to help restore the morale of its members, which had been all but shattered by the turmoil of 1942. He held that the individual directors should have knowledge of the whole Jersey business and at the same time have authority and responsibility in their own right as executives in some area or areas of the board's concern. He saw the urgent need for a broad distribution of authority and responsibility in Jersey's Board of Directors and for a type of organization that would enable the individual director to carry out his duties effectively. Under Gallagher's leadership, the board reviewed the company's administrative structure and set Jersey on a new organizational course.

Succeeding Gallagher as president in 1944, Holman served as Jersey's chief executive for sixteen years. He was a leader of unimpeachable integrity, wide horizons, and a long time-perspective. With his appreciation of the logistics of oil, he showed great foresight in appraising the company's future needs. He was also cognizant of, and sympathetic with, the worldwide movements of the time for social and economic improvement. He recognized the need for the Jersey Company, the oil industry, and business enterprise in general to weigh issues of social good in making their decisions. But as a realist he envisaged the problems involved in trying to move with this stream of change.

Essential as these and other qualities were to Holman's leadership, it was his capacity as an administrator that made him a highly effective executive. He was by nature a leader. He was clearheaded and level-headed. In the solution of a problem his rule was: analyze, organize, delegate, and supervise. Like Gallagher, he believed in extensive delegation of responsibility. He looked upon it not only as a good management tool but also as a means of testing and training executives. With his practice of this belief went what one of his associates has characterized as "an almost unerring knack of judging and attracting 'the right man for the right job.'" Holman was firm in his judgment, but he also had a basic respect for the judgment of others; he believed that consensus—after a free expression of intelligent, well-considered positions—led to the best decisions. However, on occasions when a matter of great importance or of principle was involved, he would take a strong stand and would usually convince the others by his analysis of the problem. With his keen sense of strategy in long-term planning and his ability to maintain a strong administrative organization, Holman led the Jersey Company in its outstanding accomplishments during the final years of World War II and the period of postwar recovery and expansion.

Elected chairman of the board in 1946, Abrams held this position until his retirement in 1953. As chairman, he applied on a broader scale the insights that had characterized his career as a refinery manager and chief executive of Standard Oil Company of New Jersey. He served as the main spokesman of the Jersey board in articulating in public addresses its developing concept of the company's responsibility as a corporate citizen. He was a pioneer in advocating, inside and outside the Jersey Company, that corporations generally should assume responsibilities beyond the immediate reach of their operations. Abrams played an especially important role in promoting corporate aid to education. (See Chapter 24.)

It was significant that Jersey in this crucial time should have leaders who, besides being outstanding business executives in the traditional sense, were able to see the growing importance of social and political changes then under way. These men had demonstrated in their earlier careers a basic sense of fairness in relations with people. As their own executive duties had grown, their perception of the social responsibilities of their large company had broadened. Their insight into the mutual interdependence of management and employees and of the company itself and the diverse peoples among whom it operated added a new dimension to their influence as Jersey's leading executives.

In 1943, for the first time, the Jersey Board of Directors adopted a salary schedule for the directors and officers of the company. There had formerly been a general understanding among these administrators as to the range of their salaries, but there had been no formal schedule. President Farish, cognizant of the need for an orderly handling of salaries in the interest of good stockholder relations, had proposed in 1942 that the board consider action in this matter. After some study of what other companies were doing about the remuneration of officers and executives, the board drew up a set of rules and schedules. In accordance with Jersey's existing practice, no bonuses were to be allowed. The annual salary ranges were to be as follows: president and chairman of the board, $90,000 to $125,000; vice-presidents and members of the Executive Committee, $65,000 to $90,000; other board members, $40,000 to $65,000. Within these ranges, the Board of Directors determined the salary of the president and of the chairman, the president decided that of the individual members of the Executive Committee, and the Executive Committee set the salaries of the remaining directors.[3]

IMPROVING THE ADMINISTRATIVE STRUCTURE

Basic changes in Jersey's administrative organization and procedures have usually come in response to long-term developments affecting the company's interests and operations, but not uncommonly the actual response has been precipitated by some particular event or situation. So it was in 1943. The immediate reason for moves to strengthen Jersey's top administration in 1943 was the fact that, as already noted, specific weaknesses had become disturbingly apparent—particularly as a result of the congressional investigations of 1942 and a special problem in Venezuela in the same year. There was a lack of adequate liaison between the Board of Directors and the affiliates. Also, authority and responsibility had tended to be centered to a large extent in a few officers—especially the president—and the Executive Committee. These situations had weakened the over-all coordination of the Jersey Company's widely scattered interests and operations and had also affected the morale and the unity of the Board of Directors.

The first move was to make a broad study of Jersey's administrative organization. On the basis of the findings, a general plan was drawn up. Some parts of it went into effect at once, but the whole structure was completed only over a number of years.

An innovation of basic importance was adopted in 1943: the wide distribution of the administrative burden among the directors under a system of "contact" assignments. Each director, except the two highest officers, was assigned responsibility, as principal or alternate, in some specific area or areas of the company's interests or operations. This might be for a parent company department; it might be for an operating function among the affiliates. The contact director became the official liaison between Jersey's Executive Committee and Board of Directors on the one hand and his particular contact assignment on the other. To enable the directors to devote themselves principally to long-range planning, general policy, and high-level control, a new organizational arrangement was made whereby they were relieved of essentially routine duties. The various corporate departments of the parent company served as continuous liaison with affiliates in their particular field. In 1943 a new type of department was established to provide such relations with the different branches of operations within the Jersey Company.

This new development was the system of functional coordinators and related staff departments. These coordinators were assigned regular supervisory and advisory relations with the managers of operating affiliates. Because of the war and the time required to effect such an organizational change smoothly, the process of setting up these executives with appropriate staffs for the various branches of operations extended over several years.

A general producing department, which had been established under Sadler and had been lodged in Standard Oil Company of New Jersey since 1927, was transferred in 1943 to the parent company as the Producing Coordination Department. In the same year, the functions performed by the London Council in the later 1930's were assigned to the new Foreign Marketing Coordination Department and the Foreign Refining Coordination Department. In 1944 the Office of Pipe Line Advisor was established, with a staff of engineers, to advise Jersey's administrators on domestic and foreign pipeline matters and to serve as consultant to affiliates. A step was taken toward the union of foreign and domestic marketing by setting up a new group under Dr. Frank M. Surface to coordinate marketing research for both foreign and domestic affiliates. This move was followed by the creation of the Marketing Council, with a staff unit, and finally in 1947 by the union of foreign and domestic marketing under one coordinator. In the same year also, the Foreign Refining Coordination Department was enlarged to include domestic refining, "foreign" being dropped from its name. Finally in 1950, the president of Esso Shipping

Company was appointed Marine Transport Coordinator. The joining of pipeline and marine transport under one coordinator early in the 1950's was to mark the complete victory of Sadler's drive of the 1930's for coordination by functions rather than by companies.

The responsibilities of the new functional coordinators extended in principle to all affiliates in which the parent company had a majority ownership. In practice, their relations with Humble and Imperial were less close than with companies having a smaller and less influential outside ownership. So also were relations with Anglo-American and some other affiliates in foreign countries, especially in Europe, which traditionally had had a large measure of autonomy. These coordinators had no official relations with the corporations in which the parent company had a 50 per cent or smaller ownership. Contacts with them were channeled through designated directors.

The individual coordinators and their staff departments had over-all responsibility for the particular branch of operations that they represented. They had a threefold set of duties. First, they were expected to keep informed of worldwide developments—in such areas as demand, competition, technology, and governmental relations—that were or might become of concern to their particular operating interest. Second, they constituted a continuous liaison of the parent with affiliates. The individual coordinator and his assistants advised operating managers and evaluated the management personnel, equipment, processes, finances, employee relations, and operations generally of the affiliates. They also furnished managers and gave close guidance to new affiliates. Third, according to the company's *Organization Manual*, they kept the Executive Committee and Board of Directors informed—directly or through the coordinator's contact director—"of conditions and developments in the affiliates and of significant developments and opportunities outside the Jersey group for the particular operating interest for which they individually served as coordinators."

The Coordination Committee worked closely with these coordinators. It was assigned broader duties than it had previously had. This group, which for a time during the war had served principally as a supply committee, in 1943 took up its former work in order to begin planning for postwar operations. It was then assigned full responsibility for the overall coordination of the study, discussion, and planning of Jersey's capital investments from the operational point of view. This process was preliminary to a final review by the Executive Committee or the full board.

From 1944 the chairman of the Coordination Committee was Director

had had 53,000 owners; by 1950 the stockholders numbered 222,000. The great increase was in individuals owning less than 100 shares: from 36,000 in 1927 to 180,000 in 1950. The number owning from 100 to 999 shares rose from 13,000 to 39,000. Those having a thousand or more shares increased from 2,037 to only 2,142.[5]

While the growth in numbers was making communication more and more difficult, Jersey's new problems and programs made it increasingly important. President Farish had been cognizant of this need. During his term as chief executive, the company had begun to hold luncheon meetings in selected cities to which local stockholders were invited for discussion of company matters of current importance. Under Gallagher's leadership, the practice was adopted of inviting stockholders to an informal luncheon before the annual meeting. Recognizing both the growing demand of stockholders for more information about their company and the need to inform them of important new developments and the reasons for them, the officers and directors came prepared to talk informally with individuals at the luncheon and to answer questions at the formal meeting. Because such direct personal communication was at best limited in the number it could reach, the Stockholder's Division came to perform an important role as a continuous liaison with the company's owners. In the later 1940's, this group was answering thousands of letters annually from share owners—Secretary Minton held that every inquiry should be given thoughtful consideration.[6]

The position of Government Relations Counselor was similarly created in response to growing needs. Because of the proliferation of contacts with the federal government, the old custom of leaving them entirely to the various departments or executives concerned was resulting in a great deal of duplication and confusion. It also failed to keep directors and executives well informed of important developments and trends. After a committee had studied the situation, the counselor was designated to coordinate all the parent company's contacts with the Department of State and with the Oil and Gas Division of the Department of the Interior. His function in general was to keep the directors and executives advised concerning government matters of interest to the company.[7] The counseling of affiliates in such matters remained the responsibility of Jersey's General Counsel, Edward F. Johnson, who was appointed in 1945.

The Council on Human Relations was set up within the parent company to coordinate relations with shareholders, employees, government, and the public generally. This unit was designed to serve as a study and advisory board to assist directors and high-level executives in all matters concerning such relations inside and outside the company. Directors served as chairman and vice-chairman of this group. The other members included the executive assistant to the president, the Government Relations Counselor, and the heads of the Secretary's, Employee Relations, and Public Relations departments.

These changes in the parent company's administrative organization provided a structure suited to the large and complex operations and relations of the whole Jersey Company. The combination of full-time contact directors and functional coordinators with staff departments was a significant innovation in the administration of large business concerns. Assisted by the Coordination Committee, it provided a means for making possible the more effective use of the resources of the large, multifunctional concern producing products for an expanding market in a highly competitive industry and a changing world environment. The setting up of corporate departments and other units within Jersey's own administrative organization to assist in relations with employees and with the company's multinational publics was a timely and sensitive response to developments that were of increasing importance to the Jersey Company and, indeed, to large business concerns in general.

A NEW APPROACH TO EXECUTIVE DEVELOPMENT

The growing weight of the Jersey Company's administrative burden brought the adoption in 1945 of a formal system for executive development. The old method, by which every executive was responsible for the selection and training of his own successor, was obviously no longer adequate.[8] The increasing size and complexity of Jersey investments and operations and the many special problems to be met in the different countries where affiliates operated demanded more from executives than competence in their own special fields. These added burdens on company leaders also necessitated a more certain supply of potential officers and managers than the old system provided.

It came to be recognized during the war that the Jersey group faced a shortage of executive talent, especially in oil producing and in foreign operations. The issue was formally raised in the Executive Committee in May, 1943, by the suggestion that "among the plans being made to deal with postwar problems there should be included a plan to select and train men to staff company interests' operations."[9]

There was no definite concept among Jersey's leaders at this time as to the type of men that should be looked to for promotion to larger responsibilities. Nor was there any consensus as to how to prepare them for higher posts. Hence, the usual Jersey course was chosen of appointing a committee to study the problem and to explore possible ways of solving it. A committee, headed by R. H. Lackey, Jr., of the Employee Relations Department, was appointed to conduct such study and exploration and to recommend a program.

President Gallagher, who believed that selecting men for executive positions was a paramount responsibility of company administrators, gave support and direction to the project. At the same time, he believed that in changing the existing system it was necessary to proceed with care, because existing executives might be sensitive about their prerogatives in the selection of men to succeed themselves. Gallagher approached the problem in a pragmatic way. He talked with contact directors about what man among those available might be best qualified to fill a particular prospective vacancy. Such discussion had to do not only with a man's technical competence and his experience but also with his demonstrated judgment and general executive qualities.[10] This process of evaluation was passed on down the line—to the functional coordinators, the officers of affiliates, department heads, and so on. In other words, an informal process of analysis and evaluation helped to crystallize recognition of the qualities required for leadership in different types of work and on successive levels up the managerial and administrative ladder.

In September, 1944, the Lackey committee presented a comprehensive program for executive development to the Coordination Committee conference being held at Houston.[11] The Board of Directors endorsed this proposal and appointed as temporary coordinator J. C. Richdale, president of Colonial Beacon and a progressive executive with personal qualities suited to promoting so radical a departure from traditional practice. Individual affiliates thereupon set up management committees to explore company needs and possible procedures. The movement gained both prestige and central direction when Jersey's Coordination Committee in May, 1945, was given the assignment to guide the initiation and operation of the program. This committee delegated the assignment to a subcommittee. George B. Corless of Humble was brought to New York to serve as coordinator of executive development.[12] By the end of the war, an ambitious plan had been designed, in the words of Corless, for "developing reserves of key personnel comparable to the reserves of physical assets."[13]

The program was received throughout the Jersey Company with not a little skepticism. There was some doubt concerning the feasibility of an organized system designed to select and train men for executive posts. The new system posed other problems besides encroaching upon traditional managerial prerogatives. It was especially feared that such a plan might have a bad effect on the morale of ambitious young men who were not chosen for such training. It was also foreseen that a formal program might become mechanical and thus not accomplish its intended objective.

However, progress was made. Standard Oil of Louisiana—a friendly haven for experimentation—led the way among the affiliates in putting the program into effect. Humble, Creole, Det Danske, Anglo-American, and other affiliates soon followed. Corless commented in 1948—with reference to a serious problem in European business—that a more penetrating search for talent within the European organization might go a long way toward breaking the barriers between management and workers.[14]

By 1948 comprehensive systems for executive planning and development had been put into operation by several leading affiliates and a number of smaller ones. These programs included defining the requirements for each managerial post; forecasting needs; preparing replacement tables (possible successors for managerial personnel); developing a systematic and continuing method of selecting and appraising men with potential for executive growth; and preparing plans for suitable training in the form of job rotation or formal training, or both. The strictly educational methods ranged from short courses given by the affiliates themselves to attendance at programs offered at the university level—for example, the Harvard Advanced Management Program. Interfunctional, intercompany, and even foreign experience came to be recognized as desirable in developing executives for high-level positions throughout the Jersey Company.

Parent company and affiliates worked on improving the system of executive development and on promoting its more extensive use. One result was an increasing emphasis on human relations as a concern of management. Coordinator Corless and his associates visited companies at home and abroad to study selection criteria and training needs, to observe programs in action, and to suggest improvements. The executive development subcommittee watched over the effort to select and train men for executive posts throughout the whole group.[15] The progress made by various affiliates was also discussed at the annual meetings of managers sponsored by the Coordination Committee.[16] In fact, throughout the Jersey Company the selection and training of future executives was coming to be looked upon as a matter of paramount importance.

COMMUNICATION, ECONOMIC RESEARCH, AND CONSULTANTS

Side by side with the developments in administrative organization and personnel came the improvement of certain techniques and their extensive application throughout Jersey and its affiliates.[17] These changes did not necessarily originate within the parent company itself. Some innovations came from affiliates. Others—ranging from new concepts and methods in accounting and statistics to developments in psychology and human relations—were widely astir in business and in university classrooms. Their use provided further evidence of a new level of administrative sophistication throughout the Jersey Company.

One such development after the war was the further extension and more formal organization of communication and consultation. Direct personal interchange within Jersey itself and with affiliates—as channeled through contact directors, functional coordinators, and heads of parent company departments—was carried on along broad lines. Consultation was not only vertical, however, but occurred between individuals and groups in similar work and of like rank throughout the Jersey Company. Group conferences became an increasingly important medium for discussing problems and ways to solve them and for disseminating useful knowledge throughout the whole organization.

For such conferences, delegates from affiliates would assemble from afar at a central location to spend several days discussing subjects pertinent to their particular areas of responsibility. These gatherings might be a meeting of officers and managers sponsored by the Coordination Committee, or of men concerned especially with public relations, accounting, research, or some branch of operations. Representatives of the parent company sought to act principally as catalysts in these conferences and, in the main, to leave discussion to delegates from the affiliates. Delegates, in fact, presented most of the formal papers and had a chance to tell of the difficulties and achievements of their several companies. The proceedings were later collected in a volume which was circulated widely. Thus new ideas could spread in a short time throughout the whole group of companies. And, one might suspect, the delegates with but indifferent success to report would be influenced to look more critically at their own company's methods.

The worldwide conferences initiated by the Coordination Committee in the 1930's became an especially useful instrument for achieving unity in policy and practice. In some years, annual meetings were held in centers far from headquarters, such as at Houston in 1944 (the first held outside the New York–New Jersey area) and later at Toronto, Miami, and Paris. They were attended by a number of parent company directors and executives and by high officers and managers of affiliates. These were hard-driving meetings. They were not so much concerned with special problems in operations as with larger issues to be met and with general policies and methods. They gave considerable attention to economic, social, and political developments that were having—or might in the foreseeable future have—a bearing on the operations of affiliates in different parts of the world.

An important aspect of Jersey's administrative procedures at this time was the increased use of systematic research as a preliminary to action. Such study was generally a group activity; within the company's own walls, where departmental and committee meetings were the regular order of business, Jersey was often referred to as the "Standard Meeting Company." Many standing and *ad hoc* committees, with the assistance of staff groups, carried on investigations looking toward reports of conclusions or recommendations.

Throughout this whole process of study, emphasis was placed on economic analysis, a technique which had been developing within the company for more than a decade. It was especially concerned with costs. This was not cost analysis in the old and narrow accounting sense but something far more analytical, precise, and intellectually sophisticated. The investigation of a refining problem, for instance, might involve input-output analysis and the study of joint costs, incremental costs, and the costs of alternate processes, equipment, or plants.

A new development after the war was the employment of a greater range of outside consultants. Legal advisers had been retained from the beginning of Standard Oil, as consulting scientists and engineers had been for decades. Late in the 1930's, economists as consultants had advised Jersey officers during the investigations conducted by the Temporary National Economic Committee—apparently the parent company's first use of such professional aides in this area. After World War II, regular consultants and special advisers were retained in the field of economics, social and political conditions, and general public relations. In addition, persons with special knowledge were invited to meet with the Jersey directors to discuss matters of current interest ranging from the methods of the behavioral sciences to the political situation in the Middle East.[18]

AN EXAMPLE OF ADMINISTRATIVE PROCESS: FINANCIAL METHODS

How Jersey's administrative organization worked can be illustrated by a brief survey of what was done after the war in the area of internal finance. A similar process of analyzing, planning, counseling, reporting, and checking could be described for such other aspects of the business as technology, accounting, economics, employee and public relations, and the various branches of operations. The methods employed in financial planning and control illustrate the parent company–affiliate relationship. Finance, of course, was a basic consideration in most decisions and in operations generally.[19]

The principal financial functions of the parent company were to guide the planning of capital investments, to assure that the necessary funds were available, and to see that the affiliates used their resources to the best advantage. Soundly based central planning and searching reviews were essential to the effective working of decentralized management. Hence improved financial administration on the part of the parent company had of necessity progressed hand in hand with decentralization of the management of operations.

Many Jersey executives and departments—some of long standing and others new—contributed to the management of the company's own finances and of its financial relations with affiliates. The Board of Directors had ultimate authority. The treasurer worked closely with the Executive Committee. He and his associates maintained close relations with affiliates; they made loans to them and invested their surplus funds. The comptroller, the budget director, the functional coordinators, and the contact directors also had special responsibilities in this area. The Coordination Committee had as its principal function to study operating performance and to propose plans for future investments in physical assets.

The Comptroller's Department assembled financial information—that is, it recorded the parent company's own data and consolidated those of the affiliates. After April 1, 1948, it handled all accounting matters directly with the companies. It also served as the coordinator in its field for the Jersey companies. This department must not be thought of as a vast regiment of clerks keeping innumerable routine records, but rather as a skilled team of teachers and critics. It helped new affiliates to establish sound accounting procedures and assisted established ones in improving their accounting methods; it also worked to achieve uniformity in their systems. Employing personal consultation, conferences, and the revised *Accounting Manual,* this department served as the leader in establishing a system of international accounting essential to such an organization as the Jersey Company.

The primary financial function of the parent company was to plan expenditures for capital assets; thus capital expenditures became the focal point of its budgeting. This planning meant determining—on the basis of long-range forecasts—the over-all scope of the future operations of the affiliates, the relative weight to be given to different functions and products, the geographic and corporate distribution of investments in physical assets, and the nature of the processes and equipment to be employed in the various branches of the business. At all points, consideration was given to external factors that bore upon the oil industry and to the particular condition of individual companies and groups. Far greater emphasis than formerly was placed on forecasting Jersey's financial resources and the condition of the markets for petroleum products.

A formal method of forecasting the resources available for financing capital investments was adopted after the war. This new approach substituted a systematic and a more realistic procedure for the estimating formerly based on the extrapolation of figures from earlier years. Each affiliate drafted such a financial forecast—for one, two, or even five years ahead—which aimed to project the amount and form of liquid assets available at year's end. This looking ahead made it necessary to estimate revenue and balance sheet items and called for a concerted survey of future plans by all departments. The process fostered forward thinking and cooperation on the part of those concerned. Over the years, some of the affiliates achieved a remarkable degree of precision in estimating their future financial resources. A special staff team within the Comptroller's Department studied and consolidated the financial forecasts of the affiliates. It prepared an over-all forecast for the consolidated companies,*

---

* These were domestic and foreign affiliates in which Standard Oil Company (New Jersey) owned more than 50 per cent of the common stock. Their earnings were normally consolidated with those of the parent company.

thus providing a sum total of likely future resources available for capital expenditures.

Estimating the long-term supply of and demand for crude oil and products as a basis for investment planning also became more realistic. Many affiliates had been basing their capital budgets primarily on operating figures for one or more past years and on the judgment of their top executives concerning oil industry trends. After the war, Jersey's economists studied the possible trends of conditions that would affect supply and demand and made long-range estimates based on their findings. The parent company's board submitted these forecasts to affiliates for guidance in their planning; the larger companies also prepared their own. These estimates were used, together with the over-all financial forecasts, in preparing capital budgets.

The formal budgeting system that had been developing since the 1920's was further improved. The individual affiliates prepared their budgets by departments. Especially in the larger and well-established domestic companies, the tendency after World War II was increasingly to begin the budget-making process on the lower levels of operations, a practice which had been adopted earlier by a few affiliates. Humble's Production Department, for instance, had initiated the practice of starting the preparation of its capital budget—as well as its operating budget—out in the oil fields. This department had a tradition of decentralization, but the particular reasons for adopting the new approach were the great expansion of operations and the prospect of rising costs. District managers consulted with supervisors in the fields before drawing up proposed plans and budgets. The district budgets were combined at divisional headquarters and then, in turn, in the head offices of the department. The departmental budgets of each affiliate were combined into one. The over-all budget of an affiliate became official after discussion and action by the company's board of directors. The affiliates sent their captial budgets to the parent company's Budget Department.

After the capital budget of an affiliate reached Jersey, primary responsibility for it rested with the contact director for the company. He generally delegated the sections having to do with the various operating branches to the appropriate functional coordinators. For the particular function he represented, each such executive and his staff studied the budgets by companies and with a view to the broad plans for that one operation throughout the whole Jersey group. In this process of examination, the coordinator might consult the officers or departmental managers of affiliates. He also had the budgets studied by a committee, which normally included a number of representatives of companies that were important in the particular phase of the total operation under scrutiny. After such intensive study, the individual budgets were combined and were sent, with alternative proposals, to the Coordination Committee.

The committee then studied these budgets, by functional divisions and as a whole, with special reference to the forecasts of the requirements of the entire Jersey Company for crude oil, products, transportation, and marketing facilities, and to the new investments required to supply them. The committee gave particular thought to the technical and economic soundness of each proposed project, to its location, and to how it fitted into the operations and facilities of the whole Jersey group. The Coordination Committee submitted its conclusions and recommendations to the Executive Committee.

The final review of all considerations bearing on capital budgets was made on the level of the Board of Directors by the Executive Committee, which served as the corporate investments committee. This group, in the deliberations of which all directors present at headquarters could participate, examined the various reports and recommendations, especially the alternative suggestions of the Coordination Committee. It reviewed the budgets of the larger affiliates with high officers of the individual companies. It also discussed them with representatives of appropriate departments and staff groups of the parent company itself. With the help of the Comptroller's and the Treasurer's Department, the Executive Committee reviewed capital budgets in the light of financial forecasts and in relation to over-all corporate finance.

In this process of review, Director Crane and the treasurer and his associates provided a more influential leadership after the war than their predecessors had done. Because of foreign-exchange problems, financial considerations generally were of far greater importance in the planning of capital investments than they had been earlier. This leadership in finance and also postwar financial policies and their implementation are considered in their proper contexts in later chapters.

The Executive Committee did not formally approve or disapprove of the budgets of affiliates, but it commented on them. Each company had the authority to decide whether or not to accept the recommendations implicit in these comments. That is, it could make the final decisions itself as to its own capital budget and its plans for future expenditures. Leaving the final decisions with the affiliates was a basic expression of Jersey's policy of decentralizing responsibility.

This practice of leaving budget decisions to the affiliates did not mean that they were free to do whatever they chose with their assets. Because they were dependent on other Jersey companies to purchase their products or services—and possibly on the parent company itself for the advance of funds—they might choose not to deviate too far from considerations of the general interest. Besides, the parent company's Board of Directors cast that large shareholder's vote for directors of the affiliates, a fact which virtually meant determining who would be the directors of companies in which Jersey held a majority interest. As a result, although the affiliates had operating independence, the parent company's directors generally influenced their planning. However, affiliates could and did differ with their large stockholder on specific issues and act on their own judgment, as is demonstrated by instances of independent action by Humble.[20]

The final budgets of the affiliates expressed, in terms of the funds to be invested, the best estimates which each individual concern—as advised by the parent company—could make of the future profitability of proposed investments. Budgets could be revised later, however, to adjust them to markedly changed conditions or to correct serious miscalculations. Watching how they worked became a routine responsibility of the management of the affiliates throughout the year.

In providing funds for capital expenditures, the Jersey board depended principally on depreciation and depletion charges and retained earnings. After the war, despite inflation, the parent company followed its old policy of keeping long-term fixed-interest obligations to a minimum. It might lend investment funds to an affiliate, especially to one undergoing great expansion or to a company in a foreign country where long-term loans were not available at acceptable rates or were not to be had at all. The well-established affiliates in countries with adequate capital markets —such as those in the United States and Canada—commonly borrowed on their own account.

The company's policies with regard to the financing of capital expenditures are indicated by figures compiled from the annual consolidated statements of the parent and affiliates for the five years from 1946 through 1950. Annual capital expenditures rose from $278,789,000 in 1946 to $425,667,000 in 1947 and to $529,415,000 in 1948. Jersey and its consolidated affiliates* in this period expended more than $2,000,000,000 on capital investments: $1,970,887,000 on additions to property, plant, and

---

* The consolidated affiliates in these postwar years did not include companies in Europe and North Africa whose currencies were not freely convertible into dollars.

equipment, and $74,133,000 for the stock of the Arabian American Oil Company purchased by the parent company. (In the same period, the consolidated companies increased their working capital by $267,312,000.) The largest single source of new capital was earnings: of a total of $1,774,128,000 accruing to Jersey and the minority stockholders of the affiliates, 37 per cent was paid in dividends and more than a billion dollars was reinvested. A total of $816,446,000 came from depreciation, depletion, amortization, and retirements. Only a minor portion of the capital expenditures was financed by funded or other long-term indebtedness—a net increase of only $237,894,000 over the period. At the end of 1950, the long-term indebtedness of $441,024,197 was equal to about 17 per cent of the net worth of the consolidated companies.[21]

The condition of international exchange after the war greatly complicated the flow of Jersey funds. The company had had some trouble in the 1930's with the transfer of payments from certain countries to the United States. During World War II, it had had little difficulty because its sales abroad were mainly to governments. But after the war, foreign-exchange difficulties necessitated special arrangements for the handling of capital expenditures as well as for transferring funds in the current operations of many foreign affiliates. Because this situation so seriously affected the company's operations and investments in a large part of the world, it is considered in a separate chapter.

A further function of the parent company was to keep watch over, and to assist in the improvement of, the financial aspects of current operations. The affiliates kept Jersey headquarters informed by an impressive series of reports and reviews. Each company sent a monthly estimate of net earnings, a quarterly income statement, annual accounts, and the report of the internal auditor. These various statements were studied for each operating function and for individual affiliates by appropriate Jersey staff groups; they were consolidated by the Comptroller's Department. By watching these reports regularly, Jersey executives kept themselves informed of the general financial performance of the individual affiliates. Thus they could detect and observe new trends; they would be likely to notice at an early stage anything that was going awry.

In reviewing the operating reports of the affiliates, the major concern of Jersey's functional coordination departments was with costs. In a decentralized group, the main responsibility in this area must be borne by local managers, but the coordinators scrutinized the operating costs of the affiliates with special care. Many of the companies had kept extensive cost data for decades. Like other figures, these had come to be handled on a more nearly uniform basis in the later 1930's than they had been earlier; the *Accounting Manual*'s second volume, which was devoted to operating records, prescribed general rules. Consequently, cost figures were increasingly handled in accordance with uniform patterns for like functions; hence they became more susceptible to review and comparison by Jersey. During the war, when the overwhelming concern was with greater output, the tendency was to strain for expansion regardless of expense. But as competition once more asserted itself after the war, cost control became more stringent. The functional coordinators were responsible for gathering information about the costs of the particular operations they represented.

Comparing the experience of different affiliates might indicate that a certain company was out of line with the general experience, but there were inherent limitations to this use of cost figures. For instance, comparisons were sometimes rendered nearly useless by vast differences in geological conditions affecting oil production, in labor skills and wage rates, in the pace of inflation in foreign lands, and in other factors. Fluctuations in exchange might render dollar equivalents misleading. For affiliates whose sales volume varied considerably on a seasonal basis, quarterly data might be subject to misinterpretation. And the standard cost systems, which often yielded good results elsewhere, were unsuitable for most operations of the oil industry. At a refinery, for example, standards were hard to establish: the types of crudes used varied from time to time, and there might also be sudden changes—often to meet urgent pleas from the marketers—in both the speed of flow and the ratios of the products made. All such matters had to be considered in evaluating and comparing the cost data from the affiliates.

In financial matters as in others, personal contact might at times achieve more than a penetrating statistical analysis. On occasion, Jersey's accounting experts, frequently specialists in a particular operating function, visited affiliates. On such a visit, the parent company expert discussed costs with local managers and encouraged them to talk about costs with superintendents. Such discussions stimulated the local men "to think their problems out loud" and prompted them to ask questions. The visitor also encouraged a staff or operating group that was achieving good results, and he might tell of improvements noted on visits to other affiliates. On his return to New York, he normally reported to the departments concerned and thus helped to appraise the accomplishments and needs of the individual company.

At the end of the year, the parent company made its annual appraisal of affiliates. Then the contact directors played a major role in evaluating the performance of the various companies. They directed the studies made by appropriate departments and committees, including the Coordination Committee, of the annual reports of the affiliates. Finally, the Executive Committee reviewed the operating and financial results of the individual companies. High executives of the larger affiliates then appeared before this committee to report on their stewardship and to outline their plans. For the smaller and more remotely located concerns, the appropriate contact director made a somewhat similar review. His statement was likely to be based on written reports only, except as the director or his representative had personally visited the affiliate.

The proxy review—which occurred each year when an affiliate requested the parent company to give a voting proxy for its annual meeting—provided the occasion for a final, searching examination of the affiliate. This included examining its finances by operating departments and as a whole as well as its operating and administrative personnel. It was on the basis of such reviews that Jersey's Board of Directors decided which individuals in a company to support for election. In so doing, it exercised the parent company's most effective means of influencing an affiliate.

The Jersey board was directly responsible for the parent company's budgets and expenditures, which had risen substantially since 1939. Its administrative expenses, which had been 6 per cent of net income in that year, had risen to 10.8 per cent in 1945. Obviously, the enlarging of the company's administrative organization and functions had necessitated a considerable rise in costs. But the substantial increase in the total expenditure was a matter of real concern to the directors. Despite more than a doubling of net income from 1945 to 1949, the administrative expenses in the latter year were still 10.7 per cent of the earnings.

The board set up a committee to study the situation and to make recommendations for reducing costs. The committee reported late in 1950. It recognized that higher expenditures relative to income were a necessary result of the expansion of the administrative functions of the parent company, but it nevertheless found specific ways by which Jersey should attempt to slow up its rising costs.[22] The committee's findings provided guidance for the action that the board took in the 1950's to raise the efficiency of its departments and generally to establish better control of costs within its own organization.

It is often asked how large and complex companies can remain successful in the face of the appalling difficulties and rigidities that tend to accompany the development of large-scale operations. In the case of Standard Oil Company (New Jersey), the answer may well be found in the two-way system of review, analysis, and consultation that operated within the company itself. This endless process extended to nearly every affiliate but left responsibility for management with the executives of the companies themselves. This system, if properly utilized, combines the strength of the large company, with its extensive resources and relations, and the effectiveness of on-the-spot management.

CHANGES IN CORPORATE ORGANIZATION

Lest this example of administrative process seem to oversimplify Jersey's relations with affiliates and to give the impression of a nearly automatic working of those relationships, it must be observed that they were neither simple in form nor automatic in operation. The nature of the parent company's influence on and contacts with any particular affiliate varied with time and circumstance. Laws affecting these relations clearly were of basic importance everywhere, whether it be federal and state statutes in the United States or those in foreign countries with different legal systems and varying forms of corporate law. Public opinion also was important to the Jersey-affiliate relationship in many areas—in foreign countries to an increasing extent with the growth of nationalism. Partial outside ownership of a company was another complicating factor. Moreover, Jersey normally exercised greater influence on a concern in which it had direct ownership than on one owned wholly or partly by an affiliate.

It was Jersey policy to keep such corporate relationships as simple and direct as possible. Wholly owned affiliates were preferred in principle, but it was not always either feasible economically or wise from a public relations or a managerial point of view to acquire full ownership. In principle also, the number of affiliates should be kept at the practical minimum, but in reality the range of choice might not be extensive. After the war, Jersey moved to simplify the corporate structure. In 1946 a committee set up for this purpose made a study of the situation.[23] Many changes were subsequently made.

A number of corporations that were owned directly by the parent company itself or by affiliates were eliminated by merger with others. Within the United States, laws had changed so that to incorporate separate companies in different states was no longer necessary or practicable. As already observed, pipelines of Standard of Louisiana and Oklahoma Pipe Line Company were joined in Interstate Oil Pipe Line

Company. The most important domestic change was the merger, over a number of years, of Standard of Louisiana, Standard of Pennsylvania, Colonial Beacon, and Stanco, Incorporated, with Standard Oil Company of New Jersey and its successor, Esso Standard Oil Company.[24] In Italy several small affiliates became part of the marketing company, Standard Italo-Americana Petroli-Società per Azioni. Similarly in Germany and England, refining affiliates were merged with the principal marketing affiliate. The largest union abroad was the consolidation in 1943 of Venezuelan producing and marketing operations in the Creole Petroleum Corporation.

A change of another nature was Jersey's purchase in 1948 of Imperial's holdings in International Petroleum.[25] The reasons that had originally dictated the lodging of the Peruvian properties and operations in International as an affiliate of Imperial no longer prevailed. Administratively, it was important at this time for the parent company to establish direct relations with International and also with its affiliates operating in Colombia and having concession interests in Ecuador. However, the purchase was immediately motivated by Imperial's need for capital with which to develop production in Canada in order to reduce its dependence on oil from South America and the United States.

Jersey at the same time reduced the sharing of the ownership of certain affiliates with outside interests. One such association that might have become embarrassing from an antitrust point of view—joint ownership of Intava with Socony—was eliminated by its purchase of Socony's 50 per cent interest. Intava, which handled the sale of aviation products abroad, was then merged with Standard Oil Export Corporation, a completely owned Jersey affiliate. This company handled the export sale and shipment of crude oil and products, except lubricants, purchased from Jersey affiliates or other companies at home or abroad.[26] The parent company also reduced the outside ownership in a number of other companies. It acquired nearly all the shares of Colonial Beacon before that concern was merged with Esso Standard. It increased its ownership of International's common stock from 60 per cent at the time of purchase from Imperial to 83 per cent in 1950. It added slightly to its holdings in Creole and Humble.[27]

The company also considered disposing of certain affiliates, but it accomplished little in that direction. It sold some wartime acquisitions, such as interests in pipelines serving an emergency purpose. It actually sold only one company it had owned for a considerable time: Daggett & Ramsdell, a concern that made and sold cosmetic preparations with a petroleum base.[28] This affiliate had not proved important as an outlet for petroleum products, and it had served a market outside Jersey's general interest.

Some progress was thus made, but the corporate structure remained complex.* On a given date in 1950, Jersey had a direct ownership interest in 111 affiliates, which in turn had a stock interest in 294 companies.[29] More than half of these directly and indirectly owned corporations were engaged in operations. Upward of 50 were concession-holding companies. Many were dormant, some were kept to protect corporate names and trademarks, 14 were then in process of liquidation, and 8 had been seized by foreign governments. A large percentage had outside owners—not only affiliates in which Jersey had direct ownership but also companies once or twice removed from direct affiliation. The top officers of the parent company thought it advisable, wherever possible, to reduce the number further by liquidation, sale, or other means.

An important result of Jersey's concern over its corporate make-up in the 1940's was recognition of the need for careful study with a view to further action. By 1950 the newly constituted Committee on Corporate Concentration was making such a study.[30] More changes were to be made in the 1950's, but they fall outside the scope of this account.

Developments in the years from 1943 through 1950 notably advanced the process of change that had been initiated in the 1920's to provide a system of administration suited to the needs of an expanding company undergoing great transformations in a changing social and political environment. More effective decentralization of the management of operations was achieved, and closer coordination of decentralized management was developed. The sharing of the administrative responsibilities by a system of executives and staff departments enabled the members of the Jersey Board of Directors to give attention primarily to matters of general policy, planning, and control. Advanced techniques were employed in the varied areas of administrative concern, and sophisticated socioeconomic analysis was utilized in decision-making covering affiliates in all parts of the non-Communist world. Training and education were stressed on all administrative and operating levels. The greater use of communication, consultation, and conference contributed to high performance and effective coordination in the multinational concern the Jersey Company had become.

* For a list of the principal affiliates in 1950, see the map on pages 804–805.

Chapter 23

Postwar Employee Policies and Programs

T HE SAME GENERAL objective that moved Standard Oil Company (New Jersey) to strengthen its general administrative structure and techniques also influenced it to give greater attention to employee management. The company made no basic changes in its employee policies. However, its administrators recognized that expanding operations in an intensely competitive industry and a disturbed and changing world necessitated new approaches to employee relations and a wider application among foreign affiliates of the parent company's policies.

POSTWAR PRESSURES ON EMPLOYEE MANAGEMENT

There were few essentially new developments bearing upon the Jersey Company's relations with employees in the years immediately after the war. Most of the pressures came from extensions of prewar trends: growth in the size and complexity of operations; increasing competition in the oil industry; a mounting spirit of nationalism in many countries; and the rising demands of the lower economic and social classes around the globe. The last two of these trends, especially, were accelerated by the economic chaos and the weakening of old power structures and leadership resulting from the war.

The postwar expansion, which required a substantial increase in the number of new employees of the Jersey companies, meant hiring, training, and integrating into the work force what amounted to a large percentage of the total. Within two years after the end of the conflict, the number employed by parent company and affiliates rose from 125,000 to 169,000. In some companies—notably Imperial and Creole—the expansion of operations required major additions. It was not uncommon in countries where destruction by the war had been high to have to rebuild nearly the whole organization. The many employees who normally retired or left a company for other reasons also had to be replaced. Never before had the Jersey Company had to hire so many in so short a time.

At the same time it was becoming more important to upgrade their quality, because of the rising level of oil industry technology, which even before the war had begun to require generally higher skills as well as a larger percentage of professionally trained men. Competition in the industry on a more sophisticated level also called for greater efficiency in operations. And the wide geographic spread and larger size of operations put a heavier burden of responsibility on the lower management as well as on the work crews themselves. Generally, therefore, a higher level of competence, judgment, and dependability was required of employees in all branches of operations than in the 1920's and even in the 1930's.

The upgrading of the employee force was in itself creating new problems. Engineers and scientists, who had been taught to deal with ideas, materials, and machines and who more and more were occupying leadership posts on many levels, generally lacked the kinds of skills in human relations that men risen from the ranks had gained from experience. Many professionally trained had difficulties in handling employees. Besides, their employment tended to create a sense of frustration among able and ambitious men who had been trained in the school of experience. These employees in nearly all operations felt that their promotion above certain ranks was virtually blocked by those professionally trained.

A different kind of development complicated the process of building and maintaining an efficient employee force. Nearly everywhere employees demonstrated a rising spirit of independence. This came in part from the upgrading of the quality of the employee force. It also came from an increasing loyalty to interests or institutions outside the company. This latter development, especially, made it more difficult for managers to maintain stable employee groups with the attitudes and morale that were believed essential to efficient operating organizations.

Both at home and abroad, this change in attitude and loyalty was spurred by social and political developments that had their beginnings before the war but were intensified by the disturbed postwar conditions and shifts in the locus of political power in much of the world. In many foreign countries, a new or more intense nationalism raised barriers between national employees and foreign companies. Also, the workers generally became more demanding as their expectations rose and as they looked more and more to governments and labor organizations to give them support. There were great differences, of course, from country to country and even within a given country from time to time.

Labor organizations ranged from responsible and intelligently led unions in some places to inexperienced, highly nationalistic, and politically radical ones in others. Generally they were more assertive where they were backed strongly by the government. The concept of conflict between the interests of company and employee, which was incompatible with Jersey's long-standing reliance on management-employee cooperation, dominated the labor movement nearly everywhere—at home as well as in foreign countries.

A more searching and resourceful management of employees and of relations with them was obviously required everywhere, but it was particularly urgent in foreign operations. It was difficult at any time to build up an effective working force among peoples of different cultures and stages of economic development, peoples with scarce resources in the way of workers experienced in industrial skills and disciplines and motivated to improve their lot. The difficulties were compounded after the war by the disturbed economic and political conditions and uncertainties that existed in many of the countries where Jersey affiliates operated.

THE ROLE OF THE PARENT COMPANY

The structural changes made in Jersey's administrative organization in 1943 enabled the company to provide more effective leadership in improving the whole Jersey Company's employee management and relations. Electing Frank W. Pierce to the Board of Directors and making him contact director for employee relations raised that field to the company's highest administrative level. Establishing a corporate department for employee relations provided a special managerial and staff group to aid in developing and implementing programs.

This department performed several general functions. It kept the Board of Directors and Executive Committee informed of employee problems and relations within the parent company and among the affiliates and also of new developments in employee management generally. It served as a vehicle for spreading among the affiliates knowledge of the parent company's objectives, policies, and recommended programs. And it assisted the affiliates in designing new programs and practices adapted to their own particular needs.

Basic to much of the department's work were its study and research. In

accordance with the recognized need to employ more formal and sophisticated techniques in employee management than those being generally utilized by the Jersey companies, the department made a search for
such new methods. It investigated what was being done by educational
institutions that might be helpful in the general area of human relations.
It examined methods of testing and training utilized by the military
services. It also worked closely with certain affiliates—especially with
Standard Oil Company of New Jersey (Esso Standard)—in analyzing
problems and experimenting with ways to solve them.

The Employee Relations Department assisted affiliates in various ways.
It provided leadership in setting up in the United States a training center
for managers from abroad as well as at home. R. L. Mason, head of the
department, and his associates advised affiliates in analyzing their employee problems and in developing and applying new or revised programs and techniques. They helped transfer useful experience from
one affiliate to another. The department also sponsored general meetings
of employee relations personnel in Europe and Latin America as well as
in New York. It similarly arranged conferences of overseas specialists to
consider specific matters, such as salary and wage compensation, benefits
plans, and communication. Manager Mason and others from his department also discussed employee problems and developments at the general
Coordination Committee meetings of executives of domestic and foreign
affiliates. These meetings provided opportunities for broad consideration,
on a high managerial level, of employee relations.

The parent company's department thus served as research staff, adviser, supervisor, and coordinator for the whole Jersey Company. Much
of the uniform development of effective employee management and relations throughout the affiliates derived from the continuous study, experimentation, and exchange of ideas and experience which this parent
company department facilitated.

In this broad effort, officers, directors, and high-level executives of
Jersey itself provided leadership. Not only did the Board of Directors
make policy decisions and formulate programs for the parent company
that served as patterns for affiliates. Officers and directors also addressed employee relations conferences and meetings of executives of
affiliates sponsored by the Coordination Committee. In such meetings,
they stressed the urgency of maintaining employee organizations of high
quality and morale and gave firm support to those who were working to
strengthen the affiliates' human organization.

DEVELOPMENTS AMONG DOMESTIC AFFILIATES

The domestic affiliates—especially Standard Oil Company of New Jersey and Humble—maintained their earlier position of leadership in the general area of employee management. What they did to improve their own operations also served as a pattern for affiliates operating in foreign countries. Although the composition of the employee forces and the environmental factors affecting them were different at home than in most other parts of the world, the experience of the domestic companies contributed to the asking of pertinent questions, the formulation of specific programs, and the shaping of workable standards and practices abroad.

Unlike most of the foreign affiliates, those in the United States did not have to deal to any large extent with national or industry-wide unions. When the Wagner Act made illegal Jersey's old joint councils of representatives of management and employees, the latter had begun to organize independent unions; by the end of the war, nearly all the affiliates' wage employees and some on salary were members of such unions. The Oil Workers International Union–CIO tried to gain a foothold in the Jersey companies, but in the late 1940's it did not win any of several elections held by independent unions under the auspices of the National Labor Relations Board. No doubt, however, the general movement to organize workers affected the independent employee organizations. A movement arose in the New Jersey Works to form a federation of employee unions in the various refineries of affiliates for collective bargaining with headquarters on such matters as general wage increases and company-wide benefits, but no definite progress was made toward such federation. Management continued to bargain with local employee groups.[1]

The fact that these independent unions did not join the OWIU-CIO was not because of subservience to, or pressure by, management; rather it was the result of the belief of the large majority of employees that they were better off as they were. It was generally said that they knew that working relations and employment conditions in the Jersey companies were well above the general standards of the oil industry, and that they believed the outside union of oil workers was to a large extent merely trying to obtain what the Jersey employees already possessed.

Nevertheless, these employee unions were firm negotiators. They were quick to report grievances, pressed hard for raises in pay, and strove to extend the range of matters to be bargained with management. The companies attempted to limit collective bargaining to such issues as wage rates, hours and conditions of work, and vacations. Managers would not formally enter into bargaining concerning benefits plans, but they discussed proposed changes in the plans fully with union representatives. Such discussion no doubt at times took on somewhat the character of bargaining. Management likewise did not accept limitations on its right to determine who should be hired, dismissed, or promoted. Nor would it accept the principle of seniority as ruling in dismissals and promotions; in practice, however, seniority was given special weight, particularly in layoffs for lack of work. In brief, the companies strove to retain the managerial prerogatives which they believed essential to maintaining efficient operations.[2]

The parent company and its domestic affiliates re-examined their wage policies and practices after the war. The general policy had long been to pay going wages or better in an area in order to obtain top-quality personnel and to maintain good employee morale. With their generous fringe benefits, the Jersey companies had had the reputation of actually paying a substantial plus differential compared with the general level of the oil industry. But competition in the employment market after the war and the drive of organized labor for higher wages led them to study prevailing payments among other companies and to examine their own salary and wage rates. They made adjustments that reflected changes in the cost of living, wage trends, and other current considerations.[3] Their wage rates tended to approximate more closely than formerly those paid by other companies for comparable work in a given area; the policy of parent company and affiliates was to keep their rates generally at the top of competition.

The domestic companies retained flexibility in decisions about benefits, but the differential in this area also began to shrink as other companies raised their allowances. In accordance with their old policy of helping employees to obtain as much economic security as possible—and with a view to maintaining some advantage in the employment market—the Jersey companies liberalized their benefits programs to conform to the rise in living costs. By changing disability and survivor benefit plans, they enabled the employees and their families to obtain increased protection against the financial hazards of sickness and death. The companies also modified the old Thrift Plan so that it would encourage employees to make better financial provisions for retirement.[4]

The old Thrift Plan was divided into separate annuity and savings plans. Under the latter, an employee could contribute from 2 to 10 per cent of his pay, and the company would guarantee a graduated contribution ranging from 0.5 per cent to 3 per cent, with additional contributions as determined by management from year to year. However, an employee could participate in this attractive savings plan only by subscribing to the new Annuity Plan. This arrangement made it possible for the individual to provide for a retirement annuity which, when added to the compulsory Social Security pension, would amount to an annual income of approximately 2 per cent of his total earnings for each year of participation after July 1, 1945. Both employee and company bore the cost. If the former left the company, he would be paid the balance in his Thrift Fund account, including the company's contribution. He would also receive either his own contribution to the Annuity Fund or a paid-up annuity certificate including the company's contribution. The annuity income would become effective at the retirement age specified in the Annuity Plan.

Nearly all the employees of the domestic Jersey companies chose to participate in these plans. Within the first year after the revisions had gone into effect, 97 per cent had subscribed to the maximum under the savings plan. Including the portion paid by the companies, this meant savings for the participants equivalent to 13 per cent of their earnings. In the years from 1946 through 1950, the additional contributions of the companies averaged nearly 5.5 per cent of the earnings of the contributing employees with the result that the total savings of these employees was equivalent to nearly 18.5 per cent of their earnings.[5]

The distinctly new development in Jersey's employee management in the postwar years was the search for, and utilization of, more sophisticated and more formally organized methods. The Jersey position had traditionally been that operating men should be the leaders in maintaining morale and productivity and in providing training. Now the practice came to be to enlist consultants and outside specialists and to use new techniques.

One departure from old ways was to utilize opinion surveys to obtain evidence of the attitudes of employees toward the company, their jobs, and their supervisors, and also to measure employee morale and indicate points of weakness or strength. Several affiliates had such surveys made in different branches of operations.[6] On the whole, these revealed excellent morale, but they indicated sufficient dissatisfaction in certain areas to require attention. The dissatisfaction of Negro employees at Baton Rouge with the lack of opportunities for promotion represented a deep-seated social problem of the region. Complaint of favoritism in promotions in refineries pointed to the need to find some way to obtain an objective evaluation of the individual's capacities to supplement the subjective judgment and to check any bias of the superior involved. The considerable discontent found among research personnel in Standard Oil Development—particularly the complaint that their work did not afford them opportunities to make the best use of their training and knowledge—pointed to a situation that obviously called for careful investigation.

The surveys brought into clearer focus the already recognized need, in the interest of morale and productivity, to give more attention to the placement and promotion of individual employees. The parent company and especially Standard Oil Company of New Jersey (Esso Standard), Humble, and Standard Oil Development gave considerable attention to this general area. The development company engaged an outside specialist to study the attitudes and problems of its research personnel. One source of dissatisfaction was found to be the practice of hiring high-ranking students and then giving them essentially routine work.[7]

The affiliates' employee relations managers and staffs, directed by the Employee Relations Department in New York, began searching for objective ways to measure the qualities and capabilities of individuals. These were to be used in selecting personnel for employment, in determining the position for which an individual was best suited, and in deciding what employees were fitted for promotion to specific jobs. Managers made special studies of how best to select and evaluate supervisory, technical, professional, and office employees. The Employee Relations Department of the parent company surveyed various personnel-testing methods, including those used in the military services, and Standard Oil Company of New Jersey experimented with the use of such tests.[8] The results were not encouraging. But study, experimentation, and observation brought a better understanding of the problems and of the need to find better ways than the empirical ones customarily used for measuring individual capacity and potential.

Surveys and studies also indicated that it was necessary to help the employee to get some understanding of how his work fitted into the larger pattern of his company's interests and operations. As an affiliate grew large, geographic distances and organizational complexities became too great for informal communication to take place. This left many employees with a sense of isolation and a lack of identification and also generally lowered their morale. It had become obvious that better communication was required in order to give them more of a sense of identity with their company and to inform them of its policies, plans, and accomplishments and of other matters of interest to them.

The domestic companies attacked the employee communication problem in several ways. They studied methods and media and how to measure their effectiveness. They circulated printed information about their policies and operations. They encouraged discussion of company matters of interest to employees at group meetings and collective bargaining sessions. They also arranged special forums. They all used supervisors as major and continuous channels of communication.

Jersey and its leading domestic affiliates had long looked upon the supervisory force, particularly the foremen in operations, as the key factor in maintaining satisfactory morale and performance. In order to raise the effectiveness of the supervisors, the affiliates had begun in the 1930's to give them special training. They now undertook to define clearly the authority and responsibility of each supervisory position, and they adopted pay differentials to recognize the special importance of supervision. They also arranged for more frequent contact between supervisors and higher managerial personnel, and they designed training programs to give the former a better understanding of their human relations function and to improve their own communication with employees.[9]

More than any other postwar development, the greater emphasis on training was important in the over-all efforts to maintain sound employee relations and to raise the performance level of the employees. The companies provided better organized training programs than earlier and made them more professional in character. This training, which went far beyond the old learning on the job, ranged from courses in specific skills or tasks to advanced work in the sciences, and from courses for foremen to programs for executive development. Within the affiliates, training continued to be based in the managerial organization except where men were sent to attend special programs or to pursue advanced study in universities.[10]

An especially important postwar development was the establishment of the Esso Training Center at Elizabeth, New Jersey. The plan for such a center was inspired by the success of similar educational experiments in the military organizations of the United States during World War II. In fact, two technical employees of Standard Oil Company of New Jersey— Harry D. Kolb and Dennis V. Ward—had directed large, specialized training facilities for the Army during the war. When they returned to the company at the beginning of 1946, they were given the task of planning and organizing the Esso Training Center.[11]

The center's major function was to prepare men to direct and to conduct programs within the affiliates, both domestic and foreign. It trained scores of managers from abroad, exposing them to the concepts and methods practiced by the domestic Jersey companies and to those taught in advanced management programs in universities. The center also set standards for training programs. In addition, it prepared materials for use by affiliates in their own courses or in the special training centers which a few of them established soon after the war.[12]

PROGRESS AMONG FOREIGN AFFILIATES

After the war, the parent company and the affiliates generally gave more attention to employee matters in foreign countries than previously. Much progress had been made in the 1930's in Canada and Latin America, notably in Venezuela. European managers had shown a great deal of resistance to change, but it now became necessary to make new approaches to relations with employees in many countries. The administrators in New York hence pressed harder than earlier for the adoption of policies and programs designed to improve the productivity of operating organizations abroad.

Imperial Oil Limited had previously put into practice in Canada some of the progressive ideas of the parent company, but now it advanced still further. It had early adopted the Jersey form of management-employee councils, and it had also applied wage and benefits policies similar to those of affiliates in the United States. But it had left employee relations to the local managers of operations without much assistance from staff groups. During the war, however, the large number of new employees to be trained for jobs requiring special skills and to be indoctrinated in company objectives and policies had forced Imperial to examine its employee management and relations.

In 1944 Imperial's Board of Directors decided to establish a department to assist in this general area. In organizing its Employee Relations Department, the company had the benefit of guidance by Jersey's Director Frank W. Pierce, who was then serving as an adviser to Imperial in the general reorganization of its administration. The Canadian company patterned its department after that of affiliates in the United States and adapted to its own needs and circumstances the methods they were employing.[13]

Imperial's chief executives gave firm support to these efforts to improve the company's employee management. President R. V. LeSueur made a tour of operations in 1944, which had a good effect on morale, and Henry H. Hewetson, who became president in 1945, made it his business to visit operations regularly. The latter's bluff, hearty personality, his service with the Royal Flying Corps in World War I, and his training, which had begun near the bottom at the Sarnia refinery, enhanced his standing with rank-and-file employees and supervisors. In fact, his capacity to bridge the communication gap that had long existed between Imperial's headquarters and men in the field raised the morale of the whole organization.

By 1950 the Canadian company was making full use of the methods employed by other affiliates to promote mutual understanding and cooperation between management and employees and to train men in supervision and operating skills. As a matter of policy, the company kept wages and salaries on the level of those prevailing in the communities where it had operations. It made changes in its benefits plans similar to those of affiliates in the United States. Unlike these latter affiliates, it continued to have employee-management councils in most operating units. Exceptions were the Ioco refinery in British Columbia and Pacific Coast marine operations, whose employees—under the influence of organized labor on the Pacific Coast—voted to affiliate with outside unions. At the time of a strike of the crews of ships on the Great Lakes, however, Imperial's tanker employees took the independent position of voting against striking in an election held under the supervision of the Canadian Department of Labor. It is a fair conclusion that for most of its operations this Canadian affiliate built up an employee organization and effective practices just in time to meet the strains of the postwar years and the problems accompanying its own rapid expansion.

In many countries in Europe, government or military control delayed the adoption of new employee programs. As before the war, the European affiliates had to adjust their programs to government regulations set up to provide security for employees; these generally included pensions, health measures, and collective bargaining. The postwar resurgence of union activity greatly affected the European affiliates. This movement followed the old pattern of membership in national federations which negotiated collective industry-wide contracts with representatives of employers.[14] Furthermore, in many countries the rigid class structure in business made the application of American practices difficult.

The conditions varied, of course, from country to country. The developments in Hungary and Romania were extreme. (See Chapter 21.)

In Germany and Italy, military control delayed the return of normal employee relations. Among the affiliates in other countries on the Continent, the managers in France encountered the greatest difficulties. What a company could do there to improve its employee force and its relations with employees was limited by extensive government regulation, industry-wide bargaining with five unions (insofar as collective bargaining was possible outside government controls), domination by Communists of the Confédération Générale du Travail, and strikes.[15]

Among the unusual problems in Europe was how to rehabilitate surviving employees who had been under the domination of hostile occupation forces during the war. So ingrained had become the habit of hiding facts from the enemy that it was often necessary for an affiliate to undertake an entire program of rehabilitation and re-education of those involved. To win the confidence of such men, the training programs had to be tailored to the needs of the individual.

During the immediate postwar years, the European affiliates began extensive training programs in both manager and operator categories.[16] They sent many men to the United States to be brought up to date on the technological advances made by the oil industry in this country during the war. A large number also came to spend several months in the United States or Canada to attend training courses and observe methods in use on this side of the Atlantic. When they returned to Europe, many of them gave courses themselves or directed the training given by others. Such training fostered among managers, supervisors, and rank-and-file employees generally a greater interest in the total activities of the affiliate. It also served to weaken the structural rigidities in the managerial and operating organizations, which had their base in the European system of social and economic classes. It helped materially to establish better communication between management and employees on various levels.[17]

The broadest range of challenges to employee management continued to be in the industrially underdeveloped countries, where there were little experience in large-scale and highly technological operations and limited resources for carrying them on. In parts of the Far East and Latin America, the problems were increased by the rapid expansion of affiliates as well as by political changes that affected relations with employees.

In such underdeveloped countries, officers, managers, specialized scientific personnel, and even supervisors had to be supplied largely from North America until local men were available. Jersey recognized that, as operations expanded and relations with national governments and labor became more complex, North Americans sent to such places needed not only mastery of their own fields but also competence in relations with people. To encourage qualified men to take the risks and make whatever sacrifices for their families that working abroad might entail, Jersey offered special inducements, including a revision of the Overseas Thrift Plan to enlarge pension benefits.[18] It also provided training and orientation courses for the men going into foreign operations. These courses included study of the language, culture, and general conditions of the designated countries. They gave attention to special problems in employee relations and how to meet them.

In the Far East, the breakup of the British and Dutch empires raised serious issues for Standard-Vacuum. In the new Republic of Indonesia, where the company was endeavoring to restore its oil production and refining, it applied some significant policies. It adopted comprehensive programs for the training and education of its employees. These included the extensive local training required in building up a large new employee force for operations requiring special skills. As part of the new approach to employee training in Stanvac's operations, a large number of promising young men were sent to the United States or elsewhere in the West for advanced education. The company also began to promote Indonesians to managerial positions as they became qualified.[19]

In Latin America, as in Europe and the Far East, affiliates also had to adjust to unusual conditions. This was especially true of the producing and refining affiliates, which employed many more people than the marketers and required skills that were scarce in South America and the islands of the Caribbean. Much progress was made at the refineries at Aruba and Talara. The latter carried out an impressive housing program and provided other facilities for the workers. Creole was by far the largest company and had the most progressive employee management.

Two postwar developments were especially important to Creole. The rapid expansion of the company's operations made necessary an unusually large increase in its operating force. This build-up of personnel had to be accomplished despite the relatively small number of men available in Venezuela with the necessary operating skills, training in science and technology, and experience in management. The growing tendency of Venezuelan employees to look to government and labor organization to determine the conditions of their employment created new problems. Although the attitude of the government toward the workers varied with the political orientation of successive administrations, the influence of government and organized labor became a principal factor in determining Creole's relations with its employees.

After the overthrow of Medina in 1945, the new government passed legislation to enable unions to join federations. In 1946 the oil companies for the first time signed a collective contract with the National Federation of Oil Workers. A year after Rómulo Betancourt became provisional president, union leaders demanded the closed shop and participation in certain aspects of management, but Creole refused to consider these demands as infringing too much on essential managerial prerogatives. In negotiations attended by government officials as mediators, however, the company agreed to various terms in a collective three-year contract that became effective in 1948. A group of Communists, unwilling to accept this contract, then left the federation to form a union of their own.[20]

After the overthrow of the elected president, Rómulo Gallegos, government support of labor unions declined. On the threat of a general strike in 1949, the government of Carlos Delgado Chalbaud dissolved the national federation but not the member unions. The oil companies in the spring of 1950 refused demands for the renegotiation of wage and commissary provisions in the labor contract still in force. When the Communist leaders called a general strike in protest, the government declared the strike illegal and canceled the union's charter. The oil companies continued to observe the collective contract of 1948 until its expiration in 1951.[21]

Within its own organization, Creole adjusted its employee relations programs to developing needs. The increase in the number of employees —from 10,100 to 21,000 in the three years after January 1, 1946—brought problems of housing, training, and general orientation. The employees were mostly Venezuelans; their percentage of the total at the beginning of 1946 was 93.3. The use of a more advanced technology demanded skills beyond those formerly required. And the growing assertiveness of labor in Venezuela necessitated greater attention to employee relations. To meet these new conditions and assure itself of an adequately productive labor force, the company expanded its already experienced employee relations organization, which was working in harmony with the general policies and the recommended practices of the parent company's administration in New York.

Creole added to its benefits program, which was similar to that prevailing among affiliates in North America but adapted to Venezuelan law and conditions. Its Thrift Plan, instituted earlier, had at first been viewed with suspicion by employees who were not accustomed to savings accounts and certainly not to saving under a company-sponsored plan.[22] Even so, 74 per cent of the employees were participating by 1946, and the amount to their credit at the end of that year was $4,000,000. Creole's employee programs also included a death benefit plan, sickness and accident benefits, and group insurance.[23] Although relatively few employees had previously had any knowledge of life insurance, 66 per cent of those eligible were participating by the end of 1949.[24] In 1947 Creole also adopted a retirement program, to which employees did not contribute. This plan provided for a pension for regular retirement at age sixty after fifteen years of service or even at age fifty-five for employees with twenty-five years of service.[25]

The company extended its free medical service for employees and their families. This service reached from first-aid stations in small producing operations in the jungle to cost-paid trips to specialists for cases requiring care that company medical personnel and hospitals could not give. The modest first-aid stations provided ambulance service to nearby field hospitals and airplane transportation to larger and well-equipped area hospitals. The company at the same time carried on an extensive campaign of preventive medicine. Within a few years it reduced the malaria rate among employees in eastern Venezuela from 378 to 11 cases per thousand by spraying camps and the surrounding country with DDT. Creole improved living conditions and health generally by supplying good housing, pure water, and the best quality of food in company commissaries (including frozen foods from the United States); and it brought nurses and dietitians from the United States to teach home care of the sick and the preparation of foods. "Men like to work here," said the Venezuelan head of a Creole hospital in eastern Venezuela in 1949, "because their families are safe."[26]

Late in the 1940's, the company adopted a new policy with regard to medical services: to assist in the development of professional medical personnel and facilities outside its own organization. As its first important implementation of this policy, it built a $6-million, fully equipped hospital in Maracaibo, which it leased at a nominal charge to the Medical Mission Sisters of Philadelphia.[27] Creole reserved the right to use a given number of the hospital's 165 beds for its own employees at regular charges, but the rooms not so used at any time were also to be available to the public. The Sisters agreed to staff and manage the hospital and to conduct a school for training nurses. The company thereby provided

Maracaibo with a modern hospital and Venezuela with its first school for training nurses. As before, Creole sent Venezuelan medical men to the United States for additional training.

Late in the 1940's, also, Creole began to experiment with an innovation in employee housing. To provide housing and community facilities for employees was costly—in 1946 the company built 1,642 new houses. In addition, its executives had come to believe that providing all facilities and services created too much dependence on the company. There was also the special problem that retiring employees were often reluctant to leave their camp houses and associations and return to their old way of living.

Creole looked into the possibility of encouraging and assisting employees in home ownership. This would involve a radical change in the oil industry in Venezuela, where company-owned camps had been the rule from the beginning of operations. When the new Amuay refinery required a large number of operators, the company decided to undertake an experimental program. Here, by special arrangement with the Venezuelan government, it encouraged operating employees to build their own homes and community facilities and to form a self-governing village. This was a historic innovation in Venezuela because it was contrary to Latin America's Spanish inheritance and tradition of central control of local governments. The company gave assistance with planning and financing to those who chose to build homes in this new village.[28]

Building the Maracaibo hospital and encouraging employees to own their own homes were expressions of Creole's new policy of transferring to local communities and individuals some of the activities and services auxiliary to oil operations. The company thus began late in the 1940's to shed some parts of the once necessary but inevitably paternalistic practice of providing all services for employees. It was to implement this policy more extensively in the 1950's.

At the same time, Creole greatly expanded one service to its employees: providing training in operating skills and general education for employees and their children. This became its largest auxiliary operation.

To provide schools for the children of employees was in itself a big undertaking. By 1946 Creole had sixteen elementary schools, staffed by Venezuelan teachers, with a total enrollment of 4,389 children. In that year, it instituted in its major oil camps a system of secondary schools for outstanding elementary graduates. It also continued to offer an extensive program of vocational training for the sons and daughters of employees.

This covered various trades, drafting, shop mathematics, typing, and shorthand. These schools prepared students for field and clerical jobs with the company, but the children of employees were neither assured of, nor required to take, jobs with Creole.

Advanced education also played an increasing role in Creole's educational program. It was an essential part of the company's plan to provide adequately trained nationals for its technical and managerial work in a country where the supply of teachers, engineers, scientists, and other professionally trained personnel was far below requirements. Graduates of Creole's high schools with demonstrated ability and also others from outside the families of employees were eligible for scholarships to study in Venezuela or for undergraduate and graduate study in the United States. Especially promising employees also might be sent to the United States for advanced study. In 1945 the number of young Venezuelan men and women studying in their own country or in the United States at company expense was 77; in 1947 they numbered 266. These Venezuelans studied in such different fields as teacher education, petroleum engineering, and business administration.[29]

The company at the same time continued to expand the adult-education program for its employees. Over the many years of experience with adult classes, the workers had come to value this program highly. When Creole first began to offer elementary schooling for employees in the camps of the Bolívar coastal fields in 1938, the workers had hesitated to enroll. In 1947 more than a thousand adults, including wives of workers, were attending classes. The program in the various Creole camps was at that time staffed by a total of 36 full-time teachers and 200 part-time volunteers. By attending classes on their own time for two hours, five days a week, 75 per cent of those in the adult program in two years passed the national fourth-grade tests. Such schooling enabled the parents to read and write as their children did. This in itself was a matter of parental satisfaction, but beyond that it helped employees to advance to better jobs and better pay. In fact, reading and writing had become virtual necessities for jobs above the level of common labor. During the ten years from 1938 to 1947, the literacy rate among Creole employees rose from 18 to 88 per cent. By-products of adult education in the camps were parent-teacher associations and book clubs.[30]

Creole stepped up its efforts generally in these later years to upgrade the effectiveness of its whole employee force. In 1945 it undertook a special venture: a school for expatriate employees at Maracaibo. At this center, new employees from the United States were given an intensive course in Spanish and short courses in the law, history, and customs of Venezuela. In 1948 the company adopted a personnel-testing program for use in hiring new workers and selecting others for promotion.[31] In the same year, it introduced more advanced and better organized training within its organization. It emphasized the better preparation of supervisors. In 1948 also, it made especially important additions in establishing the Caracas Training Center and division centers at Lagunillas in western Venezuela and at Quiriquire in the eastern part of the country. The next year it expanded courses designed to teach employees specific trades or skills in both the Eastern and the Western Division and instituted such training at the new Amuay refinery.[32] At the top of Creole's educational pyramid was its project for executive development, which was similar to programs adopted by many other Jersey affiliates. The company selected men to participate and sent them to the United States for university courses in advanced management.

An especially meaningful development after the war was Creole's progress in carrying out its policy of promoting nationals to all levels of operations and administration. Its objective was to substitute Venezuelans for North Americans in supervisory and managerial positions as well as in posts requiring specialized scientific and engineering training. The company obtained many such men from the ranks of the Venezuelans whom it sent to universities for advanced study and others already professionally trained who sought employment with the company. In the early postwar years, Creole promoted nationals to high operating and administrative levels. By 1950, Dr. Guillermo Zuloaga, who in the early 1940's had come to Creole from the Petroleum Bureau of the central government, was a member of Creole's Management Committee and was in charge of exploration, economics, and public relations. The next year he was elected director of the company. Dr. Siro Vasquez became Creole's Production Department manager late in the 1940's.[33] He subsequently became a director of Creole, head of the parent company's Producing Coordination Department in New York, and in 1965 a member of the Jersey Board of Directors.

Late in the 1940's the company adopted a new policy affecting activities directly auxiliary to its oil operations: it looked to outsiders to provide some of the services which employees had performed from the beginning of Jersey operations in Venezuela. It assisted men in setting up their own enterprises as importers and suppliers of equipment and provisions; it especially helped some of its own employees to become independent entrepreneurs. It also contracted such work as road building and other construction, maintenance work, trucking, and taxi services as soon as contractors became available. There were several reasons for this new policy: rising employee costs; the growing problems incident to the management of the labor force; the desirability from a public relations point of view of encouraging local enterprise; and the conviction of Jersey administrators that the growth of the middle class was essential to the development of a stable government and society in Venezuela.[34]

By such means, Jersey's basic employee policies and programs were applied more widely among affiliates and were adapted to changing conditions and needs. In many countries, the managers' freedom in labor matters was greatly limited by government regulation, employers' federations, or employee organizations—and even by all three. However, the managers of Jersey affiliates held on to their prerogatives tenaciously. At the same time, they became more sensitive to diversity and change and achieved a better understanding of the problems involved. They also devised more effective ways of dealing with employees.

At home and generally in affiliates abroad an employee-management relationship became established which contributed to effective cooperation in achieving the companies' objectives. This cooperation was not based on the old paternalism that had long characterized the relations of parent company and affiliates with employees. It came to be based rather on recognition of the mutual interests of employer and employee and on specific agreements as to employment and a system of rules and procedures which defined and protected the rights of both parties. On the whole, the Jersey Company succeeded in maintaining a human organization of comparatively high quality and morale with which to carry on its expanding and complex operations.

Chapter 24

Changing Concepts of Corporate Responsibility, 1943–1950

A SIGNIFICANT DEVELOPMENT in Jersey policy in 1943 was the decision to make the company's relations with its sociopolitical environment a matter of organized and continuous high-level concern. This decision came after a year's exploration of what was then virtually unfamiliar territory to Jersey—as indeed to business generally. (See Chapter 15.)

Because there was little experience or precedent to follow, Jersey's efforts in the next few years to improve its standing were essentially educational for itself and also experimental as a means of communicating with the public. "It may have been a shock to many," said a high-ranking Jersey executive in 1944 in reference to his associates, "to read in *Time* magazine the sober and considered statement about Standard of New Jersey" that it is "less of a business than a public trust."[1] Company executives learned that improving the relations of parent company and affiliates required not only better communication with the diverse peoples among whom they operated. It also required a clearer comprehension of their responsibilities as corporate members of the world community which they served.

This chapter deals with this process of self-education as well as with what was done to make the parent company and its affiliates better and more favorably known outside the immediate reach of their operations. It describes study of the Jersey Company's public relations problems and efforts to develop constructive company attitudes and programs. The account deals only incidentally with the effect on the Jersey Company's standing, which at best could be assessed only over the long term if it could be measured at all. Later chapters on various aspects of operations afford some insight into the effect on the Jersey Company's own policies and practices in planning and performing its industrial functions.

ORGANIZATION, POLICY, AND PROGRAM, 1943–1945

As in other areas, Jersey's directors and officers assumed primary responsibility for public relations. They were to determine general policies, make decisions as to programs, and to participate individually in appropriate activities. They established a department to serve as coordinator and staff.

The stated functions of the Public Relations Department, as announced on February 17, 1943, were to assume responsibility for assisting the board and president in public relations matters and to be available for counsel and advice to affiliates in this field.[2] The board chose R. T. Haslam to be contact director for this new department. It retained Earl Newsom and his firm to serve as outside adviser. Newsom himself was also to clear plans and programs with the Executive Committee and the Board of Directors—that is, until the department had acquired adequate leadership and experience of its own.

The department's organization and leadership crystallized over a period of several months. In conformance with Jersey policy that a company man and not an outside specialist be chosen, George H. Freyermuth, who had been transferred to the public relations staff from the Esso Marketers, became the manager. In December, 1943, an organization plan was adopted. It divided the department's expanding staff into four functional groups: (1) the press-relations division, to have responsibility for relations with all mass communications media; (2) the liaison division, to maintain contact and to work with groups inside and outside Jersey itself and its affiliates; (3) the operations division, to have charge of editorial and art work, writing, photography, newsreels, motion pictures, and periodic and special publications; and (4) the reference division, to serve as a general service staff, to provide a clipping service and a library, and to do reference work for other divisions. Specialists from inside and outside the company rounded out the staffs of these various divisions.[3]

An important part of the department's functions was to do research and planning. An enthusiastic group worked on these functions. From the first, it included Earl Newsom and two of his associates, Stewart Schackne and Edward Stanley, both of whom became regular members of the department, and also K. E. Cook, W. M. Craig, and Charlotte Lochhead (later Mrs. Browne-Mayers). This group studied opinion surveys made for the company, sent representatives to conferences to report back on attitudes and opinions, and used other means to achieve some understanding of the nature and trend of opinion in the United States. In their own meetings, they presented and discussed ideas, observations, and suggestions. They drafted statements of objectives and policies to be acted upon by the Executive Committee.[4]

A necessary preliminary was to find answers to two basic questions: (1) What is good public relations from the point of view of the company? (2) What should the company do to obtain such relations? The public relations group drafted statements which were submitted to the Executive Committee for its consideration. The following answers were agreed to by the committee:

(1) Good Public Relations is deserving and achieving a climate of opinion in which our Company can continue to exist as a privately-owned competitive business earning a reasonable profit.
(2) The objective will be:
    a. To maintain constantly the position where all the Company's acts are in the public interest.
    b. To report and explain the Company's actions so thoroughly that the public readily and continually identifies them with the public interest.[5]

These statements became an integral part of Jersey's thinking in this area, the first as a definition of ends and the second as a conception of means. In fact, the second came to be regarded as an expression of the company's basic public relations policy: to act in the public interest and to make its actions known.[6]

A third question also had to be answered: What kind of public impression did Jersey feel that it deserved and want to achieve?[7] The answer was developed through extensive discussion and the writing of memoranda by the staff and review by the Executive Committee. This was undoubtedly the company's first effort to make such a conscious examination of its own character and to draw up a statement of its concept of itself. The consensus reached was that the company proposed to be, and to be widely known as: one that always acts in the public interest; is a good "citizen"; is important to the nation's strength in peace and war; is open, friendly, and communicative; is scientific, progressive, and efficient, constantly striving to make products better, more abundant, and cheaper; has widespread ownership, reasonable earnings, and sound policies; operates in a highly competitive industry; is understanding and fair in its dealings with employees and progressive in its labor policies; and manages its affairs democratically.[8]

The Public Relations Department had responsibility for keeping the public informed about the company. It performed the day-to-day function of providing news releases about the company to the press and other news media. It had charge of *The Lamp*. E. R. Sammis, an experienced writer and editor, was employed to change this periodical from a magazine primarily for employees to one designed for stockholders and general readers and, as such, concerned largely with important industry matters. In addition, the group cooperated with other departments in making the *Annual Report* more informative. Roy E. Stryker, a director of documentary photographers, was engaged to build up a reference library of photographic and other illustrative materials for use by the press, publishers, authors, educators, and Jersey itself.

Another responsibility of the department was to have charge of planning and arranging for special events to make the Jersey Company better and more favorably known. One such event was arranged on the initiative of President Howard of Standard Oil Development Company to mark the silver anniversary of Jersey's organized research in petroleum chemistry. This was a forum on industrial research planned to marshal the views of a cross section of national leaders in a field little known to the public. Such distinguished men as Charles F. Kettering, Frank P. Jewett, Thomas Midgley, Jr., and Warren K. Lewis delivered addresses. These were published by the company in 1945 in a book entitled *The Future of Industrial Research,* which was widely distributed to schools and libraries.

A special event of a different kind was a press conference held at Baton Rouge in the summer of 1943. The underlying purpose of this occasion was to publicize aspects of Jersey's contribution to the war effort. Its particular purpose, however, was to help clear up the confusion resulting from press reports that government officials responsible for providing synthetic rubber and 100-octane gasoline for the military were competing for raw materials. Arrangements were made for two prominent government administrators concerned with this issue, Rubber Director William Jeffers and Under Secretary of War Robert Patterson, to meet with representatives of the press. Topflight reporters from virtually all parts of the country were invited to attend. The newsmen were given a preliminary briefing on synthetic rubber and aviation gasoline by company technical men and were taken on a tour of the refinery. Reports of this conference received wide notice in the nation's press.[9]

A different undertaking, entirely experimental, illustrates the diversity of methods employed, the pragmatic way in which the public relations effort grew, and the basic approach to problems. This was an experiment in group discussion suggested by Charlotte Lochhead, who urged that company executives and outside "thought leaders" could profit from getting acquainted. A trial dinner meeting was held in Boston in June, 1943; the guests included prominent university professors, leading churchmen in New England, presidents of manufacturing companies, and the executive vice-president of the New England Council. The discussion, led by Dr. S. Ralph Harlow, professor of religion and social ethics at Smith College, ranged over such subjects as the views on business held in schools and colleges, the role of the clergy in relation to business, and the working principles and practical philosophy of businessmen.[10] A second meeting in the autumn set the pattern thereafter followed.[11] The company served as sponsor and host, but the program was planned by the "members," who then included a labor leader. The discussion was lively and searching.[12] A similar group was started in Philadelphia in December, 1943. When these two experiments had proved themselves, Jersey adopted them as a regular part of its public relations program, and it organized discussion groups in two other cities.[13]

Jersey also made arrangements for three projects to be carried out outside the company. One provided for topflight artists to paint a large number of pictures of various oil industry facilities and operations, especially those involved in the war effort.[14] The main thought motivating this particular project was to establish some community of interest between the company and that part of the public with aesthetic interests. Another undertaking was for Robert Flaherty, the widely known American producer of documentary films, to produce a film illustrating some aspect of the oil industry.[15] The third was for two members of the faculty of the Harvard Graduate School of Business Administration—after being approached by representatives of the company—to explore the feasibility of writing a history of Standard Oil Company (New Jersey).[16]

Before long, affiliates also began to establish public relations staffs and organized work in this field. In May, 1944, Standard Oil Company of New Jersey added such a group to its sales organization; this soon became a corporate department headed by B. F. Meglaughlin.[17] In the same year, Imperial gave regular staff status to the public relations activities carried on in Canada under W. F. Prendergast.[18] Early in 1945, Creole established a corporate public relations department with Jersey's K. E. Cook as manager. This action followed a survey in Venezuela—including discussions with local leaders in many villages—by a party made up of H. F. Prioleau (Creole's executive vice-president in New York), Earl Newsom, and Manager Freyermuth and K. E. Cook of Jersey's Public Relations Department.[19]

A notable development was the participation of Jersey's top administrators in spreading throughout the whole company the parent company's concept of good public relations and of the responsibilities of parent and affiliates to the general public. In 1944 a director, in addressing a conference of executives of the whole Jersey Company, stressed the need to recognize that, as one of the largest companies in the world, their company had special public obligations inherent in its size.[20] This address marked the beginning of the regular practice in gatherings of high operating executives of discussing some aspect of public relations.

Indicative of the concern of Jersey's administrators with this new undertaking was the participation of officers, directors, and high-level executives in the company's public relations activities outside the company. These men not only addressed company gatherings. They also took part in relations with the press. They talked with government administrators and legislators in Washington. And they began to address meetings of various kinds on subjects of public interest.

Thus, during the war, the foundations were laid for a broad public relations effort. Specialized staff organizations were set up, objectives were defined, and an extensive effort was undertaken to bring about a closer rapport between the Jersey Company and its social and political environment. After the war, the whole effort was greatly expanded under parent company leadership and with broad participation by affiliates.

STUDY OF PUBLIC ATTITUDE AND OPINION AFTER THE WAR

The exploration of environmental conditions and trends having significance to the Jersey Company came to be regarded as basic to the whole public relations effort. To "act in the public interest," said Manager Freyermuth in 1945, "is a sincere intention; to achieve it needs study and understanding by management."[21] The company's characteristic techniques of research and analysis were utilized in the search for such understanding. An earlier objective had been to gather information about the public's attitude toward Jersey. Self-examination and study extended the range of concern to the general climate of opinion and the reasons for it, and to worldwide social, political, and economic developments.

The Executive Committee participated in the exploration of conditions and trends bearing on the company's relations with the general public. Within a year after the war, authorities in various fields met with the committee to discuss subjects of which they had special knowledge.[22] Among them were Associate Director Irving Langmuir of the research laboratories of General Electric; President James P. Baxter of Williams College; Nelson Rockefeller, who for several years had been in the Department of State; Professor Stuart C. Dodd of the American University of Beirut; former President Herbert Hoover; Donald S. Russell of the Department of State; and Joseph Barnes, foreign editor of the *Herald Tribune* (New York). The subjects considered ranged from the problems of liberal arts colleges and methods of research in the social sciences to social, economic, and political conditions in different parts of the world.

The company retained regular consultants to keep the directors and the Public Relations Department informed and advised. In the foreign field, Laurance Duggan reported on Latin America, H. B. Hoskins was consultant on the Middle East, and Milo Perkins served as consulting economist in the international field. Arthur Newmyer & Associates covered political developments in Washington of interest to the company, and Earl Newsom & Company continued to serve as adviser. Professor Richard S. Meriam of the Harvard Graduate School of Business Administration advised on economic thought as well as on matters directly related to economic planning.[23]

It was also believed necessary to gain some comprehension of the general climate of opinion within which business operated. Achieving such understanding was not regarded as a one-time effort, for public opinion was recognized as unstable and changing. It was described as "a dynamic balance at any time of all the cross-currents of influence and opinion and knowledge which exist in people's minds."[24]

The most extensive organized program was a series of surveys made for the company by various organizations employing the developing techniques of opinion research. The first such survey had been made by Elmo Roper in the summer of 1942. (See Chapter 15.) Periodic and special surveys were later made in the United States year after year. Others measured opinion in foreign countries in which Jersey affiliates operated. Some discoveries corroborated empirical observations; others called attention to aspects of opinion not recognized previously.

These studies revealed widespread ignorance and misunderstanding of the economic system of the United States. Misconceptions about corporate earnings and their distribution were common. A nationwide survey made in 1946 of a cross section of white-collar and manual workers showed a prevailing opinion that profits were much higher than they actually were[25] and that the earnings of employees were much lower than they actually were.[26]

The surveys conducted over a number of years in the United States revealed opinion concerning Jersey itself. About 10 per cent of the individuals polled in general surveys were "unfriendly" toward "Standard Oil"; and an unusually high percentage of people expressed an unfavorable attitude toward the company as compared to other corporations in the United States. However, it was discovered that the public generally believed that all Standard Oil companies still were one concern—a fact that accounted at least in part for the belief of many that Jersey was monopolistic. The company was found to have the best standing in the regions where affiliates marketed under the Esso name. The highest percentage of unfriendly responses came from the more educated segment of those questioned; in an opinion poll of college students, 45 per cent expressed an unfavorable attitude toward Standard Oil. The company apparently was still haunted by the ghosts of its early history. But there were obviously other contributing factors.[27]

One such factor became known from opinion surveys made for the American Petroleum Institute and analyzed by Dr. Claude Robinson. These studies showed that Americans knew little about the oil industry— far less than about railroads or automobile manufacture. Many of those questioned were unaware of the industry's accomplishments, but they nevertheless registered an unfavorable attitude. Those familiar with the industry expressed the more favorable judgments, but the well-informed were a minority.[28]

Another factor that affected public opinion of Jersey was difficult to evaluate but obviously important: the general attitude toward "big business." Surveys revealed a preponderance of opinion that large concerns had made vital contributions during the war and that they were efficient. Their productivity, therefore, was not particularly questioned. But their power and equity were. Elmo Roper concluded that certain patterns emerging in opinion surveys represented essentially common ways of thinking about big business by three general groups. These ranged from the "liberals," who equated the big concerns with monopoly and held that they should be broken up, to a minority who believed that large corporations performed necessary functions in our economy but that in large as in small business there were good and bad companies.[29]

Surveys made under the direction of Dr. Frank M. Surface in several European countries indicated a general uniformity of opinion, although they also registered some national differences. For instance, exaggerated ideas on profits were found in England, Sweden, and Switzerland. A considerable opinion appeared to favor the nationalization of industries. The only oil company widely known in Europe was Royal Dutch–Shell.[30]

Latin American studies revealed a great vacuum of information about the oil industry, even among the more literate and well-educated. Confused and contradictory opinion on nationalization was evident. The same individuals who expressed respect for the fairness and technical proficiency of American companies and who understood the need for foreign capital in the development of their country's resources favored not only extensive government controls but even nationalization.[31]

These surveys at home and abroad indicated that there was a considerable sentiment for increased regulation and in some countries for nationalization. "We are not afraid of strenuous competition," one Jersey director commented in 1947, referring to the situation at home. "We welcome it. But we could not survive the opposition of the American people. . . . We could be legislated out of existence."[32]

Besides these formal studies, other means were used to gauge public opinion. Newspapers and magazines were examined systematically.[33] Developments in Washington of importance to the company or the oil industry were followed regularly. Company representatives attended conferences of religious and educational groups and also meetings devoted to current social and political issues. At such gatherings, they were impressed by the lack of knowledge of business and the critical attitude toward it, notably among scholars and teachers.[34]

Because of the widely held belief in the United States that large size was adverse to the public interest, the Executive Committee in January, 1948, decided to set up a special group to study size and concentration as economic and legal issues. This decision was precipitated by the directors' discussion of the possible effects on business of recommendations made in reports prepared on modern concepts of antitrust laws and their enforcement for the Business Advisory Council of the United States Department of Commerce.[35] The Executive Committee was especially impressed by the use of the theories of monopolistic competition in these reports and also in Eugene V. Rostow's then recently published book, *A National Policy for the Oil Industry*. Directors Harden, Haslam, and Coleman were appointed to the Committee on Economic Concentration, and Professor Meriam of the Harvard Graduate School of Business Administration and members of the company's legal and economics staffs were added as specialists to direct the research.[36]

Their findings and conclusions, which were discussed with the Executive Committee as the study progressed, were recorded in formal reports. Two submitted in September, 1948, dealt with economic thought and the trend of antitrust law.[37] One, entitled "Nature and Importance of Monopolistic Competition and Workable Competition," was a detailed analysis of these different theories and an evaluation of their influence on public opinion and their usefulness to economic analysis. This report held that the basic premises of the theorists of monopolistic competition were unrealistic and that the theories themselves were inadequate for general conclusions on public issues or company policies having to do with economic concentration. It found that the doctrines of workable competition were based on a more comprehensive and realistic approach to problems of competition and monopoly and hence were more useful. The other report, "A Memorandum of Law Concerning Monopolistic Competition under the Sherman Act," examined the relationship of the theories of monopolistic competition to the "evolving interpretation of the Sherman Act." It examined legal cases and the reasoning behind them as well as pertinent writings on questions of competition and monopoly. It concluded that the theories of monopolistic competition were having a considerable influence on current thinking about antitrust law.

In such diverse ways, Jersey went about achieving some understanding of its public relations problems. The above discussion illustrates method and process but does not deal with the subject in full breadth. Relations with special groups of people—such as stockholders, employees, government, and the oil industry generally—were also given attention. Political developments abroad were followed with the same care that was taken in consideration of antitrust law at home and the thought behind it. The understanding achieved supplied guidance for attitude and action.

BLENDING NEW ATTITUDES AND ACTIVITIES INTO THE JERSEY ORGANIZATION

After the war, the parent company encouraged affiliates to set up or expand their own public relations organizations. "You can have the best intentions in the world," said President Holman in 1945, "but unless you set up a mechanism for seeing that those intentions are carried out you might as well not have them."[38] Jersey's Public Relations Department was given the responsibility to keep in touch with the progress of the ·affiliates, to counsel and assist them in determining policies and setting up staffs, and to report to the Board of Directors on the effectiveness and efficiency of their activities.

The wide establishment of public relations departments or staff units among the affiliates came after 1945. The spread of interest in this work is indicated by the representation of companies at the annual public relations conferences held in New York. At the December, 1947, meeting, 13 domestic and 14 foreign affiliates were represented; of these 27 companies, 14 had a full-time trained man assigned to public relations work, and 9 had functioning public relations staffs.[39] The next year 32 companies in the Jersey family—22 of them in foreign countries—sent representatives to the conference.[40]

These meetings provided an occasion for comparing ideas and techniques and for spreading information about them throughout the group. Public opinion was analyzed by outside consultants; policies and ideas were presented; the experience with various techniques of individual affiliates, or of Jersey itself, was described; problems in relations with particular publics were considered; and some scholar in an appropriate field gave his interpretation of, and advice on, aspects of public relations. On each occasion, President Holman, Chairman Abrams, or the current contact director for public relations, as well as other directors or high-level executives, spoke to the group. "There seems to be little doubt," said Chairman Abrams, addressing them in 1946, "that the future of American business depends to a very great extent on the intelligence and understanding with which business leadership recognizes and adapts itself to the thinking of the people of this nation and of all nations in which American companies do business." In these meetings, the thinking, policies, and activities of the parent company itself and its consultants and specialists—together with word of what was being done in Venezuela, Canada, Denmark, Chile, New Jersey, Texas, or other places where affiliates operated—contributed to the development of the group's worldwide public relations work.[41]

Two principal themes ran throughout the deliberations in these conferences: (1) that the function of a public relations organization is to serve as a liaison between company and public and to interpret each to the other; and (2) that it is the responsibility of the administrators and operating managements to maintain constantly a position in which all the company's acts are in accord with the public interest.

Blending this operational objective into the whole organization became the responsibility of executives on all levels. "Public relations," said Director Haslam, "is a way of life . . . not a group of techniques."[42] Chairman Abrams said, referring to the Jersey Board of Directors, "I think all of us are conscious of the fact that millions of people in this country and elsewhere are in a very real sense looking over our shoulders as we discuss and deliberate. Although not physically present, there are a lot of people in our Board room whenever we meet."[43]

Records of conferences, especially of the annual meetings of officers and operating managers of affiliates arranged by Jersey's Coordination Committee, show how concern for the company's standing with the public was urged upon executives throughout the whole Jersey group of companies. In these yearly gatherings—held in Houston, New Orleans, Atlantic City, Toronto, Miami, and Paris in the early postwar years— Director Chester F. Smith, chairman of the committee, reminded the successful, hard-driving executives representing the affiliates that the day had passed when they could consider their principal problems to be technical and scientific. Building "a reservoir of good will," as he expressed it on one occasion, "is just as much a management problem as, and one of no lesser magnitude than, the technical problems we face."[44]

Company executives stressed the need to understand social and political changes going on throughout the world. In addressing the Coordination Committee meeting at New Orleans in 1946, Manager Freyermuth said:

Before we can grasp the deeper significance of public opinion . . . we must understand that today we live in one of the most significant eras in all history. . . . There is great danger for us, working in an intricate and difficult business such as ours, of becoming lost in the detail of our everyday problems. But don't forget, events in the world outside are important. It's of importance to every one of you that a Chinese family starved for lack of rice; that a few months ago a Negro voted in a primary election in Georgia; that today an illiterate native in Venezuela listens to a radio on a street corner in a little country pueblo. Yes, great social movements are in progress.

The question we face is, what is our relation to these social movements? Do we deserve to ride with them or exist with them? Can we meet these movements? If we fail to gauge them properly, we'll be swept aside in the inexorable current of events.[45]

Year after year, attention was given in these conferences to movements in different parts of the world having significance to the Jersey Company. In 1948, for example, H. B. Hoskins, director of the School of Advanced

concerning information released to the press. It should be accurate and as nearly complete as possible within the limitations imposed by the need to protect legitimate business secrets. It should be given promptly and without any attempt to influence the use of it by the reporters. Word of new developments of interest to the public should be released as a matter of routine. When feasible, material should be provided to prepare newsmen and public for anticipated events in order to forestall surprise or misrepresentation from a lack of background information. In matters of public controversy, special effort should be made to provide a frank, comprehensive, and prompt presentation of facts.[53]

Press tours were arranged to acquaint newsmen with the oil industry as well as to show what the Jersey companies were doing. Among the more extensive was a tour for Brazilian publishers of the operations of affiliates in the United States. It was sponsored by the parent company and its Brazilian affiliates. A similar tour of deepwater operations off the Louisiana coast was arranged by Jersey and Humble for American newsmen. Such trips included visits to operations, lectures, question-and-answer periods, and interviews with public officials.[54]

Similar press policies and practices were followed by affiliates at home and abroad. Some companies, to be sure, already had good relations with newspapers in their regions; some were influenced by local conditions rather than by Jersey policy. In fact, at times affiliates provided examples for the parent company to recommend to others. But the effect of Jersey's over-all leadership was felt widely throughout the whole company.

Everywhere the more intelligent way of dealing with responsible members of the press brought its reward. Obviously slanted interpretations became less frequent, and a great deal of factual material was published. A striking example of the value of good relations with newsmen was the help the British press gave Anglo-American in informing a critical public about plans for the Fawley refinery near the historic New Forest in the vicinity of Southampton.[55] Better relations with the press also brought a reward within the company itself, a "self-confidence on the part of our own employees and management," according to the manager of the company's Public Relations Department in 1948. Indicative of the changed relations was the invitation to President Holman to address the National Press Club in Washington.[56]

The radio was used extensively in these later years. Jersey companies followed the policy adopted by Standard Oil Company of New Jersey and the Esso Marketers in the 1930's of giving full freedom to news broadcasting sponsored by the marketers. The parent company was handicapped in the United States by being able to use the Standard Oil name in only a limited number of states because other companies operating in different sections of the country bore a similar name. It ran into confusion over its name in connection with its sponsorship of the national broadcasting of the Sunday afternoon concerts of the New York Philharmonic Orchestra, directed by Arturo Toscanini, for the 1948–1949 season.[57] Domestic affiliates sponsored the broadcasting of news and other programs in their own operating territories. Among these was Humble's popular coverage of intercollegiate football games in the Southwest. Radio programs were especially important in foreign countries with a high illiteracy rate; in such areas news or other broadcasts could reach the large percentage of the people who could not read but who owned radios or heard them in some village.

Jersey and its larger affiliates also carried on an extensive publications program. They distributed widely company magazines, annual reports, and many special brochures and other materials.

Their periodical publications were informative and attractive. The main focus of the parent company's magazine, *The Lamp,* was on important oil industry developments and their significance to the public. Its articles were illustrated by unusual graphic materials, and the issues contained reproductions of paintings and drawings of aspects of oil operations. *The Lamp* became recognized as an outstanding company magazine. It won awards for both its editorial substance and its excellence in graphic arts. Besides having a wide circulation at home, this magazine was also distributed by affiliates outside the United States. Creole's *El Farol* was especially notable in that, although dealing with the oil industry to some extent, it was a cultural magazine of a type not published commercially in Venezuela. *El Farol, The Humble Way,* the *Imperial Oil Review,* and other company magazines were of high quality and had extensive distribution.[58]

The Public Relations Department prepared the parent company's *Annual Report* in close collaboration with other departments.[59] The format was changed after the war and the contents became far more informative. In the late 1940's the report became a booklet consisting of about forty pages. Following the trend of the times, it contained many photographs, multicolored maps, and elaborate charts. Instead of being devoted largely to brief financial statements as formerly, these later reports dealt with the different branches of operations, employee relations, and even company thought. The financial section, which occupied up to a third of the space, contained not only the traditional financial statements—greatly enlarged—but also charts and explanations. The semitechnical jargon of accounting was replaced by words more likely to be understood by the layman; for instance, "surplus" became "earnings reinvested and employed in the business."

In 1945 the parent company began to mail its *Annual Report* to college teachers and to offer copies for class use. This distribution grew until more than 60,000 copies a year were requested for over 2,000 college classes. The classes also used large quantities of the stenographic reports of Jersey's annual stockholders' meetings and of the publication, *How to Read an Annual Report*.[60]

Affiliates followed the parent company's lead in issuing annual reports. Several companies, a part of whose capital stock was owned by the general public, published attractive and informative reports. Some affiliates completely owned by Jersey did the same. In Europe, where such reports—if published at all—tended to be restricted in content and circulation, the more informative publications of the affiliates were said to be unusual.[61]

Jersey and its affiliates also issued a large number of special publications. The parent company's Public Relations Department prepared and distributed materials varying from comic and picture booklets to books on company and industry subjects. One by Wallace E. Pratt, *Oil in the Earth*, is an authoritative and readable monograph on the origin, occurrence, and geographic distribution of oil resources and on techniques with which to explore for them. Another book by Stewart Schackne and N. D'Arcy Drake, *Oil for the World*, describes in layman's language the science and technology of the various operations of the industry.[62]

Such publications were mailed to institutions and individuals on company mailing lists, but the number of copies requested was frequently far larger than the original distribution. The demand for one booklet, *Petroleum in the World*, ran to millions of copies, mainly for schools. Among other publications widely distributed were these: *Rubber from Oil; Conservation; A Generation of Industrial Peace; The Stake of Business in American Education; Developing Tomorrow's Business Leaders; Atomic Energy in the Year 2,000;* and a set of wall charts on the oil industry for school use.

Film strips and motion pictures were also used. Jersey circulated films on oil operations, such as *Oil Hunters* and *Drilling for Oil*. These were

1945 to 1950

Eugene Holman

Frank W. Abrams

President Holman and Chairman Abrams in Flemington, New Jersey, for the 1947 annual meeting.

Directors' meeting in October, 1949. From left: Secretary Minton, directors Coleman, Holma[n], Soubry, Smith, Haslam, Howard, Suman, Pierce, Abrams, Harden, and Crane. Absen[t] F. H. Bedford, Jr.

Producing well at El Centro, Colombia.

Humble rig at Weeks Island, Louisiana.

Oklahoma wells drilled on a forty-acre spacing plan.

Derrick among the sand dunes north of Abqaiq in Saudi Arabia.

Christmas tree, over Oklahoma well, is used to control the flow of oil.

Drilling in process by Imperial Oil during harvesting of oats in Alberta field.

Stanvac derrick in Sumatra oil field has a banana plant setting.

Indonesian driller on a well near the Pendopo field camp.

This 1948 Humble well in the Gulf of Mexico is seven miles offshore from Grand Isle, Louisiana.

New Guinea natives operate a handpowered rotary rig.

A few men in the automatic-control room operate a catalytic cracking unit.

Control lines on a Butyl control house roof lead from panel to plant units.

International Petroleum tank farm at the Talara refinery in Peru.

Light ends fractionators and Hortonspheres for butadiene at the Baytown refinery.

Ras Tanura marine terminal and refinery on the Persian Gulf for Aramco's Saudi Arabian oil.

Loading isobutylene into a tank car at the Baton Rouge refinery.

Night photograph of the alkylation units at the Baton Rouge refinery.

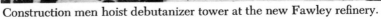
Construction men hoist debutanizer tower at the new Fawley refinery.

Refinery operators at a gasoline recovery plant.

Mississippi River pilot steering the towboat *Jack Rathbone*.

Veteran rigger at the Bayonne refinery.

Laboratory assistant in the Pittsburgh plant.

Welder at the Everett refinery in Massachusetts.

Pumper wears gas mask when he gauges tanks of high-sulfur crude.

Colombian driller on a rig where drill pipe is being pulled from the hole.

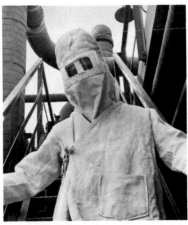

Foreman of a drilling crew at Natchez, Mississippi.

An asbestos suit is worn for protection from intense heat.

Respirator and goggles, worn where the dust flies.

Putting delivery hose in position at pipeline terminus.

Lake barge makes a gasoline delivery at the Buffalo bulk plant.

Ohio River barge arrives at the Paducah, Kentucky, landing.

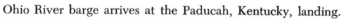

Esso Springfield at the Albany pier after voyage up the Hudson River.

Saudi Arabian pipeline between Abqaiq and Dhahran.

The *Esso Rochester* in New York Harbor.

Mississippi River oil tow near Baton Rouge.

Launching of a postwar supertanker of 26,800 deadweight tons. Capacity: 230,000 barrels.

Esso Zurich heading for harbor.

Tug approaches the tanker as it lies in quarantine

The 1947 annual meeting in Flemington, New Jersey.

used by many organizations, and special teachers' manuals to accompany them were prepared for schools. Imperial's *Search Unending* was very popular. In Chile two were in special demand: *Oil in Peru* and *Power and Octane*. The latter was used in certain night schools, in engineering courses given by the Santiago Industrial School, and in the University of Concepción.

Among the motion picture films was the documentary, *Louisiana Story*, produced by Robert Flaherty, with a musical score written by the well-known American composer Virgil Thomson.[63] This screen story was intended to show the oil industry as part of the normal day-to-day productive life of our nation's people and thus to offset a common impression that the industry was engaged in a ruthless, impersonal exploitation of a natural resource. The setting was the Louisiana bayou country, and the plot was built around a family of Acadian descent whose land Humble had leased to explore for oil. The leading character was a local lad, who was a natural actor. But the show was "stolen" from its human cast by a spectacular blowout of a wildcat well. *Louisiana Story* had its first public showing in New York in 1948 and thereafter was shown in commercial theaters throughout the country. Nowhere did Jersey's name appear, and Humble was mentioned only in the list of credits. But the critics gave Jersey publicity and the film high praise. It won many awards, including the Pulitzer Prize in 1949 for the musical score. The most important honors the picture itself received were from the British Film Academy as the best documentary of the year and at the Venice International Film Festival for "lyrical worth."[64]

The art project was of high quality as a visual interpretation of the oil industry. Sixteen of the country's leading artists painted scores of views of various wartime oil operations, facilities, and scenes of interest, such as a cat cracker at Baton Rouge, a drilling camp in the Canadian Arctic, and the unloading of gasoline at Kunming, China, from a plane that had flown over The Hump. One of the artists, Thomas Hart Benton, said of the project: "I do not know whether this is great art or not. But I do believe that, if we are to have art in our age, it will come out of this sort of background." The collection was first shown in New York in 1946, after which it went on tour to museums and colleges.[65] The pictures were used extensively in publications, and many of them were later donated to art museums around the country.[66]

In these public relations efforts, Jersey's own name and the many different names among its affiliates posed some difficulties. In the United

States, the company had to be careful in using its name in the regions where other Standard Oil companies operated. In Europe, Standard Oil Company (New Jersey), unlike Royal Dutch–Shell, apparently was not widely known to the public because it operated in different countries under different names, few of which identified the affiliates with the parent company.

It might seem that a simple solution would have been to scrap the Standard Oil name altogether and choose another for use everywhere. The Board of Directors considered this possibility and appointed a committee to study the matter. Several names were suggested, including Jersey Company, which was used rather commonly within the organization itself and in financial circles. But the directors were reluctant to give up the old name, which indeed had the prestige of a long history.

DIRECT RELATIONS WITH VARIOUS PUBLICS

Printed words and pictures could reach a large public, but their value was limited to one-way communication of factual information or impressions. Jersey's policy makers and public relations staff recognized that, in order to change public impressions of the company from the stereotype of a soul-less corporation concerned only with maximizing profits, it was also necessary to bring about person-to-person meeting and two-way communication. To promote such meeting and communication became an essential part of the company's public relations effort. Company personnel on all levels could participate in such a program. Insofar as it was organized, it was largely directed toward specific interest groups and particular issues.

Within parent company and affiliates, employees were considered invaluable as representatives to the public. In the course of his work, an employee might have contact with many outsiders, but in any case he had relatives, friends, and a varying range of acquaintances. The Jersey employees generally rated well in their home communities, but as public relations representatives they also needed to be well informed about their company. Some affiliates, especially domestic ones, had for some time followed the practice of discussing company problems, policies, and plans with employees, particularly as these related to the branch of operations in which they worked. Now, informing them also took on a public relations objective. This had been started with the sales force of Standard Oil Company of New Jersey shortly after the attack on Jersey in the Truman committee hearings in March, 1942. It later came to be practiced by other affiliates.[67]

The selection and preparation of American personnel for work overseas in the less-developed countries came to be influenced by recognition that they would be important as representatives of the company wherever they went. Accordingly, Jersey gave personnel headed overseas short but intensive instruction in the language and the current conditions of the country to which they were going. Wives were also encouraged to prepare themselves for appreciative communication with nationals among whom they were to make their homes. Although this training at best was not very extensive, it went far beyond the practice of earlier years. Then North American managers and supervisors in Latin American operations had generally learned only enough of the language of the country where they were stationed to give orders; sometimes they even posted notices for national employees in English. They lived with other expatriate employees in camps that were actually small enclaves in the host country. It is true that certain individuals had learned to speak the language well and, within the range of their time and contacts, had become interested observers of the country and friends of the people in the parts of South America where they worked. The difference at this later time was that what had once been voluntary and exceptional now became company policy.[68]

Jersey's administrators also, as noted in Chapter 22, sought to establish closer relations with the company's owners. At a time when stockholders were becoming more assertive, it was obviously important to inform them both of the company's earnings and financial condition and of its new policies and plans and the reasons for them. The stockholders themselves constituted a large "public," in 1950 approaching a quarter of a million.

Communication between the parent company and its individual stockholders took various forms. The new stockholders' division of the Secretary's Department answered letters from individual share owners. The company made a special effort to increase attendance at annual stockholders' meetings. According to available information, Jersey for several years had a larger total and percentage attendance than four other large corporations, but in 1950 General Electric caught up with it in percentage of stockholder attendance. Jersey's annual meetings at the Grange Hall in Flemington, New Jersey, gave individuals opportunities to meet company officers and directors.[69]

Operating affiliates adopted programs designed to establish closer relations with the communities where they were located. They invited individuals and groups to visit plants and to observe operations. From October, 1947, to October, 1948, some 17,000 persons—students, editors, businessmen, members of chambers of commerce—visited Esso Standard refineries. Tours conducted for visitors included talking with plant supervisors and managers, viewing film slides dealing with operations, examining graphs on such matters as wages, taxes, and company earnings, and learning something about the value of the particular operating unit to the community. Plants also provided special services to their communities, and their managers and research men were available for addressing such local organizations as school groups, farm organizations, and clubs.[70]

The discussion groups sponsored by Jersey in eastern cities were too few to have a wide influence inside or outside the company, but they indicate how far-ranging some of the public relations projects were.[71] A charter member of the Philadelphia group, Professor James H. S. Bossard of the University of Pennsylvania, in an article in *Social Forces* at the time of the group's tenth anniversary, explained its purpose and accomplishments. Noting that business does not function in a vacuum, he observed that these discussion meetings, "while serving the interests of the larger community, have also served the Esso Company in enabling its personnel to maintain direct and current contacts with the thought of the larger community."[72]

The direct person-to-person communication established with a special group referred to within Jersey as "educators" had a potentially great influence. This effort grew out of the company's realization that the lines of communication between business and the academic world were largely "down." One way to repair them was suggested by Charlotte Lochhead of the Public Relations Department in a report of her observations at a summer conference which had especially impressed upon her the lack of knowledge, group to group, in this age of specialization. As an experiment, the company in the summer of 1947 invited eight college and university professors to a two-week conference and tour of operations. The visitors reported their unanimous agreement at the end of the period that such meetings of businessmen and academic people were desirable. The next year Imperial sponsored conferences at three Canadian universities, and the "Jersey Roundtable" was again held. Other affiliates, domestic and foreign, similarly began to arrange regular or occasional conferences of academic men and women with company executives.[73]

The Jersey Roundtable was held annually for many years. These conferences, meeting in New York for three days, always involved parent company officers and directors as well as the whole Public Relations Department. The gatherings were generally made up of approximately twenty invited members of college and university faculties in the social sciences, humanities, law, and business, and of about the same number of Jersey men, including several directors. The meetings were informal, and no record was made of any of the discussion. The discussions followed a general topic made known in advance, such as the rise of big business, foreign trade, and nationalism, with attention to such matters as Jersey's views and policies, human relations within a corporation, and practical paths to cooperation between business and government. The company's participants made no effort to disguise the purpose: to inform an articulate and influential type of leader about the company's policies, problems, and operations. At first the Jersey men tended to be on the defensive, and the visitors understandably expected to be propagandized. But discussions at these conferences were characteristically marked by frankness and by efforts to be objective on the part of the company participants and by an honest search for information on the part of the visitors. According to participants from inside and outside Jersey, there was some disagreement in these meetings, but company man and educator acquired greater respect for one another and a better understanding of each other's problems and views.[74]

In 1947 Jersey entered into another new project by accepting a proposal of N. S. B. Gras and Henrietta M. Larson of the Harvard Graduate School of Business Administration for writing a history of the company. The proposal was made after a year's exploratory study of company records and discussion with officers, directors, departmental executives, and others in the parent company and several affiliates. It stipulated that the parent company should allow unrestricted access to all its records, with full freedom to publish therefrom, and should make a monetary gift to the research organization that would manage the project.[75]

The company's decision was not arrived at easily. The project obviously involved serious questions of policy and not a little risk. The officers and directors weighed the risks against the conclusions from a search by the public relations staff that nearly all the reference literature relating to Standard Oil and the oil industry itself was inaccurate, highly colored, and often damaging. The only reference work on the oil industry in many libraries was Ida M. Tarbell's *The History of the Standard Oil Company*. This work, first published as a book in 1904, contained much of value, but it could hardly be considered an objective record of Standard Oil's policies and activities even in the early decades. Miss Tarbell's views were later reflected in both scholarly and popular publications dealing with the company and the oil industry. Jersey officers and public relations staff considered various ways to correct this situation. One approach was for the company itself to increase the amount and accuracy of the available reference literature. It was finally concluded that only a detailed record, prepared by qualified scholars, would become acceptable as a reference work. In March, 1947, the Executive Committee voted favorably on the proposal to write a history of Standard Oil Company (New Jersey).[76]

Indicative of the importance attached to two-way communication was the fact that the officers, including President Holman, and directors of Jersey and affiliates themselves participated in the effort to establish person-to-person contact with the public. Chairman Abrams of the parent company's Board of Directors acted as Jersey's chief spokesman. He and others met representatives of the press and of educational and other institutions, and they personally conferred with congressmen and members of departments and of administrative agencies in Washington. Whatever the original motivation, these contacts were valuable to the company. Through them its top administrators and operating executives gained deeper insights into the problems and issues of the time that were of importance to the Jersey organization. The parent company's leaders also addressed conferences and meetings of various kinds, usually on some matter of current public concern.[77]

This personal outreach indicated something of a shift of attitude toward the public. The need for such a change was stressed in an informal address given by Chairman Abrams at the 1949 public relations conference of representatives of the Jersey companies.[78] The speaker observed with reference to American corporate officers and executives in general that "most of us come from very modest beginnings . . . but we haven't maintained our ties with the folks from whom we came." We purchase homes, he said, in "better" neighborhoods, join "a more exclusive club," and "spin ourselves a cozy social cocoon." Business leaders, he urged, must maintain contact with "the great average American people" if business is to gain their "much-needed support." He wondered whether businessmen understood that "the social order of things in this country has undergone a fundamental change" or whether "we are blinded by the way we live." This was not a sociologist speaking of the danger of forming a rigidly structured society but the chairman of the Board of Directors of one of the world's large industrial corporations in effect saying that the company could not flourish or even survive unless it was closely identified with the society of which it was a part.

IDEAS AND EXPLANATIONS PROJECTED
ON THE PUBLIC SCREEN

The *Annual Report* of Standard Oil Company (New Jersey) for the year 1948 contains this statement of the Board of Directors:

No business exists in economic isolation. It is part of the social climate of its time. Its policies and actions affect the character of that climate. In turn, that climate—which is, after all, simply the ideas and goals of large numbers of people—influences any business importantly. It can even determine whether the business is to prosper and survive or decline and disappear.

Corporate citizens have, therefore, come to accept many of the obligations traditionally imposed only upon the individual citizen. Today, companies concern themselves with employee and community welfare, and with many other activities going beyond a strictly economic concept of business functions. The management of this company is devoting an increasing share of its attention to the social problems affecting its business. We believe that in this way the continuity of the enterprise may best be assured and its economic health sustained.

This statement was obviously designed to tell the stockholders why Jersey was showing such concern for its standing with the public. It also identified the company with the values of the public it served and recognized that business and its social environment are interdependent and have mutual interests.

At no time did anyone in the company present a comprehensive exposition of Jersey's economic, social, or political thought. Its leaders were primarily men of action, and what they had to say usually had a special purpose or was associated with some particular occasion. Underlying it all, however, was something of the fervor of a new discovery and a new mission. What they said apparently described the kind of company they believed Jersey to be and the kind of world they considered favorable to its survival and growth. Over the years, their statements form a consistent pattern of thought, which may be taken to represent the company's general orientation.[79]

According to the *Annual Report* for 1945, the directors of Jersey viewed the current world confusion and struggle as two faiths in conflict: "a belief in an expanding freedom and responsibility for the individual *versus* a belief in an expanding authority of the state." Standard Oil Company (New Jersey), they stated, was "on the side of human freedom as a matter of principle and also because it believes that the prosperity of all Jersey companies is directly related to the growth of human freedom." This freedom, among other things, meant to business the right of competition, reduced restrictions on international trade, and scope for the exercise of personal initiative. "The Jersey form of decentralized organization," the statement reads, "has the great merits of every democratic system, chief among them the stimulation it gives to the development of able, courageous, energetic, self-reliant men and women." These men believed that the preservation of democracy and the survival of private enterprise were indissolubly linked—and that a viable democracy was possible only in a free industrial society.

Having advanced far beyond the old *laissez-faire* philosophy, they regarded regulation of business by government as necessary. President Holman put it this way in 1946 in addressing a conference of petroleum geologists:

A major problem facing the nation—and much of the world abroad that is not thoroughly regimented—is to find and keep the happy mean between the extremes of centralization and the anarchy of jungle-law competition. . . . The ingredient of personal freedom, incentive for use of initiative, and the spur of competition must be retained for progress, while government—the people speaking as a whole—furnishes guidance for the general welfare.[80]

Director Haslam, in addressing a Jersey public relations conference, carried this thought somewhat further. He said: "It is entirely proper and desirable that American business should operate within the general framework of rules laid down by the government, by the people. It is necessary to have order and discipline in commerce." This "does not mean regulation and supervision in detail, but it does mean general lines along which business ought to conduct its affairs to the greatest benefit of the people."[81]

However, the directors held that freedom must be earned. The *Annual Report* for 1948 contained this statement: "Freedom extends to all persons—including corporate ones—great rights and privileges. But with these come responsibilities. Our constant purpose is to meet those responsibilities. This, to us, is the surest way toward the preservation of the freedom which secures our rights and privileges." This balancing of rights and responsibilities was a logical alternative to full regimentation in a complex society that had of necessity turned away from eighteenth- and nineteenth-century theories of natural law and *laissez faire*. To men facing the realities of the time, the alternatives must have been clear: voluntary assumption of broader responsibilities or increasing control by government.

A statement made by the chairman of the Board of Directors at the annual stockholders' meeting in 1947 defined the company's conception of its responsibilities in terms of rights, or claims upon it, of four groups.[82] All these groups, the speaker said, have the right to expect efficient and sound management from a company. But each also has special claims. The stockholder "has invested his money in the expectation of a fair return, and a reasonable opportunity for appreciation of his capital as the business grows." The employee has a claim rising out of the investment of his "time and skills"; he "is entitled to a reasonable security, a fair return for his time, a chance for advancement, and the right to feel that management is interested in him as a human being." As for the customer, management has the task of keeping him "satisfied by giving him what he wants—more and better products at reasonable prices." The "last and largest group to which management is responsible is the general public." This was not only the American public: "Jersey's general public is truly international. It speaks many languages and comprises virtually every faith and political condition in the world. In the final analysis, our existence depends on our serving it better than it can be served in any other way." These obligations, said the chairman, were especially heavy for the Jersey Company as one of the outposts of American enterprise abroad and one of the important units at home. "All four of these groups," concluded the speaker, "must continually be considered and satisfied by the management of any company if it is to build soundly and to have any assurance that it can continue as a private business earning a reasonable return on its effort and its invested capital."

The company's leaders gave special attention to the question of large size, the most enduring issue they had to meet. "With our size," declared Chairman Abrams, "have grown our responsibilities as corporate citizens at home and as representatives of American business and American ideals and ability abroad." These men held that large-scale enterprise was essential for a productive and secure society. Director Haslam said in addressing a public relations conference in 1947: "The basic necessities of our modern civilization cannot be supplied except through large-scale enterprise, and without its tremendous production during the war there is some question that we would be free men today."[83]

In a letter written in 1949 in reply to questions asked by a member of the editorial staff of *Fortune* magazine, Jersey's officers and directors gave an indication of how they thought such a large commercial enterprise should operate and should balance its various responsibilities.[84] This letter—bearing the signature of Chairman Abrams but expressing the consensus of the Board of Directors—is significant as a statement on price and profit policies in particular and on the acceptance of corporate responsibilities in general. It deals with a central problem in the company's public relations claims and efforts.

The first question asked had to do with the profit motive as against considerations of public good: "Have there been in this company specific instances of consciously and deliberately foregoing opportunities for legitimate profits?"

The answer, which interpreted the question as referring to short-term profits, was affirmative. Several instances were cited of decisions by parent company and affiliates not to take action that would have maximized short-term profits. For example, during the then-recent threat of a shortage of oil products, Jersey had not taken advantage of attractive opportunities for investment because these would not have increased supplies immediately. Instead it had put the funds into projects that would bring less profit but would help meet the shortage by increasing the current supply. Price policy was another example. When demand was rising faster than anticipated after the war, Jersey executives, hoping to brake the price rise, had adopted a hold-the-line policy. Because of this action, the letter stated, Esso Standard's prices were for a time appreciably below market quotations and the actual selling prices of many of its competitors. (See Chapter 25.)

The letter explained how forgoing an immediate maximization of profits still was consistent with the company's long-range profit objective. "It can be argued, for example," it stated, "that in resisting influences a year and a half ago which might have touched off spiraling upward prices, we were motivated by a realization that if prices went unduly high they might later go unduly low and that, by avoiding wide swings, the aggregate profit over a long period would be better." A further point was made: "It can be argued that by incurring exceptional expenses to serve customers during a temporary period of difficult supply we retained the goodwill of those customers and that business received from them in the future would make such action profitable."

The second question considered by the letter was whether the judgment on profit maximization always had to be *ad hoc* or whether a kind of business philosophy could be built with regard to it. The answer contained this observation:

It seems to me [Chairman Abrams] that the elements of such a philosophy exist right now, having been developed empirically by business in its day-to-day activities. What is lacking is the formulation, and the expression in a body of business literature, of principles that at present are used by business more or less intuitively. Lacking, also, is broad public recognition of the existence of such principles.

The time element, the letter continued, is basic in the formulation of criteria for weighing the profit motive. Its explanation of the importance of time in the reconciliation of apparent conflicts between the profit motive and the public good merits quoting at length. This explanation may well be regarded as the basic justification of the broadening of Jersey's concern:

A primary motive of the corporation executive is to assure the continuance of the business. . . . The measure of his success is not alone the profit the company shows this year or next, but whether he can pass the company along to the succeeding management generation in as healthy or healthier condition than when he took over. Of course, this is not to say that he is unconcerned about current profit; he is very aware of his responsibility to the stockholders to show a return on their investment. But co-existing with that responsibility is the responsibility to the stockholders to maintain the enterprise into an indeterminate future.

Obviously, this latter goal involves profit; for if the business fails to be profitable over any considerable period, it will go bankrupt and the aim of continuity is frustrated. But there will be occasions when the goal of continuity will militate against maximum immediate profit.

As I see it, it is the goal of continuity which governs the so-called "social" actions of business. A management realizes that the continued existence of a business depends to an important degree upon its acceptance by the society of which it is a part. Such acceptance can be achieved to some degree by a company's commercial actions. But acceptance can be strengthened by doing more than that—by being, in addition, a "good citizen."

The corporate manager, thrust into some prominence by his position, seeks, both as an individual and for the company he represents, community approval. That involves more than mere observance of the letter of the law.

The goal of continuity means that the executive of a company must weigh contemplated actions on two scales—profit and public interest. Generally, I believe, the goals of long-range profit and of public interest will coincide.

Weighing contemplated action on these two scales in order to achieve an equitable and a workable balance obviously was not easy. "In daily practice," the letter stated, "decisions involving maximum short-term profits as against long-term continuity can never be automatic." The factors to be considered and their relative importance would never be the same in any two cases. Decisions, therefore, would have to come "not from rigid rules but from informed and experienced individuals exercising broad judgments."

THE CORPORATE CITIZEN

What did all this emphasis on responsibilities to the public actually mean in practice? The answer must be found primarily in the Jersey Company's policies and its day-to-day performance of its industrial functions. There was another area of concern, however, one conceived of as a general obligation of what was called corporate citizenship. This had to do with the responsibilities outside immediate industrial operations believed to be inherent in good corporate as well as good individual citizenship.

Jersey's leaders were not suddenly converted to a recognition of the company's obligations as a corporate citizen, but they clearly had not formerly thought or acted so broadly in this area, or with such a long-range perspective, as they came to do during and after World War II. The reasons for this change were no doubt many. These men were motivated by considerations of public relations; they well knew that at home and abroad it was creditable for a corporation to be associated with the public good. Moreover, they believed that a progressive and productive society provided better markets and conditions generally favorable to business enterprise. But weight must also be given to the rich, varied, and challenging experiences of parent company and affiliates that stimulated their leaders to think and act beyond the traditional boundaries of corporate concern and action.

In the United States, the company took a special interest in the improvement of education on the collegiate level. Nearly all Jersey's officers and directors were university- or college-trained men, and they were cognizant of the importance of higher education to business as well as to society in general. Soon after the war, they became actively interested as a corporate group in future educational developments in the United States. In 1946 the Executive Committee discussed the problems of liberal arts education with leaders in that important field.

Several considerations seem to have stimulated the directors' interest in education at this time. One was their belief that other fields of study besides the sciences and economics might be useful to the company. Chairman Frank W. Abrams, as a trustee of Syracuse University, was especially familiar with the needs and the contributions of private collegiate institutions. The Jersey executives, generally, were impressed by the need for a rapprochement between business and education. Dr. Frank M. Surface, executive assistant to President Holman and a former university professor, was concerned over the critical conditions generally facing institutions of higher learning after the war.

In March, 1947, Dr. Surface presented to the Executive Committee a memorandum that set in motion a course of discussion and action leading to still another innovation in public relations policy.[85] The memorandum opened with the statement that there "are probably few more important questions facing this country than the future of our educational systems." Although the writer recognized that our colleges and universities in general faced problems, he held tax-supported institutions to be the responsibility of the public. He reported that the situation was especially serious for private colleges and universities, which had no tax support and insufficient endowments to meet rising costs at a time when, because of heavy income taxes, the contributions of individuals were not adequate to meet rising needs. "I think most of us feel," he wrote in support of such institutions, "that the private and church-sponsored colleges have provided a kind of training and a development of manhood and womanhood that it is difficult, if not impossible, to attain in the mass educational system of the tax supported institutions."

Dr. Surface expressed the belief that without aid to private institutions all education on the collegiate level would eventually come under the control of government. Recognizing that there were legal obstacles to corporate contributions for general educational purposes, he raised the question whether business was not "as fully justified, from a business point of view, in supporting research work and scholarships in the social sciences as in chemistry or physics." The law had long allowed corporate support of science and engineering as of direct benefit to corporations employing science and technology.

The Executive Committee appointed a group to study the matter and to suggest policy and program, including financial aid to private educational institutions. In December, 1947, this group recommended that consideration be given to holding a forum for discussing two questions: (1) the application of scientific methods in the social sciences; and (2) the possibility of establishing a foundation to receive contributions from business and to distribute gifts to schools.[86]

Jersey in the meantime had begun to promote interest outside the company in the matter of corporate aid to education. It arranged a dinner to discuss the problems involved. This event was attended by the heads of several foundations and colleges and high executives of a number of large corporations. Most of the businessmen present expressed a willing-

ness to recommend reasonable gifts for general educational purposes by
the corporations they represented if sound legal grounds could be found
for such contributions.[87]

The company took a public stand in support of the program. In
September, 1947, Chairman Abrams addressed a meeting, inaugurating
the "Crisis in Education" campaign of the Advertising Council, on "The
Stake of Business in American Education."[88] Describing the serious
plight of American education and the general public apathy toward this
situation, Abrams stated that business corporations should give aid to
education. They should do this not only because without "a large reservoir of educated manpower, they would be handicapped in every phase
of their operations," but also because "education helps to build a more
productive society and better markets and provides the foundation of
America's greatness as a nation." He urged that corporations give financial aid and that businessmen as individuals help in their own communities and in the whole nation to overcome American indifference to the
problems of education.

Jersey's own intentions were announced in January, 1949, in an address
by Chairman Abrams at the annual meeting of the Association of American Colleges.[89] The speaker expressed the belief "that the peace, prosperity and security of this nation may depend as much on the way we
treat our teachers and religious leaders as it does on any other influence,"
and that it is "vital that we attract a substantial percentage of the best
minds of every generation into the teaching profession." He saw a special
need to assist private, independent institutions, which in addition to their
own contribution to society stimulate state-supported schools. He said
with respect to his own company:

Our Board of Directors has agreed that, if we can feel legally privileged to
do so, our Company as a corporate person, living in a great free nation and
as a long-term beneficiary of our national educational system, will be one
American corporation (we hope one of many) which will give to independent
colleges and universities for general educational purposes. We have asked our
legal department to propose to us what steps we may take to find out whether
we have that privilege.

It is our hope that we may be able to carry out our own conviction that such
a course is in the interest of our stockholders, and that in doing so we may
establish a useful precedent.

Jersey initiated action in 1949 to test the right of a corporation to make
contributions for general educational purposes, but several years were to

pass before a decisive conclusion was reached. By arrangement, the A. P. Smith Manufacturing Company, a New Jersey corporation, made a small gift to Princeton University for general educational purposes; a stockholders' suit was entered against the company to test the legality of the gift. The case was tried in the Superior Court of the state of New Jersey which ruled in favor of the company. On appeal, the state's Supreme Court in June, 1953, affirmed the judgment of the lower court. This decision, in *Smith* v. *Barlow,* as the case was called, was then appealed to the Supreme Court of the United States, but it was dismissed for want of a federal question.[90]

The favorable opinion of the New Jersey court in this suit marks an important development in the legal history of corporate contributions in the United States. Under former interpretations, corporations could make contributions to educational institutions only for specific purposes of direct benefit to the giver, such as to provide funds for scientific research of interest to the corporation itself. The concluding statement of the opinion summarizes the basis for the court's judgment:

We find that it was a lawful exercise of the corporation's implied and incidental powers under common law principles and that it came within the express authority of pertinent State legislation. As has been indicated, there is now widespread belief throughout the nation that free and vigorous nongovernmental institutions of learning are vital to our democracy and the system of private enterprise and that withdrawal of corporate authority to make such contributions within reasonable limits would seriously threaten their continuance. Corporations have come to recognize this and with their enlightenment have sought in varying measures, as has the plaintiff by its contribution, to insure and strengthen the society which gives them existence and the means of aiding themselves and their fellow citizens. Clearly then, the appellants, as individual stockholders whose private interests rest entirely upon the well being of the plaintiff corporation, ought not be permitted to close their eyes to present-day realities and thwart the long-visioned corporate action in recognizing and voluntarily discharging its high obligations as a constituent of our modern social structure.

After the court established the legal right to make such gifts, Jersey announced a program of financial aid to private colleges and universities in the United States, and in 1955 it organized the Esso Education Foundation to carry out the program.[91] Several of its foreign affiliates followed the parent company's example. Other corporations also began at once to establish foundations to provide funds for education.[92]

Because the needs were greater in certain foreign countries than at home, the Jersey affiliates abroad after the war had more opportunities for constructive action outside their own operations, especially in Latin America, the Middle East, and the Far East. Individual executives had long taken an interest in the improvement of institutions and general conditions in a number of countries, but it was during World War II that support for social and economic improvement began to crystallize into conscious corporate policy. Then action was taken in order to strengthen the company's own standing and to aid in the promotion of social and economic well-being outside its own operational reach.

The first outstanding foreign development was in Venezuela. With its larger resources, Creole could obviously afford to carry on a more extensive program than smaller companies could, and it had more at stake. But without its own and Jersey's leadership, and also an understanding Petroleum Bureau in the Venezuelan government, it would very likely not have acted so constructively. Its policies and actions were urged and guided by certain leaders in the parent company and in Creole itself—by President Eugene Holman and former Vice-President Wallace E. Pratt of the parent company, President Arthur T. Proudfit of Creole, and others.[93]

Creole's actions looked toward assisting in the development of Venezuela's material and human resources.[94] The company contributed to the Venezuelan Basic Economy Corporation, a nonprofit concern established under Rockefeller leadership with support from oil companies. Its function was to promote, at reduced costs, the production and distribution of more and better food, including fish and dairy products. The contribution of Creole to Venezuelan education was especially important. It went beyond training and schools for employees and their children; it included scholarships for advanced study in the United States or elsewhere and assistance to Venezuelan universities for improving their curriculum in such fields as geology, engineering, and business. The company also helped to raise the level of medical services in Venezuela. As noted in the preceding chapter, in addition to providing its customary medical care for its own employees and their families, late in the 1940's it built and arranged for the competent staffing of a large hospital in Maracaibo with a school for training nurses.

Many other oil companies adopted policies and practices similar to Creole's. This Venezuelan company was clearly the most progressive in public as well as in employee relations among the Jersey affiliates in Latin America, and other companies profited by its experience. Standard-Vacuum in the Far East and Arabian American Oil Company in the

Middle East likewise carried on important pioneering work in relations with governments and peoples in their operating areas.[95]

Here, then, was a large corporation whose leaders had become aware that the company was out of touch with its social and political environment and who acted to establish closer rapport with it. The steps taken were not concerned with a superficial dressing up of the company's image but rather with investigating what was wrong and seeking to remedy it.

In the process, the leaders of the parent company and affiliates envisioned new horizons in the Jersey Company's relations in a changing world. They acquired a heightened awareness of the importance of its operations to the public and of the public's importance to the company. They came to see that an enterprise of the size of their company had responsibilities beyond its own industrial functions and operational reach. At the same time, they acquired a better comprehension of the growing expectations of the masses of people around the world and of the historic shift in the relations of business and government that was taking place in the United States and other countries. They also became more conscious of the need, as a matter of concern to the company's own well-being, to examine company action in the light of the general public's interest. An example of such examination and action is presented in the next chapter.

Chapter 25

Problems in Supplying Postwar Markets

THE PRIMARY CONCERN of the directors and high-level executives of Standard Oil Company (New Jersey) during the early postwar years was to assure the affiliates adequate products at competitive costs to supply an expected long-term rise in market demand. This necessitated reexamination of some of the company's policies and redesigning of parts of the affiliates' functional structure and operations. It led to expansion and improvement in all operations with emphasis on the acquisition of new oil reserves and production.

Before Jersey and its affiliates had progressed far in implementing their plans for the long term, immediate pressures deflected some of their attention and energies to the solving of current problems. One of the urgent problems grew out of an unexpected increase in the demand for petroleum products shortly after the war. For the first time in two decades except during the war years, the oil industry had to operate under a condition of threatened and even actual shortages instead of a troublesome oversupply.

PLANNING FOR POSTWAR OPERATIONS

The Coordination Committee, and through it the various functional departments, had begun in 1943 to consider preliminary plans for the immediate postwar years. The war had so distorted the civilian market that there was little experience on which to base forecasts. It was also obviously impossible to predict when the war would end or what the rate of military demobilization would be. Jersey's leaders believed that the global commitments of the United States and its allies would permit only a gradual conversion from the military to the civilian market after the war ended. But of that there was no certainty. Plans therefore had to be kept general and flexible.

As the end of the war approached and rapid demobilization was indicated, the prevailing view among American business leaders and prominent economists came to be that economic recovery would be somewhat slow, as it had been after World War I. This view was widely held in the petroleum industry. Not all the members of Jersey's Economics Department were in agreement, but this general forecast greatly influenced the company's planning.[1] The executives assumed that military requirements for petroleum products would decline rapidly but that civilian needs would not increase fast enough to maintain the same general level of demand. This assumption was reinforced by the actual rate of demobilization of the American forces in the summer and autumn of 1945.

In October, 1945, Chairman Chester F. Smith of the Coordination Committee, in addressing a conference of company executives, stated that "our organization expects severe competition over the next few years." But for the immediate future he expressed its expectations in these words:

For a short period we anticipate there may be a fundamental lack of appreciation between supply and demand. . . . the industry is overexpanded in practically all its phases, particularly in refining and distributive facilities. . . . [It will be necessary to] make a tremendous effort to maintain a satisfactory rate of throughput to carry fixed costs. The surplus equipment, of course, will be used for improved products, and a quality race is a distinct possibility, with continued refinery additions necessary to maintain competitive advantage.[2]

The company's response to this expected condition of short-term oversupply, according to its Board of Directors, should be to raise efficiency and reduce costs in all phases of the business while improving the quality of products.[3]

In many respects, the prospect of a decline in demand was welcome. Some slackening would afford respite from the remorseless drive of the war years and allow time to repair the wear and tear of men and machines, to resume the usual process of replacement and modernization postponed by the war, and generally to restore the organization and return to normal procedures. It would also provide an opportunity to initiate the improvements in all phases of operations which had been planned for the longer term.

Jersey's directors and high-level executives had no doubt about the longer term. They foresaw a rising demand and vigorous competition once the postwar readjustment was completed. Hence, an emphasis on marketing and the improvement of the company's worldwide crude oil position would be imperative. New manufacturing facilities would also be needed to provide larger volumes of products and particularly to utilize improved techniques and methods in order to keep cost, quality, and product range competitive. Research would necessarily have to be stressed in all branches of operations. And the expansion of operations and the shortage of executive personnel would require a continuing program of training for managerial positions.[4]

Toward the end of the war, economic and scientific research groups joined with management in all phases of the business to study prospects and to plan for the next five years and to some extent for the next twenty years. Studies were made of trends in population and general economic growth in various market areas around the world to provide a basis for forecasting the rate of increase in the demand for oil products. It was concluded that the demand would probably grow at a higher rate in Latin America and Europe than in the United States, and also that in this country certain regions had a greater growth potential than others. Generally the growth rate was expected to be higher in the less-developed regions than in those already having a substantial per capita consumption. Company research indicated moreover that the entire crude production of the Western Hemisphere would before long be needed to supply the hemisphere's markets.[5] To enable Jersey to hold its relative position in the oil industry, its leaders planned capital expenditures on a scale beyond anything the company had ever experienced.[6]

A TIDAL WAVE OF DEMAND

Marketing was the front line in Jersey's postwar program for recovery and growth. To begin to restore the selling organizations in the Eastern Hemisphere and to resume competitive operations in the Americas were immediate imperatives. The marketers had to become vigorous and efficient salesmen again.

Competitive marketing was restored almost at once in the Western Hemisphere. There Jersey's plans were predicated on a plentiful supply of high-quality products. By a well-planned program of conversion, the refineries of the affiliates in the United States succeeded in providing the domestic marketers with superior products for the civilian trade. Only two weeks after gasoline rationing ended in August, 1945, they began to sell Esso Extra with an octane rating of 95 and the regular grade with a rating of 85—a boon to automobiles fueled with wartime gasolines of an octane rating ranging from 70 to 76.[7] At the very time when for several weeks in the autumn of 1945 large refineries of many competitors were affected by strikes, this early octane step-up gave the affiliates a lead in the gasoline market.

The return to serving the civilian market in much of the Eastern Hemisphere was slow. In Axis countries, oil companies could sell only to military occupation forces, which for some time controlled the distribution of whatever products were made available. In many other countries in Europe, the products supplied by the oil companies were pooled by the government and were allotted to distributors in accordance with a system of quotas. Whatever the method of regulation in a country, companies were generally allowed products in proportion to their prewar share of total national sales. However, in some countries American companies were soon affected by a shortage of dollar exchange.

Before the implementation of the plans for the Jersey Company's marketing program was well under way, and following a short recession in the demand for products, a boom struck the oil market. In 1946 the total world consumption of oil products, not including Russia, reached an all-time high, even exceeding the record wartime year. The demand rose especially fast in the Western Hemisphere. In the United States in 1946 it was 20 per cent above that of 1941, and the total Western Hemisphere demand exceeded that of the earlier year by 22 per cent. In Europe also the demand began to rise in 1946, but from a low during the war. In the world as a whole, it continued to grow in the next two years.[8]

The rate of increase was high for all major products. The demand for gasoline began to rise steeply almost at once after the end of the war. The consumption of middle distillates, especially for home heating and diesel requirements, began to increase in 1946, and in 1947 it rose at a rapid rate. Residual fuel oil consumption similarly increased, owing largely to an unsatisfactory world coal situation and the urgent need for fuel for industrial plants and ships.[9]

A summary view of Jersey's product sales during the first five postwar years is given in Table 22. These sales increased at a generally high rate over the period but with considerable variation from year to year and from country to country.

For many months after V-J Day, the affiliates met the rising demand without much difficulty, partly because of their build-up of inventories at the end of the war. But in the spring of 1946, the Esso Marketers in the northeastern section of the United States and Imperial's sales organization in eastern Canada foresaw a possible shortage of products. The

Table 22: **ANNUAL WORLDWIDE PRODUCT SALES BY AFFILI-
ATES, 1946–1950**
Standard Oil Company (New Jersey)
(In millions of 42-gallon barrels)

	1946	1947	1948	1949	1950
United States					
Esso Marketers[a] and General Office sales,[b] Standard Oil Co. of New Jersey (Esso Standard)	228.8	257.1	235.2	227.3	268.0
Standard Oil Export Corp. (Esso Export)					
Bonded fuel oil sales, American ports[c]	—	—	32.2	28.0	25.5
Total sales by the above	228.8	257.1	267.3	255.4	293.5
Humble Oil & Refining Co.	9.6	12.7	16.0	14.4	15.6
Carter Oil Co., The	5.2	5.2	6.1	5.2	5.8
Total United States	243.6	275.1	289.4	275.0	314.9
Foreign Countries					
Imperial Oil Ltd., Canada	38.1	46.1	50.6	54.7	62.0
Latin American affiliates	59.1	70.6	79.4	74.5	80.2
European and Mediterranean affiliates[d]	27.8	80.6	90.6	98.8	107.5
Standard-Vacuum Oil Co., in Asia, Africa, and Australia	22.3	28.3	32.1	38.8	40.8
Sales to nonaffiliates[e]	57.7	25.8	20.6	20.5	26.8
Total Foreign	205.1	251.4	273.2	287.2	317.2
Total World	448.7	526.5	562.6	562.2	632.2

NOTE: Because of rounding, totals are not in all cases the exact sum of the figures added. Does not include natural and cycle plant gasoline and chemical products.
[a] Sales by Marketing Department of Standard Oil Company of New Jersey (Esso Standard), Colonial Beacon Oil Company, Standard Oil Company of Pennsylvania, Stanco, Inc. (merged with Esso Standard), and Penola Inc.
[b] Contract sales include bunker sales in American ports to 1948.
[c] Handled before 1948 by Standard Oil Company of New Jersey.

[d] Sales by affiliates include their share of government pooled supplies for several years. Some of these supplies were also provided by Esso Export Corporation, which arranged the importing of petroleum products and of crude oil to be run by affiliates' refineries.
[e] Sales by Standard Oil Export to nonaffiliates in foreign countries, principally in Europe and North Africa.
Source: Statistics compiled by the Coordination and Economics Department, Standard Oil Company (New Jersey).

former also met what was considered potentially serious quality competition in the gasoline market.

This gasoline quality problem seems to have had no observable effect on the Esso Marketers' competitive position, but the possibility of losing customers because of a relative decline in quality was real. The marketers were concerned that the gasoline they had to sell might fall below the octane rating of their competitors' motor fuels and thus breach the long-held objective of Jersey—not always realized—of maintaining quality at least equal to the best competitive product. Actually the octane rating of the motor gasolines of the industry dropped because the demand outran the capacity to produce high-octane components. For a time, the leaded gasolines were at a special disadvantage because tetraethyl lead was in short supply. For much of the industry, indeed, either quality or volume had to be sacrificed until more catalytic cracking and other manufacturing facilities could be made available for producing better motor fuels in the quantity the market would take.[10]

The large increase in demand in both foreign and domestic markets eventually created problems for the Jersey Company. Some affiliates were committed by contracts to supply large military occupation needs, including aviation gasolines. The foreign affiliates had responsibilities for supplying a rising demand in certain European countries that was far beyond their expectations. Moreover, because of its worldwide operations, the company had especially large contracts for bunkering ships. One affiliate, Standard Oil Company of New Jersey, was a relatively large supplier of aviation and industrial fuels and of diesel and home-heating oils in the section of the United States where the demand for those products was greatest.[11]

The Jersey Company was able to meet its commitments well in 1946. It experienced no actual shortage of crude oil or of refinery capacity except for catalytic cracking. Despite the conversion of the government-owned Big Inch and Little Big Inch pipelines to natural gas and a consequent need for more tankers to supply Atlantic Coast refineries with crude and markets with products, the affiliates experienced no really critical transportation problems that year.

When the parent company's officers and directors in the spring of 1946 realized that the demand was rising faster than had been expected, they began to advise the affiliates to put their emphasis on immediately increasing supplies rather than on development for the long term. The producing affiliates accordingly stepped up their drilling to the limits of available manpower and materials. Humble in 1946 drilled 600 wells on proved acreage, principally in fields not fully developed during the war. Instead of reducing its production to about the 1941 level as planned, it actually raised production in 1947 to approximately twice that amount; the company's 1947 total was even slightly above that of its peak year during the war. Humble also increased its purchases.[12] Creole at the same time raised its output of crude considerably. The Western Hemisphere refineries of the affiliates increased their total crude runs by an average of more than 80,000 barrels daily, the largest additions being at Aruba and Baton Rouge. Worldwide, the group raised the number of its owned tankers (not including Standard-Vacuum's) from 157 at the end of 1945 to 191 at the end of 1946. This, however, still left the affiliates far short, in both number and tonnage, of the combined fleet of 219 ships in operation at the outbreak of war in 1939.[13]

By 1947 the Jersey companies were utilizing their equipment and manpower to the limit in nearly all operations, and they found it impossible to expand their facilities in proportion to the rise in demand. A director of the parent company noted in June: "The bridge between oil in the ground and products in the hands of the consumer is a complicated structure of well-drilling equipment, pipelines, tankers, railroads, trucks, refineries, storage tanks, and all other things necessary to produce crude, transport it, and change it into the products that the consumer needs."[14]

The transportation situation became difficult in that year. The company was hard hit by a shortage of tankers, and it made every effort to increase its tonnage. In the first eleven months of 1947, it doubled the tonnage of the United States–flag fleet by purchasing tankers from the Maritime Commission and time-chartering ships.[15] The affiliates in the United States were able to increase their pipeline mileage very little because of a shortage of steel pipe. Again, as in wartime emergencies, they shifted tank cars from short to long runs. Standard Oil Company of New Jersey, like other companies, greatly increased long-distance shipping by railroad by speeding up the unloading of cars and using trucks for the shorter hauls. By December, 1947, the affiliates were moving by rail 50,000 barrels daily to deepwater terminals. At first, tank cars were used mainly for carrying Humble's crude oil—beyond pipeline capacity—from West Texas to the Gulf for shipment by tanker. In December, tank cars also had to be used for overland shipment from Louisiana to Jersey's Atlantic Coast refineries.[16] This was an expensive type of transportation. For example, in 1947 Humble moved nearly 10,000,000 barrels of crude from West Texas to the Gulf by rail at an expenditure estimated at about $4,000,000 more than shipment by pipeline would have cost.[17]

In May, 1947, Standard Oil Company of New Jersey advised the distributors whom it was supplying that they should not plan on getting a larger volume of products in that year than they had received in 1946. However, the company informed them, they would receive supplies on the same basis as its own retail outlets. It also adopted the policy of not accepting additional heavy fuel-oil accounts, and it stopped installing new oil burners and accepting new heating oil accounts except in unusual circumstances. It instructed salesmen to relax their sales efforts in virtually all product lines—a difficult assignment for men who, as one said, "had not been taught how not to sell." At the same time, Standard Oil

Company of New Jersey reduced sales to such large marketers as Standard Oil Company of Kentucky.[18]

"Never [before] in my memory," said Howard W. Page, the manager of the parent company's Coordination and Economics Department, in June, 1947, "have the Jersey affiliates been unable to take on any commitment for major petroleum products and been unsure of supplying that business, either from their own facilities or by purchases." Now they were in a position where new orders had to be turned down, and they constantly met difficulties in supplying commitments. Page said that the affiliates were "operating at rates well above those previously considered maximum . . . and not only the Jersey affiliates but the rest of the industry has found itself without any surplus capacity."[19]

Although the prospect of shortages was widespread, the situation became most difficult in the northeastern section of the United States and in eastern Canada, both areas again being supplied largely by tankers. By December, 1947, the threat of shortages in the northeastern states—especially of heating oil—became so serious that hearings were held in Washington by a subcommittee of the Committee on Interstate and Foreign Commerce to see how the situation might be eased. President Rathbone of Standard Oil Company of New Jersey and Howard W. Page were among those who testified. The Senate committee appointed an industry committee, with Rathbone as chairman, to suggest how to meet the problem. This group recommended ways to increase the supply of products and publicity to influence customers to reduce their oil consumption. It also recommended the organization of state and local committees to assist in the allocation of supplies among users—action which the companies, under antitrust statutes, were fearful of taking on their own initiative until the passing of the so-called Taft Act late in December.[20]

According to Rathbone's testimony, his company had already taken action to prepare for the expected emergency. It had begun in November, 1947, to turn an additional 25,000 barrels of crude per day into heating oil by adjusting the refinery gasoline yields downward in order to increase distillate yields. This meant a considerable loss as compared to the production of gasoline from that oil. The company also began the expensive overland shipment of crude to Atlantic refineries by tank car. It increased its imports, even from the distant Middle East. And through publicity and salesmen, it urged customers to reduce their use of fuel oil by lowering thermostats.

Standard Oil Company of New Jersey estimated that it could supply 110 per cent of the volume provided the previous winter season, an amount it believed to be sufficient if temperatures were normal. So fine was the balance between the various factors affecting supply, however, that the company could not plan to increase supplies to meet lower temperatures. It estimated that an additional four or five tankers would provide a margin of safety, but the only vessels that could possibly become available were fifty tied up by the Maritime Commission awaiting decision as to their sale under the Ships' Sales Act—a circumstance that brought considerable criticism from both inside and outside the government.[21]

By January, 1948, in an unusually cold and stormy winter, the Jersey affiliates and other suppliers were straining their facilities to the utmost. The inventories of Standard Oil Company of New Jersey were falling. Tank cars were being rushed from the oil regions in the shortest possible time. Tanker captains, on orders from headquarters, were driving their ships hard despite excessive fuel consumption and increased expense. In the New York and Boston areas, conditions became so bad that whether or not people would have heat depended at times on when certain tankers would reach port. Managers in Esso offices, pinpointing the location of the company's ships, kept constant watch over their positions. At the unloading terminals, every man worked to shorten the turnaround time and to return the tankers to sea. The tank-truck men, on returning to the bulk plant at the end of a day of driving on icy or snow-blocked streets, might have to start out again to fill emergency orders. Overtime pay raised operating costs substantially.[22]

The company's marketers allotted their supplies among the various types of demands. They apportioned available products among the distributors and customers regularly dependent on them. They obviously had to give preference to hospitals and homes with sick people. The company kept its switchboards open around the clock, and any regular customer entirely without oil could get a small delivery within a few hours. In order to stretch the supply of fuel as far as possible, it delivered fifty gallons at a time to its retail customers instead of the scheduled larger deliveries. It also joined other integrated oil companies in making some provision for the distributors who had no regular suppliers. After the passing of the Taft Act, however, committees set up in municipalities and states, under government direction and with oil industry cooperation, allotted products to such distributors. Throughout the difficult months, by means of statements to the press, the Esso marketers kept the public regularly informed about the supply situation and what was being done to improve it.[23]

Finally the long and exceptionally cold winter drew to a close and the demand fell. For a time Esso Standard (the new name of Standard Oil Company of New Jersey) continued to bring in the maximum possible volume of fuel oil. Then the marketers began to fill the tanks of their retail customers and to restore the inventories of distributors.[24]

Although the rate of increase in world demand fell somewhat in 1948, a rise above the requirements in 1947 for a time strained an industry already stretched to the limit. Until late in the year, Jersey invested as much as possible in facilities that would increase the supply of oil products in the shortest possible time.

The parent company and its affiliates made some progress in reducing their tanker shortage. Jersey's leading marine executive, M. G. Gamble, reported in May, 1948, that in the past three months the over-all tanker requirements of the affiliates had increased about 20 per cent, partly because of having to bring more oil on the long haul from the Middle East. During those months the affiliates had chartered 144 tankers, and they were still urgently seeking to contract for more ships. The pressure had been eased somewhat by the restoration of all the Maritime Commission tankers to peacetime service. By the end of June, the general tanker situation had improved so much that charter rates were falling, but this was normal in the slack season.[25]

In 1948 the most serious bottleneck for the affiliates and in general for the Western Hemisphere oil industry was in crude supply. The affiliates' net crude production for the year was about 20 per cent more than in 1947. Creole increased its net by an average of about 50,000 barrels daily; under United States export controls it was unable to get the steel it needed for further expansion. Humble drilled all the wells for which it could get steel. Unfortunately, the fields then being developed in Texas were not so prolific as earlier ones had been, and production declined in some of the older fields. Texas wells, under state regulation, were operated at their maximum efficient rate and on every day in the year, a record that exceeded even the operating rate of the war years. Yet Humble's production in 1948 was increased an average of only 28,000 barrels per day.[26]

Shortages in the United States during the winter of 1947–1948 spurred a movement for government regulation that was to outlast the critical supply situation. In fact, one of the company's most persistent problems at that time—and also one of the industry's—came to be public criticism and government investigations, which rose primarily out of actual or feared shortages and allegations of inequities in the allocation of supplies. It was charged that the industry was creating scarcities in order to raise prices and profits. More than a score of separate congressional investigations of the oil business were started; a few lasted for many months. Bills for divorcement of the operations of integrated companies were again introduced in Congress. Strong political pressure called for export embargoes, the establishment of a synthetic oil industry, supervision of the industry by government agencies, and price regulation. On the whole, Jersey fared well in the investigations.[27]

One issue involving the company that rose in 1948 was not to be resolved for nearly a decade. On July 1, Senator Joseph C. O'Mahoney sent a telegram to President Holman, which the senator simultaneously released to the press. He requested an explanation of what was said to be the oil industry's policy of pricing Middle East oil on the basis of United States Gulf prices plus transportation from Texas ports to the Eastern Mediterranean. Under this policy, the telegram stated, the countries buying oil with funds provided by the United States' Economic Cooperation Administration (Marshall Plan) were being overcharged.

Holman's reply to the senator and letters sent in 1948 by company executives to ECA administrators in Washington explained Jersey's price policies and practices.[28] These executives maintained that the company set its prices independently and that these reflected competitive, worldwide marketing conditions and practices. They estimated that in the second half of 1948 about 10 per cent of their sales to ECA countries would be products from the Persian Gulf and another 20 per cent would be crude from the same area. They held that because of Europe's heavy dependence on the Western Hemisphere, especially for oil products, the United States Gulf or Caribbean prices had a direct competitive effect on prices for Middle East oil. Actually, the basing of Middle East prices on United States Gulf prices was an old practice that had arisen because the Gulf was the world's leading oil market.

President Holman explained the Jersey affiliates' pricing. "Our announced F.O.B. prices for crude oil supplies at the Eastern Mediterranean or Persian Gulf are equivalent to the Caribbean price for crude plus freight at published United States Maritime Commission rates from the Caribbean to Western Europe *less* freight on the same basis from either the Eastern Mediterranean or the Persian Gulf, depending on the supply point to Western Europe." Thus, Italy, he continued, because it was closer to the Eastern Mediterranean and Persian Gulf, had a delivered crude oil price of 80 cents per barrel less than the United States Gulf price *plus* freight at the United States Maritime Commission rate from the Gulf to Italy; ECA countries in Western Europe paid no more for Middle East crudes than they would have for oil purchased from the Caribbean. "For the relatively small amount of products moved from our supply sources in the Persian Gulf to European countries," President Holman explained, "our price F.O.B. Persian Gulf is either the low of *Platt's Oilgram* United States Gulf price or such lower price as will afford the purchaser as low a delivered cost as obtainable from the lowest competitive source."

This price issue was unresolved for nearly a decade. It became the subject of long discussions and investigations in Washington. In 1952 the Attorney General initiated suits against the American oil companies selling Middle East oil to purchasers financed by the Economic Cooperation Administration. The suit against Standard Oil Company (New Jersey) and Esso Export alleged overcharges totaling $36,000,000. The litigation finally ended in 1957 when the Circuit Court of Appeals upheld the decision of a District Court in a similar suit against Standard Oil Company of California and The Texas Company. The court's judgment was "that the defendant's proof showed beyond contradiction that the prices financed by ECA were in fact the lowest competitive prices." On the basis of these decisions, the suit against Jersey and Esso Export was dismissed.[29]

Jersey's leaders became apprehensive in 1948 concerning public criticism and government investigations. In September of that year, a company executive warned a conference of high officers and executives of parent company and affiliates that the current "combination of inflation, shortages, tense international relations, and a presidential election year will result in an unusual amount of political activity affecting the petroleum industry." This activity, he said, "could result in government controls which would be permanently detrimental to the public and the industry."[30]

The company had tried to counter this development in various ways. It had worked to stave off serious shortages by stretching its organization and facilities to the limit. It had kept the public informed of its investments for expanding its operating facilities and progress in increasing supplies. In addition, for nearly two years it had tried to brake the rise in the prices of crude oil and products.

PRICE POLICY IN A SELLERS' MARKET

Jersey's attempt to retard the rise in oil prices in 1947 and 1948 is of interest beyond its immediate significance to the company. It shows how complex may be the factors affecting the adjustment of supply to demand in a free market. It demonstrates the range of the considerations that influenced the company's price decisions, particularly the weighing of noneconomic and long-term economic considerations. It is an illuminating example of a corporate attempt to slow up inflation. And it throws light on the phenomenon of price leadership.

What came to be known as the company's hold-the-line policy had developed over a number of months. After the lifting of federal controls in June, 1946, the price of crude oil and products rose considerably. The increase was then justified on the grounds of low prices under federal control during the war and of increased costs and the need to enlarge supplies after the war. Although the Jersey Board of Directors was concerned that prices might go up too fast, it recognized that some increase was necessary immediately after the war to assure adequate supplies. The affiliates were not leaders in raising prices after the summer of 1946, but they raised those of both crude and products as other companies took the initiative. However, when a new round of increases seemed in prospect with the developing threat of shortages late in the winter of 1947, Jersey's directors became concerned over the effect of increases on the general inflation then gathering momentum. They discussed the matter extensively before determining what the company should do about it. They were in complete accord with President Truman's challenge in April to private enterprise "to display the leadership to make our free economy work by arresting this inflationary trend."[31]

In June, 1947, when in the judgment of the company's top administrators the supply and price situation was becoming serious, President Holman took a stand against an increase in oil prices. The occasion was an address he delivered before a meeting of the Pennsylvania Oil Producers Association at Bradford. Holman stated that under prevailing conditions the current crude prices were adequate in a majority of cases; he found it difficult to see any benefits to the public, either in greater supplies or better products, from further increases at the time. He urged upon the oil producers "an investment in the future," saying:

We have an obligation to help to stabilize an economy of which we are an important part. This dictates policies based not on short-term expediency but upon the long-term best interest of the industry as a whole. This is a time for self-discipline, for business statesmanship, for driving forward on another job the American public expects us to do.[32]

This statement was quoted widely, with mixed reactions within the industry. In the marketing territory of Standard Oil Company of New Jersey, the American Oil Company, Atlantic Refining, and Socony-Vacuum raised tank-wagon prices. And in the Gulf market, spot cargoes —that is, not contract purchases—reached the highest prices in years.[33] Jersey's domestic affiliates, however, did not raise their prices.

When the new round of increases continued to spread, the company decided that a firm public stand should be taken. On July 24, Standard Oil Company of New Jersey released to the press a statement of its policy and the reasons for it.[34] "It is our opinion," read the press release, "that under the present conditions where a shortage of fabricated steel and other materials limits the industry's ability to produce, transport, and refine more crude oil, further price increases in either crude or products will not be effective in increasing the over-all supply of petroleum products." In this situation, the statement continued, "increases would be only inflationary and should be resisted." Firmly believing that higher prices "under present conditions are not in the interest of either the oil industry or the public," the company "is following the general policy of not increasing prices unless such increases will tend to maintain or bring out additional supplies." The statement noted that the company, as before, was sharing its available supplies equitably with all its customers, and that it believed its hold-the-line policy had not worked any hardship on those independent distributors and dealers who handled Esso products.

This policy was based in large part on broad economic considerations. Obviously, motivations in a diverse group like the company's Board of Directors are never single, but in this instance these men shared a concern for the long-term economic strength of the company, the industry, and the economy. This concern was not based on their own judgment alone but also on comprehensive studies by members of the Coordination and Economics Department of conditions and trends in the economy that had a bearing on the issue. President Holman and the Jersey board were convinced that raising prices under existing conditions would only feed the fires of inflation. They foresaw that one result would be a demand for wage increases, which would tend to push prices upward again. They also held that, although higher prices would not materially affect current demand, they might in time bring about a considerable conversion to competitive fuels and the loss of outlets for the future. In brief, attempting to maximize short-run profits would not only contribute to a spiraling inflation but might also have adverse effects on the oil industry.[35]

The Jersey directors were well aware that under existing conditions raising prices would be unfortunate from a public relations viewpoint, an awareness that increased as the months went by. They believed that the public would consider increases as unwarranted attempts to take advantage of a situation in which the consumer was virtually helpless. They also believed that, because of the current reporting of high earnings by oil companies, the public would look upon such action by the industry as profiteering. This situation, as they saw it, might set in motion a demand for regulation, possibly for restoring government pricing. In brief, the oil industry seemed to face the choice of voluntary restraint or the possible imposition of federal controls.

The company's leaders were under no illusion, however, that one company's action by itself would have any significant effect on inflation. Their hope was that other companies in the oil industry would follow their example, and that, if enough did so, inflation might to some extent be checked.[36]

The price-policy statement of Standard Oil Company of New Jersey won wide commendation. On the day of its announcement, Dr. John R. Steelman, Assistant to President Truman, wired President Rathbone: "Since the wholesale commodity price index went to a new high last week, your announcement of a 'hold-the-line' policy for crude and products is a patriotic action that will be appreciated by all. Price increases at this time, unless absolutely unavoidable, are selfish and foolhardy. To hold down the price of oil is good for the country and good for business."[37] Many others in high governmental posts also sent appreciative messages. W. A. Harriman, Secretary of Commerce, stated that "widespread action in the same spirit would most certainly mitigate the danger of inflationary pressures and help to stabilize our economy at a high level of employment and output." Among others who expressed approval were General Omar Bradley, head of the Veterans Administration, Edwin G. Nourse, Chairman of the President's Council of Economic Advisers, and John J. McCloy, President of the Bank for International Reconstruction and Development. The nation's general and business press and radio gave wide attention to the policy and to the favorable comments it was receiving.[38]

Within the oil industry, however, the reception was mixed. The *National Petroleum News* on July 30 reported a storm of comments, some favorable and others highly critical. Among the favorable reactions was that of President H. S. M. Burns of Shell Oil Company, who was quoted as having characterized the price statement "as a courageous and praiseworthy declaration of policy . . . definitely in the public interest . . . as a step in curbing inflationary pressures." *Platt's Oilgram* reported that most of the majors and the independent distributors in the East disapproved of the policy.[39] The oil industry press, although itself on the whole favorable, pointed to many questions raised by the policy.

The chief executives of Jersey's domestic producing affiliates also indicated some differences of view. President Schorp of Carter Oil—who reported unfriendly reactions in the company's territory, especially among small operators and independent producers—expressed the belief that it was a mistake for Jersey to "crusade" for maintaining prices.[40] The first reaction of President Wiess of Humble was that raising prices would serve to increase supply and reduce demand, and that from a public relations point of view the effect of shortages would be worse than the effect of higher prices.[41]

Weeks passed before any definite influence on prices was observable. In September, 1947, certain large competitors reduced their prices in the marketing territory of Standard Oil Company of New Jersey. The first major to do so was The Texas Company, which on September 12 announced a reduction in the price of gasoline and fuel oils in nine states in order to meet what it called the competitive prices of Standard Oil Company of New Jersey. Only a few days later several other large companies also reduced their gasoline and certain fuel-oil prices to a level competitive with those of the Jersey affiliates. Said the *Wall Street Journal:* "It took almost two months for the 'hold-the-line' policy of Standard Oil Company of New Jersey to force competitors to lower their prices."[42]

By this time, inflation had become a matter of wide public concern. Newspapers carried stories of consumer protests, and pressure rose for the restoration of government price controls. The widely known Harvard economist, Sumner H. Slichter, in discussing the situation in *The New York Times Magazine* of September 14, wrote: "All members of the community . . . should realize that the country at the present time is going through an extraordinarily important experience. It is attempting to operate its economy at full employment, but with virtually no special controls. It remains to be seen whether full employment, absence of special controls, and stability are compatible." For prices to continue to rise 10 per cent a year, Slichter stated, would be of "profound significance." He called on business, labor, and government to act responsibly. Business, he proposed, could help by raising output per man-hour, operating at a low inventory level, postponing investments that would not immediately increase output, keeping credit extension as low as possible, financing capital needs out of earnings even at the expense of dividends, and keeping prices well below the levels that the present demand would justify.

The independent distributors in the marketing territory of Standard Oil Company of New Jersey generally opposed the hold-the-line policy and were vociferous in their opposition to it.[43] As a matter of fact, the company could enforce its price policy in the consumers' market only where it sold directly to the consumer. Its customers among jobber and retail distributors, even the independent dealers in company-owned service stations, determined their own selling prices. In the current sellers' market, distributors did not face any serious loss of customers by not following the hold-the-line policy. They would be criticized, of course, if they charged their customers the higher prices, but if they reduced their prices they were subject to criticism from other distributors. The independents tended to follow the policy of maximizing short-run profits.

Trouble also rose in the Gulf cargo market. There annual sales contracts commonly stated that prices would be those posted and published in *Platt's Oilgram* on the date of delivery. The contracts thus left the figure open, merely stipulating that the price of particular deliveries should be the lowest, the average, or any other price posted on the delivery date. The Jersey companies' refineries, however, were in a somewhat special situation in that their sales were to a limited number of customers, largely to affiliates operating abroad. Consequently, their prices were not necessarily posted and hence not published in *Platt's Oilgram*. Certain other large integrated companies similarly did not post their prices. This practice of not publicly announcing prices brought charges of discrimination from the distributors purchasing from competing refiners allegedly selling at higher prices. Because of these charges, the Jersey affiliates decided to make known what they asked for their products.[44]

The first serious challenge to the hold-the-line policy came in the crude market. Premiums—that is, amounts paid above posted prices—had for some time been paid by buyers short of crude, and pressure was gathering for a general increase. The first move was made by Phillips Petroleum Company, which on October 15, 1947, announced a general 20-cent-per-barrel increase in Texas, Oklahoma, and Kansas. This was followed by pressure from independent producers on Jersey's crude oil purchasing affiliates to raise their prices. A general advance did not get under way, however, before Sun Oil on November 28 increased its crude posting by 50 cents a barrel. Sun justified this increase on the grounds that its inventories were low and it was losing crude—reportedly some 33,000 barrels a day—to other purchasers who paid premiums above posted prices.[45] President Holman then publicly repeated the company's position that it did not believe higher prices would bring about the production of more crude. This stand was supported by the small percentage increase in crude supply after the price increase in 1947—Texas production was already at the maximum efficient rate. As to premiums, Holman considered it inevitable that a small amount of crude would go to purchasers offering more than posted prices, and he held that the increase already made had not reduced such sales.[46]

However, when some twenty major purchasers within a week followed Sun Oil's lead, Humble finally raised its crude prices. In December, 1947, the average crude price in Texas reached $2.64 a barrel, as against the previous summer's $2.00. This December price for crude was the highest since 1920.[47]

President Rathbone of Standard Oil Company of New Jersey explained in a congressional hearing why Humble raised its crude postings. It was not too serious, he said, that after Sun Oil raised its prices it bought an average of nearly 5,000 barrels per day which Humble would otherwise have purchased. But so large was the country's surplus refining capacity at the time that, after many crude buyers raised their prices, the capacity was sufficient to process a volume equal to all the oil the Jersey affiliates had been purchasing from nonaffiliated producers. Jersey could not risk losing crude needed to supply its customers. According to Rathbone, 59.2 per cent of the crude supplied by domestic affiliates represented purchases from royalty owners, minority interests, and nonaffiliated companies.[48]

This increase in the price of crude raised the question as to what the affiliates should do about their own product prices. Two weeks after Phillips raised its crude postings, the East Coast affiliate increased the price of several products, including 0.8 cent per gallon on distillates. This was its first increase in about seven months, during which time Gulf cargo prices had risen considerably and the company for several months had been selling at prices below those of some of its large competitors. After the broad crude advance at the end of November, the company followed other large marketers in a general increase in product prices. However, in order to stimulate refinery production of vitally needed fuels, its advance was proportionately higher on heating and fuel oils than on gasoline.[49]

President Rathbone later testified in the fuel-oil hearings of the House Committee on Interstate and Foreign Commerce that the "two crude price increases which occurred in 1947 subsequent to July 9 are estimated to have increased the costs of our domestic companies at the rate of approximately $88,000,000 per year." This, he said, was more "than we could afford to absorb and meet our financial obligations."[50] That is, the company would not increase its short-run profits at the expense of the consumer, but it also would not seriously penalize its owners and jeopardize its capacity to carry the mounting costs of replacing reserves and facilities by narrowing the profit margin substantially.

Available evidence suggests that the product price increases of Jersey affiliates and other large integrated companies were not so high as those of independent refiners. In an article on this hold-the-line effort, professors Harry L. Hansen and Powell Niland of the Harvard Graduate School of Business Administration show, for example, that from July 1, 1947, through February, 1948, the independent refiners' Gulf Coast cargo price range for No. 2 fuel oil tended to be higher—at times considerably higher—than that of the majors. They found evidence to suggest that the independents were at least relatively free from a price "squeeze" and that their margins tended to widen during this period.[51] Further indication that these refiners were not seriously affected by the Jersey price policy is the relative absence of complaints by them in congressional hearings.

Judging by the complaints of independent distributors, especially in the East Coast marketing territory, they were the ones who felt the effects of the hold-the-line policy the most. It is impossible, of course, to learn what the exact situation was, particularly during the winter months of fuel-oil shortages, when some distributors charged all that the traffic would bear.[52] Professors Hansen and Niland concluded that the Esso policy did lead to the exercise of some restraint by some fuel oil distributors. They also found, however, that in New York City during the winter months of 1948 the tank-wagon price per gallon of No. 2 fuel oil ranged from Esso's 12 cents per gallon to more than 15½ cents, and that individual sales were reported at even higher prices. They believed it to be significant that the distributors who complained in congressional hearings of a squeeze presented no evidence that Jersey's policies had had any effect on their profits.[53]

During February and March of 1948, attacks and investigations proliferated. Independent distributors continued to complain that their profit margins had not increased as prices of crude and products had risen. The independent crude producers were again pushing for an increase. Jersey and other large companies were being attacked as allegedly creating shortages and applying price squeezes to independents, especially to distributors. As noted previously, many investigations of the oil industry were then going on in Washington. Senator O'Mahoney requested a statement from Jersey to indicate whether or not it would follow the steel industry in raising prices.[54] In the judgment of Jersey men, raising prices at this time would lead to government controls.

They were especially concerned that crude prices might be increased still further, a development that would be especially serious for Humble as a large crude oil purchaser. In a company in which issues are discussed in committees and boards, it is difficult to follow from the records the course of the discussion among the top administrators. But a letter of Director Haslam to Chairman Abrams dated March 9, 1948, is revealing. Experience led to the belief, wrote Haslam, that a complexity of problems existed. These included keeping connections with suppliers of crude, protecting the rights of royalty owners and Humble's minority owners, and not antagonizing the independent producers too much. In addition, there were other problems connected with buying, selling, and transporting by pipelines the great quantity of crude Humble handled daily. These problems were such that the affiliate would have to raise crude prices in a week or two if other purchasers raised theirs.

Director Haslam consequently suggested that the Jersey affiliates try to check the further spiraling of crude prices by a reduction in the prices of products. He advised: "If we are sincere in wanting to stop the increase in petroleum prices and profits, at this point (with some 350 to 400 million dollars profits before us over the coming year) we should do everything possible. We should not be merely defensive in our action. We should try to bring about that which we think is best for the company, the industry, and our economy by *positive* action *ahead* of time."[55] He paraphrased the old typing-school exercise, "Now is the time for all good men to come to the aid of the country," and added, "Maybe it is!"

On March 30, 1948, Esso Standard Oil Company announced immediate price reductions on more than 350 products, including industrial and farm fuels, lubricating oils and greases, asphalt, and bottled gas. It cut the price of roofing asphalt 5 per cent and reduced the prices of industrial lubricants, cutting oils, and greases up to 25 per cent on some grades. In addition, the company offered a summer "fill-up" discount of 0.7 cent per gallon on kerosene and home heating oils. It did not reduce the prices of motor gasolines because—according to its announcement—those prices had "been held behind the general upward price trend and are low compared with the prices of almost all other commodities."

This announcement of reductions, dramatic in its timing, was carried extensively in newspapers. Senator O'Mahoney had it inserted in the *Congressional Record* of April 6 with his own comment to the press: "The price reduction recently announced by Standard Oil Company of New Jersey on several petroleum products is one of the most encouraging signs of the times so far as the battle against inflation is concerned. I should say that Esso has given the country a highly salutary example of sound industrial statesmanship." The assistant chief of the Antitrust Division of the Department of Justice congratulated Esso Standard on this evidence of "statesmanship and leadership."[56]

Whatever the cause—whether the example of Esso, concern over inflation, public opinion, government investigations, the easing up of supplies, or all of these—other large companies soon also reduced their prices. United States Steel, which had been following a cautious price policy, on April 30 announced a price reduction and its decision to "hold the line" on wages. Other large companies reduced prices at the same time.[57]

But independent distributors in Esso Standard's territory continued to be critical. In April the Federal Trade Commission was reported to be looking into the complaints of certain South Carolina jobbers. They had been protesting Esso Standard's lower prices for a year and had complained to a congressional committee that the company was creating difficulties for them by posting prices that were less than those in the Gulf market plus transportation.[58]

Esso Standard kept close watch of the effect of its policy on independent refiners and distributors. The results of a spot check, reported early in June, 1948, indicated that only about a third of the distributors of Esso products were passing the company's reductions on to consumers. Probably the company was having its strongest influence in the fuel oil market—particularly in New Jersey, Pennsylvania, and the southern states, where it sold about 80 per cent of its fuel oil directly to consumers. Its small number of company-operated service stations gave it virtually no leverage in the gasoline market. "On gasoline," according to the head of Jersey's Coordination and Economics Department, "our wholesale prices are as low as and usually lower than all others, but the station prices are equal to the market almost 100%—the dealer, in other words, gets a larger margin from us."[59]

Late in May, 1948, Esso Standard's president discussed the complex price situation at a conference of high-level operating executives of Jersey affiliates. Prices, he said, presented one of their most difficult problems. A higher price structure seemed essential to finance the required expansion of the industry, but, with the present "apparent" high earnings of oil companies, raising the charges for products would meet great opposition from the public and the government. Besides, such increases would undoubtedly generate pressure for higher prices for crude, "even though that part of the industry is relatively far better off than other branches." The solution was, of course, an adequate supply, but that seemed some time away. President Rathbone held that the company's policy undoubtedly had had a considerable dampening effect on the upward-spiraling prices, but it also had placed a considerable squeeze on the refining and marketing branches of the business and had led to much criticism of the company from nonintegrated units in the industry. "We have felt," he said, "that the lesser of two evils was to have this criticism from within the industry rather than have what might be more serious criticism from the public and the government."

The problems raised by Jersey's price policy were many, added Rathbone. It appeared that the company would have to relax the policy here and there. "We shall have to couple this," he said, "with a more generous treatment of distributors and jobbers as to margins, since this jobber group is politically the most potent and the most vociferous." The nonintegrated refiners would get the least help from such a program, but they could stand it better because they were already selling at higher prices. However, said Rathbone, "we might have to consider extending our present practice of making some crude available to independent

refiners even at the expense of our own refining operations." As for the
effect of the price policy on Esso Standard itself, the manufacturing profit
(before federal income taxes) had increased in the years 1946 through
1948 (estimated), although not enough to meet capital needs. However,
marketing profits showed little increase, "indicating that marketing profit
margins have not increased during this period of rising volume of sales
and rising prices."[60]

The price situation was a part of a larger issue, that of public relations,
which Rathbone said "might almost be termed our No. 1 problem today."
He explained:

The oil industry and our own company are certainly in the spotlight, and
are to a great extent on trial. The fuel shortage last winter brought out a host
of government investigations and a storm of public criticism. We were threatened with state control in half a dozen states and with federal control almost
daily. The industry weathered the storm with no serious trouble. We are now
facing a somewhat similar situation this summer on a potential gasoline shortage. There are at least seven congressional committees now investigating the
oil industry, and some eight or nine Department of Justice investigations are
now under way. Our earnings, our price policies, our relationship with jobbers,
our ability to supply the public, Middle East oil, national security, and other
things are under scrutiny and attack. Certainly, it is essential for us and the
industry as a whole to watch and test everything we do from the standpoint of
public and governmental reactions. Even with the utmost care, we still find
ourselves in many difficulties. It becomes increasingly hard to conduct our
business as we would like to do it and as we feel it should be conducted.[61]

In September, 1948, the demand again began to build up for a price
increase. President Holman, in addressing the National Petroleum Association, again appealed to the industry, expressing the hope that prices
would remain stable.[62] Phillips Petroleum, however, increased its crude
postings by 35 cents per barrel. It was soon followed by Sinclair and
Southern Minerals Corporation. Although under pressure from crude
producers, Humble refused to follow on the grounds of an improved
crude supply, a slackening in the rate of increase in demand, and large
additions to industry stocks. Esso Standard announced that it was not raising its crude oil postings. Humble lost lease connections to Phillips and
Sinclair averaging approximately 15,000 barrels daily. However, most
other buyers similarly refused to raise their prices, and Phillips and others
had to rescind their increase.[63]

On November 19, Esso Standard announced price adjustments on many products. These included reductions on heavy fuel oil, heating oil, and gasoline. All together, the changes added up to a substantial over-all reduction in the prices of its products.[64] A month later Esso made further reductions on heavy and diesel fuel but increased the price of gasoline.

Before the end of the year, the companies that had increased their crude prices had reduced them to competitive levels.[65] This marked the end of the domestic oil industry's rising prices and of Jersey's efforts to hold the line.

What had the company accomplished by attempting to lead a movement to brake the price rise? Certainly it had won a great deal of favorable comment from government administrators in Washington and from the press generally. Surely, also, its producing affiliates had been severely criticized by producers, and its largest marketing affiliate had been attacked by distributors. Professors Hansen and Niland concluded—on the basis of available data on the profits of jobbers during this period— that "jobbers throughout the country fared reasonably well financially." As for the consumer, they wrote: ". . . it can be said that a very large corporation, whatever its motives, served to brake an inflationary price rise. Call it business statesmanship or an error in judgment or a combination of both, Esso's action had obvious, immediate gains for the consumer." They also concluded that "on balance, Esso's hold-the-line policy probably benefited the industry and the company." The company's own profits, they believed, were "undoubtedly lower than they might have been in 1947 and 1948 had Esso raised its prices." However, "by its actions, Esso even more firmly established itself as a dependable supplier in emergencies with the ability and the willingness to supply products at prices as low as or lower than those of any other petroleum company operating in the East Coast market."[66]

This episode stands as an example of Jersey's efforts to adjust company policy and action to the economic and political realities of the postwar world. It is significant, also, as an effort of the levelheaded chief executive of the company to assume the role of industrial statesman. President Holman and his associates no doubt came through the experience with a lively appreciation of the difficulties to be met in trying to exert leadership in so complex a situation. Yet they had demonstrated that a large company would voluntarily assume the risks inherent in attempting to take constructive action under circumstances that threatened the stability of their industry and of the national economy.

such reactions, the issue was investigated by the Senate Committee on Banking and Currency.[71]

To company men, the increase in gasoline prices in the spring of 1949 seemed entirely logical and the result of the same forces—supply, demand, and costs—that cause all price changes in a free economy. Internal memoranda on Jersey's price policy give an indication of the situation and of the reasoning behind the increase. Stated one memo: "Today our efficient refineries (with our inefficient shut down) are operating at a loss. We are paying for current costs but not setting aside anything for equipment wearing out. We are back in a buyers' market where competition is tighter than for many years." The consumers were now " 'holding the line' as they always do in a buyers' market." But they were holding it below the former profit margin for Jersey refineries, which, the memo said, had "resulted in a moderate profit" during the application of the company's hold-the-line policy. They had made a profit because "our refineries were more efficient than some others" at a time when the unusual demand brought into operation the industry's least efficient refining equipment. To maintain the 1947–1949 profit margin, however, would have required Jersey to raise gasoline 2½ cents per gallon. This could not be done because the company's "price policy in a buyers' market is to set prices low enough to obtain substantial capacity outlet for our efficient facilities." The memo concluded: "These prices are not determined by us. They are determined by the buyers and competitors."[72]

The change in gasoline prices was in keeping with the usual seasonal changes in the prices of oil products and with common practice in the pricing of joint products. In the winter months when kerosene and No. 2 fuel oil were in heavy demand, Jersey affiliates and other companies normally raised their charges for these particular products relative to gasoline in order to encourage refiners to increase the percentage yield of fuel oils from a barrel of crude. In the spring, when the demand for these products fell with warmer weather but the demand for gasoline rose, the price of gasoline was increased. Thus, as was normal in the case of joint products, the individual products were priced in accordance with what the market would pay. The one in greatest demand bore the heavier share of the total cost of the processing of a barrel of oil.

The hearings on petroleum prices carried on by the Senate Committee on Banking and Currency in June, 1949, illustrate the diverse ideas about pricing that underlay the position taken by the different interest groups.[73] Jersey did not testify, but Socony was called because it had initiated the increase in gasoline prices. In these hearings were presented arguments as old in this country as the conflict in Boston of the 1630's between the supporters of Reverend John Cotton's concept of a just price and a shopkeeper, Robert Keayne, who argued for a market price—or, for that matter, as old as the controversy over just price in medieval times. Socony based its position on market conditions and on the need for profits to finance high-cost expansion to supply an expected long-term rise in demand. Representatives of a consumer organization and of independent distributors took the position that the new prices were unjust and that those who charged them were profiteering at the expense of others. The findings of the Senate committee did not sustain the April attacks in Congress. Early in the autumn, as usual at that time of the year, the increased demand brought a rise in the prices of kerosene and heavier fuels, and the normal seasonal decrease in gasoline consumption brought a reduction in the price of that product.[74]

The other controversy in which the company was involved in 1949 had to do with imports. The independent producers, especially in Texas, charged that importing oil from foreign sources caused a decline in the demand for domestic crude. They alleged that imports by the large integrated companies were weakening the independents and injuring the domestic oil industry and hence were detrimental to an essential factor in national defense. The independents urged government curbs on the bringing in of oil from abroad.

There was actually a decline in domestic production averaging nearly 500,000 barrels a day. This struck Texas oil producers especially hard: the state's production was reduced 17.3 per cent below that of 1948, while the total production of the other states fell only 1 per cent. Because the Texas proration system provided that certain marginal wells could not be restricted in their production, the prorated wells suffered an even greater reduction. Humble was especially affected because it obtained most of its crude from prorated wells and relatively little from marginal wells. The company's production in 1949 fell 25 per cent below that of 1948; its purchases from others than its royalty owners declined 35 per cent. Statistics show that compared with 1948 the production of the major oil companies was reduced proportionately more than that of the rest of the industry. Jersey's domestic producers—principally in Texas, because of Humble's large production there—had the largest reduction among the majors.[75]

The company's position on imports was presented by Eugene Holman on June 9, 1949, in hearings conducted in Washington by the Select Committee on Small Business of the House of Representatives.[76] Jersey's president maintained that his company's actions had been in full accord with the oil policy of the National Petroleum Council, which had endorsed an import policy that would both encourage exploration and development in the domestic industry and supplement the country's oil supplies on a basis that would be sound in terms of the national economy. He held that the development of oil production in this country had been beyond previous records until lately and that only in recent weeks had the number of drilling rigs at work dropped. He stated that in 1948 the United States had been a net exporter. The importing of crude and products had reached a peak late in that year, from which it had receded to the point where total imports were no higher than exports.

President Holman said that Jersey affiliates in 1948 had imported a daily average of 105,000 barrels of crude and 94,000 barrels of products—mostly residual fuel oils—but that they had exported a daily average of 225,000 barrels. In the early part of 1949, however, crude imports had not fallen equally with the decline in demand. Holman explained: "These imports were planned, and commitments made for their purchase and transportation, before mid-year 1948 when we were making every effort to assure our customers adequate heating oil. . . . If we could have known in advance that the winter would be about the warmest on record, we would not have pressed so hard to increase our supplies—it cost us plenty." The affiliates had started to cut back on imports as soon as it had become apparent that the requirements had fallen. However, because of contract commitments and the great distances from oil in the earth to the consumer, there was "a time lag between a decision to cut imports and the effect of such decision." Not until late February and early March did cutbacks become apparent in terms of receipts. But, added Holman, his company believed that "imports of special crudes and products to supplement limited domestic availability of certain grades are in the interest of our national economy."

Not imports but record stocks at the end of 1948, said the Jersey president, were primarily responsible for a reduced demand for domestic crude oil in 1949. In the previous year, production within the country had exceeded domestic consumption by 7 per cent, and 4.9 per cent of the volume produced had gone into storage.

Holman stressed the need for reserve capacity. "The idea of always selling maximum production, regardless of consumer demand," he said, "is intriguing but unworkable in any industry." He called attention to the fact that the Supply and Demand Committee of the association of the independent oil companies had estimated an average daily demand for the second half of 1949 that was 600,000 barrels above the current supply level. He referred to a report of a study made by a committee of the American Petroleum Institute which concluded that a margin of supply capacity over demand of at least 4 or 5 per cent was essential to avoid shortages. Recent shortages in fact had shown that the industry must normally have a cushion of surplus productive capacity. Also, Holman stated, figures showed that the ratio of crude oil production to reserves was far higher in the United States than in the rest of the world.

The position taken by President Holman before the congressional committee was in effect supported later by statements presented to congressional committees by various government experts in Washington. Among these experts were the State Department's Assistant Secretary for Economic Affairs, the Assistant Secretary of Commerce, the Executive Secretary of the Petroleum Committee of the Munitions Board of the Department of Defense, and a member of the Oil and Gas Division of the Department of the Interior. These men placed the issue in its larger domestic and world context. In their statements, they in substance took the position that national oil policy, especially on imports, could not safely be based on local interests alone but had to be shaped with recognition of the complexities of the world economic situation and considerations of national security.[77]

Of immediate concern to the parent company and affiliates was the need to adjust output to changes in the market. Operations had to be reduced with the decline in demand, and the Jersey Company was as hard pressed to cut down surplus operations in 1949 as it had been to remedy shortages or meet threats of shortages in 1947 and 1948.

In Venezuela, Creole's production had to be cut 7 per cent below that of 1948. This necessity came in part from the abnormal stocks on hand at the end of the year, but it was also a result of some loss of markets. The company lost most of its large outlet for both crude oil and products in Argentina because of that country's trade agreement with Britain, which virtually stopped the importing of dollar oil into that large South American market. The rapid increase in Middle East production together with British foreign-exchange restrictions also affected Creole's sales. (See Chapter 26.) To some extent the company's oil found increased outlets elsewhere, particularly because of the expansion of sales by affiliates in

Brazil, Central America, and Venezuela itself. Affiliates in the United States, principally Esso Standard, also increased their imports of heavy crude and products from Venezuela and Aruba.

Venezuela and the Caribbean refineries were in the fortunate position of providing the heavy oils that it was not economically desirable for the American refining industry, with its lighter domestic crudes, to produce in sufficient volume to supply the domestic market. This situation was especially true in Esso Standard's markets in the northeastern states, where heavy fuel oils were being used increasingly by industrial and railroad companies. Actually, however, the increase in these imports by the affiliates was proportionately less than the increase in the total United States imports from the Caribbean area.[78]

The heavy fuel had to take a severe drop in price as compared to prices for gasolines and some other light products. The Gulf Coast postings for such oil dropped from a high of $2.46 per barrel in 1948 to a low of $1.15 in May, 1949; they rose again to $1.65 in the autumn of that year, which was still far below the 1948 high. These shifts, together with the reduction in the volume of production, brought a considerable decline in Creole's earnings. The company's total income from the sale of crude fell from $491,000,000 in 1948 to $376,000,000 in 1949. Its net profit declined from $199,000,000 in the former to $116,000,000 in the latter year.[79]

This reduction in operations and income did not bring the serious reactions in Venezuela that might have developed. No doubt this came partly from the fact that the low point in the volume of production and prices came early in the year and that recovery was under way soon after midyear. But it may also have been a result of recognition by Venezuelan leaders of the importance of oil operations to their country and of the understanding that members of the government's Petroleum Bureau had of conditions affecting the prices of oil.

In the Eastern Hemisphere, the affiliates shared to some extent in the rising demand for oil products. But they experienced a relative loss compared to their European competitors because of the difficulty of obtaining payment for oil in dollars from dollar-poor countries and because of increasingly severe British trade and exchange regulations. These restrictions reduced foreign sales of crude and products about 6 per cent in 1949—mainly in the Eastern Hemisphere.[80] They also required the affiliates to purchase oil from sterling companies to supply some of the affiliates' own markets. (See Chapter 26.)

By 1950 the rate of increase in demand was again accelerating both at home and abroad. The product sales of the affiliates in that year increased 14.6 per cent above 1949 sales at home and 10.5 per cent above those abroad.[81] One reason for this upturn, especially in the United States, was the recovery from the brief recession of 1949. Another was the outbreak of war in Korea in 1950 and the consequent rise in military consumption of oil products and in military and civilian stockpiling. Still another factor was some relaxation in 1950 of restrictions on the importing of oil by American companies into Argentina and also into some countries in the Eastern Hemisphere. Moreover Jersey's affiliates made many adjustments in their operations, which gave them a better position in sterling and soft-currency markets. In 1950 the Jersey Company began to benefit from the basic changes in strategy which it had initiated soon after the war and was still in the process of carrying out.

It was in these successive periods of undersupply and oversupply in the world oil industry that Jersey put into effect its plans for expansion to prepare for an expected long-term rise in the demand for petroleum products. Before dealing with what it actually accomplished in the various branches of operations, one serious obstacle to the carrying out of the plans will be considered: the virtual postwar breakdown of the system of international finance under which commercial and capital funds moved from country to country.

Chapter 26

Postwar Problems in International Finance, 1945–1951

THE WAR LEFT the foreign trade and exchange of the non-Communist world in a chaotic condition. The old system of international trade, multilateral exchange, and free convertibility of currencies was largely gone. Between a number of countries, trade and the movement of funds became virtually normal once conversion to peacetime operations had been completed. But in a part of the Western and most of the Eastern Hemisphere foreign exchange was in serious disarray, and dollar resources were in short supply.

Jersey's administrators expected that after the war their company, with nearly all its assets representing dollar investments, would meet serious problems in countries that were short of dollar exchange. It would have difficulty in obtaining payment in dollars for crude and products and in converting interest on loans to affiliates as well as dividends into the American monetary medium. In many countries, especially in the Eastern Hemisphere, this would make risky the investment of dollars in carrying out Jersey's plans for improving its competitive stance.

What should be the company's policy in this difficult situation? Should it follow the conservative course of committing a minimum of dollars to its current operations and to the rehabilitation and expansion of its physical assets in such countries? Or should it import as much oil as it could sell and invest dollar capital in expansion even though returns in hard currency would be uncertain? The company's administrators chose what was essentially the latter course.

However, they recognized from the first that such a policy would have to be implemented with full cognizance of existing conditions and of the risks involved in any given time and place. To make wise decisions regarding current operations and investments for the future would require

694

an understanding of political and economic conditions and trends in Europe. It would also require a judicious weighing of the relations of the United States with the countries concerned. Basic, of course, would be negotiations with governments to establish the conditions under which dollar funds could be utilized and balances in foreign currencies converted into dollars.

This chapter is concerned with the process by which the company met the problems involved in operating within countries that were economically depressed and short of dollars in the early postwar years. Its focus is particularly on current operations. But the arrangements made with the various governments were similarly of importance to Jersey's capital expenditures for maintaining and improving its position in Eastern Hemisphere markets.

ECONOMIC AND INSTITUTIONAL BACKGROUND

After the war, the Jersey Company operated in what became virtually two separate worlds of international finance. Each of these had vastly different conditions affecting the company's operations and investments.[1]

One world consisted of the United States and other countries whose currency was freely convertible into dollars. Known as dollar, or hard-currency, countries, they included Central America, certain islands in the Caribbean, Venezuela, Colombia, Switzerland, Liberia, and the Philippines. Their hard-money resources came mostly from a favorable balance of trade with the United States or from the investment of this country's capital within them—or from both trade and investments. Canada was a special case inasmuch as it had considerable dollar resources although it was closely tied to British finance. Among all these countries, there was free convertibility of currencies and movement of funds.

The other world was made up of national economies short of dollar exchange and known as soft-currency countries. It included most of South America, scattered British island possessions in the Western Hemisphere, and nearly all the non-Communist part of the Eastern Hemisphere. This world consisted of two distinct groups. One, known as the sterling area, was composed of the United Kingdom and a number of other countries that, because of London's financial leadership, agreed with the British government on certain arrangements with regard to their foreign payments. The exact composition of this group varied from time to time. The members were listed on a schedule published by the British government, which indicated what was loosely called the sterling area. Besides the United Kingdom, this varying group included Eire, Australia, New Zealand, a large number of countries in southern Asia and Africa— these countries having connections with Great Britain as colonies, pro- tectorates, or members of the British Commonwealth—and others having a special treaty relationship with Britain. The remaining soft-currency countries, primarily in Western Europe and South America, were gen- erally short of dollars or balances convertible into hard currency. Al- though some of them had a comfortable position and a long tradition of trade in sterling, difficulties at the time precluded the free convertibility of their sterling into dollars.

The British government, because of London's financial position among soft-currency countries, after the war came to occupy a dominant position in most of that world. Through its agencies, notably the Exchange Con- trol Board and the Bank of England, it administered what came to be known as the sterling-area system. Under this system, trade among participating members could be financed and paid for in sterling without prior individual approval for each transaction. In practice, London banks handled most of these transactions within the framework of rules laid down by the Exchange Control Board. Each United Kingdom bank was, in fact, an agent of the board and was required to operate within its rules and regulations. If a company resident in a country that was a member of the sterling area wished to raise capital funds, it had a reasonable chance of doing so through the London market, subject to the assent of its local government, the availability of funds, and a set of priorities governing access to that market. These priorities were established by the Capital Issues Committee of the British Treasury.

The Bank of England acted as a central repository of the gold and the reserve currencies of the sterling-area countries and as a clearinghouse for their transactions. With respect to their trade with countries outside the system, each one agreed to deposit all receipts—whether from current transactions or capital movements—with the Bank of England and to receive the equivalent sterling in exchange for deposit to its account. Similarly, the needs of members for currencies of other countries to pay for imports or investments outside the sterling area were met by exchang- ing sterling deposits with the Bank of England. Of particular importance, of course, was the pool of hard currencies—notably United States dollars—thus administered by the Bank of England. The exact arrange- ments governing the amounts of hard currencies that would be made available to individual sterling-area countries were worked out between the British government and the member countries as part of their original agreements. In similar fashion, arrangements were made as to priorities for the use of these currencies and for the gradual funding over a period of years of large sterling balances that had been accumulated during the war by such countries as India and Egypt.

The commercial banks of the sterling-area countries as well as their customers found it very convenient to be able to conduct their international transactions within such a general system requiring only a limited amount of individual advance approval. This was important because, despite the lack of convertibility to hard currency, the amount of world trade carried on in sterling and centered principally in London was large and growing rapidly in the postwar period.

These financial conveniences were not made available to residents of countries outside the sterling area, on the ground that such extensions would put unacceptable pressure on hard-currency reserves. Thus, unless the prior approval of the British Exchange Control Board had been obtained, an American company could not sell goods to France and receive payment in sterling, even though the French authorities were willing to pay in that medium. To allow a British bank to transfer funds from a French-owned to an American-owned account was considered tantamount to converting French-owned sterling into United States dollars. It was held that an American resident possessing a sterling balance would seek to convert it directly into dollars or would use it for purposes in the sterling area for which he would otherwise have had to provide dollars.

Membership in the sterling-area system thus conveyed considerable advantage at a time when many countries found it easier to pay for imports in sterling than in dollars. A number of oil companies resident in the sterling area thus potentially had a commercial advantage over others—including the Jersey Company—which were not considered residents of that area.

At the same time that the international economy was being divided into two separate worlds of trade and finance, international governmental action was being mobilized in the interest of economic recovery and the restoration of world trade. The principal objectives of monetary authorities and governments were to restore full convertibility of currencies and to end the division of the economy of the non-Communist world into two separate blocs.

The United States government had decided that this country should not lapse into isolation, as it had done after World War I, but that instead it should use its influence to help bring about a peaceable and prosperous world. Viewing the restoration of international trade as an essential basis for restoring the necessities of life and a measure of order in Europe, it took the initiative in working with European countries to strengthen international trade and exchange.

First came the long and complex negotiations, beginning at Bretton Woods, New Hampshire, that led to the establishment of two major institutions: the International Monetary Fund and the International Bank for Reconstruction and Development. These institutions were designed to cope with the many problems of international trade and payments that barred the restoration of trade and the improvement of national economies, especially in Western Europe. A further development of major importance in the struggle of nations to restore economic life during the early postwar period was the General Agreement on Tariffs and Trade (GATT), which may be said to have laid improved ground rules for international trade.

Early attempts to remedy Britain's acute shortage of dollars and to alleviate the difficult exchange situation were the Anglo-American Financial Agreement of 1945, which was ratified in 1946, and a similar agreement between Canada and Britain. Under the former, the United States extended to the United Kingdom a line of credit of $3.75 billion to be repaid over a period of fifty years beginning in 1951. The British were to utilize this credit to give sterling countries freedom to use current earnings of sterling for current transactions in any currency area without discrimination and to make currently earned sterling convertible into dollars for current purposes. They were not to impose discriminating controls against imports from the United States. The credit extended under this agreement was quickly exhausted, and the experiment in limited convertibility was terminated in August, 1947.[2]

When these early institutions and arrangements were found not to have spurred recovery as much as had been hoped, the United States adopted the Marshall Plan to aid European recovery. General George C. Marshall, Secretary of State, proposed this plan in his historic commencement address at Harvard University in June, 1947. The United States established its Economic Cooperation Administration in 1948 to enlist the cooperation of countries needing help. The Organization for European Economic Cooperation, supported by billions of United States dollars, gave assurance that the countries entering it would obtain essential food and fuel as well as help in rebuilding their economies.

It was an intrinsic part of this approach to the problems of European recovery that the countries themselves should agree on other measures governing international trade and finance aimed at the earliest possible economic recovery consistent with stability. To this end, they recognized the desirability of dismantling, as soon as feasible, the restrictions and controls instituted during the war.

The development and implementation of these plans—under the Organization for European Economic Cooperation and along lines consistent with the Articles of Agreement of the International Monetary Fund and the General Agreement on Tariffs and Trade—were most encouraging to a company like Jersey that was dependent upon world trade. The company visualized its long-run interest as being essentially the same as that provided for by these and other measures for encouraging postwar recovery and stability.

NEW RESPONSIBILITIES FOR THE TREASURER'S DEPARTMENT

Long before the war was over, Jersey's administrators recognized that international finance would become a strategic factor in the process of restoring the business of affiliates in much of the Eastern Hemisphere and in carrying out plans for the expansion of operations, particularly in Europe. Since this was a relatively new situation for the parent company, it lacked personnel qualified to deal with it.*

The company had drawn its executives in finance largely from operations, and it had few men professionally trained in economics, international finance, and monetary systems—especially in the last two. One exception was Jay E. Crane, who was in charge of the foreign department of the Federal Reserve Bank of New York before joining Jersey in the 1930's. As assistant treasurer and treasurer before being elected to the Board of Directors in 1944, he had been in a position to follow closely the company's foreign financial relations and the conditions abroad affecting them.

As World War II had progressed, Crane had realized that the company must prepare for meeting postwar problems in international finance and for gauging accurately and realistically the prospects for foreign business

---

* The company, to be sure, had in the 1920's and 1930's met difficulties in foreign exchange, but these were not of a scale comparable to those of this later time.

that could be expected to develop. The Treasurer's Department needed a new type of man; the department's responsibilities were destined to involve more in the future than the long-standing professions of accounting and tax work.

Under Crane's leadership, the Board of Directors initiated preparatory moves before the war was over.[3] It decided to lodge in the Treasurer's Department the principal responsibility for advising the Jersey administrators in this complex area. It invited Leo D. Welch to join the company as treasurer on Crane's election to the board in 1944. Welch left his position as vice-president of a major New York bank, which he had served for nearly twenty years in various international assignments, principally in Latin America. As Jersey treasurer, he was in a position to observe on behalf of the company various aspects of the several measures for international recovery that were being developed late in the war.

Another major move in preparing the Treasurer's Department for its new leadership role was the appointment in 1947 of Emilio G. Collado as foreign-exchange manager. Since earning a doctorate in economics at Harvard University in 1936, Collado had been concerned with international economic matters, principally in the Department of State but also in the Federal Reserve System and the United States Treasury. He had been a participant in the negotiations leading to the establishment of the International Monetary Fund and the International Bank for Reconstruction and Development. He had also participated in the talks which resulted in the Anglo-American Financial Agreement of 1945. Immediately prior to joining Jersey, he was the United States Executive Director of the International Bank for Reconstruction and Development. His familiarity with the negotiations that had led to establishing these institutions and his personal acquaintance with many of their key people were to be of great help in his work during the ensuing years.

Director Crane had also recognized that the Treasurer's Department needed a professional analytical group to give the necessary staff support to Welch and Collado. Such a group was established. At first it was made up of a few employees who had had some experience with financial problems in international trade during the 1930's. It was rapidly augmented by young men, largely recruited from universities, most of whom had then recently been discharged from the armed services.

This new group in the Treasurer's Department had to make a prompt start as financial problems flooded in on Jersey after the war. Fortunately for Jersey, however, the resulting difficulties did not reach critical proportions until Collado and the new staff were well established.

THE DOLLAR EXCHANGE PROBLEM, AUGUST, 1945, TO MARCH, 1949

The first indication of financial trouble for Jersey in Europe appeared shortly after the war ended. Affiliates in several countries informed the company that dollar exchange was not available to pay for imported oil. (See Chapter 21.) France was in a difficult situation from the very first. The program of the British government to reduce imports, including oil, instituted in August, 1945, was an ominous development.[4] Although this measure meant interference with international trade, it was a harsh necessity caused by a shortage of dollars and it was applied to all imports regardless of source. Australia, immediately after the ending of Lend-Lease, notified Standard-Vacuum that petroleum imports would be allowed only from sterling sources.[5]

Nevertheless, Jersey began to work on restoring operations and to make tentative plans for acquiring new plants and equipment for operations in Europe and North Africa and also new sources of oil in the Middle East. In 1946 it agreed in principle to purchase vast amounts of crude oil from Anglo-Iranian Oil Company and to participate in building a pipeline from oil fields near the Persian Gulf to the Mediterranean. It also opened negotiations for affiliation with Arabian American Oil Company and the projected Trans-Arabian Pipe Line Company.

In the first three years after the war, Jersey did not encounter insurmountable difficulties in supplying its European affiliates or in carrying out its plans for their rehabilitation. Petroleum products were essential to restoring national economies and to supplying the military occupation forces on the Continent, and the worldwide shortage of oil necessitated drawing on Western Hemisphere supplies. This situation enabled oil from dollar countries to command high priority for the limited amount of dollars available in Europe. Within the sterling-area countries, government agencies set import totals for crude oil and products. Importing companies were at first granted permission to import, from whatever source they chose, a volume proportionate to their share of the market under normal competitive conditions. Since the license to import carried with it the right to dollar payment, these arrangements were satisfactory to Jersey. In fact, they conformed to traditional standards reaffirmed in the Articles of Agreement of the International Monetary Fund and the Anglo-American Financial Agreement.[6]

Somehow or other, ways of paying for dollar oil had to be found as long as European countries were largely dependent on the Western

Hemisphere for this commodity. The United States occupation forces on the Continent supplied some income in hard money in the areas where they were stationed. Such institutions as the International Monetary Fund and the International Bank for Reconstruction and Development, designed to perform specific functions, each contributed to stimulating recovery and aiding countries with foreign-exchange difficulties. So also did the Anglo-American Financial Agreement of 1945 until the funds were exhausted in the summer of 1947.

Although the Anglo-American and other agreements made soon after the war did not spur recovery as much as had been hoped, Jersey continued to plan for the restoration and even expansion of its business in the Eastern Hemisphere. Every move to restore operations was preceded by investigation and consideration from various angles. Where feasible, the affiliates, with Jersey support, resorted to local borrowing. Such recourse to local funds was possible in some countries, especially for the relatively small amounts required for restoring marketing facilities. Even in the economically more advanced countries, however, borrowing was then usually limited to the short term and was under close government regulation.[7]

Whatever hopes Jersey's administrators may have had of an early economic recovery in Europe and in other parts of the Eastern Hemisphere were fading in 1947. It was then becoming clear that monetary authorities had not realized how difficult the postwar situation would become. They had not foreseen the severe inflation that came. With much of Europe on the brink of economic, social, and political chaos, it became a serious question how far the company's leaders should go in making commitments for expenditures in that part of the world. However, they did assume risks. As a Jersey executive in Europe said in 1947, this was a time "to leaven the caution of the banker with the courage of the trader."[8]

The company was encouraged by the 1947 address of Secretary George C. Marshall and by the Marshall Plan subsequently provided for by Congress. That assistance program, made available widely in Europe, gave Jersey assurance that it could more safely commit its own funds to the rehabilitation and even expansion of its operations in Great Britain and on the Continent. Within certain limits, the aid provided dollars with which to pay for oil supplied to countries participating in the plan. The company worked out with the Economic Cooperation Administration a system for handling such shipments as were financed by that agency. The resulting payment in dollars for crude and products sold by Jersey affiliates in dollar-poor countries proved a great boon to the operations of the various companies.

Despite ECA aid to European recovery, late in 1948 two developments became of special concern to Jersey's operations in the Eastern Hemisphere and even in parts of South America: (1) the situation as to international payments became worse; and (2) the oil production of British and British-Dutch companies increased at the very time when the world shortage of oil was changing to a surplus. One of the heaviest drains on the foreign balances of the United Kingdom and of many countries on the Continent was caused by oil imports. Hence it was to be expected that those countries would purchase sterling oil as it became available in place of the dollar oil they had been buying.

Various reports in the Jersey files—of comprehensive studies and close observation of the deteriorating situation in Europe—give insight into the trend of the company's thinking about the problems of international trade and payments late in 1948 and early in 1949. The conclusion in November, 1948, from a committee's investigation was that Jersey would be able to operate as a dollar company in Europe for only a few years, and that the more important European countries could not possibly work out of their dollar deficits within that time.[9] In January, 1949, an executive of a European affiliate urged that the company establish a sterling oil circuit within the Jersey family of affiliates. This meant that the affiliates should obtain crude within the sterling area, transport it in facilities owned by affiliates in that area, and refine it in the United Kingdom and other sterling countries. The object would be to reduce dollar costs to as low a figure as that of any British company.[10]

A further report of February, 1949, by the same study committee predicted that within only a few years European refineries built with ECA funds would be in operation, and that dollar products, except some specialties, would be crowded out of European markets. The committee recommended (1) making careful studies in every country, (2) acquiring or building refining capacity in Europe to meet the requirements of markets Jersey desired to hold, and (3) making the best possible trading arrangements with individual governments. It also recommended that Jersey seek the aid of the United States government in making sterling arrangements in London. However, the company should "avoid making inappropriate demands for dollar subsidies on American petroleum industry sales in Europe." In addition, the committee suggested that the company explore other trading and exchange arrangements, including the barter business, and also the possibility of the purchase abroad of tankers, equipment, and materials of various kinds.[11]

Because more crude oil and also materials for construction and equipment were becoming available, Jersey had begun to implement its earlier plans to expand the refining facilities of its affiliates in Europe and also its European tanker fleets. However, the carrying out of its program to establish a Middle East–Europe oil circuit had to be changed somewhat in order to meet new conditions. For example, because of continued dollar shortages in sterling areas and other soft-currency countries and the building of refineries with ECA funds,[12] the company had to alter its plans so as to enlarge refineries in some countries and build new plants in a few others on the Continent.

Jersey entered negotiations with European governments concerning the financing of its projects. The company's policy continued to be to borrow locally as much as possible. For large undertakings, however, considerable dollar funds would have to be made available. The problem was to obtain some assurance from governments that the dollar capital funds advanced by Jersey would eventually be recovered and that interest and dividends would be paid in dollars.

Jersey's general policy and the implementation of its policy in building up sterling operations are summarized in a memorandum of March 19, 1949, sent to Paul G. Hoffman of the ECA. According to that statement, Jersey affiliates since 1945 had carried out, or had planned and were in the process of carrying out, "capital budgetary expenditures in more than 25 countries of Europe, North Africa, and the Middle East amounting to the equivalent of $580 million, of which $387 million represented new capital provided or to be provided by Jersey in U.S. dollars." It was Jersey policy to form "a sterling oil cycle consisting of acquiring crude oil from Anglo-Iranian and Iraq Petroleum Company, Ltd., for sterling—bringing it through Middle East Pipeline and thence to Fawley refinery [in England] to supply British requirements for sterling payment." This cycle would supply an estimated 40 per cent of the markets of Jersey affiliates in the areas involved.

This program, the memorandum stated, would be somewhat disadvantageous to Arabian American Oil Company—in which Jersey had by that time acquired an ownership interest—because the purchase of Anglo-Iranian crude would adversely affect takings from Saudi Arabia. The Aramco crude development program had already been greatly reduced. A further cutback could not "be made without incurring serious concession difficulties"—that is, difficulties with the government of Saudi Arabia, which was dependent on oil production for much of its income. Study was to be made to see what could be done to convert Aramco oil as far as possible to nondollar costs.

Jersey's objective, according to the memorandum, was to make such arrangements as would enable it to "participate in a reasonable development of production and refining in the Eastern Hemisphere generally." It was seeking a "reasonable opportunity to operate in sterling and other currencies, transferring to dollars only reasonable earnings." But, in order to do so, it "must have assurance that its unavoidable dollar costs will be met and its reasonable earnings in fact transferred to dollars." The memorandum pointed out that, regardless of the nationality of a company operating in the Middle East, there would be a certain proportion of initial dollar capital expenditures and a continuous net operating drain in the same currency. As an example, it noted the fact that the British Exchequer had to convert at least a portion of Anglo-Iranian's sterling royalty payments to dollars for the use of the government of Iran.[13]

CRISIS AND ADJUSTMENT, 1949–1951

As the early months of 1949 passed, economic conditions in Great Britain and on the Continent grew worse. The situation in Britain deteriorated to such a critical state that the government had to take strong measures to bolster the economy and to reduce its sterling exchange obligations. It took the radical method of devaluing the currency, as did most other European countries—the British pound sterling fell to nearly half its former value. Britain also attempted to reduce its sterling balances by means of trade regulations and bilateral agreements with other countries.

In April, 1949, the United Kingdom initiated a series of measures that threatened to replace American-owned oil with that of British and British-Dutch companies in markets in the Eastern Hemisphere and even in some countries in Latin America. Britain's need to narrow the gap between its dollar receipts and expenditures was critically urgent; it was, in fact, fighting to survive and to maintain its position in the economic world. But the means it used created serious problems for Jersey and other American oil companies operating abroad. Most of the oil the affiliates were selling in the sterling area came from hard-currency sources in the Western Hemisphere.

One type of measure utilized by Britain was a barter arrangement whereby the government in London undertook to supply to the other party petroleum products from British-owned sources in exchange for imports into the United Kingdom. It made such a bilateral agreement with Egypt in April, 1949. Actually, this agreement did not drive all American-owned oil out of Egypt because the British companies had insufficient supplies to meet that country's requirements. However, an agreement of Britain with Argentina—to supply oil in exchange for meat and other products—seriously affected Jersey's importing of oil to sell in that country, one of its larger South American outlets. Royal Dutch–Shell, which was granted the status of a sterling company by His Majesty's government, had plenty of Venezuelan oil for supplying Argentina; but Jersey's oil from Venezuela was shut out of that market. The effect was the reduction of the American company's sales to Argentina in 1949 by a total of nearly 12,000,000 barrels and $24,500,000.[14]

Only a little later the British Exchange Control Board established greater control over trade with soft-currency countries. It ordered British bankers to refuse to transfer funds in payment for American-supplied oil from sterling balances in London of countries outside the sterling area. Consequently, such countries as Finland, Sweden, Norway, and Denmark, which were so short of dollars as to require that all or part of their oil needs be purchased with sterling, were unable to draw on their sterling balances in the United Kingdom to pay for imports supplied by American companies. Consequently, they had to buy sterling oil. Jersey lost sales to the markets of the four Scandinavian countries totaling approximately 54,000 barrels per day.[15]

In December, 1949, Britain announced its "substitution policy." This new restriction required sterling-area affiliates of American companies to take surplus oil of companies with British ownership in lieu of supplies normally obtained from American-owned sources. The effective date of this policy was to be January 1, 1950, but because of protests from American companies and the Department of State in Washington it was postponed to February 15, 1950. When the new regulation became effective, it required the affiliates of American companies to purchase oil for import into the sterling area from British and British-Dutch companies to the extent that they had surplus oil. An American-owned affiliate thereafter could import oil from sources owned by American companies only insofar as the volume of oil required to meet its needs was beyond what the companies having sterling status could supply. Jersey oil thus became marginal in its most important Eastern Hemisphere markets. The effect of this new regulation was estimated to reduce the Jersey Company's business by nearly $85,000,000 in 1950.[16]

This latest regulation of the British government, together with the other measures of 1949, meant the probable substitution of British and British-Dutch oil for a large part of the supply that had been going into the sterling area and other soft-currency countries from American-owned companies in both hemispheres. British policy meant more than a loss of markets, which loss might well become permanent. It also meant the probable loss of important outlets for Creole's oil from Venezuela and Aramco's from Saudi Arabia. It seemed likely that, if this British restriction necessitated cutbacks in production or in programs for increasing production, it might bring complications in concession relations with those countries.[17]

Jersey's leaders had cooperated in meeting Britain's foreign-exchange problems over the years, and, although they knew that the United Kingdom was in a desperate condition, they felt that the latest restrictions represented unwarranted discrimination. These regulations, which came only after the tight supply situation had ended, could have the effect of driving American oil companies out of sterling and other markets to the advantage of British interests. In Jersey's view, such measures, insofar as they were not justified on the basis of high dollar costs, were not consistent with the principles affirmed by the Articles of Agreement of the International Monetary Fund, the General Agreement on Tariffs and Trade, and the Anglo-American Financial Agreement.

From the time of the initiation of the British regulations of 1949, the company carried on extensive discussions and negotiations with officials of His Majesty's Treasury and of the Ministry of Fuel and Power in London. Jersey kept the State Department fully informed and sought the advice of that department and of the United States Treasury. From 1949 on, Howard W. Page served as Jersey's representative in London. Trained as a chemical engineer at Stanford University and the Massachusetts Institute of Technology, since 1929 Page had served as chemical engineer with Humble, as technical adviser to Jersey interests in London and Paris, as economic analyst with its Coordination and Economics Department, and later as that department's manager. During the war, he had been successively an analyst in the Transportation Division of the Petroleum Administration for War and deputy and manager of that agency's Program Division. Page brought to negotiations with the British a rare knowledge of the world oil industry, an indefatigable search for facts, a capacity to see both sides of an issue, and an imaginative approach to solutions.[18]

In Jersey's view, the first move in these negotiations was to persuade the British authorities to change the basis of their distinction between sterling and dollar oil from the arbitrary classification according to the nationality of a company to one dependent on the actual sterling-dollar cost of the oil. Under British regulations, any oil belonging to Anglo-Iranian or Royal Dutch–Shell was considered sterling, and any owned by Jersey affiliates was classified as dollar oil. As a matter of fact, of the petroleum produced by Mene Grande Oil Company in Venezuela—of which Jersey and Royal Dutch–Shell each owned 25 per cent and Gulf Oil the remainder—only that one-fourth representing the British-Dutch company's share was classed as sterling. Similarly, Jersey's and Socony's shares of the crude oil produced by the Iraq Petroleum Company were classified by the British as dollar oil, while the shares of Anglo-Iranian and Royal Dutch–Shell were treated as sterling.[19]

Jersey based its stand on the fact that the British-owned as well as the American-owned oil produced abroad had a substantial dollar content. "Fundamentally," noted a memorandum submitted to His Majesty's Treasury on August 12, 1949, "over periods of time, the dollar and non-dollar costs of petroleum operations of British and American companies are, area by area, very similar." These costs included royalties, taxes, and other local payments in dollars and also expenditures for certain materials, supplies, equipment, and services obtainable only in the United States. An unavoidable difference in costs lay in dollar expenditures for American supervisory and technical personnel of American companies as against sterling expenditures for such personnel in British companies. A Jersey estimate of February, 1950, held that on the average sterling oil contained approximately a 50 per cent dollar content but that the dollar component of marginal sterling oil was more than 60 per cent. It was this marginal supply that would make possible the substitution of British-owned for American-owned oil. An ECA report at approximately the same time gave the estimate of the British government of the dollar cost of British oil as being 20 per cent of the total value f.o.b. in the Middle East and 60 per cent in Venezuela.[20]

One unquestionable difference between British and American companies involved the net dollar profits that might be remitted to the United States. However, Jersey urged that against such remittances should be set its own large dollar expenditures for the expansion of its affiliates. It informed the British Treasury that since the war it had carried out, or was in the process of carrying out, planned capital expenditures in Europe, North Africa, and the Middle East of which a total of more than $350,000,000 represented dollar funds.[21]

At the same time, the company maintained that dollar funds were being used by British interests to develop facilities to displace the oil in soft-currency markets of American-owned companies. Royal Dutch–Shell in 1948 borrowed $250,000,000 in the United States for use abroad. Jersey especially objected to the employment of American aid funds to help British or other foreign oil interests develop facilities for operations that would give them a competitive advantage in areas where American companies were unable to move to improve their position.[22] It held that, if the plans of the Organization for European Economic Cooperation were carried out under aid from the Economic Cooperation Administration (Marshall Plan), the resulting surplus crude and refining capacity would enable the British and other non-American companies "to supply the entire expansion in demand and have some capacity left over in duplication of existing American capacity."[23]

The company made several proposals in 1949 and 1950 to the government in London as a basis for the discussion of its problems resulting from British regulations. The Department of State also entered firmly into the controversy on behalf of the American oil companies affected by British regulations.[24]

In a formal document dated January 25, 1950, Jersey proposed (1) to make every possible effort to reduce the dollar content of oil imported into sterling or "affected" soft-currency markets, (2) to accept payment in sterling, and (3) to limit specifically its conversion to dollars. The company proposed that, in return, it be given access to the markets in normal commercial fashion and that it be permitted to use its sterling payments in sterling and other soft-currency areas for operating costs, capital investments, and the like. The latter proposal meant that the company could acquire goods or services with priorities and access to materials and equipment equal to those accorded to British and British-Dutch companies and also that it could export purchases. Jersey proposed that it set up a special method of handling such operations, believing that appropriate machinery would be a resident account in London under a so-called London entity. This entity would acquire Jersey crude and products from Creole, Lago, Aramco, Iraq Petroleum, and other companies and sell them on specified terms. The profits arising from such trade would be subject to British taxation, and the net profits, when declared as dividends, would be the property of Jersey and would be remittable in dollars.

The British in reply proposed an incentive plan to encourage American companies to reduce the dollar cost of their imports and to require them to make specified purchases within the sterling area, in return for which they would be allowed limited facilities for selling oil for convertible sterling. This plan, however, was acceptable to neither Jersey nor the United States government, a continuing point of disagreement being the dollar cost of the oil of British-owned companies.[25]

Because discussions during the winter and spring of 1950 failed to reach an over-all solution of the dollar-sterling problem, the company entered negotiations concerning certain specific matters. By following this procedure, it was able to work out with the British two agreements constituting important advances toward meeting its difficulties.[26]

One agreement was the result of a proposal, originating with Howard W. Page, for the sale of gasoline in England. Jersey proposed that, if the British would discontinue the rationing of gasoline in the United Kingdom, it would be prepared to supply all the additional gasoline requirements of its British affiliate for sterling to be utilized for purchasing goods and equipment manufactured in Britain. This offer was accepted with certain reservations, including Jersey's guarantee that the goods and services bought would be such as it would not otherwise buy and that Anglo-American would provide 25 per cent of the increased consumption until the completion of its new Fawley refinery in England. Gasoline rationing, accordingly, was discontinued in Britain on May 26, 1950. Jersey also succeeded in establishing its right to use the resulting sterling to pay Aramco for crude. This gasoline derationing arrangement was later extended to diesel-engine fuel, and the American company was allowed to use "gasoline sterling" for investment in tankers to be owned by its British affiliate.[27]

The second agreement, made in June, 1950, had to do with Jersey's share of the oil produced by Iraq Petroleum Company and the large volume to be purchased later under its contract with Anglo-Iranian. The arrangement with respect to its share of the Iraq company's production established without reservation the principle of full British-company treatment for Jersey's Iraqi oil in the sterling area. For that part of its share of the production of Iraq Petroleum sold in the sterling area, Jersey would pay that company's cost-price in sterling and sell the oil for sterling. After the payment of the British income tax, Jersey would receive the profits in dollars. The agreement also set up workable *ad hoc* arrangements with regard to sales outside the sterling area. For that part of its share sold outside the area, Jersey would pay the Iraq Petroleum Company the cost-price in the ratio of 75 per cent sterling and 25 per cent dollars. These arrangements were subject to review at the end of 1951 but without prejudice to the broad principle of British-company treatment.[28]

Agreements made at the same time with the British by companies in which Jersey's ownership interest was one-half or less further eased the situation. Arabian American Oil Company, which had been severely affected by British regulations, concluded an arrangement with respect to its own utilization of sterling. Standard-Vacuum obtained from the British government permission to convert to dollars a portion of the proceeds realized from sales in the sterling area in the Far East.[29]

In September, 1950, Jersey similarly arrived at an understanding with France covering payment for imports into that country, consisting mostly of crude, and into other areas to which France's control extended. Under this agreement, Jersey opened a special bank account in Paris, to which cargoes of oil were invoiced. The French agreed to the payment for 75 per cent of such imports in dollars; the remaining 25 per cent was to be paid for in francs to be used by Esso Export Corporation for purchases in France. The account was subject to supervision by the French Exchange Control.[30]

In the summer of 1950, the company also succeeded in improving its position with regard to the shipment of oil to Argentina. On the basis of a one-year dollar credit arrangement, that country agreed to allow the company to import enough crude to maintain its refinery operations in Argentina.[31]

The company was unable to arrive at any comprehensive agreement with the British in 1950, but it carried on discussions with them throughout the year. In the meantime, it continued to take action to place itself in a fully competitive position as to sterling and other soft-currency costs. It gradually worked out with European governments conditions for financing the building of new tankers and the construction of new and enlargement of old refineries. It succeeded in arranging considerable financing of such expenditures within the various countries, but for large projects, especially the new refinery in England, it had to provide substantial dollar capital. (See Chapters 28 and 29.)

To handle the expenditure of nondollar revenues from the sale of oil,

Jersey set up a special mechanism. It made Esso Export Corporation—which managed international cargo-lot sales of crude and products for affiliates as well as marine bunkering and aviation sales—the purchasing agent abroad for both domestic and foreign affiliates. Esso Export's functions came to be to promote and coordinate, so far as possible, the use of inconvertible currency balances in paying for services, materials, and equipment that could be used by affiliates.[32]

Esso Export, which was under the vigorous and imaginative management of President William J. Haley in New York, set up a purchasing organization in Europe. The group had its own procurement experts, who studied the special problems involved in purchasing abroad and looked for opportunities to utilize Jersey balances in inconvertible currency. These specialists familiarized themselves with actual possibilities in various fields. They traveled widely to get information concerning what could be obtained in Great Britain and on the Continent. They worked closely with the procurement personnel of the various European affiliates. They also helped manufacturers to make goods according to American specifications and standards.

Specific arrangements with individual governments determined what Esso Export could and could not buy. After the program got under way, the company purchased tubular goods, tankers, electric equipment, food products, and many other items. It encountered numerous problems, such as noncompetitive prices, uncertain delivery, the granting of priorities to nationals, the reluctance of Western Hemisphere affiliates to commit themselves to the necessity of continuing to buy spare parts abroad, and the preference of the various governments for the sale of manufactured goods with a high labor content. However, after Esso Export's purchasing personnel acquired more knowledge and skill in handling their assignments under the conditions prevailing in Europe, they established effective relations with the authorities in Britain, France, and other countries. They also learned how to arrange deals across national boundaries that were acceptable and even advantageous to the parties concerned.[33]

One series of transactions illustrates how such international operations were carried on. The Dutch affiliate needed oil products but lacked dollars, and the Aruba refinery had products to sell but required payment in hard currency. Esso Export learned that a Jersey affiliate in France wanted to have two tankers built, and that Aruba could use steel pipe. The Esso men shopped around and found that Holland was the lowest bidder for building the needed tankers. When all had been arranged, Esso Export bought oil products in Aruba for dollars and sold them to the affiliate in Holland for guilders. It used this Dutch currency to pay for the tankers, which it sold to the French affiliate for francs. It used the latter medium to pay for steel pipe purchased in France, which it exported to Aruba for dollars.[34]

In the autumn of 1950, an upturn in economic conditions began to relieve pressures in Europe. The balance-of-payments situation improved in the sterling area, and oil supplies in the hands of British companies that had been surplus to their normal requirements ceased to be burdensome. The derationing of gasoline in the United Kingdom contributed to the reduction of surplus oil, as also did a general world rise in demand and the outbreak of war in Korea.

Negotiations of Jersey and its London representative with His Majesty's Government finally brought a comprehensive settlement in February, 1951.[35] The British then agreed that thereafter Standard Oil Company (New Jersey) and its affiliates would be given equality of treatment, within certain limits, with British and British-Dutch companies. This meant, in effect, that the oil of the Jersey affiliates would be acceptable if it had as low a dollar content as competitive oils. Furthermore, the Jersey affiliates could sell for sterling in soft-currency countries and use that sterling for certain approved expenditures, including, without limitation, the purchase of goods and services within the sterling area.[36]

Jersey thus had been able to overcome many of the postwar handicaps it had met as a dollar concern in most of its old markets in Europe, North Africa, and other regions. It had done so largely by adjusting to the economic realities of the postwar world. Although there had been economic improvement in Europe, the problems in international payments were not all solved, nor could they be until a more nearly balanced trade had been restored between sterling and other soft-currency areas and hard-currency countries. But the company had substantially bridged the gulf that divided the non-Communist world into economic blocs. In so doing, it had been able to maintain itself in its Old World markets and to carry out its plans for expanding its refining in Europe as a part of its program for establishing a Middle East–Europe oil circuit.

Chapter 27

Postwar Expansion of Reserves and Production, 1946–1950

A^{T THE SAME TIME} that Standard Oil Company (New Jersey) was restoring affiliates lost during the war, strengthening its administrative organization, supplying products for the market, and overcoming its handicaps as a dollar concern in soft-currency countries, it was vigorously carrying out its plans for expansion in all branches of operations in both hemispheres. This growth was in keeping with policies adopted in the 1920's and pursued in the 1930's. It was spurred by the decision of the Board of Directors late in the war to prepare the company for holding a secure position in the growing postwar market for oil products.

In carrying out its policy of expansion, Jersey made capital investments in the five postwar years of a size far beyond its previous expenditures in any similar period of time. In the Americas in these years, it made additions to property, plant, and equipment that cost nearly $2 billion—at the end of 1945, its consolidated assets had totaled $2,531,800,000. Jersey also invested a substantial amount of new capital in the Eastern Hemisphere, where international finance was a strategic factor in the implementing of its plans for the enlargement of operations.

The Jersey Company made large additions to its petroleum reserves and production in both hemispheres. In the Americas, it invested nearly $1 billion in this branch of the business. It spent approximately half a billion on refining and the same total on transportation and marketing. In the Eastern Hemisphere, its expenditures were not as large as in the Americas, but it invested substantial amounts in both producing properties and refineries. The relatively large worldwide investments in reserves and production were a result of Jersey strategy. The Board of Directors believed it essential to increase the company's raw material resources in all oil regions in the free world in order to assure adequate supplies to serve expanding markets from the most favorable locations. The board gave special attention to increasing the company's participation in oil production in the Middle East. That region was becoming one of the world's great oil provinces and was favorably located for supplying the planned expansion of the affiliates' refining and sales in England and on the European Continent.

The Board of Directors which determined Jersey's competitive strategy for these postwar years had several members with high competence in exploration and production. Among them were President Holman, John R. Suman, and from 1949 John W. Brice, with former Vice-President Wallace E. Pratt as adviser to the board. Orville Harden, who for two decades had been concerned with the company's general interest, served as the board's principal representative in postwar negotiations having to do with Jersey's foreign oil properties. The board was assisted by the Producing Coordination Department. The coordinator until 1947 was Leonard F. McCollum, and in the next two years John W. Brice, who was succeeded by Roger H. Sherman.

TECHNOLOGY AND EXPANSION IN NORTH AMERICA

As formerly, the producing affiliates in the United States served as leaders among the Jersey companies in advancing research and technology in exploration and production. Humble's findings were made available to the other affiliates through the normal channels for spreading information about new developments. In addition to its research, Carter had the special assignment of providing personnel to assist foreign affiliates in exploration and production technology. These companies and Imperial also provided training for young men sent to North America by foreign affiliates to study operations here. In addition, the two producing companies in the United States provided those abroad with specialists and managerial personnel familiar with the most advanced methods.

The North American affiliates all followed the parent company's policy of expanding reserves and production. Increased dollar earnings made more funds available within the individual companies. However, costs were also rising. Humble and Carter found both leasing and exploration far more expensive than before the war. The competition among oil companies, and their willingness to pay much more than formerly for leases, raised bonuses, rentals, and royalties to levels that in some areas seemed to be economically unjustifiable. To find oil in the old producing regions was at the same time becoming increasingly difficult. Consequently, the search for new fields was extended into hitherto relatively unexplored areas distant from established operations and often more difficult to explore and drill.

Both Humble and Carter worked on the further improvement of exploration techniques. Although they discovered no important new oil-finding methods at this time, they made the reflection seismograph more effective for exploring geologic structures at greater depths. Humble also adapted this instrument and the gravity meter to the search for salt domes under the waters of the Gulf of Mexico. In addition, the companies improved their interpretation of geologic and geophysical data and their training of exploration personnel.[1]

Although both companies continued to lease oil lands and to drill test wells in the older oil regions, the striking feature of their search came to be its geographic spread. Carter became active on the periphery of its older operations in Utah and Wyoming and also in Michigan and Mississippi. Humble extended its search along the eastern Gulf Coast. In addition, it did reconnaissance work in Arizona and moved into California, where it made its first discovery in 1950—the Castaic Junction field. It also explored farther up the Pacific Coast, even doing some reconnaissance in Alaska. It participated extensively in the competition for leases on the continental shelf off Texas and Louisiana.[2]

Two ventures undertaken by other affiliates in 1946 reached into new areas in the United States and off the Bahamas near the Florida coast. Standard Oil Company of New Jersey entered the search for oil fields by leasing land in two eastern coastal states and drilling exploratory wells. A new affiliate, Standard Oil Company (Bahama), began to explore a concession obtained from the government of the Bahamas; it looked for likely structures in the relatively shallow offshore waters of the islands. It did extensive gravimetric mapping from data obtained by lowering gravity meters in chambers to the bottom of the sea, and carried on aerial surveying. But it drilled no test wells off the Bahamas.[3]

The widespread testing of leased lands met with fair success. Most of the wells were drilled to explore deeper structures or on land adjacent to the proved acreage of producing fields. But many were rank wildcats. They were deeper on the average and far more expensive to drill than test wells had been at any other time. In 1946, for the first time, the average depth of Humble's wildcats exceeded 9,000 feet; a decade earlier the average had been 5,500 feet. In 1948 the company drilled an East Texas wildcat to 16,347 feet, but this did not stand long as the record depth. One well drilled on land by Humble in 1946 to a depth of some 12,000 feet cost $768,200, which was then the company's record expenditure for a well.[4]

By far the most costly exploratory drilling was done in the search for oil-bearing salt domes under the waters of the Gulf of Mexico. Several companies, including Humble, had ventured onto the Gulf in the 1930's but had found no oil. In 1947 this affiliate began to construct a double-decked drilling platform in 48 feet of water in the open sea, nearly seven miles from Grand Isle, Louisiana. Measuring 206 by 110 feet and supported by 100 steel piles driven from 147 to 197 feet into the bottom of the Gulf, this platform cost $1,200,000. It was planned that seven directional wells would be drilled from this one structure. The company also built several smaller platforms and established a complete camp on Grand Isle just off the Louisiana coast.

The first well drilled from the large platform was dry, but in August, 1948, a second well struck oil. Another, drilled from a smaller platform, was completed in November. The two that discovered oil in salt domes cost $785,700 and $848,000, respectively. These high costs, estimated to be from three to five times the cost of wells of the same depth on land, at the time made questionable the profitability of oil production on the continental shelf. Offshore operations were also affected by the uncertainty, following the decision of the United States Supreme Court in *United States* v. *California*, as to whether the states or the federal government had jurisdiction over the continental shelf.[5]

The search for oil resulted in discouraging failures as well as valuable discoveries. Such was the outcome in coastal Maryland and North Carolina, where wildcatting was done for Standard Oil Company of New Jersey.[6] A costly stroke of bad luck was Humble's failure to find oil in a test well drilled in Scurry County in West Texas. The geologists had planned the well to be drilled to the geologic formation known as the Ellenburger. Oil had been discovered in that formation in several places in West Texas, and at this particular point it was found to have a structure favorable to trapping oil. When the wildcat failed to find oil in the Ellenburger, Humble abandoned the well and gave up a considerable acreage on which it had been paying rent for ten years. It was learned later that the drill bit had passed through the very edge of the Canyon reef, in which the great North Snyder field was subsequently discovered by a well drilled only a few miles east of Humble's dry well. This was the largest field found in Texas in more than a decade.[7]

The domestic companies found a number of fields in the postwar period, but these were not comparable to the spectacular discoveries of the 1930's. Humble brought in two that proved to be majors. These and Humble's and Carter's discovery of many small fields and of deeper oil-bearing structures in already developed fields, together with the extension of the producing acreage elsewhere, added up to a satisfactory record. Although they produced 683,000,000 barrels during the five years, the two companies raised their estimated crude oil reserves from 2,700,-000,000 barrels as of January 1, 1946, to 3,200,000,000 as of January 1, 1951; Humble's was by far the larger addition. They also increased their gas reserves. Humble became either the largest or one of the two largest owners of such reserves in the United States. However, the cost of the new oil and gas reserves was high. An executive of the company ventured the estimate that 10-cent-per-barrel oil reserves acquired in the 1930's were being replaced by $2.00 oil.[8]

The two companies at the same time also greatly increased their productive capacity. When shortages of materials and manpower were still acute immediately after the war and the demand for products was rising rapidly, they placed special emphasis on the development of both proved and newly discovered fields. All together, in the first five years after the war, they drilled nearly 6,000 wells. This drilling, together with the larger per-well allowables under state regulation, enabled the companies to raise their output greatly in 1947 and 1948. (See Table 23.) In the latter year Humble increased its average daily net production to 368,300 barrels. In 1949 Carter's net output grew to the daily average of 61,300 barrels.[9] Both companies had to reduce their production for a brief time because of a decline in the demand for crude oil, but they improved their potential producing capacity.

Operating in the region having the country's largest gas reserves, Humble also greatly increased its capacity to produce natural gas. In addition to its earlier Tomball and other plants for processing gas from the crude oil produced and its interest in two large cycling plants built during the war (Katy and Erath), Humble built casinghead gas plants as rapidly after the war as materials and equipment became available. It estimated that in 1950 it would produce over 500 billion cubic feet of gas. Even so, its potential was far larger than its actual production, which it held back because of uncertainty as to the conditions under which gas could be sold for transmission outside Texas.[10]

Humble and Carter raised the efficiency of their oil and gas recovery and processing and improved their drilling practices and equipment.

They did successful work on automation. For example, they designed an automatic control device to maintain uniform weight on the drilling bit and also various types of equipment for the automatic operation of wells, tank batteries, and gas-processing facilities. Their research specialists and engineers at the same time made progress in solving problems in drilling and completing wells. But as wells became deeper new difficulties appeared; among these were a greater strain on equipment, higher pressures and temperatures, and greatly increased corrosion of subsurface equipment.[11]

The affiliates also made further refinements in reservoir engineering technology. Their research groups continued to study oil recovery by gas-cap drive and the hydrodynamics of water and gas production in oil wells. They did much research on the phase behavior of hydrocarbons under reservoir conditions, and they advanced fundamental studies of fluids in reservoirs. Dr. William A. Bruce of Carter designed an automatic analyzer for calculating the efficient rate of oil recovery by water drive. The two companies also made studies of individual reservoirs. They gave attention to gas conservation and secondary recovery, Carter being especially active in the latter. Humble began to give regularly an advanced course in reservoir engineering, and it prepared a *Reservoir Engineering Manual* which in 1949 became available to its own operating organization and to other Jersey producing affiliates.[12]

By such means, Jersey affiliates were adjusting their producing operations more and more to the nature and potential of individual fields. Their objective was to produce oil and gas from them at the lowest possible cost and with the highest ultimate recovery that was economically feasible. At the end of the period, they were approaching the physical possibility of producing nearly all the oil in a reservoir, but such recovery was still far too costly to be practicable.

In most of the states in which Humble and Carter operated, the regulation of oil and gas production had gone far to aid in applying science and engineering to conserving the resource and stabilizing production. It had curbed the competitive excesses resulting from the fundamental law in the United States—the rule of capture—governing the ownership and recovery of oil in the earth. But there were still unsolved problems and unsettled controversies.[13]

Gas conservation and regulation were in the forefront of such problems and controversies. Difficulty rose especially over the gas produced with oil. The rise in the demand for crude oil increased the production of

Table 23: **DAILY AVERAGE NET CRUDE OIL PRODUCTION, PURCHASES, SALES, AND NET AVAILABLE TO AFFILIATES' REFINERIES, BY AFFILIATES AND AREAS, 1946–1950**
Standard Oil Company (New Jersey)
(In thousands of 42-gallon barrels)

WESTERN HEMISPHERE

| | North America | | | | South America | | | | | Western Hemisphere Total |
| | United States | | | Canada | Venezuela | | Peru | Colombia | Other South American[c] | |
	Humble	Carter	Standard of New Jersey[a]	Imperial	Creole	International[b]	International	Tropical		
					Net Production					
1946	309.6	57.1	—	5.3	451.2	35.4	27.5	31.4	2.3	919.7
1947	343.2	54.4	—	5.2	490.1	38.8	28.0	30.2	2.0	992.0
1948	368.3	59.6	—	10.3	540.7	40.2	31.0	22.4	2.1	1,074.6
1949	275.9	61.3	—	22.2	496.0	38.0	32.6	29.2	1.9	957.1
1950	282.5	60.0	—	32.6	555.7	43.9	31.7	32.0	1.7	1,040.1
					Purchases from Nonaffiliates and Other Outsiders					
1946	371.3	76.8	179.7	19.0	105.7	11.3	2.8	3.5	0.2	770.3
1947	466.1	81.6	235.8	18.0	103.3	9.3	1.3	3.3	0.2	918.9
1948	533.2	90.8	284.2	23.8	95.2	5.5	—	2.5	0.2	1,035.4
1949	351.3	90.4	270.7	24.8	96.5	6.8	0.2	3.8	9.9	854.4
1950	358.9	101.6	277.1	24.5	113.4	10.3	0.2	4.5	4.2	894.7
					Sales to Nonaffiliates					
1946	275.9	59.6	47.0	5.1	58.2	22.1	1.1	1.0	0.3	470.3
1947	345.1	63.8	82.8	3.8	75.2	17.1	1.2	1.1	0.1	590.2
1948	418.3	74.7	111.1	6.8	75.8	12.8	—	1.3	0.1	700.9
1949	269.4	81.9	95.5	3.6	62.0	15.0	—	1.5	0.1	529.0
1950	245.0	87.6	79.3	4.8	66.0	12.3	2.9	1.4	0.1	499.4
					Net Available to Affiliates					
1946	404.9	74.3	132.7	19.2	498.7	24.6	29.2	33.9	2.2	1,219.7
1947	464.2	72.2	153.0	19.4	518.2	31.0	28.1	32.5	2.1	1,320.7
1948	483.2	75.7	173.1	27.3	560.1	32.9	31.0	23.6	2.2	1,409.1
1949	357.8	69.8	175.2	43.4	530.5	29.8	32.8	31.5	11.7	1,282.5
1950	396.4	74.0	197.0	52.3	603.1	41.9	29.0	35.1	5.8	1,435.4

NOTE: Because of the rounding of numbers, totals are not in all cases the exact sum of those added.
[a] Esso Standard Oil Company from 1948. Includes purchases and sales of Colonial Beacon Oil Company, which was merged into the larger company in 1947, and small amounts of Middle East crude oil purchased for domestic affiliates in 1947 and 1948.
[b] International Petroleum's share of the crude oil produced by Mene Grande Oil Company.
[c] Operations of Standard Oil Company of Argentina and Standard Oil Company of Trinidad.

casinghead gas at a rate faster than equipment became available for saving it and also more rapidly than market outlets developed. As a result, much of the gas was flared, and pressure was brought by state and federal governments to conserve it.

Humble built plants for processing natural gas as fast as materials

Table 23 (cont.): **DAILY AVERAGE NET CRUDE OIL PRODUCTION, PURCHASES, SALES, AND NET AVAILABLE TO AFFILIATES' REFINERIES, BY AFFILIATES AND AREAS, 1946–1950**
Standard Oil Company (New Jersey)
(In thousands of 42-gallon barrels)

EASTERN HEMISPHERE[d]

Europe			Middle East		Far East				
Germany: Brigitta[e]	Netherlands: Nederlandse Aardolie[f]	Italy: Società Petrolifera[g]	Iraq: Iraq Petroleum[h]	Saudi Arabia: Arabian American[i]	Indonesia and New Guinea: Standard-Vacuum[j]	Esso Export Corporation[k]	Eastern Hemisphere Total	World Total	
Net Production									
0.7	0.7	0.1	9.3	—	—	—	10.7	930.4	1946
0.6	2.0	0.1	9.8	6.2	3.5	—	22.2	1,014.2	1947
0.6	4.7	0.1	6.8	99.0	43.1	—	154.3	1,228.9	1948
0.7	5.9	0.1	7.8	143.0	61.2	—	218.8	1,175.9	1949
1.1	6.7	0.1	16.9	164.0	60.2	—	249.0	1,289.1	1950
Purchases from Nonaffiliates and Other Outsiders									
n.a.[l]	—	—	0.5	—	—	7.1	7.6	777.9	1946
n.a.	—	—	0.5	1.5	0.2	11.3	13.5	932.4	1947
n.a.	—	—	0.9	0.3	—	2.2	3.4	1,038.8	1948
2.8	—	—	1.2	—	—	0.3	4.3	858.7	1949
1.1	—	1.7	0.9	—	6.5	—	10.2	904.9	1950
Sales to Nonaffiliates									
n.a.[l]	—	—	—	—	—	0.7	0.7	471.0	1946
n.a.	2.0	—	—	4.4	—	0.4	6.8	597.0	1947
n.a.	4.7	—	0.6	17.8	—	0.9	24.0	724.9	1948
n.a.	5.9	—	0.2	26.8	—	0.3	33.2	562.2	1949
n.a.	6.7	—	3.6	21.6	—	1.3	33.2	532.6	1950
Net Available to Affiliates									
0.7	0.6	0.1	9.8	—	—	6.4	17.6	1,237.3	1946
0.6	—	0.1	10.3	3.3	3.7	10.9	28.9	1,349.6	1947
0.6	—	0.1	7.1	81.5	43.1	1.3	133.7	1,442.8	1948
3.5	—	0.1	8.8	116.2	61.2	—	189.8	1,472.3	1949
2.2	—	0.1	14.2	142.4	66.7	(1.3)[m]	246.9	1,682.3	1950

d In addition to the affiliates listed was Anglo-American Oil Company, which had an average production of three barrels daily for 1946–1950, and MAORT of Hungary and Româno-Americana of Romania, the last two being under the control of the Russians for these years.

e Includes purchases by Esso A.G. in 1949 and 1950. Gewerkschaft Brigitta's purchases and sales were not reported to New York; only Jersey's half-interest in this company is shown.

f Only Jersey's half-interest in this affiliate is shown.

g Purchases in 1949 were by Stanic Industria Petrolifera S. A.

h Jersey's 11⅞ per cent interest shown. Crude from Iraq Petroleum was supplemented in 1950 by that of Petroleum Development (Qatar) Limited, in which Jersey also had about a one-eighth interest.

i Only Jersey's 30 per cent interest in affiliate shown. Actual ownership did not occur until 1948, but arrangements for purchase and for loan guarantee were signed in 1947.

j Full 100 per cent shown although Jersey's interest was only 50 per cent. Production in Sumatra was supplemented from 1948 through 1950 with that in New Guinea, growing from 100 barrels daily in 1948 to 1,900 in 1949 and 1950. Purchases of American and Iranian crude are included in 1950.

k Esso Export Corporation operated internationally. It purchased crude oil largely from the Western Hemisphere at first but shifted to Middle East for supplying affiliates in the Eastern Hemisphere. Purchases from and sales to affiliated companies are not included.

l Figures are not available; it is assumed that there were no transactions.

m Sales exceeded purchases.

Source: Standard Oil Company (New Jersey), Annual Statistical Review, 1945–1950.

perial's exploration and production organization, under Vice-President
O. B. Hopkins, drew up the new program. These men had the advice of
Jersey's leading exploration and production executives, especially G. M.
Knebel, head of the exploration staff in New York, L. G. Weeks, Jersey's
chief geologist, and L. F. McCollum, producing coordinator. M. L.
Haider was transferred from the parent company to manage the campaign. A petroleum engineer trained at Stanford University and a man of
compelling enthusiasm and drive, Haider had held managerial positions
with Carter Oil, Standard Oil Development, and the parent company
itself.* [17]

Imperial geologists in 1946 explored along the eastern geosyncline for
hundreds of miles in the general vicinity of Edmonton, Alberta. After
they had selected a likely area, seismic crews were moved to the small
village of Leduc, about twenty miles southwest of Edmonton, to make a
study of the prospect. The seismographs found a promising structure in a
reef-type formation in a deep Devonian limestone of the Paleozoic Age.
In the cold Canadian winter, late in the year, an Imperial rig began to
drill in a wheat field near the village.[18]

On February 13, 1947, when the drill bit had reached 5,066 feet, the
well was brought into production. The men in charge had expected this
to happen because a test taken higher up in the formation was saturated
with oil. Accordingly, Imperial had invited government officials, press
representatives, and others to the site. When the well "blew in," a crowd
of 500 was waiting.

The company immediately began to drill several other wells; when
three had struck pay sand, the exploration executives in Canada and New
York were convinced that Imperial had discovered a commercial field.[19]
Other companies moved in, and within a year forty wells had been
completed at Leduc—twenty-eight by Imperial. Although the limits of
the field had not been reached, it was then estimated that under the 8,000
acres already tested lay a reserve of 100,000,000 barrels of oil.[20] Fortunately, the provincial government, having learned from experience in the
Turner Valley field, had a system of regulation ready to ensure reasonably
orderly development and efficient rates of production.

Getting the oil to market was a real problem because of steel shortages
at the time. Pipe for the fifteen miles to the nearest railway was obtained
by purchasing an abandoned line in Texas. To obtain a refinery for

---

* Haider later rose to the board of Imperial and of Jersey and in 1962 to the
presidency and in 1965 to the board chairmanship of Jersey.

supplying the local market, Imperial bought from the United States government the 5,000-barrel plant built for the wartime Canol project at Whitehorse in the Yukon. This plant was dismantled, piece by piece, and moved by truck to Edmonton, approximately 1,400 miles through some of the wildest country in North America.[21]

Imperial soon made further discoveries in the vicinity of Leduc. In January, 1948, its drillers brought in the Woodbend field a few miles to

IMPERIAL PRODUCING FIELDS IN WESTERN CANADA AND PIPELINES TO LAKE SUPERIOR, AS OF DECEMBER, 1950

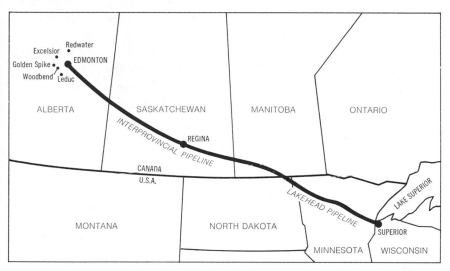

the north. In September they discovered the Redwater, fifty miles to the northeast of the first discovery. Early in 1949, they found the Golden Spike, several miles west of Woodbend. In that year, Imperial estimated that those fields had reserves totaling several hundred million barrels.[22] They were reminiscent of the great salt-dome discoveries of the 1930's on the Texas Gulf Coast. At the end of 1950, the company's reserves, which had been estimated at 27,500,000 barrels before the Leduc discovery, totaled an estimated 608,500,000 barrels.[23]

A wave of optimism ran through the entire organization as new fields were discovered. After a generation of nearly consistent failure to find oil and of large expenditure without any direct recompense, success in oil finding had finally come to Imperial and to its great north country. The company, moreover, was convinced that a large undiscovered oil treasure was still to be found in Canada and that Imperial itself would continue to locate new fields.

The plan to develop the Leduc field and the prospect of other discoveries at once raised the question of how to finance a large program of expansion. In May, 1947, Imperial's management informed the Executive Committee in New York of the need for $48,000,000 in the near future. Soon thereafter, it sold to the Royal Bank of Canada a $24,000,000 debenture series to mature in the early 1950's. An obvious solution for longerterm financing was for Imperial to sell its majority ownership in International Petroleum Company, Limited, to Jersey and others among its own stockholders. From the parent company's point of view, the original reason for putting its producing interests in Peru and Colombia under a Canadian affiliate had long since vanished, and good reasons had developed for direct relations with the Peruvian and Colombian operations. As for Imperial, its investment in International had been profitable, but now better prospects for earnings had developed at home. The two companies agreed to the sale of the Canadian affiliate's holdings in International to its own stockholders, which meant selling to Jersey its proportionate share. Imperial obtained a total of $80,299,000 for its International stock. At the same time, it also sold its interest in several small Canadian companies operating mostly in the old Turner Valley field.[24]

By such means this Canadian affiliate obtained funds to help finance the expansion that was to make it a fully integrated company in a few years. With the building of pipelines and new refineries and the enlarging and upgrading of old plants which followed the discoveries around Edmonton, the company became able to serve a rising demand for oil products at the same time that it reduced its dependence on other suppliers in the interior provinces of Canada and on imports by rail from the United States. The Montreal and Halifax refineries in eastern Canada and the Ioco on the Pacific Coast continued to process imported oil.

To several Jersey affiliates, the development of production in Canada and the sale of Imperial's holdings in International Petroleum to the parent company meant the severing of old ties or the making of new ones. To Carter Oil, it brought the loss of outlets for crude at Imperial's refineries at Regina and Sarnia. To the Canadian company, it meant the end of thirty-five years' corporate relations with International and Tropical and with their operations in Peru and Colombia. For Jersey itself, it produced changed relationships: on the one hand a greater self-sufficiency on the part of the Canadian affiliate; on the other, closer relations with International and Tropical and their operations. Jersey's direct contact with the companies operating in Peru and Colombia was especially important at the time because certain developments in these countries required careful attention on the highest administrative level.

ADVANCE AND STALEMATE IN SOUTH AMERICAN PRODUCTION

In South America, the producing activities and hopes of Jersey affiliates encountered a diversity of political conditions and popular aspirations. The general tendency in the region was toward a greater national participation in the oil industry and its benefits. This trend ran the gamut from one government's pressure for an increased share in the profits from oil production to another's refusal to grant concessions to foreign companies. In some areas, Jersey affiliates continued to operate profitably and to expand; in others, they virtually stood still or even in a measure retreated.

Creole in Venezuela was the leading oil producer among all the Jersey affiliates. This company demonstrated at its best the soundness of the parent company's policy of giving managerial autonomy to its affiliates. Under President Proudfit's leadership, Creole maintained good relations with its employees and the general public and with the Venezuelan government. It had efficient and technologically progressive operations. Despite high employee and other costs, it could produce oil at a lower unit cost than could producers in some Latin American countries and especially in certain areas in the United States.[25] This advantage was due to the generally high productivity of its oil fields and the large concessions on which it operated. The company increased its net production from a daily average of 451,200 barrels in 1946 to 555,700 in 1950.

Creole acquired no new concessions because the Venezuelan government did not issue exploratory rights during those postwar years, but it explored on extensive holdings acquired earlier and also on limited purchases from private owners. In fact, because of high rentals on lands not surveyed during the war, it carried on a large exploration campaign. When it had made sufficient surveys to select parcels for retention, it reduced these activities and allowed more than a million acres to revert to the government. At the end of 1950, however, its concessions still totaled more than 3,000,000 acres.

Utilizing the latest geophysical methods, Creole discovered new fields and extended old ones, in both acreage and depth. By probing deeper structures it added to its reserves in the Bolívar coastal fields of Lake

Maracaibo. It also struck oil in Mara, west of the northern end of the lake, in a formation in which a Royal Dutch–Shell affiliate had already found oil, and it discovered oil in a deeper formation in the Jusepin field in eastern Venezuela. Despite the large volume of production which was needed to supply the heavy demand after the war, Creole increased its estimated reserves from 5 billion barrels at the end of 1945 to approximately 5.5 billion at the end of 1950.[26]

Creole's major difficulties between 1945 and 1950 were of external origin. The political situation was then more unstable than at any time in the company's experience, except for a short period after the death of Gómez in 1935. A group of young army officers considered the reforms made under President Medina far too moderate and believed it necessary to break the hold of old *gomecista* generals on the military. They chose to work with the liberal party, Acción Democrática, and in 1945 removed the president from office and set up a revolutionary junta to administer the government of Venezuela under Rómulo Betancourt as provisional president. As they had promised, the leaders of the new regime arranged for the meeting of an assembly to draw up a new constitution and for the election of a new president and congress by universal suffrage in December, 1947. Rómulo Gallegos, an author and one of the founders of Acción Democrática, was elected president, and an overwhelming majority of the members of the new congress were of the same party.

The hope for a stable, constitutional government was not realized. The Gallegos government introduced revolutionary programs in education, labor, public health, housing, and the economy generally. It particularly undertook agrarian reform. However, the great extent of social and political reforms and the methods used by the party in power—notably its efforts to reduce the political influence of the military—stimulated the growth of opposition, which culminated in another revolution, also led by young army officers, in November, 1948. A military junta again took charge of the government. It was at first headed by Carlos Delgado Chalbaud, who dissolved the Acción Democrática but otherwise followed a policy of compromise and moderation. Differences over the type of government to be set up led to a split, and in November, 1948, with the death of Chalbaud, came a shift of power to Colonel Marcos Pérez Jiménez, who stood for military as opposed to civilian control of the Venezuelan government.[27]

Recognizing the importance of the oil industry to Venezuela and probably cognizant of the difficulties of government management of oil operations in Mexico after expropriation, these successive governments made no move to nationalize the foreign-owned industry or to make demands that might reduce its operations. But they had an effect on it. They generally supported organized labor and reinforced its demands, and they gained a larger participation by the government in the earnings of the industry.

At the time of the overthrow of the Medina government, the share of the oil companies in the industry's earnings was running slightly higher than the amount going to the government from the exploitation tax (royalty on production) and other taxes on the oil industry. The revolutionary junta claimed that, under the petroleum law of 1943, the government and the companies should share equally in the profits of the industry. Actually, the law had not explicitly provided for an equal division; it had provided for 16⅔ per cent royalty on production plus other taxes. But an equal sharing had been agreed on in principle by representatives of the government and the companies in the negotiations preceding the drafting of the law. In fact, this understanding had been incorporated in the so-called Exposition of Motives sent to the Venezuelan Congress in 1943 with the draft of the proposed new law.[28] However, price increases had later raised the companies' share of oil industry earnings above that of the government.

The first junta and the later constitutional administration under President Gallegos moved to increase the government's income from oil operations. They levied an extraordinary income tax in December, 1945, ostensibly to equalize the division of earnings. Creole's additional tax amounted to $18,700,000. When the government's participation continued to be less than that of the companies—$80,000,000 as against Creole's share of $83,000,000 from the company's earnings in 1946—the government and the foreign oil companies entered into discussions to draw up a permanent settlement of the issue. The result was an amendment to the new income tax statute of 1948, which in effect incorporated into Venezuelan law the so-called 50–50 principle. This provision stipulated that, if at the end of a year the income split between the government and an oil company favored the concessionaire, the company should make an additional payment to equalize the two shares.[29] Creole's payment to the government out of its 1950 earnings amounted to $168,000,000 as against its own profit of $167,000,000.[30]

From the long-term point of view, Creole's workable relations with the government were to the advantage of both the company and the nation.

The two parties recognized their mutual interests and interdependence, and, although differences sometimes were considerable, they found a basis for a partnership that was advantageous and profitable to both. Venezuela received a larger share of earnings from oil operations with which to "sow the petroleum" to the benefit of the country, but at the same time Creole retained enough earnings to enable it to expand and to keep its costs competitive in foreign markets. The example of this 50–50 sharing of net earnings was to have an influence far beyond the well-being of Creole and the boundaries of its host country.

In other Latin American countries, the Jersey affiliates expanded their oil production very little. This situation resulted partly from political conditions and governmental policies that discouraged foreign investments or prevented foreign-owned oil companies from expanding their operations or even entering oil production.

In Peru, the operations of the International Petroleum Company, the largest of the few oil companies operating there, remained almost static. A high feeling of nationalism at this time thwarted the granting of concessions on lands set aside as national reserves—such as the Sechura Desert, the Montaña east of the Andes, and the Lake Titacaca region. All these national reserves contained, or were adjacent to, areas where exploration had indicated favorable geologic formations. International in 1946 undertook surface geologic and gravity surveys in the Montaña, but not until 1955 was it to obtain exploration rights in that part of Peru. It expected to obtain concessions in the Sechura Desert in 1946, but the Peruvian government did not execute a contract that had been drawn up; a concession in that part of the country was obtained only after a new petroleum law had been enacted in the 1950's. Hence International in the 1940's did not expand its producing activities in Peru as much as had been anticipated; it limited its efforts to extending the proved acreage on its large La Brea estate. Its annual production rose somewhat after the war, but even in its most productive year the company produced substantially less oil than in the years from 1934 through 1938. However, because of new discoveries on La Brea and the revision of estimates, it increased its reserves modestly by the end of 1950.[31]

In Colombia Jersey faced a new experience. This had to do with the reversion to the government of the De Mares concession of The Tropical Oil Company scheduled for August 25, 1951. In December, 1948, Colombia passed a law authorizing the organization of a government company, Empresa Colombiana de Petroleos, to operate the De Mares and other concessions that might revert to the state. Under this law, 51 per cent of

Empresa's stock was to be held by the government and Colombian nationals, or by the latter alone; not more than 49 per cent could be owned by foreigners.[32]

This law raised a question of policy for Jersey. The company's preference was to remain in Colombia, and its administrators were willing to operate through a corporation partially owned by Colombians (preferably private citizens). But the American executives maintained that any operation must be strictly on a business basis and must produce a profit that could be remitted freely in dollars. They also held that Jersey must own more than half of the stock in such a company and have a contract under which to manage it. The terms Colombia offered for participation as minority owner in the management of Empresa were financially attractive, but the Jersey leaders decided not to participate for reasons of policy. Some of its executives questioned the wisdom of insisting on the ownership of more than half the stock inasmuch as a sovereign state could exert pressure to accomplish its will regardless of stock ownership. The Board of Directors held the view, however, that the legal position of an affiliate should be so clear as to be upheld by any impartial court of law.[33]

When it became apparent that no arrangement for continued operation of the De Mares concession could be made that would satisfy both the government and Jersey, each party began to prepare for the reversion of the grant. The company reorganized its Colombian business; in mid-1950 it transferred Tropical's marketing assets and operations to a new company known as Esso Colombiana, S.A. This arrangement had been made possible by a ruling of the Colombian exchange-control authorities to allow profits to be remitted abroad. The government, realizing that it was about to acquire responsibility for a large enterprise requiring specialized skills, inquired what arrangement could be made for Tropical's specialists to operate the Barrancabermeja refinery. Discussion led to an agreement under which Jersey organized International Petroleum Company (Colombia) to lease the plant for ten years.[34]

At public ceremonies on August 25, 1951, Tropical relinquished its long-held De Mares concession and the Barrancabermeja refinery. The official *Acta* recording the transfer, signed by representatives of the government and the company, contains this sentence as translated:

Both the representatives of the Nation and those of Tropical Oil Company declare, in the name of these entities, their satisfaction with the faithful manner in which both parties have carried out the contract, and with the fair and amicable form in which they have proceeded during its development and termination, thus complying with the objectives and purposes that were proposed upon its celebration.[35]

This was a notable event: the government regained possession of property in accordance with the terms of the contract between the parties and not by expropriation.

This transfer to the government ended the pioneer oil venture in Colombia, one that had been a part of Jersey's operations for more than three decades. Tropical had provided Colombia with good oil products, paid fair wages, and treated its employees well by any local standards. It had also provided the government with regular royalties and taxes; and, at the end, it turned over to the nation a field so well developed that the extraction of a large quantity of oil would be a simple operation. The advantages had not all been on the one side, however. The Colombian government had lived up to its agreements, and Tropical had recovered its capital plus a sizable increment. The amicable way in which the government and Jersey handled the De Mares matter seemed to augur well for the company should it discover another promising oil field through its explorations then being carried on in that country.

The barriers to exploration and production in other Latin American countries were virtually insurmountable. In some, even though government agencies were failing to meet growing needs for petroleum products, foreign oil companies could not obtain concessions. Such was the situation in Brazil and Argentina, whose imports to supply rising demands placed a heavy burden on their foreign payments. In Argentina, Jersey's affiliates were producing decreasing amounts of oil from old holdings, an average of only 1,600 barrels daily in 1950.[36] In Brazil, the search for oil was under the complete charge of a national company, Conselho Nacional do Petróles.[37]

CRUDE OIL FOR EASTERN HEMISPHERE MARKETS

Jersey's forecasts at the end of the war made it imperative for the long term to obtain other than predominantly Western Hemisphere oil for Eastern Hemisphere markets. Company economists estimated that the Western Hemisphere would soon require all the petroleum that the Americas would yield. In addition, oil from the Middle East had a current—and a still greater potential—cost advantage in certain parts of Europe over that from across the Atlantic. Because of the nature of the reservoirs and the efficient operations made possible by large concessions, individual wells in the Middle East yielded a far larger volume than did United States wells, and hence their unit cost of production was lower.[38] The building of more pipelines from regions near the Persian Gulf was expected to increase still further the cost handicap of American oil in certain parts of Europe.

The company started negotiations to obtain more production in the Eastern Hemisphere as soon as possible after the war. Just as after World War I, it was encouraged by the favorable attitude of the United States government. After World War II, American officials were especially concerned, in the interest of national security, that United States oil companies should obtain larger production in the Middle East.

Jersey resumed its efforts to acquire new sources of oil in Europe. Its most promising venture was a 50 per cent participation, obtained from the Royal Dutch–Shell group in 1946, in N.V. Nederlandse Aardolie Maatschappij. This company had discovered oil during the war on a large concession obtained from the Dutch government. In 1950 Jersey's share of the Schoonebeek field's production averaged 6,700 barrels daily. This black and waxy oil provided residual fuel and even gasoline for the Dutch market. An important discovery was also made at Suderbruch in Germany. In France a Jersey affiliate, after protracted negotiations with the government, applied for a concession in the Bordeaux region in what is known by geologists as the Aquitaine Basin. Reconnaissance work had found favorable indications before the war, and state-controlled companies had discovered two small oil fields in the area. Jersey's affiliate found no oil in France during the immediate postwar period; its first discovery was to come in 1954.[39]

The company also looked for oil in North Africa. An affiliate which had been doing work for more than ten years in Egypt liquidated its operations in 1949. This was done because of the unsatisfactory results of negotiations to clarify its rights under the new petroleum law of 1948. Together with changes in world petroleum supplies, this left no economic alternative to withdrawal. Elsewhere in North Africa, the results were not sufficiently encouraging for extensive investments, but what was learned in Libya was to be useful later.[40]

Standard-Vacuum Oil Company, Jersey's half-owned affiliate, endeavored to build up its production in the Far East. Lloyd W. Elliott, general manager in the Dutch East Indies before the war, became the company's president in 1946. This affiliate held a minority interest in several concerns that explored in Dutch and Australian New Guinea, Australia, and New Zealand. The only company with production—the one in Dutch New Guinea—produced a daily average of 1,900 barrels of crude in 1949 and 1950. Stanvac's principal producing interest was its wholly owned NKPM (later Standard-Vacuum Petroleum Maatschappij), which re-entered the Talang Akar and Pendopo fields in central Sumatra in 1947. These two, together with the new Lirik field, in 1950 produced a daily average of 60,200 barrels, a volume far short of meeting the needs of the company's markets. Stanvac's reserves were increased relatively little during the late 1940's. They amounted to an estimated 200,000,000 barrels at the end of 1950.[41]

Operations in the Dutch East Indies were handicapped by the disturbed conditions resulting from the setting up of the Republic of Indonesia and its efforts to gain independence. However, inasmuch as Standard-Vacuum's concession arrangements provided for sharing with the government almost half the net profits from operations within the country, no problem arose over payments at this time. The company's standing was helped by its liberal provisions for employees, its arrangements for training workers locally and for sending especially promising ones to the United States and elsewhere for advanced education, and its policy of promoting natives to higher job levels.[42]

The most dramatic move in Jersey's postwar quest for new oil was its effort to gain a place in production in Saudi Arabia. This participation was achieved through negotiations within a maelstrom of conflicting interests and forces. It came at the very time when Jersey's hold on markets in much of the Eastern Hemisphere met widespread difficulties resulting from trade and exchange regulations. Despite the risk of obtaining oil supplies for markets it might lose, the company went ahead with negotiations for a large participation in a great oil region in the Eastern Hemisphere.[43]

All the production that Jersey owned in the Middle East in 1946 was its 11⅞ per cent share, through Near East Development Corporation, of the production of Iraq Petroleum Company, Limited. Jersey's share of the company's estimated reserves at the beginning of 1946 was not over 400,000,000 barrels; its share of the crude output averaged 9,300 barrels daily in that year.[44] This was little compared with the Middle East holdings of its great foreign competitors and of the affiliates of three other American companies: Gulf Oil Corporation, Standard Oil Company of California, and The Texas Company.

Jersey's minor position in the Middle East stemmed primarily from the

Red Line Agreement of 1928 in which all the owners of Iraq Petroleum Company had bound themselves not to acquire concessions independently of the others within the boundaries of the old Turkish Empire. (See Chapter 3.) Large areas of the Middle East in consequence had been left to entry by companies other than the great international leaders of the late 1920's. Two American corporations—Standard Oil Company of California and The Texas Company—had gained firm footholds within the Red Line in the 1930's. At the end of the war, these two concerns jointly owned affiliates with oil production and proved reserves on Bahrain Islands and in Saudi Arabia: Bahrain Petroleum Company and Arabian American Oil Company (Aramco).

A favorable combination of circumstances after the war enabled Jersey to free itself from the Red Line Agreement and to acquire a share in Aramco. However, the circumstances were infinitely complex, and the process involved was long and tedious.

One basic consideration was the fact that Aramco obviously stood on the threshold of a great development. This company had concessions in Saudi Arabia covering an area equal to that of the states of Oklahoma, Arkansas, Texas, and Louisiana. By the end of the war, Aramco had discovered four major fields with proved reserves estimated in billions of barrels of oil.[45] Immense oil treasure was believed still to be undiscovered under the vast desert sands of the remainder of its concessions.

Aramco and its owners knew from experience something of the magnitude of the problems to be met in discovering and exploiting that treasure. Saudi Arabia was a country of scant rainfall, broiling heat and freezing cold, sparse vegetation, and shifting sands. Extraordinary expenditures were required to provide facilities for living and working in the region. The Saudi Arabs, moreover, were largely nomadic tribesmen without modern industrial skills and disciplines and with a social structure unsuitable for the kind of work and organization required by a large industrial concern. The country's government was centered in the all-powerful ruler, King Abdul Aziz Ibn Saud. To maintain a relationship of confidence and understanding with this sovereign, from whom the company derived its rights and privileges, was essential.[46]

Convinced that the company had concessions in the center of one of the greatest oil "plays" of all time, Aramco's owners wanted to expand operations. But expansion on the scale considered would take immense capital and would require larger foreign markets than they possessed. To increase sales in those markets against the competition of well-established

international marketers would be inordinately expensive. Reaching outlets west of Suez at competitive costs would require a pipeline spanning
desert and mountain from the Persian Gulf to the Mediterranean. Should
the two American owners of Aramco—Standard of California and Texaco
—risk the necessary capital at a time of political instability in the Near
and the Middle East and of threat of Communist aggression? Actually
they had little choice, for the Saudi government was urging immediate
expansion in order to increase its income.

The logical solution was to broaden the ownership base of Aramco.
The partners in Near East Development Corporation—Standard Oil
Company (New Jersey) and Socony-Vacuum Oil Company—were obvious prospects. They could command large capital and were willing to
assume the risks. Both needed more oil for their markets—Jersey especially, for its outlets in Europe. But the Red Line Agreement still stood in
the way, as it had done in the attempts of both companies to secure some
participation in Bahrain production in the 1930's.

Soon after the war, Jersey began to investigate how it might be freed
from the restrictions of that agreement. Its regular legal counsel in
London advised that, in their opinion, the fact that two of the owners of
Iraq Petroleum Company—Compagnie Française des Pétroles and an
individual, Calouste Sarkis Gulbenkian—had come under enemy domination by the German occupation of France in 1940 had terminated the
working agreement of 1928. As a result, the counsel held, the Red Line
restrictions were no longer in force. To obtain a broader judgment, the
head of Jersey's Law Department, Edward F. Johnson, turned to several
eminent legal firms in London. He wanted their advice concerning the
position that might be taken on this issue by the British courts, which
under the bylaws of Iraq Petroleum had jurisdiction over matters in
dispute between its owners. These British lawyers were unanimous in the
opinion that the Red Line Agreement was no longer binding on the
signatory companies.[47]

Jersey also consulted the United States Department of State. It learned
that the government would not support a new agreement incorporating
the old restrictive features.[48] In fact, the Red Line restrictions, although
agreed to in 1928 with the approval of the Department of State, were
currently contrary to the official policy of the United States regarding the
participation of American corporations in any agreements abroad that
might be in restraint of trade.[49] In fact, the United States had in 1943
entered negotiations with the British—the strongest European power in
the region—looking toward the strengthening of the American position in

the oil industry in the Middle East. These negotiations had terminated in the Anglo-American Petroleum Agreement in September, 1945. Secretary Harold Ickes, who signed it as head of the American negotiators, said with reference to one clause that it "means, among other things, that there will be no hobbling of American nationals by such devices as the Red Line Agreement." Although the agreement was not ratified by the United States Senate, and hence did not go into effect, the negotiations show that the United States was opposed to restrictive agreements and stood for what was essentially an open-door policy in the Middle East, but with safeguards for the interests of the producing countries.[50]

Although American policy was opposed to restrictive arrangements in the Middle East, the two owners of Near East Development had to deal with the other members of the Iraq group with respect to the Red Line Agreement. In the autumn of 1946, Jersey and Socony informed these other owners that, having been advised by eminent counsel that the old agreement was null and void, they were willing to negotiate a new one without the old restrictions.[51]

Discussions were then already under way between Jersey and Socony, on the one hand, and Standard of California and Texaco, on the other. In November, 1946, the first two companies sent representatives to Saudi Arabia to make a survey of Aramco's properties and operations.[52] Late in December, Jersey, Socony, and Aramco announced an agreement in principle under which the first two of these companies would acquire a 30 per cent and 10 per cent interest, respectively, in the third. They also arranged to acquire proportionate interests in Trans-Arabian Pipe Line Company (Tapline), which had been organized by Aramco's owners to build a 30-inch line from near the Persian Gulf to the Mediterranean.[53]

On the day this arrangement was made known, another with Anglo-Iranian was also announced. This was an agreement in principle, negotiated by Jersey's Director Harden, under which Jersey would purchase large quantities of crude from the British company over a period of years and would participate in a new corporation to build a pipeline from Iran and Kuwait to the Mediterranean if the building of such a line were found feasible. This contingency was dependent especially on obtaining rights of way and security of operations in Iraq and Syria. If consummated, this agreement would help the Jersey Company to meet its crude oil requirements for sterling markets from a sterling source and would give Anglo-Iranian an outlet for its expected surplus production, especially from Kuwait. Details later worked out provided for Esso Export to purchase crude at the rate of 110,000 barrels daily from Anglo-Iranian

of the other owners were compromised and their particular needs met. The restrictive provision of the Red Line Agreement was omitted.[59] These tortuous negotiations, which for three years had kept Jersey's representatives shuttling between New York, London, Paris, and Lisbon, thus finally enabled the company to take independent action in the Middle East.

Other developments followed quickly. The lawsuits were withdrawn from the British courts. In December, 1948, Jersey and Socony completed their purchase of Aramco stock.[60] Shortly thereafter a third Jersey director, John R. Suman, was elected to Aramco's board.

As agreed during the negotiations, Iraq Petroleum made plans for the construction of an additional pipeline, a 30-inch carrier from Kirkuk to the Mediterranean. Plans for increasing the company's production and that of affiliates in particular regions were also put into effect. Jersey's share of the output rose to a daily average of 16,900 barrels in 1950, and its share of reserves in Iraq and Qatar was estimated to be more than a billion barrels.[61]

Aramco's expansion program, undertaken after the agreements had been made with Jersey and Socony in March, 1947, was by this time well under way. In October, 1950, oil began to flow via an Aramco pipeline from Abqaiq, near the Persian Gulf, to Tapline at Qaisumah and thence through this pipeline to its terminal at Sidon on the Mediterranean south of Beirut, Lebanon. With new fields and mounting production, the Ras Tanura refinery, efficient crude transport by pipeline to the Mediterranean, and loading facilities for tankers carrying products to markets in Africa and Asia, Aramco was then in a position to play a major role in the oil industry of the world. In 1950 Jersey's 30 per cent share of the company's production averaged 164,000 barrels daily, and at the end of the year its portion of the estimated reserves was more than 2,800,000,000 barrels.[62]

By 1950 Aramco had accomplished vastly more in Saudi Arabia than expanding its facilities, operations, and oil reserves. Having been given wide authority by its American owners, it had conducted its relations with its employees, with the developing communities in the area of its operations, and with the Saudi government, with results that promised well for the future. Aramco's administrators recognized that its relations with Saudi Arabia depended on recognition by the host country that the relationship was advantageous to itself. They fortunately dealt with a ruler who comprehended what the company could do to help him and his people but also recognized that Aramco had to make profits if it were to continue to operate successfully and to grow.[63]

In 1950 a new agreement was made with King Ibn Saud as to the income he was to receive from Aramco's operations. The company's obligations were spelled out in the original concession contract, which in addition to other obligations provided for Aramco to pay four shillings gold per ton, or the equivalent in dollars or sterling (about 22 cents per barrel). After the war, with the increasing needs of the Saudi government and the rise in crude prices in the United States Gulf market—which at that time directly influenced the market value and prices in the Middle East—together with the artificial freezing of gold prices by the United States and British governments, King Ibn Saud pressed for a larger payment. The King's request was strengthened by the formal institution in 1948 of the 50–50 sharing of net earnings in Venezuela, the devaluation of the British pound in 1949, and the potential threat to increased outlets owing to British discrimination against oil produced by dollar companies. Aramco, indeed, faced somewhat the same dilemma as Creole had faced in 1942, and Saudi Arabia's need was similar to Venezuela's at that time. For a time King Ibn Saud required Aramco to pay its royalty in gold sovereigns, which made it necessary for the company to make special arrangements with the United States government for buying gold. Late in 1950 an equal sharing of profits was agreed upon, with the stipulation that the four-shilling gold royalty payments should be converted to dollar or sterling equivalent at International Monetary Fund rates and taxes could be paid in the monies Aramco received for the oil sold.[64]

By the end of 1950, Jersey had acquired important production in the Eastern Hemisphere. In Europe it had lost its properties in Romania and Hungary, but it had carried on a search for oil in the Netherlands, Germany, France, and North Africa that was to lead to significant developments in later years. Most important at the time was its acquisition of a large interest in Arabian American Oil Company. After more than two decades of complex negotiations and many disappointments, the company had finally obtained a position in the Middle East of a magnitude proportionate to that which it held in European markets. In Iraq, Qatar, and Saudi Arabia, its share of oil reserves was an estimated 4 billion barrels in 1950.[65]

Thus Standard Oil Company (New Jersey) had realized an objective toward which it had been moving since the 1920's. It not only had attained a strong position in its supply of crude oil from its owned reserves and production; it had also gained substantial holdings in strategic places around the globe. This assurance of raw materials from favorable locations enabled the company to develop the other branches of its foreign operations so as to meet its leading competitors on equal terms in the Eastern as well as the Western Hemisphere.

Chapter 28

Developments in Petroleum Transport
at Home and Abroad, 1946–1950

I N TRANSPORTATION, as in production, the most significant growth in the investments and operations of Standard Oil Company (New Jersey) in this period came outside the United States. Both its pipeline and tanker transport facilities were expanded far more abroad than at home. Within the United States the Jersey companies were concerned more particularly with raising operating efficiency and reducing maintenance costs than with expansion. Abroad, the replacing of wartime losses and a program of expansion enabled affiliates to acquire new transport facilities and in so doing to avail themselves of technological advances made during the war.

The parent company did not at this time have the degree of coordination in the planning and operating of transport facilities that it had developed in relation to producing, refining, and marketing. But it made progress in that direction in these postwar years. In 1951 the Board of Directors established a staff department to coordinate the company's various transportation interests.

PIPELINE INVESTMENT AND MANAGEMENT

There was no pipeline specialist on the Jersey Board of Directors. Bushrod B. Howard was contact director for oil pipeline affiliates, but his specialty was marine transport. Wallace R. Finney, who had been appointed to the Office of Pipe Line Advisor in 1944, counseled the board on matters having to do with this type of carrier and served as consultant to companies in which Jersey had a minority interest as well as to those it largely or wholly owned.

The wartime technological development which indicated the feasibility of the construction and operation of large-diameter lines had a marked effect on pipeline building in the later 1940's. The Big Inch line had demonstrated the substantial cost advantage of large lines and the feasibility of joint ownership by two or more nonaffiliated companies to make such carriers economically possible. Abroad, where production on large concessions or even in fields developed by more than one company provided enough volume to build large-diameter lines, such pipelines could be built by the company or companies producing the oil. At home, with competitive development of oil fields together with the possibility of violation of antitrust law by joint building of pipelines, it was more difficult to provide sufficient oil to make the building of large-diameter lines practicable.

The Jersey Company's investments in pipelines during the five postwar years ran into hundreds of millions of dollars. Table 24 summarizes the growth in the trunk-line mileage of its interests and the increase in the volume of oil carried. While the mileage in the United States in 1950 was only 6 per cent above that of 1946, the mileage abroad was nearly twice as large in the later as in the earlier year. The barrel-miles of oil transported grew in approximately the same proportions. However, the increase at home came early in the postwar period while that abroad came at a later time.

Creole built the first major pipeline constructed by Jersey affiliates after the war. Of 24- to 26-inch diameter, this 145-mile pipeline provided the low-cost transportation from oil fields necessary to enable the new Amuay refinery to turn out products at competitive costs. Reaching from Ulé on Lake Maracaibo to Creole's new deepwater terminal and refinery on Amuay Bay, it traversed extensive wasteland and the Gulf of Coro. Its construction was delayed nearly a year by difficulties in getting steel casing and export permits in the United States, but by December, 1948, it was ready with enough power in the initial station at Ulé to take 150,000 barrels per day. Its capacity was soon doubled by the completion of a pumping station midway on the line and by increasing the power of the Ulé station. Until the new refinery at Amuay went on stream late in 1950, special shallow-draft lake tankers carried the crude from the ocean terminal at Amuay to the Aruba refinery. This pipeline, which together with terminal facilities cost approximately $48,000,000, replaced twenty-five of the small tankers making the trip by water from the Bolívar coastal fields to Aruba. These obsolete vessels were then scrapped.[1]

The second large pipeline built in the Western Hemisphere provided economical transport to refineries for the oil produced on the prairies of Alberta, Canada, by Imperial and other companies. The building of two

Table 24: **MILEAGE AND DAILY AVERAGE AND ANNUAL THROUGHPUT OF AFFILIATES' OIL PIPELINES, 1946, 1948, AND 1950**
Standard Oil Company (New Jersey)

	Miles of Line Operated at Year End			Thousands of 42-Gallon Barrels Transported Daily			Millions of Barrel-Miles Transported		
	1946	1948	1950	1946	1948	1950	1946	1948	1950
Trunk Lines									
United States									
Humble P.L. Co.	5,769	5,757	5,987	619.0	758.6	595.1	38,344	46,830	45,185
Interstate Oil P.L. Co.	2,992	3,163	3,063	343.7	420.9	431.3	16,994	20,647	19,315
Plantation P.L. Co.[a]	1,261	1,261	1,261	59.4	97.3	103.9	13,168	20,123	20,337
Transit & Storage Co.	454	454	454	30.7	44.9	31.1	1,695	2,484	2,372
Tuscarora Oil Co.	619	623	567	27.5	44.2	46.0	1,966	2,332	2,542
Ajax P.L. Co.[b]	819	819	819	78.1	79.4	79.0	11,289	11,512	11,424
Portland P.L. Co.[c]	173	173	340	52.6	66.2	74.4	3,244	4,100	4,512
Lakehead P.L. Co.[d]	—	—	324	—	—	1.1	—	—	132
Total in United States	12,087	12,250	12,815	1,203.2	1,511.5	1,361.9	86,700	108,028	105,819
Foreign									
Andian National Corp.	667	668	668	36.6	40.5	58.2	4,469	3,717	6,282
Creole Petroleum Corp.[e]	311	443	474	327.6	341.4	783.9	8,479	9,043	24,015
Tropical Oil Co.[f]	—	66	66	—	3.6	4.9	—	88	118
Montreal P.L. Co.	76	76	149	52.5	66.2	74.0	1,453	1,836	2,051
Valley P.L. Co.[g]	96	96	—	15.9	11.7	—	185	135	—
Imperial P.L. Co.[h]	—	16	39	—	1.5	20.5	—	15	127
Interprovincial P.L. Co.[i]	—	—	803	—	—	5.9	—	—	1,318
Winnipeg P.L. Co.[j]	—	—	72	—	—	0.4	—	—	10
Iraq P.L. Co.[k]	1,153	1,153	1,064	87.6	61.3	126.5	18,426	12,483	24,557
Trans-Arabian P.L. Co.[l]	—	—	1,068	—	—	15.4	—	—	6,008
Total Foreign	2,303	2,518	4,403	520.2	526.2	1,089.7	33,012	27,317	64,486
Gathering Lines									
United States									
Humble P.L. Co.	2,666	3,068	3,367	507.9	608.5	475.8			
Interstate Oil P.L. Co.	1,227	1,408	1,396	202.7	289.5	299.2			
Total in United States	3,893	4,476	4,763	710.6	898.0	775.0			
Foreign[m]									
Imperial P.L. Co.	—	54	150	—	11.7	53.7			

[a] Total figures are given for this company; Jersey's interest was 50.4 per cent until it dropped to 48.85 per cent in 1950.
[b] Total figures for this company. Jersey affiliates, Imperial Oil Limited, The Carter Oil Company, and Esso Standard Oil Company, together owned approximately 56 per cent of the common and 40 per cent of its voting stock.
[c] Jersey sold its stock in April, 1946, to Imperial and three other Canadian companies.
[d] Fully owned affiliate of Interprovincial Pipe Line Company, which went into operation November 28, 1950.
[e] Includes lines in which it shared ownership with Mene Grande Oil Company.
[f] Products pipeline from Barrancabermeja refinery operating by the end of 1947.
[g] Properties sold February 10, 1949.
[h] Started operations October 8, 1948.
[i] Started operations October 4, 1950. Imperial Oil held 49.9 per cent of its stock.
[j] Started operations December 4, 1950. Imperial Oil held all the stock.
[k] Jersey, through half-interest in Near East Development Corporation, held almost 12 per cent of stock. Line to Haifa closed.
[l] Jersey held 30 per cent of stock of Tapline, which began operations late in 1950.
[m] Only Imperial reported gathering lines.
Source: Standard Oil Company (New Jersey), Annual Statistical Review, 1946, 1948, and 1950.

long trunk carriers was considered: one to the Pacific and the other to the Great Lakes. Jersey's Pipe Line Advisor and his staff made the studies preliminary to the planning of a line from the oil fields of Alberta over the mountains to Vancouver, but the 24-inch, 718-mile crude line to the Pacific Coast was not built until after 1950. In April, 1949, Imperial organized Interprovincial Pipe Line Company to build to the Great Lakes. It purchased just under 50 per cent of the stock and sold the majority to the public. For additional funds, $72,000,000 of 3½ per cent twenty-year bonds and $17,000,000 of twenty-one-year 4 per cent convertible debentures were sold to insurance companies and investors in Canada and the United States. Construction was begun during the winter of 1949–1950. The line ran 1,126 miles from the Redwater field via Regina to Superior, Wisconsin, at the western end of Lake Superior. The segment from the Canadian boundary to the lake was held by Lakehead Pipe Line Company, a wholly owned subsidiary of Interprovincial Pipe Line. A 75-mile spur, owned by a subsidiary of Imperial, was built from the Canadian main line to the new refinery at Winnipeg.[2]

The first delivery to the storage station and tanker terminal at Superior, Wisconsin, was made on December 5, 1950. Once the Great Lakes were open to navigation in the spring, Imperial had sufficient lake tankers, owned or chartered, to carry oil to its refinery at Sarnia, Ontario, or farther to the east. No longer did the middle provinces have to get crude by expensive rail transport from Texas and the Mid-Continent; Sarnia, also, could obtain Canadian crude to take the place of Mid-Continent oil from the United States transported long distances by pipeline.

In the Eastern Hemisphere, Jersey joined with other companies in building pipelines to provide additional low-cost transport to the Mediterranean as an alternative route to shipment by tanker from the Persian Gulf around the Arabian Peninsula and through the Suez Canal. After the war, the Iraq Petroleum Company was able to get quick approval from the British and other governments for the doubling of its line from Kirkuk to the Mediterranean. In 1945, using plans drawn up by Jersey's H. S. Austin, this company began laying a 16-inch line to Haifa, where two corporate shareholders of the Iraq company had a refinery. However, shortly before this project was completed in 1948, hostilities between the Israelis and the Arabs stopped construction. These disturbances also forced the closing of the old route to Haifa and left in operation only the 12-inch pipe to Tripoli with a daily capacity of approximately 42,000 barrels. Work was accelerated on a parallel 16-inch line of 532 miles, which went into operation in July, 1950, with a daily capacity of 95,000 barrels. The owners of Iraq Petroleum at the same time were planning another pipeline to the Mediterranean at Baniyas in Syria and connecting lines from the Mosul oil fields, and also a line from the Basrah field to a loading terminal on the Euphrates River.[3]

Late in the 1940's, Jersey participated as a 30 per cent owner in a still more ambitious undertaking by Trans-Arabian Pipe Line Company (Tapline) and Arabian American Oil Company. This was a 30- and 31-inch line reaching 1,068 miles from Abqaiq near the Persian Gulf to a terminal near Sidon, Lebanon, on the Mediterranean Sea. Besides Saudi Arabia, Tapline crossed Transjordan, Syria, and Lebanon. Jersey's Wallace R. Finney acted in a consulting capacity in the drawing up of engineering plans for this undertaking. Although delays were met in getting the necessary right of way in each transit country, deliveries to tankers at Sidon were begun in December, 1950. Tapline's capacity, after pumping stations were operating as planned, was 300,000 barrels daily. The Aramco section of 314 miles cost $50,200,000; Tapline's from Qaisumah to the terminal on the Mediterranean cost $151,200,000. These totals included pumping stations and the terminal at Sidon.[4]

Jersey was also interested in another big-inch project in the Middle East. As arranged in the American company's oil-purchase agreement with Anglo-Iranian, Middle East Pipelines, Limited, was incorporated in Great Britain in 1947 to construct and operate a pipeline to bring oil from the fields of Iran and Kuwait to the Mediterranean. The British company was to take half the stock and Jersey and Socony the remainder. However, difficulties in getting rights of way across some countries and in arranging transit payments resulted in the dropping of the project. Jersey's purchase agreement with Anglo-Iranian was then revised to provide for taking the crude from the Middle East by tanker.[5]

These long Middle East pipelines showed the increasing vitality of the oil industry of that region. It was no daydream that made American oilmen talk of the shifting of the center of gravity of the world's petroleum industry from the Gulf-Caribbean to the Middle East—or that raised concern among Western Hemisphere producers over the competition of the eastern oil even in the Atlantic seaboard markets of the United States.

Within the United States, the Jersey affiliates made no great changes in the pattern of their trunk lines. Yet the discovery of new fields and competition at home, as well as rising competition from abroad, forced them to make or plan investments for building new lines and upgrading old ones. Most of the construction was delayed by the shortage of steel until late in the decade, and it was affected by a new problem in financing improvements and additions.

This financial problem resulted from a provision of the pipeline consent decree of 1941. (See Chapter 15.) Earnings above the 7 per cent allowed for dividends could be reinvested but could not be counted in the valuation on which future dividends were based. In fact, the actual valuation of existing lines was not yet clearly determinable. It was reasonably certain that construction financed by borrowed funds could be counted in a pipeline company's valuation, but shipper-owners normally did not like to finance pipeline building by borrowing and had customarily used earnings for this purpose.

The affiliates' old lines faced handicaps in competing with younger pipelines. Because the old were of small diameter and had obsolete power systems, they were far more costly to operate, per unit of volume carried, than were the newer large-diameter lines with more efficient pumping stations. In the postwar years it was economically desirable—because of the greater efficiency of lines of larger diameter—for Jersey's domestic affiliates to participate with other companies in building certain such carriers. But joint ownership was not advisable in some circumstances, particularly for legal reasons; nor was it practicable for constructing new or rebuilding old lines that were part of an already established system.

The domestic affiliates constructed several new lines. In 1946 Humble Pipe Line Company built one to carry products from Baytown to the Dallas–Fort Worth area. The whole project, including marketing terminals, cost $6,000,000. This line carried gasoline at a considerable saving compared with tank-car and transport-truck charges.[6] When enough pipe became available in 1949, Humble also started to build a long line for moving West Texas crude, which was then being shipped by high-cost tank cars. This new carrier ran 370 miles from the convergence of several Humble pipelines at Kemper in West Texas to the main trunk at Satsuma, near Houston, whence oil was carried by pipelines to Gulf Coast refineries and tanker terminals. This 18-inch project, designed to carry 136,000 barrels daily and costing $14,500,000, was completed in 1950.[7] The Interstate Oil Pipe Line Company built several shorter lines—

one in Montana, from Elk Basin to the Billings refinery, and a feeder system to connect new fields in Mississippi with the Baton Rouge refinery.[8]

Contrary to the policy of expanding its domestic oil pipeline interests, Jersey disposed of its holdings in interstate gas transmission lines acquired late in the 1920's. The company had become concerned that the United States Department of Justice might question its participation in the gas pipelines. There was also the further consideration that investments elsewhere might yield a better return than the 6 per cent limit on gas transmission lines. In November, 1947, Jersey sold to the public its minority interests in Natural Gas Pipeline Company of America and in Colorado Interstate Gas Company. The next year it sold to a group headed by Union Securities Corporation its minority participation in Mississippi River Fuel Corporation. It retained its majority interest in Interstate Natural Gas Company until 1953, when it sold its shares to Olin Industries, Inc.[9]

The major problems of the domestic oil pipeline affiliates were obsolescence and high maintenance costs. Tuscarora, Interstate, and Humble all suffered from the aging of their lines. Consequently, their main task was to upgrade their systems. In doing so they had to choose among possible alternatives. Should old carriers be kept but modified to bring about more economical operations, such as might be achieved by the installation of pumps run by electric power? Would the saving in operating costs justify scrapping largely or wholly depreciated old facilities and incurring the long-term capital costs of building new ones? Would the future business be sufficient to justify the heavy fixed costs of new lines? Was it advisable—under the pipeline consent decree's limitation on the distribution of net earnings as dividends to 7 per cent of the Interstate Commerce Commission's valuation—to incur the capital costs necessary for construction? In order to assure capacity operations, new facilities might require the transporting of much common-carrier oil—there might not even be enough business to make efficient carriage possible.

Many old pipelines simply had to be replaced, either because their maintenance costs had become intolerably high or because they were too small to carry the required volume. The old trunk line from Moore station in northern Louisiana to Baton Rouge was rebuilt and enlarged. The Tuscarora products line in Pennsylvania, because it had to reduce costs and increase capacity, was also largely rebuilt and its capacity doubled.

The capacity of the 489-mile Portland-Montreal system was doubled by building a new line parallel to the old one. Jersey sold this system to Imperial and several other Canadian companies.[10]

Where it was not immediately urgent to increase capacity, the question of whether or not to rebuild old pipelines was given intensive study before plans were developed. This was done by Finney and his staff in New York and also by the pipeline affiliates themselves. Humble Pipe Line Company, for instance, in 1949 set up a new planning and economics division to make a thorough examination of this problem. The studies were not completed until after 1950, but they then provided a sound basis for decisions.[11]

In the same postwar years, progress was also made in reducing the maintenance and operating costs of pipelines. Jersey's Finney said in 1948: "In addition to large-diameter pipelines and wide station spacing, the Jersey pipeline group is pushing a research and development program to improve its operating methods and to lower maintenance expense. Generally, the possibilities in the pipeline field are being expanded daily by new ideas and experiments."[12]

A great deal was done to reduce corrosion in pipelines and storage tanks and the resulting loss of oil and high maintenance expense. For two decades the industry had been carrying on research on this specific problem. The installation of floating roofs on storage tanks was found to inhibit rust formation by reducing the space between the oil and the roof that was conducive to corrosion. Likewise, the introduction of cathodic protection on the pipelines, which lessened electrolytic action, decreased corrosion and cut down on the loss of oil and maintenance costs. These preventive measures became increasingly important as systems became older and as more pipelines and storage tanks were exposed to salt water—for example, in bayou country, on the continental shelf, and in Lake Maracaibo. Creole's extensive operations on this large body of water in Venezuela were subject to an especially high corrosion rate resulting from the unusual amount of electrolytic action induced by the ebb and flow of salty tidal water in the fresh water of the lake.[13]

The reduction of the costs of oil pipelines also took other forms. The installation of more efficient power in pumping stations increased the capacity of lines. Better scheduling of oil movement made some difference. Aerial inspection, instead of the old walking or riding along the lines to look for leaks, brought a considerable saving of manpower. Work on automatic controls, although not applied extensively in this period, foreshadowed the considerable application of automation that was to come in the 1950's.[14]

OIL TRANSPORT ON INLAND AND COASTAL WATERWAYS

The tankers and barges for local and long-distance movement of oil on waterways within continents, along coasts, and between islands were in great need of attention after the war. Many such carriers that had been lost during the war, especially in the Eastern Hemisphere, had to be replaced. Everywhere, old watercraft had to be improved or scrapped as obsolete. The tonnage also had to be increased in order to carry larger volumes of oil.

A great deal of replacement was necessary in the Eastern Hemisphere. On the Continent of Europe, the affiliates had lost nearly all their barges and tankers for carrying oil to terminals up rivers and along coasts. These now had to be replaced. In Great Britain also, it was necessary to build new craft—especially coastal tankers—to take the place of those lost during the war and the ones that had to be scrapped. Standard-Vacuum in the Far East had lost virtually all its regional and local oil carriers— from tankers to sampans—in the countries overcome by the enemy. Restoring the physical facilities for the distribution of oil products by water was one of the large costs of rebuilding the operations of Jersey affiliates in much of the hemisphere.

In the United States, the need was for the addition of tonnage and the reduction of costs. Better scheduling and the speeding up of loading and unloading resulted in some cost reduction. But in general the major requirements were more tonnage and the replacement of obsolescent watercraft and equipment.

This was a time of great advances in inland water transport in the United States. The federal program for dredging and damming the Ohio River and the Tennessee and for similar works on the Misssissippi increased the depth and the reliability of the water level on those great inland waterways. The design of towboats and barges was greatly changed. The old stern paddle wheel was replaced by twin screws fitted with rudders both forward and aft. The new towboats were powered by diesel engines and had vastly increased power. These improvements provided the towboats and their barges with greater maneuverability and reliability and higher speed.

Standard Oil Company of New Jersey (Esso Standard) was the largest

Marine Department. More than a score of smaller tankers were also bought.[18]

These vessels were of varied age and quality, and many had to be reconditioned. Some were among the largest and fastest wartime tankers, in particular the T-2s purchased from the Maritime Commission. These ships were each of 16,500 deadweight tons, 15-knot speed, and 138,000-barrel capacity. On most routes, they carried a barrel of oil at a cost 25 per cent less than that of the next older type of tanker of 13,000 tonnage and 12-knot speed, and at a cost from 30 to 40 per cent less than that of the still older 11,000-ton ocean tankers.[19]

Jersey participated in the oil industry's postwar movement to build newer and still larger ships, which gathered momentum as materials and shipyards became available. Late in 1948 it was reported that 280 large tankers were being built for the oil trade, many in British and Swedish yards. Jersey had ordered the construction in American shipyards—at a total cost of $75,000,000—of 12 "supertankers" of 26,800 deadweight tons, with a speed of 16 knots and a capacity of 230,000 barrels. These tankers, designed by the company's Marine Department, were twice the size of the Jersey tankers built in the late 1930's.[20]

As before the war, the United States–flag fleet was severely handicapped by operating costs that were higher than those of ships of other flags, the result in considerable part of the American seamen's higher wages. In addition, ships registered in Panama and used in international trade were exempt from income tax in that country; and in 1941 the governments of Panama and the United States had agreed to exempt shipping companies incorporated under each other's laws from taxes on income.[21] The cost difference between United States–flag and foreign tankers was such that to bring a barrel of fuel oil in 1947 by T-2 tanker from Aruba to New York cost 27 cents for a United States–flag ship but only 20.5 cents for a ship of foreign registry.[22] In the trade between points in the United States, for example from Gulf to Atlantic ports, American tankers had no such competition because foreign ships were excluded from this service.

The dollar ships—both the United States–flag vessels and the Panamanian—had to face serious sterling exchange problems. The resulting restrictions were not too burdensome so long as there was a threat of oil shortages in Europe, but the handicap became serious when Great Britain's exchange and oil import regulations became more stringent. The United States–flag ships were given some help, however, by the requirement, applied under the Marshall Plan, that at least 50 per cent of the commodities shipped in international trade financed by the United States government must be carried by ships flying this country's flag.

The long-term solution of this exchange problem was to enlarge the tanker fleets of affiliates operating in sterling countries or other areas short of dollars. Jersey began to help its foreign affiliates to rebuild their fleets as soon as possible after the war. Aside from Standard-Vacuum's shipping company, the ocean carriers of the Jersey affiliates in the Eastern Hemisphere immediately after the war were one tanker of a Belgian affiliate and the fleets of Anglo-American and Esso Transportation Company, Limited (Lago Shipping until 1946). Rebuilding and enlarging those fleets conformed to Jersey's prewar policy of registering tankers in European countries for their trade and provided tankers for carrying Middle East oil from pipeline terminals to European refineries. By far the largest increase was in the British-flag fleets, which were enlarged soon after the war by transfers from Western Hemisphere affiliates as well as by purchases from the government of the United Kingdom. Payment for transfers from dollar countries had to be arranged through negotiations with individual governments.

Getting payment for tankers transferred from dollar countries was not too difficult as long as there was a shortage of ships. In 1949, however, the shifting of Panama Transport tankers to British registry became virtually impossible even though Jersey was willing to take payment in sterling to be used by its affiliates.[23] Consequently, as far as possible orders were placed for the building of new tankers in sterling countries.

The Jersey fleets, like the tankers of the American oil industry generally, in 1949 began to suffer from the expansion of the first postwar years. As late as the middle of 1948, Gamble, then manager of Jersey's Marine Department, had likened the position of the department to that of "a man walking ahead on a fast moving treadmill and having difficulty in holding his own." Only a year later, however, the need for tankers had fallen off so greatly that, although Jersey had immobilized or otherwise disposed of sixty-seven vessels—the equal of forty-eight T-2s—there was still a prospect of a further surplus of oil-carrying ships. Not only was the lay-up program costly, especially the negotiations leading to the cancellation of period-charter contracts and those for building two supertankers; it also idled a thousand tankermen. The company's United States–flag fleet and the ships registered in Panama were most seriously affected.[24]

There were several reasons for this temporary oversupply of tankers.

volume to Great Britain. Toward the latter part of the year, the war in Korea brought some increase in the demand for products for the military services and at the same time stimulated stockpiling.[27]

When their trade again increased in 1950, the Jersey affiliates had far more efficient fleets than they had had in the early postwar boom. The oversupply of tonnage of late 1948 and 1949 had made possible and, in fact, had rendered imperative the sale for scrap of many obsolete American and foreign tankers. In 1949 and 1950, American shipyards delivered to Jersey the twelve new supertankers that the company had ordered soon after the war. The first of these vessels, the *Esso Zurich*, entered service as a United States–flag ship in January, 1949. One super-tanker went to Panama Transport and eleven to Esso Shipping Company. Orders had been placed in England for six similar ships, but they did not become available until after 1950.

Important as the development of the T-2s had been, the supertankers marked even a greater advance.* Although their deadweight tonnage was 26,800, because of their more efficient equipment they needed about the same size crew as the T-2s and even smaller tankers. The cost differential per barrel of cargo was therefore considerable. It was estimated that, if it cost 27 cents to bring a barrel of fuel oil from Aruba to New York in a United States–flag T-2 tanker, the cost by supertanker under the same registry would be 20 cents. Of course, only the largest harbors and piers could accommodate the new 628-foot ships, which had a 31.5-foot draft when fully loaded. Even so, it was cheaper to bring fuel on large tankers from Aruba to smaller North Atlantic ports by first unloading a part of the cargo in New York or at some other large port. Then with a load suffi-ciently under capacity, the ships could move on and discharge the rest of their cargoes at some secondary harbor. Most of the latter could not take ships of more than a 27-foot draft.[28]

By the end of 1950, the Jersey affiliates, not including Standard-Vacuum, had 117 ocean-going tankers totaling 2,013,000 deadweight tons; at the end of 1945, they had had 89 such tankers totaling 1,322,000 tons. Of the 117, the 52 United States–flag ships had an average age of seven and a half years, and the 49 flying the flags of the United Kingdom, Canada, and Panama averaged nine and a half years. The remaining 16 ocean tankers were registered in several countries on the European

---

* Actually, even larger tankers could have been built except that ways and drydocks were not large enough and many harbors were not sufficiently deep.

Continent.[29] The total tonnage of ocean, lake, and special-service tankers had increased more than 50 per cent. The efficiency of the British-, Panamanian-, Canadian-, and United States–flag ships owned by the affiliates had been greatly improved. In addition, fleets of Jersey companies in Europe had been restored and thus enabled to contribute to the Jersey Company's standing in sterling areas and in the soft-currency trade.

A large part of these developments in oil transport after the war was along customary lines: providing additional facilities for moving an expanding volume and raising efficiency in order to minimize costs. However, the normal process was made complicated at this time by the unusual amount of wear and obsolescence resulting from the war and by postwar difficulties in foreign exchange. There were two especially significant new developments: the reduction of unit costs by the use of larger pipelines and tankers and more efficient power; and the establishment of new routes for oil transport. The latter provided outlets for the Jersey Company's new sources of crude oil in Canada and the Middle East. In fact, such postwar developments in transportation contributed to the creation of a new framework for the worldwide movement of crude oil and products.

transshipment from shallow-draft Lake Maracaibo tankers to ocean-going vessels.

The construction of Creole's new refinery was begun in 1946 at Amuay Bay on the west coast of the Paraguaná Peninsula. Ocean tankers could load for foreign markets at Amuay; as estimated, shipment to Europe by tanker would cost only slightly more from Amuay than from Aruba. The original plan was to build a plant at a cost of $65,000,000 to process 60,000 barrels daily. But both capacity and costs rose as the plans were finally worked out and the refinery was built; the cost rose to $203,000,-000. Several plant units, including an atmospheric crude still, went into operation in January, 1950, and a vacuum still and asphalt equipment were completed later in the year. The pipeline from the Lake Maracaibo oil fields and also an ocean terminal were already in operation and were delivering crude to tankers at Amuay Bay.[7]

The building of this refinery was a beachhead operation in a barren and almost uninhabited region. Even potable water was lacking in quantity. In order to obtain an adequate supply, Creole, Royal Dutch–Shell's Caribbean Petroleum Company (which was building a refinery nearby), and the Venezuelan government built an aqueduct from mountains more than sixty miles from Amuay. Creole had to provide living quarters and the usual camp facilities for its regular employees at the refinery. But here, by special arrangement with the government, it encouraged them to build their own homes and community facilities and to form a self-governing village. The company assisted with the planning and financing of their building.[8]

With its acquisition of a large volume of crude in the Middle East, Jersey had to increase its refining capacity in the Eastern Hemisphere; in fact, its over-all plan was to set up a complete Middle East–Europe oil circuit in order to give its affiliates a firmer competitive position in European markets. However, instead of processing most of the oil near its source—as Jersey had long done in Romania and Sumatra and Aramco had done at the Ras Tanura refinery built during the war to provide products for American military forces in the Southwest Pacific[9]—the company did more refining in the countries consuming the products. By this time, the potential sales of Anglo-American were sufficient to justify large refining operations in England. However, in England, on the Continent, and in the Orient, refinery location after the war came to be determined largely by national policies and particularly by governmental exchange regulations. The latter made it imperative for the Jersey affiliates to refine within a country in order to keep import costs and dollar costs of products as low as possible.

In Europe, Jersey acquired new refineries in countries where it sold products. In Italy, which was economically exhausted at the end of the war and adopted national regulations for building up the economy, it obtained an interest in refineries at Bari and Leghorn. These had formerly been owned by the government but were turned over to an Italian company known as Anic. Since the owners had neither the capital nor the technical resources required for restoring and enlarging the plants after the war, these were placed under a new corporation, Stanic-Industria Petrolifera Società per Azioni, owned in equal parts by Jersey and the Italian company.[10] The Belgian affiliate was building a new refinery at Antwerp.[11] The one being constructed by Anglo-American was by far the most important of those planned by affiliates in the Eastern Hemisphere after the war. Although adjacent to the old Fawley plant and bearing its name, this refinery was completely new. It was located near the historic New Forest in the vicinity of Southampton.

Undertaking to build the Fawley refinery late in the 1940's involved considerable risk, but the risk was taken in order to protect Anglo-American's position in the markets of the United Kingdom. Jersey had to negotiate with the British government the conditions under which it could finance the building of the refinery and supply it with crude. It arranged to provide the plant with its own share of the oil produced by Iraq Petroleum and additional crude to be purchased from Anglo-Iranian, and it worked out acceptable plans for furnishing capital funds. Under the agreement finally made, about one-third of the investment of approximately $105,000,000 in this plant from 1949 to 1954 was in dollars and the remainder in sterling. The refinery went into operation in September, 1951. Britain's Prime Minister Clement Attlee gave an address at its dedication ceremony. With its daily capacity of 120,000 barrels, the Fawley refinery was then one of the two largest in Europe. It had the latest equipment, including a catalytic cracking unit. It also had a marine terminal where seagoing tankers discharged their cargoes and coastwise tankers took on most of the refinery's output for shipping to marine terminals throughout the British Isles.[12]

In the Orient, Standard-Vacuum located new plants within consuming countries where it had not previously carried on refining. It built a lubricating-oil and asphalt plant in Melbourne, Australia, which was completed in 1949. In that same year, it entered into negotiations for the construction of a plant at Bombay, India, and it also joined with minority Japanese interests in organizing a new concern to acquire two small refineries in Japan for processing imported crude. In 1950, it announced plans to build a 10,000-barrels-per-day refinery at Durban in the Union of South Africa.[13]

At the same time that new refineries were being planned and built, heavy investments were being made in old refineries. In this work also, there were great differences between the Eastern and the Western Hemisphere.

Most of the old plants on the European Continent and in the Orient had virtually been destroyed. These were now rebuilt, enlarged, and upgraded by the installation of the more advanced equipment. Among them were the refineries at Port Jérôme in France, Hamburg in Germany, Vallö in Norway, and Sungei Gerong in Sumatra. Because of the foreign-exchange situation, arrangements were made with the respective European governments for financing construction. These rebuilt plants, together with the new ones built or planned, in time provided Jersey affiliates with refining facilities in many countries in which they marketed in Europe and the Orient.

In the Western Hemisphere the general policy was to modernize the large refineries and increase their capacity and to abandon the small ones with obsolete equipment and without enough market potential to warrant expensive new installations. Among the plants closed by Jersey affiliates were the old Humble refineries at Ingleside and San Antonio in Texas and Creole's at La Salina in Venezuela.[14]

The companies spent large sums on old refineries. Imperial enlarged most of its plants in Canada and installed new equipment, the major investment being made at the Montreal refinery. The companies in the United States made substantial changes at Bayway, Baltimore, Baton Rouge, and Baytown. Because of the building of the new refinery at Amuay, little was spent on the Aruba refinery. The same was true of Creole's at Caripito, the four small units in Argentina, and the plant in Cuba. The Barrancabermeja refinery in Colombia was about to be turned over to the government in accordance with the De Mares concession agreement. The most important addition in Latin America was the building of new housing and community facilities for employees of the refinery at Talara, Peru. International Petroleum spent approximately $11,000,000 on this necessary and well-planned modernization project.[15]

The major portion of these postwar capital expenditures carried forward among the affiliates the developments in refining that for some time had been changing the basic character of the industry from the simple separation and finishing of oil fractions to what can rightly be called manufacturing.[16] The most important changes in equipment were the addition and enlargement of units for catalytic cracking and vacuum distillation. The role of the catalyst in refining had become especially important, and the "cat cracker" was becoming a familiar figure on the skyline of most Jersey refineries. These new cracking units ranged in size from one at Bayway with a daily capacity of 41,000 barrels to a 10,000-barrel unit at Billings. The cracking and vacuum units made possible the upgrading of gasolines and provided components for the manufacture of other valuable products.[17]

The changes in refining equipment and processes were based on the work of expanding organizations for research and development. Standard Oil Development Company (later Esso Research and Engineering) continued to play the principal and the coordinating role. Its new Esso Research Center at Linden, New Jersey, was opened in 1948 with working facilities for about 600 persons; it had the most advanced technical equipment and one of the largest industrial libraries in the country. Groups at Baton Rouge and Baytown also carried on extensive research in the general field of petroleum chemistry, and a number of foreign operations expanded work tailored to their particular needs. Esso Development Company, Limited, in England conducted and coordinated research, development, and patent work for the benefit of affiliates in Europe.[18]

These research and development groups made improvements in catalysts and catalytic cracking, isomerization, vacuum distillation, and other techniques. They made progress in the development of a new type of coking operation to convert heavy residual fuel into lighter and more valuable products, an operation that employed the fluid principle used so successfully in catalytic cracking. They also did much work on lubricants and jet fuels. They applied hydroforming to the manufacture of high-quality gasoline fractions. In the field of petrochemicals, they improved the manufacturing process and the quality of iso-octyl alcohol and made progress in work on protective coatings, additives, and detergents. Their extensive research in anticipation of future needs discovered new ways of making liquid fuels from coal, shale, and natural gas, but the plentiful supply of crude oil made these types of manufacture uneconomic at the time. Company scientists and engineers followed developments closely in atomic energy, although they did little actual research in that field in the 1940's. However, Jersey men participated in the work of the United States Atomic Energy Commission. Marion W. Boyer of Esso Standard served from 1950 to 1953 as the commission's general manager, and Eger V. Murphree of Standard Oil Development in 1950 became a member of its advisory committee.[19]

The research findings applied to the improvement of refining processes had two important results. Products were kept abreast of competition at a time when the quality race was becoming more intensive than ever; and the technologically advanced refineries produced less residual and a larger percentage of the more valuable light products—especially gasoline and middle distillates—from a barrel of crude. The less valuable fuel oil was supplied largely from the Caribbean area, where it was made from heavy Venezuelan crudes.[20]

Hand in hand with improvements in equipment, processes, and products went efforts to reduce costs. Better cost control in general made for substantial savings, while the more extensive use of automation and improved training of personnel brought some reductions. However, many costs were not subject to engineering or managerial controls. Insofar as costs rose generally throughout the industry in a country, they were not of great competitive significance locally, but differences from country to country could be of importance to the Jersey companies.

No essentially new products were introduced in the late 1940's. The Jersey refineries were principally concerned with the mass production of gasoline, kerosene, distillates, and residual fuels. Gasolines and residuals constituted nearly three-fourths of the total volume of these major products. Lubricants continued to be important, as did asphalt and—especially in the more advanced plants—such chemical products as additives for gasolines and motor oils, butadiene, Butyl rubber, and alcohols.

One policy question was discussed in this period with considerable difference of view within the parent company and the domestic affiliates: to what extent should the Jersey group increase its manufacture of chemicals from crude oil and gas, especially end products? Jersey itself is generally considered to have produced the first commercial petrochemical. This was isopropyl alcohol, which it made at Bayway in 1920 on the basis of a process developed by Carleton Ellis involving acid absorption of propylene from refinery-cracked gases followed by hydrolysis.[21] In the late 1920's and the 1930's, the manufacture of petrochemicals had been developed slowly but definitely by a few specialized chemical concerns and oil companies. Among the latter in the United States, the leaders had been Jersey—with its alcohol, gasoline and motor-oil additives, and synthetic rubbers—and Shell, which in 1929 had organized Shell Chemical Company to own and operate an ammonia plant in California and carry on any other chemical manufacture Shell might undertake in this country. World War II gave a tremendous spur to petrochemical production. At the end of the war, Jersey and Shell were still at the top among American oil companies in the manufacture of chemical products from petroleum. Jersey ranked especially high in supplying chemical companies with intermediate products in large quantities. For example, in 1945 Tennessee Eastman Corporation was taking the entire ethyl alcohol output of Bayway and Baton Rouge—some 15,500,000 gallons—and was asking for more, while Hercules and Du Pont were also wanting to purchase the same product.[22]

Although there was little peacetime experience for guidance, there was no question at the end of the war but that the petrochemical industry was here to stay. Chemicals still made up a minor part of the total investments and sales of Jersey refineries. However, they brought in higher unit profits than the average refinery product, and to a large extent their manufacture utilized by-products.

After the war more chemical concerns and oil companies began to manufacture petrochemical products on a considerable scale. Among the oil company leaders were: The Texas Company, which joined American Cyanamid Company in a corporation to specialize in such manufacture; Continental Oil, which tied up with Industrial Chemical Company; and Standard of California and Standard of Indiana, both of which established affiliates to manufacture chemical products. The Louisiana and Texas Gulf Coast region was then becoming important in the manufacture of petrochemicals.[23]

Jersey's Committee on Chemical Policy, a subcommittee of the Coordination Committee, was established during the war to study market conditions and new developments in petrochemicals and to explore alternative courses of action that Jersey might follow. The principal issue was the extent to which the Jersey Company should go into the production of end products. The minutes of the committee's meetings indicate the complexity of the issues involved in this investigation of company petrochemical policy.[24]

Many questions were debated. Would the company be wise at that

capital investments in petrochemical manufacture generally came from depreciation allowances and a portion of net earnings.[26] Progress was made, but no active coordinated program for expansion was planned. That was to come later when the decision was finally made to enter extensively into the manufacture of petrochemical products.

By 1950 the company's conservative policy was being challenged. Among the oil companies in the United States, Shell especially was moving ahead of Jersey. The petrochemicals industry was clearly on the threshold of another period of great expansion. Within Jersey, advocates of a more vigorous development in this field continued to urge a review of the company's policy.

Table 26 illustrates in terms of crude runs the postwar growth of the refining of the Jersey Company by countries, regions, and affiliates around the world. The worldwide total was approximately one-third larger in 1950 than in 1946. In the later year, by far the greater portion of the refining was in the Western Hemisphere, but the processing in the Eastern Hemisphere was making a definite recovery. Standard-Vacuum's Sungei Gerong refinery was doing especially well. The new Fawley refinery was not yet in operation in 1950, and the recovery in Europe was being restrained by governmental controls of foreign exchange. One development represented by the statistics on crude runs was especially significant: the growth of refining abroad—notably in the Caribbean area—as compared with that at home. In 1948 the total foreign crude runs exceeded domestic runs by a small margin and in 1950 by a substantial margin.

EXPANDING AND UPGRADING MARKETING

At the end of the war, Jersey planned to meet the anticipated long-term competition in the sale of oil products by entering into new markets and raising the effectiveness of the affiliates' marketing organizations. Expansion and improvement were predicated on products of high quality, new capital investments, increasing efficiency of operations, and vigorous sales promotion. The extent of the effort in the five postwar years is indicated by the fact that in the Western Hemisphere alone a total of $227,000,000 was spent on the expansion and modernization of marketing operations.[27] In the sale of products, as in other operations, recovery and growth were held back in a large part of Jersey's foreign market by depressed economic conditions and a shortage of dollars.

Three men on the parent company's Board of Directors who had had extensive experience in marketing represented a wide range of experience in that branch of operations. Director Bedford had for many years been in charge of the specialty sales of domestic affiliates. Director Haslam had been manager of the Esso Marketers when its organization and operations were greatly strengthened and its costs were reduced in the 1930's. E. E. Soubry, who became a director in 1949, had had a long career in European marketing before joining the parent company in 1943.

A series of organizational changes looking toward better coordination culminated in 1947 in the establishment of the parent company's Marketing Coordination Department. Soubry served as the marketing coordinator until he was elected to the Board of Directors in 1949. He was succeeded by Peter T. Lamont, who also had spent most of his career in European marketing. The department was designed to coordinate domestic as well as foreign operations, but its concern at first was largely with marketing abroad.

At this time Jersey also brought about a more rational corporate organization of its marketing interests. As far as possible, it merged affiliates within a country in order to eliminate the managerial duplication and territorial overlapping which had resulted, principally, from the acquisition of companies by purchase. In the United States, for example, the companies represented by the Esso Marketers were absorbed by one— Esso Standard. Jersey also placed the management of the sale of petrochemicals under Standard Alcohol Company, which then became Enjay Company. It similarly simplified certain international operations by placing them under Esso Export Corporation (later, Esso International, Inc.). This company was assigned responsibility for serving as a middleman between affiliates and between affiliated and nonaffiliated companies in the international purchase and sale of crude oil and products. In addition, when Intava was liquidated, Esso Export was given the work of handling Jersey's foreign aviation gasoline sales. It was likewise assigned responsibility for the fuel-oil bunkering business in both hemispheres.

In order to make the Jersey Company and its products better known, the policy of the late 1930's to adopt uniformity in brand names at home and abroad was now also applied to corporate names. Deutsch-Amerikanische Petroleum-Gesellschaft became Esso Aktiengesellschaft; Lago Shipping Company became Esso Transportation Company; Standard Oil Export became Esso Export Corporation; and Standard Oil Company of New Jersey was changed to Esso Standard Oil Company. This changing

WORLDWIDE OIL BUNKERING SERVICE OF JERSEY AFFILIATES IN 1949

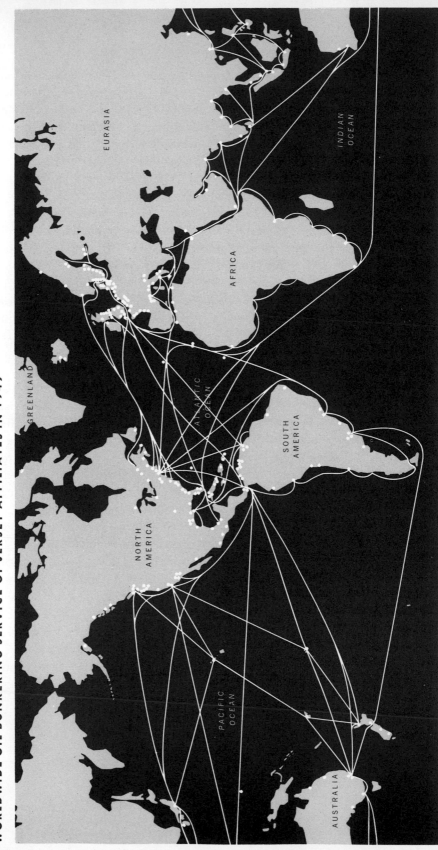

Load of hay drawn by oxen passes Esso station and general store in Maine.

Neighboring farmers in North Carolina have a friendly meeting place.

An Esso service station in northern New York State pumping gasoline.

After fueling the *Queen Mary* at her pier, the empty Esso barge rides high in the water.

Suburban tank truck delivers heating oil.

Bermudan motorcycle stops for fuel.

Tank truck in front of Parisian pastry shop is ready to deliver fuel.

A postwar service station on a major Belgian highway.

Lubricating oil for a gold mine in Honduras is being loaded for air delivery.

Swiss airliner at an international airport takes on fuel.

Diesel locomotive in a railroad yard stops at the fuel pipe.

Production research specialists gather for a conference in Tulsa, Oklahoma.

Instruction in basics of supervision at the Esso Training Center.

Creole provided education opportunities for workers after working hours.

Employment manager interviews an applicant for refinery position.

Schoolboys in the Concordia camp school, established by Creole in the La Salina area.

Labor-management conference at the Bayonne Refinery in 1946.

Aramco sponsors lessons in English and Arabic for Arab boys.

Standard Oil Development Company engineers in session at Linden, New Jersey.

This Esso Research Center in Linden was opened in 1948.

The electron microscope became a much-used instrument in the research center.

Electron photomicrograph of grease magnified 52,000 times.

of corporate names continued into the 1950's, when, for instance, Standard Oil Development Company became Esso Research and Engineering Company, and Anglo-American became Esso Petroleum Company, Limited.

But there was a limit to the extent of the altering of names at this time. Abroad, Imperial had the prestige of age, and both this Canadian company and Creole had names that were well and favorably known in their countries. At home, there was the old problem of using Standard Oil or Esso in a large part of the country. Carter could not have been changed to Esso because it operated in some of the same territory as Standard Oil Company (Indiana), which in the 1930's had prevented Jersey from expanding its marketing into Indiana's operating territory under the Esso name.[28] Here was a clear case of a company's history preventing it from doing what was rational. Generally abroad, however, the Esso name and trademark came to be widely used and served to give a common identity to affiliates and their products in different countries.

As in other branches of operations, expansion and modernization—the latter especially abroad—became the keynotes of the marketing operations of the Jersey companies in these postwar years. In much of the Eastern Hemisphere the affiliates had to await conversion to civilian control, but in the Western Hemisphere they began to implement new marketing programs soon after the end of the conflict.

Among the domestic affiliates, Humble changed from selling almost exclusively by means of large contracts to developing a considerable retail business in Texas. Its directors expected that the cargo market would shrink as oil from other regions became more competitive with Texas oil in world markets, and they believed that their own state, which was then undergoing rapid industrialization and urbanization, had a great potential for growth. Humble had undertaken in the 1920's to develop marketing in its own state, but it had met difficulty in selling light products on an economically sound basis in competition with small, low-cost inland refineries. Now, however, the smaller refineries could not afford the expensive equipment used in manufacturing the high-octane gasolines required by high-compression motors. Humble set up what was virtually a new sales organization, appointing as its manager Frank A. Watts, one of its engineers who had served during the war as director of the Materials Division of the Petroleum Administration for War.[29]

This new organization was designed especially to acquire service stations and increase Humble's sale of gasoline, the sales campaign to be based on products of high quality. The company solved the problem of the cost of long-distance transportation by building a products pipeline from Baytown to the Dallas–Fort Worth region, by organizing barge transport to Corpus Christi for the Southwest Texas division, and by purchasing gasolines manufactured to its specifications by an independent refinery in West Texas. It bought several small distributing firms, and as fast as materials and manpower were available it built additional bulk plants and service stations. In order to raise the standards of selling and service, it staffed a considerable percentage of both types of stations with its own employees instead of leasing them to independent dealers. It gave special sales training in Houston to men from commission or dealer stations as well as to its own sales force. It also carried on an extensive advertising campaign.[30]

In 1949 Humble reached second rank in the percentage it sold of the total tax-paid gasoline sales in Texas. It also achieved high percentage increases in the marketing of other products. Despite a considerable rise in wages and in the cost of materials and equipment, the Sales Department raised its earnings as a percentage of sales.[31]

Carter Oil greatly expanded its marketing territory. It did this primarily by purchasing several small companies during and after the war. By 1950 it was selling gasoline and other petroleum products in eight states extending from the Dakotas to the Pacific, and it was considering extending its marketing operations eastward to the Mississippi. Such expansion was in keeping with Jersey's general policy to extend the geographic reach of its marketing in the United States. However, Carter at this particular time had a reason of its own: it needed to obtain additional outlets for its crude oil to take the place of sales to Imperial after the Canadians discovered oil in Alberta.

Carter's Marketing Department, of which F. Warren Butler was manager, operated under conditions very different from those of the marketers in the eastern states and the South. Most of its territory was sparsely settled, which meant relatively low volume, high unit costs, and heavy reliance on distribution by consignment bulk stations and retail outlets. Because the region was western and largely rural, different sales personnel and methods were required than in most other domestic marketing areas. Carter marketers also had to compete with established brands and sales personnel already accepted in their communities. Although they worked against odds and did not reach a large volume of sales in this period, they did obtain a foothold for the company in a region believed to have a long-term growth potential.[32]

Standard Oil Company of New Jersey (Esso Standard) worked to expand an already well-established business and to reduce costs. Although its bunkering of ships was transferred to Esso Export and its petrochemical sales were assigned to Enjay, the General Office increased its total sales. That office concentrated its efforts on getting additional large contracts. The marketing organization was concerned principally with meeting a heavy demand for products until late in 1948, but it nevertheless made a beginning soon after the war in reconditioning facilities and further improving operations. The marketers also began to give special attention to promoting the sale of fuel gas, Essotane. At first this came in the South, where liquefied propane gas could be distributed in cylinders directly from Baton Rouge, but it also developed in the North after high-pressure tanks could be obtained in 1946 and 1947.

When the supplies of major products became more plentiful in 1948, these marketers started a drive to increase their sales volume and reduce selling costs. They modernized old stations, built new ones, and acquired new transport facilities. They carried on an active program to obtain more customers in all product lines, but they especially sought to obtain large-volume customers and outlets in areas of concentrated demand. They made their inventory control more efficient by better scheduling when that became possible. Also, by expanding their formal training for accountants, industrial salesmen, bulk and service-station personnel, and others, they upgraded the general performance of their organization. These efforts paid off in larger individual deliveries and total sales; the marketers increased their product sales from 123,600,000 barrels in 1946 to 149,600,000 in 1950—in both years well over half of the total sales of Esso Standard. Despite higher wages and costs of materials and equipment, they reduced unit marketing costs during this period.[33]

Although the affiliates at this time were expanding the geographic reach of their marketing, in 1950 Jersey was still far from having national distribution in the United States. Humble's entry into oil production in California[34] and Carter's expansion into several states in the Northwest meant footholds in vast regions with potential for considerable growth. But Jersey had no outlets of its own in many of the southeastern states and in the great Midwest north of the Ohio and Arkansas rivers from the Pennsylvania boundary in the East to Carter's marketing territory in the West. It had an outlet in the Southeast through the sale of products on contract to its former affiliate, Standard Oil Company (Kentucky), but there was, of course, no certainty that it would continue to hold that business. It was interested—as it had long been—in establishing marketing operations in the Middle West. However, entry there hinged on both legal and economic considerations. A formidable legal obstacle was the injunction Standard of Indiana had obtained against Jersey's entry into Indiana's operating territory in the 1930's.[35] As for economic considerations, a 1946 report of a marketing study of the Midwest states contains this statement: "In all our approaches to this problem, the competitive picture dictates that our strategy must be based primarily on that of lowest laid down cost, for only with this assurance can we proceed with confidence."[36] Entry into the great markets of the Midwest was not to come until many years later.

In Canada, Imperial, with a rising supply of oil from the Alberta fields and lower-cost transportation and operations in an expanding economy, resumed its prewar program to increase sales. New production, refineries, and pipelines made possible price reductions in the prairie provinces, which had formerly been served by oil brought by expensive railroad transportation from as far away as Texas. Because of new transportation facilities, by the end of 1950 Imperial's oil from Alberta was about to enter into refining and marketing to the eastward and thus further free the company's operations from dependence on imported crude and products.[37]

The Jersey affiliates in Latin America undertook extensive programs for expanding and modernizing their marketing. Despite inflation in some countries, dollar shortages in others, and government regulations that restricted marketing operations in several, the Jersey affiliates in a large part of Central and South America improved their selling organizations and equipment and greatly increased their sales.[38]

The producing affiliates, especially, raised the volume of their product sales in the countries where they operated. Actually, few other companies were marketing in those countries, because of the strict government regulation of the prices of petroleum products, which in some places made them lower than actual costs. The business was therefore left almost wholly to the established producing companies, mostly affiliates of Jersey and Royal Dutch–Shell. The Jersey affiliates worked to increase sales not only from immediate considerations of profit but especially because of long-term prospects in expanding economies and recognition of the public relations value of contact with the general public.

On the west coast of South America, International Petroleum enlarged its retail and wholesale distribution organization and facilities as soon as possible after the war. Its desire for larger sales was the principal motivation behind its termination of a long-standing commission arrangement with Williamson & Company; this marked a final break with the last vestige of the old system of British foreign merchants who had so long participated in the trade of the west coast of the southern continent. In Colombia, in anticipation of the expiration of the De Mares concession in 1951, Jersey organized an affiliate to take over Tropical's marketing in that country. In Venezuela, Creole carried out an extensive program to build up its facilities for selling gasoline and lubricants directly to the automobile trade, which was expanding with the building of new roads.[39]

Progress in other Latin American countries varied. As already observed, Jersey marketers for a time nearly lost their considerable volume outlet in Argentina. The government had earlier placed such restrictions on petroleum marketing by private companies, however, that there was little if any possibility of expansion. There was virtually no hope for a rise in the company's share of the market in Uruguay because the government-owned concern closely controlled the business. In Chile the marketing operations of private companies were under close government control. Brazil at this time became the largest user of Esso products in Latin America. In several countries of Central America the marketers expanded their sales so much that they had to increase their facilities and enlarge their marine terminals in order to accommodate larger tankers.[40]

Besides the increase in the sale of major products in Latin America, two other products were sold in larger quantities. One was asphalt for roads. The affiliates supplied the asphalt and also gave technical advice and assistance in its use. A boon to the Latin American housewife was "Esso gas," the liquefied petroleum gas sold in cylinders to households. Jersey salesmen also sold gas stoves, refrigerators, and hot-water heaters under the Esso oval trademark. Their sale of Esso gas and appliances was especially large in Brazil and Venezuela, but they also supplied a rising demand in many other countries. In fact, the companies established bulk terminals for filling cylinders and distributing gas in most countries in Central and South America and the West Indies.[41]

In Europe, the Communists took over large areas where affiliates had long sold their products. Besides its losses in East Germany, Romania, and Hungary, the company also lost properties and operations in Poland and the young Baltic states. It liquidated its marketing affiliate in Czechoslovakia because government controls made operations impossible. Most of these countries had come under the Soviets during the war, and the Communists continued to control them.

The Communists also gained ground on the other side of the globe.

Standard-Vacuum carried on marketing in China after the war despite inflation, which made it impossible to convert Chinese currency into dollars without a high loss. However, Stanvac was finally driven out of the country by the advance of the Chinese Communists. As in Romania and Hungary, Communists established such controls and regulations that operations became virtually impossible. In Shanghai, for example, representatives of American companies were held personally responsible for maintaining operations and meeting payrolls, and they were not permitted to liquidate any operations without the approval of Communist authorities—which was virtually unobtainable. In 1949 the company finally decided to evacuate its American staff in all Communist-held areas and to leave its properties and affairs in the hands of loyal Chinese employees. The evacuation was arranged with the Department of State in Washington, and the United States government provided a ship to pick up all the Americans—the company's employees and others—who wished to leave.[42]

By 1950 Standard-Vacuum had given up its properties and operations in all of China, and in that year the United States government ordered American companies to suspend shipments to that country.[43] The fact that the Communists were also trying to extend their control in Southeast Asia and to some of the islands made the company's operations risky and even precarious in many places.

At the same time that the affiliates' markets in extensive regions were lost or on the brink of loss, some new outlets were gained elsewhere. Jersey made a marketing survey in the Eastern Mediterranean countries from Greece and Turkey to Egypt. In 1948, on the recommendation of the Near East Marketing Committee, it purchased the Société du Naphte, S.A., from a Swiss firm. Société had bulk plants for supplying petroleum products in Lebanon, Syria, Israel, Cyprus, the Sudan, and Egypt. Jersey reorganized this company as Esso Standard (Near East), Incorporated. It was estimated that to obtain 20 per cent of the sales in those countries would require capital expenditures of $8,500,000 and five years of operations, but subsequent developments prevented the company from achieving even close to 20 per cent participation. Entry into the Near East required developing an efficient marketing organization and winning customer acceptance of the Esso brand where other distributors were firmly entrenched. In 1950 the company made its first move into Greece and Turkey by arranging to sell products to local companies and commission agents in both countries.[44]

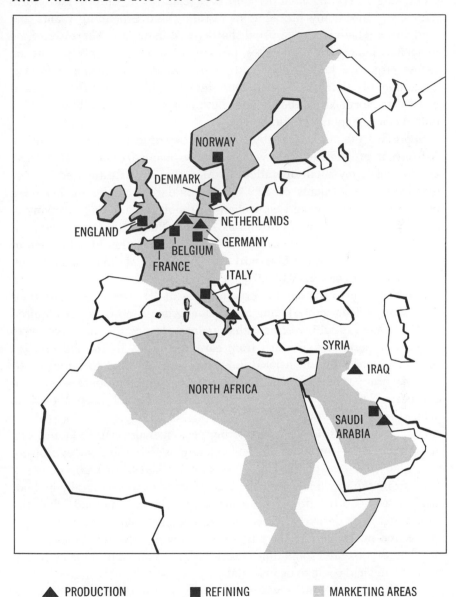

Despite depressed economies and restrictions on trade and the international flow of funds, Jersey made real progress in rehabilitating and reorienting marketing facilities and organizations in Europe and North Africa.[45] It met many problems in restoring and expanding plants and equipment. There were the usual shortages of materials. There were also difficulties in acquiring land sites, permits for service stations, permission to use large-size tank trucks, and so on, because of civic regulations, opposition of merchant associations, and the like. Nevertheless, from Norway to North Africa the affiliates built new marketing facilities and acquired efficient transport equipment.

Improving the marketers' physical assets required considerable capital. A five-year program in Italy was originally planned to cost $21,200,000. For the relatively small operations in Morocco, it was estimated in 1947 that capital investments of $2,235,000 would have to be made and a period of four years would be needed for the new marketing company to begin to "earn its living." Additions in that North African country included a modern bulk terminal to allow the importation of a full line of products. Even the small Standard Oil Company (Malta) planned projects estimated to cost $260,000.[46]

Providing funds for capital expenditures under exchange restrictions was not so difficult in marketing as in refining because marketers required relatively less capital investment than refiners. Hence the marketers were in a better position to finance from earnings and with the aid of local short-term loans. But such local financing generally had to be arranged with governments because of the scarcity of capital resources—even in advanced European countries with highly developed capital markets before the war.

Like the physical facilities, marketing personnel also had to be restored and prepared for the more efficient operations that were Jersey's objective. The employees of the European affiliates had been badly demoralized during the war. Moreover, the European managers generally had not had the competitive drive nor utilized the efficient methods that the parent company desired. Agreements abroad between competitors as to quotas and prices were of the past in the Jersey family—for the most part they had disappeared some time before the war. Now a positive approach to marketing had come to be essential.

The administrators in New York therefore promoted programs to introduce among the European affiliates the same energy and efficiency that had been developed by the marketing affiliates at home. Hence, Jersey brought key men from Europe to America for training and for observation of operations, and its representatives helped the European organizations themselves to plan and conduct training courses for men on various levels. Jersey men resident in Europe and visiting executives from New York also advised the European managers on how to improve operations. Perhaps nowhere was the teaching function of the parent company and of certain American affiliates more fully and more successfully applied after the war than in Europe.

Progress was made. Judging by the European marketers' statements at the Coordination Committee meeting of executives in Paris in 1947, effective competition was already then becoming the watchword in European operations. The European managers, reflecting a new point of view, extolled competition in service, in product quality, in costs, in volume, and in performance generally. They were adopting new methods to build larger volume and cut costs. In some affiliates in Europe special "cost and operations" managers were appointed, and suitable programs were designed and put into effect. In conferences, marketing managers from various countries compared and discussed methods and results, and they circulated statistics within their own companies in order to make comparisons and promote competition. Such comparisons were made possible by the standardization of accounting and, especially, of cost figures; it was even possible to compare European with American results. Unit costs were reduced by means of increased bulk sales, larger loads and deliveries, more rapid loading and unloading, and so on.

The European managers also put into practice new ways of raising the affiliates' standing with the public. The marketers employed more extensive advertising as business revived, and they gave special attention to public relations. The change in the corporate names of affiliates to include Standard or Esso, or both, and the use of the Esso oval identification and Esso brand names were helpful in making the affiliates' products more widely known. An especially important innovation was adopted in Britain. There Anglo-American decided to depart from the general practice in that country of selling gasoline through split dealers—that is, dealers who sold more than one company's products—and to acquire its own stations to be run by independent dealers selling only the company's own brands. This shift to exclusive-dealer outlets involved large expenditures as well as a tactful approach to offset the opposition from dealer associations, civic leaders, and others. The change was made as soon as the end of pooling made possible the selling of company-brand products.[47]

A special concern of Jersey officers and executives in New York with respect to foreign affiliates was to assure their compliance with provisions of the parent company's consent decree of 1942 requiring observance of American antitrust law in foreign operations. This effort on the part of the United States government to extend the influence of American law to the operations of affiliates incorporated in foreign countries raised problems for Jersey abroad. One objective of several parent company executives visiting Europe in the autumn of 1945—especially the head of the Law Department, Edward F. Johnson—had been to explain the meaning of the provisions of the consent decree to the affiliates' executives. General Counsel Johnson and high marketing executives had continuing responsibility for the careful promotion and cautious checking of compliance. Johnson discussed the matter with foreign executives when they came to New York, and he and an associate made trips to Europe and Latin America for similar discussions and for observations. In Europe, where outside ownership in certain affiliates was influential and there was pride in national governments and law, more than the usual tact was required as well as firmness. The Americans recognized that exceptions would have to be made where national laws and regulations were contrary to American antitrust law, as for example under pools and quotas set by governments. But they stressed the consequences to Jersey of action violative of antitrust law unless the regulations of foreign governments made conformance impossible.[48]

Every year Johnson reported to the Jersey Executive Committee on compliance with the consent decree at home and abroad. In a 1948 report he concluded that "There was not only no evidence of violation, but, on the other hand, an alertness on the part of executives to their responsibilities under the decree and a willingness on their part to comply with its spirit as well as with its letter."[49]

However, there was uncertainty as to what the actual application of American law to foreign operations might be, an uncertainty that was heightened by the Supreme Court's broadening interpretation of antitrust law late in the 1940's. As a precaution, Jersey retained outside legal counsel to examine pertinent records and to advise on the conformance of both domestic and foreign affiliates with current interpretations. Over a period of several months in 1950, two prominent New York lawyers, John W. Davis and Charles Evans Hughes, Jr., examined contracts and other records and discussed the situation with Jersey executives who had responsibility in this area. As Davis and Hughes interpreted antitrust law, they found no violations.

Jersey's great accomplishment in Eastern Hemisphere marketing, especially in England and on the European Continent, was that its affiliates' marketing operations were maintained and even strengthened under trade and exchange regulations that favored sterling as against dollar oil. The company achieved this result by assuming larger financial risks than usual, taking losses on current operations, making many changes in its operating facilities, and eventually, in effect, overcoming the barriers that limited its trade in nondollar countries. As noted in Chapter 26, Jersey in 1950 and 1951 arrived at understandings with several governments—principally with those of the United Kingdom and France—that essentially preserved its ability to supply its marketing affiliates on a competitive basis and alleviated balance-of-payments difficulties.

An immediate measure of the accomplishments of the Jersey Company in the distribution of oil products in the first five postwar years was an upward trend in its sales nearly everywhere, a trend in keeping with the worldwide rise in the consumption of petroleum products. Within the United States the total rose from 243,600,000 barrels in 1946 to 314,900,-000 in 1950. Outside this country, sales in the same years were 205,100,-000 and 317,200,000 barrels. The total sales of the affiliates in 1950 far exceeded that of any previous year. (See Table 22 in Chapter 25.)

From the point of view of its long-term prospects, the company had advanced in all branches of its operations in these early postwar years. It had expanded its capacity, and it had improved its physical facilities and administrative and operating organizations and methods. It had acquired production and refining abroad commensurate in importance with its foreign market. It had realized its long-held objective of establishing itself on an essentially equal footing with its leading competitors in all parts of the non-Communist world. It had, in fact, built up integrated operations abroad as well as at home.

Chapter 30

Growth of a Multinational Company:
A Review, 1927–1950

THE *History of Standard Oil Company (New Jersey)*, of which the present volume is the third, deals with the evolution of a vertically integrated, multinational enterprise. In its historical significance, the development of this type of business is comparable to the Commercial Revolution of the Middle Ages and the Industrial Revolution of the late eighteenth and early nineteenth centuries. The former laid the foundations of modern business in organization, practice, and underlying thought; the latter multiplied the productivity of man and enterprise by harnessing to machines the force of rivers and the energy of steam. The vertically integrated concern with affiliates in many countries has been a dynamic factor in the administrative and technological evolution of the economy of the free world.

In the petroleum industry the development of such concerns, which began late in the nineteenth century, reached a high point in the second quarter of the twentieth. This was a time of great opportunities for oil companies able to cope constructively with industrial and environmental instability and change. Driven by intense competition in the market and assisted by a general advance in science, the oil industry brought about basic transformations in its technology, structure, and administration. It discovered vast resources of raw materials in many parts of the world, greatly widened the range and improved the quality of products, and multiplied sales. The increase in sales was stimulated by the reduction of costs, which made possible prices of major products that over the long term tended not to rise in proportion to mounting costs of inputs and rising taxes.

Standard Oil Company (New Jersey) was one of the leading concerns contributing in this period to the development of the petroleum industry. Many companies, large and small, were innovative in varying ways and degrees. Most of the oil companies were regional or national in their operations. Some were specialized in function. Large vertically integrated concerns like Jersey, operating internationally, supplied consuming countries with products made from oil commonly produced in lands thousands of miles away. They were the eveners between supply and demand, nationally and internationally, and the holders of large known reserves for the future.

The year 1927 marks a turning point in the history of Standard Oil Company (New Jersey). Dismemberment by decision of the United States Supreme Court in 1911 had left the company mainly a refining and marketing concern with geographically limited operations, extensive foreign outlets supplied principally from its refineries in the United States, and a truncated top administration made up mostly of specialists in refining and sales. In subsequent years, Jersey had attempted, with only limited success, to improve its administration, to expand its production, and to increase its sales in the mass consumer market. At the same time, other large companies, at home and abroad, were acquiring a greater degree of self-sufficiency by developing functionally integrated operations. Because of the general trend in this direction, Jersey in 1927 faced the prospect of having to purchase relatively high-cost crude for its refineries and of losing its large buyers of products among oil company distributors. With the severe decline in the prices of crude oil and products then under way, the Jersey board concluded that Jersey's profits and position in the industry were in serious jeopardy and that its weaknesses in production and in marketing were no longer tolerable.

This conclusion precipitated action by the Board of Directors. It decided to move the company as rapidly as possible toward achieving a stronger functional integration by expanding its crude oil reserves and production and strengthening its position in the market. They also decided to undertake a greatly expanded program of research and development. In order to carry out these decisions effectively and to bring about better coordination of operations in the general interest, they at the same time took action to reorganize the company's administrative structure. These decisions of 1927 set Standard Oil Company (New Jersey) on courses of development which—adjusted to changing opportunities, problems, and pressures over the years—were to lead to the development of the "modern" Jersey Company.

BUILDING A VERTICALLY INTEGRATED BUSINESS AT HOME AND ABROAD

The company acted at once to carry out the decision of 1927 to expand its reserves and production. Within five years, it added greatly to its producing properties in the United States and Venezuela; it also scaled the walls of Dutch and British influence in the Far East and the Middle East by obtaining large concessions in the Dutch East Indies and a minority interest in Iraq Petroleum Company. The drive to obtain additional producing properties continued throughout the 1930's and even during World War II, especially in the United States. After the war, Imperial made a historic discovery in Canada. And by obtaining a 30 per cent ownership in Arabian American Oil Company, Jersey realized its long-held objective of obtaining a stronger position in production in the Middle East.

The accompanying chart indicates the increase in the volume of crude oil and condensate produced by affiliates at home and abroad in the years from 1927 to 1950. The Jersey Company's portion of the output of the whole industry rose from about 5 per cent of the production in the United States in 1927 to 7.3 per cent in 1950, and abroad from 8.9 per cent in the former year to 20.6 per cent in the latter.* Its world total rose from 6.5 per cent of the industry volume in 1927 to 13.7 per cent in 1950.[1]

Despite its rising output—especially the vast amounts produced annually during and just after the war—the company greatly increased its petroleum reserves. There is no record of the total holdings of the whole company in 1927, but Humble reported its gross reserves in that year at an amount that was less than 1 per cent of the estimated reserves for the whole petroleum industry in the United States.[2] At the end of 1950, the gross crude and condensate reserves of the domestic affiliates amounted to 10.8 per cent of the country's total; those of affiliates abroad were 12.5 per cent of the foreign industry's. The world total of the affiliates constituted 11.9 per cent of that of the industry. Of these reserves, approximately one-fourth was in the United States. Of the three-fourths held in foreign countries, approximately 40 per cent was in the Eastern Hemisphere, mostly in the Middle East; about the same percentage was in Venezuela. The company's estimated worldwide reserves in 1950 totaled 14 billion barrels.

---

* Such percentage figures comparing two years give only an approximate—not an exact—measure of the company's change in position relative to the whole industry.

This large increase in production and reserves was basic to Jersey's growth and strength. It gave the company assurance of raw materials at competitive costs to supply the major part of the requirements of its refineries and markets throughout the free world. Further, as was amply demonstrated during the war, these extensive resources provided large supplies in emergencies as well as for many years ahead in normal times—

**PRODUCTION OF CRUDE OIL AND CONDENSATE
BY JERSEY AFFILIATES, 1927-1950**

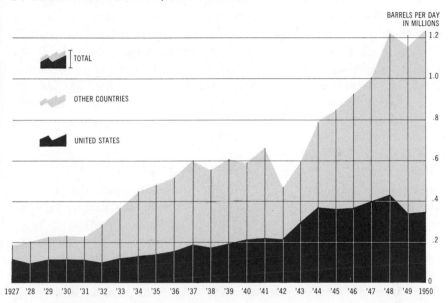

a matter of vital importance in a world that had become largely dependent on petroleum for energy.

Implementing the 1927 decision of the Board of Directors to expand the company's sale of products involved two changes. One was to extend the geographic reach of the marketing organization. The other was to expand jobbing and retailing operations vigorously in order to gain a more secure position in the expanding mass consumer market—particularly for gasoline.

The company began in 1927 to add to its marketing territory, which it was to continue to do throughout the period. Humble expanded in Texas. Principally by acquiring established marketing concerns, Jersey late in the 1920's returned to regions where it had lost affiliates in 1911. It re-entered such important oil consuming areas as the New England states, New York, and Pennsylvania at home and Great Britain abroad. By joining Socony-Vacuum in organizing Standard-Vacuum in 1934, it also regained participation in marketing in the Orient. During and after the war, it lost marketing interests in Eastern Europe to the Communists, just as Standard-Vacuum did in China. However, Jersey entered a new region by establishing marketing in several countries along the Eastern Mediterranean. And in the United States in the 1940's it resumed its policy of expansion by purchasing several small companies in the Northwest.

The company maintained approximately the same relative position in the sale of products in large volume by contract as it had held in 1927. This it did mostly by gaining new customers. Beginning late in the 1920's, the domestic affiliates sold increasing amounts of natural gas to manufacturing concerns and long-distance gas transmission lines. As oil-company distributors reduced their purchases, affiliates found other customers—among manufacturing and transportation companies and in the military services—for fuel oils, gasolines, and lubricants. An important new outlet in the 1930's was air transport, both civilian and military. During World War II, the Allies and neutral countries required all the products the oil industry could supply. After the war, the domestic affiliates sold to manufacturers a rising volume of intermediate products for making such petrochemicals as synthetic rubber and plastics.

Another significant development was expansion in the burgeoning mass market. At home the affiliates added to their own jobbing and retailing and increased their sales to independent jobbers and retail distributors; they thereby substantially raised the volume sold to the comparatively small-volume buyers of gasoline, lubricants, and heating oils. Expansion of this type came more slowly abroad—especially in the 1930's, because of depression, government regulations, and restrictive agreements with other companies. After the war, foreign affiliates, except where they were restrained by exchange difficulties, became more competitive in a growing mass market. Widely adopting the methods of affiliates in the United States, they sold to local distributors and consumers a rising volume of gasoline, heating oil, lubricants, liquefied petroleum gas, and other products.

The accompanying chart shows in terms of volume what was accomplished by the worldwide Jersey sales organizations in the years from 1927 through 1950. At the end of the period, the total sales were slightly more than four times those at the beginning. Foreign sales, which in 1927 had been less than the domestic, in 1950 slightly exceeded those at home. The total in the United States represented about the same position, relative to industry sales, in the later as in the earlier year. Abroad, however, the company had moderately improved its position.

PRODUCT SALES BY JERSEY AFFILIATES, 1927-1950

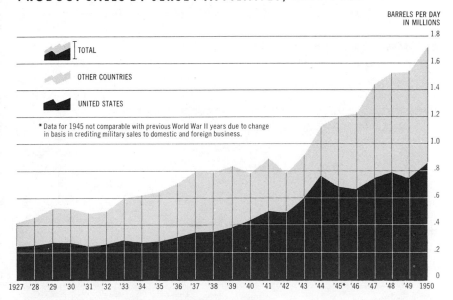

Expansion of production and sales outside the United States also led to the acquisition of additional refining capacity abroad. Especially important was the Aruba refinery acquired in 1932; being on direct tanker routes from Venezuela to Europe, it largely took the place of domestic refineries in supplying Jersey's markets across the Atlantic. Smaller plants were built abroad in the 1930's, including one in Venezuela and one in France built jointly with other American companies. The refinery in Sumatra was enlarged. After the war, the trend was to construct new refineries in consuming rather than in producing countries. This was done partly because of government regulations and the need to reduce dollar import costs in European countries. An important exception was the refinery built at the end of the period at Amuay in Venezuela to fulfill an agreement with the government to process within the country a larger percentage of Creole's production. At the same time, Anglo-American built a new refinery at Fawley in England, where a sufficiently large market for products made the operation of a plant of optimum size economically feasible.

A comparatively large refiner in 1927, the company needed to expand its over-all capacity only as its sale of products increased. The affiliates consequently raised only moderately the ratio of the amount of crude they processed to the total runs of the world refining industry: from 14.3 per cent in 1927 to 16 in 1950. In actual volume, however, the increase

REFINERY CRUDE RUNS BY JERSEY AFFILIATES, 1927-1950

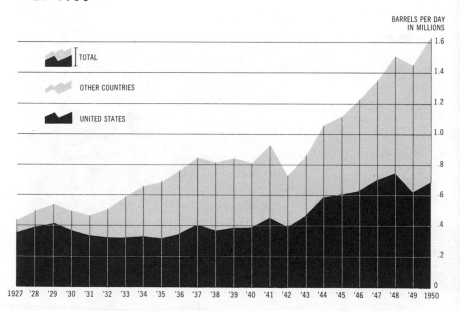

was large, as the accompanying chart shows. Both absolutely and relative to the whole industry, by far the larger gain was outside the United States. The total crude processed by Jersey refineries in the United States was only twice as large in 1950 as in 1927; their runs declined from 15.4 per cent of the industry's in 1927 to 11.9 in 1950. Outside the United States, however, the runs of the affiliates' refineries in 1950 were 11 times the earlier total, a rise from over one-tenth of the industry's runs in 1927 to slightly more than one-fifth in 1950.

To serve new and expanded operations in producing, refining, and marketing, parent company and affiliates changed their transport facilities on land and sea. Participation in the introduction of long-distance natural gas transmission and the movement of gasoline by pipelines late in the 1920's were important innovations. From time to time, affiliates built—or participated with other companies in building—lines to provide outlets for new producing fields or regions in North and South America and the Middle East. They expanded their tanker fleets although they also continued to hire considerable tonnage on long-term charters. Tanker routes followed shifts in the company's trade, but the domicile of the individual fleets was determined in large part by considerations of costs and security, government regulations, and foreign exchange. Such considerations were involved in the transfer in 1935 of the large European fleet registered in the Free City of Danzig. For reasons of security, these ships were shifted to safe and relatively low-cost registry in Panama. The high cost of building and operating tankers flying the United States flag precluded moving this foreign fleet to the United States.

The expansion of the properties and operations of Standard Oil Company (New Jersey) was paralleled by advances in technology. In fact, the company's application of science and engineering in all branches of operations was an essential element in its growth.

ADVANCING TECHNOLOGICAL CHANGE IN JERSEY OPERATIONS

Employing science, scientists, and engineers was not new to the company in 1927; what was new was the broad program undertaken. That extensive program of scientific research and technological development, especially in production and refining, was to put Standard Oil Company (New Jersey) in the forefront of a movement that brought a revolution in the oil industry's operations. For Jersey, the decision was especially important in its timing. By 1927 advances in chemistry and physics had laid the theoretical foundation for productive application to the problems of the oil industry. Jersey's early entry in a large way into research in production and refining gave it the advantages of innovation in the years of its vigorous drive to build large, integrated operations.

From late in the 1920's, Humble Oil & Refining Company was among the leaders in advancing the technology of finding and producing oil and gas which radically changed the whole petroleum industry. Humble pioneered in the use of geophysical techniques in the search for structures favorable to the trapping of oil and gas. Over the years it contributed to the improvement of the various instruments used and to the interpretation of geologic and geophysical data. In production, its most distinctive and valuable research in the early years was its quantitative studies of individual wells, especially of the relation between pressure at the bottom of the well and variations in the volume of oil produced.

Together with other oil companies engaged in research in exploration and production, Jersey's domestic affiliates in this period added to the basic knowledge of oil and gas reservoirs, their contents, and the natural energy forces within them that was essential to the improvement of production. This new knowledge also contributed to the stabilizing of the American petroleum industry. It provided a necessary basis for government regulation which greatly improved the industry in the United States. Such regulation reduced the wasteful practices that had characterized oil production in this country from its beginning, and it promoted equity among competing operators in individual fields. It also contributed to the maintaining of reserves in their natural storehouses.

The affiliates applied new reservoir concepts and producing techniques as far as possible under particular lease or concession contracts, government regulations, and economic conditions. They thereby raised the efficiency of their producing operations and increased the volume of oil ultimately recoverable from their oil fields and leases.

The 1927 decision to apply research and technology to processing on a greatly expanded scale brought fundamental changes in Jersey refining. The shift in emphasis was originally motivated by the need to obtain a larger proportion of the more valuable products—notably gasoline—from a barrel of crude and to turn out products competitive in cost and quality. The central and coordinating research organization was developed within Standard Oil Development Company. A large branch laboratory was set up at the Baton Rouge refinery, and other affiliates were encouraged to establish or add to research organizations of their own. Decentralization under the leadership of one affiliate provided for cooperation, competition, and local initiative that stimulated achievement. On these beginnings in the early years, Standard Oil Company (New Jersey) in the 1930's built a large and highly creative refining research organization.

The affiliates gradually placed engineers in managerial positions in refining. These new managers, with the assistance of staff groups for engineering and economic analysis, brought about radical changes in operations. Utilizing new or improved equipment and processes, they introduced the findings of the laboratories into the plants. The results were the improvement of old products and the production of new ones, the utilization of formerly wasted hydrocarbons, greater operating efficiency, and a rise in the economies of scale.

By the time the United States entered World War II, Jersey affiliates had made contributions to refining that had greatly advanced the company's operations and had provided processes for making products invaluable to the Allies in the war. One innovation of broad significance was fluid catalytic cracking. Others were processes for manufacturing synthetic components of aviation gasoline, TNT, and rubber. These and further advances enabled the company to contribute significantly to the manufacture of high-octane gasoline, improved lubricants, synthetic rubber, and other products for civilian and military use.

After the war, expanding company laboratories improved earlier processes and undertook new research, and refineries utilized the results in further improvement and innovation to meet increasingly intensive competition in the market. There was a growing interest in advancing the manufacture of petrochemicals. In anticipation of possible future needs, the laboratories also worked on discovering practicable ways to make liquid fuels from coal, shale, and natural gas. Refining organizations continued to carry forward developments that in the 1930's had begun to change refinery operations from the separation and finishing of oil fractions to what was essentially manufacturing—that is, breaking up petroleum molecules and joining the parts in different combinations to improve old products and make new ones.

As quality and price competition intensified in the market and the demand rose for products to serve highly specialized uses, the company also applied the new technology to its marketing operations. In 1933, the Esso Marketers made sales engineering a regular part of their organization—the first among Jersey affiliates. It was found that field representatives who had served well in the past could not judge the kinds of products needed for lubricating or fueling the newer machines and for meeting the rising competition of the later years. Salesmen trained in the technology of lubricants and fuels were better able to advise customers concerning the types and grades of products most suitable to their particular needs; they could also inform refiners more precisely of customers' requirements. The use of sales engineering increased with the greater precision and specialization of machines and with the rising demand for products tailored to particular uses under varying climatic and seasonal conditions.

Research and engineering, in fact, penetrated all aspects of the company's operations. One serious difficulty common to all functions was corrosion. Another was how to achieve the potential economies of scale. All operations had their own special problems and possibilities for improvement. In the higher managerial positions the engineer gradually replaced the practical man who had long been responsible for operations. With the use of more complex equipment and processes, special courses were established for training foremen. Even the rank-and-file worker had to have higher skills than his predecessor had needed.

RESPONDING TO A CHANGING SOCIOPOLITICAL ENVIRONMENT

The company's administrators in the 1920's had not foreseen a different need which they recognized in the 1940's: the necessity for better communication with Jersey's social and political environment. The directors and officers had generally assumed that the standing of parent company and affiliates was determined by their industrial performance and observance of governmental laws and regulations. Certain experiences late in the 1930's challenged this assumption. Several of Jersey's top leaders then came to believe that more constructive steps were required than the traditional defensive reaction to particular issues raised against the company.

The Board of Directors was shocked into reconsideration of its traditional position by certain developments in the critical war year of 1942. Most important was an attack on the company in hearings of the Senate Committee on National Defense, at which Jersey was charged with not cooperating with the government in its national defense efforts. This allegation and the resulting nationwide report in the press not only reduced the sale of products but also—in the judgment of some of Jersey's leaders—could have brought about another dissolution of Standard Oil Company (New Jersey). This development showed that industrial performance of a high order and observance of laws and cooperation with the government did not assure Jersey of good standing with the public. The directors responded at once by arranging for a group within the company to assist in its current public relations emergency and to explore possible courses of action for the future.

After some study and experimentation, in which individual directors participated, the Jersey board in 1943 decided to make public relations, at home and abroad, a matter of high-level concern. It established the Public Relations Department—with one director in charge—to assist parent company and affiliates in relations with their multinational public. The new department served as a research-and-study group. It kept the directors informed of its findings. It provided continuous liaison with public relations media and planned special events designed to acquaint people at large with the policies and operations of the Jersey Company. In addition, it assisted the affiliates in setting up similar staff groups. The Board of Directors assumed full responsibility for policies and programs, and its members participated in the company's public relations activities. Members of the board also, in conferences of representatives of the entire Jersey Company, helped to spread new attitudes concerning relations with government and public.

On the whole, Jersey's early efforts in this field were exploratory, but significant results soon began to emerge. In the United States, more factual information about the company reached the public, and relations with the press were improved. A few affiliates in foreign countries made similar progress. Self-examination produced other beneficial results. The administrators became more concerned with the effect of the company's actions on the public generally and with its responsibilities as a corporate citizen of the varied countries within which it operated. In fact, Jersey's leaders came to see that their decision-making process required consideration of the interest of the general public as well as of the company's owners, employees, and customers.

In the meantime, negotiations with the Venezuelan government had convinced Jersey's directors of the need for new approaches to public relations abroad, especially in the less-developed countries where the company had producing interests and operations. In 1942 the government of Venezuela had proposed a revision of the terms of the concession contracts of foreign companies so as to give that country a larger share of profits. This development had important implications for Jersey because of its large producing interests in Venezuela and also because revision of concessions in one country might lead to demands for change elsewhere. The Board of Directors sent one of its members to participate in negotiations with the Venezuelan government. These resulted in the solution of the issue in 1943. In the process, the company learned that in the future foreign operations would survive not only on the strength of observance of contracts and laws but also on the basis of recognition by both company and host country of a mutuality of interests.

The insights which the company gained in 1942 and 1943 from these experiences at home and abroad proved important guides to action in foreign countries, especially in the less-developed ones. The company's leaders learned that they had to consider the effect of their decisions and operations on a country as a whole, and that they must establish better communication with the general public. They came to see the need for affiliates to contribute—beyond the reach of their operations and their obligations to governments—to the improvement of the societies within which they operated. They would thereby help to bring about more stable and productive societies as well as to identify the company with the good of the people as a whole.

A new dimension was thus added to thought and action within parent company and affiliates. It is impossible to measure the effect on their standing. Perhaps the most significant achievement by 1950 was that many company executives had come to believe that the "consent" of the public was essential to the well-being and even to the survival of the company in the many countries where affiliates operated. To make the profits required for maintaining a viable company had come to require good relations with both government and public.

FINANCING GROWTH AND DEVELOPMENT

Maintaining Standard Oil Company (New Jersey) as an expanding and progressive concern required large investments. The accompanying chart indicates the annual capital expenditures of parent company and affiliates from 1928 through 1950. The trend was steeply upward throughout the period but with considerable variation from year to year. The lowest for the period was $33,100,000 in 1931; the highest was $529,400,-000 in 1948.* (Appendix 2, Table 4.)

Funds were derived from various sources. By far the larger amount came from within the company. A minor internal source was proceeds from the sale of properties. The largest came from depreciation and depletion charges and retirements; the annual total from these sources rose with the expansion of company properties and operations from $75,200,000 in 1928 to $201,100,000 in 1950. Another internal source—smaller than the above but substantial—was retained earnings. These various sources within the company contributed far more than did long-term borrowing.

---

* As noted in Tables 2, 3, 4, and 5, referred to in this section, affiliates located in Great Britain, France, Finland, Germany, and Algeria were not included in consolidated statements for the year 1939, and affiliates in Great Britain, Continental Europe, and North Africa were not included from 1940 through 1950.

Over the years, the availability of funds for growth depended first of all on profits. As an enterprise organized to employ its stockholders' capital in the petroleum business, the company had to earn more than it spent in order to reward its owners for the use of their investment and for risks they had assumed. The company obviously had to make profits in order to maintain good standing in capital markets.

In every year from 1927 through 1950, Standard Oil Company (New

ANNUAL CAPITAL EXPENDITURES BY STANDARD OIL COMPANY (NEW JERSEY), 1927-1950

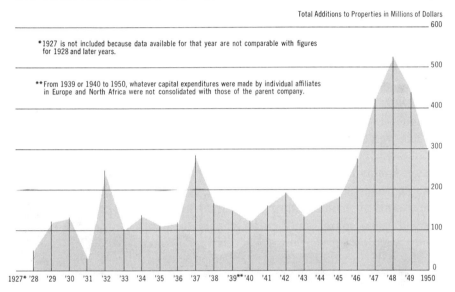

Total Additions to Properties in Millions of Dollars

*1927 is not included because data available for that year are not comparable with figures for 1928 and later years.

**From 1939 or 1940 to 1950, whatever capital expenditures were made by individual affiliates in Europe and North Africa were not consolidated with those of the parent company.

Jersey) made a profit—varying in amounts from one year to another. Its annual net dollar earnings per share, which were $1.52 in 1927, $4.43 in 1928, and the period's low of one cent in 1932, rose to $13.48 in 1950. In this period, the book value on a per-share basis rose from $41.45 in 1927 to $85.44 in 1950. (Appendix 2, Table 2.) As a percentage of net worth, the company's annual net earnings ranged from virtually nothing in 1932 to the high for the period of 16.88 per cent in 1948. The annual average for all the years from 1927 to 1950, inclusive, was 9.23 per cent. This was approximately the average of large American manufacturing concerns generally.[3]

With minor exceptions, these earnings came from oil and gas operations. Relatively little income was obtained from such miscellaneous

000 in 1950; its net worth in those same years rose from $1,008,000,000 to $2,587,500,000. (Appendix 2, Table 3.) The ratio of long-term indebtedness to net worth for the whole period was 17.5 per cent. For the year 1950 it was approximately 17 per cent.

ADJUSTING ADMINISTRATION TO NEW NEEDS

The parent company's administration was a central factor in the development of Standard Oil Company (New Jersey). Administering a company is the work of men—men who determine policies, plan the allocation of resources, and direct and coordinate their use. Effectiveness depends not only on the leaders themselves, however, but also on the suitability of the organizations through which they work and of the techniques which they employ. In the creation of the vertically integrated, multinational concern that the company became, its administration underwent transformations in organization, techniques, and leadership.

Administrative change was initiated in 1927. President Teagle and his associates then decided that, in order to carry out their plans for improving the company's competitive position, it was necessary to overcome two major administrative weaknesses: first, that most of the directors were too narrowly occupied with the management of the parent company's own refining and sales operations; and, second, that the existing coordination in the general interest of the whole company was inadequate.

The first move was to make the parent a holding company only. This was done by transferring its own operating properties and organizations to affiliates. Henceforth, the management of all operations was to be the responsibility of the officers and managers of affiliates. This freeing of the officers and directors from managerial responsibilities was designed to enable them to raise the effectiveness of their central policy making, planning, and control in the interest of the entire company.

Adjustments were needed to provide a suitable administrative structure for the performance of these holding company functions. Basic organizational changes were made in 1927, 1933, and 1943. The first of these proved brilliantly successful in strategic planning and in the addition of valuable new properties—under the leadership of a few directors, notably the superb industrial strategist, President Teagle. However, it failed to bring about the coordination in the general interest that it was intended to achieve. The reorganization of 1933 was more successful in consolidating gains, but it proved inadequate to handle the proliferating administrative load of the 1930's and the early war years. The reorganization initiated in 1943 finally established a system that was effective in the coordination of decentralized management as well as in central planning and policy making. This change was the most creative development to that time in the company's administrative structure since that designed by John D. Rockefeller and his associates in the 1880's.

This reorganization of 1943 introduced two principal changes. First of all, it distributed authority and responsibility widely among the members of the Board of Directors. All, except the president and the chairman, were assigned "contact" responsibilities on behalf of the board for particular parent-company departments or specific operating functions among affiliates. Each contact director was expected to keep himself and the board fully informed about the area for which he had been assigned responsibility.

This sharing of the top executive function gave expression to a changing concept of authority within the Board of Directors. In the early years, President Teagle had largely handled relations with affiliates through personal contact with their chief executives. To a great extent he had controlled policy and action by his own decision, although generally consulting fully with his associates. To distribute the administrative function became necessary as the company grew in size and complexity and as its problems increased. It became possible as men with broad perspectives as well as high competence in various fields were added to the board. In the 1940's the Jersey Board of Directors became a team in which each member was "supreme among equals"; the chief executive was the leader of the team. A similar change was also taking place on various levels of decision making throughout the affiliates as well as in the parent company.

The second structural change in the parent company's administration in 1943 was the establishing of new departments to assist the Board of Directors and to provide more effective liaison with affiliates. Recognizing the need for the parent company to give greater attention to two areas of rising concern, the board established the Employee Relations Department and the Public Relations Department. It also provided for a new group of executives, known as functional coordinators, to assist the contact directors for the various branches of operations. These coordinators, with their staff departments, maintained close and continuing relations with the managers of affiliates in their particular branch of operations. They and the Coordination Committee, with its Economics and Coordination Department, constituted an effective system for keeping the contact directors and Jersey's top governing bodies informed about affiliates and for assisting in planning the whole Jersey group's investments and in coordinating operations.

The administrative process was strengthened by the development and use of increasingly effective procedures and techniques. Both parent company and affiliates contributed to this growth. The former's special contribution was to provide means for spreading new attitudes, knowledge, and ways of doing things throughout the whole company. Jersey served as teacher, guide, and general coordinator for the affiliates as well as judge of their performance.

Improved techniques made essential contributions to planning and control. They included more precise accounting methods that were applied uniformly—as far as feasible—throughout the whole company. They introduced increasingly sophisticated economic analysis and cost control and made possible more realistic forecasting of the market for products and of the company's financial resources. A highly complex system, employing advanced methods, was also developed for planning capital expenditures. In the larger affiliates especially, the process of preparing capital budgets began on the lower operating levels and proceeded upward to departmental headquarters and the company's board. In the parent company, these proposed expenditures were given an intensive examination by the functional coordinators and the Coordination Committee, with the aid of professional specialists. Finally, the budgets were reviewed by the Executive Committee, which served as Jersey's investment committee. This body commented on the budgets of the affiliates. Under Jersey's system of decentralized management, each company had the authority to act as it chose upon these comments—except as it was dependent on the parent company for funds.

The parent company developed a complex system of communication— written and personal, vertical and horizontal. Communication became increasingly important as the company's investments and operations grew in size and complexity. It developed as means of travel and long-distance communication improved and as the parent company established more suitable organizations for relations with affiliates. A comprehensive number of written reports kept the parent company informed about the operations of affiliates. In the later 1930's, and especially after the organizational changes of the 1940's, two-way personal consultation tied the various departments and divisions of the parent company closer to their counterparts among affiliates. Annual conferences of high executives from around the world and periodic gatherings of representatives of like interests in parent company and affiliates became a regular part of the company's administrative process. Consultation and conference brought about a greater unity of interest and broader perspectives and helped to raise the general level of performance toward that of the more progressive units.

Similarly basic transformations were developed in relations with employees. Change in the worldwide Jersey Company, the oil industry, and the sociopolitical environment made it necessary to give increasing attention to the building and maintaining of operating forces of adequate competence and high morale. By 1927, the parent company's experience with progressive policies and programs since World War I and the creation of its small staff of specialists in employee relations had given it a foundation on which to build. At first its role was mainly advisory. The larger affiliates in the Americas made substantial progress in the 1930's in building and maintaining employee forces of the quality and morale required for effectively meeting changing conditions and needs. Most affiliates adopted variations of Jersey's benefits plans and also some form of collective bargaining. Special problems had to be met in underdeveloped countries. In anticipation of the need to apply progressive methods everywhere in the future as well as to help in solving wartime employee problems, Jersey in 1943 established its Employee Relations Department. As research staff, adviser to affiliates, and general coordinator, this department helped to improve employee management and relations throughout the whole Jersey Company.

The training and education of employees in the 1930's and 1940's became increasingly vital elements in raising the quality, performance, and morale of employees. The emphasis at first was on special programs for training in operating skills and foremanship. After World War II, in order to improve employee relations throughout the entire company, Jersey established the Esso Training Center. There, executives and directors of training from foreign and domestic affiliates were taught what research and experience had found to be the more constructive methods for improving employee management. Creole set up a similar training center in Venezuela. Creole and other affiliates in underdeveloped countries also sent hundreds of men abroad each year—principally to the United States—to study at colleges and universities.

An important new development after the war was a comprehensive program for executive development adopted by the parent company and many affiliates. Under this program, men with demonstrated executive

PRINCIPAL AFFILIATES AND AREAS OF THEIR OPERATIONS IN 1950

CONSOLIDATED COMPANIES

UNITED STATES

Esso Standard Oil Company (100%)
Refining, transportation, and marketing on Eastern seaboard

Humble Oil & Refining Company (72%)
Producing, transportation, refining, and marketing in Texas

The Carter Oil Company (100%)
Producing, refining, and marketing in central United States and Rocky Mountain area

Interstate Oil Pipe Line Company (100%)
Pipeline transportation, Oklahoma, Louisiana, and Mississippi

Interstate Natural Gas Company, Incorporated (54%)
Production of natural gas in Louisiana

Esso Shipping Company (100%)
Marine transportation

Esso Export Corporation (100%)
Marketing

Mediterranean Standard Oil Co. (100%)
Purchase and sale of Middle East crude and products

Gilbert & Barker Manufacturing Company (100%)
Manufacture and sale of oil burners and service station equipment

Enjay Company, Inc. (100%)
Marketing of chemical products

Standard Oil Development Company (100%)
Research and development

CANADA

Imperial Oil, Limited (70%)
Producing, transportation, refining, and marketing

LATIN AMERICA

Creole Petroleum Corporation (94%)
Producing, transportation, refining, and marketing in Venezuela

Lago Oil & Transport Company, Limited (100%)
Refining in Aruba, N.W.I.

International Petroleum Company, Limited (83%)
Producing, transportation, refining, and marketing in Peru, Colombia, and Venezuela

Panama Transport Company (100%)
Marine transportation

Standard Oil Company of Brazil (100%)
Marketing in Brazil

Esso, Productora de Petróleo S. A. (100%)
Producing in Argentina

Esso, Refinadora de Petróleo S. A. (100%)
Refining in Argentina

Esso, Sociedad Anónima Petrolera Argentina (100%)
Marketing in Argentina

Esso Standard Oil Company (Chile) S. A. C. (100%)
Marketing in Chile

Esso Standard Oil Company (Uruguay), S.A. (100%)
Marketing in Uruguay

Esso Standard Oil Company (Cuba) (100%)
Refining and marketing in Cuba

Esso Standard Oil Company (Puerto Rico) (100%)
Marketing in Puerto Rico and Virgin Islands

Esso Standard Oil (Antilles) S.A. (100%)
Marketing in Guianas and Lesser Antilles

Esso Standard Oil (Caribbean) S.A. (100%)
Marketing in Bermuda, the Bahamas, and Greater Antilles

Esso Standard Oil (Central America) S.A. (100%)
Marketing in Central America

Standard Oil (Canal Zone) Company (100%)
Marketing in Canal Zone

NONCONSOLIDATED COMPANIES

UNITED STATES

Ethyl Corporation (50%)
Manufacture and sale of antiknock compound

Plantation Pipe Line Company (49%)
Pipeline transportation from Louisiana to North Carolina

Solid black indicates principal affiliates' producing, refining, or marketing areas.
In the U.S.A., only the states in which affiliates had operations are indicated.

CANADA

Interprovincial Pipe Line Company (35%)
Pipeline transportation from Alberta to Wisconsin

EUROPE AND NORTH AFRICA

Anglo-American Oil Company, Limited (100%)
Refining, transportation, and marketing in the United Kingdom and Eire

Standard Française des Pétroles S. A. (55%)
Refining and marketing in France

Esso A. G. (100%)
Marketing in Western Germany

Ebano Asphalt-Werke A. G. (100%)
Refining in Western Germany

Gewerkschaft Brigitta (50%)
Producing in Western Germany

Società Petrolifera Italiana p. A. (59%)
Producing and refining in Italy

Stanic-Industria Petrolifera S. p. A. (50%)
Refining in Italy

Esso Standard Italiana, S. p. A. (90%)
Marketing in Italy

Esso Standard (Belgium) (88%)
Marketing in Belgium

Standard Amerikaansche Petroleum Cie. N.V. (66%)
Marketing in the Netherlands

N. V. Nederlandse Aardolie Mij. (50%)
Producing in the Netherlands

Det Danske Petroleums A/S (82%)
Marketing in Denmark

A/S Ostlandske Petroleumscompagni (56%)
Refining and marketing in Norway

Svenska Petroleum A/B Standard (100%)
Marketing in Sweden

O/Y Nobel-Standard A/B (67%)
Marketing in Finland

Esso Standard (Switzerland) (100%)
Marketing in Switzerland

Esso Standard Algérie S. A. (100%)
Marketing in Algeria

Esso Standard Tunisie S. A. (76%)
Marketing in Tunisia

Esso Standard (Near East), Inc. (100%)
Marketing in eastern Mediterranean

MIDDLE AND FAR EAST

Standard-Vacuum Oil Company (50%)
Producing, refining, transportation, and marketing in Far East, Australasia, and Africa

Iraq Petroleum Company, Limited (12%)
Producing, refining, and pipeline transportation in Iraq

Arabian American Oil Company (30%)
Producing and refining in Saudi Arabia

Trans-Arabian Pipe Line Company (30%)
Pipeline transportation from Saudi Arabia to Mediterranean terminal in Lebanon

NOTE: Jersey's percentage of ownership in each company, shown in parentheses, has been rounded out to the nearest whole figure. Some relatively small companies are included in order to show the worldwide areas of the affiliates' operations.

potential were selected for special training. In order to widen their experience, they were assigned to various positions in more than one company and often in more than one country. They were also sent to attend university courses in management on the advanced graduate-school level. The whole plan was designed to provide men showing high promise with the professional training and broad perspectives required for leading a complex company in the postwar world.

Behind all these developments in the company's administration was a changing leadership within the parent company—and, in fact, within the affiliates as well. At the beginning of this period, the members of Jersey's Board of Directors were typically men who had been educated principally in the school of experience and had risen from the ranks; they were relatively narrow specialists who had worked mainly in one company and in the United States. Only a few—notably Teagle and Sadler—had had an education on the collegiate level, had worked in more than one company, had served abroad as well as at home, and had acquired a wide familiarity with the world oil industry. Even these knowledgeable executives, however, looked upon their company's responsibilities as wholly industrial, except of course in times of war or of other national crisis.

The directors of the 1940's had the same general objective as their predecessors, but they brought different qualifications to their work and had a broader conception of their company's responsibilities. All but a few had earned one or more degrees in some special field, mainly in science and engineering. All had had a varied experience within the company, and several had worked in affiliates in both the United States and foreign countries. All had been tempered by depression and war. These later board members represented a wider range of specialties than the men they succeeded; they were also generalists in that they had grown beyond their particular specialty. They utilized more analytical approaches to problems than their predecessors, and they were conversant with more advanced techniques. On the whole, they also had a high capacity for teamwork. As a group, they were aware that the company's future depended not on superior industrial performance alone but also on its standing with public and government, wherever it operated. Good relations were necessary not only in the United States. As an officer of the parent company said in 1947, Jersey's general public was truly international.[5]

By 1950, the Jersey affiliates were supplying virtually a complete line of products in countries representing more than 90 per cent of the consumption of petroleum in the free world. In nearly all countries where they sold the full range of products, they were essentially nationwide marketers.[6] The outstanding exception was the United States; even there, with marketing operations in twenty-seven states instead of ten as in 1927, the company had progressed a long way toward national distribution. Of its daily average worldwide sales totaling 1,732,000 barrels in 1950, a slightly larger amount was sold abroad than at home.

The company had producing and refining operations favorably located for meeting competitors in nearly all markets on equal terms as to supply and costs. In fact, by 1950 it had several oil circuits. The domestic affiliates were then disposing of most of their products within the United States. Imperial was increasingly supplying its refineries and markets from its own producing operations within Canada. Creole in Venezuela and the refinery in Aruba had large outlets in Western Europe. Jersey's share of production in Iraq and Saudi Arabia was mainly going to refineries in the Middle East and Europe and the products to markets in Europe and Asia. Standard-Vacuum was restoring its production and refining in Sumatra to serve Oriental markets. Standard Oil Company (New Jersey), in fact, had substantial participation in all the important oil provinces of the non-Communist world.

Principally a seller of American products in foreign markets in 1927, Standard Oil Company (New Jersey) had become a truly multinational concern, with all the advantages and disadvantages of that status. The company had acquired production and refining outside the United States commensurate with its sale of products in foreign countries. The accompanying map indicates how widely scattered its operations were in 1950. Affiliates flourished in all types of climate and terrain and among peoples of all races, varied cultures, and different economic systems—and in countries with basic differences from Jersey's homeland in governments, legal systems, and national goals. Administering the company successfully not only had become a matter of farseeing competitive strategy and efficient performance. It also had come to require industrial statesmanship of a high order in the changing world of the mid-twentieth century.

Appendix 1

Directors and Officers of Standard Oil Company (New Jersey), 1927–1950

Directors[a]	From	To
Jennings, Walter	January 13, 1903	January 9, 1933[c]
Hunt, Seth B.	January 13, 1914	April 5, 1933
Jones, George H.	April 18, 1917	November 22, 1928[c]
Teagle, Walter C.	November 15, 1917[b]	November 30, 1942
Moffett, James A., Jr.	August 21, 1919	July 28, 1933
Black, Charles G.	December 27, 1920	June 6, 1933
Clark, Edgar M.	December 27, 1920	June 6, 1933
Sadler, Everit J.	December 27, 1920	November 30, 1942
Weller, Daniel R.	February 15, 1926	December 31, 1931
Farish, William S.	June 7, 1927	November 29, 1942[c]
Mowinckel, John A.	June 7, 1927	April 7, 1934
Payne, Christy	June 7, 1927	June 4, 1935
Riedemann, Heinrich	June 7, 1927	June 6, 1933
Senior, Joseph H.	June 7, 1927	June 6, 1933
Smith, G. Harrison	June 7, 1927	June 4, 1940
Swain, Chester O.	June 7, 1927	April 21, 1937[c]
Bedford, Frederick H., Jr.	October 14, 1927	December 3, 1952[c]
Hurll, Peter	November 28, 1928	May 16, 1934
Harden, Orville	April 12, 1929	December 31, 1953
Seidel, Harry G.	April 12, 1929	April 7, 1934
Powell, Francis E.	June 11, 1930	August 3, 1931
Stewart, Robert G.	June 7, 1932	February 11, 1935
Gallagher, Ralph W.	November 17, 1933	December 31, 1945
Harper, Donald L.	April 23, 1935	November 30, 1942
McCobb, Thomas C.	June 4, 1935	August 31, 1944
Pratt, Wallace E.	June 1, 1937	July 31, 1945
Abrams, Frank W.	June 4, 1940	December 31, 1953
Holman, Eugene	June 4, 1940	May 25, 1960
Haslam, Robert T.	December 1, 1942	June 7, 1950

[a] Date of retirement given through April 30, 1965.
[b] Had also been a director from 1909 to 1914; he was not a director during 1914–1917 when he served as president of Imperial Oil Limited.
[c] Died in office.

Pierce, Frank W.	December 1, 1942	March 1, 1953
Crane, Jay E.	June 6, 1944	May 22, 1957
Smith, Chester F.	June 6, 1944	May 23, 1956
Suman, John R.	February 1, 1945	March 31, 1955
Howard, Bushrod B.	August 31, 1945	November 1, 1954
Coleman, Stewart P.	January 1, 1946	March 31, 1961
Soubry, Emile E.	January 1, 1949	May 24, 1961
Brice, John W.	November 1, 1949	June 8, 1951
Rathbone, Monroe J.	November 1, 1949	May 19, 1965
Hewetson, Henry H.	June 7, 1950	May 27, 1959

Chairmen of the Board

Jones, George H.	November 16, 1925	November 22, 1928
Farish, William S.	June 6, 1933	June 1, 1937
Teagle, Walter C.	June 1, 1937	November 30, 1942
Gallagher, Ralph W.	December 1, 1942 and	January 6, 1943
	June 12, 1944	December 31, 1945
Abrams, Frank W.	January 1, 1946	December 31, 1953

Presidents

Teagle, Walter C.	November 15, 1917	June 1, 1937
Farish, William S.	June 1, 1937	November 29, 1942
Gallagher, Ralph W.	January 6, 1943	June 12, 1944
Holman, Eugene	June 12, 1944	December 31, 1953

Vice-Presidents

Hunt, Seth B.	August 21, 1919	April 5, 1933
Jones, George H.	December 27, 1920	November 16, 1925
Moffett, James A., Jr.	June 9, 1924	July 28, 1933
Reed, Frank A.	February 25, 1927	June 4, 1931
Black, Charles G.	May 16, 1930	June 6, 1933
Clark, Edgar M.	May 16, 1930	June 6, 1933
Sadler, Everit J.	May 16, 1930 and	December 24, 1931
	January 18, 1932 and	August 1, 1933
	August 30, 1933	November 30, 1942
Payne, Christy	June 6, 1933	June 4, 1935
Harden, Orville	April 4, 1935	December 31, 1953
Swain, Chester O.	June 4, 1935	April 21, 1937
Gallagher, Ralph W.	April 27, 1937	November 30, 1942
Howard, Frank A.	July 19, 1940	January 5, 1945
Pratt, Wallace E.	December 1, 1942	January 31, 1945
Holman, Eugene	December 1, 1942	June 12, 1944

Abrams, Frank W.	June 12, 1944	December 31, 1945
Suman, John R.	February 1, 1945	March 31, 1955
Haslam, Robert T.	January 1, 1946	October 1, 1950
Smith, Chester F.	December 1, 1946	August 11, 1955
Crane, Jay E.	October 19, 1950	September 6, 1956

Treasurers

Hunt, Seth B.	November 16, 1925	April 5, 1933
Payne, Christy	April 5, 1933	June 4, 1935
Resor, Reuben P.	June 4, 1935	August 9, 1938
Crane, Jay E.	August 10, 1938	October 16, 1944
Welch, Leo D.	October 16, 1944	May 27, 1954

Secretaries

White, Charles T.	December 4, 1911	June 6, 1933
Minton, Adrian C.	June 6, 1933	February 24, 1955

Appendix 2

Selected Financial and Operating Statistics

Table 1: **ANALYSIS OF OWNERSHIP OF COMMON STOCK**
Standard Oil Company (New Jersey), 1927–1950

	Holdings Under 1,000 Shares		Holdings of 1,000 Shares or More		Total Holdings of Shares	
	No. of holders	No. of shares	No. of holders	No. of shares	No. of holders	No. of shares
1927	50,802	4,046,463	2,037	20,244,170	52,839	24,290,633
1928	60,539	4,309,194	1,581	20,135,134	62,120	24,444,328
1929	91,051	4,379,479	1,707	20,473,908	92,758	24,853,459
1930	110,288	5,421,154	1,664	20,080,142	111,952	25,501,296
1931	125,478	5,803,682	1,563	19,873,664	127,041	25,677,346
1932	139,465	6,647,076	1,950	19,093,793	141,415	25,740,869
1933	131,763	6,470,635	1,951	19,270,242	133,714	25,740,877
1934	125,048	6,307,647	1,978	19,548,350	127,026	25,855,997
1935	123,894	6,607,651	2,015	19,248,346	125,909	25,855,997
1936	118,546	6,542,456	2,082	19,682,227	120,628	26,224,683
1937	120,447	6,717,715	2,082	19,506,968	122,559	26,224,683
1938	124,319	6,992,326	2,064	19,599,150	126,383	26,591,476
1939	128,677	7,307,644	2,100	19,942,989	130,777	27,250,633
1940	134,273	7,609,056	2,082	19,674,531	136,355	27,283,587
1941	141,374	8,226,590	2,109	19,056,997	143,483	27,283,587
1942	145,181	8,492,374	2,119	18,791,213	147,300	27,283,587
1943	147,098	8,678,309	2,110	18,605,278	149,208	27,283,587
1944	152,924	9,031,760	2,124	18,301,982	155,048	27,333,742
1945	157,896	9,344,326	2,129	17,989,416	160,025	27,333,742
1946	161,914	9,605,350	2,101	17,728,392	164,015	27,333,742
1947	168,624	9,900,417	2,068	17,433,325	170,692	27,333,742
1948	197,992	11,284,367	2,066	18,101,068	200,058	29,385,435
1949	212,867	11,451,718	2,143	18,731,676	215,010	30,183,394
1950	219,922	11,623,329	2,142	18,662,217	222,064	30,285,546

NOTE: Does not include shares issuable for scrip certificates, except for years 1948–1950. Figures for 1927–1933 are as of November, the closest to the year end that information as to the size of individual holdings is available. The remainder are as of the year end, with a very slight difference from published figures because they include a few shares of $100 par value not exchanged for $25 shares in the change of 1922.
Source: Stock records of Standard Oil Company (New Jersey).

Table 2: **CONSOLIDATED EARNINGS, DIVIDENDS, RETAINED EARNINGS, AND BOOK VALUE, AS REPORTED PER SHARE, 1927–1950**
Standard Oil Company (New Jersey)

Year	Earnings	Dividends Cash	Dividends Stock	Retained earnings	Book value	Number of shares (year end)
1927	$ 1.52	$1.50	16⅔%[a]	$ 0.02	$41.45	24,317,219
1928	4.43	1.50		2.93	44.52	24,484,219
1929	4.75	1.87		2.88	46.61	25,418,968
1930	1.65	2.00		(0.35)[b]	46.52	25,518,468
1931	0.34	2.00		(1.66)	48.02	25,735,468
1932	0.01	2.00		(1.99)	45.22	25,740,965
1933	0.97	1.25		(0.28)	44.71	25,761,465
1934	1.76	1.25		0.51	42.37	25,856,081
1935	2.43	1.96[c]		1.18	42.33	25,856,081
1936	3.73	2.00		1.73	43.73	26,224,767
1937	5.64	2.50		3.14	46.45	26,224,767
1938	2.86	1.50	1½%[d]	1.36	46.15	26,618,065
1939	3.26	1.25	2½%[e]	2.01	46.74	27,285,919
1940	4.54	1.75		2.79	47.65	27,283,587
1941	5.15	2.50		2.65	48.32	27,283,587
1942	3.06	2.00		1.06	48.53	27,283,587
1943	4.45	3.76[f]		2.45	49.65	27,283,587
1944	5.69	2.50		3.19	52.85	27,333,742
1945	5.64	2.50		3.14	56.33	27,333,742
1946	6.50	3.00		3.50	60.56	27,333,742
1947	9.83	4.00		5.83	66.50	27,333,742
1948	12.44	2.00	5%[g]	10.44	73.68	29,385,435
1949	8.91	4.00	2%[h]	4.91	77.10	30,183,394
1950	13.48	5.00		8.48	85.44	30,285,546

[a] 1 share for 6.
[b] ( ) means amount paid per share in excess of the year's earnings.
[c] 4 shares Mission Corporation for 75 shares of Jersey worth 71 cents per Jersey share book value, plus $1.25 in cash.
[d] 3 shares for 200.
[e] 5 shares for 200.
[f] 1 share Consolidated Natural Gas Co. for 10 shares of Jersey worth $1.76 per Jersey share book value, plus $2 in cash.

[g] 2 shares for 40.
[h] 1 share for 50.
NOTE: The year 1939 excludes affiliates located in Great Britain, France, Finland, Germany, and Algeria; the years 1940 through 1950 exclude affiliates located in Great Britain, Continental Europe, and North Africa.
Source: Comptroller's Department, Standard Oil Company (New Jersey).

Table 3: **CONSOLIDATED BALANCE SHEET, 1927–1950**
Standard Oil Company (New Jersey)
(In thousands of dollars)

Year	Current Assets	Property, Plant, and Equipment Less Reserves	Investments and Other Assets	Total Assets	Current Liabilities
		Assets			
1927	$ 615,098	$ 656,645	$154,858	$1,426,601	$ 98,702
1928	713,070	651,603	207,595	1,572,268	144,731
1929	783,188	776,589	207,601	1,767,378	170,109
1930	730,987	851,823	188,184	1,770,994	169,094
1931	671,155	1,129,911	117,944	1,919,010	85,916
1932	574,782	1,148,831	164,396	1,888,009	127,631
1933	557,678	1,060,449	294,108	1,912,235	150,501
1934	608,940	1,082,380	250,390	1,941,710	201,774
1935	641,470	1,054,520	198,924	1,894,914	216,133
1936	611,264	1,041,421	189,165	1,841,850	178,926
1937	672,068	1,193,535	195,213	2,060,816	237,139
1938	667,346	1,172,252	205,037	2,044,635	177,662
1939	595,718	1,121,061	318,210	2,034,989	129,111
1940	606,040	1,078,224	387,274	2,071,538	120,185
1941	693,621	1,059,679	449,052	2,202,352	187,347
1942	685,549	1,121,476	413,153	2,220,178	189,812
1943	859,800	1,108,310	359,699	2,327,809	273,941
1944	1,027,712	1,118,508	344,090	2,490,310	330,633
1945	1,043,898	1,142,230	345,680	2,531,808	264,080
1946	1,023,080	1,277,763	359,145	2,659,988	284,049
1947	1,100,563	1,526,062	369,365	2,995,990	410,494
1948	1,184,288	1,860,334	481,421	3,526,043	524,450
1949	1,246,682	2,087,371	481,992	3,816,045	399,418
1950	1,542,211	2,127,032	518,752	4,187,995	495,079

NOTE: The year 1939 excludes affiliates located in Great Britain, France, Germany, Algeria, and Finland; the years 1940 through 1950 exclude all affiliates located in Great Britain, Continental Europe, and North Africa.

Table 3 (*Cont.*): **CONSOLIDATED BALANCE SHEET, 1927–1950**
Standard Oil Company (New Jersey)
(In thousands of dollars)

Liabilities			Shareholders' Equity		Total Liabilities and Shareholders' Equity
Long-Term Indebtedness	Minority Interest	Reserves and Other Liabilities	Capital Stock	Surplus	
$169,239	$119,978	$ 30,609	$607,930	$ 400,143	$1,426,601
167,197	134,063	36,129	612,105	478,043	1,572,268
170,133	163,661	78,778	635,474	549,223	1,767,378
169,014	163,551	82,120	637,962	549,253	1,770,994
173,442	327,353	96,419	643,387	592,493	1,919,010
271,048	284,960	40,290	643,524	520,556	1,888,009
251,106	282,710	76,035	644,037	507,846	1,912,235
217,830	344,310	82,332	646,402	449,062	1,941,710
163,631	334,834	85,786	646,402	448,128	1,894,914
178,989	249,327	87,897	655,619	491,092	1,841,850
221,973	251,833	131,682	655,619	562,570	2,060,816
276,082	242,749	119,827	665,452	562,863	2,044,635
270,670	244,367	115,366	682,148	593,327	2,034,989
270,768	228,321	152,086	682,090	618,088	2,071,538
283,883	242,915	169,928	682,090	636,189	2,202,352
253,036	245,859	207,310	682,090	642,011	2,220,178
232,158	246,179	220,857	682,090	672,584	2,327,809
214,855	262,906	237,264	683,344	761,308	2,490,310
203,130	279,002	245,965	683,344	856,287	2,531,808
198,207	294,390	228,020	683,344	971,978	2,659,988
213,298	319,001	235,374	683,344	1,134,479	2,995,990
225,098	344,056	267,338	734,636	1,430,465	3,526,043
475,710	351,032	262,643	754,585	1,572,657	3,816,045
441,024	367,622	296,756	757,139	1,830,375	4,187,995

Source: Comptroller's Department, Standard Oil
Company (New Jersey).

Table 4: **SOURCES AND USES OF FUNDS, 1928–1950**
Standard Oil Company (New Jersey)
(In millions of dollars)

				Sources of Funds				
	Net Income Accruing to Jersey	**Net Income Accruing to Minority Interests in Affiliated Companies**	**Deprecia-tion, Depletion, and Retire-ments**	**Cash Income Total**	**Proceeds from Sale of Prop-erties**	**Net Change in Long-Term Debt**	**Other (Net)**	**Total Sources of Funds**
1928	$108.5	$17.4	$ 75.2	$201.1		$ (2.0)	$(58.2)	$140.9
1929	120.9	24.0	79.5	224.4		2.9	(11.2)	216.1
1930	42.2	14.7	84.2	141.1		(1.1)	(6.3)	133.7
1931	8.7	11.9	109.8	130.4		4.4	(27.1)	107.7
1932	.3	15.3	111.3	126.9		97.6	(62.2)	162.3
1933	25.1	13.7	112.0	150.8		(19.9)	42.1	173.0
1934	45.6	22.3	111.6	179.5		(33.3)	25.5	171.7
1935	62.9	24.1	118.3	205.3		(54.2)	11.6	162.7
1936	97.8	28.6	113.7	240.1		15.4	(75.5)	180.0
1937	148.0	40.7	110.8	299.5		59.6	(5.0)	354.1
1938	76.1	32.4	111.5	220.0		55.6	8.1	263.5
1939	89.1	24.6	98.7	212.4		(3.9)	(47.7)	160.8
1940	123.9	21.1	95.8	240.8		(3.5)	(45.5)	191.8
1941	140.6	26.7	90.9	258.2		6.3	(14.9)	249.6
1942	83.4	20.8	87.3	191.5	$56.3	(20.0)	28.0	255.8
1943	121.3	25.8	110.9	258.0	16.7	(15.9)	38.9	297.7
1944	155.4	36.3	119.6	311.3	22.8	(17.3)	45.9	362.7
1945	154.2	35.4	137.5	327.1	12.8	(11.7)	28.4	356.6
1946	177.6	34.1	120.0	331.7	12.5	(4.9)	.4	339.7
1947	268.6	52.5	143.0	464.1	28.6	15.1	7.3	515.1
1948	365.6	79.3	168.1	613.0	17.4	11.8	(51.7)	590.5
1949	268.9	56.3	184.3	509.5	16.5	250.6	6.1	782.7
1950	408.2	63.0	201.1	672.3	33.4	(34.7)	8.3	679.3

NOTE: 1927 is not included because data available for that year are not comparable with figures for 1928 and later years. From 1928 through 1941 "Proceeds from sale of properties" and "Cash dividends paid to minority interests" do not appear under those headings but are included in "Other (net)" under "Sources of funds."

Table 4: (*cont.*):   **SOURCES AND USES OF FUNDS, 1928–1950**
Standard Oil Company (New Jersey)
(In millions of dollars)

							Cash Dividends Paid to Jersey Shareholders	Cash Dividends Paid to Minority Interests in Affiliates	Total Uses of Funds	Increase (Decrease) in Funds
			Additions to Properties							
	Producing	Refining	Marketing	Transportation	Other	Total				
1928						$ 52.4	$ 36.6		$ 89.0	$ 51.9
1929						124.9	46.5		171.4	44.7
1930						134.0	50.9		184.9	(51.2)
1931						33.1	51.2		84.3	23.4
1932						249.8	50.6		300.4	(138.1)
1933						101.0	32.0		133.0	40.0
1934						139.8	31.9		171.7	—
1935						112.2	32.3		144.5	18.2
1936						120.6	52.4		173.0	7.0
1937						286.0	65.5		351.5	2.6
1938						169.4	39.3		208.7	54.8
1939						150.4	33.5		183.9	(23.1)
1940						124.9	47.7		172.6	19.2
1941						161.0	68.2		229.2	20.4
1942	$ 49.3	$ 76.1	$ 7.9	$56.1	$5.9	195.3	54.6	$ 16.5	266.4	(10.6)
1943	61.4	42.1	3.6	24.0	4.5	135.6	54.6	17.3	207.5	90.2
1944	100.6	12.4	7.6	33.2	9.4	163.2	68.3	20.0	251.5	111.2
1945	134.7	13.4	15.2	20.3	1.8	185.4	68.3	20.2	273.9	82.7
1946	151.9	37.6	36.5	49.8	3.0	278.8	82.0	19.7	380.5	(40.8)
1947	187.5	96.8	50.7	86.2	4.5	425.7	109.3	29.1	564.1	(49.0)
1948	272.2	137.1	42.0	72.7	5.4	529.4	55.9	35.4	620.7	(30.2)
1949	210.3	107.2	43.1	77.6	3.7	441.9	119.8	33.6	595.3	187.4
1950	159.0	54.6	37.6	41.9	2.0	295.1	151.0	33.3	479.4	199.9

Data are not included in 1939 for affiliates in Great Britain, France, Finland, Germany, and Algeria, or in 1940 through 1950 for affiliates in Continental Europe, Great Britain, and North Africa.

"Additions to properties" by functions are not available before 1942.
Source: Comptroller's Department, Standard Oil Company (New Jersey).

Table 5: **CONSOLIDATED INCOME STATEMENT, 1927–1950**
Standard Oil Company (New Jersey)
(In thousands of dollars)

Year	Revenues		Costs and Other Deductions				Net Income Accruing To	
	Sales and Operating	Non-operating	Operating Costs and Expenses (Exclusive of Those Shown Separately)	Deprecia-tion, Depletion, and Retire-ments	Income Taxes	Interest and Other Financial Charges	Minority Interests	Jersey Share-holders
1927[a]	$1,256,505	$18,081	$1,141,425	$ 74,899	[d]	$ 8,518	$ 9,321	$ 40,423
1928[a]	1,302,779	17,361	1,110,524	75,220	[d]	8,533	17,377	108,486
1929[a]	1,523,386	26,076	1,315,921	79,543	[d]	9,088	23,997	120,913
1930[a]	1,381,879	29,395	1,261,211	84,221	[d]	8,903	14,788	42,151
1931[a]	1,084,926	32,615	977,739	109,824	[d]	9,361	11,913	8,704
1932[a]	1,080,026	209	943,405	111,334	[d]	9,847	15,366	283
1933	779,766	2,058	623,221	111,977	[d]	7,840	13,702	25,084
1934	1,017,973	18,973	825,641	111,634	$ 14,111	17,678	22,263	45,619
1935	1,076,215	26,289	864,733	118,339	17,600	14,840	24,128	62,864
1936	1,162,121	24,959	908,622	113,747	26,052	12,315	28,571	97,773
1937	1,308,900	23,995	988,914	110,763	35,791	8,737	40,698	147,992
1938	1,173,730	25,478	939,162	111,468	30,797	9,345	32,382	76,054
1939[b]	933,766	21,073	708,804	98,717	23,904	9,683	24,602	89,129
1940[c]	821,684	34,027	572,144	95,832	33,277	9,432	21,140	123,886
1941[c]	978,365	38,443	658,805	90,942	60,609	39,212[e]	26,668	140,572
1942[c]	1,039,339	14,818	795,618	87,302	50,000	18,628[f]	20,799	81,810
1943[c]	1,302,812	19,339	956,382	110,910	93,000	14,729[f]	25,803	121,327
1944[c]	1,638,706	14,100	1,205,730	119,559	115,000	20,777[f]	36,344	155,396
1945[c]	1,618,075	17,811	1,229,324	137,535	69,000	10,447[f]	35,424	154,156
1946[c]	1,622,339	22,473	1,246,259	120,006	73,000	(6,222)[f]	34,159	177,610
1947[c]	2,354,917	31,750	1,781,402	143,003	135,000	6,155[f]	52,481	268,626
1948[c]	3,300,786	31,402	2,495,887	168,081	203,000	20,296	79,319	365,605
1949[c]	2,891,945	42,741	2,297,994	184,274	115,000	12,270	56,279	268,869
1950[c]	3,134,558	63,709	2,299,115	201,082	207,000	19,891	62,956	408,223

[a] Includes intercompany sales and purchases.
[b] Excludes affiliates located in Great Britain, France, Germany, Algeria, and Finland.
[c] Excludes affiliates located in Great Britain, Continental Europe, and North Africa.
[d] Income taxes are included in operating costs and expenses.
[e] Includes a provision of $30,000,000 for losses on foreign investments.

[f] Includes provisions for wartime and postwar contingencies of $7,000,000 in 1942, $6,000,000 in 1943, $12,000,000 in 1944, and $1,000,000 in 1945. The major portion of these reserve provisions was not required and was later restored to income: $15,500,000 in 1946 and $9,046,000 in 1947.

Source: Comptroller's Department, Standard Oil Company (New Jersey).

Table 6: **NUMBER OF EMPLOYEES, 1927—1950**
Standard Oil Company (New Jersey) and Affiliates[a]

As of Dec. 31	United States[b]	Canada[c]	Latin America	Total Western Hemisphere	Eastern Hemisphere[d]	Total
1927	51,808	17,200	8,611	77,619	32,978	110,597
1928	49,898	18,354	10,516	78,768	33,277	112,045
1929	57,865	20,282	9,986	88,133	41,684	129,817
1930	54,681	17,517	11,214	83,412	57,691	141,103
1931	46,197	13,414	7,994	67,605	47,051	114,656
1932	46,388	13,058	14,182	73,628	46,841	120,469
1933	47,171	13,778	19,638	80,587	49,854	130,441
1934	50,179	15,393	20,070	85,642	44,061	129,703
1935	49,612	16,100	21,414	87,126	42,853	129,979
1936	49,424	16,996	20,808	87,228	43,000	130,228
1937	51,846	7,901	35,954	95,701	41,456	137,157
1938	50,621	7,648	34,304	92,573	41,394	133,967
1939	48,654	7,580	35,233	91,467	35,095	126,562
1940	48,441	8,083	32,829	89,353	27,754	117,107
1941	50,765	8,204	33,369	92,338	10,706	103,044
1942	50,346	8,507	33,034	91,887	9,914	101,801
1943	52,674	10,332	35,244	98,250	10,817	109,067
1944	48,907	11,571	37,837	98,315	11,612	109,927
1945	52,924	11,459	41,984	106,367	18,693	125,060
1946	57,775	10,881	48,610	117,266	32,284	149,550
1947	61,444	12,659	53,859	127,962	41,334	169,296
1948	63,018	12,864	55,115	130,977	29,142	160,119
1949	60,324	12,725	49,267	122,316	30,105	152,421
1950	58,735	12,454	45,610	116,799	30,811	147,610

[a] Companies in which Jersey had more than a 50 per cent stock interest.
[b] Casual employees not included.
[c] Employees in Newfoundland are included but not those of Imperial's affiliates in Latin America.

[d] For the years 1939–1950 figures for Europe are not complete. Does not include employees in the Far East after merger in Standard-Vacuum in 1934.
Source: Employee Relations Department, Standard Oil Company (New Jersey).

Table 7: **WORLDWIDE SALES OF PRODUCTS, 1927–1950**
Standard Oil Company (New Jersey)
(Thousands of barrels daily)

	Major Products						
	Total Gasolines[a]						
Year	Aviation Fuels[b]	Motor Gasolines[c]	Kerosenes[d]	Distillates[e]	Residual Fuels[e]	Total Major Products	Total Products[f]
1927	176.5		47.1	44.5	122.0	390.1	428.5
1928	186.6		45.4	46.3	146.1	424.4	464.4
1929	223.0		46.1	54.7	161.8	485.6	530.6
1930	226.4		43.7	58.2	158.1	486.4	527.9
1931	213.5		44.3	51.2	137.7	446.7	487.9
1932	218.2		42.9	51.8	163.0	475.9	512.4
1933	233.0		56.0	62.7	216.4	568.1	607.2
1934	227.5		56.3	72.6	231.5	587.9	628.2
1935	238.2		56.3	81.9	235.5	611.9	657.2
1936	257.5		60.3	103.8	248.2	669.8	719.3
1937	281.2		64.3	129.1	275.2	749.8	803.7
1938	10.0	278.7	61.5	140.3	256.0	746.5	798.5
1939	12.8	289.2	68.3	153.0	263.8	787.1	846.0
1940	13.5	254.7	62.6	142.4	266.1	739.3	785.2
1941	23.5	288.4	62.5	167.4	304.1	845.9	898.5
1942	41.9	228.2	47.6	156.8	279.7	754.2	796.5
1943	80.3	228.3	48.5	167.4	362.1	886.6	927.6
1944	120.9	274.3	48.2	188.3	461.4	1,093.1	1,140.4
1945	81.3	314.1	64.9	204.2	486.6	1,151.1	1,205.5
1946	15.3	368.6	99.7	221.2	457.2	1,162.0	1,229.4
1947	27.9	415.3	121.0	253.3	541.9	1,359.4	1,442.4
1948	36.8	456.3	123.8	296.3	540.1	1,453.3	1,537.2
1949	41.1	491.9	116.8	286.9	519.5	1,456.2	1,540.3
1950	45.0	534.5	130.7	332.6	591.4	1,634.2	1,732.0

NOTE: Includes 100 per cent of sales of Standard-Vacuum.
[a] Total gasolines not separated into aviation fuels and motor gasolines, 1927–1937.
[b] Aviation fuels includes jet fuels, 1947–1950.
[c] Motor gasolines includes LPG, 1927–1944, and special naphthas in all years but excludes natural gasolines and cycle plant products.
[d] Kerosenes includes tractor fuel sales, 1946–1950.

Prior to 1946 tractor fuels are included in distillates sales.
[e] Distillates and residual fuels includes total land and international bunker sales.
[f] Excludes chemical products.
Sources: Coordination and Planning Department and Comptroller's Department, Standard Oil Company (New Jersey).

Table 8: **PERCENTAGE OF GASOLINE MARKET BY STATES**
Standard Oil Company (New Jersey) and Domestic Affiliates
(For Selected Years)

	1910	1926	1933	1936	1939	1946	1950
New Jersey			27.1	27.0	28.7	30.6	29.9
Maryland			22.9	21.7	23.2	24.8	26.2
District of Columbia			29.6	28.5	28.0	30.7	27.8
West Virginia	77.0	43.2	37.4	33.8	36.2	36.0	32.1
Virginia			28.5	29.9	29.6	30.2	28.6
North Carolina			28.1	27.2	29.1	30.4	30.1
South Carolina			31.6	30.4	29.6	28.7	28.5
Louisiana			23.8	24.2	26.2	26.9	25.8
Tennessee	81.7	35.5	25.8	23.8	30.7	28.5	25.4
Arkansas			18.3	20.1	21.8	24.9	23.2
Delaware			13.7	14.5[a]	17.5	18.1	17.8
Pennsylvania			9.4	11.4	14.0	14.8	15.3
Maine			2.8	4.1	8.0	12.3	15.6
New Hampshire			5.6	7.2	10.6	12.0	12.0
Vermont			5.9	5.8	7.7	12.5	13.2
Massachusetts			8.5	8.5	9.8	12.3	13.5
Rhode Island			6.6	6.8	7.7	9.3	13.3
Connecticut			6.5	10.1	11.2	12.0	12.9
New York			7.1	8.7	10.2	11.3	12.3
Texas		5.9	5.9	5.7	5.8	9.5	13.1
Colorado			—	—	—	2.5	3.8
Idaho			—	—	—	1.4	3.2
Montana			—	—	—	9.1	13.4
Nebraska			—	—	—	0.2	0.3
North Dakota			—	—	—	2.6	.5.9
South Dakota			—	—	—	1.9	0.8
Washington			—	—	—	0.2	0.2
Wyoming			—	—	—	2.7	2.8
Percentage of United States Gasoline Market			6.0	6.6	6.9	7.5	8.1

[a] Estimate.   Source: Marketing Coordination Department, Standard Oil Company (New Jersey).

Notes

Nearly all the unpublished records cited in the notes were located in the offices and vaults of Standard Oil Company (New Jersey) and some of its affiliates. The company source of the records of the parent company is not indicated except where necessary to avoid uncertainty. The abbreviation then used is SONJ. The company sources of the other unpublished records are given. In the case of affiliates whose records are cited frequently, the abbreviations below are used to indicate their location as of the time the research was done:

CARTER: The Carter Oil Company records. This company was merged with Humble Oil & Refining Company in the reorganization initiated in 1959.

COL. BEACON: Colonial Beacon Oil Company records. This company was merged in 1947 with Standard Oil Company of New Jersey, which in 1959 was merged with Humble.

CREOLE: Creole Petroleum Corporation records. Standard Oil Company of Venezuela and Lago Petroleum Corporation were merged with Creole in 1943.

ESSO: Esso Standard Oil Company records. The name of this company before February, 1948, was Standard Oil Company of New Jersey. This company was merged with Humble Oil & Refining Company in the reorganization initiated in 1959.

ESSO SH: Esso Shipping Company records. This company, established in 1950 and merged in 1958 with Esso Standard Oil Company, was preceded, in this order, by Standard Shipping Company (organized in 1927), the Marine Department of Standard Oil Company of New Jersey, and the Marine Department of Standard Oil Company (New Jersey).

HUMBLE: Humble Oil & Refining Company records.

IMPERIAL: Imperial Oil Limited records.

INTERNATIONAL: International Petroleum Company, Limited, records.

INTERSTATE: Interstate Oil Pipe Line Company records. This company was the successor in 1944 of Oklahoma Pipe Line Company and the Pipeline Department of Standard Oil Company of Louisiana.

SOC of LA: Standard Oil Company of Louisiana records. This company was merged in 1944 with Standard Oil Company of New Jersey, which in 1959 was merged with Humble.

SODC: Standard Oil Development Company records. This company in 1954 became Esso Research and Engineering Company.

TROPICAL: The Tropical Oil Company, Limited.

CHAPTER 1

1. For the years prior to 1927, see these volumes in the series entitled *History of Standard Oil Company (New Jersey):* Ralph W. Hidy and Muriel E. Hidy, *Pioneering in Big Business, 1882–1911* (New York, 1955), and George Sweet Gibb and Evelyn H. Knowlton, *The Resurgent Years, 1911–1927* (New York, 1956).

2. Gibb and Knowlton, *The Resurgent Years,* chaps. 4, 11, 12, 13, and 14.

3. Henrietta M. Larson and Kenneth Wiggins Porter, *History of Humble Oil & Refining Company, A Study in Industrial Growth* (New York, 1959), 71–77; Gibb and Knowlton, *The Resurgent Years,* 410–412.

4. John G. McLean and Robert Wm. Haigh, *The Growth of Integrated Oil Companies* (Boston, 1954), 344f, 377–379, 682–687; Gibb and Knowlton, *The Resurgent Years,* 453–457.

5. SONJ, *The Lamp,* Feb., 1927.

6. Gibb and Knowlton, *The Resurgent Years,* 435–456, *passim;* Larson and Porter, *History of Humble,* chap. 8.

7. McLean and Haigh, *Integrated Oil Companies,* chap. 8.

8. Gibb and Knowlton, *The Resurgent Years,* 328–358, 563.

9. McLean and Haigh, *Integrated Oil Companies,* 101–108; Gibb and Knowlton, *The Resurgent Years,* 487; Larson and Porter, *History of Humble,* 227f; Paul H. Giddens, *Standard Oil Company (Indiana), Oil Pioneer of the Middle West* (New York, 1955), 281–329; Kendall Beaton, *Enterprise in Oil, A History of Shell in the United States* (New York, 1957), 269–287, 300–310; U.S. Federal Trade Commission, *Petroleum Industry, Prices, Profits, and Competition* (1928), 56.

10. Larson and Porter, *History of Humble,* 227–235; Gibb and Knowlton, *The Resurgent Years,* 483–496.

11. Gibb and Knowlton, *The Resurgent Years,* 674f.

12. Larson and Porter, *History of Humble,* chap. 11, shows how President Teagle of Jersey and President Farish of Humble came to this conclusion.

13. Gibb and Knowlton, *The Resurgent Years,* 617–619.

14. *Ibid.,* 630–664, contains brief notes on individual companies in which Jersey had an ownership interest in the years 1912–1927.

15. *The Lamp,* Oct., 1927.

16. Gibb and Knowlton, *The Resurgent Years,* 619. See index for individuals.

17. *Ibid.,* 618f.

18. *Ibid.,* 610–617.

19. *Ibid.,* 617–619.

20. See Charles Wilson, *The History of Unilever, a Study in Economic Growth and Social Change* (London, 1954).

21. See Alfred P. Sloan, Jr., *My Years with General Motors* (New York, 1964).

CHAPTER 2

1. Many officers, executives, and other employees, current and retired, within the Jersey Company in the years 1945 through 1962 discussed company administration and operations for the period 1927 to 1939 with representatives of the Business History Foundation, Inc. Among the latter were N. S. B. Gras, Henrietta M. Larson, George S. Gibb, John S. Ewing, Evelyn H. Knowlton, Charles S. Popple, and William T. Baxter. Among the large number of company personnel interviewed were the following: directors or officers of the Jersey Company—Frank W. Abrams, Frederick H. Bedford, Jr., John W. Brice, Stewart P. Coleman, Ralph W. Gallagher, Robert T. Haslam, Eugene Holman, Bushrod B. Howard, Frank A. Howard, Peter T. Lamont, Christy Payne, Frank W. Pierce, Wallace E. Pratt, Arthur T. Proudfit, Heinrich Riedemann, Everit J. Sadler, David A. Shepard, G. Harrison Smith, Emile E. Soubry, John R. Suman, and Walter C. Teagle; other officers, executives, specialists, or secretaries to top men—Henry E. Bedford, Jr., Edward F. Johnson, Gordon Michler, Adrian C. Minton, Frank Mott, Thomas W. Palmer, Richardson Pratt, Estelle B. Sexton, Frank M. Surface, Mrs. Mary Williams, and Wesley Zane.

2. Stockholders' Minutes, June 7, 1927; *The New York Times,* June 8, 1927.

3. Corporate records; *The Lamp,* June and Oct., 1927; SONJ, *Annual Report,* 1927 and 1928; *The New York Times,* Aug. 2, 1927.

4. Directors' Minutes, 1927–1933; Corp. recs.; Personnel recs.; SONJ, *Annual Report,* 1927; *The Lamp,* June and Oct., 1927, Dec., 1928, Apr., 1929, June, 1930, June, 1933, and Feb. and June, 1934. Comments concerning particular directors are drawn from many sources, including correspondence files and interviews.

5. Personnel recs.; Notes on W. C. Teagle, compiled by E. Lyman, about 1946. Jerome Beatty, "Walter C. Teagle, Giant of Oil," *American Magazine,* Dec., 1931.

6. W. C. Teagle to Henri Deterding, Dec. 21, 1925; Personnel recs.; Notes on Teagle, compiled by E. Lyman.

7. Henrietta M. Larson and Kenneth Wiggins Porter, *History of Humble Oil & Refining Company, A Study in Industrial Growth* (New York, 1959), 245–511, *passim.*

8. Heinrich Riedemann to C. T. White, June 20, 1932, and letter with short biographical sketch, Apr. 4, 1934; Personnel recs.; *The Lamp,* June, 1933. Interviews of H. M. Larson with Riedemann, Oct., 1947. For a detailed record of the business life of Riedemann's father, see Ernst Hieke, *Wilhelm Anton Riedemann* (Hamburg, 1963).

9. E. J. Sadler to Secretary White, Dec. 9, 1935; Personnel recs.

10. Directors' Minutes, June 6, 1927; Stockholders' Minutes, June 4, 1929; Memo to Executive Committee from special committee, F. W. Pierce, chairman, Jan. 13, 1933.

11. Directors' Minutes, June 7 and Nov. 28, 1928; June 4, 1929; May 16 and June 3, 1930; June 4, 1931; June 4, 1932; and Apr. 5, 1933.

12. Correspondence between directors and others: W. C. Teagle to G. H. Jones, July 20, 1927; F. E. Powell to Teagle, Apr. 25, 1928; Heinrich Riedemann to Teagle, May 17, Sept. 30, Oct. 9 and 19, 1928, and Jan. 3, 1929; Teagle to S. B.

Hunt, Aug. 24, 1928; Teagle to C. O. Swain, Aug. 24 and Sept. 10, 1928; Peter Hurll to Hunt, Dec. 10, 1929; Teagle to Hurll, Dec. 17, 1929; Teagle to K. R. Kingsbury, Apr. 24, 1931; W. E. Pratt to W. S. Farish, Aug. 8, 1931. Also: Memo on merger with California Standard (unsigned), Mar. 27, 1931; Farish to Teagle, Oct. 17, 1931; Memo by Farish for Jersey board, Jan. 10, 1933. HUMBLE: Release by the Federal Oil Conservation Board, May 11, 1927, with excerpts from letter of Teagle and Farish to Hon. Hubert Work, May 2, 1927; Teagle to Farish, May 13, 1927; Teagle to Riedemann, with copy to Farish, Mar. 7, 1928.

13. Memo to Executive Committee from special committee, F. W. Pierce, chairman, Jan. 13, 1933; Memo on Jersey holding company (undated and unsigned, but probably by member of Law Dept. late in 1932 or early in 1933); Memo on organization (also undated and unsigned and probably late in 1932 or early in 1933); *The Lamp,* Oct., 1927.

14. Memo on parent company organization and functions by E. J. Sadler, May 17, 1933; Memo to Executive Committee from special committee, F. W. Pierce, chairman, Jan. 13, 1933.

15. Memo on organization (undated and unsigned); Memo to Executive Committee from special committee, F. W. Pierce, chairman, Jan. 13, 1933; Memo to Executive Committee by E. J. Sadler, Sept. 7, 1933.

16. Peter Hurll to W. C. Teagle and J. A. Moffett, Jr., June 21, 1929; Hurll to Teagle, May 1, 1931; Teagle to Heinrich Riedemann, Hurll, J. A. Mowinckel, and H. G. Seidel, Oct. 7, 1931; Hurll to Moffett, Apr. 20, 1932; Memo by E. J. Sadler, Mar. 22, 1934.

17. Memo on responsibilities and duties of the Coordination Committee and Coordination Dept. (unsigned), Oct. 28, 1927; E. M. Clark to W. C. Teagle, Apr. 2, 1928; Secretary White to heads of depts. and cos. in New York, Mar. 19, 1930; Coordination Committee membership, 1931–1932, by H. L. Shoemaker, Jan. 17, 1952; Draft of memo for administration, by C. G. Black and Christy Payne, June 2, 1933.

18. Heinrich Riedemann to W. C. Teagle, Apr. 8, 1931.

19. Report of Manufacturing Dept., 1926; W. C. Teagle to E. M. Clark, Dec. 26, 1926, Jan. 4, 1927, and Mar. 20, 1929; Clark to Teagle, Dec. 22 and 31, 1926; Teagle to Clark, C. G. Black, and D. R. Weller, Feb. 15, 1927; Clark to Orville Harden, Jan. 5, 1927, Aug. 5 and Oct. 7, 1929; Memo on proposed refinery at Cartagena by Harden, Jan. 20, 1927; Report on future manufacturing activities at New York seaboard as compared to Gulf refineries by committee headed by Harden, July 19, 1927; Harden to G. W. Gordon, Apr. 18, 1928; Memo about Atlantic Coast refineries by Harden, Jan. 22, 1929.

20. Memo on accounting differences, Aug. 25, 1931; Memo on production and reserves, Aug. 27, 1931; W. C. Teagle to Heinrich Riedemann, Aug. 27, 1931; H. L. Shoemaker to Teagle, W. S. Farish, Orville Harden, and T. C. McCobb, Dec. 10, 1935; SONJ, *Annual Report*, 1934. Gibb and Knowlton, *The Resurgent Years*, 610–617. Report on research in the history of annual accounts, independent audits, and the comptroller, prepared by William T. Baxter.

21. W. C. Teagle to heads of depts. and cos. in New York, June 16, 1932.

22. Memo to the Exec. Com. from special committee, F. W. Pierce, chairman, Jan. 13, 1933; Pierce to Teagle, Aug. 30, 1936. COL. BEACON: E. N. Wrighting-ton to E. F. Johnson, July 6, 1936.

23. W. C. Teagle to J. A. Moffett and C. O. Swain, with memorandum, May 9, 1933.

24. *Ibid.;* W. C. Teagle to C. O. Swain, May 12, 1933.

25. E. J. Sadler to W. C. Teagle, May 24 and 29, 1933; Teagle to C. O. Swain, with suggestions from E. M. Clark, May 26, 1933; Draft of memo by C. G. Black and Christy Payne, June 2, 1933; Teagle to individual directors in New York, June 6, 1933.

26. E. J. Sadler to W. C. Teagle, May 24, 1933.

27. W. C. Teagle to individual directors in New York, June 6, 1933; Teagle to directors in New York, with memo, June 7, 1933.

28. *The New York Times,* June 7, 1933.

29. *The Lamp,* Aug., 1933; Telephone directory for New York offices, Jan., 1935, Jan., 1937, and June, 1938; Report of office-space committee to F. W. Abrams, Apr. 1, 1941.

30. Teagle's memo to the directors, June 7, 1933, hereafter referred to as the Memo of 1933; Directors' Minutes, June 6, 1933; Memo by C. O. Swain, June 30, 1933.

31. Directors' Minutes, May 1 and Dec. 14, 1933; Memo on retirement policy, May 19, 1933; SONJ, *Annual Report,* 1933; *The Lamp,* Aug., 1933.

32. E. M. Clark to W. C. Teagle, Apr. 13, 1933; Teagle to Clark, Apr. 18, 1933; Stockholders' and Directors' Minutes, June 6, 1933; Personnel recs.; Corp. recs.; *The Lamp,* Aug., 1933.

33. Directors' Minutes, July 28 and Nov. 17, 1933; *The Lamp,* Aug., 1933; *New York Herald Tribune,* Jan. 12, 1934.

34. Directors' Minutes, May 25, 1934; Memo *in re* foreign holding company (undated and unsigned, but probably by member of Law Dept. in 1934); Memo (unsigned), Aug. 28, 1934; Status memo on the International Association (Petroleum Industry) Limited, by M. E. McDowell, May 29, 1934; Memo by E. J. Sadler, Mar. 22, 1934; McDowell to W. S. Farish, Sept. 13, 1934; F. W. Pierce to W. C. Teagle, Aug. 30, 1936; *The Lamp,* Feb. and June, 1934.

35. Personnel recs.; SONJ, *Annual Report,* 1935, 1936, and 1937; *The Lamp,* June, 1932.

36. Larson and Porter, *History of Humble,* 85–89, 328f, 335, 416–418.

37. Memo of 1933.

38. *Ibid.*

39. *Ibid.*

40. *Ibid.*

41. Directors' Minutes, Apr. 4, 1935.

42. Directors' Minutes and Exec. Com. Minutes, 1933–1939; Memo of 1933.

43. Exec. Com. Minutes, 1933–1936, *passim;* Exec. Com. memoranda, 1937–1939.

44. Exec. Com. Minutes, 1933–1939, *passim;* Many interviews with Jersey directors and officers.

45. Memo of 1933.

46. *Ibid.;* Personnel recs.; *The Lamp,* Aug., 1933, and June, 1934.

47. Exec. Com. Minutes, 1933–1939, *passim;* Directors' Minutes, May 25, 1934; Memo on International Association by E. J. Sadler, Mar. 22, 1934; Montagu Piesse to E. F. Johnson, Aug. 31, 1934; Proposed organization of the International Association, July 29, 1936; F. W. Pierce to W. C. Teagle, Aug. 30, 1936; Personnel recs.

48. E. J. Sadler to Exec. Com., Sept. 17, 1933; Memo on relations of Humble with Jersey, S.O. Co. of N.J., and other companies in the Jersey group, Oct. 6, 1938; Corp. recs.

49. F. W. Pierce to W. C. Teagle, Aug. 30, 1936.

50. Exec. Com. Minutes, Feb. 19, 1937.

51. Memo of 1933.

52. E. M. Clark to W. C. Teagle, Apr. 13, 1933; Teagle to Clark, Apr. 18, 1933; F. A. Howard to R. W. Gallagher, Oct. 12, 1944; Coordination Committee membership, by H. L. Shoemaker, Jan. 17, 1952; Personnel recs.; *The Lamp,* Aug., 1933.

53. An illustration of the methods used by Humble is given in a report of May 28, 1932, of J. W. Harrell and H. W. Ferguson to S. P. Coleman on "Determination of the Cost of the Products from the Refining of Crude Petroleum." This report, from Humble records, describes a method of figuring the costs of joint products. The major premise of the method was that all petroleum fractions could be converted into gasoline and fuel oil and that the gasoline and fuel equivalent of the fraction could be used as a measure of its value. Two types of costs were recognized: total costs and increment costs. A knowledge of increment costs led to the determination of the relative desirability of different product yields from a given crude. The same concept of increment costs could be used for production and transportation as well

as refining. See also Larson and Porter, *History of Humble,* 545f.

54. S. P. Coleman, "Coordination in the Jersey Family," a paper presented at an international petroleum conference in Rome in March, 1957.

55. E. J. Sadler to Northrop Clarey, Feb. 20, 1940.

56. Memo of 1933; Memos by E. J. Sadler, May 28 and June 12, 1936, and Mar. 16, 1937; H. L. Shoemaker to members of the Coordination Committee, May 24, 1939, and Jan. 8, 1940; Sadler to members of Coord. Com., Feb. 15, 1941; Coord. Com. group meetings, Agenda and Minutes, 1934–1939.

57. A. C. Minton to heads of departments and companies in New York, Sept. 19, 1934; H. L. Shoemaker to W. C. Teagle, W. S. Farish, Orville Harden, and T. C. McCobb, Dec. 10, 1935. Report on budgets by William T. Baxter.

58. Unsigned memorandum, dated Aug. 31, 1936, explaining the responsibilities and procedures of the Coord. Com.; Memos by E. J. Sadler, May 28 and June 12, 1936, and Mar. 16, 1937; S. P. Coleman, a paper delivered at the Coord. Com. Meeting, San Juan, Puerto Rico, June 3, 1957, dealing partly with the history of coordination in Jersey; interview of H. M. Larson with Coleman, Apr. 19, 1962. Also report on the development of economic analysis in Jersey prepared for the authors by William T. Baxter.

59. Eugene Holman to H. L. Shoemaker, Jan. 30, 1936.

60. Coord. Com. Group Meetings, Minutes, May 10–14, 1937; Eugene Holman to H. L. Shoemaker, Jan. 30, 1937; E. L. Estabrook to Holman, Apr. 9, 1936.

61. A. C. Minton to heads of depts. and cos. in New York, Mar. 19, 1940.

62. Coord. Com. Group Meetings, Agenda and Minutes, 1934–1939; Memos by E. J. Sadler, May 28 and June 12, 1936, and Mar. 16, 1937.

63. Remarks prepared by E. J. Sadler, Agenda, Coord. Com. Group Meeting, May 15–19, 1939.

CHAPTER 3

1. On producing before 1927, see Ralph W. Hidy and Muriel E. Hidy, *Pioneering in Big Business, 1882–1911* (New York, 1955), and George Sweet Gibb and Evelyn H. Knowlton, *The Resurgent Years, 1911–1927* (New York, 1956).

2. The authors of this volume and other members of the staff of the Business History Foundation from 1945 to 1958 discussed the production history of the Jersey companies in the late 1920's and the 1930's with many men and women then or formerly connected with the parent company or its affiliates. Among them were E. J. Sadler, W. E. Pratt, Eugene Holman, J. R. Suman, Alice Carruthers, H. T. Eagles, E. L. Estabrook, H. H. Hill, G. M. Knebel, H. H. Baker, C. D. Mill, J. Miller, T. V. Moore, I. S. Salnikov, W. P. Haynes, and M. A. Wright.

3. Annual Statistical Review, 1950. The sales figures for the company and the whole industry are not exactly comparable, but the difference is so small that the percentage range stated unquestionably covers it.

4. W. C. Teagle to Jersey directors, with statement of production for the year 1927 for the twenty leading oil companies, Mar. 16, 1928.

5. *Ibid.*

6. On these problems of domestic production, the authors of this volume have drawn on Henrietta M. Larson and Kenneth Wiggins Porter, *History of Humble Oil & Refining Company* (New York, 1959).

7. This account is based principally on information contained in letters of W. E. Pratt to F. M. Surface, Aug. 10, 1963, and Feb. 16, 1965. No written record was found of the offer to the Producing Department in New York; presumably, no such record was made of the matter. The offer was not submitted to the Board of Directors. Pratt's letter of Feb. 16, 1965, adds information obtained from checking his own knowledge of the matter with C. Stuart Morgan in Tucson, Arizona, in the winter of 1965. *Origin of American Oil Concessions in Bahrain, Kuwait, and Saudi Arabia* by Frederick Lee Moore,

Jr. (a privately printed thesis presented at Princeton University in 1948); also, Stephen Hensley Longrigg, *Oil in the Middle East* (New York, 1961), 98–102.

8. CREOLE: W. C. Teagle had taken this position in a letter to E. J. Sadler of Apr. 1, 1926.

9. CREOLE: Directors' Minutes, 1920–1927.

10. CREOLE: Plan of Merger and Reorganization, June 30, 1928; *Annual Report,* 1928; *Supplemental Report,* 1928; Short Survey and History and Present Status of Standard Oil Co. of Venezuela, Mar. 1, 1933.

11. CREOLE: *Annual Report,* 1928.

12. C. M. Leonard to E. J. Sadler, Sept. 20 and Oct. 22, 1928; Agreement between Trinidad Oil Fields, Inc., and Beacon Oil Co., Sept. 10, 1928. American Petroleum Institute (API), *Petroleum Facts and Figures,* 1928, p. 34f; Wallace E. Pratt and Dorothy Good, eds., *World Geography of Petroleum* (Princeton, N.J., 1950), 80–94.

13. Gibb and Knowlton, *The Resurgent Years,* 305f.

14. *Ibid.,* 278–305. Also, letter of Wallace E. Pratt to Frank M. Surface, Feb. 16, 1965, following conversations with C. Stuart Morgan, who was an executive from 1928 in Near East Development Corporation.

15. Copy of an agreement between D'Arcy Exploration Co., Ltd., the Anglo-Persian Oil Co., Ltd., Compagnie Française des Pétroles, S. A., Near East Development Corp., Participation and Investments (Gulbenkian), and Turkish Petroleum Co., dated July 31, 1928 (the Red Line Agreement); Guy Wellman to Eugene Holman, Oct. 26, 1934, memo on group agreement.

16. W. S. Farish to W. C. Teagle, Oct. 17, 1930; E. J. Sadler to Teagle, June 15, 1931; G. S. Walden to Sadler, July 29 and Aug. 31, 1931; Heinrich Riedemann to Teagle, Aug. 18, 1931, and Nov. 2, 1934; Teagle to Riedemann, Aug. 27 and Oct. 6 and 7, 1931.

17. W. C. Teagle to John W. Davis, Apr. 1, 1929; Davis to Teagle, Mar. 28, 1930;

Teagle to K. R. Kingsbury, Mar. 20, 1930.

18. 47F. 2d 228 (E. D., Mo., 1931). J. A. Moffett, Jr., to W. C. Teagle, Jan. 21, 1930; K. R. Kingsbury to Teagle, Mar. 7, 1930, Feb. 10 and June 12, 1931; Teagle to Kingsbury, Mar. 20 and Apr. 24, 1930, and Feb. 13, 1931.

19. Press release, W. C. Teagle to Northrop Clarey, Aug. 25, 1931.

20. This discussion is based on a large number of letters and memoranda in the Jersey Company records as well as on information provided by W. E. Pratt, one of the participants in the negotiations. The memoranda had to do with a variety of matters, particularly production and reserves and accounting values and differences. The correspondence, dated from August, 1931, to October, 1933, was mostly internal correspondence—that is, between Jersey officers and directors— and a few letters by Humble officers. Especially revealing were certain letters in the Teagle-Kingsbury correspondence: Kingsbury to Teagle, Sept. 15, 1931, and Dec. 1, 1932; Teagle to Kingsbury, Sept. 5 and 12, 1931, and Oct. 17, 1933, with press release.

21. Balance sheet of Pan American Petroleum & Transport Company, Dec. 31, 1927, and Dec. 31, 1929; data on domestic and foreign properties of Standard of Indiana, Apr. 1, 1929, and Oct. 1, 1930; Eugene Holman to H. E. Linam, May 12, 1932; E. F. Johnson to C. O. Swain, Aug. 17, 1932; copy of letter to B. O. Seaver, May 11, 1937, without sender's name.

22. Paul H. Giddens, *Standard Oil Company (Indiana), Oil Pioneer of the Middle West* (New York, 1955), 489.

23. *Ibid.*, 461f, 489.

24. *Ibid.*, 489f.

25. On Stewart: Giddens, *Standard Oil Company (Indiana)*, chaps. 9, 13, and 14. On Doheny: U.S. Senate, Committee on Public Lands and Surveys, hearings in 1924, under Senate Resolutions 282 and 294, published as *Leases upon Naval Oil Reserves* (Washington, 1929). On Mexican companies: interviews of H. M. Larson with Burton Wilson and other men who had worked in Mexico.

26. Memos by E. J. Sadler, Mar. 11 and 16, 1932; C. B. Ware to Sadler, Mar. 14, 1932; Memos (unsigned), Mar. 17 and 23, 1932; L. C. Booker to Eugene Holman, Apr. 7, 1932; Cable to Creole Pet. Corp., New York, from Caracas, Apr. 14, 1932.

27. Memo by Richardson Pratt, Mar. 14, 1932; Memo (unsigned), Mar. 17, 1932.

28. Memo by E. J. Sadler, Mar. 11, 1932.

29. Eugene Holman to E. J. Sadler, Mar. 14, 1932; Report entitled Companies of Importance in the Middle East.

30. Eugene Holman to H. E. Linam, May 12, 1932; Memo of special meeting of the stockholders of Pan American, May 23, 1932.

31. E. J. Sadler to W. C. Teagle, Mar. 15, 1932; Memos by Sadler, Mar. 16 and 18, 1932; Memos (unsigned), Mar. 17 and 23, 1932; Memo of special meeting, May 23, 1932; E. F. Johnson to C. O. Swain, July 20, 1933; Annual reports of producing subsidiaries of Pan American, 1930, 1931, and 1932; Giddens, *Standard Oil Company (Indiana)*, 490f.

32. Annual reports of producing subsidiaries of Pan American, 1931.

33. Giddens, *Standard Oil Company (Indiana)*, 493.

34. M. H. Eames to Eugene Holman, Aug. 1, 1933; Directors' Minutes, 1932–1935, *passim;* Corporation records. Larson and Porter, *History of Humble,* 527f.

35. Memo by E. J. Sadler, June 12, 1936.

36. Heinrich Riedemann to W. C. Teagle, Nov. 2, 1934.

37. Extract in SONJ records of minutes of a meeting of the directors of Iraq Petroleum Company, Oct. 30, 1928; H. G. Seidel to G. S. Walden, June 3, 1932. Also information obtained by H. M. Larson from Wallace E. Pratt; Moore, *Origin of American Oil Concessions in Bahrain, Kuwait, and Saudi Arabia.*

38. G. S. Walden to E. J. Sadler, Sept. 8, 1932.

39. H. G. Seidel to E. J. Sadler, Sept. 8, 1932; Sadler to Seidel, Sept. 22, 1932.

40. G. S. Walden to E. J. Sadler, Sept. 7, 1932; W. E. Pratt to F. M. Surface, Aug. 11, 1963, and Feb. 16, 1965. Arabian American Oil Company, *Aramco Handbook* (Dhahran, Saudi Arabia, 1968), 107–111; Longrigg, *Oil in the Middle East,* 110–112.

41. G. S. Walden to Prod. Dept., Apr. 5, 1929; Walden to E. J. Sadler, Feb. 9, 1931; Memo by Sadler, June 16, 1933; *The Lamp,* Aug., 1936. *The New York Times,* Sept. 1, 1933.

42. W. C. Teagle to E. J. Sadler, June 27, 1934; Memo, G. S. Walden, July 26, 1934; Memo, Eugene Holman to Orville Harden, Aug. 17, 1934; Holman to Teagle, Oct. 8, 1934; Eugene Stebinger to Holman, Oct. 18, 1934.

43. E. J. Sadler to H. G. Seidel, Sept. 8, 1932; H. L. Shoemaker to Guy Wellman, Jan. 30, 1934.

44. H. L. Shoemaker to Guy Wellman, Jan. 30, 1934; E. J. Sadler to H. G. Seidel, Feb. 1, 1934; Seidel to W. C. Teagle, June 14, 1934; C. O. Swain to Teagle, June 26, 1934; Seidel to Teagle, Oct. 2, 1934; J. A. Brown to Teagle, Feb. 20, 1935; Teagle to Wellman, Feb. 21, 1935; Wellman to Teagle and W. S. Farish, May 22, 1935.

45. W. C. Teagle to G. S. Walden, Nov. 21, 1935.

46. H. G. Seidel to W. C. Teagle, Oct. 2, 1934. *Economist* (London), May 19, 1934, p. 1092.

47. G. S. Walden to J. A. Brown, Nov. 19, 1935.

48. *Ibid.*

49. W. C. Teagle to A. C. Corwin and G. S. Walden, Aug. 2, 1934; W. Fraser to H. G. Seidel, Oct. 1, 1934; Seidel to Teagle, Oct. 2, 1934; Teagle to Eugene Holman, Nov. 13, 1934; Skliros (a resident representative of Iraq Petroleum in Iraq) to Iraq groups, Dec. 12, 1934.

50. Report on Bahrein and Arabian Properties of Standard Oil Company of California, Aug. 17, 1934; J. A. Brown to W. C. Teagle, Feb. 20, 1935; Guy Wellman to Teagle and W. S. Farish, May 22, 1935; Teagle to K. R. Kingsbury, Aug. 10, 1935; G. S. Walden to Brown, Nov. 19, 1935.

51. G. S. Walden to J. A. Brown, Nov. 19, 1935; Eugene Holman to H. G. Seidel, Jan. 29, 1936; Andrew Agnew to Seidel, Mar. 10, 1936; John Cadman to Seidel, Mar. 11, 1936; Seidel to W. C. Teagle, Mar. 12, 1936; Holman to Teagle, Mar. 17, 1936; Teagle to Holman, Mar. 23, 1936.

52. G. S. Walden to E. J. Sadler, Nov. 24, 1936; Extracts from 1937 registration statement of Texaco with Securities Exchange Commission; Walden to J. A. Brown, W. C. Teagle, W. S. Farish, and other Jersey and Socony directors, Jan. 18, 1937.

53. G. S. Walden to W. C. Teagle, Feb. 3, 1937; Teagle to Walden, Feb. 8, 1937.

54. INTERNATIONAL: Directors' Minutes, Dec. 24, 1937, and Feb. 4 and Nov. 28, 1938; Report for eighteen months ending Dec. 31, 1937; Agreement between Mene Grande Oil Co., S.A., and International Pet. Co., Limited, Dec. 15, 1937; Agreement between Mene Grande Oil Co., International, and Compañía Shell de Venezuela, Nov. 5, 1957, to clarify previous agreement.

55. Contract between the Royal Hungarian Minister of Finance and the European Gas & Electric Co. of London and New York, June 8, 1933; Supplementary contract, June 24, 1938; Agreement, June 8, 1933; Supplementary agreement, June 10, 1937; Eugene Holman to E. J. Sadler, Dec. 2, 1938; Paul Ruedemann to R. P. Bolton, Mar. 28, 1939; Memo by Bolton, Dec. 13, 1940; History of operations of Magyar Amerikai Olajipari R. T. (MAORT) in Hungary.

56. Pratt and Good, eds., *World Geography of Petroleum,* 262f. SONJ, Statistics on foreign production, 1928–1939.

57. E. J. Sadler to Eugene Holman, June 2, 1939.

58. *Coordination Com. Group Meeting,* 1947; Pratt and Good, eds., *World Geography of Petroleum,* 261.

59. E. J. Sadler to Eugene Holman, Jan. 2, 1939.

60. W. E. Pratt to Eugene Holman, July 15, 1939.

61. National Industrial Conference Board (NICB), *Petroleum Almanac,* 1946, pp. 21, 35, 295, 298.

62. W. C. Teagle to directors of SONJ, Mar. 16, 1928.

63. Copy of Achnacarry statement of principles, Sept. 17, 1928.

64. Annual reports of producing subsidiaries of Pan American, 1930 and 1931; SONJ *Annual Report,* 1929–1933. CREOLE: H. I. Fry to Prod. Dept., Apr. 11, 1929; Annual report of general manager for 1930; General manager's review for 1932. API, *Petroleum Facts and Figures,* 1929, pp. 234–246.

65. Hidy and Hidy, *Pioneering in Big Business,* 178, 671–676; Larson and Porter, *History of Humble,* 176–185.

66. E. J. Sadler, Memo, Pipe Line Rates, Gathering Charges, and Selling Commissions, Jan. 28, 1927.

67. Digests of the development of state laws and federal cooperation are given in two volumes published by the American Bar Association (ABA): *Legal History of Conservation of Oil and Gas, A Symposium* (Chicago, 1938); and B. M. Murphy, ed., *Conservation of Oil and Gas, A Legal History* (Chicago, 1948). For a brief résumé of early law, see Larson and Porter, *History of Humble,* 298–300.

68. Larson and Porter, *History of Humble,* chap. 11; Federal Oil Conservation Board, *Report I* (Sept., 1926); *Report II* (Jan., 1928).

69. Larson and Porter, *History of Humble,* 259–263.

70. HUMBLE: E. J. Sadler to W. S. Farish, June 6, 1927.

71. HUMBLE: Copy of a letter from W. C. Teagle and W. S. Farish to Hubert Work, May 2, 1927. Also, *The Lamp,* June, 1927; Larson and Porter, *History of Humble,* 309f.

72. Larson and Porter, *History of Humble,* 307–309; *The Lamp,* June, 1927.

73. ABA, *Report of the Fifteenth Annual Meeting* (1927), address entitled "Legislative Control of the Business of Producing Oil and Gas."

74. Larson and Porter, *History of Humble,* 317f.

75. Robert E. Hardwicke, *Antitrust Laws . . . vs. Unit Operation of Gas and Oil Pools* (New York, 1948), 32, 54, 123n; API, *Petroleum Facts and Figures,* 1929, pp. 224–245.

76. SONJ, *Annual Report,* 1931 and 1932. Larson and Porter, *History of Humble,* 469 and chap. 18, 47n; ABA, *Legal History of Conservation of Oil and Gas, A Symposium,* 151–182, 220–234; NICB, *Petroleum Almanac,* 1946, p. 11; Murphy, ed., *Conservation of Oil and Gas, A Legal History,* 549–555.

77. Memo of The Standard Oil Company (Ohio) *re* oil industry code (undated); Telegram to N.Y. from W. S. Farish, Sept. 7, 1933; W. C. Teagle to H. L. Ickes, Sept. 8, 1933; W. G. Skelly to N. R. Margold, Oct. 2, 1933; F. H. Flour to Margold, Oct. 4, 1933; Memo for the oil administration *re* price control, by Margold, Oct. 5, 1933. *The Secret Diary of Harold L. Ickes: The First Thousand Days, 1933–1936* (New York, 1953), 9–14, 73, 81–86, 95, 97–99, 102, 106–108, 233; *New York Herald Tribune,* Jan. 12, 1934; U.S. House, 73rd Cong., *Hearings before a Subcommittee of the Committee on Interstate and Foreign Commerce* (Washington, 1934), pt. 1, p. 673.

78. W. S. Farish to N. R. Margold, Oct. 2, 1933.

79. *Amazon Petroleum Corporation* v. *Ryan,* 55 S. Ct. 241; *Panama Refining Company* v. *Ryan,* 55 S. Ct. 241; *A. L. A. Schechter Poultry Co.* v. *United States,* 55 S. Ct. 837; Murphy, ed., *Conservation of Oil and Gas,* 564.

80. Murphy, ed., *Conservation of Oil and Gas,* 571–702, surveys the development.

81. API, *Petroleum Industry Hearings Before the Temporary National Economic Committee* (New York, 1942), 536–539.

82. Petroleum Engineering Reports, 1929–1933; H. H. Hill to Eugene Holman, July 16, 1935.

83. M. H. Eames to Eugene Holman, Aug. 1, 1933; Directors' Minutes, 1932–1935; Corp. recs.

84. Eugene Holman to presidents of companies and heads of departments, with memo and organization chart of the Prod. Dept., Jan. 5, 1939.

85. *Ibid.;* Telephone directories for New York offices, Jan., 1935, Jan., 1937, June, 1938, and Aug., 1940; Payroll of the Prod. Dept., 1927–1934; E. J. Sadler to W. S. Farish, May 24, 1935; F. H. Kay to Eugene Holman, July 16, 1935; H. H. Hill to Holman, July 16, 1935; Memo by Holman, Aug. 16, 1935; Holman to L. Wilson, Nov. 8, 1935; Eugene Stebinger to Holman, Apr. 20, 1939; S. P. Coleman to Gordon, Hill, Holman, and Shoemaker, Apr. 5, 1940; C. H. Lieb to Holman, Dec. 26, 1940; Résumé of Exploration Activities, by Wiedenmeyer, July 11, 1946.

86. General Coordination Committee Meetings, Agenda and Minutes, for the years 1934 to 1939, inclusive.

CHAPTER 4

1. Information on Humble in this section is from the *History of Humble Oil & Refining Company* (New York, 1959), by Henrietta M. Larson and Kenneth Wiggins Porter, pp. 139–142, 267–278, and 390–425. Specific references to Humble records as sources of data are given in the Humble history.

2. On Pratt's contribution, see *ibid.*, 335, 417f.

3. *Ibid.*, 139–141. Also, W. E. Pratt to F. M. Surface, Aug. 21, 1963.

4. American Petroleum Institute (API), *Finding and Producing Oil* (New York, 1939), 10; API, *Petroleum Facts and Figures*, 1941, p. 76.

5. Larson and Porter, *History of Humble,* 141. The authors are indebted to Wallace E. Pratt for the statement about the geology of Carter's territory (W. E. Pratt to F. M. Surface, Aug. 21, 1963).

6. Larson and Porter, *History of Humble,* 272–277, 391. Résumé of Exploration Activities, by Wiedenmeyer, July 11, 1946. *Bulletin of the American Association of Petroleum Geologists,* vol. XVII, 1, 362, article on "Sugarland Oil Field," by W. B. Carter and P. H. O'Bannon.

7. Larson and Porter, *History of Humble,* 276, 391f, 413.

8. *Ibid.*, 392, 410, 413, 415f. General Coordination Meeting, Agenda, May 9, 1938, Review of Production Research Programs; *ibid.*, May 13, 1940, Reorganization of Jersey Geophysical Services.

9. General Coordination Meeting, Agenda, May 9, 1938, Review of Production Research Programs; *ibid.*, May 13, 1940, Reorganization of Jersey's Geophysical Services; *ibid.*, June 14–16, 1945, Loudon Pool.

10. Larson and Porter, *History of Humble,* 277, 395–397, 447–449. Résumé of Exploration Activities, by Wiedenmeyer, July 11, 1946.

11. Larson and Porter, *History of Humble,* 413.

12. *Ibid.*, 139, 267–278, 390–411.

13. General Coordination Meeting, Agenda, May 9, 1938, Standard Oil Co. of La.; *ibid.*, June 14–16, 1945, Loudon Pool. Larson and Porter, *History of Humble,* 411–425.

14. Larson and Porter, *History of Humble,* 267–278, 399–403, 408, 410, 413–416. CARTER: Background data on representative pools, by "J. C. K.," Feb. 8, 1950.

15. Larson and Porter, *History of Humble,* 405–408.

16. General Coordination Meeting, Agenda, June 9, 1938, Standard Oil Co. of La.; *ibid.*, June 14–16, 1945, Loudon Pool. Larson and Porter, *History of Humble,* 394.

17. Larson and Porter, *History of Humble,* 394. CARTER: Net reserves of Carter and Louark, by Economics Dept., June 6, 1947. National Industrial Conference Board (NICB), *The Petroleum Almanac,* 1946, p. 42.

18. Larson and Porter, *History of Humble,* 278–296 and chaps. 17 and 19.

19. George Sweet Gibb and Evelyn H. Knowlton, *History of Standard Oil Company (New Jersey), The Resurgent Years, 1911–1927* (New York, 1956), 449f. Interview of H. M. Larson with C. D. Watson, Apr. 10, 1945.

20. Larson and Porter, *History of Humble*, 279–285.

21. *Ibid.*, 284.

22. *Ibid.*, 280–286, 441. API, Div. of Production, *Proceedings*, 1930, pp. 18–122; *ibid.*, 1934, p. 158.

23. Larson and Porter, *History of Humble*, 285.

24. Published in the 1929 *Transactions* of the Petroleum Division of American Institute of Mining and Metallurgical Engineers (AIMME).

25. Larson and Porter, *History of Humble*, 310–312.

26. *Ibid.*, 437–440.

27. *Ibid.*, 434–445.

28. *Ibid.*, 286f, 292–295, 489–492.

29. *Ibid.*, 573f, 576f.

30. CARTER: Background data on representative oil pools, by "J. C. K.," Feb. 8, 1940. Larson and Porter, *History of Humble*, 322.

31. A good digest of the development of state laws is given in two volumes published by the American Bar Association (ABA): *Legal History of Conservation of Oil and Gas, A Symposium* (Chicago, 1938); Blakely M. Murphy, ed., *Conservation of Oil and Gas, A Legal History* (Chicago, 1948).

32. "Legislative Control of the Business of Producing Oil and Gas," *Report of the Fifteenth Annual Meeting of the American Bar Association*, 1927, pp. 576–630.

33. Larson and Porter, *History of Humble*, 298, 301–316, 318–325, 450–452, 456–458.

34. ABA, *Legal Hist. of Cons. of Oil and Gas*, 1–15.

35. Larson and Porter, *History of Humble*, 298–306. Various issues of the SONJ, *Annual Report* and *The Lamp* contain statements on law and regulation, especially in the years 1927–1935. On the development of regulation, see ABA, *Legal Hist. of Cons. of Oil and Gas*, 110–151, 214–219.

36. Larson and Porter, *History of Humble*, 306–310.

37. *Ibid.*, 309–315. *General and Special Laws of the State of Texas Passed by the Forty-first Legislature at the Regular Session* (1929), chap. 313, pp. 694–696.

38. Larson and Porter, *History of Humble*, 315f. API, *Bulletin*, Jan. 12, Oct. 31, and Dec. 2 and 9, 1927, and Jan. 6, 1928; Robert E. Hardwicke, *Antitrust Law . . . vs. Unit Operation of Gas and Oil Pools* (New York, 1948), 41–44; Fed. Oil Cons. Board, *Report III*, Feb. 25, 1929; ABA, *Legal Hist. of Cons. of Oil and Gas*, 219f; AIMME, Pet. Div., *Transactions*, 1930, pp. 101–104.

39. Larson and Porter, *History of Humble*, 316–318.

40. *Ibid.*, 320. ABA, *Legal Hist. of Cons. of Oil and Gas*, 200.

41. ABA, *Legal Hist. of Cons. of Oil and Gas*, 28f, 152–160, 220f; Larson and Porter, *History of Humble*, 318f. CARTER: Outline of Oklahoma Conservation Law, by V. H. Taylor, Dec. 8, 1949. API, *Petroleum Facts and Figures*, 1929, pp. 225, 246, and 1930, p. 141.

42. API, *Petroleum Facts and Figures*, 1929, pp. 223–248; Larson and Porter, *History of Humble*, 321.

43. Larson and Porter, *History of Humble*, 449–459; *Texas Acts*, 42nd leg., 4th called sess., chap. 2, p. 3; ABA, *Legal Hist. of Cons. of Oil and Gas*, 228–247; *World Petroleum*, Sept., 1931; *The Lamp*, June, 1931.

44. U.S. House of Repres., 73rd Cong., *Hearings Before a Subcommittee of the Committee on Interstate and Foreign Commerce* (Washington, 1934), pt. I, p. 748.

45. Larson and Porter, *History of Humble*, 462–469.

46. A survey of the development of support for regulation and of regulation itself may be found in *ibid.*, 459–487.

47. 52 S. Ct. 559.

48. 5 F. Supp. 633.

49. ABA, *Legal Hist. of Cons. of Oil and Gas*, 241–247, 556f, 696f.

50. Larson and Porter, *History of Humble*, 489–501.

51. API, *Petroleum Industry Hearings Before the Temporary National Economic Committee* (New York, 1942), 536–539. For a recent statement on pro-

ration, see pages 536f of *The American Petroleum Industry, The Age of Energy, 1899–1959* (Evanston, 1963) by Harold F. Williamson, Ralph L. Andreano, Arnold R. Daum, and Gilbert C. Klose. This volume was published after this and other chapters had been written.

52. *Ibid.* (Williamson *et al.*), 431–433. Interview of H. M. Larson with C. D. Watson of Carter, April 10, 1945.

53. Larson and Porter, *History of Humble,* 429–431, 433f.

54. *Ibid.,* 288–299. General Coordination Meeting, Agenda, June 14–16, 1945, Carter Activity in the Rocky Mountain Area. CARTER: Directors' Minutes, July 29, 1929; J. J. Conry to Eugene Holman, Sept. 22, 1938; M. J. Rathbone to Conry, June 30, 1938; Background Data on Representative Oil Pools, by J. C. K., Feb. 9, 1950.

55. Memo on net crude production in the U.S., 1924–1938, dated Apr. 7, 1939; Study of domestic and foreign production and reserves, by companies and countries, 1936–1948. NICB, *The Petroleum Almanac,* 1946, p. 33; John G. McLean and Robert Wm. Haigh, *The Growth of Integrated Oil Companies* (Boston, 1954), 682f.

56. Memo on departmental operations, 1934–1939, by C. L. Burrill, Sept. 10, 1940. NICB, *The Petroleum Almanac,* 1946, p. 42. Humble's relatively larger potential was amply demonstrated in World War II (Larson and Porter, *History of Humble,* 576f).

57. For accounts of the experience of the Jersey affiliates' largest purchaser, see Larson and Porter, *History of Humble,* 316–326, 462, 477, 515–518, 529–535.

58. Memos by E. J. Sadler, June 12, 1936, and Mar. 16, 1937. Larson and Porter, *History of Humble,* 477, 515–517, 529, 534.

59. NICB, *The Petroleum Almanac,* 1946, p. 11. Memo by C. L. Burrill, Sept. 10, 1940. Larson and Porter, *History of Humble,* 453, 516, 535.

60. Larson and Porter, *History of Humble,* 322f, 454, 456, 472, 521, 530–533.

61. Humble's price policy and practice are discussed in many places in *ibid.*

Attention is called especially to pages 322f, 461f, 472–474, 477, and 516f.

62. *Ibid.,* 473.

63. Gibb and Knowlton, *The Resurgent Years,* 70–73 and 635–640.

64. SONJ, *Annual Report,* 1926; a manuscript by Miller, Corporate Histories of Natural Gas Companies, prepared in 1944 and revised in 1946. U.S. Senate, 70th Cong., 1st sess., Doc. 92, *A Monthly Report on the Electric Power and Gas Utilities Industry,* Dec. 15, 1935 (Washington, 1936), pt. 83, p. 247f.

65. Miller, Corporate Histories of Natural Gas Companies. U.S. Senate, 70th Cong., 1st sess., Doc. 92, *A Monthly Report . . . ,* pt. 83, p. 247f; Louis Stotz, *History of the Gas Industry* (New York, 1938), 376–378.

66. SONJ, Directors' Minutes, 1927, 1933, and 1937; W. C. Teagle, Memo of June 7, 1933; *The Lamp,* Aug., 1933. American Gas Association, *Monthly,* Sept., 1952.

67. General Coordination Meeting, Agenda, May 10, 1937, The Oriskany Sand in the Appalachian States; SONJ, *Annual Report,* 1939; *The Lamp,* Dec., 1941, and Feb., 1943.

68. SONJ, Red Books.

69. Letter of R. W. Gallagher to Jersey stockholders, Nov. 1, 1943; SONJ, *Annual Report,* the years from 1935 to 1943, inclusive; *The Lamp,* Feb. and Aug., 1942. Murphy, ed., *Conservation of Oil and Gas,* 652–655.

70. SONJ, *Annual Report,* for the years 1927 to 1939, inclusive; Orville Harden, chairman, Report on the future Manufacturing Activities at N.Y. Seaboard as compared to Gulf Refineries, July 19, 1927; Christy Payne to C. T. White, Oct. 23, 1931. SOC of LA, Annual Report, 1944.

71. ABA, *Legal Hist. of Cons. of Oil and Gas,* 67–74.

72. Miller, Corporate Histories of Natural Gas Companies; SONJ, *Annual Report,* 1939. U.S. Senate, 70th Cong., 1st sess., Doc. 92, *A Monthly Report . . . ,* pt. 83, pp. 195–238, and pt. 84–II, pp. 3595–3599; Stotz, *History of the Gas Industry,* 374f.

73. SONJ, *Annual Report,* 1928 and 1929; Miller, Corporate Histories of Natural Gas Companies. Stotz, *History of the Gas Industry,* 378–380.

74. SONJ, *Annual Report,* 1930 and 1939; Miller, Corporate Histories of Natural Gas Companies. Stotz, *History of the Gas Industry,* 381f; ABA, *Legal Hist. of Cons. of Oil and Gas,* 269.

75. Stotz, *History of the Gas Industry,* 309–336, 342–353, 384–388; U.S. Senate, 70th Cong., 1st sess., Doc. 92, *A Monthly Report . . . ,* pt. 84–II, pp. 1802–3591.

76. Larson and Porter, *History of Humble,* 501f, 504.

77. *Ibid.,* 502–503.

78. *Ibid.,* 502–504.

79. *Ibid.,* 504.

80. *Ibid.,* 505f.

81. *Ibid.,* 506.

82. *Ibid.,* 507.

83. NICB, *The Petroleum Almanac,* 1946, p. 249; API, *Petroleum Facts and Figures,* 1941, pp. 91, 93.

84. Larson and Porter, *History of Humble,* 649; U.S. House, 80th Cong., 1st sess., *Hearings Before the Committee on Interstate and Foreign Commerce* (Washington, 1947), 162–171, 187–198; Murphy, ed., *Conservation of Oil and Gas,* 852f.

CHAPTER 5

1. Data in this paragraph were obtained from the Directors' Minutes of Jersey and Imperial and from official lists of officers and directors of International Petroleum and Tropical.

2. George Sweet Gibb and Evelyn H. Knowlton, *The Resurgent Years, 1911–1927* (New York, 1956), 422f.

3. W. E. Pratt to F. M. Surface, Aug. 7, 1963.

4. The discussion of Imperial's production effort that follows is based largely on the research of J. S. Ewing in the company's records.

5. Gibb and Knowlton, *The Resurgent Years,* 89–91, 422. IMPERIAL: Corporate records; Memorandum prepared for

C. O. Stillman on Imperial's subsidiaries in Turner Valley; A. E. Burns to A. M. McQueen, Nov. 25, 1927.

6. Quoted in *Toronto Globe,* Dec. 9, 1929.

7. Committee report, Ottawa, Jan. 8, 1930.

8. *The Lamp,* Oct., 1929.

9. Statement by A. M. McQueen in *Toronto Globe,* Dec. 9, 1929.

10. IMPERIAL: C. O. Stillman to A. M. McQueen, Dec. 30, 1930; McQueen to Stillman, Jan. 2, 1931.

11. IMPERIAL: A. M. McQueen to C. O. Stillman, Oct. 8, 15, and 28, 1931; *Albertan* (Calgary), Sept. 10, 1931.

12. IMPERIAL: J. H. McLeod to R. V. LeSueur, Aug. 25, 1936; Vernon Taylor, "Development of the Turner Valley Gas and Oil Field," in *Technical Publication* #1099 of Amer. Inst. of Mining and Metallurgical Engineers.

13. IMPERIAL: J. H. McLeod to R. V. LeSueur, Sept. 13, 1937.

14. *Imperial Oil Review,* Fall-Winter, 1939, 15–18.

15. F. K. Beach and J. L. Irwin, *The History of Alberta Oil* (Dept. of Lands and Mines, Edmonton, 1939), 26.

16. IMPERIAL: J. H. McLeod to G. H. Smith, Oct. 1, 1937.

17. Gibb and Knowlton, *The Resurgent Years,* 366–380.

18. INTERNATIONAL: L. N. Stone to B. Dunlap, July 1, 1926; R. V. LeSueur to Montagu Piesse, June 12, 1931; Memo of A. Iddings to A. Norcutt, May 9, 1941; Memo on Public Relations, to W. F. Prendergast by A. H. Clark, June 26, 1941. TROPICAL: H. A. Metzger to G. H. Smith, June 16, 1926; Memo on some of the conditions established by Tropical for workingmen, Nov., 1926; P. F. Shannon to R. I. Dodson, Mar. 24, 1934; Shannon to Metzger, June 4, 1935; Annual Report, 1926, 1934, 1935, and 1940.

19. INTERNATIONAL: E. Pombo to G. H. Smith, June 2, 1926, and Sept. 30, 1930; R. V. LeSueur to Smith, Apr. 19 and May 7, 1927; Smith to Orville Harden, Aug. 10, 1934; A. Iddings to

LeSueur, Oct. 28, 1941; Memo on Public Relations, to W. F. Prendergast by A. H. Clark, June 26, 1941.

20. G. H. Smith to Eugene Holman, Apr. 28, 1937. Interview of E. H. Knowlton and H. M. Larson with H. A. Metzger, June 20, 1956.

21. This paragraph is based largely on interviews in Venezuela, especially with a publisher of oil reports in Maracaibo and with a former Colombian newspaperman who was head of Creole's public relations in Maracaibo. It would be easy to conclude that British colonial tradition was at work in Colombia, but the situation apparently was far too complex to allow of any single explanation.

22. Producing Department Memo on eastern Peru, Sept. 10, 1943; W. E. Pratt to E. L. Estabrook, Sept. 15, 1942.

23. Memo by E. J. Sadler to W. C. Teagle, May 28, 1936.

24. INTERNATIONAL: Report of operations for 18-month period ending Dec. 31, 1939.

25. Eugene Holman to R. V. LeSueur, Jan. 12, 1938.

26. Statements in SONJ Red Books.

27. T. R. Armstrong to E. J. Sadler, July 27, 1935.

28. *El Universal* (Mexico City), Feb. 8, 1928; Richardson Pratt to P. E. Pierce, Feb. 10, 1928.

29. G. S. Walden, Report on inspection trip to Argentina and Bolivia, 1926; Walden to J. B. Eskeson, Jan. 5, 1938.

30. Samuel Flagg Bemis, *The Latin American Policy of the United States: An Historical Interpretation* (New York, 1943), 285f.

31. Memo on status of investments in Argentina, by G. F. Howard, May 31, 1935.

32. Interview, G. S. Gibb and C. S. Popple with W. A. Watkins, Tulsa, Okla., Oct. 24, 1949.

33. Statement of Standard Oil Co., S. A., Argentina, by F. C. Schultz, to Buenos Aires press, Apr. 19, 1927; Draft of memo for U.S. State Dept. in 1935; Review of Prod. Dept. operations in Argentina, by Schultz, June 19, 1934; T. S. Armstrong to E. J. Sadler, July 27, 1935.

34. Memo on Argentina, prepared for submission to Cordell Hull (Secretary of State), May 31, 1935.

35. Background Memo on Argentina, prepared by Prod. Dept. for the use of Eugene Holman, July, 1935.

36. Review of Prod. Dept. operations in Argentina, by F. C. Schultz, June 19, 1934.

37. Memo on Argentina, prepared by F. C. Pannill, Jan. 14, 1948.

38. See Bryce Wood, *The Making of the Good Neighbor Policy* (New York, 1961), chap. 7.

39. A. Corwin to W. C. Teagle, Sept. 23, 1918, enclosing report on inspection tour of Bolivia; Report of Eugene Stebinger, Nov. 5, 1920.

40. Concession contract between Bolivia and the Standard Oil Company (New Jersey), July 27, 1922.

41. Report of G. S. Walden on inspection trip to Argentina and Bolivia, 1926.

42. T. R. Armstrong to F. C. Schultz, Nov. 13, 1926; Armstrong to Cordell Hull, Mar. 15, 1939.

43. *Confiscation: A History of the Oil Industry in Bolivia* (a pamphlet published by SONJ, N.Y., 1939), 3f.

44. *Ibid.*, 14f.

45. Harris Gaylord Warren, *Paraguay, An Informal History* (Norman, Okla., 1949), 295.

46. *Ibid.*

47. T. W. Palmer to Laurence Duggan (State Department), Mar. 18, 1937; F. C. Schultz to Eugene Holman, Apr. 6, 1936; *Confiscation: A History of the Oil Industry in Bolivia*, 4f.

48. Warren, *Paraguay*, 294.

49. Wood, *The Making of the Good Neighbor Policy*, 169.

50. Robert J. Alexander, *The Bolivian National Revolution* (New Brunswick, N.J., 1958), 22–26; Robert J. Alexander, *Communism in Latin America* (New Brunswick, N.J., 1957), 213–215.

51. T. W. Palmer to Laurence Duggan, Mar. 18, 1937. *Confiscation: A History of the Oil Industry in Bolivia,* 6.

52. How is this sudden change explained? A driller on Bolivian operations at the time said it started with the firing of a Bolivian roughneck from a drilling crew (interview of H. M. Larson with G. McKee, La Salina, Venezuela, Feb. 16, 1949). Whether or not this was the spark that set off the blast, it indicates how sensitive the situation was.

53. Translation of the Bolivian decree of Mar. 13, 1937; T. W. Palmer to Laurence Duggan, Mar. 18, 1937; Col. G. Rodrigues to SOC of Bolivia, Mar. 18, 1937.

54. Summary of events, by F. C. Schultz, Apr. 6, 1937; E. Aramber to C. W. Gillespie, June 28, 1937. *Confiscation: A History of the Oil Industry in Bolivia,* 6–8.

55. Concession contract between Bolivia and Standard Oil Company (New Jersey), July 27, 1922.

56. Wood, *The Making of the Good Neighbor Policy,* 169.

57. F. C. Schultz to T. R. Armstrong, Feb. 25, 1926; Telegram, Armstrong to Schultz, Feb. 26, 1926; Schultz to F. J. Conway, Feb. 26, 1926; Schultz to J. P. Arner, Mar. 16, 1926; Schultz to R. C. Wells, Oct. 16, 1926; Armstrong to Schultz, Nov. 13, 1926; Conway to Producing Dept., Oct. 19, 1927; Armstrong to Schultz, Jan. 12, 1928; Armstrong to Cordell Hull, Mar. 15, 1939.

58. Wood, *The Making of the Good Neighbor Policy.* Published in 1961, this is the most recent work dealing at some length with the Bolivian expropriation. Chapter 7 is devoted to this case, the author's interest being in the State Department's response as a part of the process of developing and applying the Good Neighbor Policy. This chapter, together with its notes, presents a full and objective account of the contents of the department's files on this Bolivian issue in the National Archives of the United States. These files were examined by H. M. Larson after the Jersey Standard manuscript was ready for the press.

59. *Ibid.,* 169.

60. *Ibid.,* 169–171.

61. Bemis, *The Latin American Policy of the United States,* 276–294.

62. Wood, *The Making of the Good Neighbor Policy,* 171.

63. *Ibid.* For the State Department's cautious moves under its new commitment and the results with regard to the Good Neighbor Policy, see chap. 7.

64. Interview of H. M. Larson with F. C. Pannill in 1957. On Pannill's failure to reach any understanding with Minister Finot, see Wood, *The Making of the Good Neighbor Policy,* 173f.

65. Wood, *The Making of the Good Neighbor Policy,* 174 and 176f.

66. *Ibid.,* 176–179. Telegram, Eugene Holman to J. Taylor Fly, Mar. 18, 1938.

67. Wood, *The Making of the Good Neighbor Policy,* 174, 178f.

68. *Confiscation: A History of the Oil Industry in Bolivia,* 10f; Wood, *The Making of the Good Neighbor Policy,* 178–181. The quotation was printed in *El Debato* (La Paz), Feb. 19, 1939.

69. Translation of decision of Bolivian Supreme Court rejecting Standard Oil Company of Bolivia's suit for recovery, Mar. 8, 1939. *The New York Times,* Mar. 10, 1939; Wood, *The Making of the Good Neighbor Policy,* 181.

70. Gibb and Knowlton, *The Resurgent Years,* 359–366; Bemis, *The Latin American Policy of the United States,* 217f.

71. J. Reuben Clark, Jr., "The Oil Settlement in Mexico," *Foreign Affairs,* vol. VI, no. 4 (1928); Bemis, *The Latin American Policy of the United States,* 218.

72. J. Kennalley, Jr., to C. H. Lieb, June 15, 1928.

73. Memorandum by Richardson Pratt, July 9, 1928, in a letter of C. H. Lieb on land policy in Mexico, June 21, 1928.

74. Bemis, *The Latin American Policy of the United States,* 344–346.

75. Robert J. Alexander, *Communism in Latin America,* 330–335, 337.

76. *Diario Oficial,* Nov. 25, 1936.

77. Bemis, *The Latin American Policy of the United States*, 346.

78. Copy of proposed contract presented to Huasteca and Transcontinental by Central Oil Workers Syndicate of Mexico, Nov. 3, 1936. Roscoe B. Gaither, *Expropriation in Mexico* (New York, 1940), 10–13.

79. Memo prepared by the Law Department for submission to the U.S. State Department, Mar., 1938.

80. Translation of the award of the Mexican Labor Board, Dec. 18, 1937; Translation of the petition of the oil companies to the Supreme Court of Mexico, Dec. 29, 1937; Decision of the Supreme Court rejecting the petition of the oil companies, Mar. 1, 1938. Gaither, *Expropriation in Mexico*, 14, 17–19; Bemis, *The Latin American Policy of the United States*, 347.

81. Wood, *The Making of the Good Neighbor Policy*, 203–205.

82. *Diario Oficial*, March 19, 1938. SONJ: J. B. Burnett to Eugene Holman, Mar. 21, 1938; *Annual Report*, 1937. Gaither, *Expropriation in Mexico*, chap. 8.

83. Wood, *The Making of the Good Neighbor Policy*, 203f; Gaither, *Expropriation in Mexico*, 27. Bemis gives the impression that Cárdenas' objective was expropriation (*The Latin American Policy of the United States*, 345–347).

84. *Mexico, Expropriation of Foreign-Owned Oil Properties*, 1938 (published by Huasteca Petroleum Co., N.Y., 1938), pp. 88–98, translation of note handed to the Ambassador of Mexico in Washington by Cordell Hull, July 21, 1938. Samuel Bemis, as quoted in *The Christian Science Monitor* of Feb. 13, 1964, stated that "The trouble with our Latin American policy stems directly from the doctrine of nonintervention." For an account of the relations of the Department of State and the Mexican government over this issue, see Wood, *The Making of the Good Neighbor Policy*, 203–259.

85. Wood, *The Making of the Good Neighbor Policy*, 249.

86. *Gazette Oficial*, July 18, 1922.

87. Several Creole employees, from member of Creole Executive Committee to local supervisor, interviewed by H. M. Larson in January and February, 1949, in Venezuela.

88. CREOLE: Record for the Ministry of Fomento, Venezuela, Dec. 16, 1942.

89. Wallace E. Pratt and Dorothy Good, eds., *World Geography of Petroleum* (Princeton, N.J., 1950), 64. CREOLE: Interview with Superintendent Hood of the Quiriquire field, February, 1949.

90. CREOLE: *Annual Report*, 1928; Directors' Minutes, Feb. 18, 1931; A Brief Corporate History of Creole Petroleum Corporation (manuscript).

91. According to company men interviewed who knew H. E. Linam and his work as a manager, he had the job of upgrading the working organization, especially the expatriate supervisory force. He succeeded, but his authoritarian methods made many enemies for him.

92. CREOLE: *Annual Report*, 1928–1932.

93. CREOLE: Report on Operations in Eastern Venezuela During the Year, 1928; Annual Review of General Manager, 1928–1931.

94. Information concerning exploration, production, and transportation was obtained either from the manager's operating reviews of the Creole Petroleum Corporation, submitted to the New York office, or from Creole's *Annual Report* for the various years.

95. CREOLE: T. R. Armstrong to H. E. Linam, Sept. 7, 1933.

96. CREOLE: Gen. Man. Review, Standard Oil of Venezuela and Lago Petroleum, for the years 1932 to 1939, inclusive; Directors' Minutes, May 9, 1934; Eugene Holman to H. E. Linam, Mar. 1, 1937; Holman to T. R. Armstrong, June 14, 1937; Memo on Linam, June 30, 1932. Interview of H. M. Larson with Mr. Regan, a geologist, in Venezuela, Jan. 31, 1949.

97. CREOLE: File on pooling agreements.

98. The frequent reports of Creole from Venezuela to headquarters in New York,

and also interviews in 1949 with early company employees in Venezuela, give a vivid picture of transportation difficulties and how they were overcome.

99. Several veteran employees who were interviewed by H. M. Larson in Venezuela in 1949 described the early conditions and the gradual development of oil camp communities. Some vivid experiences of life in the camps were recalled. For example, in 1930 French escapees from Devil's Island who were employed as cooks in the Quiriquire camp had to be discharged because they fought each other dangerously. Or, there were the experiences of the lone geologist who spent months surveying with the faithful help of two natives, one to cook (he was not a good tinned-food cook, but he could gather considerable food in the countryside) and one to look after the pack mules and equipment. Among those interviewed were Messrs. Hood, Latham, Magnuski, McKee, Peake, Porterfield, Prince, Regan, Skeie, and Soper.

100. CREOLE: Eugene Holman to C. H. Lieb, Mar. 25, 1930.

101. This incident was related to E. H. Knowlton and H. M. Larson by Eugene Holman, who gave the experience as an example of the capacity of the illiterate Venezuelan for advancement.

102. The difficulty of developing national foremen was especially stressed by Superintendent Hood of Quiriquire in telling of his experiences to H. M. Larson in Feb., 1949. He had then been superintendent of this field for seventeen years.

103. CREOLE: Gen. Man. Rev., Standard Oil of Venezuela, 1936.

104. CREOLE: File on labor troubles following the death of Gómez; Gen. Man. Rev., Standard Oil of Venezuela and Lago Pet., 1936; Review of Labor Organization in Venezuela, presented at General Coordination Meeting, Miami, Feb. 8, 1946.

105. CREOLE: Gen. Man. Rev., Standard Oil of Venezuela and Lago Pet., 1936.

106. CREOLE: Gen. Man. Rev., Standard Oil of Venezuela, 1937. Interview of H. M. Larson with Manager Hagen of

the Creole Ind. Rel. Dept. in Caracas, Feb. 4, 1949.

107. CREOLE: Eugene Holman to F. C. Laurie, Jan. 12, 1937.

108. CREOLE: T. R. Armstrong to L. C. Booker, Feb. 8, 1937.

109. CREOLE: File on 1936 Labor Law, including reports on sources of its provisions as well as the contents of the law itself. Interview with Manager Hagen, Creole's Ind. Rel. Dept., Feb. 4, 1949.

110. Interview with Manager Hagen, Feb. 4, 1949.

111. CREOLE: Gen. Man. Rev., Lago Pet., 1936.

112. CREOLE: Gen. Man. Rev., Standard Oil of Venezuela, 1936.

113. CREOLE: File on *Utilidades.*

114. CREOLE: *Annual Report,* 1928–1939. SONJ, Red Books; Memo by C. L. Burrill, Sept. 10, 1940; Records on gross crude oil reserves.

115. Interview of H. M. Larson with J. J. Conry, Tulsa, Apr. 6, 1945.

116. Annual Report of Româno-Americana, 1929–1937; T. J. E. Umbeck, Historical Report of Româno-Americana from the Date of Inception.

117. *Ibid.;* SONJ, Red Books; Heinrich Riedemann to W. C. Teagle, Nov. 16, 1936; E. J. Sadler to Teagle, Nov. 25, 1936.

118. E. J. Sadler to Orville Harden, Jan. 3, 1931; General Report on Poland, Mar. 5, 1935; SONJ, Red Books.

119. Cable, R. P. Bolton to SONJ, Nov. 26, 1935; E. J. Sadler to Eugene Holman, June 2, 1939.

120. Contract between Royal Hungarian Minister of Finance and European Gas & Electric Company, June 8, 1933; Supp. Contract, June 24, 1938; Agreement, June 8, 1933; Supp. agreement, June 10, 1937; Eugene Holman to E. J. Sadler, Dec. 2, 1938; Paul Ruedemann to R. P. Bolton, Dec. 13, 1940.

121. SONJ, Records on gross crude reserves.

122. Gibb and Knowlton, *The Resurgent Years,* 391–394.

123. G. S. Walden to E. J. Sadler, Oct. 31, 1927; Sadler to W. C. Teagle, May 11, 1928; Frederick Horstmann to Sadler, July 17, 1928; Walden to Prod. Dept., Apr. 5, 1929; Guy Wellman to Campbell, May 4, 1929; Walden to Teagle, Apr. 18, 1930; Memo by Walden, May 30, 1930.

124. Memo by G. S. Walden, May 30, 1930; Walden to E. J. Sadler, Feb. 9, 1931; Notice to Stockholders of Socony-Vacuum, Nov. 6, 1933.

125. Brief Summary of Nederlandsche Koloniale Petroleum Maatschappij, June 12, 1945.

126. Departmental Operations, 1934–1939, by C. L. Burrill, Sept. 10, 1940.

127. SONJ, Records on gross crude reserves.

CHAPTER 6

1. On the development of the company's refining research before 1927, see George Sweet Gibb and Evelyn H. Knowlton, *The Resurgent Years, 1911–1927* (New York, 1956). Information was also obtained from interviews of N. S. B. Gras with the following: E. M. Clark, June 16, 1946; N. E. Loomis, Aug. 23, 1946; F. A. Howard, Sept. 12, 1946; R. P. Russell, Aug. 22, 1946.

2. Henrietta M. Larson and Kenneth Wiggins Porter, *History of Humble Oil & Refining Company* (New York, 1959), 204–209, 216.

3. Gibb and Knowlton, *The Resurgent Years*, 532–547; Larson and Porter, *History of Humble*, 207f.

4. Gibb and Knowlton, *The Resurgent Years*, 546f. Interview of N. S. B. Gras with R. P. Russell, Aug. 22, 1946.

5. IMPERIAL: Mutualization Contract of Jan. 1, 1929. Larson and Porter, *History of Humble*, 217. Interview of H. M. Larson with E. H. Dickson of SODC, June 18, 1945.

6. Gibb and Knowlton, *The Resurgent Years*, 544–546.

7. Frank A. Howard, *Buna Rubber, The Birth of an Industry* (New York, 1947), 11–18.

8. *Ibid.*, 15–17.

9. *Ibid.*, 20–24; Gibb and Knowlton, *The Resurgent Years*, 546. SONJ Secretary's Department, Contract dated September 7, 1927, Standard Oil Company (New Jersey) and I. G. Farbenindustrie. A memorandum of a meeting of Jersey and Farben executives in New York late in 1926 is reproduced in U.S. Senate, 77th Cong., 1st sess., *Hearings Before a Special Committee Investigating the National Defense Program*, pt. 11, *Rubber* (Washington, 1942), 4581–4583. This and other references below to this publication are to exhibits from Jersey files.

10. Contract dated Sept. 7, 1927, between SONJ and I. G. Farben.

11. Howard, *Buna Rubber*, 25–27. Testimony of F. A. Howard in U.S. Circuit Court of Appeals for the Second District, *Standard Oil Company (New Jersey) et al. v. Tom Clark, Attorney General . . .*, Transcript of Record filed Nov. 4, 1946; 64 Fed. Supp. 646.

12. Howard, *Buna Rubber*, 27–32. *The Lamp*, Dec., 1929. Agreement of Nov. 9, 1929, between I. G. Farbenindustrie Aktiengesellschaft, S.I.G. Company, Standard Oil Company [New Jersey], and Standard Oil Company of New Jersey. This agreement, filed in the SONJ Secretary's Dept., is reproduced in U.S. Senate, 77th Cong., 1st sess., *Hearings . . . National Defense Program*, pt. 11, pp. 4561–4568. A memorandum of a preliminary meeting of Jersey and Farben officials in New York, March 21, 1929, is in *ibid.*, 4591–4596.

13. Agreement of Nov. 9, 1929, between I. G. Farbenindustrie and Standard Oil Company [New Jersey] is reproduced in U.S. Senate, 77th Cong., 1st sess., *Hearings . . . National Defense Program*, pt. 11, pp. 4572–4580. Howard, *Buna Rubber*, 28f, 249–251; *The New York Times*, Dec. 2, 1929.

14. U.S. Senate, 77th Cong., 1st Sess., *Hearings . . . National Defense Program*, pt. 11, pp. 4583f. The agreement is reproduced in Howard, *Buna Rubber*, 252–260.

15. SONJ, *Annual Report*, 1931, 1932, and 1933; *The Lamp*, Feb., 1930, and Sept., 1944. ESSO: *Salesmotor*, Jan., 1938; Tabulation of Refinery Processes,

by Draughton, Mar. 23, 1945. Larson and Porter, *History of Humble,* 545; *Chemical and Engineering News,* June 25, 1943 (vol. 21), 950–959.

16. Records in SONJ files on the organizing of the companies. U.S. Circuit Court of Appeals for the Second District, *Standard Oil Company (New Jersey) et al.* v. *Tom Clark, Attorney General . . . ,* Transcript of Record filed Nov. 4, 1946, pp. 1093–1097.

17. SONJ: *Annual Report,* 1932 and 1933; General Coordination Committee Meeting, Agenda, Jan. 24, 1935, Baton Rouge Hydro Plant, and minutes of meeting of Apr. 20, 1936. Larson and Porter, *History of Humble,* 545.

18. SONJ, *Annual Report,* 1931, 1932, and 1933; R. T. Haslam to F. M. Surface, Feb. 3, 1958. ESSO: *Salesmotor,* Dec., 1931, Dec., 1933, and Mar., May, and Sept., 1934; *Esso Marketer,* Sept., 1927. SODC: History of Lubricating Oil Additives, by J. G. McNab, Sept. 17, 1945. U.S. Senate, 77th Cong., 1st sess., *Hearings . . . National Defense Program,* pt. 11, pp. 4711f.

19. SONJ, *Annual Report,* 1933–1935. SODC: History of Lubricating Oil Additives, by J. G. McNab, Sept. 17, 1945.

20. IMPERIAL: History of the Development of the Technical and Research Department (manuscript prepared by the department, 1947). SOC of LA: Annual Report, 1935, 1937, and 1938. ESSO: Tabulation of Refinery Processes, by C. R. Draughton. SONJ, Data on Foreign Refineries of Subsidiaries and Affiliates, compiled by H. L. Shoemaker, May 19, 1944.

21. Larson and Porter, *History of Humble,* 561f.

22. *Ibid.,* 562.

23. Gibb and Knowlton, *The Resurgent Years,* 539–541; Howard, *Buna Rubber,* 51; Alfred P. Sloan, Jr., *My Years with General Motors* (Garden City, N.Y., 1964), 221–226.

24. Graham Edgar, "Measurement of Knock Characteristics of Gasoline in Terms of Standard Fuel Oil," *Industrial and Engineering Chemistry,* Feb., 1927.

25. Howard, *Buna Rubber,* 51–53.

26. *Industrial Bulletin of Arthur D. Little, Inc.,* May, 1944.

27. E. V. Murphree to M. J. Rathbone, Aug. 29, 1944; G. Freyermuth, Production and Requirements of 100-Octane Gasoline, Aug. 14, 1942. Howard, *Buna Rubber,* 52; Charles Sterling Popple, *Standard Oil Company (New Jersey) in World War II* (New York, 1952), 23; Kendall Beaton, *Enterprise in Oil: A History of Shell in the United States* (New York, 1957), 564f.

28. Popple, *SONJ in W. W. II,* 21.

29. Beaton, *Enterprise in Oil,* 535, 560–562; Popple, *SONJ in W. W. II,* 22.

30. SONJ, *Annual Report,* 1935; G. Freyermuth, Prod. and Req. of 100-Octane Gasoline. Howard, *Buna Rubber,* 53; Larson and Porter, *History of Humble,* 558f.

31. Freyermuth, Prod. and Req. of 100-Octane Gasoline. Popple, *SONJ in W. W. II,* 23; Beaton, *Enterprise in Oil,* 561. ESSO: Sales records, 1935.

32. Beaton, *Enterprise in Oil,* 562–563, contains a summary of the controversy between Wright Field and the General Staff.

33. *Ibid.,* 565f; Popple, *SONJ in W. W. II,* 23; Larson and Porter, *History of Humble,* 559.

34. SONJ, *Annual Report,* 1938; Manufacturing records, Chemical Products Division. Popple, *SONJ in W. W. II,* 24, 27f; Larson and Porter, *History of Humble,* 559.

35. Larson and Porter, *History of Humble,* 559f.

36. *Ibid.* ESSO: Tabulation of Refinery Processes, by Draughton. SONJ: *Annual Report,* 1940; Summary of Refinery Operations in Sumatra, H. M. Davidson, Apr. 4, 1947. Popple, *SONJ in W. W. II,* 24, 27f; Beaton, *Enterprise in Oil,* 567–569; Larson and Porter, *History of Humble,* 560.

37. ESSO: Tabulation of Refinery Processes, by Draughton. SONJ, Article (manuscript) by Cooke, Oct. 2, 1940. Larson and Porter, *History of Humble,* 559.

38. Popple, *SONJ in W. W. II*, 24, 26–28.

39. SONJ, Annual Statistical Review, 1946; Chronology of Aviation Fuels Development by Standard Oil Company (New Jersey). National Industrial Conference Board, *Petroleum Almanac*, 1946, pp. 152, 275.

40. John Lawrence Enos, *Petroleum Progress and Profits: A History of Process Innovation* (Cambridge, 1962), 192f.

41. F. A. Howard to Orville Harden, Jan. 20, 1938. Popple, *SONJ in W. W. II*, 13.

42. SODC: Research and development records on catalytic cracking. Popple, *SONJ in W. W. II*, 13; U.S. Senate, 77th Cong., 1st sess., *Hearings . . . National Defense Program*, pt. 11, pp. 4665–4667; Howard, *Buna Rubber*, 77f. The quotation is from Enos, *Petroleum Progress and Profits*, 196.

43. Enos, *Petroleum Progress and Profits*, 196, 200f.

44. ESSO: Technical Report No. 504, Baton Rouge laboratories, Dec. 8, 1938. General Coordination Committee Meeting, May, 1945, Patents and Competitive Situation. U.S. Senate, 77th Cong., 1st sess., *Hearings . . . National Defense Program*, pt. 11, p. 4665.

45. R. T. Haslam to Lt. Col. Charles G. Mettler, Jan. 23, 1933.

46. Popple, *SONJ in W. W. II*, 100.

47. Larson and Porter, *History of Humble*, 564, 596; Popple, *SONJ in W. W. II*, 103f.

48. An account of the early interest of Jersey in I. G. Farben's work on synthetic rubber may be found in Howard, *Buna Rubber*, 40–76. A short account of Jersey's interest in synthetic rubber and efforts to develop processes for its manufacture appears in Popple, *SONJ in W. W. II*, 49–55.

49. Howard, *Buna Rubber*, 36f.

50. General Coordination Committee Meeting, Agenda, 1934. ESSO: Tabulation of Refinery Processes, by Draughton. Howard, *Buna Rubber*, 35–37.

51. Records of the interrogation of high Farben officials in 1945 and 1946 in connection with the Nuremberg trials (U.S. Archives, Record group 238, Interrogation Files) reveal how close the relationship became between Farben and the German government after Hitler came into power, especially after the German four-year plan went into effect in 1936. Among those who gave information on the relations of Farben with government agencies, notably the *Wehrmacht*, were Denker, Schmitz, Schnitzler, and Struss. Farben's research expenditures, which came to be subsidized by the government, rose from 900,000 RM in 1934 to 2,000,000 in 1935, and 8,700,000 in 1938. Dr. Herman Schmitz, the Farben official in charge of the building of new plants useful to the military, said that, after the four-year plan went into effect in 1936, Farben's investments were mostly tied up with the *Wehrmacht*. For information from Jersey records, see U.S. Senate 77th Cong., 1st sess., *Hearings . . . National Defense Program*, pt. 11, pp. 4598–4602.

52. U.S. Archives, Documents of the U.S. District Court of New York in connection with *Standard Oil Company (New Jersey) . . . v. . . . Alien Property Custodian*, (64 Fed. Supp. 656), Hunter Exhibits nos. 58 and 59.

53. *Ibid.*, nos. 65 and 80; U.S. Senate, 77th Cong., 1st sess., *Hearings . . . National Defense Program*, pt. 11, pp. 4602, 4639, and 4730; Howard, *Buna Rubber*, 41–44, 60–62, 68–73, and 93–96.

54. Howard, *Buna Rubber*, 44–46.

55. *Ibid.*, 77–91.

56. SONJ, *Annual Report*, 1939. SODC: Records of Butyl research and development. U.S. Senate, 77th Cong., 1st sess., *Hearings . . . National Defense Program*, pt. 11, pp. 4465f and 4479f; Howard, *Buna Rubber*, 47–51.

57. Howard, *Buna Rubber*, 65–68; 77th Cong., 1st sess., *Hearings . . . National Defense Program*, pt. 11, p. 4724.

58. Howard, *Buna Rubber*, 261f; 77th Cong., 1st sess., *Hearings . . . National Defense Program*, pt. 11, p. 4725.

59. Howard, *Buna Rubber*, 113–115; Beaton, *Enterprise in Oil*, 590; U.S. Senate, 77th Cong., 1st sess., *Hearings . . . National Defense Program*, pt. 11, pp. 4384, 4396f, 4725–4731.

60. ESSO: Esso Laboratories, Operating Costs at Baton Rouge, 1927–1948, prepared by R. Melum, Mar. 22, 1949. SODC: R. W. Burkhardt to C. S. Popple, Nov. 14, 1946. HUMBLE: Annual Report of Refinery and Technical Research Department, 1937–1939. Howard, *Buna Rubber*, 55.

CHAPTER 7

1. For the history of Jersey refining to 1927, see Ralph W. Hidy and Muriel E. Hidy, *Pioneering in Big Business, 1882–1911* (New York, 1955), and George Sweet Gibb and Evelyn H. Knowlton, *The Resurgent Years, 1911–1927* (New York, 1956). See especially the table on pages 678f of the latter.

2. Report of Manufacturing Department for 1926; Report of committee on future manufacturing activities at N.Y. seaboard as compared to Gulf refineries, by Orville Harden, chairman, July 19, 1927; Memo by E. G. Barber, Apr. 8, 1927; W. C. Teagle to E. M. Clark, June 7, 1927; Memo on organization (unsigned and undated, but probably prepared by special committee late in 1932 or early 1933); Memo concerning lubricating oil purchases by Socony-Vacuum, June 30, 1932. ESSO: H. A. Wilkinson to G. W. Mayer, Jan. 7, 1925; Memo of meeting of H. L. Pratt, Judge Speer, Teagle, and C. O. Swain, by the last-named, Oct. 1, 1926; Total domestic sales of petroleum products, Marketing Department and General Office sales by companies, compiled in 1935 and subsequent years. SODC: C. A. Straw to F. A. Howard, Feb. 28, 1925. Henrietta M. Larson and Kenneth Wiggins Porter, *History of Humble Oil & Refining Company* (New York, 1959), 215f.

3. Undated manuscript entitled Historical Account of Anglo-American Oil Co., Limited.

4. C. H. Haupt to E. M. Clark, Dec. 21, 1928; Memo by Orville Harden concerning future of Everett refinery and New Jersey Works, Jan. 22, 1929; H. L. Shoemaker to Coordination Committee concerning supplies and outlets of the Everett refinery, September 17, 1930. COL. BEACON: Chronology prepared

from company records, by J. A. Fair in 1947 and 1948.

5. Larson and Porter, *History of Humble*, 190–197, 233–238, 545.

6. C. M. Leonard to E. J. Sadler, Sept. 20 and Oct. 28, 1928; Memo for Sadler, by Eugene Holman, Aug. 20, 1931; Statistics on crude runs of refineries; *The Lamp*, Aug., 1929. CREOLE: L. C. Booker to Creole Pet. Corp., Sept. 24, 1928; C. H. Lieb to Creole Pet. Corp., Feb. 18 and Mar. 16, 1929; Statistics on refineries in the Dutch West Indies and Venezuela as of Jan. 1, 1931.

7. Report of operations of producing subsidiaries of Pan American Petroleum & Transport for 1931. CREOLE: Memo on Pan American Foreign Corp., Mar. 17, 1932; Manager's Review for 1935.

8. Report of operations of producing subsidiaries of Pan Am. Pet. & Trans. for 1931; Oil refining at the world's crossroads, Aruba, N.W.I., draft of article, dated Aug. 29, 1939; Draft of article by T. S. Cooke, Oct. 2, 1940; General Coordination Meeting, Agenda, June 24, 1935, Advisability of Further Expansion of Aruba in View of Nationalistic Tendencies in Foreign Countries.

9. Report of operation of producing subsidiaries of Pan Am. Pet. & Trans. for 1931; Report of producing operations of Lago Petroleum for 1932, by F. C. Laurie, Feb. 28, 1933; Statistics on crude runs of refineries. CREOLE: W. R. Finney to T. R. Armstrong, Mar. 27, 1934; L. C. Booker to Armstrong, July 30, 1934; Eugene Holman to Laurie, July 19, 1935.

10. Oil refining at the world's crossroads, Aruba, N.W.I., Aug. 29, 1939; Draft of article on Aruba, by T. S. Cooke, Oct. 2, 1940; Map of Aruba refinery, Jan. 1, 1954. On combination units, see p. 607 of *The American Petroleum Industry: The Age of Energy, 1899–1959* (Evanston, 1963), by Harold F. Williamson, Ralph L. Andreano, Arnold R. Daum, and Gilbert C. Klose.

11. Oil refining at the world's crossroads, Aruba, N.W.I., Aug. 29, 1939. National Industrial Conference Board (NICB), *The Petroleum Almanac*, 1946, pp. 334–337.

12. CREOLE: Statistics on refineries in Venezuela and the N.W.I., as of Jan. 1, 1931; Manager's annual review by H. E. Linam, from 1934 to 1938, inclusive; *Annual Report,* 1939; Brief corporate history of Creole Pet. Corp., by N. J. Beals, Feb., 1945. American Petroleum Institute (API), *Petroleum Facts and Figures,* 1941, p. 81; Edwin Lieuwen, *Petroleum in Venezuela, A History* (Berkeley, 1955), 67–74; John Lawrence Enos, *Petroleum Progress and Profits: A History of Process Innovation* (Cambridge, 1962), 260.

13. Data on foreign refineries, by H. L. Shoemaker, May 19, 1944. IMPERIAL: *Imperial Oil Review,* June, 1947.

14. Data on foreign refineries, by H. L. Shoemaker, May 19, 1944; SONJ, *Annual Report,* 1934. Standard Oil Company of Bolivia, *Confiscation: A History of the Oil Industry in Bolivia* (New York, 1939); J. R. Powell, *The Mexican Petroleum Industry, 1938–1950* (Berkeley, 1956), 71–86; API, *Petroleum Facts and Figures,* 1941, p. 18; NICB, *The Petroleum Almanac,* 1946, p. 335.

15. Memo by W. J. Haley, Mar. 5, 1935; Memo by G. H. Michler for D. L. Harper (undated); Memo on Brazilian supply (unsigned), Feb. 6, 1936; S. P. Coleman to Harper, Jan. 25, 1937; Haley to G. W. Gordon, Feb. 4, 1937; H. L. Shoemaker to Harper, Nov. 10, 1937; Michler to Harper, Dec. 3, 1937; Haley to E. H. Barlow, Dec. 5, 1937; W. Simonson to Harper, Apr. 29, 1938; Memo on history of installation of refinery at São Paulo (unsigned and undated); Harper to A. C. Minton, Sept. 9, 1940. *Bulletin of the Pan-American Union,* vol. 62 (July, 1938), 426; *Oil & Gas Journal,* April 9, 1948.

16. Copy of decree covering importation of petroleum products into France, Mar. 30, 1929; Memo on the French refining situation (unsigned and undated); H. E. Bedford to D. L. Harper, Apr. 24, 1929; Bedford to W. C. Teagle, Apr. 10 and 12, 1929.

17. 40 *Stat.* 516 (1918).

18. Memo on merger (unsigned), Aug. 2, 1929; H. E. Bedford to C. O. Swain, Oct. 11, 1929; Memo on merger, by George Michler for Swain, May 20, 1930.

19. C. H. Haupt to Guy Wellman, June 30, 1931; E. H. Barlow to Wellman, July 10, 1931; Wellman to F. A. Howard, Dec. 19, 1932; Data on foreign refineries, by H. L. Shoemaker, May 19, 1944; *The Lamp,* June, 1931, and June, 1934.

20. H. E. Bedford to W. C. Teagle, Apr. 12, 1929; Bedford to Guy Wellman, Sept. 30, 1930. *Oil & Gas Journal,* Dec. 29, 1932; *The Petroleum Times,* Mar. 27 and June 12, 1937.

21. *The Petroleum Times,* Mar. 27 and June 12, 1937, and Feb. 28, 1939; API, *Petroleum Facts and Figures,* 1937, p. 8, and 1941, p. 18; NICB, *The Petroleum Almanac,* 1946, p. 335.

22. *The Petroleum Times,* July 24, Aug. 7, Oct. 2, and Nov. 27, 1937, and Jan. 1 and 22, 1938.

23. API, *Petroleum Facts and Figures,* 1928, pp. 47–50, and 1941, p. 18; NICB, *The Petroleum Almanac,* 1946, p. 335.

24. *The Petroleum Times,* Feb. 19, 1938.

25. *Ibid.,* Feb. 19 and Mar. 12, 1938.

26. Data on foreign refineries, by H. L. Shoemaker, May 19, 1944; *The Lamp,* June, 1941; History of DAPG (manuscript), by F. Bachof. API, *Petroleum Facts and Figures,* 1941, p. 18; NICB, *The Petroleum Almanac,* 1946, p. 335; *The Petroleum Times,* July 24 and Nov. 27, 1937, and Feb. 26, 1938.

27. Data on foreign refineries, by H. L. Shoemaker, May 19, 1944. API, *Petroleum Facts and Figures,* 1941, p. 18; NICB, *The Petroleum Almanac,* 1946, p. 335; *The Petroleum Times,* Feb. 26 and May 5, 1938.

28. General Coordination Meeting, Agenda, June 24, 1935, Advisability of Further Expansion of Aruba in View of Nationalistic Tendencies in Foreign Countries; Coordination Committee Minutes, Apr. 20, 1936, discussion of manufacturing operations in foreign countries, and May 9–13, 1938, discussion of foreign growth; Data on foreign refineries, by H. L. Shoemaker, May 19, 1944.

29. Data on foreign refineries, by H. L. Shoemaker, May 19, 1944; Summary of

refinery operations in Sumatra, by H. M. Davidson, Apr. 4, 1947. NICB, *The Petroleum Almanac,* 1946, p. 335.

30. Memo by P. W. Parker, Mar. 19, 1934; W. C. Teagle to Henri Deterding, Aug. 31, 1934; Cable of Orville Harden to Teagle and J. A. Brown, Oct. 26, 1934; Résumé of position between Standard-Vacuum and Mitsui, commented on by Parker in letter to Brown, May 29, 1935; G. S. Walden to Parker, June 25, 1935; Memo on Japanese situation by "J. C. G.," Oct. 10, 1935; Résumé of meeting in N.Y. in letter of H. Wilkinson to Teagle, Oct. 29, 1935; Teagle to Wilkinson, Oct. 30, 1935.

31. NICB, *The Petroleum Almanac,* 1946, p. 93.

32. ESSO: Total domestic sales of petroleum products, Marketing Department and General Office sales by companies, compiled in 1935 and subsequent years.

33. SONJ statistics on refinery operations, U.S. and foreign, 1927–1939. NICB, *The Petroleum Almanac,* 1946, p. 70.

34. Interviews of H. M. Larson with many older operating managers and supervisors suggested that correspondence schools had provided virtually the only special training of many of that generation who had risen above the rank and file. This is a phase of American education about which little is known but which merits investigation.

35. Circular letter to heads of departments and companies, July 3, 1929. SOC of LA: Records of officers and directors.

36. Personnel records of these companies and Jersey's press releases of Oct. 6, 1949, and Apr. 26, 1950; *The Lamp,* Feb. 1934, and Apr., 1942. Also, interviews with several men in high positions in the companies, including Lloyd G. Smith and Brian Mead.

37. Larson and Porter, *History of Humble,* 208, 556.

38. Interviews: H. M. Larson with Dr. N. E. Loomis of SODC, June 18, 1945; with Dr. H. G. M. Fischer, SODC, June 20, 1945; and with E. W. Luster, SODC, June 21, 1945. Also: Gibb and Knowlton, *The Resurgent Years,* 520–531; Larson and Porter, *History of Humble,* 216f.

39. Gibb and Knowlton, *The Resurgent Years,* 526, 537f; Larson and Porter, *History of Humble,* 204, 208, 216, 218.

40. Interviews of H. M. Larson and E. H. Knowlton with Brian Mead, July 9 and 19, 1956. General Coordination Meeting, Agenda, Oct., 1934, Operating and Cost Control; Memo by E. J. Sadler, Oct. 7, 1932.

41. General Coordination Meeting, Agenda, Oct., 1934, Operating and Cost Control. SOC of LA: Annual Report, 1936. Larson and Porter, *History of Humble,* 554. Interview of H. M. Larson with Dr. H. G. M. Fischer, of SODC, June 20, 1945.

42. Hidy and Hidy, *Pioneering in Big Business,* 35f, 89–108.

43. E. M. Clark to W. C. Teagle, Dec. 22 and 31, 1926, and Jan. 20 and May 26, 1927; Teagle to Clark, Dec. 26, 1926, and Jan. 4, 1927; F. W. Abrams to G. W. McKnight, Jan. 3, 1927; C. H. Haupt to McKnight, Jan. 6, 1927; McKnight to C. G. Black and Clark, Jan. 25, 1927; Clark to C. E. Graff, Feb. 2, 1927; Teagle to Clark, Black, and D. R. Weller, Feb. 15, 1927; Review of the Manufacturing Dept. for 1926, by Graff; Report of committee on future of manufacturing activities at N. Y. seaboard as compared to Gulf refineries, by Orville Harden as chairman, July 19, 1927.

44. Larson and Porter, *History of Humble,* 544–547.

45. SODC: E. M. Clark to Orville Harden, Oct. 6, 1929; Louis Link to D. R. Weller, Sept. 17, 1929; J. L. Finley to H. C. Wiess, Oct. 9, 1929; C. I. Fiero to Clark, Nov. 5, 1930. ESSO: Tabulation of Refinery Processes, by C. R. Draughton, Baton Rouge, Mar. 23, 1949; Baton Rouge expansion and development, by "A. F. R.," Mar. 8, 1949; Memo by H. J. Voorhies, Baton Rouge, Apr. 4, 1949; A brief history of the Bayonne Works; A short history of the Eagle Works, Apr. 10, 1939; Plant inventory cards of Bayway. HUMBLE: List of investments in refinery equipment, 1921–1950.

46. ESSO: Plant records of Bayway and Bayonne; Tabulation of Refinery Processes, by C. R. Draughton, Mar. 23, 1949; Baton Rouge expansion and devel-

opment, by "A. F. R.," Mar. 8, 1949; Memo by H. J. Voorhies, Apr. 4, 1949. Larson and Porter, *History of Humble*, 205–207, 213–215.

47. 283 U.S. 163–183. *Oil & Gas Journal*, Jan. 15, 1931; *The New York Times*, Apr. 14, 1931; API, *Petroleum Industry Hearings Before the Temporary National Economic Committee* (New York, 1942), 353–386.

48. API, *Petroleum Facts and Figures*, 1937, p. 119.

49. SONJ, *Annual Report*, 1927–1931. ESSO: Bayonne inventory cards; Tabulation of Refinery Processes, by C. R. Draughton, Mar. 23, 1949. Larson and Porter, *History of Humble*, 215.

50. Memo by G. W. Gordon, Sept. 10, 1934; General Coordination Meeting, Agenda, Oct., 1934, Combination Topping and Cracking Unit; and June, 1935, Economies of Combination Units versus Jersey's present Refinery Equipment.

51. On the economy of these units, see John G. McLean and Robert Wm. Haigh, *The Growth of Integrated Oil Companies* (Boston, 1954), 572f.

52. General Coordination Meeting, Agenda: June 20, 1935, Modernization of Refinery Equipment Necessary for Rehabilitation of the Baytown Refinery; May 10, 1937, Industry Refinery Capacity, Worldwide and Local Trends; May 13, 1937, Manufacturing Problems and Need for Flexibility and Spare Capacity in U.S. Refineries; May 15–19, 1939, Obsolescence of Equipment. Also, Data on foreign refineries, by H. L. Shoemaker, May 19, 1944; Memo by E. J. Sadler, June 12, 1936; Richardson Pratt to Eugene Holman, Apr. 19, 1944; SONJ, *Annual Report*, 1939.

53. Larson and Porter, *History of Humble*, 561f.

54. ESSO: Tabulation of Refinery Processes, by C. R. Draughton, Mar. 23, 1949. Larson and Porter, *History of Humble*, 559.

55. Departmental Operations, 1934–1939, by C. L. Burrill, Sept. 18, 1940; Richardson Pratt to Eugene Holman, Apr. 19, 1944.

56. SONJ, Annual Statistical Review, 1950.

57. *Ibid.*

58. NICB, *The Petroleum Almanac*, 1946, pp. 334–337; Williamson *et al.*, *The American Petroleum Industry: The Age of Energy, 1899–1959*, 646f; McLean and Haigh, *The Growth of Integrated Oil Companies*, 682–687.

59. Memo concerning discussions of proposed products sales agreement between Humble and Standard of New Jersey, Aug. 7, 1934; Memo of H. H. Baker, Sept. 18, 1934. Larson and Porter, *History of Humble*, 549f.

60. CREOLE: Sales agreement, Aug. 1, 1935; Brief corporate history of Creole, by Beals, Feb., 1948.

61. SONJ, Red Books, 1927 to 1935, inclusive.

62. Memo by C. L. Burrill, Sept. 10, 1940.

63. Memo by E. J. Sadler, June 12, 1936.

CHAPTER 8

(Manuscript records herein cited were from the files of Esso Shipping Company unless otherwise indicated.)

1. Annual Report of Standard Shipping Company, 1927; Statistics of Fleets of Large Companies on Oct. 1, 1927.

2. Ann. Report of Standard Shipping Co., 1927.

3. U.S. Department of Commerce, Bureau of Marine Inspection and Navigation, *Navigation Laws of the United States* (Washington, 1940), 116f.

4. Ann. Report of Standard Shipping Co., 1927.

5. George Sweet Gibb and Evelyn H. Knowlton, *The Resurgent Years, 1911–1927* (New York, 1956), 476–481.

6. Ann. Rep. of Standard Shipping Co., 1927–1931; H. L. Shoemaker to R. L. Hague, Mar. 11, 1937, and Mar. 11, 1938; Hague to Shoemaker, Apr. 13, 1937, and Apr. 14, 1938. SONJ: Eugene Holman to heads of departments and committees, Apr. 5, 1938. *The Ships' Bulletin*, Mar.–Apr., 1939. Views concerning the management of marine activities in this period have been gathered from interviews with men active in marine operations.

7. *Register of Tank Vessels of the World,* 1928.

8. Ann. Report of Standard Shipping Co., 1929.

9. *Ibid.,* for the years 1929 to 1931, inclusive.

10. *Ibid.,* 1930; *The Bulletin,* May, 1931.

11. Ann. Report of Standard Shipping Co., 1930; *The Bulletin,* May, 1931, and Jan., Sept., and Oct., 1933.

12. COL. BEACON: *Annual Report,* 1929.

13. Ann. Report of Standard Shipping Co., 1929–1931; Annual Report of Marine Activities, 1932 and 1933.

14. R. L. Hague to Peter Hurll, Aug. 7, 1929; Hague to A. Maclean, Sept. 6, 1929.

15. Ann. Report of Standard Shipping Co., 1927–1931.

16. Ann. Report of Standard Shipping Co., 1927–1929; History of Schedule Freight Rates, United States, Consortium, and Latin America, 1927–1950, by G. A. Gumbs, Jr., Mar. 15, 1950. SONJ: J. A. Moffett, Jr., to W. C. Teagle, June 4, 1928; R. F. Hand to C. G. Black, Mar. 8, 1929; R. L. Hague to E. M. Clark, Apr. 3 and Sept. 13, 1929, Aug. 23, 1930; Clark to W. S. Farish, Apr. 8, 1929; Hand to E. J. Sadler, Nov. 12, 1929; H. L. Shoemaker to Clark, Aug. 22, 1930; Clark to Shoemaker, Aug. 25, 1930; Hand to Clark, Jan. 30, 1931.

17. SONJ: Red Books, 1929.

18. Ann. Report of Marine Activities, 1932, 1933, and 1934. *World Petroleum,* Nov., 1931, Feb., May, June, and July, 1932; *The Petroleum Times,* Jan. 2, 1932. SONJ: Executive Committee Minutes, Jan. 5, 1934. 76th Cong., 2nd sess., *Hearings Before the Temporary National Economic Committee,* pt. 14 (Washington, 1940), 7334f.

19. Ann. Report of Standard Shipping Co., 1927–1933; *The Bulletin,* June, 1932, and June, 1934. *Register of Tank Vessels of the World,* 1931, 1932, and 1933.

20. SONJ: Historical Account of Anglo-American Oil Co., Ltd. (a manuscript, undated and unsigned). *Register of Tank Vessels of the World,* 1928 and 1932.

21. Annual Report of the Marine Activities of Jersey's Affiliates, 1932–1934; *The Bulletin,* Sept., 1932, and July, 1933. SONJ: Unsigned memo of Mar. 17, 1932; E. F. Johnson to C. O. Swain, Aug. 16, 1932, and July 20, 1935. *The Lamp,* June, 1932.

22. *The Bulletin,* Sept., 1932, and July, 1933. SONJ: Unsigned memo dated Mar. 17, 1932; E. F. Johnson to C. O. Swain, Aug. 16, 1932, and July 30, 1933; *The Lamp,* June, 1932.

23. Ann. Report of Standard Shipping Co., 1930 and 1931; *The Bulletin,* Jan., 1931. SONJ: E. M. Clark to H. L. Shoemaker, Aug. 25, 1930; Shoemaker to Clark, Aug. 22, 1930; R. L. Hague to Clark, Aug. 23, 1930.

24. Ann. Report of Standard Shipping Co., 1930; History of Schedule Freight Rates . . . , by G. A. Gumbs, Jr., Mar. 15, 1950; R. L. Hague to B. B. Howard, Mar. 26, 1931; R. F. Hand to Howard, Jan. 27, 1931; Memo on Insurance of Tankers, by "H. D." [Dodge], Jan. 12, 1927.

25. History of Schedule Freight Rates . . . , by G. A. Gumbs, Jr., Mar. 15, 1950.

26. This figure is based on the data for Dec. 31, 1935, minus acquisitions in the year 1935.

27. SONJ: Red Books.

28. History of Schedule Freight Rates . . . , by G. A. Gumbs, Jr., Mar. 15, 1950.

29. R. L. Hague to D. L. Harper (undated but apparently in 1932); Hague to W. C. Teagle, Apr. 10, 1935.

30. R. L. Hague to W. C. Teagle, Apr. 10, 1935.

31. *Ibid.*

32. *Ibid.*

33. Boleslaw Adam Boczek, *Flags of Convenience: An International Legal Study* (Cambridge, 1962), 6–10.

34. Memo for R. L. Hague by H. D. Dodge, May 15, 1935; Weekly newsletter by R. F. Hand, June 10, 1935; Hand to W. C. Teagle, Mar. 23, 1936, and to F. Breme, Apr. 24, 1936. Boczek, *Flags of Convenience,* 40, 45, 53–61.

35. *The Bulletin,* June, 1935. SONJ: Corporation records; unsigned letter to B. D. Seaver, May 11, 1937; Eugene Holman to stockholders of Pan American Foreign Corporation, Nov. 23, 1936; Exec. Com. Minutes, Dec. 8, 1936. *Register of Tank Vessels of the World,* 1934 and 1939.

36. SONJ: "H.C." to E. J. Sadler, May 14, 1928; P. J. Gallagher to D. L. Harper, Feb. 21, 1929; Annual Report of Standard-Vacuum, 1939; Annual Statistical Review, 1943; *The Lamp,* Feb., 1934. Also, *Register of Tank Vessels of the World,* 1928, 1932, and 1934.

37. SONJ: Heinrich Riedemann to W. C. Teagle, Oct. 16, 1923, and to Guy Wellman, May 30, 1925; R. L. Hague to C. G. Black, Jan. 5, 1927; R. F. Hand to Piesse & Sons, Jan. 8, 1927; Montagu Piesse to Hand, Feb. 25, 1929; J. S. Hansen to R. H. Steyer, Feb. 3, 1956. *The Ships' Bulletin,* Mar.–Apr., 1941. *World Petroleum,* Feb., 1932; National Industrial Conference Board, *The Petroleum Almanac,* 1946, pp. 64, 307, 314, 319–321, 325–328.

38. Ann. Report of Marine Activities, 1932–1939. *Register of Tank Vessels of the World,* 1934 and 1939.

39. Ann. Report of Marine Activities, 1936–1939. *The Ships' Bulletin,* 1936–1939, various issues. *Register of Tank Vessels of the World,* 1928, 1932, and 1934.

40. SONJ: *Annual Report,* 1935.

41. *The Ships' Bulletin,* July and Aug., 1936; R. L. Hague to W. C. Teagle, Apr. 28, 1936.

42. *The Ships' Bulletin,* Dec., 1936, Sept. and Dec., 1937, Jan.-Feb., Mar.-Apr., May-June, and Aug., 1938; Ann. Report of Marine Activities, 1938. SONJ: *Annual Report,* 1935.

43. Ann. Report of Marine Activities, 1937 and 1938; History of the Marine Department. SONJ: General Coordination Committee Meeting, May 9–13, 1938, B. B. Howard's program; *The Lamp,* Feb., 1938. Charles Sterling Popple, *Standard Oil Company (New Jersey) in World War II* (New York, 1952), 186f.

44. History of the Marine Dept.; *The Ships' Bulletin,* issues from January to September, 1939, and July-Aug., 1942. SONJ: Exec. Com. Minutes, Jan. 4, 1938, and Feb., 1939; *Annual Report,* 1937–1939; *The Lamp,* Feb., 1936, and Oct., 1940.

45. Memo by H. L. Shoemaker concerning foreign tankers, May 5, 1938; Shoemaker to R. L. Hague, Mar. 11, 1937, and Mar. 11, 1938; Hague to Shoemaker, Apr. 13, 1937, and Apr. 14, 1938; *The Ships' Bulletin,* July-Aug., 1939. *Register of Tank Vessels of the World,* 1939. SONJ: Eugene Holman to heads of departments and companies, Aug. 5, 1938.

46. SONJ: Ann. Stat. Review, 1945; Article on Aruba, by T. S. Cooke, Oct. 2, 1940; Annual Report of Standard Oil Co. of Venezuela, 1935, 1936, and 1939; Annual Report of Operations of Lago Petroleum Corp., 1932, 1933, 1935, and 1937; Annual Review by F. C. Laurie for 1935. CREOLE: *Annual Report,* 1935–1939; E. L. Estabrook to Eugene Holman, Nov. 4, 1939.

47. SONJ: Ann. Stat. Review, 1946. *Register of Tank Vessels of the World,* 1939.

48. History of Schedule Freight Rates . . . , by Gumbs, Mar. 15, 1950.

49. *Ibid.*

50. *Ibid.*

51. *Ibid.*

52. *Ibid.*

53. Ann. Rep. of Standard Shipping Co., 1927–1931; *The Bulletin,* 1927 to 1936, *passim; The Ships' Bulletin,* 1936 to 1939, *passim.* Various other sources were used, including National Labor Relations Board, *Written Trade Agreements in Collective Bargaining* (Washington, 1940), and John J. Collins, "The Jersey Standard Tanker Officers Association, 1938–1957, A Study in Independent Unionism" (a manuscript Ph.D. thesis presented at Fordham University, 1958).

54. Philip Taft, *The Structure and Government of Labor Unions* (Cambridge, 1954), 189–199.

55. Collins, "The Jersey Standard Tanker Officers Association. . . ."

56. *Ibid.* SONJ: General Coordination Committee Meeting, Minutes, May 15, 1939, and May 13, 1940; Ann. Report of Marine Activities, 1939–1941.

57. Ann. Report of Marine Activities, 1941. Collins, "The Jersey Standard Tanker Officers Association. . . ."

58. Collins, "The Jersey Standard Tanker Officers Association. . . ." Ann. Report of Marine Activities, 1939–1940.

59. Collins, "The Jersey Standard Tanker Officers Association. . . ." Ann. Report of Marine Activities, 1941.

60. SONJ: Red Books for the years 1935 to 1939, inclusive; Departmental Operations, 1934–1939, by C. L. Burrill, Sept. 10, 1940.

61. *The Ships' Bulletin,* Mar.-Apr., May-June, and Nov.-Dec., 1939.

CHAPTER 9

1. For the history of the pipelines of Jersey affiliates before 1927, see the following: Ralph W. and Muriel E. Hidy, *Pioneering in Big Business, 1880–1911* (New York, 1955); George Sweet Gibb and Evelyn H. Knowlton, *The Resurgent Years, 1911–1927* (New York, 1956); Henrietta M. Larson and Kenneth Wiggins Porter, *History of Humble Oil & Refining Company* (New York, 1959); John L. Loos, *Oil on Stream: A History of Interstate Oil Pipe Line Company, 1909–1959* (Baton Rouge, 1959).

2. National Industrial Conference Board (NICB), *The Petroleum Almanac,* 1946, p. 58. SONJ, *Annual Report,* 1926 to 1931, inclusive; *The Lamp,* Dec., 1930. U.S. House, 72nd Cong., 2nd sess., *Report on Pipelines* (Washington, 1933), pt. I, pp. 217, 222f, 228.

3. For information about these three lines in producing regions see: Loos, *Oil on Stream,* and Larson and Porter, *History of Humble.*

4. For one company's rates, see Larson and Porter, *History of Humble,* 523.

5. *Ibid.,* 698; Loos, *Oil on Stream,* 125, 152f. SONJ, Red Books.

6. Larson and Porter, *History of Humble,* 151–158, 698.

7. Loos, *Oil on Stream,* 104, 106, 112.

8. *Ibid.,* 134f.

9. Paul H. Giddens, *Standard Oil Company (Indiana): Oil Pioneer of the Middle West* (New York, 1955), 444–446.

10. Loos, *Oil on Stream,* 134–136, 139f.

11. Memo by Orville Harden, Oct. 21, 1929; Harden to H. M. Dawes, May 20, 1930; E. J. Sadler to O. Donnell, July 8, 1930; W. C. Teagle to Peter Hurll, Sept. 10, 1930; Sadler to Teagle, Sept. 17, 1930; Harden to Teagle, Nov. 18, 1930; Contract between SONJ, Ohio Standard, and Pure Oil Co., Dec. 20, 1930; Operating agreement of Oklahoma Pipe Line and Ajax Pipe Line, Dec. 29, 1932. U.S., 72nd Cong., 2nd sess., *Report on Pipelines,* pt. I, pp. 92, 152, 270–272; Loos, *Oil on Stream,* 136–138.

12. Report on pipelines of affiliates, 1931–1938, by H. L. Shoemaker, Feb. 15, 1937. U.S., 72nd Cong., 2nd sess., *Report on Pipelines,* pt. II, pp. 182, 187–190, 272–304, 316.

13. H. S. Austin to E. J. Sadler, Apr. 3 and July 9, 1929; E. F. Johnson to E. W. Dean, Apr. 12, 1929; Johnson to F. J. Faulks, Apr. 13, 1929; Memo on Tuscarora, Feb. 19, 1930. 72nd Cong., 2nd sess., *Report on Pipelines,* pt. I, pp. 9–16, 75f, 81f, 123–126, 244–250; Gibb and Knowlton, *The Resurgent Years,* 469.

14. Larson and Porter, *History of Humble,* 155–157, 161, 169, 698; Loos, *Oil on Stream,* 106, 115, 117–121, 135, 144–147.

15. Loos, *Oil on Stream,* 125, 152f; John G. McLean and Robert Wm. Haigh, *The Growth of Integrated Oil Companies* (Boston, 1954), 244.

16. HUMBLE: W. C. Teagle to W. S. Farish, Sept. 12, 1928, and Nov. 2 and 14, 1928. The quotation is from the letter of Nov. 2.

17. HUMBLE: W. S. Farish to W. C. Teagle, Nov. 8, 1928.

18. Larson and Porter, *History of Humble,* 450–453, 483. Chapter 18 deals with

the East Texas field and the efforts to establish regulation of its production.

19. *Ibid.*, 520.

20. *Ibid.*, 521.

21. See Chapter 4 of this volume and Larson and Porter, *History of Humble*, chaps. 18 and 20.

22. Hidy and Hidy, *Pioneering in Big Business*, 671–698.

23. Arthur M. Johnson, *Petroleum Pipelines and Public Policy, 1906–1959* (Cambridge, 1967), 215f, 227.

24. *Ibid.*, 216; Larson and Porter, *History of Humble*, 522f.

25. U.S. House of Representatives, 73rd Congress, *Hearings Before a Subcommittee of the Committee on Interstate and Foreign Commerce* (Washington, 1934), pt. I; 74th Cong., 1st sess., *House Report* no. 2 (1935); *A. L. A. Schecter Poultry Co.* v. *United States*, 55 S. Ct., 837; Larson and Porter, *History of Humble*, 485; Johnson, *Petroleum Pipelines and Public Policy*, 223, 229–235.

26. SONJ: Table of gathering and trunkline rates, July, 1932–May, 1933. Loos, *Oil on Stream*, 322.

27. W. S. Farish to W. P. Cole, Jr., Dec. 21, 1934; Analysis of Ajax Corp. in reference to reduction in tariffs, Aug. 2, 1935. HUMBLE: Rate tables compiled by Humble Pipe Line Co. Larson and Porter, *History of Humble*, 522; Loos, *Oil on Stream*, 322.

28. Loos, *Oil on Stream*, 143; Larson and Porter, *History of Humble*, 519.

29. Loos, *Oil on Stream*, 125, 153; Larson and Porter, *History of Humble*, 547–550, 698.

30. Larson and Porter, *History of Humble*, 698.

31. Loos, *Oil on Stream*, 125, 152f.

32. 49 U.S. Statutes, 33C, 18. See *Legal History of the Conservation of Oil and Gas, A Symposium* (American Bar Association, 1938) and Blakely M. Murphy, ed., *Conservation of Oil and Gas, A Legal History* (American Bar Association, 1948). Also, Larson and Porter, *History of Humble*, 484–486.

33. Interview of H. M. Larson with Smith Day, Mar. 26, 1945.

34. Loos, *Oil on Stream*, 209f.

35. *Ibid.*, 183.

36. *Ibid.*

37. *Ibid.*, 210.

38. *Ibid.*, 188. SONJ: W. R. Finney to Eugene Holman, May 9, 1939, asking for jobs for Ajax employees; C. F. Smith to H. L. Shoemaker, Jan. 13, 1939; J. A. Veasey to W. E. Pratt, Oct. 20, 1939.

39. Loos, *Oil on Stream*, 187f.

40. This account of Oklahoma's employee relations is based on pages 189 to 195 of Loos, *Oil on Stream*.

41. *Ibid.*, 195.

42. *Ibid.*, 121–123.

43. *Ibid.*, 125, 156, 160, 179.

44. Larson and Porter, *History of Humble*, 519, 696, 698.

45. *Ibid.*, 523–525.

46. *Ibid.*, 380–382; *The Lamp*, June, 1936, and Oct., 1939.

47. Johnson, *Petroleum Pipelines and Public Policy*, 248f; Larson and Porter, *History of Humble*, 380–382, 692f.

48. Larson and Porter, *History of Humble*, 522; Loos, *Oil on Stream*, 179f, 212f. INTERSTATE: Manuscript History, 1904–1944.

49. Loos, *Oil on Stream*, 125, 152, 179f, 212f; Larson and Porter, *History of Humble*, 698. SONJ: Red Books; Departmental Operations, 1934–1939, by C. L. Burrill, Sept. 10, 1940.

50. 76th Cong., 2nd sess., *Hearings before the Temporary National Economic Committee*, pt. 14 (Washington, 1940), Sec. 2, and pt. 15, Sec. 2; Amer. Pet. Institute, *Petroleum Industry Hearings Before the Temporary National Economic Committee* (New York, 1942). On the investigations by the Interstate Commerce Commission: Johnson, *Petroleum Pipelines and Public Policy*, 241–250.

51. For a survey of the complex issues involved, see Johnson, *Petroleum Pipelines and Public Policy*, 270–288. For a review by a member of the Antitrust Division of the Department of Justice, see Roy C. Cook, *TNEC Monograph, No. 39*, entitled *Control of the Petroleum Industry by Major Oil Companies*

(Washington, 1941). On the issue as to the independent refiners' access to crude and markets, see pages 70 to 75 of Daniel C. Hamilton, *Competition in Oil, The Gulf Coast Refinery Market, 1935–1950* (Cambridge, 1958). On pipeline costs see Leslie Cookenboo, Jr., *Costs of Operating Crude Oil Pipe Lines* (Houston, 1954). The general movement to regulate pipelines in the 1930's is described in Williamson *et al., The American Petroleum Industry: The Age of Energy, 1899–1959* (Evanston, 1963), and in George S. Wolbert, Jr., *American Pipe Lines: Their Industrial Structure, Economic Status, and Legal Implications* (Norman, 1952).

52. For a summary of the position taken by various oil industry representatives, see Johnson, *Petroleum Pipelines and Public Policy,* 272–278.

53. Larson and Porter, *History of Humble,* 522.

54. *Ibid.,* 698; Loos, *Oil on Stream,* 125, 152, 179f, 212f. Also, SONJ, Red Books.

55. Figures presented by Sun Oil Company at the TNEC hearings in 1939 suggest the relative costs of the different kinds of transport serving the oil industry. Sun Oil's average costs were 4.873 cents per ton-mile by truck, 1.640 by railroad, 0.526 by gasoline pipeline, 0.477 by crude oil pipeline, 0.259 by barge, and 0.063 by tanker (API, *Petroleum Industry Hearings,* 274).

56. SOC of LA: Annual Report, 1934–1937. *The Lamp,* Apr., 1936.

57. ESSO SH: Annual Report, 1927–1931; *The Bulletin,* Feb., Apr., and July, 1927, Jan., 1930, and July and Sept., 1932.

58. D. S. Harper to E. M. Clark, Aug. 25, 1932; R. L. Hague to Clark, Oct. 7, 1932; General Coordination Meeting Minutes, May 10, 1937. COL. BEACON: Report of Visit of Coordination Committee in fall of 1939.

59. SOC of LA: Annual Report, 1936–1939 and 1944; S. B. Short to W. W. Tennant, Feb. 25, 1939.

60. General Coordination Meeting Minutes, Transportation Committee Activities, May 10, 1937.

61. SOC of LA: A. G. Phelps to R. N. Keppel, Apr. 30, 1937; Phelps to E. J. Sadler, Sept. 26, 1938; Copy of statement made by R. T. Haslam before the Cole Committee, Apr. 1, 1941.

62. TNEC, *Hearings,* Part 15, Sec. 2, 8559–8561.

63. Annual Report for the Dutch East Indies, 1927; Report of NKPM, 1930, 1936, and 1937; G. S. Walden to E. J. Sadler, Jan. 27, 1930; Annual Review by L. W. Elliott, 1935, 1936, and 1939.

64. Report on Andian National Corporation's proposed pipeline, Nov. 13, 1924; A. A. Eberly to E. J. Sadler, May 25, 1925; *The Lamp,* Feb., 1929, and June, 1930. INTERNATIONAL: Copy of publicity for Andian for Barranquilla newspaper, Feb. 20, 1926; address delivered by J. W. Flanagan, Apr. 27, 1928.

65. A. M. McQueen to W. C. Teagle, July 15, 1925; Teagle to G. H. Smith, Mar. 2 and Apr. 9, 1929; H. L. Shoemaker to Eugene Holman, Sept. 7, 1939; Gross and net income of Andian National Corp. for the years 1933–1939, and earnings and dividends paid, 1937–1946; Annual report of International for the year ending June 30, 1937; Semiannual reports of pipelines for 1935–1938. INTERNATIONAL: G. H. Smith to J. W. Flanagan, Apr. 25, 1929; Flanagan to Smith, May 14, 1929; Extract of Memoria del Ministerio de Industrias al Congreso Nacional en las sesiones ordinarias de 1929; Memo by "F. V. L.," Oct. 17, 1929; Flanagan to Teagle, Apr. 6, 1933.

66. INTERNATIONAL: A. M. McQueen to E. J. Sadler, Oct. 21, 1930; Report of A. Iddings, Sept. 23, 1930; Memo on F. B. Bimel's visit to Peru, Mar. 16–Apr. 4, 1945.

67. R. W. Estabrook to W. R. Finney, Feb. 5, 1936; Annual Report of Standard Oil Co. of Venezuela, 1931, 1935, 1936, and 1938; *The Lamp,* Apr., 1931. CREOLE: *Annual Report,* 1930–1939.

68. Crude Oil Situation of Imperial Oil Co., Ltd., by "A. C. R.," Aug. 26, 1946; Report of Trinidad Oil Fields Operating Co., Ltd., 1936; *The Lamp,* Aug. and Oct., 1929; Annual reports for Huasteca and Transcontinental, 1935, 1936, and 1937; Annual Report of Standard Oil Co.,

S.A.P., Argentina, 1937 and 1939, and Manager's Review, 1930. On expropriation in Bolivia and Mexico, see Chapter 5 of this volume.

69. *The Lamp,* Feb. and Aug., 1932, Oct., 1933, and June, 1934; Monthly report of Iraq Pet. Co. for meeting, Jan. 19, 1933; Annual Report, Iraq Pet. Co., 1934–1939; R. W. Estabrook to Eugene Holman, Dec. 15, 1937.

70. Annual Report, Iraq Pet. Co., 1934–1939; Balance sheet of Iraq Pet. Co., June 30, 1932, and June 30, 1934; Minutes of Group Meeting, Jan. 20, 1937.

71. Annual Report, Soc. Petrolifera Italiana, 1935; Annual Report, Standard-Nobel, Producing Dept., 1933; Annual Report, Romàno-Americana, 1935–1938; Annual Report, MAORT, 1939; Review of Romàno-Americana, June, 1938; Eugene Holman to T. R. Armstrong, Oct. 28, 1935; *The Lamp,* June, 1934.

72. Departmental operations, 1934–1939, by C. L. Burrill, Sept. 10, 1940.

73. Report by committee on future manufacturing activities at N.Y. seaboard as compared to Gulf refineries, by Orville Harden, chairman, July 19, 1927; Annual Report, International Petroleum Co., year ending June 30, 1935, through 1939; Report of Standard Oil Co., S.A.P., Argentina, 1937 and 1939; General Coordination Meetings, Minutes, on Tropical's marine operations in Colombia, Oct. 23–26, 1945. ESSO SH: *The Ships' Bulletin,* Aug., 1938, and Sept.-Oct., 1938.

74. Summary of affiliates in Great Britain, France, and Germany in 1938 and 1939 (unsigned); Report of Standard-Vacuum, 1939; Annual Review of NKPM, 1935, 1936, and 1937; Annual Review of Standard-Vacuum, 1938 and 1939; *The Lamp,* Feb., 1934. ESSO SH: *The Ships' Bulletin,* Sept.-Oct., 1938, and Jan.-Mar., 1945.

CHAPTER 10

1. Harold F. Williamson, Ralph L. Andreano, Arnold R. Daum, and Gilbert C. Klose, *The American Petroleum Industry: The Age of Energy, 1899–1959* (Evanston, 1963), chaps. 12 and 13.

2. Annual Statistical Review, 1950; Deliveries into consumption in 1927; Memo on total deliveries of lubricants to Socony-Vacuum, June 30, 1932; Report of committee on future manufacturing activities at N.Y. seaboard as compared to Gulf refineries, by Orville Harden, 1927; Memo on organization (probably by special committee late in 1932 or early in 1933); General Coordination Meeting Minutes, May 9, 1938, Percentage of gasoline consumption enjoyed by the Esso Marketers, Standard of Kentucky, and major competitors in recent years, and significant changes in position. ESSO: Contract sales statistics, 1930–1939; Memo on meeting of H. L. Pratt, Judge Speer, W. C. Teagle, and C. O. Swain, by the last-named, Oct. 1, 1926. Estimates for domestic general office sales and those of the marketing companies, Jersey and Standard Oil Company of New Jersey and Standard of Louisiana, are based on these data and on statements in earlier years that about half of the domestic business was on a contract basis.

3. George Sweet Gibb and Evelyn H. Knowlton, *The Resurgent Years, 1911–1927* (New York, 1956), 496.

4. *Ibid.,* 487–492; Henrietta M. Larson and Kenneth Wiggins Porter, *History of Humble Oil & Refining Company* (New York, 1959), 230–232.

5. Compiled from the following sources: SONJ, Changes in Share of the Gasoline Market, 1926–1945, and Supplements and Other Studies, 1948–1952, by N. H. Seubert; Ralph W. Hidy and Muriel E. Hidy, *Pioneering in Big Business, 1882–1911* (New York, 1955), chaps. 10 and 15; District Court of the United States for the Northern District of Illinois, Eastern Division, *United States* v. *Standard Oil Company (Indiana), et al.,* No. 4131, vol. VIII, Book of Exhibits, 5235; Federal Trade Commission, *Report on the Pacific Coast Petroleum Industry,* pt. 2, *Prices and Competitive Conditions* (Washington, 1922), 244f, 248f, and *Prices, Profits and Competition in the Petroleum Industry* (Washington, 1928), 57, 225–227; Marquis James, *The Texaco Story* (The Texas Company, 1953), 108; Tide Water Oil Company, *Tide Water*

Topics, "Autobiography of an Oil Company," Nov.–Dec., 1923; National Industrial Conference Board, *The Petroleum Almanac,* 1946, p. 96; John G. McLean and Robert Wm. Haigh, *The Growth of Integrated Oil Companies* (Boston, 1954), 78–80, 384, 682f. Also letters to E. H. Knowlton from Robert I. Marshall, Cities Service Company, Jan. 19 and 31, 1955; and from James S. Cross, Jan. 11, 1955, and Philip D. Crell, Jan. 21, 1955, both of Sun Oil Company.

6. Compiled from sources in Note 5, above.

7. Corp. recs.; Changes in Share of the Gasoline Market in the United States, 1926–1945, by N. H. Seubert. ESSO: *The Salesmotor,* Oct.-Nov., 1927.

8. Corp. recs. ESSO: *The Salesmotor,* July and Aug.-Sept., 1928.

9. ESSO: E. F. Johnson to E. W. Dean, Apr. 12, 1929; Johnson to F. J. Faulks, Apr. 12, 1929; H. S. Austin to E. J. Sadler, July 9, 1929; copy of ICC valuation docket 1252, Tuscarora Oil Co., Ltd., 1940. *Oil & Gas Journal, Oil City Derrick, Petroleum Industry,* Diamond Jubilee Number, "Depicting 75 Years of Development of the Petroleum Industry, 1859–1934."

10. Changes in Share of the Gasoline Market in the United States, 1926–1945, by N. H. Seubert. Views of W. S. Farish, president of Jersey, on the marketing of petroleum products presented before the House Judiciary Committee in its hearings on the Harrington bill for the divorcement of marketing from other petroleum operations, Washington, D.C., June 23, 1939. Paul H. Giddens, *Standard Oil Company (Indiana): Oil Pioneer in the Middle West* (New York, 1955), 244.

11. H. A. Wilkinson to G. W. Meyer, Jan. 7, 1925; Memo of meeting, by C. O. Swain, Oct. 1, 1926.

12. COL. BEACON: History and development of Colonial Beacon Oil Company, by A. F. Whiting, Apr. 1, 1946; List of company's properties as of Nov. 14, 1928.

13. *Ibid.*

14. Corp. recs.; circular letters.

15. Memo of Orville Harden, Jan. 22, 1929; Changes in Share of the Gasoline Market . . . , by Seubert. COL. BEACON: History and Development . . . , by Whiting; Notes on marketing companies acquired through 1935.

16. W. C. Teagle to Northrop Clarey, Aug. 25, 1931.

17. F. H. Bedford, Jr., to W. C. Teagle, Jan. 20, 1933.

18. Heinrich Riedemann to W. C. Teagle, Sept. 15, 1933.

19. Orville Harden to W. C. Teagle, Mar. 21, 1929. Giddens, *Standard Oil Company (Indiana),* 285, 580–582, 708; McLean and Haigh, *The Growth of Integrated Oil Companies,* 210, 259f.

20. Sales statistics. Larson and Porter, *History of Humble,* 233–244.

21. Federal Trade Commission, *Prices, Profits, and Competition in the Petroleum Industry.*

22. W. C. Teagle to E. M. Clark, Mar. 20, 1929, with memo on sales research and marketing analysis; J. H. Senior to Teagle, Aug. 16, 1929, with report of special committee on marketing analysis and sales research; Report of special committee to Teagle, Sept. 18, 1929.

23. ESSO: Compilation of data, obtained from the American Petroleum Institute, which had been supplied by The Texas Company, Jan., 1955.

24. *Ibid.*

25. Interviews with several former members of the marketing organization.

26. Corp. recs. SOC of LA: List of officers and directors, 1909–1940. COL. BEACON: List of officers and directors. ESSO: *The Salesmotor,* Aug., 1932.

27. Number of Employees of Domestic Companies, 1927–1932; SONJ, *Annual Report,* 1930, 1931, and 1932.

28. J. H. Senior to W. C. Teagle, Aug. 16, 1929; General Coordination Meetings, Minutes, May 9, 1938, Study of principal petroleum product prices over the past ten years and comparison of these prices with general price index of other commodities. ESSO: *The Salesmotor,* Jan., 1930, Apr., July, and Dec., 1931. COL. BEACON: Memo on marketing, Apr. 29,

1930; Report of Marketing Dept. for the year 1929, by E. N. Wrightington. HUMBLE: *Humble Dealer,* Mar., 1931.

29. ESSO: *The Salesmotor,* June and Nov., 1930, Mar. and Dec., 1931, and July, 1932. COL. BEACON: Memo on marketing, Apr. 29, 1930. HUMBLE: *Sales Lubricator,* May, 1931.

30. Memo on marketing policy, by F. H. Bedford, Jr., May 2, 1929; J. H. Senior to W. C. Teagle, Aug. 16, 1929; Report of special committee to Teagle, Sept. 18, 1929. Gibb and Knowlton, *The Resurgent Years,* 489–491; Larson and Porter, *History of Humble,* 227f.

31. Report of special committee to Teagle, Sept. 18, 1929; General Coordination Meetings, Minutes, May 15, 1939, Cost-reduction programs in domestic marketing. ESSO: *The Salesmotor,* Nov. and Dec., 1928.

32. ESSO: Compilation of data obtained from the American Petroleum Institute, which had been furnished by The Texas Company, Jan., 1955.

33. Report of special committee to Teagle, Sept. 18, 1929; General Coordination Meetings, Minutes, May 15, 1939, Cost-reduction programs in domestic marketing. ESSO: *The Salesmotor,* Nov. and Dec., 1928, and Jan., 1930. McLean and Haigh, *The Growth of Integrated Oil Companies,* 106–108.

34. Larson and Porter, *History of Humble,* 236, 539.

35. *Ibid.,* 233–235.

36. Report of special committee to Teagle, Sept. 18, 1929. ESSO: Memo on service-station history (not dated, but probably 1938); Summary statistics by L. B. Gatchell, Apr. 6, 1933; Memo from E. S. Hall to F. M. Surface (not dated, but probably 1938).

37. Memo on marketing policy, by F. H. Bedford, Jr., May 2, 1929; C. G. Sheffield to various marketers, May 4, 1929; SONJ, *Annual Report,* 1928 and 1929. ESSO: *The Salesmotor,* Jan.-Feb. and July-Aug., 1929, Sept., 1930, and Apr. and Sept., 1931.

38. F. H. Bedford, Jr., to W. C. Teagle, Apr. 16, 1929; Teagle to directors in the U.S., Apr. 15, 1929; *The Lamp,* Aug.,

1930; Memo by S. C. Hope for F. H. Bedford, Jr., June 13, 1947. ESSO: *The Salesmotor,* Aug., 1930.

39. ESSO: *The Salesmotor,* Feb. and Dec., 1931, and Feb. and Mar., 1932.

40. *Ibid.*

41. General Coordination Committee Meeting, data presented at the Seaview Conference, May 12, 1941.

42. Larson and Porter, *History of Humble,* 541f, 545.

43. SONJ, Red Books for the years 1927 to 1933, inclusive.

44. ESSO: Contract sales statistics.

45. Corp. recs.; SONJ, *Annual Report,* 1929. ESSO: *The Salesmotor,* July, 1928, and Sept.-Oct., 1929.

46. Larson and Porter, *History of Humble,* 242.

47. *Ibid.,* 547f.

48. *Ibid.,* 548f.

49. *Ibid.,* 548–550.

50. *Ibid.,* 551f.

51. *Ibid.,* 542f, 550–553.

52. *Ibid.,* 537, 553.

53. Personnel records; Corp. recs. *The New York Times,* Feb. 12, 1935; Giddens, *Standard Oil Company (Indiana),* 208, 248, 431, 492.

54. Directors' Minutes, June 6 and July 28, 1933; Memo by W. C. Teagle, June 7, 1933; A. C. Minton to A. C. Bedford, Aug. 2, 1933; Teagle to H. L. Ickes, Sept. 8 and Nov. 15, 1933; Ickes to Teagle, Nov. 15, 1933; W. S. Farish to N. R. Margold, Oct. 2, 1933; E. J. Sadler to Farish, Nov. 18, 1933; Margold's memo for the oil administration *re* price control, Oct. 5, 1933; *The Lamp,* Aug., 1933. *Oil & Gas Journal,* Aug. 3, 1933.

55. Statement on price fixing by W. C. Teagle, Nov., 1933; E. J. Sadler to W. S. Farish, Nov. 29, 1933; Marketing agreement of forty-one companies in eastern section of U.S., Dec. 1, 1934; *The Lamp,* Aug., 1933, and Feb., 1934. *Oil & Gas Journal,* June, 1933–Mar., 1934, *passim;* Harold L. Ickes, *Secret Diary of Harold L. Ickes: First Thousand Days, 1933–1936* (New York, 1953), 84–86, 95–99, 106–

108, 158f; Williamson, Andreano, Daum, and Klose, *The American Petroleum Industry: The Age of Energy, 1899–1959,* 693.

56. Memo by W. C. Teagle, June 7, 1933. ESSO: *The Salesmotor,* June, 1933.

57. COL. BEACON: E. N. Wrightington to E. F. Johnson, July 6, 1936.

58. ESSO: *The Salesmotor,* June, 1933.

59. *Ibid.,* Feb. and June, 1933, and June, 1934.

60. *Ibid.,* June, 1933, and Feb. and June, 1934.

61. *Ibid.,* Aug.-Sept., 1928, Nov., 1933, and June, 1934; *The Esso Marketer,* Jan. 3, 1936. The change in the function of field managers was emphasized by several men in the New Orleans sales office interviewed by H. M. Larson in March, 1945.

62. *The Salesmotor,* June, 1934. SONJ, Executive Committee Minutes, Apr. 9, 1934.

63. ESSO: *The Salesmotor,* July, 1933. Memo by F. M. Surface for E. H. Knowlton, Nov. 24, 1954. *National Petroleum News,* Mar. 3, 10, and 17, 1943.

64. ESSO: Cost surveys, 1934–1939.

65. ESSO: Consumer surveys, 1935–1939.

66. ESSO: *The Salesmotor,* July, 1933, to Jan., 1935, *passim.*

67. *Ibid.,* Mar., 1934. The unfavorable reaction to this effort was stressed by sales managers interviewed by H. M. Larson in New Orleans in March, 1945.

68. ESSO: *The Salesmotor,* June, 1931, May, 1932, Feb. and Dec., 1933, Feb., Aug., and Dec., 1934, and May, 1935, *passim.* Memo by F. M. Surface for E. H. Knowlton, Nov. 24, 1954.

69. ESSO: *The Salesmotor,* June, 1933, and Nov., 1934. General Coordination Meetings, Minutes, May 15, 1939, on domestic sales of naphthas and gasoline; R. T. Haslam to F. M. Surface, Oct. 29, 1957.

70. SONJ, Red Books, 1927 to 1939, inclusive.

71. Executive Committee Minutes, Feb. 11 and 19, 1935; F. W. Pierce to W. C.

Teagle, Aug. 30, 1936; Letters of R. T. Haslam to W. S. Farish and Teagle, 1935–1939. *The New York Times,* Apr. 26, 1932, and Apr. 23 and 24, 1935.

72. For a survey of changes in market demand and in the market for oil products in the 1930's, see Williamson, Andreano, Daum, and Klose, *The American Petroleum Industry: The Age of Energy, 1899–1959,* chaps. 18 and 19.

73. ESSO: *The Esso Marketer,* Oct. 11 and Nov. 9, 1935. Memo by F. M. Surface for E. H. Knowlton, Nov. 24, 1954. The effect of Haslam on the salesmen was stressed by men in sales at the time, especially T. M. Gordon and P. V. Rome, interviewed by H. M. Larson in New Orleans in March, 1945.

74. ESSO: *The Salesmotor,* June and July, 1935; *The Esso Marketer,* Oct. 11 and Dec. 20, 1935.

75. *The Lamp,* Aug., 1936. McLean and Haigh, *The Growth of Integrated Oil Companies,* 289–294; Giddens, *Standard Oil Company (Indiana),* 313f, 548–554.

76. Larson and Porter, *History of Humble,* 551f; Williamson, Andreano, Daum, and Klose, *The American Petroleum Industry: The Age of Energy, 1899–1959,* 706.

77. Larson and Porter, *History of Humble,* 552.

78. SONJ, *Annual Report,* 1936. ESSO: Summary statistics by Gatchell, Apr. 6, 1953. SOC of LA: T. M. Milling to M. J. Rathbone, Feb. 17, 1937. Larson and Porter, *History of Humble,* 551f.

79. Guy Wellman to W. C. Teagle and W. S. Farish, Mar. 21, 1934; Teagle to Farish, Aug. 14, 1934; E. C. Seubert to Teagle, Mar. 28, June 18, and Oct. 1, 1934; Farish to Teagle, June 4 and 15, 1934. Giddens, *Standard Oil Company (Indiana),* 708.

80. E. S. Hall to W. S. Farish, July 21, 26, 27, and Aug. 24, and Sept. 21, 1938. Giddens, *Standard Oil Company (Indiana),* 708; 98F 2nd, Decision of the Circuit Court of Appeals, 8th Circuit, July 18, 1938, in *Esso, Inc.* v. *Standard Oil Co.*

81. ESSO: *The Esso Marketer,* July, 1936. Memo by F. M. Surface to E. H. Knowlton, Dec. 7, 1953.

82. ESSO: *The Esso Marketer,* July, 1938; Telephone directory for the offices in New York, June, 1938.

83. ESSO: *The Esso Marketer,* various issues in the years from 1936 to 1940.

84. *Ibid.,* various issues in the years from 1935 to 1940.

85. General Coordination Meetings, Minutes, May 10, 1937, on trends in domestic consumption and sales.

86. General Coordination Meetings, Minutes, May 15, 1939, on premium gasoline, domestic; F. A. Howard to F. W. Abrams and R. T. Haslam, Apr. 13, 1939; Howard to W. S. Farish, May 8, 1939; Executive Committee Minutes, May 2, 1939. ESSO: *The Esso Marketer,* Jan., 1940.

87. Exec. Com. Minutes, Sept. 6, 1935; R. T. Haslam to F. M. Surface, Oct. 29, 1957; Memo by Surface for E. H. Knowlton, Nov. 12, 1957. ESSO: *The Salesmotor,* 1928–1935, *passim; The Esso Marketer,* 1935–1939, *passim.*

88. ESSO: *The Esso Marketer* reported such courses and meetings.

89. R. T. Haslam to A. C. Bedford and J. E. Skehan, Jan. 29, 1940; General Coordination Meeting, Minutes, May 15, 1939, on cost-reduction programs in domestic marketing.

90. ESSO: Cost surveys, 1934–1939; Summary statistics, by Gatchell, Apr. 6, 1953. R. T. Haslam to A. C. Bedford and J. E. Skehan, Jan. 29, 1940.

91. W. C. Teagle to T. C. McCobb, Apr. 7, 1936.

92. Memo by C. L. Burrill, Sept. 10, 1940; Memo by F. M. Surface for E. H. Knowlton, Nov. 24, 1954.

93. General Coordination Meetings, Minutes, May 10, 1937, on transportation committee activities, and May 13, 1940, on Jersey's position in the gasoline pipeline industry.

94. Williamson, Andreano, Daum, and Klose, *The American Petroleum Industry: The Age of Energy, 1899–1959,* 649; American Petroleum Institute, *Petroleum Facts and Figures,* 1959, pp. 114, 117, 125, 128.

95. R. T. Haslam to W. S. Farish, May 12, 1939.

96. Memo by C. L. Burrill, Sept. 10, 1940.

97. R. T. Haslam to A. C. Bedford and J. E. Skehan, Jan. 29, 1940.

98. ESSO: Contract sales statistics, 1939.

99. *Ibid.,* 1933–1939. Giddens, *Standard Oil Company (Indiana),* 491. Jersey also arranged for Humble to process large amounts for Pan American Petroleum & Transport Co., but these were *processing* not *sales* contracts (Larson and Porter, *History of Humble,* 548f; Giddens, *Standard Oil Company (Indiana),* 497–500).

100. Memo on operations of Lago Oil & Transport Co., Ltd., for 1938 and 1939.

101. Larson and Porter, *History of Humble,* 553.

102. ESSO: Contract sales statistics, 1933–1939.

103. M. H. Eames to heads of departments and companies, Sept. 12, 1933. Gibb and Knowlton, *The Resurgent Years,* 639.

104. ESSO: *The Salesmotor,* various issues in the years 1933–1935; *The Esso Marketer,* also issues in 1935–1939.

105. SONJ, Red Books for the years 1928–1939.

106. *Ibid.,* 1939.

107. ESSO: Cost surveys, 1934–1939; Summary statistics, by Gatchell, Apr. 6, 1953; R. T. Haslam to A. C. Bedford and J. E. Skehan, Jan. 29, 1940.

108. ESSO: Compilation of price data obtained from the American Petroleum Institute.

109. NICB, *The Petroleum Almanac,* 1946, p. 275. Williamson, Andreano, Daum, and Klose, *The American Petroleum Industry: The Age of Energy, 1899–1959,* p. 685, contains a chart representing the wholesale price index for petroleum products. Daniel C. Hamilton's *Competition in Oil: The Gulf Coast Refinery Market, 1925–1950* (Cambridge, 1958), p. 216, presents a series of annual

prices for regular-grade gasoline in terms of 1926 dollars—10.211 cents per gallon in 1926 and 6.283 cents in 1939.

CHAPTER 11

1. On foreign marketing by Jersey and affiliates before 1927, the reader is referred to the earlier volumes in the history of Standard Oil Company (New Jersey): Ralph W. Hidy and Muriel E. Hidy, *Pioneering in Big Business, 1882–1911* (New York, 1955); George Sweet Gibb and Evelyn H. Knowlton, *The Resurgent Years, 1911–1927* (New York, 1956). Information about foreign marketing and executives of Jersey and affiliates has been gathered through many interviews by H. M. Larson, E. H. Knowlton, and J. S. Ewing, between the years 1948 and 1961, with present and past employees of Jersey and affiliates. Those interviewed included P. T. Lamont, G. H. Smith, E. E. Soubry, H. E. Bedford, Jr., M. K. Blood, W. R. Carlisle, C. W. Hunt, E. F. Johnson, A. C. Minton, Frank Mott, H. A. Metzger, G. H. Michler, T. W. Palmer, D. W. Ramsey, Jr., W. Simonson, and many others.

2. W. C. Teagle to the directors, Mar. 16, 1928. *The Economist,* Dec. 21, 1929, pp. 1196f.

3. W. C. Teagle to the directors, Mar. 16, 1928, with data on production for the year 1927 for the 20 leading oil companies; Peter Hurll to Teagle, Feb. 21, 1928; John Cadman to Teagle, Feb. 22, 1928.

4. W. C. Teagle to the directors, Mar. 16, 1928.

5. *Ibid.;* Heinrich Riedemann to W. C. Teagle, Sept. 13, 1928, and Jan. 3, 1929.

6. W. C. Teagle to the directors, Mar. 16, 1928; Peter Hurll to Teagle, Feb. 21, 1928; Memo, Mar. 23, 1928.

7. National Industrial Conference Board (NICB), *The Petroleum Almanac,* 1946, pp. 146, 340.

8. 40 *Stat.* 516 (1918). Copy of letter of Vernon W. Van Fleet to C. F. Kelly, July 31, 1924.

9. Address by G. H. Montague before the American Mining Congress, Washing-ton, D.C., on "Lawful Combinations in Industry," Dec. 2, 1927, as reported in release for newspapers, Dec. 3, 1927; Montague to E. A. McCullock, July 11, 1929; E. F. Johnson to Montague, Mar. 27 and May 22, 1929.

10. Peter Hurll to W. C. Teagle, Feb. 21, 1928; John Cadman to Teagle, Feb. 22, 1928; Teagle to Heinrich Riedemann, Mar. 23, 1928; Teagle to C. O. Swain, Mar. 7, Apr. 9, Sept. 24, and Oct. 29, 1928; G. H. Montague to Swain, Apr. 11 and 19 and May 18, 1928; Memos about export association by Riedemann, May 7 and Nov. 10, 1928; Drafts of Association (unsigned), May 16, June 21 and 27, and Sept. 25, 1928; Riedemann to Teagle, G. H. Jones, J. A. Moffett, Jr., and Swain, May 10, 1928; Redraft by Riedemann and Montague, May 18, 1928; Riedemann to Teagle, May 18, Sept. 30, and Oct. 8 and 19, 1928; Teagle to Moffett and Swain, Oct. 30, 1928; Draft of by-laws of Export Petroleum Association, Apr. 18 and Dec. 15, 1928; Montague to R. C. Holmes, Dec. 19, 1928; Certificate of incorporation of Export Petroleum Association, Dec. 27, 1928; Notes on Chicago meeting, Dec. 7, 1928; Export Trade Section of Legal Division of Federal Trade Commission to Montague, May 18, 1929; Memo by Montague, Dec. 10, 1930; Teagle to Guy Wellman, Mar. 29, 1932.

11. Peter Hurll to W. C. Teagle, Feb. 21, 1928; John Cadman to Teagle, Feb. 22, 1928; F. E. Powell to Teagle, Oct. 19, 1928; Heinrich Riedemann to Teagle, Jan. 3, 1929.

12. Copy of letter from directors of Anglo-American to N. M. Smith, June 21 and 22, 1928. Gibb and Knowlton, *The Resurgent Years,* chap. 12.

13. For a discussion of the role of large companies in international business, see Adolf A. Berle, Jr., *The 20th Century Capitalist Revolution* (New York, 1954), chap. 3.

14. W. C. Teagle to C. O. Swain, Aug. 24 and Sept. 10, 1928.

15. Copy of the "Achnacarry Agreement," Sept. 17, 1928.

16. *Ibid.*

17. Memo by G. H. Montague, Dec. 10, 1930; Notes for Montague to discuss with Holmes Committee, Dec. 10, 1930.

18. Copy of "Achnacarry Agreement," Sept. 17, 1928; H. E. Cole to C. F. Meyer, July 26, 1929; Copy of minutes of Meeting of Export Petroleum Association and appendices A, B, and C, sent by G. H. Montague to C. O. Swain, Nov. 8, 1929; Memo for European markets, Jan. 20, 1930; Addendum and Memorandum No. 1, Jan. 20, 1930.

19. Copy of minutes of meeting of Export Petroleum Association and appendices A, B, and C sent by G. H. Montague to C. O. Swain, Nov. 8, 1929; Memo of meeting at Sir Henri Deterding's house, May 4, 1929; H. E. Cole to C. F. Meyer, July 26, 1929; G. S. Walden to E. J. Sadler, Mar. 21, 1930, and Aug. 4, 1931; W. C. Teagle to J. A. Moffett, Jr., and Peter Hurll, Mar. 11, 1930; Heinrich Riedemann to Teagle, Aug. 18, 1931; Memo of Sadler, June 15, 1931; H. E. Pratt to Teagle, Oct. 4, 1932; C. E. Arnott to Teagle, Feb. 17, 1932.

20. Memo for European Markets, Jan. 20, 1930; Addendum and Memorandum No. 2, Jan. 20, 1930; Heads of Agreement, Dec. 15, 1932; Minutes of meetings, Oct. 24, 25, and 26, Nov. 17 and 19, and Dec. 15 and 16, 1932; F. J. Wolfe to D. L. Harper, Oct. 4, 1933; Harper to Wolfe, Oct. 4, 1933; Agreement between Continental Oil Co. and Anglo-American, Oct. 7, 1932. Federal Trade Commission, *International Petroleum Cartel* (Washington, 1952), 236–249.

21. D. L. Harper to Orville Harden, Dec. 17, 1934. NICB, *The Petroleum Almanac,* 1946, pp. 113, 340. Federal Trade Commission, *International Petroleum Cartel,* 251.

22. H. G. Seidel to Eugene Holman, Sept. 8, 1932; Guy Wellman to E. J. Sadler, Dec. 15, 1932; Wellman to W. C. Teagle, June 13, 1933; Copy of *Official Journal* of the League of Nations, Dec., 1933, pp. 1653–1660.

23. Draft Memo of Principles (1934), and Addendum, Oct., 1935. For a brief survey of these efforts at international cooperation, see Harold F. Williamson, *et al., The American Petroleum Industry,*

The Age of Energy, 1899–1959 (Evanston, 1963), 736–743.

24. Circular amendment to Addendum IV of Draft Memo of Principles, Jan. 13, 1938; Statistics on deliveries into consumption in 1938; R. H. Porters to D. L. Harper, Jan. 26, 1939.

25. SONJ, *Annual Report,* 1939.

26. Stockholders' Minutes, June 1, 1943. *The Times* (London), Feb. 6, 1939; *World Petroleum,* May, 1951.

27. CREOLE: *Annual Report,* 1943. NICB, *The Petroleum Almanac,* 1946, p. 305.

28. Guy Wellman to Montagu Piesse, May 8, 1928; Heinrich Riedemann to W. C. Teagle, May 18, 1928; F. H. Bedford, Jr., to C. O. Swain, Sept. 10, 1928; F. E. Powell to Teagle, Dec. 21, 1928. Transcript of Records, *United States* v. *Standard Oil Company of New Jersey et al.,* U.S.D.C., Mo. (Washington, 1908), Testimony, VII, 7, 33, 80, 101, 104.

29. Guy Wellman to Montagu Piesse, May 8, 1928; Heinrich Riedemann to W. C. Teagle, May 18, 1928; John G. Milburn to C. O. Swain, May 21, 1928; Memo by Montagu Piesse for Teagle, Sept. 3, 1928; Milburn and John W. Davis to directors of Anglo-American and Standard Oil Export Corp., Nov. 2, 1929; Swain to Attorney General and FTC, Nov. 21, 1929.

30. F. E. Powell to W. C. Teagle, Apr. 3 and 25, and Dec. 21, 1928; W. W. Oswald to Teagle, Apr. 24, 1928; Teagle to Powell, May 8, 1928; Heinrich Riedemann to Teagle, May 9, 1928; Memo by Montagu Piesse for Teagle, Sept. 3, 1928; Memo on value of Anglo-American, Nov. 16, 1928; Peter Hurll to Teagle, Mar. 11, 1929; Hurll to Teagle and J. A. Moffett, Jr., June 21, 1929; Teagle to S. B. Hunt, Moffett, and C. O. Swain, July 1, 1929; Teagle to Hurll, Aug. 13, and Dec. 17, 1929, and May 11, 1931; D. L. Harper to Anglo-American, Nov. 6, 1929; Powell to stockholders of Anglo-American, Nov. 25, 1929; Harper to Powell, Nov. 25, 1929; Hurll to Hunt, Dec. 10, 1929; Hunt to Teagle, Jan. 22 and 31, 1930; Memo by Hurll, July 10, 1931; Notice of Redemption of Preferred Stock by W. R. Mook, June 30, 1936.

31. Frederick Horstmann to W. C. Teagle, Nov. 2, 1927, and Feb. 8, 1928; Heinrich Riedemann to Teagle, Mar. 13, 1928; E. J. Sadler to Teagle, May 11, 1928; Horstmann to Sadler, July 17, 1928; G. S. Walden to Production Dept., Apr. 5, 1929; Walden to Sadler, May 13, July 2, and Dec. 19, 1929, Oct. 1, 1930, and Feb. 7, 1931; Walden to Teagle, Apr. 18, 1930; Memo by Walden on Bataafsche's method of selling, May 30, 1930; Teagle to Walden, Feb. 16, 1931; Cable, C. O. Swain to Teagle, Mar. 30–31, 1931; Memo on discussion of Far Eastern situation, Mar. 31, 1931.

32. W. C. Teagle to G. S. Walden, Feb. 16, 1931; Cable, C. O. Swain to Teagle, Mar. 30–31, 1931; H. E. Pratt to Teagle, Oct. 4, 1932.

33. G. S. Walden to E. J. Sadler, Mar. 30, 1932; Walden to J. A. Moffett, Jr., Aug. 1, 1932; Walden to D. L. Harper, Aug. 10, 1932; Memo of conversation with Minister of Colonies, Sept. 15, 1933; Memo on merger, June 16, 1933; Annual Report of Standard-Vacuum, 1934.

34. Stockholders' Minutes, June 7, 1927; Directors' Minutes, Apr. 22, 1940; W. C. Teagle's Memo of 1933; Personnel recs.; Corp. recs.; Memo by E. J. Sadler, Mar. 22, 1934.

35. Stockholders' Minutes, June 7, 1927, and June 6, 1933; Directors' declaration of policy on retirement, May 19, 1933; Corp. recs.; Personnel recs.; Memo by E. J. Sadler, Mar. 22, 1934.

36. Stockholders' Minutes, June 7, 1927; Corp. recs.; Personnel recs.

37. Directors' Minutes, Nov. 28, 1928, Apr. 12, 1929, June 11, 1930, Aug. 3, 1931, and June 6, 1933; W. C. Teagle's Memo of 1933; *The Lamp,* June, 1934.

38. W. C. Teagle's Memo of 1933; Orville Harden to T. C. McCobb, Nov. 17, 1933; Memo by E. J. Sadler, Mar. 22, 1934; Memo on reorganization in Latin America (1934); Status memo by M. E. McDowell, May 29, 1934; Memo and articles of association of the International Association (Petroleum Industry) Ltd., Aug. 29, 1934; Guy Wellman to Harden, May 7, 1935; F. W. Pierce to Teagle, Aug. 30, 1936; *The Lamp,* Aug., 1934, Apr., 1935, and Oct., 1936.

39. WEST INDIA OIL CO.: Minutes of Directors' Meetings, 1934 and 1937, *passim.* SONJ: Corp. recs.; Memo on restrictive practices in various Latin American countries by M. E. McDowell for W. S. Farish, Sept. 13, 1934.

40. E. F. Johnson to C. O. Swain, July 31, 1930; Johnson to Montagu Piesse, May 14, 1931, and July 3, 1934; Directors' Minutes, May 25, 1934; Memo *re* interview with G. S. Engel of Shell, Apr. 13, 1934; Memo by Piesse and Johnson, Apr. 26, 1934; Memo by M. E. McDowell, May 29, 1934; Memo concerning foreign companies, Aug. 28, 1934; Memo concerning the aluminum case; Memo *re* foreign holding company; Memo and articles of association of the International Association (Petroleum Industry) Ltd., Aug. 29, 1934; Piesse to Johnson, Aug. 31, 1934; Résumé by McDowell for W. S. Farish, Sept. 13, 1934; Memo on reorganization in Latin America (1934); Guy Wellman to Orville Harden, Mar. 15, 1935, with memorandum *re* setup for European coordination, Paris, Mar. 5, 1935; Memo by Piesse, May 18, 1935; W. C. Teagle to Harden, Apr. 1, 1936; Memo on the International Association (Petroleum Industry) Ltd., July 29, 1936; F. W. Pierce to Teagle, Aug. 30, 1936; T. J. E. Umbeck to Harden, Nov. 23, 1936.

41. J. H. Shaw to Montagu Piesse, June 28, 1934; Guy Wellman to Orville Harden, Mar. 15, 1935, with memo *re* setup for European coordination, Paris, Mar. 5, 1935; Memo on London setup by F. A. Howard, Apr. 6, 1936; Council of Management of the International Association (Petroleum Industry) Ltd., Nov. 1, 1936.

42. Memo on International Association (Petroleum Industry) Ltd., Aug. 26, 1934; Memo by F. A. Howard, Apr. 6, 1936; Draft Memo of Principles; W. C. Teagle to Orville Harden, Apr. 1, 1936; Guy Wellman to Teagle, Apr. 23, 1936; Memo on income-tax position in the United Kingdom, Mar. 23, 1936; F. W. Pierce to Teagle, Aug. 30, 1936; General Coordination Meetings, Minutes, on changing brand names, May 15, 1939.

43. H. G. Seidel to W. S. Farish, Sept. 5, 1939.

44. IMPERIAL: Statistics of sales research section. SONJ: Red Books.

45. IMPERIAL: Memo, tariff protection on gasoline, Sept. 23, 1930; W. C. Teagle, to G. H. Smith, Feb. 28 and Dec. 24 and 28, 1931; Statistics of sales research section; Review of operations, 1930–1938, by H. H. Hewetson. SONJ: Red Books.

46. Thomas Palmer to Guy Wellman, Oct. 8, 1927; G. H. Smith to Eugene Holman, Apr. 28, 1937; Memo on marketing in Colombia, by "N.A.N.," Mar. 22, 1945; Memo on Tropical Oil Co. by "M.P.M.," Oct. 6, 1946; Marketing in Peru, Nov. 20, 1946; Memo, Nov. 25, 1941; Memo on Tropical, 1938–1939. INTERNATIONAL: Memo on taxes, by E. E. Vanderfeen, 1942. TROPICAL: H. A. Metzger to Minister of Industries, July 16, 1929.

47. INTERNATIONAL: Agreement with Balfour, Williamson & Co., etc., Feb. 2, 1915, May 1, 1916, Nov. 25, 1920, and July 1, 1930; G. H. Smith to W. C. Teagle, Jan. 7, 1927; Memo by R. J. Bennett for Smith, May 15, 1928; W. S. Reid to Smith, June 16, 1932; Smith to Orville Harden, Aug. 27, 1934; Milne & Co. to International, Nov. 21, 1934.

48. INTERNATIONAL: R. J. Bennett to Williamson & Co., Feb. 14 and Apr. 26, 1927; Part of letter of Williamson & Co., May 13, 1929; G. H. Smith to H. C. R. Williamson, Dec. 1, 1931; Smith to Orville Harden, Aug. 27, 1934; Minute Book, No. 3, giving power of attorney, Feb. 14, 1938.

49. INTERNATIONAL: R. V. LeSueur to M. F. Frey, Aug. 22, 1930; Frey to LeSueur, Aug. 29, 1930; E. Pombo to G. H. Smith, June 11, 1931; Memo on LeSueur's trip to Peru in 1933; W. S. Reid to Smith, Mar. 1, 1934; Memo by R. J. Bennett for LeSueur, Mar. 13, 1934; The Petroleum Industry in Peru, by E. E. Vanderfeen, 1941. Interview with R. J. Bennett by Helen Cowan in Jan., 1949. SONJ: Red Books for the years 1931–1938, inclusive. Available figures, beginning in 1931, are on earnings before administrative and other charges.

50. Directors' Minutes; Personnel recs.

51. Corp. recs.; Sales statistics; Summary of Venezuela by Dr. Guillermo Zuloaga, Dec., 1951; Memo on restrictive measures in various Latin American countries (undated and unsigned); M. E. McDowell to W. S. Farish, Sept. 13, 1934; General Coordination Meetings, Minutes, on keeping prices low in marketing end, May 10–14, 1937; Red Books; Sales statistics.

52. General Coordination Meetings, Minutes, on Latin American market consumption outlook, May 12, 1941; Sales statistics.

53. Memo on restrictive measures of various Latin American countries (undated and unsigned); Annual Report of Huasteca Petroleum Corp., 1935–1938; Sales statistics; Red Books.

54. Memo on restrictive measures of various Latin American countries (undated and unsigned); Memo by H. E. Bedford, Jr. (undated).

55. Memo by H. E. Bedford, Jr. (undated).

56. Memo on restrictive measures of various Latin American countries (undated and unsigned); General Coordination Meetings, Minutes, Report on Latin American marketing, May 9–13, 1938, Chilean monopoly law, May 13–19, 1939, and Latin American market consumption outlook, May 12, 1941; Sales statistics; Red Books.

57. Memo on restrictive measures of various Latin American countries (undated and unsigned); General Coordination Meetings, Minutes, Report on Latin American marketing, May 9–13, 1938, Latin American market consumption outlook, May 12, 1941, and marketing in Argentina, Feb. 8–13, 1946; Corp. recs.

58. Memo on restrictive measures of various Latin American countries (undated and unsigned); Draft of memo to the U.S. State Dept. after Eugene Holman's trip to the Argentine in 1934; Memo on companies in Argentina, Mar. 17, 1947; Summary of Argentina, by W. W. Hall, July 10, 1944; Memo on reorganization of corporate structure in Argentina, by Thomas Palmer for C. O. Swain, Feb. 4, 1932.

59. Memo on restrictive measures of various Latin American countries (undated and unsigned); St. John Garwood to Thomas Palmer, Jan. 18, 1933; Memo on intercompany relations, prepared by St. John Garwood, B. B. Edmunds, R. C. Reynolds, and G. A. Kent, June 24, 1929; T. R. Armstrong to E. J. Sadler, July 27, 1935; Orville Harden to W. C. Teagle, Oct. 27 and Nov. 12, 1936; Harden to Heinrich Riedemann, Jan. 14, 1937; J. T. Fly to E. F. Johnson, Feb. 12, 1937; Harden to G. H. Michler, Mar. 15, 1937; Memo on Argentina, by R. P. Bolton, Sept., 1942; Memo on companies in Argentina, July 29, 1949; Memo on Argentina, by F. W. Surface, July 29, 1943; Summary of Argentina, by R. C. Horne, Dec., 1951.

60. R. G. Wells to T. R. Armstrong, Mar. 12, 1936; Thomas Palmer to U.S. Dept. of State, Division of Latin American Affairs, Mar. 18, 1937; Eugene Holman to M. K. Blood, Jan. 5, 1937; J. L. Cluley to C. H. Lieb, Apr. 21, 1942; Agreement, Jan. 27, 1942; Marketing in Peru, by "W. F. M.," Nov. 20, 1946.

61. Deliveries into consumption, 1927, 1928, and 1938; Red Books. NICB, *The Petroleum Almanac,* 1946, p. 342.

62. A historical account of Anglo-American Oil Co. (not dated). *The New York Times,* Oct. 24, 1929.

63. Peter Hurll to S. B. Hunt, Jan. 20, 1931; Hurll to W. C. Teagle, July 22, 1931; Press release, Nov. 29, 1951.

64. A historical account of Anglo-American Oil Company (not dated); F. J. Wolfe to D. L. Harper, Oct. 4, 1933; Harper to Wolfe, Oct. 5, 1933; Guy Wellman to Montagu Piesse, Oct. 7, 1933; Agreement between Continental Oil Co. and Anglo-American, Oct. 7, 1933.

65. Corp. recs.; Notice of redemption of preferred stock of Standard Oil Export Corp., by W. R. Mook, June 30, 1936; Guy Wellman to G. H. Montague, June 10, 1935; Memo by R. W. Burkart, June 29, 1936; Marketing coordination notes, received by F. W. Abrams, Aug. 1, 1948.

66. Deliveries into consumption, 1927, 1928, and 1938; Marketing coordination notes, received by F. W. Abrams, Aug. 1, 1948; W. W. Hall to E. E. Soubry, May 15, 1952.

67. Deliveries into consumption, 1927, 1928, and 1938; Marketing in the United Kingdom and Ireland, by "W. F. M.," Oct. 25, 1946; Marketing coordination notes, received by Abrams, Aug. 1, 1948. *The Petroleum Times,* Oct. 2, 1937, and subsequent issues.

68. General Coordination Meetings, Minutes, Apr. 20, 1936, May 9–13, 1938, and May 15–19, 1939; Summary of operations and general information of Jersey's European and North African affiliated companies, received by F. W. Abrams, May 5, 1947. Interview of C. S. Popple with Adrian C. Minton, Aug. 23, 1951.

69. R. F. McKenna to A. L. Mellar, Nov. 1, 1934; C. B. Millard to J. R. Clarke, Oct. 30, 1939; Marketing in Germany in 1938, by "W. F. M."; Corp. recs.; Summary of operations and general information on Jersey's European and North African affiliated companies, received by F. W. Abrams, May 5, 1947.

70. Summary of operations . . . received by F. W. Abrams, May 5, 1947; Corp. recs.; Sales statistics; Deliveries into consumption, 1927, 1928, and 1938.

71. General Coordination Meetings, Minutes, Review of foreign exchange situation, May 9, 1938.

72. Copy of decree covering importation of petroleum products, in *Journal Official,* Mar. 30, 1929; Memo on French refining situation in 1929; H. E. Bedford, Jr., to D. L. Harper, Apr. 24, 1929, to W. C. Teagle, Apr. 10, 1929, and to C. O. Swain, Oct. 11, 1929; E. E. Soubry to E. R. Stettinius, May 24, 1945.

73. G. H. Michler to C. O. Swain, May 20, 1930; General Coordination Meetings, Minutes, May 15, 1939; Marketing coordination notes, received by F. W. Abrams, Aug. 1, 1948; Summary of France, by S. Scheer, Nov., 1951; Corp. recs.; Deliveries into consumption, 1927, 1928, and 1939; *The Lamp,* June, 1934.

74. Copy of royal decree, Law No. 1684, of Aug. 28, 1935, published in *Official Gazette,* Sept. 12, 1935; Marketing coordination notes, received by F. W. Abrams, May 5, 1947.

75. H. G. Seidel to W. S. Farish, Sept. 5, 1935; Guy Wellman to Orville Harden, Oct. 11, 1935; Wellman to W. C. Teagle, Oct. 31, 1935.

76. Marketing coordination notes, received by F. W. Abrams, May 5, 1947; General Coordination Meetings, Minutes, 1947; W. C. Teagle to F. A. Howard, Mar. 5, 1936; Sales statistics; Corp. recs.

77. Marketing coordination notes, received by F. W. Abrams, May 5, 1947; General Coordination Meetings, Minutes, 1947; Marketing coordination notes, received by Abrams, Aug. 1, 1948; Sales statistics; Corp. recs.; Deliveries into consumption, 1927, 1928, and 1938.

78. Marketing coordination notes, received by F. W. Abrams, Aug. 1, 1948; Sales statistics; Corp. recs.; Deliveries into consumption, 1927, 1928, and 1938.

79. Marketing coordination notes, received by F. W. Abrams, Aug. 1, 1948; Corp. recs.; Sales statistics.

80. Marketing coordination notes, received by F. W. Abrams, May 5, 1947; H. E. Bedford, Jr., to Guy Wellman, Nov. 24, 1932; Sales statistics; Deliveries into consumption, 1927, 1928, and 1938; Memo by I. Willis, May 26, 1939.

81. Marketing coordination notes, received by F. W. Abrams, May 5, 1947; Sales statistics; Corp. recs.

82. General report of Standard-Nobel w Polsce, Mar. 5, 1935; Corp. recs.

83. Marketing coordination notes, received by F. W. Abrams, May 5, 1947; Sales statistics; Corp. recs.

84. Cable, H. E. Bedford, Jr., to D. L. Harper, Oct. 20, 1927; Memo of conversation between an official of the State Department and P. P. Campbell regarding Jersey's Spanish interests, Oct. 25, 1927; Bedford to Harper, Dec. 6, 1928; Marketing coordination notes, received by F. W. Abrams, May 5, 1947. *The New York Times,* Oct. 25, 1927.

85. Annual Report, Standard-Vacuum Oil Co., 1945; Corp. recs.; *The Lamp,* Feb., 1934. Magnolia Petroleum Co., *Magnolia Oil News,* Founders' Number, Apr., 1931.

86. Résumé of position between Standard-Vacuum Oil Co. and Mitsui regard-

ing a partnership arrangement in Japan (undated); Memo on Japanese Petroleum Industry Control Law, Aug. 21, 1934; Notes on trade quotas, Oct. 30, 1934.

87. Notes on trade quotas, Oct. 30, 1934; Memo on Japanese Petroleum Industry Control Law, Aug. 21, 1934; Message from U.S. Embassy in Tokyo, Aug. 15, 1935; Memo of understanding reached Apr. 13, 1935; Notes on meeting, Sept. 20, 1935; Memo on situation in China and Japan, Oct. 9, 1935; Japanese situation, by "J. C. G.," Oct. 10, 1935; Japanese policy, excerpt from letter of H. Wilkinson to W. C. Teagle, Oct. 29, 1935.

88. Memo of Oct. 23, 1935; H. M. McLarin to C. O. Swain, Mar. 23, 1936; McLarin to D. L. Harper, Sept. 11, 1936; T. J. E. Umbeck, Jr., to Harper, Apr. 20, 1937; McLarin to W. R. Mook, Aug. 19, 1937; H. E. Bedford, Jr., to Harper, June 1, 1939; Corp. recs.

89. Sales statistics; Red Books.

90. SONJ, Red Books.

CHAPTER 12

1. Philip Cabot, *Addresses, 1935–1941* (Cambridge, 1942). This book, compiled after Cabot's death, is provocative in its consideration of the forces at work throughout the world in the 1930's.

2. For the employee relations of Jersey and its affiliates before 1927, see Ralph W. Hidy and Muriel E. Hidy, *Pioneering in Big Business, 1882–1911* (New York, 1955); George Sweet Gibb and Evelyn H. Knowlton, *The Resurgent Years, 1911–1927* (New York, 1956); and Henrietta M. Larson and Kenneth Wiggins Porter, *History of Humble Oil & Refining Company* (New York, 1959).

3. These points are given in full in Clarence J. Hicks, *My Life in Industrial Relations* (New York, 1941), and in the 1925 edition of a Jersey publication entitled *Industrial Representation in the Refineries of Standard Oil Company (New Jersey).*

4. *The Lamp,* Oct., 1927. Information on industrial relations of Jersey and its affiliates has been obtained through interviews with present and former employ-

ees—including T. H. A. Tiedemann, Frank W. Pierce, Ralph L. Mason, Charles E. Shaw, R. L. B. Roessle, W. M. Dassler, O. E. Gredler, W. B. Maloney, H. E. Linam, Brian Mead, L. G. Smith, H. E. Bedford, Jr., C. E. Lanning, Ray H. Horton, David B. Harris, W. P. Raymond, Jr., A. H. Mitchell, and many others—by members of the Business History Foundation. The latter included the N. S. B. Gras, H. M. Larson, K. W. Porter, C. S. Popple, and E. H. Knowlton.

5. Larson and Porter, *History of Humble,* 102–104.

6. *Industrial Representation in the Refineries of Standard Oil Company (New Jersey),* edition of 1925; *Employee Representation and Collective Bargaining,* A Report to the Business Advisory and Planning Council for the Department of Commerce, by W. C. Teagle, chairman of the Committee on Industrial Relations [1933?]; Employee representation, 1918 to 1946, copy of report by Harry R. Clark, Bayonne refinery; History of the Union Development in the Bayonne Refinery, by W. L. Johnson, Mar. 11, 1946; *The First Day in April, 1918* (New York, 1956). Stuart Chase, *A Generation of Industrial Peace* (New York, 1946). For conditions in Humble Oil & Refining Company, see Larson and Porter, *History of Humble.*

7. J. W. Myers and C. R. Dooley to C. J. Hicks, Oct. 23, 1926; C. T. White to heads of departments and companies, Nov. 18 and 26, 1926, Dec. 1, 1927, and Nov. 21, 1928; Hicks to C. G. Black, Aug. 2, 1927; White to W. C. Teagle, Nov. 19, 1928; individual salary cards.

8. W. C. Teagle to E. M. Clark, May 7, 1929, and to F. H. Bedford, Jr., June 7, 1929.

9. W. C. Teagle to F. H. Bedford, Jr., Aug. 1, 1930.

10. SONJ, *Annual Report,* 1929, 1930, 1931; C. T. White to heads of departments and companies, Apr. 25, 1929, and May 21, 1930; Directors' Minutes, Feb. 27, 1931; Presidents of companies to employees, July 13, 1931; Report covering annuity plans in 1932; J. W. Myers to

W. C. Teagle, May 17, 1933; Memo by A & B Committee, Sept. 4, 1934; T. C. McCobb to J. L. Cluley, Jan. 19, 1939; High Lights of Company Plans and Policies, by K. N. Rackley, Apr. 22, 1949.

11. SONJ, Directors' Minutes, Nov. 24, 1931; Report covering annuity plans in 1932; J. W. Myers to W. C. Teagle, May 17, 1933; Memo by A & B Committee, Sept. 4, 1934; High Lights of Company Plans and Policies, by K. N. Rackley, Apr. 22, 1949; SONJ, *Annual Report,* 1932, 1933, 1934, and 1935.

12. SONJ, Directors' Minutes, Apr. 26, 1928, and Apr. 23, 1931; C. T. White to heads of departments and companies, Oct. 2, 1931; C. O. Swain to W. C. Teagle, Feb. 1, 1932; Report on company contributions to five stock plans, 1921–1935; F. W. Pierce to R. W. Gallagher, Dec. 10, 1935; SONJ, *Annual Report,* 1928 to 1935, inclusive. Larson and Porter, *History of Humble,* 98, 345f, 361.

13. SONJ, Directors' Minutes, Apr. 28, 1928, May 6, 1929, and Apr. 23, 1931; Profit-sharing plan for management, for voting on June 4, 1929, in letter to stockholders from W. C. Teagle, May 8, 1929; SONJ, *Annual Report,* 1932.

14. A. C. Minton to presidents of companies, June 26, 1934; SONJ, *Annual Report,* 1932, 1933, and 1934.

15. C. J. Hicks to S. B. Hunt, Jan. 4, 1932; F. W. Pierce to Christy Payne, Nov. 27, 1933.

16. A. C. Minton to heads of companies, Aug. 6, 1934; General Coordination Meetings, Minutes, Medicine in Industry, May 24–27, 1948. ESSO: Memo on the Stanocola Employees' Medical and Hospital Association, by B. H. Farrier, Nov. 12, 1948.

17. W. S. Farish to E. M. Clark, Apr. 8, 1926; J. W. Myers to C. J. Hicks, Feb. 29, 1928; High Lights of Company Plans and Policies, by K. N. Rackley, Apr. 22, 1949; Summary of important industrial relations developments during 1934, 1935, and 1939; Annual reports of various affiliates, such as NKPM, Creole, and Lago Oil & Transport in the period up to 1939. Larson and Porter, *History of Humble,* 101–104, 351–353.

18. Larson and Porter, *History of Humble*, 354f. Also interviews with W. P. Raymond, Jr., of Standard of Louisiana, Mar. 9, 1945, and with A. H. Mitchell of Carter, Apr. 12, 1945.

19. C. R. Dooley to E. M. Clark, June 6, 1928; C. T. White to heads of departments and companies, Jan. 31, 1929, June 18, 1930, and Mar. 29, 1932; C. J. Fiero to Clark, July 1, 1930; R. M. Young to Clark, June 28, 1930; W. C. Teagle to F. H. Bedford, Jr., Aug. 1, 1930; Historical Review of Executive Development, exhibit A (undated). ESSO: High Points and Trends in Personnel and Employee Relations Developments, Baton Rouge Refinery, 1909–1949, by "W. W. W.," Mar. 30, 1949. Larson and Porter, *History of Humble*, 354f.

20. Statistics on number of regular and temporary employees, 1923–1947; C. T. White to heads of departments and companies, June 5, 1929, and Nov. 19, 1930; C. J. Hicks to W. C. Teagle, Sept. 26, 1930; Teagle to directors, Sept. 27, 1930; Teagle to heads of departments and companies, Sept. 30, 1930; Teagle to E. M. Clark, Sept. 30, 1931, and Apr. 4, 1932; Teagle to S. B. Hunt, Jan. 30, 1932; E. J. Sadler to Teagle, Jan. 25, 1932. SONJ, *Annual Report*, 1931. Larson and Porter, *History of Humble*, 157, 355f, 358f, and 382.

21. W. C. Teagle to C. J. Hicks, May 22, 1931, including extract from letter received from Heinrich Riedemann.

22. W. C. Teagle to S. B. Hunt, Jan. 20, 1932. HUMBLE: R. H. Horton to J. R. Suman, May 12, 1959; Work Schedules and General Rates of Pay, 1918–1957. Larson and Porter, *History of Humble*, 356f.

23. E. J. Sadler to W. C. Teagle, Jan. 25, 1932; Christy Payne to C. O. Swain, Jan. 26, 1932; Swain to Teagle, Feb. 1, 1932; Teagle to Payne, Apr. 4, 1932.

24. W. C. Teagle to E. M. Clark, Apr. 4 and June 16, 1932, and to Christy Payne, Apr. 4, 1932; Teagle to C. J. Hicks, May 10, 1932; M. S. Florsheim to Teagle, May 14, 1932; Memo on wages, June 7, 1932; Teagle to heads of departments and companies, June 14 and 16, 1932; C. T. White to heads of departments and companies, June 21, 1932; *The Lamp*, June, 1932. Larson and Porter, *History of Humble*, 356.

25. A. P. Sloan, Jr., to W. C. Teagle, July 1, 1932; R. L. Hague to E. M. Clark, Sept. 14, 1932; C. T. White to heads of departments and companies, Sept. 30, 1932; Clark to Teagle, Nov. 29, 1932; SONJ, *Annual Report*, 1932; *The Lamp*, Aug., 1933. *Oil & Gas Journal*, Sept. 8, 15, and 22, Oct. 13 and 20, 1932; *The New York Times*, July 17 and 18, Aug. 26 and 28, 1932.

26. Declaration of policy on retirement by directors, May 19, 1933; *The Lamp*, Oct., 1933, and Feb., 1943.

27. U.S. Dept. of Commerce, *Statistical Abstract of the United States* (1951), 173.

28. *Ibid.*

29. Base-rate history of representative classifications, by "RHH and PRS," Apr. 14, 1948; General Coordination Meetings, Minutes, Hourly wage rates, May 12, 1941; Average hourly rates, scheduled hours of work, average weekly pay at the Bayway refinery, and index of cost of living, 1915–1938, June 29, 1938.

30. Summary of important industrial relations developments during 1934 and 1935; Average hourly rates . . . at the Bayway refinery . . . , June 29, 1938; W. C. Teagle to presidents of domestic companies, June 6, 1935; A. C. Minton to presidents of domestic companies, May 23, 1935, and Nov. 30, 1936; General Coordination Meetings, Minutes, Hourly wage rates, May 12, 1941.

31. Summary of important industrial relations developments during 1934, 1935, and 1939; A. C. Minton to heads of companies and departments, Nov. 23, 1935, July 27, and Nov. 30, 1936, and Feb. 9, 1939.

32. E. J. Sadler to W. C. Teagle, Jan. 25, 1932; Memo covering Sadler's point about higher salaried executives, Sept. 12, 1935; F. W. Pierce to R. W. Gallagher, Sept. 12, 1935.

33. Copy of address by W. C. Teagle at the Academy of Political Science, Ithaca, N.Y., Nov. 2, 1933; SONJ, *Annual Report*, 1934; Stockholders' Minutes, June 6, 1939.

34. Summary of important industrial relations developments during 1934, 1935, and 1939; Statement of industrial relations policies to presidents of domestic companies by W. C. Teagle (not dated, but in 1934 or 1935); F. W. Pierce to Eugene Holman, Nov. 7, 1936; SONJ, *Annual Report*, 1933, 1934, and 1937. ESSO: F. W. Abrams to C. F. Smith, Apr. 23, 1937. Larson and Porter, *History of Humble*, 373f.

35. Summary of important industrial relations developments during 1934, 1935, and 1939; High Lights of Industrial Relations Conference, Sept. 18–20, 1939; Chronological history of the Jersey Co., prepared for F. W. Abrams in 1938; SONJ, *Annual Report*, 1941. Stuart Chase, *A Generation of Industrial Peace*. ESSO: Abrams to C. F. Smith, Apr. 23, 1937; Background memo of Employee Relations Dept. (undated, but about 1944). *United States of America before the National Labor Relations Board, Second Region, in the matter of Standard Oil Company of New Jersey and Congress of Industrial Organizations*, Case No. II C 2449; *Memorandum for the Trial Examiner on behalf of respondent Standard Oil Company of New Jersey*, Jan. 19, 1942; *Brief for Trial Examiner on behalf of respondent Standard Oil Company*, Jan. 19, 1942; U.S. Circuit Court of Appeals, for the second circuit, *National Labor Relations Board v. Standard Oil Company and Standard Oil Company of New Jersey: Answer of Intervenor, Bayonne Refinery Employees' Association*, Nov. 13, 1942; *Brief for Bayonne Refinery Employees' Association on petition for enforcement of order of the NLRB.*

36. Summary of important industrial relations developments during 1934, 1935, and 1939. Larson and Porter, *History of Humble*, 359f, 362–375.

37. F. W. Pierce to W. C. Teagle, Oct. 3, 1934, and Jan. 25, 1935; Pierce to Christy Payne, Oct. 6, 1934; Pierce to W. S. Farish, Mar. 11, 1935; A. T. Wisner to Pierce, July 31, 1935; Teagle to R. W. Gallagher (not dated); Teagle to Pierce, Feb. 7, and May 27, 1936; Summary of important industrial relations developments during 1934, 1935, and 1939;

Memo on employees' thrift plan, Jan. 1, 1936; A. C. Minton to heads of companies and departments, Nov. 18, 1936, Oct. 13 and 26, 1937, Jan. 30 and Nov. 1, 1938, July 3 and Nov. 1, 1939; Notice about vacations for salaried employees, Jan. 13, 1938; Memo for files about vacations, by M. H. Eames, May 13, 1938.

38. Statistics of regular employees, 1923–1947; Labor turnover, 1922–1942; SONJ, Directors' Minutes, Nov. 14, 1933. ESSO: *Esso Marketer*. ESSO SH: *The Ships' Bulletin*, and other publications for specialized groups, various issues, 1927–1939.

39. See Larson and Porter, *History of Humble*, pp. 375–388, for an example of the development of a more cognitive handling of employee relations in the later 1930's.

40. SONJ: Summary of important industrial relations developments during 1939; General Coordination Meetings, Minutes, on labor relations, May 9–13, 1938. Larson and Porter, *History of Humble*, 375–387.

41. This account is based mostly on the research of John S. Ewing in Imperial's Employee Relations Department and his interviews with members of the department and men at the Imperial refineries in August, 1949.

42. IMPERIAL: *Imperial Oil Review*, Mar.–Apr., 1930. The gift was noted by many newspapers in Canada and the United States.

43. IMPERIAL: G. H. Smith to C. A. Eames, Dec. 28, 1933; *Imperial Oil Review*, July–Aug., 1932. Also interviews by John S. Ewing.

44. *Imperial Oil Review*, various issues, 1937–1939.

45. Inasmuch as relatively little material on industrial relations of Jersey's affiliates in Europe has been kept in New York, information has been sought on general labor conditions from various published sources such as: Henry W. Ehrmann, *Organized Business in France* (Princeton, 1957); Walter Galenson, editor, *Comparative Labor Movements* (New York, 1950); Frank E. Gannett, editor, *Industrial and Labor Relations in Great Britain: A Symposium* (New York, 1939); In-

dustrial Relations Counselors, Inc., and others, *Administration of Public Employment Offices and Unemployment Insurance* (New York, 1935); W. L. Mackenzie King, *Industry and Humanity* (Toronto, 1947); Val R. Lorwin, *The French Labor Movement* (Cambridge, 1954); Maurice F. Neufeld, *Labor Unions and National Politics in Italian Industrial Plants* (Ithaca, 1954).

46. Organization chart of International Association (Petroleum Industry) Limited, Nov. 1, 1936; Memo summarizing group industrial relations discussions, with details of various jobs and schedule of meetings in 1939, by C. E. Shaw; Agenda for four-day London conference on industrial relations (not dated but probably June, 1938); Minutes of second industrial relations conference in London in June, 1939; Summary of important industrial relations developments during 1939.

47. Agenda for four-day London conference in June, 1938, including material prepared by Standard Française des Pétroles. For general conditions see: Galenson, ed., *Comparative Labor Movements,* 313–347; Industrial Relations Counselors, Inc., *Administration of Public Employment Offices and Unemployment Insurance,* 97–174; Lorwin, *The French Labor Movement,* 1–84; Ehrmann, *Organized Business in France,* 1–57.

48. Agenda for four-day London conference in June, 1938, including material prepared by Standard Française des Pétroles; Minutes of second industrial relations conference in London, June, 1939; Summary of important industrial relations developments during 1939.

49. Agenda for four-day London conference in June, 1938, including material prepared by Standard Française des Pétroles; Minutes of second industrial relations conference in London, June, 1939; Summary of important industrial relations developments during 1939.

50. Galenson, ed., *Comparative Labor Movements,* 1–103; Gannett, ed., *Industrial and Labor Relations in Great Britain,* 193–339.

51. R. H. Porters to W. S. Farish, Oct. 5, 1938; Summary of important industrial

relations developments during 1939; Minutes of second industrial relations conference in London, June, 1939; Eugene Holman to Heinrich Riedemann, July 11, 1946; Review of Anglo pension and insurance and social security department, Dec. 1, 1947; Pension plan of Anglo-American, Mar. 17, 1950.

52. Minutes of second industrial relations conference in London, June, 1939; Summary of important industrial relations developments during 1939.

53. Galenson, ed., *Comparative Labor Movements,* 104–172. Industrial Relations Counselors, Inc., *Administration of Public Employment Offices and Unemployment Insurance,* 181–254.

54. ESSO SH: Annual Report, Standard Shipping Co., 1927–1930. Galenson, ed., *Comparative Labor Movements,* 243–312.

55. Translation of booklet, containing agreement between the government and employees of DAPG, Sept. 15, 1934; Eugene Holman to Heinrich Riedemann, July 11, 1946. Galenson, ed., *Comparative Labor Movements,* 243–312.

56. Galenson, *Comparative Labor Movements,* 410–479; Neufeld, *Labor Unions and National Politics in Italian Industrial Plants,* 14f.

57. Manager of SIAP to Willis, July 20, 1937; Willis to E. E. Soubry, July 24, 1937.

58. Annual Report of Romăno-Americana, 1927 to 1933, inclusive.

59. *Ibid.,* 1934 to 1937, inclusive.

60. *Ibid.,* 1934 to 1938, inclusive; General Coordination Meetings, Minutes, Labor relations in Romania and Central Europe, May, 1938; Summary of important industrial relations developments during 1939; Minutes of second industrial relations conference in London, June, 1939.

61. Annual Report of Romăno-Americana, 1934–1938; General Coordination Meetings, Minutes, Labor relations in Romania and Central Europe, May, 1938; Summary of important industrial relations developments during 1939; Minutes of second industrial relations conference in London, June, 1939.

62. Statistics of employees, 1923–1947; Eugene Holman to Heinrich Riedemann, July 11, 1946.

63. *The Medical Bulletin,* "Doctors in Oil," by A. W. Schoenleber, in issues of 1948 and 1949.

64. G. S. Walden to E. J. Sadler, May 28 and July 17, 1928, July 30 and Dec. 20, 1929, and Mar. 24, Aug. 21, and Oct. 17, 1931; Walden to H. Dodge, Mar. 5, 1930; Walden to T. R. Armstrong, Apr. 7, 1931; Walden to S. Resor, July 30, 1939; J. H. Weitermann to Walden, Jan. 26, 1932; Frederick Horstmann to Walden, July 4, 1933; C. J. Hicks to NKPM (not dated); two- and three-year temporary contract forms; J. L. Cluley to W. C. Magarity, Nov. 12, 1931; J. W. Myers to Cluley, Aug. 27, 1931; General Coordination Meetings, Minutes, Training of native employees to fill skilled and unskilled positions otherwise requiring imported foreign personnel, May 10, 1937.

65. Summary of important industrial relations developments during 1935 and 1939; Memoranda summarizing group industrial relations discussions with details of jobs in 1939; Minutes of second industrial relations conference in London, June, 1939.

66. Medical Report of NKPM for July-Dec., 1928; Annual Medical Dept. report for NKPM for 1929, by A. W. Schoenleber for E. J. Sadler, July 23, 1930; L. W. Elliott to Production Dept., May 24, 1929; Annual Report of NKPM, 1928–1933.

67. G. S. Walden to E. J. Sadler, Oct. 31, 1927, Oct. 11, 1929, and Aug. 6, 1930; Walden to Production Dept. in New York, Apr. 1, 1931; Walden to L. W. Elliott, Apr. 7, 1930; Walden to Eugene Holman, Nov. 26, 1929; Holman to Walden, Dec. 17, 1930; Elliott to Production Dept. in New York, May 31, 1929; Cable from NKPM to Production Dept. in New York, May 31, 1929; W. C. Teagle to Sadler, Aug. 5, 1928; Annual Review of NKPM for 1928; Annual Review of Standard-Vacuum, 1938 and 1939.

68. Corp. recs.; Personnel recs.; Annual Report of Standard-Vacuum, 1938 and 1939.

69. A. W. Schoenleber to E. J. Sadler, July 18, 1929; G. S. Walden to Sadler, Sept. 30 and Oct. 11, 1929, and Nov. 17, 1931; Walden to L. W. Elliott, Sept. 3, 1929, and July 9, 1931; Elliott to Walden, Oct. 21, 1929; Memo by Walden, Apr. 15, 1930; General medical rules (undated); General medical policy, 1929; H. F. Prioleau to G. H. Gordon, Aug. 28, 1931; Walden to C. J. Hicks, Apr. 4, 1932.

70. Summary of important industrial relations developments during 1935 and 1939; General Coordination Meetings, Minutes, Public and industrial relations, Colombia and Peru, May 10, 1937. INTERNATIONAL: Monthly statement, Dec. 31, 1927, and Apr. 30, 1928; B. Dunlop to A. M. McQueen, Dec. 18, 1928; W. S. Reid to G. H. Smith, Dec. 15, 1930; R. V. LeSueur to McQueen, Apr. 19, 1932; A. Iddings to E. Pombo, Apr. 9, 1931; Copy of translation of laws 7505 and 7735; copy of translation of decrees, July 26, 1934, and Aug. 31, 1935; Annual Report of International Petroleum, 1939.

71. INTERNATIONAL: A. Fleming to A. M. McQueen, Sept. 29, 1930; E. Pombo to G. H. Smith, Sept. 5 and Nov. 20, 1930; A. Iddings to McQueen, July 2, 1931; Agreement between International and Lobitos and delegates of Federation of Workmen, Dec. 27, 1930; Cable of Iddings, Feb. 20, 1931; Iddings to Pombo, June 26, 1931; Fleming to T. W. Palmer, Nov. 16, 1932; Smith to P. F. Shannon, Dec. 19, 1933; Medical report of medical care and population, 1931–1940.

72. General Coordination Meetings, Minutes, Public and industrial relations, Colombia and Peru, May 10, 1937. INTERNATIONAL: Annual Report, 1936 and 1937; Copy of translation of laws 8433 and 8509 and decrees of Nov. 14 and 20, 1936, and Feb. 23, 1937; Minutes concerning employees thrift plan effective Mar. 1, 1939.

73. INTERNATIONAL: Medical reports of A. W. Schoenleber, Dec. 19, 1933, and Jan. 8, 1939; Annual Report, 1939; Monthly labor statement, Jan. 31 and Apr. 30, 1928; Schoenleber, on housing, to Eugene Holman, Apr. 22, 1937.

74. TROPICAL: J. A. Montalvo to manager, Apr. 18, 1928; R. V. LeSueur to Minister of Industries, May 8, 1929; Annual Report, 1926, 1936, and 1940; F. B. Bimel on housing to P. F. Shannon, Nov. 7, 1935.

75. General Coordination Meetings, Minutes, Public and industrial relations, Colombia and Peru, May 10, 1937, and Relations with labor organizations, Colombia, Feb. 8–13, 1946; G. H. Smith to W. C. Teagle, Dec. 10, 1935. TROPICAL: R. Dodson to P. F. Shannon, July 12 and Oct. 6, 1934; H. A. Metzger to Smith, Dec. 29, 1935; Shannon to Smith, Dec. 14, 1934, Jan. 4 and Mar. 30, 1936; Dodson to Smith, Dec. 28, 1935.

76. General Coordination Meetings, Minutes, Collective bargaining, May 15, 1949. TROPICAL: Petition to company from Federación de Empleados, Dec. 5, 1935; Annual Report, 1934–1938; Memo of C. W. Wilcox to G. H. Smith, Mar. 17, 1936.

77. TROPICAL: Annual Report, 1934–1939; H. A. Metzger to J. W. Myers, Dec. 18, 1931; Scanlon to Metzger, May 4 and July 1, 1934; Old-age retirement fund for workmen and second-class employees, adopted in July, 1934; R. Dodson to G. H. Smith, Mar. 24, 1936; P. F. Shannon to Smith, Mar. 30, 1936; Memo of C. W. Wilcox to Smith, Mar. 16, 1936, and July 26, 1938. INTERNATIONAL: J. K. Oldfield to F. M. Surface, Apr. 15, 1959; Law 10 regulated by Colombian Decree 652 of 1935.

78. INTERNATIONAL: J. K. Oldfield to F. M. Surface, Apr. 15, 1959.

79. *Ibid.*

80. A. W. Schoenleber to G. S. Walden, Aug. 2, 1929. TROPICAL: History of the De Mares Concession, in E. E. Vanderfeen's office; Manager's Summary of Annual Report for 1934; Report on accidents by C. W. Wilcox, May 9, 1929; Report of R. S. Bonsib to G. H. Smith, Sept. 28, 1929.

81. TROPICAL: H. A. Metzger to J. W. Flanagan, Nov. 27, 1934; L. P. Maier to Flanagan, Feb. 7, 1935.

82. For various accounts of Mexico's relations with the oil industry in those years see Harlow S. Person, *Mexican Oil:*

Symbol of Recent Trends in International Relations (New York, 1942); J. Richard Powell, *The Mexican Petroleum Industry, 1938–1950* (Berkeley, 1956); Standard Oil Co. (N.J.), *Present Status of the Mexican Oil "Expropriations"* (New York, n.d.); Samuel Flagg Bemis, *The Latin American Policy of the United States: An Historical Interpretation* (New York, 1943).

83. Summary of important industrial relations developments during 1935 and 1939; *The Medical Bulletin,* June, 1948, 56–61.

84. Medical report for NKPM for July-Dec., 1928; A. W. Schoenleber to G. S. Walden, Aug. 2, 1928. CREOLE: *Annual Report,* 1928 to 1932, inclusive.

85. General Coordination Meetings, Minutes, Lago Oil & Transport Co., Ltd., and training of native employees to fill skilled and semiskilled positions and others requiring imported foreign personnel, May 10, 1937; Summary of important industrial relations developments during 1935 and 1939.

86. General Coordination Meetings, Minutes, Company cooperation in a home-owning plan for employees, May 13, 1940; Summary of important industrial relations developments during 1939.

CHAPTER 13

1. Executive Committee Minutes, June 22 and Aug. 8, 1939, May 9, July 24 and 31, and Aug. 7, 1940, Feb. 20, Apr. 14, Sept. 5, Oct. 1, Nov. 7 and 19, 1941; R. H. Porters to D. L. Harper, Jan. 26 (with translation of new German company law) and 27, 1939; Orville Harden to C. B. Rayner, Mar. 30, 1945; E. F. Johnson to Harden, Jan. 24, 1945; Synopsis of report on German government organization by C. M. Pollock, May 26, 1945; W. S. Culbertson to SONJ, Mar. 19, 1942; A. G. May to Harden, Sept. 25, 1944; J. N. Bohannon to T. R. Armstrong, July 26, 1940; W. S. Reed to Secy. of State, July 29 and Oct. 29 and 31, 1940; Guy Wellman to Secy. of State, Aug. 7, 1940; E. L. Estabrook to C. H. Lieb, Dec. 26, 1940; Report on Activities of Standard Française des Pétroles, by R. B. Young, Feb. 10, 1943. U.S. Strategic Bombing

Survey, Oil Division, *Final Report, German Oil, Chemical, Rubber, Explosives and Propellants Industries* (Washington, 1945), 10, 14, and fig. 11; U.S. Senate, 79th Cong., 1st sess., *Hearings Before a Subcommittee of the Committee on Military Affairs, Elimination of German Resources for War*, pt. 3 (Washington, 1945), 204, 295, 343–352, 415f, 442, 452, 485f, 490f, 504–508, 517f, 524f, and pt. 7 (Washington, 1945), 953, 956; Henry W. Ehrmann, *Organized Business in France* (Princeton, 1957), 58–100.

2. Memo on Jersey's sales to Germany and Italy in 1939 and 1940, by D. L. Harper, Feb. 21, 1941; Memo on Jersey's sales to Germany and Italy, 1935–1940, by Harper, Mar. 21, 1941; E. J. Sadler to W. D. Puleston, Dec. 13, 1939. U.S. Strategic Bombing Survey, Oil Division, *Final Report*, 25f.

3. Exec. Com. Minutes, June 21 and Sept. 10, 1940, Feb. 5 and Sept. 23, 1941. U.S. Senate, 77th Cong., 1st sess., *Hearings Before a Special Committee Investigating the National Defense Program*, pt. 11, *Rubber* (Washington, 1942), 4372f, 4516–4519, 4668–4671, 4721–4723 (contains many exhibits from company records).

4. Text of speech of W. S. Farish at annual stockholders' meeting, June 3, 1941; SONJ, *Annual Report*, 1940.

5. Report on Activities of Standard Française, Feb. 10, 1943. *National Petroleum News*, Jan. 31, 1945; U.S. Strat. Bombing Survey, Oil Div., *Final Report*, 25–28; U.S. Senate, 79th Cong., 1st sess., *Hearings . . . Elimination of German Resources for War*, pt. 3, pp. 294f.

6. Exec. Com. Minutes, June 22, 1939; Draft of a letter about Italian producing affiliate to U.S. Secy. of State, Nov. 29, 1940; Report of T. W. Palmer to L. F. McCollum, Nov. 30, 1940; Annual Stat. Rev., 1940 and 1941; Chart of producing and pipeline interests, W. E. Pratt's copy, Oct. 15, 1943; Memo on international claims, Oct. 27, 1944; Summary of Romanian operations during war period, by Econ. Dept., Dec. 1, 1944; Orville Harden to W. G. Wood, Apr. 12, 1945; Harden to K. C. Krentz, Aug. 31, 1945; W. A. Greeven to G. H. Michler, Oct. 10, 1945; Harden to J. A. Loftus, Oct. 25,

1945; G. H. Keatley to L. F. McCollum, June 5, 1945; Historical Report of Româno-Americana from Date of Inception, by T. J. E. Umbeck, Jan. 14, 1947; American Petroleum Institute (API), *Petroleum Facts and Figures*, 1950 (New York, 1951), 446f; U.S. Strat. Bombing Survey, Oil Div., *Final Report*, 21.

7. Heinrich Riedemann to W. C. Teagle, Jan. 20, 1937; Bert Teagle to G. W. Gordon, Sept. 27, 1937; Memo by W. J. Haley, Apr. 25, 1938; F. A. Howard to W. S. Farish, Mar. 14, 1940; W. C. Asbury to Howard, Apr. 9, 1940; Exec. Com. Minutes, Oct. 17, 1940; Report of Activities of Standard Française, Feb. 10, 1943; A. G. May to Orville Harden, Sept. 25, 1944; Harden to W. G. Wood, Apr. 12, 1945; Harden to J. A. Loftus, Oct. 25, 1945; Hist. Report of Româno-Americana, by Umbeck. U.S. Strat. Bombing Survey, Oil Div., *Final Report*, 10–22; U.S. Senate, 79th Cong., 1st sess., *Hearings . . . Elimination of German Resources for War*, pt. 7, pp. 945, 961, 966.

8. S. P. Coleman to Eugene Holman, Sept. 27, 1940; D. H. West to E. E. Soubry, Nov. 22, 1943; Summary of Romanian operations during war period, by Econ. Dept., Dec. 1, 1944; Notes on vessels of "La Columbia," by L. Marianai, Feb. 14, 1945; Synopsis of report by C. M. Pollock, May 26, 1945; Hist. Report of Româno-Americana, by Umbeck. ESSO SH: Annual Report of Marine Operations of Standard Oil Co. of N.J., 1940, 1941, and 1942. *The Lamp*, Feb., 1941. U.S. Strat. Bombing Survey, Oil Div., *Final Report*, 31–52; *National Petroleum News*, Jan. 31, 1945.

9. Exec. Com. Minutes, Mar. 21, 1941; Ann. Stat. Rev., 1940 and 1941; Synopsis of report by C. M. Pollock, May 26, 1945; Report on Activities of Standard Française, Feb. 10, 1943. U.S. Senate, 79th Cong., 1st sess., *Hearings . . . Elimination of German Resources for War*, pt. 3, pp. 504–508; U.S. Strat. Bombing Survey, Oil Div., *Final Report*, 14, 25–28, fig. 11; *National Petroleum News*, Jan. 31, 1945.

10. *American Business and World Trade*, by R. T. Haslam, Oct. 6, 1943; *The Lamp*, Oct., 1942.

11. Exec. Com. Minutes, Sept. 5 and 8, 1939; L. Sinclair to Orville Harden, Nov. 16, 1939, with memo on Petroleum Board and subcommittees; A. G. May to G. S. Walden, May 1, 1940; O. G. Holmden to Harden, May 29, 1940; H. G. Seidel to Harden, June 13, 1940. *National Petroleum News,* Nov. 8, 15, and 22, 1944; John W. Frey and H. Chandler Ide, eds., *A History of the Petroleum Administration for War, 1941–1945* (Washington, 1946), 23; W. K. Hancock and M. N. Gowing, *British War Economy* (London, 1949), 62–72, 88–95; Ehrmann, *Organized Business in France,* 53–57.

12. A. G. May to G. S. Walden, May 1, 1940; Walden to Orville Harden, May 21, 1940; H. G. Seidel to Harden, June 13, 1940. *The Lamp,* Apr., 1942; *National Petroleum News,* Nov. 8, 15, and 22, 1945; *The Oil Weekly,* Jan. 29, 1945.

13. Memo in connection with the shipping problem, Sept. 19, 1939; E. J. Sadler to D. L. Harper, Oct. 27, 1939; Eugene Holman to H. L. Shoemaker, Jan. 18, 1940, with papers prepared by C. H. Lieb and H. H. Hill. ESSO SH: Ann. Rep. of Marine Oper., 1940.

14. Memo in connection with the shipping problem, Sept. 19, 1939; B. B. Howard to E. J. Sadler, Sept. 22, 1939. *The Lamp,* Feb., 1941. Samuel Flagg Bemis, *The United States as a World Power* (New York, 1952), 359–381; Hancock and Gowing, *British War Economy,* 104–135.

15. S. P. Coleman to Eugene Holman, Jan. 28, 1941; H. L. Shoemaker to D. L. Harper, Mar. 26, 1940; E. E. Soubry to J. E. Lindroth, June 27, 1945; Annual Stat. Rev., 1940 and 1941; Summary of operations, for F. W. Abrams, May 5, 1947. ESSO SH: Ann. Rep. of Marine Oper., 1940 and 1941.

16. Exec. Com. Minutes, June 30, 1939; Minutes of meetings of Iraq group in 1939; Annual Report from Iraq Petroleum Co., 1939.

17. Annual Report from Iraq Petroleum Co., 1940 and 1941; Annual Statistical Review, 1940 and 1941; Summary of Middle East Developments, by Aramco, in 1948.

18. Ann. Stat. Rev., 1940 and 1941; Annual Report from Iraq Petroleum Co., 1940, 1941, and 1942; Memo on group agreement, July 31, 1940.

19. Exec. Com. Minutes, Nov. 22, 1940; Ann. Stat. Rev., 1940 and 1941; Annual Report from Standard-Vacuum, 1939 and 1940.

20. Annual Report from Standard-Vacuum, 1939 and 1940; H. L. Shoemaker to Eugene Holman, July 11, 1941. ESSO SH: Ann. Rep. of Marine Oper., 1940, 1941, and 1942.

21. On this subject, see Nicholas R. Clifford, *Retreat from China: British Policy in the Far East, 1937–1941* (Seattle, 1967).

22. Exec. Com. Minutes, Nov. 12, 1940; G. S. Walden to S. K. Hornbeck, Oct. 24, 1940; Memo by Walden, June 18, 1941; Annual Report from Standard-Vacuum, 1939, 1940, and 1941; W. S. Farish's speech to stockholders, June 3, 1941. Samuel Flagg Bemis, *A Diplomatic History of the United States* (New York, 1955), 821–827; *Hearings . . . National Defense Program,* pt. 11, pp. 4672–4675; T. Harry Williams, Richard N. Current, and Frank Freidel, *A History of the United States* (New York, 1959), 546f.

23. Dexter Perkins, *The Evolution of American Foreign Policy* (New York, 1948), 151.

24. *Ibid.,* 150; Samuel Flagg Bemis, *The Latin American Policy of the United States* (New York, 1943), 359–362. See for example: C. Hartley Grattan, *Why We Fought* (New York, 1929); Walter Millis, *The Road to War* (New York, 1935); and Edwin M. Borchard and W. L. Page, *Neutrality for the United States* (New Haven, 1937). See also the hearings of Nye Committee (Special Senate Committee Investigating the Munitions Industry, pursuant to S. Res. 206, 73rd Cong.).

25. Bemis, *Latin American Policy,* 354–366; Bemis, *Diplomatic History,* 771–775, 834–843.

26. National Industrial Conference Board, *The Petroleum Almanac,* 1950, pp. 334–337.

27. ESSO SH: Annual Report of Marine Operations, 1940.

28. Exec. Com. Minutes, May 24 and Aug. 24, 1939; Memo in connection with the shipping problem, Sept. 19, 1939; E. J. Sadler to D. L. Harper, Oct. 27, 1939; H. L. Shoemaker to Harper, Mar. 26, 1940; Shipments by Jersey's affiliates of 100-octane and base stock, 1939–1942; Shoemaker to T. C. McCobb, Jan. 2, 1940; Memo on available tonnage, Mar. 4, 1940; Orville Harden to Right Hon. Lord Chatterfield, Cabinet Office, Whitehall, Nov. 15, 1939. ESSO SH: Ann. Rep. of Marine Oper., 1940. Hancock and Gowing, *British War Economy,* 120–135, 151–196.

29. Shipments by Jersey's affiliates of 100-octane gasoline, 1939–1942; United Kingdom requirements for 1941, Apr. 29, 1941; Estimated 100-octane aviation gasoline and blending agent situation, 1940–1942, by H. L. Shoemaker, Oct. 20, 1939; Ann. Stat. Rev., 1941. Petroleum Administration for War, World-Wide Petroleum Supply Survey, 4th quarter 1945 and year 1946 (Nov., 1945), Table 1-B, 2-B.

30. Estimated 100-octane aviation gasoline and blending agent situation, 1940–1942, by H. L. Shoemaker, Oct. 20, 1939; R. T. Haslam, *American Business and World Trade,* Oct. 6, 1943; *The Lamp,* Apr. and Aug., 1942.

31. Frey and Ide, eds., *A History of PAW,* 3.

32. *Ibid.,* 193.

33. For a "feeling" of the ordeal of England at this time and for information on Anglo-American relations, see W. S. Churchill, *The Second World War: Their Finest Hour* (Boston, 1949).

34. G. Gordon-Bell to D. L. Harper, Apr. 19, 1937; F. W. Abrams to H. L. Shoemaker, May 7, 1937.

35. Memo on available tonnage, Mar. 4, 1940; H. L. Shoemaker to Eugene Holman, July 3, 1940; E. E. Soubry to Orville Harden, Dec. 21, 1940; Memo by F. C. Laurie, July 4 and Nov. 25, 1940. ESSO SH: Ann. Rep. of Marine Oper., 1940 and 1941.

36. E. E. Soubry to D. L. Harper, Oct. 24, 1940; A. Agnew to H. Wilkinson, Nov. 29 and Dec. 19, 1940; Wilkinson to Agnew, Dec. 24, 1940; Wilkinson to F. Godber, June 26, 1940; Godber to Wilkinson, May 29, June 5, June 28 and Aug. 24, 1940; Soubry to Orville Harden, Dec. 21, 1940; Harper to Soubry, July 1, 1940; H. G. Seidel to Harden, Aug. 22, 1940; Harden to Seidel, Sept. 6, 1940; S. P. Coleman to Eugene Holman, Jan. 28 and Mar. 25, 1941; Analysis of tonnage and business, by H. L. Shoemaker, Jan. 30, 1941; Memo by Harden, Feb. 13, 1941; Shoemaker to C. M. Davison, Mar. 14, 1941; B. B. Howard to Holman, Oct. 16, 1941; C. E. Klitgaard to Harper, Feb. 26, 1940; Holman to P. Harwood, Mar. 27, 1941; Howard to K. J. Balsillie, Sept. 26, 1940; Harden to H. E. Bedford, Feb. 13, 1940. ESSO SH: Ann. Rep. of Marine Oper., 1940, 1941, and 1942.

37. H. L. Shoemaker to A. C. Minton, May 9, 1941; Estimated U.S. and Western Hemisphere tanker tonnage balance, Jan., 1941–Mar., 1942, by J. A. Cogan, May 12, 1941; Memo on U.S. tanker tonnage situation during the remainder of 1941 and first quarter of 1942, May 22, 1941; Eugene Holman to W. S. Farish, June 12, 1941; S. P. Coleman to Holman, June 20 and Aug. 27, 1941; Proposed plan of handling tanker transportation, East Coast, July 24, 1941; Holman to R. K. Davies, July 30, 1941; Estimated western tonnage balance, 1941–1942, by Cogan, Aug. 7, 1941; Holman to Davies, Aug. 29, 1941; B. B. Howard to Farish, Sept. 25, 1941; Shoemaker to Orville Harden, Jan. 15, 1941; L. C. McClosky to E. J. Sadler, May 22 and June 2, 1941; Memo for Holman and Coleman by Cogan, June 27, 1941; Shoemaker to Holman, July 30, 1941; Agnew and Heath-Eaves to Harden, Nov. 9, 1945. ESSO SH: Ann. Rep. of Marine Oper., 1941 and 1942. Frey and Ide, eds., *A History of PAW,* 84f.

38. ESSO SH: Ann. Rep. of Marine Oper., 1941.

39. Charles Sterling Popple, *Standard Oil Company (New Jersey) in World War II* (New York, 1952), 193–195.

CHAPTER 14

1. W. S. Farish to H. L. Ickes, July 3, 1941; Memo prepared for inspection trip of N.J. Works by Jersey directors, Nov., 1942; Manager's review, of Lago Petroleum and of Standard Oil Co. of Venezuela, 1940, 1941, and 1942; Annual Report of Standard Oil Co. of N.J., 1940 and 1941.

2. Annual Statistical Review, 1940 and 1941; R. T. Haslam to W. S. Farish, June 27 and July 16, 1941. John W. Frey and H. Chandler Ide, eds., *A History of the Petroleum Administration for War* (Washington, 1946), 39–42. Petroleum Administration for War, District One History, Petroleum Industry Committee, May, 1941, to November, 1945 (mimeographed), v. 2, 206; Harold L. Ickes, *Fightin' Oil* (New York, 1943), 48–53.

3. Ann. Stat. Rev., 1940 and 1941; Executive Committee Minutes, Jan. 21, 1941; C. H. Lieb to H. E. Linam, Nov. 25, 1942; Manager's review of Lago Petroleum and of Standard Oil Co. of Venezuela, 1940 and 1941. INTERNATIONAL: Annual Report, 1939, 1940, and 1941; O. B. Hopkins to L. W. Wiedley, May 10, 1940. TROPICAL: A. S. Clarke to C. W. Wilcox, Jan. 2, 1941, summarizing 30-year contract period of the De Mares concession. CREOLE: *Annual Report,* 1940 and 1941. Henrietta M. Larson and Kenneth Wiggins Porter, *History of Humble Oil & Refining Company* (New York, 1959), 423–425, 508; National Industrial Conference Board (NICB), *The Petroleum Almanac,* 1950, p. 11.

4. Ann. Stat. Rev., 1940 and 1941; R. T. Haslam to W. S. Farish, Nov. 27, 1941; Manager's review of Lago Petroleum and of Standard Oil Co. of Venezuela, 1940 and 1941; Memo prepared for trip to Venezuela of group in New York, Oct. 18–29, 1943. IMPERIAL: Review of Operations, 1930–1942, by H. H. Hewetson. CREOLE: *Annual Report,* 1940 and 1941. Frey and Ide, eds., *A History of PAW,* 39–42.

5. Eugene Holman to F. H. Howard, Sept. 27, Oct. 2, Nov. 25, and Dec. 9, 1940; Final report of committee on marine costs, Mar. 27, 1941. ESSO SH:

Ann. Rep. of Marine Oper., 1940 and 1941.

6. C. E. Klitgaard to B. B. Howard, Apr. 3, 1940; Klitgaard to Eugene Holman, July 17, 1940; Howard to Holman, June 18, 1940; Holman to Howard, July 1, 1940; Klitgaard to W. S. Farish, Oct. 21, 1940; E. G. Grace to Farish, Dec. 17, 1940; S. P. Coleman to Holman, Mar. 25 and Aug. 20, 1941; *The Lamp,* Oct., 1941. ESSO SH: Ann. Rep. of Marine Oper., 1940, 1941, and 1942. NICB, *The Petroleum Almanac,* 1950, p. 317.

7. W. S. Farish to H. L. Ickes, July 3, 1941; A. G. Phelps to H. L. Shoemaker, Mar. 19, 1941; Farish to R. K. Davies, Aug. 27, 1941; Eugene Holman to Davies, Aug. 29, 1941; Ann. Stat. Rev., 1940 and 1941.

8. Memo on rental for right of way, by M. C. Mallon, Aug. 21, 1939; Analysis of inland transportation possibilities, by J. E. Lindroth, May 7, 1941; W. R. Finney to A. G. Phelps, Apr. 11, 1941; Statement of R. T. Haslam before Cole Committee, Apr. 1, 1941; E. J. Sadler to Office of Chief of Engineers, War Dept., July 29, 1941; Ann. Stat. Rev., 1940 and 1941; Memo, H. L. Shoemaker, Pipe Line Activities of Jersey Affiliates to Improve District One Supply Position, Apr. 28, 1945.

9. A. G. Phelps to H. L. Shoemaker, Mar. 19, 1941; W. R. Finney to Phelps, Apr. 11, 1941; Analysis of inland transportation possibilities, by J. E. Lindroth, May 7, 1941; W. S. Farish to H. L. Ickes, July 3, 1941; Ann. Stat. Rev., 1941; SONJ, *Annual Report,* 1942. Larson and Porter, *History of Humble,* 587.

10. G. E. Bubar to R. T. Haslam, May 12, 1941; Eugene Holman to M. W. Bowen, May 21, 1941; Supplies of crude and products for District #1, by H. L. Shoemaker, Nov. 10, 1942; Directors' Minutes, Sept. 5, 1941.

11. Supplies of crude and products for District #1, by H. L. Shoemaker, Nov. 10, 1942; Annual Report of Standard Oil Co. of N.J., 1940 and 1942.

12. ESSO SH: Ann. Rep. of Marine Oper., 1940 and 1941.

13. This account is based on the following sources: U.S. Senate, 77th Cong., 1st sess., *Hearings Before a Committee Investigating the National Defense Program,* pt. 11 (Washington, 1942), 4373–4376, 4583–4587; E. V. Murphree, *Adventures in Applied Chemistry,* a Jersey publication of Jan. 6, 1950; Frank A. Howard, *Buna Rubber: The Birth of an Industry* (New York, 1947), 59–91 and 265–273. Many of the references to the above *Hearings* in this and other notes below are to exhibits from the files of Standard Oil Company (New Jersey). Also, U.S. Archives, Nuremberg Trial Records, film roll 143, Memorandum by Dr. Friedrich Ringer, Jan. 12, 1940.

14. Hutz and Joslin to W. E. Currie, Dec. 15, 1939, enclosing assignments received by this law firm from I. G. Farben. Translations of the Farben records referred to are in U.S. Archives, Exhibits in Standard Oil Company (New Jersey) . . . v. Markham . . . , GIG/43: I.G. Farbenindustrie A.G. (signed by ter Meer and Loehr) to Reich Minister of Economics, Oct. 5, 1939; I. G. Farbenindustrie A.G. (signed by ter Meer and Butefisch) to Economic Defense Staff, Oct. 6, 1939.

15. F. A. Howard to W. S. Farish, Oct. 12, 1939; Howard to A. C. Minton, Oct. 16, 1939; Executive Committee Memoranda, Oct. 18, 1939 (reproduced on page 3223 of the report of the Bone Committee hearings, U.S. Senate, 77th Cong., 2d sess., *Hearings Before the Committee on Patents,* Washington, 1942).

16. Memorandum of Sales Department, dated Sept. 28, 1942, Washington, D.C. U.S. Senate, 77th Cong., 1st sess., *Hearings . . . National Defense Program,* pt. 11, pp. 4725–4736.

17. Larson and Porter, *History of Humble,* 564. SODC: Major J. P. Harris to F. A. Howard, Dec. 9, 1939; Howard to Harris, Dec. 22, 1939.

18. Exec. Com. Minutes, Aug. 14 and Sept. 25, 1940, and Jan. 30, 1941. *The Lamp,* Feb., 1944. HUMBLE: Development Dept., Five-year Laboratory Look-ahead, Aug. 14, 1945; Annual Report of Refining Technical and Research Dept., 1940. U.S. Senate, 77th Cong., 1st sess., *Hearings . . . National Defense Pro-*

gram, pt. 11, pp. 4363–4364; Larson and Porter, *History of Humble,* 596.

19. H. C. Wiess to E. J. Sadler, Aug. 19, 1940. Larson and Porter, *History of Humble,* 596. U.S. Senate, 77th Cong., 1st sess., *Hearings . . . National Defense Program,* pt. 11, pp. 4364 and 4367.

20. Larson and Porter, *History of Humble,* 596; Kendall Beaton, *Enterprise in Oil* (New York, 1957), 599–662; C. S. Popple, *Standard Oil Company (New Jersey) in World War II* (New York, 1952), 112f.

21. Memo, G. H. Freyermuth, Production and Requirements of 100-Octane Gasoline, Aug. 12, 1942; G. Gordon-Bell to D. L. Harper, Apr. 19, 1937.

22. Frey and Ide, eds., *A History of PAW,* 194f.

23. Exec. Com. Minutes, Mar. 6, May 9, July 7 and 11, and Sept. 30, 1941, and Mar. 15, 1943; Memo on aviation-gasoline blending-agent plants operating or under construction, Mar. 1, 1940; H. L. Shoemaker to Eugene Holman and F. W. Abrams, Oct. 17, 1940; Abrams to W. S. Farish, Apr. 16, 1941; Equivalent production of 100-octane aviation gasoline by Jersey affiliates, 1935–1945, by "R.M.S.B." of Coord. & Econ. Dept., Apr. 11, 1946; Review of Baton Rouge refinery for visit of Holman and R. T. Haslam, May 8, 1943; Memo for trip to N.J. Works, Nov., 1942; E. S. Hall to Farish, Mar. 30, 1942; Shipments by Jersey's affiliates of 100-octane gasoline or base stock from the United States, 1939–1942. Larson and Porter, *History of Humble,* 558–560; U.S. Senate, 77th Cong., 1st sess., *Hearings . . . National Defense Program,* pt. 11, pp. 4626f.

24. Exec. Com. Minutes, Jan. 8, May 9, and Oct. 9, 1940; Review of Baton Rouge refinery for visit of Eugene Holman and R. T. Haslam, May 8, 1943. Larson and Porter, *History of Humble,* 594.

25. *New York World Telegram,* Dec. 30, 1940. Popple, *SONJ in W. W. II,* 31f.

26. Popple, *SONJ in W. W. II,* 194f.

27. Frey and Ide, eds., *A History of PAW,* 194f.

28. F. W. Abrams to W. S. Farish, Oct. 16, 1941; Copy of press release by Office of Petroleum Coordinator, Dec. 1, 1941. ACAS-4, *Report of the Aviation Petroleum Branch,* 1941–1945.

29. Frank A. Howard's *Buna Rubber,* while focusing on the part played by Jersey in the development and manufacture of synthetic rubber, places the Jersey story in the larger context of the whole development, with a wealth of detail as observed by the author as an officer of Standard Oil Development Co. from 1927 onward. Many quotations from documents are given. Popple's *SONJ in W. W. II* contains a chapter dealing principally with the company's contribution. Beaton's *Enterprise in Oil,* pp. 588–598, contains a succinct summary, which focuses on Shell's work in synthetic rubber. Another brief account, which emphasizes the government's part, may be found in *A History of PAW,* 222–225.

30. Howard, *Buna Rubber,* 164f.

31. *Ibid.,* 109–111. U.S. Senate, 77th Cong., 1st sess., *Hearings . . . National Defense Program,* pt. 11, pp. 4405, 4731–4733.

32. U.S. Senate, 77th Cong., 1st sess., *Hearings . . . National Defense Program,* pt. 11, pp. 4413, 4734–4736 (copies of memoranda and correspondence).

33. *Ibid.,* 4417; U.S. Senate, 77th Cong., 1st sess., *Hearings Before the Committee on Patents,* pt. 6 (Washington, 1942), 2987–2992; Popple, *SONJ in W. W. II,* 56.

34. M. W. Boyer, Wartime Developments in the Baton Rouge Area, a paper delivered at a Coordination Committee meeting at Sarnia, Ontario, on Oct. 23, 1945; Memo by E. V. Murphree, Acetic Acid and other Acetylene Products, May 25, 1942; M. H. Eames to Richardson Pratt, Aug. 30, 1940; A. C. Minton to H. L. Shoemaker, Feb. 11, 1941; Memo prepared at Baytown, Nov. 25, 1941; Technical Orientation Program for Baton Rouge Refinery, Aug., 1947.

35. SONJ, *Annual Report,* 1940 and 1941. U.S. Senate, 77th Cong., 1st sess., *Hearings . . . National Defense Program,* pt. 11, pp. 4417, 4422–4429, 4460–4461; Howard, *Buna Rubber,* 100–104, 115, 137f, and 274–285; Beaton, *Enterprise in Oil,* 590.

36. Memos on discussions in Washington and elsewhere; F. A. Howard to E. R. Stettinius, Jr., June 11, 1940. U.S. Senate, 76th Cong., 3rd sess., *Hearings Before the Committee on Military Affairs* (Washington, 1940), June 14, 1940.

37. U.S. Senate, 77th Cong., 1st sess., *Hearings . . . National Defense Program,* pt. 11, pp. 4284f, 4297f, 4300, 4588, 4746–4748; Howard, *Buna Rubber,* 115–130.

38. F. A. Howard to W. S. Farish, Oct. 9, 1940; Memo from Howard to M.B.H. [Hopkins] and H.W.F. [Fisher], Nov. 6, 1940; Exec. Com. Minutes, Jan. 12, 1942; Memo on W. L. Clayton's (RFC) report to Jesse Jones of Feb. 20, 1941, on the rubber situation; Howard to S. T. Crossland (RFC), June 6 and 27, 1941. U.S. Senate, 76th Cong., 3rd sess., *Hearings Before the Committee on Military Affairs,* June 14, 1940; U.S. Senate, 77th Cong., 1st sess., *Hearings . . . National Defense Program,* pt. 11, pp. 4285–4287, 4289, 4295, 4303, 4306, 4471, 4490, 4530–4553 (*passim*).

39. F. A. Howard to R. R. Deupree (OPM), Apr. 16, 1941; Howard to E. R. Weidlein (OPM), Apr. 15, 1941; Weidlein to Howard, Apr. 21, 1941; Howard to Deupree, Apr. 25 and June 26, 1941. Howard, *Buna Rubber,* 135f and 143f.

40. Exec. Com. Minutes, Jan. 8, 14, and 25, Feb. 13 and 25, Apr. 25, June 11 and 20, July 3, Aug. 5 and 30, Sept. 17, and Oct. 27, 1941; F. A. Howard to M. J. Rathbone, June 27, 1941; Howard to S. T. Crossland, July 11, 1941; Review of Baton Rouge refinery for visit of Holman and Haslam, May 8, 1943; Annual Report from Standard of La., 1944. SONJ: *Annual Report,* 1940 and 1941. Howard, *Buna Rubber,* 166f; Rubber Reserve Company, *Report on the Rubber Program,* 1940–1945 (Washington, 1945), 5–6, 18–23; *Hearings . . . National Defense Program,* pt. 11, pp. 4463–4465.

41. Technical Orientation Program for Baton Rouge Refinery, Aug., 1947;

Memo prepared at Baytown, Nov., 1941. Howard, *Buna Rubber,* 146.

42. *Hearings . . . National Defense Program,* pt. 11, pp. 4465, 4771; Howard, *Buna Rubber,* 167f. SONJ: Defense Supplies Corporation, to M. J. Rathbone, Jan. 13, 1942.

43. Howard, *Buna Rubber,* 56–58; Popple, *SONJ in W. W. II,* 58f; Larson and Porter, *History of Humble,* 598.

44. M. W. Boyer, Wartime Developments in the Baton Rouge Area, Oct. 23, 1945. See Beaton's *Enterprise in Oil,* 592f, for an account of Shell's substantial accomplishments.

45. Exec. Com. Minutes, July 11, 1940. ESSO SH: Ann. Rep. of Marine Oper., 1940. Popple, *SONJ in W. W. II,* 190f; Frey and Ide, eds., *A History of PAW,* 18–20.

46. W. S. Farish to H. L. Ickes, July 3, 1941; Eugene Holman to R. K. Davies, Aug. 23, 1941. ESSO SH: Ann. Rep. of Marine Oper., 1941. Frey and Ide, eds., *A History of PAW,* 378–382.

47. Frey and Ide, eds., *A History of PAW,* 14 and 39.

48. *Ibid.,* 56f, 61f, and 327–342.

49. *Ibid.,* 196f.

50. Directors' Minutes, Apr. 22, 1940, and Nov. 12, 1942; Personnel records.

51. Exec. Com. Minutes, June 7, 1939, June 4, 1940, and June 4, 1941; H. L. Shoemaker to members of the Coordination Committee, May 24, 1939; Memo to members of the Board of Directors and of the Coordination Committee, Jan. 8, 1940; Memo on coordination, by E. F. Johnson, Feb. 13, 1940; Memo on coordination, sent by E. J. Sadler to Northrop Clarey, Feb. 2, 1940; Memo on coordination, by F. W. Abrams, Jan. 12, 1943.

52. A. C. Minton to heads of depts. and cos., Mar. 19, 1940; Memo on chemical products sales, Nov. 26, 1940; Eugene Holman to R. K. Davies, Aug. 29, 1941; Members of the Coordination Committee, 1931–1952, by H. L. Shoemaker, Jan. 17, 1952; Memo on domestic refining reports, Nov. 29, 1940; S. P. Coleman to C. F. Smith, Nov. 28, 1940; F. W. Abrams to Minton, June 27, 1940.

CHAPTER 15

1. John W. Frey and H. Chandler Ide, eds., *A History of the Petroleum Administration for War* (Washington, 1946), 1.

2. Samuel Flagg Bemis, *The Latin American Policy of the United States: An Historical Interpretation* (New York, 1943), 348–359.

3. Executive Committee Minutes, Jan. 21 and 27 and Feb. 27, 1942; Copy of agreement, dated Jan. 27, 1942; Comptroller's Department, consolidated accounts, 1938, and Green Book, 1942; *Annual Report,* 1941.

4. Bemis, *Latin American Policy,* 347–349.

5. Exec. Com. Minutes, Nov. 21, 1941, and Aug. 25, 1943; Directors' Minutes, Oct. 1, 1943; *Annual Report,* 1941, 1942, and 1943; Green Book, 1943. *The New York Times,* Apr. 22, 1942, and Oct. 2, 1943. The commission and its report and also editorial comments are discussed in pages 247–259 of Bryce Wood's *The Making of the Good Neighbor Policy* (New York, 1961).

6. W. S. Farish, President, to the stockholders, Feb. 10, 1942; *Annual Report,* 1943. 49 Stat., 803; Standard Oil Co., 10 SEC, 1122 (1942).

7. *U.S.* v. *Atlantic Refining Company et al.,* Civil Action No. 14060 (D. District of Columbia), 1941; *National Petroleum News,* Dec. 24, 1941, p. 3. George S. Wolbert, *American Pipelines, Their Industrial Structure, Economic Status, and Legal Implications* (Norman, Okla., 1952), 142–160. Arthur M. Johnson, *Petroleum Pipelines and Public Policy, 1906–1959* (Cambridge, 1967), chap. 16. For earnings of a large domestic pipeline affiliate in the 1930's, see Henrietta M. Larson and Kenneth W. Porter, *History of Humble Oil & Refining Company* (New York, 1959), 525f.

8. Memo for Orville Harden by E. F. Johnson, Aug. 20, 1941; *Annual Report,* 1941; *The Lamp,* Apr. and Aug., 1942. *Standard Oil Co.* v. *U.S.,* 163 U.S. (1931), 283; *Ethyl Gasoline Corp.* v. *U.S.,* 308 U.S. (1940), 436.

9. George E. Polk, *Patents and Industrial Progress* (New York, 1942). 75th Cong., *Hearings Before the Temporary National Economic Committee, Investigation of Concentration of Economic Power*, pts. 2, 3, and 14, Monograph, no. 21, 22, and 31, and *Final Report* (Washington, 1940, 1941, and 1942). 78th Cong., 1st sess., *Message from the President of the United States, June 18, 1945, Transmitting Report of the National Planning Commission* (Washington, 1943).

10. Directors' Minutes, Mar. 25, 1942; Exec. Com. Minutes, Jan. 6 and 26, Feb. 17, and Mar. 1 and 25, 1942. *United States of America* v. *Standard Oil Company (New Jersey) et al.*, Complaint and Consent Decree, Civil 2091 (D.N.J., 1942); C.C.H., *1940–1943 Trade Cases*, 933; U.S. Senate, 77th Cong., 1st sess., *Hearings Before a Special Committee Investigating the National Defense Program*, pt. 11 (Washington, 1942), 4677–4687.

11. *Hearings . . . National Defense Program*, pt. 11, pp. 4321, 4328, 4345–4347.

12. U.S. Senate, 77th Cong., 2d sess., *Hearings Before the Committee on Patents*, pt. 9 (Washington, 1942), 5235.

13. Interview of E. H. Knowlton and H. M. Larson with W. R. Carlisle, June 5, 1956.

14. *Hearings . . . National Defense Program*, pt. 11, pp. 4307, 4560f.

15. *Hearings Before the Committee on Patents*, pt. 9, p. 5236.

16. *Hearings . . . National Defense Program*, pt. 11, pp. 4307–4309, 4311f. Press release by W. S. Farish, Mar. 27, 1942.

17. The Union's officers included Frank Kingdon, Reinhold Niebuhr, and Albert Sprague Coolidge.

18. Copy of press release, Jan. 30, 1942.

19. Press release to International News, Jan. 30, 1942.

20. *Hearings . . . National Defense Program*, pt. 11, pp. 4283–4306, *passim* (quotation on 4306).

21. *Ibid.*, 4308–4358, *passim* (quotation on 4308). It is pertinent to note that the Nuremberg Tribunal stated, in its judgment in the trial of twenty-three Farben officials, that it could not assume, in the absence of more specific evidence, that the failure of the United States to develop the production of synthetic rubber was due to the withholding of information by Farben (pages 58f of mimeographed record of the trial in the Library of Congress).

22. *Hearings . . . National Defense Program*, pt. 11, pp. 4308–4311.

23. For an example, see *The Christian Science Monitor*, Mar. 28, 1942.

24. Copies in SONJ files of reports and editorials of some of the newspapers and magazines which carried an account of these hearings in great detail during late March and early April, 1942; a collection of letters received and sent by W. S. Farish, Apr.-July, 1942; Memo, by R. T. Haslam, Mar. 28, 1942; Memo for Haslam, by Earl Newsom, May 1, 1942. *The Christian Science Monitor*, Mar. 28, 1942.

25. *Hearings . . . National Defense Program*, pt. 11, pp. 4360f.

26. *Ibid.*, 4359–4497, *passim*.

27. For example, *ibid.*, 4318, 4631f.

28. *Ibid.*, 4499–4516.

29. *Hearings . . . National Defense Program*, pt. 11, p. 4318.

30. *Ibid.*, 4391–4394, 4846–4848. *Hearings Before the Committee on Patents*, pt. 1, p. 526, and pt. 6, p. 2804.

31. Statement of F. A. Howard to the authors, July 26, 1961. Also, Frank A. Howard, *Buna Rubber* (New York, 1947), 24f; and *Hearings Before the Committee on Patents*, pt. 9, pp. 5179–5181.

32. *Ibid.*, 77–91. *Hearings . . . National Defense Program*, pt. 11, pp. 4835–4838.

33. *Ibid.*, 4521–4553, *passim*.

34. *Hearings Before the Committee on Patents*, pt. 1, pp. 5f.

35. *Hearings . . . National Defense Program*, pt. 11, pp. 4830–4834.

36. *Hearings Before the Committee on Patents*, pt. 1, title page.

37. *Ibid.*, 11.

38. *Ibid.*, 627, 651, and 656.

39. *Ibid.*, 627.

40. Interview of E. H. Knowlton and H. M. Larson with Earl Newsom, June 2, 1959; and H. M. Larson with Stewart Schackne, Aug. 24, 1961. R. T. Haslam to F. M. Surface, Feb. 12, 1960. George Sweet Gibb and Evelyn H. Knowlton, *The Resurgent Years, 1911–1927* (New York, 1956), 571f.

41. R. T. Haslam to F. M. Surface, Feb. 12, 1960. Interview of H. M. Larson with Charlotte Browne-Mayers, Nov. 18, 1960. *Hearings Before the Committee on Patents*, pt. 6, pp. 2643f.

42. R. T. Haslam to F. M. Surface, Feb. 12, 1960. Interview of H. M. Larson with Earl Newsom, Sept. 20, 1961.

43. Gibb and Knowlton, *The Resurgent Years*, 249–251, 258f, and 613f.

44. Interview of H. M. Larson with Earl Newsom, Sept. 20, 1961.

45. *Hearings Before the Committee on Patents*, pt. 5, pp. 2111f, 2136.

46. U.S. Senate, 77th Cong., 2nd sess., *Hearings Before a Subcommittee of the Committee on Agriculture and Forestry, Utilization of Farm Crops, Industrial Alcohol and Synthetic Rubber*, pt. 1 (Washington, 1942), 409, 417–419.

47. *Hearings Before the Committee on Patents*, pt. 6, pp. 2621–3277.

48. Memo, Earl Newsom to R. T. Haslam, May 20, 1942, and Newsom to Haslam, May 21, 1942. Interview of H. M. Larson with Newsom, Sept. 20, 1961. *The New York Times*, May 22, 1942.

49. *Additional Report of the Special Committee Investigating the National Defense Program, Rubber*, 27–42.

50. *Hearings . . . National Defense Program*, pt. 11, p. 4808.

51. It was stated in the Bone Committee hearings (pt. 6, pp. 2644 and 2649) that such a statement had been prepared.

52. *Hearings . . . National Defense Program*, pt. 11, pp. 4806f.

53. *Ibid.*, 4806–4932.

54. Interview of H. M. Larson with Earl Newsom, Sept. 20, 1961.

55. Confidential Memorandum Covering Considerations Underlying Public Relations of Standard Oil Company (New Jersey), by Earl Newsom, enclosed in a letter of R. T. Haslam to E. F. Johnson, July 2, 1942.

56. *Hearings Before a Subcommittee of the Committee on Agriculture . . .*, pt. 3, pp. 1057–1082.

57. Testimony on SONJ and Standard Oil Development appears in *Hearings Before the Committee on Patents*, pts. 1, 3, 4, 6, 7, 8, 9. The testimony of Jersey executives is in pt. 9, pp. 5033–5258.

58. *Time*, Aug. 31, 1942.

59. *Hearings Before the Committee on Patents*, pt. 9, pp. 5038–5060, 5081f.

60. The validity of the release, and consequently its admissibility as evidence, was questioned by Chairman Bone until a member of the press offered a copy which he said he himself had obtained from the State Department. No written evidence of this has been found in Jersey's records, but an account of it was in a letter of R. T. Haslam to F. M. Surface, Feb. 12, 1960.

61. *Hearings Before the Committee on Patents*, pt. 9, pp. 5130f. This explanation is consistent with that of P. J. Anderson in an interview with him on this matter by H. M. Larson in May, 1962. Anderson was in charge of the sales to Brazilian airlines in 1941. He said the Jersey executives in Brazil worked closely with U.S. Ambassador Jefferson Caffery.

62. Executive Committee Minutes, Sept. 21, 1942.

63. Public Relations Department files, Oct., 1942, to Jan., 1943.

64. Personnel records; W. M. Craig, Memo on Public Relations, Jan. 17, 1943; K. E. Cook to C. Webb, Jan. 28, 1943.

65. *The Lamp*, Feb., 1943.

66. Report by Earl Newsom, Nov. 2, 1942.

CHAPTER 16

1. John W. Frey and H. Chandler Ide, Editors, *A History of the Petroleum Administration for War, 1941–1945* (Washington, 1946), 2.

2. This section is based mostly on *ibid.*, 1f. The quotations are from those pages.

3. *Ibid.*, 15f, 22, 24f; H. Duncan Hall, *North American Supply* (London, 1955), 336–383; D. D. Eisenhower, *Crusade in Europe* (Garden City, 1948), 4, 27.

4. Frey and Ide, eds., *A History of PAW*, 43–54.

5. *Ibid.*, 22–34 (organization chart on 27), 301–316, and 347–349.

6. *Ibid.*, 55–69 (organization chart on 57) and 327–347.

7. Executive Committee Minutes, Mar. 16, 1945. Charles Sterling Popple, *Standard Oil Company (New Jersey) in World War II* (New York, 1952), 280.

8. Frey and Ide, eds., *A History of PAW*, 327–341.

9. S. P. Coleman to J. E. Lindroth, May 9, 1945. Frey and Ide, eds., *A History of PAW*, 328.

10. Frey and Ide, eds., *A History of PAW*, 80.

11. *Ibid.*, 309.

12. *Ibid.*, 70–75, 309, 328.

13. H. L. Ickes to Eugene Holman, Jan. 16, 1945; R. K. Davies to Holman, Jan. 12, 1945; S. P. Coleman to J. E. Lindroth, May 9, 1945. Frey and Ide, eds., *A History of PAW*, 75–80.

14. Frey and Ide, eds., *A History of PAW*, 55.

15. Directors' Minutes, June 3 and 11, 1942.

16. SONJ, *Organization Manual*, Apr. 20, 1943.

17. Directors' Minutes, Nov. 12 and 20, 1942; Exec. Com. Minutes, Sept. 16 and Nov. 12, 1942; *The Lamp*, Dec., 1942, and Feb., 1943.

18. Directors' Minutes, Nov. 30, 1942; *The Lamp*, Dec., 1942. For W. S. Farish's career before he joined the parent company, see Henrietta M. Larson and Kenneth Wiggins Porter, *History of Humble Oil & Refining Company* (New York, 1959).

19. Directors' Minutes, Nov. 30, 1942, Jan. 6, 1943, June 12 and Oct. 14, 1944; *The Lamp*, Dec., 1942, and June, 1944.

20. SONJ, *Organization Manual*, Apr. 20, 1943; M. H. Eames to presidents of companies and heads of departments, Feb. 26, 1943.

21. R. L. Mason to C. F. Smith, Mar. 10, 1942; SONJ, *Annual Report*, 1943. Frey and Ide, eds., *A History of PAW*, 146–157.

22. A. C. Minton to presidents of domestic subsidiary companies and to heads of departments, Aug. 23, 1940; M. H. Eames to pres. of dom. sub. and heads of depts., May 21 and Dec. 10, 1943.

CHAPTER 17

1. John W. Frey and H. Chandler Ide, eds., *A History of the Petroleum Administration for War, 1941–1945* (Washington, 1946), 331, 340.

2. SONJ, Annual Statistical Review, 1946 and 1948. Henrietta M. Larson and Kenneth Wiggins Porter, *History of Humble Oil & Refining Company* (New York, 1959), 662, 695.

3. Annual Statistical Review, 1942–1945; PAW, Program Division, World-Wide Petroleum Supply Survey, Nov., 1945. Frey and Ide, eds., *A History of PAW*, 169–185, 257–259.

4. Press release, about Sept. 7, 1943; W. E. Pratt to J. J. Lienhard, Nov. 3, 1943; *The Lamp*, Oct., 1943.

5. Frey and Ide, eds., *A History of PAW*, 185f. American Petroleum Institute, *Petroleum Facts and Figures*, 1951, p. 364. B. P. Brown to H. L. Ickes, May 1, 1943.

6. Ann. Stat. Rev., 1946 and 1948.

7. Annual Review of Carter for 1942 and 1943. CARTER: List of officers and directors; Directors' Minutes, Sept. 11 and Dec. 31, 1942, and Dec. 4, 1943; Net reserves, acquisitions, and production, 1910–1946.

8. Résumé of Northwest Purchases of The Carter Oil Company; General Coordination Meeting, Agenda, Carter's Operating Territory, June 14–16, 1945.

9. Memo on Canol Project, Apr. 13, 1945. IMPERIAL: *Annual Report*, 1939–1945; *Imperial Oil Review*, fall, 1943. U.S. Senate, 77th Cong., 1st. sess. *Hear-*

ings Before a Special Committee Investigating the National Defense Program, The Canol Project (Washington, 1944), 22.

10. E. L. Estabrook to W. E. Pratt, July 28, 1942; Pratt to Estabrook, Sept. 15, 1942; Memo on Eastern Peru, Sept. 10, 1943; Memo on Eastern Peru, by L. F. McCollum, Nov. 4, 1943; Ann. Stat. Rev., 1942–1945. INTERNATIONAL: Annual Report, 1940–1945.

11. TROPICAL: Directors' Minutes, Mar. 6, 1944; Copy of decision of Supreme Court of Justice, Sept. 19, 1944; L. P. Maier to G. H. Smith, Oct. 18, 1943; Memo on subsidiaries to hold concessions, 1944.

12. Executive Committee Minutes, Jan. 27, Feb. 27, Mar. 16, and Apr. 27, 1942, Aug. 23 and 25, and Oct. 1, 1943; Ann. Stat. Rev., 1942–1945.

13. General Coordination Meeting, Agenda, Carter's Operating Territory, June 14–16, 1945.

14. Ann. Stat. Rev., 1944.

15. *Ibid.*, 1948.

16. The discussion of Humble's production in this section is based principally on *History of Humble* by Larson and Porter. For references to Humble records, see the pages indicated below.

17. *Ibid.*, 267f, 490–493, 662, 695.

18. *Ibid.*, 498, 576f, 583.

19. *Ibid.*, 577.

20. *Ibid.*, 571, 578.

21. *Ibid.*, 578f.

22. *Ibid.*, 571.

23. *Ibid.*, 579.

24. *Ibid.*

25. *Ibid.*, 577, 579, 583f.

26. *Ibid.*, 580, 610.

27. *Ibid.*, 580–582, 695.

28. *Ibid.*, 573f, 696; Kendall Beaton, *Enterprise in Oil: A History of Shell in the United States* (New York, 1957), 627, gives Shell's wartime increase in the United States as 30 per cent. Humble's figures include condensate, which was a small percentage of the total.

29. Larson and Porter, *History of Humble,* 588.

30. *Ibid.*, 574, 696.

31. *Ibid.*, 574.

32. *Ibid.*, 588.

33. Creole Petroleum Corporation, *Annual Report,* 1941 and 1942.

34. *Ibid.*

35. CREOLE: *Annual Report,* 1938 and 1939. Bryce Wood, *The Making of the Good Neighbor Policy* (New York, 1961), 263.

36. CREOLE: Manager's Annual Review, 1940; *Annual Report,* 1943. Interview of C. S. Popple with H. E. Linam, June 13, 1949.

37. W. E. Pratt to A. T. Proudfit, Nov. 19, 1947. Interview of C. S. Popple with H. E. Linam, June 13, 1949. Letter of W. E. Pratt to H. M. Larson, Oct. 7, 1968. Wood, *Making of the Good Neighbor Policy,* 270f.

38. Wood, *Making of the Good Neighbor Policy,* 272–274.

39. *Ibid.*, 264–269, 274.

40. Interview of H. M. Larson with W. E. Pratt, Feb., 1956. Wood, *Making of the Good Neighbor Policy,* 274.

41. Exec. Com. Minutes, Sept. 24 and Oct. 1, 1942.

42. Copy of Minutes of Directors' Meeting, Creole Pet. Corp., Nov. 20, 1942; W. E. Pratt to Arthur T. Proudfit, Nov. 19, 1947. Interviews of H. M. Larson with W. E. Pratt, Feb., 1956, and Nov., 1959, and interview of E. H. Knowlton and H. M. Larson with W. E. Pratt, Oct., 1956. Letter of W. E. Pratt to H. M. Larson, Oct. 7, 1968.

43. This statement is based on conversations with several men who had known and worked with W. E. Pratt over a considerable period of time and also on extensive research in the records of Humble Oil & Refining Company of which company Pratt had long been an officer. See Larson and Porter, *History of Humble,* 416–418.

44. Interview of H. M. Larson with W. E. Pratt, Feb., 1956, and Nov., 1959.

45. Exec. Com. Minutes, Dec. 15, 18, 23, 24, and 28, 1942, and Jan. 4, 1943. Interviews with W. E. Pratt, noted above, and with Arthur T. Proudfit, June 5, 1956.

46. Exec. Com. Minutes, Feb. 4, 5, 14, and 19, and Mar. 1 and 15, 1943; W. E. Pratt to Arthur T. Proudfit, Nov. 19, 1947. CREOLE: Circular letters to stockholders, Mar. 11 and 31, 1943; *Annual Report*, 1942.

47. See Samuel Flagg Bemis, *The Latin American Policy of the United States: An Historical Interpretation* (New York, 1943), 251–294, *passim*.

48. Personnel records; Exec. Com. Minutes, Jan. 14 and Feb. 17, 1943.

49. Personnel records; Exec. Com. Minutes, Dec. 24, 1942; *The Lamp*, Dec., 1942.

50. Exec. Com. Minutes, Mar. 24, Apr. 20 and 29, May 12, June 22, and Aug. 12, 1943. CREOLE: Directors' Minutes, Mar. 29, June 23, July 28, and Aug. 24, 1943; Stockholders' Minutes, Apr. 22, May 6, and Aug. 17, 1943; *Annual Report*, 1943 and 1944.

51. Exec. Com. Minutes, Aug. 12, 1943; *Annual Report*, 1943 and 1944. CREOLE: Directors' Minutes, Aug. 24, 1943; Stockholders' Minutes, Aug. 12, 1943; Manager's Annual Review, 1943–1945; *Annual Report*, 1943.

52. CREOLE: Manager's Annual Review, 1943–1945; *Annual Report*, 1944 and 1945.

53. Ann. Stat. Rev., 1945. CREOLE: *Annual Report*, 1944 and 1945.

54. Agenda, Miami Public Relations Conference, 1946, Relations with Labor Organizations—Venezuela.

55. CREOLE: C. H. Lieb to F. W. Pierce, July 24, 1942; Bimonthly Report on Industrial Relations, Mar.-Apr., 1942; Manager's Annual Review, 1942–1945; *Annual Report*, 1944.

56. Agenda, Miami Public Relations Conference, 1946, Relations with Labor Organizations—Venezuela.

57. K. E. Cook, Memo dated Mar. 1, 1945. Interview with K. E. Cook, Nov. 19, 1960.

58. CREOLE: *El Farol,* 1939 to 1945, *passim*. Interviews of H. M. Larson in Venezuela and New York with several of President Proudfit's associates and others who knew him.

59. Ann. Stat. Rev., 1950. Frey and Ide, eds., *A History of PAW,* 440.

CHAPTER 18

1. John W. Frey and H. Chandler Ide, editors, *A History of the Petroleum Administration for War* (Washington, 1946), 197f. C. F. Smith to B. K. Brown (OPC), Feb. 4, 1942; H. L. Shoemaker to R. T. Haslam, Aug. 13, 1942; Report by R. G. Sloane, Aug. 13, 1945; Review of Baton Rouge Refinery for Visit of Eugene Holman and Haslam, May 8, 1943.

2. E. J. Sadler to C. F. Smith, Oct. 1, 1942. Charles S. Popple, *Standard Oil Company (New Jersey) in World War II* (New York, 1952), 44.

3. Standard-Vacuum Oil Company, Annual Report, 1941; Annual Statistical Review, 1942; *The Lamp*, Apr., 1942. Interview of C. S. Popple with L. W. Elliott, Oct. 30, 1947. U.S. Senate, 77th Cong., 2d sess., *Hearings Before the Committee on Patents*, pt. 9 (Washington, 1942), 5122f.

4. PAW, Program Division, World-Wide Petroleum Supply Survey, Nov., 1945. National Industrial Conference Board, *The Petroleum Almanac*, 1946, pp. 334–337.

5. Frey and Ide, eds., *A History of PAW,* 301, 328–340. R. K. Davies to Eugene Holman, Dec. 11, 1944; Davies to W. W. White, Dec. 11, 1944; Memo entitled Foreign Operations Committee, dated Nov. 29, 1944; Personnel recs.

6. Information supplied by Brian Mead, who was Secretary of the Caribbean Area Petroleum Committee.

7. Agenda, Coordination Committee Group Meeting, in Canada, Oct. 23–25, 1945, M. W. Boyer, Wartime Developments in the Baton Rouge Area, and M. J. Rathbone, Trends in Refinery Operation; Domestic Memo of "R.S.P." (on process-control system), Dec. 17, 1943. Popple, *SONJ in W. W. II,* 40.

8. Ann. Stat. Rev., 1942–1945; C. F. Smith to B. K. Brown, Feb. 4, 1942; H. L. Shoemaker to R. T. Haslam, Aug. 13, 1942; Contract between Standard Oil Company of New Jersey and Defense Supplies Corporation, Jan. 13, 1942; Coordination Committee Group Meeting, 1945, Wartime Developments in the Baton Rouge Area, by M. W. Boyer. Popple, *SONJ in W. W. II*, 240f; Frey and Ide, eds., *A History of PAW*, 193, 367–369.

9. As told to E. H. Knowlton and H. M. Larson by one of the engineers. Also, E. V. Murphree, *Adventures in Refining*, a pamphlet containing an address delivered on Jan. 6, 1950; Renegotiation Report for 1943, dated Jan. 31, 1945. John Lawrence Enos, *Petroleum Progress and Profits* (Cambridge, 1962), 203f.

10. Coordination Committee Group Meeting, Oct., 1945, Wartime Developments in the Baton Rouge Area, by M. W. Boyer.

11. War Achievement Booklet, Everett Refinery; Standard Oil Co. of N.J., News Letter No. 226, Oct., 1943, and No. 235, July, 1944. Henrietta M. Larson and Kenneth Wiggins Porter, *History of Humble Oil & Refining Company* (New York, 1959), 592.

12. Employee Representation, 1918 to 1946, by H. R. Clark; History of Union Development in the Bayonne Refinery, by W. L. Johnson, Mar. 11, 1945; Annual Report from Standard Oil Co. of N.J., 1942. Frey and Ide, eds., *A History of PAW*, 146–157; *Brief for Trial Examiner on Behalf of Respondent, Standard Oil Company*, Jan. 19, 1942, and *Memorandum for Trial Examiner*, Jan. 19, 1942, before the NLRB, second region, *In the Matter of Standard Oil Company of New Jersey, and Congress of Industrial Organizations* (Case No. II-C-2449).

13. CARTER: J. C. Lovelady to A. W. Brown, June 3, 1959. SONJ: Executive Committee Minutes, Nov. 17, 1944, and June 6, 1945; Ann. Rep., Standard Oil Company of N.J., from 1942 to 1945, inclusive.

14. Larson and Porter, *History of Humble*, 600–606.

15. Coordination and Economics Dept., Chronological Record of Supplies into District One; Ann. Stat. Rev., 1942. Popple, *SONJ in W. W. II*, 93f.

16. Information submitted to the RFC Price Adjustment Board, for the year 1945; Renegotiation Report for 1943, dated Jan. 31, 1945. Interviews.

17. Statistics of Refinery Crude Runs, Coordination and Economics Dept. PAW, Program Division, World-Wide Petroleum Supply Survey, Nov., 1945.

18. H. L. Shoemaker to F. W. Abrams, Oct. 28, 1943; E. V. Murphree, *Adventures in Applied Chemistry*. HUMBLE: Annual Report of Refining Technological and Research Dept., 1939 to 1945, inclusive. Larson and Porter, *History of Humble*, 597; Kendall Beaton, *Enterprise in Oil: A History of Shell in the United States* (New York, 1957), 602.

19. Review of Baton Rouge Toluene Operations, May 8, 1943. Beaton, *Enterprise in Oil*, 601f; Paul H. Giddens, *Standard Oil Company (Indiana): Oil Pioneer of the Middle West* (New York, 1955), 619.

20. Larson and Porter, *History of Humble*, 597; Popple, *SONJ in W. W. II*, 113; Beaton, *Enterprise in Oil*, 601f; Giddens, *Standard Oil Company (Indiana)*, 619.

21. Memo on Baton Rouge Toluene Plant, June 20, 1945.

22. Popple, *SONJ in W. W. II*, 112f, based on figures supplied by Humble and by the Ordnance Dept., Washington, D.C.; Beaton, *Enterprise in Oil*, 602.

23. Frey and Ide, eds., *A History of PAW*, 201f.

24. *Ibid.*, 193–213, contains an excellent summary of the industry's manufacture of 100-octane gasoline during the war and of the part played by various government agencies and industry groups.

25. E. V. Murphree to M. J. Rathbone, Aug. 29, 1944; Renegotiation Report for 1942, dated Feb. 21, 1944, p. ix. Larson and Porter, *History of Humble*, 559f; Beaton, *Enterprise in Oil*, 567–569.

26. H. L. Shoemaker to W. S. Farish, Oct. 21, 1941; Shoemaker to R. T. Haslam, Aug. 13, 1942; C. F. Smith to Shoemaker, Sept. 17, 1942; Ann. Rep.

from Standard Oil Co. of N.J., 1942; L. B. Freeman to C. S. Popple, Feb. 21, 1947.

27. Frey and Ide, eds., *A History of PAW*, 200. Ann. Rep. from Standard Oil Co. of N.J., 1942; R. W. Gallagher to Robert P. Patterson, June 22, 1943; G. H. Mettam to J. R. Carringer, Aug. 23, 1944; M. W. Boyer to M. J. Rathbone, June 20, 1944. Beaton, *Enterprise in Oil*, 581–583.

28. E. V. Murphree, Contributions to the War Effort of Research and Development and Engineering Work of Standard Oil Development Company, dated Jan. 30, 1946; M. J. Rathbone to C. F. Smith, Jan. 31, 1944; L. B. Freeman to C. S. Popple, Feb. 21, 1947; *The Lamp*, June, 1944. *The New York Times*, June 8, 1942; Popple, *SONJ in W. W. II*, 35; Beaton, *Enterprise in Oil*, 586f.

29. Report to Navy Dept., Price Adjustment Board, by Standard Oil Group, dated Feb. 21, 1944. Frey and Ide, eds., *A History of PAW*, 455; Popple, *SONJ in W. W. II*, 37.

30. Contract between Standard Oil Co. of N.J. and Defense Supplies Corp., Jan. 13, 1942. Larson and Porter, *History of Humble*, 594; Popple, *SONJ in W. W. II*, 37f.

31. Ann. Stat. Rev., 1943. Frey and Ide, eds., *A History of PAW*, 212; Popple, *SONJ in W. W. II*, 36, 47.

32. H. L. Shoemaker, Memo prepared for the Coordination Committee, Apr. 25, 1944. Popple, *SONJ in W. W. II*, 45; Frey and Ide, eds., *A History of PAW*, 212f.

33. Frey and Ide, eds., *A History of PAW*, 213.

34. M. J. Rathbone to Harold L. Ickes, Aug. 12, 1944. Popple, *SONJ in W. W. II*, 45.

35. Popple, *SONJ in W. W. II*, 47; Frey and Ide, eds., *A History of PAW*, 213 and 455.

36. Frey and Ide, eds., *A History of PAW*, 455. Report to the Navy Dept., Price Adjustment Board, by the Standard Oil Group, dated Feb. 21, 1944; Renegotiation Report for the year 1943, dated Jan. 31, 1945; *ibid.* for 1944, dated

Aug. 15, 1946; Standard Oil Co. of N.Y., News Letter, May, 1945; C. B. Henderson to Standard Oil Co. of N.J., Oct. 8, 1945 (this letter was written for the RFC). Larson and Porter, *History of Humble*, 213.

37. Rubber Reserve Company, *Report on the Rubber Program*, 1940–1945 (Feb. 24, 1945), 59f; U.S. Senate, 77th Cong., 1st sess., *Hearings Before the Committee on Patents*, pt. 9, pp. 5167f.

38. Rubber Res. Co., *Report on the Rubber Program*, 20f, 28f, 31f.

39. *Ibid.*, 30–32, 70f, 76–80; Frank A. Howard, *Buna Rubber* (New York, 1947), 172–177.

40. Howard, *Buna Rubber*, 182–184; Rubber Res. Co., *Report on the Rubber Program*, 23.

41. Rubber Res. Co., *Report on the Rubber Program*, 21; U.S. 77th Cong., 2nd sess., *Hearings Before a Subcommittee of the Committee on Agriculture and Forestry* (Washington, 1942).

42. Rubber Res. Co., *Report on the Rubber Program*, 34; Howard, *Buna Rubber*, 212f, quoting from the President's veto message.

43. Rubber Res. Co., *Report on the Rubber Program*, 42; 77th Cong., 2nd sess., House Doc. 837, *The Rubber Situation*, *Report of the Rubber Survey Committee*, Sept. 10, 1942 (Washington, 1942).

44. At this time, Thurman W. Arnold again raised the old cartel issue in a hearing before a congressional committee: 78th Cong., 1st sess., *Hearings Before a Subcommittee of the Committee on Military Affairs of the U.S. Senate*, *Scientific and Technological Mobilization* (Washington, 1943), pt. 1, pp. 626–662; pt. 3, pp. 286f.

45. Rubber Res. Co., *Report on the Rubber Program*, 34; Howard, *Buna Rubber*, 223–226.

46. Rubber Res. Co., *Report on the Rubber Program*, 34f, 41–43.

47. Howard, *Buna Rubber*, 183.

48. Directors' Minutes, Apr. 15, 1943; Renegotiation Report for 1943, p. 70. Rubber Res. Co., *Report on the Rubber*

Program, 31f, 71–76; Howard, *Buna Rubber,* 231–238.

49. Report of H. L. Shoemaker on War Projects, July 21, 1944; Coordination Committee Group Meeting, Oct., 1945, M. W. Boyer, Wartime Developments in the Baton Rouge Area.

50. Ann. Rep. from Standard Oil Co. of N.J., 1942–1945; Ann. Rep. from S.O. Co. of La., 1944. HUMBLE: Annual Report of Refining Tech. and Res. Dept., 1942–1945. Larson and Porter, *History of Humble,* 598; Rubber Res. Co., *Report on the Rubber Program,* 38–40; Howard, *Buna Rubber,* 297f.

51. Report of H. L. Shoemaker on War Projects, June 12, 1942; Memo on Butyl Rubber, Per K. Frolich, undated; Notes on Butyl Project, Chemical Products Division, undated but apparently Feb., 1943; Memo on Plancor, 572, Baton Rouge, H. W. Fisher, Chemical Products Division, Aug. 20, 1943. Rubber Res. Co., *Report on the Rubber Program,* 30, 43; Howard, *Buna Rubber,* 186.

52. Rubber Res. Co., *Report on the Rubber Program,* 29f, 43f; Larson and Porter, *History of Humble,* 598; Popple, *SONJ in W. W. II,* 66–69.

53. Rubber Res. Co., *Report on the Rubber Program,* 58f.

54. *The New York Times,* June 6, 1943.

55. These percentages are based on statistics in Rubber Res. Co., *Report on the Rubber Program,* 58f, and on figures obtained from U.S. Rubber Company by SONJ.

56. Agenda of Chemical Policy Committee meeting, July 28 and Aug. 1, 1944. Rubber Res. Co., *Report on the Rubber Program,* 30; Howard, *Buna Rubber,* 241–243.

57. Jersey Petroleum Group, Preliminary Renegotiation Report for 1943, dated Jan. 31, 1945; *ibid.* for 1944, dated Aug. 15, 1946; Jersey Specialty Group, Preliminary Renegotiation Report for 1943, dated Jan. 23, 1945.

58. Exec. Com. Minutes, Jan. 13, 1942; Renegotiation Report for 1942, dated Feb. 21, 1944, p. xiv; Ann. Rep. from Standard Oil Co. of N.J., 1942 and 1943; H. L. Shoemaker, Summary Chart, Mar.

11, 1943; Memo by W. V. Rathbone, Dec. 31, 1946. Rubber Res. Co., *Report on the Rubber Program,* 59.

59. Humble Oil & Refining Co. to SONJ, Feb. 25, 1943. Larson and Porter, *History of Humble,* 561f, 598f.

60. Popple, *SONJ in W. W. II,* 117.

61. Renegotiation Report for 1943, dated Jan. 31, 1945; Ann. Rep. from Standard Oil Co. of N.J., 1943. 77th Cong., 1st sess., *Hearings Before the Senate Committee on Patents,* pt. 9, p. 5137.

62. Renegotiation Report for 1943, dated Jan. 31, 1945; Exec. Com. Minutes, Jan. 7, 1947; Orville Harden to C. Rayner, May 31, 1944.

63. Historical Sketch on Rust Ban, S.O. Co. of Penn., Jan. 31, 1947; Report, Stanco, Inc., and Stanco Distributors, Inc., to Navy Dept. Price Adjustment Board for Year 1942, dated Feb. 21, 1944.

64. C. W. Bohmer, Technical History of Beacon Lubricants, Jan. 17, 1947, and Andok Lubricant C, Dec. 27, 1946. *Oilways,* June, 1942, pp. 17–19.

65. Memorandum for D. C. Jennings on Emergency Grease Supply for Army Ordnance Department, by H. E. Bloomsburg, June 15, 1943; *The Lamp,* Oct., 1943; *Oilways,* Aug. 1943, 18–20; information supplied by the Baltimore refinery; interview of H. M. Larson in 1945 with men in the Baltimore grease works. *Time,* July 26, 1943, p. 80.

66. Exec. Com. Minutes, Feb. 4, 1942; Gilbert & Barker Manufacturing Company, Renegotiation Report to U.S. Navy Department, Year 1942, p. 10; Gilbert & Barker, Renegotiation Report to RFC Price Adjustment Board, 1943, section K, item 14.

67. Renegotiation Report for the year 1944, dated Aug. 15, 1946; *ibid.,* 1945, dated June 5, 1947; Standard Oil Development Company, Contributions to the War Effort (undated); *The Lamp,* Apr., 1944.

68. Renegotiation Report for the Year 1944, dated Aug. 15, 1946; *ibid.,* 1945, dated June 15, 1947; *The Lamp,* Sept., 1944. Popple, *SONJ in W. W. II,* 126, 128f.

69. Renegotiation Report for the Year 1944, dated Aug. 15, 1946; *The Lamp*, Sept., 1944. Popple, *SONJ in W. W. II*, 129f.

70. Larson and Porter, *History of Humble*, 570f; Popple, *SONJ in W. W. II*, 313.

71. Jersey Petroleum Group, Preliminary Renegotiation Report for 1945, dated June 5, 1947; *The Lamp*, Dec., 1944; Press release, Mar. 23, 1945; Vannevar Bush to R. P. Russell, Feb. 5, 1943; J. B. Conant to Russell, Feb. 3, 1943; Exec. Com. Minutes, Feb. 10, 1944. Howard, *Buna Rubber*, 126f; Frey and Ide, eds., *A History of PAW*, 311, 328.

CHAPTER 19

1. Eugene Holman to R. K. Davies, Aug. 29, 1941; W. J. Edmonds to F. W. Abrams, Nov. 4, 1943; H. L. Shoemaker to Members of the Coordination Committee, August 22, 1944; M. G. Gamble to Holman, Jan. 25, 1944. *Ships of the Esso Fleet in World War II* (New York, 1946), 405. ESSO SH: Annual Report of Marine Operations, Standard Oil Company of New Jersey, 1942–1945. Frey and Ide, eds., *A History of PAW*, 327–334. One member of the Marine Department of Standard Oil Company of New Jersey, who had supervised shipbuilding for that company, was put in charge of the Maritime Commission shipbuilding at South Portland, Maine (Frederic Chapin Lane, *Ships for Victory*, Baltimore, 1951, p. 514).

2. ESSO SH: Ann. Rep. of Marine Oper., 1942–1945.

3. *Ibid.*

4. Charles Sterling Popple, *Standard Oil Company (New Jersey) in World War II* (New York, 1952), 195.

5. *Ibid.*, 311.

6. *Ships of the Esso Fleet*, 76–80.

7. ESSO SH: Ann. Rep. of Marine Operations, 1941 and 1942. See John W. Frey and H. Chandler Ide, eds., *A History of the Petroleum Administration for War* (Washington, 1946), 87–88, on early submarine campaign against Atlantic Coast shipping.

8. *Ships of the Esso Fleet*, 15–24. On the early months of the conflict with the Japanese in the East, see Winston S. Churchill, *The Hinge of Fate* (Boston, 1950).

9. *Ships of the Esso Fleet*, 35–39.

10. *Ibid.*, 522f.

11. *Ibid.*, 149f.

12. *Ibid.*, 496–502.

13. Interview of H. M. Larson with J. J. Winterbottom, Nov., 1959. Popple, *SONJ in W. W. II*, 192f, 202; Lane, *Ships for Victory*, 30, 102.

14. Popple, *SONJ in W. W. II*, 311. ESSO SH: Ann. Rep. of Marine Operations, 1941–1945.

15. Eugene Holman to Nelson Rockefeller, Apr. 18, 1941. ESSO SH: *The Ships' Bulletin*, Nov.–Dec., 1941, and July–Aug., 1942; Ann. Rep. of Marine Operations, 1942–1945. Lane, *Ships for Victory*, 38; H. D. Hall, *North American Supply*, 425; Frey and Ide, eds., *A History of PAW*, 462; National Industrial Conference Board, *The Petroleum Almanac*, 1946, p. 311; Stanton Hope, *Tanker Fleet* (London, 1948), 16f.

16. *The Ships' Bulletin*, July–Aug., 1942.

17. *Ships of the Esso Fleet*, 83–88, 106–110, 252–254. ESSO SH: Ann. Rep. of Marine Operations, 1942–1945.

18. ESSO SH: Ann. Rep. of Marine Operations, 1941–1945. Total figures of losses of foreign affiliates are not available. Popple, *SONJ in W. W. II*, 208.

19. ESSO SH: Ann. Rep. of Marine Operations, 1942–1945.

20. Popple, *SONJ in W. W. II*, 229f.

21. Popple, *SONJ in W. W. II*, 208; Frey and Ide, eds., *A History of PAW*, 110.

22. ESSO SH: Ann. Rep. of Marine Operations, 1942–1945. Frey and Ide, eds., *A History of PAW*, 90, 97–100, 449–452.

23. Memo by A. G. Phelps to H. L. Shoemaker, Feb. 15, 1943; Annual Statistical Review, 1942–1945; *The Lamp*, Feb., 1943. Frey and Ide, eds., *A History of PAW*, 90–97, 449–452; Popple, *SONJ in W. W. II*, 311.

24. Memo by H. L. Shoemaker, Rail Activities of Jersey Affiliates to Improve

District One Supply Position, Sept. 27, 1943.

25. *Ibid.;* Memo by A. G. Phelps to H. L. Shoemaker, Feb. 15, 1943.

26. Memo by A. G. Phelps to H. L. Shoemaker, Feb. 15, 1943. Frey and Ide, eds., *A History of PAW,* 111.

27. H. L. Shoemaker, Emergency Installations of Tank Car Loading and Unloading Facilities, Jan. 27, 1944; The Bayway Industrial Tank Car Unloading Facilities, 1942–1945, Mar., 1946; A. G. Phelps, Memo, Feb. 15, 1943. Henrietta M. Larson and Kenneth Wiggins Porter, *History of Humble Oil & Refining Company* (New York, 1959), 585f.

28. SONJ, Ann. Stat. Rev., 1942–1945; A. G. Phelps, Memo, Feb. 15, 1943; Phelps to H. L. Shoemaker, July 16, 1943. Frey and Ide, eds., *A History of PAW,* 92, 96, 109, 116f; PAW District One History (MS.), vol. III, pp. 43–47.

29. W. R. Finney to J. E. Lindroth, Aug. 21, 1944. Frey and Ide, eds., *A History of PAW,* 102–108, 328.

30. Chronological Background and Current Data concerning Pipe Line Contributions to Alleviation of Industry Transportation Problem, District No. 1, 1939 through 1943, by W. R. Finney's office.

31. Pipe Line Activities of Jersey Affiliates . . . , Apr. 28, 1945; Ann. Stat. Rev., 1942–1945; *The Lamp,* Dec., 1942, and Feb., 1943. Frey and Ide, eds., *A History of PAW,* 102–104; John L. Loos, *Oil on Stream! A History of Interstate Oil Pipe Line Company, 1909–1959* (Baton Rouge, La., 1959).

32. Chronological Background and Current Data . . . 1939 through 1943; H. L. Shoemaker, Pipe Line Activities of Jersey Affiliates . . . , Apr. 28, 1945; Ann. Stat. Rev., 1942–1945. Larson and Porter, *History of Humble,* 587.

33. Interview of H. M. Larson with Prof. R. S. Meriam of the Harvard Business School, Sept. 29, 1961. U.S. Senate, 78th Cong., 1st sess., *Hearings Before a Special Committee Investigating the National Defense Program,* Part 17 (Washington, 1943), Exhibit No. 69a, pp. 7116–7129.

34. W. R. Finney to J. E. Lindroth, Aug. 21, 1944; Chronological Background and Current Data . . . 1939 through 1943; *The Lamp,* Dec., 1942. Frey and Ide, eds., *A History of PAW,* 104–109, 452–454.

35. Larson and Porter, *History of Humble,* 586.

36. SONJ, *Annual Report,* from 1942 to 1944, inclusive; L. F. Kahle to W. R. Finney, Jan. 15, 1945; Pipe Line Engineering and Operating Report for 1945, by Office of Pipe Line Advisor; Personnel recs.

37. SONJ, Ann. Stat. Rev., 1942–1945.

38. W. R. Finney to J. E. Lindroth, Aug. 21, 1944; *The Lamp,* Oct., 1943. IMPERIAL: *Imperial Oil Review,* fall, 1943. U.S. Senate, 77th Cong., 1st sess., *Hearings Before the Committee on National Defense,* pt. 22, *The Canol Project* (Washington, 1944).

39. E. D. Graffen to W. R. Finney, Apr. 27, 1944; Finney to J. E. Lindroth, Aug. 18, 1944; K. Smith (U.S. Navy) to Finney, Aug., 1944; Memo by J. B. Adoue, Jr., July 16, 1943. *The Lamp,* Dec., 1941, Oct., 1943, Sept., 1944, and Oct., 1945. Loos, *Oil on Stream,* 209; Frey and Ide, eds., *A History of PAW,* 271.

40. *The Lamp,* Apr., 1942, Apr., June, and Dec., 1944; Chronological Background and Current Data . . . 1939 through 1943, and 1944 to Mar., 1945, W. R. Finney's office.

CHAPTER 20

1. John W. Frey and H. Chandler Ide, Editors, *A History of the Petroleum Administration for War, 1941–1945* (Washington, 1946), 330–333. E. E. Soubry to A. C. Minton, May 4, 1944; Walter Schaefer to C. S. Popple, Dec. 29, 1947. *The Lamp,* Feb., 1943.

2. Product Sales, World, 1912–1950, compiled by the Coordination and Economics Department; Annual Statistical Review, 1942–1945; Walter Schaefer to C. S. Popple, Dec. 29, 1947.

3. Charles S. Popple, *Standard Oil Company (New Jersey) in World War II* (New York, 1952), 246–248.

4. Frey and Ide, eds., *A History of PAW*, 120–124, 129–136, 140, 144; PAW District One History (MS.), II, pp. 21, 28–29. *The Lamp*, Apr. and Oct., 1942.

5. Frey and Ide, eds., *A History of PAW*, 129–136. ESSO: J. B. Darby, Petroleum Directive No. 59.

6. Ann. Stat. Rev., 1942–1945. *The Lamp*, June, 1944. CARTER: Résumé of Northwest Purchases, by R.B.C., Dec. 13, 1949. Henrietta M. Larson and Kenneth Wiggins Porter, *History of Humble Oil & Refining Company* (New York, 1959), 606–609.

7. Frey and Ide, eds., *A History of PAW*, 124–126. SONJ, Ann. Stat. Rev., 1942–1945.

8. Popple, *SONJ in W. W. II*, 157f.

9. Frey and Ide, eds., *A History of PAW*, 144.

10. *Ibid.*, 121, 129, 137–139, 144. *The Lamp*, Aug. and Oct., 1942; Ann. Stat. Rev., 1942; *The Esso Marketer* for the years 1942–1945, *passim*.

11. Ann. Stat. Rev., 1942–1945; N. H. Seubert, Changes in Share of the Gasoline Market in the U.S., 1926–1945.

12. Product Sales, Foreign, compiled by the Coordination and Economics Department of Standard Oil Company (New Jersey).

13. IMPERIAL: Statistics compiled by the sales research section of the Marketing Department; H. H. Hewetson, Review of Operations, 1930–1942; *Annual Report*, 1942–1945.

14. Ann. Stat. Rev., 1942–1945; F. R. Hawkins to J. E. Lindroth, Sept. 19, 1944; Memo by G. H. Michler for Southern Division (undated); Summary of Argentina's Oil Policy, by W. W. Hall, July 10, 1944; Memorandum prepared for visit of Jersey men to Venezuela, Oct. 18–29, 1943; Coordination Committee Group Meeting, Sarnia, Oct., 1945, Marketing of Peruvian and Colombian Products in 1944. TROPICAL: C. W. Wilcox to T. W. King, Sept. 22, 1944. INTERNATIONAL: Minutes, Sept. 12, 1944; *Annual Report*, 1942–1945.

15. Executive Committee Minutes, July 28, 1942, and July 19, and Aug. 15, 1944; A. C. Minton to heads of departments and companies, July, 1944; SONJ, *Annual Report*, 1942–1945; Ann. Stat. Rev., 1942–1945; Annual Report of Standard-Vacuum, 1942, 1943, and 1944. *National Petroleum News*, Nov. 8, 15, and 22, and Dec. 6, 1944; Popple, *SONJ in W. W. II*, 267f.

16. Frank Knox, Secretary of the Navy, to W. S. Farish, Jan. 24, 1942; Col. G. F. Lewis, Air Transport Command, to R. W. Gallagher, June 30, 1943; *The Lamp*, Dec., 1943, and Feb., 1944. Popple, *SONJ in W. W. II*, 292, 295f.

17. Popple, *SONJ in W. W. II*, 271–273.

18. *Ibid.*, 273f.

19. *Ibid.*, 269f.

20. *Ibid.*, 268.

21. Interviews of C. S. Popple with R. I. Worssam and C. K. Gamble. Popple, *SONJ in W. W. II*, 271.

22. SONJ, Ann. Stat. Rev., 1950. Frey and Ide, eds., *A History of the PAW*, 440.

CHAPTER 21

1. R. W. Gallagher, "Leadership in American Business," an address delivered in October, 1945, and reprinted in 79th Cong., 1st sess., *Congressional Record*, 91, pt. 13, A 4851.

2. SONJ, *Annual Report*, 1945. John W. Frey and H. Chandler Ide, eds., *A History of the Petroleum Administration for War* (Washington, 1946), 289–291.

3. Frey and Ide, eds., *A History of PAW*, 291–293.

4. *Ibid.*, 296–298.

5. SONJ, *Annual Report*, 1947.

6. Henrietta M. Larson and Kenneth Wiggins Porter, *History of Humble Oil & Refining Company* (New York, 1959), 623.

7. ESSO: Louisiana Division, Report of Operations, 1945. Larson and Porter, *History of Humble*, 623.

8. ESSO: Directors' Minutes, Mar. 16, 1946. Larson and Porter, *History of Humble*, 623.

9. SONJ, *Annual Report*, 1945. ESSO: Annual Report of S.O.C. of N.J., 1945.

Larson and Porter, *History of Humble,* 624f. See Chapter 25 of this volume for later difficulties in supplying the demand.

10. Pipe Line Engineering and Operating Report, 1945; *The Lamp,* Sept., 1950.

11. Harvey O'Connor, *History of Oil Workers International Union (CIO)* (Denver, 1950), 52–55.

12. P. J. McCroskey, circular letter to Heads of Departments . . . , Oct. 1, 1945.

13. Larson and Porter, *History of Humble,* 606.

14. SONJ, *Annual Report,* 1945.

15. ESSO: Annual Report of S.O.C. of N.J., 1945; *The Lamp,* Oct., 1945.

16. ESSO: Annual Report of S.O.C. of N.J., 1945.

17. SONJ, *Annual Report,* 1946.

18. 40 Stat. 461.

19. *Standard Oil Company (N.J.) et al.* v. *Markham,* 57 Fed. Supp. 332.

20. 61 Fed. Supp. 813.

21. 64 Fed. Supp. 656. U.S. Circuit Court of Appeals for the Second District, *Standard Oil Company (New Jersey), Standard Oil Development Company, Standard Catalytic Company, and Jasco, Incorporated,* v. *Tom Clark, Attorney General, as Successor to the Alien Property Custodian. . . .* Transcript of Record filed, Nov. 4, 1946, Joint Appendix to the Briefs . . . , vol. I, 36–69, 215–237.

22. U.S. Circuit Court of Appeals, *Standard Oil Company (New Jersey)* . . . v. *Tom Clark* . . . , 238–241; 163 Fed. 2d 917.

23. 333 U.S. 873.

24. Executive Committee Minutes, Apr. 20, 1948; *The Lamp,* June–Sept., 1948; SONJ, *Annual Report,* 1948.

25. SONJ, *Annual Report,* 1946.

26. IMPERIAL: Minutes of the General Marketing Committee, Mar., 1947.

27. *Ibid.,* Aug. 26, 1947.

28. IMPERIAL: Statement of R. V. Le-Sueur released for publication on Aug. 18, 1945.

29. SONJ, *Annual Report,* 1946.

30. R. A. Carder and L. Sinclair, "United Kingdom," *Coordination Committee Group Meeting,* Paris, 1947, pp. 11, 115, and 125. ESSO SH: Annual Report of Marine Operations, for the years 1945–1950.

31. SONJ, *Organization Manual,* July 1, 1946; Notes on European and Far Eastern Refineries, by Coordination & Economics Dept., Mar. 11, 1948; SONJ, *Annual Report,* 1946.

32. Memo, Condition of the French Operating Organization, Mar. 14, 1945; C. G. Irish to E. E. Soubry, Apr. 3, 1945; Copy of resolution of Board of Directors of United Petroleum Securities Corp., May 17, 1945; Cable, Soubry to Irish, May 18, 1945; Memo, French Financial Situation, May 18, 1945; *The Lamp,* Sept., 1951.

33. R. T. Haslam to W. E. Pratt, Aug. 31, 1945.

34. R. T. Haslam to W. E. Pratt, July 2 and Aug. 19, 1945; Exec. Com. Minutes, Aug. 31 and Sept. 7, 18, 1945; D. A. Shepard to F. M. Surface, Oct. 31, 1962. Interview of H. M. Larson with D. A. Shepard, Oct., 1962.

35. Orville Harden to the United States Department of State, Oct. 16, 1945; Dept. of State to Harden, Nov. 16, 1945.

36. R. T. Haslam to W. E. Pratt, Nov. 19, 1945.

37. S. D. Turner to G. S. Walden, Nov. 16, 1949; Minutes of the Marketing Council, Nov. 27, 1951; Papers presented at the Coordination Committee Group Meeting at Paris, 1947 and 1952; SONJ, *Annual Report,* 1946. ESSO SH: Annual Report of Marine Operations, for the years 1945–1950. Also, Henry W. Ehrmann, *Organized Business in France* (Princeton, 1957); Val R. Lorwin, *The French Labor Movement* (Cambridge, 1954); Duke University, School of Law, series on *Law and Contemporary Problems,* vol. 16 entitled *War Claims* (Summer, 1951).

38. *Coordination Committee Group Meeting,* Paris, 1947, p. 408; Statement of P. T. Lamont quoted in letter of Mary Neumany to F. M. Surface, Aug. 14, 1963.

39. D. H. West to G. H. Michler, May 22 and June 14, 1945; Report of Società to SONJ, Jan., 1949.

40. Cable, F. W. Abrams to Società, June 8, 1948; Report of Società to SONJ, Jan., 1949.

41. G. H. Michler to C. B. Raynor, Jan. 18, 1946; P. T. Lamont to Michler, Apr. 9, 1946.

42. John Boesch (P.O.W.) to SONJ, Apr. 25, 1945.

43. Memos, Board of Managers of DAPG to SONJ, June 25 and Aug. 14, 1945.

44. P. T. Lamont to G. H. Michler, Apr. 8, 1946.

45. H. L. Preuss to P. T. Lamont, Jan. 17, 1946.

46. Exec. Com. Minutes, Aug. 29, 1946, and Jan. 31, 1947; J. E. Lindroth to E. E. Soubry, Dec. 6, 1946; W. T. Meyer to O. K. Taylor, Aug. 11, 1948.

47. SONJ, *Annual Report,* 1947; P. T. Lamont to E. E. Soubry, Apr. 2, 1946; W. Greeven to W. R. Carlisle, Mar. 15, 1948; Greeven to Soubry, Sept. 7, 1948; Report of Operations of DAPG, Jan., 1949.

48. Exec. Com. Minutes, Sept. 2, 1948.

49. George Koegler to Orville Harden, May 24, 1945; Cable, D. A. Shepard to E. E. Soubry, June 9, 1945.

50. Exec. Com. Minutes, Nov. 15, 1946. Ely Maurer, "Protection of Non-Enemy Interests in Enemy External Assets," 428–429, in *Law and Contemporary Problems,* vol. 16, *War Claims.*

51. L. F. McCollum to Eugene Holman, Sept. 13, 1946.

52. H. L. Shoemaker to L. F. McCollum, Apr. 10, 1947; Exec. Com. Minutes, Apr. 14, 1947; V. C. Georgescu to McCollum, May 19, 1947.

53. V. C. Georgescu to SONJ, Apr. 30, 1947.

54. Memo, Romania, by V. C. Georgescu, July 16, 1947.

55. R. P. Bolton to J. R. Suman, Aug. 26, 1947.

56. *Ibid.,* Oct. 7, 1947.

57. Exec. Com. Minutes, Mar. 22 and 31, Apr. 26, and May 9, 1948; T. J. E. Umbeck, Supplement dated Oct. 15, 1948, to Historical Report of Româno-Americana, Jan. 14, 1947; Eugene Holman to P. Groze (Prime Minister of Romania), May 5, 1948.

58. George Koegler to U.S. Dept of State, July 22, 1948.

59. Exec. Com. Minutes, June 18 and 28 and Sept. 2, 1948; J. W. Brice to Producing Dept., June 17, 1948; SONJ, *Annual Report,* 1948 and 1949.

60. Copy in SONJ records of Hungarian government decree returning MAORT to its owners, Aug. 9, 1945. This decree and other documents having to do with MAORT in the references below are printed in a book published by the company in 1949 entitled *Standard Oil Company (New Jersey) and Oil Production in Hungary by MAORT, 1931–1945.* On conditions in Hungary: Paul Ruedemann, "Hungary," *Coordination Committee Group Meeting,* Paris, 1947, pp. 167–171.

61. George Bannantine to L. F. McCollum, Feb. 23, 1946.

62. Translation in SONJ records of document signed by Marshal of the Soviet Union K. Voroshilov, Jan. 17, 1946.

63. Paul Ruedemann to Hon. H. F. Arthur Schoenfeld, United States Minister, Budapest, Hungary, Nov. 18, 1946.

64. Exec. Com. Minutes, Feb. 8, 1946; *Standard Oil Company (New Jersey) and Oil Production . . . by MAORT,* 6–8.

65. Paul Ruedemann, "I Learned About Communism the Hard Way," *Saturday Evening Post,* May 28, 1948 (vol. 221).

66. Copy in SONJ records of letter from minister of industries appointing Paul Szekely controller of MAORT, May 8, 1948; Paul Ruedemann to the Hon. Selden Chapin, American Minister, Budapest, June 3, 1948, in *Standard Oil Company (New Jersey) and Oil Production . . . by MAORT.*

67. *Standard Oil Company (New Jersey) and Oil Production . . . by MAORT,* 11. Pages 56–60 contain a 1947 report of an investigation under the non-Communist government recommending

the practices the Communist government alleged to be wrong.

68. Exec. Com. Minutes, Sept. 15, 1948. *Standard Oil Company (New Jersey) and Oil Production . . . by MAORT,* vii.

69. Exec. Com. Minutes, Sept. 20, 1948; Associated Press news dispatch, Vienna, dated Sept. 20, 1948.

70. Copy in SONJ records of statement of Paul Ruedemann, sworn to before Harrison Lewis, U.S. Consul, Vienna, Austria, Sept. 27, 1948 (also pp. 46–48 in *Standard Oil Company (New Jersey) and Oil Production . . . by MAORT*). Paul Ruedemann, "I Learned About Communism the Hard Way," *Saturday Evening Post,* May 28, 1948.

71. Copy in SONJ records of decrees by which the Hungarian government expropriated MAORT, Sept. 24, 1948. Also, pp. 33f of *Standard Oil Company (New Jersey) and Oil Production . . . by MAORT.*

72. Copy in SONJ records of *Report of the Hungarian Ministry of Home Affairs on the MAORT Sabotage,* Sept. 28, 1948.

73. John W. Brice to the Secretary of State, Washington, D.C., Nov. 23, 1948; Exec. Com. Minutes, Jan. 24, 1949; SONJ, *Annual Report,* 1948 and 1949. Text of U.S. note to Hungarian Ministry of Foreign Affairs is on pp. vii–xi of *Standard Oil Company (New Jersey) and Oil Production . . . by MAORT.*

74. Marketing Review of Standard-Vacuum Oil Company, 1945.

75. *Ibid.*

76. Page 1 of *Stanvac in Indonesia,* by the Center for International Studies at Massachusetts Institute of Technology (National Planning Association, 1957). In SONJ records, Operating Review of Standard-Vacuum Oil Company, 1945.

77. Operating Review of Standard-Vacuum, 1946 and 1947.

78. Memo, Condition of Standard-Vacuum Employees in Occupied Countries, Jan., 1947.

79. Oper. Rev. of Standard-Vacuum, 1947.

80. *Ibid.,* 1946 and 1947; L. W. Elliott to Orville Harden, Jan. 20, 1949; Annual Report of Standard-Vacuum Oil Co., 1948.

81. ESSO SH: Ann. Rep. of Marine Oper., for the years 1942–1945. Memo in SONJ records, Information on War Losses of European and North African Companies and Marine Losses of SONJ, Panama Transport, and Imperial, 1950. Information obtained from H. W. Kull and F. A. Hook, Sept. 20, 1961, and on 1962 legislation from the SONJ Law Department, Feb. 4, 1964.

82. Nehemiah Robinson, "War Damage Compensation and Restitution in Foreign Countries," *Law and Contemporary Problems,* vol. 16, *War Claims,* pp. 351–355, contains a statement on provisions for compensation in occupied countries in Europe. Memo, Information on War Losses . . . 1950; Memo prepared for U.P.S.C. meeting by W. J. Haley, Dec. 3, 1945; H. L. Shoemaker to J. E. Lindroth, Aug. 28, 1946; Haley to R. T. Haslam, Oct. 1, 1946; Memo by Haley, Oct. 7, 1946; Data presented to F. W. Abrams, Sept. 27, 1948; Haley to E. E. Soubry, Mar. 14, 1950; SONJ, *Annual Report,* 1947 and 1950; Annual Report (English translation) of Société Anonyme Française, for the years 1953–1956; Information received from R. O. Anderson, Mar. 21, 1960, and May 8, 1961.

83. SONJ, *Annual Report,* 1946. C. Joseph Stetler, "To What Extent Should Congress Appropriate to Distribute the Burden of War Loss, Given the Insufficiency of War Reparation," *Law and Contemporary Problems,* vol. 16, *War Claims,* 477–481; Malcolm S. Mason, "Relationship of Vested Assets to War Claims," *ibid.,* 400–403. Information on payments under 1962 legislation received from the SONJ Law Department, July 3 and Oct. 1, 1968.

84. J. E. Lindroth to E. E. Soubry, Dec. 6, 1946; SONJ, *Annual Report,* 1947; W. Greeven to W. R. Carlisle, Mar., 1948; W. T. Meyer to O. K. Taylor, Aug. 11, 1948; Eugene Holman to Secretary of State of U.S., June 13, 1951; Memo, Information on War Losses . . . , 1950; Memo on War Losses, Dec., 1956; also information from R. O. Anderson, Mar.

21, 1960, and May 8, 1961. C. Joseph
Stetler, *op. cit.*, 479f; Walter Sterling
Surrey, "Problems of the Italian Peace
Treaty: Analysis of Claims Provisions
and Description of Enforcement," *Law
and Contemporary Problems*, vol. 16,
War Claims, 437–447. Samuel Herman,
"War Damage and Nationalization in
Eastern Europe," *Law and Contempo-
rary Problems*, vol. 16, *War Claims*, 498–
507.

85. Memo, Information on War Losses
. . . , 1950; Foreign Claims Settlement
Commission of the United States, Claims
for MAORT and Romăno-Americana,
1956–1958. Data on awards furnished by
the SONJ Law Department in September, 1968.

86. Information furnished by SONJ Law
Department, Feb. 4, 1964, and July 3 and
Oct. 1, 1968.

87. Information furnished by general
counsel of Esso Standard Eastern, Inc.,
Aug. 7, 1968.

88. *Law and Contemporary Problems*,
vol. 16, *War Claims*, C. Joseph Stetler,
op. cit., 477f.

89. Information furnished by general
counsel of Esso Standard Eastern, Inc.,
Aug. 7, 1968.

CHAPTER 22

1. Specific data in this section on retirements, elections, and appointments are
based on the parent company's personnel
records, Directors' Minutes, and its *Annual Report* for the years covered.

2. The following statements about these
officers are based on the authors' own
research and observations and on discussions and correspondence with several of
the officers' associates on the Board of
Directors and others who worked closely
with them.

3. Directors' Minutes, Mar. 25, 1943.

4. Circular letter from Secretary's Department to heads of departments, Feb.
9, 1945.

5. Statistics on shareholders supplied by
Assistant Secretary Muriel E. Reynolds.

6. Memo by A. C. Minton, undated,
1945; Interview with Muriel E. Reynolds,

Oct. 31, 1961, and with A. C. Minton,
June 11, 1968. Also, Adrian C. Minton,
"Company-Stockholder Relations," pp.
51–61 of *Science, Engineering, Public
Relations: A Symposium* (Massachusetts
Institute of Technology, 1949).

7. Memorandum for Executive Committee, Report of Special Committee to Investigate Government Relations, Feb. 7,
1947; Executive Committee Minutes,
Mar. 13, 1947.

8. W. C. Teagle to F. H. Bedford, Jr.,
Aug. 1, 1930.

9. Executive Committee Minutes, May
21, 1943.

10. Interview with A. C. Minton, June
11, 1968.

11. Outline of Program for Executive
Development, Sept. 6, 1944.

12. Circular letter, H. L. Shoemaker to
members of the Coordination Committee,
May 23, 1945; G. B. Corless, Memo on
Executive Development, Jan. 23, 1946.

13. G. B. Corless, Memo on Executive
Development, Jan. 23, 1946.

14. Executive Development, in Agenda,
Coordination Committee Group Meeting,
1946; *ibid.*, 1947 and 1948.

15. Minutes of the Executive Development Subcommittee, for the years 1946–
1949; "Developing Tomorrow's Business
Leaders," *The Lamp*, Feb., 1946.

16. Coord. Com. Group Meeting, reports
for the years 1946–1949.

17. This section is based primarily on
company reports and on interviews with
men concerned with these developments.

18. There were frequent references to
consultants and experts in the Executive
Committee Minutes, notably for the year
1946.

19. This section on finance is based
largely on a study made in the offices of
Standard Oil Company (New Jersey) by
Professor William T. Baxter. Materials
from affiliates have been added to Baxter's findings. An example of an affiliate's
financial procedures may be found in
Henrietta M. Larson and Kenneth Wiggins Porter, *History of Humble Oil &
Refining Company* (New York, 1959),
615–617.

20. See Larson and Porter, *History of Humble*, 213f, 547–550.

21. SONJ, *Annual Report*, 1945 to 1950, inclusive; Exec. Com. Minutes, Aug. 7, 1944, Feb. 14, Nov. 3, and Dec. 17, 1947, and Jan. 28, July 26, and Oct. 31, 1948.

22. Report of the Committee for Review of Departmental Expenses, Nov. 3, 1950.

23. Memo on Corporate Organization, Oct. 3, 1946; *Coordination Committee Group Meeting*, 1947, pp. 434f.

24. Exec. Com. Minutes, June 10, Nov. 1, and Dec. 17 and 31, 1948; Annual Report of Standard Oil Company of New Jersey (Esso Standard) for 1945 and 1948.

25. Exec. Com. Minutes, May 27 and June 13, 1947, and Feb. 18, 1948.

26. *Ibid.*, Jan. 23, 1946.

27. *Ibid.*, Jan. 15, Feb. 18, Mar. 11, 16, and 23, Aug. 30, Sept. 30, 1948, and Feb. 2, 1949.

28. *Ibid.*, Jan. 28, 1948.

29. J. O. Larson to the Directors, May 16, 1950.

30. Minutes of the Committee on Corporate Concentration, 1950.

CHAPTER 23

1. Interview of H. M. Larson with R. L. Mason, retired manager of the Employee Relations Department, Nov. 1, 1961.

2. *Ibid.* Henrietta M. Larson and Kenneth Wiggins Porter, *History of Humble Oil & Refining Company* (New York, 1959), 619–623.

3. SONJ, *Annual Report*, 1946–1949; interview of H. M. Larson with R. L. Mason, Nov. 1, 1961. Larson and Porter, *History of Humble*, 619f.

4. Larson and Porter, *History of Humble*, 618f. SONJ, *Annual Report*, 1946–1950.

5. SONJ, *Annual Report*, 1946, 1947, and 1949; R. L. Mason, Management Prerogatives, General Trends and Developments, Coordination Committee Group Meeting, 1948; *Know Your Benefits*, a descriptive booklet issued in 1950. Larson and Porter, *History of Humble*, 618.

6. SONJ, *Annual Report*, 1947; R. L. Mason, Composite View of Employee Opinion Surveys, Coord. Com. Group Meeting, 1946; Reports of surveys; Interview of H. M. Larson with R. L. Mason, Nov. 1, 1961.

7. Discussion with Professor R. M. Hower of the Harvard Graduate School of Business Administration, Nov., 1962.

8. SONJ, *Annual Report*, 1950; Annual Report of Standard Oil Company of New Jersey (Esso Standard), 1946 and 1948; William Naden, Employee Relations Problems, Coord. Com. Group Meeting, 1946; Matthew Radom, Testing, Employment, and Counseling, Coord. Com. Group Meeting, 1948.

9. Annual Report of S.O.C. of N. J., 1946; V. O'Rourke, Organizational Planning, Coord. Com. Group Meeting, 1948.

10. SONJ, *Annual Report*, 1946. Larson and Porter, *History of Humble*, 621f.

11. "Design for Training," *The Lamp*, Jan., 1947; H. D. Kolb to W. P. Headden, Jan. 23, 1964.

12. "Design for Training," *The Lamp*, Jan., 1947.

13. These paragraphs on Imperial's employee relations are based mainly on a report written by John S. Ewing from research in the company's records.

14. W. M. Hall to E. E. Soubry, Sept. 20, 1945; P. T. Lamont to Soubry, Apr. 2, 1946; J. E. Lindroth to Soubry, Dec. 6, 1946; data presented by Standard Française to F. W. Abrams, Sept. 27, 1948; *Coord. Com. Group Meeting*, 1947, pp. 221–236.

15. *Coord. Com. Group Meeting*, 1947, p. 222. Val R. Lorwin, *The French Labor Movement* (Cambridge, 1954); Henry W. Ehrmann, *Organized Business in France* (Princeton, 1957).

16. SONJ, *Coord. Com. Group Meeting*, 1947, pp. 127, 224.

17. This observation about the weakening of class differences came from conversations with several Jersey executives.

18. SONJ, *Annual Report*, 1946.

19. An excellent description of Standard-Vacuum's employee relations is given in *Stanvac in Indonesia*, a study made by

the Center for International Studies at Massachusetts Institute of Technology and published by the National Planning Association in 1957.

20. CREOLE: *Annual Report*, 1945–1948. SONJ: Coord. Com. Group Meeting, 1946. Edwin Lieuwen, *Petroleum in Venezuela* (London, 1961), 90–110.

21. CREOLE: *Annual Report*, 1948, 1949, and 1950. Papers delivered at the Coord. Com. Group Meeting, Caracas, Venezuela, Feb. 19–21, 1951.

22. The experience in saving is interesting and meaningful. It was discussed in interviews of H. M. Larson in February, 1949, with M. C. Hagen, then head of Creole's Employee Relations Department, and with C. I. Babin of the Western Division.

23. CREOLE: *Annual Report*, 1946.

24. *Ibid.*, 1949.

25. *Ibid.*, 1947.

26. Dr. A. Lacorte, head of the Creole Hospital at Quiriquire, in conversation with H. M. Larson in February, 1949.

27. Observations and interviews of H. M. Larson with Creole executives in Maracaibo in February, 1949.

28. CREOLE: *Annual Report*, 1946 and 1950. Interview of H. M. Larson with L. G. Smith (Creole director) in New York.

29. CREOLE: *Annual Report*, 1945 and 1947. H. M. Larson participated in 1950–1951 in giving a course at the Harvard Business School in which a young Venezuelan employee of Creole was a student. A decade later this man was a member of the company's board of directors.

30. "The Three R's," *The Lamp*, Mar., 1947. CREOLE: *Annual Report*, 1945. H. M. Larson visited Creole camp schools in 1949, talked with several teachers, and discussed Creole education with a school principal and several executives of the company.

31. CREOLE: *Annual Report*, 1948.

32. *Ibid.*, 1945, 1946, and 1949. "The Three R's," *The Lamp*, Mar., 1947.

33. CREOLE: *Organization Manual*, 1949, 1950, and 1951.

34. Based on H. M. Larson's observations in Venezuela and discussions with Creole executives in 1949. An excellent description of Creole's employee relations is presented in a study published by the National Planning Association: Wayne C. Taylor, John Lindeman, and Victor Lopez R., *The Creole Petroleum Corporation in Venezuela* (Washington, 1955).

CHAPTER 24

1. R. T. Haslam, "Public Relations Requirements and Activities," Agenda, Coordination Committee Group Meeting, 1944.

2. M. H. Eames to Presidents of Subsidiary Companies and Heads of Departments, Feb. 17, 1943.

3. Memo, G. H. Freyermuth to R. T. Haslam, Dec. 30, 1943; draft of circular letter issued Feb. 17, 1943. Among the records of earlier discussions are: E. B. Lyman to Earl Newsom, Feb. 4, 1943; Report on Public Relations Conference, dated Feb. 4, 1943; Freyermuth to R. P. Russell, Feb. 25, 1943; W. M. Craig to Staff, Sept. 3, 1943.

4. Public Relations Department files, 1943–1945.

5. The earliest complete version of this statement is undated but appears in a memo at the end of the department's file for 1943.

6. For example, F. W. Abrams in Notes on the North American Public Relations Conference, 1952, p. 2.

7. Memo on Standard Oil Company Public Relations Policy, June 14, 1943.

8. Statement of objectives suggested in discussions filed with a letter of Dec. 31, 1943; letter of Stewart Schackne to G. H. Freyermuth, Oct. 14, 1944, which presents a later statement of aims in public relations; an elaborate statement entitled Writing Group Responsibilities, dated Feb. 12, 1945, repeating the list of company characteristics contained in the Oct. 14, 1944, statement, which became the department's official guide.

9. Stewart Schackne to F. M. Surface, Aug. 1, 1961.

10. L. E. Ulrope to J. C. Richdale, May 11, 1942; Charlotte Lochhead to J. C.

Richdale, June 8, 1942; Lochhead to R. S. Meriam, Apr. 16, 1943; Lochhead to Richdale, Apr. 16, 1943; Richdale to Lochhead, Apr. 19, 1943; Warren T. Powell to Lochhead, Apr. 22, 1943; Lochhead to S. Ralph Harlow, Apr. 23, 1943; Report on Boston trip, Apr. 25–28, 1943; Lochhead to R. T. Haslam, Apr. 30, 1943; Report on Boston Business-men's and Clergymen's Group Dinner Meeting—Algonquin Club, June 15, 1943; L. D. Hartman to Lochhead, June 23, 1943; F. M. Surface to Lochhead, June 30, 1943. Interview of H. M. Larson with Mrs. Charlotte Browne-Mayers, Nov. 18, 1960.

11. Memo on dinner meeting at Algonquin Club, Oct. 6, 1943; R. S. Meriam to Charlotte Lochhead, Oct. 23, 1943.

12. J. C. Richdale to Charlotte Lochhead, Nov. 2, 1943.

13. Interview of H. M. Larson with Mrs. Charlotte Browne-Mayers, Nov. 18, 1960.

14. Memo on Art Project, Edward Stanley to G. H. Freyermuth, Jan. 17, 1944; *Public Relations Conference, Standard Oil Company (New Jersey) and Affiliated Companies,* 1948, p. 83.

15. Interview of H. M. Larson with Robert Flaherty in Baton Rouge, La., March, 1945.

16. Earl Newsom to G. H. Freyermuth, May 22, 1944; Freyermuth to R. T. Haslam, June 27, 1944; Haslam to Freyermuth, June 28, 1944. BUSINESS HISTORY FOUNDATION: Freyermuth to H. M. Larson, June 19, 1944, and June 29, 1944; N. S. B. Gras, Preliminary Proposal for a History of Standard Oil Company (New Jersey), Oct. 24, 1944; Copy of letter of A. C. Minton, Secretary, Standard Oil Company (New Jersey), to D. K. David, Dean, Harvard Business School, Feb. 23, 1945. Also, Larson, "Danger in Business History," *Harvard Business Review,* Apr., 1944; discussion with Freyermuth and Stewart Schackne in June, 1944, and with various officers, directors, and managers in Aug., 1944.

17. B. F. Meglaughlin, "Delaware's Plans for Public Relations," *Public Rel. Conf.,* 1945, p. 42.

18. *Public Rel. Conf.,* 1946, pp. 100–104.

19. G. H. Freyermuth to F. M. Surface, July 12, 1961; *Public Rel. Conf.,* 1945, p. 80. Interview of H. M. Larson with Earl Newsom, Sept. 20, 1961.

20. R. T. Haslam, Public Relations Requirements and Activities, Coordination Committee Group Meeting, 1944.

21. G. H. Freyermuth, Public Support—Deserving It and Getting It, Coord. Com. Group Meeting, 1945.

22. Executive Committee Minutes, Jan., 1946–Jan., 1947, *passim.*

23. *Ibid.,* Sept. 12, 1946; Apr. 10, 1947; Apr. 19, 1947; Mar. 2, 1948; July 9, 1949; July 25, 1949. Also, *Public Rel. Conf.,* 1945, p. 25.

24. G. H. Freyermuth, Public Relations Developments—General Remarks, Coord. Com. Group Meeting, New Orleans, 1946.

25. F. M. Surface in *Public Rel. Conf.,* 1946, pp. 10–22. Also, F. M. Surface, *Penalties of Economic Ignorance,* an address published in a booklet by the company.

26. F. M. Surface, *Penalties of Economic Ignorance.*

27. F. M. Surface in *Public Rel. Conf.,* 1945, pp. 8–20; Garland Davis in *ibid.,* 1946, pp. 16–23; G. H. Freyermuth, *ibid.,* 1947, pp. 15–30; *ibid.,* 1948, pp. 34–45; J. L. Woodward, *ibid.,* 1948, pp. 25–33; Elmo Roper in *ibid.,* 1949, pp. 21–31; Freyermuth, Public Relations Developments—General Remarks, Coord. Com. Group Meeting, 1946.

28. Claude Robinson in *Public Rel. Conf.,* 1946, pp. 24–34; Leo Bogart, *ibid.,* 1949, pp. 7–20. U.S. Senate, 79th Cong., 1st sess., *Hearings Before a Special Committee Investigating Petroleum Resources* (Washington, 1946), 53f.

29. Elmo Roper in *Public Rel. Conf.,* 1949, pp. 25–29.

30. F. M. Surface in *Public Rel. Conf.,* 1948, pp. 10–21; "Public Opinion, England, Sweden, Switzerland," Market Research Bulletin, Sept. 9, 1948, Marketing Coordination Department.

31. F. M. Surface, "What People Are Thinking Abroad," *Public Rel. Conf.,* 1948; Leo Bogart, Memo to W. B. Brown

on Surveys of Public Opinion in Latin America, Feb. 1, 1949.

32. R. T. Haslam in *Public Rel. Conf.,* 1947, p. 3.

33. Stewart Schackne in *Public Rel. Conf.,* 1945, pp. 23–26.

34. Interviews of H. M. Larson with Mrs. Charlotte Browne-Mayers. One of the conferences that influenced the group's thinking was the Wellesley Summer Institute for Social Progress.

35. Exec. Com. Minutes, Jan. 29, 1948.

36. *Ibid.,* Mar. 8, 1948, and July 25, 1948.

37. These reports are dated Sept. 3, 1948, and are signed "For the Committee" by R. S. Meriam, Chairman, and J. C. Moroney, Secretary.

38. *Public Rel. Conf.,* 1945, p. 30.

39. *Ibid.,* 1947, p. 1.

40. *Ibid.,* 1948, p. 1; also, *ibid.,* 1947, pp. 90 and 92.

41. *Ibid.,* for the years 1945–1950, *passim.*

42. *Ibid.,* 1946, p. 117.

43. *Ibid.,* 1947, pp. 105f.

44. *Coord. Com. Group Meeting,* Paris, 1947, p. 440.

45. *Ibid.,* New Orleans, 1946, G. H. Freyermuth, Public Relations Developments.

46. *Ibid.,* Atlantic City, 1948, Remarks in Connection with General Political and Economic Trends and Their Effect upon the Jersey Affiliates' Operations, by H. B. Hoskins, A. T. Proudfit, P. W. Lambright, D. A. Shepard, and others; and Congressman Herter as quoted by C. F. Smith in his Closing Remarks.

47. R. T. Haslam, Public Relations Requirements and Activities, Coord. Com. Group Meeting, 1944.

48. C. F. Smith, summarizing Dean Mason's points in Closing Remarks, Coord. Com. Group Meeting, 1949.

49. *Ibid.*

50. *Ibid.,* Opening Remarks.

51. *Public Rel. Conf.,* 1946, p. 107.

52. *Ibid.*

53. G. H. Freyermuth, Current Public Relations Developments and Activities, Coord. Com. Group Meeting, 1948.

54. J. W. Crayhon, "Press Activities," *Public Rel. Conf.,* 1945, pp. 54–58; G. H. Freyermuth, Current Public Relations Developments and Activities, Coord. Com. Group Meeting, 1948; W. N. Finnegan, Jr., *Public Rel. Conf.,* 1948, pp. 91–94; F. R. Hall, "Nationalism and Oil in Brazil," *Public Rel. Conf.,* 1949, pp. 163–170.

55. Arthur Palmer, "The Fawley Refinery Project," *Public Rel. Conf.,* 1949, pp. 133–147.

56. J. W. Crayhon, "Giving a Plus to Release Material," *Public Rel. Conf.,* 1946, pp. 88–91; G. H. Freyermuth, Current Public Rel. Dev. and Act., Coord. Com. Group Meeting, 1948.

57. Exec. Com. Minutes, Aug. 12, 1948; *Public Rel. Conf.,* 1948, pp. 80f; *The Lamp,* Nov., 1948.

58. *Public Rel. Conf.,* 1947, p. 91; W. F. Prendergast, "Report on Imperial's Public Relations," *ibid.,* 1946, p. 104.

59. The 1948 *Annual Report* was selected by a board of judges as the best American petroleum company report and the best of all industry reports (Exec. Com. Minutes, Sept. 7, 1949).

60. Information obtained from C. E. Springhorn.

61. Mimeographed copy of address delivered by Eugene Holman at the Second Annual Convention of the Export Advertising Association, Oct. 5, 1950.

62. E. R. Sammis, "Direct Mail Activities," *Public Rel. Conf.,* 1945, pp. 62–67; publications in the Public Relations Department; information provided by C. E. Springhorn.

63. *Yale Review,* Autumn, 1961, p. 72.

64. *The New York Times,* Sept. 26, 1948, p. 5X, and Sept. 29, 1948, p. 36L. Stewart Schackne, "Some Considerations Underlying Jersey's Public Relations Activities," *Public Rel. Conf.,* 1948, pp. 79–81, 83; *Yale Review,* Autumn, 1961, p. 72. Letter from Flaherty International Seminar, Aug. 17, 1962.

65. "Art's Place in Industry," *The Lamp,* Dec., 1945; *Public Rel. Conf.,* 1948, p. 83; Carl Maas, Memo on Art Exhibition Program, Jan. 31, 1950; 40-page catalog of the collection entitled, *Oil: 1940–1945.*

66. G. H. Freyermuth to F. M. Surface, Jan. 4, 1963.

67. Coord. Com. Group Meeting, 1946, reports on public relations efforts in domestic affiliates. *Public Rel. Conf.,* 1951, contains reports of such activities by European affiliates. The authors observed this development in Jersey and a few affiliates.

68. Memo, Stewart Schackne to W. M. Craig, July 12, 1943; Memo, Edward Stanley to A. M. Bailey, July 19, 1943. Interviews of H. M. Larson with company executives and supervisors in Venezuela, Aruba, N.W.I., and the United States.

69. Memo by A. C. Minton, undated, 1945; a looseleaf binder entitled Historical Data on Annual Meetings of Standard Oil Co. (N.J.). The authors of *New Horizons* attended stockholders' meetings in the late 1940's.

70. B. F. Meglaughlin, "Delaware's Plans for Public Relations," *Public Rel. Conf.,* 1945, pp. 42–45; Meglaughlin, "The Plant Tour as a Public Relations Technique," *ibid.,* 1948, pp. 89–91.

71. The brochure prepared for the meeting of the Philadelphia group celebrating its tenth anniversary contains a statement of its membership and the topics discussed over the years. The membership consisted of doctors, lawyers, university professors, labor leaders, and businessmen, including a few Jersey men. A local company executive served as host, but the programs were planned and the discussions were run by the self-perpetuating membership. Subjects of public significance were discussed.

72. James H. S. Bossard, "Experiment in Intergroup Relations—a Ten-Year Summary," *Social Forces,* vol. 32 (1954), 218. Another evaluation of the discussions of this group is given by Stuart Chase, in his *Roads to Agreement* (New York, 1951), 112f.

73. *Public Rel. Conf.,* 1947, pp. 5 and 49; Charlotte Lochhead, "A Proposal for

a Joint Conference with Educators," *ibid.,* 50–53; W. F. Prendergast, "Imperial's Conferences with Educators," *ibid.,* 1948, pp. 97–99.

74. No records have been kept of discussions at the conference, but H. M. Larson has discussed the meetings with Mrs. Charlotte Browne-Mayers, Dr. F. M. Surface, and several of the guests at the Jersey Roundtables.

75. The Business History Foundation, Inc., was organized to carry on the project and to facilitate other research and publication in the history of business.

76. Exec. Com. Minutes, Mar. 3, 1947; F. W. Abrams to N. S. B. Gras, May 12, 1947; Gras to Abrams, May 14, 1947; *Public Rel. Conf.,* 1947, pp. 48f.

77. *Public Rel. Conf.,* 1945, p. 38; F. W. Abrams, "Public Relations Responsibility of the Individual," *ibid.,* 102–105. Two addresses delivered by directors in 1945 were printed in the *Congressional Record:* R. T. Haslam, "United We Stand," in *ibid.,* 79th Cong., 1st sess., 91, pt. 1, 1214–1217; and R. W. Gallagher, "Leadership in American Business," in *ibid.,* 79th Cong., 1st sess., 91, pt. 3, A4851f.

78. F. W. Abrams, "Closing Remarks," *Public Rel. Conf.,* 1949, pp. 175–178.

79. It is obvious, of course, that the administrators and executives generally had the assistance of writers in the preparation of statements or addresses. The more important of these were discussed with associates, even in meetings of the Executive Committee or Board of Directors. Any formal statement ostensibly expressed the position not only of the administrator who made it but of his associates as well.

80. Copy of address by Eugene Holman at annual meeting of American Association of Petroleum Geologists, Apr. 2, 1946.

81. R. T. Haslam, "Private Business in America Today," *Public Rel. Conf.,* 1947, p. 5.

82. *Stenographic Report of the Annual Meeting of the Stockholders of Standard Oil Company (New Jersey),* June 3, 1947, pp. 13–16, 21.

83. *Ibid.; Public Rel. Conf.*, 1947, p. 5.

84. F. W. Abrams to Russell W. Davenport, Aug. 2, 1949.

85. F. M. Surface, The Responsibilities of Business in the Field of Education, Mar. 5, 1947.

86. Exec. Com. Minutes, Dec. 17, 1947.

87. Report on the dinner meeting, including a list of those present. Also, interview of H. M. Larson with F. M. Surface, April 7, 1959.

88. Pamphlet with the same title and an article in *The Lamp*, Nov., 1947. According to Earl Newsom, this address was read to the Jersey board before it was delivered.

89. Address of F. W. Abrams, delivered on Jan. 11, 1949, on "How Can American Business Help American Education?"

90. The decisions in the courts are recorded in: 26 New Jersey Superior, 106, and 97 Atlantic 2nd, 186; 13 New Jersey, 145; 98 Atlantic 2nd, 508; 346 U.S., 861. Irving S. Olds of the United States Steel Corporation, President Harold W. Dodds of Princeton University, Frank W. Abrams of Jersey, and others testified in the lower court. Their testimony is given in a printed pamphlet: *Supreme Court of New Jersey, No. A-160, September Term, 1952. The A. P. Smith Manufacturing Company* v. *Ruth F. Barlow . . . and Theodore D. Parsons, Attorney General of New Jersey. Opinion Argued June 8, 1953; decided June 25, 1953.*

91. The *Annual Report* of the Esso Education Foundation, beginning in 1957, gives details as to the range and amount of gifts.

92. *Saturday Review*, Sept. 12, 1964, p. 59, contains an informative article on *Smith* v. *Barlow* and on the formation of educational foundations and their gifts to higher education.

93. Interviews of H. M. Larson with individual executives in Venezuela, Aruba, and New York. These interviews indicated that Creole's public relations activity was a result of the experiences of perceptive men with certain values as well as a response to the necessities of the situation.

94. This brief survey was drawn from a number of sources. It is based, especially, on H. M. Larson's observations and interviews with individuals, inside and outside of Creole, on a tour of Creole's operations in 1949, as well as on research in the company's records in New York and interviews with individuals there, including Henry E. Pelkey, K. E. Cook, and Lloyd Smith, who had had long experience in Venezuela or Aruba. Another source is a study entitled *The Creole Petroleum Corporation in Venezuela* by Wayne C. Taylor and John Lindeman, with the collaboration of Victor Lopez R. of Caracas University, published by the National Planning Association. "Creole Petroleum: Business Embassy," *Fortune,* Feb., 1949, also deals with Creole's public relations.

95. See: David H. Finnie, *Desert Enterprise: The Middle East Oil Industry in Its Local Environment* (Cambridge, 1958); *Stanvac in Indonesia* (National Planning Association, 1957), by Center for International Studies at MIT.

CHAPTER 25

1. U.S. Senate, 78th Cong., 1st sess., *Hearings Before Special Committee Investigating Petroleum Resources* (Washington, 1946), testimony of S. P. Coleman.

2. Opening Remarks, Coordination Committee Group Meeting, 1945.

3. *Ibid.*

4. *Ibid.*, 1945 and 1946, *passim.*

5. *Ibid.*, 1946: H. W. Page, Industry and Jersey Affiliates' Five-Year Operating Survey; Page and others, Crude Supply and Product Requirements . . . , 1950–1965; J. W. Connolly, Shifts in U.S. Population and Industry and Its Effect on Petroleum Markets.

6. *Ibid.*, 1946, Opening Remarks by C. F. Smith; SONJ, *Annual Report*, 1945.

7. Henrietta M. Larson and Kenneth Wiggins Porter, *History of Humble Oil & Refining Company* (New York, 1959), 626.

8. *Coord. Com. Group Meeting*, 1947, pp. 2f; *ibid.*, 1948, No. 2, p. 5; Annual Statistical Review, 1947 and 1948.

9. Ann. Stat. Rev., 1947.

10. A. C. Bedford, Importance of Product Quality, Coord. Com. Group Meeting, 1946. Interview of H. M. Larson with S. P. Coleman, Apr. 19, 1962.

11. Ann. Stat. Rev., for the years 1946–1950.

12. Larson and Porter, *History of Humble*, 635, 642, and 696f.

13. Ann. Stat. Rev., 1946.

14. *Coord. Com. Group Meeting*, 1947, p. 3.

15. U.S. Senate, 80th Cong., 1st sess., *Hearings Before Subcommittee of the Committee on Interstate and Foreign Commerce on Oil Shortage* (Washington, 1948), Dec. 9, 1947, p. 49.

16. *Ibid.*, 46.

17. Larson and Porter, *History of Humble*, 645.

18. U.S. Senate, 80th Cong., 1st sess., *Hearings . . . Subcom. . . . on Oil Shortage,* Dec. 9, 1947, pp. 46 and 54; *ibid.,* June 29, 1948, p. 13. *Coord. Com. Group Meeting*, 1947, pp. 438f.

19. H. W. Page, *Coord. Com. Group Meeting*, 1947, p. 10.

20. The Taft Act (P. L. 395, 80th Cong.) was signed Dec. 30, 1947. U.S. Senate, 80th Cong., 1st sess., *Hearings . . . Subcom. . . . on Oil Shortage,* Dec. 9, 1947, pp. 10–20, 45–49, 118–129.

21. *Ibid.,* 21–30, 47–56, 59–62; U.S. Senate, 81st Cong., 1st sess., Special Committee to Study Problems of Small Business, *Final Report, Oil Supply and Distribution Problems* (Washington, 1949), 23.

22. The authors of this volume were doing research in Jersey's offices at the time.

23. U.S. Senate, 80th Cong., 1st sess., *Hearings . . . Subcom. . . . on Oil Shortage,* June 9, 1948, pp. 1–3, 10f, 52. Two of the authors of this volume were Esso customers at the time and hence observed at first hand something of what the company was doing.

24. *Ibid.*

25. Executive Committee Minutes, Mar. 29, May 18, June 22, Sept. 26, 1948;

Ann. Stat. Rev., 1948; *Ships' Bulletin,* March-April and July-August, 1948; M. G. Gamble, Review of the Jersey Affiliates' World-wide Anticipated Tanker . . . Facilities, Coord. Com. Group Meeting, 1948. U.S. Senate, 80th Cong., 1st sess., *Hearings . . . Subcom. . . . on Oil Shortage,* June 29, 1948, p. 4.

26. Ann. Stat. Review, 1948; General Oil Situation, Coord. Com. Group Meeting, 1948. U.S. Senate, 80th Cong., 1st sess., *Hearings . . . Subcom. . . . on Oil Shortage,* June 29, 1948, pp. 6f. 81st Cong., 2nd sess., Report of the Subcom. on Oil Imports to the House Select Com. on Small Business, *Effects of Foreign Imports on Independent Domestic Producers* (Washington, 1950), 101. Larson and Porter, *History of Humble*, 634.

27. Among the more important federal committees and agencies investigating the industry were these: Subcom. on Oil Shortage of Senate Com. on Interstate and For. Com.; Senate Com. on Banking and Currency; Subcom. of Senate Com. on Small Business; Subcom. on Govt. Procurement of House Com. on Military Supplies; House and Senate Joint Econ. Com.; Federal Trade Commission.

28. Eugene Holman to P. G. Hoffman (ECA administrator), July 1, 1948; Telegram, Holman to Senator O'Mahoney, July 1, 1948; Press release, July 1, 1948; Orville Harden to Robert Dechert (ECA), Oct. 14, 1948.

29. *U.S. of A. v. Standard Oil Company of California et al.,* 155 F. Supp. 121, and 270 F. 2nd 50; *United States v. Standard Oil Company (New Jersey) et al.,* U.S. District Court for the Southern District of New York, Civil Action No. 78–154.

30. H. W. Page, Résumé of Recent Pol. Dev., Coord. Com. Group Meeting, 1948.

31. Board of Directors' Minutes, July 3, 1946; Statement for internal circulation, July 25, 1946; Exec. Com. Minutes, Nov. 18, 1946; Press releases, S.O.C. of N.J., July 25, 1946, and Feb. 27, 1947. *The Commercial and Financial Chronicle,* Apr. 24, 1947, p. 2216. Conversation of H. M. Larson on Sept. 27, 1962, with R. S. Meriam, consultant to Standard Oil Company (New Jersey) at that time.

32. Exec. Com. Minutes, July 2, 1947. *Business Week,* Aug. 2, 1947.

33. *National Petroleum News,* July 30, 1947, p. 9; *Business Week,* Aug. 8, 1947.

34. Press release, S.O.C. of N.J., July 24, 1947.

35. Correspondence and memoranda, June, 1947–May, 1949.

36. *Ibid.*

37. Telegram, John R. Steelman to M. J. Rathbone, July 24, 1947.

38. Arthur Newmyer & Associates to G. H. Freyermuth, July 25, 28, 30, and 31, 1947; reports from Radio Reports, Inc.

39. B. F. Meglaughlin to A. Clarke Bedford and R. N. Keppel, Aug. 1, 1947.

40. L. F. McCollum to J. R. Suman, Aug. 1, 1947, reporting telephone conversation.

41. G. H. Freyermuth to F. W. Abrams, Aug. 15, 1947.

42. The price reductions were noted in newspapers and radio broadcasts across the country for about a week from Sept. 13. They received special notice from such commentators as Sylvia Porter (*N.Y. Post,* Sept. 16, 1947) and W. M. Jablonski (*Journal of Commerce,* Sept. 20, 1947).

43. Harry L. Hansen and Powell Niland, "Esso Standard: A Case Study in Pricing," *Harvard Business Review,* May-June, 1952, pp. 122–126.

44. *Ibid.,* May-June, 1952, pp. 118–120; *National Petroleum News,* Aug. 20, 1947.

45. *Oil & Gas Journal,* Dec. 6, 1947, p. 53; U.S. Senate, 80th Cong., 1st sess., Spec. Com. to Study Problems of Small Business, *Hearings on Oil Supply and Distribution Problems,* pt. 9 (1948), 2847f.

46. *National Petroleum News,* Dec. 3, 1947, p. 11; Melvin G. de Chazeau and Alfred E. Kahn, *Integration and Competition in the Petroleum Industry* (New Haven, 1959), 189.

47. Larson and Porter, *History of Humble,* 642.

48. U.S. House, 80th Cong., 2nd sess., Subcom. of Com. on Interstate and Foreign Com., *Hearings on Fuel Investiga-tion,* pt. 2 (Feb., 1948), 1017, 1064–1066.

49. Press releases on price changes, Oct. 28 and Dec. 19, 1947. Hansen and Niland, *op. cit.,* page 125, gives successive dates on which companies raised tankwagon prices.

50. U.S. House, 80th Cong., 2nd sess., Subcom. of Com. on Interstate and Foreign Com., *Hearings on Fuel Investigation,* pt. 2, p. 1064.

51. Hansen and Niland, *op. cit.,* 128.

52. *The New York Times* reported on distributors' prices on Jan. 1, 5, 8, and 25, 1948.

53. Hansen and Niland, *op. cit.,* 125 and 129.

54. Telegram, Joseph C. O'Mahoney to Eugene Holman, Mar. 5, 1948.

55. R. T. Haslam to F. W. Abrams, Mar. 9, 1948.

56. Message from Assistant Chief Sonnett relayed by Arthur Newmyer & Associates to G. H. Freyermuth, Apr. 5, 1949. 80th Cong., 2nd sess., *Cong. Record,* vol. 94, pt. 10, p. A 2130.

57. *The New York Times,* 1948: Apr. 28, L 1; Apr. 30, L 33; May 2, F 1.

58. U.S. Senate, 80th Cong., 1st sess., Special Com. to Study Problems of Small Business, *Hearings on Oil Supply and Distribution Problems,* pt. 9, p. 2721.

59. H. W. Page to Eugene Holman, June 2, 1948.

60. Esso Standard Territory, Coord. Com. Group Meeting, 1948.

61. M. J. Rathbone in *ibid.*

62. Press release, Sept. 14, 1945.

63. Larson and Porter, *History of Humble,* 642. Esso Standard press release, Sept. 29, 1948.

64. Esso Standard press release, Nov. 19, 1948.

65. Larson and Porter, *History of Humble,* 642.

66. Hansen and Niland, *op. cit.,* 130.

67. H. W. Page to Frank M. Surface, July 2, 1962.

68. Ann. Stat. Rev., 1948 and 1949.

69. Esso Standard press release, Apr. 5, 1949.

70. Arthur Newmyer & Associates to G. H. Freyermuth, Apr. 6, 1949; *ibid.,* Apr. 7, 1949. *Congressional Record,* Apr. 5, 1949, p. 3900.

71. W. Kerr Scott to Eugene Holman, Apr. 20, 1949. U.S. Senate, 81st Cong., 1st sess., Subcom. of the Com. on Banking and Currency, *Hearings on an Investigation into the Cause of Price Increases in Petroleum Products,* June 29 and 30, 1949 (Washington, 1949).

72. Memoranda on pricing dated Apr. 26 and May 2, 1949.

73. Hearings referred to in note 71, above, *passim.*

74. Esso Standard press releases, Sept. 13 and Nov. 25, 1949.

75. U.S. House, 81st Cong., 2nd sess., Report of Subcom. on Oil Imports of the Select Committee on Small Business, *Effects of Foreign Oil Imports on Independent Domestic Producers* (Washington, 1950), 98. Ann. Stat. Rev., 1949.

76. U.S. House, 81st Cong., 1st sess., Select Com. on Small Business, *Effects of Foreign Oil Imports on Independent Domestic Producers* (Washington, 1949), 110–115, 167–187.

77. U.S. House, 81st Cong., 2nd sess., Report of Subcom. on Oil Imports . . ., *Effects of Foreign Oil Imports on Independent Domestic Producers,* 92–104.

78. CREOLE: *Annual Report,* 1949. SONJ, *Annual Report,* 1949; Ann. Stat. Rev., 1949; Second Report of the Subcom. to Study the Effect of the Dollar Problem on Jersey's Foreign Business, Feb. 28, 1949.

79. CREOLE: *Annual Report,* 1949.

80. SONJ, *Annual Report,* 1949; *The Lamp,* March, 1950.

81. SONJ, *Annual Report,* 1950; Ann. Stat. Rev., 1950.

CHAPTER 26

1. The classification below is based on one in the *London Financial Times* of Sept. 16, 1948, as revised in the November, 1948, Report of the Subcommittee to Study the Effect of the Dollar Problem on Jersey's Foreign Business.

2. Raymond F. Mikesell, *Foreign Exchange in the Postwar World* (New York, 1954), 23, 27, 30f, 42f; Charles E. Kindleberger, *The Dollar Shortage* (New York, 1950), 1, 242, 252.

3. For information on the building of a professional group to deal with postwar problems of international finance, the authors are indebted to David J. Jones of Standard Oil Company (New Jersey), who was a member of the group.

4. B. G. Ellis, Ministry of Fuel and Power, to Standard Oil Company (New Jersey), Aug. 8, 1945.

5. Standard-Vacuum Marketing Review, 1945.

6. Memorandum submitted by Standard Oil Company (New Jersey) to His Majesty's Treasury, Aug. 12, 1949.

7. This and other statements as to Jersey's financial policy in foreign operations in the early postwar period have been drawn from a variety of Jersey's records, including the following addresses given by Emilio G. Collado: "Foreign Financial Operations of American Oil Companies," Nov. 8, 1956; "Financial Problems of International Petroleum Operations," Oct. 1, 1957; "The Role of the Treasurer in a Large International Company," Oct. 7, 1958; and "Problems in International Oil Operations," Apr. 29, 1960.

8. R. H. Porters as quoted in *Coordination Committee Group Meeting,* 1947, p. 423.

9. Report of the Subcommittee to Study the Effect of the Dollar Problem on Jersey's Foreign Business, Nov. 10, 1948.

10. Memo, R. H. Porters to SONJ, Jan. 3, 1949.

11. Report of the Subcommittee . . ., Feb. 28, 1949.

12. In the Coordination Committee Group Meeting in 1949, P. T. Lamont reported that the committee governing the aid programs had received applications for financial aid for the construction of refining capacity in European countries totaling well over a million barrels per day. This was far more than was actually built.

13. Eugene Holman to P. G. Hoffman, Mar. 9, 1949, enclosing the memorandum.

14. Memorandum Submitted by Standard Oil Company (New Jersey) to His Majesty's Treasury, Aug. 12, 1949.

15. *Ibid.;* Eugene Holman to John W. Snyder, Secretary of the Treasury, Sept. 9, 1949.

16. SONJ, *Annual Report,* 1949; Memos of the Jersey Treasurer's Department on British Exchange Control Problems, Dec. 30, 1949, and on Dollar-Sterling Oil Problem, Jan. 25, 1950; Proposal, submitted Jan. 25, 1950, to His Majesty's Government . . . by Standard Oil Company (New Jersey). Also, Roger R. Sharp, "America's Stake in World Petroleum," *Harvard Business Review,* Sept., 1950, pp. 25–41.

17. Treasurer's Dept., Memorandum on Dollar-Sterling Oil Problem, Jan. 25, 1950; Orville Harden to Dean Acheson, Secretary of State, Feb. 2, 1950; John R. Suman to Charles Sawyer, Secretary of Commerce, Feb. 8, 1950.

18. This statement is based on correspondence in the SONJ records between H. W. Page and men at headquarters in New York. Page's approach was specifically spelled out in a letter to E. E. Soubry, Dec. 18, 1950.

19. Memorandum Submitted by Standard Oil Company (New Jersey) to His Majesty's Treasury, Aug. 12, 1949; Eugene Holman to John W. Snyder, Secretary of the Treasury, Sept. 9, 1949; Proposal, submitted, Jan. 25, 1950, to His Majesty's Government . . . by Standard Oil Company (New Jersey).

20. Memorandum Submitted . . . to His Majesty's Treasury, Aug. 12, 1949; Memorandum in a letter of E. G. Collado to Victor Butler, British Ministry of Fuel and Power, Nov. 29, 1949; Orville Harden to Dean Acheson, Feb. 2, 1950. Horst Mendershausen, "Dollar Shortage and Oil Surplus in 1949–1950," No. 11, in *Essays in International Finance* (Princeton, N.J., Nov., 1950), 10.

21. Memorandum Submitted . . . to His Majesty's Treasury, Aug. 12, 1949.

22. Eugene Holman to P. G. Hoffman, Mar. 9, 1949; Memorandum on Dollar-Sterling Oil Problem, Jan. 25, 1950.

23. Memorandum on Dollar-Sterling Oil Problem, Jan. 25, 1950; Memorandum Submitted . . . to His Majesty's Treasury, Aug. 12, 1949.

24. Memorandum Submitted . . . to His Majesty's Treasury, Aug. 12, 1949; Memorandum in letter of E. G. Collado to Victor Butler, British Ministry of Fuel and Power, Nov. 29, 1949; Proposal, submitted Jan. 25, 1950, to His Majesty's Government . . . by Standard Oil Company (New Jersey).

Halford L. Hoskins' *Middle East Oil in United States Foreign Policy* (Library of Congress Legislative Reference Service, Public Affairs Bulletin No. 89, Dec., 1950) deals with this issue and the position taken by the Department of State. Hoskins states (page 53) that "there is considerable evidence that the British oil industry, with the active support of its government, found the opportunity very tempting not only to exclude dollar competition from their own domestic market through import curbs, but also to take over certain other world oil markets that had been in part supplied in terms of American dollar oil." Also (pages 54–55), "the conviction grew in Washington that British oil restrictions were designed more for commercial advantage than for economy and hence were out of keeping with American efforts to assist in European economic recovery." There is no statement of these views in the Jersey correspondence examined by the authors.

25. Memorandum by United Kingdom, Feb., 1950, on Dollar-Sterling Oil Problem; Oliver Franks to Orville Harden, Mar. 24, 1950; R. H. S. Eakens, U. S. Department of State, to Eugene Holman, Mar. 31, 1950.

26. Orville Harden to R. H. S. Eakens, July 19, 1920. Also, Sharp, *Harvard Business Review,* Sept., 1950, pp. 25–41.

27. Victor Butler, British Ministry of Fuel and Power, to H. W. Page, May 20, 1950; Page to Butler, May 22, 1950, referring to proposal made by E. E. Soubry, May 8, 1950; Page to Butler, May 25, 1950, defining types of purchases; Orville Harden to R. H. S. Eakens, State Dept., July 19, 1950; Page to W. J. Haley, Aug. 2, 1950.

28. E. G. Collado to Henry Wilson Smith, His Majesty's Treasury, May 11, 1950; Smith to Collado, May 24, 1950; Collado to Smith, May 26, 1950; Orville Harden to R. H. S. Eakens, July 19, 1950.

29. Orville Harden to R. H. S. Eakens, July 19, 1950; Victor Butler to R. L. Brougham (Aramco), July 3, 1950; L. M. Snyder (Aramco) to R. H. S. Eakens, U.S. Dept. of State, July 3, 1950; H. W. Page to W. J. Haley, July 18, 1950. *New York Times,* Apr. 27, 1950, pt. I, p. 15. Information about the Stanvac agreement was furnished by V. H. Grigg.

30. Translation of letter of July 13, 1951, from Ministère des Finances & des Affaires Economiques, Direction des Finances Exterieures, to "Mr. President," Esso Export Corporation. This letter refers to the Ministry's letters of Sept. 5, 1950, and Jan. 5, 1951. Also R. H. Porters to W. J. Haley, July 17, 1951.

31. Orville Harden to R. H. S. Eakens, July 30, 1950.

32. Executive Committee Minutes, Mar. 21 and June 16, 1950.

33. Esso Export, in reports of Coordination Committee Group Meeting, 1950; interview with David J. Jones, Apr. 24, 1965. *New York World Telegram,* June 16, 1951, "Esso Export Conquers Exchange Difficulties."

34. *New York World Telegram,* June 16, 1951, *loc. cit.*

35. H. W. Page to E. E. Soubry, Dec. 18, 1950.

36. Victor Butler, British Ministry of Fuel and Power, to H. W. Page, Jan. 19, 1951; Page to Butler, Jan. 22, 1951; Butler to Page, Feb. 1, 1951.

CHAPTER 27

1. Henrietta M. Larson and Kenneth Wiggins Porter, *History of Humble Oil & Refining Company* (New York, 1959), 653–657.

2. *Ibid.,* 655–659. Coordination Committee Group Meeting, 1946, Crude Supply and Products Requirements—U.S. . . . Industry and Jersey . . . (Humble and Carter); and *ibid.,* 1948, Long-Range Possibilities of Oil Supplies . . . (Carter). HUMBLE: *Annual Report,* 1950.

3. Annual Report of Standard Oil Company of New Jersey, 1946 and 1947; *The Lamp,* Oct., 1946. Wallace E. Pratt and Dorothy Good, eds., *World Geography of Petroleum* (Princeton, 1950), 48.

4. Larson and Porter, *History of Humble,* 658.

5. *Ibid.,* 657–659; 332 U.S. 19; Ernest R. Bartley, *The Tidelands Oil Controversy* (Austin, Texas, 1953), 162–181.

6. Annual Report of Standard Oil Co. of N.J., 1947.

7. Larson and Porter, *History of Humble,* 659–661. This failure in West Texas, where it was believed oil would be found in the Ellenburger, demonstrates the importance in the search for new oil of men's judgment concerning where it may or may not be found. See *Oil's First Century* (Boston, 1959), 64, for Wallace E. Pratt's observations on this point.

8. Annual Statistical Review, 1946–1950. Larson and Porter, *History of Humble,* 661f.

9. Ann. Stat. Rev., 1946–1950.

10. H. H. Baker, Natural Gas Outlook, Coord. Com. Group Meeting, 1949. Larson and Porter, *History of Humble,* 647–653.

11. Larson and Porter, *History of Humble,* 636–638.

12. *Ibid.,* 638. "Electronics Tells How Oil Pools Behave," *The Lamp,* Feb., 1946.

13. For the development of such regulation, with particular emphasis on Texas, see Larson and Porter, *History of Humble,* chaps. 11, 13, 18, and 19.

14. *Ibid.,* 649–653; 156 F. 2d 949. H. H. Baker, Natural Gas Outlook, Coord. Com. Group Meeting, 1949.

15. Larson and Porter, *History of Humble,* 640f; 331 U.S. 791; 193 S. W. 2nd 824.

16. For the earlier history of Imperial's exploration, see Chapter 5; also George

Sweet Gibb and Evelyn H. Knowlton, *The Resurgent Years, 1911–1927* (New York, 1956), 89–91 and 422, and Wallace E. Pratt, *Oil in the Earth* (Lawrence, Kan., 1943), 39–41. Examples of Theodore Link's contributions to the knowledge of the geology of Western Canada before 1947 are articles in the *Bulletin of the American Association of Petroleum Geologists*, vols. XV, XVI, XVIII, and XIX.

17. The brief account that follows of Imperial's exploration and production after the war is based principally on John S. Ewing's research in the records of Imperial and Jersey. On the planning of the exploration campaign that led to the Leduc discovery, Dr. F. M. Surface contributed information from conversations in the fall of 1963 with President Michael L. Haider of Jersey and Wallace E. Pratt.

18. L. F. McCollum to H. H. Hewetson, Jan. 9, 1947; *Imperial Oil Review*, Feb., 1947, p. 21.

19. *Imperial Oil Review*, Apr., 1947, pp. 3–5, and Aug., 1947, pp. 2–5.

20. *Ibid.*, Feb., 1948, pp. 11–13.

21. Producing Department Memo on Imperial Pipe Line; "Trek by Truck," *The Lamp*, Sept., 1948.

22. M. L. Haider, Current Exploration Activities and Results—Canadian Northwest, Coord. Com. Group Meeting, 1949.

23. Ann. Stat. Rev., 1950.

24. IMPERIAL: Directors' Minutes, Oct. 17, 1947, Mar. 17, May 31, and June 7 and 10, 1948; *Annual Report*, 1948 and 1949. SONJ: Executive Committee Minutes, May 2 and June 13, 1947, and Feb. 18, 1948; M. E. MacDowell to Orville Harden, Dec. 16, 1948; *Annual Report*, 1948.

25. H. H. Hill, Trends in Cost of Finding and Producing Crude Oil (Chart 2), Coord. Com. Group Meeting, 1946.

26. Reserve records; Ann. Stat. Rev., 1946 and 1950. CREOLE: *Annual Report*, 1950.

27. Edwin Lieuwen, *Petroleum in Venezuela* (London, 1961), 64–91.

28. The pertinent clause of the Exposition of Motives sent to the Venezuelan Congress with the proposed 1943 Law of Hydrocarbons, copied from the *Diary of Debates of the National Congress* (Chamber of Deputies), Volume II, Extraordinary Session, 1943, was sent with free and literal translations to H. M. Larson by R. S. Lombard of Creole in Caracas.

29. Chapter XI, Income Tax Law of 1948, published in *Gaceta Oficial*, 216 Extraordinary, Nov. 12, 1948.

30. H. F. Prioleau to L. F. McCollum, Sept. 25, 1946; W. E. Pratt to A. T. Proudfit, Nov. 19, 1947; Memo of J. T. Fly to J. W. Brice, Nov. 24, 1947; Prioleau to Brice, Jan. 19, 1948, with memo of Jan. 16; Memo of Fly, Apr. 22, 1948; Memo, 50–50 Tax in Venezuela, Dec. 20, 1948; S. P. Coleman to F. A. Davies, Mar. 26, 1952. CREOLE: *Annual Report*, 1945–1950. *The New York Times*, Jan. 25, 1946.

31. INTERNATIONAL: Memo by "F. C. P.," July 10, 1945; H. A. Grimes to L. F. McCollum, Feb. 7, 1946; Memo Aug. 25, 1946; S. C. Hope to McCollum, Sept. 11 and 18, 1946, and Jan. 4, 1947; J. K. Oldfield to H. W. Page, June 1, 1947; Grimes to L. P. Maier, Nov. 13, 1948; Annual Report, 1946 and 1947. SONJ, Ann. Stat. Rev., 1945–1950.

32. Memo, De Mares Concession, Feb. 16, 1949.

33. Memo, Colombia, Mar. 8, 1949; R. T. Haslam to Orville Harden, Mar. 14, 1949; Eugene Holman to James Bruce, July 5, 1949.

34. News release, July 11, 1950; C. T. Helm to J. W. Brice, June 12, 1951; Record of incorporation of International Petroleum Company (Colombia) in Secretary's Department.

35. Photostatic copy of the *Acta* of Aug. 25, 1951, with translation, from the records of International Petroleum Company, Limited.

36. Historical Memo on Argentina, by "F. C. P.," Jan. 14, 1948; Memo on Argentina, by E. J. Reeves, Oct. 11, 1947; Ann. Stat. Rev., 1950.

37. Pratt and Good, eds., *World Geography of Petroleum*, 128.

38. Coordination Committee Group Meeting, 1947, p. 38.

39. *Ibid.*, 399f; Ann. Stat. Rev., 1950. "Dutch Oil," *The Lamp*, Nov., 1949; "The Discovery in France," *The Lamp*, Nov., 1954; SONJ, *Annual Report*, 1949. Pratt and Good, eds., *World Geography of Petroleum*, 259f.

40. C. L. Lockett, Middle East and Far East, *Coord. Com. Group Meeting*, 1947; *ibid.*, A. L. Owens, Egypt and Libya; SONJ, *Annual Report*, 1949.

41. Annual Report of Standard-Vacuum, 1945–1950; Operating Review of Standard-Vacuum, 1945–1950; Ann. Stat. Rev., 1950.

42. For an exposition of Standard-Vacuum's employee and public relations, see *Stanvac in Indonesia*, a study made by the Center for International Studies at MIT and published by the National Planning Association in 1957.

43. S. P. Coleman, Middle East Production Possibilities, *Coord. Com. Group Meeting*, 1947, p. 26.

44. Ann. Stat. Rev., 1946.

45. Federal Trade Commission, *Report on International Petroleum Cartel* (Washington, 1952), 119.

46. An excellent book on the Middle East oil industry, with considerable detail on Arabia and Aramco, is David H. Finnie's *Desert Enterprise: The Middle East Oil Industry in Its Local Environment* (Cambridge, 1958). *The Texaco Star*, Saudi Arabian Number, 1946, describes the situation in Arabia.

47. D. N. Pritt to SONJ, July 17, 1946; E. F. Johnson, Recent Iraq Petroleum Company Agreement, *Coord. Com. Group Meeting*, 1947, pp. 37f.

48. Johnson, Recent Iraq Petroleum Company Agreement, *Coord. Com. Group Meeting*, 1947.

49. *Report on Int. Pet. Cartel*, 101f, quoting President Eugene Holman.

50. U.S. 80th Cong., 1st sess., *Petroleum Agreement with Great Britain and Northern Ireland: Hearings before the Committee on Foreign Relations*, June 2–25, 1947 (Washington, 1947); Herbert Feis, *Petroleum and American Foreign Policy* (Palo Alto, 1944), chap. 8; John W. Frey and H. Chandler Ide, eds., *A History of the Petroleum Administration for War* (Washington, 1946), 279–307, particularly 285; George Lenczowski, *Oil and State in the Middle East* (Ithaca, 1960), 167–172.

51. One such notice: Standard Oil Company (New Jersey) to Participations and Investments, Ltd., C. S. Gulbenkian, president, Oct. 3, 1946. *Report on Int. Pet. Cartel*, 101–103.

52. Notes on Trip to Arabia, Jan. 2, 1947.

53. Draft of Agreement between Arabian American Oil Company and Standard Oil Company (New Jersey), Nov. 14, 1946; SONJ, *Annual Report*, 1946; E. F. Johnson, *Coord. Com. Group Meeting*, 1947, pp. 37f. *Report on Int. Pet. Cartel*, 102.

54. Press releases, Dec. 26, 1946, and Mar. 6, 1947. *Report on Int. Pet. Cartel*, 145–152.

55. Denton, Hall & Burgin to Messrs. Piesse & Sons, Jan. 8, 1947; Press release, Jan. 10, 1947. *The New York Times*, Jan. 10, 1947; *Report on Int. Pet. Cartel*, 103f.

56. Press release, Mar. 6, 1947. *Report on Int. Pet. Cartel*, 122–124.

57. *Report on Int. Pet. Cartel*, 103.

58. Draft of statement for release by President Holman, May 29, 1947.

59. Orville Harden to Eugene Holman, Nov. 4, 1948; SONJ, *Annual Report*, 1948.

60. SONJ, *Annual Report*, 1948.

61. Copies of minutes of Iraq group meetings.

62. Report of operations of Aramco, 1948–1950.

63. On Aramco-Saudi government relations see David H. Finnie, *Desert Enterprise*. For an informative article on Aramco's contribution to Saudi Arabian community and economic development, see C. S. Coon, "Operation Bultiste—Promoting Industrial Development in Arabia," in H. M. Teaf and P. G. Franck, eds., *Hands Across Frontiers: Case Studies in Technical Cooperation* (Ithaca, N.Y., 1955), 307–361. Another informative work is *The Arabia of Ibn Saud*

(New York, 1952) by Roy Lebkicher, George Reutz, and Max Steinecke.

64. J. E. Crane to Eugene Holman, May 16, 1947; W. L. Butte to Orville Harden and J. R. Suman, Jan. 19, 1949; J. P. Lockhard to M. A. Wright, Nov. 9, 1950; Review of Operating Highlights of Aramco, Feb. 23, 1951. *New York Times*, Jan. 4, 1951. Also interview of H. M. Larson with S. P. Coleman, director of Jersey and of Aramco.

65. Ann. Stat. Rev., 1950.

CHAPTER 28

1. W. R. Finney to B. B. Howard, Dec. 17, 1948; Finney, Review of the Jersey Affiliates' World-Wide Anticipated Pipe Line Transportation Facilities, Coordination Committee Group Meeting, 1948. "Shortcut to Amuay Bay," *The Lamp*, Nov., 1949. CREOLE, *Annual Report*, 1948 and 1949.

2. Executive Committee Minutes, Aug. 8 and Dec. 19, 1949; Office of the Pipe Line Advisor, Notes and Records on Interprovincial; W. R. Finney, Review of the Jersey Affiliates' World-Wide Anticipated Pipe Line Transportation Facilities, Coord. Com. Group Meeting, 1948; Memo, Imperial Pipe Line Co., Ltd., June 15, 1949; Interprovincial, Report for 1949; Addition to Imperial Budget, June 12, 1950; Annual Statistical Rev., 1950; SONJ, *Annual Report*, 1949 and 1950.

3. SONJ, *Annual Report*, 1950; Iraq group meeting minutes, 1945–1950; Ann. Stat. Rev., 1950.

4. ARAMCO: *Annual Report*, 1948, 1949, and 1950. SONJ: *Annual Report*, 1950; W. R. Finney, Review of . . . Pipe Line Transportation Facilities, Coord. Com. Group Meeting, 1948; Finney to Frank M. Surface, Apr. 3, 1964. SONJ: Comptroller's Green Book, 1951, pp. 25f.

5. W. L. Butte to L. F. McCollum, Sept. 4, 1947; Canfield to B. B. Howard, O. Harden, J. R. Suman, and S. P. Coleman, Mar. 2, 1950; Canfield to Harden and Howard, Apr. 19, 1950.

6. Larson and Porter, *History of Humble*, 628.

7. *Ibid.*, 646. HUMBLE, *Annual Report*, 1949 and 1950. SONJ, *Annual Report*, 1950.

8. John L. Loos, *Oil on Stream! A History of Interstate Oil Pipe Line Company, 1909–1959* (Baton Rouge, 1959), 215–279. W. R. Finney, Review of . . . Pipe Line Transportation Facilities, Coord. Com. Group Meeting, 1948.

9. SONJ, *Annual Report*, 1947, 1948, and 1953.

10. Finney, Review of . . . Pipe Line Transportation Facilities, Coord. Com. Group Meeting, 1948; SONJ, *Annual Report*, 1950.

11. HUMBLE PIPE LINE: Reports of Planning and Economics Division. Larson and Porter, *History of Humble*, 646–649.

12. W. R. Finney, Review of . . . Pipe Line Transportation Facilities, Coord. Com. Group Meeting, 1948.

13. Larson and Porter, *History of Humble*, 644f. Observations of one of the authors on a tour of Lake Maracaibo operations and interviews with executives. Also, discussions with a corrosion engineer of Humble Pipe Line Company.

14. Larson and Porter, *History of Humble*, 643f. Interviews by H. M. Larson with Humble pipeline executives and engineers.

15. "Big Mamma," *The Lamp*, Sept., 1947; "Moving 1,700,000 Tons of Oil a Day," *ibid.*, Nov., 1947; M. G. Gamble, The World-Wide Ocean Tanker Outlook and Remarks on Inland Waterways Equipment, *Coord. Com. Group Meeting*, 1947, and Coord. Com. Group Meeting, 1948; Annual Report of Esso Standard, 1946–1950.

16. "Lake Tankers," *The Lamp*, June, 1951.

17. ESSO SH: Annual Report of Marine Operations, 1945–1948. J. J. Collins, "The Jersey Tanker Officers Association, 1948–1957: A Study in Independent Unionism" (a manuscript thesis).

18. ESSO SH: Annual Rep. of Marine Oper., 1945–1948.

19. M. G. Gamble, The World-Wide Ocean Tanker Outlook . . . , *Coord. Com. Group Meeting*, 1947.

20. ESSO SH: Annual Report of Marine Oper., 1947–1948; *Ships' Bulletin,* March-April, 1948, pp. 5–7, July-August, 1948, p. 5, and January–February, 1949, p. 3. SONJ, *Annual Report,* 1949.

21. Boleslaw Adam Boczek, *Flags of Convenience: An International Study* (Cambridge, 1962), 58.

22. M. G. Gamble, The World-Wide Ocean Tanker Outlook . . . , *Coord. Com. Group Meeting,* 1947.

23. Exec. Com. Minutes, July 6, 19, and 25, 1949.

24. M. G. Gamble, A Review of the World-Wide Anticipated Ocean Transport Situation, Coord. Com. Group Meeting, 1949.

25. SONJ, *Annual Report,* 1949.

26. M. G. Gamble, A Review of . . . Ocean Transport Situation, Coord. Com. Group Meeting, 1949.

27. SONJ: *Annual Report,* 1950; J. J. Winterbottom, Jersey's Overall Ocean Tanker . . . Activities and Outlook, Coord. Com. Meeting, 1952.

28. M. G. Gamble, The World-Wide Ocean Tanker Outlook . . . , *Coord. Com. Group Meeting,* 1947.

29. SONJ: *Annual Report,* 1949 and 1950; Ann. Stat. Rev., 1946 and 1950. ESSO SH: Ann. Rep. of Marine Oper., 1949 and 1950.

CHAPTER 29

1. SONJ, *Organization Manual,* for the years 1943 to 1950, inclusive.

2. Summary of Changes in Working Capital . . . by Comptroller's Department, Oct. 27, 1959; SONJ, *Annual Report,* 1945–1950; W. J. Haley to C. F. Smith, Mar. 19, 1948; Haley to E. E. Soubry, Mar. 14, 1950.

3. Memo for Wm. J. Haley *re* Manufacturing Group Meeting, May 15–17, 1945.

4. SONJ, *Annual Report,* 1948 and 1949.

5. *Ibid.,* 1948 and 1949.

6. CREOLE, *Annual Report,* 1942.

7. *Ibid.,* 1945–1950. H. L. Shoemaker to members of the Coordination Committee, Apr. 24, 1944; Memo on Location of Refinery, July 7, 1945; W. J. Haley to C. F. Smith, July 24, 1946; Haley to department heads, June 24, 1946; L. G. Smith to C. F. Smith, Sept. 8, 1948; Haley to C. F. Smith, Apr. 12, 1949; C. E. Lanning to C. F. Smith, Jan. 6, 1950.

8. CREOLE, *Annual Report,* 1950. L. G. Smith to W. J. Haley, Jan. 24, 1947.

9. Interview of H. M. Larson with L. G. Smith. Arabian American Oil Company, *Aramco Handbook, Oil in Middle East* (Dhahran, Saudi Arabia, 1968), 123.

10. W. J. Haley to C. F. Smith, Dec. 20, 1948.

11. Press release, Sept. 6, 1949; SONJ, *Annual Report,* 1950.

12. SONJ, *Annual Report,* 1949–1951. Executive Committee Minutes, Apr. 27, May 6, July 22, and Aug. 2, 1949, and June 15, 1950; Press release, May 26, 1950; H. L. Desmoulins, United Kingdom—Refining Operations, *Coordination Committee Group Meeting,* 1947; *The Lamp,* Sept., 1950, "Refinery Going Up" and "Fawley Will Produce for a Varied Market." The financial figures on total cost were obtained from the Refining Coordination Department.

13. Executive Committee Minutes, June 16, 1948; Annual Report of Standard-Vacuum, 1945–1950; SONJ, *Annual Report,* 1950.

14. Henrietta M. Larson and Kenneth Wiggins Porter, *History of Humble Oil & Refining Company* (New York, 1959), 623. SONJ, *Annual Report,* 1949. CREOLE, *Annual Report,* 1949.

15. SONJ, *Annual Report,* 1946–1950; Annual Report for Standard Oil Company of New Jersey, 1946–1948, and Annual Review, 1947–1950. HUMBLE, *Annual Report,* 1946 and 1948.

16. Same sources as in note 15.

17. Memo on Refining Study, H. W. Fisher to S. P. Coleman, Aug. 23, 1950.

18. SONJ, *Annual Report,* 1948, 1949, and 1950; H. Tett, Esso Development Company, Ltd., *Coord. Com. Group Meeting,* 1947; "Science Looks Ahead," *The Lamp,* Nov., 1947.

19. SONJ, *Annual Report,* 1948, 1949, and 1950; E. V. Murphree, Atomic Power, Coord. Com. Group Meeting, 1945; Murphree, H. W. Ferguson, and G. L. Stewart, Gas Synthesis Process, and H. G. M. Fischer, Standard Oil Development—Progress Report on Refining Techniques, Coord. Com. Group Meeting, 1946; *ibid.,* 1947, Murphree, Review of the More Important Phases of the Development Company's Activities—General Review, and M. J. Rathbone, Some Trends in Modern Petroleum Refining in American Plants; *ibid.,* 1949, Murphree, Synthetic Fuels—from Natural Gas, Coal, and Oil Shale and Review of the 1949 Spring Tech. Com. Meeting; S.O.C. of N.J. (Esso Standard), Annual Report, 1946–1948, and Annual Review, 1947–1950. *Who's Who in America,* 1960.

20. Memo on Refining Study, H. W. Fisher to S. P. Coleman, Aug. 23, 1950.

21. M. B. Hopkins, Recent Chemical Developments, Coord. Com. Group Meeting, 1945; *Petroleum Engineering Course,* Esso Research and Engineering Co., sec. 6, bk. 1, 1960, p. 1. *Tirk-Othmer Encyclopedia of Chemical Technology,* vol. X, 184; *Business Week,* Sept. 3, 1960, pp. 55–78, containing a useful survey of the development and current condition of the petrochemical industry. Also, Kendall Beaton, *Enterprise in Oil: A History of Shell in the United States* (New York, 1957), 513–547.

22. M. B. Hopkins, Recent Chemical Developments, Coord. Com. Group Meeting, 1945. Kendall Beaton, *Enterprise in Oil,* 502–547, 615–617, 676–679; Larson and Porter, *History of Humble,* 564, 596–598.

23. Larson and Porter, *History of Humble,* 596–598.

24. Chemical Policy Committee, Minutes; M. J. Rathbone, Trends in Refining Operations, Coord. Com. Group Meeting, 1945.

25. O. V. Tracy, Esso and the Petrochemical Industry, Coord. Com. Group Meeting, 1954.

26. Exec. Com. Minutes, Aug. 9, 1946; H. W. Fisher, Jersey Affiliates' Chemical Business—Present Status and Future Plans, Coord. Com. Group Meeting,

1946; E. V. Murphree, New Developments in the Oil Industry, *ibid.,* 1948; O. V. Tracy, Review of the Oil Chemical Business in the Gulf Coast Area, *ibid.,* 1949; Tracy, Esso and the Petrochemical Industry, *ibid.,* 1954. Also, *The Lamp,* "Wider Horizons in Plastics," Sept., 1947, and "Science Looks Ahead," Nov., 1947.

27. SONJ, *Annual Report,* 1946–1950; Summary of Changes in Working Capital . . . , by Comptroller's Department, Oct. 27, 1959. ESSO: Annual Review, 1947–1950.

28. 98 F 2d, 1–8.

29. F. A. Watts, Domestic Marketing . . . Humble Oil & Refining Company, Coord. Com. Group Meeting, 1949. Larson and Porter, *History of Humble,* 625.

30. F. A. Watts, Marketing Trends and Problems . . . Humble, Coord. Com. Group Meeting, 1946. Larson and Porter, *History of Humble,* 625–633.

31. Larson and Porter, *History of Humble,* 632–633. Ann. Stat. Rev., 1946–1950.

32. Ann. Stat. Rev., 1946–1950; F. W. Butler, Marketing Trends and Problems . . . Carter, Coord. Com. Group Meeting, 1946; E. R. Smith, Domestic Marketing . . . The Carter Oil Company, *ibid.,* 1949.

33. R. N. Keppel, Marketing Trends and Problems . . . Esso Marketing, Coord. Com. Group Meeting, 1946; F. H. Billups, Status of . . . Liquefied Petroleum Gas Program and Future Plans . . . Delaware, *ibid.,* 1946; W. R. Goodwin and E. R. Smith, Competitive Factors Threatening Market Position, *ibid.,* 1948; L. E. Ulrope, Domestic Marketing, Policies and Objectives . . . Esso Standard Oil Company, *ibid.,* 1949. ESSO: Annual Report, 1946–1948; Annual Review, 1947–1950.

34. Larson and Porter, *History of Humble,* 657.

35. 98 F 2d, 1–8.

36. R. N. Keppel, Proposed Expansion of Domestic Sales Activities into the Mid-West, Coord. Com. Group Meeting, 1946.

37. Based on a report on the history of Imperial's marketing written by John S.

Ewing from research in the company's records.

38. SONJ, *Annual Report*, 1946–1950; A. T. Proudfit, P. W. Lambright, and C. T. Helm, Remarks in Connection with General Political and Economic Trends and Their Effect upon the Jersey Affiliates' Operations . . . Venezuela . . . Peru and Colombia . . . Balance of Latin America, Coord. Com. Group Meeting, 1948. INTERNATIONAL, *Annual Report*, 1946–1948. CREOLE, *Annual Report*, 1946–1950.

39. INTERNATIONAL, *Annual Report*, 1945–1948.

40. Exec. Com. Minutes, Nov. 29 and Dec. 2, 1948, and July 27, Aug. 1, and Nov. 1, 1949; SONJ, *Annual Report*, 1948–1950.

41. SONJ, *Annual Report*, 1948–1950.

42. SONJ, *Annual Report*, 1948, 1949; Operating Report of Standard-Vacuum for 1949 and 1950; Exec. Com. Minutes, Aug. 3 and 25, 1949, and Aug. 10, 1950.

43. Exec. Com. Minutes, Aug. 10, 1950; SONJ, *Annual Report*, 1950.

44. SONJ, *Annual Report*, 1948; Marketing Coordination Notes, Aug. 1, 1948; D. W. Ramsey, Summary Report of the Middle East Marketing Committee, *Coord. Com. Group Meeting*, 1947, pp. 163–165; Marketing Council Meeting, Minutes, Nov. 27, 1951.

45. This and the following paragraphs on Eastern Hemisphere marketing are based primarily on the following SONJ records: Reports on marketing in Europe and North Africa and along the Eastern Mediterranean, *Coord. Com. Group Meeting*, 1947; Summary of Operations and General Information, Jersey's European and North African Affiliated Companies, May 5, 1947; Marketing Coordination Notes, Aug. 1, 1948; Marketing Council Meeting, Minutes, Nov. 27, 1951. ESSO PETROLEUM, *Annual Report*, 1951 and 1952. STANDARD–VACUUM, *Annual Report*, 1945–1950.

46. *Coord. Com. Group Meeting*, 1947, pp. 87, 134f, 303; SONJ, *Annual Report*, 1949–1951.

47. ESSO PETROLEUM, *Annual Report*, 1952. *Coord. Com. Group Meeting*, 1947, p. 121.

48. R. T. Haslam to W. E. Pratt, Nov. 19, 1945; E. F. Johnson, Consent Decree—Standard Oil Company (New Jersey)—1942, *Coord. Com. Group Meeting*, 1947, pp. 427–432 (an especially illuminating discussion of the matter as presented to a large meeting of executives of Jersey companies in Paris'); E. F. Johnson, reports to Executive Committee.

49. E. F. Johnson, reports to Exec. Com., dated July 7, 1947, Jan. 24, and Feb. 9, 1948, and July 31, 1950.

CHAPTER 30

1. The statistical series used for comparisons of production, refining, and sales in 1927 and 1950 were obtained largely from the Annual Statistical Review of Standard Oil Company (New Jersey). The industry and company figures on sales are not exactly comparable because the company figures consist of only actual product sales but the industry series includes fuel oil burned at refineries, losses at refineries, losses in the handling of crude and products, and estimates for Communist countries. Other sources utilized were various editions of *Petroleum Facts and Figures*, issued by the American Petroleum Institute, and *The American Petroleum Industry, 1899–1959, The Age of Energy* (Evanston, 1963), by Harold F. Williamson, Ralph L. Andreano, Arnold R. Daum, and Gilbert C. Klose.

2. Henrietta M. Larson and Kenneth Wiggins Porter, *History of Humble Oil & Refining Company* (New York, 1959), 695.

3. Daniel C. Hamilton, *Competition in Oil: The Gulf Coast Refinery Market, 1925–1950* (Cambridge, 1958), 218.

4. For a chart, together with its sources, showing the general trend, see p. 86 of *The Growth of Integrated Oil Companies* (Boston, 1954) by John G. McLean and Robert Wm. Haigh. On the related issue of competition in the American oil industry, see the following: Melvin G. de Chazeau and Alfred E. Kahn, *Integration and*

Competition in the Petroleum Industry (New Haven, 1959); Daniel C. Hamilton, *Competition in Oil: The Gulf Coast Refinery Market, 1925–1950* (Cambridge, 1959); Edmund G. Learned and Catherine C. Ellsworth, *Gasoline Pricing in Ohio* (Boston, 1959).

5. *Stenographic Report of the Annual Meeting of the Stockholders of Standard Oil Company (New Jersey), June 3, 1947.*

6. Data supplied by the Marketing Coordination Department of Standard Oil Company (New Jersey).

Index

Abadan refinery (Iran): 304, 310, 490
Abrams, Frank W.: 30, 35, 167, 190-191, 194, 760; as administrator, 585-586; background, 583; elected to board, 422; on employee relations, 346-347; as president of S.O. of N.J., 355, 357; principal responsibilities of, 466, 582; public relations role, 448, 638-639, 650, 653, 656, 658
Accidents: compensation for, 350, 374; on pipelines, 244; prevention of, 351; rate of, abroad, 371, 377-378; refinery, wartime, 496-497. *See also* Safety
Accounting: 604, 644; extra, for rationing system, 547; marine, 401; practices of affiliates, 20, 202, 258, 261, 286, 321, 598-599; shortcomings in methods, 20; standardization of, 781, 802
Accounting Manual: 20, 32, 599, 604
Acetylene: 170-171, 173
Acetylene process: 156, 406
Achnacarry Agreement: 60, 308-309, 313, 327. *See also* Deterding, Sir Henri
Acrylonitrile: 172
Additives: 159-160, 514, 766-768. *See also specific products*
Administration: changes in corporate organization, 13, 606-608, 800-807; by contact directors, 588, 605; decentralization of, 12-13, 16-17, 20, 24, 28-30, 35-36, 346, 792, 801-802; evolution of new, 12-36; of fleets, 205, 208-211, 215-226; functional coordinators, 589, 593, 603-604; integration of operations, 113; Memorandum of 1933, 23-24, 26, 28, 30, 580-608; weaknesses in, 6-11, 465, 587, 785, 800. *See also* Affiliates; Board of Directors; Finance; *specific committees, departments, functions*
Adoue, J. B., Jr.: 550
Advertising: 283, 293, 301, 774, 781
Advertising Council: Crisis in Education campaign, 658

Advisory Commission to the Council of National Defense: 415, 417, 419, 434, 460. *See also* War Production Board
Affiliates: acquisition, transfer, and mergers of, 48-50, 95, 771, 773; change in corporate names, 781; committee systems of, 195; compensation for war losses, 576-579; corporate network of, 6-7; crude oil production by, 38, 108, 115, 148-149, 473, 488, 720-721; crude oil runs and reserves, 95-99, 342, 499, 667, 769, 786; dividends to SONJ, 798; employee relations, 344, 345-381, 613-627; executive development programs, 595; foreign, compliance with consent decree, 782; foreign, transport methods, 253-259; list of, 804-805; marketing, 284-285, 303-342; number of, 608; pipeline operations, 229, 234-235, 237, 240-241, 248-251, 537-538, 745; postwar operations, 557-561, 563-576, 704, 715-726; pricing policy, 672-685; producing coordination, 68-70; public relations, 632-633, 637-638; publications of, 643-644; refineries, net value of, 199; relations to SONJ, 17, 28-29, 589, 603-608, 800-802; research, 76-77, 84, 150-175; sales, 277-278, 296, 298, 330-331, 541-544, 666; tanker operations of, 204-226, 392-396, 402, 523, 526, 758; war's impact on European, 383-387
AFL. *See* American Federation of Labor
Africa: 58, 338, 538-539. *See also* North Africa *and specific countries*
Agentia Americana: 338
Agreements: Aramco and Saudi Arabia, 50/50, 741; on cross-licensing of patents, 507, 510; on dollar-sterling exchange, 698, 701-702, 706, 710-711; Morrow-Calles, 378; Mutualization, 152; pooling, 478; Potsdam, 568, 571;

909

71 72 73 10 9 8 7 6 5 4 3 2 1